Hawaii

Ned Friary
Glenda Bendure

LONELY PLANET PUBLICATIONS
Melbourne • Oakland • London • Paris

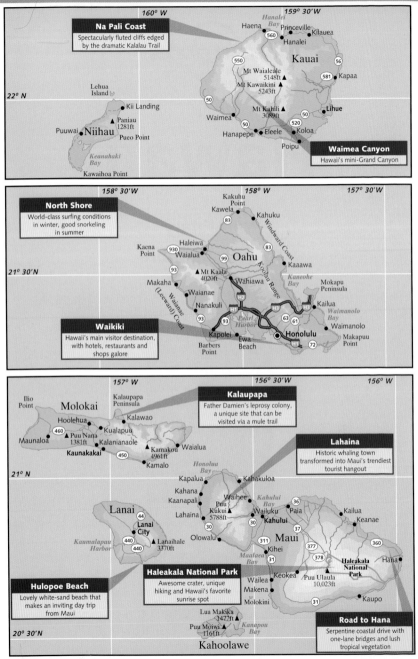

Na Pali Coast
Spectacularly fluted cliffs edged by the dramatic Kalalau Trail

160° W
159° 30'W

Hanalei Bay
Haena
Princeville
Kilauea
560
Hanalei

550
Kauai
56

Mt Waialeale ▲
5148ft
Mt Kawaikini ▲
5243ft
581
Kapaa

22° N

Lehua Island
Kii Landing
50
Mt Kahili ▲
3089ft
Lihue

Paniau ▲
1281ft
Waimea
50
50
520
Koloa
Puuwai ● **Niihau**
Pueo Point
50
Hanapepe ● Eleele
Poipu

Keanahaki Bay

Kawaihoa Point

Waimea Canyon
Hawaii's mini-Grand Canyon

North Shore
World-class surfing conditions in winter, good snorkeling in summer

158° 30'W
158° W
157° 30'W

Kakuhu Point
Kawela
Kahuku
83

Windward Coast

Kaena Point
Haleiwa
930
Waialua
99
Oahu
83

93
Mt Kaala ▲
4020ft
Wahiawa
Kaaawa

21° 30'N

Makaha
Waianae
Nanakuli
Koolau Range
Kaneohe Bay
Mokapu Peninsula
Kailua

H2
H1
H3
H3
Waimanolo Bay

63 61
Waimanolo

93
93
Pearl Harbor
Kapolei
Ewa Beach
● **Honolulu**
Makapuu Point

Barbers Point
H1
72

Waikiki
Hawaii's main visitor destination, with hotels, restaurants and shops galore

Waianae (Leeward) Coast

157° W
156° 30'W
156° W

Ilio Point
Molokai
Kalaupapa Peninsula

Kalaupapa
Father Damien's leprosy colony, a unique site that can be visited via a mule trail

Hoolehua
Kalawao
460
Puu Nana ▲
1381ft
Kualapuu
Maunaloa
Kalanianaole
Kaunakakai
450
Kamakou ▲
4961ft
Waialua
Kamalo

Lahaina
Historic whaling town transformed into Maui's trendiest tourist hangout

21° N

Honolua Bay
Kapalua
Kahakuloa

Kahana
Waihee
Kahului Bay
36
Kaanapali
Puu Kukui ▲
5788ft
Wailuku
Paia
Kailua
Lanai
Lahaina
30
Kahului
Keanae

44
Lanai City ●
Olowalu
311
37
360

440
Lanaihale ▲
3370ft
Maui
377
Kaumalapau Harbor
440
Kihei
378
Haleakala National Park
Hana

Hulopoe Beach
Lovely white-sand beach that makes an inviting day trip from Maui

Haleakala National Park
Awesome crater, unique hiking and Hawaii's favorite sunrise spot

Maalaea Bay
31
Wailea
Keokea
Puu Ulaula ▲
10,023ft
Makena
31
Kaupo
Molokini

Road to Hana
Serpentine coastal drive with one-lane bridges and lush tropical vegetation

20° 30'N

Lua Makika ▲
1477ft
Puu Moiwi ▲
1116ft
Kanapou Bay

Kahoolawe

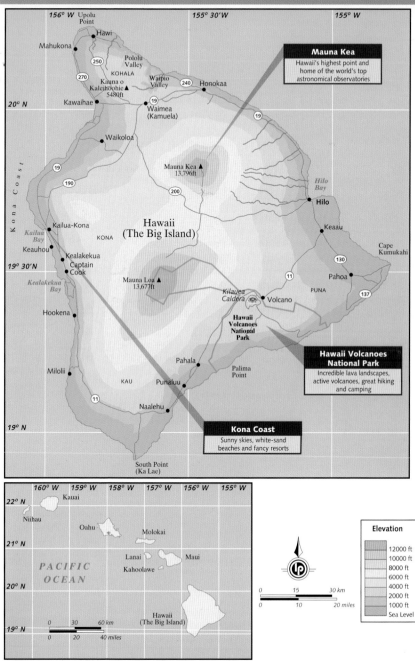

Mauna Kea
Hawaii's highest point and home of the world's top astronomical observatories

Hawaii Volcanoes National Park
Incredible lava landscapes, active volcanoes, great hiking and camping

Kona Coast
Sunny skies, white-sand beaches and fancy resorts

Hawaii
(The Big Island)

Mauna Kea ▲
13,796ft

Mauna Loa ▲
13,677ft

Kilauea
Caldera

Hawaii
Volcanoes
National
Park

156° W   Upolu Point
Hawi
Mahukona
Pololu Valley
KOHALA
Kauna o Kaleihoohie ▲ 5480ft
Waipio Valley
Honokaa
250
270
240
Kawaihae
19
Waimea (Kamuela)
19
Waikoloa
20° N
155° 30'W
155° W

Kona Coast
19
190
200
Kailua-Kona
KONA
Keauhou
Kealakekua
Captain Cook
Kealakekua Bay
Kailua Bay
Hookena
Milolii
11
KAU
19° 30'N

Hilo Bay
Hilo
Keaau
Cape Kumukahi
130
Pahoa
11
PUNA
137
Volcano

Pahala
Palima Point
Punaluu
Naalehu

South Point
(Ka Lae)

19° N

Elevation

	12000 ft
	10000 ft
	8000 ft
	6000 ft
	4000 ft
	2000 ft
	1000 ft
	Sea Level

160° W   159° W   158° W   157° W   156° W   155° W
22° N
Kauai
Niihau
Oahu
Molokai
21° N
Lanai
Kahoolawe
Maui
PACIFIC
OCEAN
20° N
Hawaii
(The Big Island)
19° N

0   15   30 km
0   10   20 miles

0   30   60 km
0   20   40 miles

Hawaii
5th edition – March 2000
First published – August 1990

Six-monthly upgrades of this title available free on
www.lonelyplanet.com/upgrades

Published by
Lonely Planet Publications Pty Ltd ABN 36 005 607 983
90 Maribyrnong St, Footscray, Victoria 3011, Australia

Lonely Planet Offices
Australia Locked Bag 1, Footscray, Victoria 3011
USA 150 Linden St, Oakland, CA 94607
UK 10a Spring Place, London NW5 3BH
France 1 rue du Dahomey, 75011 Paris

Photographs
Ann Cecil, Ron Dahlquist, Ned Friary, Robert Fried, Lee Foster, BJ
Formento, Christopher Gallagher, Kim Grant, Robert Leon, Casey
Mahaney, Douglas Peebles, Eric L Wheater, Astrid Witte
Many of the images in this guide are available for licensing from
Lonely Planet Images.
email: lpi@lonelyplanet.com.au
Web site: www.lonelyplanetimages.com

Illustrations
Mark Butler, Hugh D'Andrade, Shelley Firth, Hayden Foell, Rini
Keagy, Justin Marler, Hannah Reineck, Wendy Yanagihara

Front cover photograph
Evening light over Kalalau Valley, Kauai (Ann Cecil)

ISBN 1 86450 047 6

text & maps © Lonely Planet Publications Pty Ltd 2000
photos © photographers as indicated 2000

Printed by The Bookmaker International Ltd
Printed in China

Contents

INTRODUCTION   11

FACTS ABOUT HAWAII   13

History 13
Geography 30
Geology 30
Climate 31
Ecology & Environment . . 33

Flora & Fauna 34
Government & Politics . . . 38
Economy 39
Population & People 40
Education 40

Arts 40
Society & Conduct 41
Religion 42
Language 42

FACTS FOR THE VISITOR   46

Highlights 46
Planning 46
Tourist Offices 47
Visas & Documents 48
Customs 52
Money 52
Post & Communications . 54
Internet Resources 56
Books 56
Films 59
Newspapers & Magazines 59
Radio & TV 60
Photography & Video . . . 60

Time 60
Electricity 60
Weights & Measures 61
Laundry 61
Health 61
Women Travelers 65
Gay & Lesbian Travelers . 65
Disabled Travelers 66
Senior Travelers 67
Travel with Children 67
Useful Organizations 67
Libraries 68
Dangers & Annoyances . . 68

Emergency 71
Legal Matters 72
Business Hours 72
Public Holidays & Special
Events 72
Work 75
Accommodations 75
Food 80
Drinks 83
Entertainment 84
Spectator Sports 84
Shopping 84

OUTDOOR ACTIVITIES   86

Surfing 86
Windsurfing 86
Diving 87
Snorkeling 87

Kayaking 87
Fishing 89
Whale Watching 89
Hiking 89

Running 91
Mountain Biking 92

GETTING THERE & AWAY   93

Air 93

Sea 101

Organized Tours 102

GETTING AROUND   103

Air 103
Bus 105
Car 106

Bicycle 108
Hitchhiking 108
Boat 108

Taxi 108
Organized Tours 108

OAHU   110

History 110
Geography 111

Climate 111
Flora & Fauna 111

Government 114
Economy 114

2   Contents

Population & People . . . 114
Orientation 114
Information 115
Activities 117
Organized Tours 123
Accommodations 123
Entertainment 125
Shopping 125
Getting There & Away . . 126
Getting Around 126
Honolulu **129**
Downtown Honolulu . . . 130
Chinatown 138
Ala Moana &
University Area 142
Elsewhere in Honolulu . . 145
Waikiki **161**
Pearl Harbor Area **186**
USS Arizona Memorial . . 187
Pearl City 188

Hawaii's Plantation
Village 188
Keaiwa Heiau State Park 189
Southeast Oahu **190**
Diamond Head 190
Hanauma Bay
Beach Park 192
Koko Head
Regional Park 193
Makapuu Point 195
Waimanalo 196
Pali Hwy 196
Windward Coast **198**
Kailua 198
Kaneohe 203
Waiahole & Waikane . . . 205
Kualoa 206
Kaaawa 206
Kahana Valley 207
Punaluu 208
Sacred Falls State Park . . 208

Hauula 208
Laie 209
Malaekahana State
Recreation Area 210
Kahuku 210
Central Oahu **211**
Hwy 750 212
Wahiawa 213
North Shore **214**
Waialua 216
Mokuleia 216
Haleiwa 217
Waimea 220
Waianae Coast **224**
Kahe Point 224
Nanakuli 224
Maili 226
Waianae 226
Makaha 226
North of Makaha 228
Kaena Point State Park . . 229

HAWAII (THE BIG ISLAND)   231

History 233
Geography 235
Climate 235
Flora & Fauna 236
Government & Politics . . 236
Economy 236
Population & People . . . 237
Orientation 237
Information 237
Activities 238
Organized Tours 244
Accommodations 245
Entertainment 247
Shopping 247
Getting There & Away . . 247
Getting Around 248
Kona **249**
Kailua-Kona 249
Keauhou 262
Holualoa 265
South Kona **267**
Honalo 268
Kainaliu 269
Kealakekua 269
Kealakekua Bay 270
Captain Cook 272

Honaunau 274
Puuhonua o Honaunau
National Historical Park   275
Hookena 277
Milolii 277
**North Kona &
South Kohala** **277**
Honokohau Harbor 278
Honokohau Beach 278
Kaloko-Honokohau National
Historical Park 280
Keahole Point/
OTEC Beach 280
Onizuka Space Center . . 281
Lava Tube 281
Kona Coast State Park . . 281
Kua Bay 281
Kaupulehu 281
Kiholo Bay 283
Waikoloa Beach Resort . 283
Waikoloa 285
Mauna Lani Resort 286
Puako 288
Hapuna Beach State Park 288
Mauna Kea Beach 289
Spencer Beach Park 289

Puukohola Heiau 289
Kawaihae 290
North Kohala **290**
Waimea to Hawi
(Hwy 250) 290
Kawaihae to Pololu
Valley (Hwy 270) 292
Mookini Heiau 293
Hawi 294
Kapaau 295
Makapala 295
Pololu Valley 296
Waimea (Kamuela) **297**
Around Waimea 301
Hamakua Coast **302**
Honokaa 302
Kukuihaele 304
Waipio Valley 305
Kalopa State
Recreation Area 308
Laupahoehoe Point 309
Kolekole Beach Park . . . 309
Akaka Falls 309
Pepeekeo 4-Mile
Scenic Drive 310
Saddle Rd **311**

Mauna Kea 311
Mauna Loa's
Northern Flank 315
Hilo **316**
Downtown Hilo 318
Around Hilo 321
Puna **329**
Keaau 329
Pahoa 331
Lava Tree State Park . . . 332
Kapoho 332
Ahalanui Beach Park . . . 333
Isaac Hale Beach Park . . 334

MacKenzie State
Recreation Area 334
Opihikao 334
Kehena Beach 335
Kalapana 335
Kalapana to Pahoa 335
Kau **336**
Manuka State
Wayside Park 336
Hawaiian Ocean View
Estates 336
South Point 338
Waiohinu 339
Naalehu 340

Whittington Beach Park   340
Punalu 341
Pahala 341
Wood Valley 341
Pahala to Hawaii
Volcanoes National Park   342
Hawaii Volcanoes
National Park **342**
Crater Rim Drive 345
Chain of Craters Rd 348
Mauna Loa Rd 349
Hiking Trails 351
Volcano 354

MAUI   357

History 357
Geography 360
Climate 360
Flora & Fauna 360
Government 361
Economy 361
Population & People . . . 361
Orientation 361
Information 362
Activities 363
Organized Tours 369
Accommodations 370
Entertainment 372
Shopping 372
Getting There & Away . . 372
Getting Around 374
Northwest Maui **375**

Lahaina 375
Lahaina to Maalaea 387
Lahaina to Kaanapali . . . 388
Kaanapali 389
Honokawai 395
Kahana 396
Napili 397
Kapalua 398
Honolua &
Mokuleia Bays 399
Kahului-Wailuku Area . . 400
Kihei **410**
Wailea & Makena **418**
Wailea 418
Makena 422
Road To Hana **424**
Paia 424

Hwy 360 429
Hana 433
Hana to Kipahulu 438
Upcountry **441**
Paia to Makawao 441
Makawao 443
Haiku 444
Pukalani 445
Kula 446
Polipoli Spring
State Recreation Area . . 448
Keokea 449
Ulupalakua Ranch 450
Piilani Hwy 450
Haleakala National Park **452**
Hiking the Crater 457

MOLOKAI   460

History 460
Geography 462
Climate 463
Flora & Fauna 463
Government 463
Economy 464
Population & People . . . 464
Orientation 464
Information 465
Activities 465
Organized Tours 467
Accommodations 467
Shopping 468

Getting There & Away . . 468
Getting Around 469
Kaunakakai **470**
East Molokai **474**
Kawela 474
Kamalo 474
Ualapue 475
Kaluaaha 476
Iliiliopae Heiau 476
Pukoo 476
Waialua 477
Halawa Valley 478
Central Molokai **478**

Kualapuu 478
Kalae 479
Palaau State Park 479
Kalaupapa Peninsula . . . 480
Kamakou 483
Hoolehua 486
Moomomi Beach 487
West End **488**
Maunaloa 488
Molokai Ranch 489
Kaluakoi Resort 490
West End Beaches 491

LANAI   494

History 494
Geography 497
Climate 497
Flora & Fauna 498
Government 498
Economy 498
Population & People . . . 498
Orientation 499

Information 499
Activities 500
Getting There & Away . . 500
Getting Around 500
Around Lanai 501
Lanai City 501
Shipwreck Beach &
Keomuku 504

Manele Bay &
Hulopoe Bay 506
Kaunolu 508
Kaumalapau Harbor . . . 508
Northwest Lanai 508
Munro Trail 509

KAHOOLAWE   511

History 511   Geography 514   Getting There & Away . . 514

KAUAI   515

History 515
Geography 518
Climate 518
Flora & Fauna 518
Government 520
Economy 520
Population & People . . . 520
Orientation 520
Information 520
Activities 522
Organized Tours 527
Accommodations 528
Entertainment 530
Shopping 530
Getting There & Away . . 531
Getting Around 531
East Side 532
Lihue 533

Wailua 540
Waipouli 549
Kapaa 550
Kapaa to Kilauea 552
North Shore 554
Kilauea 554
Kalihiwai 557
Anini 558
Princeville 559
Hanalei Valley 562
Hanalei 562
Hanalei to Wainiha 567
Haena 567
Na Pali Coast 570
South Shore 574
Koloa 574
Poipu 577
West Side 583

Kalaheo 583
Hanapepe Valley
Lookout 585
Eleele, Numila &
Port Allen 586
Hanapepe 586
Olokele 587
Makaweli 587
Russian Fort Elizabeth . . 587
Waimea 587
Kekaha 590
Barking Sands 590
Polihale State Park 591
Waimea Canyon 591
Waimea Canyon
State Park 592
Kokee State Park 593

NIIHAU   597

History 598   Geography 599   Getting There & Away . . 599

NORTHWESTERN HAWAIIAN ISLANDS   600

Fauna 601
French Frigate Shoals . . 602

Laysan Island 602
Necker & Nihoa 603

Midway Islands 603

GLOSSARY   605

ACKNOWLEDGMENTS   608

INDEX   613

MAP INDEX

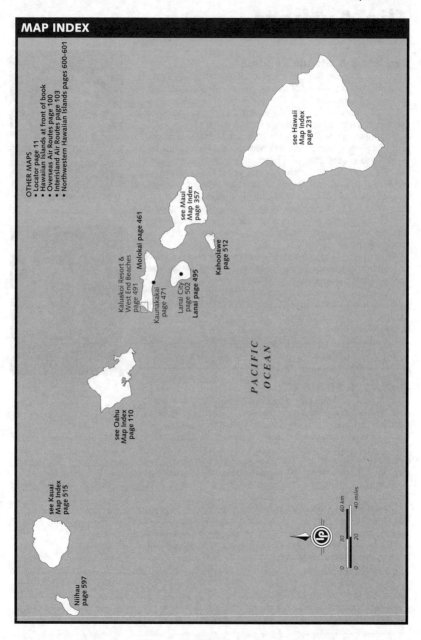

OTHER MAPS
• Locator page 11
• Hawaiian Islands at front of book
• Overseas Air Routes page 100
• Interisland Air Routes page 103
• Northwestern Hawaiian Islands pages 600–601

see Hawaii
Map Index
page 231

see Maui
Map Index
page 357

Molokai page 461

Kaluakoi Resort &
West End Beaches
page 491

Kaunakakai
page 471

Lanai City
page 502
Lanai page 495

Kahoolawe
page 512

see Oahu
Map Index
page 110

see Kauai
Map Index
page 515

Niihau
page 597

PACIFIC
OCEAN

0   30   60 km
0   20   40 miles

The Authors

Ned Friary & Glenda Bendure

Ned grew up near Boston, studied Social Thought & Political Economy at the University of Massachusetts in Amherst and, upon graduating, headed west.

Glenda grew up in California's Mojave Desert and first traveled overseas as a high school exchange student to India.

They met in Santa Cruz, California, where Glenda was completing her university studies. In 1978, with Lonely Planet's first book (*Across Asia on the Cheap*) in hand, they took the overland trail from Europe to Nepal. For the next six years, they explored Asia and the Pacific while maintaining a home base in Japan, where Ned taught English and Glenda edited a monthly magazine.

On the first of many extended trips to Hawaii, they went straight from Osaka to the green lushness of Kauai, a sight so soothing for concrete-weary eyes that a two-week vacation stretched into a four-month sojourn.

Ned and Glenda have a particular fondness for islands and tropical climates. In addition to this *Hawaii* guide, they have authored Lonely Planet's guidebooks to *Oahu*, *Eastern Caribbean* and *Bermuda*. Their writing duties have also taken them north on occasion; they're responsible for LP's guide to *Denmark*, as well as the Norway and Denmark chapters of LP's *Scandinavian & Baltic Europe* book.

They now live on Cape Cod in Massachusetts – at least when they're not on the road.

FROM THE AUTHORS

Many thanks to the people who have helped us on this project: Allen Tom, Sanctuary Program Manager at Hawaiian Islands Humpback Whale National Marine Sanctuary; Andrea Kaawaloa, Park Ranger at Hawaii Volcanoes National Park; Curt A Cottrell, Na Ala Hele Trails & Access Program Manager; Linda Delaney from the Office of Hawaiian Affairs; Andrea Perala, Communications Director for the WM Keck Observatory; Karen Reebok of the UH Astronomy program; Jon Giffin of the Division of Forestry & Wildlife; and Roy Damron of the Kona Reefers Dive Club.

Thanks also to those friends and travelers who have shared insights and experiences with us along the way. We'd especially like to acknowledge Rich, Shelly and Catie Hausman and Glenn Thering and Ted Brattstrom, who have joined us in exploring many of Hawaii's more remote corners and back trails.

This Book

This fifth edition of *Hawaii* was written by Ned Friary & Glenda Bendure.

FROM THE PUBLISHER

Hawaii is a product of Lonely Planet's US office. Valerie Sinzdak and Julie Connery edited the book, and senior editor Jacqueline Volin shepherded this edition all the way. Valerie, Don Root and Roxane Buck-Ezcurra proofread the book, and Ken DellaPenta did the indexing. Special thanks to editor Maria Donohoe for helping with the glossary. Sean Brandt served as the lead cartographer for much of the project, with assistance from Tracey Croom Power, Guphy, Mary Hagemann, Patrick Huerta and Monica Lepe, under the guidance of senior cartographer Amy Dennis. Wendy Yanagihara and Josh Schefers designed the book, with help from Susan Rimerman and Margaret Livingston. Valerie, Jacqueline, Kevin Anglin, Wade Fox and Elaine Merrill assisted with layout review. Rini Keagy designed the cover, with production help from Simon Bracken.

THANKS

Many thanks to the travelers who used the last edition and wrote to us with helpful hints, advice and interesting anecdotes. Your names appear in the back of this book.

Foreword

ABOUT LONELY PLANET GUIDEBOOKS

The story begins with a classic travel adventure: Tony and Maureen Wheeler's 1972 journey across Europe and Asia to Australia. Useful information about the overland trail did not exist at that time, so Tony and Maureen published the first Lonely Planet guidebook to meet a growing need.

From a kitchen table, then from a tiny office in Melbourne (Australia), Lonely Planet has become the largest independent travel publisher in the world, an international company with offices in Melbourne, Oakland (USA), London (UK) and Paris (France).

Today Lonely Planet guidebooks cover the globe. There is an ever-growing list of books, and there's information in a variety of forms and media. Some things haven't changed. The main aim is still to help make it possible for adventurous travelers to get out there – to explore and better understand the world.

At Lonely Planet we believe travelers can make a positive contribution to the countries they visit – if they respect their host communities and spend their money wisely. Since 1986 a percentage of the income from each book has been donated to aid projects and human-rights campaigns.

Updates Lonely Planet thoroughly updates each guidebook as often as possible. This usually means there are around two years between editions, although for more unusual or more stable destinations the gap can be longer. Check the imprint page (following the color map at the beginning of the book) for publication dates.

Between editions, up-to-date information is available in two free newsletters – the paper *Planet Talk* and email *Comet* (to subscribe, contact any Lonely Planet office) – and on our website at www.lonelyplanet.com. The *Upgrades* section of the website covers a number of important and volatile destinations and is regularly updated by Lonely Planet authors. *Scoop* covers news and current affairs relevant to travelers. And, lastly, the *Thorn Tree* bulletin board and *Postcards* section of the site carry unverified, but fascinating, reports from travelers.

Correspondence The process of creating new editions begins with the letters, postcards and emails received from travelers. This correspondence often includes suggestions, criticisms and comments about the current editions. Interesting excerpts are immediately passed on via newsletters and the website, and everything goes to our authors to be verified when they're researching on the road. We're keen to get more feedback from organizations or individuals who represent communities visited by travelers.

Lonely Planet gathers information for everyone who's curious about the planet – and especially for those who explore it firsthand. Through guidebooks, phrasebooks, activity guides, maps, literature, newsletters, image library, TV series and website, we act as an information exchange for a worldwide community of travelers.

Research Authors aim to gather sufficient practical information to enable travelers to make informed choices and to make the mechanics of a journey run smoothly. They also research historical and cultural background to help enrich the travel experience and allow travelers to understand and respond appropriately to cultural and environmental issues.

Authors don't stay in every hotel because that would mean spending a couple of months in each medium-size city and, no, they don't eat at every restaurant because that would mean stretching belts beyond capacity. They do visit hotels and restaurants to check standards and prices, but feedback based on readers' direct experiences can be very helpful.

Many of our authors work undercover; others aren't so secretive. None of them accept freebies in exchange for positive write-ups. And none of our guidebooks contain any advertising.

Production Authors submit their raw manuscripts and maps to offices in Australia, the USA, the UK or France. Editors and cartographers – all experienced travelers themselves – then begin the process of assembling the pieces. When the book finally hits the shops, some things are already out of date, we start getting feedback from readers and the process begins again....

WARNING & REQUEST

Things change – prices go up, schedules change, good places go bad and bad places go bankrupt – nothing stays the same. So, if you find things better or worse, recently opened or long since closed, please tell us and help make the next edition even more accurate and useful. We genuinely value all the feedback we receive. Julie Young coordinates a well-traveled team that reads and acknowledges every letter, postcard and email and ensures that every morsel of information finds its way to the appropriate authors, editors and cartographers for verification.

Everyone who writes to us will find their name in the next edition of the appropriate guidebook. They will also receive the latest issue of *Planet Talk*, our quarterly printed newsletter, or *Comet*, our monthly email newsletter. Subscriptions to both newsletters are free. The very best contributions will be rewarded with a free guidebook.

Excerpts from your correspondence may appear in new editions of Lonely Planet guidebooks, the Lonely Planet website, *Planet Talk* or *Comet*, so please let us know if you *don't* want your letter published or your name acknowledged.

Send all correspondence to the Lonely Planet office closest to you:

Australia: Locked Bag 1, Footscray, Victoria 3011
USA: 150 Linden St, Oakland, CA 94607
UK: 10A Spring Place, London NW5 3BH
France: 1 rue du Dahomey, 75011 Paris

Or email us at: talk2us@lonelyplanet.com.au

For news, views and updates, see our website: www.lonelyplanet.com

HOW TO USE A LONELY PLANET GUIDEBOOK

The best way to use a Lonely Planet guidebook is any way you choose. At Lonely Planet, we believe the most memorable travel experiences are often those that are unexpected, and the finest discoveries are those you make yourself. Guidebooks are not intended to be used as if they provided a detailed set of infallible instructions!

Contents All Lonely Planet guidebooks follow the same format. The Facts about the Country chapters or sections give background information ranging from history to weather. Facts for the Visitor gives practical information on issues like visas and health. Getting There & Away gives a brief starting point for researching travel to and from the destination. Getting Around gives an overview of the transport options available when you arrive.

The peculiar demands of each destination determine how subsequent chapters are broken up, but some things remain constant. We always start with background, then proceed to sights, places to stay, places to eat, entertainment, getting there and away, and getting around information – in that order.

Heading Hierarchy Lonely Planet headings are used in a strict hierarchical structure that can be visualized as a set of Russian dolls. Each heading (and its following text) is encompassed by any preceding heading that is higher on the hierarchical ladder.

Entry Points We do not assume guidebooks will be read from beginning to end, but that people will dip into them. The traditional entry points are the list of contents and the index. In addition, however, some books have a complete list of maps and an index map illustrating map coverage.

There may also be a color map that shows highlights. These highlights are dealt with in greater detail later in the book, along with planning questions. Each chapter covering a geographical region usually begins with a locator map and another list of highlights. Once you find something of interest in a list of highlights, turn to the index.

Maps Maps play a crucial role in Lonely Planet guidebooks and include a huge amount of information. A legend is printed on the back page. We seek to have complete consistency between maps and text, and to have every important place in the text captured on a map. Map key numbers usually start in the top left corner.

Although inclusion in a guidebook usually implies a recommendation, we cannot list every good place. Exclusion does not necessarily imply criticism. In fact, there are a number of reasons why we might exclude a place – sometimes it is simply inappropriate to encourage an influx of travelers.

Introduction

Hawaii's natural beauty is extraordinarily grand. Mark Twain fittingly called the Hawaiian chain 'the loveliest fleet of islands that lies anchored in any ocean.' Volcanic in origin, the Hawaiian Islands are high and rugged, lushly green and cut by spectacular gorges and valleys. The beaches are beautiful, ranging from bleached white to jet black. The terrain is amazingly varied, climbing from lowland deserts to alpine mountaintops, with everything from barren lava flows to tropical rain forests in between.

Hawaii is the world's most isolated archipelago, 2500 miles from the nearest landmass. Its isolation is so great that more than 90% of the thousands of animal and plant species that have evolved here exist nowhere else on earth.

Geologically, the islands are also unique. Hawaii (commonly called the 'Big Island') contains the world's most active volcano (Kilauea) and the highest mountain when measured from the sea floor (Mauna Kea), while Maui includes the largest dormant volcano on earth (Haleakala). On Molokai, the sea cliffs stand taller than anywhere else on the planet.

As one of the world's leading visitor destinations, Hawaii does have the expected mass tourism, high-rise hotels and crowded beaches. But that's only one side of the place.

You can also find scores of tourist-free areas and secluded beaches to explore, while your accommodation options include upland lodges, isolated resorts and cozy, island-style B&Bs. And the best the islands have to offer is still free for hikers and backcountry campers.

The Hawaiian Islands include some of the world's top surfing and windsurfing spots

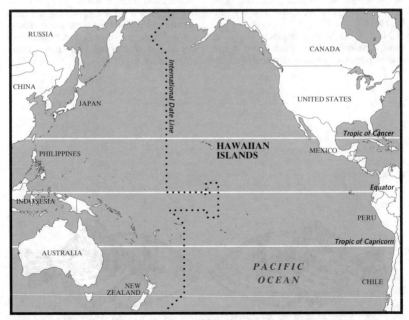

and enjoy excellent conditions for snorkeling, swimming, diving, kayaking and most other water sports.

Hawaii's climate is unusually pleasant for the tropics, as near-constant trade winds prevail throughout the year. Much of the time, the rain comes only in short daytime showers that are accompanied by rainbows.

Hawaii's six main islands all feature lovely beaches and splendid scenery. Their leeward coasts are sunny, dry and desert-like, with white sands and turquoise waters. The mountainous windward sides have tropical jungles, cascading waterfalls and pounding surf. The uplands are cool and green, with rolling pastures, small farms and ranches.

Oahu is the most crowded and developed of the islands, with Waikiki still providing nearly half of the tourist accommodations in Hawaii. Honolulu has all the pluses and minuses of urban life, from good museums and lively nightlife to congested traffic. The state's capital contains wonderful restaurants, with both inexpensive ethnic foods and gourmet cuisines. Oahu also has the best surf.

Maui is the second largest and second most developed of the islands, but it still boasts plenty of unspoiled places well off the beaten path. The scenic coastal drive to Hana and the sunrise at Haleakala are two of the island's highlights. Maui is also the best island for watching humpback whales.

The Big Island has two things the other islands don't: snow and erupting volcanoes. There's room to move, with space enough for cowboys, astronomers and traditional fishing villages, as well as alternative communities that have settled on the side of lava flows.

Kauai has Hawaii's greenest scenery, a deeply cut canyon resembling a mini-Grand Canyon and the famous razorback cliffs of the Na Pali Coast. The least developed of the four largest islands, it's a mecca for hikers, kayakers and other outdoor enthusiasts.

Molokai, the most Hawaiian of the islands, is rural, slow-paced and only lightly visited by tourists. Lanai, the smallest island, has recently reinvented itself, changing from a rural plantation that revolved around pineapple growing to a luxury resort destination.

Hawaii is ethnically diverse, with an appealing collage of East, West and Pacific peoples and cultures. While less than 1% of the population is pure Hawaiian, almost a quarter of the islanders boast some Hawaiian ancestry, and there's a resurgence of interest in traditional Hawaiian culture among islanders of all races.

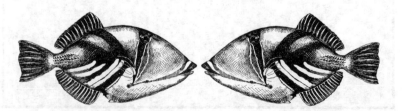

Facts about Hawaii

HISTORY

Hawaii is the northern point of the huge triangle of Pacific Ocean islands known as Polynesia. The other two points of the triangle are Easter Island to the southeast and New Zealand to the southwest.

The original settlers of Polynesia, which means 'many islands,' apparently followed a long migratory path through Southeast Asia, down through Indonesia and across Melanesia, before settling the Polynesian islands of Tonga and Samoa in about 1000 BC. Over the next 1500 years, they migrated to the more far-flung islands of Polynesia, with Hawaii being one of the last areas settled.

Archaeological evidence indicates the first Polynesians arrived in Hawaii from the Marquesas Islands between 500 and 700 AD. Among the links are ancient stone statues found on Hawaii's now-uninhabited Necker Island; these have striking similarities to statues found on the Marquesas Islands.

When the first wave of Tahitians arrived in Hawaii in about 1000 AD, they apparently fought and subjugated the Marquesans, who were forced to build temples, irrigation ditches and fishponds for the conquerors.

Hawaiian legends about a tribe of little people called *menehune* may well refer to the Marquesans. Indeed, the word 'menehune' is very similar to the Tahitian word for 'outcast.'

Ancient Hawaii

The earliest Hawaiians had simple animistic beliefs. Good fishing, a safe journey and a healthy child were all the result of being in tune with the spirits of nature. Offerings to the gods consisted of prayers and a share of the harvest.

Around the 12th century, in a later wave of migration, a powerful Tahitian *kahuna* (priest), Paao, arrived on the Big Island. Convinced that the Hawaiians were too lax in their worship, Paao introduced the concept of offering human sacrifice to the gods and he built the first *luakini heiau*, a type of temple where these sacrifices took place. He also established the *kapu* system, a practice of taboos that strictly regulated all social interaction.

Kapus forbade commoners from eating the same food or even walking the same ground as the *alii*, or royalty. A commoner who crossed the shadow of a king could be put to death. Kapus prohibited all women from eating coconuts, bananas, pork and certain varieties of fish.

Paao also decided that Hawaii's blue blood was too diluted and summoned the chief Pili from Kahiki (Tahiti) to establish a new royal lineage. With Pili as chief and Paao as high priest, a new ruling house was formed. Their dynasty was to last 700 years.

King Kamehameha the Great, like all the Big Island chiefs, traced his lineage to Pili. Likewise, Kamehameha's *kahuna nui* (high priest) descended from Paao.

Religion In the old Hawaiian religion there were four main gods: Ku, Lono, Kane and Kanaloa.

Ku was the ancestor god for all generations of humankind, past, present and future. He presided over all male gods while his wife, *Hina*, reigned over the female gods. When the sun rose in the morning, it was said to be Ku; when it set in the evening, it was Hina. Like yin and yang, they were responsible for heaven and earth.

Ku had many manifestations, one as the benevolent god of fishing, *Ku-ula* (Ku of the abundant seas), and others as the god of forests and the god of farming. People prayed to Ku when the harvest was scarce. At a time of drought or other such disaster, a temple would be built to appease Ku.

One of the most fearful of Ku's manifestations was *Kukailimoku* (Ku, the snatcher of land), the war god whom Kamehameha the Great worshipped. At the temples built

Petroglyphs

The ancient Hawaiians had no written history, although they did cut petroglyphs into smooth lava rock. Many of these carved pictures are stylized stick figures depicting warriors with spears, barking dogs, birds, canoes and other decipherable images. Some are linear marks, which may have been made to record important events or represent calendars or genealogical charts.

The meanings and purposes behind Hawaiian petroglyphs are not well understood. Some may have been intentionally cryptic, while others may just be random graffiti or the carvings of a budding artist.

Most petroglyphs are found along ancient footpaths and may have been clustered at sites thought to have spiritual power, or *mana* in Hawaiian.

The Big Island has the greatest concentration of petroglyphs, with several large fields full of carvings just a few minutes' walk from the main roads.

NED FRIARY

for the worship of Kukailimoku, the sacrificial offerings included not only food, pigs and chickens but also human beings.

Lono was the god in charge of the elements, bringing rain and an abundant harvest. He was also the god of fertility and peace.

Kane created the first man out of the dust of the earth and breathed life into him (the Hawaiian word for man is *kane*), and it was from Kane that the Hawaiian chiefs were said to have descended.

Ku, Lono and Kane together created the earth, the moon, the stars and the ocean.

Kanaloa, the fourth major god, was often pitted in struggles against the other three gods. When heaven and earth separated, it was Kanaloa who was placed in charge of the spirits on earth. Forbidden from drinking the intoxicating beverage *kava*, these spirits revolted and along with Kanaloa were driven to the underworld, where Kanaloa became the ruler of the dead.

Below the four main gods, there were 40 lesser gods. The best known of them was *Pele*, goddess of volcanoes. Her sister *Laka* was goddess of the hula, and another sister, *Poliahu*, was the goddess of snow.

The Hawaiians had gods for all occupations and natural phenomena. There was a god for the *tapa* (cloth) maker and a god for the canoe builder, as well as shark gods and mountain gods.

Heiaus The temples erected in ancient Hawaii, called *heiaus*, were built in two basic styles, both of which were constructed of lava rock. One was a simple rectangular enclosure of stone walls built directly on the ground. The other was a more substantial structure built of rocks piled high to form raised terraced platforms. (The remains of both types can still be found throughout the islands today, and this book points the way to many of them.)

Inside the heiaus were prayer towers, taboo houses and drum houses. These structures were made of native ohia wood, thatched with pili grass and tied with cord from the native olona shrub. Tikis, or god images, called *kii*, were carved of wood and placed around the prayer towers.

The heiaus were most commonly dedicated to Lono, the god of harvest, or Ku, the god of war. Those built in honor of Ku were called *luakini heiaus* and were the only ones where human sacrifices took place.

Heiaus were built in auspicious sites, often perched on cliffs above the coast or in other places thought to have *mana*, or 'spiritual power.' A heiau's significance lay not in the structure itself but in the mana of the site. When a heiau's mana was gone, it was abandoned.

The Makahiki

According to legend, the god Lono rode a rainbow down from the heavens to a breadfruit grove above Hiilawe Falls in the Big Island's Waipio Valley, where he discovered Kaikilani, a beautiful princess, in a paradise-like setting. They fell in love, married and moved across the island to Kealakekua Bay on the Kona Coast.

When Lono discovered that a chief was lusting after Kaikilani, he became enraged and beat Kaikilani, who, as she lay dying, professed her faithful love for Lono alone. In his grief, Lono traveled restlessly around the island challenging every man he met to a wrestling match and other competitions.

After four months, a still disheartened Lono set sail on a canoe with a tall mast hung with sails made of finely woven Niihau mats. The huge canoe was laden with so much food that it took 40 men to carry it down to Kealakekua Bay. Lono pledged to return one day on a floating island covered with trees and full of pigs and chickens.

The Hawaiians remembered Lono each year with a harvest festival, called the *makahiki*, which lasted from October to February. Numerous interisland competitions similar to the Olympics were held, including outrigger canoe races, fishing and surfing tournaments, foot races, wrestling matches and *holua* (sled) racing contests. Even during wartime, fighting would be suspended for the four months of the makahiki, so that the games and festivities dedicated to Lono could proceed.

Hawaiian Sports & Games

Holua (sled) racing was ancient Hawaii's most exciting spectator sport. Racers would ride prone on narrow wooden sleds, racing at high speed down steep hills along furrows that had been covered with pili grass or ti leaves to make the surface smooth. Many of the holua slide paths were a mile or two long.

Hawaiians were heavy bettors and often wagered on the holua races, as well as on foot races, surfing competitions and many other sports.

Surfing is a Hawaiian creation that was as popular in old Hawaii as it is today. When the waves were up, everyone was out. There were royal surfing grounds and spots for commoners as well. Boards used by commoners were made of breadfruit or *koa* wood and were about 6 feet long. Only the *alii* (royals) were free to use the long *olo* boards, which were up to 16 feet in length and made of *wiliwili*, the lightest of native woods. The boards were highly prized possessions and were carefully wrapped in *tapa* (cloth made from pounded bark) and suspended from the ceilings of homes.

Other popular Hawaiian games included *ulu maika*, in which rounded stone discs were rolled between two stakes, somewhat resembling bowling, and *moa pahee*, a similar game using a large wooden dart.

For the more passive, there was *konane*, a strategy game similar to checkers. Indentations were carved into a stone board to hold the pebbles of white coral and black lava that were used as playing pieces.

Captain Cook

The Hawaiian Islands were the last of the Polynesian islands to be 'discovered' by the West. This was due in large part to the fact that early European explorers who entered the Pacific around the tips of either Africa or South America centered their explorations in the Southern Hemisphere.

Although the English were the first known Western explorers to set foot on Hawaiian shores, there is speculation that Spanish sailors, whose galleons had been making annual runs between Mexico and the Philippines since 1565, may have stumbled upon Hawaii and kept the discovery a secret.

British explorer Captain James Cook spent the better part of a decade exploring and charting most of the South Pacific before chancing on Hawaii as he sailed from Tahiti in search of a northwest passage to the Atlantic.

On January 18, 1778, Cook spotted the islands of Oahu, Kauai and Niihau. The winds favored approaching Kauai, and on January 19, Cook's ships, the *Discovery* and the *Resolution*, sailed into Kauai's Waimea Bay. Cook named the Hawaiian archipelago the Sandwich Islands, in honor of the Earl of Sandwich.

Cook was surprised to find that the islanders showed a strong Tahitian influence in their appearance, language and culture. They sailed out in their canoes to welcome Cook's ships and were eager to trade fish and sweet potatoes for nails. The islanders were not interested in the useless beads and trinkets that Cook had used successfully as barter elsewhere in the Pacific. Metal, which was totally absent from the islands, was the only thing they wanted in exchange.

After two weeks of stocking provisions on Kauai and Niihau, Cook's expedition continued its journey north. Failing to find the fabled passage through the Arctic, Cook sailed back to Hawaii. By coincidence, he arrived on virtually the same date as his first visit the year before.

This time he discovered the remaining Hawaiian Islands. On January 17, 1779, Cook sailed into Kealakekua Bay on the Big Island, where a thousand canoes came out to greet him.

When Cook went ashore the next day, he was met by the high priest and guided to a temple lined with skulls. Everywhere the English captain went, people fell face down on the ground in front of him to the chant of 'Lono.'

As fate would have it, Cook had landed during the makahiki festival. The tall masts and white sails of Cook's ships – even the way he had sailed clockwise around the island – all fitted the legendary descriptions of how the god Lono would reappear.

Whether the priests actually believed Cook was the reincarnated Lono or whether they just used his appearance to enhance their power and add a little flair to the festivities is unknown. What is clear is that Cook never realized that both of his arrivals to Hawaii had coincided with the makahiki festivals – he assumed this was the way things were in everyday Hawaii.

There's little wonder Cook had a favorable impression of the islands. The islanders treated his crew with gracious hospitality. Hawaiian men invited the sailors to boxing matches and other competitions, and the women performed dances for the visitors and readily bedded down with them.

For men who had just spent months roaming inhospitable frozen tundra, this was paradise indeed.

The expedition's skilled artist, John Webber, was allowed to move freely in the villages. Today his detailed drawings of native people, costumes and village life constitute the best visual accounts of life in old Hawaii.

A few weeks after their arrival, the crews had restocked all the supplies needed except firewood. Rather than scour the hillsides for wood, Cook directed his men to haul onboard the temple railings and wooden images from the harborside temple dedicated to Lono. As Cook had been mistaken for Lono himself, the priests didn't attempt to stop Cook's men.

On February 4, the English vessels and their crews sailed north out of Kealakekua Bay headed for Maui. En route they ran into a storm off the northwest coast of the Big

Island, where the *Resolution* broke a fore-mast. Uncertain of finding a safe harbor in Maui, Cook decided to go back to Keala-kekua to repair the mast – a decision that would prove to be a fatal mistake.

When Cook and his crew arrived back at Kealakekua Bay on February 11, the islanders quickly appeared with the usual provisions to barter. The ruling alii, however, seemed upset with the ships' reappearance.

Apparently, the makahiki had ended, and not only was Cook's timing inauspicious, but so were the conditions of his return. This time he had arrived in a counter-clockwise direction and with a broken sail.

Thievery became a big problem, and after a boat was stolen, Cook ordered a blockade of Kealakekua Bay and then set off with a party of 11 men to the main village at the northern point of the bay. His intention was to capture the high chief Kalaniopuu and hold him until the cutter was returned. This was a tactic that Cook had used elsewhere in the Pacific and that he saw as reasonable diplomacy.

While Cook was en route to the village, a Hawaiian canoe attempting to sail out of the bay was fired upon by the English sailors. Unbeknownst to Cook's crew, the canoe was transporting a lower chief, Noekema, who was killed in the musket fire.

In the meantime, Cook had reached Kalaniopuu's house, and the chief had agreed to go with him. But as they walked down to the shore, Kalaniopuu's wailing wife ran after him, and the old chief suddenly balked and attempted to get away. In the midst of it all, word of Noekema's death reached the village, where a crowd quickly gathered.

Hoping to prevent bloodshed, Cook let the chief go, but the situation continued to escalate. As Cook was walking toward his boat, he shot at one of the armed Hawaiians who tried to block his way. The pistol mis-fired and the bullet bounced off the man's chest. The Hawaiians began to throw stones, and Cook ordered his men onshore to fire more shots.

Cook had always assumed, as had been the case on other Pacific islands, that if

trouble developed his men could fire a few shots and the natives, upon seeing the blood, would quickly disperse. That assumption proved wrong, however, and the Hawaiians, who were now in an angry frenzy, attacked rather than retreated.

The sailors in the boats fired another round as their captain began to make his way toward them over slippery rocks. Before they could reload, the crowd of Hawaiians moved in and Cook was struck on the head. Stunned by the blow, he staggered into the shallows, where the Hawaiians beat and stabbed him, passing the daggers to share in the kill. Four other sailors also died in the battle.

In this freak melee on a shore of the Sandwich Islands, Cook's last discovery, the life of the greatest explorer and navigator of the 18th century came to a bloody end.

Cook's men, shocked by his death, went on a rampage. They burned a village, be-headed two of their victims and rowed across the bay with the heads on poles.

Eventually, Kalaniopuu made a truce and returned those parts of Cook's dismem-bered body he was able to find. The skull was returned, but it had been stripped of its skin – a common practice bestowed upon great chiefs.

Cook's remains were buried at sea in a military funeral, at which time the Hawaiians

Captain Cook's death, by John Webber

placed a kapu on the bay and also held ceremonies of their own.

A week after Cook's February 14 death, the two English ships set sail, landing briefly on Oahu, Kauai and Niihau before finally leaving Hawaiian waters on March 15, 1779.

Cook and his crew left the Hawaiians a costly legacy: the iron that was turned into weapons, the introduced diseases that decimated the natives, and the first children of mixed blood. The crews also returned home with charts and maps that would allow others to follow in their wake, and in Britain and Europe their stories and drawings were published, stirring the public's keen sense of adventure.

Some of Cook's crew returned to the Pacific, leading their own expeditions. Among them was Captain George Vancouver, who brought the first cattle and horses to Hawaii, and the ill-fated William Bligh, who captained the *Bounty*.

Kamehameha the Great

At the time of Cook's arrival in Hawaii in 1778, the islands were divided into separate warring chiefdoms. Kamehameha the Great, who by 1791 had become sole chief of the Big Island, was to become the first to unite all the Hawaiian Islands under one rule.

In 1795, after conquering Maui and Molokai, Kamehameha successfully invaded Oahu and established his reign there as well.

Kamehameha then made two attempts to invade Kauai, the only island not yet under his control. In 1796 his canoes were caught in a storm at sea and forced to turn back before ever reaching the island. In 1804, while Kamehameha was in Oahu again preparing for an invasion of Kauai, his warriors were struck by a deadly outbreak of a feverish disease, probably cholera, and the invasion plans were scrapped. The luck of the draw may have been Kauai's at the time, but Kamehameha's power was too obvious to ignore, so in 1810 Kauai agreed by treaty to accept Kamehameha's overlordship.

The Sandalwood Trade

By the mid-1780s, Hawaii was becoming a popular port of call for Yankee traders plying the seas between North America and China.

In the early 1790s, American sea captains discovered that Hawaii had great stocks of fragrant sandalwood, worth a premium in China. When the captains showed interest in it, Hawaiian chiefs readily began bargaining the wood away in exchange for foreign weapons.

A lucrative three-way trade developed. From Hawaii, the ships sailed to Canton and traded loads of sandalwood for Chinese silks and porcelain, which were then carried back to New England ports and sold at a high profit. In New England, the ships were reloaded with goods to be traded to the Hawaiians.

Hawaii's forests of sandalwood were so vast at this time that the Chinese name for Hawaii was Tahn Heong Sahn, the 'Sandalwood Mountains.'

Trying to maintain the resource, Kamehameha eventually put a kapu on all sandalwood forests, giving himself total control over the trade. Even under his relatively shrewd management, the bulk of the profits ended up in the sea captains' fat pockets. Payment for the sandalwood was made in overpriced goods, originally cannons and rifles, and later exotic items such as European furniture.

While Kamehameha was careful not to devastate all his forests or overburden his subjects, his successor, Liholiho, partially lifted the royal kapu, allowing island chiefs to get in on the action. The chiefs began purchasing foreign luxuries by signing promissory notes to be paid in future shipments of sandalwood.

To pay off the rising 'debts,' Hawaiian *makaainana* (commoners) were forced into virtual servitude. Used like packhorses to haul all the wood, with sandalwood logs strapped to their backs with bands of ti leaves, the men who carted the wood were called *kua leho*, literally 'calloused backs' after the thick permanent layer of calluses that they developed. It was not uncommon for them to carry heavy loads 20 miles from the interior to ships waiting on the coast. During the height of the trade, missionaries recorded seeing caravans of as many as 3000 men carting wood.

In a few short years after Kamehameha's death, Hawaii's sandalwood forests were exhausted. In a futile attempt to continue the trade, Oahu's Governor Boki, who had heard of vast sandalwood reserves in the New Hebrides Islands, set sail in November 1829 with 500 men on an ill-conceived expedition to harvest the trees. Boki's ship was lost at sea, and the expedition's other ship, not too surprisingly, received a hostile welcome in New Hebrides.

In August 1830, 20 emaciated survivors sailed back into Honolulu Harbor. Boki had been a popular, if troubled, leader in a rapidly changing Hawaii. Hawaiians grieved in the streets of Honolulu when they heard of Boki's tragedy, and his death marked the end of the sandalwood trade.

End of the Old Religion

King Kamehameha died in 1819 at his Kamakahonu residence on the Big Island. The crown was passed to his reluctant son, Liholiho, who was proclaimed Kamehameha II. In reality, the power was passed to Kaahumanu, who had been the favorite of Kamehameha's 21 wives.

Kaahumanu was an ambitious woman, determined to break down the ancient kapu system of taboos that restricted her powers. Less than six months after Kamehameha's death, Kaahumanu threw a feast for women of royalty at the sacred Kamakahonu compound. Although one of the most sacred taboos strictly forbade men from eating with women, Kaahumanu forcefully persuaded Liholiho to sit beside her and join in the meal.

It was an otherwise uneventful meal; no angry gods manifested themselves. But in that one act, the old religion was cast aside, along with 600 years of taboos and restrictions. Hawaiians no longer had to fear being put to death for violating the kapu, and a flurry of temple-smashing and idol-burning quickly followed.

Those chiefs and kahuna who resisted were easily squelched by Liholiho, using the powerful army that Kamehameha had left behind. It was the end of an era.

The Missionaries

On April 19, 1820, the brig *Thaddeus* arrived from Boston with the first of the Christian missionaries to Hawaii. By a twist of fate, they landed in Kailua Bay, a stone's throw from Kamakahonu, where Kaahumanu had feasted the overthrow of the old religion six months earlier.

It was a timely arrival for the missionaries. The loss of their native religion and social structure had left the Hawaiians with a spiritual void into which the Christians zealously stepped.

The *Thaddeus* carried 23 Congregationalists, the first of 12 groups to be sent in the next three decades by the New England-based American Board of Commissioners of Foreign Missions. The leader of this initial group of missionaries was Hiram Bingham.

Hawaii's Alii

Hawaii is the only state in the USA to have once been ruled by a monarchy. Beginning with Kamehameha the Great's 1795 unification of the islands, the reign of Hawaii's *alii* (royalty) continued until the overthrow of Queen Liliuokalani by *haole* (Caucasian) businessmen in 1893. The following are the dates that each of Hawaii's monarchs lived.

Kamehameha the Great
c1758-1819
Kamehameha II (Liholiho)
1797-1824
Kamehameha III (Kauikeauoli)
1813-54
Kamehameha IV (Alexander Liholiho)
1834-63
Kamehameha V (Lot Kamehameha)
1830-72
Lunalilo (William C Lunalilo)
1832-74
Kalakaua (David Kalakaua)
1836-91
Liliuokalani (Lydia Liliuokalani)
1838-1917

The missionaries befriended Hawaiian royalty and made inroads quickly. After Queen Kaahumanu became seriously ill, Sybil Bingham, Hiram's wife, nursed her back to health. Shortly after, Kaahumanu showed her gratitude by passing a law forbidding work and travel on the Sabbath.

Up until this time, the Hawaiians had no written language. Using the Roman alphabet, the missionaries established a written Hawaiian language that allowed them to translate the Bible. They taught the Hawaiians to read and write and established the first 'American' high school west of the Rocky Mountains.

With encouragement from the missionaries, the Hawaiians quickly took on Western ways, Western clothing and Western laws.

Liholiho (Kamehameha II)

With Kaahumanu holding the real power, in November 1823 a floundering Liholiho set sail for England with his favorite wife to pay a royal visit to King George – although he failed to inform anyone in England of his plans.

When Liholiho arrived unannounced in London, misfitted in Western clothing and lacking in royal etiquette, the British press roasted him with racist caricatures. He never met King George. While being prepped in the social graces for an audience with the king, Liholiho and his wife came down with measles. They died in England within a few weeks of each other in July 1824.

The Whalers

Within a year of the missionaries' arrival, whalers began calling on Hawaiian ports. The first of these visitors were mostly New England Yankees, with a sprinkling of Gay Head Indians and former slaves. As more and more ships arrived, men of all nationalities roamed Hawaiian ports. Most were in their teens or twenties, ripe for adventure.

Towns sprang up with shopkeepers catering to the whalers, and saloons, brothels and hotels boomed. Honolulu and Lahaina became bustling ports of call.

From 1825 to 1870, Hawaii was the whaling center of the Pacific. It was a convenient way station for whalers hunting both the Arctic and Japanese whaling grounds. At the peak, between 500 and 600 whaling ships were pulling into Hawaiian ports each year.

Whaling brought big money to Hawaii, and the dollars spread beyond the whaling towns. Many Maui farmers got their start supplying the whaling ships with potatoes, Big Island cattle ranches grew with the rising demand for beef and even the average Hawaiian could earn a little money by turning in sailors who had jumped ship.

The Hawaiians themselves made good whalers, and sea captains gladly paid a $200 bond to the Hawaiian government for each *kanaka* (native Hawaiian) allowed to join their crew. Kamehameha IV even set up his own fleet of whaling ships that flew under the Hawaiian flag.

The whaling industry in the Pacific peaked in the mid-19th century. In a few short years, all but the most distant whaling grounds were depleted, with whalers forced to go farther afield to make their kills. By 1860, whale oil prices were dropping as an emerging petroleum industry began to produce a less expensive fuel for lighting.

The last straw for Pacific whaling came in 1871, when an early Arctic storm caught more than 30 ships by surprise, trapping them in ice floes above the Bering Strait. Although more than 1000 seamen were rescued, half of them Hawaiian, the fleet itself was lost.

Sugar Plantations

Ko, or sugarcane, arrived in Hawaii with the early Polynesian settlers. While the Hawaiians enjoyed chewing the cane for its juices, they never refined it into sugar.

The first known attempt to produce sugar in Hawaii was in 1802, when a Chinese immigrant in Lanai boiled crushed sugarcane in iron pots. Other Chinese soon set up small sugar mills on the scale of neighborhood bakeries.

In 1835, a young Bostonian, William Hooper, saw bigger possibilities in sugar and set out to establish Hawaii's first sugar plantation. Hooper convinced Honolulu investor Ladd & Company to put up the money for his venture and then worked out a deal with

Kamehameha III to lease 980 acres of land on Kauai for $300. His next step was to negotiate with Kauai's alii for the right to use Hawaiian laborers.

In the mid-1830s, Hawaii was still largely feudalistic. Commoners fished, farmed and lived on land that was under the domain of the local alii; in exchange, the commoners worked for the alii when needed. Therefore, before Hooper could hire any hands for his plantation, he had to first pay the alii a stipend to free the Hawaiians from their traditional work obligations.

The new plantation system, which introduced the concept of growing crops for profit rather than subsistence, marked the advent of capitalism and the introduction of wage labor in Hawaii.

The sugar industry emerged at the same time that whalers began arriving in force. Together, they became the foundation for Hawaii's moneyed economy.

By the 1850s, sugar plantations were established on Maui, Oahu and the Big Island, as well as on Kauai.

Sugarcane, a giant grass, only flourishes with abundant water, so plantations were limited to the rainier parts of Hawaii and even then were vulnerable to drought. In 1856, an 11-mile irrigation ditch was dug to bring mountain water to some Kauai cane fields, which were suffering from a drought. While this Kauai ditch was intended only as a rescue procedure, its success showed plantation owners the possibilities for irrigating heretofore unsuitable lands.

In the 1870s, the 17-mile Hamakua Ditch was dug on Maui, the first of several extensive aqueducts that would carry millions of gallons of water daily from upland rain forests to water-thirsty plantations. These artificial waterways turned dry central plains into drenched cane fields. Today, Hawaii is still crisscrossed with hundreds of miles of working ditches and aqueducts built a century ago.

In addition to the irrigation systems, the sugar companies built flumes and railroads to carry the cane from the fields to the mills. For over 100 years, sugar formed the backbone of the Hawaiian economy.

Hawaii's Immigrants

As the sugar industry boomed, Hawaii's native population declined, largely as the result of diseases introduced by foreigners.

To expand their operations, plantation owners began to look overseas for a labor supply. They needed immigrants accustomed to working long days in hot weather – and for whom the low wages would still seem like an opportunity.

In 1852, plantation owners began recruiting laborers from China. In 1868, recruiters went to Japan, and in the 1870s they brought in Portuguese from Madeira and the Azores. After Hawaii's 1898 annexation to the USA resulted in restrictions on Chinese immigration, plantation owners turned to Puerto Ricans and Koreans. Filipinos were the last group of immigrants brought to Hawaii to work the fields; the first wave came in 1906, the last in 1946.

Although these six ethnic groups made up the bulk of the field hands, a number of South Seas islanders, Scots, Scandinavians, Germans, Galicians, Spaniards and Russians all came in turn as well.

Each group brought its own culture, food and religion. Chinese clothing styles mixed with both Japanese kimonos and European bonnets. A dozen languages filled the air, and a unique pidgin English developed as a means for the various groups to communicate with one another.

Conditions varied with the ethnic group and the period. At the end of the 19th century, Japanese contract laborers were being paid $15 a month. After annexation, the contracts were considered indentured servitude and were declared illegal under US law. Still, wages as low as a dollar a day were common up until the 1930s.

In all, approximately 350,000 immigrants came to Hawaii to work on the sugar plantations. The continuous flow of immigrant workers replaced those who invariably found better options elsewhere. Although some workers came for a set period to save money and return home, others worked out their contracts and then moved off the plantations to farm their own plots or start their own businesses.

Plantation towns like Koloa, Paia and Honokaa grew up around the mills, with barber shops, fish markets, beer halls and bathhouses catering to the workers.

The major immigrant populations – Japanese, Chinese, Filipino and Western European – came to outnumber the native Hawaiians. Together, they created the unique blend of cultures that would continue to characterize Hawaii for generations to come.

Kamehameha III

The last son of Kamehameha the Great, Kamehameha III ruled for 30 years, from 1825 until his death in 1854. In 1840, he introduced Hawaii's first constitution, both to protect his powers and to adjust to changing times. The new constitution established Hawaii's first national legislature and provided for a Supreme Court.

Kamehameha III was also responsible for passing the Great Mahele land act, establishing religious freedom and giving all male citizens the right to vote.

Hawaii's only 'invasion' by a foreign power took place during Kamehameha's reign. In 1843, George Paulet, an upstart British commander upset about a petty land deal involving a British national, sailed into Honolulu commanding the British ship *Carysfort* and seized Oahu for six months. In that short period, he Anglicized street names, seized property and began to collect taxes.

To avoid bloodshed, Kamehameha III stood aside as the British flag was raised and the ship's band played 'God Save the Queen.' Queen Victoria herself wasn't flattered. After catching wind of the incident, she dispatched Admiral Richard Thomas to restore Hawaiian independence. Admiral Thomas re-raised the Hawaiian flag at the site of what is today Honolulu's Thomas Square. As the flag was raised, Kamehameha III uttered the words '*Ua mau ke ea o ka aina i ka pono*,' meaning 'The life of the land is perpetuated in righteousness,' which remains Hawaii's official motto.

The Great Mahele

The Great Mahele of 1848, which was introduced under the urging of influential missionaries, permanently altered Hawaiian concepts of land ownership. For the first time, land became a commodity that could be bought and sold.

Through the provisions of the Great Mahele, the king, who had previously owned all land, gave up title to the majority of it. Island chiefs were allowed to purchase some of the lands that they had controlled as fiefdoms for the king. Other lands, which were divided into 3-acre farm plots called *kuleana*, were made available to all Hawaiians. In order to retain title, chiefs and commoners alike had to pay a tax and register the land.

The chiefs had the option of paying the tax in property, and many did so. Commoners had no choice but to pay the taxes in cash. Although the act was intended to turn Hawaii into a country of small farms, in the end only a few thousand Hawaiians carried through with the paperwork and received kuleana.

In 1850, land purchases were opened to foreigners. Unlike the Hawaiians, the Westerners jumped at the new opportunity, and before the native islanders could clearly grasp the concept of private land ownership, there was little land left to own.

Within a few decades, the Westerners, who were much more adept at wheeling and dealing in real estate, owned 80% of all privately held lands. Even many of the Hawaiians who had gone through the process of getting their own kuleana eventually ended up selling it to the *haole* (white men) for a fraction of its real value.

Although the missionaries had painted an appealing picture for Kamehameha III (persuading him that that the majority of Hawaiians would come to own small farms), the Hawaiians suddenly became a landless people, drifting into ghettos in the larger towns. With a bitter twist, many of the missionaries themselves ended up with sizable tracts of land, and more than a few of them left the church to tend their new estates.

Although Hawaiian commoners had no rights to the land prior to the Great Mahele, they were free to move around and work the property of any chief. In return for their personal use of the land, they paid the chief in labor or with a percentage of their crops. In this way, they lived off the land. After the Great Mahele, they were simply *off* the land.

Kamehameha IV

Kamehameha IV had a short and rather confusing reign that lasted from 1855 to 1863. Some of his acts, whether intentional or not, contributed to a further eroding of native culture. He tried to give his rule an element of European regality, à la Queen Victoria, and he and Queen Emma, his consort, established a Hawaiian branch of the Church of England. He also passed a law mandating all children be given a Christian name along with their Hawaiian name, a statute that stayed on the books until 1967.

Struggles between those wanting to make the monarchy stronger and those wishing to weaken it marked Kamehameha IV's reign.

Kamehameha V

The most significant accomplishment of Kamehameha V, who reigned from 1863 to 1872, was the establishment of a controversial constitution that gave greater power to the king at the expense of elected officials. It also restricted the right to vote.

Kamehameha V, who suffered a severe bout of unrequited love, was the last king from a royal lineage that dated back to the 12th century. From childhood, he was enraptured by Princess Bernice Pauahi, who in the end turned down his proposals, opting instead to marry American Charles Reed Bishop. Jolted by the rejection, Kamehameha V never married, yet he also never gave up on the beloved princess. Even on his deathbed, he offered Princess Bernice his kingdom, which she declined.

As the bachelor king left no heirs, his death in December 1872 brought an end to the Kamehameha dynasty. Subsequent kings would be elected.

Lunalilo

King Lunalilo's short reign lasted from 1873 to 1874. His cabinet, made up largely of Americans, was instrumental in paving the way for a treaty of reciprocity with the USA.

Although the USA was the biggest market for Hawaiian sugar, US sugar tariffs ate heavily into profit margins. As a means of eliminating the tariffs, most plantation owners favored the annexation of Hawaii to the USA.

The US government was cool to the idea of annexation, but it warmed to the possibility of establishing a naval base on Oahu. In 1872, General John Schofield was sent to assess Pearl Harbor's strategic value. He was impressed with what he saw – the largest anchorage in the Pacific – and reported his enthusiasm back to Washington.

Although native Hawaiians protested in the streets and the Royal Troops even staged a little mutiny, there would eventually be a reciprocity agreement that would cede Pearl Harbor to the USA in exchange for duty-free access for Hawaiian sugar.

King Kalakaua

King David Kalakaua (1874-91) turned out to be Hawaii's last king. Although known as the 'Merrie Monarch,' he ruled in troubled times.

The first challenge to his reign came on election day. His contender had been the dowager Queen Emma, and when election results were announced, her followers rioted in the streets, requiring Kalakaua to request aid from US and British warships that happened to be in Honolulu Harbor at the time.

Despite the initial turmoil, Kalakaua went on to reign as a great Hawaiian revivalist. He brought back the hula, turning around decades of missionary repression against the 'heathen dance,' and penned the lyrics for the national anthem, *Hawaii Ponoi*, now the state song. He also tried to ensure some self-rule for native Hawaiians, who had become a minority in their own land.

When Kalakaua left for his first trip overseas, scores of Hawaiians came to the waterfront weeping. The last king to leave the islands, Kamehameha II, had come back in a coffin.

While in the USA, Kalakaua met with President Ulysses S Grant and persuaded him to accept Lunalilo's reciprocity treaty, which the US Congress had been resisting. Kalakaua also managed to postpone the ceding of Pearl Harbor for eight years. He returned to Hawaii a hero – to the business community for the treaty, and to the Hawaiians for simply making it back alive.

The king became a world traveler, visiting India, Egypt, Europe and Southeast Asia. Kalakaua was well aware that Hawaii's days as an independent Polynesian kingdom were numbered. To counter the Western powers that were gaining hold of Hawaii, he made a futile attempt to establish a Polynesian-Pacific empire. On a visit with the emperor of Japan, he even proposed a royal marriage between his niece, Princess Kaiulani, and a Japanese prince, but the Japanese declined.

Visits with other foreign monarchs gave Kalakaua a taste for royal pageantry. He returned home to build Iolani Palace for what the haole business community thought was an extravagant $360,000. Many influential whites saw the king as a lavish spender, fond of partying and hosting public luaus.

King David Kalakaua brought back the hula.

As Kalakaua incurred debts, he became increasingly less popular with the sugar barons, whose businesses were now the backbone of the economy. They formed the Hawaiian League in 1887 and developed their own armies, which stood ready to overthrow Kalakaua. The league presented Kalakaua with a list of demands and forced him to accept a new constitution strictly limiting his powers. The new law of the land also limited suffrage to property owners, excluding the vast majority of Hawaiians.

On July 30, 1889, a group of about 150 Hawaiians attempted to overthrow the new constitution by occupying Iolani Palace. Called the Wilcox Rebellion after its part-Hawaiian leader, it was a confused and futile attempt, and the rebels were forced to surrender.

Kalakaua died in San Francisco in 1891.

Queen Liliuokalani

Kalakaua was succeeded by his sister, Liliuokalani, wife of Oahu governor John O Dominis.

Queen Liliuokalani (1891-93) was even more determined than Kalakaua to increase the power of the monarchy. She charged that the 1887 constitution had illegally been forced upon King Kalakaua; the Hawaii Supreme Court upheld her contention.

In January 1893, as Liliuokalani was preparing to proclaim a new constitution that restored royal powers, a group of armed haole businessmen occupied the Supreme Court and declared the monarchy overthrown. The white men announced a provisional government, led by Sanford Dole, son of a pioneer missionary. A contingent of US sailors came ashore, ostensibly to protect the property of US citizens, but instead the troops marched on the palace and positioned their guns at the queen's residence. Realizing it was futile to oppose US forces, the queen opted to avoid bloodshed and stepped down.

The provisional government immediately appealed to the USA for annexation, while the queen appealed to the USA to restore the monarchy. To Dole's dismay, the timing of events was to the queen's advantage. US

President Grover Cleveland, a Democrat, had just replaced a Republican administration and his sentiments clearly favored the queen.

Cleveland sent an envoy, James Blount, to investigate the situation and determine what course of action the US government should take.

In the meantime, Cleveland received Queen Liliuokalani's niece, Princess Kaiulani, who, at the time of the coup, had been in London being prepared for the Hawaiian throne. The beautiful 18-year-old princess eloquently pleaded the monarchy's case. She also made a favorable impression with the American press, which largely caricatured those involved in the coup as dour, greedy buffoons.

Cleveland ordered the US flag be taken down and the queen restored to her throne. However, the provisional government, now firmly in power, turned a deaf ear, declaring that Cleveland was meddling in 'Hawaiian' affairs.

The new government, with Dole as president, inaugurated itself as the Republic of Hawaii on July 4, 1894. Although Cleveland initially favored reversing the situation, he also knew that ousting a government of white Americans and replacing them with native Hawaiians could endanger his own political future. His subsequent actions were largely limited to rhetoric.

Weary of waiting for outside intervention, in early 1895 a group of Hawaiian royalists attempted a counter-revolution that was easily squashed in a fortnight. Liliuokalani was accused of being a conspirator and placed under arrest.

To humiliate her, the provisional authorities tried her in her own palace and referred to her only as Mrs John O Dominis. She was fined $5000 and sentenced to five years of hard labor, later reduced to nine months of house arrest at the palace.

Liliuokalani spent the rest of her life in her husband's residence, Washington Place, one block from the palace. When she died in November 1917, all of Honolulu came out for the funeral procession. To most islanders, Liliuokalani was still their queen.

Annexation

With the Spanish-American War of 1898, Americans acquired a taste for expansionism.

Along with Pearl Harbor, Hawaii took on a new strategic importance, being midway between the USA and its newly acquired possession, the Philippines. The annexation of Hawaii passed in the US Congress on July 7, 1898. Hawaii entered the 20th century as a territory of the USA.

In just over a century of Western contact, the native Hawaiian population had been decimated by foreign diseases to which they had no immunities. Captain Cook's crew introduced venereal disease in 1778. The whalers followed with cholera and smallpox, and the Chinese immigrants who replaced Hawaiian laborers brought leprosy. By the end of the 19th century, the native Hawaiian population had been reduced from an estimated 300,000 to less than 50,000.

Descendants of the early missionaries had taken over first the land and now the government. Without ever having fought a single battle against a foreign power, Hawaiians had lost their islands to ambitious foreigners. All in all, as far as native Hawaiians were concerned, annexation was nothing to celebrate.

The Chinese and Japanese were also uneasy. One of the reasons for the initial reluctance of the US Congress to annex Hawaii had been the racial mix of the islands' population. There were already restrictions on Chinese immigration to the USA, with restrictions on Japanese immigration expected to follow.

In a rush to avoid a labor shortage, the sugar plantation owners quickly brought 70,000 Japanese immigrants into Hawaii. By the time the immigration wave was over, the Japanese accounted for more than 40% of Hawaii's population.

In the years since the reciprocity treaty with the US, signed in the 1870s, sugar production had increased tenfold. Those who ruled the land ruled the government, and closer bonding with the USA didn't change the formula. In 1900, US President McKinley appointed Sanford Dole the first territorial governor.

World War I

Soon after annexation, the US Navy established a huge Pacific headquarters at Pearl Harbor and built Schofield Barracks, the largest US army base anywhere. The military quickly became the leading sector of Oahu's economy.

The islands were relatively untouched by WWI, even though the first German prisoners of war 'captured' by the USA were in Hawaii. They were escorted off the German gunboat *Grier*, which had the misfortune to be docked at Honolulu Harbor when war broke out.

The war affected people in Hawaii in other ways. Heinrich Hackfeld, a German sea captain long settled in the islands, had established Hawaii's most successful merchandise stores, BF Ehler's & Company. He had also developed a real estate empire rooted in sugar, by purchasing Lahaina's Pioneer Mill, among other properties. He lost it all during WWI.

Anti-German sentiments forced Hackfeld to liquidate his holdings, and American Factors (Amfac) took over his properties, renaming the stores Liberty House. Today you'll find a Liberty House on most of the islands.

Pineapples & Planes

In the early years of the 20th century, pineapple emerged as Hawaii's second major export crop. James Dole, a cousin of Sanford Dole, purchased the island of Lanai in 1922 and turned it into the world's largest pineapple plantation. Although sugar remained Hawaii's most lucrative crop in export value, the more labor-intensive pineapple eventually surpassed it in terms of employment.

In 1936, Pan American flew the first passenger flights from the US mainland to Hawaii, an aviation milestone that ushered in the transpacific air age. Hawaii was now only hours away from the US West Coast.

World War II

On December 7, 1941, a wave of Japanese bombers attacked Pearl Harbor, forcing the USA into WWII. The attack caught the US fleet totally by surprise, even though there had been warnings, some of which were far from subtle.

At 6:40 am, the USS *Ward* spotted a submarine's conning tower approaching the entrance of Pearl Harbor. The *Ward* immediately attacked with depth charges and sank what turned out to be one of five midget Japanese submarines launched to penetrate the harbor. At 7:02 am, a radar station on the North Shore of Oahu reported some planes approaching. Even though they were coming from the wrong direction, they were assumed to be US planes from the mainland.

At 7:55 am, Pearl Harbor was hit. Within minutes, the USS *Arizona* went down in a fiery inferno, trapping 1177 men beneath the surface. Twenty other US ships were sunk or damaged, along with 347 aircraft. More than 2500 people were killed.

It wasn't until 15 minutes after the bombing started that US anti-aircraft guns began to shell the Japanese warplanes. The Japanese lost 29 aircraft in the attack.

After the smoke cleared, Hawaii was placed under martial law, and Oahu took on the face of a military camp. Already heavily militarized, vast tracts of Hawaii's land were turned over to the US armed forces for expanded military bases, training and weapons testing. Much of that land would never be returned. Throughout the war, Oahu served as the command post for the USA's Pacific operations.

Following the attack on Pearl Harbor, a wave of suspicion landed on the *nisei* (people of Japanese descent) in Hawaii. While sheer numbers prevented the sort of internment practices that took place on the mainland, the Japanese in Hawaii were subject to interrogation, and their religious and civic leaders were sent to mainland internment camps.

Japanese language schools were closed, and many of the teachers were arrested. Posters were hung in restaurants and other public places warning islanders to be careful about speaking carelessly in front of anyone of Japanese ancestry. Nisei were dismissed from their posts in the Hawaiian National Guard and prevented from joining the armed services.

The Japanese sank a battleship like this one at Pearl Harbor.

Eventually, Japanese-Americans were allowed to volunteer for a segregated regiment, although they were kept on the mainland and out of action for much of the war.

During the final stages of the war, when fighting was at its heaviest, the nisei were given the chance to form a combat unit. Volunteers were called, and more than 10,000 nisei signed up, forming two distinguished Japanese-American regiments. One of these, the 442nd Second Regimental Combat Team, which was sent into action on the European front, became the most decorated fighting unit in US history.

The veterans returned to Hawaii with different expectations. Many went on to college using the 'GI Bill' and then became some of Hawaii's most influential lawyers, judges and civic leaders. Among the veterans of the 442nd is Hawaii's senior US senator, Daniel Inouye, who lost an arm in the fighting.

Unionizing Hawaii

The feisty mainland-based International Longshoremen's and Warehousemen's Union (ILWU) began organizing Hawaiian labor in the 1930s.

After WWII, the ILWU organized an intensive campaign against the 'Big Five' – C Brewer, Castle & Cooke, Alexander & Baldwin, Theo Davies and Amfac – Hawaii's biggest businesses and landholders, all of which had roots in sugar.

The ILWU's six-month waterfront strike in 1949 virtually halted all shipments to and from Hawaii. The union went on to organize plantation strikes that resulted in Hawaii's sugar and pineapple workers becoming the world's highest paid.

The new union movement helped develop a political opposition to the staunchly Republican big landowners, who had maintained a stronghold on the political scene since annexation.

In the 1950s, McCarthyism, the fanatical wave of anti-Communism that had swept the mainland, spilled over to Hawaii. In the fallout, the leader of the ILWU in Hawaii, Jack Hall, was tried and convicted of being a Communist.

Postwar Hawaii

WWII brought Hawaii closer to the center stage of American culture and politics.

The prospect of statehood had long been the central topic in Hawaiian politics. Three decades had passed since Hawaii's first delegate to the US Congress, Prince Jonah Kuhio Kalanianaole, introduced the first statehood bill in 1919. The bill had received a cool reception in Washington at that time, and there were mixed feelings in Hawaii as well. However, by the time the war was over, opinion polls showed that two out of three Hawaiian residents favored statehood.

Still, Hawaii was too much of a melting pot for many politicians to support statehood, particularly those from the rigidly segregated southern states. To the overwhelmingly white and largely conservative Congress, Hawaii's multiethnic community was too exotic and foreign to be thought of as 'American.'

Congress was also concerned with the success of Hawaiian labor strikes and the growth of membership in the ILWU. It all combined to keep statehood at bay until the end of the 1950s.

Statehood

In March 1959, the US Congress finally passed legislation to make Hawaii a state. On June 27, a plebiscite was held in Hawaii, with more than 90% of the islanders voting for statehood. The island of Niihau was the only precinct to vote against it.

On August 21, 1959, after 61 years of territorial status, Hawaii became the 50th state of the USA.

Hawaiian Sovereignty

Over the past decade, a Hawaiian sovereignty movement, intent on righting some of the wrongs of the past century, has become a forefront political issue in Hawaii. The success of the Protect Kahoolawe movement (see the Kahoolawe chapter), growing discontent over the mismanagement of Hawaiian Home Lands (see the boxed text) and the heightened consciousness created by the 1993 centennial anniversary of Queen Liliuokalani's overthrow have all served as rallying points. Things are still in a formative stage, and a consensus on what form sovereignty should take has yet to emerge.

Ka Lahui Hawaii, the largest of the many Hawaiian sovereignty groups, has adopted a constitution for a Hawaiian nation within the USA, similar to that of 300 Native American groups on the mainland who have their own tribal governments and lands. Ka Lahui Hawaii wants all Hawaiian Home Lands, as well as the title to much of the crown land taken during annexation, turned over to native Hawaiians. These lands include nearly 1¾ million acres that were held by the Hawaiian Kingdom at the time of the 1893 overthrow. On Kauai alone, the crown lands represent nearly half of the island, including extensive park lands, such as those along the Na Pali Coast.

Other native Hawaiian groups are also calling for self-determination. Some favor the restoration of the monarchy while others focus on monetary reparations, but the majority are looking at some form of a nation-within-a-nation model.

One sovereignty demand was addressed in 1993, when US president Bill Clinton signed a resolution apologizing 'to Native Hawaiians for the overthrow of the Kingdom of Hawaii on January 17, 1893, with participation of agents and citizens of the United States, and the deprivation of the rights of Native Hawaiians to self-determination.' The apology went on to 'acknowledge the ramifications of the overthrow' and expressed a commitment to 'provide a proper foundation for reconciliation.'

Ka Lahui introduced state legislation to establish itself as the steward of a new Hawaiian nation, and two other sovereignty bills were also introduced. In part to sort out the disparity between the three bills, the state legislature established the Hawaiian Sovereignty Advisory Commission as a mechanism for native Hawaiians to determine what form sovereignty should take. The commission itself, however, became a source of conflict, as all 20 of the commission members were chosen by the governor, and only 12 of those were selected from nominees submitted by native Hawaiian organizations. Consequently, some groups, such as Ka Lahui and Nation of Hawaii, refused to participate in the commission.

In the summer of 1996, a commission-sponsored mail-in vote, open to all people of Hawaiian ancestry, was held on the ballot question: 'Shall the Hawaiian People elect delegates to propose a native Hawaiian government?' It was a first-step vote to determine if native Hawaiians wanted to establish a sovereignty process that would be based on electing delegates and holding a convention to chart out their future.

Of the 80,000 ballots mailed to native Hawaiians worldwide, some 30,000 people voted. The initiative passed, with 73% voting yes and 27% against, but in many ways it was a far more divided vote. Some native Hawaiians, including members of Ka Lahui, felt the process was co-opted by the state, which had provided funding for the ballot, and they boycotted the vote. The controver-

sial commission itself disbanded after the vote, and the state declared it would not provide funding for the delegate elections and convention. A nonprofit group, Ha Hawaii, which includes former members of the commission, then spent two years raising funds for that purpose.

In January 1999, the election organized by Ha Hawaii took place, with voters selecting 85 delegates to form a Hawaiian Convention aimed at charting the sovereignty course. However, many groups boycotted this election as well, claiming the Ha Hawaii vote was influenced by the state and the process itself was flawed. Consequently, the

Hawaiian Home Lands

In 1920, under the sponsorship of Prince Jonah Kuhio Kalanianaole, the Territory of Hawaii's congressional delegate, the US Congress passed the Hawaiian Homes Commission Act. The act set aside almost 200,000 acres of land for homesteading by native Hawaiians, who were by this time the most landless ethnic group in Hawaii. Despite this apparently generous gift, the land was but a small fraction of the crown lands that were taken from the Kingdom of Hawaii when the USA annexed the islands in 1898.

Under the legislation, people of at least 50% Hawaiian ancestry were eligible to apply for 99-year leases at $1 a year. Originally, most of the leases were for 40-acre parcels of agricultural land, although more recently residential lots as small as a quarter of an acre have been allocated under the plan.

Hawaii's prime land, already in the hands of the sugar barons, was excluded from the act. Much of what was designated for homesteading was on far more barren turf.

Indeed, the first homesteading village, at Kalanianaole on Molokai, failed when the wells drew brackish waters and destroyed the newly established crops. Still, many Hawaiians were able to make a go of it, settling homesteads on Oahu, the Big Island, Kauai, Maui and Molokai. Presently, there are about 6500 native Hawaiian families living on about 30,000 acres of homestead lands.

As with many acts established to help native Hawaiians, administration of the Hawaiian Home Lands has been riddled with abuse. The majority of the land has not been allocated to native Hawaiians but has been leased out to big business, ostensibly as a means of creating an income for the administration of the program.

Parker Ranch on the Big Island has about 30,000 acres of Hawaiian Home Lands under lease at just a few dollars an acre. Kekaha Sugar, an Amfac subsidiary, leases the lion's share of Kauai's 18,569 acres of Hawaiian Home Lands, while less than 5% is made available to native Hawaiians.

In addition, the federal, state and county governments have illegally, and with little or no compensation, taken large tracts of Hawaiian Home Lands for their own use. The Lualualei Naval Reservation alone constitutes one-fifth of all homestead lands on Oahu, where more than 5000 native Hawaiians remain on the waiting list – some for as many as 30 years.

voter turnout was only 8.7% – fewer than 9,000 of the 102,000 eligible voters participated. With so few people embracing the election, the future of the convention remains in doubt, and there's still no clear consensus on a forum for debating sovereignty issues.

Although attitudes may change once the movement takes shape, polls show that a significant majority of all Hawaii residents support the concept of Hawaiian sovereignty if it's within the framework of a nation-within-a-nation. Interestingly, the support doesn't vary greatly along ethnic lines.

Incidentally, the Hawaiian flag flown upside down as a sign of distress has come to symbolize the Hawaiian sovereignty movement.

GEOGRAPHY

The Hawaiian Islands stretch 1523 miles in a line from Kure Atoll in the northwest to the Big Island in the southeast. Ka Lae, on the Big Island, is the southernmost point of the USA.

The equator is 1470 miles south of Honolulu, and all the main islands are in the tropic of Cancer. Hawaii shares the same latitude with Hong Kong, Bombay and Mexico's Yucatán Peninsula.

Hawaii's eight major islands are, from largest to smallest, Hawaii (the Big Island), Maui, Oahu, Kauai, Molokai, Lanai, Niihau and Kahoolawe. Together, they have a total land area of 6470 sq miles, which includes 96 small nearshore islands with a combined area of less than 3 sq miles.

The Northwestern Hawaiian Islands lie scattered across a thousand miles of ocean west of Kauai. They consist of 33 islands in 10 clusters with a total land area of just under 5 sq miles.

In total, Hawaii is smaller than Fiji but a bit larger than the US state of Connecticut.

Hawaii's highest mountain is Mauna Kea on the Big Island, which is 13,796 feet above sea level. According to the *Guinness Book of Records*, it's the world's highest mountain (33,476 feet) when measured from the ocean floor. Mauna Loa, also on the Big Island, is Hawaii's second highest mountain, at 13,677 feet.

GEOLOGY

The Hawaiian Islands are the tips of massive mountains, created by a crack in the earth's mantle that has been spewing out molten rock for more than 25 million years. The hot spot is stationary, but the ocean floor is part of the Pacific Plate, which is moving northwest at the rate of about 3 inches a year. (The eastern edge of this plate is California's San Andreas Fault.)

As weak spots in the earth's crust pass over the hot spot, molten lava bursts through as volcanoes, building underwater mountains. Some of them finally emerge above the water as islands.

Every new volcano eventually creeps northward past the hot spot that created it. The farther from the source, the lower the volcanic activity, until the volcano is eventually cut off completely and turns cold.

Once the lava stops, it's a downhill battle. The forces of erosion – wind, rain, waves – slowly wash the mountains away. In addition, the settling of the ocean floor causes the land to gradually recede.

Thus, the once mountainous Northwestern Hawaiian Islands, the oldest in the Hawaiian chain, are now low, flat atolls that in time will be totally submerged.

The Big Island, Hawaii's southernmost island, is still in the birthing process. Its most active volcano, Kilauea, is directly over the hot spot. In its latest eruptive phase, which began in 1983 and still continues, Kilauea has pumped out more than 2 billion cubic yards of lava, making this the largest known volcanic eruption in Hawaii's history.

Less than 30 miles southeast of the Big Island, a new seamount named Loihi has already risen 15,000 feet on the ocean floor. The growing mounds of lava are expected to break the ocean surface within 10,000 years – however, if the volcano were to become hyperactive, it could emerge within a century or two.

In 1987, the Woods Hole Oceanographic Institution explored Loihi with *Alvin*, the same deepwater mini-sub that had discovered the *Titanic* wreck the year before. The scientists measured Loihi's summit to be 3117 feet below the surface of the water.

Hawaii's volcanoes are shield volcanoes, which form not by explosion but by a slow build-up of layer upon layer of lava. They rise from the sea with gentle slopes and a relatively smooth surface. It's only after eons of facing the elements that their surfaces become sharply eroded. It's for this reason that the Na Pali cliffs on Kauai, the oldest of the main islands, are the most jagged in Hawaii.

Hawaii's active volcanoes are Kilauea and Mauna Loa, both on the Big Island. The Big Island's Mauna Kea and Hualalai and Maui's Haleakala are dormant, with future eruptions possible. The volcanoes on all the other Hawaiian Islands are considered extinct.

CLIMATE

Overall, Hawaii has great weather. It's balmy and warm, with northeasterly trade winds prevailing most of the year.

Average temperatures differ only about 7°F from winter to summer. Near the coast, daily temperatures average a high of about 83°F and a low of around 68°F.

The rainiest time of the year is from December to March. Not only does winter have about twice the rainfall of summer, but winter storms can also hang around for days. In summer, the rain is more likely to fall as passing showers. This doesn't mean winter is a bad time to go to Hawaii; it just means the weather is more of a gamble.

Rainfall varies even more with location than with season. In places like Kailua-Kona on the Big Island, you can sunbathe on the beach for all but a few days a year. At the same time, you can watch typical afternoon showers pour on the hill slopes just a mile or two inland and know you're well beyond reach.

Hawaii's high volcanic mountains trap the trade winds that blow from the northeast, blocking moisture-laden clouds and bringing abundant rainfall to the windward side of the islands. Hilo, the rainiest city in the USA with 130 inches annually, is on the windward side of the Big Island.

Conversely, the same mountains block the wind and rain from the southwesterly, or leeward, side of the islands, so it's there

The Creation Myth

The early Hawaiians were astutely tuned in to geological forces and were well aware of the order in which the islands were created. Their creation story goes something like this:

Pele, the goddess of volcanoes and fire, was born of the marriage of earth and sky. She is both Creator and Destroyer (not unlike the Hindu god Shiva). Her eruptions of molten lava both build the mountains and wreak havoc over everything in their path.

Pele was driven from her home in the northwestern shoals by a jealous older sister, Na Maka o Kahai, goddess of the seas. Pele fled to the southeast and built her home in a crater on Niihau, then on Kauai, then Oahu, and each island in turn. Each time she dug down into the fiery earth deeper than the time before, and each time she was chased away by her sister, the sea.

After being forced from her home on Haleakala on Maui, Pele crossed over to the Big Island. There she built her highest mountains yet and, in their volcanic recesses, made a home far from the reaches of Na Maka o Kahai.

The sea goddess, however, is still never far from Pele's doorstep. She persistently wears away at Pele's home, her waves taking on the lava, eroding it and crushing it into sand.

In time, Pele will again be forced to move on, but for now she makes her home deep in Kilauea, the most active volcano on earth.

✿ ✿ ✿ ✿ ✿ ✿ ✿ ✿ ✿ ✿ ✿ ✿ ✿ ✿

you'll find the driest, sunniest conditions and the calmest waters. Leeward areas generally receive only 10 to 25 inches of rain a year.

During *kona* weather, the winds blow from the south, a shift from the typical northeast trades. The ocean swell pattern also changes at this time – snorkeling spots suddenly become surfing spots and vice

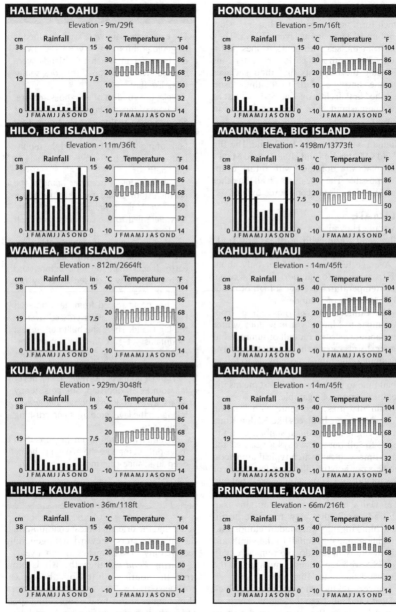

HALEIWA, OAHU
Elevation - 9m/29ft

HONOLULU, OAHU
Elevation - 5m/16ft

HILO, BIG ISLAND
Elevation - 11m/36ft

MAUNA KEA, BIG ISLAND
Elevation - 4198m/13773ft

WAIMEA, BIG ISLAND
Elevation - 812m/2664ft

KAHULUI, MAUI
Elevation - 14m/45ft

KULA, MAUI
Elevation - 929m/3048ft

LAHAINA, MAUI
Elevation - 14m/45ft

LIHUE, KAUAI
Elevation - 36m/118ft

PRINCEVILLE, KAUAI
Elevation - 66m/216ft

versa. Kona storms usually occur in winter and are very unpredictable.

The summits of Mauna Kea and Mauna Loa on the Big Island receive snow each winter, and in some years Haleakala on Maui sports a short-lived snow cover as well. The lowest temperature ever recorded on Mauna Kea, Hawaii's coldest spot, was 11°F, while the highest temperature there was 66°F.

ECOLOGY & ENVIRONMENT

Hawaii's native ecosystems have been greatly stressed by the introduction of exotic flora and fauna species. Erosion caused by free-ranging cattle and goats and the monocrop cultures of sugarcane and pineapple have destroyed native ground covers, resulting in washouts that sweep prime topsoil into the sea and choke nearshore reefs. Tourism-related development has long taken its toll, particularly the proliferation of large resort hotels and golf courses, which commonly are built on fragile coastal lands.

On the plus side, Hawaii has no polluting heavy industry, roadside billboards are not allowed and environmental awareness is more advanced than on much of the US mainland.

There are more than 150 environmental groups in Hawaii, ranging from chapters of international organizations fighting to save the rain forest to neighborhood groups working to protect local beaches from impending development.

One of the broadest-based is the Hawaii chapter of the Sierra Club, which has groups on all the main islands. Its activities range from political activism on local environmental issues to weekend outings aimed at eradicating invasive plants from native forests.

The nonprofit Earthjustice Legal Defense Fund (which until recently was called the Sierra Club Legal Defense Fund) is in the forefront, pressing legal challenges against abuses to Hawaii's fragile environment. In conjunction with Greenpeace Hawaii, the group has forced the state of Hawaii to prohibit jet skis in waters used by endangered humpback whales. On behalf of several environmental groups, the Legal Defense

Fund filed legal challenges halting a geothermal energy project on the Big Island that would have carved up one of Hawaii's last remaining lowland rain forests.

In still another challenge, the Legal Defense Fund took on both the National Rifle Association and the state to force the removal of introduced mouflon game sheep from the slopes of Mauna Kea. The sheep were found to be the primary cause for the decline of the *palila*, a native honeycreeper. A landmark case, it marked the first time that habitat destruction was successfully defined as the 'taking' (meaning killing, harming or harassing) of an endangered species under the US Endangered Species Act.

In 1999, the Legal Defense Fund, together with the Center for Marine Conservation and the Sea Turtle Restoration Project, filed a lawsuit to stop the ongoing killing of endangered sea turtles by an emerging longline fishing industry. Most of the 100 longline ships in Hawaii's waters arrived in the past decade after depleting fishing stocks in the Atlantic Ocean. Although these operations target swordfish or tuna, they lay fishing lines up to 30 miles long, carrying thousands of baited hooks that catch anything that goes for the bait, including seabirds, marine mammals and hundreds of endangered sea turtles.

The Nature Conservancy of Hawaii has opted for a different approach; it protects Hawaii's rarest ecosystems by buying up vast tracts of land and working out long-term stewardships with some of Hawaii's biggest landholders. One project included purchasing the Kipahulu Valley on Maui in conjunction with the state and turning the 11,000 acres over to the federal government to become part of Haleakala National Park.

On Molokai, the Nature Conservancy manages the rain forest at Kamakou Preserve and at Pelekunu Valley on the island's wet northeast coast, as well as the windswept Moomomi dunes on the dry northwest coast. The group also manages a crater above Hanauma Bay on Oahu, the Waikamoi rain forest on Maui, a native dryland forest in Lanai and a Kauai nesting site for

'Agricultural' Golf Courses

In the late 1980s, the state passed a controversial bill that allowed golf courses to be built on agriculture-zoned land. This bill led to the gobbling up of major tracts of farmland by Japanese developers and the eviction of small leasehold farmers.

Hawaii is one of the few Pacific island chains where island-grown produce has been relatively abundant, and the eviction of farmers who have been growing crops on the land for generations has the potential to make the islands more reliant on imported foods. One of the slogans of the resistance movement is: 'No can eat golf balls.'

Currently, the state has about 80 golf courses, but the proposed courses on the drawing board could double that number in the not-too-distant future.

Not surprisingly, attempts to control the development of new golf courses is one of the forefront issues for island environmentalists.

the *ao* (Newell's shearwater), a threatened bird species once thought extinct. In addition, the Nature Conservancy has jurisdiction over a few other areas, including an undisclosed spot on Maui that harbors a lava tube ecosystem with insects that exist solely at this site.

FLORA & FAUNA

The Hawaiian Islands chain, 2500 miles from the nearest continental land mass, is the most geographically isolated place in the world.

All living things that reached Hawaii's shores were carried across the ocean on the wind or the waves – seeds clinging to a bird's feather, a floating hala plant, or insect eggs in a piece of driftwood. Probably the first life forms to arrive on the newly emerged volcanic islands were fern and moss spores, able to drift thousands of miles in the air.

It's estimated that before human contact, a new species managed to take hold in Hawaii only once every 100,000 years. New arrivals found specialized habitats ranging from desert to rain forest and elevations climbing from sea level to nearly 14,000 feet. Each species evolved to fit a specific niche in its new environment.

More than 90% of Hawaii's native flora and fauna are found nowhere else on earth. Some still resemble their ancestors. The *nene*, for instance, looks like its cousin, the Canada goose, but its feet have adapted to walking on lava by losing most of its webbing. The majority of Hawaiian birds, however, have evolved so thoroughly that it's not possible to trace them to any continental ancestors.

Many of Hawaii's birds may have evolved from a single species, as is thought to have been the case with more than 30 species of native honeycreeper.

At the time of Western contact, Hawaii had 70 native bird species. Of those, 24 are now extinct and an additional 36 are threatened with extinction.

Having evolved with limited competition and few predators, Hawaii's native species generally fare poorly among the more aggressive varieties of introduced flora and fauna. The native species are also highly sensitive to habitat destruction.

When the first Polynesian settlers arrived, they weren't traveling light. They brought food and medicinal plants, chickens, dogs and pigs.

The pace of introducing exotic species escalated with the arrival of Westerners, starting with Captain Cook, who dropped off goats and left melon and pumpkin seeds. The next Western visitors left cattle and horses.

Prior to human contact, Hawaii had no land mammals save for the monk seals and hoary bats. The introduction of free-ranging pigs, cattle and goats, who all grazed and foraged at will, devastated Hawaii's fragile ecosystems and spelled extinction for many plants.

Some introduced songbirds and game birds spread avian diseases to which native Hawaiian birds had no immunity. Erosion, deforestation and thousands of introduced plants that compete with and choke out native vegetation have all taken their toll.

Today, more than 25% of all endangered species in the USA are Hawaiian plants and animals. Of approximately 2400 different native plants, half are either threatened or endangered.

Flora

Because Hawaii's climate varies from dry desert conditions to lush tropical rain forests, you'll find a wide variety of vegetation.

The most prevalent native forest tree is the *ohia lehua*, which is one of the first plants to colonize old lava flows; recognizable by its red pom-pom flowers, it grows in barren areas as a shrub and on more fertile land as a tree.

Koa, endemic to Hawaii, is commonly found at higher elevations, such as Kokee State Park in Kauai; it grows up to 100 feet high and is unusual in that the young saplings have fernlike compound leaves, while mature trees have flat, crescent-shaped phyllodes. The *kukui* tree, which was brought by the early Polynesian settlers, has oily nuts that Hawaiians used for candles – hence its common name, the candlenut tree; it's easily identifiable in the forest by its light silver-tinged foliage.

Two trees found along the coast that proved useful in old Hawaii are the *hala*, also called pandanus or screw pine, whose spiny leaves were used for thatching and weaving; and the coconut palm, called *niu*, which thrives in coral sands and produces about 75 coconuts a year.

Kiawe, a non-native tree readily found in dry coastal areas, is a member of the mesquite family that's useful for making charcoal but is a nuisance for beachgoers, as its sharp thorns easily pierce soft sandals.

Common native coastal plants include *pohuehue*, a beach morning glory with pink flowers that's found on the sand just above the high-tide line; and beach *naupaka*, a shrub with oval leaves and a small, white, five-petaled flower that looks as if it's been torn in half. The native *ilima*, with its delicate yellow-orange flowers, can grow at higher elevations but is commonly found along beaches, where it has adapted to harsh winds by growing as a ground cover.

More than 5000 varieties of hibiscus bushes grow in Hawaii; on most, the colorful flowers bloom only for a day. The variety most frequently used in landscape hedges is the red (or Chinese) hibiscus, which was introduced to Hawaii. There are also a number of native hibiscus, including the *hau* tree, whose flowers open as yellow and change to dark orange as the day goes on. The *kokio keokeo*, a native Hawaiian white hibiscus tree that thrives in moderately moist forests and grows up to 60 feet high, is the only Hawaiian hibiscus with a fragrance. The pink butterfly hibiscus, another popular hedge variety, is believed to be a cross between the native white hibiscus and the introduced coral hibiscus.

Hawaii, of course, is abloom with scores of other tropical flowers, most introduced, including blood-red anthuriums, brilliant orange birds of paradise, colorful bougainvilleas, red ginger, torch ginger, shell ginger and various heliconias with bright orange and red bracts. There are also hundreds of varieties of orchids, all but four of which are introduced.

Fauna

Hawaiian Monk Seal The Hawaiian monk seal, so named for the cowl-like fold of skin at its neck and for its solitary habits, exists only in Hawaii. The Hawaiian name for the animal is ilio holo kai, meaning 'the dog that runs in the sea.'

This species has remained nearly unchanged for 15 million years, though in the past century it has been in danger of dying out completely. Fortunately, conservation efforts, including the translocation of some seals to create a better male-female ratio, appear to be bringing the seals back from the edge of extinction. The Hawaiian monk seal population has risen about 15% in the past decade to a total of approximately 1300 seals.

Hawaiian monk seals, which are sensitive to human disruption, breed and give birth primarily in the Northwestern Hawaiian Islands. In recent years, however, sightings of

The Hawaiian monk seal is coming back from the brink of extinction.

monk seals hauling themselves onto beaches on the main islands – primarily in Kauai, but also on the northern shores of Oahu, Maui and Molokai – have increased.

The annual birth rate for the monk seal pups is between 150 and 175 a year, though because of shark attacks and other predators, the majority fail to reach maturity. Monk seals feed on reef fish, eels, octopus and lobster.

Of the world's two other monk seal species, the Caribbean monk seal is extinct and the Mediterranean monk seal numbers only in the hundreds.

Whales Whales are air-breathing, warm-blooded, placental mammals that lactate and nurse their young. Basically there are two types: toothed whales, which use their teeth to catch and rip apart their prey, and baleen whales, which have rows of a horny elastic material, called baleen or whalebone, that hangs from the upper jaw and acts as a filter to extract food from the water.

Hawaii's year-round resident whales, which are all toothed whales, include the sperm whale, false killer whale, pigmy killer whale, beaked whale, melon-head whale and, most common of all, the pilot whale. The pilot whale is a small whale that often travels in large pods and, like most whales, prefers deep offshore waters.

Several types of migrating baleen whales occasionally pass through Hawaiian waters, including the fin whale, minke whale and right whale. But it is the islands' most frequent visitor – the migrating humpback – that everyone wants to see.

The fifth largest of the great whales, the humpback, which has long white flippers and a knobby head, can reach a length of 45 feet and weigh 40 to 45 tons. The toothless humpbacks gulp huge quantities of water, trapping krill and small fish in their filterlike baleen. Each whale can eat close to a ton of food a day.

Once one of the most abundant of the great whales, humpbacks were hunted almost to extinction and are now an endangered species. Around the turn of the 20th century, an estimated 15,000 humpbacks remained. They were still being hunted as late as 1966, when the International Whaling Commission enforced a ban on their slaughter.

The entire population of North Pacific humpbacks is now thought to be about 4000. An estimated two-thirds of those winter in Hawaii, while most of the others migrate to Mexico.

Humpbacks spend the summer feeding in the plankton-rich waters off Alaska, developing a layer of blubber that sustains them through the winter, when the adults go without eating.

Come November, humpbacks begin filtering into Hawaii. During a romantic winter sojourn in the warm tropical waters, the whales mate and give birth. The gestation period is 10 to 12 months.

Mothers stay in shallow waters once their calves are born, apparently as protection from shark attacks. At birth, calves are about 12 feet long and weigh 3000 pounds. They are nursed for about six months and can put on 100 pounds a day in the first few weeks.

Despite their size, humpbacks often put on an amazing acrobatic show, which includes arching dives, breaching and fin splashing. In breaching, humpbacks jump almost clear out of the water and then splash down with tremendous force.

They save the best performances for breeding time. Sometimes several of the bull whales will do a series of crashing breaches to gain the favor of a cow, often bashing into one another, even drawing blood, before the most impressive emerges as the winner.

Luckily for whale watchers, humpbacks are coast-huggers, preferring waters with depths of less than 600 feet. They can be found throughout the islands, but their most frequented wintering spot is the shallow area between Maui, Lanai, Molokai and Kahoolawe.

Whales are highly sensitive to human activity and noise and seek out quiet coastal spots. They have abandoned areas where human activities have picked up and seem to have a particular distaste for jet skis.

Humpbacks are protected by US federal law under the Marine Mammal Protection Act and the Endangered Species Act. Coming within 100 yards of a humpback (300 yards in cow/calf waters) is prohibited and can result in a $25,000 fine. The rules apply to everyone, including swimmers, kayakers and surfers, and they are strictly enforced – whether violators are aware of the law or not.

Although the early Hawaiians seem to have paid little attention to whales – there are no petroglyph drawings of whales and virtually no legends about them – the state's current residents have designated the humpback whale as Hawaii's official marine mammal.

Dolphins Dolphins, which like whales are marine cetaceans, are common to Hawaii. Spinner, bottlenose, slender-beaked, spotted, striped and rough-toothed varieties can all be found in Hawaiian waters.

Dolphins are nocturnal feeders who often come into calm bays during the day to rest.

Whale Songs

Humpbacks are remarkable not only for their acrobatics but also for their singing. They are the only species of large whales known to do either.

Each member of the herd sings the same set of songs, in the same order. Whale songs last anywhere from six to 30 minutes and evolve as the season goes on, with new phrases added and old ones dropped, so that the songs the whales sing when they arrive in Hawaii become different songs by the time they leave.

It's thought that the humpbacks don't sing in their feeding grounds in Alaska. When they return to Hawaii six months later, however, they recall the songs from the last season and begin where they left off. The humpback's complex songs include the full range of frequencies audible to the human ear.

Although it may seem tempting to swim out and join them, approaching the dolphins can apparently disturb their rest; in addition, it will subject swimmers to a hefty fine under the Marine Mammal Protection Act. This is a current controversy in Hawaii, as swimmers who claim that dolphins enjoy playing in the surf with humans are at odds with federal officials bent on enforcing laws against the harassment of marine mammals.

Incidentally, the *mahimahi* or 'dolphin' that you may come across on menus in Hawaii is not the marine mammal but a fish.

National Parks

Hawaii has two national parks: Hawaii Volcanoes National Park on the Big Island and Haleakala National Park on Maui. Among the most unique places in the US National Parks system, both Haleakala and Hawaii Volcanoes center around volcanic craters. Both have awesome scenery and include several types of terrain, from sea level to more than 10,000 feet, and from barren lava landscapes to lush tropical rain forests. They also have unique flora and fauna and are the main habitat for the nene, a number of endangered forest birds and a host of native flora. The parks offer incredible hikes, some across crater floors, and a variety of camping options. For full details on both parks, see the Big Island and·Maui chapters.

GOVERNMENT & POLITICS

Hawaii has three levels of government: federal, state and county. The seat of state government is in Honolulu.

Hawaii has a typical state government with executive power vested in the governor, who is elected to a four-year term. The present governor, Benjamin Cayetano, who has been in office since December 1994, is the first state governor in the USA to be of Filipino ancestry.

The state's lawmaking body is a bicameral legislature. The Senate includes 25 members, elected for four-year terms from the state's 25 senatorial districts. The House of Representatives has 51 members, each elected for a two-year term.

The legislature has a typical Hawaiian casualness. The regular legislative session, which convenes on the third Wednesday of January, meets for a mere 60 days a year. Special sessions of up to 30 days can be convened by the governor, but otherwise, 60 days is it.

Hawaii is divided into four county governments, but unlike the mainland states, it has no municipal government. The city of Honolulu is part of Honolulu County, which governs all of Oahu; Hawaii County oversees the Big Island; Kauai County governs Kauai and Niihau; and Maui County presides over Maui, Molokai and Lanai.

While the leprosy colony of Kalaupapa on Molokai is called the 'county' of Kalawao, in actuality it has no county government and is under the jurisdiction of the Hawaii State Department of Health.

Official Hawaii

State nickname: The Aloha State

State flower: *pua aloalo* – hibiscus

State tree: *kukui* – candlenut tree

State bird: *nene* – Hawaiian goose

State marine mammal: humpback whale

State fish: *humuhumunukunukuapuaa* – rectangular triggerfish

State motto: *Ua mau ke ea o ka aina i ka pono* – 'The life of the land is perpetuated in righteousness.'

State song: *Hawaii Ponoi* – written by King Kalakaua

State flag: Designed for King Kamehameha I prior to 1816, it has the UK's Union Jack in the upper left-hand corner. Eight stripes of red, white and blue represent the eight largest islands.

State seal: The state seal incorporates the state motto and a heraldic shield flanked by Kamehameha I on one side and the Goddess of Liberty holding the Hawaiian flag on the other. It also has taro and banana leaves, ferns, a phoenix and the statehood year of 1959.

Each county has a mayor and county council. The counties provide services, such as police and fire protection, that on the mainland are usually assigned to cities. Development issues are usually decided at county level and are the central issue of most mayoral campaigns.

ECONOMY

Tourism is Hawaii's largest industry and accounts for about one-third of the state's income. Hawaii welcomes about 6.7 million visitors a year. In total they spend about $10 billion in the state, but not all at the same rate. The 3.7 million visiting Americans spend an average of $150 a day, while the 1.8 million Japanese spend nearly double that. Since the onset of the Asian economic downturn, dubbed the 'Asian flu,' visitor arrivals from Japan and other Asian nations have dropped 10%. Although there's been a 4% rise in the number of North American and European tourists coming to Hawaii, that hasn't been enough to offset stagnation in Hawaii's tourism industry.

Hawaii now spends a whopping $60 million a year to promote tourism, though ironically much of the advertising money is gleaned from its ever-rising room tax (now 11.41%), which itself may contribute to discouraging visitors.

The second largest sector in the economy is the US military, pumping out $3 billion annually. Agriculture is a distant third.

Sugar and pineapple, which once formed the backbone of Hawaii's economy, have been scaled back dramatically in recent years. Pineapple production has ceased on Lanai, which until the early 1990s was nicknamed the 'Pineapple Island,' and sugar, which is still being grown on Kauai and Maui, has recently disappeared from the landscape of both the Big Island and Oahu. Today, the two crops account for $175 million in sales, less than half of their value a decade ago.

Meanwhile, diversified crops, defined as all crops except sugar and pineapple, have increased two-fold over the past decade and have a combined sales value of nearly $300 million. Of this, Hawaii's 750 farms and nurseries sold nearly $70 million in flowers, while macadamia nuts brought in another $40 million. Other sizable crops include vegetables, tropical fruit, coffee and seed corn. Bananas, which have faltered for years because of blight, are now once again being commercially harvested for export.

Hawaii's former agribusiness-based economy is in the midst of change. Hawaii's 'Big Five' companies – Amfac, Castle & Cooke, C Brewer, Theo Davies and Alexander & Baldwin – all had their origins in sugar, now on the wane. The Big Five hold onto their plantations not so much for what's being produced on them, but for the potential they hold as future golf courses and condo developments – and bit by bit they're being sold off for those purposes. The biggest buyers in recent years have been Japanese developers; more than a third of all Japanese investment in the USA is now in Hawaii.

Hawaii's unemployment rate hovers around 6%, which is nearly 2% higher than the US average. The cost of living is 20% higher in Honolulu than in the average US mainland city, while wages are 9% lower. For those stuck in service jobs, the most rapidly growing sector of the economy, it's tough to get by.

Native Hawaiians have the lowest median family income in Hawaii and are at the bottom of most health and welfare indicators, including high school drop-out rates, suicide rates and tragic death and major disease statistics. They also make up a disproportionately high percentage of Hawaii's homeless.

The Military Presence

Hawaii is the most militarized state in the nation.

In total, the military has a grip on about 250,000 acres of Hawaiian land. The greatest holding is on Oahu, where nearly 25% of the island is controlled by the armed forces and where there are more than 100 installations, from ridge-top radar stations to Waikiki's Fort DeRussy Beach.

Oahu is the hub of the Pacific Command, which directs military activities from the

West Coast of the USA to the eastern coast of Africa. The US Navy, which accounts for 40% of Hawaii's military presence, is centered at Pearl Harbor, home of the Pacific Fleet.

Despite the ending of the Cold War, the military still spends about $3 billion annually in the state. It pays out $500 million in contracted services, and it employs 19,000 civilians directly. There are 45,000 military personnel and an additional 50,000 military dependents living on the islands.

The state's politicians, while otherwise liberal-leaning, generally embrace the military presence. The Chamber of Commerce of Hawaii even has a special military affairs council that lobbies in Washington, DC to draw still more military activity (and all the revenue that goes with it) to Hawaii.

POPULATION & PEOPLE

The population of Hawaii is an estimated 1,193,000. In the island breakdown, approximately 880,000 people live on Oahu, 141,000 on the Big Island, 106,000 on Maui, 56,100 on Kauai, 6800 on Molokai, 3000 on Lanai and 190 on Niihau.

There is no ethnic majority in Hawaii – everyone belongs to a minority. Some 32% of the population claims 'mixed ethnicity,' with a majority of those having some Hawaiian blood. As for the rest, Caucasians and Japanese each account for approximately 22% of the population, followed by Filipinos (12%), Chinese (5%), African Americans, Koreans, Samoans and Puerto Ricans. There are about 9000 full-blooded Hawaiians, less than 1% of the population.

Hawaii's people are known for their racial harmony. Race is generally not a factor in marriage. Islanders have a 50/50 chance of marrying someone of a race different than their own and the majority of children born in Hawaii are *hapa*, or mixed-blood.

EDUCATION

Hawaii is the only US state to have a public education system run by the state rather than county or town education boards. Education accounts for approximately one-third of the state budget.

Under Hawaii state law, all children between the ages of six and 18 are expected to attend school. More than 80% of all students are enrolled in Hawaii's public school system, with the remainder in private schools.

Schools operate on a two-semester system; the first semester is from the first week of September to late December, the second from early January to the first week in June.

ARTS
Hula

Hawaii's most distinctive native art form is the hula, a graceful dance combining facial expressions and body movements to convey stories of historical and legendary importance.

Taught at a *halau* (school), the art of hula has attracted an influx of new students in recent years. Some classes practice in public places, such as school grounds and parks, where visitors are welcome to watch. Although many of the halau rely on tuition fees, others receive sponsorship from hotels and shopping centers and give weekly public performances in return.

There are also numerous islandwide hula competitions; two of the biggest are the Prince Lot Hula Festival held each July in Oahu and the week-long Merrie Monarch Festival, which begins on Easter Sunday in Hilo. For more on hula, see the boxed text 'Dance & Music.'

Music

Contemporary Hawaiian music gives center stage to the guitar, which was first introduced to the islands by Spanish cowboys in the 1830s. The Hawaiians made it uniquely their own, however. In 1889, Joseph Kekuku, a native Hawaiian, designed the steel guitar, one of only two major musical instruments invented in what is now the USA. (The other is the banjo.) The steel guitar is usually played with slack-key tunings and carries the melody throughout the song.

Slack-key guitar, a type of tuning in which some strings are slackened from the conventional tuning to produce a harmonious soulful sound, is also a 19th-century Hawaiian creation and one that has come back into the spotlight in recent times. Some of Hawaii's more renowned slack-key guitar players are Cyril Pahinui, Keola Beamer, Raymond Kane, Peter Moon and Atta Isaacs Jr, and the late Gabby Pahinui and Sonny Chillingworth.

The ukulele, so strongly identified with Hawaiian music, was actually derived from the braginha, an instrument from Portugal introduced to Hawaii in the 19th century. In the Hawaiian language, the word 'ukulele' means 'jumping flea.'

Both the ukulele and the steel guitar were essential to the lighthearted, romantic music popularized in Hawaii from the 1930s to the 1950s. 'My Little Grass Shack,' 'Lovely Hula Hands' and 'Sweet Leilani' are classic examples. Due in part to the 'Hawaii Calls' radio show, which for more than 30 years was broadcast worldwide from the Moana Hotel in Waikiki, this music became instantly recognizable as Hawaiian, conjuring up images of beautiful hula dancers swaying under palm trees in a tropical paradise. Among the current-day masters of the ukulele are Troy Fernandez and Ledward Kaapana.

A current sound in Hawaii is Jawaiian, a blending of Hawaiian music and Jamaican reggae. One hot new group with an emphasis on Jawaiian is the Oahu-based Kulana, but many other well-known musicians incorporate elements of Jawaiian, including Bruddah Waltah, the Kaau Crater Boys and Hoaikane. Other popular contemporary Hawaiian musicians include vocalist-composer Henry Kapono; Hapa, the duo of Kelii Kanealii and Barry Flanagan, who fuse folk, rock and traditional Hawaiian elements; the Hawaiian Style Band, which merges Hawaiian influences with rock; and Kealii Reichel, a charismatic vocalist and hula dancer who sings Hawaiian ballads, love songs and poetic chants.

Art

Many artists draw inspiration from Hawaii's rich cultural heritage and natural beauty.

The well-known Hawaiian painter Herb Kawainui Kane creates detailed oil paintings focusing on the early Polynesian settlers and King Kamehameha's life. His works are mainly on display in museums and at gallery collections in resorts.

Another notable native Hawaiian artist is Rocky Kaiouliokahihikoloehu Jensen, who does wood sculptures and drawings of Hawaiian gods, ancient chiefs and early Hawaiians, with the aim of creating sacred art in the tradition of *makaku*, or 'creative artistic mana.'

Pegge Hopper paints traditional Hawaiian women in relaxed poses using a distinctive graphic design style and bright washes of color. Her work has been widely reproduced on posters and postcards.

Some of Hawaii's most impressive crafts are ceramics, bowls made of native woods and baskets woven of native fibers. The goddess Pele is a source of inspiration for many Big Island artists – some even use molten lava as a sculpting material.

Hawaiian quilting is another unique art form. The concept of patchwork quilting was introduced by the early missionaries, but the Hawaiians, who had only recently taken to Western cotton clothing, didn't have a surplus of cloth scraps – and the idea of cutting up new lengths of fabric simply to sew them back together again in small squares seemed absurd. Instead, the Hawaiian women created their own designs using larger cloth pieces, typically with stylized tropical flora on a white background.

A more transitory art form is the creation of the *lei* (garland). Although the leis most widely worn by visitors are made of fragrant flowers such as plumeria and tuberose, traditional leis of mokihana berries and maile leaves were more commonly worn in old Hawaii. Both types are still made today.

SOCIETY & CONDUCT

In many ways, contemporary culture in Hawaii resembles contemporary culture in the rest of the USA.

Hawaiians listen to the same pop music and watch the same TV shows as Americans on the mainland. Hawaii has discos and ballroom dancing, rock bands and classical orchestras, junk food and nouvelle cuisine. But the wonderful thing about Hawaii is that the mainland influences largely stand beside, rather than engulf, the culture of the islands.

Not only is traditional Hawaiian culture an integral part of the social fabric, but so are the customs of the ethnically diverse immigrants who have made Hawaii their home. Hawaii is more than just a meeting place of East and West; it's also a place where the cultures merge, typically in a manner that brings out the best of both worlds.

The 1970s saw the start of a Hawaiian cultural renaissance that continues today. Hawaiian language classes are thriving, and there is a concerted effort to reintroduce Hawaiian words into modern speech. Hula classes concentrate more on the nuances of hand movements and facial expressions than on the dramatic hip-shaking that sells dance shows. Many Hawaiian artists and craftspeople are returning to traditional mediums and themes.

Certainly, the tourist centers have long been overrun with packaged Hawaiiana, from plastic leis to theme-park luaus, that practically parodies island culture. But fortunately for the visitor, the growing interest in traditional Hawaiiana is having an impact on the tourist industry, and authentic performances by hula students and contemporary Hawaiian musicians are increasingly easier to find.

RELIGION

Hawaii's population is religiously diverse.

Christianity has the largest following, with Catholicism being the predominant religious denomination in Hawaii. Interestingly, the United Church of Christ, which includes the Congregationalists who initially converted the islands, claim only about half as many members as the Mormons and one-tenth as many as the Catholics.

In addition, Hawaii has about 100 Buddhist temples, scores of Shinto shrines and two dozen Hindu temples. There are also Taoist, Tenrikyo, Jewish and Muslim houses of worship.

LANGUAGE

The unifying language of Hawaii is English, but it's liberally peppered with Hawaiian phrases, loan words from the various immigrant languages and pidgin slang.

It's not uncommon to hear islanders speaking in other languages, however, as the main language spoken in one out of every four homes in Hawaii is a mother tongue other than English. The Hawaiian language itself is still spoken among family members by about 9000 people, and Hawaiian is, along with English, an official state language.

Closely related to other Polynesian languages, Hawaiian is melodic, phonetically simple and full of vowels and repeated syllables.

Some 85% of all place names in Hawaii are in Hawaiian, and as often as not they have interesting translations and stories behind them.

The Hawaiians had no written language until the 1820s, when Christian missionaries arrived and wrote down the spoken language in roman letters.

Pronunciation

The written Hawaiian language has just 12 letters. Pronunciation is easy and there are few consonant clusters.

Vowel sounds are about the same as in Spanish or Japanese, more or less like this:

a   ah, as in 'father,' or uh, as in 'above'
e   ay, as in 'gay' or eh, as in 'pet'
i   ee, as in 'see'
o   oh, as in 'go'
u   oo, as in 'noon'

Hawaiian has diphthongs, created when two vowels join together to form a single sound. The stress is on the first vowel, although in general if you pronounce each vowel separately, you'll be easily understood.

The consonant *w* is usually pronounced like a soft English *v* when it follows the letters *i* and *e* (the town Haleiwa is pronounced Haleiva) and like the English *w* when it follows *u* or *o*. When *w* follows *a*, it can be pronounced either *v* or *w* – thus you will hear both Hawaii and Havaii.

The other consonants – h, k, l, m, n, p – are pronounced about the same as in English.

Glottal Stops & Macrons Written Hawaiian uses both glottal stops and macrons, although in modern print they are often omitted.

The glottal stop (') indicates a break between two vowels, which produces an effect similar to saying 'oh-oh' in English. A macron, a short straight line over a vowel, stresses the vowel.

Glottal stops and macrons not only affect pronunciation, but can give a word a completely different meaning. For example, *ai* can mean 'sexual intercourse' or 'to eat,' depending on the pronunciation.

All this takes on greater significance when you learn to speak Hawaiian in depth. If you're using Hawaiian words in an English-language context (this *poi* is *ono*), there shouldn't be much of a problem.

Compounds Hawaiian may seem more difficult than it is because many proper names are long and look similar. Many begin with ka, meaning 'the,' which over time simply became attached to the beginning of the word.

When you break each word down into its composite parts, some of which are repeated, it all becomes much easier. For example: *Kamehameha* consists of the three compounds Ka-meha-meha. *Humuhumunukunukuapuaa*, which is Hawaii's state fish, is broken down into humu-humu-nuku-nuku-a-pu-a-a.

Some words are doubled to emphasize their meaning. For example: *wiki* means 'quick,' while *wikiwiki* means 'very quick.'

There are some easily recognizable compounds repeatedly found in place names, and it can be fun to learn a few. For instance, *wai* means 'freshwater' – Waikiki means 'spouting water,' so named for the freshwater springs that were once there. *Kai* means 'seawater' – Kailua means 'two seas.' *Lani* means 'heavenly' – Lanikai means 'heavenly sea.' *Hana* means 'bay' – Hanalei means 'crescent bay.'

Common Hawaiian Words

Learn these words first: *aloha* and *mahalo*, which are everyday pleasantries; *makai* and

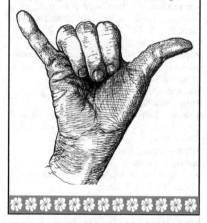
mauka, commonly used in giving directions; and *kane* and *wahine*, often on bathroom doors.

aina – land
akamai – clever
alii – chief, royalty
aloha – love, welcome, goodbye
aloha aina – love of the land
hale – house
hana – work; or bay, when used as a compound in place names
haole – Caucasian
hapa – half; or person of mixed blood
hapa haole – half-white, used for a person, thing or idea
Hauoli Makahiki Hou – Happy New Year
Hawaii nei – all the Hawaiian Islands, as distinguished from the Big Island
heiau – ancient Hawaiian temple
holoholo – to walk, drive or ramble around for pleasure
holoku – a long dress similar to the *muumuu*, but more fitted and with a yoke

hui – group, organization
hula – traditional Hawaiian dance
imu – underground earthen oven used in traditional *luau* cooking
kahuna – wise person in any field; commonly a priest, healer or sorcerer
kalua – traditional method of baking in an underground oven
kamaaina – native-born Hawaiian or a longtime resident; literally, 'child of the land'
kane – man
kapu – taboo, part of strict ancient Hawaiian social system; today often used on signs, meaning 'Keep Out'
kaukau – food
keiki – child, children
kokua – help, cooperation; 'Please Kokua' on a trash can is a gentle way of saying, 'Don't litter'
kona – leeward; or a leeward wind
lanai – veranda
lei – garland, usually of flowers, but also of leaves, shells or feathers
lolo – stupid, crazy
lomilomi – massage
luau – traditional Hawaiian feast
mahalo – thank you
makai – toward the sea
malihini – newcomer, visitor
manini – convict tang (a reef fish); also used to refer to something small or insignificant
mano – shark
mauka – toward the mountains, inland
mele – song, chant
Mele Kalikimaka – Merry Christmas
muumuu – long, loose-fitting dress introduced by the missionaries
nene – a native goose; Hawaii's state bird
ohana – family, extended family
ono – delicious; also the name of the wahoo fish
pakalolo – marijuana; literally, 'crazy smoke'
pali – cliff
paniolo – Hawaiian cowboy
pau – finished, no more; *pau hana* means quitting time
puka – any kind of hole or opening
pupu – snack food, hors d'oeuvres; shells
puu – hill, cinder cone
tutu – aunt, older woman

ukulele – stringed musical instrument
wahine – woman
wikiwiki – hurry, quick

Pidgin

Hawaii's early immigrants communicated with each other in pidgin, a simplified, broken form of English. It was a language born of necessity, stripped of all but the most needed words.

Modern pidgin is better defined as local slang. It is an extensive language, lively and ever-changing. Whole conversations can take place in pidgin, or often just a word or two is dropped into a more conventional English sentence.

Even Shakespeare's *Twelfth Night* has been translated (by local comedian James Grant Benton) to *Twelf Nite O Wateva*. Malvolio's line 'My masters, are you mad?' becomes 'You buggahs crazy, o wat?'

Short-term visitors will rarely win friends by trying to speak pidgin. It's more like an insider's code that you're allowed to use only after you've lived in Hawaii long enough to understand the nuances.

Some characteristics of pidgin include: a fast staccato rhythm, two-word sentences, dropping the soft 'h' sound from words that start with 'th', use of loan words from many languages (often Hawaiian) and double meanings that trip up the uninitiated.

Some of the more common words and expressions:

blalah – big Hawaiian fellow
brah – brother, friend; also used for 'hey you'
broke da mouth – delicious
buggah – guy
chicken skin – goose bumps
coconut wireless – word of mouth
cockaroach – steal
da kine – that kind of thing, whatchamacallit, etc; used whenever you can't think of the word you want but you know the listener knows what you mean
gee vem – go for it, beat them
grinds – food, eat; ono grinds is good food
haolefied – become like a haole (white man)

howzit? – hi, how's it going?
how you stay? – how are you?
humbug – a real hassle
like beef? – wanna fight?
mo' bettah – much better, the best
slippahs – flip-flops, thongs

stick – surfboard
stink eye – dirty look, evil eye
talk story – any kind of conversation, gossip, tales
tanks – thanks; more commonly, tanks brah
tree – three

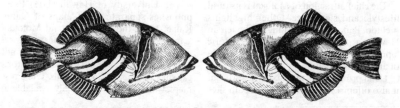

Facts for the Visitor

HIGHLIGHTS

Hawaii is a spectacular place with each island offering its own unique highlights.

On **Oahu**, renowned visitor attractions include Waikiki, Pearl Harbor and the North Shore with its huge winter surf. Honolulu's historic downtown, with the only royal palace in the USA, and the adjacent Chinatown offer a fascinating glimpse of Hawaii's multi-ethnic society. Other things not to be missed include Kailua's superb beach, the scenic drive around the southeast coast and the view from Diamond Head summit.

On **Maui**, the must-do's include a trip to Haleakala summit for the sunrise, the serpentine coastal drive to Hana and a visit to historic Lahaina. Maui also has lovely beaches, top-notch windsurfing and excellent winter whale-watching opportunities.

On the **Big Island**, don't miss Hawaii Volcanoes National Park, with its fascinating landscape of steaming craters and lava flows. Rural Waipio Valley and the cascading Akaka Falls also offer splendid natural scenery. Remnants of ancient Hawaiian culture are plentiful, including *heiaus* (ancient temples) at Puuhonua o Honaunau, more widely known as the Place of Refuge, and numerous petroglyph fields.

Kauai is a favorite of naturalists and is known for its lush mountainous scenery, especially the Na Pali Coast and Kokee State Park, both of which offer excellent backcountry hiking trails. It also has the impressive Waimea Canyon, dubbed the 'Grand Canyon of the Pacific,' and numerous waterways that provide excellent kayaking opportunities.

The chief attraction of **Molokai** is its rural lifestyle and slow pace. Other highlights include Papohaku, the longest beach in Hawaii, a mule trail down to the historic leprosy colony of Kalaupapa and a shoreline of ancient fishponds.

Lanai promotes its two luxury resorts but it also offers a few off-the-beaten-path sites to explore. Its south coast has a lovely beach, Hulopoe Bay, with fine diving and snorkeling.

PLANNING

When to Go

Hawaii is a great place to visit any time of the year.

Although the busiest tourist season is in winter, that has more to do with weather *elsewhere*, as many visitors are snowbirds escaping cold winters back home. Essentially the weather in Hawaii is agreeable all year round. It's a bit rainier in the winter and a bit hotter in the summer, but there are no extremes, and cooling trade winds modify the heat throughout the year.

In terms of cost, spring through fall can be a bargain, as many hotel prices drop around April 1 and most don't climb back up again until mid-December.

Naturally, certain activities have their peak seasons. For instance, if you're a board surfer, you'll find the biggest waves in winter, whereas if you're a windsurfer, you'll find the best wind conditions in summer.

Maps

If you're renting a car, the guide booklets handed out by the car rental agencies have simple maps showing the main roads. However, if you really want to explore, a more detailed road map can be invaluable.

Gousha and Rand McNally both publish good Oahu street maps with detailed Honolulu sections. The American Automobile Association (AAA) puts out a good Honolulu road map and an all-Hawaii map, which it distributes free to its members.

The University of Hawaii (UH) Press publishes separate relief maps of Oahu, Kauai, Maui, the Big Island and Molokai/Lanai. Overall, they're the best general maps for the Neighbor Islands as they not only cover roads but also beaches, historical sites and major hiking trails. UH Press maps, which cost $4, are readily available in

Hawaii bookstores and in shops frequented by tourists.

The United States Geological Survey (USGS) publishes topographical maps of Hawaii. Both full-island and detailed sectional maps are available, and there's also an individual USGS map for Hawaii Volcanoes National Park. Maps can be ordered from the US Geological Survey (☎ 800-435-7627, fax 303-202-4693, infoservices@usgs.gov), PO Box 25286, Denver Federal Center, Denver, CO 80225. Maps cost $4 per sheet, plus a $3.50 mailing fee per order.

USGS maps can also be purchased at several places in Hawaii, including on Kauai at the Kauai Museum in Lihue and the Kokee State Park museum; on Oahu at the Pacific Map Center, 560 N Nimitz, Honolulu; and on the Big Island at the Middle Earth Bookshoppe in Kailua-Kona, Basically Books in Hilo and Hawaii Volcanoes National Park.

Nautical charts published by the National Oceanic and Atmospheric Administration can be ordered from the NOAA Distribution Division (☎ 301-436-6990), National Ocean Service, 6502 Lafayette Ave, Riverdale, MD 20737. Upon request, NOAA will send a complete list of charts available and addresses where charts can be purchased around the world. In Hawaii, you can find NOAA nautical charts at the Pacific Map Center in Honolulu, Basically Books in Hilo and some larger marine supply companies.

What to Bring

Hawaii has balmy weather and a casual attitude towards dress, so for the most part packing is a breeze.

At the lower elevations it's summer all year. Shorts, sandals and a T-shirt or cotton shirt are the standard day dress. If you don't intend to spend time at higher elevations, a light jacket or sweater will be the warmest clothing you'll need.

Pack light. You can always pick up something with a tropical Hawaiian print when you get there and dress island-style.

An aloha shirt and lightweight slacks for men, and a cotton dress for women, is pretty much regarded as 'dressing up' on the islands. Only a few of the most exclusive restaurants require anything dressier.

Hawaii does, however, have highland areas (called 'upcountry' on the islands) as well as mountains, and most people get at least as far as the former. The upcountry can be a good 20°F cooler than the coast, and when the fog blows in and the wind picks up, it gets quite nippy. If you intend to spend any time in the upcountry, plan on another layer of clothing.

The temperature on the mountain summits on the Big Island and Maui can dip below freezing. If you're going to be camping at high elevations, you need to be prepared for cold weather; a tent, winter-rated sleeping bag, rain gear and layers of warm clothing are a must.

Camping on the beach is another matter entirely. A very lightweight cotton bag is the most you'll need. Public campgrounds require campers to use tents – a good idea anyway because of mosquitoes. If you don't want to pack camping gear, you can rent it on Oahu, Kauai and the Big Island.

For hiking, bring footwear with good traction. Many people just wear sneakers, although walking on lava can be tough on the ankles. Serious hikers should consider lugging along their hiking boots.

You won't regret bringing binoculars for watching whales and birds, and a flashlight is useful for exploring caves. Snorkel gear may come in handy too, but you don't need to worry too much about what to bring, as just about anything you forget to pack you can easily buy in Hawaii.

TOURIST OFFICES

The Hawaii Visitors and Convention Bureau (HVCB) provides free tourist information on the state. On request, the bureau will mail you some general, Hawaii-wide tourist information and a booklet listing member hotels and restaurants.

On the US mainland, HVCB maintains an office (☎ 415-248-3800, 800-353-5846, fax 415-248-3808) at 180 Montgomery St, suite 2360, San Francisco, CA 94104.

You can also call the following toll-free numbers from the mainland to order free glossy tourism magazines, though these can take as long as a month or two to arrive. For a magazine on all of Hawaii, call ☎ 800-464-2924. For similar booklets about Maui, call ☎ 800-525-6284; for Kauai, call ☎ 800-245-2824; for the Big Island, call ☎ 800-648-2441; and for Oahu, call ☎ 800-624-8678.

HVCB material can also be viewed at www.gohawaii.com on the Web.

Local Tourist Offices

The HVCB main office (☎ 923-1811, fax 924-0290) is in the Waikiki Business Plaza, suite 801, 2270 Kalakaua Ave, Honolulu, HI 96815.

Tourist offices on Oahu, Maui, Kauai, the Big Island and Molokai can provide information more specific to their islands; phone numbers and addresses are in the individual island chapters.

Tourist Offices Abroad

For some odd reason, the Hawaii Visitors and Convention Bureau frequently changes its overseas agents. The following are the current addresses for HVCB representatives abroad.

Australia
   (☎ 02-9955-2619, fax 02-9955-2171)
   c/o The Sales Team, suite 2, level 2,
   34 Burton St, Milsons Point, NSW 2061

Canada
   (☎ 604-669-6691, fax 604-669-6075)
   c/o Comprehensive Travel Industry Services,
   suite 104, 1260 Hornby St,
   Vancouver, BC V6Z 1W2

China
   (☎ 21-6466-1077, fax 21-6466-7501)
   c/o East-West Marketing, 38 Da Pu Rd,
   Hai Hua Garden, No 4 Building 27C,
   Shanghai 200023

Germany
   (☎ 610-272-2411, fax 610-272-2409)
   c/o American Venture Marketing,
   Siemenstrasse 9, 63263 Neu Isenburg

Japan
   (☎ 3-3201-0430, fax 3-3201-0433)
   Kokusai Building, 2nd floor, 1-1
   Marunouchi 3-chome, Chiyoda-ku, Tokyo 100

Korea
   (☎ 2-773-6719, fax 2-757-6783)
   c/o Travel Press, Seoul Center Building,
   12th floor, 91-1 Sokong-dong, Chung-ku,
   Seoul 100-070

New Zealand
   (☎ 9-379-3708, fax 9-309-0725)
   c/o Walshes World, Dingwall Building,
   2nd floor, 87 Queen St, Auckland

Taiwan
   (☎ 22-506-7043, fax 22-507-5816)
   c/o Federal Transportation Company, 8th floor,
   61 Nanking East Rd, Section 3, Taipei

UK
   (☎ 0181-941-4009, fax 0181-941-4011)
   Box 208, Sunbury on Thames,
   Middlesex TW16 5RJ

VISAS & DOCUMENTS

The conditions for entering Hawaii are the same as for entering any state in the USA.

Passport & Visas

Canadians must have proper proof of Canadian citizenship, such as a citizenship card with photo ID or a passport. Visitors from other countries must have a valid passport, and most visitors also need a US visa.

However, a reciprocal visa-waiver program allows citizens of certain countries to enter the USA for stays of 90 days or less without first obtaining a US visa. Currently these countries are: Andorra, Argentina, Australia, Austria, Belgium, Brunei, Denmark, Finland, France, Germany, Iceland, Ireland, Italy, Japan, Liechtenstein, Luxembourg, Monaco, Netherlands, New Zealand, Norway, Portugal, San Marino, Singapore, Spain, Sweden, Switzerland, the UK and Uruguay. Under this program, you must have a roundtrip ticket that is nonrefundable in the USA, and you will not be allowed to extend your stay beyond the 90 days.

Other travelers will need to obtain a visa from a US consulate or embassy. In most countries the process can be done by mail.

Your passport should be valid for at least six months longer than your intended stay in the USA, and you'll need to submit a recent photo (37 x 37mm) with the application. Documents of financial stability and/or guarantees from a US resident are sometimes required, particularly for visitors from third-world countries.

Visa applicants may be required to 'demonstrate binding obligations' that will ensure their return home. Because of this requirement, those planning to travel through other countries before arriving in the USA are generally better off applying for their US visa while they are still in their home country – rather than while on the road.

The validity period for US visitor visas depends on what country you're from. The length of time you'll be allowed to stay in the USA is ultimately determined by US immigration authorities at the port of entry.

Visa Extensions If you want to stay in the USA longer than the date stamped on your passport, apply for an extension by contacting the Honolulu office of the Immigration & Naturalization Service (☎ 532-3721), 595 Ala Moana Blvd, *before* the stamped date.

Travel Insurance

Foreign visitors should be aware that health care in the USA is expensive. It's a good idea to take out a travel insurance policy, which usually covers medical expenses, luggage theft or loss, and cancellation or delays in your travel arrangements. Policies vary widely in coverage, so get your insurer or travel agent to explain the details.

Check the small print because some policies exclude 'dangerous activities,' which can include scuba diving, motorcycling, anything to do with parachutes and even trekking.

While you may find a policy that pays doctors or hospitals directly, be aware that many doctors and medical clinics in Hawaii will demand payment at the time of service. If you have to make a claim later, be certain to keep all documentation.

It's best to purchase travel insurance as early as possible. If you buy it the week before you fly, you might find, for instance, that you're not covered for delays to your flight caused by a strike that may have been in force before you took out the insurance.

Paying for your ticket with a credit card often provides travel accident insurance and may also give you the right to reclaim your payment if the operator doesn't deliver. Ask your credit card company, or the issuing bank, for details.

Documents

Visitors should keep in mind that all US airlines, including Hawaii's interisland carriers, now require passengers to present a photo ID as part of the airline check-in procedure.

HIV & Entering the USA

Everyone entering the USA who isn't a US citizen is subject to the authority of the Immigration & Naturalization Service (INS). The INS can keep people from entering or staying in the USA by excluding or deporting them. This is especially relevant to travelers with HIV (human immunodeficiency virus). Though being HIV-positive is not grounds for deportation, it is a 'ground of exclusion' and the INS can invoke this rule to refuse admission.

Although the INS doesn't test people for HIV at customs, it may try to exclude anyone who answers 'yes' to this question on the nonimmigrant visa application form: 'Have you ever been afflicted with a communicable disease of public health significance?' INS officials may also stop people if they seem sick, are carrying AIDS/HIV medicine or, sadly, if the officer happens to think the person 'looks gay,' though sexual orientation is not legally a ground of exclusion.

It's imperative that visitors know and assert their rights. Immigrants and visitors who may face exclusion should discuss their rights and options with a trained immigration advocate before applying for a visa. For legal immigration information and referrals to immigration advocates, contact the National Immigration Project of the National Lawyers Guild (☎ 617-227-9727, fax 617-227-5495), 14 Beacon St, suite 602, Boston, MA 02108; or the Immigrant HIV Assistance Project (☎ 415-782-8995), 685 Market St, suite 700, San Francisco, CA 94105.

Embassies & Consulates

US Embassies Abroad
US embassies around the world include the following:

Australia
(☎ 02-6214-5600)
21 Moonah Place
Canberra, ACT 2600

Canada
(☎ 613-238-5335)
100 Wellington St
Ottawa, ON K1P 5T1

Denmark
(☎ 35 55 31 44)
Dag Hammarskjolds Allé 24
2100 Copenhagen

France
(☎ 01-43-12-22-22)
2 avenue Gabriel
75382 Paris Cedex 08

Germany
(☎ 030-832-9233)
Clayallee 170
14195 Berlin

Ireland
(☎ 1-668-8777)
42 Elgin Rd
Ballsbridge, Dublin

Japan
(☎ 3-224-5000)
10-5, Akasaka 1-chome
Minato-ku, Tokyo 107-8420

Korea
(☎ 2-397-4114)
82 Sejong-Ro, Chongro-ku
Seoul 110-050

Malaysia
(☎ 3-248-9011)
376 Jalan Tun Razak
50400 Kuala Lumpur

Netherlands
(☎ 70-310-9209)
Lange Voorhout 102
2514 EJ, The Hague

New Zealand
(☎ 4-472-2068)
29 Fitzherbert Terrace
PO Box 1190
Thorndon, Wellington

Singapore
(☎ 476-9100)
27 Napier Rd
Singapore 258508

Thailand
(☎ 2-205-4000)
120 Wireless Rd
Bangkok

UK
(☎ 0171-499-9000)
24/31 Grosvenor Square
London W1A 1AE

Your Own Embassy

As a tourist, it's important to realize what your own embassy – the embassy of the country of which you are a citizen – can and can't do.

Generally speaking, it won't be much help in emergencies if the trouble you're in is remotely your own fault. Remember that you are bound by the laws of the country you are in. Your embassy will not be sympathetic if you end up in jail after committing a crime locally, even if such actions are legal in your own country.

In genuine emergencies you might get some assistance, but only if other channels have been exhausted. For example, if you need to get home urgently, a free ticket home is exceedingly unlikely – the embassy would expect you to have insurance. If you have all your money and documents stolen, the embassy might assist in getting a new passport, but a loan for onward travel is out of the question.

Embassies used to keep letters for travelers or have a small reading room with home newspapers, but these days the mail-holding service has been stopped, and even newspapers tend to be out of date.

Embassies & Consulates

Foreign Consulates in Hawaii
Honolulu hosts the following consulates and government liaison offices:

American Samoa
American Samoa
Office-Hawaii
(☎ 847-1998)
1427 Dillingham Blvd
suite 210

Australia
Consulate-General
of Australia
(☎ 524-5050)
1000 Bishop St

Austria
Consulate of Austria
(☎ 923-8585)
1314 S King St, suite 1260

Belgium
Consulate of Belgium
(☎ 533-6900)
745 Fort St Mall, 18th floor

Brazil
Consulate of Brazil
(☎ 235-0571)
44-166 Nanamoana

Chile
Consulate of Chile
(☎ 949-2850)
1860 Ala Moana Blvd
suite 1900

Denmark
Consulate of Denmark
(☎ 545-2028)
1001 Bishop St, suite 2626

**Federated States
of Micronesia**
Federated States of
Micronesia Office
(☎ 836-4775)
3049 Ualena
suite 408

Germany
Consulate of Germany
(☎ 946-3819)
2003 Kalia Rd

India
Consulate-General of India
(☎ 262-0292)
306 Hahani St

Italy
Consulate of Italy
(☎ 531-2277)
735 Bishop St, suite 201

Japan
Consulate-General of Japan
(☎ 523-7495)
1742 Nuuanu Ave

Kiribati
Consulate of Kiribati
(☎ 521-7703)
850 Richards St, suite 503

Korea
Consulate-General of Korea
(☎ 595-6109)
2756 Pali Hwy

Mariana Islands
Hawaii Liaison Office
(☎ 592-0300)
1221 Kapiolani Blvd.

Mexico
Consulate of Mexico
(☎ 524-4390)
677 Ala Moana Blvd
suite 501

Netherlands
Consulate of the Netherlands
(☎ 535-8450)
700 Bishop St, 21st floor

Norway
Consulate of Norway
(☎ 593-1240)
1314 S King St, suite G4

Papua New Guinea
Consulate-General
of Papua New Guinea
(☎ 524-5414)
1154 Fort St Mall, suite 300

Philippines
Consulate-General
of the Philippines
(☎ 595-6316)
2433 Pali Hwy

Sweden
Consulate of Sweden
(☎ 528-4777)
737 Bishop St, suite 2600

Switzerland
Consulate of Switzerland
(☎ 737-5297)
4231 Papu Circle

Thailand
Royal Thai
Consulate-General
(☎ 845-7332)
287A Kalihi

Tonga
Tonga Consular Agency
(☎ 521-5149)
220 S King St, suite 1230

All foreign visitors (other than Canadians) must of course bring their passport. US citizens and Canadians may want to bring along a passport as well, in the event they are tempted to extend their travels beyond Hawaii.

All visitors should bring their driver's license and any health insurance or travel insurance cards.

Members of senior citizen organizations such as the American Association of Retired Persons (AARP) can get an occasional hotel or car rental discount by showing their cards.

Members of Hostelling International (HI) will be able to take advantage of lower rates at the three HI hostels in Hawaii by bringing their membership card.

Members of the American Automobile Association (AAA) or other affiliated automobile clubs can get car rental, airfare and some sightseeing admission discounts with their membership cards.

Divers should bring their certification cards.

Photocopies

All important documents (passport data page and visa page, credit cards, travel insurance policy, air tickets, driver's license etc) should be photocopied before you leave home. Leave one copy with someone at home and keep another with you, separate from the originals.

CUSTOMS

US Customs allows each person over the age of 21 to bring one US quart of liquor and 200 cigarettes duty-free into the USA. Most fresh fruits and plants are restricted from entry into Hawaii, and there's a strict quarantine on animals.

MONEY
Currency

As is true throughout the USA, the US dollar is the only currency used in Hawaii.

The US dollar is divided into 100 cents. Coins come in denominations of one cent (penny), five cents (nickel), 10 cents (dime), 25 cents (quarter) and 50 cents (half dollar). Notes come in one-, five-, 10-, 20-, 50- and 100-dollar denominations. Also legal tender but only occasionally seen are a one-dollar coin that the government has tried unsuccessfully to bring into mass circulation and a two-dollar note that is out of favor.

Exchange Rates

At press time, exchange rates were:

country	unit		dollar
Australia	A$1	=	US$0.65
Canada	C$1	=	US$0.68
Euro	€1	=	US$1.07
France	1FF	=	US$0.16
Germany	DM1	=	US$0.55
Hong Kong	HK$1	=	US$0.13
Japan	¥100	=	US$0.94
New Zealand	NZ$1	=	US$0.54
UK	UK£1	=	US$1.65

Exchanging Money

Cash If you're carrying foreign currency, it can be exchanged for US dollars at larger banks, such as the ubiquitous Bank of Hawaii, or at Honolulu International Airport.

Traveler's Checks The main benefit of traveler's checks is to provide protection from theft. Large companies such as American Express and Thomas Cook generally offer efficient replacement policies.

Keeping a record of the check numbers and those you have used is vital when it comes to replacing lost checks. You should keep this information separate from the checks themselves.

Foreign visitors who carry traveler's checks will find it much easier if the checks are in US dollars.

Restaurants, hotels and most stores accept US dollar traveler's checks and treat them just like cash, so if that's what you're carrying, odds are you'll never have to use a bank or pay an exchange fee.

Credit Cards Major credit cards are widely accepted throughout Hawaii, including at car rental agencies and most hotels, restaurants, gas stations, shops and larger grocery stores. Most recreational and tourist activities in Hawaii can also be paid for by credit card. Note, however, that many B&Bs and some condominiums, particularly those handled through rental agencies, do not accept credit cards.

The most commonly accepted cards in Hawaii are Visa, MasterCard and American Express, although JCB, Discover and Diners Club cards are also accepted by a fair number of businesses.

ATMs Automatic teller machines (ATMs) are another handy alternative. We long ago stopped taking traveler's checks to Hawaii, choosing instead to withdraw money from a bank account back home using ATMs. The small service charge works out cheaper than the 1% fee charged for traveler's checks, and there's no need to carry a bundle of checks around.

Major banks such as Bank of Hawaii and First Hawaiian Bank have extensive ATM networks throughout Hawaii that will give cash advances on major credit cards (MasterCard, Visa, American Express, Discover and JCB) and allow cash withdrawals with affiliated ATM cards. Most ATM machines in Hawaii accept bank cards from both the Plus and Cirrus systems, the two largest ATM networks in the USA.

Look for ATMs outside banks, in most large grocery stores, in mall-style shopping centers and in a growing number of convenience stores.

International Transfers Transferring money from your home bank will be easier if you've authorized someone back home to access your account. Specify the town, the bank and the branch to which you want your money directed, or ask your home bank to tell you where there's a suitable one, and make sure you get the details right. You can find some of the necessary information on the websites of Hawaii's two largest banks: Bank of Hawaii (www.boh.com) and First Hawaiian Bank (www.fhb.com).

Costs

How much money you'll need for your visit to Hawaii depends on your traveling style.

Some people get by quite cheaply while others rack up huge balances on their American Express card.

Airfare to Hawaii is usually one of the heftier parts of the budget. Fares vary greatly, particularly from the US mainland, so shop around. (Note that Hawaii stopovers are often thrown in free, or for a nominal charge, on trips between North America and Asian or Pacific countries.)

Interisland flights cost about $50 to $95 one way, depending on how you buy your tickets. Hawaii has just one interisland ferry service, which operates between Lanai and Maui and costs $25 each way.

It can be a bit challenging to explore the islands without renting a car, except on Oahu, where there's a good inexpensive bus system. Renting a car usually costs between $150 and $200 a week.

Camping is an alternative to paying for a hotel. Every island except Lanai has at least one state park with free camping as well as inexpensive county campgrounds. In addition, Maui and the Big Island have excellent national parks with free camping.

Each of the four main islands has at least a couple of hostel-style places with dormitory beds for around $15 and either B&Bs or spartan hotels in the $40 to $50 range. For hotels with more standard middle-class amenities expect to pay nearly double that, and if you've got your mind set on a 1st-class beachfront hotel, get ready to pay upwards of $125 a night. For a splurge on a luxury hotel – and Hawaii has some of the world's finest – rates generally begin around $250.

If you're staying awhile, there are ways to cut accommodation costs. Weekly and monthly condo rental rates can beat all but the cheapest hotels. Besides having more space, most condos are turnkey, meaning that they're equipped with virtually everything you'll need, from towels and beach mats to a kitchen stocked with pots and pans. Being able to prepare your own meals in a condo can save a bundle on your food costs.

Another cost-cutter is to travel in the low season, generally from April to mid-December, when accommodation rates are often discounted as much as 30%.

Since much of Hawaii's food is shipped in, grocery prices average 25% higher than on the mainland. Because of the shipping costs, bulky items like cereal have the highest markups, while compact items such as canned tuna have the lowest. Food in local neighborhood restaurants is a good value in Hawaii, with prices generally as cheap as you'll find on the mainland.

The good news for visitors is that lots of things in Hawaii are free. There are no parking or entrance fees at beaches or state parks, for instance, and most of Hawaii's historical sights can be explored for free.

Tipping

Tipping practices are the same as in the rest of the USA. In restaurants, waiters expect a tip of about 15%, while 10% is generally sufficient for taxi drivers, hairstylists and the like. Hotel bellhops are typically tipped about $1 per bag.

Taxes

Hawaii has a 4.17% state sales tax that is tacked onto virtually everything, including all meals, groceries, car rentals and accommodations. An additional 7.24% room tax brings the total tax added to accommodation bills to 11.41%. Another tax targeted at visitors is a $2-a-day 'road use' tax imposed upon all car rentals.

POST & COMMUNICATIONS
Postal Rates

Postage rates for 1st-class mail sent and delivered within the USA are 33¢ for letters up to 1oz (22¢ for each additional ounce) and 20¢ for standard-size postcards. First-class mail between Hawaii and the mainland goes by air and usually takes three to four days.

International airmail rates are 60¢ for a half-ounce letter and 55¢ for a postcard to any foreign country with the exception of Canada (48¢ for a half-ounce letter and 45¢ for a postcard) and Mexico (40¢ for a half-ounce letter and 40¢ for a postcard).

The cost for parcels airmailed anywhere within the USA is $3.20 for 2lb or less. For heavier items, rates differ according to the distance mailed.

Receiving Mail

You can have mail sent to you c/o General Delivery at most post offices in Hawaii. An exception is on Oahu, where all general delivery mail addressed to Honolulu or Waikiki is delivered to the main post office, adjacent to Honolulu International Airport. Domestic mail is generally held for 10 days, international mail for 30 days. Most hotels will also hold mail for incoming guests.

Telephone

The telephone area code for all of Hawaii is 808. You don't need to use the area code when making calls on the same island, but you must use it when calling from one island to another and when calling Hawaii from outside the state.

All phone numbers listed in this book beginning with 800, 877 or 888 are toll-free calls from the US mainland, unless otherwise noted. The same numbers are sometimes toll-free from Canada as well.

Pay phones can be found throughout Hawaii in public places such as shopping centers and beach parks. Local calls cost 35¢ at pay phones. Any call made from one point on an island to any other point on that island is a local call. Calls from one island to another are long-distance.

A number of companies provide pay-phone service. From a GTE pay phone (the most common), direct-dialed calls from one Hawaiian island to another cost $1.45 for the first minute and 15¢ for each additional minute. The rate drops to $1.35 for the first minute and 10¢ for each extra minute every day from 5 pm to 8 am and all day on Saturday and Sunday. No matter which telephone company owns the pay phones, however, you can always call your own long-distance carrier and have the operators put your calls through at your own company's rates.

Most hotels add on a service charge of 50¢ to $1 for each local call made from a room phone, and most also impose hefty surcharges on long-distance calls. Public coin phones, which can be found in most lobbies, are always cheaper. You can pump in coins, use a phone card or make collect calls from pay phones. In Hawaii, as elsewhere in the

US, you can make toll-free calls (those that begin with 800, 877 or 888) from pay phones without inserting any money.

For directory assistance on the same island, dial ☎ 1-411; for other islands, dial ☎ 1-808-555-1212. To find out if there's an interisland toll-free number for a business, dial ☎ 1-800-555-1212.

International Calls To make an international call direct from Hawaii, dial ☎ 011 + country code + area code + number. (If you're calling Canada, though, you just have to dial ☎ 1 + area code + number.) For international operator assistance dial ☎ 0. The operator can give specific rate information and tell you which time periods are the cheapest for calling; these vary with the country being called.

When calling Hawaii from overseas, you must precede the 808 area code with 1, the international country code for the USA.

Phone Cards There's a wide range of local and international phone cards. Lonely Planet's eKno Communication Card is aimed specifically at travelers and provides cheap international calls, a range of messaging services and free email. For local calls, you're usually better off with a local card. You can join online at www.ekno.lonelyplanet.com, or by phone from Hawaii by dialing ☎ 1-800-294-3676. Once you have joined, to use eKno from Hawaii, dial ☎ 1-800-527-6786.

Fax
Faxes can be sent and received through the front desk of most hotels. There are also business centers throughout Hawaii, such as Kinko's, that offer reasonably priced fax services.

Email & Internet Access
Traveling with a portable computer is a great way to stay in touch with home, but unless you know what you're doing, it's fraught with potential problems. If the power-supply voltage in your home country is different than in Hawaii (see Electricity), bring a universal AC adapter, which will enable you to plug it in without frying the innards. You may also need a plug adapter, which is often easiest to buy before you leave home.

Also, your PC-card modem may not work once you leave your home country – but you won't know for sure until you try. The safest option is to buy a reputable 'global' modem before you leave home. Keep in mind that the telephone socket may be different from that at home as well, so ensure that you have at least a US RJ-11 telephone adapter that works with your modem. You can almost always find an adapter that will convert from RJ-11 to the local variety. For more information on traveling with a portable computer, see www.teleadapt.com or www.warrior.com.

Major Internet service providers such as AOL (www.aol.com) and CompuServe (www.compuserve.com) have dial-in nodes throughout the USA; it's best to download a list of the dial-in numbers before you leave home. If you access your Internet email at home through a smaller ISP, your best option is either to open an account with a global ISP, like those mentioned above, or to rely on public access points to collect your mail.

To use public access points to get your email, you'll need to know your incoming (POP or IMAP) mail server name, your account name and your password. A final option to collect mail through public access points is to open a free Web-based email account such as HotMail (www.hotmail.com) or Yahoo! Mail (mail.yahoo.com). You can then access your mail from anywhere in the world from any Internet-connected machine running a standard Web browser.

Internet cafes where you can check your email do exist in Hawaii, but they're scarce

and tend to be short-lived. Kinko's (www
.kinkos.com), a 24-hour business center with
offices throughout Hawaii, offers computers
with Internet access for 20¢ a minute, with
no minimum charge. Many public libraries
are also online, though officially you need to
have a Hawaii library card (see Libraries
later in this chapter).

If you're carrying a laptop, you may want
to check in advance with your hotel to see if
the room has a phone jack that can accommodate modem hookups; these are becoming more common as hotels upgrade and
renovate.

INTERNET RESOURCES

The World Wide Web is a rich resource for
travelers. You can research your trip, hunt
down bargain airfares, book hotels, check on
weather conditions or chat with locals and
other travelers about the best places to visit
(or avoid!).

There's no better place to start your Web
explorations than the Lonely Planet website
(www.lonelyplanet.com). Here you'll find
succinct summaries on traveling to most
places on earth, postcards from other travelers and the Thorn Tree bulletin board, where
you can ask questions before you go or dis-
pense advice when you get back. You can
also find travel news and updates to many
of our most popular guidebooks, and the
subWWWay section links you to the most
useful travel resources elsewhere on the Web.

In addition, www.planet-hawaii.com is a
useful website that has links to a wealth of
Hawaii information. Other websites are given
throughout this book under specific topics.

BOOKS

A great many books have been written
about Hawaii and its people, landscapes,
history, culture and unique flora and fauna.
The books that follow are just a few of the
recommended titles. Note that 'UH Press'
in this section refers to the University of
Hawaii Press in Honolulu.

Lonely Planet

If your travels will take you only to Waikiki,
Honolulu or elsewhere on the island of
Oahu, pick up Lonely Planet's *Oahu* guide,
which provides the most in-depth coverage
available to that island.

Activity Guides

*Diving and Snorkeling Guide to the Hawai-
ian Islands* by Doug Wallin (Lonely Planet/
Pisces Books) is an excellent guide to both
diving and snorkeling in the Hawaiian
Islands. It includes color photos illustrating
sites and fish.

The Beaches of Oahu, *The Beaches of
Maui County*, *Beaches of the Big Island* and
Beaches of Kauai and Niihau are by John
Clark (UH Press). These comprehensive
books detail each island's coastline and every
one of its beaches, including water conditions, shoreline geology and local history.
The Maui edition includes Maui, Molokai,
Lanai and Kahoolawe. Clark also has a new
book, *Hawaii's Best Beaches*, that covers 50
of the best beaches in the state. If you're
going to be spending a lot of time exploring
beaches, these books are the ones to have.

*Surfer's Guide to Hawaii: Hawaii Gets All
the Breaks* by Greg Ambrose (Bess Press)
describes the top surfing spots throughout
the islands. Written in an entertaining style,
it's packed with everything you need to
know about surfing in Hawaii.

Kathy Morey's *Kauai Trails*, *Maui Trails*,
Oahu Trails and *Hawaii Trails*, the last to the
Big Island, all by Wilderness Press, are comprehensive hiking guides with good maps
and clear directions.

Hawaiian Hiking Trails by Craig Chisholm
(The Fernglen Press) is a good statewide
hiking guide to Hawaii's best-known trails.
Chisholm illustrates each hike with a USGS
map of the route.

Six Islands on Two Wheels by Tom Koch
(Bess Press) is a comprehensive guide to cycling in Hawaii. Koch encourages you to bring
your own bike to Hawaii and tells you how
to outfit it, where to ride and what to expect.

Mountain Biking the Hawaiian Islands
by Oahu resident John Alford (Ohana Publishing) is an excellent resource for mountain bikers, covering the public trails open
to bikers on six islands, with maps and
descriptions.

History & Politics

Hawaiian Antiquities by David Malo (Bishop Museum Press), written in 1838, was the first account of Hawaiian culture written by a Hawaiian. It gives an in-depth history of Hawaii before the arrival of the missionaries.

Shoal of Time by Gavan Daws (UH Press) is a comprehensive and colorful history covering the period from Captain Cook's 'discovery' of the islands to statehood.

Fragments of Hawaiian History by John Papa Ii (Bishop Museum Press), translated by Mary Kawena Pukui, is a firsthand account of old Hawaii under the *kapu* (taboo) system. Ii lived in Kailua-Kona at the time of Kamehameha I.

Hawaii's Story by Hawaii's Queen by Queen Liliuokalani (Mutual Publishing), written in 1897, is an autobiographical account of Liliuokalani's life and the circumstances surrounding her 1893 overthrow.

The Betrayal of Liliuokalani: Last Queen of Hawaii, 1838-1917 by Helena G Allen (Mutual Publishing) is an insightful account not only of the queen's life but also of missionary activity and foreign encroachment in Hawaii.

Kauai, the Separate Kingdom by Edward Joesting (UH Press) is the authoritative history book on Kauai, the only Hawaiian island never conquered in battle.

The Hawaiian Kingdom by Ralph S Kuykendall (UH Press) is a three-volume set that covers Hawaiian history from 1778 to 1893 and is considered the definitive work on the period.

Merchant Prince of the Sandalwood Mountains by Bob Dye (UH Press) tells the story of Chun Afong, Hawaii's first Chinese millionaire, in the context of the turbulent social and economic changes of the 18th century.

Natural History

Hawaii: The Islands of Life (Signature Publishing) has strikingly beautiful photos of the flora, fauna and landscapes being protected by the Nature Conservancy of Hawaii. The text is by respected Pacific author Gavan Daws.

The Many-Splendored Fishes of Hawaii by Gar Goodson (Stanford University Press) is one of the better of several small, inexpensive fish-identification books on the market and has good descriptions and 170 color drawings.

Hawaii's Fishes: A Guide for Snorkelers, Divers and Aquarists by John P Hoover (Mutual Publishing), a more expensive and comprehensive field guide, covers more than 230 reef and shore fishes of Hawaii. It's fully illustrated with color photographs and gives insights on island dive sites.

Hawaii's Birds (Hawaii Audubon Society) is the best pocket-size guide to the birds of Hawaii. It includes color photos and descriptions of all the native birds and many of the introduced species.

For something more comprehensive, there's *A Field Guide to the Birds of Hawaii & the Tropical Pacific* by H Douglas Pratt, Phillip L Bruner and Delwyn G Berrett (Princeton University Press). The book contains nearly 50 pages of color plates.

Mammals in Hawaii by P Quentin Tomich (Bishop Museum Press) is an authoritative book on the mammals in Hawaii, with interesting stories on how they arrived in the islands. He includes all species of whales and dolphins found in Hawaiian waters.

Trailside Plants of Hawaii's National Parks by Charles H Lamoureux (Hawaii Natural History Association) covers common trailside plants and trees in some depth. It's a good book to have if you'll be spending time hiking in the national parks.

Plants and Flowers of Hawaii by SH Sohmer and R Gustafson (UH Press) has quality color photos and descriptions of more than 130 native plants of Hawaii, including information on their habitat and evolution.

The new *Manual of the Flowering Plants of Hawaii* by Warren L Wagner, Derral R Herbst and SH Sohmer (Bishop Museum Press) has in-depth information on Hawaiian flora, including rare and endangered species that have recently been categorized.

Practical Folk Medicine of Hawaii by LR McBride (Petroglyph Press) has descriptions of many native medicinal plants and their uses.

People

Keneti by Bob Krauss (UH Press) is a biography of Kenneth 'Keneti' Emory, the esteemed Bishop Museum archaeologist who over the years sailed with writer Jack London, worked with anthropologist Margaret Mead and surfed with Olympian Duke Kahanamoku. Emory, who died in 1992, spent much of his life uncovering the ruins of villages and temples throughout the Pacific, recording them before they disappeared forever.

Paddling My Own Canoe by Audrey Sutherland (UH Press) details the author's adventures and ruminations while kayaking solo along the rugged, isolated North Shore of Molokai. The book helped popularize wilderness kayaking in Hawaii.

Father Damien, the priest who worked in the leprosy colony on Molokai, is the subject of many books, including *Holy Man: Father Damien of Molokai* by Gavan Daws, *Damien the Leper* by John Farrow and others.

Aloha Cowboy by Virginia Cowan-Smith and Bonnie Domrose Stone (UH Press) is an illustrated account of 200 years of *paniolo* (cowboy) life in Hawaii.

Hawaiian Culture

The Kumulipo by Martha Beckwith (UH Press) is a translation of the Hawaiian chant of creation. The chant of 2077 lines begins in the darkness of the spirit world and traces the genealogy of an *alii* (royal) family, said to be the ancestors of humankind.

Hawaiian Mythology by Martha Beckwith (UH Press) has comprehensive translations of Hawaii's old myths and legends.

Nana I Ke Kumu (Look to the Source) by Mary Kawena Pukui, EW Haertig and Catherine A Lee (Hui Hanai) is a fascinating two-volume collection of information on Hawaiian cultural practices, social customs and beliefs.

The Legends and Myths of Hawaii (Mutual Publishing) is a collection of legends as told by King David Kalakaua. It has a short introduction to Hawaiian culture and history as well.

Niihau Shell Leis by Linda Paik Moriarty (UH Press) explains the development of the unique Hawaiian craft of shell lei-making by Niihauans and illustrates the various styles.

Hawaiian Petroglyphs by J Halley Cox (Bishop Museum Press) lists petroglyph sites and includes extensive photos and illustrations.

Legacy of the Landscape by Patrick Vinton Kirch (UH Press) details 50 of the most important Hawaiian archaeological sites, including ancient heiaus, fishponds and petroglyphs.

Fiction

A Hawaiian Reader, edited by A Grove Day and Carl Stroven (Mutual Publishing), is an excellent anthology with 37 selections, both fiction and nonfiction. It starts with a log entry by Captain James Cook and includes writings from early missionaries as well as Mark Twain, Jack London, Somerset Maugham, David Malo, Isabella Bird, Martha Beckwith and others. If you only have time to read one book about Hawaii, this inexpensive paperback is a great choice.

Stories of Hawaii (Mutual Publishing) is a collection of 13 of Jack London's yarns about the islands.

OA Bushnell is one of the best-known contemporary authors writing about Hawaii. UH Press has published his titles *The Return of Lono*, a historical novel of Captain Cook's final voyage; *Kaaawa*, about Hawaii in the 1850s; *Molokai*, about life in the leprosy colony at Kalaupapa; *The Stone of Kannon*, about the first group of Japanese contract laborers to arrive in Hawaii, and its sequel, *The Water of Kane*.

Talking to the Dead by Sylvia Watanabe is an enjoyable read that portrays a sense of growing up as a second-generation Japanese American in postwar Hawaii.

Hawaii is James Michener's ambitious novel of the islands, from their volcanic origins to their emergence as a state. This sweeping saga traces the Polynesian settlers, the arrival of the missionaries and whalers, the emergence of the sugar barons and the development of Hawaii's multi-ethnic society.

Reference

The recently revised 350-page *Atlas of Hawaii* by the Department of Geography, University of Hawaii (UH Press), is loaded with data, maps and tabulations covering everything from land ownership to seasonal ocean wave patterns.

Place Names of Hawaii by Mary Kawena Pukui, Samuel H Elbert and Esther T Mookini (UH Press) is a glossary of 4000 Hawaiian place names. The meaning and background of each name is explained.

Hawaiian Dictionary by Mary Kawena Pukui and Samuel H Elbert (UH Press) is the authoritative work on the Hawaiian language. It's in both Hawaiian-English and English-Hawaiian, with 30,000 entries. There's also an inexpensive pocket-size version with 10,000 Hawaiian words.

There are many other Hawaiian-language books on the market, including grammar texts, conversational self-study guides and books on pidgin.

Bookstores

The four largest islands all have good bookstores with extensive Hawaiiana sections. Bookstore locations are listed under Information in each island chapter.

Ordering by Mail Island Bookshelf (☎ 503-297-4324, 800-967-5944, fax 503-297-1702, www.islandbookshelf.com), PO Box 91003, Portland, OR 97291, specializes in books on Hawaii and will mail out a comprehensive catalog on request.

The following publishers will send catalogs of their own titles that can be ordered by mail.

Bess Press
(☎ 734-7159, 800-910-2377, fax 732-3627, www.besspress.com)
3565 Harding Ave, Honolulu, HI 96816

Bishop Museum Press
(☎ 848-4134, fax 841-8968)
1525 Bernice St, Honolulu, HI 96817

University of Hawaii Press
(☎ 956-8255, 888-847-7377, fax 988-6052, www2.hawaii.edu/uhpress)
2840 Kolowalu St, Honolulu, HI 96822

FILMS

Dozens of feature movies have been filmed in Hawaii and scores of others have used footage of Hawaii as backdrops. One of the few that has insightfully delved into island life is *Picture Bride* (1993), starring Yuki Kudoh, with a cameo by Toshiro Mifune; filmed on Oahu, it depicts the blunt realities of 19th-century Hawaiian plantation life for a Japanese mail-order bride.

Classic movies filmed at least partially on Hawaii include: *Song of the Islands* (1942), filmed on the Big Island, starring Betty Grable and Victor Mature; *From Here to Eternity* (1953), filmed in Oahu, starring Burt Lancaster and Deborah Kerr; *Miss Sadie Thompson* (1953), filmed on Kauai, starring Rita Hayworth; *South Pacific* (1958), filmed on Kauai, with Mitzi Gaynor and Rossano Brazzi; *The Old Man and the Sea* (1958), filmed on the Big Island, starring Spencer Tracy; *Blue Hawaii* (1961), filmed on Kauai, starring Elvis Presley and Angela Lansbury; *Hawaii* (1966), filmed on Oahu and Kauai, starring Julie Andrews and Max von Sydow; *Tora! Tora! Tora!* (1970), filmed on Oahu, starring Jason Robards; *King Kong* (1976), filmed on Kauai, with Jessica Lange and Jeff Bridges; and *Raiders of the Lost Ark* (1981), filmed on Kauai, with Harrison Ford.

In the 1990s, a couple of blockbusters used Hawaii as their main base. Steven Spielberg's *Jurassic Park* (1993) was filmed in remote valleys on Kauai, while Kevin Costner's big washout *Waterworld* (1995) was filmed in the waters off the Big Island.

NEWSPAPERS & MAGAZINES

Hawaii's main paper is the *Honolulu Advertiser*, which is published daily each morning. The Honolulu paper is sold throughout Hawaii, but the Neighbor Islands also have their own newspapers. The *Hawaii Tribune-Herald* in Hilo, *West Hawaii Today* in Kailua-Kona, the *Maui News* in Wailuku and the *Garden Island* in Lihue are each published at least five times a week.

Several mainland newspapers are also widely available, including *USA Today*, the *Wall Street Journal* and the *Los Angeles Times*. Look for them in the lobbies of larger hotels and in convenience stores. You can get international newspapers at Borders bookstores, which carry an impressively wide selection.

Honolulu and *Aloha* are the largest general interest magazines about Hawaii. *Honolulu* is geared more towards residents and is published monthly. *Aloha* has more visitor-oriented feature articles and is published six times a year.

The numerous tourist magazines distributed free on the islands are well worth perusing. They usually have simple maps, a bit of current event information, lots of ads and discount coupons for everything from hamburgers to sunset cruises.

RADIO & TV

Hawaii has a total of about 50 AM and FM radio stations, including some that feature Hawaiian music. Programming varies widely across the dial; for specific details, see the Information headings in the individual island chapters.

On Hawaiian TV you'll find stations representing the major US networks, as well as cable channels offering tourist information, Japanese-language programs and more. Almost anything you can watch on the mainland you can watch in Hawaii.

For some local flavor, the evening news on Channel 2 ends with some fine slack-key guitar music by Keola and Kapono Beamer and clips of people waving the *shaka* sign.

PHOTOGRAPHY & VIDEO
Film & Equipment

Both print and slide film are readily available on all the islands. If you're going to be in Hawaii for any length of time, consider having your film developed there, as the high temperature and humidity of the tropics greatly accelerates the deterioration of exposed film. The sooner it's developed, the better the results.

Kodak and Fuji have labs in Honolulu, and island drugstores and camera shops usually send customer orders to those labs. Longs Drugs is one of the cheapest places for both purchasing film and having it developed. All the tourist centers have one-hour print processing shops as well.

Technical Tips

Don't leave your camera in direct sun any longer than necessary. A locked car can heat up like an oven in just a few minutes.

Sand and water are intense reflectors, and in bright light they'll often leave foreground subjects shadowy. You can try compensating by adjusting your f-stop or attaching a polarizing filter, or both, but the most effective technique is to take all of your beach photos in the gentler light of early morning and late afternoon.

Video Systems

Videotapes can be readily purchased throughout Hawaii. But foreign visitors should be aware that North America uses the NTSC system, which is incompatible with the PAL system used in Europe.

TIME

Hawaii does not observe daylight saving time. When it's noon in Hawaii, it's 1 pm in Anchorage, 2 pm in Los Angeles, 5 pm in New York, 10 pm in London, 11 pm in Bonn, 7 am the next day in Tokyo, 8 am the next day in Sydney and Melbourne and 10 am the next day in Auckland. That's assuming none of those other places is observing daylight saving time either.

The time difference is one hour greater during those months when other countries *are* observing daylight saving. For example, from April to October when it's noon in Hawaii it's 3 pm in Los Angeles and 6 pm in New York; and from November to March when it's noon in Hawaii it's 9 am in Melbourne and 11 am in Auckland.

Hawaii has about 11 hours of daylight in midwinter and almost 13^1/$_2$ hours in midsummer. In midwinter, the sun rises at about 7 am and sets at about 6 pm. In midsummer, it rises before 6 am and sets after 7 pm.

And then there's 'Hawaiian Time,' which is either a slow-down-the-clock pace or a euphemism for being late.

ELECTRICITY

Electricity is 110/120 V, 60 cycles. Most outlets accept a flat, two-pronged plug, as elsewhere in the USA, but some grounded outlets also allow you to use items with three-pronged plugs.

WEIGHTS & MEASURES
Hawaii uses the US system of measurement. Distances are measured in feet, yards and miles; weights are tallied in ounces, pounds and tons. Those unaccustomed to the US system can consult the metric conversion table on the inside back cover of this book.

LAUNDRY
Many hotels, condominiums and hostels have coin-operated washers and dryers. If there's not one where you're staying, you can find commercial coin-operated laundries on all the islands. The average cost is about $1 to wash a load of clothes and another dollar to dry. Laundry locations are listed under Information in each island chapter.

HEALTH
Hawaii is a very healthy place to live and to visit. As it's 2500 miles from the nearest industrial center, there's little air pollution – other than that caused by volcanic activity. Hawaii ranks first of all the 50 US states in life expectancy, which is currently about 76 years for men and 81 years for women.

Everyday Health

Normal body temperature is up to 98.6°F (37°C); more than 4°F (2°C) higher indicates a high fever. The normal adult pulse rate is 60 to 100 beats per minute (children 80 to 100, babies 100 to 140). As a general rule, the pulse increases about 20 beats per minute for each 2°F (1°C) rise in fever.

Respiration (breathing) rate is also an indicator of illness. Count the number of breaths per minute: between 12 and 20 is normal for adults and older children (up to 30 for younger children, 40 for babies). People with a high fever or serious respiratory illness breathe more quickly than normal. More than 40 shallow breaths a minute may indicate pneumonia.

There are few serious health concerns. The islands have none of the tropical nasties like malaria, cholera or yellow fever, and you can drink water directly out of the tap, although all stream water needs to be boiled or treated.

No immunizations are required to enter Hawaii or any other port in the USA.

Be aware that there are many poisonous plants in Hawaii, so you should never taste a plant that you cannot positively identify as edible.

If you're new to the heat and humidity, you may find yourself easily fatigued and more susceptible to minor ailments. Acclimatize yourself by slowing down your pace and setting your body clock to the more kicked-back 'Hawaiian Time.' Drink plenty of liquids.

If you're planning on a long outing or anything strenuous, take enough water and don't push yourself.

Medical Problems & Treatment
Hawaii has 25 acute-care hospitals, 2600 physicians and 1200 dentists. While the rural islands of Molokai and Lanai have limited medical facilities, the other islands have fully staffed hospitals with modern facilities. Still, for specialized care and serious illnesses, many islanders have more confidence in Honolulu hospitals than in Neighbor Island facilities.

Some travel insurance policies cover medical expenses. For more information, see Travel Insurance under Visas & Documents, earlier in this chapter.

Leptospirosis Visitors to Hawaii should be aware of leptospirosis, a disease caused by bacteria found in freshwater streams and ponds on the islands.

Animals such as rats, mongooses and wild pigs carry the disease. Humans most often pick up leptospirosis by swimming or wading in water contaminated by animal urine. Leptospires can exist in any freshwater source, including idyllic-looking waterfalls and jungle streams, because the water may have washed down the slopes through animal habitats.

The bacteria enter the body through the nose, eyes, mouth or cuts in the skin. Symptoms can occur within two to 20 days after exposure and may include fever, chills, sweating, headaches, muscle pains, vomiting and diarrhea. More severe symptoms include blood in the urine and jaundice. Symptoms may last from a few days to several weeks.

A few dozen cases statewide are confirmed each year; wetland taro farmers, swimmers and backcountry hikers account for the majority of them. Because symptoms of leptospirosis resemble the flu and hepatitis, other cases probably go unconfirmed. Although deaths have been attributed to the disease, they are relatively rare.

Some precautions include wearing waterproof *tabis* (reef walkers) when hiking and avoiding unnecessary freshwater crossings, especially if you have open cuts.

Leptospirosis can be serious, yet thousands of people swim in Hawaiian streams without contracting it. The state has posted warnings at many trailheads and freshwater swimming areas. Islanders have differing opinions on leptospirosis – some never swim in freshwater because of it, while others consider it such a long shot that they take no precautions at all.

Sunburn Sunburn is always a concern in the tropics, as the closer you get to the equator, the fewer of the sun's rays are blocked out by the atmosphere. Don't be fooled by what appears to be a hazy overcast day – you can get sunburned surprisingly quickly, even through clouds.

Sunscreen with an SPF (sun protection factor) of 10 to 15 is recommended if you're not already tanned. If you're going into the water, use a water-resistant sunscreen. Snorkelers may want to wear a T-shirt if they plan to be out in the water a long time. You'll not only be protecting against sunburn but also against potential skin cancer and premature aging of the skin.

Fair-skinned people can get both first- and second-degree burns in the hot Hawaiian sun, and wearing a sun hat for added protection is a good idea. The most severe sun is between 10 am and 2 pm.

Prickly Heat Prickly heat is an itchy rash caused by excessive perspiration trapped under the skin. It usually strikes people who have just arrived in a hot climate and whose pores have not yet opened sufficiently to cope with greater sweating. Keeping cool by bathing often or resorting to air-con may help until you acclimatize.

Heat Exhaustion Dehydration or salt deficiency can cause heat exhaustion. Take time to acclimatize to high temperatures and make sure you get sufficient liquids. Salt deficiency is characterized by fatigue, lethargy, headaches, giddiness and muscle cramps, and in this case salt tablets may help. Vomiting or diarrhea can deplete your liquid and salt levels.

Heat Stroke This serious, sometimes fatal condition can occur if the body's heat-regulating mechanism breaks down and the body temperature rises to dangerous levels. Long, continuous periods of exposure to high temperatures can leave you vulnerable to heat stroke. Avoid strenuous activity in

Medical Kit

A small first-aid kit is a sensible thing to carry, especially if you plan on camping or hiking into the backcountry.

A basic kit should have things such as aspirin or Panadol for pain or fever; an antihistamine (such as Benadryl) for use as a decongestant, to relieve the itch from insect bites or to help prevent motion sickness; an antiseptic ointment for cuts and scratches; calamine lotion or aluminum sulfate spray to ease the irritation from bites and stings; bandages and Band-Aids; scissors; tweezers; insect repellent; and a good sunblock.

Also, be sure to bring adequate supplies of prescription medicine or contraceptive pills you may already be taking.

open sun (such as lengthy hikes or bike rides across lava fields) when you first arrive.

The symptoms of heat stroke include very little perspiration and a high body temperature (102°F to 106°F). Where sweating has ceased, the skin becomes flushed and red. Severe, throbbing headaches and lack of coordination will also occur, and the sufferer may be confused or aggressive. Eventually the victim may become delirious or convulse. Hospitalization is essential, but in the meantime, you can help those suffering from heat stroke by getting them out of the sun, removing their clothing, covering them with a wet sheet or towel and then fanning them continually.

Fungal Infections The same climate that produces lush tropical forests also promotes a prolific growth of skin fungi and bacteria. Hot weather fungal infections are most likely to occur between the toes or fingers or in the groin.

To prevent fungal infections, it's essential to keep your skin dry and cool and allow air to circulate. Choose loose cotton clothing rather than artificial fibers, and sandals rather than shoes. If you do get an infection, wash the infected area daily with a disinfectant or medicated soap. Rinse and dry well and then apply an antifungal powder.

Altitude Sickness On the Big Island, people planning to go to the summits of Mauna Kea or Mauna Loa need to be aware of the possibility of Acute Mountain Sickness (AMS), which occurs at high altitudes due to lack of oxygen. It can be fatal. While AMS can generally be avoided by making gains in elevation at a slow pace, Hawaii presents an unusual situation, as most people who visit Mauna Kea summit do so by car. Many of those visitors drive straight up to nearly 14,000 feet from their hotels on the coast, a mere two-hour ride that offers no time to acclimatize. As a result, AMS is a common problem for summit visitors, even though most cases are on the mild side.

AMS symptoms include headaches, nausea, dizziness and shortness of breath, while confusion and lack of coordination and balance are real danger signs. With all but the mildest of symptoms, travelers experiencing signs of AMS should immediately descend to a lower elevation. For more information, see Dangers & Annoyances in the Mauna Kea section of the Big Island chapter.

Motion Sickness Eating only lightly before and during a trip will reduce your chances of getting motion sickness. If you are prone to the condition, try to find a place that minimizes disturbance – near the wing on aircraft or close to midships on boats. Fresh air usually helps; reading or cigarette smoke doesn't. Commercial anti-motion-sickness preparations, which can cause drowsiness, have to be taken before the trip commences; when you're feeling sick it's too late. Ginger is a natural preventative and is available in capsule form.

Jet Lag When we travel long distances rapidly, our bodies take time to adjust to the 'new time' of our destination and we may experience fatigue, disorientation, insomnia, anxiety, impaired concentration and loss of appetite. These effects will usually be gone within three days of arrival, but there are ways of minimizing the impact of jet lag:

- Rest for a couple of days prior to departure; try to avoid late nights and last-minute dashes for traveler's checks and the like.

- Try to select flight schedules that minimize sleep deprivation; arriving late in the day means you can go to sleep soon after you arrive. For very long flights, try to organize a stopover.

- Avoid excessive eating (which bloats the stomach) and alcohol (which causes dehydration) during the flight. Instead, drink plenty of noncarbonated, nonalcoholic drinks such as fruit juice or water.

- Make yourself comfortable by wearing loose-fitting clothes and perhaps bringing an eye mask and earplugs to help you sleep.

HIV & AIDS Infection with the human immunodeficiency virus (HIV) may lead to acquired immune deficiency syndrome (AIDS), which is a fatal disease. Any exposure to blood, blood products or body fluids may put the individual at risk. The disease is often transmitted through sexual contact or dirty needles – vaccinations, acupuncture, tattooing and body-piercing can be potentially as dangerous as intravenous drug use.

If you have any questions regarding AIDS while in Hawaii, contact the AIDS/STD Hotline at ☎ 922-1313 on Oahu or ☎ 800-321-1555 from the Neighbor Islands.

Cuts & Scratches Cuts and skin punctures are easily infected in Hawaii's hot and humid climate, and infections can be persistent. Keep any cut or open wound clean and treat it with an antiseptic solution. Keep the area protected, but where possible avoid bandages, which can keep wounds wet.

Coral cuts are even more susceptible to infection because tiny pieces of coral can get embedded in the skin. These cuts are notoriously slow to heal, as the coral releases a weak venom into the wound.

Pesky Creatures Hawaii has no land snakes, but it does have its fair share of annoying mosquitoes as well as centipedes that can give an unpleasant bite. The islands also have bees and ground-nesting wasps, which, like the centipede, generally pose danger only to those who are allergic to their stings. (For information on stinging sea creatures, see Ocean Safety under Dangers & Annoyances, later.)

This being the tropics, cockroaches are plentiful; although they don't pose much of a health problem, they do little for the appetite. Condos with kitchens have the most problems. If you find that the place you're staying is infested, you can always call the manager or the front desk and have them spray poisons – which are no doubt more dangerous than the roaches!

While sightings are not terribly common, there are two dangerous arachnids on the islands: the black widow spider and the scorpion.

Black Widow Spiders Found in much of the USA, the black widow is glossy black and has a body that's a half-inch in diameter with a characteristic red hourglass mark on its abdomen. It weaves a strong, tangled web close to the ground and inhabits brush piles, sheds and outdoor privies.

Its bite, which resembles the prick of a pin, can be barely noticeable, but is followed in about 30 minutes by severe cramping in which the abdominal muscles become board-like and breathing becomes difficult. Other reactions include vomiting, headaches, sweating, shaking and a tingling sensation in the fingers. In severe cases the bite can be fatal. If you think you've been bitten by a black widow, seek immediate medical help.

Scorpions The scorpion, confined principally to warm dry regions, is capable of inflicting a painful sting by means of its caudal fang. Like the black widow, the venom contains neurotoxins. Severity of the symptoms generally depends on the age of the victim; stings can even be fatal for very young children. Symptoms are shortness of breath, hives, swelling or vomiting. Apply diluted household ammonia and cold compresses to the area of the sting and seek immediate medical help.

While the odds of encountering a scorpion are quite low in Hawaii, campers should always check inside their hiking boots before putting them on!

Ciguatera Poisoning Ciguatera is a serious illness caused by eating fish affected by ciguatoxin, which herbivorous fish can pick up from marine algae. There is no ready way of detecting ciguatoxin, and it's not diminished by cooking. Symptoms of food poisoning usually occur three to five hours after eating.

Ciguatoxin is most common among reef fish (which are not commonly served in restaurants) and hasn't affected Hawaii's deep-sea fish, such as tuna, marlin and mahimahi. The symptoms, if you do eat the wrong fish, can include nausea; stomach cramps; diarrhea; paralysis; tingling and numbness of the face, fingers and toes; and a reversal of temperature sensations, so that hot things feel cold and vice versa. Extreme cases can result in unconsciousness and even death. Vomit until your stomach is empty and get immediate medical help.

Dance & Music

Ancient Hula

Perhaps nothing is more uniquely Hawaiian than the hula. There are many different schools of hula, all very disciplined and graceful in their movements. Before Western contact, students spent years training in hula schools, sometimes moving to other islands to enroll with the masters.

ROBERT FRIED

Most ancient hula dances expressed historical events, legendary tales and the accomplishments of the great *alii* (royal rulers). Facial expressions, hand gestures, hip sway and dance steps all conveyed the story. Hulas were performed to rhythmic chants and drum beatings, which served to connect the dancers with the world of spirits. Eye movement was very important: If the story told about the sun, the eyes would gaze upward; if about the netherworld, they would gaze downward.

One school, the *hula ohelo*, was very sensual, with movements suggesting the act of procreation.

Hula dancers wore *tapa* (cloth made from pounded bark), not the grass skirts that were introduced from Micronesia only a hundred years ago.

The Christian missionaries thought it all too licentious for their liking and suppressed it. The hula might have been lost forever if not for King Kalakaua, the 'Merrie Monarch,' who revived it in the latter half of the 19th century.

ROBERT FRIED

Musical Instruments

The *pahu hula*, a knee drum carved from a breadfruit or coconut log, with a sharkskin drum head, was used solely at hula performances. Other hula musical instruments include *ke laau* sticks, used to keep the beat for the dancers; *iliili*, stone castanets; *puili*, rattles made from split bamboo; and *uliuli*, gourd rattles decorated with colorful feathers.

The early Hawaiians were a romantic lot, and some instruments were used for courting, including the *ohe*, a nose flute made of bamboo, and the *ukeke*, a musical bow with a couple of strings.

Ancient Crafts

Tapa Weaving

In ancient Hawaii, women spent much of their time beating *kapa* (tapa cloth) or preparing *lauhala* for weaving.

Tapa made from the *wauke* (paper mulberry tree) was the favorite. The bark was carefully stripped, then pounded with wooden beaters that were carved with different patterns, which then became the pattern of the tapa. Dyes were made from charcoal, flowers and sea urchins.

Tapa had many uses in addition to clothing, from food containers to burial shrouds. After the missionaries introduced cotton cloth and western clothing, the art of tapa making slowly faded away. These days, the tapa for sale in Hawaii is usually Samoan or Fijian tapa, which can be identified by the bold designs. Hawaiian tapa was different, with more delicate patterns.

Lauhala Weaving

Lauhala weaving uses the *lau* (leaves) of the *hala*, or pandanus, tree. Preparing the leaves for weaving is hard, messy work, as there are razor-sharp spines along the leaf edges and down the center.

In old Hawaii, lauhala were woven into mats and floor coverings, but these days smaller items like hats, place-mats and baskets are most common.

ROBERT FRIED

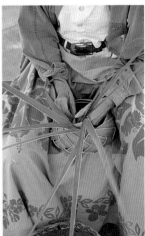

NED FRIARY

WOMEN TRAVELERS

Women travelers are no more likely to encounter problems in Hawaii than anywhere else in the USA. We advise everyone – especially women traveling alone – against hitchhiking. If you do thumb a ride, size up the vehicle's occupants carefully and don't hesitate to turn down anyone who makes you feel uncomfortable. If you're camping, opt for popular, well-used camping areas, rather than more remote locales where you might be the only camper; the lesser-used spots sometimes become impromptu drinking hangouts.

Women who have been abused or sexually assaulted can call the Sex Abuse Treatment Center's 24-hour hotline on Oahu at ☎ 524-7273. Similar Neighbor Island hotlines are: ☎ 245-4144 on Kauai, ☎ 935-0677 on the Big Island and ☎ 242-4357 on Maui, Molokai and Lanai.

Recommended reading for first-time women travelers is the *Handbook for Women Travellers* by M and G Moss, published by Judy Piatkus Books.

GAY & LESBIAN TRAVELERS

Gay marriages in Hawaii? In recent years, it has looked as if travelers of all persuasions might soon be able to tie the knot in Hawaii, as the state moved center stage in the movement to legalize same-gender marriages.

In December 1996, a state circuit court judge ruled that Hawaii's prohibition of same-sex marriage violated the equal protection clause of the state constitution, which explicitly bans gender discrimination. Implementation of the ruling, however, was postponed pending appeal of the case to the Hawaii Supreme Court – and that ruling has yet to come down.

In the meantime, two related events have taken place. In July 1997, Hawaii became the first US state to extend broad rights to domestic partners. To appease the vocal conservatives who oppose gay marriages, the law was written to cover any two adults who cannot legally marry, including a range of pairings beyond same-sex couples, such as a mother and adult child or two siblings living together. Those who register are covered on an umbrella of items ranging from medical insurance to survivorship rights.

In the eyes of Hawaii legislators, the new domestic partnership law was a compromise, meant to quiet both the pro and con voices in the controversy over gay marriages.

As the domestic partnership law was being established, the state legislature proceeded to put forth an amendment to Hawaii's state constitution allowing the legislature 'to reserve marriage to opposite-sex couples' only. This amendment was overwhelmingly passed by Hawaii voters in the November 1998 elections.

The issue, however, is far from buried. The Hawaii Supreme Court could still rule favorably on the original prohibition against same-sex marriage, or even be asked to void the new state constitutional amendment under the US Constitution's equal protection clause. So the final battle in this protracted struggle may still be years away.

Gay marriages aside, Hawaii is as popular a vacation spot for gays and lesbians as it is for straights. The state has strong minority protections and a constitutional guarantee of privacy that extends to sexual behavior between consenting adults.

Still, most of the gay scene is very low-key, especially on the Neighbor Islands; public hand-holding and other outward signs of affection between gays is not commonplace. Certainly in terms of nightlife, the main gay club scene is centered in Waikiki.

The following information sources can help gay and lesbian visitors get oriented to the islands.

Pacific Ocean Holidays (☎ 923-2400, 800-735-6600, fax 923-2499), PO Box 88245, Honolulu, HI 96830, arranges vacation packages for gay men and women. The company also produces a booklet called *Pocket Guide to Hawaii*, which is geared to the gay community and costs $5 when ordered by mail.

The volunteer-run Gay & Lesbian Community Center (☎ 951-7000), 1566 Wilder Ave, Honolulu, HI 96822, is a good source of information on local issues for both women and men. It also has recorded information on the latest gay entertainment venues and

Hawaiian Weddings

Many visitors come to Hawaii not only for their honeymoon, but to exchange their wedding vows as well. Getting married in Hawaii is a straightforward process. The state requires that the prospective bride and groom appear in person together before a marriage license agent and pay $50 for a license, which is given out on the spot. There's no waiting period and no residence, citizenship or blood-test requirement. The legal age for marriage is 18, or 16 with parental consent.

Full information and forms are available from the Department of Health (☎ 586-4544), Marriage License Office, PO Box 3378, 1250 Punchbowl St, Honolulu, HI 96813. The office is open from 8 am to 4 pm Monday to Friday.

Numerous companies provide wedding services. One of these, Affordable Weddings of Hawaii (☎ 923-4876, 800-942-4554, fax 396-0959), PO Box 26475, Honolulu, HI 96825, will mail out a brochure with tips on planning your wedding, choosing a location and securing photography services. The Reverend KC Russ of Affordable Weddings can provide a nondenominational service, starting at $95 for a simple weekday ceremony and going up to $800 for more elaborate packages.

For something more romantic, there's Captain Ken of the *Love Boat*, a private 40-foot yacht sailing off Honolulu at sunset. One reader recommending the service reported that the captain made the day a lot of fun and was appropriately serious when it came to the ceremony. The whole thing, with flowers, champagne, dinner, limousine service and a three-hour cruise, costs around $1000. It's arranged through Tradewind Charters-Wedding at Sea (☎ 973-0311, 800-829-4899, fax 396-5094, captken@pixi.com), 1098 Kumukumu St, suite E, Honolulu, HI 96825.

will mail a visitor information packet to travelers for $5.

For general information on gay issues, browse the websites www.tnight.com and www.gayhawaii.com; both have links to a variety of gay and lesbian sites that cover items from travel and entertainment to politics.

DISABLED TRAVELERS

Overall, Hawaii is an accommodating destination for travelers with disabilities, and Waikiki in particular is considered one of the more handicapped-accessible destinations in the USA. Many of the larger hotels in Hawaii have wheelchair-accessible rooms, and as more of them renovate their facilities, accessibility improves.

The Commission on Persons with Disabilities (☎ 586-8121), 919 Ala Moana Blvd, Room 101, Honolulu, HI 96814, distributes the three-part *Aloha Guide to Accessibility*, which contains detailed travel tips for physically disabled people. Part I contains general information and covers airport access on the major islands; this section can be obtained free by mail, and with it you'll get an order form for purchasing Parts II and III, which detail accessibility to beaches, parks, shopping centers and visitor attractions and list hotels with wheelchair access or specially adapted facilities. The entire set costs $15, postage included, or $5 if you just want the section on hotels.

Wheelers of Hawaii (☎ 879-5521, 800-303-3750), 186 Mehani Circle, Kihei, HI 96753, is a well-regarded organization that books accessible accommodations, rents accessible vans and arranges various activities for disabled travelers.

If you have a physical disability, you may want to get in touch with your national support organization (preferably the 'travel officer' if there is one) before leaving home.

Wooden Bowls

The Hawaiians had no pottery and made their containers using either gourds or wood. Wooden food bowls were mostly of *kou* or *milo*, two native woods that didn't leave unpleasant tastes. Bowls used for other purposes were sometimes made of *koa*, a beautifully grained reddish hardwood.

Ornamentation played no role in traditional Hawaiian bowls, which were free of designs and carvings. Their beauty lay in the natural qualities of the wood and in the shape of the bowl alone. Cracked bowls were often expertly patched with dovetailed pieces of wood. Rather than decrease the value of the bowl, patching suggested heirloom status, and such bowls were among the most highly prized.

Featherwork & Leis

The Hawaiians were known for their elaborate featherwork. The most impressive pieces were the capes worn by chiefs and kings. The longer the cape, the higher the rank. Those made of the yellow feathers of the now-extinct *mamo* bird were the most desired.

The mamo was a predominantly black bird with a yellow upper tail. An estimated 80,000 mamo birds were caught to create the cape that King Kamehameha wore. It's said that bird catchers would capture the birds,

pluck the desired feathers and release them unharmed. The ancient Hawaiians used feathers when making helmets and *leis* (garlands). Other leis were made of fragrant *mokihana* berries, *maile* leaves and a variety of flowers.

The *lei palaoa*, a Hawaiian necklace traditionally worn by royalty, is made of finely braided human hair that's hung with a smoothly carved whale tooth pendant shaped like a curved tongue. Before foreign whalers arrived, many of these pendants were made of bone.

Fishponds

The early Hawaiians had a well-developed aquaculture system with numerous coastal fishponds.

There were essentially two kinds of fishponds. One type was inshore and totally closed off from the sea, although generally close enough to have brackish water. These inshore ponds would be stocked with fry (small fish). Hawaiians took advantage of the varying salinity levels by cultivating different varieties of fish in different parts of the pond.

The other kind was a shoreline fishpond, created by building a long stone wall that paralleled the beach and curved back to shore at both ends. For these walled ponds, the Hawaiians built *makaha*, or sluice gates, which allowed young fish to swim in but kept fattened fish from swimming back out. The fish in the pond could be easily netted at any time.

Amaama (mullet) and *awa* (milkfish) were the two varieties of fish most commonly raised in these fishponds. Most fishponds were strictly for the alii, and commoners were not allowed to eat the fish raised in them.

They often have libraries devoted to travel, and can put you in touch with travel agents who specialize in tours for the disabled.

In the USA, the Society for the Advancement of Travel for the Handicapped (SATH; ☎ 212-447-7284), 347 Fifth Ave, suite 610, New York, NY 10016, publishes a quarterly magazine for $13 a year and has various information sheets on travel for the disabled. You can also browse the SATH website at www.sath.org.

SENIOR TRAVELERS

Hawaii is a popular destination for retirees, and lots of senior discounts are available. The applicable age has been creeping lower as well.

For instance, Hawaii's biggest hotel chain, Outrigger, offers across-the-board discounts of 20% to anyone 50 years old or older, and if you're a member of the American Association of Retired Persons (AARP), you'll get an additional 5% off. AARP discounts are available from other hotels as well, so whenever you book a reservation, be sure to inquire.

The nonprofit AARP itself is a good source for travel bargains. For information on joining this advocacy group for Americans aged 50 and older, contact AARP (☎ 800-424-3410), Membership Center, 3200 E Carson St, Lakewood, CA 90712.

US citizens who are 62 or older are eligible to purchase a Golden Age Passport for just $10, which allows unlimited lifetime entry into all US National Park sites, including those in Hawaii.

Information on Elderhostel study vacations is under Organized Tours in the Getting There & Away chapter.

TRAVEL WITH CHILDREN

Families with children will find lots to do in Hawaii. In addition to beaches, swimming pools and a range of water sports, Hawaii has lots of other outdoor activities and cool sightseeing attractions for kids of all ages.

Successful travel with young children requires planning and effort. Try not to overdo things; even for adults, packing too much into the time available can cause problems. Include children in the trip planning; if they've helped to work out where you will be going, they will be much more interested when they get there.

For those vacationing with children, Lonely Planet's *Travel with Children* by Maureen Wheeler has lots of valuable tips and interesting anecdotal stories.

If you're traveling with infants and come up short, Baby's Away (www.csd.net/~babyaway) rents cribs, strollers, playpens, infant seats, high chairs, gates and more on Oahu (☎ 395-2929), Maui (☎ 875-9030), Kauai (☎ 245-6259) and the Big Island (☎ 329-7475).

USEFUL ORGANIZATIONS
State Parks

The Division of State Parks (☎ 587-0300), PO Box 621, Honolulu, HI 96809, provides a free brochure to Hawaii's state parks, including camping information and a brief description of each park.

Environmental Groups

The Sierra Club offers guided hikes, maintains trails and is involved in conservation projects throughout Hawaii. You can get recorded information on upcoming hikes by dialing ☎ 538-6616. For other information on Sierra Club activities, write Sierra Club, PO Box 2577, Honolulu, HI 96803.

Earthjustice Legal Defense Fund plays a leading role in protecting Hawaii's fragile environment through court action. To learn more about the organization's present struggles, contact Earthjustice Legal Defense Fund (☎ 599-2436, www.earthjustice.org), 223 S King St, 4th floor, Honolulu, HI 96813.

The Nature Conservancy of Hawaii protects some of Hawaii's endangered ecosystems by acquiring land and arranging long-term stewardships with landowners. The group offers guided hikes into some of its preserves, most notably Kamakou on Molokai and Waikamoi in the Haleakala area on Maui. For the upcoming hike schedule or to find out more about current projects, contact the Nature Conservancy of Hawaii (☎ 537-4508, www.tnc.org), 1116 Smith St, Honolulu, HI 96817.

American Automobile Association

The American Automobile Association (AAA), which has its only Hawaii office (☎ 593-2221) at 1270 Ala Moana Blvd in Honolulu, can provide AAA members with information on motoring in Hawaii, including detailed Honolulu and Hawaii road maps. Members are also entitled to discounts on car rentals, Aloha Airlines tickets and some hotels and sightseeing attractions.

For information on joining AAA on the mainland before arrival in Hawaii, call ☎ 800-564-6222. Membership dues vary by state but average $55 the first year, $40 for subsequent years.

LIBRARIES

Hawaii has a statewide system of public libraries, with nearly 50 branches. Visitors can check out books only after applying for a Hawaii library card; a visitor's card valid for three months costs $10 and can be issued on the spot. As the system is unified, not only is the card good at all branches, but you can borrow a book at one branch and return it at another branch – even on another island.

Most of the libraries have good Hawaiiana sections, with lots of books on culture, history, flora and fauna. Most also subscribe to Hawaii's daily newspapers as well as a few mainland newspapers such as the *Wall Street Journal* and *USA Today*.

Most, but not all, branches have computers that are online. Although a few librarians will sometimes bend the rules, officially you need a library card to use the computers. At many libraries you need to sign up for a particular time slot – sometimes this must be done in advance, and at other times you may be able to walk in and find a computer vacant.

DANGERS & ANNOYANCES
Ocean Safety

Drowning is the leading cause of accidental death for visitors. An average of 45 people drown each year in Hawaii.

If you're not familiar with water conditions, ask someone. If there's no lifeguard around, local surfers are generally helpful – they'd rather give you the lowdown on water conditions than pull you out later. It's best not to swim alone in any unfamiliar place.

Shorebreaks Shorebreaks – waves that break close to or directly on shore – form when ocean swells pass abruptly from deep to shallow waters. If only a couple of feet high, they're generally fine for novice bodysurfers to try their hand, but otherwise they're for experienced bodysurfers only.

Large shorebreaks can hit hard with a slamming downward force. Broken bones, neck injuries, dislocated shoulders and loss of wind are the most common injuries, although anyone wiped out in the water is a potential drowning victim as well.

Rip Currents Rip currents, or rips, are fast-flowing ocean currents moving from shallow nearshore areas out to sea. They are most common in conditions of high surf, forming when water from incoming waves builds up near the shore. Essentially the waves are coming in faster than they can flow back out.

The water then runs along the shoreline until it finds an escape route out to sea, usually through a channel or out along a point. Swimmers caught up in the current can be ripped out to deeper water.

Although rips can be powerful, they usually dissipate 50 to 100 yards offshore. Anyone caught in one should either go with the flow until it loses power or swim parallel to shore to slip out of it. Trying to swim against a rip current can exhaust even the strongest of swimmers.

Undertows Undertows are common along steeply sloped beaches when large waves backwash directly into incoming surf. The outflowing water picks up speed as it flows down the slopes. When it hits an incoming wave it pulls under it, creating an undertow. Swimmers caught up in an undertow can be pulled beneath the surface. The most important thing is not to panic. Go with the current until you get beyond the wave.

Rogue Waves Never turn your back on the ocean. Waves don't all come in with equal height or strength. An abnormally high 'rogue

STRONG CURRENT   MAN-OF-WAR   SHARP CORAL

HIGH SURF   DANGEROUS SHOREBREAK   WAVES ON LEDGE

wave' can sweep over shoreline ledges such as those circling Hanauma Bay on Oahu or tear up onto beaches like Lumahai on Kauai. Over the years, numerous people have been swept into the ocean from both.

You need to be particularly cautious during high tide and in conditions of stormy weather or high surf.

Some people think rogue waves don't exist because they've never seen one. But that's the point – you don't always see them.

Coral Most coral cuts occur when swimmers are pushed onto the coral by rough waves and surges. It's a good idea to wear diving gloves when snorkeling over shallow reefs. Avoid walking on coral, which can not only cut your feet but can also damage the coral.

Jellyfish Take a peek into the water before you plunge in to make sure it's not jellyfish territory. These gelatinous creatures, with saclike bodies and stinging tentacles, are fairly common around Hawaii. They're most apt to be seen eight to 10 days after the full moon, when they come into shallow near-shore waters in places such as Waikiki.

Jellyfish are not keen on the sun, and as the day heats up they retreat from shallow waters, so encounters between jellies and beachgoers are most common in the morning. The pain from a sting varies from mild to severe, depending on the variety of jellyfish. Unless you have an allergic reaction to their venom, though, the stings are not dangerous.

Portuguese Man-of-War The Portuguese man-of-war is a colonial hydrozoan, or a colony of coelenterates, rather than a solitary coelenterate like the jellyfish. Its body consists of a translucent, bluish, bladderlike float, which in Hawaii generally grows to four or five inches long. Known locally as 'bluebottles,' they're most often found on the windward coasts, particularly after storms.

The sting of a Portuguese man-of-war is very painful, similar to a bad bee sting except that you're likely to get stung more than once from clusters of long tentacles containing hundreds of stinging cells. These tentacles can reach up to 50 feet in length. Even touching a bluebottle a few hours after it's washed up onshore can result in burning stings.

If you do get stung, quickly remove the tentacles and apply vinegar or a meat tenderizer containing papain (derived from papaya) to neutralize the toxins – in a pinch, you could use urine as well. For serious reactions, including chest pains or difficulty in breathing, seek medical attention immediately.

Fish Stings Encounters with venomous sea creatures in Hawaiian waters are rather rare. You should, however, learn to recognize scorpionfish and lionfish, two related fish that can inject venom through their dorsal spines if touched. Both are sometimes found in quite shallow water.

The Hawaiian lionfish, which grows up to 10 inches long, is strikingly attractive with vertical orange and white stripes and feathery appendages that contain poisonous spines; it likes to drift along the reef, particularly at night. The scorpionfish is more drab in appearance, has shorter and less obvious spines, is about six inches in length, and tends to sit immobile on the bottom or on ledges.

The sting from either can cause a sharp burning pain, followed by numbness around the area, nausea and headaches. Immediately stick the affected area in water that is as hot as bearable (take care not to unintentionally scald the area due to numbness) and go for medical treatment.

Cone Shells Cone shells should be left alone unless you're sure they're empty. There's no safe way of picking up a live cone shell, as the animal inside has a long harpoonlike tail that can dart out and reach anywhere on its shell to deliver a painful sting. The wound should be soaked in hot water and medical attention sought.

A few species, such as the textile cone, whose shell is decorated with brown diamond or triangular shapes, have a venom so toxic that in extreme cases the sting could even be fatal.

Sea Urchins The *wana*, or spiny sea urchin, has long brittle spines that can puncture the skin and break off, causing burning and possible numbness. The spines sometimes inflict a toxin and can cause an infection. You can try to remove the spines with tweezers or by soaking the area in hot water, although more serious cases may require surgical removal.

Eels The *puhi*, or moray eel, is often spotted by snorkelers around reefs and coral heads. The eels constantly open and close their mouths to pump water across their gills, which makes them look far more menacing than they actually are.

Eels don't attack, but will protect themselves if they feel cornered by fingers jabbing into the reef holes or crevices they occupy. Eels have sharp teeth and strong jaws and may clamp down if someone sticks a hand in their door.

Sharks More than 35 varieties of sharks are found in Hawaiian waters, including the nonaggressive whale shark and basking sharks, which can reach lengths of 50 feet. As Hawaiian waters are abundant with fish, sharks in Hawaii are well fed and most pose little danger to humans.

Sharks are curious and will sometimes investigate divers, although they generally just check things out and continue on their way. If they start to hang around, however, it's probably time for you to go.

Outside of the rarely encountered great white shark, the most dangerous shark in Hawaiian waters is the tiger shark, which averages about 20 feet in length and is

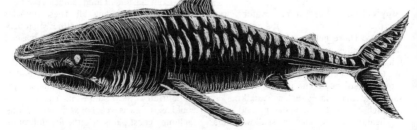

Divers need to look out for the tiger shark.

identified by vertical bars along its side. The tiger shark is not terribly particular about what it eats and has been known to chomp down on pieces of wood (including surfboards) floating on the ocean surface.

Should you come face to face with a shark, the best thing to do is move casually and quietly away. Don't panic, as sharks are attracted by things that thrash around.

Some aquatic officials suggest thumping an attacking shark on the nose or sticking your fingers into its eyes, which may confuse it long enough to give you time to escape. Indeed, some divers who dive in shark waters carry a billy club or bang stick.

Avoid murky waters. After heavy rains, sharks sometimes come in around river mouths.

Sharks are attracted by blood. Some attacks on humans are related to spearfishing; when a shark is going after a diver's bloody catch, the diver sometimes gets in the way. Sharks are also attracted by shiny things and by anything bright red or yellow, which might influence your choice of swimsuit color.

Unpleasant encounters with sharks are extremely unlikely, however. According to the University of Hawaii Sea Grant College, only about 30 unprovoked shark attacks were known to have occurred in Hawaii between 1900 and 1990; about a third of these were fatal. Nevertheless, in recent years, increasing numbers of both sharks and shark attacks have been reported in Hawaii, with attacks now occurring on average at a rate of about two or three per year.

Tsunamis

Tsunamis, or tidal waves, are not common in Hawaii, but when they do hit they can be severe.

Tsunamis can be generated by earthquakes, typhoons or volcanic eruptions. The largest to ever hit Hawaii was in 1946, the result of an earthquake in the Aleutian Islands. Waves reached a height of 55.8 feet, entire villages were washed away and 159 people died. Since that time, Hawaii has installed a modern tsunami warning system, which is aired through yellow speakers mounted on telephone poles around the islands. They're tested on the first working day of each month at 11:45 am for about one minute.

Although tsunamis traveling across the Pacific can take hours to arrive, others can be caused by earthquakes or volcanic eruptions within Hawaii. For these there may be little warning. Any earthquake strong enough to cause you to grab onto something to keep from falling is a natural tsunami warning. If you're in a low-lying coastal area when one occurs, immediately head for higher ground.

Tsunami inundation maps, which can be found in the front of island telephone books, show susceptible areas and safety zones.

Theft & Violence

For the most part, Hawaii is a relatively safe place. But the islands are notorious for rip-offs from parked rental cars. The people who break into these cars are good at what they do; they can pop a trunk or pull out a lock assembly in seconds to get to your loot. What's more, they do it not only when you've left your car in a secluded area to go for a long hike, but also in crowded parking lots where you'd expect safety in numbers.

It's certainly best not to leave anything of value in your car any time you walk away from it. If for some reason you feel you must, at least pack things well out of sight *before* you've pulled up to the place where you're going to leave the car.

Other than rip-offs, most hassles encountered by visitors are from drunks. Be tuned in to the vibes on beaches at night and in places where young men hang out to drink.

Overall, violent crime is lower in Hawaii than in most mainland cities. However, there are some pockets of resentment against tourists as well as against off-islanders moving in. Oahu tends to be worse than the other islands.

EMERGENCY

For police, fire and ambulance emergencies, dial ☎ 911. The inside front covers of island phone books list other vital service agencies, such as poison control, Coast Guard rescue and suicide and crisis lines.

If you lose your passport, contact your consulate in Honolulu; a complete list of consulate phone numbers can be found in the telephone book yellow pages.

For refunds on lost or stolen American Express traveler's checks, call ☎ 800-221-7282; for MasterCard traveler's checks, dial ☎ 800-223-9920.

LEGAL MATTERS

Anyone arrested in Hawaii has the right to have the representation of a lawyer, from the time of their arrest to their trial. The Hawaii State Bar Association (☎ 537-9140) can make referrals; foreign visitors may want to call their consulate for advice.

In Hawaii, anyone driving with a blood alcohol level of .08% or greater is guilty of driving 'under the influence.'

As with most places, the possession of marijuana and nonprescription narcotics is illegal in Hawaii. Be aware that US Customs has a zero-tolerance policy for drugs; federal authorities have been known to seize boats after finding even minute quantities of marijuana onboard.

Hawaii's Department of Commerce & Consumer Affairs offers a handy recorded information line for consumer issues. Dial ☎ 587-1234 for information on your rights regarding refunds and exchanges, time-share contracts, car rentals and similar topics.

BUSINESS HOURS

While there's a variance of half an hour in either direction, the most common office hours in Hawaii are 8:30 am to 4:30 pm Monday to Friday. Shops in central areas and malls, as well as large chain stores, are usually open into the evenings and on weekends, and some grocery stores are open 24 hours.

PUBLIC HOLIDAYS & SPECIAL EVENTS

With its multitude of cultures and good year-round weather, Hawaii has a seemingly endless number and variety of holidays, festivals and events. The list that follows includes the highlights.

As dates for many events change a bit from year to year, check local newspapers or inquire at one of the island tourist offices for exact schedules. Water-sport events are particularly reliant on the weather and the surf, so any schedule is tentative.

January

New Year's Day
On New Year's Eve, the night before this national holiday, fireworks displays take place in some of the larger towns and resorts.

Chinese New Year
Festivities begin at the second new moon after the winter solstice (mid-January to mid-February) with lion dances and strings of firecrackers. Honolulu's Chinatown is the center stage.

Narcissus Festival
Part of the Chinese New Year celebrations, this festival runs for about five weeks and includes arts and crafts, food booths, a beauty pageant and coronation ball.

Hula Bowl
This classic East/West college all-star football game is held at Oahu's Aloha Stadium on a Saturday in January.

Morey Bodyboards World Championships
The world's top bodyboarders hit the Banzai Pipeline's towering waves on Oahu's North Shore.

Sony Open in Hawaii
This PGA tour golf tournament takes place in Oahu in mid-January at Oahu's Waialae Country Club.

Ka Molokai Makahiki
A modern-day version of the ancient makahiki festival takes place in Kaunakakai on Molokai in mid-January. The weeklong celebration features a tournament of traditional Hawaiian games and sporting events, an outrigger-canoe fishing contest and Hawaiian music and hula dancing.

Martin Luther King Jr Day
This national holiday is observed on the third Monday of the month.

Senior Skins Game
This senior PGA tour golf tournament takes place in late January at Mauna Lani Resort on the Big Island.

February

NFL Pro Bowl
The National Football League's annual all-star game takes place at Oahu's Aloha Stadium near the beginning of the month.

Cherry Blossom Festival
This Japanese celebration, which covers the entire month and spills over into March,

features tea ceremonies, mochi pounding and taiko drumming. Most activities occur on Oahu.

Hawaiian Ladies Open
This PGA tour golf tournament takes place in mid-February at Oahu's Kapolei Golf Course.

Presidents' Day
This national holiday is observed on the third Monday of the month.

Great Aloha Run
Honolulu's popular 8.2-mile fun run from Aloha Tower to Aloha Stadium takes place on Presidents' Day.

March

Hawaii Pro Am Windsurfing Tournament
Contestants take to the big waves off Maui's Hookipa Beach.

St Patrick's Day
The March 17 festivities include a parade down Waikiki's Kalakaua Ave.

Prince Kuhio Day
On March 26, a state holiday honors Jonah Kuhio Kalanianaole, Hawaii's first delegate to the US Congress. On his native island of Kauai there's a weeklong festival, including canoe races, music and dance.

Easter
This Christian holiday falls in March or April. Many business offices are closed on Good Friday (the Friday before Easter Sunday).

Merrie Monarch Festival
Named after King David Kalakaua, this is Hawaii's biggest hula competition and Hawaiiana festival. Held in Hilo on the Big Island, it starts on Easter Sunday and lasts for a week.

April

Da Kine Hawaiian Pro Am
Held at Maui's Hookipa Beach in April, this is the world's top international windsurfing competition.

The Ulupalakua Thing
Held on a Saturday in late April at Maui's Tedeschi Vineyards, this fairlike trade show offers the chance to sample food prepared by Maui's top chefs.

International Bed Race
Held on Oahu, this offbeat wheeled-bed race runs along Kalakaua Ave to Kapiolani Park in late April.

May

May Day
Known as Lei Day in Hawaii, the first day of May finds everyone wearing leis. The festivities

include lei-making competitions on several islands, and Oahu crowns a lei queen at Kapiolani Park.

Molokai Ka Hula Piko
Held on Molokai in mid-May, this weeklong festival celebrates the birth of the hula, with traditional dance performances, Hawaiian food, cultural demonstrations and visits to sacred sites.

Molokai Challenge
Held in late May, this 32-mile kayak race crosses the treacherous Kaiwi Channel, from Kaluakoi Resort on Molokai to Koko Marina, Oahu.

Keauhou-Kona Triathlon
Starting at the Big Island's Keauhou Bay, this grueling competition (a half-Ironman) includes a 56-mile bike race, 13-mile run and 1.2-mile swim. The contest takes place on the last Sunday in May.

Memorial Day
The last Monday in May is a national holiday that honors soldiers killed in battle.

50th State Fair
Complete with games, rides and exhibits, the fair runs for four weekends from late May into June at Oahu's Aloha Stadium.

June

King Kamehameha Day
This state holiday is celebrated on June 11 or the nearest weekend, with events on all islands. On Oahu, the statue of Kamehameha is ceremoniously draped with leis, and there's a parade from downtown Honolulu to Kapiolani Park. On the Big Island, the Kamehameha statue in the king's hometown of Kapaau is also draped with leis.

Bankoh Kihoalu
This Hawaiian slack-key guitar festival takes place at the Maui Arts & Cultural Center in mid-June.

King Kamehameha Hula Competition
One of Hawaii's biggest hula contests takes place in Honolulu near the end of the month.

July

Puuhonua o Honaunau Cultural Festival
Always held at Puuhonua o Honaunau National Historical Park on the Big Island, this festival includes a 'royal court,' a *hukilau* (net-fishing event), hula and traditional craft displays. It takes place on the weekend closest to July 1.

Independence Day
On all the islands, fireworks and festivities mark this national holiday on July 4.

Parker Ranch Rodeo

A Hawaiian-style rodeo and horse race, sponsored by Hawaii's largest cattle ranch, takes place on the Big Island on July 4.

Transpacific Yacht Race

In odd-numbered years, sailboats leave Southern California on the July 4 weekend and arrive in Honolulu 10 to 14 days later. The race has been held for nearly a century.

Prince Lot Hula Festival

Held at Oahu's Moanalua Gardens on the third Saturday of the month, this festival attracts hula competitors from Hawaii's major hula schools.

Kilauea Volcano Wilderness Marathon & Rim Runs

This set of contests, held at Hawaii Volcanoes National Park on the Big Island, includes a 10-mile run around the rim of Kilauea, a 5.5-mile race into Kilauea Iki Crater and a 26.2-mile marathon through the Kau Desert. The event happens at the end of July and draws an international crowd.

August

Obon

This special season, which is celebrated around the islands in July and August, is marked by traditional Japanese dances to honor deceased ancestors. The final event is a floating lantern ceremony at Waikiki's Ala Wai Canal on the evening of August 15.

Hawaiian International Billfish Tournament

The world's number-one marlin tournament takes place in Kailua-Kona on the Big Island. It lasts two weeks, usually beginning in early August, and includes a parade and fun events.

Admission Day

This state holiday, on the third Friday of August, observes the anniversary of Hawaiian statehood.

September

Labor Day

This is a national holiday observed on the first Monday of the month.

Hana Relay

A 54-mile relay run from Kahului to Hana takes place in mid-September on Maui.

Aloha Week

This celebration of all things Hawaiian includes parades, cultural events, contests, canoe races and Hawaiian music. Festivities are staggered from mid-September to early October, depending on the island.

Na Wahine o Ke Kai

Hawaii's major annual women's outrigger canoe race starts at sunrise at Kaluakoi on

Molokai, and ends 40 miles later at Waikiki's Fort DeRussy Beach. It's held near the end of the month.

The Haleakala Run to the Sun

Maui's 36.2-mile ultramarathon begins at dawn at sea-level Paia and climbs 10,000 feet to the top of Haleakala. It's usually held in late September or early October.

October

Columbus Day

This national holiday is observed on the second Monday of the month.

Na Molokai Hoe

Hawaii's major men's outrigger canoe race starts shortly after sunrise on Molokai and finishes at Waikiki's Fort DeRussy Beach about five hours later. Teams from Australia, Germany and the US mainland join Hawaiian teams in this annual competition, first held in 1952. It takes place near the middle of the month.

Ironman Triathlon

Considered by many to be the ultimate endurance race, this is the triathlon that started it all and remains the world's best known. The 2.4-mile swim, 112-mile bike race and 26.2-mile marathon begins and ends at the Big Island's Kailua Pier on the Saturday in October closest to the full moon.

Kona Coffee Cultural Festival

This weeklong event features a parade, a coffee-picking contest and cultural events. It takes place in Kailua-Kona on the Big Island in late October or early November.

Xterra Championship

This off-road triathlon includes a 30km bike ride up the slopes of Haleakala, an 11km trail run and a 1.5km ocean swim. It's held in late October on Maui.

Aloha Classic World Wavesailing Championship

The final event of the Pro Boardsailing Association's world tour features top international competitors. The contest takes place in late October and early November at Maui's Hookipa Beach.

November

Election Day

The second Tuesday of the month is a state holiday during election years.

Veterans Day

November 11th is a national holiday honoring veterans of the armed services.

The PGA Grand Slam of Golf

This championship playoff takes place in mid-November in Poipu on Kauai.

Hawaii International Film Festival
About 150 films from Pacific Rim and Asian nations are screened in theaters throughout the islands. The festival begins in Oahu in mid-November and continues on the Neighbor Islands the following week.

Ka Hula Lea Festival
This statewide hula festival takes place in mid-November in Waikoloa on the Big Island.

The Triple Crown of Surfing
These three professional competitions draw the world's top surfers to Oahu's North Shore. The events begin in November and run through December, with the exact dates depending on when the surf's up.

Thanksgiving
This national holiday is celebrated on the fourth Thursday of the month.

December

Bodhi Day
The Buddhist Day of Enlightenment is celebrated on the 8th, with ceremonies at Buddhist temples.

Honolulu Marathon
The second-biggest marathon in the USA is run midmonth along a 26.2-mile course from Aloha Tower to Kapiolani Park.

Christmas Day
December 25 is a national holiday. Christmas festivals and craft fairs take place on all the islands throughout December.

First Night Honolulu
Held on New Year's Eve, this is an alcohol-free evening of music, dance, art and family-oriented activities at 50 venues in Honolulu.

WORK

US citizens can pursue employment in Hawaii as they would in any other state. Foreign visitors who are in the USA for tourist purposes are not legally allowed to take up employment.

As Hawaii has had a relatively slow economy for the past few years, the job situation is not particularly rosy. Much of the economy is tied into the service industry, with wages hovering close to the minimum wage. For visitors, the most common work to land is waiting on tables, and if you're young and energetic there are possibilities in restaurants and clubs.

If you're hoping to find more serious 'professional' employment, note that Hawaii is considered a tight labor market, with a lack of diversified industries and a relatively immobile labor force. Those jobs that do open up are generally filled by established Hawaii residents. One good resource is to go online to www.surfhawaii.com to view the 'help wanted' ads in the *Honolulu Advertiser*.

For more information on employment in Hawaii, contact the State Department of Labor & Industrial Relations (☎ 586-8700) at 830 Punchbowl St, Honolulu, HI 96813.

ACCOMMODATIONS

Hawaii has a wide variety of accommodations, including B&Bs, hotels and condominiums in all price ranges. There are also a handful of hostels and state park cabins that are quite inexpensive.

In Waikiki, hotels far outnumber condos, while in Kihei and Kona the opposite is true. In most other major tourist destinations in Hawaii, hotels and condos exist in roughly equal numbers.

More than 75,000 hotel and condo rooms cover the state. Oahu, which once boasted all of Hawaii's visitor accommodations and until 20 years ago still had 75%, has now slipped to about 50% as development continues full speed ahead on the Neighbor Islands.

Many places to stay in Hawaii have different rates for high season and low season (also called peak season and off-season). High season most commonly applies to the winter period of December 15 to March 31. During this time, many of the places offering the best deals, particularly the smaller hotels and condos, are booked up well in advance. During the low-season period of April to mid-December, many places drop their rates by 10% to 30%, and getting the room of your choice without advance reservations is far easier.

If you are traveling with children, be aware that some B&Bs and historic inns prohibit children from staying, so it's important to inquire about their policies before making reservations.

Except where noted, the rates given in this book are the same for either singles or doubles. Rates do not include the combined

Travel Clubs

Travel clubs can provide handsome discounts on accommodations. Essentially, hotels and condos try to fill last-minute vacancies by offering cut rates to members of these clubs. In many cases, you aren't allowed to book more than 30 days in advance, and rooms are limited during the busiest periods. A few places even black out winter dates altogether.

Many of Hawaii's largest hotel chains, including Outrigger, participate in the two travel clubs listed below. Both clubs allow members to book hotels directly, so they're easier to use than travel clubs that act more like reservation services.

By far the most prominent is the Entertainment program, which produces an annual book on Hawaii listing scores of hotels that offer members 50% off the standard published rates. It also has about 100 restaurants with two-for-one meals (or 50% off meals for single diners) and numerous coupons for other discounts. The books, which include a membership card, can be ordered by mail (☎ 800-374-4464) for $40 or purchased in Hawaii at bookstores and a few other places (☎ 737-3252 for Hawaii locations).

Another popular club, Encore (☎ 800-638-0930), offers the same 50% room discounts and a similar list of hotels as Entertainment, but the dining benefits are more marginal. Annual membership costs $60.

One important difference between the two clubs is that Entertainment membership is valid for a one-year period beginning and ending December 1 – a problem for travelers who arrive in November and stay into December. Encore, on the other hand, is valid for 12 months from the time you enroll.

Keep in mind that the number of businesses participating in these programs varies significantly with the economy. When hotel occupancy is low, participation booms, and when the economy is brisk, more businesses pull out of the clubs or add restrictions.

Certainly these clubs will work out best for those who are in Hawaii for longer periods of time, have flexibility with hotel preferences and dates, and are planning to travel during the months outside of the peak winter season.

room and sales tax of 11.41%, which is added to the price of all accommodations, including B&Bs.

Reservations

A reservation will guarantee you a room on the specific dates you want to stay at a place. Be aware, however, that most reservations require deposits. Once you have either sent a deposit or guaranteed it with a credit card, there may be restrictions on getting a refund if you change your mind.

Many B&Bs, hotels and condominiums will only refund your money if they receive your cancellation a set number of days in advance; three days for a hotel and 30 days for a condominium is typical, but this varies widely among places. In some instances

you'll forfeit your entire deposit, while other places will issue a partial refund. Be certain to clearly establish the cancellation policies and other restrictions before making a deposit.

Camping

Hawaii has numerous public campgrounds but no full-service private campgrounds of the KOA type found on the US mainland.

In general, camping in the national parks is better than in the state parks, and the state parks are better choices than the county parks.

Over the years there have been some assaults and numerous thefts targeted at off-island campers. The violence has decreased in most places, though a few campgrounds in rough areas, including the entire Waianae Coast of Oahu, are best avoided. People traveling alone, especially women, need to be particularly cautious.

In terms of theft, generally the less you look like a tourist, the less likely you are to be targeted; always be careful with your valuables.

Pick your park carefully, especially the county parks. Some are well established, with caretakers, and attract other campers, while others are pit stops along the road frequented mostly by drinkers.

For the most part, the farther you are from population centers, the less likely you are to run into hassles. Thieves and drunks aren't big on hiking. Backcountry camping is generally safe on all the islands; your biggest safety concern might be a twisted ankle or an encounter with a wild boar or cross-eyed hunter.

More information on all the following parks can be found in the individual island chapters.

National Parks There are two national parks in Hawaii that allow camping: Haleakala National Park on Maui and Hawaii Volcanoes National Park on the Big Island. These two parks offer some of the finest camping opportunities in Hawaii and also provide spectacular hiking. There are no camping fees at either, and the parks have both drive-up and wilderness camping areas; getting a space is seldom a problem.

State Parks The five largest islands have state park campgrounds. These range from wilderness areas that you need to backpack into to developed roadside campsites. Some also have cabins that can be rented (see the following Cabins section for details). State parks often have caretakers and better security than county parks.

Camping is allowed in the following places: on Kauai in Kokee, Na Pali Coast and Polihale State Parks; on Oahu in Keaiwa Heiau, Malaekahana and Sand Island State Recreation Areas and Kahana Valley State Park; on Molokai in Palaau State Park; on Maui in Polipoli Spring State Recreation

Area and Waianapanapa State Park; and on the Big Island in Kalopa State Park and MacKenzie State Recreation Area.

Camping in the state parks is free, though a permit is required. Developed campgrounds generally have picnic tables, barbecue grills, drinking water, toilets and showers, though the maintenance of the facilities varies greatly.

The maximum length of stay allowable at any one state park is five nights. Another camping permit for the same park will not be issued until 30 days have elapsed. Campgrounds are open seven nights a week, except on Oahu where they are closed on Wednesday and Thursday nights. In addition, parks in forested areas may be closed during periods of drought due to extreme fire danger.

Permit applicants must be at least 18 years old and provide their address and phone number as well as an identification number (driver's license, passport or social security number) for each camper in the group. Applications are not accepted earlier than 30 days before the intended camping date on Oahu or one year on the Neighbor Islands. As permits are issued on a first-come, first-served basis, it's best to apply as soon as possible; if you have a change of plans, be sure to cancel so other campers get a chance to use the space.

Camping permits can be obtained on weekdays from any of the following Division of State Parks offices, either in person, by mail or by phone.

Big Island
   (☎ 974-6200) PO Box 936,
   75 Aupuni St, Room 204, Hilo, HI 96721
Kauai
   (☎ 274-3444)
   3060 Eiwa St, Room 306, Lihue, HI 96766
Maui
   (☎ 984-8109) 54 S High St, Wailuku, HI 96793
Oahu
   (☎ 587-0300) PO Box 621,
   1151 Punchbowl St, Honolulu, HI 96809

County Parks All the counties have parks with camping areas, although not all are of equal standard. Some county parks have wonderful white-sand beaches and good facilities, while others are little more than unappealing roadside rest areas that have been turned into 'beach parks' simply by plopping down rest rooms. Just because camping is allowed doesn't mean you'd want to camp there, or even use the beach.

Maui, which has the lion's share of Neighbor Island hotels and condos, seems more dedicated to getting your dollar than encouraging camping. Camping is allowed at only one county park, with a three-night limit. The fee is $3 per person per night.

Molokai has two county parks with camping areas, one of which is delightfully set on Hawaii's largest white-sand beach. The fee is $3 per person per night.

The Big Island has 11 county campgrounds, each with a fee of $3 per person per night and a maximum stay of two weeks (one week in summer).

Kauai has seven county campgrounds, including a couple of the nicest beachside camping spots in Hawaii. The fee is $3 per person per night and the maximum stay is one week at each park.

Oahu has a dozen county campgrounds, a couple of which are recommendable and safe. There are no fees.

Cabins

The state has housekeeping cabins on the Big Island at Kalopa State Park and Mauna Kea State Recreation Area, and on Maui at Polipoli Spring State Recreation Area and Waianapanapa State Park.

These cabins are generally simple places, each with a kitchen, a common area, a bathroom, one to three bedrooms, basic furnishings, bedding, a hot shower and limited cooking and eating utensils. Polipoli, the most remote, has neither electricity nor refrigerators and you'll need a 4WD vehicle or good hiking boots to reach it. The cabins cost $45 per night for one to four people, $50 for five people or $55 for six people.

In addition to the housekeeping cabins, the state also rents simple, enclosed A-frame shelters at Hapuna Beach State Park on the Big Island; the cost is $20 for one to four people.

People staying in the cabins are subject to the same five-day limit as tent campers.

Reservations can be made at any of the state park offices (listed above under Camping) and should be done as early as possible as the cabins are in high demand. Summer is the busiest time, but reservations can book up well in advance throughout the year. Cancellations do occur, however, and if someone with a reservation doesn't pay their deposit in time, the computer automatically bounces them and the site opens again.

Reservations can be made in person, by phone or by mail, with 50% of the fee due within two weeks of making the reservation. Personal checks are accepted if you're paying more than 30 days in advance, but otherwise you'll need a bank check or postal money order. The remainder is due in cash when you check in. Refunds require at least 15 days notice prior to the camping date.

In addition to the state-maintained cabins, there are concession-run cabins at Malaekahana State Recreation Area on Oahu and at Kokee State Park on Kauai (see the destination chapters for more information).

Hostels

Hawaii has three hostels associated with Hostelling International (HI). Two are on Oahu; one is right in Waikiki and the other is a few miles away near the Honolulu campus of the University of Hawaii. The third is a small hostel near Hawaii Volcanoes National Park on the Big Island.

In addition, a number of private hostel-style places offering inexpensive accommodations have sprung up in recent years. Most are in Waikiki on Oahu, but you'll also find a handful of others on the Neighbor Islands. Look for them in Kapaa on Kauai; in Wailuku on Maui; and in Kailua-Kona, Hilo and Keeaau on the Big Island. Some of the places are quite nice, while others are mere crash pads. Rates for a dorm bed range from about $14 to $17, and more expensive private rooms are often available as well.

B&Bs

Hundreds of B&Bs are scattered around Hawaii. Some are modest spare bedrooms in family households, others are romantic and private hideaways and a few are full-fledged inns. B&Bs generally begin around $50, although the average is closer to $75 and the most exclusive properties are $100 to $150. Many require a minimum stay of two or three days, and some give discounts for stays of a week or more. B&Bs vary greatly, but for the most part they offer some of the best lodging bargains in Hawaii.

Because Hawaii state codes place restrictions on serving home-cooked meals, many B&Bs offer a continental breakfast or provide food for guests to cook their own meals. Some places do provide full home-cooked breakfasts – they just don't advertise it.

Keep in mind that Hawaiian B&Bs are small scale – most have only a few guest rooms. Out of consideration for their neighbors and guests, the B&B hosts, who are often not home during the day, discourage unannounced drop-ins. Because of this, B&Bs do not appear on maps in the destination chapters. Even if you're hoping to book for the same day, you'll need to call first, though same-day reservations are usually hard to get.

In this book, we recommend a number of B&Bs that you can book directly. Many other home-based B&Bs don't handle their own reservations but sign up with B&B reservation services. Some of these agencies book whole houses, condos and studio cottages as well. All require at least part of the payment in advance and have cancellation penalties. The following are reputable services that don't tack on needling booking fees:

Affordable Paradise Bed & Breakfast
(☎ 261-1693, fax 261-7315, afford@aloha.net, www.aicomm.com/hawaii), 226 Pouli Rd, Kailua, HI 96734, books reasonably priced cottages, studios and B&Bs throughout the islands, with a particularly good selection on Oahu. Proprietor Maria Wilson speaks German.

Bed & Breakfast Hawaii
(☎ 822-7771, 800-733-1632, fax 822-2723, reservations@bandb-hawaii.com, www.bandb-hawaii.com), PO Box 449, Kapaa, HI 96746, is one of the larger services. You can contact the company in advance to receive by mail a free listing of all the properties it books, or you can simply call and book by phone.

Anne's Three Bears Bed & Breakfast
(☎/fax 325-7563, three.bears@pobox.com), 72-1001 Puukala St, Kailua-Kona, HI 96740, books B&Bs throughout Hawaii, including many moderately priced ones. The amiable operators – Anne and Art Stockel – speak German.

All Islands Bed & Breakfast
(☎ 263-2342, 800-542-0344, fax 263-0308, carlina001@hawaii.rr.com, www.hawaiialohaspirit.com/alisbnb), 823 Kainui Drive, Kailua, HI 96734, books scores of host homes throughout Hawaii. There's a 3% fee if you use a credit card.

Condos

Condominiums are individually owned apartments that are fully furnished with everything a visitor needs, from linen and towels to dishes and cutlery. Condos have more space than hotel rooms, generally with a living room and full kitchen, and many also have washer/dryers, sofa beds and a *lanai* (veranda). Unlike hotels, most condos don't have a daily room-cleaning service.

Although some condo complexes operate similarly to hotels, with a front desk, most condos are booked through rental agents. If you're staying awhile or are traveling with several people, condos almost always work out cheaper than all but the bottom-end hotels. However, most condo units booked through rental agents have a three- to seven-day minimum stay, require deposits and have hefty cancellation fees.

Condos often offer weekly and monthly rates. The general rule is that the weekly rate is six times the daily rate and the monthly is three times the weekly.

As condo rental agencies generally deal with specific destinations, they are listed in the individual island chapters.

Hotels

In Hawaii, as elsewhere, hotels commonly undercut their standard published rates to remain as close to capacity as possible. While some hotels simply offer discounted promotional rates to pick up the slack, a few of the larger chains, such as Outrigger and Hawaiian Pacific Resorts, often throw in a free rental car. Before booking any hotel, it's worth asking if any specials are currently available – some places actually have room/car packages for less than the 'standard' room rate!

While a good travel agent at home may know about some of these discounts, many of the best deals are advertised only in Hawaii, and to find them you'll need to pick up a Honolulu newspaper. The travel section of the Sunday *Honolulu Advertiser* is best.

At most hotels the rooms are basically the same, with rates usually corresponding to two variables: the view and the floor. An ocean view often costs 50% to 100% more than a parking lot view, which is sometimes euphemistically called 'garden view.' And the higher you go, the higher the tariff; the higher floors are generally quieter, especially on busy roads.

The toll-free numbers given in this book are for calls from the mainland and usually can't be dialed within Hawaii. However, some hotels will accept collect calls from the Neighbor Islands – it never hurts to try.

If you have a Hawaii driver's license, always ask about *kamaaina* (longtime locals) rates, as many middle- and top-range hotels give Hawaii residents big discounts.

The Hawaii Visitors Bureau (see Tourist Offices, earlier) will mail out on request a free annual accommodations guide listing member hotels with addresses and prices. It includes virtually all of Hawaii's resort hotels and most of those in the moderate price range.

FOOD

Eating in Hawaii can be a real treat, as the islands' ethnic diversity has given rise to hundreds of different cuisines. You can find every kind of Japanese food, regional Chinese cuisines, spicy Korean specialties, native Hawaiian dishes and excellent Thai and Vietnamese food.

Although you could spend a bundle eating out, you don't need to, as there are good, cheap neighborhood restaurants to explore on all the islands.

Hawaii also has many restaurants run by renowned chefs that feature gourmet foods of all type, including traditional continental fare. Some of the best restaurants are at the top-end hotels, although a fair number of the more successful chefs have moved on to open their own places.

Many of these 'renegade chefs' specialize in what's been dubbed 'Pacific Rim' or 'Hawaii Regional' cuisine, which incorporates fresh island ingredients and borrows liberally from the islands' various ethnic groups. It's marked by creative combinations such as grilled freshwater shrimp with taro chips, wok-charred *ahi* (yellowfin tuna) with island greens, and Peking duck in ginger-*lilikoi* (passion fruit) sauce.

Fresh fish is readily available throughout the islands. Seafood is generally expensive at places catering to tourists, but can be quite reasonable at neighborhood restaurants.

Fruit

Hawaii has an abundance of fruit, including avocado, banana, breadfruit, star fruit, coconut, guava, lychee, mango, papaya, passion fruit and pineapple. Sweet Kau oranges are grown on the Big Island.

Watermelons grown on Molokai are so famous throughout the islands that the airlines had to create special regulations for passengers carrying them out of Molokai to prevent loose melons from bombing their way down the aisles.

Wild fruits can be sometimes be found along trails; these include strawberry guava, common guava, thimbleberries, mountain apples, Methley plums and ohelo berries.

Hawaiian Food

The traditional Hawaiian feast marking special events is the *luau*. Local luaus are still commonplace in modern Hawaii for events such as baby christenings. In spirit, these luaus are far more authentic than any of the commercial tourist luaus, but they're family affairs and the short-stay visitor would be lucky indeed to get an invitation to one.

The main course at a luau is *kalua* pig, which is roasted in a pitlike earthen oven known as an *imu*. The imu is readied for cooking by building a fire and heating rocks in the pit. When the rocks are glowing red, layers of moisture-laden banana trunks and green ti leaves are placed over the stones. A pig that has been slit open is filled with some of the hot rocks and laid on top of the bed. Other foods wrapped in ti and banana leaves are placed around it. It's all covered with more ti leaves and a layer of mats and topped off with dirt to seal in the heat, which then bakes and steams the food. Anything cooked in this style is called *kalua*.

The process takes about four to eight hours, depending on the amount of food. A few of the hotel luaus still bake the pig outdoors in this traditional manner and you can often go in the morning and watch them prepare and bury the pig.

Wetland taro is used to make *poi*, a paste pounded from cooked taro corms. Water is added to make it puddinglike, and its consistency is measured as one-, two- or three-finger poi – which indicates how many fingers are required to bring it from bowl to mouth. Poi is highly nutritious and easily digestible, but it's an acquired taste. It is sometimes fermented to give its flavor more zing.

Laulau is fish, pork and taro wrapped in a ti leaf bundle and steamed. *Lomi* salmon (sometimes called *lomilomi* salmon) is made by marinating thin slices of raw salmon with diced tomatoes and green onions.

Fish

Some of the most popular locally caught fish include:

Hawaiian Name	Common Name
ahi	yellowfin tuna
aku	skipjack tuna
au	swordfish, marlin
kaku	barracuda
mahimahi	a fish called 'dolphin' (not the mammal)
mano	shark
onaga	red snapper
ono	wahoo
opah	moonfish
opakapaka	pink snapper
papio or *ulua*	jack fish
uhu	parrotfish
uku	gray snapper

Other Hawaiian foods include baked *ulu* (breadfruit), *limu* (seaweed), *opihi* (tiny limpet shells that fishers pick off the reef at low tide) and *pipikaula* (beef jerky). *Haupia*, the standard dessert to a Hawaiian meal, is a stiff pudding made of coconut cream thickened with cornstarch or arrowroot.

In Hawaiian food preparation, ti leaves are indispensable, functioning like a biodegradable version of both aluminum foil and paper plates: food is wrapped in it, cooked in it and served upon it.

Many visitors taste traditional Hawaiian food only at expensive luaus or by sampling a dollop of poi at one of the more adventurous hotel buffet meals. Although Hawaiian food is harder to find than other ethnic foods, a few restaurants throughout the islands serve the real thing, and it's some of the cheapest food in Hawaii.

Local Food

The distinct style of food called 'local' usually refers to a fixed-plate lunch with 'two scoop rice,' a scoop of macaroni salad and a serving of beef stew, mahimahi or teriyaki chicken, generally scarfed down with chopsticks. A breakfast plate might have Spam, eggs, kimchee and, always, two scoops of rice.

Another popular item is 'loco moco,' which consists of rice topped with a hamburger, a fried egg and a generous ladleful of brown gravy.

These local-style meals are the standard fare at diners and lunch wagons. If it's full of starches, fats and gravies, you're probably eating local.

Snacks

Pupu is the word for all kinds of munchies or hors d'oeuvres. Boiled peanuts, soy-flavored rice crackers called *kaki mochi* and sashimi are common pupus.

Poke A local favorite is *poke*, which is raw fish marinated in soy sauce, oil, chili peppers, green onions and seaweed. It comes in many varieties – sesame ahi is a particularly delicious one – and all make a nice accompaniment with beer.

Tropical Fruit

Pineapple Hawaii's number-one fruit crop is the pineapple. Most Hawaiian pineapples are of the smooth cayenne type and weigh a good 5 lbs. Pineapples are unique among fruits in that they don't continue to ripen after they're picked. Although they're harvested year-round, the long sunny days of summer produce the sweetest pineapples.

Papaya Papayas come in several varieties. One of the best of those found in grocery stores is the Solo, a smallish variety with pale strawberry-colored flesh. The flavor of papayas depends largely on where they're grown. Some of the most prized are from the Kapoho area of Puna on the Big Island and the Kahuku area of Oahu. Papayas, which are a good source of calcium and vitamins A and C, are harvested year-round.

Mango Big old mango trees are abundant in Hawaii, even in remote valleys. The juicy oblong fruits are about 3 inches in diameter and 4 to 6 inches long. The fruits start out green but take on deeper colors

Pineapple

as they ripen, usually reddening to an apricot color. Mangoes are a good source of vitamins A and C. Two popular varieties, Pirie and Haden, are less stringy than those usually found in the wild. Mangoes are mainly a summer fruit.

Avocado Hawaii has three main types of avocado: the West Indian, a smooth-skinned variety that matures in summer and autumn; the rough-skinned Guatemalan, which matures in winter

Papaya

and spring; and the Mexican variety, which has a small fruit and smooth skin. Many of the avocados now in Hawaii are a hybrid of the three. Local avocados tend to be larger and more watery than those grown in California.

Crack Seed Crack seed is a Chinese snack food that can be sweet, sour, salty or some combination of the three. It's often made from dried fruits, such as plums and apricots, although more exotic ones include sweet-and-sour baby cherry seeds, pickled mangoes and *li hing mui*, one of the sour favorites. Crack-seed shops often sell dried cuttlefish, roasted green peas, candied ginger, beef jerky and rock candy as well.

Shave Ice Shave ice is similar to mainland snow cones, only better. The ice is shaved as fine as powder snow, packed into a paper cone and drenched with sweet fruit-flavored syrups. Many islanders like the ones with ice cream and/or sweet azuki beans at the bottom, while kids usually opt for rainbow shave ice, which has colorful stripes of different syrups.

Grocery Stores

You can save money by buying some of your food from grocery stores and preparing your own meals. You don't even have to have kitchen facilities – most of Hawaii's grocery stores have deli sections with food geared for takeout, with everything from fried chicken and sliced cold cuts to fresh-made poke and salads.

Tropical Fruit

Star Fruit The carambola, or star fruit, is a translucent yellow-green fruit with five ribs like the points of a star. It has a crisp, juicy pulp and can be eaten without being peeled.

Guava The common guava is a yellow, lime-shaped fruit, about 2 to 3 inches in diameter. It has a moist, pink, seedy flesh, all of which is edible. Guavas can be a little tart but tend to sweeten as they ripen. They're a good source of vitamin C and niacin and can be found along roadsides and trails.

Lilikoi Passion fruit is a vine with beautiful flowers that grow into small round fruits. The thick skin of the fruit is generally purple or yellow and wrinkles as it ripens. The pulp inside is juicy, seedy and slightly tart. The slimy texture can be a bit of a put-off the first time, but once you taste it you'll be hooked.

Mountain Apple The mountain apple is a small oval fruit a couple of inches long. The tree is related to the guava, though the fruit is completely different, with a crispy white flesh and a pink skin. The tree bears fruit in the summer and is common along trails.

Lilikoi

Ohelo These berries grow on low shrubs common in lava areas. The ohelo is a relative of the cranberry, similar in tartness and size. The fruit is red or yellow and is used in jellies and pies.

Breadfruit The Hawaiian breadfruit is a large, round, green fruit. It's comparable to potatoes in carbohydrates and is prepared much the same way. In old Hawaii, as in much of the Pacific, breadfruit was one of the traditional staples.

Breadfruit

One important tip is to get a membership card when you first shop at a supermarket. As is the trend in the rest of the USA, Hawaii's main supermarket chains have initiated a two-tier pricing system. Members get discounted prices, while the rest of the public gets gouged with higher prices – and the difference in the two prices can be significant. Although the chains don't advertise it, short-term visitors can get these free membership cards on the spot simply by asking. Of the two biggest statewide chains, Foodland will usually issue its card (called a Makai Card) right at the checkout counter without paperwork, while Safeway requires you to fill out a simple form at the customer service desk first.

DRINKS
Nonalcoholic Drinks

Tap water is safe to drink, but water from freshwater streams should be boiled.

Cans of Hawaiian-made fruit juices such as guava-orange or passion fruit are stocked at most stores. If you're going for a hike and want to toss a couple of drinks in your daypack, the juices make a good alternative to sodas, as they don't explode when shaken and they taste good even when they're not kept cold.

Alcoholic Drinks

The drinking age in Hawaii is 21. It's illegal to have open containers of alcohol in motor vehicles and, although it's commonplace, drinking in public parks or on the beaches is also illegal. All grocery stores sell liquor, as do most of the smaller food marts. People in their early twenties – or those who look like they are – will need to show a driver's license, passport or similar photo ID to purchase alcohol.

Tedeschi Vineyards, a local winery on Maui, makes a good pineapple wine, grape wines and champagne.

There are microbreweries on Oahu, Kauai and the Big Island, producing a variety of British- or German-influenced ales and lagers. Although most sell in their own brewpubs only, the Big Island's Kona Brewing Company bottles its ales for sale in grocery stores and restaurants.

And then there are those ubiquitous tropical drinks topped with a fruit garnish and paper umbrella. Three favorites are: piña colada, with rum, pineapple juice and cream of coconut; mai tai, a mix of rum, grenadine and lemon and pineapple juices; and Blue Hawaii, a vodka drink colored with blue curaçao.

ENTERTAINMENT

Hawaii has an active and varied entertainment scene, and you won't suffer for want of nightlife. Big-name musicians from the mainland like to vacation in Hawaii, and folks like Hootie & the Blowfish, Janet Jackson, Leann Rimes and Celine Dion have included Hawaii in recent tours.

There's plenty of Hawaiian entertainment as well, including contemporary Hawaiian music, slack-key guitar performances and hula shows. For detailed information, see the Entertainment sections in the island chapters.

SPECTATOR SPORTS

In part because of its isolation and relatively low population, Hawaii doesn't have major league sports teams. From October through December, however, players from Japanese, Korean and US minor-league baseball organizations come to Hawaii to hone their skills as participants in a winter baseball league. There are four teams: the Honolulu Sharks, who use the University of Hawaii's Rainbow Stadium as their home field; the West Oahu Canefires, at Hans L'Orange Field in Waipahu; the Maui Stingrays, at the War Memorial Stadium in Wailuku; and the Hilo Stars at the Wong Stadium in Hilo. Tickets cost around $5; schedules are printed in the sports pages of local newspapers.

Honolulu's Aloha Stadium hosts three nationally televised football events each winter: the NFL Pro Bowl, an all-star game of the National Football League; the Hula Bowl, an all-star East/West college football game; and the Aloha Bowl, another major collegiate football game. For ticket information, contact the Aloha Stadium ticket office (☎ 486-9300) as far in advance as possible.

Still, some of the most popular spectator sports in Hawaii aren't mainland imports. Surfing, boogie boarding and windsurfing contests attract some of the world's top wave riders and bring out scores of onlookers.

For information on specific sporting events, see the Public Holidays & Special Events section earlier in this chapter.

SHOPPING

Hawaii has a lot of fine craftspeople, and quality handicrafts can be readily found on all the islands.

Woodworkers use beautifully grained native Hawaiian hardwoods, such as *koa*, to create calabashes and bowls. Hawaiian bowls are not decorated or ornate, but rather are shaped to bring out the natural beauty of the wood. The thinner and lighter the bowl, the finer the artistic skill and the greater the value.

There are some excellent island potters, many influenced by Japanese styles and aesthetics. Good raku work in particular can be found throughout the islands at reasonable prices.

Lauhala, the leaves of the pandanus tree that were once woven into the mats that Hawaiians slept on, are now woven into placemats, hats and baskets.

Music shops carry recorded traditional and contemporary Hawaiian music. Hula musical instruments such as nose flutes and gourd rattles are uniquely Hawaiian and make interesting gifts.

Niihau shell *leis*, garlands made from the tiny shells that wash up on the island of Niihau, are one of the most prized Hawaiian souvenirs. Elaborate pieces can cost thousands of dollars.

Hawaii's island-style clothing is colorful and light, often with prints of tropical flowers. The classiest aloha shirts are of lightweight cotton with subdued colors (like those of reverse fabric prints). Women might want to buy a *muumuu*, a loose, comfortable, full-length Hawaiian-style dress.

Foods are popular purchases. The standard souvenir is macadamia nuts, either canned or covered in chocolate. Kona coffee, macadamia nut butters, lilikoi or *poha* berry preserves and mango chutney all make convenient, compact gift items.

Pineapples are not a great choice in the souvenir department. Not only are they heavy and bulky, but they're likely to be just as cheap at home.

For those who enjoy Japanese food, Hawaii is a good place to pick up ingredients that might be difficult to find back home. Most grocery stores have a wide selection of things like dried seaweed, *mochi* and *ume* plums.

Flowers such as orchids, anthuriums and proteas make good gifts if you're flying straight home. Proteas stay fresh for about 10 days and then can be dried. Foreign visitors should check with their airline in advance, however, as there are commonly restrictions against bringing agricultural products across international borders.

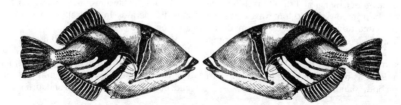

Outdoor Activities

Hawaii has an exhaustive variety of sports and recreational activities available to visitors. In addition to top conditions for practically all water sports, there are also fine opportunities for hiking, biking, jogging, tennis, golf, horseback riding – you name it. There's even snow skiing on the Big Island in winter.

Hawaii is a great place to learn to dive, surf or windsurf. Equipment rental is available on the main islands, and most places that rent the equipment also give lessons to beginners. Hawaii has 750 miles of coastline, and all of its 283 beaches are public up to the high-water mark.

Except for sports competitions or specialized tours, few activities require advance planning before you get to Hawaii.

More detailed information on all activities – including shops, prices and phone numbers – is given in each island chapter.

SURFING
Hawaii lies smack in the path of all the major swells that race unimpeded across the Pacific, so it comes as no surprise that the sport of surfing got its start in these islands hundreds of years ago.

Hawaii has good surfing throughout the year, with the biggest waves hitting from November to February along the north shores of the islands. Summer swells, which break along the south shores, are usually not as frequent and not nearly as large as the north-side winter swells.

Oahu's North Shore has Hawaii's top surf action, attracting championship surfers from around the world. The winter swells at Waimea, Sunset Beach and the Banzai Pipeline can bring in towering 30-foot waves, creating the conditions that legends are made of. Waikiki has Oahu's top south shore surfing.

Maui and Kauai also have some excellent surfing spots. The Big Island and Molokai are not as notable, but it is possible to surf on both islands.

H30, a monthly magazine that interviews surfers and reports on surfing events and surf conditions, can be picked up at surf shops around Oahu. By mail, annual subscriptions cost $36 in the USA, $72 in other countries; contact H30 (☎ 488-7873, fax 488-7584, www.h30.com), 99-061 Koaha Way, suite 206, Aiea, HI 96701.

WINDSURFING
Maui has some of the world's best windsurfing action, with Hookipa Beach near Paia hosting top international windsurfing competitions. Hookipa's death-defying conditions, which include dangerous shorebreaks and razor-sharp coral, are for expert windsurfers only, but tamer spots that are well suited for beginners can be found on other parts of Maui, such as Kihei.

Oahu also has lots of windsurfing activity, with some spots ideal for beginners and other locales boasting advanced wave-riding conditions. Oahu's Kailua Beach attracts the biggest crowd with its excellent year-round wind.

Although Maui and Oahu are by far the top two islands for windsurfing, Kauai also has some fairly good windsurfing spots, most notably Anini Beach on the North Shore, which has conditions good for both beginners and more advanced windsurfers. The Big Island doesn't rate as a windsurfing destination, although if you're there and want to windsurf, you can find a couple of beaches with reasonable conditions. It's possible to rent gear and take lessons on all four islands.

Although there are good windsurfing conditions in Hawaii year-round, winter can have flat periods. In general, the best winds are from June to September.

Most of the major windsurfing shops in Kailua on Oahu and in Kahului on Maui can arrange tours that package together windsurfing gear rental, accommodations and, in some cases, car rental and airfare.

DIVING

There's good year-round diving in Hawaii. Under normal conditions, the leeward shores of the islands have the best diving most months of the year. The north shores are usually best in the summer.

Hawaiian waters have excellent visibility, with water temperatures ranging from 72°F to 80°F.

The marine life around the islands is superb. Almost 700 fish species live in Hawaiian waters, with nearly one-third of those found nowhere else in the world. Divers often see spinner dolphins, green sea turtles, manta rays and moray eels. Although it's rare for divers to see humpback whales underwater, they do sometimes hear them singing.

Hawaii has underwater caves, canyons, lava tubes, vertical walls and sunken ships. There are all sorts of colorful sponges and corals, including the gemlike black coral.

The four largest islands all have some excellent diving opportunities and numerous dive shops. Complete gear can be rented, and prices are quite competitive.

If you want to experience diving for the first time, some of the dive operations offer a short beginner's 'try scuba' course for nondivers that includes a brief instruction, followed by a shallow beach or boat dive. The cost generally ranges from $60 to $90, depending upon the operation and whether a boat is used.

For those who want to jump into the sport wholeheartedly, a number of shops also offer full open-water certification courses in either PADI or NAUI. The cost generally ranges from $300 to $400, equipment included, and the entire course usually takes the better part of a week.

Snuba

If you want to get beneath the surface but aren't ready for a dive course, snuba offers an experience in between snorkeling and diving. Snuba divers breathe through a long air hose attached to an air tank on an inflatable raft that floats on the water's surface. They simply wear a mask and weight belt and can dive down as far as the air hose allows.

All snuba programs include elementary dive instruction that essentially explains how to clear your face mask and equalize ear pressure. An instructor is in the water with you during the entire dive. Generally, the best snuba experiences are those from boats, as you can get to better dive sites, but snuba from the beach is also available.

Snuba makes for a quick and easy introduction to the underwater world and can certainly whet one's appetite for more serious diving.

SNORKELING

Donning a mask and snorkel allows you to turn the beach into an underwater aquarium. Numerous snorkeling sites throughout Hawaii offer splendid coral gardens and varied and abundant reef fish. Hawaii's nearshore waters harbor some 20 different kinds of butterfly fish, large rainbow-colored parrotfish, numerous varieties of wrasses, bright yellow tangs, odd-shaped filefish and ballooning puffers, just to list a few.

Some travelers cart along their own mask, snorkel and fins, but these can be rented on the islands from dive shops for around $15 a week or from water sports huts on some of the busier beaches, though rates tend to be higher there.

KAYAKING

Kayaking is becoming increasingly popular in Hawaii, spurred in part by the newer types of stable kayaks that are suitable for beginners.

By far the most popular kayaking destination is Kauai, which offers both navigable rivers leading to scenic natural sights and ocean kayaking along the spectacular Na Pali Coast. In winter, when the surf along the north side of the island gets rough, ocean kayaking moves to the less spectacular but still pleasant south side.

Ocean kayaking is also picking up in Maui, primarily along the southwest coast – a splendid whale-watching area in winter. On both Kauai and Maui, you can join guided tours or rent kayaks to head off on your own.

Considerations for Responsible Diving

The popularity of diving is placing immense pressure on many sites. Please consider the following tips when diving and help preserve the ecology and beauty of reefs.

- Do not use anchors on the reef, and take care not to ground boats on coral. Encourage dive operators and regulatory bodies to establish permanent moorings at popular dive sites.
- Avoid touching living marine organisms with your body or dragging equipment across the reef. Polyps can be damaged by even the gentlest contact. Never stand on coral, even if they look solid and robust. If you must hold on to the reef, only touch exposed rock or dead coral.
- Be conscious of your fins. Even without contact, the surge from heavy fin strokes near the reef can damage delicate organisms. When treading water in shallow reef areas, take care not to kick up clouds of sand. Settling sand can easily smother the delicate organisms of the reef.
- Practice and maintain proper buoyancy control. Major damage can be done by divers descending too fast and colliding with the reef. Make sure you are correctly weighted and that your weight belt is positioned so that you stay horizontal. If you have not dived for a while, have a practice dive in a pool before taking to the reef. Be aware that buoyancy can change over the period of an extended trip: Initially you may breathe harder and need more weight; a few days later you may breathe more easily and need less weight.
- Take great care in underwater caves. Spend as little time within them as possible, as your air bubbles may be caught within the roof and thereby leave previously submerged organisms high and dry. Taking turns to inspect the interior of a small cave will lessen the chances of damaging contact.
- Resist the temptation to collect or buy coral or shells. Aside from the ecological damage, taking home marine souvenirs depletes the beauty of a site and spoils the enjoyment of others. The same goes for marine archaeological sites (mainly shipwrecks). Respect their integrity; some sites are protected from looting by law.
- Ensure that you take home all your rubbish and any litter you may find as well. Plastics in particular are a serious threat to marine life. Turtles can mistake plastic for jellyfish and eat it.
- Resist the temptation to feed fish. You may disturb their normal eating habits, encourage aggressive behavior or feed them food that is detrimental to their health.
- Minimize your disturbance of marine animals. In particular, do not ride on the backs of turtles, as this causes them great anxiety.

On Oahu, the most popular kayaking spot is the Kailua area, where visitors can rent kayaks right on the beach and paddle across the bay to a deserted island.

On the Big Island, the main kayaking destination is Kealakekua Bay, a haven for dolphins, a splendid snorkel locale and the site of the monument marking the spot where Captain Cook met his end.

Molokai, whose undeveloped North Shore boasts the world's highest sea cliffs, is an overlooked but unsurpassed kayaking destination for those seeking solitude. Suitable for kayaking only in the calm summer months, it takes about five days to explore and is certainly not for the faint of heart.

FISHING

Hawaii has some of the world's best deep-sea fishing, with the Kona region of the Big Island holding most of the world records for Pacific blue marlin. Not surprisingly, Kona has the biggest charter fishing-boat industry, although charters can be arranged on other islands as well.

In addition to ocean fishing, the state maintains four public freshwater fishing areas: in Kokee on Kauai, in Wahiawa and Nuuanu on Oahu and at Waiakea on the Big Island. Stocked fish include rainbow trout, largemouth and smallmouth bass, bluegill sunfish, channel catfish, tilapia and carp.

Licenses are required for freshwater fishing. A 30-day license for nonresidents costs $3.75 (free for seniors 65 and older).

No licenses are required for saltwater fishing when the catch is for private consumption. There are, however, seasons, size limits and/or other restrictions on taking *ula* (spiny lobster), crab, octopus *(hee* in Hawaiian, and also called tako or squid), *opihi* (a kind of limpet), *limu* (seaweed) and certain species of fish. Clams and oysters cannot be taken.

Also, seek local advice before eating your catch, as ciguatera poisoning (see Health in the Facts for the Visitor chapter) has become more common in recent years.

The booklets *Hawaii Fishing Regulations* and *Freshwater Fishing in Hawaii* can be obtained free from the Division of Aquatic Resources (☎ 587-0100), Department of Land & Natural Resources, 1151 Punchbowl St, room 330, Honolulu, HI 96813.

WHALE WATCHING

Approximately two-thirds of the North Pacific's estimated 4000 humpback whales winter in Hawaiian waters, providing visitors with some fantastic whale-watching opportunities.

Humpbacks begin filtering in to Hawaii around November and some stay as late as May, with most in residence from January to March. They prefer waters with depths of less than 600 feet, which means that they come relatively close to the shore in Hawaii. At times, they can be spotted off any of the Hawaiian Islands, but the largest numbers congregate in the shallow waters between Maui, Lanai, Molokai and Kahoolawe. The Kona Coast of the Big Island is another favored spot, as is the Penguin Bank west of Molokai.

Whales can often be seen right from shore, with the best possibilities along the west coast of Maui. To get even closer, take one of the seasonal whale-watching cruises, which depart from all the main islands. Other possibilities for whale watching include kayaking along the shoreline or hopping on the Maui-Lanai ferry, which cruises past prime humpback territory.

See also Whales under Flora & Fauna in the Facts about Hawaii chapter.

HIKING

Hawaii has many first-rate hiking opportunities. Like the islands themselves, the hiking options are incredibly varied, from desert treks to lush rain-forest walks, and from beach strolls to snowy ridgeline trails.

Hikes range from short family-style nature strolls that can be walked in an hour to backcountry treks that can last several days and require backpacking in your own food, water and gear.

Despite all the development on Hawaii, it's amazing how much land is still in a natural state. There are places where you could walk for days without seeing another soul.

The hiking trails of Hawaii's two national parks have no parallels anywhere. Both have

Na Ala Hele

Of special interest to hikers and naturalists is the work of Na Ala Hele, a group affiliated with Hawaii's Division of Forestry & Wildlife.

Na Ala Hele was established in 1988 with the task of documenting public access to trails as part of a movement to preserve Hawaii's natural environment and cultural heritage. Throughout the state, the group has negotiated with private landowners and the military to gain access to previously restricted areas and reestablish abandoned trails.

The Na Ala Hele logo signpost is marking an increasing number of trailheads as the organization's work continues. Na Ala Hele is headquartered at the Division of Forestry & Wildlife, 567 S King St, suite 132, Honolulu, HI 96813.

barren lunarlike landscapes as well as lush, tropical forests.

Hawaii Volcanoes National Park on the Big Island has the distinction of containing both the world's most active volcano and the world's largest mountain mass. The park offers breathtaking hikes down into steaming craters and others that climb the snow-capped summit of Mauna Loa.

At Haleakala National Park on Maui, the volcano is sleepier but equally awe-inspiring, boasting the world's largest crater. Hikes into the caldera can take half a day, while hikes across its floor can take half a week.

Still, the premier hike in all of Hawaii is on Kauai's Na Pali Coast, where the Kalalau Trail follows an ancient Hawaiian footpath along the edges of the most spectacularly fluted coastal cliffs in Hawaii. The trail winds down into lush valleys where camping is allowed and waterfalls and ruins can be explored.

There are also hiking trails into other ancient valleys, such as Waipio on the Big Island. On Maui and the Big Island you can follow old 'king's trails' along footpaths worn through the lava over hundreds of years by the bare feet of travelers.

Every island has ridgeline trails with panoramic views, as well as trails to secluded beaches and waterfalls. Some islands have trails through nature preserves, where you can observe native plants and birds and enjoy lots of solitude.

Of the organizations that offer guided hikes on the major islands, the most active is the Sierra Club, with branches on Oahu, Maui, Kauai and the Big Island. Local newspapers list hiking schedules.

Safety

A number of Hawaii's hiking trails take you into steep, narrow valleys with gullies that require stream crossings. The capital rule here is that if the water begins to rise it's not safe to cross, as a flash flood may be imminent. Instead, head for higher ground and wait it out.

Flash floods are the biggest dangers on trails, followed by falling rocks. Be wary of swimming under high waterfalls, as rocks can dislodge from the top, and be careful on the edge of steep cliffs, as cliffside rock in Hawaii tends to be crumbly.

Darkness sets in soon after sunset in Hawaii, and ridgetop trails are not the place to be caught unprepared in the dark. It's a good idea to carry a flashlight when you're hiking, just in case. Jeans will protect your legs from the overgrown parts of the trail, and sturdy footwear with good traction is advisable on most hikes. Hawaiian trails tend to be quite slippery when wet, so a walking stick always makes a good companion.

Hawaii has no snakes, no poison ivy, no poison oak and few dangers from wild animals. There's a slim possibility of meeting up with a large boar in the backwoods, but they're unlikely to be a problem unless cornered.

RUNNING

Running and jogging are popular activities in Hawaii. More than 100 road races, ranging from 'fun runs' to triathlons, are held in the islands each year.

Hawaii's best-known races are the Honolulu Marathon, held in December, which has mushroomed into a huge event in recent years, and the world-renowned Ironman Triathlon, held in Kona on the Big Island in October.

Other well-attended races include the Great Aloha Run, an 8.2-mile jaunt held in Honolulu every February; the Oahu Perimeter Relay, a 133-mile relay race around Oahu in late February; the Maui Marathon, a marathon from Kahului to Kaanapali in late March; and the Kilauea Volcano Wilderness Marathon & Rim Runs, which includes a marathon and shorter races at Hawaii Volcanoes National Park on the Big Island in July.

The Department of Parks & Recreation of the City & County of Honolulu (650 S King St, Honolulu, HI 96813) compiles a schedule of annual running events that it will mail out upon request.

Ironman Triathlon

The Ironman, the first and foremost of all triathlons, takes place each October on the sunny Kona Coast, starting and ending in Kailua-Kona. It's a grueling, nonstop combination of a 2.4-mile swim, 112-mile bike race and 26.2-mile run that draws the world's top triathletes. Competitors have 17 hours to finish the race, though the top athletes cross the finish line in about half that time. The current men's record, set by Luc Van Lierde of Belgium in 1996, is eight hours and four minutes, while the women's record, set by Paula Newby-Fraser of the USA in 1992, is eight hours and 55 minutes.

The total prize purse is $250,000, with the top male and female finishers receiving $35,000 each. The next nine men and women across the finish line share the remainder of the purse, with the second-place finisher receiving $25,000, third-place $20,000 and fourth-place $15,000.

The Ironman began in 1978 with just 15 participants. The following year, the event was covered by *Sports Illustrated*, which labeled it 'lunatic.' By 1980, the Ironman was drawing enough participants to receive TV coverage on ABC's *Wide World of Sports*, and since that time its popularity has continued to grow by leaps and bounds.

These days, some 25,000 triathletes compete in 22 worldwide qualifiers in hopes of earning one of the 1500 entry berths in the Ironman event. The athletes who participate in the Ironman represent each US state and Canadian province and approximately 50 other countries.

Harsh Kona conditions make the event the ultimate endurance test, even by triathlon standards. Heat reflected off the lava landscape crossed by the race commonly exceeds 100°F, making dehydration and heat exhaustion major challenges. Many contenders arrive weeks before the race just to acclimate themselves. On the day of the race, nearly 5000 volunteers line up along the 140-mile course to offer water to passing racers; in all, they hand out some 12,500 gallons of water – more than 8 gallons for each triathlete!

To learn more about the race, including qualifying requirements, contact the Ironman Triathlon World Championship (☎ 329-0063, fax 326-2131), 75-5722 Kuakini Hwy, suite 101, Kailua-Kona, HI 96740, or visit the organization's website at www.ironmanlive.com.

The comprehensive bimonthly magazine *Hawaii Race* (☎/fax 922-4222, mjaffe@aloha.net), 3442 Waialae Ave, suite 6, Honolulu, HI 96816, includes upcoming statewide race schedules, qualification details and actual entry forms for the major races. Subscriptions are $18 a year; a single sample copy will usually be sent free on request.

MOUNTAIN BIKING

Mountain biking is gaining popularity in Hawaii, and mountain bikes can now be rented on all the main islands. While cycling along roads isn't a problem – other than the shortage of bike lanes – getting off the beaten path is a bit more complicated, since access to public forests and trails is limited.

On Maui, which just a few years ago had no legally accessible off-road trails, the Maui Mountain Bike Club has worked out an agreement with the state for bike access to some of the hiking trails in Polipoli Spring State Recreation Area; in return for access, the club helps maintain the trails.

On the Big Island, which is big on space, the county has designated a number of areas that bikers can use and has funded the publication of a new mountain-biking trail map. The routes include the 45-mile Mana Rd loop that circles around Mauna Kea and the 6½-mile beach trail to Pine Trees on the Kona Coast.

On Kauai, the state forestry department has opened 18 of its trails to mountain bikers, including the 13-mile Powerline Trail, a picturesque ridgetop route from Wailua to Princeville, and the Waimea Canyon Trail.

On densely populated Oahu, where mountain bikers are often pitted against hikers, there are fewer options. Bikes have been banned from the Tantalus trails because tire tracks were causing trail erosion. The state is considering opening the trails in the dry summer months but keeping them closed to cyclists in the rainier winter season. In the meantime, the paved Tantalus Drive, which is also open to vehicle travel, remains a popular biking route.

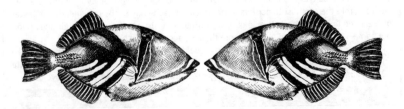

Getting There & Away

AIR

Almost all visitors to Hawaii arrive by air. Hawaii is a major Pacific hub and an intermediate stop on many flights between the US mainland and Asia, Australia, New Zealand and the South Pacific. Passengers on these routes can usually make a free stopover in Honolulu. Virtually all international flights, and the vast majority of domestic flights, arrive at Honolulu International Airport.

Honolulu International Airport

Honolulu International is a modern airport that's recently completed an extensive upgrade and expansion. Although it's a busy place, it's not particularly difficult to get around.

The airport has all the expected services, including fast-food restaurants, lounges, newsstands, sundry shops, lei stands, gift shops, duty-free shops, a 24-hour medical clinic and a mini-hotel for naps and showers.

You'll find a visitor information booth, car rental counters and hotel/condo courtesy phones in the baggage claim area.

If you arrive early for a flight and are looking for something to do, check out the Pacific Aerospace Museum ($3) in the main departure lobby. The museum features some multimedia displays on aviation.

Money Thomas Cook has foreign exchange booths spread around the airport, including in the international arrival area and in the central departure lobby next to the barber shop. On the opposite side of the same barber shop, ATMs belonging to American Express and Bank of Hawaii give cash advances on major credit cards and permit withdrawals using Cirrus- and Plus-system ATM cards. Thomas Cook adds on hefty transaction fees, so using the ATM may be a better option.

If you're in no hurry, you can avoid transaction fees by going to the Bank of Hawaii on the ground level across the street from baggage claim D. It's open 8:30 am to 4 pm Monday to Thursday and to 6 pm on Friday.

Baggage Storage Coin-operated lockers in front of gates 13, 14 and 24 cost 50¢ per hour, or $3 per 24 hours, up to a maximum of 24 hours; coin-changing machines are next to the lockers.

On the ground floor of the parking structure, opposite the main overseas terminal, a baggage storage service will hold items for $3 to $10 a day, depending on the size. It's open 24 hours a day; for information call ☎ 836-6547.

Airport Shuttle The free Wiki Wiki airport shuttle connects the main terminals with the interisland terminals from 6 am to 10:30 pm

---

Warning

The information in this chapter is particularly vulnerable to change: Prices for international travel are volatile, routes are introduced and canceled, schedules change, special deals come and go, and rules and visa requirements are amended. Airlines and governments seem to take a perverse pleasure in making price structures and regulations as complicated as possible. You should check directly with the airline or a travel agent to make sure you understand how a fare (and any ticket you may buy) works. In addition, the travel industry is highly competitive, and many hidden costs and benefits exist.

The upshot of this is that you should get opinions, quotes and advice from as many airlines and travel agents as possible before you part with your hard-earned cash. All the details given in this chapter should be regarded as pointers and are not a substitute for your own careful, up-to-date research.

---

daily. You can pick it up along the curb in front of the airport's main lobby (on the upper level), and in front of the various interisland gates as well.

Airlines

The following airlines have scheduled flights to Honolulu International Airport on Oahu. The seven-digit numbers listed are local Oahu numbers; those that begin with 800 are toll-free numbers.

Air Canada	☎ 800-776-3000
Air New Zealand	☎ 800-262-1234
All Nippon Airways	☎ 800-235-9262
America West Airlines	☎ 800-235-9292
American Airlines	☎ 800-223-5436
Canadian Airlines	☎ 681-5000
China Airlines	☎ 955-0088
Continental Airlines	☎ 800-523-3273
Delta Air Lines	☎ 800-221-1212
Garuda Indonesia	☎ 947-9500
Hawaiian Airlines	☎ 838-1555
Japan Airlines	☎ 521-1441
Korean Air	☎ 800-438-5000
Northwest Airlines	☎ 955-2255
Philippine Airlines	☎ 800-435-9725
Qantas Airways	☎ 800-227-4500
Singapore Airlines	☎ 800-742-3333
TWA	☎ 800-221-2000
United Airlines	☎ 800-241-6522

Buying Tickets

Numerous airlines fly to Hawaii and a variety of fares are available. Rather than just walking into the nearest travel agent or airline office, it pays to do a bit of research and shop around first.

You might want to start by perusing the travel sections of magazines and large newspapers, like the *New York Times*, the *San Francisco Chronicle* and the *Los Angeles Times* in the USA; the *Sydney Morning Herald* or Melbourne's *Age* in Australia; and *Time Out* or *TNT* in the UK.

Airfares are constantly in flux. Fares vary with the season you travel, the day of the week you fly, your length of stay and the flexibility the ticket provides for flight changes and refunds. Still, nothing determines fares more than business, and when things are slow, regardless of the season, airlines drop fares to fill the empty seats.

The airlines each have their own requirements and restrictions, which also seem to be constantly changing. For the latest deals, browse travel services on the Internet, visit a knowledgeable travel agent or simply start calling the different airlines and compare.

When you call, it's important to ask for the lowest fare, as that's not always the first one you'll be quoted. Each flight has only a limited number of seats available at the cheapest fares. When you make reservations, the agents will generally tell you the best fare that's still available on the date you give them, which may or may not be the cheapest fare that the airline is currently offering. If you make reservations far enough in advance and are a little flexible with dates, you'll usually do better.

In addition to a straightforward roundtrip ticket, Hawaii can also be part of a Round-the-World or Circle Pacific ticket.

Unless otherwise noted, all of the fares quoted in this chapter are in US dollars. In some cases, when fares are quoted in foreign currencies, the US-dollar equivalent is noted in parentheses.

Round-the-World Tickets Round-the-World (RTW) tickets, which allow you to fly on the combined routes of two or more airlines, can be an economical way to circle the globe.

RTW tickets are valid for one year and you must travel in one general direction without backtracking. Although most airlines restrict the number of sectors that can be flown within the USA and Canada to four, and a few heavily traveled routes (such as Honolulu to Tokyo) are sometimes blacked out, stopovers are otherwise generally unlimited on most airlines. However, in recent years some airlines have been capping the number of free stopovers and charging a fee for additional stops.

In most cases a 14-day advance purchase is required. After the ticket is purchased, dates can usually be changed without penalty and tickets can be rewritten to add or delete stops for $25 to $75 each, depending upon the carrier.

There's an almost endless variety of possible airline and destination combinations. Because of Honolulu's central Pacific location, Hawaii can be included on most RTW tickets. As a general rule, travel solely in the Northern Hemisphere will be notably cheaper than travel that includes destinations in the Southern Hemisphere.

British Airways and Qantas Airways offer a couple of RTW tickets that allow you to combine routes covering the southern and central Pacific regions, Asia and Europe. One version, the One World Explorer, is based on the number of continents you visit, requires traveling to a minimum of three continents and allows three stops in each continent visited; extra stops can be added for an additional $100 each. The One World Explorer costs $2800 in the USA, A$2599 in Australia and £860 in the UK. A second version is the Global Explorer, which is based instead on the total miles flown, allowing 28,500 miles of travel. The Global Explorer, which allows six free stops (additional stops can be added for $83 each), costs $3089 in the USA, A$2949 in Australia and £999 in the UK. Because Qantas has a code-sharing partnership with American Airlines (meaning you can book a flight – such as New York-Los Angeles – through Qantas, using a Qantas ticket coupon, but you'll actually fly on American), these RTW tickets also allow some travel within the USA.

As another example, Continental Airlines offers standard RTW tickets that allow unlimited stops at one set fare, linking up with either Malaysia Airlines, Singapore Airlines or Thai Airways for $2650. With these airlines an itinerary could take you from the US mainland to Honolulu, Guam and Bali or Manila. From there, one possible routing would be to continue through Hong Kong, Saigon, Calcutta, Delhi, Istanbul, Rome and Paris before returning to North America.

Circle Pacific Tickets A variety of tickets allow wide-ranging travel within the Pacific Rim area, including a stop in Hawaii.

With the best known, the Circle Pacific ticket, two airlines link up to allow stopovers along their combined Pacific Rim routes. Rather than simply flying from Point A to Point B, these tickets allow you to swing through much of the Pacific and eastern Asia, taking in a variety of destinations as long as you keep traveling in the same circular direction.

Circle Pacific routes essentially have the same fares: $2789 when purchased in the USA and A$3385 when purchased in Australia, for instance. Circle Pacific fares include four stopovers with the option of adding additional stops at $50 each. There's typically a seven-day advance purchase requirement and a maximum stay of six months.

The routes and airline combinations are numerous, and your itinerary can be selected from scores of potential destinations. For example, a Qantas-United ticket could take you from Los Angeles to Honolulu, on to Tokyo, south to Singapore, followed by Sydney and then back to Los Angeles.

Some variations to Circle Pacific tickets have more attractive fares. Air New Zealand, in conjunction with Singapore Airlines, offers a Pacific Escapade fare that allows unlimited stops as long as you don't travel more than 22,000 miles, and it's about 10% cheaper than the regular Circle Pacific fares.

If you're coming from the USA and don't want to go all the way to Asia, Air New Zealand also offers a Coral Explorer fare that allows travel from Los Angeles to New Zealand, Australia and a number of South Pacific islands with a return from Honolulu. The base price ranges from $1050 to $1600, depending on the season, but stops beyond two cost an additional $150 each.

Another interesting option, the Circle Micronesia pass with Continental Airlines, departs from Los Angeles or San Francisco and combines Honolulu with the islands of Micronesia. The price depends on how much of Micronesia you opt to see. If you only go as far as Guam it's $1230; if you go to Palau, at the westernmost end of Micronesia, it's $1650. The pass allows four stops; additional stops can be added for $50 each.

Baggage Allowance – This will be written on your ticket. For international travelers, it's usually one 20kg item to go in the hold, plus one item of hand luggage. With most US airlines, however, passengers are allowed to check in two bags, each weighing up to 70lb.

Bucket Shops – These are unbonded travel agencies specializing in discounted airline tickets.

Bumped – Just because you have a confirmed seat doesn't mean you're going to get on the plane (see Overbooking).

Cancellation Penalties – If you have to cancel or change a discounted ticket, you'll often incur heavy penalties; insurance can sometimes be taken out against these penalties. Some airlines impose penalties on regular tickets as well, particularly against 'no-show' passengers.

Check-In – Airlines ask you to check in a certain time ahead of the flight departure (usually one to two hours). If you fail to check in on time and the flight is overbooked, the airline can cancel your booking and give your seat to somebody else.

Confirmation – Having a ticket written out with the flight and date you want doesn't mean you have a seat until the agent has checked with the airline that your status is 'OK' or confirmed. Meanwhile you could just be 'on request.'

Electronic Ticket – If you're flying from the US mainland to Hawaii, it's possible to book your flight with an electronic ticket (also called E-ticket or ticketless travel). Essentially you get a receipt, but no ticket, from your airline or travel agent; you merely show identification at the ticket counter to get your boarding pass. One big advantage is the impossibility of losing your ticket.

ITX – An ITX, or 'independent inclusive tour excursion,' is often available on tickets to popular holiday destinations. Officially it's a package deal combined with hotel accommodations, but many agents will sell you one of these for the flight only and give you phony hotel vouchers in the unlikely event that you're challenged at the airport.

Lost Tickets – If you lose your airline ticket, an airline will usually treat it like a traveler's check and, after inquiries, issue you another one, though there may be a fee involved. Legally, however, an airline is entitled to treat a lost ticket like cash – if you lose it, then it's gone forever. Take good care of your tickets.

No-Shows – No-shows are passengers who fail to show up for their flight. Full-fare passengers who fail to turn up are sometimes entitled to travel on a later flight. The rest are penalized (see Cancellation Penalties).

Air Travel Glossary

On Request – This is an unconfirmed booking for a flight.

Onward Tickets – An entry requirement for many countries is that you have a ticket out of the country. If you're unsure of your next move, the easiest solution is to buy the cheapest onward ticket to a neighboring country or a ticket from a reliable airline that can later be refunded if you do not use it.

Open Jaw Tickets – These are return tickets where you fly out to one place but return from another. If available, this can save you backtracking to your arrival point.

Overbooking – Airlines hate to fly empty seats and since every flight has some passengers who fail to show up, airlines often book more passengers than they have seats. Usually excess passengers make up for the no-shows, but occasionally somebody gets bumped. Guess who it is most likely to be? The passengers who check in late.

Point-to-Point Tickets – These are discount tickets that can be bought on some routes in return for passengers waiving their rights to a stopover.

Reconfirmation – With some airlines, it's necessary to reconfirm your reservation at least 72 hours prior to the departure time of an onward or return flight. If you don't do this, the airline can delete your name from the passenger list and you could lose your seat.

Restrictions – Discounted tickets often have various restrictions on them, such as advance payment, minimum and maximum periods you must be away (eg, a minimum of one week or a maximum of six months) and penalties for changing the tickets.

Round-the-World Tickets – RTW tickets give you a limited period (usually a year) in which to circumnavigate the globe. You can go anywhere the carrying airlines go, as long as you don't backtrack. The number of stopovers or total number of separate flights is decided before you set off, and they usually cost more than a basic return flight.

Standby – This is a discounted ticket where you only fly if a seat is empty at the last moment. Standby fares are usually available only on domestic routes, but they are largely a thing of the past in the USA.

Travel Periods – Ticket prices vary with the time of year. There is a low (off-peak) season and a high (peak) season, and often a low-shoulder season and a high-shoulder season as well. Usually the fare depends on your outward flight – if you depart in the high season and return in the low season, you pay the high-season fare.

Discount Fares from Hawaii Hawaii is a good place to get discounted fares to virtually anywhere around the Pacific. Fares vary according to the season, airline and demand, but often you can find a roundtrip fare to Los Angeles or San Francisco for around $275; to Tokyo for $400; to Hong Kong, Manila or Singapore for $550; to Saigon or Sydney for $650; and to Auckland or Bali for $700.

If you don't have a set destination in mind, you can sometimes find some great on-the-spot deals. The travel pages of the Sunday *Honolulu Advertiser* have scores of ads by travel agencies advertising discounted overseas fares.

The following agencies specialize in discount travel.

Cheap Tickets
    (☎ 947-3717, 800-377-1000, www.cheaptickets.com), Kapiolani Blvd at Atkinson Drive, Honolulu

King's Travel
    (☎ 593-4481, 800-801-4481, www.kingstravel.com), Imperial Plaza Building, 725 Kapiolani Blvd, Honolulu

Panda Travel
    (☎ 734-1961), 1017 Kapahulu Ave, Honolulu

Travelers with Special Needs

If you have special needs of any sort – you require a vegetarian diet, are taking a baby or have a medical condition that warrants special consideration – you should let the airline know as soon as possible so its personnel can make arrangements accordingly. Remind them when you reconfirm your booking and again when you check in at the airport. It may also be worth calling around the airlines before you make your booking to find out how each of them can handle your particular needs.

Most international airports, including Honolulu International Airport, will provide an escorted cart or wheelchair from check-in desk to plane when needed, and have ramps, lifts, accessible toilets and reachable phones. Aircraft toilets, on the other hand, are likely to present a problem for some disabled passengers; travelers should discuss this with the airline at an early stage and, if necessary, with their doctor.

As a general rule, children under two travel for 10% of the standard fare (or free on some airlines) as long as they don't occupy a seat. They don't get a baggage allowance either. 'Skycots,' baby food and diapers should be provided by the airline if requested in advance. Children between two and 12 can usually occupy a seat for half to two-thirds of the full fare, and they do get a baggage allowance.

Departure Tax

There are no departure taxes to pay when leaving Hawaii.

US Mainland

Competition is high among airlines flying to Honolulu from the major mainland cities, and at any given time any airline could have the cheapest fare. Sometimes package tour companies offer the best airfare deals, even if you don't want to buy the whole 'package.' Check with your travel agent.

Typically, the lowest roundtrip fares from the US mainland to Honolulu are about $550 to $850 from the East Coast and $250 to $450 from the West Coast. For those flying from the East Coast, it may be cheaper to buy two separate tickets – one to the West Coast with a low-fare carrier such as Southwest Airlines, and a separate ticket from the West Coast to Hawaii.

Although conditions vary, the cheapest fares are generally for midweek flights and have advance purchase requirements and other restrictions. These are usually nonrefundable and nonchangeable, at least on the outbound flight (although most airlines make allowances for medical emergencies).

Most mainland flights fly into Honolulu, but there are also direct flights to Maui, Kauai and the Big Island. The service varies with the island. Only one major airline – United – flies straight from the mainland to Kauai, while four airlines currently offer service between the mainland and Maui.

The following airlines fly to Honolulu from both the US East and West Coasts.

American	☎ 800-433-7300
Continental	☎ 800-525-0280
Delta	☎ 800-221-1212
Northwest	☎ 800-225-2525
TWA	☎ 800-221-2000
United	☎ 800-241-6522

In addition, Hawaiian Airlines (☎ 800-367-5320) has nonstop flights to Honolulu from Seattle, Portland, San Francisco and Los Angeles; it also has a new nonstop flight from Los Angeles to Maui that continues on to Kona. Depending on the season and current promotional fares, a roundtrip ticket from Portland or Seattle is usually around $450. The standard fares from Los Angeles and San Francisco are also in the $450 range, although Hawaiian commonly offers discounted fares from those cities for about $300.

As we go to press, the other interisland carrier, Aloha Airlines (☎ 800-367-5250), is planning to initiate its first-ever service to the mainland, with daily flights from Oakland, California, to Honolulu and Maui beginning in early 2000.

The flight time to Honolulu is about 5¹/₂ hours from the West Coast, 11 hours from the East Coast.

Canada
Both Air Canada and Canadian Airlines offer flights to Honolulu from Vancouver and from other Canadian cities via Vancouver. The cheapest roundtrip fares to Honolulu are around C$550 ($349) from Vancouver, C$675 ($429) from Calgary or Edmonton and C$1000 ($635) from Toronto. These fares are for midweek travel, generally allow a maximum stay of either 30 or 60 days and have a 14-day advance purchase requirement.

Central & South America
Most flights to Hawaii from Central and South America go via Houston or Los Angeles, though a few of those from the eastern cities go via New York.

United Airlines offers flights from numerous cities in Mexico and Central America, including San José, Guatemala City, Mexico City, Guadalajara and Cancún. United's lowest roundtrip fare from Mexico City to Honolulu is $850 and allows a maximum stay of 30 days.

UK & Continental Europe
The most common route to Hawaii from Europe is west via New York, Chicago or Los Angeles. If you're interested in heading east with stops in Asia, it may be cheaper to get a Round-the-World ticket instead of returning the same way.

American Airlines has a roundtrip fare from London to Honolulu for $1200 that allows a stay of up to 60 days. American's cheapest roundtrip fare from Paris to Honolulu is $900 and allows a stay of up to three months. From Frankfurt to Honolulu the lowest fare is $950 for a stay of up to 21 days.

United, Delta and Continental airlines have similarly priced service to Honolulu from a number of European cities.

You can usually beat the published airline fares at 'bucket shops' and other travel agencies specializing in discount tickets. London is arguably the world's headquarters for bucket shops, and they are well advertised. Two good, reliable agents for cheap tickets in the UK are Trailfinders (☎ 0171-937-5400), 215 Kensington High St,

---

Agricultural Inspection

All luggage and carry-on bags leaving Hawaii for the US mainland are checked by an agricultural inspector using an X-ray machine. You cannot take out gardenia, jade vines or roses, even those in leis, although most other fresh flowers and foliage are permitted. You can bring home pineapples and coconuts, but most other fresh fruits and vegetables are banned. Other things not allowed to enter mainland states include plants in soil, fresh coffee berries, cactus and sugarcane. Seeds, fruits and plants that have been certified and labeled for export aren't a problem.

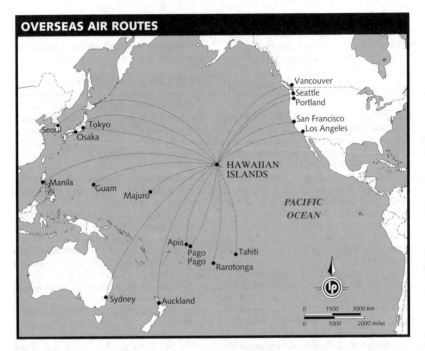

OVERSEAS AIR ROUTES

Vancouver
Seattle
Portland
San Francisco
Los Angeles
Seoul
Tokyo
Osaka
HAWAIIAN
ISLANDS
Manila
Guam
Majuro
PACIFIC
OCEAN
Apia
Pago
Pago
Tahiti
Rarotonga
Sydney
Auckland

0   1500   3000 km
0   1000   2000 miles

London, and STA Travel (☎ 0171-361-6144), 117 Euston Rd, London.

Australia

Qantas flies to Honolulu from Sydney or Melbourne (via Sydney but with no change of plane), with roundtrip fares ranging from A$999 ($631 at the current exchange rate) to A$1479 ($934), depending on the season. These tickets have a minimum stay of four days and a maximum stay of 60 days. No US carriers currently provide service between Australia and Honolulu, though United and Continental have both done so in the past.

New Zealand

Air New Zealand has Auckland-Honolulu roundtrip fares for NZ$1449 ($772). These tickets, which have to be purchased at least seven days in advance, allow stays of up to six months. One free stopover is allowed and others are permitted for an additional NZ$100 per stop. The one-way fare, which

also allows you a free stopover in Fiji, is NZ$1079 ($575).

South Pacific Islands

Air New Zealand has a one-way fare from Nadi (on Fiji) to Honolulu for F$994 ($478) and a six-month excursion ticket, with no advance purchase requirement, for F$1346 ($681).

Hawaiian Airlines flies to Honolulu from Tahiti and American Samoa. From Pago Pago in American Samoa, the fare is $403 one way, with no advance purchase required, and $578 and up roundtrip, with a 21-day advance purchase. From Tahiti to Honolulu the standard one-way fare is a steep $1014, but there's a seven-day 'Shoppers Special' excursion ticket with a seven-day advance purchase requirement that costs $685.

Air New Zealand flies to Honolulu from Tonga, the Cook Islands and Western Samoa. The lowest roundtrip fare from Tonga to Honolulu costs T$1159 ($729), requires a seven-day advance purchase and allows a stay of up to 45 days. A one-way ticket costs T$667 ($420).

From Rarotonga on the Cook Islands, Air New Zealand's cheapest roundtrip fare to Honolulu is NZ$1319 ($703), has a seven-day advance purchase and allows a stay of up to one year, while the one-way fare costs NZ$1049 ($559), with a two-week advance purchase.

From Apia in Western Samoa, Air New Zealand's roundtrip fare to Honolulu costs WS$1396 ($469) with no advance purchase requirement and a 90-day maximum stay. The one-way fare, which also has no advance purchase requirement, is WS$969 ($326).

Micronesia

Continental flies nonstop from Guam to Honolulu with roundtrip fares starting at $850. But a more exciting way to connect those two endpoints is via Continental's island hopper, which stops en route at the Micronesian islands of Chuuk, Pohnpei, Kosrae and Majuro before reaching Honolulu. It costs $717 one way with no advance purchase requirement and has free unlimited stopovers. If you're coming from Asia, this is a good alternative to a nonstop transpacific flight and a great way to see some of the Pacific's most remote islands without having to spend a lot of money.

Japan

Fares in this section are in yen; there are approximately 120 yen to one US dollar.

Japan Airlines flies to Honolulu from Tokyo, Osaka, Nagoya, Fukuoka and Sapporo. Excursion fares vary a bit with the departing city and the season, but, except at busier holiday periods, they're generally about ¥140,000 for a ticket valid for three months. The one-way fare from Tokyo is ¥149,700.

Two American carriers, Continental Airlines and Northwest Airlines, also have flights to Honolulu from Japan with fares that are competitive with JAL's.

An interesting alternative if you're only going one way would be to fly from Japan to Guam (¥72,950) and then pick up a Conti-nental Airlines ticket that would allow you to island hop through much of Micronesia on your way to Honolulu – for less than the cost of a direct one-way Japan-Honolulu ticket.

Southeast Asia

Numerous airlines fly directly to Hawaii from Southeast Asia. The fares given below are standard published fares, though bucket shops in places like Bangkok and Singapore should be able to come up with much better deals. Also, if you're traveling to the USA from Southeast Asia, tickets to the US West Coast are not that much more than tickets to Hawaii, and many allow a free stopover in Honolulu.

Northwest Airlines flies to Honolulu from Hong Kong, Bangkok, Manila, Seoul and Singapore. Thai Airlines, Korean Air and Philippine Airlines also offer numerous flights between Southeast Asian cities and Honolulu. Seasonal variations exist, but the standard roundtrip fares average about $1100 from Manila, $1200 from Seoul and Bangkok, $1500 from Hong Kong and $1800 from Singapore.

SEA

In recent years, a handful of cruise ships have begun offering tours that include Hawaii. Many of these trips are referred to as 'repositioning tours,' as they typically visit Hawaii during April, May, September and October on ships that are otherwise used in Alaska during the summer and in the Caribbean in the winter.

Most of these cruises last 10 to 12 days and have fares that begin around $150 a day per person, based on double occupancy, though discounts and promotions can bring that price down. Airfare to and from the departure point is extra.

Princess Cruises (☎ 800-568-3262) offers cruises that generally go between Honolulu and Tahiti, or between Honolulu and Vancouver, Canada. Both Royal Caribbean Cruise Line (☎ 800-327-6700) and Holland America Cruise Line (☎ 800-426-0327) typically depart for Honolulu from Ensenada in Mexico or from Vancouver. Norwegian Cruise Line (☎ 800-327-7030) commonly goes between Honolulu and Kiribati. Most of the cruises include stopovers in Kailua-Kona, Hilo, Maui and Kauai.

Because US federal law bans foreign-flagged ships from offering cruises that carry passengers solely between US ports, a foreign port is included on all trips. Curiously, the only cruise ship in the USA that currently flies under a US flag is the *Independence*, which travels solely within the Hawaiian Islands. See the Getting Around chapter for information on the *Independence* cruise.

ORGANIZED TOURS

Package tours to Hawaii abound. The basic ones just include airfare and accommodations, while others can include car rentals, sightseeing tours and all sorts of recreational activities. If you're interested, travel agents can help you sort through the various packages.

For those with limited time, package tours can be the cheapest way to go. Costs vary, but one-week tours with airfare and no-frills hotel accommodations usually start around $500 from the US West Coast, $800 from the US East Coast, based on double occupancy. If you want to stay somewhere fancy or island hop, the price can easily be double that.

For information on multi-island tours within Hawaii, see the Getting Around chapter of this book.

Specialized Tours

In addition to traditional package tours, some study and environmental tours to Hawaii are available.

Earthwatch International (☎ 800-776-0188, fax 617-926-8532, www.earthwatch.org), PO Box 9104, Watertown, MA 02272, sends volunteers to work on scientific and conservation projects worldwide. Hawaii projects focus on such activities as restoring mountain streams and assisting in humpback whale research. The cost is $2000 for programs that last about two weeks. Meals and accommodations are included, but airfare is not.

Elderhostel (☎ 617-426-8056, 877-426-8056, www.elderhostel.org), 75 Federal St, Boston, MA 02110, is a nonprofit organization offering educational programs for those aged 55 or older. The organization has its origins in the youth hostels of Europe and the folk schools of Scandinavia. It offers a full range of ongoing programs, some on the Big Island in conjunction with the Lyman House Memorial Museum in Hilo and the Volcano Art Center, and others throughout Hawaii affiliated with Hawaii Pacific University. Many programs focus on Hawaii's people and culture, while others explore the natural environment. The fee is about $600 for one-week programs, $1200 for two weeks, including accommodations, meals and classes but excluding airfare.

For information on Oceanic Society Expeditions tours to Midway Islands, see the Northwestern Hawaiian Islands chapter.

Volunteer Programs

The National Park Service has a program allowing volunteers to work at Haleakala National Park on Maui and at Hawaii Volcanoes National Park on the Big Island. Duties may be as varied as staffing information desks, leading hikes, trapping predatory animals or controlling invasive plants.

Competition is stiff; out of hundreds of applications, only about 25 people can be selected each year. Candidates with a background in natural sciences and a knowledge of practicalities like first aid are preferred. A three- to six-month (40 hours a week) commitment is required. Volunteers receive no salary or help with airfare, though barracks-style housing and a stipend of about $10 a day to help pay for food are provided. For information, write to Volunteers in Parks, Haleakala National Park, PO Box 369, Makawao, HI 96768, or Volunteers in Parks, Hawaii Volcanoes National Park, PO Box 52, Hawaii National Park, HI 96718.

Another group, the Student Conservation Association (☎ 603-543-1700), PO Box 550, Charlestown, NH 03603, sends a handful of people each year to work for three months as volunteers at Haleakala National Park. Positions range from interpretive assistants who work directly with visitors to habitat restoration aides. Roundtrip airfare to Hawaii, a weekly stipend of about $75 and accommodations are provided. Anyone over 18 with a high school degree may apply.

Getting Around

AIR

The major airports handling interisland traffic are at Honolulu (on Oahu), Lihue (on Kauai), Kahului (on Maui), Kona and Hilo (both on the Big Island).

Smaller airports with scheduled commercial flights are: Lanai; Molokai Airport (at Hoolehua) and Kalaupapa, both on Molokai; Kapalua West Maui and Hana, both on Maui; and Waimea-Kohala, on the Big Island.

Aloha Airlines and Hawaiian Airlines, the two major interisland carriers, both offer frequent flights in full-bodied jet aircraft between the five major airports.

The smaller airports are served by commuter airlines using prop planes. Island Air, an affiliate of Aloha Airlines, is the largest of the commuter airlines and offers the most extensive schedule.

Airfares

Interisland air travel is competitive in Hawaii and the fares commonly adjust up and down to reflect the competition. Unfortunately for travelers, Mahalo Air, an upstart company that had an extensive network and cut-rate prices, went out of business recently and fares are once again on the high end.

The two largest carriers, Hawaiian Airlines and Aloha Airlines, both have a standard one-way fare for all flights between any two airports that they serve. That fare is currently $93.

Island Air, the largest of the commuter airlines, also charges $93 one way.

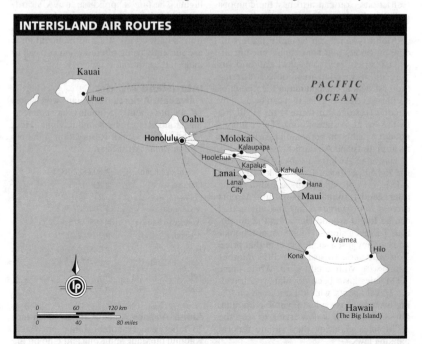

INTERISLAND AIR ROUTES

If a connection is required on any inter-island flight with any of the airlines, an additional $2 is charged.

Roundtrip fares on all these airlines are double the one-way fares.

All said and done, there's little need to ever pay a standard fare, as some handsome discounts are readily available.

Coupons You can save a bundle by using discount coupons instead of purchasing full-fare tickets. The coupons don't have any advance purchase requirements, and you can make reservations ahead of time before buying them.

Hawaiian Airlines sells coupon booklets containing six tickets good for interisland flights between any two destinations it serves. The booklets cost $333 when purchased directly from the airline at the airport ticket counter. These tickets can be used by any number of people and on any flight without restrictions. You can also buy the coupons individually from discount travel agents around the islands for around $50.

Aloha Airlines can be more fickle with coupon books and sometimes, but not always, restricts them to use by local residents only. Still, as we go to press Aloha is offering the best deal at the counter: a $315 book of six unrestricted coupons that can be used by anyone (resident or tourist) on all flights by the airline. A similar book of six coupons good for flights on both Aloha Airlines and its affiliate Island Air costs $450.

Hawaiian Airlines also sells its coupons for $54.50 per ticket from Bank of Hawaii ATMs, one of which can be found in the interisland terminal at Honolulu Airport (across from Burger King) and others that can be found around Hawaii at the ubiquitous 7-Eleven stores. Unlike coupon books, you can buy just a single ticket at that price. You will need to use your PIN number along with your credit card. While these ATM sales have been popular with travelers, travel agents, who are not keen on losing business, have a less favorable opinion. One Oahu agent is now trying to stop the ATM sales, claiming they violate federal banking laws.

Air Passes Hawaiian Airlines offers air passes allowing unlimited air travel for a specified number of consecutive days. You can go anywhere you please as often as you want. Reservations can be made in advance and you're free to revise your itinerary at will. Passes are nonrefundable and will not be replaced if lost or stolen.

The biggest drawback is that the air-pass costs have recently skyrocketed and for most people the aforementioned coupons will work out better. The current fare is: $299 for five days, $315 for one week, $369 for 10 days and $409 for two weeks.

Other Discounts Aloha Airlines offers American Automobile Association (AAA) members a 25% discount off the standard ticket fare on all of its interisland flights. Aloha's sister airline, Island Air, offers the same discount on all point-to-point flights (ie, those that don't require a connecting flight). The fare is applicable to AAA cardholders and those traveling with them.

Other schemes come up from time to time, so always ask what promotional fares are currently being offered when you call to make a reservation.

Interisland Airlines

Hawaiian Airlines Hawaiian, which flies DC-9s, has about 175 flights a day connecting Honolulu, Lihue, Kahului, Kona, Hilo, Molokai and Lanai. Reservation numbers for Hawaiian Airlines are:

Neighbor Islands	☎ 800-882-8811
Oahu	☎ 838-1555
US mainland & Canada	☎ 800-367-5320
American Samoa	☎ 699-1875
Australia	☎ 2-9244-2111
Japan	☎ 3-3214-4774
New Zealand	☎ 09-379-3708
Tahiti	☎ 4215-00
UK	☎ 1753-664406

Aloha Airlines Aloha Airlines, which flies 737s between Honolulu, Lihue on Kauai, Kahului on Maui, and Kona and Hilo on the

Big Island, schedules more than 200 inter-island flights a day. Reservation numbers for Aloha Airlines are:

Big Island	☎ 935-5771
Kauai	☎ 245-3691
Maui	☎ 244-9071
Oahu	☎ 484-1111
US mainland & Canada	☎ 800-367-5250
Hong Kong	☎ 2826-9118
Osaka	☎ 06-341-7241
Tokyo	☎ 03-3216-5877

Island Air Island Air serves Hawaii's smaller airports using 18-passenger DeHavilland Dash 6 or 37-passenger Dash 8 aircraft. As these prop planes fly lower than jet aircraft, you often get better views en route. Island Air is part of the Aloha Airgroup, so bookings can be made through Aloha Airlines as well.

Island Air has flights to Honolulu, Molokai, Kalaupapa, Kahului, Hana, Kapalua West Maui and Lanai. To some of the more remote sectors, flights are only twice daily, while the more popular routes have around eight flights a day.

Reservation numbers for Island Air are:

Oahu	☎ 484-2222
Neighbor Islands	☎ 800-652-6541
US mainland	☎ 800-323-3345

Pacific Wings This little airline, which recently relocated from Nevada, flies eight-passenger Cessna 402 prop planes. Its home base is Kahului, Maui. It flies to Honolulu, Molokai, Kalaupapa, Hana and Waimea-Kohala. Pacific Wings' most remote destinations, Waimea-Kohala and Kalaupapa, have only one flight scheduled a day while the other routes have three or four. Keep in mind that with this and other small airlines the schedules are a bit elastic – if there aren't advance bookings for a flight, the flight is often canceled.

The one-way fare for non-Hawaii residents is $75 on most routes. Reservation numbers for Island Air are ☎ 873-0877 on Maui and 888-574-4546 elsewhere in the USA. If you have a small group, ask Pacific Wings about its three-passenger plane, which can sometimes be chartered for less than the cost of flying on one of the company's scheduled flights.

Other Airlines Smaller commuter airlines, sometimes consisting of just a single plane, come and go with some frequency in Hawaii.

Molokai Air Shuttle (☎ 545-4988) flies a five-passenger Piper between Honolulu and Molokai; the flights are on demand, leaving when enough passengers arrive at the airport. Unlike other airlines, the company charges tourists the same as locals, and offers a roundtrip fare of just $55, less than half of any competitor's fare.

Paragon Air (☎ 800-428-1231) flies six-seater prop planes on demand to Molokai from both the Kahului and Kapalua West Maui airports. The flights typically head over to Molokai in the morning and back in the afternoon, but there's no regular schedule and you may have to be flexible. Paragon charges $50 one way and $89 roundtrip.

BUS

Oahu's excellent islandwide public bus system, called TheBus, makes that island the easiest one to get around without a car. You can get almost anywhere on Oahu via TheBus, and the fare is just $1 regardless of your destination.

The Big Island has limited public bus service between Kona and Hilo and between Hilo and Hawaii Volcanoes National Park. A couple of other routes serve the Hilo area, but they're geared primarily for commuters and the service is infrequent. While these buses can get you between major towns, they're not practical for short sightseeing hops.

Kauai's limited public bus service can take visitors between island towns but doesn't cover the main tourist destinations, such as Waimea Canyon or the Kilauea lighthouse.

Maui has no county-operated buses. However, a limited and rather expensive private bus service operates between the Kihei and

Kaanapali areas. And inexpensive shuttles connect Kaanapali with Lahaina and the Napili/Kapalua area.

Molokai has no buses, but there's a mule train!

For detailed information on these services, see the Getting Around sections in the appropriate destination chapters.

CAR

The minimum age for driving in Hawaii is 18 years, though car rental companies usually have higher age restrictions. If you're under age 25, you should call the car rental agencies in advance to check their policies regarding restrictions and surcharges.

You can legally drive in the state as long as you have a valid driver's license issued by a country that is party to the United Nations Conference on Road & Motor Transport – which covers virtually everyone.

However, car rental companies will generally accept valid foreign driver's licenses only if they're in English. Otherwise, most will require renters to show an international driver's license along with their home license.

Gasoline is about 25% more expensive in Hawaii than on the US mainland, with the price for regular unleaded gasoline averaging about $1.70 a gallon.

Road Rules

As with the rest of the USA, driving is on the right-hand side of the road.

Drivers at a red light can turn right after coming to a full stop and yielding to oncoming traffic, unless there's a sign at the intersection prohibiting the turn.

Hawaii requires the use of seat belts for drivers and front-seat passengers. State law also strictly requires the use of child-safety seats for children aged three and under, while four-year-olds must either be in a safety seat or secured by a seat belt. Most of the car rental companies rent child-safety seats, usually for around $5 a day, but they don't always have them on hand so it's advisable to reserve one in advance.

Speed limits are posted and enforced. If you're stopped for speeding, expect to get a ticket, as the police rarely just give warnings.

Cruising unmarked police cars come in the most unlikely models and colors!

Horn honking is considered rude in Hawaii unless required for safety.

Rental

Rental cars are available on all of the islands. With most companies the weekly rate works out far cheaper per day than the straight daily rate. For a small car, the daily rate with unlimited mileage ranges from around $25 to $45, while typical weekly rates are $150 to $200.

Rates vary a bit from company to company and within each company depending on season, time of booking and current promotions. If you belong to an automobile club, a frequent-flier program or a travel club, you'll often be eligible for some sort of discount, so always ask.

One thing to note when renting a car is that rates for midsize and full-size cars are often only a few dollars more per week than the rate for a small car. And because some promotional discounts exclude economy-size cars, at times the lowest rate available may actually be on a larger car.

At any given time any one of the rental companies could be offering the best rates, so you can save money by shopping around. Be sure to ask the agent for the cheapest rate, as the first quote given is not always the lowest.

It's a good idea to make reservations in advance for each island you plan on visiting. Walking up to the counter without a reservation will not only subject you to higher rates, but during busy periods, which can include weekends year-round, it's not uncommon for cars to be sold out altogether.

Another advantage of advance reservations is that if you have a bottom-line car reserved and none are in the yard when you show up, the upgrade is free.

On daily rentals, most cars are rented on a 24-hour basis, so you could get two days' use by renting at midday and driving around all afternoon, then heading out to explore somewhere else the next morning before the car is due back. Most companies even have an hour's grace period.

In Hawaii, rental rates generally include free unlimited mileage, though if you drop off the car at a different location from where you picked it up, there's usually an additional fee and sometimes a mileage charge.

Having a major credit card greatly simplifies the rental process. Without one, some agents simply will not rent vehicles, while others will require prepayment by cash or traveler's checks as well as a deposit of around $300; some actually do an employment verification and credit check, while others don't do background checks but reserve the right for the station manager to decide whether to rent to you or not. If you intend to rent a car without plastic, it's wise to make your plans well in advance.

Be aware that many car rental companies are loathe to rent to people who list a campground as their address on the island, and a few specifically add 'No Camping Permitted' to their rental contracts. Most typically require that you fill in the name and phone number of the place where you're staying.

Most car rental companies officially prohibit use of their cars on dirt roads.

In addition to the rates, you're charged a $2-a-day state tax on all car rentals.

Rental Agencies The following are international companies operating in Hawaii whose cars can be booked from offices around the world. The toll-free numbers given are valid from the US mainland.

Alamo (☎ 800-327-9633) has locations at the Kona, Hilo, Kahului and Lihue airports and near the Honolulu and Kapalua West Maui airports.

Avis (☎ 800-321-3712) is at the main airports on Oahu, Maui, Kauai and the Big Island as well as at four locations around Waikiki. If you're visiting at least two islands, Avis has a multi-island deal that allows you to rent a car at the rate of $32 a day as long as you rent for a minimum of five days on the combined islands.

Budget (☎ 800-527-0700) is at the main airports on Oahu, Kauai, Molokai, Maui and the Big Island as well as about 35 other locations around Hawaii. All other things being equal, Budget is probably the best choice for bargain-hunters, as renters are given coupons that allow free admission for one person to participating

Where's the Highway?

The word 'highway' is used very liberally in Hawaii. Just about every road of any distance gets to be called a highway, including some insignificant secondary roads and even a dirt road or two.

In this book we've given priority to using highway numbers because that's what you'll see on road signs. However, if you're asking directions, keep in mind that islanders generally refer to roads by name and few pay attention to the route numbers – many wouldn't even be able to tell you the route number of the road on which they live.

❀ ❀ ❀ ❀ ❀ ❀ ❀ ❀ ❀ ❀ ❀ ❀ ❀

tourist attractions – it's a particularly good deal on Oahu.

Dollar (☎ 800-800-4000) is at the airports on Oahu, Kauai, Molokai, Maui and the Big Island as well as numerous locations in Waikiki. It's one of the more liberal agencies for renting to people under the age of 25.

Hertz (☎ 800-654-3131) is at the main airports on Oahu, Maui, Kauai and the Big Island as well as the Kapalua West Maui airport.

National (☎ 800-227-7368) is at the main airports on Oahu, Kauai, Maui and the Big Island and at a couple of locations in Waikiki.

There are a handful of smaller rental agencies in Hawaii as well, but this is one area in which smaller is not necessarily better. For the most part, the big companies offer newer, more reliable cars and fewer hassles.

Insurance Rental companies in Hawaii have liability insurance, which covers people and property that you might hit with their vehicles. Damage to the rental vehicle itself is not covered. For this, a collision damage waiver (CDW) is available from car rental agencies, typically for an additional $15 to $17 a day.

The CDW is not really insurance per se, but rather a guarantee that the rental company won't hold you liable for any damages to their car (though even here there are exceptions). If you decline the CDW, you are usually held liable for any damages up to the full value of the car. If damages do occur and you find yourself in a dispute with the rental company, you can call the state Department of Commerce & Consumer Affairs at ☎ 587-1234 and then key in 7222 for recorded information on your legal rights.

If you have collision coverage on your vehicle at home, it might cover damages to car rentals in Hawaii. Check with your insurance company before your trip.

Some credit cards, including most 'gold cards' issued by Visa and MasterCard, offer reimbursement coverage for collision damages if you rent the car with that credit card and decline the CDW. If yours doesn't, it may be worth changing to one that does. Be aware that most credit-card coverage isn't valid for rentals of more than 15 days or for exotic models, jeeps, vans and 4WD vehicles.

BICYCLE

It's possible to cycle around all the Hawaiian Islands. However, when you get away from coastal routes, you'll face some pretty hefty climbs. Exploring the islands thoroughly by bicycle is an option best suited for well-conditioned cyclists.

Hawaii has been slow to adopt cycle-friendly traits. A few new road projects now include cycle lanes, but such lanes are still relatively rare on the islands. Hawaii's roads also tend to be narrow, and many of the main coastal routes are heavily trafficked.

You'll find places to rent bicycles on Oahu, Maui, Kauai, Molokai and the Big Island. If you bring your own bike to Hawaii, you can transport it on interisland flights for $20. The bicycle can be checked at the counter, the same as any baggage, but you'll need to prepare the bike first by either wrapping the handlebars and pedals in foam or fixing the handlebars to the side and removing the pedals.

For island-specific cycling information, see the Activities and Getting Around sections in the destination chapters. See also Mountain Biking under Outdoor Activities.

HITCHHIKING

Hitchhiking is not common in Hawaii. In Maui County it's outright illegal, while on other islands it's more of a gray area and tolerance varies. All in all, hitchhiking results are mixed at best. Hitchhikers should size up each situation carefully before getting in cars, and women should be especially wary of hitching alone.

Hitchhiking is never entirely safe anywhere in the world, and Lonely Planet does not recommend it. Travelers who decide to hitchhike should understand that they are taking a potentially serious risk. People who do choose to hitchhike will be safer if they travel in pairs and let someone know where they are planning to go.

BOAT

The only regularly scheduled interisland ferry in Hawaii is a small 24-passenger boat that operates five times a day between Lahaina on Maui and Manele Boat Harbor on Lanai. The crossing, which takes an hour, costs $25 each way.

Another commercial vessel, the 118-foot *Maui Princess*, goes from Lahaina to Kaunakakai, Molokai, on Saturday mornings and back to Lahaina in the afternoon. But the boat is also used for charters so this once-weekly service occasionally gets rescheduled. The fare is $69 either one way or roundtrip.

TAXI

All the main islands have taxis, with the fares based on mileage regardless of the number of passengers. Rates vary, as they're set by each county, but average about $10 per 5 miles.

ORGANIZED TOURS

A number of companies operate half-day and full-day sightseeing bus tours on each island. Also readily available are specialized adventures, such as whale-watch cruises, bicycle tours down Haleakala, snorkel trips to Lanai and cruises along the Kona Coast, just to mention a few. All these tours can be booked after arrival in Hawaii. For details, see the Organized Tours sections of each chapter.

Overnight Tours

If you want to visit another island while you're in Hawaii but only have a day or two to spare, it might be worth looking into 'overnighters,' which are mini-packaged tours to the Neighbor Islands that include round-trip airfare, car rental and hotel accommodations. Rates depend on the accommodations you select, with a one-night package typically starting at $130 per person, based on double occupancy. You can add on additional days for an additional fee, which is usually about $60 per person.

If you have an air pass, the same tour companies also sell room/car packages minus the airfare – though the room/car packages offered directly by some hotels may work out cheaper.

The largest companies specializing in overnighters are: Roberts Hawaii (☎ 523-9323 on Oahu, 800-899-9323 from the Neighbor Islands and the mainland) and Pleasant Island Holidays (☎ 922-1515 on Oahu, 800-654-4386 from the Neighbor Islands).

Cruises

American Hawaii Cruises (☎ 800-765-7000), 2100 Nimitz Hwy, Honolulu, HI 96819, operates the cruise ship *Independence*, which makes a seven-day tour around Hawaii. The ship leaves Honolulu each Saturday year-round and visits Kauai (Nawiliwili Harbor), Maui (Kahului Harbor) and the Big Island (Hilo and Kona) before returning to Honolulu.

Rates start at $1400 for the cheapest inside cabin and go up to $3550 for an outside suite. Fares are per person, based on double occupancy, and you'll pay an additional $85 in port charges.

Although more modest than the ultra-modern mammoths that cruise the Caribbean, the *Independence* is a full-fledged cruise ship, 682 feet long, with lavish buffet meals, swimming pools and the like. The ship carries a crew of 325, along with 1021 passengers.

Helicopter Tours

Helicopter tours are readily available from a number of companies on the main islands. They go to some amazing places, with flights over active volcanoes, along towering coastal cliffs and above inaccessible waterfalls. Prices vary depending on the destination and the length of the flight, with a 30-minute tour averaging about $125 per passenger.

Before you book one, be ready to make some inquiries. Be aware, for instance, that not every seat in all copters is a window seat. A common configuration is two passengers up front with the pilot, and four people sitting across the back. The two back middle seats simply don't give the photo opportunities proclaimed in the brochures. It's like being a midseat rear passenger on a scenic drive – only there's no getting out at viewpoints! People are usually seated according to weight, so if you're dishing out a lot of money, make sure you know in advance where you'll be sitting.

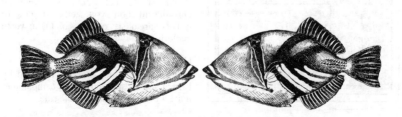

Oahu

The images most commonly conjured up of Hawaii are those of Oahu – places like Waikiki, Pearl Harbor and Sunset Beach.

Oahu is by far the most developed of the Hawaiian islands and, quite appropriately, has long been nicknamed 'The Gathering Place.' It's home to 880,000 people – nearly 75% of the state's population. The scene here is urban, with highways, high-rises and crowds. If you're looking for a getaway vacation, you'd best continue on to one of the Neighbor Islands.

Still, despite all its development, in terms of scenic beauty Oahu holds its own. It has fluted mountains, aqua-blue bays and valleys carpeted with pineapple fields.

Oahu has excellent beaches. Hanauma Bay, east of Waikiki, is the most visited snorkeling spot in the islands. The North Shore sees Hawaii's top surfing action, and windward Kailua is Hawaii's most popular becah for windsurfing.

Honolulu is a modern city with an intriguing blend of Eastern and Western influences. Cultural offerings range from Chinese lantern parades and traditional *hula* (Hawaiian dance) performances to ballet and good museums. Honolulu has the only royal palace in the USA, fine city beaches and parks and some great hilltop views. The city is also a diner's delight, with a wonderful array of good ethnic restaurants.

Oahu can be the cheapest Hawaiian island to visit. It's the only one you can get around easily without your own car, thanks to the inexpensive, islandwide bus system. Oahu also has some of Hawaii's cheapest accommodations, including a growing number of hostels and Ys.

Almost all of Oahu's hotels and tourist facilities are centered in Waikiki. Waikiki resembles a hybrid mix of Miami Beach and Tokyo, with a population density rivaling the latter. There's a lot happening in Waikiki, but to get a better feel for what Hawaii's all about, you need to step out of it. There are plenty of places on Oahu worth exploring.

Highlights

- Enjoying sunset hula shows at Waikiki Beach
- Visiting the throne room of Iolani Palace, former home to Hawaiian royalty
- Riding the waves at the North Shore's Banzai Pipeline
- Reliving history at Pearl Harbor's military memorial
- Windsurfing in the turquoise waters off Kailua Beach

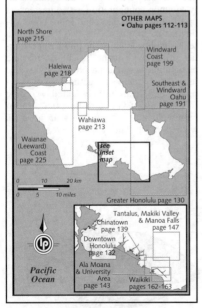

HISTORY

Oahu was the final island conquered by Kamehameha the Great in his campaign to unite all Hawaii under his sole rule.

Prior to that, however, it was not Kamehameha but Kahekili, the aging king of Maui, who seemed the most likely candidate to grasp control of the entire island chain. Kahekili already ruled neighboring Molokai and Lanai when in the 1780s he killed his own stepson to take Oahu.

After Kahekili died at Waikiki in 1794, a power struggle ensued and his lands were divided between two quarreling relatives. His son, Kalanikupule, got Oahu and his half brother, King Kaeokulani of Kauai, took Maui, Lanai and Molokai. The two ambitious heirs immediately went to battle with each other, creating a rift that Kamehameha readily moved into.

In 1795, Kamehameha swept through Maui and Molokai, conquering those islands before crossing the channel to Oahu. On the quiet beaches of Waikiki he landed his fleet of canoes and marched up toward Nuuanu Valley to battle Kalanikupule, the king of Oahu.

The Battle of Nuuanu

The Oahu warriors were no match for Kamehameha's troops. The first heavy fighting took place around the Punchbowl, where Kamehameha's forces quickly circled the fortresslike crater and drove out the Oahuan defenders. Scattered fighting continued up Nuuanu Valley, with the last big battle taking place near the current site of Queen Emma's summer palace.

The Oahuans, only ready for the usual spear-and-stone warfare, panicked when they realized Kamehameha had brought in a handful of Western sharpshooters. The foreigners picked off the Oahuan generals and blasted into their ridge-top defenses.

What should have been the advantage of high ground turned into a death trap for the Oahuans when they found themselves wedged up into the valley, unable to spread out. Fleeing up the cliffsides in retreat, they were forced to make their last stand at the narrow, precipitous ledge along the current-day Nuuanu Pali Lookout. Hundreds of Oahuans were driven over the top of the *pali* (cliff) to their deaths.

Some Oahuan warriors, including King Kalanikupule, escaped into the upland forests. When Kalanikupule surfaced a few months later, he was sacrificed by Kamehameha to the war god Ku. Kamehameha's taking of Oahu marked the last battle ever fought between Hawaiian troops.

GEOGRAPHY

Oahu, which covers 594 sq miles, is the third-largest Hawaiian island. It basically has four sides, with distinct windward and leeward coasts and north and south shores. The island's extreme length is 44 miles, its width 30 miles.

Two separate volcanoes arose to form Oahu's two mountain ranges, Waianae and Koolau, which slice the island from the northwest to the southeast. Oahu's highest point, Mt Kaala at 4020 feet, is in the Waianae Range.

CLIMATE

In Honolulu, the average daily maximum temperature is 84°F and the minimum is 70°F. Temperatures are a bit higher in summer and a few degrees lower in winter. The highest temperature on record is 94°F and the lowest is 53°F.

Waikiki has an average annual rainfall of only 25 inches, whereas the Lyon Arboretum in the upper Manoa Valley, north of Honolulu, averages 158 inches. Mid-afternoon humidity averages 56%.

Average afternoon water temperatures in Waikiki are 77°F in March, 82°F in August.

FLORA & FAUNA

Most of the islets off Oahu's windward coast are sanctuaries for seabirds, including terns, noddies, shearwaters, Laysan albatrosses, tropicbirds, boobies and frigate birds. Moku Manu ('Bird Island') off Mokapu Peninsula has the greatest variety of species.

Oahu has an endemic genus of tree snail, the *Achatinella*. In former days the forests were loaded with these colorful snails, which clung like gems to the leaves of trees. They were too attractive for their own good, however, and hikers collected them by the

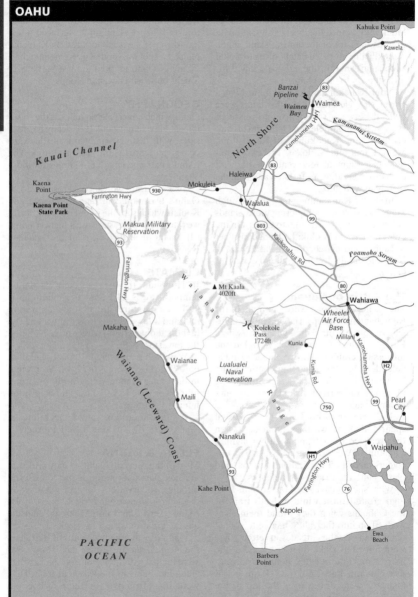

OAHU

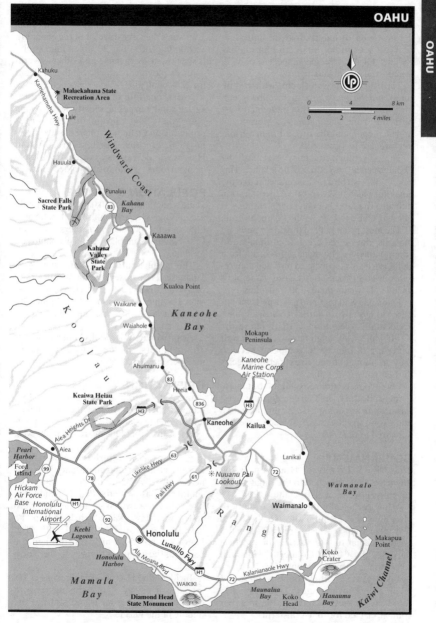

handfuls around the turn of the 20th century. Even more devastating has been the deforestation of habitat and the introduction of a cannibal snail and predatory rodents. Of 41 *Achatinella* species, only 19 remain and all are endangered.

The *elepaio*, a brownish bird with a white rump, and the *amakihi*, a small yellow-green bird, are the most common endemic forest birds on Oahu. The *apapane*, a vibrant red honeycreeper, and the *iiwi*, a bright vermilion bird, are less common.

The only other endemic forest bird, the Oahu creeper, may already be extinct. This small yellowish bird looks somewhat like the amakihi, which makes positive identification difficult. The last Oahu creeper sighting was of a single bird in 1985 on the Poamoho Trail.

The most prominent of the urban birds are pigeons, doves, red-crested cardinals and common mynas. The myna, introduced from India, is a brown, spectacled bird that congregates in noisy flocks. Introduced game birds include pheasants, quails and francolins.

Oahu has wild pigs and goats in its mountain valleys. Brush-tailed rock-wallabies, accidentally released in 1916, reside in the Kalihi Valley. Although rarely seen, the wallabies are of interest to zoologists because they are thought to be an extinct subspecies in their native Australia.

Oahu boasts some excellent botanical gardens. Both Foster Garden and the Lyon Arboretum are home to some unique native and exotic species, some of which have disappeared in the wild.

GOVERNMENT

The 'City & County of Honolulu' is the unwieldy name attached to the single political entity governing all of Oahu.

While technically the City & County of Honolulu also includes the Northwestern Hawaiian Islands, which stretch 1300 miles beyond Kauai to Kure Atoll, for practical purposes the City & County of Honolulu refers to the island of Oahu.

Like Hawaii's other counties, there are no municipal governments. Oahu is administered by a mayor and a nine-member council, elected for four-year terms.

ECONOMY

Oahu has a 5% unemployment rate. Tourism is the largest sector of the economy, accounting for about 30% of Oahu's jobs. It's followed by defense and other government employment, which together account for 22% of all jobs.

Nearly one-fifth of Oahu is still used for agricultural purposes, mostly for growing pineapples. Sugar production, no longer profitable on Oahu, was phased out entirely in 1996. On the North Shore, around Haleiwa and Waialua, coffee trees have been introduced into former cane fields.

POPULATION & PEOPLE

Oahu's population is 880,000, with Honolulu accounting for nearly half of the total. Some other sizable population centers are Pearl City, Kailua, Kaneohe, Aiea, Waipahu and Mililani.

The population is 24% Caucasian, 21% Japanese, 17% mixed ancestry other than part-Hawaiian, 16% part-Hawaiian (less than 1% pure Hawaiian), 7% Filipino and 6% Chinese, with numerous other Pacific and Asian minorities.

Approximately 13% of Oahu's residents are members of the armed forces or members' dependents.

ORIENTATION

Almost all visitors to Oahu land at Honolulu International Airport, the only civilian airport on the island. It's at the western outskirts of the Honolulu district, 9 miles west of Waikiki.

H-1, the main south-shore freeway, is the key to getting around the island. H-1 connects with Hwy 72, which runs around the southeast coast; with the Pali (61) and Likelike (63) Hwys, which go to the windward coast; with Hwy 93, which leads up the leeward Waianae Coast; and with H-2, Hwys 99 and 750, which run through the center of the island on the way to the North Shore.

Incidentally, H-1 is designated as a US *interstate* freeway – an amusing term to describe a road on an island state in the middle of the Pacific.

Rush-hour traffic is heavy heading toward Honolulu in the mornings and away from it in the evenings.

Directions on Oahu are often given by using landmarks, in addition to the Hawaii-wide *mauka* (inland side) and *makai* (seaward side). If someone tells you to go 'Ewa' (a land area west of Honolulu) or 'Diamond Head' (east of Honolulu), it simply means to head in that direction.

Maps
There are simple island maps in the free tourist magazines, but if you're going to be renting a car and doing any exploring at all, it's worth picking up a good road map, especially for navigating around Honolulu. Detailed Gousha road maps (which are recommended, since they show the numbered highway exits) and Rand McNally road maps are sold in stores throughout Oahu for a couple of dollars. Members of the American Automobile Association or an affiliated automobile club can get a free Gousha road map from the AAA office (☎ 593-2221), 1270 Ala Moana Blvd. Most comprehensive – but more detailed than most visitors will need – is the 200-page *Bryan's Sectional Maps Oahu* atlas, which shows and indexes virtually every street on the island.

INFORMATION
Tourist Offices
The administrative office of the Hawaii Visitors and Convention Bureau (☎ 923-1811, fax 924-0290), in Waikiki at 2270 Kalakaua Ave, suite 801, Honolulu, HI 96815, can mail out general tourist information on Oahu and the rest of the state.

To pick up tourist brochures in person, go to the HVCB's visitor information office (☎ 924-0266), which is in Waikiki's Royal Hawaiian Shopping Center, 2201 Kalaukaua Ave, suite A401A.

Money
There are nine banks with around 150 branches throughout Oahu, so it's never a problem finding a bank in the major towns. The Bank of Hawaii, Hawaii's largest bank,

has a branch at the airport and at 2220 Kalakaua Ave in central Waikiki.

Banks are generally open from 8:30 am to 4 pm Monday to Thursday and from 8:30 am to 6 pm on Friday.

Automatic teller machines (ATMs) that accept major credit cards and Cirrus and Plus system debit cards can be found at banks, the airport, larger shopping centers, most supermarkets and numerous other locations.

Post & Communications
There are 35 post offices on Oahu. The main Honolulu post office is not in central Honolulu but is at the side of the airport at 3600 Aolele St, opposite the interisland terminal. It's open from 7:30 am to 8:30 pm Monday to Friday and 8 am to 2:30 pm on Saturday.

All general delivery mail sent to you in Honolulu must be picked up at the main post office. Keep in mind that any mail sent general delivery to the Waikiki post office or other Honolulu branches will either go to the main post office or be returned to the sender. If you're receiving mail in Honolulu, have it addressed to you c/o General Delivery, Main Post Office, 3600 Aolele St, Honolulu, HI 96820-3600.

Email & Internet Access Cybercafes in Honolulu have about the life expectancy of a fly. Most of those that have sprung up in the last few years have now fallen by the wayside.

One exception is Coffee Haven (☎ 732-2090, sip@coffee-haven.com), 1026 Kapahulu Ave near the H-1 overpass, which owes its success to providing good coffee and homemade pies along with Internet access. There are four Macs available for $4 an hour and one IBM for $6 an hour. The minimum charge is 50¢, which covers five to seven minutes. It's open from 8 am to 10 pm Monday to Thursday, 8 am to midnight on Friday and Saturday and 9 am to 5 pm on Sunday.

Kinko's (943-0005), 2575 S King St, near the University of Hawaii, provides email access, as well as computer work stations, for $12 an hour, but there's no minimum so you pay only for the minutes you use. It's open 24 hours a day.

A cheaper and more casual setting near the UH campus can be found at the Coffee Cove On Line (☎ 955-2683, online@ coffeecove.com), 2600 S King St, where you can get coffee and muffins while you check your email. The cost is $1.50 per 15 minutes. It's open from 7 am to midnight on weekdays, 10 am to midnight on weekends.

In addition, a couple of the hostels in Waikiki have computers with Internet access.

Newspapers & Magazines

The main newspaper is the *Honolulu Advertiser* (www.honoluluadvertiser.com), published daily. Oahu also has numerous weekly or monthly newspapers, many of which can be picked up free around the island. These include the *Honolulu Weekly* (www .honoluluweekly.com), a progressive paper with an extensive entertainment section; the *Waikiki News*, with Waikiki-related news and upcoming events; and other regional rags such as the *Windward Oahu News* and the *Kailua Sun Press*.

Numerous free tourist magazines are available at the airport and all around Waikiki. They can be a good source of visitor information, although most of it is paid advertising. *This Week Oahu* and *Spotlight's Oahu Gold* usually have the best discount coupons.

Radio & TV

Honolulu has 17 commercial AM radio stations, 12 FM stations and three noncommercial, public radio stations. Radio station Da KINE (105.1 FM) plays classic Hawaiian music. Hawaii Public Radio is on KHPR (88.1 FM), KKUA (90.7 FM) and KIPO (89.3 FM).

There are a dozen network-affiliated TV stations and numerous cable TV stations. Channels 8 and 10 feature ongoing visitor information and ads geared to tourists.

Bookstores

All of the following bookstores have good collections of Hawaiiana books, travel guides and general fiction.

Borders has a Honolulu branch in the Ward Centre on Ala Moana Blvd and another in the Waikele Center in Waipahu. There's a Barnes & Noble bookstore in Honolulu at 4211 Waialae Ave.

Another national chain, Waldenbooks, has shops in the Kahala Mall, Windward Mall, Pearlridge Center and in Waikiki at the Waikiki Shopping Plaza.

For a well-stocked bookstore in downtown Honolulu, there's Bestsellers, on the corner of Bishop and S Hotel Sts.

Rainbow Books & Records, 1010 University Ave at S Beretania St, near the University of Hawaii, is a good place to look for used books, as well as current travel guides.

Libraries

Hawaii's statewide library system has its main library in downtown Honolulu, next to Iolani Palace. There are also 21 other public

---

Official Oahu

Oahu's nickname is 'The Gathering Place.' Its flower is the delicate native *ilima,* whose yellow-orange blossoms are the inspiration behind the island's official color.

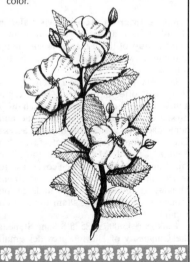

libraries around Oahu, including ones in Waikiki, Kailua and Kaneohe.

Weather Hotlines

The National Weather Service provides recorded weather forecasts for Honolulu (☎ 973-4380) and all of Oahu (☎ 973-4381). The weather service also offers recorded tide and surf conditions (☎ 973-4383) and a marine forecast (☎ 973-4382).

Emergency

Dial ☎ 911 for all police, fire and ambulance emergencies.

Oahu has several hospitals with 24-hour emergency services. Two in the Honolulu area are Queen's Medical Center (☎ 538-9011), 1301 Punchbowl St, and Straub Clinic & Hospital (☎ 522-4000), 888 S King St at Ward. In Kailua, Castle Medical Center (☎ 263-5500), 640 Ulukahiki, is open 24 hours.

Divers with the bends are brought to the UH Hyperbaric Treatment Center (☎ 587-3425), 347 N Kuakini St, Honolulu.

A suicide and crisis line (☎ 521-4555) operates 24 hours a day.

ACTIVITIES
Swimming

Oahu boasts more than 50 beach parks, most of which include rest rooms and showers. Twenty-three are patrolled by lifeguards. The island's four distinct coastal areas have their own peculiar seasonal water conditions. When it's rough on one side, it's generally calm on another, so you can find places to swim year-round.

Oahu's south shore extends from Barbers Point to Makapuu Point and encompasses the most popular beaches on the island, including the extensive white sands of Waikiki and Ala Moana. The sapphire waters of Hananuma Bay attract swimmers as well.

The windward coast extends from Makapuu Point to Kahuku Point. Lovely Kailua Beach Park, Oahu's busiest windsurfing spot, also has good swimming conditions and is the best all-around beach on the windward side. Other nice windward beaches are at Waimanalo, Kualoa and Malaekahana.

The North Shore extends from Kahuku Point to Kaena Point. Although the North Shore has spectacular waves in winter, it can be as calm as a lake during the summer months. There are attractive sandy strands at Haleiwa, Waimea and Sunset Beach.

The leeward Waianae Coast extends from Kaena Point to Barbers Point. It's the driest, sunniest side of Oahu, with long stretches of white sands. The most popular beach on this side is Makaha, which sees big surf in the winter but has suitable swimming conditions in summer.

Swimming Pools The county maintains 18 community swimming pools on Oahu, including ones in Kailua, Kaneohe, Pearl City, Wahiawa and Waipahu. Pools in the greater Honolulu area are at Palolo Valley District Park (☎ 733-7362), 2007 Palolo Ave; Manoa Valley District Park (☎ 988-6868), 2721 Kaaipu Ave; Booth District Park (☎ 522-7037), 2331 Kanealii Ave; and McCully District Park (☎ 973-7268), 831 Pumehana.

Surfing

Oahu has 594 defined surfing sites, nearly twice as many as any of the other Hawaiian islands. In winter, the North Shore gets some of Hawaii's most spectacular surf, with swells reaching 20 to 30 feet. This is the home of the Banzai Pipeline, Sunset Beach and some of the world's top surfing competitions.

Makaha is the top winter surf spot on the Waianae Coast.

The south shore sees its finest surfing waves in summer, when scores of surfers head to Waikiki and Diamond Head for some of the best breaks.

Surf News Network (☎ 596-SURF) has a recorded surf line reporting winds, wave heights and tides, updated three times a day. The National Weather Service (☎ 973-4383) also provides surf reports. For a live video surf report, visit www.seewaves.com.

The county's Haleiwa Surf Center (☎ 637-5051), at Haleiwa Alii Beach Park on the North Shore, holds free surfing lessons from 9:30 am to noon on most Saturdays and

Sundays between early September and late May. Surfboards are provided – all you need to bring is a swimsuit and suntan lotion!

Surf-N-Sea (☎ 637-9887) in Haleiwa rents surfboards for $5 the first hour, $3.50 each additional hour, or $24 a day. Surf-N-Sea gives two-hour surfing lessons for $65. This and a few other shops in Haleiwa also sell new and used boards.

In Waikiki, surfing lessons are available through beachside concession stands like Star Beach Boys behind the police station or Aloha Beach Services behind Duke's Canoe Club. The going rate is $35 for a one-hour lesson. These Waikiki concession stands also rent surfboards for around $8 an hour or $25 a day.

Planet Surf (☎ 924-9050), at 159 Kaiulani Ave in Waikiki and opposite Pupukea Beach Park in Waimea, rents boards for $20 a day.

H30, a monthly magazine that interviews surfers and reports on surfing events and surf conditions, is free at surf shops around the island.

Bodysurfing & Boogie Boarding

On the windward coast, Waimanalo Beach Park and nearby Bellows Field Beach Park have gentle shorebreaks good for beginning bodysurfers.

The two hottest (and most dangerous) spots for expert bodysurfers are Sandy and Makapuu Beach Parks in southeast Oahu. Other top shorebreaks are at Makaha on the Waianae Coast, Waimea Bay on the North Shore, Kalama Beach in Kailua and Pounders in Laie on the windward coast.

The most popular boogie-boarding place in Waikiki is at Kapahulu Groin.

Rentals If you're going to be doing much boogie boarding, you may be better off purchasing your own equipment. However, there are plenty of places to rent boards.

The concession stands on Waikiki Beach generally charge about $5 an hour, $15 a day for boogie board rentals.

A cheaper option, Planet Surf (☎ 924-9050), at 159 Kaiulani Ave in Waikiki, rents boogie boards for $8 a day, $20 a week. You can also buy a used board there. There's

another branch opposite Pupukea Beach Park on the North Shore.

Surf-N-Sea (☎ 637-9887) in Haleiwa rents boards for $4 for the first hour, $3 for each additional hour.

Kailua Sailboards & Kayaks (☎ 262-2555), 130 Kailua Rd in Kailua, rents boogie boards for $12 a half day.

Windsurfing

Kailua Bay is Oahu's number one windsurfing spot. It has good year-round trade winds and both flat-water and wave conditions in different sections of the bay. Windsurfing shops set up vans at Kailua Beach Park on weekdays and Saturday mornings, renting boards and giving lessons. It's a great place for beginners to try the sport.

Other good spots include Diamond Head for speed and jumps and Backyards for North Shore challenges. Fort DeRussy Beach is Waikiki's main windsurfing spot.

Naish Hawaii (☎ 262-6068, 800-767-6068) – as in windsurfing champion Robbie Naish – sells and rents equipment. The shop is in downtown Kailua, at 155A Hamakua Drive, Kailua, HI 96734, but you can also arrange to have your equipment delivered to Kailua Beach. Rental rates vary with the board and rig: Beginner equipment costs $20 for two hours or $30 a full day; intermediate and advanced equipment is $35 a half day, $40 to $45 a full day. Naish gives introductory group lessons for $35 for three hours. For $55 you can get a 1½-hour private lesson that includes an additional 2½ hours of board use.

Kailua Sailboards & Kayaks (☎ 262-2555, watersports@aloha.net), 130 Kailua Rd, Kailua, HI 96734, rents beginner equipment for $29 a half day, $39 a full day or $160 a week; high-performance boards cost $39 a half day, $49 a day or $199 a week. Three-hour beginner's lessons cost $49.

Waikiki Pacific Windsurfing (☎ 949-8952), at the Prime Time concession stand on Fort DeRussy Beach, rents windsurfing equipment for $30 an hour, $80 for a half day; add $10 more for a lesson.

In Haleiwa, Surf-N-Sea (☎ 637-9887) rents windsurfing equipment for $12 for the first hour and $8 for each additional hour. Two-hour windsurfing lessons cost $65.

Diving

Top summer dive spots include the caves and ledges at Three Tables and Shark's Cove on the North Shore and the Makaha Caverns on the Waianae Coast. On the south shore, Hanauma Bay has calm diving conditions most of the year. There are a number of other popular dive spots between Hanauma and Honolulu that provide good winter diving. Two-tank dives average around $85. PADI certification courses, which can sometimes be given in as little as three days, cost around $400. If you're staying in Waikiki, many dive shops will provide transportation from your hotel.

There are numerous dive shops on Oahu. The following are all five-star PADI operations.

Aaron's Dive Shop
(☎ 262-2333, aarons@aloha.com)
602 Kailua Rd, Kailua, HI 96734

Aloha Dive Shop
(☎ 395-5922)
Koko Marina Shopping Center
Honolulu, HI 96825

Aquatic Lifestyles
(☎ 396-9738, aloha@hawaii-dive.com)
377 Keahole St, Hawaii Kai, HI 96825

Bojac Aquatic Center
(☎ 671-0311)
94-801 Farrington Hwy, Waipahu, HI 96796

Breeze Hawaii Diving Adventure
(☎ 735-1857, aloha@breezehawaii.com)
3014 Kaimuki Ave, Honolulu, HI 96816

Dan's Dive Shop
(☎ 536-6181)
660 Ala Moana Blvd, Honolulu, HI 96813

Dive Authority-Honolulu
(☎ 596-7234)
333 Ward Ave, Honolulu, HI 96814

Hawaii Dive College
(☎ 843-2882)
24 Sand Island Access Rd, Honolulu, HI 96819

Hawaiian Island Aquatics
(☎ 622-3483)
1640 Wilikina Drive, Wahiawa, HI 96786

Honolulu Diving Academy
(☎ 941-4369)
512-A Atkinson Drive, Honolulu, HI 96814

Island Quest
(☎ 422-5551, iq@oceanconcepts.com)
Building 1511, Scott Pool
Pearl Harbor, HI 96860

Ocean Concepts
(☎ 696-7200, ocw@oceanconcepts.com)
85-371 Farrington Hwy, Waianae, HI 96792

South Sea Aquatics
(☎ 922-0852)
2155 Kalakaua Ave, Honolulu, HI 96815

Sunshine Scuba
(☎ 593-8865, sunshine@lava.net)
642 Cooke St, Honolulu, HI 96813

Waikiki Diving Center
(☎ 922-2121)
424 Nahua St, Honolulu, HI 96815

Windward Dive Center
(☎ 263-2311, wdc@divehawaii.com)
789 Kailua Rd, Kailua, HI 96734

Snuba Snuba Tours of Oahu (☎ 396-6163) offers snuba, a sort of scuba diving for snorkelers, at Hanauma Bay for $85 or at Maunalua Bay in the Hawaii Kai area for $75. Both of these prices include roundtrip transportation from Waikiki; if you get there on your own, the cost for either outing drops to $65. This is a nice way to get introduced to the underwater world. All programs include elementary dive instruction. An instructor stays in the water with you during your dive, which lasts about 30 minutes. For more information on snuba, see the Outdoor Activities chapter, earlier in this book.

Snorkeling

For snorkeling, Hanauma Bay on the south shore is the best year-round spot. In summer, Pupukea Beach Park on the North Shore provides excellent snorkeling.

If you plan on doing a lot of snorkeling, it may be cheaper for you to buy your own equipment. For those who only want to try it a few times, plenty of places offer rentals by the day or week.

Prime Time Sports (☎ 949-8952), a concession stand at Fort DeRussy Beach, rents snorkel sets for $8 for three hours.

A cheaper option, Planet Surf (☎ 924-9050), at 159 Kaiulani Ave in Waikiki, rents snorkel sets for $5 a day, $13 a week. There's

OAHU

another branch opposite Pupukea Beach Park on the North Shore.

Snorkel Bob's (☎ 735-7944), 702 Kapahulu Ave, about a mile out of Waikiki, rents elementary snorkel sets from $3.50 a day, $9 a week, and better sets with silicone masks for $7 a day, $19 to $29 a week. You can arrange to return them on one of the Neighbor Islands for no extra charge.

Surf-N-Sea (☎ 637-9887) in Haleiwa rents snorkel sets for $6.50 for a half day, $9.50 for 24 hours. Kailua Sailboards & Kayaks (☎ 262-2555), 130 Kailua Rd in Kailua, charges $9 a day for snorkel set rentals.

Kayaking

Kailua Beach, which has a nearshore island that you can paddle to, is one of the most popular destinations for kayaking on Oahu. Waikiki, while not as interesting, also has a fair amount of kayaking activity simply because of its high tourist density.

Twogood Kayaks Hawaii (☎ 262-5656), 345 Hahani St in Kailua, has kayak sales, rentals and lessons. One-person kayaks rent for $25 a half day or $32 a full day; two-person kayaks cost $32/42. Kailua Sailboard & Kayaks (☎ 262-2555), 130 Kailua Rd in Kailua, has one- and two-person kayaks at the same rates.

Kayak Oahu Adventures (☎ 923-0539) rents kayaks from the New Otani Kaimana Beach Hotel on Waikiki's Sans Souci Beach. Rates for one/two-person kayaks are $10/20 an hour, $30/40 a half day.

At the other end of Waikiki is Prime Time Sports (☎ 949-8952), on Fort DeRussy Beach, which rents one-person kayaks for $10 an hour, two-person kayaks for $20.

Hiking

The trail that leads three-quarters of a mile from inside the crater of Diamond Head up to its summit is the most popular hike on Oahu. It's easy to reach from Waikiki and ends with a panoramic view of greater Honolulu.

Another nice, short hike is the Manoa Falls Trail, just a few miles above Waikiki, where a peaceful path through an abandoned arboretum of lofty trees leads to a waterfall.

The Tantalus and Makiki Valley area has the most extensive trail network around Honolulu, with fine views of the city and surrounding valleys. Amazingly, although it's just 2 miles above the city hustle and bustle, this lush forest reserve is unspoiled and offers quiet solitude.

On the western edge of Honolulu, the Moanalua Trail goes deep into the Moanalua Valley. You can hike it on your own or join a guided Sunday walk.

At Keaiwa Heiau State Park, northwest of Honolulu, the Aiea Loop Trail leads 4½ miles along a ridge that offers views of Pearl Harbor, Diamond Head and the Koolau Range.

The Kaena Point Trail is a coastal hike through a natural area reserve on the westernmost point of Oahu. There are also longer forestry trails in the same area.

On the windward side, there's a pleasant hour-long hike out to Makapuu lighthouse and a longer trail at Sacred Falls State Park that follows a narrow mountain valley to a waterfall.

There are short walks from the Nuuanu Pali Lookout, within Hoomaluhia Park and along many beaches.

For details on these and other hikes, see the respective sections of this chapter.

Hitchhiking Weeds

All hikers who have explored Oahu should scrub their shoes and wash their socks and long pants before hiking on other islands to avoid transferring clinging *Clidemia hirta* seeds, which are practically invisible. This weed has infested much of Oahu, overrunning trails and choking out native plants, but it's not yet widely established on the Neighbor Islands. It's presumed that the patches of this invasive plant that are now found along trails on Molokai and Maui hitchhiked there on the boot of an Oahu hiker.

Guided Hikes Notices of hiking club outings can usually be found in the Honolulu Advertiser's Friday 'TGIF' insert and the Honolulu Weekly's 'Scene' section.

By joining these outings, you can meet and hike with ecology-minded islanders. It may also be a good way to get to the backwoods if you don't have a car, as the hikers often share rides. Wear sturdy shoes and, for the longer hikes, bring lunch and water.

Naturalists from the Hawaii Nature Center (☎ 955-0100), at the forestry baseyard camp in Makiki, lead hikes on either Saturday or Sunday most weekends. The cost is $7 for nonmembers. Trails range from the easy 2½-mile Makiki Loop Trail to a strenuous 6-mile hike up Mt Kaala, Oahu's highest point. Reservations are required.

The Sierra Club (☎ 538-6616) leads hikes and other outings on Saturdays and Sundays. These range from easy 2-mile hikes to strenuous 10-mile treks. Most outings meet at 8 am at the Church of the Crossroads, 2510 Bingham St, Honolulu. The hike fee is $3.

The Hawaii Audubon Society (☎ 528-1432) leads bird-watching hikes once a month, usually on a weekend. The suggested donation is $2. Binoculars and a copy of *Hawaii's Birds* are recommended.

Running

Oahuans are big on jogging. In fact, it's estimated that Honolulu has more joggers per capita than any other city in the world. Kapiolani Park and Ala Moana Park are two favorite jogging spots. There's also a well-beaten 4.8-mile run around Diamond Head crater.

Oahu has about 70 road races each year, from 1-mile fun runs and 5-mile jogs to competitive marathons, biathlons and triathlons. For an annual schedule of running events with times, dates and contact addresses, write to the Department of Parks & Recreation, City & County of Honolulu, 650 S King St, Honolulu, HI 96813.

Oahu's best-known race, the Honolulu Marathon, held in mid-December, is the second-largest marathon in the USA. For information send a self-addressed, stamped envelope to Honolulu Marathon Associa-

tion, 3435 Waialae Ave, No 208, Honolulu, HI 96816. Those writing from overseas are asked to include two international response postage coupons.

The Department of Parks & Recreation holds a Honolulu Marathon Clinic at 7:30 am most Sundays at the Kapiolani Park Bandstand. It's free and open to everyone from beginners to seasoned marathon runners. Runners join groups of their own speed.

Going for the gold in the Honolulu Marathon

Horseback Riding

Kualoa Ranch (☎ 237-8515), opposite Kualoa Regional Park on the windward coast, has 40-minute trail rides for $28 and 1½-hour rides for $45.

The Turtle Bay Hilton (☎ 293-8811) in Kahuku has 45-minute trail rides for $35 and 1½-hour sunset rides for $65.

Tennis

Oahu has 181 county tennis courts spread around the island. If you are staying in Waikiki, the most convenient locations are the 10 lighted courts at Ala Moana Beach Park; the 10 unlit courts at the Diamond Head Tennis Center, at the Diamond Head end of Kapiolani Park; and the four lighted Kapiolani Park courts, opposite the Waikiki Aquarium. Court time is free on a first-come, first-served basis.

With ground space at a premium, few Waikiki hotels have room for tennis courts. The Ilikai Hotel (☎ 944-6300), 1777 Ala Moana Blvd, and the Pacific Beach Hotel (☎ 922-1233), 2490 Kalakaua Ave, each have two courts and charge $5 per hour per person for hotel guests, $8 for nonguests; rackets can be rented for $4.

Planet Surf (☎ 924-9050), 159 Kaiulani Ave in Waikiki, rents tennis rackets for $5 a day, $20 a week.

Outside Waikiki, the Turtle Bay Hilton in Kahuku (☎ 293-8811) charges $12 per person per day, with one-hour playing time guaranteed; rackets rent for $8 a day. The resort has a pro shop and gives lessons.

Golf

Oahu has five 18-hole municipal golf courses: Ala Wai Golf Course (☎ 733-7387) on Kapahulu Ave, on the inland side of the Ala Wai Canal, near Waikiki; Pali Golf Course (☎ 266-7612), 45-050 Kamehameha Hwy, Kaneohe; Ted Makalena Golf Course (☎ 675-6052), Waipio Point Access Rd, Waipahu; Ewa Villages Golf Course (☎ 681-0220) in Ewa; and West Loch Golf Course (☎ 675-6076), 91-1126 Okupe St, Ewa Beach.

Greens fees for 18 holes at any of these municipal courses are $40 per person, plus an optional $14 for a gas-powered cart. The county also maintains the nine-hole Kahuku Golf Course (☎ 293-5842) in Kahuku.

The reservation system is the same at all municipal courses: call (☎ 296-2000) and key information into the recorded system as prompted. The earliest bookings are accepted just three days in advance for visitors, but one week in advance for resident golfers.

The only municipal course near Waikiki is the Ala Wai Golf Course, which lays claim to being the 'busiest in the world.' Local golfers who may book earlier in the week usually take all the starting times, leaving none for visitors. However, visiting golfers who don't mind a wait may show up at the Ala Wai window and put their names on the waiting list; as long as the entire golfing party waits at the course, they'll usually get a chance to golf before the day is over. If you come without clubs, you can rent them for about $20.

At last count, Oahu also had seven military and 23 private, public or resort golf courses, but the number is rising, fueling many a conflict between environmentalists and overseas developers.

Skydiving & Gliding

For around $200, Skydive Hawaii (☎ 945-0222) will attach you to the hips and shoulders of a skydiver so you can jump together from a plane at 13,000 feet, free-fall for a minute and finish off with 10 to 15 minutes of canopy ride. The whole process, including some basic instruction, takes about 1½ hours. Participants must be over 18 years of age and weigh less than 200 pounds. If you're an experienced skydiver, you can make arrangements for a solo jump. Flights take off daily, weather permitting, from Dillingham Airfield in Mokuleia.

Glider Rides (☎ 677-3404) offers 20-minute flights on engineless piloted glider craft, towed by a small airplane and then released to slowly glide back to earth. Flights leave daily, weather permitting, from Dillingham Airfield in Mokuleia between 10:30 am and 5 pm. The cost is $100 for one person or $120 for two.

At the same location, Soar Hawaii (☎ 637-3147) offers 30-minute glider rides for $120 for either one or two people – though a single person can often negotiate $20 off the rate. For thrill seekers, the company also offers acrobatic rides with barrel rolls, spirals and wingovers.

ORGANIZED TOURS

For conventional sightseeing tours by van or bus, there's E Noa Tours (☎ 591-2561), Polynesian Adventure Tours (☎ 833-3000) or Roberts Hawaii (☎ 539-9400).

All of these companies offer full-day, circle-island tours, which average $55 and generally encompass southeast Oahu, the windward coast and the North Shore.

For those who actually want to get into the water and relax along the way, a good alternative island tour is offered by Alala EcoAdventures. These owner-led tours, which are small-scale and personable, include visits to Diamond Head and the major southeast Oahu sights, as well as some time at Haleiwa and Sunset Beach. Tours operate a few times a week, last all day and cost just $25. Make reservations through Hostelling International Honolulu (☎ 946-0591).

Waikiki Trolley

The Waikiki Trolley is a tourist trolley bus that runs along two fixed routes. The 'red line,' between Waikiki and Honolulu, has about two dozen stops, including the Ala Moana Center, Honolulu Academy of Arts, Iolani Palace, Hawaii Maritime Center, Bishop Museum, Chinatown and the Ward Centre. The 'green line' is more limited, with stops at the zoo and aquarium in Waikiki, Hanauma Bay, Halona Blowhole and Sea Life Park.

Sightseeing narration is provided en route and passengers can get off at any stop and then pick up the next trolley. Both lines depart from the Royal Hawaiian Shopping Center in Waikiki; the red line every 20 minutes and the green line once an hour, between 8:30 am and 6:30 pm. One-day passes cost $18 for a single line, $30 for both lines, making it a pricey alternative to the public bus.

Cruises

There are numerous sunset sails, dinner cruises and party boats leaving daily from Kewalo Basin, just west of Ala Moana Park. Rates range from $20 to $100, with dinner cruises averaging about $50. Many provide transport to and from Waikiki and advertise various come-ons and specials; check the free tourist magazines for the latest offers.

A handful of catamarans depart from Waikiki Beach, including the *Manu Kai* (☎ 946-7490), which docks behind the Duke Kahanamoku statue and charges $10 for one-hour sails. The green-sailed *Mai Ta'i* catamaran (☎ 922-5665), which departs from the beach in front of the Sheraton Waikiki, offers 1½-hour sails for $20 and longer sunset sails for $30.

Royal Hawaiian Cruises (☎ 848-6360) runs two-hour whale-watching cruises from January to April aboard the *Navatek I*, a sleek, high-tech catamaran designed to minimize rolling. There's a morning cruise at 8:30 am that costs $39 for adults and $24 for children ages three to 11. The boat leaves from Pier 6, near the Aloha Tower.

Atlantis Submarines (☎ 973-9811) has a 65-foot, 48-passenger sightseeing submarine that descends to a depth of 100 feet. The tour lasts 1¾ hours, including boat transport to and from the sub. About 45 minutes are spent cruising beneath the surface around a ship and two planes that were deliberately sunk to create a dive site. Tours leave from Hilton Hawaiian Village on the hour from 8 am to 4 pm daily and cost $89 for adults, though if you book the 2 pm sailing there's a $59 special. All dives are $39 for children 12 and under.

ACCOMMODATIONS

Some 90% of Oahu's 40,000 visitor rooms are in Waikiki. Unlike on the Neighbor Islands, where there are multiple destinations, all but two of Oahu's resort hotels are found in Honolulu.

The Waikiki-Honolulu area contains a wide range of accommodations. The least-expensive places are the two HI-affiliated youth hostels and the handful of private hostel-type lodgings; all of them have dorm beds for about $16. After that, there are rooms at Ys for $30 and a few budget Waikiki hotels that start around $50. Waikiki has lots of mid-range hotels in the $75 to $125 range, as well as high-priced luxury hotels.

Unless otherwise noted, the rates given throughout this chapter are the same for either singles or doubles and don't include the 11.41% room tax.

Some hotels have different rates for the high and low seasons. The high season is generally from December 15 to April 15, but it can vary by hotel a few weeks in either direction. The rest of the year is the low season, though a few hotels switch to high-season rates in midsummer.

To lure customers, some large chains like Outrigger offer a free rental car if you request it at the time of booking. A few independent hotels occasionally throw in a car as well; it never hurts to ask whenever you book any hotel. If you had planned on renting a car, it can be a tidy savings.

Camping

Camping is allowed at numerous county beach parks, one botanical garden and four state parks.

All county and state campgrounds on Oahu are closed on Wednesday and Thursday nights, ostensibly for maintenance, but also to prevent permanent encampments.

Although thousands of visitors use these campsites each year without incident, Oahu has more of a reputation for problems than other islands. Rip-offs, especially at roadside and beachfront campgrounds, are not unknown. Camping along the Waianae Coast is not recommended.

State Parks Camping is free by permit at Sand Island and Keaiwa Heiau, both in the greater Honolulu area, and at Malaekahana State Recreation Area and Kahana Valley State Park, both on the windward coast.

Keaiwa Heiau is a good choice for an inland park. The best choice for a coastal state park is the Malaekahana State Recreation Area, which is also the only public park on Oahu with cabins (see the Windward Coast section).

Camping is limited to five nights per month in each park. Permit applications can be made no more than 30 days before the first camping date. Applications may be made to the Division of State Parks by mail (PO Box 621, Honolulu, HI 96809), by phone (☎ 587-0300) or in person (1151 Punchbowl St, room 131) between 8 am and 3:30 pm Monday to Friday.

County Beach Parks Camping is free at the county beach parks, but permits are required. Permits are not available by mail but can be picked up between 7:45 am and 4 pm Monday to Friday at the Department of Parks & Recreation (☎ 523-4525) on the ground floor of the Honolulu Municipal Building, 650 S King St in downtown Honolulu, the tall gray building on the corner of King and Alapai Sts.

Permits are also available from satellite city halls, including one at the Ala Moana Center (☎ 973-2600), where permits are issued 9 am to 4:30 pm Monday to Thursday, 9 am to 5:45 pm Friday, 8 am to 4 pm Saturday. Other satellite city halls are in Kailua, Kaneohe and Wahiawa.

Camping is allowed at Mokuleia and Kaiaka Beach Parks on the North Shore; Hauula, Swanzy, Kualoa, Bellows Field, Waimanalo and Waimanalo Bay Beach Parks on the windward side; and Nanakuli, Lualualei (summer only) and Keaau Beach Parks on the Waianae Coast.

Camping is allowed from 8 am Friday to 8 am Wednesday, except at Swanzy and Bellows Field Beach Parks, which are open only on weekends.

Kualoa, in one of Oahu's nicest beach settings, has an on-site caretaker and gates that are locked at night. Kaiaka, Bellows Field and Waimanalo Bay also have caretakers, but other beach parks don't.

For more information about the facilities available at county beach parks, see the Accommodations section of the Facts for the Visitor chapter.

County Botanical Garden Hoomaluhia Park (☎ 233-7323), an inland park in Kaneohe at the base of the Koolau Range, is unique among the county campgrounds in that it's operated by the botanical gardens division. With a resident caretaker and gates that close to noncampers at 4 pm, Hoomaluhia Park is one of the safest places to camp on Oahu. What's more, like other county campgrounds, there's no fee.

The five grassy camping areas, each of which has rest rooms, cold showers and drinking water, can accommodate up to 650 people, but often only a couple of the areas need to be opened.

Camping is allowed on Friday, Saturday and Sunday nights only. You can get a permit in advance at any satellite city hall, or simply come up to the park between 9 am and 4 pm Monday to Saturday to get a permit; if you take the latter route on the same day you intend to camp, call first to be sure space is available.

Backcountry Camping The state forestry allows backcountry camping along a number of valley and ridge trails, including in Hauula on the windward coast.

All backcountry camping requires a permit from the Division of Forestry & Wildlife (☎ 587-0166), 1151 Punchbowl St, room 325, Honolulu, HI 96813. Permits are issued between 7:45 am and 4 pm Monday to Friday. There are no fees.

Fellow hikers on backcountry trails are likely to be pig hunters.

Camping Supplies The Bike Shop (☎ 596-0588), 1149 S King St, rents internal-frame backpacks and two-person lightweight tents. The rate for each supply is $15/35/70 per day/weekend/week.

Omar The Tent Man (☎ 677-8785), 94-158 Leoole St, Waipahu, HI 96797, has weekly rates of $30 for lightweight two-person dome tents, $20 for sleeping bags or external-frame backpacks and $18 for stoves or lanterns. Three-day rates for those items are $25, $15 and $14 respectively.

ENTERTAINMENT

The vast majority of Oahu's entertainment takes place in Honolulu, which includes but is certainly not limited to Waikiki.

The best place to look for up-to-date entertainment information is in the free *Honolulu Weekly* newspaper and the 'TGIF' insert in the Friday edition of the *Honolulu Advertiser*. Oahu has numerous movie theaters showing first-run movies. There are also a handful of theater companies that perform everything from 'South Pacific' and Broadway musicals to Mamet satires and pidgin fairy tales. Check the newspapers for current movies and plays.

More detailed information is located in the Entertainment sections under specific destinations. For festivals, fairs and sporting events, see the Special Events section in the Facts about Hawaii chapter.

Luaus

Oahu's two main luaus, *Paradise Cove* (☎ 973-5828) and *Germaine's Luau* (☎ 949-6626), are both huge, impersonal affairs held nightly near the Barbers Point area. Both cost around $50, which includes the bus ride from Waikiki hotels (about one hour each way), a buffet dinner, drinks, a Polynesian show and related hoopla. Children pay about half price.

SHOPPING

Honolulu is a large, cosmopolitan city with plenty of sophisticated shops selling designer clothing, jewelry and the like. For general crafts, the best deals are usually found at one of the craft shows that are periodically held in city parks (check the newspapers).

For kitsch souvenirs, there are scores of shops selling fake Polynesian stuff, from Filipino shell hangings and carved coconuts to cheap seashell jewelry and wooden tiki statues. The largest single collection of such shops is at the International Market Place in Waikiki.

If you just want to buy a carton of macadamia nuts, Longs Drugs has better prices than most places in Waikiki. The Ala Moana Center, which has been billed as the 'largest open-air shopping center in the world,' includes a Longs, as well as 200 other stores (see the Ala Moana section).

For local flavor, the Aloha Flea Market (☎ 486-1529), at Aloha Stadium near Pearl

Harbor, has some 1500 vendors and is open from 6 am to 3 pm on Wednesday, Saturday and Sunday. A private shuttle bus to the flea market picks shoppers up at Waikiki hotels about once every half hour from 7 am to noon. The cost is $5 roundtrip; call ☎ 455-7300 for reservations.

Hawaiiana Souvenirs

The Hula Supply Center (☎ 941-5379), 2346 S King St in Honolulu, sells feather *leis* (garlands), calabash gourds, bamboo sticks, hula skirts, Tongan *tapa* (cloth made from pounded bark) and the like. Although they're intended for Hawaiian musicians and dancers, some of the items would make interesting souvenirs or gifts and prices are reasonable.

Quilts Hawaii (☎ 942-3195), 2338 S King St, next to Hula Supply Center, has high-quality Hawaiian quilting, including bedcovers, pillows and wall hangings. It also carries other Hawaiian crafts such as hats, *koa* (native hardwood) chests and dolls. Prices are high but reasonable for the quality.

Kamaka Hawaii (☎ 531-3165), at 550 South St in Honolulu, specializes in handcrafted ukuleles, with prices starting at $235.

For antique and previously worn aloha shirts, Bailey's Antique Shop (☎ 734-7628), 517 Kapahulu Ave, near Waikiki, has the island's widest selection, with prices from $10 to $3000. Bargain-hunters can sometimes find used aloha shirts and *muumuus* (long, loose-fitting dresses) at thrift shops around the island, including the Goodwill store at 780 S Beretania St in Honolulu and the small shop (open 10 am to 2 pm Monday, Tuesday, Thursday and Friday) at the Waikiki Community Center, 310 Paoakalani Ave.

CDs and cassettes of Hawaiian music also make good souvenirs. You'll find an excellent collection of both classic and contemporary Hawaiian music at Borders, which has a branch at the Ward Centre in Honolulu, and at Tower Records, which has shops behind the Ala Moana Center and at Waikiki's International Market Place. Both companies allow you to listen to various CDs before you buy.

GETTING THERE & AWAY

The vast majority of flights into Hawaii land at Honolulu International Airport, the only commercial airport on Oahu. See also the Getting There & Away chapter in the front of the book for information on flights to Oahu and airport facilities.

All interisland airlines that serve the Neighbor Islands also use Honolulu International Airport. For details on flying to the Neighbor Islands, see the Getting Around chapter in the front of the book and the Getting There & Away sections of individual Neighbor Island chapters.

GETTING AROUND

Oahu is an easy island to get around, whether you travel by public bus or private car.

Traffic in Honolulu can get quite jammed during rush hour, from 7 to 9 am and 3 to 6 pm weekdays. Expect heavy traffic in both directions on H-1 during this time, as well as when heading toward Honolulu in the morning and away in the late afternoon on the Pali and Likelike Hwys. If you're heading to the airport during rush hour, give yourself plenty of extra time.

To/From the Airport

From the airport you can get to Waikiki by local bus (if your baggage is limited), by airport shuttle services, by taxi or by rental car. A taxi to Waikiki from the airport will cost about $20. The main car rental agencies have booths or courtesy phones in the airport baggage claim area.

The easiest way to drive to Waikiki from the airport is to take Hwy 92, which starts out as Nimitz Hwy and turns into Ala Moana Blvd, leading directly into Waikiki. Although this route hits more local traffic, it's hard to get lost on it.

If you're into life in the fast lane, connect instead with the H-1 Fwy heading east.

On the return to the airport from Waikiki, take note not to miss the poorly marked interchange where H-1 and Hwy 78 split; if you're not in the right-hand lane at that point, you could easily end up on Hwy 78. It takes about 20 minutes to get from Waikiki to the airport via H-1 *if* you don't hit traffic.

Bus Travel time is about an hour between the airport and the far end of Waikiki on city bus Nos 19 and 20; the fare is $1. The bus stops at the roadside median on the 2nd level, in front of the airline counters. There are two stops; it's best to wait for the bus at the first one, which is in front of Lobby 4. Luggage is limited to what you can hold on your lap or store under your seat, the latter space comparable to the space under an airline seat.

Shuttles Super Shuttle (☎ 841-2928) and Airport Express (☎ 949-5249) offer shuttle service between the airport and Waikiki hotels. The ride takes about 45 minutes. These buses are picked up at the roadside median on the ground level in front of the baggage claim areas. The charge is $6 one way or $10 roundtrip. You don't need a reservation from the airport to Waikiki, but you do need to call at least a few hours in advance for the return van to the airport. Shuttles operate from 6 am to 10 pm.

Bus

Oahu's public bus system, called TheBus, is extensive and easy to use.

TheBus has some 80 routes, which collectively cover most of Oahu. You can take the bus to watch windsurfers at Kailua or surfers at Sunset Beach or Makaha, visit Chinatown or the Bishop Museum, snorkel at Hanauma Bay or hike Diamond Head. However, some of the island's prime viewpoints are beyond reach: TheBus doesn't stop at the Nuuanu Pali Lookout, go up to Tantalus or out to Kaena Point.

Taking TheBus in downtown Honolulu is the best way to get around on weekdays, when traffic congestion can make driving a bit overwhelming for visitors. Lots of bus routes converge downtown – so many that Hotel St, which begins downtown and crosses Chinatown, is restricted to bus traffic only.

Buses stop only at the marked bus stops. Each route can have a few different destinations. The destination is written on the front of the bus next to the number.

Buses generally keep the same number when inbound and outbound. For instance, bus No 8 can take you into the heart of Waikiki or out away from it toward Ala Moana – so take note of both the number and the written destination before you jump on.

If you're in doubt, ask the bus drivers. They're used to disoriented visitors, and most drivers are patient and helpful.

Overall, the buses are in excellent condition – if anything, they're too modern. Newer buses are air-conditioned, with sealed windows and climate-control that sometimes seems so out of 'control' that drivers and passengers wear jackets to keep from freezing!

Currently, about half of the buses are equipped with wheelchair lifts and most have bike racks that cyclists can use for free.

Although TheBus is convenient enough, this isn't Tokyo – if you set your watch by the bus here, you'll come up with 'Hawaiian Time,' a distinctly laid-back pace. In addition to not getting hung up on schedules, buses can sometimes bottleneck, with one packed bus after another cruising right by crowded bus stops. Saturday nights between Ala Moana and Waikiki can be a particularly memorable experience.

Still, TheBus usually gets you where you want to go and, as long as you don't try to cut anything close or schedule too much in one day, it's a great deal.

Fares The one-way fare for all rides is $1 for adults, 50¢ for children ages six to 18. Children under the age of six ride free. You can use either coins or $1 bills; bus drivers don't make change.

Transfers, which always have a time limit stamped on them, are given for free when more than one bus is required to get to a destination. If needed, ask for one when you board.

Visitor passes valid for unlimited rides over four consecutive days cost $10 and can be purchased at any of the ubiquitous ABC Stores.

Monthly bus passes valid for unlimited rides in a calendar month cost $25 and can be purchased at satellite city halls, 7-Eleven convenience stores and Foodland and Star supermarkets.

Seniors 65 years and older can buy a $20 bus pass valid for unlimited rides during a two-year period. Senior passes are issued at satellite city halls upon presentation of an identification card with a birthdate.

Schedules & Information TheBus has a great telephone service. As long as you know where you are and where you want to go, you can call ☎ 848-5555 anytime between 5:30 am and 10 pm and find out not only which bus to catch, but also when the next one will be there. This same number also has a TDD service for the hearing impaired and can provide information on which buses are wheelchair accessible.

You can pick up free printed timetables for individual routes and a handy schematic route map at any satellite city hall, including the one at the Ala Moana Center. They can also be found in the downtown Honolulu library and a few places in Waikiki, including the Waikiki Beach police station, the International Market Place food court and the McDonald's at the Waikiki Tower hotel.

Common Routes Bus Nos 8, 19, 20 and 58 run between Waikiki and the Ala Moana Center, Honolulu's central transfer point. There's usually a bus every 10 minutes or less. From Ala Moana you can connect with a broad network of buses to points inland and Ewa.

Bus Nos 2, 19 and 20 will take you between Waikiki and downtown Honolulu.

Bus No 4 runs between Waikiki and the University of Hawaii.

Circle-Island Route It's possible to circle the island by TheBus, beginning at the Ala Moana Center. The No 52 Wahiawa-Circle Island bus goes clockwise up Hwy 99 to Haleiwa and along the North Shore. At the Turtle Bay Hilton, on the northern tip of Oahu, it switches signs to No 55 and comes down the windward coast to Kaneohe and down the Pali Hwy back to Ala Moana. The No 55 Kaneohe-Circle Island bus does the same route in reverse. If you do it nonstop, it takes about four hours.

To make the loop around southeast Oahu from Waikiki, it's bus No 58 to Sea Life Park and then No 57 up to Kailua and back into Honolulu.

Because you'll need to change buses, ask for a transfer when you first board. Transfers have time limits and aren't meant to be used as stopovers, but you can usually grab a quick break at Ala Moana. Anytime you get off to explore along the route, you'll need to pay a new $1 fare when you reboard.

Car

Budget (☎ 537-3600), National (☎ 831-3800), Hertz (☎ 831-3500), Avis (☎ 834-5536) and Dollar (☎ 831-2330) all have desks at Honolulu International Airport and car lots on the airport grounds. Alamo (☎ 833-4585) has its operations about a mile outside the airport, on the corner of Nimitz Hwy and Ohohia St.

All things being equal, try to rent from a company with its lot inside the airport; not only is it more convenient to do so, but more importantly, on the way back, all the highway signs lead to the in-airport car returns.

The international car rental companies also have numerous branch locations in Waikiki, many in the lobbies of larger hotels. General rental information and toll-free numbers are in the Getting Around chapter in the front of this book.

Budget gives renters a coupon booklet that allows one free admission to a few of Oahu's tourist attractions; although the participants have been scaling back, those offering discounts still include the Polynesian Cultural Center and the Bishop Museum. The coupons aren't two-for-one deals (you don't have to buy a second admission to use the coupon), so for a single traveler it's all free.

Moped

State law requires mopeds to be ridden by one person only and prohibits their use on sidewalks and on freeways.

Blue Sky Rentals (☎ 947-0101), on the ground floor of Inn on the Park Hotel, 1920 Ala Moana Blvd, is a good Waikiki spot to rent a moped. The rates, which include tax, are $20 from 8 am to 6 pm, $25 for 24 hours and $105 for a week.

Mopeds can also be rented at similar rates from Diamond Head Mopeds (☎ 921-2899), at the corner of Lewers St and Kuhio Ave.

Taxi

Metered taxis charge a flag-down fee of $2 to start with, and then fares click up in 25¢ increments at a rate of $2 per mile. There's an extra charge of 35¢ for each suitcase or backpack.

Taxis are readily available at the airport and larger hotels but generally are otherwise hard to find. To phone for one, try Sida (☎ 836-0011), Charley's (☎ 955-2211), Americabs (☎ 591-8830) or City Taxi (☎ 524-2121). If you're at a phone booth but have no coins, you can reach City Taxi toll-free by dialing (☎ 800-359-2121).

Bicycle

There's a lot more traffic on Oahu than on the other islands, which makes cycling less appealing. The state's Department of Transportation publishes a *Bike Oahu* map with possible routes divided into those for novice cyclists, those for experienced cyclists and routes that are not bicycle-friendly. The map can usually be found at the HVCB visitor information center in Waikiki and at bike shops.

Planet Surf (☎ 924-9050), at 159 Kaiulani Ave in Waikiki and opposite Pupukea Beach Park in Waimea, rents bikes from $10 a day. Blue Sky Rentals (☎ 947-0101), 1920 Ala Moana Blvd in Waikiki, has mountain bikes, road bikes and hybrids for $15 from 8 am to 6 pm, $20 for a 24-hour period.

The Hawaii Bicycling League (☎ 735-5756), 3442 Waialae Ave, No 1, Honolulu, HI 96812, holds bike rides around Oahu nearly every Saturday and Sunday, ranging from 10-mile jaunts to 60-mile treks. The rides are free and open to the public.

Honolulu

In 1793, the English frigate *Butterworth* became the first foreign ship to sail into what is now called Honolulu Harbor. Its captain, William Brown, named the harbor Fair Haven. Ships that followed called it Brown's Harbor. But over time the name Honolulu, which means 'Sheltered Bay,' came to be used for both the harbor and the adjacent seaside district that the Hawaiians had called Kou.

As more and more foreign ships found their way to Honolulu, a harborside village of thatched houses sprouted up and the town became Hawaii's center of trade.

In 1809, Kamehameha I moved his royal court to Honolulu from nearby Waikiki. On what today is the southern end of Bethel St, Kamehameha set up residence to keep an eye on all the trade that moved in and out of the harbor. From there, Hawaiian sandalwood was shipped to Canton in exchange for weapons and luxury goods, which Kamehameha loaded into his harborside warehouses.

In the 1820s, whaling ships began pulling into Honolulu for supplies, liquor and women. At the same time, Christian missionaries began coming ashore to save souls. The Protestant mission and Episcopal and Catholic churches all established their Hawaiian headquarters in downtown Honolulu.

Both the whalers and the missionaries, a number of whom turned into businessmen, left their mark. Downtown Honolulu contains the offices of the 'Big Five' corporations that controlled most of Hawaii's commerce by the end of the 19th century. It's no coincidence that their lists of corporate board members – Alexander, Baldwin, Cooke and Dole – read like rosters from the first mission ships. The whalers left a different legacy. Hotel St, a line of bars and strip joints a few blocks from the harbor, is still the city's red-light district.

By the early years of the 20th century, Honolulu had expanded into a sprawling cosmopolitan city, but the downtown area remains the heart of the place. Today, Honolulu is the only major city in Hawaii. It has a population of nearly 400,000 and is the state's center of business, culture and politics. It's been the capital of Hawaii since 1845. Honolulu International Airport and

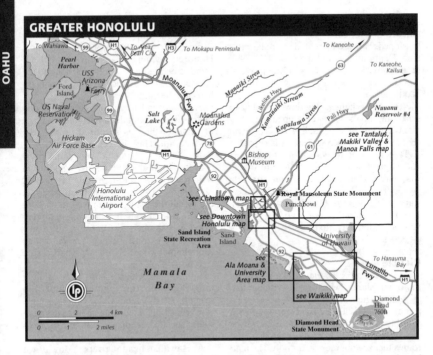

GREATER HONOLULU

Honolulu Harbor are Hawaii's two busiest ports.

Honolulu is home to many people from throughout the Pacific region, with immigrants from Japan, the Philippines and China, among other countries. It's a city of minorities, with no ethnic majority.

Honolulu's ethnic diversity can be seen on almost every corner – the sushi shop next door to the Vietnamese bakery, the Catholic church around the block from the Chinese Buddhist temple, and the rainbow of school children waiting for the bus.

The major federal, state and county offices and the state's highest concentration of historic buildings are found in downtown Honolulu.

DOWNTOWN HONOLULU

Downtown Honolulu is a hodgepodge of past and present, with both sleek highrises and stately Victorian-era buildings. A royal palace, a modern state capitol, a coral-block New England missionary church and a Spanish-style city hall all lie within sight of one another.

The downtown area is intriguing to explore. In addition to sightseeing, you can take in a Friday noon band concert on the palace lawn or browse through Hawaiiana books in the library's courtyard.

Information

The downtown branch of the Honolulu post office is on the Richards St side of the Old Federal Building. It's open from 8 am to 4:30 pm weekdays.

A number of airlines have ticket offices in the downtown Honolulu area. Within a two-minute walk of the intersection of Bishop and S Hotel Sts, you'll find United Airlines, Northwest Airlines, Delta Air Lines, Aloha Airlines and Hawaiian Airlines.

There's metered parking along Punchbowl St and on Halekauwila St opposite the federal building. There are also a limited number of metered spaces in the basement of the state office building on the corner of Beretania and Punchbowl Sts.

Walking Tour

Downtown Honolulu's most handsome buildings are all within walking distance. A good starting place for a self-guided walking tour is Iolani Palace, the area's most pivotal spot both historically and geographically. From there, you can walk out back to the state capitol and continue to S Beretania St to visit the war memorial, Washington Place and St Andrew's Cathedral, and then go down Richards St past No 1 Capitol District and the YWCA and Hawaiian Electric buildings. If you want to make the walk longer, head north on Merchant St to see the historic buildings that were erected to house Hawaii's largest corporations and the highrises that have sprung up around them. Otherwise, continue southeast along S King St where the old federal building, Aliiolani Hale, Kawaiahao Church and the Mission Houses Museum line one side of the street, the state library and city hall the other.

Iolani Palace

Iolani Palace is the only royal palace in the USA. It was the official residence of King Kalakaua and Queen Kapiolani from 1882 to 1891 and of Queen Liliuokalani, Kalakaua's sister and successor, for two years after that.

Following the overthrow of the Hawaiian kingdom in 1893, the palace became the capitol – first for the republic, then for the territory and later for the state of Hawaii.

It wasn't until 1969 that the current state capitol was built and the legislators moved out of their cramped quarters. The Senate had been meeting in the palace dining room and the House of Representatives in the throne room. By the time the legislators left, the palace was in shambles, the grand koa staircase termite-ridden and the Douglas fir floors pitted and gouged.

After extensive renovations topping $7 million, the palace was largely restored to its former glory and opened as a museum in 1978. These days, visitors must wear booties over their shoes to protect the highly polished wooden floors.

Iolani Palace was modern for its day. Every bedroom had its own full bath with hot and cold water running into copper-lined tubs, a flushing toilet and a bidet. According to the tour guides, electric lights replaced the palace gas lamps a full four years before the White House in Washington got electricity.

The throne room, decorated in red and gold, features the original thrones of the king and queen and a *kapu* (taboo) stick made of the long, spiral ivory tusk of a narwhal. In addition to celebrations full of pomp and pageantry, it was in the throne room that King Kalakaua danced his favorite Western dances – the polka, the waltz and the Virginia reel – into the wee hours of the morning.

Not all the events that took place there were joyous ones. Two years after she was dethroned, Queen Liliuokalani was brought back to the palace and tried for treason in the throne room. In a move calculated to humiliate the Hawaiian people, she spent nine months as a prisoner in Iolani Palace, her former home.

Guided tours of the palace leave every 15 minutes from 9 am to 2:15 pm Tuesday to

KIM GRANT

Iolani Palace

DOWNTOWN HONOLULU

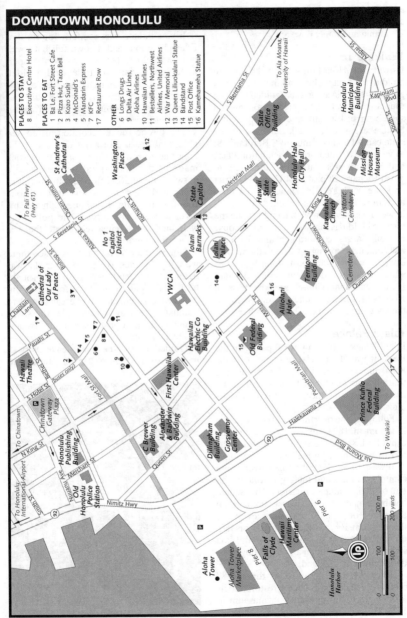

PLACES TO STAY
8 Executive Centre Hotel

PLACES TO EAT
1 Ba Le, Fort Street Cafe
2 Pizza Hut, Taco Bell
3 Kozo Sushi
4 McDonald's
5 Mandarin Express
7 KFC
17 Restaurant Row

OTHER
6 Longs Drugs
9 Delta Air Lines, Aloha Airlines
10 Hawaiian Airlines
11 Bestsellers, Northwest Airlines, United Airlines
12 War Memorial
13 Queen Liliuokalani Statue
14 Bandstand
15 Post Office
16 Kamehameha Statue

Saturday and cost $8 for adults, $3 for children ages five to 12. Children under five are not admitted. The admission price includes a 15-minute video on palace history that's shown in the barracks. The tours themselves last 45 minutes. Sometimes you can join up on the spot, but it's advisable to make advance reservations by phoning (☎ 522-0832). The palace is wheelchair accessible.

Palace Grounds The palace grounds have a lengthy history. Before Iolani Palace was built, there was a simpler house on these grounds that King Kamehameha III used when he moved the capital from Lahaina to Honolulu in 1845. Prior to that, it was the site of a *heiau* (temple).

The palace ticket window and a gift shop are in the former **barracks** of the Royal Household Guards, a building that looks oddly like the uppermost layer of a medieval fort that's been sliced off and plopped on the ground.

The **domed pavilion** on the grounds was originally built for the coronation of King Kalakaua in 1883 and is still used for the inauguration of governors and for concerts by the Royal Hawaiian Band.

The **grassy mound** surrounded by a wrought iron fence was the site of a royal tomb until 1865, when the remains of King Kamehameha II and Queen Kamamalu (who both died of measles in England in 1824) were moved to the Royal Mausoleum in Nuuanu.

The huge **banyan tree** between the palace and the state capitol is thought to have been planted by Queen Kapiolani.

Hawaii State Library

The central branch of the statewide library system lies near the corner of King and Punchbowl Sts. Located in a beautifully restored historic building, its collection of over half a million titles is the state's best and includes comprehensive Hawaii and Pacific sections.

It's open from 9 am to 5 pm on Monday, Friday and Saturday; 9 am to 8 pm on Tuesday and Thursday; and 10 am to 5 pm on Wednesday.

The **Hawaii State Archives** next door holds official government documents and an extensive photo collection. It's open to the public for research.

Queen Liliuokalani Statue

The statue of Hawaii's last queen stands between Iolani Palace and the capitol. It faces Washington Place, Liliuokalani's home and place of exile for more than 20 years. The bronze statue is holding the Hawaii constitution that Liliuokalani wrote in 1893, in fear of which US businessmen overthrew her; *Aloha Oe*, a popular hymn that she composed; and *Kumulipo*, the Hawaiian chant of creation.

State Capitol

Hawaii's state capitol is not your standard gold dome. Constructed in the late 1960s, it was a grandiose attempt at a 'theme' design.

Its two legislative chambers are cone-shaped to represent volcanoes; the rotunda is open-air to let gentle trade winds blow through; the supporting columns represent palm trees; and the whole structure is encircled by a large pool symbolizing the ocean surrounding Hawaii.

Unfortunately, the building not only symbolizes the elements but has been quite effective in drawing them in. The pool tends to collect brackish water; rain pouring into the rotunda has necessitated the sealing of skylights; and Tadashi Sato's 'Aquarius' floor mosaic, meant to show the changing colors and patterns of Hawaii's seas, got so weathered it had to be reconstructed.

After two decades of trying unsuccessfully to deal with all of the problems on a piecemeal basis, the state put the facility through a thorough renovation, completed in 1997. Visitors are free to walk through the rotunda, and from there peer through viewing windows into the two flanking legislative chambers.

In front of the capitol is a **statue of Father Damien**, the Belgian priest who volunteered to work among the lepers of Molokai and died of leprosy 16 years later, at age 49. The stylized sculpture was created by Venezuelan artist Marisol Escubar.

War Memorial

The war memorial is a sculptured eternal torch dedicated to soldiers who died in WWII. It sits between two underground garage entrances on S Beretania St, directly opposite the state capitol.

Washington Place

Washington Place, the governor's official residence, is a large colonial-style building with stately trees, built in 1846 by US sea captain John Dominis. The captain's son John married the Hawaiian princess who later became Queen Liliuokalani. After the queen was dethroned, she lived at Washington Place in exile until her death in 1917.

A plaque near the sidewalk on the left side of Washington Place is inscribed with the words to *Aloha Oe*.

The large tree in front of the house on the right side of the walkway is a *pili* nut tree, recognizable by the buttresslike roots that extend from the base of its trunk. (In Southeast Asia the nuts of these trees are used to produce oil.)

St Andrew's Cathedral

King Kamehameha IV, who was attracted by the royal trappings of the Church of England, decided to build his own cathedral in the capital. He and his consort, Queen Emma, founded the Anglican Church of Hawaii in 1858.

The cathedral's cornerstone was finally laid in 1867 by King Kamehameha V. Kamehameha IV had passed away four years earlier on St Andrew's Day – hence the church's name.

St Andrew's is on the corner of Alakea and S Beretania Sts. The building is of French Gothic architecture and was shipped in pieces from England. Its most striking feature is the impressive window of hand-blown stained glass that forms the western facade and reaches from the floor to the eaves. In the right section of the glass you can see the Reverend Thomas Staley, the first bishop sent to Hawaii by Queen Victoria, alongside King Kamehameha IV and Queen Emma.

No 1 Capitol District

The elegant five-story building on Richards St opposite the state capitol houses some of the offices of the state legislature.

This structure has something of the appearance of a Spanish mission, with courtyards and ceramic tile walls. Built in 1928, it served as the YMCA Armed Services building for more than five decades.

Fort Street Mall

Fort Street is a pedestrian shopping mall lined with benches and an ever-growing number of high-rise buildings. While the mall is not interesting in itself, if you're downtown it's a reasonable place to eat – not as good as Chinatown, but a few blocks closer. Hawaii Pacific University, a small but growing private institution, has much of its campus at the north end of the mall.

A block from the Fort Street Mall, on the corner of Bishop and S King Sts, is the new 30-story **First Hawaiian Center**, the headquarters of the First Hawaiian Bank. It has some modern sculpture on the lawn and a worthwhile gallery featuring contemporary Hawaiian art; the gallery is free and open during banking hours.

Cathedral of Our Lady of Peace

The center of the Roman Catholic church in Hawaii is the Cathedral of Our Lady of Peace, at the S Beretania St end of Fort St Mall. Constructed of coral blocks in 1843, it's older and more ornate than nearby St Andrew's Cathedral.

Father Damien, who later ministered to Molokai's leper colony, was ordained at the cathedral in 1864.

Aliiolani Hale

Aliiolani Hale ('House of Heavenly Kings') was the first major government building built by the Hawaiian monarchy. It has housed the Supreme Court since its construction in 1874 and was once also home to the legislature. The building has a distinctive clock tower and was originally designed by Australian architect Thomas Rowe to be a royal palace, although it never was used as such.

It was on the steps of Aliiolani Hale, in January 1893, that Sanford Dole proclaimed the establishment of a provisional government and the overthrow of the monarchy.

Kamehameha Statue

The statue of Kamehameha the Great stands in front of Aliiolani Hale, opposite Iolani Palace. It was cast by Thomas Gould in 1880. This one is actually a recast, as the first statue was lost at sea near the Falkland Islands. The original statue, recovered after this second version was dedicated, now stands in Kohala, the Big Island birthplace of Kamehameha.

On June 11, a state holiday honoring Kamehameha, the statue is ceremoniously draped with layer upon layer of 12-foot leis.

Honolulu Hale

City Hall, also known as Honolulu Hale, is largely of Spanish mission design with a tiled roof, decorative balconies, arches and pillars. Built in 1927, it bears the initials of CW Dickey, Honolulu's most famous architect of the day. The open-air courtyard in the center of the building is sometimes used for concerts and art exhibits.

Kawaiahao Church

Oahu's oldest church, on the corner of Punchbowl and S King Sts, was built on the site where the first missionaries constructed a grass thatch church shortly after their arrival in 1820. The original, impressive structure measured 54 by 22 feet and seated 300 people on *lauhala* mats, woven from hala leaves.

Still, thatch wasn't quite what the missionaries had in mind, so they designed a more typically New England-style Congregational church with simple Gothic influences.

Built between 1838 and 1842, the church is made of 14,000 coral slabs, many weighing more than 1000 pounds. Hawaiian divers chiseled the immense blocks of coral out of Honolulu's underwater reef.

The clock tower was donated by Kamehameha III and the clock, built in Boston and installed in 1850, still keeps accurate time. Inside the church is breezy and cool. The rear seats, marked by *kahili* (feather staffs) and velvet padding, were for royalty and are still reserved for the descendants of royalty today. The church is usually open to visitors from 8 am to 4 pm.

The **tomb of King Lunalilo**, the successor to Kamehameha V, is on the church grounds at the main entrance. Lunalilo ruled for only one year before his death in 1874 at the age of 39.

Around the back is a **cemetery** where many of the early missionaries are buried, including members of the Baldwin and Bingham families.

Mission Houses Museum

Three of the original buildings that once comprised the Sandwich Islands Mission headquarters still stand: the Frame House (built in 1821), the Chamberlain House (1831) and the Printing Office (1841).

They're open to the public as the Mission Houses Museum, 553 S King St. The houses are authentically furnished with handmade quilts on the beds, settees in the parlor and iron pots in the big stone fireplaces.

Coral blocks make up Kawaiahao Church.

The coral-block **Chamberlain House** was the early mission storeroom – a necessity, as Honolulu had few shops stocking supplies in those early days. Upstairs are hoop barrels, wooden crates packed with dishes, and a big office desk with pigeon-hole dividers and the quill pen that Levi Chamberlain used to work on accounts. Levi was the person appointed by the mission to buy, store and dole out supplies to the missionary families, which each had an allowance. His account books show that in the late 19th century, 25¢ would buy either 1 gallon of oil, one pen knife or two slates.

The first missionaries packed more than their bags when they left Boston – they actually brought a prefabricated wooden house around the Horn with them! Designed to withstand cold New England winter winds, the small windows instead block out Honolulu's cooling trade winds, keeping the two-story house hot and stuffy. The **Frame House**, as it's now called, is the oldest wooden structure in Hawaii.

The **Printing Office** housed the lead-type press that was used to print the Bible in the Hawaiian language.

The Mission Houses Museum (☎ 531-0481) is open from 9 am to 4 pm Tuesday to Saturday. Admission is $6 for adults and $2 for children (under age six free). While you can explore the visitor center and the Chamberlain House on your own, the Printing Office and the Frame House can only be seen with a guide. Guided tours, which last an hour, are usually given at 9:30 and 11 am and 1 and 2:30 pm, but the schedule can vary so it's best to call ahead.

Other Historic Buildings

The **Hawaiian Electric Company's** four-story administration building on the corner of Richards and S King Sts is of Spanish colonial design. It has an arched entranceway and ornate period lamps hanging from hand-painted ceilings. The entrance leads into the customer service department so you can easily walk in to take a look at the architectural details.

Diagonally opposite on Merchant St is the **Old Federal Building**, another interesting edifice with Spanish colonial features. Completed in 1922, it holds a post office and customs house.

Also noteworthy, the three-story **YWCA** at 1040 Richards St was built in 1927 by Julia Morgan, the renowned architect who designed William Randolph Hearst's San Simeon estate in California.

The **Old Honolulu Police Station** (1931) on the corner of Bethel and Merchant Sts has beautiful interior ceramic tile work in earthen tones on its counters and walls. It now is home to the state departments of Housing and Finance. Also worth a look is the old **Honolulu Publishing building** across the street.

The four-story **Alexander & Baldwin building** on the corner of Bishop and Queen Sts was built in 1929. The columns at the Bishop St entrance are carved with tropical fruit and the Chinese characters for prosperity and long life. Inside the portico are ceramic tile murals of Hawaiian fish. Samuel Alexander and Henry Baldwin, both sons of missionaries, vaulted to prominence in the sugar industry and created one of Hawaii's 'Big Five' controlling corporations. The other four corporations – Theo Davies, Castle & Cooke, Amfac and C Brewer – also built their headquarters within a few blocks of here.

The four-story, 70-year-old **Dillingham Building,** on the corner of Bishop and Queen Sts, is of Italian Renaissance-style architecture, with arches, marble walls, elaborate elevator doors and an arty brick floor. Seeing this ornate structure mirrored in the reflective glass of the 30-story Grosvenor Center next door provides a study in contrasts.

Hawaii Theatre

The neo-classical Hawaii Theatre, 1130 Bethel St, first opened in 1922 with silent films playing to the tune of a pipe organ. It ran continuous shows during World War II, but the development of mall cinemas in the 1970s was its undoing.

After closing in 1984, the theater's future looked dim, even though it was on the Register of Historic Buildings. Theater buffs came to the rescue, however, forming a non-profit group and purchasing the property from the Bishop Estate. They raised enough money to undertake a $10 million restoration.

The 1400-seat theater, which has a lovely interior with Shakespearean bas-reliefs and trompe l'oeil mosaics, has now reopened for dance, drama and music performances.

Honolulu Academy of Arts

The Honolulu Academy of Arts (☎ 532-8700), 900 S Beretania St, is an exceptional museum, with permanent Asian, European, American and Pacific art collections from ancient times to the present.

Just inside the door and to the right is a room with works by Matisse, Cézanne, Gauguin, van Gogh and Picasso. There is a welcoming place to sit in the middle of the room to take it all in.

This airy museum has numerous small galleries around six garden courtyards. The Spanish Court has a small fountain surrounded by Greek and Roman sculpture and Egyptian reliefs dating back to 2500 BC. There are sculptures and miniatures from India, jades and bronzes from ancient China, Madonna and Child oils from 14th-century Italy and high-quality changing exhibits.

The Hawaiian section is small but choice, with feather leis, tapa beaters, poi pounders and koa calabashes. The adjacent collection from Papua New Guinea, Micronesia and the South Pacific includes ancestor figures, war clubs and masks.

The museum is open from 10 am to 4:30 pm Tuesday to Saturday and 1 to 5 pm on Sunday. Admission is $5 for adults, $3 for senior citizens and students, free for children 12 and under. There's a gift shop, library and lunch cafe.

The museum is off the tourist track and seldom crowded. Bus No 2 from Waikiki stops out front; there's metered parking behind the museum.

Aloha Tower

Built in 1926, the 10-story Aloha Tower is a Honolulu landmark that for years was the city's tallest building. In the days when all tourists arrived by ship, this icon of pre-wartime Hawaii – with its clock tower inscribed with the word 'Aloha' – greeted every visitor. These days, visiting cruise ships still disembark at the terminal beneath the tower. Take a peek through the terminal windows to see colorful murals depicting Honolulu of bygone days.

The Aloha Tower is at Pier 9, off Ala Moana Blvd at the harbor end of Fort St. The tower's top-floor observation deck offers a sweeping 360° view of Honolulu's big commercial harbor and downtown area. An elevator zips visitors (free of charge) to the top from 9 am to sunset daily.

Beneath the tower is the Aloha Tower Marketplace, a shopping center with numerous kiosks, stores and eateries.

Hawaii Maritime Center

The Hawaii Maritime Center (☎ 536-6373) is at Honolulu Harbor's Pier 7 on the Diamond Head side of the Aloha Tower. The center has a maritime museum; the *Falls of Clyde*, said to be the world's last four-masted four-rigged ship; and the berth for the double-hulled sailing canoe *Hokulea*.

The 60-foot *Hokulea* was built to resemble the type of ship used by Polynesians in their migrations. It has made a number of voyages from Hawaii to the South Pacific, retracing the routes of the early Polynesian seafarers using age-old methods of navigation, most notably wave patterns and the position of the stars. When in port, the canoe is docked beside the museum.

Permanently on display is the 266-foot iron-hulled *Falls of Clyde*, built in Glasgow, Scotland, in 1878. In 1899, Matson Navigation bought the ship and added a deck house, and the *Falls* began carrying sugar and passengers between Hilo and San Francisco. It was later converted into an oil tanker and eventually stripped down to a barge.

After being abandoned in Ketchikan, Alaska, where it had been relegated to the function of a floating oil storage tank, the *Falls* was towed to Seattle. A group of Hawaiians raised funds to rescue the ship in 1963, just before it was scheduled to be sunk to create a breakwater off Vancouver. With the aid of the Bishop Museum, the *Falls* was eventually transported to Honolulu and restored. Visitors can stroll the deck and walk down into the cargo holds.

The main museum has an interesting mishmash of maritime displays and artifacts, including a good whaling-era section and model replicas of ships. There's a reproduction of a Matson liner stateroom and interesting old photos of Waikiki in the days when just the Royal Hawaiian and the Moana hotels shared the horizon with Diamond Head. Both hotels belonged to Matson, who had spearheaded tourism in Hawaii and ironically sold out to the Sheraton chain in 1959, just before the jet age and statehood launched sleepy tourism into a booming industry.

The museum is open from 8:30 am to 5 pm daily. Admission is $7.50 for adults, $4.50 for children ages six to 17, free under six.

To get there, take bus No 19 or 20 from Waikiki. By car, it's off Ala Moana Blvd, about a mile west of Ward Warehouse. There's free parking for museum visitors on Richards St, just east of the museum.

Sand Island

Sand Island is a 500-acre island on the western side of Honolulu Harbor. About a third of the island has been set aside as a state recreation area.

The park is heavily used by locals who camp, fish and picnic there on weekends, but it has little appeal to the casual visitor. (For information on obtaining a camping permit, see also Camping in the Accommodations section near the beginning of this chapter.)

Sand Island cannot be reached from the downtown area, but by an access road a few miles west, off the Nimitz Hwy. Sand Island Access Rd leads 2½ miles down to the park through an industrial area with a wastewater treatment plant, oil tanks, scrap metal yards and the like. The airport is directly across the lagoon and Sand Island is on the flight path.

The park has showers, rest rooms and a sandy beach, which, while cleaner than it's been in years past, is still far from pristine.

CHINATOWN

A walk through Chinatown is like a trip to Asia. Although it's predominantly Chinese, it has Vietnamese, Thai and Filipino influences as well.

Chinatown is busy and colorful. It has a market that could be right off a back street in Hong Kong; fire-breathing dragons curl their way up the red pillars outside the Bank of Hawaii; and good, cheap Asian restaurants abound. You can get tattooed, consult with an herbalist, munch on moon cakes or slurp a steaming bowl of Vietnamese soup. There are temples, shrines, noodle factories, antique shops and art galleries to explore.

Chinatown has seen some urban renewal, particularly on its downtown edge. The spiffed-up image includes a new 'entranceway' at the intersection of S Hotel and Bethel Sts, marked by a small park, two marble lions and a new high-rise complex. Yet despite creeping gentrification, Chinatown still has its seamy side. Just a block away on S Hotel St, you'll find darkened doorways advertising 'video peeps' for 25¢ and bawdy nightspots with names like Risqué Theatre and Paradise Lost.

Places to eat in Chinatown are listed near the end of the Honolulu section.

History

Chinese immigrants who had worked off their sugarcane plantation contracts began settling in Chinatown and opening up small businesses around 1860.

In December 1899, the bubonic plague broke out in the area. The 7000 Chinese, Hawaiians and Japanese who made the crowded neighborhood their home were cordoned off and forbidden to leave. As more plague cases arose, the Board of Health decided to conduct controlled burns of infected homes. On January 20, 1900, the fire brigade set fire to a building on the corner of Beretania St and Nuuanu Ave. The wind suddenly picked up and the fire spread out of control, racing toward the waterfront. To make matters worse, police guards stationed inside the plague area attempted to stop quarantined residents from fleeing.

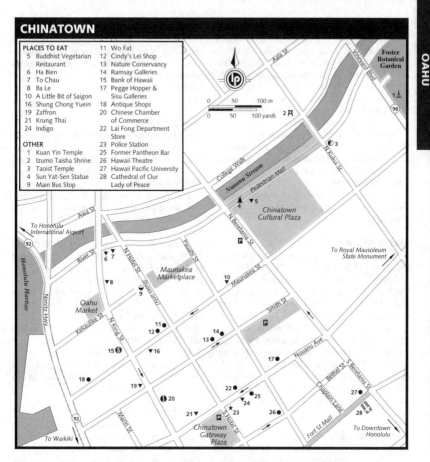

CHINATOWN

PLACES TO EAT		11	Wo Fat
5	Buddhist Vegetarian	12	Cindy's Lei Shop
	Restaurant	13	Nature Conservancy
6	Ha Bien	14	Ramsay Galleries
7	To Chau	15	Bank of Hawaii
8	Ba Le	17	Pegge Hopper &
10	A Little Bit of Saigon		Sisu Galleries
16	Shung Chong Yuein	18	Antique Shops
19	Zaffron	20	Chinese Chamber
21	Krung Thai		of Commerce
24	Indigo	22	Lai Fong Department
			Store
OTHER		23	Police Station
1	Kuan Yin Temple	25	Former Pantheon Bar
2	Izumo Taisha Shrine	26	Hawaii Theatre
3	Taoist Temple	27	Hawaii Pacific University
4	Sun Yat-Sen Statue	28	Cathedral of Our
9	Main Bus Stop		Lady of Peace

Nearly 40 acres of Chinatown burned to the ground on that fateful day.

Not everyone thought the fire was accidental. Just the year before, Chinese immigration into Hawaii had been halted by the US annexation of the islands, and Chinatown itself was prime real estate on the edge of the burgeoning downtown district.

Despite the adverse climate, the Chinese held their own and a new Chinatown arose from the ashes.

In the 1940s, thousands of US GIs walked the streets of Chinatown before being shipped off to Iwo Jima and Guadalcanal.

Many spent their last days of freedom in Chinatown's 'body houses,' pool halls and tattoo parlors.

Orientation & Information

Chinatown proper is immediately north of downtown Honolulu, roughly bounded by Honolulu Harbor, Bethel St, Vineyard Blvd and River St. To get there by car from Waikiki, take Ala Moana Blvd and turn at Bethel St or Smith St. Or take Beretania St and head down Nuuanu Ave or Maunakea St, toward the ocean. Hotel St is open to bus traffic only.

Chinatown is full of one-way streets, traffic is tight and it can be difficult to find a parking space. Your best bet for metered parking ($1 an hour, three-hour limit) is the lot off Smith St between Pauahi and N Beretania Sts. There are parking garages on N Beretania St just west of Maunakea St and at Chinatown Gateway Plaza on Nuuanu Ave that have similar rates.

Parking hassles can be avoided by taking the bus. From Waikiki, you can take bus No 2 to Hotel St and the center of Chinatown, or bus No 20 to River St on the western edge of Chinatown.

Note that Chinatown, particularly on its River St end, is not a place to be walking after dark.

Oahu Market

The heart of Chinatown is Oahu Market, the corner of Kekaulike and N King Sts.

Everything the Chinese cook needs is on display: pig heads, jasmine rice, ginger root, fresh octopus, quail eggs, slabs of tuna, long beans and salted jellyfish.

Oahu Market has been an institution since 1904. In 1984, the tenants organized and purchased the market themselves to save it from falling into the hands of developers. These days it gets a lot of competition from the bustling Maunakea Marketplace, which is newer, larger and has a hot-food section.

Maunakea St

On the corner of N Hotel and Maunakea Sts is **Wo Fat**, a former restaurant whose facade resembles a Chinese temple. Although its glory days have faded, it stands as one of Chinatown's oldest buildings, erected just after the fire of 1900.

If you're up for a snack, **Shung Chong Yuein**, 1027 Maunakea St, sells delicious moon cakes, almond cookies and other pastries at reasonable prices. This is the place to buy dried and sugared foods – everything from candied ginger and pineapple to candied squash and lotus root. The shop also offers boiled peanuts, which are quite good if you can resist comparing them to the roasted variety.

Across the street is **Cindy's Lei Shop**, a friendly place with leis made of *maile* (a native twining plant), lantern *ilima* (native ground cover) and Micronesian ginger, in addition to the more common orchids and plumeria. Prices won't break the bank, starting at just $3.50 for a lei of tuberose flowers.

Nuuanu Ave

The **Chinatown Police Station**, on the corner of S Hotel St and Nuuanu Ave in the Perry Block Building (circa 1888), has enough 1920s atmosphere to resemble a set from *The Untouchables*.

Just down the street is the **Pantheon Bar**, now abandoned but still noteworthy as the oldest watering hole in Honolulu and a favorite of sailors in days past.

Across the street, **Lai Fong Department Store** sells antiques, knickknacks and old postcards of Hawaii dating back to the first half of the 20th century. Even walking into the store itself is a bit like stepping back into the 1940s. Lai Fong's, which has been in the same family for 70 years, also sells Chinese silks and brocades by the yard and makes silk dresses to order.

Incidentally, the **granite-block sidewalks** along Nuuanu Ave were made from the discarded ballast of ships that brought tea from China in the 19th century.

Antiques & Arts

Chinatown has a number of antique shops and art galleries. **Pegge Hopper**, whose prints of voluptuous Hawaiian women adorn many a wall in the islands, has her gallery at 1164 Nuuanu Ave. Next door at 1160 Nuuanu Ave is **Sisu Gallery**, which features changing exhibits of avant-garde photo art, glass work and metal sculptures. Also notable is **Ramsay Galleries**, 1128 Smith St, featuring finely detailed pen-and-ink drawings by the artist Ramsay and changing collections of high-quality works by other local artists.

A good place to browse for antiques is at **Aloha Antiques** and the adjacent **Mahalo Antique Mall**, at 926 and 930 Maunakea St. At this site, about 20 vendors have set out their eclectic collections, which include everything from jewelry and Art Deco items to Asian statues and ceramics.

Chinatown Cultural Plaza

This plaza covers the better part of a block along N Beretania St from Maunakea St to River St.

The modern complex doesn't have the character of Chinatown's older shops, but inside it's still quintessential Chinatown, with tailors, acupuncturists and calligraphers alongside travel agents, restaurants and a Chinese newspaper. There's also a small produce and meat market and a post office.

At a small courtyard statue of the goddess Kuan Yin, elderly Chinese people light incense and leave mangoes.

River St Pedestrian Mall

The River St pedestrian mall has covered tables beside Nuuanu Stream, where old men play mahjongg and checkers. A statue of Chinese revolutionary leader Sun Yat-sen stands watch at the end of the pedestrian mall near N Beretania St.

There are eat-in and takeout restaurants all along the mall, including a couple of Chinese options and the peculiarly named Kent's Drive In, a hole-in-the-wall eatery serving plate lunches on the *pedestrian* walkway!

Taoist Temple

Organized in 1889, the Lum Sai Ho Tong Society was one of more than 100 societies started by Chinese immigrants in Hawaii to help preserve their cultural identity. This one was for the Lum clan, who hail from west of the Yellow River. At one time the society had more than 4000 members, and even now there are nearly a thousand Lums in the Honolulu phone book.

The society's Taoist temple on the corner of River and Kukui Sts honors the goddess Tin Hau, a Lum child who rescued her father from drowning and was later deified. Many Chinese claim to see her apparition when they travel by boat. The elaborate altar inside the temple is open for viewing when the street-level door is unlocked, which is typically from 8:30 am to 2 pm daily.

Izumo Taisha Shrine

The Izumo Taisha Shrine, across the river on Kukui St, is a small wooden Shinto shrine built by Japanese immigrants in 1923. During WWII, the property was confiscated by the city of Honolulu and wasn't returned to its congregation until 1962.

Incidentally, the 100-pound sacks of rice that sit near the altar symbolize good health, while the ringing of the bell placed at the shrine entrance is considered to be an act of purification for those who come to pray.

Foster Botanical Garden

The Foster Botanical Garden covers 12½ acres at the northern end of Chinatown. The entrance is on Vineyard Blvd, opposite the end of River St. The garden took root in 1850 when German botanist William Hillebrand purchased 5 acres of land from Queen Kalama and planted the trees that now tower in the center of the property.

Captain Thomas Foster bought the property in 1867 and continued planting the grounds. In the 1930s, the tropical garden was bequeathed to the city of Honolulu and is now a city park.

The garden is arranged in groupings, including sections of palms, orchids, plumerias and poisonous plants.

If you've ever wondered how nutmeg, allspice or cinnamon grow, stroll through the Economic Garden. In this section there's also a black pepper vine that climbs 40 feet up a gold tree, a vanilla vine and other herbs and spices.

The herb garden was the site of the first Japanese language school in Oahu. Many Japanese immigrants sent their children here to learn to read Japanese, hoping to maintain their cultural identity and the option of someday returning to Japan. During the bombing of Pearl Harbor, a stray artillery shell exploded into a room full of students. A memorial marks the site.

At the other end of the park the wild orchid garden can be a good place for close-up photography. Unfortunately, this side of the garden is skirted by the H-1 Fwy, which detracts from what otherwise would be a peaceful stroll.

Foster Garden holds many extraordinary plants. For instance, the garden's own East African *Gigasiphon macrosiphon*, a tree with white flowers that open in the evening, is thought to be extinct in the wild. The tree is so rare that it doesn't have a common name.

The native Hawaiian *loulu* palm, taken long ago from Oahu's upper Nuuanu Valley, may also be extinct in the wild. The garden's chicle tree, New Zealand kauri tree and Egyptian doum palm are all reputed to be the largest of their kind in the USA. Oddities include the cannonball tree, the sausage tree and the double coconut palm that's capable of producing a 50-pound nut.

Foster Garden is open from 9 am to 4 pm daily. Admission costs $5 for those ages 13 and over, $1 for children. Trees are labeled, and a free corresponding self-guided tour booklet is available at the entrance.

The Friends of Foster Garden provides volunteer guides who conduct hour-long walking tours at 1 pm Monday to Friday. Call ☎ 522-7066 for reservations.

Herbs & Noodles

Chinatown herbalists are both physicians and pharmacists, with walls full of small wooden drawers each filled with a different herb. They'll size you up, feel your pulse and listen to you describe your ailments before deciding which drawers to open, mixing herbs and flowers and wrapping them for you to take home and boil up together. The object is to balance yin and yang forces. You can find herbalists at the Chinatown Cultural Plaza and along N King and Maunakea Sts.

There are also half a dozen noodle factories in Chinatown. If you look inside, you'll see clouds of white flour hanging in the air and thin sheets of dough running around rollers and coming out as noodles. One easy-to-find shop, Yat Tung Chow Noodle Factory, next to Ba Le at 150 N King St, makes nine sizes of noodles, from skinny golden thread to fat udon.

❀❀❀❀❀❀❀❀❀❀❀❀❀❀

Kuan Yin Temple

The Kuan Yin Temple, on Vineyard Blvd near the entrance of Foster Garden, is a bright red Buddhist temple with a green ceramic-tile roof. The ornate interior is richly carved and filled with the sweet pervasive smell of burning incense.

The temple is dedicated to Kuan Yin Bodhisattva, goddess of mercy, whose statue is the largest in the prayer hall. Devotees burn paper 'money' for prosperity and good luck. Offerings of fresh flowers, oranges and other items are placed at the altar. The large citrus fruit that is stacked pyramid-style is the pomelo, considered a symbol of fertility because of its many seeds.

Hawaii's multiethnic Buddhist community worships at the temple, and respectful visitors are welcome.

Organized Tours

Two organizations offer Chinatown walking tours. Keep in mind, however, that Chinatown is a fun place to poke around on your own, and it can feel a bit touristy being led around in a group. Still, the guides provide a commentary with historical insights and often take you to a few places you're unlikely to walk into otherwise.

The Hawaii Heritage Center (☎ 521-2749) offers walking tours of Chinatown from 9:30 to 11:30 am on Friday for $5. Reservations are not taken; meet in front of Ramsay Galleries at 1128 Smith St.

The Chinese Chamber of Commerce (☎ 533-3181) leads walking tours of Chinatown from 9:30 am to noon on Tuesday for $5. Meet at the chamber office at 42 N King St.

ALA MOANA & UNIVERSITY AREA

Ala Moana means 'Path to the Sea.' Ala Moana Blvd (Hwy 92) connects the Nimitz Hwy and the airport with downtown Honolulu and Waikiki. Ala Moana is also the name of a land area just west of Waikiki, which includes Honolulu's largest beach.

Ala Moana Center Ala Moana Center is Hawaii's biggest shopping center, with some 200 shops. Whenever outer islanders fly to

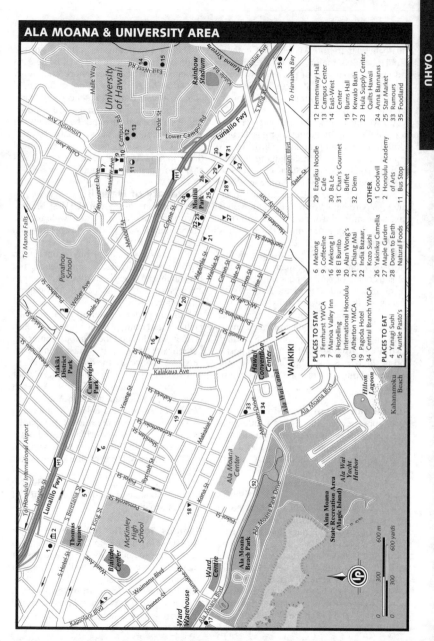

ALA MOANA & UNIVERSITY AREA

PLACES TO STAY
3   Fernhurst YWCA
7   Manoa Valley Inn
8   Hostelling
     International Honolulu
10 Atherton YMCA
19 Pagoda Hotel
34 Central Branch YMCA

PLACES TO EAT
4   Yanagi Sushi
5   Auntie Pasto's

6   Mekong
9   Coffeeline
16 Mekong II
18 El Burrito
20 Alan Wong's
21 Chiang Mai
22 India Bazaar,
     Kozo Sushi
26 Yakiniku Camellia
27 Maple Garden
28 Down to Earth
     Natural Foods

29 Ezogiku Noodle
     Cafe
30 Ba Le
31 Chan's Gourmet
     Buffet
32 Diem

OTHER
1   Goodwill
2   Honolulu Academy
     of Arts
11 Bus Stop

12 Hemenway Hall
13 Campus Center
14 East-West
     Center
15 Burns Hall
17 Kewalo Basin
23 Hula Supply Center,
     Quilts Hawaii
24 Anna Bannanas
25 Star Market
33 Rumours
35 Foodland

Honolulu to shop, they go to Ala Moana. Tourists wanting to spend the day at a mall usually head there too. Ala Moana Center is also Honolulu's major bus transfer point, and tens of thousands of passengers transit through daily, so even if you weren't planning to go to the shopping center you're likely to end up there!

Ala Moana has a Sears, Liberty House, Neiman Marcus, JCPenney, Longs Drugs, Foodland supermarket and Shirokiya, a department store with a Japanese food market. You'll also find local color at the Crack Seed Center, where you can scoop from jars full of pickled mangoes, rock candy, salty red ginger, cuttlefish and banzai mix. (For more information about crack seed, see the Food section of the Facts for the Visitor chapter).

There's a shop selling Molokai kites, another selling old Hawaiian stamps and coins, a couple of banks and airline offices, a travel agency and a good food court with dozens of ethnic fast-food stalls.

On the inland side of the center, near Sears, is a post office open from 8:30 am to 5 pm on weekdays, to 4:15 pm on Saturday. Also at the ground level, but at the opposite end of the row, is a satellite city hall where you can get bus schedules and county camping permits.

Ala Moana Beach Ala Moana Beach Park, opposite the Ala Moana Center, is a fine city park with much less hustle and bustle than Waikiki. The park is fronted by a broad golden-sand beach, nearly a mile long, that's buffered from the traffic noise of Ala Moana Blvd by a grassy lawn with shade trees.

This is where Honolulu residents go to jog after work, play volleyball and enjoy weekend picnics. The park has full beach facilities, several softball fields and tennis courts and free parking. It's a very popular park yet big enough to feel uncrowded.

Ala Moana is generally a safe place to swim and is a good spot for distance swimmers. However, the deep channel that runs the length of the beach can be a hazard at low tide to poor swimmers who don't realize

it's there. A former boat channel, it drops off suddenly to overhead depths.

The 43-acre peninsula jutting from the Diamond Head side of the park is the **Aina Moana Recreation Area**, more commonly known as Magic Island. During the school year, you can find high school outrigger teams practicing here in late afternoon. There's a nice walk around the perimeter of Magic Island and sunsets can be picturesque, with sailboats pulling in and out of the adjoining Ala Wai Yacht Harbor. This is also a hot summer surf spot.

University of Hawaii

The University of Hawaii (UH) at Manoa, the central campus of the statewide university system, is east of downtown Honolulu and 2 miles north of Waikiki.

The university has strong programs in astronomy, geophysics, marine sciences and Hawaiian and Pacific studies. The campus attracts students from islands throughout the Pacific.

Manoa Garden restaurant in Hemenway Hall is a gathering place for many students. Hemenway Hall and the Campus Center are behind Sinclair Library, which fronts University Ave opposite the bus stop.

Two outside walls of the Campus Center have grand Hawaiiana murals, with scenes based on photos from a classic August 1981 *National Geographic* article on Molokai.

Ka Leo O Hawaii, the student newspaper, lists lectures, music performances and other campus happenings. It can be picked up free at the university libraries and other places around campus.

To get to the campus by bus, take Bus No 4 from Waikiki. Bus No 6 runs between UH and Ala Moana.

Campus Tours The Information Center (☎ 956-7235) in the university's Campus Center can provide campus maps and answer questions. Free one-hour walking tours of the campus, emphasizing the school's history and architecture, leave from the Campus Center at 2 pm on Monday, Wednesday and Friday; to join one, simply arrive 10 minutes before the tour begins.

East-West Center At the east side of the UH campus is the East-West Center (☎ 944-7111), 1777 East-West Rd, a federally funded educational institution established in 1960 by the US Congress. The center's stated goal is the promotion of mutual understanding among the people of Asia, the Pacific and the USA. Some 2000 researchers and graduate students work and study at the center, examining development policy, the environment and other Pacific issues.

Changing exhibitions on Asian art and culture are displayed in **Burns Hall**, on the corner of Dole St and East-West Rd. It's open from 8 am to 5 pm weekdays; admission is free. The center occasionally has other multicultural programs open to the public, such as music concerts or scholastic seminars. For current happenings call the center.

ELSEWHERE IN HONOLULU
Upper Manoa Valley

The Upper Manoa Valley, inland from the university, ends at forest reserve land in the hills above Honolulu. The road into the valley runs through a well-to-do residential neighborhood before reaching the trailhead to Manoa Falls and the Lyon Arboretum.

The **Manoa Falls Trail** is a beautiful hike, especially for one so close to the city. The trail runs for three-quarters of a mile above a rocky streambed before ending at the falls. It takes about 30 minutes one way.

Surrounded by lush damp vegetation and moss-covered stones and tree trunks, you get the feeling you're walking through a thick rain forest a long way from anywhere. The only sounds come from chirping birds and the rushing stream and waterfall. All sorts of trees line the path, including tall *Eucalyptus robusta*, with their soft, spongy, reddish bark; flowering orange African tulip trees; and other lofty varieties that creak like wooden doors in old houses. Many of them were planted by the Lyon Arboretum, which at one time held a lease on the property.

Wild purple orchids and red ginger grow up near the falls, adding to the tranquility found there. The falls are steep and drop about 100 feet vertically into a small shallow pool. The pool is not deep enough for swimming, and occasional falling rocks make it inadvisable anyway.

The trail is usually a bit muddy but not too bad if it hasn't been raining lately. Be careful not to catch your foot in exposed tree roots – they're potential ankle breakers, particularly if you're moving with any speed. The packed clay can be slippery in some steep places, so take your time and enjoy the walk.

About 75 feet before Manoa Falls, an inconspicuous trail starts to the left of the chain-link fence. Well worth a little 15-minute side trip, the **Aihualama Trail** offers a broad view of the Manoa Valley, just a short way up the path.

Attending University

You can get information on undergraduate studies at the University of Hawaii from the Admissions and Records Office (☎ 956-8975), 2600 Campus Rd, Room 001, Honolulu, HI 96822, and on graduate studies from the Graduate Division (☎ 956-8544), Spalding Hall, 2540 Maile Way, Room 354, Honolulu, HI 96822.

The summer session consists primarily of two six-week terms. Tuition is $392 per credit for nonresidents and $122 per credit for residents. For the summer catalog, contact the Summer Session (☎ 956-7221), 2500 Dole St, Krauss Building, Room 1001, Honolulu, HI 96822.

There are also shorter, noncredit recreation and craft classes organized through Campus Leisure Programs (☎ 956-6468) that are open to the general public. Most classes, such as beginning hula, lei-making, slack-key guitar and ceramics, meet once or twice a week and cost around $50 for a monthlong session. More useful to short-term visitors are the outdoor programs, such as hiking outings that cost $10 and sailing classes for around $100.

After about five minutes of walking, you'll enter a bamboo forest with some massive old banyan trees. When the wind blows, the forest releases eerie crackling sounds. It's an engaging forest – enchanted or spooky, depending on your mood.

You can return to the Manoa Falls Trail or go on another mile to Pauoa Flats where the trail connects with the Puu Ohia Trail in the Tantalus area.

Lyon Arboretum The Lyon Arboretum, 3860 Manoa Rd, is a great place to go after hiking to Manoa Falls if you want to identify trees and plants you've seen along that trail.

Dr Harold Lyon, after whom the arboretum is named, is credited with introducing 10,000 exotic trees and plants to Hawaii. Approximately half of these are represented in this 193-acre arboretum, which is under the auspices of the University of Hawaii.

This is not a landscaped tropical flower garden, but a mature and largely wooded arboretum, where related species are clustered in a semi-natural state.

The Hawaiian ethnobotanical garden contains mountain apple, breadfruit and taro, as well as *ko*, the sugarcane brought by early Polynesian settlers; *kukui* (candlenut tree), which produced lantern oil; and *ti*, used medicinally since ancient times and for moonshine after Westerners arrived.

The arboretum also has herbs, spices and cashew, cacao, papaya, betel nut, macadamia nut, jackfruit and calabash trees, as well as greenhouses and classrooms.

A good choice among the arboretum's many short trails is the 20-minute walk up to **Inspiration Point**, which offers a view of the hills that enclose the valley. En route you'll encounter wonderful scents, inviting stone benches and lots of birdsong. The path loops through ferns, bromeliads and magnolias and passes by tall trees, including a bo tree, a descendant of the tree under which Gautama Buddha sat when he received enlightenment.

The arboretum is open from 9 am to 3 pm Monday to Saturday. A $1 donation is appreciated. Free guided tours (call ☎ 988-0464 for reservations) are given at 1 pm on the first Friday and third Wednesday of each month and at 10 am on the third Saturday of the month.

The reception center has a book and gift shop as well as helpful staff members who can give you a map of the garden and information on the arboretum's organized hikes, workshops and children's programs.

Getting There & Away From Ala Moana Center, take the No 5 Manoa Valley bus to the end of the line at the junction of Manoa Rd and Kumuone St. From there, it's a 10-minute walk to the road's end, where the Manoa Falls Trail begins. Lyon Arboretum is at the end of the short drive off to the left just before the trailhead.

To get there by car, simply drive to the end of Manoa Rd. There's room to park at the trailhead, but it's not a very secure place so don't leave anything valuable in the car. Lyon Arboretum has a parking area adjacent to its gardens that's reserved for arboretum visitors only.

Tantalus & Makiki Valley

Just 2 miles from downtown Honolulu, a narrow switchback road cuts its way up the lush green forest reserve land of Tantalus and the Makiki Valley. The road climbs up almost to the top of 2013-foot Mt Tantalus, with swank mountainside homes tucked in along the way.

Although the road is one continuous loop, the western side is called Tantalus Drive and the eastern side is Round Top Drive. The 8½-mile circuit is Honolulu's finest scenic drive, offering splendid views of the city below.

The route is winding, narrow and steep, but it's a good paved road. Among the profusion of dense tropical growth, bamboo, ginger, elephant-ear taro and fragrant eucalyptus trees are easily identified. Vines climb to the top of telephone poles and twist their way across the wires.

A network of hiking trails runs between Tantalus Drive and Round Top Drive and throughout the forest reserve, with numerous trailheads off both roads. The trails are seldom crowded, which seems amazing considering how accessible they are. Perhaps

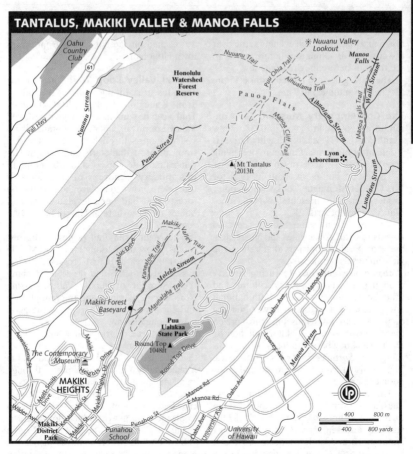

TANTALUS, MAKIKI VALLEY & MANOA FALLS

because the drive itself is so nice, the only walking most people do is between their car and the scenic lookouts.

The Makiki Heights area below the forest reserve is one of the most exclusive residential areas in Honolulu and the site of a museum of contemporary art (see below). There's bus service as far as Makiki Heights, but none around the Tantalus-Round Top loop drive.

Puu Ualakaa State Park From Puu Ualakaa State Park you can see an incredible panorama of all Honolulu. The park

entrance is 2½ miles up Round Top Drive from Makiki St. It's half a mile in to the lookout; bear to the left when the road forks.

The sweeping view from the lookout extends from Kahala and Diamond Head on the far left, across Waikiki and downtown Honolulu, to the Waianae Range on the far right. To the southeast is the University of Hawaii at Manoa, easily recognized by its sports stadium; to the southwest you can see clearly into the green mound of Punchbowl Crater; the airport is visible on the edge of the coast and Pearl Harbor beyond that.

Although the best time to be here is during the day if you're taking photos, this is also a fine place to watch evening settle over the city. Arrive 30 minutes before sunset to see the hills before they're in shadow.

The park gates are locked from 6:45 pm (7:45 pm in summer) to 7 am.

The Contemporary Museum The Contemporary Museum (☎ 526-0232, www.tcmhi.org), 2411 Makiki Heights Drive, is a delightful modern art museum occupying an estate with 3½ acres of wooded gardens.

The estate house was built in 1925 for Mrs Charles Montague Cooke, whose other former home is the present site of the Honolulu Academy of Arts.

You enter the museum through a covered courtyard with bronze gates and an arrangement of parabolic mirrors that reflect the view hundreds of times over.

Inside are galleries featuring quality changing exhibits of paintings, sculpture and other contemporary work by both national and international artists. A newer building on the lawn holds the museum's most prized piece, a vivid environmental installation by David Hockney based on his sets for *L'Enfant et les Sortilèges*, Ravel's 1925 opera. There's also a cafe serving lunch and afternoon desserts.

The museum is open from 10 am to 4 pm Tuesday to Saturday and from noon to 4 pm on Sunday. Admission is $5 for adults, $3 for students and senior citizens, and free for children 12 and under. Docent-led tours, conducted at 1:30 pm, are included in the price of admission.

Rolling Sweet Potatoes

In olden times, the slopes of Puu Ualakaa ('Rolling Sweet Potato Hill') were planted with sweet potatoes, which were said to have been dug up and then rolled down the hill for easy gathering at harvest time. The hill's other name, Round Top, dates to more recent times.

The museum, near the intersection of Mott-Smith and Makiki Heights Drives, can be reached on the No 15 bus from downtown Honolulu.

Makiki Valley Loop Trail Three of the Tantalus area hiking trails – Maunalaha Trail, Kanealole Trail and Makiki Valley Trail – can be combined to make the Makiki Valley Loop Trail, a popular 2½-mile hike.

The loop is through a lush and varied tropical forest that starts and ends in Hawaii's first state nursery and arboretum. In this nursery, hundreds of thousands of trees were grown to replace the sandalwood forests that had been leveled in Makiki Valley and elsewhere in Hawaii in the 19th century.

The **Maunalaha Trail** begins at the rest rooms below the parking lot of the Makiki Forest base yard. It first crosses a bridge, passes taro patches and proceeds to climb the east ridge of Makiki Valley, passing Norfolk pine, bamboo and fragrant allspice and eucalyptus trees. There are some good views along the way.

After three-quarters of a mile, you'll come to a four-way junction, where you'll take the left fork and continue on to the **Makiki Valley Trail**. The trail passes through small gulches and across gentle streams with patches of ginger. Near the Moleka Stream crossing are mountain apple trees (related to allspice and guava), which flower in the spring and fruit in the summer. Edible yellow and strawberry guavas also grow along the trail. There are some fine views of the city below.

The **Kanealole Trail** begins as you cross Kanealole Stream and then follows the stream back to the base yard, three-quarters of a mile away. The trail leads down through a field of Job's tears; the beadlike bracts of the female flowers of this tall grass are often picked to be strung in leis. Halfway down, a grove full of introduced mahogany grows. Because Kanealole Trail tends to be muddy, be sure to wear shoes with good traction and pick up a walking stick.

To get to the Makiki Forest base yard, turn left off Makiki St and go half a mile up

Makiki Heights Drive. Where the road makes a sharp bend, proceed straight ahead through a green gate into the Makiki Forest Recreation Area and continue until you reach the base yard. There's a parking lot on the right just before the office.

You can also take the No 15 bus, which runs between downtown and Pacific Heights. Get off near the intersection of Mott-Smith Drive and Makiki Heights Drive and walk down Makiki Heights Drive to the base yard. It's a mile-long walk between the bus stop and the trailhead.

An alternative is to hike just the Makiki Valley Trail, which you can reach by following Tantalus Drive 2 miles past its intersection with Makiki Heights Drive. As you come around a sharp curve, look for the wooden post marking the trailhead on the right. You can take this route in as far as you want and backtrack out or link up with other trails along the way.

Puu Ohia Trail The Puu Ohia Trail, in conjunction with the Pauoa Flats Trail, leads up to a lookout with a view of Nuuanu reservoir and valley. It's nearly 2 miles one way and makes a hardy hike.

The trailhead is at the very top of Tantalus Drive, 3.6 miles up on the left from its intersection with Makiki Heights Drive. There's a large turnoff opposite the trailhead where you can park.

The Puu Ohia Trail starts up reinforced log steps and leads past ginger, bamboo groves and lots of eucalyptus, a fast-growing tree that was planted to protect the watershed. About half a mile up, the trail reaches the top of 2013-foot Mt Tantalus (Puu Ohia).

From Mt Tantalus, the trail leads into a service road. Continue on the road to its end, where there's a Hawaiian Telephone building. The trail picks up again behind the left side of the building.

Continue down the trail until it leads into the **Manoa Cliff Trail**, which you'll go left on for a short distance until you come to another intersection, where you'll turn right onto the **Pauoa Flats Trail**. The trail leads down into Pauoa Flats and onward to the

lookout. The flats area can be muddy; be careful not to trip on exposed tree roots.

You'll pass two trailheads before reaching the lookout. The first is **Nuuanu Trail**, on the left, which runs three-quarters of a mile along the western side of Upper Pauoa Valley and offers broad views of Honolulu and the Waianae Mountains.

The second is **Aihualama Trail**, a bit farther along on the right, which takes you 1¼ miles to Manoa Falls through bamboo groves and huge old banyan trees. If you were to follow this route, you could then hike down the Manoa Falls Trail, a distance of about a mile, to the end of Manoa Rd and from there catch a bus back to town (see the Upper Manoa Valley section).

Punchbowl

Punchbowl (see the Greater Honolulu map) is the bowl-shaped remains of a long-extinct volcanic crater. At an elevation of 500 feet, it sits a mile above the downtown district and offers a fine view of the city out to Diamond Head and the Pacific beyond.

The early Hawaiians called the crater Puowaina, the 'hill of human sacrifices.' It's believed there was a heiau at the crater and that the bodies of slain kapu breakers were brought to Punchbowl to be cremated upon the heiau altar.

Today, it is the site of the 115-acre National Memorial Cemetery of the Pacific. The remains of Hawaiians sacrificed to appease the gods now share the crater floor with the bodies of more than 25,000 soldiers, more than half of whom were killed in the Pacific during WWII.

The remains of Ernie Pyle, the distinguished war correspondent who covered both world wars and was hit by machine gun fire on Ie Shima during the final days of WWII, lies in section D, grave 109. Five stones to the left, at grave D-1, is the stone for astronaut Ellison Onizuka, the Big Island native who perished in the 1986 *Challenger* disaster. Their resting places are marked with the same style of flat granite stone that marks each of the cemetery's graves.

A huge memorial at the head of the cemetery has eight marble courts representing different Pacific regions and is inscribed with the names of the 26,289 Americans missing in action from WWII and the Korean War. Two additional half courts have the names of 2489 soldiers missing from the Vietnam War.

For the best view of the city, walk to the lookout 10 minutes south of the memorial.

The cemetery is open 8 am to 5:30 pm in winter and to 6:30 pm from March through September.

The entrance into Punchbowl is off Puowaina Drive. There's a marked exit as you start up the Pali Hwy from H-1; watch closely, as it comes up quickly! From there, drive slowly and follow the signs as you wind through a series of narrow streets on the short way up to the cemetery.

By bus, take a No 2 from Waikiki to downtown Honolulu and get off at Beretania and Alapai Sts, where you transfer to a No 15 bus. Ask the driver where to get off. It's about a 15-minute walk to Punchbowl from the bus stop.

Royal Mausoleum State Monument

The Royal Mausoleum (see the Greater Honolulu map) contains the remains of kings Kamehameha II, III, IV and V as well as King David Kalakaua and Queen Liliuokalani, the last reigning monarchs.

Not here are the remains of Kamehameha I, the last king to be buried in secret in accordance with Hawaii's old religion.

The original mausoleum building, which is usually locked, is now a chapel; the caskets are in nearby crypts. Other gravestones honor Kamehameha I's British confidante John Young and American Charles Reed Bishop, husband of Princess Bernice Pauahi Bishop.

The royal mausoleum, at 2261 Nuuanu Ave (just before the avenue meets the Pali Hwy), is open 8 am to 4:30 pm Monday to Friday.

The **Hsu Yin Temple**, just across Nuuanu Ave from the mausoleum on Kawananakoa Place, is a Buddhist temple that's worth a quick look if you're visiting the mausoleum. At the altar are the standard offerings of oranges and burning incense, while prints on the walls depict the Buddha's life story.

Bishop Museum

The Bishop Museum (☎ 847-3511, www.bishop.hawaii.org), 1525 Bernice St, is considered by many to be the best Polynesian anthropological museum in the world.

One side of the main gallery, the Hawaiian Hall, has three floors covering the cultural history of Hawaii. The 1st floor, dedicated largely to pre-Western-contact Hawaii, has a full-size pili-grass thatched house and numerous other displays from carved temple images to calabashes and weapons.

One of the museum's most impressive holdings is a feather cloak that was worn by Kamehameha I. It was created entirely of the yellow feathers of the now-extinct *mamo*, a predominantly black bird with a yellow upper tail. Around 80,000 birds were caught, plucked and released to create this cloak. You can see a taxidermic mamo at the left of the nearby Queen Liliuokalani exhibit; it gives a sense of just how few feathers each of these birds had to sacrifice.

The 2nd floor is dedicated to the varied influences of 19th-century Hawaii. Here you'll find traditional tapa cloth robes, as well as missionary-inspired quilt work and barter items that Yankee traders brought to the islands; there's also a small whaling exhibit. The top floor has displays on the various ethnic groups that comprise present-day Hawaii. Like Hawaii itself, it has a bit of everything, including samurai armor, Portuguese festival costumes, Taoist fortune-telling sticks and a Hawaiian ukulele made of two coconut shell halves.

The Polynesian Hall contains masks from Melanesia, stick charts from Micronesia and weapons and musical instruments from across Polynesia.

The Kahili Room, a small gallery on the 1st floor of the main hall, is dedicated to Hawaiian royalty. It houses the horse carriage used by Queen Liliuokalani and a display of *kahili*, the feathered staffs that were used at official events such as coronations and royal funerals.

In the Hawaiian Hall lobby, craftspeople demonstrate Hawaiian quilting, lauhala weaving, lei-making and other traditional crafts from 9 am to 2:30 pm weekdays. A

Hawaiian music and dance demonstration is given at 11 am and 2 pm daily.

The museum also has a modern wing called the Castle Building with interactive natural history displays that will be of particular interest to kids. Here one can listen to dolphins, see through the eyes of a frog or enter a reconstructed lava tube. Be forewarned, though – since these displays attract children, you may find a lot of the exhibits marked 'out of order.'

The Bishop Museum is open from 9 am to 5 pm daily. Admission is $14.95 for adults, $11.95 for children ages four to 17, free for children under four.

The museum is also home to Oahu's only planetarium, but shows are temporarily off as the antiquated facility is being replaced with a new state-of-the-art planetarium that is expected to be completed in the year 2001.

The museum shop sells many books on the Pacific not easily found elsewhere as well as quality Hawaiiana gift items. There's also a snack shop that's open to 4 pm.

To get to the Bishop Museum from Waikiki or downtown Honolulu take the No 2 School St bus to Kapalama St, walk toward the ocean and turn right on Bernice St. By car, take exit 20B off H-1, go inland on Houghtailing St and turn left on Bernice St.

Moanalua

In olden times, the Moanalua Valley (see the Greater Honolulu map) was a stopover for people who were traveling between Honolulu and Ewa, as well as a vacation spot for Hawaiian royalty. In 1884, Princess Pauahi Bishop willed the valley to Samuel M Damon, and it's now privately owned by the Damon estate.

Moanalua Gardens Moanalua Gardens, maintained by the Damon Estate, is a large grassy park with grand shade trees. The park is the site of Kamehameha V's gingerbread-trimmed summer cottage, which overlooks a taro pond. Beyond it a Chinese-style hall is fronted by carp ponds and stands of golden-stemmed bamboo. The center of the park has a grassy stage where the Prince Lot Hula Festival is held on the third Saturday in July.

This is not a must-see spot, except during the festival, but it is a pleasant place to stroll. To get there, take the Puuloa Rd/Tripler Hospital exit off Hwy 78 and then make an immediate right-hand turn into the gardens.

Moanalua Trail The trail up Moanalua Valley, once cobblestoned, is now a gravel and dirt road. It's a dry area, and there is only partial shade along the trail. There are both native and introduced plants, and lots of birds. Seven stone bridges remain along the path in various stages of disrepair.

The nonprofit Moanalua Gardens Foundation (☎ 839-5334) works to preserve Moanalua Valley in its natural state. The foundation's efforts to raise public awareness of the valley's history and environmental uniqueness helped defeat plans that would have routed the new H-3 Fwy through Moanalua Valley.

The foundation gives interpretive walks into Moanalua Valley at least one Sunday each month. The easy 5-mile walks begin at 9 am, finish around 1 pm and cost $3. Reservations can be made in advance.

If you want to hike the trail on your own, the Damon Estate requests that you first call ahead for permission to enter.

If you follow the road all the way in, it's about 4 miles. Numbered posts along the first half of the trail correspond to a self-guided brochure available for $5 from the foundation's office at 1352 Pineapple Place, Honolulu, HI 96819; add $4 for shipping to get it by mail.

To get to the trailhead, take the Moanalua Valley/Red Hill exit off Hwy 78 (one exit past Moanalua Gardens). Stay to the right and then follow the Moanalua Valley sign uphill 1¹/₂ miles on Ala Aolani St to where the road ends at a parking lot.

PLACES TO STAY
In Honolulu

Budget A small hostel, *Hostelling International Honolulu* (☎ 946-0591, fax 946-5904, 2323A Seaview Ave, Honolulu, HI 96822) is in a quiet residential neighborhood near the University of Hawaii. There are seven dorms with bunk beds that can accommodate 42 travelers, with men and women in separate dorms. Rates are $12.50 for HI members and $15.50 for nonmembers. There are also two rooms for couples that cost an extra $10. If you're not a member, there's a three-night maximum stay. HI membership is sold on site; the cost is $25 for Americans, $18 for foreign visitors. Credit cards are accepted. Office hours are from 8 am to noon and 4 pm to midnight. There's a TV lounge, common-use kitchen, laundry room, lockers and bulletin boards with useful information for new arrivals. From Ala Moana, catch bus No 6 or 18 (University or Woodlawn), get off at the corner of University Ave and Metcalf St, and walk one block uphill to Seaview Ave. By car, take exit 24B off the H-1 Fwy, head inland on University Ave and turn left at Seaview Ave.

The **Central Branch YMCA** (☎ 941-3344, fax 941-8821, 401 Atkinson Drive, Honolulu, HI 96814), on the east side of the Ala Moana Center, is the most conveniently located of the YMCAs. There are 114 rooms in all. The rooms with shared bath, which are available to men only, are small and simple and resemble those in a student dorm, with a simple desk, a single bed, a lamp, a chair and linoleum floors. The cost is $29 for a single or $40 for a room with an extra, rollaway bed. Rooms with private bath, which are a bit nicer but still small and basic, are open to both men and women and cost $36.50/51.50 for singles/doubles. There's a coin laundry, a TV lounge and a snack bar. Credit cards are accepted.

Fernhurst YWCA (☎ 941-2231, fax 949-0266, fernywca@gte.net, 1566 Wilder Ave, Honolulu, HI 96822) has rooms for women only in a three-story building about a mile from the university. There are 60 rooms, each intended for two guests, with two single beds, two lockable closets, two dressers and a desk. Two rooms share one bathroom. The cost is $25 per person. If you get a room to yourself, which is easier during the low season, it costs $5 more. Rates include breakfast and dinner except on weekends and holidays; there are limited kitchen facilities on each floor. Payment is required in advance; guests must be YWCA members

($30 a year if you're not a member elsewhere). Rented linen costs an additional $20, but you can bring your own. Although the YWCA accepts tourists, most guests are local, as Fernhurst provides transitional housing for women in need. There's a laundry room, TV room and a garden courtyard with a small pool. Fernhurst is at the intersection of Wilder Ave and Punahou St on the No 4 and 5 bus lines.

The **Nuuanu YMCA** (☎ 536-3556, 1441 Pali Hwy, Honolulu, HI 96813), at the intersection of Pali Hwy and Vineyard Ave, has mostly long-term tenants but rents some rooms for $25 a day, $143 a week. Accommodations are for men only. Rooms are small and spartan, with louvered windows, a single bed and a small metal desk and chair. Bathrooms are shared. Guests have access to a TV lounge, the weight room and pool.

During the school year, the **Atherton YMCA** (☎ 946-0253, fax 941-7802, 1810 University Ave, Honolulu, HI 96822) operates as a dorm for full-time University of Hawaii students only. During the summer holidays (mid-May to mid-August) it's usually open on a space-available basis to nonstudents, although some years it's full with students year-round. Rates are $20 per day for a room with a bed, dresser, desk and chair; there's also a $25 processing fee. Reservations are made by application, which is available by mail or fax. The Y is directly opposite the university.

Mid-Range The Pagoda Hotel (☎ 941-6611, 800-367-6060, fax 955-5067, reservations@ hthcorp.com, 1525 Rycroft St, Honolulu, HI 96814), north of the Ala Moana Center, has two sections. There are studios with kitchenettes in a nearby apartment complex, but they can feel a bit too removed from the main hotel, especially if you're checking in at night. The rooms in the hotel itself are quieter and have the usual amenities, including air-con, TV, phone, refrigerator and a central lobby. The hotel rooms cost $90 and the studios cost $95. There's no extra charge for children under 18 occupying the same room as their parents. There's nothing distinguished about this hotel other than a restaurant with a carp pond, but it is one way to avoid jumping into the Waikiki scene. For more information, visit the hotel's website at www.pagodahotel.com.

Top End The Executive Centre Hotel (☎ 539-3000, 800-949-3932, fax 523-1088, 1088 Bishop St, Honolulu, HI 96813) is Honolulu's only downtown hotel. Geared for business-people, it comprises 116 suites, each large and comfortable with modern amenities that include three phones, private voice mail, two TVs, a refrigerator, room safe and whirlpool bath. As the hotel's on the upper floors of a high-rise, most of the rooms have fine city views. There's a heated lap pool, a fitness center and a business center with computers and secretarial services. Standard rates, which include continental breakfast, range from $170 for a mountain view to $195 for an executive ocean-view suite, the latter with kitchen facilities and a washer/dryer. Business travelers qualify for corporate rates that begin at $121; otherwise there are promotions and discounts, including 50% off for members of the Entertainment travel club.

Manoa Valley Inn (☎ 947-6019, 800-535-0085, fax 946-6168, marc@aloha.net, 2001 Vancouver Drive, Honolulu, HI 96822), on a quiet side street near the University of Hawaii, is an authentically restored Victorian inn that's on the National Register of Historic Places. The inn's common areas and the eight guest rooms are furnished with antiques and there's complimentary evening wine, a common parlor and a billiard room. Rates, which include continental breakfast, are $99 for rooms with shared bath and $140 to $190 for rooms with a private bath. The inn is managed by Marc Resorts.

Kahala Mandarin Oriental (☎ 739-8888, 800-367-2525, fax 739-8800, sales@mohg .com, 5000 Kahala Ave, Honolulu, HI 96816) is on its own quiet stretch of beach in the exclusive Kahala area east of Diamond Head. This is where the rich and famous go when they want to avoid the Waikiki scene, a 10-minute drive away. The guest list is Hawaii's most regal: Britain's Prince Charles, King Juan Carlos and Queen Sofia, and the last six US presidents. Formerly the Kahala Hilton, the 370-room hotel has undergone a $75 million facelift. Rates start at $295 for garden-view rooms and $420 for rooms on the hotel's enclosed lagoon where dolphins swim just beyond the lanais. The presidential suite tops off at $3530. The hotel can be booked through Mandarin Oriental Hotels worldwide.

Near the Airport

If you have some dire need to be near Honolulu International, there are three hotels outside the airport along a busy highway and beneath flight paths. All provide free 24-hour transport to and from the airport, which is about 10 minutes away.

In addition, for long layovers or midnight flights there are two cheaper places where you can catnap or just take a shower.

The more attractive option is *Sleep & Shower* (☎ 836-3044, fax 834-8985, Terminal PO Box 42, Honolulu, HI 96819), right in the airport's main terminal between lobbies five and six. It has 17 small private rooms, each with a single bed and its own bathroom and shower. The place is clean, modern and relatively quiet, although there is some vibration from the shuttle bus that runs overhead. Overnight (eight-hour) stays are $30, a two-hour daytime nap and shower costs $17.50; additional hours are $5. Only one person is allowed to stay in each room. The five dorm beds at the side of the lobby cost $19 overnight, but they're not suited for light sleepers, as they're located in a semi-open part of the lobby. If you want to stop by for a shower only, the cost is $7.50, with towels, shampoo and shaving cream provided. It's open 24 hours. Reservations are taken for the overnight stays, except in the dorm, and MasterCard and Visa cards are accepted.

Nimitz Shower Tree (☎ 833-1411, 3085 N Nimitz Hwy) occupies a converted warehouse in an industrial area not far from the airport hotels. The facilities are basic: the private 'roomettes' are rows of little cubicles with louvered doors and an open wall at the top so it's a bit like being in a dorm. The cost is $24 to $33 for an overnight sleep. You can also go there just to take a shower for $7.50. It's open 24 hours. The Nimitz Shower Tree also offers rooms by the week for $110, which attracts a fair number of local boarders.

The most comfortable option near the airport is the **Best Western Plaza Hotel-Honolulu Airport** (☎ 836-3636, 800-528-1234, fax 834-7406, 3253 N Nimitz Hwy, Honolulu, HI 96819), a modern hotel with 274 pleasant rooms, each with a king or two double beds, TV and refrigerator. The only drawback is the heavy traffic noise from the nearby highway, which has an overpass adjacent to the front of the hotel; be sure to ask for a rear room. Rack rates are $97, but there's often a 'manager's special' for $85; non-smoking rooms are available. The hotel has a pool, lounge and restaurant; there are fast-food places within walking distance.

Holiday Inn-Honolulu Airport (☎ 836-0661, 800-800-3477, fax 833-1738, 3401 N Nimitz Hwy, Honolulu, HI 96819), on the corner of Rodgers Blvd, has 308 rooms and a standard rate of $112. The rooms are on the small side and relatively bland, but this four-story hotel has typical Holiday Inn amenities, including a lounge, pool and restaurant. Guests have a choice of a king or two double beds; nonsmoking rooms are available. There's commonly a promotional rate, dubbed the 'manager's special,' that discounts the standard rate by about 20%.

Pacific Marina Inn (☎ 836-1131, fax 833-0851, 2628 Waiwai Loop, Honolulu, HI 96819) is a mile farther east in an industrial area, but on the plus side it has the least traffic noise. This three-decker motel has small, straightforward rooms for $88, but there's usually an 'airport special' of $55 to $65; it can be reached on the courtesy phone in the baggage claim area. The rooms have air-con, TVs and phones, and there's a pool on the grounds.

PLACES TO EAT

Honolulu has an incredible variety of restaurants that mirror the city's multiethnic composition, and if you know where to look it can also be quite cheap. The key is to get out of the tourist areas and eat where the locals do.

Around the University

Not surprisingly, the area around the University of Hawaii at Manoa supports an interesting collection of reasonably priced ethnic restaurants, coffee shops and health food stores. The following places are all within a 10-minute walk of the three-way intersection of King St, Beretania St and University Ave.

Coffeeline (☎ 947-1615), at the corner of University and Seaview Aves, is a student hangout best known for its coffees and vegetarian meals. Vegan soup costs $2.50; omelettes, sandwiches and salads are around $4; and a few hot dishes such as spinach lasagna cost $5. Coffeeline is open 7 am to 4 pm Monday to Friday and 7 am to noon on Saturday.

Ezogiku Noodle Cafe (1010 University Ave), on the corner of Beretania St, dishes up ramen for $6.50, gyoza (grilled garlic-and-pork-filled dumplings) for $3.75 and a handful of other dishes, including curries and fried rice. While it's nothing memorable, it is on par with similar fast-food noodle shops in Japan. Ezogiku is open 11 am to 11 pm daily.

Across the street, a branch of the Vietnamese restaurant **Ba Le** (1091 University Ave) sells good inexpensive French rolls, croissants and sandwiches. A tasty vegetarian sandwich costs $2, while a roast beef version goes for $4.

Diem (☎ 941-8657, 2633 S King St), near the corner of University Ave, is a small Vietnamese restaurant with $5 lunch specials served until 3 pm daily. Dinner specials that include an entree, salad, rice and appetizer cost $9. Diem is open 11 am to 3 pm and 5 to at least 9 pm daily.

Chan's Gourmet Buffet (☎ 949-1188, 2600 S King St) is a long-established Chinese restaurant that has thrown away its menu and switched to buffet meals. It now caters to students and other value-oriented diners with a generous $6 lunch buffet (available 10:30 am to 4 pm Sunday to Friday) of about 50 items, mostly Chinese food but also some Japanese and American dishes. At dinner (served from 4:30 to 10:30 pm daily), the price goes up to $8 but includes seafood dishes. On Saturday, there's a dim sum brunch (9 am to 4 pm) for $9.

India Bazaar (☎ 949-4840), in a little shopping center at 2320 S King St, is a small cafe selling inexpensive Indian food. You can get a vegetarian thali that includes spiced rice and three curry items for $6 and a chicken thali for $7. Side orders of papadams, chapatis and raita are each under $1. India Bazaar is open 11 am to 9 pm Monday to Saturday.

In the same complex is a branch of **Kozo Sushi**, a local chain that specializes in good inexpensive sushi. An excellent choice is the California maki, a crab and avocado version that comes eight pieces to the set for $3.50. Although it's mostly takeout, the shop has a couple of tables where you can sit and eat. Kozo is open 9 am to 7 pm Monday to Saturday, 9 am to 6 pm Sunday.

Maple Garden (☎ 941-6641, 909 Isenberg St), around the corner from S King St, is a popular local Sichuan Chinese restaurant with good food at reasonable prices. Vegetarian entrees, which include a delicious eggplant in hot garlic sauce, average $6.50, while most meat dishes cost about a dollar more. At lunch there are a couple of multi-item plate specials that include hot sour soup and an almond tofu dessert for just $6. Maple Garden is open 11 am to 2 pm and 5:30 to 10 pm daily.

Chiang Mai (☎ 941-1151, 2239 S King St) serves northern Thai food, including a wonderful sticky rice. The menu features two dozen vegetarian dishes and a range of meat dishes for around $7. Chiang Mai is open 11 am to 2 pm Monday to Friday and 5:30 to 10 pm nightly.

Yakiniku Camellia (☎ 946-7595, 2494 S Beretania St) has a tasty all-you-can-cook Korean lunch buffet for $9.95 from 11 am to 3 pm. It's quality food and if you've worked up an appetite, it's a fine deal. The mainstay is pieces of chicken, pork and beef that you select and grill at your table. Accompanying this are 18 marinated side dishes, miso and seaweed soups, simple vegetable salads and a few fresh fruits. When selecting kimchis, keep in mind that the redder they are, the hotter they are.

Dinner, from 3 to 10 pm, costs $15.75 and adds on sashimi. Everything is authentic, right down to the vending machine selling Korean-language newspapers.

Down to Earth Natural Foods (2525 S King St) is a large natural foods supermarket with everything from Indian chapatis to local organic produce and a dozen varieties of granola sold in bulk. It's a great place to shop and the healthier yogurts and wholegrain breads that some of Honolulu's more with-it supermarkets sell are substantially cheaper here. The store's open 7:30 am to 10 pm daily. The vegetarian deli on the premises features a salad bar and hot dishes such as vegan chow fun or vegetable curry for $5 a pound.

Ala Moana Center

Ala Moana Center's food court is a circus, with neon signs, hundreds of tiny tables crowded together and nearly 50 fast-food stands circling it all. There's something for everyone, from salads to daiquiris, ice cream to pizza, and Chinese, Japanese, Korean, Hawaiian, Filipino, Thai and Mexican specialties.

If you have the munchies, this is a good place to stop when you're between buses. It's like window-shopping – you can walk through, preview the food and select what you want. Called Makai Market, the food court is on the ground floor, on the side of the center closest to the ocean. It's open 8 am to 9 pm Monday to Saturday and 9 am to 6 pm on Sunday.

Panda Express has good MSG-free Mandarin and Sichuan food, with dishes like spicy chicken, broccoli beef and eggplant with garlic sauce. Combination plates with fried rice or chow mein and two entrees are $5, three entrees $6. The food is fresh and you can select what looks best from the steamer trays.

Yummy Korean BBQ is a similar concept, with Korean selections that include rice and a number of tasty pickled veggies and kimchis. At lunch and dinner, you can expect to pay $5.50 to $7 for a plate.

Patti's Chinese Kitchen is a big-volume restaurant with a few dozen dishes to choose from. It costs $5 for two selections, $6 for three selections, including rice or noodles. If you really want to indulge, you can get a whole roast duck for $11. There's also a limited selection of dim sum and desserts, such as almond cookies and *haupia* (coconut pudding).

Naniwa Ya Ramen dishes up steaming bowls of authentic Japanese ramen noodles for around $6 and has gyoza, a tasty grilled dumpling that goes great with beer, for $3.

Cactus Jack's offers tacos, tostadas or fajitas with rice and beans for around $6. At nearby *Little Cafe Siam,* two tasty skewers of chicken satay in peanut sauce cost $2.25, and at *Sbarro* a big slice of pizza costs around $3.

Paradise Bakery & Café makes nice muffins and bagels while the nearby *Twisted Pretzel* sells fresh pretzels and the locally popular malasada, a Portuguese-style fried doughnut that's served warm.

Also in the Ala Moana Center is a *Foodland* supermarket that's open from 7 am to 11 pm daily and branches of the *McDonald's, Pizza Hut, Häagen-Dazs* and *Dunkin' Donuts* fast-food chains.

Ward Centre

Ward Centre, a shopping complex at 1200 Ala Moana Blvd, has a couple of coffee shops and delis, a branch of *Keo's* Thai restaurant and about a dozen other dining spots.

Mocha Java/Crepe Fever, on the center's ground level, is a popular hangout serving good fresh-fruit smoothies, coffees, crêpes, omelettes, sandwiches, desserts and other light eats. It's open 7 am to 9 pm Monday to Saturday, 8 am to 4 pm on Sunday.

Scoozee's (☎ 597-1777), also located on the ground level, is a trendy nouveau Italian cafe with good pastas, pizzas and calzones for $10 and sandwiches for just a tad less. Scoozee's is open from 11 am daily, closing at 10 pm Sunday to Thursday and at 11 pm on Friday and Saturday.

The food is a bit too Americanized at *Compadres* (☎ 591-8307), but this busy Mexican restaurant still draws a crowd and wins plenty of local awards. Combination

plates with rice and beans average $10 to $15. It's on the center's upper level and is open from 11 am to 11 pm weekdays, until 10 pm on Sunday and to midnight on Friday and Saturday.

A trendy high-energy place is the new *Brew Moon* (☎ 593-0088), a branch of a small Boston-based chain of microbreweries. It specializes in ales ranging from a low calorie 'moonlight' brew to a copper-colored 'Hawaii 5' malt; a 20-ounce sampler of five different ales cost $5.50, a single brew $4.75. Brew Moon serves a wide variety of snacks, including nachos, *poke* (marinated fish) and shrimp rolls for around $8; burgers and sandwiches with fries are also within that price range. Meals such as jambalaya chicken or ginger sesame stir-fry are around $10 at lunch and $15 at dinner. It's open from 11 am to 1 am daily.

At the top end is *A Pacific Cafe Oahu* (☎ 593-0035), a branch of Jean-Marie Josselin's well-regarded Pacific Rim restaurant on Kauai. The menu here features calamari tempura, fresh fish carpaccio and similar appetizers for around $10. Entrees such as blackened *ahi* (yellowfin tuna) with hearts of palm or rack of lamb average $25. The lunch menu has similar but lighter servings and prices that are about 40% less. On the center's upper level, A Pacific Cafe is open 11:30 am to 2 pm Monday to Friday and 5:30 to 9 pm daily.

Ward Warehouse The following places are at Ward Warehouse, the shopping complex on the corner of Ala Moana Blvd and Ward Ave. There's free garage parking and bus Nos 8, 19 and 20 stop out front. The two restaurants are on the upper level and have harbor views, so when making reservations be sure to ask for a window table.

For cheap eats, the *Old Spaghetti Factory* (☎ 591-2513) is hard to beat. This family-style restaurant has an elaborate decor, chock-full of antiques, heavy woods, Tiffany stained glass – even an old streetcar. At lunch (11:30 am to 2 pm Monday to Friday), you can get spaghetti with tomato sauce for $3.75, with clam sauce for $4.65 or with meatballs for $5.85. All meals come with bread and a simple green salad. Meals are about a dollar more at dinner, which is served from 5 to 10 pm weekdays, from 11:30 am to 10:30 pm Saturday and from 4 to 9:30 pm Sunday. The food itself is not special, but the price is right and the setting is interesting.

Kincaid's Fish, Chop & Steak House (☎ 591-2005) is a pleasant place serving good moderately priced seafood and steaks. A favorite lunch spot for downtown businesspeople, the lunch entrees include such things as spicy Cajun fettuccine for $10, oven-roasted garlic prawns for $13 and ahi with pineapple salsa for $15. At dinner, fresh fish entrees and steaks cost $17 to $24. Kincaid's is open 11 am to 5 pm for lunch and 5 to 10 pm for dinner daily.

On the ground level of Kincaid's is *Coffee Works*, a pleasant little cafe that has coffee, espresso, scones and bagels. It's open 9 am to 9 pm daily, except on Sunday, when it's open 8 am to 5 pm.

Restaurant Row

Restaurant Row, a rather sterile complex on the corner of Ala Moana Blvd and Punchbowl St, caters largely to the downtown business crowd. There's a *Burger King*, a *Subway*, a *Bad Ass Coffee Co* coffee shop, a pizzeria, an ice cream shop and several restaurants.

Payao (☎ 521-3511), a Thai eatery related to the popular university-area Chiang Mai restaurant, has an extensive menu, with vegetarian offerings for around $7, curries, beef, chicken and noodle dishes for around $8 and seafood dishes for a bit more. Payao is open 11 am to 2 pm Monday to Saturday and 5 to 9:30 pm nightly.

Island Salsa (☎ 536-4777) takes its name from its salsa table, where customers can select from a variety of fresh-made sauces, ranging from the tame to the fire-eater. While there's no lard in the food, in other ways it's near-authentic Mexican fare. Two tacos or a hefty burrito, in either tofu, grilled vegetable or chicken versions, cost $8 to $9, while combo plates with black beans and rice cost $12. Island Salsa is open 11 am to 11 pm daily.

The best top-end choice at Restaurant Row is *Sunset Grill* (☎ 521-4409), which features grilled fresh fish and meats from around $20 at dinner and salads, calamari and sandwiches for half that price at lunch. It also periodically runs an all-you-can-eat ribs deal ($10.95), starting at 5 pm and ending when the ribs run out. In addition to good food, the restaurant boasts an extensive wine list, including numerous selections by the glass. Sunset Grill is open 11 am to 11 pm weekdays and 5 pm to at least 10 pm weekends.

There's also a branch of *Ruth's Chris Steak House* (☎ 599-3860), a pricey mainland chain restaurant offering quality à la carte steaks for around $25; add $5 for a baked potato or salad. It's open 5 to 10 pm nightly.

Fort St Mall

The Fort St Mall, a pedestrian street right on the edge of the downtown district, has a number of cheap restaurants within walking distance of Iolani Palace. It's convenient for downtown workers and sightseers, but certainly not a draw if you're elsewhere around town.

Taco Bell, *McDonald's*, *Burger King*, *KFC*, *Subway* and *Pizza Hut* are all near the intersection of Hotel St and Fort St Mall.

A good local option is *Ba Le*, a branch of the Chinatown restaurant, which has inexpensive Vietnamese sandwiches, as well as shrimp rolls, green papaya salads and French coffees. There are plenty of vegetarian options and the highest priced item, a seafood sandwich, is just $4. Ba Le is open 7 am to 7 pm Monday to Friday and 8:30 am to 4 pm on Saturday.

Adjacent to Ba Le is the *Fort Street Cafe*, an ever-popular student hangout with plate lunches, Vietnamese *pho* (beef) soups and various types of *saimin* (a Japanese noodle soup) for around $5. It's open 7 am to 7 pm weekdays and 7 am to 4 pm on Saturday.

For Chinese fast food there's *Mandarin Express* (116 S Hotel St). While the food is served from steamer trays, it tends to be fresh at meal times and you can eat heartily for around $5; after 3 pm, there's a 20%

discount. Mandarin Express is open 9 am to 6 pm, weekdays only.

Kozo Sushi *(1150 Bishop St)*, a block south of the Fort St Mall, has good inexpensive sushi for takeout. It's open from 9 am to 5 pm Monday to Thursday, to 5:30 pm on Friday.

Chinatown

For a quintessentially local dining option head to the food court in the *Maunakea Marketplace* on N Hotel St. Here you'll find about 20 stalls with mom-and-pop vendors dishing out homestyle Chinese, Thai, Vietnamese, Korean and Filipino food. You can get a solid meal for $5 and chow down at tiny wooden tables crowded into the central walkway. The marketplace is open from around 7 am to 3:30 pm daily.

Ba Le *(150 N King St)* is another good place for a quick inexpensive bite. Crispy baguettes can be purchased for 40¢ or as sandwiches for $2 vegetarian style, $3 with meat. The vegetarian sandwich is a tangy mixture of crunchy carrots, daikon and cilantro. For a caffeine jolt, there's sweet, strong French coffee with milk for $1.75 hot or cold. The kitchen also prepares good croissants, shrimp rolls and tropical tapioca puddings. Ba Le is open from 6 am to 5 pm Monday to Saturday, from 6 am to 3 pm on Sunday.

Krung Thai *(☎ 599-4803, 1028 Nuuanu Ave)* is a good-value little Thai eatery on the edge of Chinatown. Lunch, the only meal served, is geared to the business community's 30-minute lunch breaks, with food ready in steamer trays. You can choose from a dozen hot dishes such as chicken Panang, beef eggplant and vegetarian curry. One item costs $4, two items $4.89, and all are served with rice or noodles. Krung Thai is open 10:30 am to 2:30 pm Monday to Friday. There are tables in a rear courtyard where you can eat.

One of the best Chinatown eateries is the Vietnamese restaurant *To Chau* *(1007 River St)*, where the specialty is pho, a delicious soup of beef broth with rice noodles and thin slices of beef garnished with cilantro and green onion. It comes with a second plate of fresh basil, mung bean sprouts and slices of hot chili pepper. It's a bargain at just $3.85 for a regular bowl or $5.20 for an extra-large one. The shrimp rolls with a spicy peanut sauce ($3) are recommendable, and the restaurant also serves rice and noodle dishes, but just about everybody comes for the soup. This spot is open 8 am to 2:30 pm daily. It's so popular that even at 10 am you may have to line up outside the door for one of the 16 tables. It's well worth the wait – though if you're daunted by the line, there's also good inexpensive Vietnamese food at *Ha Bien* next door.

There's a run of small Vietnamese restaurants on Maunakea St near its intersection with Pauahi St, including *A Little Bit of Saigon* *(1160 Maunakea St)*, which serves a decent pho for $5, good fried tofu or chicken noodle dishes for $7 and various combination plates for under $10. It's open 10 am to 10 pm daily.

The *Buddhist Vegetarian Restaurant* *(☎ 532-8218)*, facing the River St pedestrian mall inside the Chinatown Cultural Plaza, is a health-oriented Chinese dining spot that uses tofu and gluten in place of meats. The menu is both imaginative and extensive, with most dishes priced from $7 to $10. There's also a dim sum service available at lunch. The restaurant's open 10:30 am to 2 pm and 5:30 to 9 pm daily except Wednesday.

Zaffron *(☎ 533-6635, 69 N King St)*, a small family-run Indian restaurant, offers a choice of $7 plate lunches, including vegetarian, tandoori chicken and meat or fish curry. Each comes with chole, aloo sabiz, rice and nan. Lunch is served 11 am to 2:30 pm Monday to Saturday. Zaffron is also open from 6 to 9:30 pm on Friday and Saturday, at which time there's a buffet dinner for $12.50.

For upscale dining there's *Indigo* *(☎ 521-2900, 1121 Nuuanu Ave)*, which has an open-air courtyard and good Asian-Pacific food. A special treat is the creative dim sum appetizers, such as tempura ahi rolls and goat cheese wontons. Dinner features duck, steak and fish dishes for $17 to $20. Popular at lunch are the gourmet pizzas ($8.50) that come in vegetarian, duck and spicy chicken varieties. Indigo is open 11:30 am to 2 pm Tuesday to Friday and 5:30 to 9:30 pm Tuesday to Saturday.

Elsewhere in Honolulu

Helena's Hawaiian Foods (☎ 845-8044, 1364 N King St) is a friendly family-run operation that's been serving good, inexpensive Hawaiian food since 1946. It's a thoroughly local restaurant, with 10 simple Formica-top tables and a mix of vinyl chairs and stools. The elderly women who run the restaurant make a delicious *kalua* pig, which has been baked in an underground oven; also notable are the *pipikaula* (a kind of broiled beef) and the *lomi* salmon (diced, marinated fish). Helena's is a survivor, and walking in the door is a bit like stepping back 50 years. Nearly everything on the à la carte menu is under $2.50, while complete meals with rice or poi (the Hawaiian taro paste is served fresh, day-old or sour) are $5.50 to $9. Helena's is open from 11 am to 7:30 pm Tuesday to Friday.

Auntie Pasto's (☎ 523-8855, 1099 S Beretania St) offers good Italian food at honest prices. Pasta dishes cost $5.50 with tomato sauce, $8 with pesto or $7 heaped with fresh vegetables in butter and garlic. The Parmesan cheese is freshly grated and the Italian bread is served warm. Although it's off the tourist track, this popular spot attracts a crowd and you may have to wait for a table, particularly on weekends. Auntie Pasto's is open 11 am to 10:30 pm Monday to Friday and 4 to 10:45 pm on Saturday and Sunday.

Mekong (☎ 591-8841, 1295 S Beretania St) is not only home to the original Keo's, but it still has the original Thai chef. It also has a similar menu to that more upscale spinoff, but in this tiny eatery posters replace the artwork, you bring your own booze and prices are about a third less. The tasty spring rolls cost $6, while most beef, chicken and vegetarian main dishes are a dollar more. Nothing on the menu is over $10. Mekong is open 11 am to 2 pm on weekdays and 5 to 9:30 pm nightly. Parking is available in the lot at the west side of the building, next to a florist. There's also a *Mekong II* (☎ 941-6184, 1726 S King St), which has essentially the same menu.

El Burrito (☎ 596-8225, 550 Piikoi St), near the Ala Moana Center, could be a neighborhood restaurant on a back street in Mexico City. This hole-in-the-wall squeezes in about a dozen tables and serves Honolulu's most authentic Mexican food. Two tamales, enchiladas or chile rellenos with rice and beans average $9. El Burrito is open from 11 am to 8 pm Monday to Thursday, from 11 am to 9 pm on Friday and Saturday. Expect lines at dinnertime, especially on weekends.

Pagoda Restaurant (☎ 941-6611, 1525 Rycroft St), at the Pagoda Hotel, has only average food but a pleasant setting with a carp pond. The breakfast menu (available 6:30 to 10:30 am) is extensive, with many choices for around $5. From 11 am to 2 pm on weekdays, there's a lunch buffet of Japanese and American dishes for $11. There's also a nightly dinner buffet (4:30 to 9:30 pm), which costs $19 ($17 on Monday and Tuesday) and features an array of dishes including prime rib, Alaskan snow crab, sashimi, tempura, a salad bar and a dessert bar.

On the waterfront, the *Gordon Biersch Brewery Restaurant* (☎ 599-4877) is the most popular spot at the Aloha Tower Marketplace on Ala Moana Blvd. Hawaii's first microbrewery restaurant, it features its own German-style lagers accompanied by Hawaiian *pupu* (snacks). Some creative salads, sandwiches and pizzas are available for under $10, while hot pastas, Louisiana gumbo seafood or New York steaks run from $10 to $20. Gordon Biersch is open 10:30 am to 10 pm daily (to 11 pm on weekends). There's also live entertainment Wednesday to Saturday nights.

Although it overlooks the parking lot and not the water, *Chai's Island Bistro* (☎ 585-0011) at the Aloha Tower Marketplace also has a following. Under the same management as the popular Singha Thai restaurant in Waikiki, Chai's features Pacific Rim cuisine, with appetizers such as crispy duck lumpia, ahi tempura and organic salads for under $10. The lunch entrees range from chicken satay for $11 to brandy-glazed lamb chops for $20, while at dinner the same dishes jump $5. Chai's is open 11 am to 4 pm weekdays and 4 to 10 pm nightly.

Alan Wong's (☎ 949-2526, 1857 S King St) is one of Hawaii's top restaurants – a high-energy place specializing in upscale Hawaii Regional cuisine. Chef Wong, who won accolades at the Big Island's exclusive Mauna Lani Resort before striking out on his own, prepares a creative menu with an emphasis on fresh local ingredients. Appetizers such as tempura ahi or duck salad cost $7.50 to $10, while entrees average $30 for spicy seafood paella, beef tenderloin with Kona lobster or ginger-crusted *onaga* (red snapper). Each night there's also a five-course 'tasting menu' for $65 and a three-course vegetarian menu for $45. Alan Wong's is open 5 to 10 pm nightly; reservations are often essential.

Yanagi Sushi (☎ 537-1525, 762 Kapiolani Blvd), is one of Honolulu's most popular places for moderately priced sushi. It's open 11 am to 2 pm daily and 5:30 pm to 2 am (to 10 pm on Sunday).

At the county-run People's Open Market program, farmers sell local produce for one hour a week at 22 locations around Oahu. Mondays and Wednesdays are set aside for the greater Honolulu area. Call ☎ 522-7088 for current times and locations or pick up a schedule at any satellite city hall.

ENTERTAINMENT

Honolulu has a lively entertainment scene. The best updated listings are in the free *Honolulu Weekly*, which is readily found throughout the city.

Theater & Concerts

Honolulu boasts a symphony orchestra, an opera company, ballet troupes, chamber orchestras and numerous community theater groups.

The *Hawaii Theatre* (☎ 528-0506, 1130 Bethel St) is a major venue for dance, music and theater. Performances range from top contemporary Hawaiian musicians such as Hapa and Hookena to modern dance and film festivals.

The *Blaisdell Center* (☎ 591-2211, 777 Ward Ave) presents concerts, Broadway shows and some family events, such as the Honolulu Symphony, the Ice Capades, the Brothers Cazimero (well-known Hawaiian performers) and the occasional big-name rock musicians.

The *Academy Theatre* (☎ 532-8768) of the Honolulu Academy of Arts, 900 S Beretania St, and to a lesser degree the *East-West Center* (☎ 944-7111), adjacent to the University of Hawaii, both present multicultural theater and concerts.

Cinemas

Honolulu has several movie theaters showing first-run feature films, including a nine-screen multiplex cinema at *Restaurant Row* (☎ 526-4171).

The *Academy Theatre* (☎ 532-8768) at the Honolulu Academy of Arts showcases American independent cinema, foreign films and avant-garde shorts. Tickets cost $5.

Music & Dancing

Anna Bannanas (☎ 946-5190, 2440 S Beretania St), not far from the university, features blues, rock or reggae bands from 9:30 pm to 2 am Thursday to Sunday. There's usually a cover charge of $4.

The *Pier Bar* (☎ 536-2166), at the Aloha Tower Marketplace, features live music from 7 pm to 2 am Tuesday to Saturday, including top-name contemporary Hawaiian musicians such as Willie K and Henry Kapono. There's no cover on Tuesday; other nights are usually $3.

Rumours (☎ 955-4811, 410 Atkinson Drive), at the Ala Moana Hotel, has DJ dancing from 9 pm to 4 am on weekends, with top 40 music on Friday and '70s to '90s music on Saturday. The cover is $5.

Free Entertainment

In the *Ala Moana Center*, a courtyard area called Centerstage is the venue for free performances by high school choirs, gospel groups, ballet troupes, local bands and the like. There's something happening almost daily; look for the schedule in Ala Moana's free shopping magazine.

Plumeria

Vanda orchid

Heliconia

The shadow of a chameleon on a heliconia leaf

NED FRIARY

Canoeing along the Honolulu coastline

ROBERT FRIED

LEE FOSTER

Surfing at Poipu on Kauai

Hiking in Maui's lush northwest valleys

ASTRID WITTE & CASEY MAHANEY

Snorkeling with lemon butterflyfish in the Molokini crater

The aptly named Sunset Beach, on Oahu's North Shore

Slow down, dude, at Haleiwa on Oahu.

Hula dancers at Oahu's Aloha Festival

Offerings at the Puu o Mahuka Heiau, Oahu

Hanauma Bay, Oahu

Chinatown produce market, Honolulu

Sunrise over Oahu's Lanikai Beach

The Royal Hawaiian Band performs from 12:15 to 1:15 pm on Friday (except August) at the bandstand on the lawn of the Iolani Palace.

The Mayor's Office of Culture & Arts sponsors a number of free performances, exhibits and events, ranging from street musicians in city parks to band concerts in various locales around Honolulu. Call ☎ 527-5666 for current events.

Waikiki

Once Hawaii's only tourist destination, Waikiki still accounts for nearly half of the visitor accommodations in the entire state, with an amazing density of high-rise hotels clustered along an attractive stretch of white-sand beach.

Waikiki is crowded with package tourists from both Japan and the US mainland. It has 25,000 permanent residents and some 65,000 visitors on any given day, all in an area roughly 1½ miles long and half a mile wide. Waikiki has 450 restaurants, 350 bars and clubs, and more shops than you'd want to count. All in all it boasts some 33,000 hotel and condo rooms.

While the beaches are packed during the day, at night most of the action is along the streets, where window-shoppers, time-share touts and prostitutes all go about their business. A variety of live music, from mellow Hawaiian to rock, wafts from streetside clubs and hotel lounges.

Visitors who are into city lights or singles scenes often find what they're looking for here, while many seasoned travelers and a fair number of Oahu residents avoid Waikiki like the plague.

Waikiki Beach has wonderful orange sunsets, with the sun dropping down between cruising sailboats. It's the one time of day that the area approaches the romantic image that the travel brochures like to portray.

Just beyond Waikiki is Diamond Head, a landmark so dominant that it's used as a directional marker – islanders say 'go Diamond Head' instead of 'head east.'

Orientation

Waikiki is bounded on two sides by the Ala Wai Canal and on another by the ocean. The eastern boundary varies according to who's drawing the line, but it's usually considered to be Kapahulu Ave.

There are two main roads: The beach road is Kalakaua Ave, named after King David Kalakaua; the main drag for Waikiki's buses is Kuhio Ave, named after Prince Jonah Kuhio Kalanianaole, a distinguished Hawaiian statesman.

City buses are not allowed on Kalakaua Ave, and trucks are prohibited at midday. Traffic on this four-lane road is one way so it's relatively smooth for driving, but pedestrians need to be cautious as cars tend to zoom by fast.

Walking along the beach is an alternative to using the crowded sidewalks. It's possible to walk the full length of Waikiki along the sand and the seawalls. Although it's rather hot and crowded at midday, it's pleasant at other times. The beach is quite romantic to stroll along at night, enhanced by both the city skyline and the surf lapping at the shore, and it's dark enough to see the stars.

Information

Tourist Offices The Hawaii Visitors and Convention Bureau has its visitor information office (☎ 924-0266) in the Royal Hawaiian Shopping Center, 2201 Kalakaua Ave, suite A401A (Building A, 4th floor), at the Lewers St end of the center. It is open 8 am to 5 pm Monday to Friday.

Free tourist magazines, such as *This Week Oahu*, *Spotlight's Oahu Gold* and *Guide to Oahu*, can readily be found on street corners and in hotel lobbies throughout Waikiki.

Money There's a Bank of Hawaii at 2220 Kalakaua Ave and a First Hawaiian Bank at 2181 Kalakaua Ave, the latter with some interesting Hawaiiana murals by the renowned artist Jean Charlot.

There are numerous ATMs around Waikiki that accept major bank and credit cards. Those at Food Pantry on Kuhio Ave and the nearby 7-Eleven convenience store are both accessible 24 hours.

OAHU

WAIKIKI

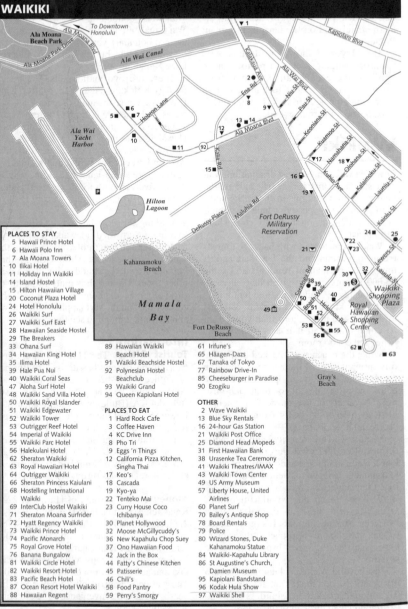

To Downtown
Honolulu

Ala Moana
Beach Park

Kapiolani Blvd

Ala Moana Park Drive

Ala Moana Blvd

Ala Wai Canal

Ala Moana Blvd

Kalakaua Ave

Ala Wai Blvd

▼ 1

2 ●

Ena Rd

8

Niu St

Pau St

9 ▼

● 6

5 ■   ■ 7

Hobron Lane

Keoniana St

13 ■ ■ 14

Kuamoo St

12
▼

Ala Moana Blvd

Namahana St

Ala Wai
Yacht
Harbor

■ 10

Kalia Rd

92

■ 11

▼17

18 ▼
■

Olohana St

Kalaimoku St

15 ■

16 ▷

19 ▼

Kuhio Ave

Launiu St

Kanekapolei St

P

Hilton
Lagoon

Maluhia Rd

DeRussy Place

Fort DeRussy
Military
Reservation

24 ■

25
●

▼22
▼23

21 ◁

Kahanamoku
Beach

Saratoga Rd

29 ■

32

30 ▼

Lewers St

Lauula St

31

Waikiki
Shopping
Plaza

Beach Walk

38
39

Helumoa Rd

40

50

49 血

51
52

Royal
Hawaiian
Shopping
Center

Mamala
Bay

53 ■

54 ■

55 ■

56 ■

62 ■

■ 63

Fort DeRussy
Beach

Gray's
Beach

PLACES TO STAY
5 Hawaii Prince Hotel
6 Hawaii Polo Inn
7 Ala Moana Towers
10 Ilikai Hotel
11 Holiday Inn Waikiki
14 Island Hostel
15 Hilton Hawaiian Village
20 Coconut Plaza Hotel
24 Hotel Honolulu
26 Waikiki Surf
27 Waikiki Surf East
28 Hawaiian Seaside Hostel
29 The Breakers
33 Ohana Surf
34 Hawaiian King Hotel
35 Ilima Hotel
39 Hale Pua Nui
40 Waikiki Coral Seas
47 Aloha Surf Hotel
48 Waikiki Sand Villa Hotel
50 Waikiki Royal Islander
51 Waikiki Edgewater
52 Waikiki Tower
53 Outrigger Reef Hotel
54 Imperial of Waikiki
55 Waikiki Parc Hotel
61 Halekulani Hotel
62 Sheraton Waikiki
63 Royal Hawaiian Hotel
64 Outrigger Waikiki
66 Sheraton Princess Kaiulani
68 Hostelling International
     Waikiki
69 InterClub Hostel Waikiki
71 Sheraton Moana Surfrider
72 Hyatt Regency Waikiki
73 Waikiki Prince Hotel
74 Pacific Monarch
75 Royal Grove Hotel
76 Banana Bungalow
81 Waikiki Circle Hotel
82 Waikiki Resort Hotel
83 Pacific Beach Hotel
87 Ocean Resort Hotel Waikiki
88 Hawaiian Regent

89 Hawaiian Waikiki
     Beach Hotel
91 Waikiki Beachside Hostel
92 Polynesian Hostel
     Beachclub
93 Waikiki Grand
94 Queen Kapiolani Hotel

PLACES TO EAT
1 Hard Rock Cafe
3 Coffee Haven
4 KC Drive Inn
8 Pho Tri
9 Eggs 'n Things
12 California Pizza Kitchen,
     Singha Thai
17 Keo's
18 Cascada
19 Kyo-ya
22 Tenteko Mai
23 Curry House Coco
     Ichibanya
30 Planet Hollywood
32 Moose McGillycuddy's
36 New Kapahulu Chop Suey
37 Ono Hawaiian Food
42 Jack in the Box
44 Fatty's Chinese Kitchen
45 Patisserie
46 Chili's
58 Food Pantry
59 Perry's Smorgy

61 Irifune's
65 Häagen-Dazs
67 Tanaka of Tokyo
77 Rainbow Drive-In
85 Cheeseburger in Paradise
90 Ezogiku

OTHER
2 Wave Waikiki
13 Blue Sky Rentals
16 24-hour Gas Station
21 Waikiki Post Office
25 Diamond Head Mopeds
31 First Hawaiian Bank
38 Urasenke Tea Ceremony
41 Waikiki Theatres/IMAX
43 Waikiki Town Center
49 US Army Museum
57 Liberty House, United
     Airlines
60 Planet Surf
70 Bailey's Antique Shop
78 Board Rentals
79 Police
80 Wizard Stones, Duke
     Kahanamoku Statue
84 Waikiki-Kapahulu Library
86 St Augustine's Church,
     Damien Museum
95 Kapiolani Bandstand
96 Kodak Hula Show
97 Waikiki Shell

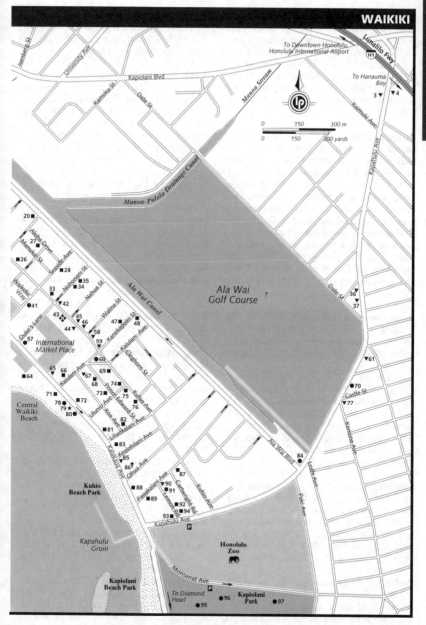

WAIKIKI

Post & Communications The main post office in Waikiki, 330 Saratoga Rd, is open from 8 am to 4:30 pm on weekdays, except on Wednesday, when it's open from 8 am to 6 pm. Saturday hours are 9 am to noon.

There's a branch post office at the Hilton Hawaiian Village, 2005 Kalia Rd, that's open from 8 am to noon and 1 to 4 pm Monday to Saturday.

Photography Fox Photo, with Waikiki branches in the Royal Hawaiian Shopping Center and the Sheraton Moana hotel, does one-hour photo processing.

To buy film and to have slides processed, Longs Drugs is a good choice. It offers processing by Kodak and Fuji and relatively rapid turnaround: slides generally take two to three days, prints a day or two. What's more, the cost of developing is significantly cheaper than at camera shops. While there are no branches in Waikiki, there's a Longs Drugs on the upper level of the Ala Moana Center.

Bookstores & Libraries Waldenbooks, which has a good collection of Hawaiiana books, travel guides and paperback fiction, is at the Waikiki Shopping Plaza, 2270 Kalakaua Ave.

The Waikiki-Kapahulu Public Library, 400 Kapahulu Ave, is open from 10 am to 8 pm on Tuesday and Wednesday and 10 am to 5 pm on Monday, Thursday, Friday and Saturday. It's a relatively small library, but it does have the daily Honolulu newspapers as well as the *New York Times* and *Wall Street Journal*.

Laundry Many Waikiki accommodations have on-site laundry facilities. If yours doesn't, there are public coin laundries open from 6:30 am to 10 pm daily at the following hotels: Waikiki West, 2330 Kuhio Ave; the Waikiki Coral Seas, 250 Lewers St; and the Outrigger Waikiki, 2335 Kalakaua Ave.

Parking Finding cheap parking in Waikiki can be a hassle and may be more trouble than it's worth. Many of the hotels charge $8 to $15 a day for guest-parking in their garages.

At the west end of Waikiki the best bet is the public parking lot at the end of the Ala Wai Yacht Harbor, which has free parking up to a maximum of 24 hours.

At the east end of Waikiki, the zoo parking lot on Kapahulu Ave has meters that cost just 25¢ an hour with a four-hour parking limit. If you like taking chances, you can try your luck parking overnight at the zoo; however, if you don't move out early enough in the morning you may be greeted with the sight of a police officer placing a $25 ticket on your window.

Emergency Dial ☎ 911 for all police, fire and ambulance emergency services.

Doctors On Call (☎ 971-6000) has a 24-hour clinic with X-ray and lab facilities at 2222 Kalakaua Ave, room 212. The approximate charge for an office visit is $85 to $150. The doctors also make house calls, though this is apt to run more than twice the office visit cost. Smaller branch clinics, with more typical business hours, are located at the Hilton Hawaiian Village (☎ 973-5252), the Royal Hawaiian Hotel (☎ 923-4499) and the Hyatt Regency Waikiki (☎ 971-8001).

Dangers & Annoyances There's been a clampdown on the hustlers who used to push time-shares and other con deals from every other street corner in Waikiki. They're not totally gone; there are just fewer of them (and some have metamorphosed into 'activity centers'). If you see a sign touting car rentals for $5 a day, you've probably found one.

Time-share salespeople will offer you all sorts of deals, from free luaus to sunset cruises, if you'll just come to hear their 'no obligation' pitch. Caveat emptor.

Beaches

The 2-mile stretch of white sand that runs from the Hilton Hawaiian Village to Kapiolani Park is commonly called Waikiki Beach, although different sections along the way have their own names and characteristics.

In the early morning, the beach belongs to walkers and joggers, and it's surprisingly quiet. Strolling down the beach toward

Diamond Head at sunrise can actually be a meditative experience.

By mid-morning it looks like a normal resort beach, with boogie-board and surfboard concessionaires setting up shop and catamarans pulling up on the beach offering $15 sails. By noon it is packed, and the challenge is to walk down the beach without stepping on anyone.

Most of Waikiki's beautiful white sands are not its own. Tons of sand have been barged in over the years, much of it from Papohaku Beach on Molokai.

As the beachfront developed, landowners haphazardly constructed seawalls and offshore barriers to protect their property. In the process, they blocked the natural forces of sand accretion, and erosion has long been a serious problem at Waikiki.

Sections of the beach are still being replenished with imported sand, although much of it ends up washing into the ocean, where it fills channels and depressions and alters the surf breaks.

Waikiki is good for swimming, boogie boarding, surfing, sailing and other beach activities most of the year. Between May and September, summer swells can make the water a little rough for swimming, but they also make it the best season for surfing. As a consequence of all the activity and alterations, Waikiki beaches simply aren't that good for snorkeling; the best of them is Sans Souci.

There are lifeguards and showers at many places along the beach.

Kahanamoku Beach Kahanamoku Beach, fronting the Hilton Hawaiian Village, is the westernmost section of Waikiki. It was named for Duke Kahanamoku, a surfer and swimmer who won Olympic gold in the 100-meter freestyle in 1912 and went on to become a Hawaiian celebrity.

Kahanamoku Beach is protected by a breakwater at one end and a pier at the other, with a coral reef running between the two. It's a calm swimming area.

Fort DeRussy Beach One of the least-crowded Waikiki beaches, Fort DeRussy Beach borders 1800 feet of the Fort De-

Russy Military Reservation. Like all beaches in Hawaii, it's public; the federal government provides lifeguards. This beach offers an alternative to frying on the sand, as it has a grassy lawn partially shaded by trees, as well as arbored picnic shelters.

The water is usually calm and good for swimming. When conditions are right, the beach is used by windsurfers, boogie boarders and board surfers. There are two beach huts, open daily, that rent windsurfing equipment, boogie boards, kayaks and snorkel sets.

Gray's Beach Gray's Beach, the local name for the beach near the Halekulani Hotel, was named for a boarding house called Gray's-by-the-Sea that stood on the site in the 1920s. On the same stretch of beach was the original Halekulani, a lovely low-rise mansion that was converted into a hotel in the 1930s. In more recent times, the mansion gave way to the present high-rise hotel.

Because the seawall in front of the Halekulani was built so close to the waterline, the part of the beach fronting the hotel is often totally submerged.

The section of beach that stretches between the Halekulani and the Royal Hawaiian Hotel varies in width from season to season, changing with the tides. The waters off the beach are shallow and calm.

Central Waikiki Beach The area between the Royal Hawaiian Hotel and the Waikiki Beach Center is the busiest section of the whole beach and has a nice spread of sand for sunbathing.

Most of the beach has a shallow bottom with a gradual slope. While the swimming's pretty good here, there are also a lot of catamarans, surfers and plenty of other swimmers in the water. Keep your eyes open.

Queen's Surf and Canoe's Surf, Waikiki's best-known surf breaks, are offshore.

Waikiki Beach Center The area opposite the Hyatt Regency Waikiki is the site of the Waikiki Beach Center, which includes rest rooms, showers, a police station, surfboard lockers and rental concessions.

The **Wizard Stones of Kapaemahu** – four boulders on the Diamond Head side of the Waikiki police station – are said to contain the secrets and healing powers of four sorcerers, named Kapaemahu, Kinohi, Kapuni and Kahaloa, who visited from Tahiti in ancient times. Before returning to their homeland, they transferred their powers to these stones.

Just east of the stones is a bronze **statue of Duke Kahanamoku** (1890-1968), Hawaii's most decorated athlete, standing with one of his longboards. Considered the 'father of modern surfing,' Duke, who lived in Waikiki, gave surfing demonstrations on beaches around the world, from Sydney, Australia, to Rockaway Beach, New York. Many local surfers took issue with the placement of the

From Swamp to Resort

At the turn of the century, Waikiki was almost entirely wetlands. It had more than 50 acres of fishponds as well as extensive taro patches and rice paddies. Fed by mountain streams from the upland Manoa and Makiki Valleys, Waikiki was one of Oahu's most fertile and productive areas, generating high yields for the region's farmers.

By the late 19th century, Waikiki's narrow beachfront was lined with gingerbread-trimmed cottages, built by Honolulu's more well-to-do citizens.

Robert Louis Stevenson, who frequented Waikiki in those days, wrote:

If anyone desires such old-fashioned things as lovely scenery, quiet, pure air, clear sea water, heavenly sunsets hung out before his eyes over the Pacific and the distant hills of Waianae, I recommend him to Waikiki Beach.

Tourism took root in 1901, when the Moana opened its doors as Waikiki's first real hotel. A tram line was constructed to connect Waikiki to downtown Honolulu, and city folk crowded aboard for the beach. Tiring quickly of the pesky mosquitoes that thrived in the wetlands, these early beachgoers petitioned to have Waikiki's 'swamps' brought under control.

In 1922, the Ala Wai Canal was dug to divert the streams that flowed into Waikiki. Old Hawaii lost out, as farmers had the water drained out from under them. Coral rubble was used to fill the ponds, creating what was to become Hawaii's most valuable piece of real estate. Water buffaloes soon were replaced by tourists.

Waikiki's second hotel, the Royal Hawaiian, was built in 1927 and became the crown jewel of the Matson Navigation Company. The Royal was the land component for cruises on the *Malolo*, one of the premier luxury ships of the day. The $7.5-million ship, built while the $2-million hotel was under construction, carried 650 passengers from San Francisco to Honolulu each fortnight. The Pink Palace, as the Royal Hawaiian was nicknamed, opened with an extravagant $10-a-plate dinner.

Hotel guests ranged from the Rockefellers to Charlie Chaplin, Babe Ruth to royalty. Some of the guests brought dozens of trunks, their servants and even their Rolls Royces.

The Great Depression put a damper on things, and WWII saw the Royal Hawaiian turned into an R&R center for servicemen.

Waikiki had 1400 hotel rooms in 1950. In those days, surfers could drive their cars to the beach and park on the sand. In the 1960s, tourism took over in earnest and by 1968 Waikiki had 13,000 hotel rooms. By 1988, that number had more than doubled.

The lack of available land has finally halted the boom. In a desperate attempt to squeeze in one more high-rise, St Augustine's Catholic Church, standing on the last speck of uncommercialized property along busy Kalakaua Ave, was nearly sold to a Tokyo developer for $45 million. It took a community uproar and a petition to the Vatican to nullify the deal.

statue, as Duke is standing with his back to the sea, a position they say he never would have assumed in real life. In response, the city moved the statue as close to the sidewalk as possible.

Kuhio Beach Park Kuhio Beach Park is marked on its east end by Kapahulu Groin, a walled storm drain with a walkway on top that juts out into the ocean.

A low breakwater seawall runs about 1300 feet out from Kapahulu Groin, paralleling the beach. It was built to control sand erosion, and in the process two nearly enclosed swimming pools were formed. Local kids walk out on the breakwater, which is called The Wall, but it can be dangerous to the uninitiated due to a slippery surface and breaking surf.

The pool closest to Kapahulu Groin is best for swimming, with the water near the breakwater reaching depths of 5 feet and greater. However, because circulation is limited the water gets murky with a noticeable film of suntan oil. The 'Watch Out Deep Holes' sign refers to holes in the pool's sandy bottom that can be created by swirling currents. Those who can't swim should be cautious in the deeper areas of the pool, as the holes can take waders by surprise.

The park, incidentally, is named after Prince Kuhio, who maintained his residence on this beach. His house was torn down in 1936, 14 years after his death, in order to expand the beach. Between the old-timers who gather each afternoon to play chess and cribbage at Kuhio's sidewalk pavilions and the kids boogie boarding off the Groin, this section of the beach has as much local color as tourist influence.

The city has recently approved a controversial plan to remove one lane of Kalakaua Ave along this area and bring in more sand to extend Kuhio Beach Park inland a few more feet. If city officials follow through with it, expect plenty of noise and disruption during the project.

Kapahulu Groin Kapahulu Groin is one of Waikiki's hottest boogie-boarding spots. If the surf's high enough, you're sure to find a few dozen boogie boarders, mostly teenage boys, riding the waves.

The kids ride straight for the wall and then veer away at the last moment, drawing 'oohs' and 'ahs' from the tourists who gather to watch them. Kapahulu Groin is also a great place to catch sunsets, so you might consider taking a stroll at dusk.

Kapiolani Beach Park Kapiolani Beach Park starts at Kapahulu Groin and extends down to the Natatorium, beyond Waikiki Aquarium.

Queen's Surf is the name given to the wide midsection of Kapiolani Beach. The stretch in front of the pavilion is a popular beach with the gay community. It's a pretty decent area for swimming, with a sandy bottom. The beach between Queen's Surf and Kapahulu Groin is shallow and has a lot of broken coral.

LEE FOSTER

Duke Kahanamoku and his beloved board

Kapiolani Beach Park is a relaxed place with little of the frenzy of activity found in front of the central strip of Waikiki hotels. It's a popular weekend picnicking spot for local families who unload the kids to splash in the water as they line up the barbecue grills.

There's a big grassy field, good for spreading out a beach towel and unpacking a picnic basket. Free parking is available near the beach along Kalakaua Ave. There are rest rooms and showers at the Queen's Surf pavilion. The surfing area offshore is called Public's.

Natatorium The run-down Natatorium, at the Diamond Head end of Kapiolani Beach, is a 100-meter-long saltwater swimming pool built after WWI as a memorial for soldiers who died in that war. There were once hopes of hosting an Olympics on Oahu, with this pool as the focal point. Although that never happened, two Olympic gold medalists – Johnny Weissmuller and Duke Kahanamoku – both trained in this tide-fed pool.

The Natatorium, which is listed on the National Register of Historic Places, has long been closed and in disrepair, but after years of debate the city has recently allocated $11 million to restore the facility.

Sans Souci Beach Down by the New Otani Kaimana Beach Hotel, Sans Souci is a nice little sandy beach away from the main tourist scene. Despite being off by itself, it too has outdoor showers and a lifeguard station.

Many residents come to Sans Souci to swim their daily laps. A shallow coral reef close to shore makes for calm, protected waters and provides reasonably good snorkeling. More coral can be found by following the Kapua Channel as it cuts through the reef, although beware of currents that can pick up in the channel. Check conditions with the lifeguard before venturing out.

Royal Hawaiian Hotel
The Royal Hawaiian, Hawaii's first luxury hotel, is worth a look even if you're not staying there. With its pink turrets and

Moorish architecture, it's a throwback to the era when Rudolph Valentino was *the* romantic idol and travel to Hawaii was by luxury liner.

The hotel was originally on a 20-acre coconut grove, but over the years the grounds have been chipped away by a huge shopping center on one side and a gigantic high-rise hotel on the other. The Royal Hawaiian is a survivor.

Inside, the hotel is lovely and airy, with high ceilings and chandeliers and everything in rose colors. The small garden at the rear is filled with birdsong, a rare sound in most of Waikiki.

Fort DeRussy
Fort DeRussy Military Reservation is a US Army post used mainly as a recreation center for the armed forces. This large chunk of Waikiki real estate was acquired by the US Army a few years after Hawaii was annexed to the USA. Prior to that it was swampy marshland and a favorite duck-hunting spot for Hawaiian royalty. The Hale Koa Hotel on the property is open only to military personnel, but there's public access to the beach and the adjacent military museum. The section of Fort DeRussy between Kalia Rd and Kalakaua Ave has public footpaths that provide a shortcut between the two roads.

US Army Museum of Hawaii Battery Randolph, a reinforced concrete building erected in 1911 as a coastal artillery battery, houses the army museum at Fort DeRussy. The battery once held two formidable 14-inch disappearing guns with an 11-mile range that were designed to recoil down into the concrete walls for reloading after each firing. A 55-ton lead counterweight would then return the carriage to position.

The battery now exhibits a wide collection of weapons, from Hawaiian shark-tooth clubs to WWII tanks, as well as exhibits on military history as it relates to Hawaii told through dioramas, scale models and period photos. There are historic displays on King Kamehameha and Hawaii's role in WWII. It's open from 10 am to 4:15 pm daily, except

Monday, Christmas and New Year's Day. Admission is free.

Oceanarium
The Pacific Beach Hotel, 2490 Kalakaua Ave, houses a very impressive three-story 280,000-gallon aquarium that forms the backdrop for two of the hotel restaurants. Even if you're not dining there, you can view the aquarium quite easily from the hotel lobby. Divers enter the Oceanarium to feed the tropical fish daily at noon and 1, 6:30 and 8:15 pm.

Damien Museum
St Augustine's Church, off Kalakaua Ave and Ohua Ave, is a quiet little sanctuary in the midst of the hotel district. In the rear of the church a second building houses the modest Damien Museum, honoring Father Damien, the Belgian priest famed for his work at the leprosy colony on Molokai. It has a video presentation on the colony, some interesting historical photos and a few of Damien's personal possessions.

As a befitting tribute to Father Damien's life, the building also houses a lunchtime soup kitchen. Museum hours are 9 am to 3 pm Monday to Friday; entry is free.

Ala Wai Canal
Every dawn, people jog and power-walk along the Ala Wai Canal, which forms the northern boundary of Waikiki. Late in the afternoon, outrigger canoe teams can be seen paddling up and down the canal and out to the Ala Wai Yacht Harbor, offering photo opportunities for passersby.

Kapiolani Park
The nearly 200-acre Kapiolani Park, at the Diamond Head end of Waikiki, was a gift from King Kalakaua to the people of Honolulu in 1877. Hawaii's first public park, it was dedicated to Kalakaua's wife, Queen Kapiolani.

In its early days, horse racing and band concerts were the park's big attractions. Although the racetrack is gone, the concerts continue and Kapiolani Park is still the venue for a range of community activities.

The park contains the Waikiki Aquarium, the Honolulu Zoo, Kapiolani Beach Park, the Kodak Hula Show grounds, the Kapiolani Bandstand and the Waikiki Shell, an outdoor amphitheater that serves as a venue for symphony, jazz and rock concerts. It has sports fields, tennis courts, huge lawns and tall banyan trees.

The Royal Hawaiian Band presents free afternoon concerts nearly every Sunday at the Kapiolani Bandstand. Dance competitions, Hawaiian music concerts and other activities occur at the bandstand throughout the year.

A pleasant park, it's a large enough area to have a lot of quiet space despite all the activity.

Waikiki Aquarium This interesting aquarium (☎ 923-9741), 2777 Kalakaua Ave, dates to 1904 and has recently completed a $3-million makeover.

The aquarium has interactive displays, a mini-theater and an auditorium where visitors can look through a 14-foot glass window at circling sharks.

Outrigger canoes still navigate the Ala Wai Canal.

Tanks re-create various Hawaiian reef habitats, making this a great place to identify fish you've seen while snorkeling or diving. There are black-tip sharks, moray eels, flash-back cuttlefish wavering with pulses of light and rare Hawaiian fish with names like the bearded armorhead and the slingjawed wrasse. There's an interesting variety of exotic marine life as well. In 1985, the aquarium was the first to breed the Palauan chambered nautilus in captivity. A couple of these sea creatures, with their unique spiral chambered shell, are on display. There are also some giant clams from Palau that were less than an inch long when acquired in 1982 and now measure over 2 feet, the largest in the USA.

There's also a touch tank for children, a green sea turtle and three Hawaiian monk seals.

The aquarium is open from 9 am to 5 pm daily, although entry is not allowed after 4:30 pm. Admission is $6 for adults, $4 for senior citizens over 60 and students with ID, $2.50 for children ages 13 to 17 and free for children 12 and under.

Honolulu Zoo The Honolulu Zoo (☎ 971-7171) has undergone extensive renovations that have upgraded it into a respectable city zoo, with some 300 species spread across 42 acres. The highlight is the nicely naturalized African Savanna section, which has lions, cheetahs, white rhinos, giraffes, zebras, hippos and monkeys. The zoo also has an interesting reptile section, a good selection of tropical birds (including some native Hawaiian birds) and a small petting zoo.

It's open from 9 am to 4:30 pm daily except Christmas and New Year's Day. Admission is $6 for adults, $1 for children ages six to 12.

In front of the zoo, there's a large banyan tree that is home to hundreds of white pigeons – escapees from a small group brought to the zoo in the 1940s.

Art in the Park Local artists have been hanging their paintings on the fence that surrounds the zoo for more than 25 years. If you're looking for a painting, this is a good opportunity to buy directly from the artist. The work is on display from 10 am to 4 pm on Saturday and Sunday and from 9 am to noon on Tuesday.

Kodak Hula Show The Kodak Hula Show, off Monsarrat Ave near the Waikiki Shell, is a staged photo opportunity of hula dancers, ti-leaf skirts and ukuleles. The musicians are a group of older ladies who performed at the Royal Hawaiian Hotel in days gone by.

This is the scene in postcards where hula dancers hold up letters forming the words 'Hawaii' and 'Aloha.' The whole thing is quite touristy, although entertaining if you're in the mood, and it's free.

Kodak has been hosting this show since 1939. The benches are set up stadium-style around a grassy stage area with the sun at your back. The idea is for everyone to shoot a lot of film – and it works. Even though Kodak no longer monopolizes the film market, the tradition continues.

Shows are held from 10 to 11:15 am on Tuesday, Wednesday and Thursday. Make an effort to be on time, because once the show starts, latecomers can only enter between acts.

Places to Stay

Waikiki's main beachfront strip, Kalakaua Ave, is largely lined with high-rise hotels and $150-plus rooms. As is the norm in resort areas, most of these hotels cater to package tourists, driving the prices up for individual travelers.

Better values are generally found at the smaller hostelries on the back streets. There are hotels in the Kuhio Ave area and up near the Ala Wai Canal that are as nice as some of the beachfront hotels but half the price. If you don't mind walking 10 minutes to the beach, you can save yourself a bundle.

In many hotels the rooms themselves are the same, with only the views varying; generally the higher the floor, the higher the price. If you're paying extra for a view, you might want to ask to see the room first, as Waikiki certainly doesn't have any truth-in-labeling laws governing when a hotel can call a room 'ocean-view.' While some 'ocean-views' are the real thing, others are merely glimpses of the water as seen through a series of high-rises.

Waikiki has many more hotel rooms than condos. Most of Waikiki's condos are filled with long-term residents and there isn't the proliferation of vacation rental agents as on the Neighbor Islands. The best way to find a condo in Waikiki is to look in the 'Vacation Rentals' section of the daily paper, although the listings can be meager, particularly in the winter.

Places to Stay – Budget

Hostels In addition to the one Hostelling International (HI) hostel, there are a number of private businesses providing hostel-style dormitory accommodations around Waikiki. They all cater to backpackers and draw a fairly international crowd. There are no curfews or other restrictions, except that some of these places, in an effort to avoid taking on local boarders, may require travelers to show a passport or an onward ticket.

Most of the hostels are small-scale, but the newest place to jump into the fray, the Banana Bungalow, is a large operation, with as much capacity as all the other private hostels combined. Whether there will now be enough business to keep all of these hostels operational remains to be seen. And just how the additional competition will play out – whether the smaller places will compete by improving, or take the opposite route and cut back on spending – is another unknown. One thing that is reasonable: expect changes to some of the places that follow.

Banana Bungalow Waikiki Beach (☎ 924-5074, 888-246-7835, fax 924-4119, hires@bananabungalow.com, 2463 Kuhio Ave, Honolulu, HI 96815) is hands-down the most cushy hostel in Hawaii. It occupies a modern mid-rise building on Kuhio Ave, convenient to the bus and about a five-minute walk from the beach. Run by a small mainland chain, the place is a cross between a hostel and a hotel, with about 25 rooms that each have six to eight dorm beds and 35 other rooms set aside as private accommo-

dations. All rooms, whether dorm or private, have a bathroom, balcony, phone, cable TV and air-con. There's a choice of coed or same-sex dorms. Guests have use of kitchen facilities, a big-screen TV, a coin laundry and computers with Internet access ($1 per 10 minutes). Inexpensive barbecues are held three nights a week and there's a daily tour to Hanauma Bay, Pearl Harbor or a hiking destination for $3 to $7. Boogie boards, surfboards and snorkel gear can be borrowed for free. Dorm beds cost $16, while private rooms, with one king or two twin beds, start at $60; tax is included. MasterCard and Visa are accepted. Free airport transportation is available. For more information, visit the website www.bananabungalow.com.

Hostelling International Waikiki (☎ 926-8313, fax 922-3798, 2417 Prince Edward St, Honolulu, HI 96815) is a 60-bed hostel on a back street a few short blocks from Waikiki Beach. Like many of the Waikiki hostels, it's in an older low-rise apartment complex with the units converted for hosteling mainly by adding extra beds – often in what used to be the living room. Dorm beds cost $16. There are also four rooms for couples at $40, with small refrigerators and private bathrooms. For the private rooms, paid reservations or a credit card hold are required. The hostel office stays open from 7 am to 3 am. Unlike most HI hostels, there's no daytime dormitory lockout and a group kitchen is accessible throughout the day. Four parking spaces are available at $5 a day. Occasionally, you can get a bed as a walk-in, but at busy times reservations are often necessary two to three weeks in advance. There's a maximum stay of seven nights and a $3 surcharge if you're not an HI member; HI membership can be purchased on-site for $25 for Americans, $18 for foreign visitors. MasterCard and Visa credit cards are accepted.

InterClub Hostel Waikiki (☎ 924-2636, fax 922-3993, 2413 Kuhio Ave, Honolulu, HI 96815) is a well-established private hostel that has recently scaled back its capacity. Bunk beds are arranged five to eight to a room; each room has its own refrigerator and bathroom. To stay here, you officially need a passport and an onward ticket out of Hawaii. There's a lounge and TV room, a washer/dryer and lockers. One drawback is that the building is right on heavily trafficked Kuhio Ave so it may be noisy for light sleepers. Dorm beds cost $15. The hostel also has a few simple private rooms for $45 with linoleum floors, refrigerators, balconies and private baths.

Hawaiian Seaside Hostel (☎ 924-3306, fax 923-2110, reservations@hawaiianseaside .com, 419 Seaside Ave, Honolulu, HI 96815) occupies an aging two-story apartment building set back in an alley off Seaside Ave. The place is run-down and the mattresses are seasoned, but it has a travelers' atmosphere and cheap rates. Small dorm rooms with six bunk beds cost $12 per bed, or you can opt for a semiprivate room that accommodates two people for $15 per person. Discounts, equivalent to roughly one night free, are available on weekly stays. There's an open-air courtyard with a pool table, cable TV and a common kitchen; limited watersports equipment can be borrowed for free. The hostel has three online computers ($3 per 30 minutes) with fast cable connections to the Internet. It's only about a 10-minute walk from Waikiki Beach. You can make reservations with the hostel at the website www.hawaiianseaside.com.

A short walk from the beach is the *Polynesian Hostel Beachclub* (☎ 922-1340, fax 923-4146, reservation@hostelhawaii.com, 2584 Lemon Rd, Honolulu, HI 96815), which occupies a small three-story apartment complex on a side street behind the Queen Kapiolani Hotel. There are a variety of sleeping arrangements. You can get a bunk bed in a small dorm (four to six people) for $16.75; a bedroom in a two-bedroom apartment at $32/38 for singles/doubles; or a fully private studio with a kitchen for $50 a double. Each apartment has its own bathroom, but only the studios have private kitchens. There's a common room with a full kitchen, a laundry area and occasional activities. Boogie boards and snorkel sets can be borrowed for free. Parking is available for $5. The biggest drawback is the noise – particularly the garbage trucks that make their

clangorous rounds on Lemon Rd around dawn. For more details, visit the website www.HostelHawaii.com.

The nearby *Waikiki Beachside Hostel* (☎ 923-9566, fax 923-7525, hokondo@ aol.com, 2556 Lemon Rd, suite B101, Honolulu, HI 96815) is another small condo complex that's been converted into hostelstyle accommodations. It has dorm beds from $15 to $18 and private rooms for around $55. The units each have a refrigerator, oven and private bath. It's not fancy but it has a higher standard of cleanliness than most of the other small hostels.

On the opposite end of Waikiki is *Island Hostel* (☎/fax 942-8748, 1946 Ala Moana Blvd, Honolulu, HI 96815), which has about 20 studio rooms in Hawaiian Colony, an apartment building that's been tidied up after years of neglect. All of the hostel rooms have TV, hot plates and a private bath. The dorm beds are in older rooms that can feel a bit confined, but there are only four people to a room and they're a notch above some of the competition. Nearly half of the rooms have been upgraded with new tile floors and fresh paint; these have been converted into private rooms, most with one single and one double bed, though at least one has bunk beds. The cost for a dorm bed is $16.50, tax included; there's a small discount for weekly stays. The renovated private rooms cost $55, while older rooms cost $50; private room prices can fluctuate a bit with the season and if things are slow you might be able to work out a better deal. Although a bit farther than other hostels from the beach, it's still within walking distance and, on the plus side, the beach at this end of Waikiki is less crowded. Credit cards are accepted.

Hotels *Hale Pua Nui* (☎ 923-9693, fax 923-9678, 228 Beach Walk, Honolulu, HI 96815) is an older four-story building with 22 studio apartments. It's strictly a budget place, and the rooms are wearworn, but each has two twin beds, a kitchenette, fan, air-con, TV and phone – and the beach is but a five-minute walk away. Rates are $45/57 in the low/high season and there are discounts for stays of two weeks or more. When things are slow, boarders are divided between locals and tourists, but in winter it packs full with visitors, particularly Canadians.

So many retirees return each winter to the 85-room **Royal Grove Hotel** (☎ 923-7691, fax 922-7508, rghawaiii@gte.net, 151 Uluniu Ave, Honolulu, HI 96815) that it can be a challenge to get a room in the high season without advance reservations. In the oldest wing there are small $43 rooms that have no air-con and are streetside and exposed to traffic noise. The main wing has $57 rooms that are straightforward but perfectly adequate with air-con and *lanais* (verandas). Both types of rooms have a double and two single beds, TV, kitchenette and private bath. This is an older, no-frills hotel, but unlike other places in this category it has a small pool.

A decent low-end value is the **Waikiki Prince Hotel** (☎ 922-1544, fax 924-3712, 2431 Prince Edward St, Honolulu, HI 96815), which has 24 units in a six-story building just next door to Hostelling International Waikiki. The rooms are simple but clean and have air-con, TV and private bath. There are small double rooms for $40 and larger rooms with kitchenettes for $55. In the low season, the seventh night is free. There's no pool but it's just a couple of minutes' walk to the beach.

Hawaii Polo Inn (☎ 949-0061, 800-669-7719, fax 949-4906, 1696 Ala Moana Blvd, Honolulu, HI 96815), a member of the Marc Resorts chain, is at the westernmost end of Waikiki. The 66 motel-style rooms are lined up in rows with their entrances off a long outdoor corridor. The rooms have been renovated, but they're still straightforward. All have small refrigerators, coffeemakers, phones and TVs; some have lanais, although generally the lanai area is at the expense of room space. The published rates start at $98/109 in the low/high season, but when things are slow, the Polo Inn commonly offers a more attractive discounted rate of $55 to $65, which is certainly a good deal. Request a room in back to minimize the traffic noise from busy Ala Moana Blvd.

Places to Stay – Mid-Range
Waikiki Sand Villa Hotel (☎ 922-4744, 800-247-1903, fax 923-2541, 2375 Ala Wai Blvd, Honolulu, HI 96815) is on the Ala Wai Canal, a 10-minute walk from Waikiki Beach. The 223 rooms are compact and rather ordinary but have TV, refrigerators, air-con, room safes, bathtubs and small lanais, some with views across the golf course toward Manoa Valley. Ask for one of the corner units, which have the best views. Children under 12 stay free, and most rooms have both a double and a twin bed. Standard rooms, which are on the lower floors, cost $74/85 in the low/high season, while upper floors are about $10 more. There are also poolside studios with kitchenettes that can sleep up to four people for $133/148. Rates include a simple continental breakfast. The hotel can be booked from overseas by calling 1800-127-756 in Australia, 0800-440-712 in New Zealand and 0031-11-2858 in Japan.

The nearby **Aloha Surf Hotel** (☎ 923-0222, 800-423-4514, fax 924-7160, 444 Kanekapolei St, Honolulu, HI 96815) should only be considered as a last option, as the rooms are overdue for a renovation. They're also on the small side and lack refrigerators. All 202 rooms have air-con, TVs, phones and room safes. Standard rooms on the two lower floors cost $76/86 in the low/high season. Higher-floor rooms with lanais cost $10 more. There's a swimming pool.

Hotel Honolulu (☎ 926-2766, 800-426-2766, fax 922-3326, hotelhnl@lava.net, 376 Kaiolu St, Honolulu, HI 96815), a quiet oasis set back from busy Kuhio Ave, is Waikiki's only gay hotel. It has the character of an unhurried inn, with helpful management and lots of hanging ferns. The 19 main units are decorated with flair, each with its own theme, and these are large and comfortable, with lanais, kitchens, ceiling fans and air-con. Studios cost $89 to $99, one-bedroom units cost $109 to $119. There are also five smaller, non-theme studios in an adjacent building for $75. Coffee is free and there's a sundeck but no pool.

The 451-room **Ocean Resort Hotel Waikiki** (☎ 922-3861, 800-367-2317, fax 924-1982, 175 Paoakalani Ave, Honolulu, HI 96815), a former Quality Inn, hosts a fair number of people on low-end package tours. Nonetheless the rooms have the same amenities as more expensive hotels, with air-con, cable TV, phones, refrigerators and room safes. Nonsmoking rooms are available on request and there are two pools. The published rate for the standard rooms is $93/103 in the low/high season, while moderate rooms, which are larger and on higher floors, cost $125/135. When things are slow, the hotel sometimes offers walk-in rates that can drop as low as $55.

Ilima Hotel (☎ 923-1877, 800-367-5172, fax 924-8371, mail@ilima.com, 445 Nohonani St, Honolulu, HI 96815) is a smaller hotel in a less hurried section of Waikiki, about a 10-minute walk from the beach. All 99 units are roomy and light with large lanais, two double beds, tasteful rattan furnishings, cable TV with HBO and kitchens with an oven, microwave and full-size refrigerator. The staff is friendly, the lobby has interesting Hawaiiana murals and there's a small heated pool and fitness room. Popular with business travelers and other return visitors, the Ilima offers free local phone calls and free parking, a rarity in Waikiki. Rates vary according to the floor, although the rooms themselves are the same. High-season rates start at $102/107 for singles/doubles in studios on the 4th floor and rise to $122/127 for studios on the 10th to 16th floors. There are also some one- and two-bedroom suites for $152 and $197 respectively. All rates are $12 less from April to mid-December. To see pictures of the hotel, go to www.ilima.com online.

Patrick Winston owns 14 pleasant units in the *Hawaiian King Hotel* (☎ 922-3894, 800-545-1948 (daytime), winston@iav.com, 417 Nohonani St, suite 409, Honolulu, HI 96815). Each has one bedroom with either a queen or two twin beds, a living room, TV, phone, air-con, ceiling fans, a lanai and a kitchen with microwave, refrigerator and hot plate. Many also have an oven, some have a washer/dryer and all include thoughtful touches. Although it's an older complex, a lot of money has gone into these units, and the spiffy decor places the hotel on a par with pricier

places. There's a courtyard pool. Rates are $109 to $119 in the high season and $20 less in the low season; ask about discounts, as Patrick can sometimes fill last-minute vacancies at lower rates. There's a four-day minimum stay. There are also some unrenovated rooms that are cheaper at $65/85 in the low/high season.

The Breakers (☎ 923-3181, 800-426-0494, fax 923-7174, 250 Beach Walk, Honolulu, HI 96815) is a friendly, older low-rise hotel with 64 units surrounding a courtyard pool. While some of the units are a bit wearworn, they are otherwise comfortable. The regular rooms each have a double bed, a single bed and a kitchenette and cost $91 on the ground floor without a lanai or $97 on the 2nd floor with a lanai. There are also large suites that have a separate bedroom with a queen bed, a living room that resembles a studio with two twin beds, a full kitchen and a table for four; these cost $130 for two people, $146 for four. Both categories have air-con, TV, room safes and phones. Avoid the rooms closest to Saratoga Rd, which has lots of traffic.

A member of Castle Resorts & Hotels, the 313-room *Queen Kapiolani Hotel* (☎ 922-1941, 800-533-6970, fax 922-2694, 150 Kapahulu Ave, Honolulu, HI 96815) is a 19-story hotel at the quieter Diamond Head end of Waikiki. This older hotel has an aging regal theme: chandeliers, high ceilings and faded paintings of Hawaiian royalty. Standard rooms cost $107/120 in the low/high season. However, rooms are anything but standard and vary greatly in size, with some very pleasant and others so small they barely accommodate a bed. The simplest way to avoid a closet-size space is to request a room with two twin beds instead of a single queen. Also, be sure to get a room without interconnecting doors, which can act like a sound tunnel to the next room. Some of the ocean-view rooms, which cost $40 more, have lanais with fine unobstructed views of Diamond Head.

The 20-story *Waikiki Resort Hotel* (☎ 922-4911, 800-367-5116, fax 922-9468, 2460 Koa Ave, Honolulu, HI 96815) is a Korean-owned hotel with a Korean restaurant. Not surprisingly, it books heavily with Korean travelers on package tours. Its clean, modern rooms have mini-refrigerators, TVs, phones, air-con, room safes and lanais. The regular rates begin at $108; a room and car deal is available for an additional $10.

The 200-room *Holiday Inn Waikiki* (☎ 955-1111, 888-924-5454, fax 947-1799, 1830 Ala Moana Blvd, Honolulu, HI 96815) is a recommendable mid-range hotel at the western end of Waikiki. Rooms are modern and comfortable with either two double beds or one king bed, a desk, room safe, TV, refrigerator, coffeemaker and a bathroom with a tub and hair dryer. Some also have lanais. Rates depend on the floor and range from $117 to $130, but there are numerous discounts including an ongoing promotion called 'Great Rates' that takes 15% off. There's a pool and sundeck, and the beach is about a 10-minute walk away. Unlike most hotels on busy Ala Moana Blvd, the Holiday Inn is set back from the road, so it tends to be notably quieter. For more information, visit the hotel's website at www.holiday-inn-waikiki.com.

An interesting, little-known option is *Imperial of Waikiki* (☎ 923-1827, 800-347-2582, fax 923-7848, 205 Lewers St, Honolulu, HI 96815), a pleasant all-suite time-share that rents out unfilled rooms on a space-available basis. It's a good value, especially considering it's directly opposite the Halekulani, Waikiki's most exclusive hotel, and just a two-minute walk from the beach. A studio with a double pull-down bed, queen sofa bed, toaster, coffeemaker, microwave and refrigerator costs $99 for up to two people. A small one-bedroom suite with a kitchenette, a queen bed in the bedroom and a pull-down bed and queen sofa bed in the living room costs $119 for up to four people. There are also roomier one-bedroom suites with two baths and full kitchens for $20 more and well-equipped two-bedroom, two-bath units for $189 for up to five people. There's a pool and a 24-hour front desk. All prices are $10 less in the low season.

The *Coconut Plaza Hotel* (☎ 923-8828, 800-882-9696, fax 923-3473, 450 Lewers St, Honolulu, HI 96815) is a quiet 80-room hotel near Ala Wai Blvd. The rooms have contemporary decor and are comfortable enough, though they're on the small side. Rooms with refrigerators, microwaves, TV, air-con and lanais cost $110, while those that add on a two-burner stove cost $160. There are various promotions, including senior discounts, that can lower these rates. A simple continental breakfast is provided. To see pictures of the hotel, visit www.coconutplaza.com online.

Waikiki Circle Hotel (☎ 923-1571, 800-922-7866, fax 926-8024, 2464 Kalakaua Ave, Honolulu, HI 96815), booked through the Aston chain, is a small hotel with a good central location opposite the beach. It has 104 rooms on 13 floors, all with lanais, two double beds, room safes, phones, TVs and air-con. The hotel is older but has been renovated and the rooms are comfortable. This circular building has a back room on each floor that's called 'city view' and costs $120; while you can't see the ocean, these are farther from the road and quieter. Each floor also has two rooms with partial ocean views for $135 and five rooms with unobstructed ocean views for $150. All rates are $20 more from Christmas through March and in July and August. Request one of the upper-floor rooms, which have the same rates but better views.

Waikiki Grand (☎ 923-1511, 800-535-0085, fax 923-4708, marc@aloha.net, 134 Kapahulu Ave, Honolulu, HI 96815) is a 173-room hotel opposite the zoo. The rooms are rather small and ordinary, but they have the standard amenities: TV, phone, air-con, mini-refrigerator and coffeemaker. The hotel has a pool. The rack rates listed in the hotel brochure are a pricey $129 for a standard room or $149 for a room with a kitchenette, but there are sometimes hefty discounts. The hotel is a member of the Marc Resorts chain.

Pacific Monarch (☎ 923-9805, 800-922-7866, fax 924-3220, 142 Uluniu Ave, Honolulu, HI 96815) is a 34-story condominium hotel. While some of the 216 units are a bit lackluster, they're otherwise adequate spots. The studios are roomy, each with a table, desk, double bed, sofa bed, small refrigerator and two-burner hot plate. The one-bedroom units have a small bedroom and a living space with a full kitchen, a dining table for four, a sofa bed and a large lanai. Aston is the rental agent for more than half of the units, with low-/high-season rates set at $125/145 for a studio and $160/180 for a one-bedroom unit. Up to four people can stay at these rates. Ask about promotions, as this property sometimes has rates as low as $85, at which time it's a more attractive option. Aston's website is www.aston-hotels.com.

The *New Otani Kaimana Beach Hotel* (☎ 923-1555, 800-356-8264, fax 922-9404, kaimana@pixi.com, 2863 Kalakaua Ave, Honolulu, HI 96815) is right on Sans Souci Beach on the quieter Diamond Head side of Waikiki. Popular with return visitors, it's a pleasantly low-key place with 125 units. Room rates start at $125/140 in the low/high season; studios with kitchenettes start at $150/165. All have air-con, TV, refrigerators and lanais.

Outrigger Hotels Over the years, the Outrigger (PO Box 88559, Honolulu, HI 96830) chain has snapped up and renovated many of Waikiki's middle-range hotels; at last count it had 21. Overall it's a well-run and fairly good-value chain, although there's a wide range in both price and quality. At any rate, with one phone call you can check on the availability of 25% of the hotel rooms in Waikiki!

Ask about promotional deals when making reservations – currently, these include a 'Free Ride' program, which provides a free Budget rental car when you book at the regular room rate; a 'First Night Free' on stays of six nights; and a 20% 'Island Hopper' discount on stays of seven consecutive nights at any combination of the chain's Waikiki and Neighbor Island hotels. Travelers aged 50 and older are entitled to a discount of 20% (25% for AARP members). In addition, some Outrigger hotels offer 50% discounts to members of the Encore and Entertainment travel clubs.

All Outrigger rooms have air-con, phone, cable TV, room safe and coffeemaker, and most also have refrigerators. Nonsmoking

rooms are available and children under 18 stay free.

Note that Outrigger is now planning to regroup its low-end properties under the label Ohana Hotels, but these will remain under the same Outrigger umbrella. Reservation details should remain the same.

To book rooms at any Outrigger, you can call ☎ 303-369-7777 or fax 303-369-9403. Outrigger also has the following toll-free numbers: ☎ 800-688-7444 and fax 800-622-4852 from the USA and Canada; ☎ 1-800-688-74443 and fax 1-800-622-48522 from Australia, New Zealand, Hong Kong and the United Kingdom; ☎ 0800-181-8598 from Germany; and ☎ 1-800-688-74443 from Japan. Additional toll-free numbers, via AT&T USA Direct 800 service, are available from many other countries; the local AT&T representative can provide the access number.

To email Outrigger, write reservations@outrigger.com; the chain maintains a web site at www.outrigger.com.

The 303-room *Waikiki Surf* (☎ 923-7671, 2200 Kuhio Ave) has recently been renovated and is one of Outrigger's better deals in the Kuhio area. Standard hotel rooms cost $90 and are small but otherwise quite pleasant; each has a mini-refrigerator, lanai and either one queen or two twin beds. The kitchenette units are a good value; they cost just $5 more but are roomier and have a king or two double beds, a larger refrigerator and either a two-burner hot plate or a microwave. There are also one-bedroom units for up to four people for $140.

If preparing your own meals is a consideration, the *Waikiki Surf East* (☎ 923-7671, 422 Royal Hawaiian Ave), a block north of the Waikiki Surf, is a recommendable place with kitchenettes in all its units. Both the studios and one-bedroom units are large and most have a sofa bed, as well as a regular king or two double beds. Prices are the same for up to four people: $100 for the studios and $140 for the one-bedroom units. The accommodations are superior to many higher-priced Outriggers – the lower price simply reflects the distance from the beach and the fact that the hotel is a converted apartment building with no restaurant or other lobby facilities.

The recently renovated **Ohana Surf** (☎ 922-5777, 2280 Kuhio Ave) has 251 pleasant rooms, each with a lanai, refrigerator and two-burner stove. Rates are $90 on the lower floors and $100 on the higher floors, the latter less prone to catch the drone of traffic on busy Kuhio Ave. Although it's a couple of blocks inland, the rooms are otherwise on par with many beachside hotels charging nearly twice the price.

A curious mid-range option is the **Ala Moana Towers** (☎ 942-7722, 1700 Ala Moana Blvd), a tall, thin high-rise hotel at the western end of Waikiki. Set back a little from Ala Moana Blvd, there's some buffer from traffic noise, and with only four units per floor this narrow 40-story complex is less bustling than most of Waikiki's hotels. The rooms are a bit compact but pleasant and have kitchenettes with a microwave, refrigerator, oven and hot plates. Request one of the upper floors, as these have a splendid view of either the yacht harbor or city. The rate is $100 for a city view and $120 for a ocean view. There's also a fun glass-walled outdoor elevator.

There are a number of Outrigger hotels closer to the water, including the 109-room **Waikiki Coral Seas** (☎ 923-3881, 250 Lewers St), a small hotel popular with return guests. Although Outrigger gives the property its low-end economy rating, the rooms are comfortable and adequately furnished with either one queen or two double beds and even have a lanai. Regular rooms cost $90, kitchenette units $100 and one-bedroom units $130.

Just a stone's throw from the beach is the 184-room **Waikiki Edgewater** (☎ 922-6424, 2168 Kalia Rd). This is an older property with simple but sufficient rooms, each with a small refrigerator and either two twins or a queen bed. Rates are $90 for a standard room and $100 for a kitchenette. Ask for one of the rear rooms, as they tend to be quieter.

The **Waikiki Royal Islander** (☎ 922-1961, 2164 Kalia Rd) is a smaller hotel with 100 rooms, a friendly staff and a good location

just across from Fort DeRussy Beach. The rooms in this 12-story hotel are on the small side but are pleasant and have all the standard amenities. For ocean views, the best rooms are the upper-floor corner ones, all of which end in the numbers 01. The only drawback is that the hotel is on a busy intersection so roadside rooms on the lower floors can be noisy. Rates are $90 to $115, depending upon the view.

The 439-room **Waikiki Tower** (☎ 922-6424, 200 Lewers St) is a high-rise hotel a few minutes' walk from the beach. The rooms are comfortable with a lanai, a small refrigerator and either two doubles or a king bed. The cheapest rates are for rooms from the 12th floor down, which cost $115. Rooms on floors 14 and above are essentially the same but cost $15 more. There are also kitchenette rooms with a microwave starting at $120.

Right on the beach, the 885-room **Outrigger Reef Hotel** (☎ 923-3111, 2169 Kalia Rd) has undergone a $50 million renovation. As might be expected, the rooms are spiffy, albeit without much character, and have the usual 1st-class amenities. Wheelchair-accessible rooms are available and some floors have been designated for nonsmokers only. Rates, which are the same year-round, range from $160 for a non-view room to $325 for an oceanfront room.

Places to Stay – Top End

The following hotels all have standard 1st-class amenities and in-house restaurants. All are on the beach or across the street from it and all have swimming pools.

A good-value top-end hotel is the 298-room **Waikiki Parc Hotel** (☎ 921-7272, 800-422-0450, fax 923-1336, 2233 Helumoa Rd, Honolulu, HI 96815), which is across the street from its more upscale sister, the Halekulani. The hotel has a pleasantly understated elegance. Rooms are average in size but have nice touches like ceramic-tile floors, shuttered lanai doors and bathtubs. Standard rooms cost $175, while the upper-level ocean-view rooms top out at $270. If you book in the mid-range, request the 8th floor, which has larger lanais. The hotel often

OAHU

runs cheaper promotional rates, including a 'park and sunrise' deal that includes breakfast and free parking for $146; a room and car package for $158; and a 25% room-rate discount for those over age 55. For more information, browse the hotel's website at www.waikikiparc.com.

The **Pacific Beach Hotel** (☎ 922-1233, 800-367-6060, fax 922-0129, 2490 Kalakaua Ave, Honolulu, HI 96815) is a high-rise hotel with 831 rooms. The accommodations, while not distinguished, are pleasant with comfortable beds, TVs, phones, room safes, minirefrigerators, lanais and bathrooms with tubs. Nonsmoking rooms are available. There are tennis courts and a fitness center, and the hotel has an impressive three-story aquarium filled with tropical fish. Room rates range from $180 to $300.

The **Hawaiian Regent** (☎ 922-6611, 800-367-5370, fax 921-5222, hwnrgnt@aloha.net, 2552 Kalakaua Ave, Honolulu, HI 96815) is one of Waikiki's largest hotels, with 1346 rooms inside a huge mazelike complex. However, rooms are quite ordinary for the money, with rates ranging from $165 to $270.

The 713-room **Hawaiian Waikiki Beach Hotel** (☎ 922-2511, 800-877-7666, fax 923-3656, 2570 Kalakaua Ave, Honolulu, HI 96815) looks almost like a reflection of the larger Hawaiian Regent across the street, and the rooms are comparable although cheaper. Prices start at $120. The best value is the Mauka Tower, an annex off to the side of the main building, where the rates are at the low end and the rooms are larger and quieter than in the main hotel.

The **Sheraton** pretty much owns a little stretch of the beach, boasting 4400 rooms in its four Waikiki hotels. The toll-free numbers for all of Sheraton's Hawaii hotels are ☎ 800-325-3535 from the USA and Canada, 008-07-3535 from Australia and 1-120-003535 from Japan.

The 1150-room **Sheraton Princess Kaiulani** (☎ 922-5811, fax 923-9912, 120 Kaiulani Ave, Honolulu, HI 96815) is the Sheraton's cheapest Waikiki property. One of Waikiki's older hotels, it was built in the 1950s by Matson Navigation to help develop Waikiki into a middle-class destination, and from the outside it looks rather like an apartment complex. However, the interior is more appealing and the rooms are modern. Rates begin at $195. It's in the busy heart of Waikiki across the street from the beach.

The big, 793-room **Sheraton Moana Surfrider** (☎ 922-3111, fax 923-0308, 2365 Kalakaua Ave, Honolulu, HI 96815) is a special place for those fond of colonial hotels. Erected in 1901, the Moana was Hawaii's first beachfront hotel. It's undergone a $50 million historic restoration, authentic right down to the carved columns on the porte cochere. Despite the fact that modern wings (the 'Surfrider' section) have been attached to the main hotel's flanks, the Moana has survived with much of its original character intact. The lobby is open and airy with high plantation-like ceilings, reading chairs and Hawaiian artwork. The rooms in the original building have been closely restored to their early 1900s appearance. The furnishings are made from a different wood on each floor (koa on the 5th, cherry on the 6th), with TVs and refrigerators hidden behind armoire doors. Rates in the historic wing range from $265 for city views to $405 for ocean views.

The pink Moorish-style **Royal Hawaiian Hotel** (☎ 923-7311, fax 923-8999, 2259 Kalakaua Ave, Honolulu, HI 96815), now a Sheraton property, was Waikiki's first luxury hotel. It's still a beautiful building, cool and airy, and loaded with charm. The historic section maintains a classic appeal, with some of the rooms having quiet garden views. This section is easier to book too, since most guests prefer the modern high-rise wing with its ocean views. Character comes at a price; rates begin at a steep $305 in the historic wing, $475 in the high-rise tower.

Sheraton Waikiki (☎ 922-4422, fax 922-9567, 2255 Kalakaua Ave, Honolulu, HI 96815) is an 1850-room giant hotel that looms over the Royal Hawaiian Hotel. The bustling lobby resembles an exclusive Tokyo shopping center, as it's lined with expensive jewelry stores and boutiques with French names and designer labels. The hotel has central elevators that deposit guests at some of the longest corridors in Hawaii. Rates range from $250 for a city view to $465 for a luxury ocean-view unit.

The beachfront *Hilton Hawaiian Village* (☎ 949-4321, 800-445-8667, fax 947-7898, 2005 Kalia Rd, Honolulu, HI 96815) is Hawaii's largest hotel, with 2545 rooms. The ultimate in mass tourism, it's practically a package-tour city unto itself – entirely self-contained for people who never want to leave the hotel grounds. It's quite a busy place, right down to the roped-off lines at the front desk, which resembles an airline check-in counter. The Hilton is on a nice beach, has some good restaurants and offers free entertainment including Friday-night fireworks. The rooms are modern and comfortable with rates starting at $210 for a garden view, $325 for an ocean view.

Hyatt Regency Waikiki (☎ 923-1234, 800-233-1234, fax 923-7839, 2424 Kalakaua Ave, Honolulu, HI 96815) has twin 40-story towers with 1230 rooms. There's a maximum of 18 rooms per floor, so it's quieter and feels more exclusive than other hotels its size. Rooms are pleasant with rattan furnishings and cost from $240 to $400, depending on the view. Between the towers there's a large atrium with cascading waterfalls and tropical vegetation.

The *Halekulani Hotel* (☎ 923-2311, 800-367-2343, fax 926-8004, 2199 Kalia Rd, Honolulu, HI 96815) is considered by many to be Waikiki's premier hotel. The 456 rooms, which are pleasantly subdued rather than posh, have large balconies, marble vanities, deep tubs for soaking and little touches like bathrobes and fresh flowers. Rooms with garden views cost $295, while those fronting the ocean are $425. Suites start at $700. The hotel has a website at www.halekulani.com.

Places to Eat

Waikiki has no shortage of places to eat, although the vast majority of the cheaper ones are easy to pass up. Generally, the best inexpensive food is found outside Waikiki, where most Honolulu residents live and eat. Waikiki's top-end restaurants, on the other hand, are some of the island's best, though they can quickly burn a hole in your wallet.

Places to Eat – Budget

For inexpensive bakery items, try the *Patisserie*, which has a branch at 2330 Kuhio Ave beside the Wakiki West hotel, and another at 2168 Kalia Rd in the lobby of the Waikiki Edgewater. Both are open from at least 6:30 am to 9 pm daily and have reasonably priced pastries, croissants, bread and coffee. If you want to eat in, there's a small sit-down area where you can get standard breakfast items, sandwiches and deli salads.

Fatty's Chinese Kitchen (2345 Kuhio Ave) is a hole-in-the-wall eatery in an alley at the west side of the Miramar hotel. It serves up some of the cheapest food to be found in these parts, with rice or chow mein plus one hot entree for only $3.50. Add $1 for each additional entree. Despite the low cost, the food is good – on par with Chinese restaurants elsewhere charging twice the price. The atmosphere is purely local, with a dozen stools lining a long bar and the cook on the other side chopping away. Fatty's is open from 10:30 am to 10:30 pm daily.

At the northwest corner of the *International Market Place* there's a food court with about two dozen stalls selling cinnamon buns, shave ice, frozen yogurt, pizza, sandwiches and various plate lunches, including Korean, Chinese, Mexican and Greek – nothing really notable, but it is cheap. There's a *Häagen-Dazs* ice cream shop on Kalakaua Ave just east of the International Market Place.

Moose McGillycuddy's (310 Lewers St) has 20 types of omelettes for $4.95 each, but the best deal is the early-bird special (7:30 to 8:30 am) of two eggs, bacon and toast for $1.99. The restaurant also has an extensive menu of burgers, sandwiches, Mexican food, salads and drinks at moderate prices. It's open for meals from 7:30 am to 9:30 pm daily, with breakfast served to 11 am. There's music and dancing nightly until at least 2 am.

Tenteko Mai (2126 Kalakaua Ave) is an unpretentious little place with good authentic Japanese ramen for $7.50. The tasty grilled dumplings called gyoza cost $4 a half dozen. The scene feels like a neighborhood eatery in Tokyo, with the seating at stools around a U-shaped bar and fellow diners chatting away in Japanese. Tenteko Mai is open from 11 am to midnight daily.

A bit cheaper, but also a notch down in quality, is the nearby *Curry House Coco Ichibanya (2136 Kalakaua Ave)*, which has Japanese-style curry-rice dishes for $5 to $7. It's open 11 am to midnight daily.

The two *Perry's Smorgy* restaurants, one at the Waikiki Coral Seas hotel at 250 Lewers St and the other at 2380 Kuhio Ave on the corner of Kanekapolei St, offer inexpensive all-you-can-eat buffets. Breakfast (7 to 11 am) includes pancakes, eggs, ham, coffee and fresh fruit. It's a tourist crowd

Breakfast Ideas

Signs draped from buildings advertising breakfast specials for $2 to $4 are commonplace. *Eggs 'n Things (1911 Kalakaua Ave)* and *Moose McGillycuddy's (310 Lewers St)* both have perennial breakfast specials.

Food Pantry (2370 Kuhio Ave) has a doughnut counter, while the nearby *Patisserie (2330 Kuhio Ave)* has a full bakery that serves various pastries and a few inexpensive egg dishes.

Fast-food chains like *Jack in the Box*, *McDonald's* and *Burger King* offer quick, cheap breakfasts from just about every other corner. If you're really hungry and not too demanding of quality, the $5 all-you-can-eat breakfast buffet at *Perry's Smorgy* (250 Lewers St and 2380 Kuhio Ave) is a good deal.

For $10 to $20, you can try one of the all-you-can-eat breakfast buffets that many of the larger hotels offer, but few are worth the money. A couple of noteworthy exceptions, both with ocean-view dining, are the simple breakfast buffet ($7) at the *Shore Bird Broiler (2169 Kalia Rd)*, in the Outrigger Reef Hotel, and the more elaborate spread ($10) at *Duke's Canoe Club (2335 Kalakaua Ave)*, in the Outrigger Waikiki Hotel.

and the food is cafeteria quality, but it's hard to beat the $4.99 price. Lunch, which includes a reasonable fruit and salad bar as well as simple hot dishes like fried chicken, is served from 11:30 am to 2:30 pm and costs $5.99. Dinner (5 to 9 pm) adds on a round of beef and costs $8.99. If it's convenient, opt for the Kuhio Ave location, as it has a surprisingly pleasant gardenlike setting.

Eggs 'n Things (1911 Kalakaua Ave) is a busy all-nighter, open from 11 am to 2 pm daily. It specializes in breakfast fare, with a variety of waffles, pancakes, crepes and omelettes priced from $5 to $8, though the most popular deal is the 'early riser' special of three pancakes and two eggs that's offered from 5 to 9 am for just $3.

Also at the west side of Waikiki is *Pho Tri (478 Ena Rd)*, which specializes in pho, a Vietnamese noodle soup spiced with fresh green basil. A large bowl of chicken or beef pho costs $6, as do various rice plates. Pho Tri is open 10 am to 10 pm daily.

Ezogiku (2546 Lemon Rd, but entered on Paoakalani) is a little noodle shop that's part of a Tokyo chain eatery. The food is not spectacular, but the prices are reasonable, with ramen from $6.50, gyoza for $3.75. Ezogiku is open 11 am to midnight daily.

American fast-food chains are well represented in Waikiki: there are three *Burger King*, four *McDonald's* and six *Jack in the Box* restaurants, the latter open 24 hours. In addition to the usual menus, they add some island touches, such as passion-fruit juice, saimin and Portuguese sausage. All three chains usually have discount coupons in the free tourist magazines.

Kapahulu Ave There's a group of cheap neighborhood restaurants along Kapahulu Ave, the road that starts in Waikiki near the zoo and runs up to the H-1 Fwy.

One favorite is *Irifune's* (☎ 737-1141, 563 Kapahulu Ave), a funky little joint decorated with Japanese country kitsch. Alcohol is not served, but you can bring in beer from the nearby liquor store. The gyoza is a good appetizer at $3.50. The combination dinners (around $10) include tempura and options such as tataki ahi, a delicious fresh tuna that's seared lightly on the outside, sashimi-like inside, and served with a tangy sauce. Lunch specials begin at $7.50. Although few tourists come up this way, the restaurant is locally popular. You might have to wait 30 minutes to be seated at dinner, but it's well worth it. Irifune's is open 11:30 am to 1:30 pm and 5:30 to 9:30 pm Tuesday to Saturday.

Ono Hawaiian Food (726 Kapahulu Ave) is *the* place in the greater Waikiki area to sample Hawaiian food served Hawaiian-style. It's a simple diner, but people line up outside waiting to get in. For $7.75, you can select plates of either kalua pig or *laulau*, pork or beef that has been wrapped in ti leaves and steamed. Both come with pipikaula, lomi salmon and haupia with rice or poi. Ono is open 11 am to 7:30 pm Monday to Saturday.

New Kapahulu Chop Suey (730 Kapahulu Ave) serves big plates of Chinese food. The combination special lunch plate costs just $4.15, the special dinner $5, while a score of other dishes are under $6. While it's certainly not gourmet, it's a lot of food for the money. New Kapahulu is open 11 am to 9 pm daily.

KC Drive Inn (1029 Kapahulu Ave), farther up the road near the freeway, features Ono Ono malts (a combination of chocolate and peanut butter that tastes like a liquefied Reese's Peanut Butter Cup) for $2.50 and waffle dogs (a hot dog wrapped in a waffle) for $2, as well as inexpensive plate lunches, breakfast fare, burgers and saimin for either eat-in or takeout. A local favorite since the 1930s, this spot is open from 6 am to at least 11:30 pm daily.

If you're on foot, *Rainbow Drive-In*, at the intersection of Kapahulu and Kanaina Aves, is much closer to central Waikiki, has similar fast food and just as much of a following. It's open daily from 7:30 am to 9 pm.

Coffee Haven (☎ 732-2090, sip@coffee-haven .com, 1026 Kapahulu Ave) is a friendly little Internet cafe that makes a pleasant breakfast stop even if you don't need to check your email. It has coffee, scones, salads and sandwiches, as well as delicious homemade cherry and apple pies for $1.85 a slice. Internet

access costs $4 an hour on Macs, $6 an hour on PCs, with a 50¢ minimum.

Grocery Stores The best place to get groceries in Waikiki is the Food Pantry (2370 Kuhio Ave), which is open 24 hours a day. Its prices are higher than those of the chain supermarkets, which are all outside Waikiki, but lower than those of the smaller convenience stores. Food Pantry, like most grocery stores, accepts credit cards.

Beyond Waikiki, the easiest supermarket to get to without a car is the *Foodland* at the Ala Moana Center. If you have a car, there's a *Foodland* north of Waikiki close to the eastern intersection of King and Kapiolani Sts. There are grocery stores along Beretania St as well, including a *Star Market* in the university area at the intersection of Beretania and S King Sts.

Places to Eat – Mid-Range

Shore Bird Beach Broiler (☎ 922-2887, 2169 Kalia Rd), at the Outrigger Reef Hotel, is an enjoyable place for beachside dining that doesn't break the budget. At one end of the open-air dining room there's a big common grill where you cook your own order; *mahimahi* ('dolphin' fish), sirloin steak or teriyaki chicken costs $13. Meals come with an all-you-can-eat buffet bar that includes salad, chili, rice and fresh fruit. The buffet alone costs $8. Dinner is served from 4:30 to 10 pm nightly; get seated before 6 pm and you can enjoy the sunset and take advantage of cheaper early-bird prices as well. It's a busy place, so unless you get there early, expect to wait for a table – however, this is scarcely a hardship, as you can hang out on the beach in the meantime. Shore Bird also has a breakfast buffet from 7:30 to 11 am daily, with simple pastries, fruit, eggs and ham for $7. Look for coupons in the free tourist magazines that knock a dollar off all meal prices.

Duke's Canoe Club (☎ 922-2268), at the Outrigger Waikiki on Kalakaua Ave, also has a nice waterfront view. The restaurant takes its name from the late surfing king Duke Kahanamoku and the outrigger canoe club that was on the beach here in earlier days. While it's a big operation, the food is fine for the money. From 7 to 10:30 am there's a good breakfast buffet with granola, omelettes to order and fresh fruit and pastries for $10, or you can pay $8 and select from just the cold dishes. At lunch (11:30 am to 2:30 pm), there's a buffet with a salad bar and hot main dishes such as chicken and mahimahi for $10. At dinner (5 to 10 pm), fresh fish dishes cost $20, while chicken and steak meals are priced from $15. All dinners come with a full salad bar that includes cold pastas, greens, fruit and muffins. There's also a children's menu with burgers, chicken or spaghetti for $5.

The Honolulu branch of the **Hard Rock Cafe** (☎ 955-7383, 1837 Kapiolani Blvd), is just over the Ala Wai Canal beyond Waikiki. It's enlivened with loud rock music and decorated with old surfboards and a 1959 Cadillac 'woody' wagon hanging precariously over the bar. The menu features good burgers with fries for around $8 and other all-American food, including barbecued ribs and milkshakes, but it's the atmosphere as much as the food that draws the crowd. The Hard Rock Cafe is open 11:30 am to 11 pm daily (to 11:30 pm on weekends).

Competing for a similar audience is **Planet Hollywood** (☎ 924-7877, 2155 Kalakaua Ave), which has a flashy celluloid motif, with Hollywood memorabilia lining the walls and flicks playing on big-screen TVs. Part of the attraction is the hope, however seldom realized, of catching a glimpse of one of the restaurant's Hollywood shareholders, who include Arnold Schwarzenegger and Whoopi Goldberg. Sandwiches, burgers and thin-crust pizzas cost around $10, while pastas and fajitas average $13. There's also a $4 kids' menu that includes pizza, pasta or burgers and fries. Planet Hollywood is open from 11:30 am to 11 pm daily; the bar stays open until midnight.

Cheeseburger in Paradise (☎ 923-3731, 2500 Kalakaua Ave) is the latest theme eatery, this one boasting a tropical motif. It's open air and some of the tables look out (across Kalakaua Ave) at the beach. It features decent sandwiches, including Black Angus burgers, Cajun chicken and vegetarian burgers, for $7 to $10. The menu also includes similarly priced salads. Diners can enjoy live entertainment from 7 to 10 pm nightly.

Chili's (☎ 922-9697, 2350 Kuhio Ave) is a popular Tex-Mex chain restaurant from the mainland that serves soft tacos with rice and beans or burgers with fries for around $8, grilled chicken for $10 and baby-back ribs for $18. Chili's also has decent salads. It's open 11 am to 11 pm daily.

The **Oceanarium Restaurant** (☎ 922-1233, 2490 Kalakaua Ave), in the Pacific Beach Hotel, has standard fare with anything but standard views, as the dining room wraps around an impressive three-story aquarium filled with colorful tropical fish. At breakfast, you can order waffles or French toast for $7 or a full buffet for $13. At lunch, sandwiches average $8, while dinners begin at $16. The more expensive **Neptune's Garden**, a seafood restaurant in the same hotel, also has views of the aquarium.

A fun place to dine is **Tanaka of Tokyo**, which has branches in the Waikiki Shopping Plaza (☎ 922-4702, 2250 Kalakaua Ave) and King's Village (☎ 922-4233, 131 Kaliulani Ave). Both restaurants have about 20 U-shaped *teppanyaki* tables, each with a central grill that's presided over by a chef with 'flying knives,' who cooks and serves the meals to the diners at his table. Meals are set courses that include salad, miso soup, rice, shrimp appetizer and dessert; the price, which is determined by the entree selected, ranges at dinner from $18 for chicken to $36 for lobster tail. Lunch costs $10 to $15. Look for coupons in the free tourist magazines good for half off one meal when two people dine together. Both restaurants are open from 11:30 am to 2 pm weekdays and from 5:30 to 10 pm nightly.

California Pizza Kitchen (☎ 955-5161, 1910 Ala Moana Blvd) serves up a good thin-crust pizza cooked in a wood-fired brick oven. One-person pizzas range from $8 for a traditional tomato and cheese to $10 for more intriguing creations, such as the tandoori chicken pizza with mango chutney. This mainland chain restaurant also has a variety of pasta dishes, both traditional and exotic, for $8 to $12 and good green salads, with generous half-order portions for $5. The restaurant's open 11:30 am to 10 pm Monday to Thursday, 11:30 am to 11 pm Friday and Saturday, noon to 10 pm Sunday.

In the same building, *Singha Thai (☎ 941-2893, 1910 Ala Moana Blvd)* has award-winning Thai food and a troupe of Thai dancers that performs nightly. For starters, the grilled beef salad and the hot-and-sour tom yum soup are tasty house specialties and cost $8 each. Entrees, such as spicy chicken shiitake-mushroom stir-fry and various curry and noodle dishes, average $14. Singha Thai is open for dinner only, from 4 to 11 pm nightly.

Keo's (☎ 943-1444, 2028 Kuhio Ave), Waikiki's other top-rated Thai restaurant, has similarly good food and slightly cheaper prices. The one drawback is that its new location, roadside on busy Kuhio Ave, can be noisy. Nonetheless Keo's, which has long been a favorite with visiting celebs such as Jimmy Carter and Kevin Costner, continues to have a loyal following. Owner Keo Sananikone liberally spices the dishes with organically grown herbs from local farms. House specialties include various curries, Evil Jungle Prince (a spicy dish with basil and coconut milk), spring rolls and green papaya salad. Main dishes can be ordered in vegetarian ($10), chicken ($11) or shrimp ($13) versions. Keo's opens at 5 pm nightly.

Places to Eat – Top End

For fine Chinese dining, the *Golden Dragon (☎ 946-5336)* in the Hilton Hawaiian Village has both excellent food and a good ocean view. While the varied menu has some expensive specialties, there are many dishes, including oyster beef and a deliciously crispy lemon chicken, that cost around $15. The Golden Dragon is open for dinner only, 6 to 9 pm Tuesday to Sunday.

Banyan Veranda (☎ 922-3111) at the Sheraton Moana Surfrider features buffets on the hotel's historic courtyard veranda. While the food is not gourmet quality, it is good, and the setting is a gem. Every night there's a sunset buffet from 6 to 10 pm,

accompanied by Hawaiian music and hula dancing until 7:30 pm and a classical pianist after that. The meal, which costs $25, features Chinese dim sum, Vietnamese summer rolls, sushi, salads, oysters on the half shell, hot fish and meat dishes and tempting desserts. More extravagant still is the Sunday brunch, which lasts from 9 am to 1 pm and costs $32.50. All in all, it's a class act that's hard to beat.

The *Surf Room (☎ 931-7194)* at the Royal Hawaiian Hotel has outdoor beachside dining but the food is pricey. There's a $21 breakfast buffet from 6:30 to 10 am and a $23 lunch buffet from 11:30 am to 2:30 pm. The dinner menu changes nightly, with meat and seafood entrees for $25 to $30.

David Paul's Diamond Head Grill (☎ 922-3734, 2885 Kalakaua Ave), in the Colony Surf Hotel, is a swank place with splashy contemporary paintings and a full wall of windows looking out to Diamond Head. Paul offers a menu similar to the one in his well-regarded Maui restaurant, with appetizers such as Kula corn chowder, Maui onion soup or Kona lobster crab cakes for $8 to $13, and entrees, including his signature tequila shrimp, priced from $25 to $30. David Paul's is open for lunch from 11:30 am to 2:30 pm weekdays and for dinner from 5:30 to 10 pm nightly. There's entertainment, typically jazz, from 9 pm to midnight Tuesday to Saturday.

La Mer (☎ 923-2311) in the Halekulani Hotel offers Oahu's finest French food along with an ocean view and fastidious service. The dining is formal; men are required to wear jackets (loaners are available). The four-course fixed-price dinner of the day costs $85, the six-course version $105. Otherwise, appetizers such as tartar of ahi with caviar or grilled lobster salad average $25, while à la carte entrees range from $36 to $45 and include dishes such as roasted duck, bouillabaisse and filet mignon. La Mer is open 6 to 9:30 pm nightly.

Waikiki's most renowned Sunday brunch buffet is at *Orchid's (☎ 923-2311)* at the Halekulani Hotel. The grand spread includes sashimi, sushi, prime rib, smoked salmon, roast suckling pig, roast turkey, an array of salads and fruits and a rich dessert bar. There's a fine ocean view, orchid sprays on the tables and a soothing flute and harp duo. The buffet costs $34 (more on holidays) and lasts from 9:30 am to 2:30 pm. It's best to make advance reservations or you may encounter a long wait.

Other top-end Waikiki restaurants include *Bali* (☎ 941-2254) at the Hilton Hawaiian Village, for Hawaiian-influenced continental cuisine; *Cascada* (☎ 945-0270, 440 Olohana St) at the Royal Garden at Waikiki, for Euro-Asian specialties; and *Kyo-ya* (☎ 947-3911, 2057 Kalakaua Ave), for traditional Japanese food served by kimono-clad waitresses.

Entertainment

Waikiki has a varied entertainment scene. For updated schedule information, check the free tourist magazines and the daily newspapers.

Concerts The *Waikiki Shell* in Kapiolani Park hosts both classical and contemporary music concerts. For current schedule information, call the Blaisdell Center box office at ☎ 591-2211.

Hawaiiana Waikiki has lots of Hawaiian-style entertainment, from Polynesian shows with beating drums and hula dancers to mellow duos playing ukulele or slack-key guitar.

There's a free city-sponsored hula show at *Kuhio Beach Park* near the Duke Kahanamoku statue at 5:30 pm every Saturday and Sunday. The performers are different each week, varying from accomplished adult dancers to troupes of young children just learning the art. All in all, it's a very pleasant scene.

From 8 to 10 pm on Friday, the city also sponsors a group of musicians and hula dancers who stroll along Kalakaua Ave between the Royal Hawaiian Shopping Center and the Duke Kahanamoku statue, performing as they go.

The Keolalaulani *halau* (hula school) performs a free hula show on the 2nd floor of the *Waikiki Town Center* (2301 Kuhio Ave)

at 7 pm on Monday, Wednesday, Friday and Saturday.

The beachside courtyard at *Duke's Canoe Club* (☎ 922-2268) at the Outrigger Waikiki on Kalakaua Ave has become Waikiki's most popular place to hear contemporary Hawaiian music. There's entertainment from 4 to 6 pm and 10 pm to midnight daily, with the biggest names – including Brother Noland, Henry Kapono and Kapena – appearing on weekend afternoons.

At the Sheraton Moana Surfrider's *Banyan Veranda* (☎ 922-3111), you can listen to music beneath the same old banyan tree where 'Hawaii Calls' broadcast its nationwide radio show for four decades beginning in 1935. The performance schedule varies, but typically there's Hawaiian music and a hula dance show from 5:30 to 7:30 pm nightly, followed by a classical pianist from 8 to 10:45 pm.

An older, genteel crowd gathers daily at the Halekulani Hotel's open-air *House Without a Key* restaurant for sunset cocktails, Hawaiian music and hula dancing.

The *Royal Hawaiian Hotel* (☎ 923-7194) has a $78 beachside luau from 6 to 8:30 pm on Monday, with an open bar, buffet-style dinner and Polynesian show; the price for children ages five to 12 is $48.

Cinemas *Waikiki Theatres* (☎ 971-5133), on Seaside Ave near Kalakaua, has three screens showing first-run movies.

Hawaii IMAX Theatre (☎ 923-4629, 325 Seaside Ave) shows a 40-minute movie of Hawaii vistas several times a day on a 70-foot-wide screen, with three-dimensional visual effects. It costs $8.50 for adults and $6 for children ages three to 11.

Dance Clubs *Wave Waikiki* (☎ 941-0424, 1877 Kalakaua Ave) has an emphasis on alternative music and is one of Honolulu's hottest dance clubs. Hours are 9 pm to 4 am nightly, the minimum age is 21 and there's no dress code. There's typically a cover charge of about $5, though it's sometimes waived if you come in before 10 pm.

At *Moose McGillycuddy's* (☎ 923-0751, 310 Lewers St) live bands play rock and roll from 8 pm to at least 1 am nightly except Sunday. There's a $3 cover charge on weekends and you have to be 21 to get in.

In addition, a good number of the larger Waikiki hotels have nightclubs, some with dancing, some without.

Gay Venues *Hula's Bar & Lei Stand* (☎ 923-0669, 134 Kapahulu Ave), which has long been Waikiki's main gay venue, has moved to the 2nd floor of the Waikiki Grand hotel. This is a popular place for gays to meet, dance and have a few drinks.

Other gay spots in Waikiki are *Angles Waikiki* (☎ 926-9766, 2256 Kuhio Ave), a nightclub with dancing, pool and darts; *Fusion Waikiki* (☎ 924-2422, 2260 Kuhio Ave), which has DJ music and female impersonator shows; and *In-Between* (☎ 926-7060, 2155 Lauula St), a gay bar open until 2 am nightly.

Free Entertainment A pleasant way to pass the evening is to stroll along Waikiki Beach at sunset and sample the outdoor Hawaiian shows that take place at the beachfront hotels. You can wander past the musicians playing at the Sheraton Moana Surfrider's Banyan Veranda, watch bands performing beachside at Duke's Canoe Club, see the poolside performers at the Sheraton Waikiki and so on down the line.

Hilton Hawaiian Village shoots off fireworks from the beach at around 7:30 pm on Friday, preceded at 6:15 pm by a torch-lighting ceremony and a hula show at the hotel pool. At 6 pm from Sunday to Thursday, there's a brief torch-lighting ceremony with Hawaiian music. All are free.

The Royal Hawaiian Band performs from 2 to 3:15 pm most Sundays, with the exception of August, at the *Kapiolani Park Bandstand*. It's a quintessential Hawaiian scene that caps off with the audience joining hands and singing Queen Liliuokalani's *Aloha Oe* in Hawaiian.

At 11 am and 5:15 pm daily the *Sheraton Moana Surfrider* offers free hour-long historical tours of the old Moana Hotel, which is on the National Register of Historic Places. Tours leave from the concierge desk

and are open to the public; reservations are not necessary. You can also stroll through on your own. The 2nd floor has a display of memorabilia from the early hotel days, with scripts from 'Hawaii Calls,' period photographs and a short video.

The *Royal Hawaiian Shopping Center* (☎ 922-0588) occasionally offers free events, including Polynesian 'mini-shows' and other streetside entertainment. In addition, you can join in various activities. Hula lessons take place from 10 to 11 am on Monday, Wednesday and Friday; lei-making lessons happen from 11 am to noon on Monday and Wednesday; both coconut-frond weaving and Hawaiian quilting lessons occur from 9:30 to 11:30 am on Tuesday and Thursday; and hour-long ukulele lessons start at 10 am on Tuesday and Thursday and at 11:30 am on Monday, Wednesday and Friday. All the classes are free, though supplies must be purchased for the quilting class, and it's wise to call to confirm the schedule.

Other free things, including the Kodak Hula Show, the Damien Museum, the Oceanarium and the US Army Museum, are

---

Tea Ceremony

The Urasenke Foundation of Hawaii, 245 Saratoga Rd, offers tea-ceremony demonstrations on Wednesday and Friday, bringing a rare bit of serenity to busy Saratoga Rd. Students dressed in kimonos perform the ceremony on tatami mats in a formal tea room; for those participating, it can be a meditative experience.

It costs $2 to be served green tea and sweets, or you can watch the ceremony for free. Demonstrations take place at 10 am and 11 am; each lasts about 45 minutes. Although reservations are not always essential, they can be made by calling ☎ 923-3059. Because guests must leave their shoes at the door, the foundation appreciates it if all visitors wear socks. The building is diagonally across the street from the Waikiki post office.

detailed under Waikiki sights. In addition, see Hawaiiana in this same Entertainment section.

Shopping

Waikiki has no shortage of souvenir stalls, swimsuit and T-shirt shops, quick-stop convenience marts or fancy boutiques.

The prolific ABC discount marts (33 in Waikiki at last count) are often the cheapest places to buy more mundane items, such as macadamia nuts, beach mats, sunblock and other vacation necessities.

International Market Place, in the center of Waikiki, is a collection of ticky-tacky shops and stalls set beneath a sprawling banyan tree. Although few of the stalls carry high-quality goods, if you're looking for inexpensive jewelry or T-shirts, it's worth a stroll. The market place also has a Tower Records shop with an extensive Hawaiian music section and a set-up that allows you to listen to the CDs before you buy.

The Royal Hawaiian Shopping Center, Waikiki's biggest shopping center, spans three blocks along Kalakaua Ave. It has a few dozen clothing and jewelry shops as well as numerous gift shops, the most interesting of which is The Little Hawaiian Craft Shop with a range of Hawaii-made crafts.

Liberty House, a somewhat upscale department store with good quality clothing, is at the Waikiki Beachcomber Hotel on Kalakaua Ave.

Still, for the best deals on most items, you'll need to leave Waikiki. Try the Ala Moana Center, the Aloha Flea Market or one of the frequent craft shows that pop up around the city.

Pearl Harbor Area

On December 7, 1941, a wave of more than 350 Japanese planes attacked Pearl Harbor, home of the US Pacific Fleet.

Some 2335 US soldiers were killed during the two-hour attack. Of those, 1177 died in the battleship USS *Arizona*, which took a direct hit and sank in less than nine minutes.

Honolulu Star-Bulletin 1st EXTRA

Evening Bulletin, Est. 1882 No. 11587
Hawaiian Star, Vol. XLVIII No. 11559

HONOLULU, TERRITORY OF HAWAII, U. S. A., SUNDAY, DECEMBER 7, 1941

★ PRICE FIVE CENTS

WAR!

(Associated Press by Transpacific Telephone)

SAN FRANCISCO, Dec. 7.—President Roosevelt announced this morning that Japanese planes had attacked Manila and Pearl Harbor.

OAHU BOMBED BY JAPANESE PLANES

SIX KNOWN DEAD, 21 INJURED, AT EMERGENCY HOSPITAL

Twenty other ships were sunk or seriously damaged and 188 airplanes were destroyed.

USS ARIZONA MEMORIAL

Over 1.5 million people 'remember Pearl Harbor' each year with a visit to the USS Arizona Memorial (see the Greater Honolulu map). Operated by the National Park Service, the memorial is Hawaii's most-visited attraction.

The visitor center includes a museum and theater as well as the offshore memorial at the sunken USS *Arizona*. The park service provides a 75-minute program that includes a 23-minute documentary film on the attack followed by a boat ride out to the memorial and back. Everything is free. The memorial and all facilities are accessible to the disabled.

The 184-foot memorial, built in 1962, sits directly over the *Arizona* without touching it. It contains the ship's bell and a wall inscribed with the names of those who perished onboard. The average age of the ship's enlisted men was 19.

From the memorial, the battleship can be viewed 8 feet below the surface. The ship rests in about 40 feet of water and even now oozes a gallon or two of oil each day. In the rush to recoup from the attack and prepare for war, the navy exercised its option to leave the men in the sunken ship buried at sea. They remain entombed in its hull.

The visitor center (☎ 422-2771; 24-hour recorded information 422-0561) is open from 7:30 am to 5 pm daily except Thanksgiving, Christmas and New Year's Day. There's a snack bar and a souvenir/book store.

Weather permitting, the programs run every 15 or 20 minutes from 8 am to 3 pm (from 7:45 am in summer) on a first-come, first-served basis. As soon as you arrive, pick up a ticket at the information booth (each person in the party must pick up his or her own ticket); the number on the ticket corresponds to the time the tour begins. Generally the shortest waits are in the morning; if you arrive before the first crowds, you might get in within half an hour, but waits of a couple of hours are not unknown. Summer months are busiest, with an average of 4500 people taking the tour daily, and the allotment of tickets is sometimes gone by 11 am.

Pearl Harbor survivors, who act as volunteer historians, are sometimes available to give talks about the day of the attack.

There's a little open-air museum to keep you occupied while you're waiting. It has interesting photos from both Japanese and US military archives showing Pearl Harbor before, during and after the attack. One photo depicts Harvard-educated Admiral Yamamoto, the brilliant military strategist who planned the attack on Pearl Harbor even though he personally opposed going to war with the USA. Rather than relish the victory, Yamamoto stated after the attack that he feared Japan had 'awakened a sleeping giant and filled him with a terrible resolve.'

Bowfin Park

If you have to wait an hour or two for your USS Arizona Memorial tour to begin, you might want to stroll over to the adjacent Bowfin Park.

The park contains a moored WWII submarine, the USS *Bowfin*, and the Pacific Submarine Museum, which traces the development of submarines from their early origins to the nuclear age.

Commissioned in May 1943, the *Bowfin* sank 44 ships in the Pacific before the end of the war. Visitors can take a self-guided tour using a 30-minute recorded cassette tape (included in the admission fee) that corresponds with items seen along the walk through the submarine. Admission of $8 for adults, $3 for children ages four to 12, includes entry to both the submarine and the museum.

There's no charge to enter the park and view the missiles and torpedoes spread around the grounds, look through the periscopes or inspect the Japanese *kaiten*, a suicide torpedo.

The kaiten is just what it looks like: a torpedo with a single seat. As the war was closing in on the Japanese homeland, the kaiten was developed in a last-ditch effort to ward off an invasion. It was the marine equivalent of the kamikaze pilot and his plane. A volunteer was placed in the torpedo before it was fired. He then piloted it to its target. At least one US ship, the USS *Mississinewa*, was sunk by a kaiten. It went down off Ulithi Atoll in November 1944.

The park and museum are open 8 am to 5 pm daily.

Battleship Missouri Memorial

In 1998, the decommissioned battleship USS *Missouri*, nicknamed 'Mighty Mo,' was brought to Ford Island by the nonprofit USS Missouri Memorial Association to provide a third element to Pearl Harbor's WWII commemorative sites.

The 887-foot-long ship, part of a powerful group of battleships launched near the end of WWII, served as a flagship during the battles of Iwo Jima and Okinawa. On September 2, 1945, the formal Japanese surrender that ended WWII took place on the battleship's deck. The *Missouri* is now docked just a few hundred yards from the sunken remains of the USS *Arizona*; together, the ships provide a unique set of historical bookends.

In 1999, the USS *Missouri* was opened to visitors, who can take a self-guided tour for $10 or join a group tour for $14. Children's prices are $4 less.

You can not drive directly to Ford Island, which is a military base. Instead, a shuttle bus takes visitors to the *Missouri* from Bowfin Park, where the tickets are sold. The battleship site (☎ 877-644-4896) is open from 9 am to 5 pm daily.

Getting There & Away

The USS Arizona Memorial visitor center and Bowfin Park are off Kamehameha Hwy (Hwy 99) on the Pearl Harbor Naval Base just south of Aloha Stadium. If coming from Honolulu, take H-1 west to exit 15A (Stadium/Arizona Memorial). Make sure you follow highway signs for the Arizona Memorial, not Pearl Harbor.

The private Arizona Memorial Shuttle Bus (☎ 839-0911) picks up people from Waikiki hotels a few times a day, with the first run at around 7 am; the last bus returns at 4:15 pm. The ride takes around 40 minutes and costs $3 one way or $5 roundtrip. Call to make arrangements.

You can get there by public transport as well, but it takes longer. The most direct of the public buses from Waikiki to the USS Arizona Memorial is the No 47 Waipahu, which usually takes one to 1¼ hours. Bus No 20 also covers the same route, but it makes an en route stop at the airport, adding about 15 minutes to the travel time.

There are also private boat cruises to Pearl Harbor leaving from Kewalo Basin for about $25, but they should be avoided, as passengers are not allowed to board the memorial.

PEARL CITY

Pearl City is the largest urban area in Hawaii outside of Honolulu. It's home to about 45,000 people, including a lot of military personnel and civilians who work on the bases, but it offers little of interest to visitors.

If you're just passing through and not going into Pearl City itself, stay on H-1 and avoid the parallel Kamehameha Hwy, as it's all stop-and-go traffic through blocks of fast-food restaurants and shopping malls.

Pearlridge Shopping Center is a massive mall that runs between H-1 and Kamehameha Hwy. A swap meet is held a block west of the shopping center on weekends at the drive-in theater.

HAWAII'S PLANTATION VILLAGE

A visit to Hawaii's Plantation Village (☎ 677-0110) in Waipahu will reward you with a glimpse of plantation life and insights into Hawaii's multiethnic heritage.

This site encompasses 30 homes and buildings set up to recreate a plantation village of the early 20th century. The cookhouse was originally on this site and the shrine was moved here; the other structures have been newly built but authentically replicate the architecture of the time.

The houses are set up with period furnishings that portray the lifestyles of the eight different ethnic groups – Hawaiian, Japanese, Okinawan, Chinese, Korean, Portuguese, Puerto Rican and Filipino – that worked Hawaii's sugar plantations. One-hour guided tours of the village are given on the hour between 9 am and 3 pm.

The setting is particularly evocative, as Waipahu was one of Oahu's last plantation towns, and its sugar mill, which operated until 1995, still looms on a knoll directly above this site. There's also a small museum detailing the lives and cultural backgrounds of plantation workers. Artifacts on display, such as an ofuro bath, Korean flute, straw slippers and various tools, are accompanied by insightful interpretive write-ups. All in all, it's a quality community-based production.

It's open from 9 am to 4 pm Monday to Saturday. Admission costs $5 for adults, $4 for seniors and children five to 17.

To get there, head west on H-1, take exit 7, turn left at the end of the off-ramp onto Paiwa St, then turn right onto Waipahu St, drive past the mill and turn left into the complex. The distance from H-1 is about 1⅓ miles.

KEAIWA HEIAU STATE PARK
This park in Aiea, north of Pearl Harbor, covers 334 acres and contains an ancient medicinal temple, campgrounds, picnic facilities and a scenic loop trail. The park is open from 7 am to sunset for day visitors. As with all state parks there are no fees.

At the park entrance is **Keaiwa Heiau**, a 100-by-160-foot single-terraced stone structure built in the 1600s and used by *kahuna lapaau* (herbalist healers). The kahunas used hundreds of medicinal plants and grew many on the grounds surrounding the heiau. Among those still found here are *noni* (Indian mulberry), whose pungent yellow fruits were used to treat heart disease; kukui, whose nuts were an effective laxative; *ulu* (breadfruit), whose sap soothed chapped skin; and ti leaves, which were wrapped around a sick person to break a fever. Not only did the herbs have medicinal value, but the heiau itself was considered to possess life-giving energy. The kahuna was able to draw from the powers of both.

People wishing to be healed still place offerings within the heiau. The offerings reflect the multiplicity of Hawaii's cultures: rosary beads, New Age crystals and sake cups sit beside flower leis and rocks wrapped in ti leaves.

To get to Keaiwa from Honolulu, head west on Hwy 78 and take the Stadium/Aiea turnoff onto Moanalua Rd. Turn right onto Aiea Heights Drive at the second traffic light. The road winds up through a residential area 2½ miles to the park.

Aiea Loop Trail
The 4½-mile Aiea Loop Trail begins at the top of the park's paved loop road next to the rest rooms and comes back out at the campground, about a third of a mile below the start of the trail. The trail starts off in a forest of eucalyptus trees and runs along the ridge. Other trees along the way include ironwood, Norfolk Island pines, edible guava and native *ohia lehua*, which has fluffy red flowers.

There are vistas of Pearl Harbor, Diamond Head and the Koolau Range. About two-thirds of the way along, the wreckage of a C-47 cargo plane that crashed in 1943 can be spotted through the foliage on the east ridge. The hike takes 2½ to three hours and is a fairly easy walk.

Camping
The park's camping area can accommodate 100 campers. Most sites have their own picnic table and barbecue grill. Sites are not crowded together, but because many of them are largely open there's not a lot of privacy either. There's a distant view of Honolulu's airport a couple of miles to the south.

If you're camping in winter, make sure your gear is waterproof, as it rains a lot at this 880-foot elevation, although the temperature is usually pleasant. There are rest rooms, showers, a pay phone and drinking water.

For Oahu, it's a good choice for a campground. There's a resident caretaker by the front gate, and the gate is locked at night for security. As with all Oahu public campgrounds, no camping is permitted on Wednesday and Thursday. Camping permits must be obtained in advance; see Camping in the Accommodations section at the start of this chapter.

Southeast Oahu

Some of Oahu's finest scenery is along the southeast coast, which curves around the tip of the Koolau Mountains. Diamond Head, Hanauma Bay and the island's most famous bodysurfing beaches are all just a 20-minute ride from Waikiki.

East of Diamond Head, H-1 turns into the Kalanianaole Hwy (Hwy 72), passing the exclusive Kahala residential area, a run of shopping centers and some housing developments that creep into the mountain valleys.

The highway rises and falls as it winds its way around the Koko Head area and Makapuu Point, with beautiful coastal views along the way. The area is geologically fascinating, with boldly stratified rock formations, volcanic craters and lava sea cliffs.

DIAMOND HEAD

Diamond Head is a tuff cone and crater that was formed by a violent steam explosion deep beneath the surface long after most of Oahu's volcanic activity had stopped. As the backdrop to Waikiki, it's one of the best-known landmarks in the Pacific. The summit is 760 feet high.

The Hawaiians called it Leahi and built a *luakini heiau* (temple for human sacrifices) on the top. But ever since 1825, when British sailors found calcite crystals sparkling in the sun and mistakenly thought they'd struck it rich, it's been called Diamond Head.

In 1909, the US Army began building Fort Ruger at the edge of the crater. Soldiers built a network of tunnels and topped the rim with cannon emplacements, bunkers and observation posts. Reinforced during WWII, Fort Ruger has been a silent sentinel whose guns have never fired.

Today, there's a Hawaii National Guard base inside the crater as well as Federal Aviation Administration and civil defense facilities. Diamond Head is a state monument with picnic tables, rest rooms, a pay phone and drinking water. The best reason to visit is to hike the trail to the crater rim for the panoramic view. The gates are open 6 am to 6 pm daily.

Hiking

The trail to the summit was built in 1910 to service the military observation stations along the crater rim.

It's a fairly steep hike, with a gain in elevation of 560 feet, but it's only three-quarters of a mile to the top and plenty of people of all ages hike up. It takes about 30 minutes one way. The trail is open and hot, so you might want to take along something to drink.

As you start up the trail, you can see the summit ahead a bit to the left, at roughly eleven o'clock.

The crater is dry and scrubby with kiawe and koa trees, grasses and wildflowers. The little yellow-orange flowers along the way are native ilima, Oahu's official flower.

About 20 minutes up the trail, you enter a long, dark tunnel. Because the tunnel curves you don't see light until you get close to the end. It's a little spooky, but the roof is high enough for you to walk through without bumping your head, there is a hand rail and your eyes should adjust enough to make out shadows in the darkness. Nevertheless, to prevent accidents, the park advises hikers to tote along a flashlight.

The tunnel itself seems like it should be the climax of this long climb, but upon coming out into the light you're immediately faced with a steep 99-step staircase. Persevere! After this there's a shorter tunnel, a narrow spiral staircase inside an unlit bunker and the last of the trail's 271 steps. Be careful when you reach the top – there are some steep drops.

From the top there's a fantastic 360° view taking in the southeast coast to Koko Head and Koko Crater and the leeward coast to Barbers Point and the Waianae Mountains. Below is Kapiolani Park and the Waikiki Shell. You can also see the lighthouse, coral reefs, sailboats and sometimes even surfers waiting for waves at Diamond Head Beach.

To reach Diamond Head from Kuhio Ave in Waikiki, take bus No 22 or 58, both of which run about twice an hour. It's a 20-minute walk from the bus stop to the trailhead at the parking lot. Once you get through the tunnel, you're in the crater.

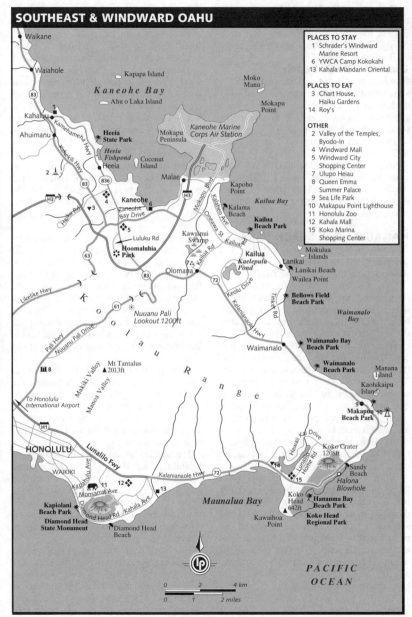

SOUTHEAST & WINDWARD OAHU

PLACES TO STAY
1 Schrader's Windward
   Marine Resort
6 YWCA Camp Kokokahi
13 Kahala Mandarin Oriental

PLACES TO EAT
3 Chart House,
   Haiku Gardens
14 Roy's

OTHER
2 Valley of the Temples,
   Byodo-In
4 Windward Mall
5 Windward City
   Shopping Center
7 Ulupo Heiau
8 Queen Emma
   Summer Palace
9 Sea Life Park
10 Makapuu Point Lighthouse
11 Honolulu Zoo
12 Kahala Mall
15 Koko Marina
   Shopping Center

Waikane
Waiahole
Kapapa Island
Kaneohe Bay
Ahu o Laka Island
Kahaluu
Ahuimanu
Kamehameha Hwy
Kahekili Hwy
Heeia
State Park
*Heeia
Fishpond*
Heeia
Coconut
Island
Malae
Mokapu
Peninsula
Kaneohe Marine
Corps Air Station
Moko
Manu
Mokapu
Point
Kapoho
Point
Kalaheo Ave
Kalama Beach
Kaneohe
Kaneohe
Bay Drive
Luluku Rd
Hoomaluhia
Park
Kawainui
Swamp
Onewa St
Kailua Rd
Kailua Rd
Kailua St
Kailua Bay
Kailua
Beach Park
Kailua
Mokulua
Islands
Lanikai
Lanikai Beach
Wailea Point
*Kaelepulu
Pond*
Olomana
Keolu Drive
Kalanianaole Hwy
Tinker Rd
**Bellows Field
Beach Park**
*Waimanalo
Bay*
**Waimanalo Bay
Beach Park**
Pali Hwy
Nuuanu Pali Drive
Nuuanu Pali
Lookout 1200ft
Likelike Hwy
K o o l a u
Makiki Valley
Manoa Valley
Mt Tantalus
▲2013ft
R a n g e
Waimanalo
**Waimanalo
Beach Park**
Manana
Island
Kaohikaipu
Island
**Makapuu
Beach Park**
To Honolulu
International Airport
HONOLULU
Lunalilo Fwy
WAIKIKI
Kalakaua Ave
Monsarrat Ave
Kalanianaole Hwy
Kahala Ave
Hawaii Kai Drive
Lunalilo Home Rd
Koko Crater
1208ft
Sandy
Beach
*Halona
Blowhole*
**Kapiolani
Beach Park**
**Diamond Head
State Monument**
Diamond Head Rd
Diamond Head
Beach
Maunalua Bay
Koko
Head
642ft
Kawaihoa
Point
**Hanauma Bay
Beach Park**
**Koko Head
Regional Park**

*PACIFIC
OCEAN*

0   2   4 km
0   1   2 miles

By car from Waikiki, take Monsarrat Ave (which begins by the zoo) to Diamond Head Rd and then take the right turn after Kapiolani Community College into the crater.

Diamond Head Beach

Conditions at Diamond Head Beach are suitable for intermediate to advanced windsurfers, and when the swells are up it's a great place for wave riding. Even as a spectator sport it's exhilarating.

The beach has showers but no other facilities.

To get there from Waikiki, follow Kalakaua Ave to Diamond Head Rd. There's a parking lot just beyond the lighthouse. Walk east past the end of the lot and you'll find a paved trail down to the beach.

HANAUMA BAY BEACH PARK

Hanauma, which means 'Curved Bay,' is a wide, sheltered bay of sapphire and turquoise waters set in a rugged volcanic ring.

Once a popular fishing spot, it had nearly been fished out when it was designated a marine life conservation district in 1967. Now that the fish are fed instead of eaten, they swarm in by the thousands.

From the overlook, you can peer into crystal waters and view the entire coral reef that stretches across the width of the bay. You're bound to see schools of glittering silver fish, the bright blue flash of parrotfish and perhaps a sea turtle. To see an even more colorful scene, put on a mask, jump in and view it from beneath the surface.

Hanauma seems to get as many people as fish. With over a million visitors a year, it's often busy and crowded.

While it's for good reason that everyone's there, the heavy use of the bay has taken its toll. The coral on the shallow reef has been damaged by all the action, and the food that snorkelers feed the fish has increased fish populations in Hanauma well beyond what it can naturally support. In fact, many of the fish in the bay are not common to Hanauma but are more aggressive types that have been drawn in by the feeding.

A master plan is under way that aims to normalize the fish distribution and reduce the number of beachgoers from 10,000 a day to just 2000. Fish feeding will also be phased out – in the meantime, snorkelers shouldn't feed the fish anything but fish food, which can be bought at the beach concession stand.

Hanauma is both a county beach park and a state underwater park. It has a grassy picnic area, lifeguards, showers, rest rooms, changing rooms and access for the disabled. The bay is closed on Tuesday but is otherwise open from 7 am until 6 pm in winter daily, until 7 pm in summer. There's a $3 admission fee for non-Hawaii residents.

The snack bar sells hot dogs, ice cream and soda. Snorkel sets can be rented at the beach concession stand from 8 am to 4:30 pm for $6; you'll need to either hand over $30, a credit card or your car rental keys as a deposit.

Paths lead along low ledges on both sides of the bay; the eastern one goes to the Toilet Bowl, the western one to Witches Brew. When the surf is up, which includes most high-wind days, the paths are gated shut and entry to the ledges is prohibited. At other times you can walk out along the ledges, but you should still be cautious; whenever the tide is high, waves can wash over the ledges, and of course a rogue wave can occur at any time.

More people drown at Hanauma than at any other beach on Oahu. Although the figure is high largely because there are so many visitors at this beach, people drowning in the Toilet Bowl or being swept off the ledges have accounted for a fair number of deaths over the years.

Hanauma Bay is about 10 miles from Waikiki along Hwy 72. There's a large parking lot, although it sometimes fills in the middle of the day and on weekends. It costs $1 to drive into the parking area but if you're unable to find a space, the fee will be refunded. Parking outside a marked space will result in a parking ticket.

Bus No 22, called the Beach Bus, goes to Hanauma Bay (and on to Sea Life Park). On weekdays, the first buses leave Waikiki from the corner of Kuhio Ave and Namahana St at 8:15 and 9:15 am, with subsequent buses leaving at 55 minutes past the hour until

3:55 pm, and then a final bus at 4:25 pm. Buses leave Hanauma for Waikiki at least once every hour from 11:10 am to 5:40 pm. On weekends, the buses are more frequent (roughly twice an hour), though the schedule is more sporadic.

Toilet Bowl

A 15-minute walk out to the point on the left side of the bay brings you to the Toilet Bowl, a small natural pool in the lava rock. The Toilet Bowl is connected to the sea by an underwater channel, which enables water to surge into the bowl and then flush out from beneath.

People going into the pool for the thrill of it can get quite a ride as it flushes down four to 5 feet almost instantly. However, the rock around the bowl is slippery and hard to grip, and getting in is far easier than getting out. It definitely should not be tried alone.

Witches Brew

A 10-minute walk along the right side of the bay will take you to a rocky point. The cove at the southern side of the point is the treacherous Witches Brew, so named for its swirling, turbulent waters.

There's a nice view of Koko Crater from there, and green sand made of olivine can be found along the way.

Diving & Snorkeling

Snorkeling is good at Hanauma Bay year-round. Mornings are better than afternoons, because swimmers haven't yet stirred up the sand.

The large, sandy opening in the middle of the coral, known as the Keyhole, is an excellent place for novice snorkelers. The deepest water is 10 feet, though it's very shallow over the coral, so if you have diving gloves, bring them. The Keyhole is well protected and usually swimming-pool calm.

Hanauma's biggest attraction is the sheer number and variety of fish. It's got big rainbow parrotfish crunching off chunks of coral, moray eels, bright yellow butterfly fish, goatfish, Moorish idols and numerous other tropicals.

For confident snorkelers, the snorkeling is better on the outside of the reef, where there are larger coral heads, bigger fish and fewer people; to get there follow the directions on the signboard near the snack bar or ask the lifeguard at the southwest end of the beach. Keep in mind that because of the channel current it's generally easier getting out than it is getting back in. Don't attempt to swim outside the reef when the water is rough or choppy. Not only will the channel current be strong, but the sand will be stirred up and the visibility poor anyway.

Divers have the whole bay to play in, with clear water, coral gardens, sea turtles and lots of fish. Beware of currents when the surf is up; surges near the Witches Brew, on the right-hand side; and the Molokai Express, a treacherous current that runs just outside the mouth of the bay.

KOKO HEAD REGIONAL PARK

The entire Koko Head area is a county regional park. It includes Hanauma Bay, Koko Head, Halona Blowhole, Sandy Beach and Koko Crater.

Koko Head is backed by Hawaii Kai, an expansive development of condos, houses, shopping centers, a marina and a golf course – all meticulously planned and rather sterile in appearance.

Koko Crater and Koko Head are both tuff cones created about 10,000 years ago in Oahu's last gasp of volcanic activity.

Koko Head

Koko Head, not to be confused with Koko Crater, overlooks and forms the southwest side of Hanauma Bay.

There are two craters atop Koko Head, as well as radar facilities on the 642-foot summit. The mile-long summit road is closed to casual visitors.

The Nature Conservancy maintains a preserve inside the shallow Ihiihilauakea Crater, the larger of the two craters. The crater has a unique vernal pool and a rare fern, the *Marsilea villosa*. For information on work parties or weekend excursions to the preserve, call the Nature Conservancy (☎ 537-4508).

Halona Blowhole Area

About three-quarters of a mile past Hanauma is a **lookout** with a view of striking coastal rock formations and crashing surf.

A little less than a mile farther is the parking lot for the **Halona Blowhole**, where water surges through a submerged tunnel in the rock and spouts up through a hole in the ledge. It's preceded by a gushing sound, created by the air that's being forced out by the rushing water. The action depends on water conditions – sometimes it's barely discernible, while at other times it's a show-stopper.

Down to the right of the parking lot is **Halona Cove**, the little beach where the risqué love scene with Burt Lancaster and Deborah Kerr in *From Here to Eternity* was filmed in the 1950s.

Right before the blowhole, a small **stone monument** sits atop Halona Point. It was erected by Japanese fishers to honor those lost at sea.

Sandy Beach

Sandy Beach is one of the most dangerous beaches on the island, if measured in terms of lifeguard rescues and broken necks. It has a punishing shorebreak, a powerful backwash and strong rip currents.

Nevertheless, the shorebreak is extremely popular with bodysurfers who know their stuff. It's equally popular with spectators, who gather to watch the bodysurfers being tossed around in the transparent waves.

Sandy Beach is wide, very long and, yes, sandy. It's frequented by sunbathers, young surfers and admirers of both. When the swells are big, board surfers hit the left side of the beach.

Red flags flown on the beach indicate hazardous water conditions. Even if you don't notice the flags, always check with the lifeguards before entering the water.

Not all the action is in the water. The grassy strip on the inland side of the parking lot is used by people looking skyward for their thrills – it's both a hang-glider landing site and a popular locale for kite-flying.

The park has rest rooms, showers and a pay phone. Local Chef, a food wagon, sets up in the parking lot from around 11:30 am to 4 pm daily, selling cheap burgers, beef stew and $5 plate lunches.

Koko Crater

According to Hawaiian legend, Koko Crater is the imprint left by the vagina of Pele's sister Kapo, which was sent here from the Big Island to lure the pig-god Kamapuaa away from Pele.

Inside the crater there's a simple dryland botanical garden of plumeria trees, oleander and cacti that's maintained by the county. To get there, take Kealahou St off Hwy 72 opposite the northern end of Sandy Beach. Just over half a mile in, turn left onto the one-lane road to Koko Crater Stables and continue a third of a mile to the garden, which is open from 9 am to 4 pm daily; admission is free.

Places to Eat

Koko Marina Shopping Center, on the corner of Lunalilo Home Rd and Hwy 72, has a *Foodland* supermarket, standard fast-food eateries, a few sit-down restaurants, a bagel place and a shave ice shop. The best choice for local flavor is *Yummy Korean BBQ*, which offers $6 barbecued meat dishes (the chicken is a good, lean choice) with 'two-scoop rice' and four tasty marinated vegetable dishes or kimchis. You can enjoy your meal at the waterfront tables adjacent to the marina.

The best upscale option in Southeast Oahu is *Roy's* (☎ 396-7697, Hawaii Kai Corporate Plaza, Hwy 72). Chef Roy Yamaguchi is a creative force behind the popularity of Hawaii Regional cuisine, which emphasizes fresh local ingredients and borrows liberally from Asian influences. An exhibition kitchen sits in the center of the dining room, where Roy orchestrates an impressive troupe of sous-chefs. Starters include salads, spring rolls and pizzas that have been baked in an *imu* (underground oven) for around $8. The crispy Thai stuffed chicken, topped with a tasty chutney and macadamia curry sauce, costs $16 and makes a delightful main dish. Most other meat dishes cost around $20, while fresh fish specials average $25. Roy's is a top choice for a night out – the food is attractively presented, the service attentive and the servings good-sized. It's open from 5:30 pm (5 pm on Saturday and Sunday) to 10 pm; reservations are advised.

MAKAPUU POINT

About 1⅓ miles north of Sandy Beach, the 647-foot Makapuu Point and its coastal **lighthouse** mark the easternmost point of Oahu. The mile-long service road to the lighthouse was recently deeded by the federal government to Hawaii, thus opening this site to the public. The gate into the service road is locked to keep out private vehicles, but you can park off the highway just beyond the gate and walk in from there. There are fine coastal views along the way and at the lighthouse lookout.

Back on the highway, about a third of a mile farther along, there's a scenic **roadside lookout** with a view down onto Makapuu Beach, with its aqua-blue waters outlined by white sand and black lava. It's an even more spectacular sight when hang gliders are taking off from the cliffs, which serve as Oahu's top hang-gliding spot.

From the lookout you can see two offshore islands, the larger of which is **Manana Island**, also known as Rabbit Island. This aging volcanic crater is populated by feral rabbits and burrowing wedge-tailed shearwaters. They coexist so closely that the birds and rabbits sometimes even share the same burrows. The island looks vaguely like the head of a rabbit, and if you try hard you may see it, ears folded back. If that doesn't work, you could also try to imagine it as a whale.

In front of it is the smaller **Kaohikaipu Island**, which won't tax the imagination – all it looks is flat.

There's a coral reef between the two islands that divers sometimes explore, but to do so requires a boat.

Makapuu Beach Park

Makapuu Beach is one of the island's top winter bodysurfing spots, with waves reaching 12 feet and higher. It also has the island's best shorebreak. As with Sandy Beach, Makapuu is strictly the domain of experienced bodysurfers who can handle rough water conditions and dangerous currents. Surfboards are prohibited.

In summer, when the wave action disappears, the waters can be calm and good for swimming.

The beach is opposite Sea Life Park in a pretty setting, with cliffs in the background and a glimpse of the lighthouse. Two native Hawaiian plants are plentiful – naupaka by the beach and yellow-orange ilima by the parking lot.

Sea Life Park

Sea Life Park (☎ 259-7933) features a big, 300,000-gallon aquarium with sea turtles, eels, eagle rays, hammerhead sharks and thousands of reef fish. A spiral ramp circles the 18-foot-deep aquarium, allowing you to view the fish from different depths.

In one of two outdoor amphitheaters, jumping dolphins and waddling penguins perform the standard park tricks.

In the other, the Whaler's Cove, a group of Atlantic bottlenose dolphins give a choreographed performance. The dolphins tail walk, do the hula and give rides to a 'beautiful island maiden' – all bordering on kitsch.

There's a large pool that contains California sea lions and a smaller pool with harbor seals. There's also a section with rare Hawaiian monk seals, comprised largely of abandoned or injured pups that have been rescued from the wild; once they reach maturity, they're released back into their natural habitat. The turtle lagoon holds green sea turtles, while another section of the park has red-footed boobies, albatrosses and great frigate birds, all seabirds that are indigenous to Hawaii.

Hanging from the ceiling of the park's little **Whaling Museum** is the skeleton of a 38-foot sperm whale that was washed up off Barbers Point in 1980. The rest of the museum consists of a continuously playing video on marine life and some posters on marine life and sanctuaries, much of it relating to the mainland.

Sea Life Park is open from 9:30 am to 5 pm daily. Admission is a steep $25 for adults, $12.50 for children ages four to 12 (free for children under four). There's a $3 parking fee in the main lot; however, if you continue past the ticket booth to the area marked 'additional parking,' there's no fee.

You can visit the whaling museum and the park restaurant (sandwiches, salads and other cafeteria-style food) without paying admission. You also get a free look at the seal and sea lion pools along the walk to the museum.

Public bus Nos 22, 57 Kailua/Sea Life Park and 58 Hawaii Kai/Sea Life Park stop at Sea Life Park.

WAIMANALO

Waimanalo Bay has the longest continuous stretch of beach in Oahu: 5½ miles of white sand running north from Makapuu Point to Wailea Point. A long coral reef about a mile out breaks up the biggest waves, protecting much of the shore.

Waimanalo has three beach parks with camping. The setting is scenic, although the area isn't highly regarded for safety.

Waimanalo Beach Park

Waimanalo Beach Park has an attractive beach of soft white sand and the water is excellent for swimming.

It's an in-town county park with a grassy picnic area, rest rooms, changing rooms, showers, ball fields, basketball and volleyball courts and a playground. Camping is allowed in an open area near the road. (For information on obtaining camping permits, see Camping in the Accommodations section near the beginning of this chapter.)

The park has ironwood trees, but overall it's more open than the other two parks to the north. The scalloped hills of the lower Koolau Range rise up on the inland side of the park, and Manana Island and Makapuu Point are visible to the south.

Waimanalo Bay Beach Park

This county park, about a mile north of Waimanalo Beach Park, has Waimanalo Bay's biggest waves and thus is popular with board surfers and bodysurfers.

Locals call the park Sherwood Forest because hoods and car thieves used to hang out there in days past. The park has not totally shaken its reputation, so keep an eye on your belongings.

The park itself is quite appealing, with beachside campsites shaded with ironwood trees. (For information on obtaining camping permits, see Camping in the Accommodations section near the beginning of this chapter.) There's a lifeguard station, barbecue grills, drinking water, showers and rest rooms.

Bus No 57 stops on the main road in front of the park, and from there it's a third of a mile walk to the beach and campground. The gate is open from 6 am to 7:45 pm.

Bellows Field Beach Park

The beach fronting Bellows Air Force Base is open to civilian beachgoers and campers on weekends only, from noon on Friday until 8 am on Monday. This long beach has fine sand and a natural setting backed by ironwood trees. The small shorebreak waves are good for beginning bodysurfers and board surfers.

There's a lifeguard, showers, rest rooms and water; the 50 campsites are set out among the trees. Although it's military property, camping permits are issued through the county Department of Parks & Recreation. For information on obtaining permits, see Camping in the Accommodations section near the beginning of this chapter.

The marked entrance is a quarter of a mile north of Waimanalo Bay Beach Park. Bus No 57 stops in front of the entrance road, and from there it's 1½ miles to the beach.

Places to Eat

Just north of Waimanalo Beach Park, you'll find a *7-Eleven* convenience store; *Keneke's*, a local plate-lunch eatery; and *Leoni's Ristorante*, a pizza and sub joint.

There's a *food mart* and a *McDonald's* just south of Waimanalo Bay Beach Park. About a mile north of Bellows Field is a shopping cluster with *Jack in the Box*, *Subway* and *Dave's Ice Cream*.

PALI HWY

The Pali Hwy (Hwy 61) runs between Honolulu and Kailua, cutting through the spectacular Koolau Range. It's a scenic little highway, and if it's been raining heavily every fold and crevice in the mountains will have a lacy waterfall streaming down it.

Many Kailua residents commute to work over the Pali, so Honolulu-bound traffic can be heavy in the morning and outbound traffic heavy in the evening. It's less of a problem for visitors, however, as most day-trippers will be traveling against the traffic. Public buses travel the Pali Hwy, but none stop at the Nuuanu Pali Lookout.

Past the 4-mile marker, look up and to the right to see two notches cut about 15 feet deep into the crest of the pali. These notches are thought to have been dug as cannon emplacements by Kamehameha I.

The original route between Honolulu and windward Oahu was via an ancient footpath that wound its way perilously over these cliffs. In 1845, the path was widened into a horse trail and later into a cobblestone carriage road.

In 1898, the Old Pali Hwy (as it's now called) was built following the same route. It was abandoned in the 1950s after tunnels were blasted through the Koolau Range and the present multilane Pali Hwy opened.

You can still drive a loop of the Old Pali Hwy (called Nuuanu Pali Drive) and hike another mile of it from the Nuuanu Pali Lookout.

Queen Emma Summer Palace

At the Pali Hwy's 2-mile marker sits the Queen Emma Summer Palace, which once belonged to Queen Emma, the consort of Kamehameha IV.

Emma was three-quarters royal Hawaiian and a quarter English, a granddaughter of the captured sailor John Young, who became a friend and adviser of Kamehameha I. The house is also known as Hanaiakamalama, the name of John Young's home in Kawaihae on the Big Island, where he served as governor.

After their deaths, the Youngs left the home to Queen Emma, who often slipped away from her formal downtown home to spend time at this cooler retreat. It's a bit like an old Southern plantation house, with a columned porch, high ceilings and louvered windows to catch the breeze.

The home was forgotten after Emma's death in 1885 and was scheduled to be razed in 1915, as the estate was being turned into a public park. The Daughters of Hawaii rescued it and now run it as a museum.

The house has period furniture collected from five of Emma's homes. Some of the more interesting pieces are a cathedral-shaped koa cabinet made in Berlin and filled with a set of china from Queen Victoria; feather cloaks and capes; and Emma's necklace of tiger claws, a gift from a maharaja of India.

It's open from 9 am to 4 pm daily except holidays. Admission is $5 for adults, $1 for children under age 12.

Nuuanu Pali Drive

For a scenic side trip through a shady green forest, turn off the Pali Hwy onto Nuuanu Pali Drive, half a mile past the Queen Emma Summer Palace. The 2-mile road runs parallel to the Pali Hwy and then comes back out to it before the Nuuanu Pali Lookout, so you don't miss anything by taking this side loop – in fact, quite the opposite.

The drive is through mature trees that form a canopy overhead, all draped with hanging vines and wound with philodendrons. The lush vegetation along Nuuanu Pali Drive includes banyan trees with hanging aerial roots, tropical almond trees, bamboo groves, impatiens, angel trumpets and golden cup – a tall climbing vine with large golden flowers.

Nuuanu Pali Lookout

Whatever you do, don't miss the Nuuanu Pali Lookout with its broad view of the windward coast from a height of 1200 feet. From the lookout you can see Kaneohe straight ahead, Kailua to the right and Mokolii Island and the coastal fishpond at Kualoa Park to the far left.

This is *windward* Oahu – and the winds that funnel through the pali are so strong that you can sometimes lean against them. It gets cool enough to appreciate having a jacket.

In 1795, Kamehameha I routed Oahu's warriors up the Nuuanu Trail during his invasion of the island. On these steep cliffs Oahu's warriors made their last stand. Hundreds were thrown to their death over the pali by Kamehameha's troops. A hundred years later, during the construction of the Old Pali Hwy, more than 500 skulls were found at the base of the cliffs.

The abandoned Old Pali Hwy winds down from the right of the lookout, ending abruptly at a barrier near the current highway about a mile away. Few people realize the road is here, let alone venture down it. It makes a nice walk and takes about 20 minutes one way. There are good views looking back up at the jagged Koolau Mountains and out across the valley.

As you get back on the highway, it's easy to miss the sign leading you out of the parking lot, and instinct could send you in the wrong direction. Go to the left if you're heading toward Kailua, to the right if heading toward Honolulu.

Windward Coast

Windward Oahu, the island's eastern side, follows the Koolau Range along its entire length. The mountains looming inland are lovely, with scalloped folds and deep valleys. In places, they come so near to the shore that they almost seem to crowd the highway into the ocean.

The windward coast runs from Kahuku Point in the north to Makapuu Point in the south. (For the Waimanalo to Makapuu area, see the Southeast Oahu section.)

The two main towns are Kaneohe and Kailua, both largely nondescript bedroom communities for workers who commute to Honolulu, about 10 miles away.

North of Kaneohe, the windward coast is rural Hawaii, where many Hawaiians toil close to the earth, making a living with small papaya, banana and vegetable farms. It's generally wetter on the windward side and the vegetation is lush and green.

The windward coast is exposed to the northeast trade winds. This is a popular area

for anything that requires a sail – from windsurfing to yachting.

There are some attractive swimming beaches on the windward coast – notably Kailua, Kualoa and Malaekahana – although many other sections of the coast are too silted for swimming. Swimmers should keep an eye out for stinging Portuguese men-of-war that are sometimes washed in during storms.

Most of the offshore islets that you'll see along this coast have been set aside as bird sanctuaries. These tiny islands are vital habitat for ground-nesting seabirds, which have largely been driven off the populated islands by the introduction of mongooses, cats and other predators.

Two highways cut through the Koolau Range from central Honolulu to the windward coast. The Pali Hwy (Hwy 61) goes straight into Kailua center. The Likelike Hwy (Hwy 63) runs directly into Kaneohe, and, although it doesn't have the scenic stops the Pali Hwy has, it is in some ways more dramatic. Driving away from Kaneohe it feels as if you're heading straight into tall fairy-tale mountains – then you suddenly shoot through a tunnel and emerge on the Honolulu side, the drama gone.

If you're heading both to and from windward Oahu through the Koolau Range, take the Pali Hwy up from Honolulu and the Likelike Hwy back for the best of both. (See the Pali Hwy section for details on that drive.)

KAILUA

In ancient times, Kailua was a place of legends. It was home to a giant turned into a mountain ridge, the island's first *menehunes* (legendary little people) and numerous Oahuan chiefs.

But that's all history. Kailua today would be an ordinary middle-class community if not for being endowed with one of Oahu's finest beaches and splendid windsurfing conditions.

Kailua is the third-largest city in Oahu, with a population of 38,000.

Ulupo Heiau

Ulupo Heiau is a sizable open-platform temple, made of stones piled 30 feet high and

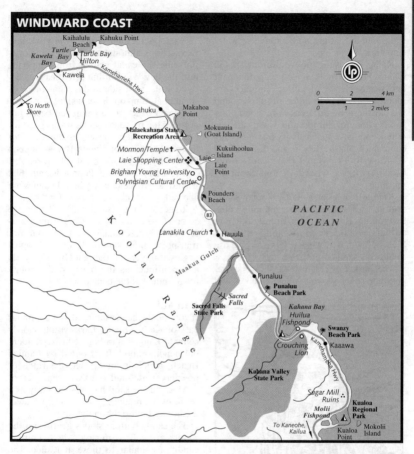

WINDWARD COAST

Kaihalulu Beach
Kahuku Point
Turtle Bay
Kawela Bay
Turtle Bay Hilton
Kawela
Kamehameha Hwy
To North Shore
Kahuku
Makahoa Point
Malaekahana State Recreation Area
Mokuauia (Goat Island)
Mormon Temple
Kukuihoolua Island
Laie Shopping Center
Laie
Brigham Young University
Laie Point
Polynesian Cultural Center
Pounders Beach
83
Lanakila Church
Hauula
Koolau Range
Maakua Gulch
PACIFIC OCEAN
Punaluu
Sacred Falls
Punaluu Beach Park
Sacred Falls State Park
Kahana Bay
Huilua Fishpond
Swanzy Beach Park
Crouching Lion
Kaaawa
Kamehameha Hwy
Kahana Valley State Park
Sugar Mill Ruins
Kualoa Regional Park
Molii Fishpond
To Kaneohe, Kailua
Kualoa Point
Mokolii Island

0   2   4 km
0   1   2 miles

140 feet long. Its construction is attributed to menehunes, the little people who legends say created much of Hawaii's stonework, finishing each project in one night. Fittingly, Ulupo means 'night inspiration.'

In front of the heiau, which is thought to have been a luakini type used for human sacrifices, is an artist's rendition of how the site probably looked in the 18th century, before Westerners arrived.

If you walk the path across the top of the heiau, you get a view of Kawainui Swamp, one of Hawaii's largest habitats for endangered waterbirds. Legends say the swamp's

ancient fishpond had edible mud at the bottom and was home to a *moo*, or lizard spirit.

Ulupo Heiau is a mile south of Kailua Rd. Coming up the Pali Hwy from Honolulu, take Uluoa St, the first left after passing the Hwy 72 junction. Then turn right on Manu Aloha St and right again onto Manuoo St. The heiau is behind the YMCA.

Kailua Beach Park

Kailua Beach Park is at the southeastern end of Kailua Bay. This glistening white-sand beach is long and broad with lovely turquoise waters. The park is popular for long walks, family outings and a range of water activities.

Kailua Bay is the top windsurfing spot in Oahu. Onshore trade winds are predominant and windsurfers can sail at Kailua every month of the year. In different spots around the bay there are different water conditions, some good for jumps and wave surfing, others for flat-water sails. Two windsurfing companies, Naish Hawaii and Kailua Sailboards, give lessons and rent boards at the beach park on weekdays and Saturday mornings.

Kailua Beach has a gently sloping sandy bottom with waters that are generally calm. Swimming is good year-round, but sun bathers should keep in mind that the breezes favored by windsurfers also give rise to blowing sand.

The park has rest rooms, showers, lifeguards, a snack shop, a volleyball court and

Beware of the Portuguese man-of-war.

large grassy expanses partly shaded with ironwood trees.

Kaelepulu Canal divides the park into two sections, although a sandbar sometimes prevents the canal waters from emptying into the bay. Windsurfing activities are centered at the west side of the canal; there's a small boat ramp on the east side.

Kalama Beach, an unimproved beach just north of the park, has gentle waves good for novice bodysurfers. Surfers usually head for the northern end of Kailua Bay at **Kapoho Point** or farther still to a break called **Zombies**.

The island offshore, **Popoia Island** (Flat Island), a bird sanctuary where landings are allowed, is a popular destination for kayakers.

To get to Kailua Beach Park, take bus No 56 or 57 from Ala Moana Center and transfer to No 70 in Kailua. If you have your own transport, simply stay on Kailua Rd, which begins at the end of the Pali Hwy (Hwy 61) and continues as the main road through town, ending at the beach.

Lanikai

If you follow the coastal road as it continues east of Kailua Beach Park, you'll shortly come to Lanikai, a rather exclusive residential neighborhood. It's fronted by Lanikai Beach, which is an attractive stretch of powdery white sand – at least what's left of it. Much of the sand has washed away as a result of the retaining walls built to protect the homes built right on the shore.

The sandy bottom slopes gently and the waters are calm, offering safe swimming conditions similar to those at Kailua. The twin **Mokulua islands** sit directly offshore.

From Kailua Beach Park, the road turns into the one-way Aalapapa Drive, which comes back around as Mokulua Drive to make a 2½-mile loop. There are 11 narrow beach access walkways off Mokulua Drive. For the best stretches of beach, try the one opposite Kualima Drive or any of the next three.

Places to Stay

Kailua has no hotels, but there are many furnished beachfront cottages, studios and B&B-style rooms in private homes. While the majority are handled by reservation services, the following places can be booked directly with the owners.

A short walk from Kailua Beach, **Sheffield House** (☎ 262-0721, sheffieldhouse@poi.net, 131 Kuulei Rd, Kailua, HI 96734), consists of two cozy rental units in the home of Paul and Rachel Sheffield. There's a guest room with a wheelchair-accessible bathroom for $55 and a one-bedroom suite that has a queen bed and a separate sitting area with a queen futon for $75. Each unit has a private entrance, TV, microwave, toaster oven, coffeemaker, small refrigerator and ceiling fan. The Sheffields, who have three young children of their own, welcome kids. There's a three-day minimum stay; breakfast is not included in the rates, but coffee and tea are provided.

Akamai Bed & Breakfast (☎/fax 261-2227, 800-642-5366, akamai@alohoa.net, 172 Kuumele Place, Kailua, HI 96734) has two pleasant studio units in a private home about 10 minutes' walk from Kailua Beach. Each is modern and comfortable and has a refrigerator, microwave, coffeemaker, bathroom, cable TV and private entrance. Both have a king bed as well as a sofa bed. The rate of $75 includes a fruit basket and breakfast items. There's a laundry room ($1 per load) and a quiet courtyard with a pool. The minimum stay is three days; smoking is limited to the outdoors. To see photos of the accommodations, visit the website www.planet-hawaii.com/akamaibnb.

Papaya Paradise Bed & Breakfast (☎/fax 261-0316, 395 Auwinala Rd, Kailua, HI 96734) is a 15-minute walk from Kailua Beach. Bob and Jeanette Martz, retired from the army and home most of the time, rent two rooms off the side of their home. One room has a queen bed and a trundle bed, the other two twin beds; each has a private entrance, bathroom, phone, air-con, ceiling fan and TV. The rates are $75 for singles or doubles, including a continental breakfast. Guests have access to a refrigerator and microwave. There's a pool and Jacuzzi. Boogie boards and snorkel gear can be borrowed for free. There's usually a three-day minimum stay.

Kailua Tradewinds (☎ 262-1008, fax 261-0316, 391 Auwinala Rd, Kailua, HI 96734), a vacation rental next door to Papaya Paradise, consists of two studio units at the home of Jona Williams, Jeanette's daughter. Breakfast is not provided, but each unit has a refrigerator, microwave, coffeemaker and toaster as well as a private entrance, queen bed, bathroom, TV and phone. One of the units also has a double futon. The rate is $70 for singles or doubles, plus $10 for each additional person. There's a swimming pool. Beach gear is available for guests to use. For more details, visit cyberrentals.com/hi/willaoahu.html on the Web.

Manu Mele Bed & Breakfast (☎/fax 262-0016, manumele@pixi.com, 153 Kailuana Place, Kailua, HI 96734) consists of two attractive guest rooms in the contemporary home of English-born host Carol Isaacs. The largest, the Hibiscus Room, has a king bed and costs $80, while the smaller but perfectly suitable Pikake Room has a queen bed and costs $70. Each has a private entrance, bathroom, refrigerator, microwave, coffeemaker, air-con, ceiling fan and cable TV. There's a shared guest phone in the hall. A generous basket of fruit and baked goods is provided for the first morning. There's a two-night minimum stay. The house has a pool and there's a short footpath to the beach nearby. Smoking is not allowed in the units. The owner maintains a website at www.pixi.com/~manumele.

Most of the statewide B&B agencies have listings in Kailua. The two that follow are based in Kailua and book more than 50 different Kailua-area accommodations.

Affordable Paradise Bed & Breakfast (☎ 261-1693, fax 261-7315, afford@aloha.net, 226 Pouli Rd, Kailua, HI 96734) books studios and B&Bs from $55 a double and cottages from $65. Maria Wilson, who speaks German, can also arrange rooms in private homes starting at $45. For a list of available spots, browse online at www.aicomm.com/hawaii.

All Islands Bed & Breakfast (☎ 263-2342, 800-542-0344 carlina001@hawaii.rr.com, 823 Kainui Drive, Kailua, HI 96734) has B&B rooms from $55 to $70, studio apartments from $65 to $90 and a few cottages from $85. The agency maintains a website at www.hawaiialohaspirit.com/alisbnb.

In addition, **Naish Hawaii** (☎ 262-6068, 800-767-6068, fax 263-9723, 155A Hamakua Drive, Kailua, HI 96734) specializes in windsurfing vacations with accommodations in Kailua but can also book places for non-windsurfing travelers.

Places to Eat

Near the Beach Kalapawai Market, on the corner of Kailua Rd and Kalaheo Ave, is a popular place to stop for coffee on the way to the beach. You have a choice of fresh brews, with a 12-ounce cup costing just $1. The market also has a few cheap eats, including bagels or chili and rice, and a good selection of wine and beer. It's open from 6 am to 9 pm daily.

Kailua Beach Restaurant (130 Kailua Rd), in the Kailua Beach Center, has $3.75 pancake or omelette breakfasts, served with bacon and toast, until 10:30 am. At other times there are about 40 Chinese plate-lunch options, such as chicken with broccoli, kung pao shrimp or stir-fry noodles, for $5 to $7. For dessert, try some of the Honolulu-made Dave's Ice Cream. The restaurant is open 7 am to 9 pm daily.

Also in the Kailua Beach Center is **Island Snow**, a popular shave ice shop with tropical flavors such as Maui mango and banzai banana. It's open from 10 am to at 6 pm daily.

Buzz's (☎ 261-4661, 413 Kawailoa Rd), opposite Kailua Beach Park, has lunchtime fresh fish burgers or sandwiches with fries, as well as Caesar or spinach salads, each for around $8. However, it's most popular as an evening steak house, with cuts of beef from $14 to $25, salad bar included. Buzz's is open daily; lunch is served from 11 am to 2:30 pm, dinner from 5 to 10 pm. Trivia buffs can find a plaque on one of the lanai tables marking the spot where Bill and Hillary Clinton ate dinner during one of their Hawaii visits. Credit cards are not accepted.

Town Center All of the following eateries are in the town center, within a mile of each other.

On Hoolai St, just north of Kailua Rd, **Boston's North End Pizza** (☎ 263-7757) makes good pizza; for $10 to $16, a whole pie

can easily feed three or four people. The huge slices, a full quarter of a pizza, cost $2.50 to $4, depending on the number of toppings. The spinach and fresh garlic version is awesome. The shop is open 11 am to 8 pm weekdays and 11 am to 9 pm weekends.

You can check your email nearby at **Stir Crazy.com** (☎ 261-8804, 45 Hoolai St). This friendly little cafe makes lattes and other coffees as well as soups, salads and tortilla-rolled sandwiches, including lots of vegetarian options; everything costs $5 or less. Internet access costs $2.25 for 15 minutes. The cafe is open 7 am to 9 pm weekdays, 8 am to 9 pm on Saturday and 8 am to 4 pm on Sunday.

Agnes Bake Shop, opposite Stir Crazy. com, is a good little bakery that makes whole-grain breads, inexpensive pastries, and Portuguese malasadas to order. The malasadas, which are intended to be eaten hot, take about 10 minutes to fry up and cost 55¢ each. You can also order coffee, tea and Portuguese bean soup and sit down to eat at one of the half-dozen cafe tables. The bake shop is open 6 am to 6 pm daily except Monday.

A popular dining spot is **Jaron's** (☎ 261-4600, 201 Hamakua Drive), which has a jazzy decor and a varied menu. Lunch prices range from $6 to $9, including blackened ahi Caesar or Thai chicken salads, and vegetarian, fish or meat sandwiches with soup. Dinner emphasizes pastas, seafood and steaks from $12 to $20. A good deal are the sunset dinners ($9 to $11.50), nightly from 4 to 7 pm, that offer a choice of seven entrees, such as chicken piccata or salmon, with salad and sourdough bread. Jaron's is open for lunch from 11 am to 4 pm (Monday to Saturday) and for dinner from 4 to at least 9 pm. Sunday brunch takes places from 9 am to 2 pm. Jaron's has contemporary Hawaiian music, rock or reggae bands on Friday and Saturday; there's a dance floor and a small cover charge.

The bustling little **Zia's Caffe** (☎ 262-7168, 201 Hamakua Drive), an open-air place next to Jaron's, has excellent Italian fare at honest prices. Various pastas, veggie lasagna, shrimp scampi and a delicious eggplant parmesan cost $7 to $10. There are also soups, salads and sandwiches. Zia's is open 11 am to 9 pm weekdays and 4:30 to 9 pm on weekends.

Cisco's Cantina *(☎ 262-7337, 123 Hekili St)*, an unpretentious Mexican restaurant, serves generous portions at reasonable prices. You can get a taco for $6, a burrito for $8.50 or a two-item combination plate for $10, all served with rice and beans. Cisco's is open 11 am to 10 pm Sunday to Thursday, to 11 pm on weekends.

The Source *(32 Kainehe St)* is a natural food store with bulk herbs and spices, vitamins, general food items and a small produce section. The Source is open 9 am to 9 pm weekdays, 10 am to 5 pm on weekends.

Kailua also has numerous fast-food eateries in the town center, including ***Burger King, Pizza Hut, McDonald's, KFC, Jack in the Box*** and ***Taco Bell***.

KANEOHE

Kaneohe, with a population of 36,000, is Oahu's fourth-largest city.

Kaneohe Bay, which stretches from Mokapu Peninsula all the way up to Kualoa Point, 7 miles north, is the state's largest bay and reef-sheltered lagoon. Although inshore it's largely silted and not good for swimming, the near-constant trade winds that sweep across the bay are ideal for sailing.

Two highways run north to south through Kaneohe. Kamehameha Hwy is closer to the coast and goes by Heeia State Park. Kahekili Hwy runs inland from the outskirts of Kaneohe, where it intersects the Likelike Hwy and continues north past Byodo-In. The highways merge into a single route, Kamehameha Hwy (Hwy 83), a few miles north of Kaneohe.

Kaneohe Marine Corps Air Station occupies the whole of Mokapu Peninsula. The H-3 Fwy terminates at its gate.

Hoomaluhia Park

The county's youngest and largest botanical garden is Hoomaluhia, a 400-acre park in the uplands of Kaneohe. The park is planted with groups of trees and shrubs from tropical regions around the world.

It's a peaceful, lush green setting, with a stunning pali backdrop. Hoomaluhia is not a landscaped flower garden, but more of a natural preserve. A network of trails wind through the park and up to a 32-acre lake (no swimming allowed).

The little visitor center (☎ 233-7323) has displays on flora and fauna, on Hawaiian ethnobotany and on the history of the park, which was originally built by the US Army Corps of Engineers as flood protection for the valley below.

The park is at the end of Luluku Rd, which starts 2¼ miles down Kamehameha Hwy from the Pali Hwy. Bus Nos 55 and 56 stop at the Windward City Shopping Center, opposite the start of Luluku Rd. It's

H-3

The recently opened H-3 Fwy, which got its impetus during the Reagan era, owes its existence in no small way to the heated Cold War mania of the day. Fought bitterly by environmentalists, the highway slices across formerly pristine valleys to connect military bases on both sides of the island, with the Kaneohe Marine Corps Air Station at one end and the Pearl Harbor Naval Base at the other. As the post-Cold War military presence in Hawaii downsizes, the freeway's cost of $1.25 billion stands out as the biggest pork-barrel project in Hawaii's history.

1½ miles up Luluku Rd from the highway to the visitor center and another 1½ miles from the visitor center to the far end of the park – so if you use the bus, expect to do some walking.

The park is open from 9 am to 4 pm daily and admission is free. Guided two-hour nature hikes are held at 10 am on Saturday and 1 pm on Sunday; call the visitors' center for registration.

Weekend camping is allowed in Hooma-luhia Park. For information on obtaining camping permits, see Camping in the Accommodations section at the front of this chapter.

Valley of the Temples & Byodo-In

The Valley of the Temples is an interdenominational cemetery in a beautiful setting just off the Kahekili Hwy, 1½ miles north of Haiku Rd. For visitors the main attraction is Byodo-In, the 'Temple of Equality,' which is a replica of the 900-year-old temple of the same name in Uji, Japan. This one was dedicated in 1968 to commemorate the 100th anniversary of Japanese immigration to Hawaii.

Byodo-In sits against the Koolau Range. The rich red of the temple against the verdant fluted cliffs is strikingly picturesque, especially when mist settles in on the pali.

The temple is meant to symbolize the mythical phoenix. Inside the main hall is a nine-foot-tall gold-lacquered buddha sitting on a lotus. Wild peacocks roam the grounds and hang their tail feathers over the upper temple railings.

Fronting the temple is a carp pond with cruising bullfrogs and cooing doves. The three-ton brass bell beside the pond is said to bring tranquility and good fortune to those who ring it.

It's all very Japanese, right down to the gift shop selling sake cups, daruma dolls and happy buddhas. This scene is as close as you'll get to Japan without having to land at Narita.

Admission to the temple, which is collected from 8 am to 4:30 pm daily, is $2 for adults, $1 for children under 12. There are no fees to visit outside these hours and, as with most cemeteries, the grounds are usually accessible from sunrise to sunset.

On the way out, you might want to head up to the hilltop mausoleum with the cross on top and check out the view.

Heeia State Park

Heeia State Park is on Kealohi Point, just off Kamehameha Hwy. It has a good view of Heeia Fishpond on the right and Heeia-Kea Harbor on the left.

Before Western contact, stone-walled fishponds used to raise mullet and other fish for royalty were common along the coast throughout Hawaii. The **Heeia Fishpond** is an impressive survivor that remains largely intact despite the invasive mangrove that grows along its walls and takes root between the rocks.

Coconut Island, just offshore to the southeast of the fishpond, was a royal playground in times past. It was named for the coconut trees planted there by Princess Bernice Pauahi Bishop. In the 1930s it was the estate of Christian Holmes, heir to the Fleischmann Yeast fortune, who dredged the island, doubling its size to 25 acres. During the war the estate served as an R&R facility and had a brief stint as a hotel. Air-brushed shots of Coconut Island were used in opening scenes for the *Gilligan's Island* TV series. The Hawaii Institute of Marine Biology of the University of Hawaii occupies a niche on the island, while the rest is privately owned.

You can walk around the grounds of Heeia State Park and take in the view, but otherwise there's not much to do here.

Places to Stay

YWCA Camp Kokokahi (☎ 247-2124, *kokokahi@gte.net, 45-035 Kaneohe Bay Drive, Kaneohe, HI 96744)* is a budget option 1½ miles northeast of Kaneohe center. Although the camp gives priority to groups, it also accepts individual travelers. Accommodations are in simple cabins. You can opt for a tiny cabin all to yourself for $20, a double cabin with two single beds for $15 per person or a dorm bed in a five-person cabin for $15. Rates include a pillow, sheets and a blanket, as well as access to kitchen, lounge and laundry facilities. You can also pitch a tent on the site for $8 per person. Though Camp Kokokahi overlooks Kaneohe Bay, the water is too silted for swimming, but there's a heated pool on the grounds. Two things to keep in mind: The place sometimes books out completely, so call ahead to make reservations before coming all the way out, and check-in isn't allowed after 8 pm, so arrive early. Bus No 56 (1¼ hours from Ala Moana Center) stops out front. The office is open from 8 am to 5 pm weekdays and 8:30 am to 5 pm weekends; after 5 pm, the on-site caretaker can be reached by dialing pager ☎ 549-4540 or ☎ 571-4407.

Alii Bluffs Windward Bed & Breakfast (☎/fax 235-1124, 800-235-1151, donm@ lava.net, 46-251 Ikiiki St, Kaneohe, HI 96744) has two bedrooms in a cozy home filled with Old World furnishings, oil paintings, antique toys and collectibles. The Victorian Room has one double bed and costs $75, while the Circus Room has two twin beds and costs $60. Each room has a private bathroom. Originally from the Scottish Highlands, where his mother ran a B&B, host Don Munro gives guests the run of the house and provides beach towels and coolers. Breakfast and afternoon tea are included in the rates. There's a small pool and a view of Kaneohe Bay. For more information, visit Don's website at www.hawaiiscene.com/aliibluffs.

The 57-unit *Schrader's Windward Marine Resort* (☎ 239-5711, 800-735-5711, fax 239-6658, 47-039 Lihikai Drive, Kaneohe, HI 96744) is a spread of simple low-rise wooden buildings in a residential neighborhood. Despite the name, the ambiance is more like a local motel than a resort. So many of the guests are military families that the resort offers free transport to the Kaneohe Marine Corps base. One-bedroom units range from $79 to $116, two-bedroom units from $110 to $200. All have refrigerators, microwaves, TVs, air-con and phones.

Places to Eat
Chart House (☎ 247-6671) at Haiku Gardens has a romantic, open-air setting with a picturesque view of a lily pond tucked beneath the Koolau Mountains. Open from 5:30 pm nightly, the restaurant features standard steak and seafood dishes ($17 to $30) accompanied by a nice salad bar, though the real attraction is the setting. The gardens are floodlit at night.

You can also drop by Haiku Gardens in the daytime and take a 10-minute stroll around the pond. To get there from Kamehameha Hwy, turn west on Haiku Rd just past Windward Mall; after crossing Kahekili Hwy, continue on Haiku Rd a quarter of a mile farther.

Chao Phya Thai Restaurant, in the Windward City Shopping Center at the corner of Kamehameha Hwy and Kaneohe Bay Drive, is a family-run restaurant serving good Thai food. Most dishes on the extensive menu cost $6 to $8. Chao Phya is open for lunch from 11 am to 2 pm and for dinner from 5 to 9 pm daily. The restaurant doesn't serve liquor, but you can bring your own.

The Windward City Shopping Center also has *Kimo's Bagelman*, with 75¢ bagels; *Kozo Sushi*, with good, inexpensive takeout sushi; a *Foodland* supermarket; *KFC* and *McDonald's*. *Burger King* and *Pizza Hut* are on the opposite side of the Kamehameha Hwy.

The Windward Mall, on Kamehameha Hwy at its intersection with Haiku Rd, is a large, two-level mall with a bank, chain department stores and numerous other shops. The *Windward Mall Food Court* is sort of a mini Ala Moana, with a line of food stalls selling hot cinnamon rolls, deli items, pizza by the slice and Japanese, Chinese, Mexican and Korean meals.

WAIAHOLE & WAIKANE
Waiahole and Waikane mark the beginning of rural Oahu. The area is home to family-run orchid nurseries and small coconut, banana, papaya and lemon farms.

Large tracts of Waikane Valley were taken over for military training and target practice during WWII, a use that continued until the 1960s. The government now claims the land has so much live ordnance that it can't be returned to the families it was leased from. This is a source of ongoing contention with

OAHU

local residents, who are upset that much of the inner valley remains off-limits.

KUALOA
Kualoa Regional Park
Kualoa Regional Park, a 153-acre county park on Kualoa Point, is bounded on its southwestern side by Molii Fishpond. From the road southwest of the park the fishpond is visible through the trees as a distinct green line in the bay.

Kualoa is a nice beach park in a scenic setting. The mountains looming precipitously across the road are, appropriately enough, called Pali-ku, meaning 'vertical cliff.' When the mist settles, it looks like a scene from a Chinese watercolor.

The main offshore island is **Mokolii**. In Hawaiian legend, Mokolii is said to be the tail of a nasty lizard or a dog – depending on who's telling the story – that was slain by a god and thrown into the ocean. Following the immigration of Chinese laborers to Hawaii, this conical-shaped island also came to be called Papale Pake, Hawaiian for 'Chinese hat.'

Apua Pond, a 3-acre brackish salt marsh on the point, is a nesting area for the endangered *aeo* (Hawaiian stilt). If you walk down

Sacred Ground

In ancient times, Kualoa was one of the most sacred places on Oahu. When a chief stood on the point, passing canoes lowered their sails in respect. The children of chiefs were brought here to be raised, and it may also have been a place of refuge where *kapu* (taboo) breakers and escaped warriors could seek reprieve from the law.

It was at Kualoa that the double-hulled canoe *Hokulea* landed in 1987, following a two-year rediscovery voyage through Polynesia that retraced the ancient migration routes. Because of its rich significance to Hawaiians, Kualoa Regional Park is listed in the National Register of Historic Places.

❀ ❀ ❀ ❀ ❀ ❀ ❀ ❀ ❀ ❀ ❀ ❀ ❀

the beach beyond the park, you'll see a bit of **Molii Fishpond**, but it's hard to get a good perspective on it from there. The rock walls are covered with mangrove, *milo* (a native shade tree) and pickleweed.

The park is largely open lawn with a few palm trees. It has a long, thin strip of beach with shallow waters and safe swimming. There are picnic tables, rest rooms, showers, a pay phone and a lifeguard. Camping is free from Friday to Tuesday nights with a permit from the county; a caretaker locks the gates at night. For information on obtaining camping permits, see Camping in the Accommodations section near the beginning of this chapter.

Kualoa Ranch
The horses grazing on the green slopes across the road from Kualoa Regional Park belong to Kualoa Ranch. Part of the ranch property was used as a backdrop for the movies *Jurassic Park* and *Godzilla*. The ranch offers all sorts of activities, including horseback riding, kayaking and target shooting, with much of it packaged for Japanese tourists who are shuttled in from Waikiki.

Back in 1850, Kamehameha III leased about 625 acres of this land for $1300 to Dr Judd, a missionary doctor who became one of the king's advisers. Judd planted the land with sugarcane, built flumes to transport it and imported Chinese laborers to work the fields. His sugar mill trudged along for a few decades but went under just before the reciprocity agreement with the USA opened up mainland sugar markets.

You can still see the remains of the mill's stone stack and a bit of the crumbling walls half a mile north of the beach park, right alongside the road.

KAAAWA
In the Kaaawa area, the road hugs the coast and the pali moves right on in, with barely enough space to squeeze a few houses between the base of the cliffs and the road.

Swanzy, a neighborhood beach park used mainly by fishers, is fronted by a shore wall. Across the road is a 7-Eleven store and a gas station – pretty much the commercial center of town, such as it is.

Crouching Lion

The crouching lion is a rock formation at the back of the restaurant of the same name, which comes up shortly after the 27-mile marker.

In Hawaiian legend, the rock is said to be a demigod from Tahiti who was cemented to the mountain during a jealous struggle between Pele, the volcano goddess, and her sister Hiiaka. When he tried to free himself by pulling into a crouching position, he was turned to stone.

To find him, stand at the Crouching Lion Inn sign with your back to the ocean and look straight up to the left of the coconut tree. The figure, which to some people resembles a lion, is on a cliff in the background.

The inn itself has standard sandwiches, salads and a few hot plates for $7 to $12 at lunch. Dinners are about double that, although there's usually a cheaper early-bird special.

Continuing north, just past the inn on the right, you get a glimpse of **Huilua Fishpond** on the coast.

KAHANA VALLEY

In old Hawaii, the islands were divided into *ahupuaa* – pie-shaped land divisions reaching from the mountains to the sea that provided everything the Hawaiians needed for subsistence. Kahana Valley, 4 miles long and 2 miles wide, is the only publicly owned ahupuaa in Hawaii.

Kahana is a wet valley. Annual rainfall ranges from about 75 inches along the coast to 300 inches in the mountains. Before Westerners arrived, Kahana Valley was planted with wetland taro. The overgrown remnants of more than 130 terraces and irrigation canals have been uncovered in the valley.

In the early 20th century, the area was planted with sugarcane, which was hauled north to the Kahuku Mill via a small railroad. During WWII, the upper part of Kahana Valley was taken over by the military and used for training in jungle warfare.

In 1965, the state bought Kahana Valley from the Robinson family of Kauai (the owners of Niihau) in order to preserve it from development.

Kahana Valley State Park

The entrance to Kahana Valley State Park is located a mile north of the Crouching Lion Inn.

When the state purchased Kahana it also acquired tenants, many of whom had been living in the valley for a long time. Rather than evict a struggling rural population, the state created a plan allowing the 140 residents to stay on the land. The concept is to eventually incorporate the families into a 'living park,' with the residents acting as interpretive guides. The development of the park has been a slow process, but after two decades of planning and negotiating, the 'living park' concept has inched forward. A simple orientation center inside the park entrance has been opened and tours are being provided to school children and local organizations.

While there are no tours for individual travelers, you can walk through the valley on your own. The orientation center, which is open from 7:30 am to 4 pm weekdays, has the latest information on trail conditions. Keep in mind that the trails can be slippery when wet, especially since this is the wettest side of Oahu.

The most accessible of the park trails is a 1¼-mile loop trail that begins at the orientation center. It starts along the old railroad route, passes a fishing shrine called Kapaeleele Koa, and leads to Keaniani Kilo, a lookout that was used in ancient times for spotting schools of fish in the bay. The trail then goes down to the bay and along the highway back to the park entrance. You can find a trail map at the orientation center.

The park also takes in Kahana Bay and its tree-lined beach. The bay is set deep and narrow, and the protected beach provides safe swimming, with a gently sloping sandy bottom. The 10 beachside campsites are used primarily by island families, and there may be some turf issues for tourists. To camp here, you must obtain a permit in person from the park orientation center (☎ 237-8858) or from the main state parks office in Honolulu. For more information on obtaining permits, see Camping in the Accommodations section near the beginning of this chapter.

PUNALUU

Punaluu is a scattered little seaside community. At Punaluu Beach Park, a narrow beach provides fairly good swimming, as the offshore reef protects the shallow inshore waters in all but stormy weather. Be cautious near the mouth of the Waiono Stream and in the channel leading out from it, as currents are strong when the stream is flowing quickly or the surf is high.

Ahi's (53-146 Kamehameha Hwy), north of the 25-mile marker, specializes in fresh shrimp, with most meals around $10; it's open from 11 am to 9 pm Monday to Saturday.

SACRED FALLS STATE PARK

Sacred Falls is a 1374-acre state park with a 2-mile trail leading up the narrow Kaliuwaa Valley, which folds deeply into the Kooulau Mountains.

The moderately difficult hike, which follows Kaluanui Stream through a narrow canyon, takes about 1½ hours, involves a couple of stream crossings and ends at an 80-foot waterfall beneath high, rocky cliffs.

The falls may be sacred, but the hike isn't blessed. Because the canyon is narrow, it's subject to flash floods, and over the years a number of hikers have been swept to their deaths after quick rainstorms have unleashed sudden swells of water without warning.

Falling rocks pose another hazard and account for the site's single worst disaster. In May 1999, on a sunny Sunday afternoon, more than 50 people who were swimming and sunbathing at the base of the falls were injured when a landslide let loose directly above them. Eight people were killed by falling boulders and debris, and a dozen others had to be hospitalized.

Although the trail to the falls has weathered other disasters, the instability that caused the landslide has cast doubts on the park's future. Until geologists can make a positive

determination about the soundness of the cliff face, it's unlikely the falls will reopen.

If Sacred Falls State Park does reopen, the trail will still be closed any day when the weather is sufficiently bad or the water level is high. Entering when the gate is locked will not only subject hikers to potential natural hazards but also to hefty fines. The Division of State Parks (☎ 587-0300) will post a sign at the trailhead noting whether the trail is open or closed.

The park is on the inland side of Kamehameha Hwy, about a third of a mile north of the 23-mile marker.

HAUULA

Hauula is a rather tired-looking town graced with a fine backdrop of hills and Norfolk pines. There's a 7-Eleven convenience store and a few small eateries.

The in-town beach is none too appealing for swimming, but it occasionally gets waves big enough for local children to ride. The beach is actually a county park that allows camping, although it's mostly local families that camp there. For information on obtaining camping permits, see Camping in the Accommodations section near the beginning of this chapter.

The stone ruins of **Lanakila Church** (circa 1853) sit perched on a hill opposite Hauula Beach, next to the newer Hauula Congregational Church.

Trails

The Division of Forestry & Wildlife maintains three trails in the forest reserve behind Hauula: **Hauula Loop Trail** (2½ miles), **Maakua Gulch Trail** (3 miles) and **Maakua Ridge Trail** (2½ miles). All three trails are through a hunting area and head into some beautiful hills. Hauula Loop and Maakua Ridge trails have good views, while the Maakua Gulch Trail crosses a stream and leads to a waterfall and pool.

As flash flooding is a potential problem, the Maakua Gulch Trail should not be hiked in rainy weather or when the stream is high.

The trailhead to all three is at a bend in Hauula Homestead Rd, about a quarter of a mile up from Kamehameha Hwy. Camping is allowed along the route. Call the Division of Forestry (☎ 587-0166) for information, trail maps and the required camping permits.

LAIE

Laie is thought to be the site of an ancient *puuhonua* – a place where kapu breakers and fallen warriors could seek refuge. Today, Laie is the center of the Mormon community in Hawaii.

The first Mormon missionaries to Hawaii arrived in 1850. After an attempt to establish a Hawaiian 'City of Joseph' on Lanai failed amidst a land scandal, the Mormons moved to Laie. In 1865, they purchased 6000 acres of land in the area and slowly expanded their influence.

In 1919, the Mormons constructed a **temple**, a smaller version of the one in Salt Lake City, at the foot of the Koolau Range. This stately temple, at the end of a wide promenade, appears like nothing else on the windward coast. Although there's a visitors' center where eager guides will tell you all about Mormonism, tourists are not allowed to enter the temple itself.

Nearby is the Hawaii branch of **Brigham Young University**, with scholarship programs bringing in students from islands throughout the Pacific.

Information

Laie Shopping Center, about half a mile north of the Polynesian Cultural Center, has restaurants, a Foodland supermarket, a coin laundry and a Bank of Hawaii.

Polynesian Cultural Center

The Polynesian Cultural Center (☎ 293-3333), called PCC by locals, is a 'nonprofit' organization belonging to the Mormon Church. The center draws about 900,000 tourists a year, more than any other attraction on Oahu with the exception of the USS Arizona Memorial.

The park's seven theme villages represent Samoa, New Zealand, Fiji, Tahiti, Tonga, the Marquesas and Hawaii. They have authentic-looking huts and ceremonial houses, many elaborately built with twisted sennit ropes and hand-carved posts. The huts hold weavings, tapa cloth, feather work and other handicrafts.

People of Polynesian descent in native garb demonstrate poi pounding, coconut frond weaving, dances, games and the like. There's also a re-creation of an old mission house and a missionary chapel representative of those found throughout Polynesia in the mid-19th century.

Most of the people working here are Pacific Island students from the nearby Brigham Young University, who pay their college expenses by providing PCC with a source of inexpensive labor. Not all students end up at the 'village' of their home islands. At times there are more Samoans than Hawaiians, for instance, so you may well find a Samoan student demonstrating Hawaiian weavings. People are amiable and you could easily spend a few hours wandering around chatting or trying to become familiar with a craft or two.

The admission price includes boat rides along the waterway that winds through the park; the Pageant of the Long Canoes, a sort of trumped-up floating talent show at 2:30 pm; and 35-minute van tours of the Mormon temple grounds and BYU campus. PCC is open from 12:30 to 9 pm daily except Sunday, though the theme-park activities cease by 6 pm.

Although it can be interesting, PCC is also very touristy and hard to recommend at an admission price of $27 for adults and $16 for children ages five to 11.

The 'Admission-Buffet-Show' package, which costs $47 for adults and $30 for children, adds on a buffet dinner and evening Polynesian song and dance show. The show, which runs from 7:30 to 9 pm, is partly authentic, partly Hollywood-style and much like an enthusiastic college production, with elaborate sets and costumes.

Beaches

The 1½ miles of beach fronting the town of Laie between Malaekahana State Recreation Area and Laie Point are used by surfers, bodysurfers and windsurfers.

Pounders, half a mile south of the main entrance to PCC, is an excellent bodysurfing beach, but the shorebreak, as the name of the beach implies, can be brutal. There's a strong winter current. The area around the old landing is usually the calmest. Summer swimming is generally good and the beach is sandy.

From **Laie Point** there's a good view of the mountains to the south and of tiny offshore islands. The one to the left with the hole in it is Kukuihoolua, otherwise known as Puka Rock. To get to Laie Point, head seaward on Anemoku St, opposite the Laie Shopping Center, then turn right on Naupaka St and go straight to the end.

Places to Stay

Rodeway Inn Hukilau Resort (☎ 293-9282, 800-526-4562, fax 293-8115, 55-109 Laniloa St, Laie, HI 96762), right outside the Polynesian Cultural Center, is a two-story motel with 49 rooms surrounding a courtyard pool. While not special, it's comfortable enough and each room has a lanai, cable TV, air-con and mini-refrigerator. Rates start at $84, including a continental breakfast.

Places to Eat

Laie Chop Suey in the Laie Shopping Center is a local-style eatery with standard Chinese fare. Most main dishes cost $5 to $6, as do set lunch and dinner plates. This spot is open 10 am to 9 pm Monday to Saturday.

The shopping center also has a grocery store, a *Subway* sandwich shop and *Domino's Pizza*.

Laie's *McDonald's*, on the highway at the north end of PCC, has a little more character than the usual McDonald's. Originally built as a restaurant for the hotel next door, the building resembles a Polynesian longhouse with a peaked roof, and there's even a small waterfall inside. The only Laie eatery open on Sunday, McDonald's operates 6:30 am to at least 10 pm daily.

MALAEKAHANA STATE RECREATION AREA

Malaekahana Beach stretches between Makahoa Point to the north and Kalanai Point to the south. The long, narrow, sandy beach is backed by ironwoods. Swimming is generally good year-round, although there are occasionally strong currents in winter. This popular family beach is also good for many other water activities, including bodysurfing, board surfing and windsurfing. Kalanai Point, the main section of the state park, is less than a mile north of Laie and has picnic tables, barbecue grills, camping, rest rooms and showers.

Mokuauia (Goat Island), a state bird sanctuary just offshore, has a nice sandy cove with good swimming and snorkeling. It's possible to wade over to the island – best when the tide is low and the water's calm, but be sure to ask the lifeguard about water conditions and the advisability of crossing. Be careful of the shallow coral and sea urchins.

You can also snorkel across to Goat Island and off its beaches. Beware of a rip current that's sometimes present off the windward end of the island, where the water is deeper.

Camping

Malaekahana has the best campgrounds at this end of the windward coast. You can pitch a tent in the park's main Kalanai Point section for free if you have a state park permit. For information on obtaining permits, see Camping in the Accommodations section near the beginning of this chapter.

You can also rent a cabin or camp for a fee in the Makahoa Point section of the park, which has a separate entrance off the highway three-quarters of a mile north of the main park entrance. Friends of Malaekahana (☎ 293-1736 after 10 am), a local nonprofit group working on cultural preservation projects, maintains this end and has gates that are locked to vehicles between 7 pm and 7 am. Rustic cabins that can accommodate a small group cost $66 on weekdays and $80 on weekends, tax included. Tent camping in this section costs $5 per person.

KAHUKU

Kahuku is a former sugar town with little wooden cane houses lining the road. The mill in the center of town belonged to the Kahuku Plantation, which produced sugar here from 1890 until it closed in 1971. The operation was a relatively small concern, unable to keep up with the increasingly mechanized competition of Hawaii's bigger mills. When the mill shut down, Kahuku's economy skidded into a slump that still lingers today.

A fledgling shopping center has been set up inside the old **Kahuku Sugar Mill**, with small shops ringing the old machinery. The mill's enormous gears, flywheels and pipes have been painted in bright colors to help visitors visualize how a sugar mill works. The steam systems are red, the cane-juice systems light green, hydraulic systems dark blue and so forth. It looks like something out of *Modern Times* – you can almost imagine Charlie Chaplin caught up in the giant gears.

The center has not been wildly successful, but there's a local plate-lunch eatery, food mart, gas station, post office, bank and a few other shops in the complex.

The shallow **Kuilima Cove**, which is one of the area's best swimming spots, is fronted by the Turtle Bay Hilton, the sole hotel in Kahuku. You can park at one of the free spaces for beachgoers, which are on the right just before the guard booth, and walk 10 minutes to the beach. Alternatively, there's parking inside the hotel lot at very reasonable rates.

Kaihalulu Beach is a beautiful, curved, white-sand beach backed by ironwoods. Although a shoreline lava shelf and rocky bottom make the beach poor for swimming, it's good for beachcombing – you can walk east about a mile to Kahuku Point. Local fishers cast throw nets from the shore and pole fish from the point. The dirt road just inland of the beach is also used as a horse trail.

To get to the beach, turn into the Turtle Bay Hilton. Just before the guard booth, turn right into an unmarked parking lot, where there are free spaces for beachgoers. It's a five-minute walk out to the beach. There are no facilities.

Places to Stay

Turtle Bay Hilton & Country Club (☎ 293-8811, 800-445-8667, fax 293-9147, Kahuku, HI 96731) is a self-contained resort and the only major hotel on the windward and north shores. The Hilton is perched on Kuilima Point, between Turtle Bay and Kuilima Cove. All 485 rooms have ocean views. Room rates range from $165 to $265, suites from $400 to $1500. There are two golf courses, two pools, horse stables and 10 tennis courts – which means there's never a shortage of activities.

You can find a better deal with *Turtle Bay Condos* (☎ 293-2800, fax 293-2169, PO Box 248, Kahuku, HI 96731), which handles the units at Kuilima Estates, the modern condominium complex on the grounds fronting the Hilton. Rates are $90 for a regular studio, $100 for a studio with a loft and from $110/150 for a unit with one/two bedrooms. In addition there's a $50 cleaning fee tagged on to all rentals, no matter how long you stay. Each unit has a complete kitchen, washer/dryer, TV, phone and lanai.

Places to Eat

If you like shrimp, look for *Giovanni's Aloha Shrimp*, a truck that parks along the highway just south of the Kahuku Sugar Mill. Popular with both locals and weekend sightseers from Honolulu, Giovanni's offers a choice of tasty shrimp scampi, conventional grilled shrimp or an ultra-fiery spicy shrimp. A plate with half a pound of jumbo shrimp and two scoops of rice costs $11. There's a covered picnic area where you can sit and eat. It's open from 10:30 am to 6:30 pm daily.

There are also a few restaurants at the Turtle Bay Hilton. The *Palm Terrace* has buffets for around $14 at lunch and $20 at dinner. The *Sea Tide Room* has a Sunday brunch for $27, while *The Cove* is the hotel's fine-dining restaurant.

Central Oahu

Central Oahu forms a saddle between the Waianae Mountains on the west and the Koolau Mountains on the east.

Three routes lead north from Honolulu to Wahiawa, the town smack in the middle of Oahu. The freeway, H-2, is the fastest route, whereas Hwy 750, the farthest west, is the most scenic. The least interesting of the options, Hwy 99, catches local traffic as it runs through Mililani, a modern, nondescript residential community.

Most people just zoom up through central Oahu on their way to the North Shore. If your time is limited this isn't a bad idea. There are a few sights along the way, but Wahiawa, the region's commercial center, doesn't really warrant much more than a zip through anyway.

From Wahiawa two routes, Hwy 803 (Kaukonahua Rd) and Hwy 99 (Kamehameha Hwy), lead down through pineapple country to the North Shore. Hwy 803 is a slightly shorter way to reach Mokuleia than Hwy 99 and about the same distance to Haleiwa. Both are fine scenic roads, and if you're not circling the island, you might as well go up one and down the other.

HWY 750

Hwy 750 (Kunia Rd) adds a few miles to the drive through central Oahu but if you have the time it's worth it. Follow H-1 to the Kunia/Hwy 750 exit, 3 miles west of where H-1 and H-2 divide.

After you turn up Hwy 750 the first mile is through creeping suburbia but then you enter plantation lands. The route runs along the foothills of the Waianae Range and the countryside remains solidly agricultural all the way to Schofield Barracks.

Up the road 2 miles you'll come to a strip of corn fields planted by the Garst Seed Company. Three generations of corn are grown here each year, which makes it possible to develop hybrids of corn seed at triple the rate it would take on the mainland. The little bags placed over each ear of corn prevent them from being cross-pollinated.

A bit farther north begins one of the most scenic pineapple fields in Hawaii. There are no buildings and no development – just red earth carpeted with long green strips of pineapples stretching to the edge of the mountains.

From the Hawaii Country Club, just up the road on the right, there's a distant view of Honolulu all the way to Diamond Head.

Kunia

Kunia, a little town in the midst of the pineapple fields, is home to the field workers employed by Del Monte. If you want to see what a current-day plantation village looks like, turn west off Hwy 750 onto Kunia Drive, which makes a 1¼-mile loop through the town.

Rows of grey-green wooden houses with corrugated tin roofs stand on low stilts. People take pride in their little yards, with bougainvillea and other flowers adding a splash of brightness despite the wash of red dust that blows in from the surrounding pineapple fields.

Kunia Drive intersects the highway at about 5½ miles north of the intersection of Hwy 750 and H-1 (there's a store and post office near the turnoff) and again at the 6-mile marker.

Kolekole Pass

Kolekole is the gap in the Waianae Mountains that Japanese fighter planes once flew through on their way to bomb Pearl Harbor. The landscape may look familiar, as the flight scene was recreated here 30 years later for the shooting of the popular war film *Tora! Tora! Tora!*

Kolekole Pass, at an elevation of 1724 feet, sits above Schofield Barracks on military property. It can be visited as long as the base isn't on some sort of military alert.

Access the pass through Foote Gate, on Hwy 750, a third of a mile south of its intersection with Hwy 99. After passing through the gate, take the first left onto Road A, then the first right onto Lyman Rd. The drive is 5¼ miles up past the barracks, golf course and bayonet assault course. The parking lot is opposite the hilltop with the big white cross that's visible from miles away.

The five-minute walk to the top of the pass ends at a clearing with a view straight down to the Waianae (Leeward) Coast. In Hawaiian mythology, the large, ribbed stone that sits atop the ridge here is said to be the embodiment of a woman named Kolekole who took the form of this stone in order to become the perpetual guardian of the pass. Along the side of the stone are a series of ridges, one of them draining down from a bowl-like depression on the top. Shaped perfectly for a guillotine, the depression has given rise to a more recent 'legend' that Kolekole served as a sacrificial stone for the beheadings of defeated chiefs and warriors. The fact that military bases flank both sides of the pass has no doubt had a little influence on this violent story.

Just west of the pass the road continues through a Navy base down to the Waianae Coast, but you can't take it. The Navy base is a stockyard for nuclear weapons, and there's no public access through that side.

WAHIAWA

Wahiawa is a GI town. Just about every fast-food chain you can think of is there. Tattoo parlors and pawn shops are the town's main refinements, and if you're looking for a little excitement, there are some rough-and-tumble bars.

To go through town and visit the botanical garden, healing stones and royal birthstones, take Kamehameha Hwy (which is Hwy 80 as it goes through town, although it's Hwy 99 before and after Wahiawa). To make the bypass around Wahiawa, stick with Hwy 99.

Wahiawa Botanical Garden

The Wahiawa Botanical Garden, 1396 California Ave, is a mile east of the Kamehameha Hwy. What started out in the 1920s as a site for forestry experiments by the Hawaii Sugar Planters' Association is now a 27-acre city park with grand old trees around a wooded ravine.

The park is a nice shady place to take a stroll. Interesting 70-year-old exotics such as cinnamon, chicle and allspice are grouped in one area. Tree ferns, loulu palms and other Hawaiian natives are in another. The trees are identified by markers, and the air is thick with birdsong.

The garden is open from 9 am to 4 pm daily. Admission to the park is free, as is a brochure describing some of the trees.

Healing Stones

One of the stranger sights to be labeled with a Hawaii Visitors Bureau marker, the

'Healing Stones' are caged inside a small stone 'temple' next to the Methodist church on California Ave, half a mile west of its intersection with Kamehameha Hwy.

The main stone is thought to have been the gravestone of a powerful Hawaiian chief. Although the chief's original burial place is in a field a mile away, the stone was moved long ago to a graveyard at this site. In the 1920s, people thought the stone had healing powers and thousands made pilgrimages to the supposedly miraculous rock before interest waned. The housing development and church came later, taking over the graveyard and leaving the stones sitting on the sidewalk.

A local group with roots in India, who sees a spiritual connection between Hawaiian and Indian beliefs, now visits the temple, so you may see flowers or little elephant statues placed around the stones. The story is actually more interesting than the site, however.

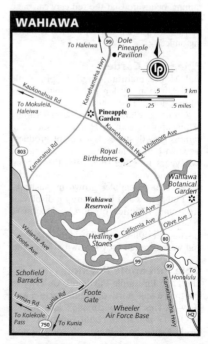

WAHIAWA

Royal Birthstones

Kukaniloko, a group of royal birthstones where queens gave birth, is just north of Wahiawa. The stones are thought to date back to the 12th century. It was said that if a woman lay properly against the stones while giving birth, her child would be blessed by the gods, and indeed, many of Oahu's great chiefs were born at this site.

These stones are one of only two documented birthstone sites in Hawaii (the other's in Kauai). Many of the petroglyphs on the stones are of recent origin, but the eroded circular patterns are original.

To get to them from town, go three-quarters of a mile north on Kamehameha Hwy from its intersection with California Ave. Turn left onto the red dirt road that's directly opposite Whitmore Ave. The stones, marked with a state monument sign, are a quarter of a mile down through a pineapple field, among a stand of eucalyptus and coconut trees. If it has been raining, be aware that the red clay can cake onto your car tires, and once back on the paved road the car may slide as if it's driving on ice.

Pineapple Garden

Del Monte maintains a little pineapple demonstration garden in a triangle at the intersection of Hwys 99 and 80.

Smooth cayenne, the commercial variety of pineapple grown in Hawaii, is shown in various growth stages. Each plant produces just two pineapples. The first takes nearly two years to reach maturity, the second about one year more. Other commercial varieties of pineapples grown in Australia, the Philippines and Brazil are on display, as are some varieties of purely decorative bromeliads.

You can pull off to the side of the road and walk through on your own at any time.

Dole Pineapple Pavilion

The Dole Pineapple Pavilion is on Hwy 99 less than a mile north of its intersection with Hwy 80. This touristy complex, in the heart of Oahu's pineapple country, consists of a bustling gift shop along with some simple bromeliad gardens and a hibiscus hedge maze out back. Dole's processing plant sits across the street and miles of pineapple fields surround the area.

At the Dole gift shop you can purchase pineapple juice, pineapple freezes, pineapple pastries and pineapples boxed to take home. Expect things to be a bit pricey, but the gardens are free and it makes a nice opportunity to get out and stretch. If you feel like getting lost, you can wander through the maze for $4.50 but there's really not much thrill to it. Hours are from 9 am to 6 pm daily.

North Shore

Oahu's North Shore is synonymous with surfing and prime winter waves. Sunset Beach, the Banzai Pipeline and Waimea Bay are among the world's top surf spots and attract some of the best international surfers.

Other North Shore surf breaks may be less well known, but with names like Himalayas and Avalanche, they're not exactly for neophytes.

On winter weekends, convoys of cars make the trip up from Honolulu to watch the action from the beach. You can beat much of the traffic simply by coming up on a weekday.

It's believed that the earliest Polynesians to arrive on Oahu were drawn to the North Shore by the region's rich fishing grounds, cooling trade winds and moderate rain. The areas around Mokuleia, Haleiwa and Waimea all once had sizable Hawaiian settlements. Abandoned taro patches still remain in their upland valleys.

By the early 1900s, the Oahu Railroad & Land Company had extended the railroad around Kaena Point and along the entire North Shore, linking the area with Honolulu and bringing in the first beachgoers from the city. Hotels and private beach houses sprang up, but when the railroad stopped running in the 1940s the hotels shut down for good. Sections of abandoned track are still found along many of the beaches.

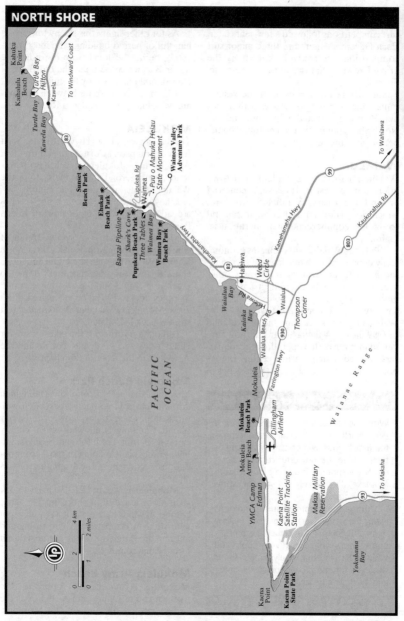

NORTH SHORE

Kahuku Point
Kaihalulu Beach
Turtle Bay Hilton
Turtle Bay
Kawela Bay
Kawela

To Windward Coast

83

Sunset Beach Park
Ehukai Beach Park
Banzai Pipeline
Shark's Cove
Pupukea Beach Park
Three Tables
Waimea Bay
Waimea Bay Beach Park

Pupukea Rd
Waimea
Puu o Mahuka Heiau State Monument
Waimea Valley Adventure Park

To Wahiawa

99

Kaukonahua Rd

803

Kamehameha Hwy

83 Haleiwa
Weed Circle
Kamehameha Hwy

Waialua Bay
Kaiaka Bay

Haleiwa Rd
Waialua Beach Rd

Waialua
Thompson Corner

930

Farmington Hwy

PACIFIC OCEAN

Mokuleia

Mokuleia Beach Park

Dillingham Airfield

Waianae Range

Mokuleia Army Beach

Makua Military Reservation

YMCA Camp Erdman

Kaena Point Satellite Tracking Station

93

To Makaha

Kaena Point
Kaena Point State Park

Yokohama Bay

4 km
2 miles

0 2
0 1

OAHU

Waikiki surfers started taking on North Shore waves in the late 1950s and big-time surf competitions followed a few years later. Each December there are three major surf competitions, collectively known as the Triple Crown, with prize purses reaching six figures.

Surf mania prevails even in the restaurants, which serve up omelettes with names like 'Pumping Surf' and 'Wipe Out.' Half the North Shore population can be found on the beach when the surf's up.

WAIALUA

Waialua, a little former plantation town about a mile west of Haleiwa, is centered around the dusty Waialua Sugar Mill, which closed down in 1996, bringing an end to the last commercial sugar operation on Oahu.

While the Waialua area remains economically depressed, with much of the surrounding fields taken over by feral cane, other sections are newly planted in coffee – a labor-intensive crop that holds out promise for new jobs. Indeed, the first harvest of Waialua coffee is reaching the market, and in 1999 the old Waialua Sugar Mill, now converted into the coffee operation's headquarters, opened a small visitor center. There's not much to see, and the center sells cups of

coffee rather than doling out samples, but it is open free.

As for other sights, this sleepy town has a handful of period buildings, the most interesting being the local watering hole, the Sugar Bar, which occupies the old Bank of Hawaii building down by the mill.

The most scenic route between Haleiwa and Waialua is along Haleiwa Rd.

MOKULEIA

The Farrington Hwy (Hwy 930) runs west from Thompson Corner to Dillingham Airfield and Mokuleia Beach. (Both this road and the road that travels along the Waianae Coast are called Farrington Hwy, but they don't connect, as each side reaches a dead end about 2½ miles short of Kaena Point.)

Mokuleia Beach is a 6-mile stretch of white sand running from Kaiaka Bay toward Kaena Point. Although some GIs and locals come this way, the beaches don't draw too much of a crowd and the area has sort of a 'boonies' feel to it. The only beach facilities are at Mokuleia Beach Park, and the nearest store is back in Waialua.

Dillingham Airfield is the take-off site for glider rides and skydiving. For details, see Activities in the front of this chapter.

Mokuleia Beach Park

Mokuleia Beach Park, opposite Dillingham Airfield, has a large open grassy area with picnic tables, rest rooms, showers and a pay phone. Camping is allowed with a county camping permit. For information on obtaining permits, see Camping in the Accommodations section near the beginning of this chapter.

Mokuleia is sandy but has a lava rock shelf along much of its shoreline. The fairly consistent winds here make it a popular spot with windsurfers, particularly in spring and autumn. In winter, the strong currents turn it into a dangerous area.

Mokuleia Army Beach

Mokuleia Army Beach, opposite the western end of Dillingham Airfield, has the widest stretch of sand on the Mokuleia

---

North Shore Water Conditions

With the exception of Haleiwa Beach Park, North Shore beaches are notorious for treacherous winter swimming conditions. There are powerful currents along the entire shore. If it doesn't look as calm as a lake, it's probably not safe for swimming or snorkeling.

During the summer, surf conditions along the whole North Shore can mellow right out. Shark's Cove then becomes a prime snorkeling and diving spot, and Waimea Bay, internationally famous for its winter surf, turns into a popular swimming and snorkeling beach.

shore. Once reserved exclusively for military personnel, the beach is now open to the public, although it is no longer maintained and there are no facilities.

The beach is unprotected and has very strong rip currents, especially during winter high surf. Surfing is sometimes good.

Army Beach to Kaena Point

From Army Beach, you can proceed another 1 1/2 miles down the road, passing still more white-sand beaches with aqua waters. You'll usually find someone shore-casting and occasionally a few local people camping.

The paved road goes past YMCA Camp Erdman and then ends at a locked gate. The terrain is scrub land reaching up to the base of the Waianae Range, while the shoreline is wild and windswept. The area is not only desolate, but can also be a bit trashed, and this is certainly not a must-do drive.

From road's end, it's possible to walk the 2 1/2 miles to Kaena Point along state park lands, but it's more attractive from the other side (for details, see Kaena Point State Park in the Waianae Coast section).

HALEIWA

Haleiwa is the gateway to the North Shore and the main town catering to the multitude of day-trippers who make the circle-island ride.

The 2500 townspeople are a multiethnic mix of families who have lived in Haleiwa for generations and more-recently-arrived surfers, artists and New Age folks.

Most of Haleiwa's shops are lined up along Kamehameha Ave, the main drag through town.

Haleiwa has a picturesque boat harbor, bounded on both sides by beach parks. One side is known for its winter surfing, the other for the North Shore's safest year-round swimming.

The Anahulu River, which flows out along the boat harbor, is spanned by the Rainbow Bridge, so nicknamed for its distinctive arches. Take a glimpse up the river from the bridge. It's still a lushly green scene, and it's easy to imagine how it must have looked in ancient Hawaii, when the riverbanks were lined with taro patches.

Information

There's a Bank of Hawaii in the Haleiwa Shopping Plaza and a First Hawaiian Bank farther north on Kamehameha Ave.

The post office, on the south side of town, is open from 8 am to 4 pm on weekdays, from 9 am to noon on Saturday.

Surf-N-Sea (☎ 637-9887), 62-595 Kamehameha Ave, just north of the Rainbow Bridge, rents surfboards, boogie boards, windsurfing equipment, dive gear and snorkel sets. The staff also give surfing and windsurfing lessons, run a dive operation, and sell new and used surfboards and sailboards. Hawaiian Surf, Strong Current and Raging Isle, all in the North Shore Marketplace, also carry surfboards.

North Shore Surf & Cultural Museum

You can get a sense of how integral surfing is to the town's character by visiting the North Shore Surf & Cultural Museum, in the North Shore Marketplace, which has a collection of vintage surfboards, period photos and surf videos. Admission is by donation. Run by volunteers, it's usually open from 9 am to 6 pm Monday to Saturday and from 10 am to 6 pm on Sunday.

Matsumoto's

For many people the circle-island drive isn't complete without lining up at Matsumoto's tin-roofed general store for shave ice. Hawaiian shave ice is a bit like a snow cone, although better because the ice is finer. The cloyingly sweet syrups are no different, however. Shave ice at Matsumoto's costs from $1.20 for the small plain version to $2 for a large with ice cream and sweetened azuki beans.

Liliuokalani Church

The Protestant church opposite Matsumoto's takes its name from Queen Liliuokalani, who spent summer on the shores of the Anahulu River and attended services here. Although the church dates from 1832,

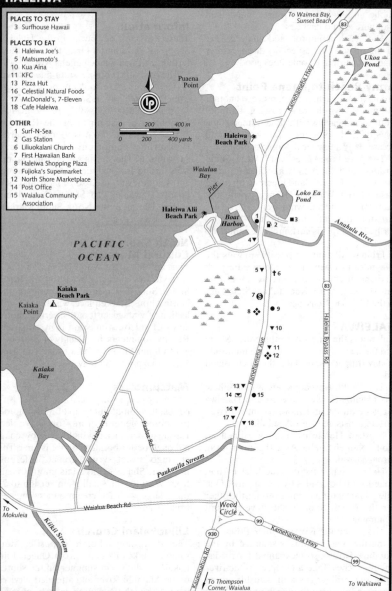

HALEIWA

PLACES TO STAY
3 Surfhouse Hawaii

PLACES TO EAT
4 Haleiwa Joe's
5 Matsumoto's
10 Kua Aina
11 KFC
13 Pizza Hut
16 Celestial Natural Foods
17 McDonald's, 7-Eleven
18 Cafe Haleiwa

OTHER
1 Surf-N-Sea
2 Gas Station
6 Liliuokalani Church
7 First Hawaiian Bank
8 Haleiwa Shopping Plaza
9 Fujioka's Supermarket
12 North Shore Marketplace
14 Post Office
15 Waialua Community
    Association

the current building was built in 1961. As late as the 1940s, services were held entirely in Hawaiian.

Of most interest is the unusual **seven-dial clock** that Queen Liliuokalani gave the church in 1892. The clock shows the hour, day, month and year, as well as the phases of the moon. The queen's long 12-letter name replaces the numerals on the clock face. The church is open whenever the minister is in, which is typically in the mornings.

Kaiaka Beach Park

The 53-acre Kaiaka Beach Park is on Kaiaka Bay, about a mile west of town. This is a good place for a picnic, as there are shady ironwood trees, but the in-town beaches are better choices for swimming. Two streams empty out into Kaiaka Bay, muddying up the beach after heavy rainstorms. Kaiaka has rest rooms, picnic tables, showers and seven campsites. Camping is free with a permit from the county. For information on obtaining such permits, see Camping in the Accommodations section near the beginning of this chapter.

Haleiwa Alii Beach Park

Surfing is king at Haleiwa Alii Beach Park. This is the site of several tournaments in the winter, when north swells can bring waves as high as 20 feet.

When waves are 5 feet and under, lots of younger kids bring their boards out. Any time the waves are 6 feet or better, there are also strong currents, and the water conditions are more suited to experienced surfers. The county (☎ 637-5051) offers free surfing lessons here on weekend mornings during winter.

The 20-acre beach park has rest rooms, showers, picnic tables and a lifeguard tower. The shallow areas on the southern side of the beach are generally the calmest for swimming.

Haleiwa Beach Park

Haleiwa Beach Park is on the north side of Waialua Bay. As the beach is protected by a shallow shoal and a breakwater, the waters are usually very calm and see little wave action, though north swells occasionally ripple into the bay.

While the beach isn't Haleiwa's most appealing, this 13-acre county park has full beach facilities as well as basketball and volleyball courts, an exercise area and a softball field. It also has a good view of Kaena Point.

Places to Stay

Surfhouse Hawaii (☎ 637-7146, surfhouse@ aol.com, 62-203 Lokoea Place, Haleiwa, HI 96712) is a budget place to stay at the north side of Haleiwa. Situated on 2 acres at the back of Lokoea Pond, Surfhouse Hawaii offers three accommodation options. One is dormitory-style in a cabin with a lanai, a kitchen and six beds for $15 per person. Outside, there's a half-dozen tenting sites, some of which have platforms, at a cost of $9 for one camper or $15 for two. The third option is a $45 private room with a double bed and shared bath in the home of Lee and Sofie, the couple who run the place. All guests have access to kitchen facilities. Bicycles and watersports gear are available for rent; if you don't have a tent, you can rent that as well, for a small fee. The location, on a quiet side road immediately north of Rainbow Bridge, is within walking distance of both the beach and town center. For more information, visit www.surfhouse .com online.

Haleiwa's other camping option is at Kaiaka Beach Park, where the county allows camping from Friday to Tuesday nights. For details on obtaining a permit, see Camping

---

House of the Frigate Bird

In the summer of 1832, John and Ursula Emerson, the first missionaries to the North Shore, built a grass house and missionary school beside the Anahulu River. They called the school Haleiwa, meaning house (hale) of the great frigate bird (iwa). Over time, the name came to refer to the entire village.

under Accommodations in the Facts for the Visitor chapter.

In addition, people occasionally rent out rooms in their homes. You can usually find room-for-rent notices on the bulletin boards at the Coffee Gallery, Celestial Natural Foods and Haleiwa Super Market.

Places to Eat

Cafe Haleiwa, at the south side of town, is an unpretentious eatery serving good food. An institution of sorts on the North Shore, it has long been a haunt for local surfers. A large burrito served with terrific home fries costs $6, while two large pancakes loaded with blueberries cost $3.50. Lunch is predominantly sandwiches and Mexican fare, averaging $7 to $8. The cafe is open 7 am to 2 pm daily, with breakfast available until 12:30 pm (2 pm on Sunday).

Celestial Natural Foods, opposite Cafe Haleiwa, has bulk foods, granolas, fresh produce, yogurts and just about everything else you'd expect to find in a good health food store. There's a cafe in the back of the store selling vegetable chili over brown rice for $3, sandwiches and salads for around $5 and a few Middle Eastern dishes for a tad more. The store is open 9 am to 6:30 pm Monday to Saturday and 10 am to 6 pm on Sunday; the cafe has slightly shorter hours daily.

The popular *Kua Aina* in the center of town makes the North Shore's best burgers and fish sandwiches, each about $5. It's open 11 am to 8 pm daily.

The *Coffee Gallery* in the North Shore Marketplace is a fine alternative to the burger and plate-lunch scene. This shop offers steamed coffees, scones and bagels at reasonable prices. Breakfast fare, such as granola with yogurt and fruit, costs around $5, as do soups, sandwiches, quiche and salads at lunchtime. There's open-air seating at the side of the cafe, and food can be ordered for takeout. The Coffee Gallery is open 8 am to 8:30 pm daily.

Cholo's in the North Shore Marketplace has good Mexican fare, though finding a free table on a busy day can be a challenge. You can order a variety of combination plates for $7 to $10. A good choice when they're available are the fresh ahi tacos, which cost $3.50. Cholo's is open 8 am to 9 pm daily.

There's a more expensive Mexican restaurant, *Rosie's Cantina*, as well as a pizza place, *Pizza Bob's*, in the Haleiwa Shopping Plaza.

If you're looking for generic fast-food fare, there's a *McDonald's*, *Pizza Hut*, *KFC* and *7-Eleven*, all on Kamehameha Ave at the south side of town.

The local favorite for a more upscale meal is *Haleiwa Joe's* (☎ 637-8005), which has a pleasant harborview setting at the north side of town. It features meat and seafood dinners from $13 to $20. You can add a green salad for $1.50 or tempting ahi spring rolls, sushi or sashimi for $5 to $10. Dinner is served from 5:30 pm nightly. Lunch, available from 11:30 am to 4:30 pm, includes burgers, fish sandwiches and salads in the $6 to $10 range.

Haleiwa has two main grocery stores: *Haleiwa Super Market*, in the Haleiwa Shopping Plaza, and *Fujioka's Supermarket*, across the street.

WAIMEA

The Waimea Valley was once heavily settled. The lowlands were terraced in taro, the valley walls dotted with house sites and the ridges topped with heiaus. Just about every crop grown in Hawaii thrived in the valley, including a rare pink taro favored by Hawaiian royalty.

Waimea River, now blocked at the beach, originally opened into the bay and was a passage for canoes traveling to villages upstream. The sport of surfing was immensely popular here centuries ago, with the early Hawaiians taking to Waimea's huge waves on their long boards.

When Captain Cook's ships sailed into Waimea to collect water in 1779, shortly after Cook's death on the Big Island, an entry in the ship's log noted that the valley was uncommonly beautiful and picturesque.

However, Western contact wasn't kind to the area. Deforestation above the valley, from logging and the introduction of plantations, contributed to a devastating flood in Waimea in 1894. In addition to water damage, a large quantity of mud washed through the valley, so much so that it permanently altered the shape of Waimea's shore. After the flood, most residents abandoned the valley and resettled elsewhere.

Waimea Bay Beach Park

Waimea Bay is a beautiful, deeply inset bay with turquoise waters and a wide white-sand beach almost 1500 feet long. Ancient Hawaiians believed its waters were sacred.

Waimea Bay's mood changes with the seasons; it can be tranquil and as flat as a lake in summer, then savage with incredible surf and the island's meanest rip currents in winter. Waimea boasts Hawaii's biggest surf and holds the record for the highest waves ever ridden in international competition. As at Sunset Beach, the huge north swells bring out crowds of spectators who throng to watch Waimea surfers perform their near-suicidal feats on waves of up to 35 feet.

On winter's calmer days the boogie boarders are out in force, but even then sets come in hard and people get pounded. Winter water activities here are not for novices.

Usually the only time the water is calm enough for swimming and snorkeling is from June to September. The best snorkeling is around the rocks on the left of the bay.

Waimea Bay Beach Park is the most popular North Shore beach. There are showers, rest rooms, picnic tables and a pay phone, and a lifeguard is on duty daily. Parking is often tight.

Waimea Valley Adventure Park

Waimea Valley Adventure Park (☎ 638-8511), across the highway from Waimea Bay Beach Park, is a combined botanical garden and cultural theme park.

The main park road leads three-quarters of a mile up the Waimea Valley to a waterfall, passing extensive naturalized gardens that include sections of ginger, hibiscus, heliconia and medicinal plants. Many of the plants are labeled for identification, and there are several rare species under propagation.

The park has ancient stone platforms and terraces and a few replicas of thatched buildings similar to those used by early Hawaiians. Traditional hula dances, Hawaiian games and other demonstrations are given during the day. A cliff diver plunges 60 feet into the waterfall pool five times a day to thrill spectators.

The valley's natural beauty is nicely preserved, and the park is pleasant to wander through, but the cost of admission is quite steep at $24.95 for adults, $12.50 for children ages four to 12. Children three and under are admitted free.

A cheaper deal is to come at 4:15 pm, when the rate drops to $10 for adults and $5 for children. Although the demonstrations stop around this time, the grounds are less crowded and more pleasant for strolling. The park is open from 10 am to sunset daily. There's a simple in-park eatery with sandwiches and burgers.

Public bus No 52 stops on the highway in front of the park, from where it's a half-mile walk to the park entrance.

St Peter & Paul Church

The church of St Peter & Paul stands beneath the tall yet unassuming tower on the

Human Sacrifices

In 1792, Captain Vancouver, who had been an officer on one of Captain Cook's vessels a decade earlier, anchored in Waimea Bay. While three of his men were collecting water on shore, they were attacked and killed. It's thought that their bodies were taken up to Puu o Mahuka Heiau on the ridge above the beach and sacrificed.

When Vancouver returned a year later demanding justice, the high chief turned over three islanders. Although Vancouver doubted that these particular men had anything to do with the earlier murders, he had come to set an example so he ordered their execution anyway.

northern side of Waimea Bay. The structure was originally a rock-crushing plant, built to supply gravel for the construction of the highway in the 1930s. After it was abandoned, the Catholic church converted it into Oahu's most unlikely chapel.

Puu o Mahuka Heiau

Puu o Mahuka Heiau State Monument is a long, low-walled platform temple perched on a bluff above Waimea. The largest heiau on Oahu, its construction is attributed to the legendary menehunes.

The terraced stone walls are a couple of feet high, although most of the heiau is now overgrown. This was an excellent site for a temple, and it's well worth the drive up for the view. It can also be a fine place to watch the sunset.

Walk up above the left side of the heiau from the parking lot for a view of Waimea Valley and Waimea Bay. To the west, you can see all the way out along the coast to Kaena Point.

To get to the heiau, turn up Pupukea Rd at the Foodland supermarket. The marked turnoff to the heiau is about half a mile up the road, and from there it's three-quarters of a mile in. On the drive up there's a good view of Pupukea Beach Park.

Pupukea Beach Park

Pupukea Beach Park is a long beach along the highway that includes Three Tables on the left and Shark's Cove on the right. In the middle is Old Quarry, where a wonderful array of jagged rock formations and tide pools are exposed at low tide. This is a very scenic beach, with deep-blue waters, a varied coast and a mix of lava and white sand. The rocks and tide pools are tempting to explore, but be careful – they're razor sharp, and if you slip it's easy to get a deep cut.

The waters off Pupukea Beach are a marine-life conservation district.

There are showers and rest rooms in front of Old Quarry. The beach entrance is opposite an old gas station; bus No 52 stops out front. Snorkel sets and other water sports equipment can be rented from Planet Surf, at the side of the Foodland supermarket.

Three Tables Three Tables, at the western end of the beach, gets its name from the ledges rising above the water. In summer when the waters are calm, Three Tables has good snorkeling and diving. It's possible to see some action by snorkeling around the tables, but the best coral and fish as well as some small caves, lava tubes and arches are in deeper water farther out. This is a summer-only spot, however. In winter, dangerous rip currents flow between the beach and the tables. Beware of sharp rocks and coral.

Shark's Cove Shark's Cove is beautiful both above and below the water's surface. The naming of the cove was done in jest – sharks aren't a particular problem.

In the summer, when the seas are calm, Shark's Cove offers good snorkeling and swimming conditions as well as Oahu's most popular cavern dive. A fair number of beginning divers take lessons here, while the underwater caves will thrill advanced divers.

To get to the caves, swim out of the cove and around to the right. Some of the caves are very deep and labyrinthine, so caution should be used exploring them. There have been a number of drownings in these caves.

The large boulders out on the end of the point to the far right of the cove are said to be followers of Pele, the volcano goddess. As an honor, she gave them immortality by turning them to stone.

Ehukai Beach Park

The main reason people come to Ehukai Beach Park is to watch the pros surf the world-famous **Banzai Pipeline**, a few hundred feet to the left of the park. The Pipeline breaks over a shallow coral reef and can be a death-defying wave to ride.

At Ehukai Beach itself, many board riders and bodysurfers brave a hazardous current to ride the waves. Water conditions mellow out in summer, when it's good for swimming.

The entrance to Ehukai Beach Park is opposite the Sunset Beach Elementary School. The beach has a lifeguard, rest rooms, showers and a pay phone.

Sunset Beach Park

Sunset Beach Park, just south of the 9-mile marker, is a pretty beach that invites sunbathing, but the main action is in the water. This beach is Oahu's classic winter surf spot, with incredible waves and challenging breaks.

Winter swells create powerful rips. Even when the big waves have mellowed in the summer, there's still an along-shore current for swimmers to deal with. Toilets and a lifeguard tower are the only facilities.

Backyards, the surf break off Sunset Point at the northern end of the beach, draws a lot of top windsurfers. There's a shallow reef and strong currents to contend with, but Backyards has the island's biggest waves for sailing.

Places to Stay

Because Waimea has no post office, these accommodations have been assigned either Haleiwa or Kakuhu mailing addresses, although they are in the Waimea area.

Backpackers (☎ 638-7838, fax 638-7515, 59-788 Kamehameha Hwy, Haleiwa, HI 96712), opposite Three Tables, is pretty much a surfers' hangout. A durable place that's been in business for 20 years, it has a few different set-ups, most of it beach-house casual. The main house has four bunks to a room for $15 a bed, while a three-story house behind it has simple double rooms for $50. Both houses have shared bathrooms and kitchens. Expect spartan decor and aging furniture, but if you're looking for a place to crash between waves, then it's an option that doesn't bite the wallet deeply.

A small beachfront motel across the road has eight studios with TVs, kitchens and great views. Units on the bottom floor have dorm beds for $17, while those on the top are rented out like hotel rooms for $80 to $95.

The third property, a few hundred yards away on the inland side of the road, consists of nine cottages with either two or three bedrooms. Dorm beds are $15 while an entire cottage, which sleeps six to eight people, costs $110 to $150. Backpackers makes daily airport runs at around noon – the ride is free, and you can get dropped off in Waikiki as well. For more details, visit the website www.backpackers-hawaii.com.

Debbie Rezent (☎ 638-9402, 58-335 Mamao Place, Haleiwa, HI 96712) rents a pleasant studio unit above the garage at her home in a residential area close to Sunset Beach. It has a deck with a peek of the ocean, two twin beds, TV, bathroom with tub and limited kitchen facilities that include a refrigerator, microwave and hot plate. The cost is a reasonable $50.

Thomsen's Bed & Breakfast (☎ 638-7947, fax 638-7694, 59-420 Kamehameha Hwy, Haleiwa, HI 96712) is one large studio unit set above the garage of a private home near Ehukai Beach Park. It has a king bed, queen sofa bed, bathroom, kitchen area, private entrance, phone, TV and a lanai facing the mountains. It's a good value at $65, but despite the name, breakfast is not included.

Ironwoods (☎ 293-2554, fax 293-2603, 57-531 Kamehameha Hwy, Kahuku, HI 96731) is a studio in the beachside home of Ann and Richard McMann, just 2 miles north of scenic Sunset Beach. It has a loft bedroom with one king or two twin beds that's reached by steep ladder stairs and a downstairs sitting area with a kitchenette, cable TV and bathroom. This room costs $65 a night, with a simple breakfast, or $400 a week with no breakfast; there's a three-night minimum stay. Expect to hear traffic noise, though it's usually drowned out by the sound of surf.

The bulletin board at Pupukea Foodland has notices of roommates wanted and the occasional vacation rental listing.

Places to Eat

You can get burgers, sandwiches and $6 plate lunches at *Sunset Diner*, opposite Sunset Beach Park, from 9:30 am to 8 pm daily. Food supplies can be picked up at *Kammie's Market*, next to Sunset Diner, or at *Sunset Beach Store*, just north of Sunset Beach.

However, the best grocery prices and selection on the North Shore are at the

OAHU

Foodland supermarket opposite Pupukea Beach Park, which also has a deli with good inexpensive fried chicken. *Starbucks* coffee shop, inside Foodland, has bagels, scones and brownies for under $2, but if don't want to eat in you can find cheaper bakery items at Foodland itself.

The popular *Oceanside Grill*, a little white trailer that parks along the highway 100 yards north of Foodland, has beef or vegetarian burgers for around $4 and a few tables where you can sit and eat. This unassuming spot is open 11 am to about 5:30 pm daily.

Waianae Coast

The Waianae Coast is the arid, leeward side of Oahu.

In 1793, English captain George Vancouver, the first Westerner to drop anchor here, found a barren wasteland with only a few scattered fishing huts. Just two years later, in 1795, Kamehameha invaded Oahu and the population density along the Waianae Coast swelled with Oahuans who were forced to flee from their homes elsewhere on the island. This isolated western extreme of Oahu became their permanent refuge.

Today, leeward Oahu still stands separate from the rest of the island. There are no gift shops or sightseeing buses on the Waianae Coast. When you get right down to it, other than watching surfers at Makaha, there aren't a whole lot of sights to see.

Although developers are beginning to grab Waianae farmland for golf courses, leeward Oahu remains the island's least-touristed side. The area has a history of resisting development and a reputation for not being receptive to outsiders. In the past, visitors have been the targets of assaults and muggings. There's still a problem with thefts from cars and campsites, and although things aren't as hostile as they used to be, some locals aren't keen on sharing their space with tourists. Overall, you need to be attuned to the mood of the people.

Farrington Hwy (Hwy 93) runs the length of the leeward coast. There are long stretches of white-sand beaches, some quite attractive, others a bit trashed. In winter, most have treacherous swimming conditions, but at that time they also have some of the island's more challenging surfing. Although the towns themselves are ordinary, the cliffs and valleys cutting into the Waianae Range form a lovely backdrop.

At road's end, there's an undeveloped mile-long beach and a fine nature hike out to scenic Kaena Point.

KAHE POINT

Despite its name, the **Kahe Point Beach Park** doesn't include a beach, just the rocky cliffs of Kahe Point. The park has running water, picnic tables and rest rooms, but little else to recommend it.

The smokestacks of the nearby electric power plant punctuate the small park's backdrop. Along the road in front of the beach park a sign welcomes visitors to the Waianae Coast.

Hawaiian Electric Beach Park, the sandy beach north of Kahe Point, is more commonly known as Tracks, the name given to it by beachgoers who used to go there by train before World War II. In summer, this is a fairly calm place to swim, while in winter it's frequented by surfers.

To get there, take the first turnoff after the power plant and drive over the abandoned railroad tracks. There are rest rooms and a lifeguard station.

NANAKULI

Nanakuli, with a population of 9500, is the biggest town on the Waianae Coast. The site of a Hawaiian Homesteads settlement, Nanakuli also has one of the largest native Hawaiian populations on the island of Oahu. The town has supermarkets, the Waianae District Court, a bank and a few fast-food eateries.

Nanakuli is lined by a broad sandy beach park. There's swimming, snorkeling and diving during the calmer summer season. In winter, high surf can create rip currents and dangerous shorebreaks.

WAIANAE (LEEWARD) COAST

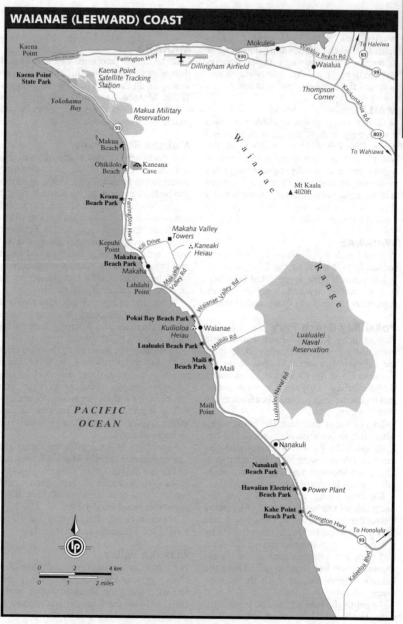

To get to the beach park, turn left at the traffic lights on Nanakuli Ave. This is a community park, with a playground, sports fields, full beach facilities and campsites. For information on obtaining camping permits, see Camping in the Accommodations section near the beginning of this chapter.

MAILI

Maili has a long, grassy roadside park with a seemingly endless stretch of white-sand beach. Like other places on this coast, the water conditions are often treacherous in winter but are usually calm enough for swimming in summer. There's a lifeguard station, a playground, beach facilities and a few castrated coconut palms to provide limited but safe shade.

WAIANAE

Waianae, with a population of 8800, is the second-largest town on the leeward coast. It has a beach park, a protected boat harbor, a satellite city hall, a police station, supermarkets and lots of fast-food places.

Pokai Bay Beach Park

Protected by Kaneilio Point and a long breakwater, Pokai Bay Beach Park features the calmest year-round swimming on the Waianae Coast. Waves seldom break inside the bay, and the sandy seafloor slopes gently, making the beach a popular spot for families with children.

Snorkeling is fair near the breakwater, where fish gather around the rocks. The bay is also used by local canoe clubs, and you can watch them rowing in the late afternoon. There are showers, rest rooms and picnic tables, and a lifeguard is on duty daily.

Kaneilio Point, which runs along the south side of the bay, is the site of **Kuilioloa Heiau**. Partly destroyed by the army during WWII, the heiau has been reconstructed by a Waianae group. Because part of the point had been lost, some sections of the temple reconstruction had to be modified from the heiau's original design to fit the smaller space.

To get to the beach park and heiau, turn onto Lualualei Homestead Rd, heading seaward, at the traffic light immediately after the Waianae post office.

MAKAHA

Makaha means 'ferocious,' and in days past the valley was notorious for the bandits who waited along the cliffs for travelers to pass. Today, Makaha has world-class surfing as well as Oahu's best-restored heiau, a golf course and a few condos.

Makaha Beach Park

Makaha Beach is broad, sandy and crescent-shaped, with some of the most daunting winter surf in the islands. Experienced surfers and bodysurfers both hit the waves here.

The beach is home to some major surf competitions. The most colorful is Buffalo's Big Board Surfing Classic held in February using old-style surfboards called 'tankers,' which are sometimes 15 feet long and weigh more than 80 pounds. As surfers today favor small, light boards, most competitors are of an older generation of surfers.

When the surf's not up, Makaha is a popular swimming beach. When the surf is up, rip currents and a strong shorebreak make swimming hazardous.

In summer the slope of the beach is relatively flat, while in winter the wave action results in a steeper drop. The beach sand is slightly coarse and of calcareous origin, with lots of mollusk-shell fragments. As much as half of it temporarily washes away during winter erosion, but even then Makaha is still an impressive beach.

Snorkeling is good offshore during the calmer summer months. Makaha Caves, out where the waves break farthest offshore, feature underwater caverns, arches and tunnels at depths of 30 to 50 feet. It's a popular leeward diving spot.

Makaha Beach has showers and rest rooms, and lifeguards are on duty daily.

Makaha Valley

For a little loop drive, turn inland from Kili Drive, opposite Makaha Beach Park, where the road skirts up along scalloped green cliffs into Makaha Valley. If you're there at midday, you can visit one of Hawaii's most authentically restored heiaus, which sits high in Makaha Valley at the back of a private residential estate.

An estimated 3000 wild peacocks live in the valley, including about two dozen white ones. They can be spotted, or at least heard, throughout the upper valley, and if you visit the heiau, it's not unusual to see them performing their courting rituals in the field adjacent to the parking lot.

To get to the heiau, take Kili Drive to the Makaha Valley Towers condominium complex and turn right onto Huipu Drive. Half a mile down on the left is Mauna Olu St, which leads a mile into Mauna Olu Estates and up to Kaneaki Heiau.

To get to the Makaha Valley Country Club golf course, stay on Huipu Drive. Makaha Valley Rd, which intersects with Huipu Drive near the golf course, completes the loop, connecting back with the Farrington Hwy.

Kaneaki Heiau Kaneaki Heiau was originally a Lono temple, dedicated to the god of agriculture. It was later transformed into a luakini temple, and it's thought that Kamehameha used it as a place of worship after he conquered Oahu. Kaneaki Heiau remained in use until the time of Kamehameha's death in 1819.

Restoration, undertaken by the Bishop Museum and completed in 1970, added two prayer towers, a taboo house, drum house, altar and god images. The heiau was authentically reconstructed in the traditional manner using ohia tree logs and pili grass shipped over from the Big Island. For those interested in early Hawaiian culture, it's a special place; the immediate setting surrounding the heiau remains undisturbed, even though the site is in the midst of a residential estate.

The guard at the Mauna Olu Estates gatehouse usually lets visitors go through to the heiau, a three-minute signposted drive past the gatehouse, between the hours of 10 am and 2 pm Tuesday to Sunday. However, you might want to call the gatehouse (☎ 695-8174) in advance to inquire, as the guards can be a bit inconsistent in

providing access. Also, you'll need to show your rental vehicle contract and driver's license, and there's typically no access if it's raining. There's no admission charge.

Places to Stay

Makaha doesn't have many accommodations for short-term visitors. There are a handful of condos geared primarily to permanent residents, but none are terribly appealing and they generally require you to stay for at least a week.

Makaha Surfside (☎ 695-9574 or 524-3455, riess@aloha-cafe.com, 85-175 Farrington Hwy, Makaha, HI 96792) is a four-story cinder-block apartment complex a mile south of Makaha Beach. Although it's predominantly residential, some of the 450 units are rented out on a weekly basis for around $300 for studios, $400 for one-bedroom units, both with full kitchens. It's an ordinary complex, although there are pools and barbecue grills.

Makaha Shores (☎ 696-8415, fax 696-1805, Hawaii Hatfield Realty, 85-833 Farrington Hwy, suite 201, Waianae, HI 96792) is a condo right on the northern end of Makaha Beach, with lanais overlooking the water. Studios cost $450 for one week, $650 for two weeks or $900 a month, with a $50 cleaning fee tacked on. There are one-bedroom units as well for around 20% more.

Hawaii Hatfield Realty also handles units for the same price in *Makaha Valley Towers*, the high-rise complex that's tucked into the valley.

Places to Eat

Makaha Valley Country Club, overlooking the golf course at the east end of Makaha Valley Rd, is a popular lunch spot with a varied menu that includes fried chicken or teriyaki beef plates for around $7 and sandwiches for about half that.

For something on the run, the *7-Eleven* store on the corner of Farrington Hwy and Makaha Valley Rd sells inexpensive doughnuts, turnovers and simple fast-food items.

Opposite the beach, about 150 yards north of the 7-Eleven, is *Makaha Drive-In*, which serves up $5 plate lunches and burgers, chili and sandwiches for around $2.

NORTH OF MAKAHA
Keaau Beach Park

Keaau Beach Park is another long, open, grassy strip, this time bordering a rocky shore, with campsites, showers, drinking water, picnic tables and rest rooms. A sandy beach begins at the very northern end of the park, although a rough reef, sharp drop and high seasonal surf make swimming uninviting. Enter the water at your own risk.

For information on obtaining camping permits, see Camping in the Accommodations section near the beginning of this chapter.

Driving north along the coast, you'll see low lava sea cliffs, white-sand beaches and patches of kiawe. On the inland side, you'll get a glimpse into a run of little valleys.

Kaneana Cave

Kaneana Cave, a massive cave on the right-hand side of the road about 2 miles north of Keaau Beach Park, was once underwater. Its impressive size is the result of wave action that wore away loose rock around an earthquake crack and expanded the cavern over the millennia as the ocean slowly receded.

Nanaue the Shark Man

Hawaiian legend tells of a child named Nanaue, who was born with an open space between his shoulders. Unknown to his mother, the child's father was the king of sharks in the guise of a man. Nanaue was born half human, half shark. He was human on land, but when he entered the ocean, the opening on his back became a shark's mouth. After a nasty spell in which many villagers were ripped to shreds by a mysterious shark, Nanaue's secret was discovered, and he was forced to swim from island to island as he was hunted down. For a while, he lived near Makua and took his victims into Kaneana Cave via an underwater tunnel.

✿✿✿✿✿✿✿✿✿✿✿✿

It's a somewhat uncanny place – often a strong wind gusts near the cave while it's windless just down the road.

Hawaiian kahunas once performed their rituals inside the cave's inner chamber. Older Hawaiians consider it a sacred place and won't enter for fear it's haunted by the spirits of deceased chiefs. From the collection of broken beer bottles and graffiti inside, it's obvious not everyone shares their sentiments.

From Ohikilolo Beach, below the cave, you can see Kaena Point to the north. Ohikilolo Beach is sometimes called Barking Sands, as the sand is said to make a 'woofing' sound if it's walked on when very dry.

Makua Valley

Scenic Makua Valley opens up wide and grassy, backed by a fan of sharply fluted mountains. Ironically, this very picturesque expanse serves as the ammunition field of the Makua Military Reservation.

The ocean-side road opposite the south end of the reservation leads to a little grave-yard shaded by yellow-flowered be-still trees. This is all that remains of the Makua Valley community, forced to evacuate during WWII, when the US military took over the entire valley for bombing practice. War games still take place in the valley, which is fenced off with barbed wire and signs that warn of stray explosives.

Makua Beach, the white-sand beach opposite the military reservation, was a canoe landing in days past. A movie set of Lahaina as it appeared during the 19th century was built on Makua Beach for the 1966 movie *Hawaii*, starring Julie Andrews and Max von Sydow. No trace of the set remains.

Satellite Tracking Station

Immediately before the gate to Kaena Point State Park, a road leads up to Kaena Point Satellite Tracking Station, operated by the US Air Force. The tracking station's antennas and domes sit atop the mountains above the point, a couple of them appearing like giant white golf balls perched on the ridge.

There are hiking trails above the tracking station, including a 2½-mile ridge trail that leads to Mokuleia Forest Reserve. You'll need to obtain a hiking permit in advance from the Division of Forestry & Wildlife (☎ 587-0166) to get past the air force's guard station.

KAENA POINT STATE PARK

Kaena Point State Park is an undeveloped 853-acre coastal strip that runs along both sides of Kaena Point, the westernmost point of Oahu.

Until the mid-1940s the Oahu Railroad ran up here from Honolulu and continued around the point, carrying passengers on to Haleiwa on the North Shore.

The attractive mile-long sandy beach on this side of the point is Yokohama Bay, named for the large numbers of Japanese fishers who came here during the railroad days.

Winter commonly brings huge pounding waves, making Yokohama a popular seasonal surfing and bodysurfing spot. It is, however, best left to the experts because of the submerged rocks, strong rip currents and dangerous shorebreak.

Swimming is pretty much limited to the summer, and then only during calm conditions. When the water's flat, it's possible to snorkel; the best spot and easiest access is at the south side of the park. There are rest rooms, showers and a lifeguard station.

In addition to being a state park, Kaena Point has been designated a natural area reserve because of its unique ecosystem. The extensive dry, windswept coastal dunes that rise above the point are the habitat of many rare native plants. The endangered Kaena akoko that grows on the talus slopes is found nowhere else.

More common plants are the beach naupaka, with white flowers that look like they've been torn in half; pau-o-Hiiaka, a vine with blue flowers; and beach morning glory, sometimes found wrapped in the parasite plant kaunaoa, which looks like orange plastic fishing line.

Seabirds common to the point include shearwaters, boobies and the common noddy, a dark-brown bird with a grayish crown. You can often see schools of spinner dolphins off the beach, and in winter humpback whale sightings are not uncommon.

Dirt bikes and 4WD vehicles once created a great deal of disturbance in the dunes, but after Kaena Point became a natural area reserve in 1983, vehicles were restricted and the situation improved. The reserve has once again become a nesting site for the Laysan albatross, and Hawaiian monk seals occasionally bask in the sun here.

Kaena Point Trail

A 2½-mile (one way) coastal hike runs from the end of the paved road at Yokohama Bay to Kaena Point, following the old railroad bed. Along the trail are tide pools, sea arches, fine coastal views and the lofty sea cliffs of the Waianae mountain range. The

Kaena Point Legends

Early Hawaiians believed that when people went into a deep sleep or lost consciousness, their souls would wander. Souls that wandered too far were drawn west to Kaena Point. If they were lucky, they were met here by their *aumakua* (ancestral spirit helper), who led their souls back to their bodies. If unattended, their souls would be forced to leap from Kaena Point into the endless night, never to return.

On clear days, Kauai can be seen from the point. According to legend, it was at Kaena Point that the demigod Maui attempted to cast a huge hook into Kauai and pull it next to Oahu to join the two islands. But the line broke and Kauai slipped away, with just a small piece of it remaining near Oahu. Today, this splintered rock, off the end of Kaena Point, is known as Pohaku o Kauai.

hike is unshaded (Kaena means 'the heat'), so take plenty of water.

Don't leave anything valuable in your car. Telltale mounds of shattered windshield glass can be found at the road's-end parking area used by most hikers; parking closer to the beach rest rooms or leaving your doors unlocked can decrease the odds of having your car windows smashed. Unfortunately, you can't always escape crime in paradise.

Hawaii (The Big Island)

The island of Hawaii, commonly called the Big Island, is nearly twice the size of all the other Hawaiian Islands combined. Geographically, it's so incredibly varied that it resembles a mini-continent. Climates range from tropical to subarctic. Landscapes include one of just about everything: desolate lava flows, lush coastal valleys, high sea cliffs, rolling pastures, deserts and rain forests.

Geologically, it's the youngest Hawaiian island and the only one still growing. Kilauea, the most active volcano on earth, has added 550 acres of coastal land to the island since its latest series of eruptions began in 1983.

The Big Island has Hawaii's highest mountains, which rise almost 14,000 feet above sea level. Some people liken them to icebergs, not only for their seasonal snowcaps but because their summits are merely the tips of mountain masses that rise 32,000 feet from the ocean floor.

The mountains create a huge barrier that blocks the moist northeasterly trade winds and makes the leeward side of the Big Island the driest region in Hawaii. The Kona and Kohala Coasts, on this sunny western side, have the island's best beaches and water conditions.

The windward east coast catches the rain and has a predominantly rugged coastline with pounding surf, lush tropical rain forests, deep ravines and majestic waterfalls.

Still, the island's most impressive scenery is at Hawaii Volcanoes National Park, which encompasses incredible volcanic sites. The park offers excellent hiking and camping in locales that range from tropical beaches to the icy 13,677-foot summit of Mauna Loa. You can drive or cycle around the rim of Kilauea's huge caldera and walk across still-steaming crater floors.

The Big Island has many noteworthy historical sites, including Hawaii's best petroglyphs and some of its most important *heiaus* (ancient temples). It also boasts the largest privately owned cattle ranch in the USA and the world's top collection of astronomical observatories. The latter dot the summit of Mauna Kea, Hawaii's highest point at 13,796 feet.

Hilo and Kona are the two distinct population centers on the Big Island. Hilo, on the lush, rainy east coast, is the island's only

Highlights

- Glimpsing a volcano's awesome power
- Gazing at the stars atop Mauna Kea, Hawaii's highest point
- Swimming with schools of tropical fish at Kahaluu Beach
- Hiking through the jungle to lush Akaka Falls
- Touring an ancient temple at Puuhonua o Honaunau

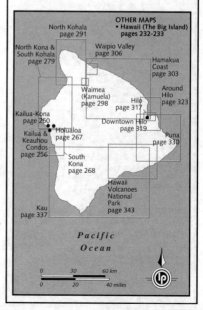

HAWAII (THE BIG ISLAND)

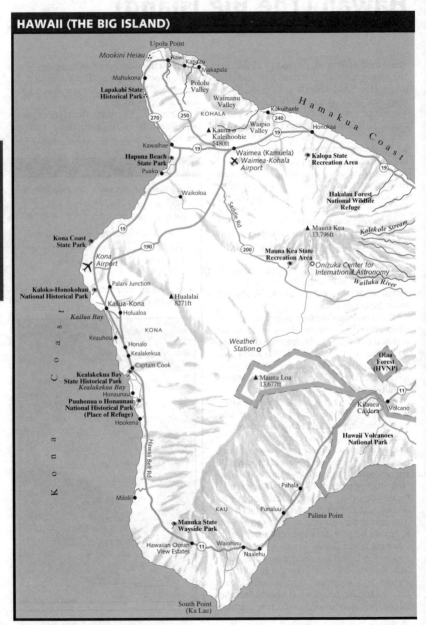

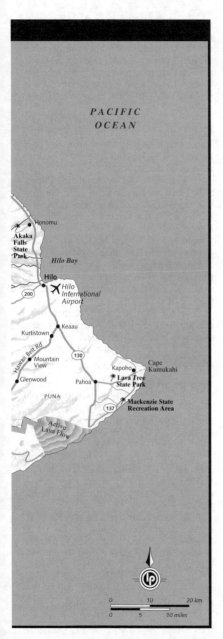

real city. It is the oldest city in Hawaii, and it shows its age with character. But it is Kona, on the dry, sunny west coast, that attracts the visitors. The Kona region has the lion's share of the island's accommodations and is the center of most recreational activities, including excellent diving and deep-sea fishing.

The Big Island is big on space, and few places feel crowded. It attracts a lot of adventurous people. It's got cowboy country, traditional fishing villages, valleys with taro farmers and wild horses, and a fair number of alternative folks living off the land.

HISTORY

By and large, the history of the Big Island is the history of Hawaii. It's widely believed that the first Polynesian settlers to Hawaii landed on this island. It was on the Big Island that the first *luakini heiau* (temple of human sacrifice) and the *kapu* system of strict taboos regulating all aspects of daily life came into being – both introduced by the Tahitian high priest Paao, who migrated here in the 12th century. It was also on the Big Island, seven centuries later, that the old Hawaiian gods were overthrown and replaced by those of the Christians.

This was where English explorer Captain Cook died (in 1779, a year after 'discovering' Hawaii), and this was where Kamehameha the Great rose to power.

Kamehameha the Great

Kamehameha the Great was born on the Big Island in 1758. As a young boy, he was brought to Kealakekua Bay to live at the royal court of his uncle, Kalaniopuu, high chief of the island.

Kamehameha went on to become Kalaniopuu's fiercest general, and the chief appointed him guardian of the war god, Kukailimoku, the 'snatcher of land.'

This war god was embodied in a coarsely carved wooden image with a bloody red mouth and a helmet of yellow feathers. Kamehameha carried it into battle with him, and it was said that during the fiercest fighting the image would screech out terrifying battle cries.

THE BIG ISLAND

Kamehameha the Great

Immediately after Kalaniopuu's death in 1782, Kamehameha led his warriors against Kalaniopuu's son, Kiwalao, who had taken the throne. Kiwalao was killed, and Kamehameha emerged as ruler of the Kohala region and one of the ruling chiefs of the Big Island. Kamehameha's cousin, Keoua, also presided over the island.

Kamehameha's ambitions extended well beyond sharing control of the island. In 1790, with the aid of a captured foreign schooner and two shipwrecked sailors, Isaac Davis and John Young, whom he used as gunners, Kamehameha attacked and conquered the island of Maui.

Shortly after that, Kamehameha was in Molokai preparing for an invasion of Oahu when word reached him that Keoua, chief of the Kau region, was attacking the Hamakua Coast. Keoua boldly pillaged Waipio Valley, which was the most sacred area on the Big Island and the site where Kamehameha had ceremoniously received his war god a decade earlier.

As an angry Kamehameha set sail for home, Keoua's soldiers beat a quick retreat back to Kau. But when the withdrawing troops passed beneath the slopes of Kilauea Crater, the volcano suddenly erupted, and many of the warriors were instantly killed as toxic fumes and ashes swept over them. It is the only known volcanic explosion in Hawaiian history to have resulted in mass fatalities. Casts of the soldiers' footprints, imprinted in volcanic mud and ash, remain on the trail to this day.

In the midst of these power struggles, Kamehameha was told by a prophet from Kauai that if he built a new heiau to honor his war god, Kukailimoku, he would become ruler of all the islands.

Kamehameha did so, completing Puukohola Heiau in Kawaihae in 1791. He then sent word to Keoua that his appearance was requested at the heiau for reconciliation. Keoua, well aware that this was a luakini temple, probably knew his fate was sealed, but he sailed to Kawaihae anyway.

Upon landing, Keoua and his party became the heiau's first sacrifices. With Keoua's death, Kamehameha became sole ruler of the Big Island.

Over the next few years, Kamehameha conquered all the islands (except for Kauai, over which he established suzerainty) and named the entire kingdom after his home island, Hawaii.

End of an Era

Kamehameha the Great established his kingdom's royal court in Lahaina on Maui, but he later returned to his Kamakahonu residence, on the north side of Kailua Bay, where he died in May 1819.

The crown was passed to his hesitant son, Liholiho, and Kamehameha's favorite wife, Kaahumanu, a spirited woman who wasn't content to be kept in her place by the old traditions.

In Kamakahonu, six months after Kamehameha's death, Kaahumanu sat down with Liholiho to eat a meal, something strictly forbidden under the kapu system. This breaking of the kapus by royalty marked the demise of the old religion. Almost immediately, temples throughout the islands were abandoned and their idols burned.

On April 4, 1820, the ship *Thaddeus* sailed into Kailua Bay with Hawaii's first Christian missionaries aboard. They landed beside Kamehameha's recently desecrated heiau at Kamakahonu. Their timing was propitious, as the recent abandonment of the old religion had left a vacuum into which the missionaries readily moved.

GEOGRAPHY

The Big Island has an area of 4036 sq miles and is growing as new lava spews into the sea. It's 93 miles long and 76 miles wide. The Big Island is the youngest of the Hawaiian Islands and the farthest east. Its southern tip, called South Point or Ka Lae, is the southernmost point in the USA.

The island was formed by five large shield volcanoes: Kohala, Hualalai, Mauna Kea, Mauna Loa and Kilauea. The last two are still active, with Kilauea having the distinction of being the most active volcano on earth.

At 13,796 feet, Mauna Kea ('White Mountain') is the highest point in the Hawaiian Islands. It extends an additional 19,680 feet below sea level to the ocean floor and when measured from its base is the highest mountain in the world.

Mauna Loa ('Long Mountain'), just slightly lower at 13,677 feet above sea level, makes up more than half the landmass of the Big Island and, when measured from the ocean floor, is the largest mountain mass in the world.

CLIMATE

Rainfall and temperatures vary more with location than with the seasons. The leeward northwest coast between Lapakahi and Waikoloa is the driest region in the state. Kawaihae, in the center of this strip, averages less than 10 inches of rain a year.

On the windward side of Mauna Kea, near the 2500-foot elevation, around 300 inches of rain fall annually. So much rain is squeezed out of the clouds as they rise up Mauna Kea and Mauna Loa that only about 15 inches of precipitation reaches the summits, much of it as snow. Heavy subtropical winter rainstorms in Hilo occasionally bring blizzards to the mountains as low as the 9000-foot level.

Elevation makes enough of a difference that even within the city of Hilo, annual rainfall ranges from some 130 inches on the shore to 200 inches on the higher slopes. Trivia buffs may be interested to know that Hilo has the world's largest raindrops, measuring up to 8mm in diameter!

Average annual rainfall in Volcano, just north of Hawaii Volcanoes National Park, is 101 inches. At Kailua-Kona it's 25 inches. Although winter is wetter than summer, location again is the key. In Kona, seasonal

Vog

'Vog' is a word coined on the Big Island to define the volcanic haze that has been hanging over the island since Kilauea's latest eruptive phase began in 1983. It usually blows toward Kona, and conditions can resemble city smog when the trade winds falter. Vog consists of water vapor, carbon dioxide and significant amounts of sulfur dioxide.

In the early 1990s, an average of 275 tons of sulfur dioxide were being emitted from Kilauea daily, causing air quality problems on the Big Island and haze throughout Hawaii. The sulfur dioxide level exceeds standards set by the US Environmental Protection Agency an average of 22 days a year. While this shouldn't present health problems for short-term visitors, scientists are currently studying the link between vog and respiratory problems for residents.

rainfall variations are marginal, while at Volcano, the winter sees about twice as much rain as the summer.

In January, the average daily high temperature is 65°F at Hawaii Volcanoes National Park, 79°F in Hilo and 81°F in Kailua-Kona. In August, those readings rise to 71°F, 83°F and 85°F, respectively. Nighttime lows are about 15° less.

FLORA & FAUNA

The *nene*, the endangered goose that is Hawaii's state bird, lives on the upland slopes of Mauna Kea, Mauna Loa and Hualalai. As recently as a hundred years ago, an estimated 25,000 nene lived on the Big Island. Today, there may be just 375 of the birds left in the wild. Still, the nene are friendly, and you might come across them, particularly at Hawaii Volcanoes National Park.

Other native birds include the endangered *palila*, a small yellow bird that survives solely on Mauna Kea's slopes, and the *io* (Hawaiian hawk), which also occupies the mountain slopes and lives only on the Big Island. Another endangered bird endemic to the Big Island is the *alala* (Hawaiian crow), which hangs on precariously with a single flock of fewer than a dozen birds.

Wild horses roam Waipio Valley, and feral cattle graze on the slopes of Mauna Kea. Wild pigs, goats and sheep – all nonnative species – take a toll on the Big Island's environment and are hunted. Still, the most insidious of all introduced species is the mongoose, a commonly seen ferretlike creature whose appetite for native birds and their eggs has led to a drastic decline in endemic avian populations.

Two rare varieties of silversword grow on the Big Island – one on Mauna Kea and the other on Mauna Loa. Related to their better-known Maui cousin, these distant relatives of the sunflower grow in remote areas well off the beaten path.

GOVERNMENT & POLITICS

The Big Island is one county unto itself with an elected mayor and a nine-member council.

Hilo is the county seat and political center. Rivalry is ongoing between old established Hilo and boomtown Kona; there's even a simmering separatist movement, based in Kona, aimed at dividing the island into two counties. The biggest political issue on the island, as elsewhere in Hawaii, is rampant development.

ECONOMY

The Big Island's unemployment rate is 8%. Employment is fairly diversified, with retail trade, government, hotels and construction industries employing about half of the workforce.

Although the last Big Island sugar company ceased operations in 1996, agriculture still accounts for a significant sector of the economy. The island continues to produce the vast majority of Hawaii's macadamia nuts, coffee and tropical flowers, as well as four-fifths of the state's fruit, including papayas, bananas and oranges.

The nene, Hawaii's state bird

The island's illicit underground agriculture in *pakalolo* (marijuana) has declined greatly as the result of strict police surveillance. But the majority of all marijuana confiscated in Hawaii still comes from the Big Island's Puna and Kau districts.

The Big Island has several sizable cattle ranches, which collectively produce the majority of the beef marketed in the state.

POPULATION & PEOPLE

The population of the Big Island is approximately 141,000. Hilo holds about a third of the island's population, but the Big Island's demographics are changing rapidly.

Between 1970 and 1980, North Kona (which includes Kailua-Kona) became the fastest-growing district in the state, with a growth rate of 185%. Between 1980 and 1990, neighboring South Kohala took the honors as the state's most rapidly growing district, with its population doubling.

The Big Island's ethnic breakdown is 26% part-Hawaiian, 25% Caucasian, 21% Japanese, 15% mixed non-Hawaiian and 9% Filipino. Full-blooded Hawaiians make up just 1% of the population.

ORIENTATION

The Big Island has airports in Hilo and Kona. The Hilo Airport is in town. However, most visitors land at Kona Airport, which is between the island's main resort areas of Kailua-Kona and Waikoloa.

From the Kona Airport, you follow Hwy 19 along the Kona Coast, 7 miles south to Kailua-Kona or 12 miles north to Waikoloa.

The Hawaii Belt Rd circles the island, taking in the main towns and many of the sights. Different segments of the road have different highway numbers and names, but it's easy to follow.

From Kona to Hilo, the northern half of the belt road is 93 miles, and the journey takes about two hours nonstop. The southern Kona-Hilo route is 125 miles and takes approximately three hours.

Maps

The best general map of the Big Island is the one published by the University of Hawaii Press; it's sold in numerous shops around the island for $4. The chamber of commerce publishes a pretty good foldout map that you can get free at the tourist office and from some businesses.

INFORMATION
Tourist Offices

The Big Island Visitors Bureau has two offices: 250 Keawe St, Hilo, HI 96720 (☎ 961-5797, fax 961-2126); and 75-5719 W Alii Drive, Kailua-Kona, HI 96740 (☎ 329-7787, fax 326-7563).

You can receive a tourist information packet by calling ☎ 800-648-2441 and leaving your mailing address on the answering machine, or you can browse www.bigisland .org to find much of the same information online.

Newspapers & Magazines

West Hawaii Today (☎ 329-9311), which is the Kona Coast newspaper, and Hilo's *Hawaii Tribune-Herald* (☎ 935-6621) are both published daily except Saturday. *West Hawaii Today* is online at www.westhawaii .com, where you can find its classified ads and top news stories.

Free tourist magazines such as *This Week Big Island* and *Spotlight's Big Island Gold* are readily available at the airport, in hotel lobbies and around town. They're good sources of general information and include discount coupons for activities and eateries around the island. Look also for the free *Coffee Times*, which has fewer ads and more articles of cultural interest.

Radio & TV

The island has five AM and 11 FM radio stations. KAHU (1060 AM) and KWXX (94.7 FM) play Hawaiian music. Network, public TV and major cable TV stations are relayed from Honolulu. Channel 7 on cable TV features visitor information programs.

Libraries

There are public libraries in Kailua-Kona, Kealakekua, Holualoa, Hilo, Waimea, Pahoa, Pahala, Naalehu, Mountain View, Laupahoehoe, Kapaau, Honokaa and Keaau.

THE BIG ISLAND

Official Hawaii

The island of Hawaii is nicknamed the Big Island. Its official flower is the *ohia lehua*, from a native tree that flourishes around lava flows; ceremonial leis are made from its fluffy red pom-pom blossoms. The island's official color is red.

Weather Hotlines

The National Weather Service provides recorded forecasts for the Big Island (☎ 961-5582); for Hilo and vicinity (☎ 935-8555); and for water conditions (☎ 935-9883).

Hawaii Volcanoes National Park (☎ 985-6000) offers recorded information on current volcano eruptions and viewing points.

Emergency

For police, ambulance or fire emergencies, dial ☎ 911. There's also a crisis hotline (for less urgent problems) at ☎ 935-3393.

The two main hospitals are the Hilo Medical Center (☎ 974-6800) in Hilo and the Kona Community Hospital (☎ 322-9311) in Kealakekua. Waimea contains the smaller North Hawaii Community Hospital (☎ 885-4444).

ACTIVITIES

The vast majority of the Big Island's recreational activities take place on the west coast. Most of the Waikoloa-area resorts offer their guests a variety of water activities, including cruises and dive trips. Usually, these are open to the public as well, but the rates are generally higher than average.

Swimming

The Big Island has 313 miles of shoreline, but it doesn't have the grand expanses of sandy beach you'll find on Maui or Oahu. Instead, most of the Big Island's beaches are sandy pockets bordering bays and coves.

The best swimming spots are on the west coast. Kailua-Kona has a few good beaches, although the better ones are farther up the Kona Coast around Waikoloa and Kohala. Of these, Anaehoomalu and Hapuna are both beautiful and easily accessible public beaches. The west coast is also dotted with a number of isolated gems that require a hike to reach but are well worth the effort.

Hilo is not as well endowed with beaches, but you'll find a few decent places to swim and snorkel on the east side of Hilo Bay.

The Puna and Kau districts have interesting black-sand beaches but generally unfavorable swimming conditions.

Swimming Pools The county has public pools at Honokaa High School in Honokaa, Kamehameha Park in Kapaau, Konawaena High School in Kealakekua, Kau High School in Pahala, Laupahoehoe High School in Laupahoehoe and Hoolulu Complex in Hilo. The pools schedule certain hours for lap swims and others for open use. For information, call ☎ 961-8694.

Surfing

The Big Island is not one of the better islands for surfing, although local surfers do manage to catch waves in a number of places. Many of the island's surf spots are rocky, so surfers new to the area should check conditions thoroughly before hitting the waves.

On the eastern side of the island, Honolii Cove, 2 miles north of Hilo, is popular. Favorite Kona Coast surfing locales include Kahaluu Beach, in Keauhou, and Banyans, near the banyan tree north of White Sands Beach.

White Sands Beach is also one of the best places on the Kona Coast for boogie boarding and bodysurfing.

Windsurfing

The Big Island is not a real hot spot for windsurfing. Most windsurfers head to Anaehoomalu Bay in Waikoloa, which has some of the island's better wind and water conditions. You can rent boards from Ocean Sports (☎ 886-6666), the beach hut in front of the Royal Waikoloan, for $20 an hour and get a one-hour lesson for $45. The best winds are usually between 10 am and 2 pm.

Kawaihae Harbor and Hilo Bay are other spots that occasionally see some windsurfing activity.

Diving

The Big Island has excellent diving on the leeward Kona and Kohala Coasts; the best conditions are in spring and summer, but good, calm dive spots can be found year-round. Diving is far more limited on the Hilo side, where the season is basically from April to September.

Shore dives along the Kona Coast take in steep nearshore drop-offs with lava tubes, caves and diverse marine life. Farther out are about 40 popular boat-dive areas, including an airplane wreck off Keahole Point.

One well-known dive spot is Red Hill, an underwater cinder cone about 10 miles south of Kona. It has beautiful lava formations – including ledges and lots of honeycombed lava tubes nicely lit by streaks of sunlight – as well as coral pinnacles and many brightly colored nudibranchs (types of mollusks).

Another good spot is off Kaiwi Point, south of Honokohau Harbor, where sea turtles, large fish and huge eagle rays swim around some respectable drop-offs. Nearby is Suck-em-up, a couple of lava tubes you can swim into and let the swell pull you through, like an amusement park ride.

Coral and other marine life flourish in Kealakekua Bay, a protected cove that's calm year-round.

Dive Operations Kona has numerous dive operations. The cost of a two-tank dive averages $85 in the day and $95 at night. The night dives typically center around viewing manta rays. Introductory dives range from $45 for a one-tank shore dive with Jack's Diving Locker to around $100 for a two-tank boat dive with several of the dive shops. The five-star PADI operations offer certification courses for around $400.

The more established dive operations include the following:

Jack's Diving Locker
 (☎ 329-7585, 800-345-4807, divejdl@gte.net, www.divejdl.com), 75-5819 Alii Drive, Kailua-Kona, HI 96740, at the Coconut Grove Marketplace, is one of the best outfits for introductory dives. It's rated five stars by PADI.

Dive Makai
 (☎/fax 329-2025, dmakai@divemakai.com, www .divemakai.com), PO Box 2955, Kailua-Kona, HI 96745, is a personable little operation run by husband-and-wife team Tom Shockley and Lisa Choquette. They are conservation oriented and have a good word-of-mouth reputation.

Eco-Adventures of Kona
 (☎ 329-7116, 800-949-3483, ecodive@kona.net, www.eco-adventure.com), 75-5660 Palani Drive, Kailua-Kona, HI 96740, at King Kamehameha's Kona Beach Hotel, is a well-regarded, five-star PADI operation.

Kona Coast Divers
 (☎ 329-8802, divekona@ilhawaii.net), 75-5614 Palani Rd, Kailua-Kona, HI 96740, is also a five-star PADI operation and one of the largest on the Big Island.

Sea Paradise Scuba
 (☎ 322-2500, 800-322-5662), PO Box 580, Kailua-Kona, HI 96745, is based at Keauhou Bay and tends to head south, often to Red Hill or Kealakekua Bay.

Kohala Divers
 (☎ 882-7774, theboss@kohaladivers.com), PO Box 44940, Kawaihae, HI 96743, at the shopping center in Kawaihae, is a five-star PADI operation in the Kohala area. Guides organize trips up the Kohala Coast.

Nautilus Dive Center
 (☎ 935-6939), 382 Kamehameha Ave, Hilo, HI 96720, organizes dives in the Hilo area.

Live-Aboard Boat The *Kona Aggressor* (☎ 329-8182, 800-344-5662, fax 329-2628, livedive@compuserve.com), Live-Dive Pacific, 74-5588 Pawai Place, Building F, Kailua-Kona, HI 96740, is an 85-foot live-aboard dive boat that accommodates up to 10 guests. All-inclusive one-week trips cost $1895 and start each Saturday.

Dive Club The Kona Reefers Dive Club meets on the third Friday of the month and holds shore dives (and sometimes boat

THE BIG ISLAND

dives) open to the public on weekends once a month. Look for announcements in *West Hawaii Today*, or inquire at any of the dive shops.

Snorkeling

Snorkelers will find some good spots south of Kailua-Kona. The area's most popular easy-access snorkeling haunt is Kahaluu Beach in Keauhou, which is teeming with colorful fish and makes a good place for beginners to try out the sport. The north side of the Place of Refuge is another fine drive-up snorkeling spot, although it's best suited for those with a bit more experience. There's also terrific snorkeling in the calm, clear, 30-foot-deep waters near Captain Cook's monument at the north end of Kealakekua Bay – however, it takes a hike, horseback ride or boat to reach this area.

Snorkeling Cruises
The most popular snorkeling cruise is to Kealakekua Bay. Prices for the following tours include snorkeling gear, beverages and food.

Fairwind (☎ 322-2788, 800-677-9461, www .fair-wind.com) makes trips to Kealakekua Bay aboard a 60-foot catamaran. The trips leave from Keauhou Bay, which allows for more snorkeling time than other boats. You can choose either a 4½-hour morning tour that costs $79/44 for adults/children (six to 17), or a 3½-hour afternoon tour that costs $48/31 for adults/children.

Captain Zodiac (☎ 329-3199, 800-422-7824) offers four-hour tours aboard bouncy Zodiac rubber rafts. The rafts depart from Honokohau Harbor at 8 am and 1 pm daily, with pick-up possible at the Kailua-Kona and Keauhou piers. The cost of $65/52 for adults/children (four to 12), includes about an hour of snorkeling time at Kealakekua Bay followed by visits to sea caves.

Kamanu Sail and Snorkel (☎ 329-2021) takes a 36-foot catamaran out of Honokohau Harbor for snorkeling at Pawai Bay, just north of the Old Kona Airport. The boat, which motors down and sails back, takes a maximum of 24 people. It departs daily at 9 am and 1:30 pm. Cost is $48/29 for adults/children (under 12).

Snorkelers can sometimes tag along with divers on dive tours if space is available. The cost typically ranges from $25 to $45. Keep in mind, however, that ideal dive conditions don't always make good snorkeling conditions.

Snorkeling Gear Rentals
A couple of places in Kailua-Kona rent snorkel sets for around $7 a day, $15 a week; try Morey's Scuba Hut at the south end of the Kona Inn Shopping Village or the beach hut at King Kamehameha's Kona Beach Hotel.

The ubiquitous Snorkel Bob's (☎ 329-0770), which has a branch off Alii Drive by the Royal Kona Resort, rents snorkel gear for around $15 to $30 a week.

In Hilo, Planet Ocean Watersports (☎ 935-7277), 200 Kanoelehua Ave (Hwy 11) in the same complex as Fiascos restaurant, rents snorkel gear for $6/24 a day/week.

Many of the dive shops also rent snorkel gear, though prices tend to be higher.

Kayaking

The most common kayaking destination on the Big Island is Kealakekua Bay. Kayakers generally launch from Napoopoo Beach and paddle across the bay to the Captain Cook Monument, where they can then add on a little snorkeling and exploring.

Although there are no longer kayak rental operations at the bay, you can rent kayaks a few miles away in the hillside town of Honalo. Aloha Kayak Company (☎ 322-2868), on Hwy 11 opposite Teshima's restaurant in Honalo, rents single/double kayaks for $25/40 a day, including all equipment, life vests and a car rack. You can rent snorkel gear for an additional $4. The company also can arrange five-hour guided kayak tours for $75 per person, with a minimum of three people.

If you just want to paddle around Kailua Bay, the beach hut at King Kamehameha's Kona Beach Hotel in Kailua-Kona rents kayaks for $15 for the first hour, $5 for each additional hour.

In Hilo, kayakers usually launch from Richardson Ocean Park on the east side of town. Planet Ocean Watersports (☎ 935-

7277), on Hwy 11 near Fiascos, rents single/double kayaks for $25/30 a day and can also arrange kayak tours starting at $40.

Fishing

Deep-sea fishing is big on the Kona Coast; this is the world's number-one spot for catching Pacific blue marlin, a spectacular fighting fish with a long swordlike bill. Most of the world records for catches of these fish belong to Kona fishers, with at least one marlin weighing 1000lb or more reeled in virtually every year. Kona is also known for its record catches of *ahi* (yellowfin tuna) and spearfish.

Near the Chart House restaurant at Kailua's Waterfront Row, there's an interesting 'Granders Wall' lined with photos of anglers next to their 1000lb marlin catches.

You can watch the boats come in and see the fish weighed at Honokohau Harbor from 11 am to noon for the morning charters and from around 3:30 to 5 pm for the afternoon and full-day charters.

Kona has more than 100 charter fishing boats. The standard cost, if you join an existing party, is $75 to $100 per person for half a day, sharing a boat with three to five other fishers. You can also charter a whole boat and take up to six people at a cost of $225 to $400 for half a day, $325 to $600 for a full day, depending upon the boat. You might want to first take a look at the tourist magazines, which often advertise a few renegade boats at discount rates – though those boats will need to be booked directly with the skippers. Prices include all fishing equipment but not food or drink.

The following centers each book numerous boats:

Kona Charter Skippers Association
   (☎ 329-3600, 800-762-7546)
   75-5663 Palani Rd, Kailua-Kona, HI 96740
Kona Activities Center
   (☎ 329-3171, 800-367-5288)
   75-5799-B5B Alii Drive, Kailua-Kona, HI 96740

Of the numerous fishing tournaments held in Kona, the granddaddy of them all is the Hawaiian International Billfish Tournament (☎ 329-6155, billfish@lava.net), held in early August and accompanied by a week of festive activities.

Hiking

There is excellent hiking all around the Big Island. Some of the best and most varied hikes are inside Hawaii Volcanoes National Park, where trails lead across steaming crater floors, through lush native forests and up to the peak of Mauna Loa.

On the northern tip of the island, steep coastal cliffs and deep valleys reach down from the Kohala Mountains. From the road's end on the northwest side of the range, it's a 30-minute hike down to the beach at the bottom of Pololu Valley. On the southeast side, you can take a 30-minute walk down into verdant Waipio Valley or backpack deep into remote Waimanu Valley.

North of Kona, you can hike in from the highway to secluded beaches, or explore portions of ancient footpaths and petroglyph fields. Na Ala Hele, a state-sponsored group composed mostly of volunteers, is currently working to reestablish the entire 50-mile historic trail system that once ran between Kailua-Kona and Kawaihae. Mauna Lani Resort and Lapakahi State Park have easy trails, marked with interpretive plaques, around ancient fishponds and through abandoned villages.

South of Kona, a trail leads to the spot where Captain Cook died at Kealakekua Bay. In the center of the island, a strenuous hike leads to the summit of Mauna Kea, while on the slopes below, Kalopa State Recreation Area has short, easy forest trails.

All hikes are detailed in their respective sections.

Cycling

The Big Island Mountain Bike Association (☎ 961-4452), based at Hilo Bike Hub in Hilo, sponsors fun rides, races and trail-maintenance outings. In conjunction with the county, the group has published a free brochure detailing off-road trails that are open to the public. These range from easy jaunts along beaches to a strenuous 45-mile circle around Mauna Kea. You can pick up the brochure at island tourist offices and bike shops, or browse www.interpac.net/~mtbike for online information.

For bike rental information, see Bicycle in the Getting Around section of this chapter.

Horseback Riding

Kings' Trail Rides O'Kona (☎ 323-2388), in Kealakekua, takes a maximum of six horseback riders per outing down the Captain Cook Trail to Kealakekua Bay for lunch and snorkeling. As the trail is a bit rocky and steep, prior riding experience is required. The cost is $95 per person.

Kohala Naalapa (☎ 889-0022), at the intersection of Hwy 250 and Kohala Ranch Rd, offers 2½-hour trail rides that cross the pastures of Kahua Ranch in Kohala and afford fine views of the coast. The rides depart at 9 am and cost $75. A 1½-hour afternoon ride is available in the same area; it leaves at 1 pm and costs $55.

Paniolo Riding Adventures (☎ 889-5354), on Hwy 250 in Kohala, offers 2½-hour horseback rides for $85 and four-hour rides for $125. Horses are selected according to the rider's experience, but they're all real riding horses, not trail horses, and you can canter with the lead wrangler.

Dahana Ranch Roughriders (☎ 885-0057), just off the Old Mamalahoa Hwy between Waimea and Honokaa, is owned and operated by native Hawaiians. Horses cross the open range of a working cattle ranch rather than following trails. Rides are by appointment only at 9 and 11 am and 1 and 3 pm daily; they last 1½ hours, cost $55 and are open to both novice and experienced riders aged three and up. Also, with a minimum of four people, a 'city slicker adventure' can be arranged; beginning at either 8 am or 3 pm, you'll help drive about 100 head of cattle for around 2½ hours. The cost is $100.

For horseback rides in Waipio Valley, see the Waipio section.

Tennis

Many county parks on the Big Island have tennis courts. The Old Kona Airport Beach Park in Kailua-Kona has four lighted outdoor tennis courts, and if you show up with racket in hand, there's a fair chance you'll find a partner.

Hilo's Hoolulu Complex has four lighted outdoor courts and three indoor courts. The indoor courts are open 8 am to 10 pm daily (to 6 pm on Saturday) and cost $2 an hour per court before 4 pm, or $4 an hour thereafter; reservations are required. There's no fee or reservation system for the outdoor courts.

Other county courts lighted for night play are at Kailua Playground in Kailua-Kona, Greenwell Park in Captain Cook, Waimea Park in Waimea, Lincoln Park in Hilo, Papaaloa Park in the North Hilo district, Honokaa Park in Honokaa, Kamehameha Park in Kapaau, and Naalehu Park and Pahala School in the Kau district. All are free to the public.

Many of the larger hotels and resorts have tennis courts for their guests; some are also available to nonguests. The Royal Kona Resort (☎ 329-3111), in Kailua-Kona, opens its four courts to the public for $4 per person per hour ($5 at night when it's lit) and rents rackets for $3.

Kings Sport & Racquet Club (☎ 329-2911), at King Kamehameha's Kona Beach Hotel in Kailua-Kona, has four courts (two lighted) open to the public. The club charges $5 per person per day and rents rackets for $5.

The Royal Waikoloan Hotel Tennis Center (☎ 885-6789 ext 7286) has six courts and charges $8 per person a day for guests or nonguests. Rackets rent for $5 a day; ball machines and lessons are available.

Elsewhere in the Waikoloa area, the Mauna Kea Beach Hotel (☎ 882-7222) has 13 courts open to the public, and the Orchid at Mauna Lani (☎ 885-2000) has 10 courts open to the public; both charge higher rates than the Royal Waikoloan Hotel Tennis Center.

Golf

The Big Island has more than a dozen golf courses, including some world-class courses in the Waikoloa area that are laid out on top of lava flows.

The courses that follow are all 18-hole courses, with the exception of the Naniloa Country Club, which has nine holes.

The island's top courses are: Mauna Kea Golf Course (☎ 882-5400), near Mauna Kea Beach; Francis Ii Brown South Course and North Course, at Mauna Lani Resort (☎ 885-6655); Waikoloa Beach Course (☎ 886-6060) and Waikoloa Kings' Course (☎ 886-7778), at the Waikoloa Beach Resort; Hapuna Golf Course (☎ 880-3000), at the Hapuna Beach Prince Hotel; and the Four Seasons Hualalai Golf Club (☎ 325-8000), a PGA-tour course that's open only to members and hotel guests.

Nonguests are charged $175 at the Mauna Lani's Francis Ii courses, $175 at Mauna Kea, $135 at Hapuna and $120 at the two Waikoloa Beach Resort courses. However, you can beat these fees substantially by waiting until midafternoon to tee off – most of the courses then cut fees at least 50% and sometimes more. All of the greens fees at these resorts include mandatory carts. Guests staying at the resorts typically get discounts ranging from 20% to 50% off the standard rates.

For the island's most reasonably priced turf, head for the Hilo Municipal Golf Course (☎ 959-7711), 340 Haihai St in Hilo, which charges $25, plus $15 for a cart.

Other courses around the Big Island include the following:

Kona Country Club and Alii Country Club
(☎ 322-2595), Keauhou; the standard cost is $150, including cart, but discounts are available during off hours.

Makalei Hawaii Country Club
(☎ 325-6625), off Hwy 190 northeast of Kailua; the standard cost is $110, including cart, but steep discounts are often available for after-noon play.

Naniloa Country Club
(☎ 935-3000), Hilo; the cost varies with the day, but is around $25, plus a cart fee of $7.

SeaMountain Golf Course
(☎ 928-6222), Punaluu; the cost of $40 includes a cart.

Volcano Golf and Country Club
(☎ 967-7331), Hawaii Volcanoes National Park; the cost of $50 includes a cart.

Waikoloa Village Golf Club
(☎ 883-9621), Waikoloa village; the regular cost is $75, cart included, but afternoon discounts are sometimes offered.

Skiing & Snowboarding

Skiing in Hawaii is primarily a curiosity event. Snow does fall each winter on the upper slopes of Mauna Kea, though the timing is unpredictable. The ski season usually starts anywhere from early January to late February and can run for several months. There are bad years when there's virtually no skiing and good years when the season can extend through June.

Skiing Mauna Kea is not your standard sort of skiing. The altitude can be tough, and the slopes can have exposed rocks. There are no ski lodges, lifts or other facilities.

When there's snow, Ski Guides Hawaii (☎ 885-4188), PO Box 1954, Kamuela, HI 96743, based in Waimea, can provide a full day of skiing or snowboarding for around $250 per person. The cost includes use of ski equipment, transportation to Mauna Kea from Waimea, lunch and a 4WD shuttle service up the mountain after each run.

Sporting Competitions

The renowned Ironman Triathlon, held in Kailua-Kona each October, combines a 2.4-mile ocean swim, 112-mile bike race and 26.2-mile marathon into one exhaustive endurance race. Some 1500 men and women from 50 countries compete in the Ironman each year, drawing worldwide media coverage. The Ironman usually takes place on the Saturday nearest the full moon, so that late-finishing racers won't have to run along the highway in the dark. It begins and ends near Kailua Pier. Start time is 7 am, and the first triathletes cross the finish line shortly after 3 pm; the other contenders follow throughout the afternoon and evening, with the finish line remaining open until midnight. For information on the race, contact Ironman Triathlon World Championship (☎ 329-0063), 75-5722 Kuakini Hwy, suite 101, Kailua-Kona, HI 96740, or visit the organization's website at www.ironman.com.

The Kilauea Volcano Wilderness Runs are held at Hawaii Volcanoes National Park in July. There are four separate events: a 10-mile run around the rim of Kilauea Caldera; both a 5-mile run and a 5-mile walk that go down into Kilauea Iki Crater; and a

26.2-mile marathon through the Kau Desert. For information, contact the Volcano Art Center (☎ 967-8222), PO Box 104, Hawaii Volcanoes National Park, HI 96718.

ORGANIZED TOURS

Roberts Hawaii (☎ 329-1688) and Polynesian Adventure Tours (☎ 329-8008) both offer daylong circle-island bus tours that cost $55 to $65. Both companies pick up passengers at hotels in Waikoloa, Kailua-Kona and Keauhou; the exact time depends on where you're staying, but expect to leave around sunrise and get back around sunset. Among the sights visited are Kailua-Kona, Hawaii Volcanoes National Park (focusing on the main Crater Rim Drive sights), Punaluu black-sand beach, Hilo and Waimea. However, because the island is so big and there's so much to cover, you'll only get a quick glimpse of most places.

If you're in Hilo, Arnott's Lodge (☎ 969-7097), the local hostel, offers recommendable day tours on a rotating schedule to Mauna Kea, Puna, South Point (and Green Sands Beach) and Hawaii Volcanoes National Park. These are geared for active people who prefer to do some hiking and/or swimming during their outings rather than just sitting on a bus. The cost for each outing is $36 (except for the national park, which costs $41) for those staying at Arnott's and $50 to $75 for nonguests.

Information on tours into Waipio Valley or up to Mauna Kea summit is detailed in those sections.

Helicopter & Plane

The most popular Big Island helicopter tour is a flight over Kilauea Volcano – especially when the volcano is acting up.

The cost largely depends on your departure point. Flights from the Volcano Golf Course or Hilo are about $150, from Kona about $225 and from Waikoloa about $300. However, as it's a competitive market, it's worth checking the free tourist magazines for discount coupons and calling around to compare prices.

Companies include Sunshine Helicopters (☎ 882-1223, 800-469-3000), Volcano Heli-

Tours (☎ 967-7578), Hawaii Helicopters (☎ 329-4700, 800-994-9099), Mauna Kea Helicopters (☎ 885-6400, 800-400-4354), Blue Hawaiian Helicopters (☎ 961-5600, 800-745-2583) and Safari Helicopters (☎ 969-1259, 800-326-3356).

A cheaper way to see the sights is to fly by small prop plane. Island Hoppers (☎ 969-2000) offers 'flightseeing' tours that begin at $70 from Hilo, $150 from Kona, while Big Island Air (☎ 329-4868, 800-303-8868) leaves from Kona on one-hour tours to the volcano ($135) and longer tours circling the island ($185).

Keep in mind that the volcano area is often rainy even when it's sunny in Kona. If it's raining, it's not worth going up, so if you're coming from the Kona side, call first to see what the weather's like.

Dinner Cruise

Capt Beans' Cruises (☎ 329-2955), the high-profile boat with the yellow lights and orange sails, has a touristy dinner cruise in the evening for ages 21 and over. It leaves at 5:15 pm daily from Kailua Pier, takes two hours and costs $49, including food, drinks and a Polynesian show.

Whale Watching

Although the best whale watching is off Maui, you can spot whales from the Big Island as well. The season for humpback whales, which are the most popular attraction, usually starts around January and runs through March or April. However, pilot, sperm, beaked and false killer whales – and five dolphin species – can be found in Kona waters year-round.

Marine mammal biologist Dan McSweeney of Whale Watch (☎ 322-0028) leads three-hour whale-watching cruises leaving from Honokohau Harbor daily. Hydrophones allow passengers to hear whale songs. The cost is $45/30 for adults/children 11 and under. The tours have a 24-hour nonrefundable cancellation policy.

A couple of the snorkeling tour boats and fishing boats also do whale watches during humpback season, so it's worth taking a look at listings in the tourist magazines.

Submarine & Glass-Bottom Boats

Atlantis Submarines (☎ 329-6626, 800-548-6262) gives 45-minute submarine rides that dive down about 100 feet in a coral crevice in front of the Royal Kona Resort. The sub has 26 portholes, carries 46 passengers and departs five times a day from 10 am to 2:30 pm. The outing lasts two hours, including the boat ride to and from the sub, and costs $79/39 for adults/children.

A cheaper option is *Nautilus II* (☎ 326-2003), a 33-passenger semisubmersible. Passengers sit in a glass-windowed room beneath the surface of the water and look out at the fish as the boat edges along the reef. It leaves from Kailua Pier daily at 9:30, 10:30 and 11:30 am and at 1 pm; the tour takes about 50 minutes and costs $39/19 for adults/children.

Cheaper still is the Kailua Bay Charter Company's (☎ 324-1749) 36-foot glass-bottom boat, which leaves Kailua Pier hourly and circles around Kailua Bay. Trips cost $20/10 for adults/children (under five free).

ACCOMMODATIONS

The Big Island has a wide range of accommodation options. As the island is so big, it's worth considering moving around and exploring from a couple of different bases.

Most of the island's accommodations are centered around Kailua-Kona, with the majority of the rooms in condos – though some of these are run like hotels with a front desk and daily rates. If you're staying a week or more, condos are usually a better deal than hotels.

At the bottom end, Kailua-Kona has a hostel-style place with dormitory beds. Otherwise, the cheapest places in the Kona area are *mauka* (inland) of Kailua-Kona in small local hotels in the towns of Holualoa and Captain Cook.

The Waikoloa area, north of Kailua-Kona, has the island's most expensive beach resorts. The Mauna Kea and Mauna Lani resorts attract wealthy tourists who want an elegant hideaway and not much excitement. Kona Village is even more low-key, playing out the getaway fantasy in comfortable Polynesian-style thatched huts, while the Hilton Waikoloa Village stands in sharp contrast, with splashy high-tech toys and constant titillation.

Rainy Hilo doesn't see a great many visitors, and its lodging choices aren't as numerous as you might expect for a city. But Hilo does have a number of good budget to midrange options, including a friendly hostel.

In the uplands, Volcano and Waimea have pleasant B&Bs and a couple of larger places. Other B&Bs and guest houses – some in fine country settings – are scattered around the island. These types of accommodations have become increasingly popular throughout the Big Island and offer some excellent midrange lodging values.

Unless otherwise noted, the rates given in this chapter are the same for either singles or doubles and don't include the 11.41% tax.

Camping

At first glance, the list of Big Island campgrounds seems to read like some sort of 'Camping Guide to Hell': Laupahoehoe Beach, where a village was washed away in a tidal wave; Halape Beach, where an earthquake sank the shoreline 30 feet; and Kamoamoa Beach, which is now buried under a lava flow.

Despite all that, there's really little to worry about. Hawaii's lava isn't the rushing type that sweeps through campgrounds overnight, and tsunami speakers have been set up to warn of approaching tidal waves.

In fact, some of the best and safest camping on the island can be found in Hawaii Volcanoes National Park. More detailed descriptions of specific sites can be found throughout the chapter.

State Parks Tent camping is allowed at Kalopa State Recreation Area, which has good facilities and a caretaker, and at MacKenzie State Recreation Area, which is a bit forsaken. Both are free, but permits are required.

In addition, there are A-frame shelters at Hapuna Beach and self-contained housekeeping cabins at Mauna Kea State Recreation Area and Kalopa State Recreation Area.

The booking system is computerized, and reservations can be made at state park offices on any island. The Big Island office (☎ 974-6200) is at 75 Aupuni St (PO Box 936), Hilo, HI 96721. The maximum length of stay at any state park is five nights a month.

The aging A-frame shelters at Hapuna Beach are one-room setups, each equipped with screened windows, a picnic table and wooden sleeping platforms for up to four people. Shared facilities include rest rooms, cold showers and a pavilion with refrigerator, electric range and sink. Although the shelters are elementary and offer little privacy, the area is maintained and the cost is just $20 per night.

Cabin prices at Mauna Kea are $45 for up to four people, while prices at Kalopa are $55 for up to eight people. These cabins have kitchens with limited cookware and bathrooms with hot showers.

The cabins and shelters are popular with island families and commonly require booking well in advance. Cancellations do occur, however, and if you're flexible with dates, you might be able to get one without advance reservations.

County Beach Parks The county allows camping at 11 of its beach parks: Kolekole and Laupahoehoe, north of Hilo; Isaac Hale in Puna; Spencer, Keokea, Kapaa, Mahukona, Hookena and Milolii, all on the western side of the island; and Whittington and Punaluu, both in Kau.

With the exception of Spencer, which is patrolled by a security guard, all of the county parks can be rough and noisy areas, as they're popular among late-night drinkers.

Camping permits are required and can be obtained by mail or in person from the Department of Parks & Recreation (☎ 961-8311), 25 Aupuni St, Hilo, HI 96720. Office hours are 7:45 am to 4:30 pm Monday to Friday, but don't cut it too close to closing time.

You can also make reservations by phone through the Hilo office and then pick up the camping permit at Park & Recreation branch offices around the island. In Kailua-Kona, the office is at Hale Halawai Park (☎ 327-3560) and is open weekdays 7:45 am

to 4 pm. In Captain Cook, the office is at the Yano Center (☎ 323-3060), opposite the Manago Hotel; it's generally staffed noon to 2 pm on weekdays. In Waimea, the office is at the community center (☎ 885-5454) at Waimea Park, and is officially staffed 8:30 to 10:30 am on weekdays. In Naalehu, the office is at the community center (☎ 929-7028) and is open 2 to 3 pm Monday to Thursday, 1 to 2 pm Friday. Except for the Kailua-Kona office, it's best to call ahead to confirm that someone will indeed be in the offices, as they're only lightly staffed.

Daily camping fees are $3 for adults, $1 for children 13 to 17 and 50¢ for children 12 and under. Camping is allowed for up to two weeks in each park, except in June, July and August, when it's limited to one week in each park.

Only Laupahoehoe, Keokea, Spencer and Punaluu have drinking water. Some of the others have catchment water that can be treated for drinking, while others have only brackish water that can be used for showers but is unsuitable for drinking.

Campers should also be aware that beach parks in the Puna and Kau areas are sometimes closed during winter storms.

Hawaii Volcanoes National Park The Hawaii Volcanoes National Park section of this chapter has details on the park's two drive-up campgrounds and on trail shelters and tenting sites for backcountry hikers. They're all free and rarely filled.

Camping Supplies Pacific Rent-All (☎ 935-2974), 1080 Kilauea Ave, Hilo, HI 96720, rents three-person tents for $22 for two days or $44 a week and lightweight sleeping bags for $7/21. The shop also rents Coleman stoves, lanterns, water jugs and a few other supplies. The selection is limited and is generally geared more for drive-up camping than backcountry use.

Hilo Surplus Store (☎ 935-6398), 148 Mamo St in Hilo, sells camping supplies including rain gear, stoves, sleeping bags, army-surplus pup tents, commercial dome tents and Eureka backpacks. You can also try one of the discount department stores, such as Kmart or Wal-Mart in Kailua-Kona or Sears in Hilo.

ENTERTAINMENT

The Big Island entertainment scene is largely centered around the hotels in the Kona and Waikoloa areas. Most offer Hawaiian music of some type, often duos strumming guitars in the early evening, and a few hotels have dance bands, jazz groups and nightclubs as well.

Although it's a more local scene, Hilo also has a few places with music and dancing. In addition, each spring Hilo hosts the week-long Merrie Monarch Festival, the state's largest hula festival, which starts on Easter Sunday and features hula troupes from all the islands.

First-run feature films are shown at Kress Cinemas, Prince Kuhio Plaza and Waiakea Shopping Plaza in Hilo and at Hualalai Theatres and Kona Marketplace Cinemas in Kailua.

For the latest entertainment listings, check *West Hawaii Today*, especially its Friday entertainment page.

Luaus

The Kona Village Resort, one of the most expensive hotels on the Big Island, offers one of Hawaii's more authentic luaus. It's held on Friday night and costs $70. As the luau is complimentary for all of the resort's guests, seating for the general public is limited and sometimes is booked up weeks in advance.

In Kailua-Kona, King Kamehameha's Kona Beach Hotel holds a popular luau on Sunday, Tuesday, Wednesday and Thursday, and in Waikoloa, the Royal Waikoloan has a luau on Sunday and Wednesday. Both cost $53.

All Big Island luaus include a dinner buffet, cocktails and a Polynesian show.

SHOPPING

Kona coffee and macadamia nuts are the Big Island's most popular souvenir items. If you're buying coffee, note that 'Kona blend' is only 10% Kona coffee, so if you want the real thing, make sure what you pick up is labeled 100%. Prices change with the market, but Kona coffee is one of the more expensive gourmet beans, priced from around $10 a pound.

Supermarkets and discount stores, such as Longs Drugs, usually have the best deals on coffee and macadamia nuts.

Shops selling local arts and crafts are plentiful. Notable ones include the Volcano Art Center in Hawaii Volcanoes National Park and the handful of galleries in the hillside village of Holualoa.

GETTING THERE & AWAY
Air

The Big Island has commercial airports in Kona (near Kailua-Kona) and Hilo. While there are frequent flights into both, Kona is the busier of the two. United Airlines offers nonstop flights from California to Kona, and Japan Air Lines offers nonstop service from Tokyo to Kona.

Hawaiian Airlines (☎ 800-882-8811) and Aloha Airlines (☎ 800-652-6541) connect both Big Island airports with the other Hawaiian Islands. On the Honolulu-Kona route, both Hawaiian and Aloha fly an average of once hourly from around 5 am to 7:30 pm, while on the Honolulu-Hilo route the schedule is slightly lighter. Both airlines also offer a couple of nonstop flights from Maui to both Kona and Hilo; for most other interisland destinations, you'll need to go via Honolulu. On both Aloha and Hawaiian, the one-way fare for a flight between the Big Island and any other Hawaiian Island is currently $93.

Island Air (☎ 800-652-6541) offers one flight a day from Kona to Lanai and from Kona to Kapalua West Maui Airport. The one-way fare to either destination is $93.

For more information on interisland air travel and ticketing, see the Getting Around chapter in the front of this book.

Kona Airport The Kona Airport is on Hwy 19, about 7 miles north of Kailua-Kona. It has a visitor information booth, lei stand, restaurant, gift shop, taxi stand, car rental booths and a newsstand that sells the University of Hawaii (UH) Big Island map and mainland newspapers.

Lava Wasteland?

Flying into Kona Airport can be a shock if you're expecting to see tropical greenery and waving palm trees. Instead, the view from the airplane looks more like a black lava wasteland, as if the island had been paved over in asphalt. Don't panic! This is but one face of the Big Island – and even here, if you look closer, you can catch a glimpse of some fine secluded white-sand beaches squeezed between the lava and the turquoise waters. And, of course, once you get on the ground, there's a great deal more to the island than lava landscapes.

For a relatively busy airport, it's surprisingly casual, and it's all open-air (there's not enough rain to justify sealing it up!).

Hilo Airport The Hilo Airport is off Hwy 11, just under a mile south of the Hwy 11 and Hwy 19 intersection. It has the same visitor services as the Kona Airport (see above).

GETTING AROUND
To/From the Airport

At both the Hilo and Kona Airports, taxis can be picked up curbside, and car rental booths line the road just outside the arrival areas.

Shuttle bus services from the Kona Airport pop up from time to time, so you might want to inquire at the information booth – but don't expect much, as they typically charge nearly as much as a taxi.

Bus

Hele-On, the county public bus, offers limited islandwide service.

Buses between Kona and Hilo run along the northern route of the Hawaii Belt Rd once in each direction Monday to Saturday. The bus leaves the South Kona town of Kealia at 5:45 am. Stops along the way include the Kona Surf Resort in Keauhou at 6:25 am, the Lanihau Center in Kailua-Kona

at 6:45 am, Parker Ranch Shopping Center in Waimea at 8:05 am and the Dairy Queen in Honokaa at 8:30 am. The bus arrives in Hilo at the Mooheau Bus Terminal, on Kamehameha Ave, at 9:45 am.

The return trip leaves Hilo at 1:30 pm and arrives in Kailua-Kona at 4:30 pm. One-way fares are $5.25 between Kailua-Kona and Hilo, $3 between Kailua-Kona and Waimea and $4.50 between Waimea and Hilo.

Another route connects Kailua-Kona (Lanihau Center) and Captain Cook four times a day, weekdays only. Fare for the one-hour trip is $1.50.

The four other major routes are: Pahoa to Hilo, Honokaa to Hilo, Waiohinu to Hilo via Volcano, and Hilo to the Waikoloa hotels via Honokaa and Waimea. Each route runs at least once a day in each direction Monday to Friday. The Waikoloa bus is the only bus to operate daily, leaving Hilo early every morning and returning in the late afternoon. It's mostly used by commuting hotel workers, but if you're staying in Hilo and feel up for a 5:30 am departure, then it's good for a day's outing at the beach. The return buses leave the Hilton Waikoloa for Hilo at 2:30 and 4:25 pm. The ride takes about two hours.

There's also limited weekday service around the city of Hilo for 75¢ per ride, but it mainly connects the downtown area with the outlying malls and has little practical value for most visitors.

You can get detailed schedule information by calling ☎ 961-8744 on weekdays between 7:45 am and 4:30 pm.

Drivers accept only the exact fare. You can buy a sheet of 10 bus tickets for $6.75; each ticket is valid for 75¢ in fare, so you get a little discount this way and don't have to carry a lot of change. Luggage and backpacks cost $1 extra per piece. Some of the buses are equipped to carry up to four bicycles for an additional $1 in fare.

For information on shuttle service between Kailua-Kona and Keauhou, see Getting Around in the Kailua-Kona section.

For information on commercial bus tours, see Organized Tours under Activities earlier in this chapter.

Car & Motorcycle

The following companies have car rental booths at both the Kona and Hilo Airports.

Agency	Kona Airport	Hilo Airport
Alamo	☎ 329-8896	☎ 961-3343
Avis	☎ 327-3000	☎ 935-1290
Budget	☎ 329-8511	☎ 935-6878
Dollar	☎ 329-2744	☎ 961-6059
Hertz	☎ 329-3566	☎ 935-2896
National	☎ 329-1674	☎ 935-0891

For more information on car rentals, see the Getting Around chapter in the front of the book.

Harper Car & Truck Rentals, on Kalanianaole Ave in Hilo (☎ 969-1478) and at the airport in Kona (☎ 329-6688), has 4WD vehicles adjusted for use at Mauna Kea's high altitude. Unlike other rental agencies, Harper puts no restrictions on going to Mauna Kea's summit, or most anywhere else on the island, with the exception of Waipio Valley and Green Sands Beach, which are off-limits. Isuzu Troopers, Toyota 4-Runners and Jeep Cherokees all cost $111 a day, $665 a week; even if you purchase the optional CDW ($20), there's still a $5000 deductible should you damage the vehicle. Harper's toll-free number is ☎ 800-852-9993.

DJ's Rentals (☎ 329-1700), in a kiosk opposite King Kamehameha's Kona Beach Hotel in Kailua-Kona, rents mopeds starting at $25 a day and two-person motor scooters starting at $45. The company also rents motorcycles, including Harley Davidsons, for $120 to $145 a day.

Hilo is a good place to gas up on the Big Island, as gas is cheaper there than in Kona.

Taxi

The taxi flag-down fee is $2, and it costs $2 a mile after that. The approximate fare from Kona Airport to Kailua-Kona is $18 to $20; to Waikoloa it's about $40.

Bicycle

Hawaiian Pedals (☎ 329-2294), in the Kona Inn Shopping Village in Kailua-Kona, rents mountain bikes for $20/70 a day/week, performance bikes for $25 a day, tandem bikes for $35 a day and car bike racks for $5 a day.

Dave's Triathlon Shop (☎ 329-4522), in the rear of Kona Square on Alii Drive in Kailua-Kona, rents road bikes for around $25/60 a day/week and bike racks that can hold up to three bikes for $5/15.

As Kona is the center of activity for the Ironman Triathlon, a few area bike shops sell and repair high-caliber equipment. Two such places are Dave's Triathlon Shop, mentioned above, and B&L Bike & Sports (☎ 329-3309), off Hwy 11 near the Kopiko Plaza.

Hilo Bike Hub (☎ 961-4452), 318 E Kawili St in Hilo, rents mountain bikes from $20 to $65 a day and hybrid road bikes starting at $30 a day; the cost depends on each bike's age and condition. The weekly rate is four times the daily rate.

Kona

Kona literally means 'leeward.' The Kona Coast refers to the dry, sunny west coast of the Big Island. However, to make matters a little more confusing, the name Kona is also used to refer to Kailua, the largest town on the Kona Coast. The town's name is compounded Kailua-Kona by the post office and other officialdom to avoid confusion with Kailua on Oahu.

The weather is so consistent on this side of the island that the local paper commonly alternates two forecasts: 'Sunny morning. Afternoon clouds with upslope showers' or 'Sunny morning. Cloudy afternoon with showers over the slopes.'

The afternoon showers that hit the higher slopes rarely touch the coastline just a couple of miles below. Because it sees so little rain, Kona is also dubbed the Gold Coast. It's a good bet for a sunny vacation any time of the year.

KAILUA-KONA

In the 19th century, Kailua-Kona was a favorite vacation retreat for Hawaiian royalty. These days, it's the largest vacation destination on the Big Island.

THE BIG ISLAND

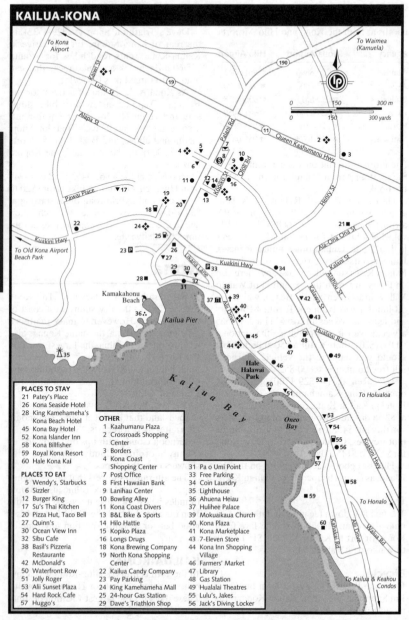

KAILUA-KONA

To Kona Airport

To Waimea (Kamuela)

Kailua Bay

Oneo Bay

Kamakahonu Beach

Kailua Pier

Hale Halawai Park

To Old Kona Airport Beach Park

To Holualoa

To Honalo

To Kailua & Keahou Condos

PLACES TO STAY
21 Patey's Place
26 Kona Seaside Hotel
28 King Kamehameha's
   Kona Beach Hotel
45 Kona Bay Hotel
52 Kona Islander Inn
58 Kona Billfisher
59 Royal Kona Resort
60 Hale Kona Kai

PLACES TO EAT
5 Wendy's, Starbucks
6 Sizzler
12 Burger King
17 Su's Thai Kitchen
20 Pizza Hut, Taco Bell
27 Quinn's
30 Ocean View Inn
32 Sibu Cafe
38 Basil's Pizzeria
   Restaurante
42 McDonald's
50 Waterfront Row
51 Jolly Roger
53 Alii Sunset Plaza
54 Hard Rock Cafe
57 Huggo's

OTHER
1 Kaahumanu Plaza
2 Crossroads Shopping
   Center
3 Borders
4 Kona Coast
   Shopping Center
7 Post Office
8 First Hawaiian Bank
9 Lanihau Center
10 Bowling Alley
11 Kona Coast Divers
13 B&L Bike & Sports
14 Hilo Hattie
15 Kopiko Plaza
16 Longs Drugs
18 Kona Brewing Company
19 North Kona Shopping
   Center
22 Kailua Candy Company
23 Pay Parking
24 King Kamehameha Mall
25 24-hour Gas Station
29 Dave's Triathlon Shop

31 Pa o Umi Point
33 Free Parking
34 Coin Laundry
35 Lighthouse
36 Ahuena Heiau
37 Hulihee Palace
39 Mokuaikaua Church
40 Kona Plaza
41 Kona Marketplace
43 7-Eleven Store
44 Kona Inn Shopping
   Village
46 Farmers' Market
47 Library
48 Gas Station
49 Hualalai Theatres
55 Lulu's, Jakes
56 Jack's Diving Locker

It's got a lot to make it a drawing card. The weather is good, the setting on the leeward side of Mt Hualalai is pretty, and a number of ancient Hawaiian and missionary-era historic sites are scattered in and around town. Even though its period character is a bit stifled by trinket shops and mini-malls, Kailua-Kona is still a fun place to poke around. It has lots of places to stay and eat, as well as activities ranging from world-class deep-sea fishing to snorkeling cruises. And thanks to its central location, the town makes a good base for exploring the entire Kona Coast.

Most of Kailua-Kona's condos are lined up along Alii Drive, the 5-mile coastal road that runs from the town center at Kailua Bay south to Keauhou. This strip sees a lot of power-walkers and joggers, particularly in the early morning hours, but the hottest activity occurs here in October when the road serves as the finish line of the world-famous Ironman Triathlon.

Kailua-Kona has a few swimming, snorkeling and surfing spots, although the island's best beaches are up the coast to the north.

Information

Tourist Offices The Big Island Visitors Bureau (☎ 329-7787) has a branch office in the Kona Plaza on Alii Drive. It's open 8 am to noon and 1 to 4:30 pm Monday to Friday.

Money Bank of Hawaii and First Hawaiian Bank both have branches at Lanihau Center on Palani Rd. You'll find ATMs at the banks and at numerous places around town, including the 7-Eleven on Kuakini Hwy, the Kona Inn Shopping Village on Alii Drive and larger grocery stores.

Post & Communications The post office is in the Lanihau Center on Palani Rd. It's open 8:30 am to 4:30 pm on weekdays and 9:30 am to 1:30 pm on Saturday.

Zac's Business Center (☎ 329-0006, fax 329-1021), at the North Kona Shopping Center on Kuakini Rd, has computers with Internet access for $8 an hour, or $2.75 for 15 minutes. You can also receive faxes for 50¢ a page and send faxes at varying rates. It's

open 8 am to 7 pm Monday to Friday, 9 am to 6 pm Saturday and 10 am to 4 pm Sunday.

Travel Agencies Cut Rate Tickets (☎ 326-2300), in the Kona Coast Shopping Center on Palani Rd, sells discounted tickets for interisland travel. It's open 8 am to 7 pm weekdays, 9 am to 5 pm Saturday and 9 am to 2 pm Sunday.

Bookstores Middle Earth Bookshoppe, in the Kona Plaza on Alii Drive, is a well-stocked central bookstore with Hawaiiana and general travel sections. Borders, on Hwy 19, is the area's largest bookstore and also carries a wide selection of US and foreign newspapers, including the *London Times* and *Le Monde*.

Libraries Kona's modern public library, on Hualalai Rd, subscribes to both Neighbor Island and mainland newspapers, including the *Los Angeles Times* and *USA Today*. It also sells used paperback books for just 25¢. It's open 10 am to 8 pm on Tuesday, 9 am to 6 pm on Wednesday and Thursday, 11 am to 5 pm on Friday and 9 am to 5 pm on Saturday.

The local daily, *West Hawaii Today*, and the Hilo and Honolulu papers are available at numerous places around town.

Photography Longs Drugs, in the Lanihau Center on Palani Rd, sells cameras and film and handles processing by major developers, including Kodak and Fuji. With its own darkroom, Longs also offers same-day print processing ($8 for 24 prints). However, if you can wait two days, the send-out service costs only $5 for 24 prints.

Laundry There are coin laundries in the North Kona Shopping Center on Kuakini Rd and on Kuakini Hwy east of its intersection with Henry St. In addition, most condos have either washers and dryers in the units or a laundry room on site.

Parking The center of Kailua-Kona gets quite congested, and finding a parking space in town can be a challenge.

Free public parking is available in the lot behind Kona Seaside Hotel, between Likana Lane and the Kuakini Hwy. The Kona Inn Shopping Village provides complimentary parking for patrons in the lot behind the Kona Bay Hotel. Patrons of Kona Marketplace can park free at the rear of that center.

At the north end of Alii Drive, the big parking lot behind King Kamehameha's Kona Beach Hotel offers free parking for the first 15 minutes; it costs $1 per half hour after that. If you purchase something in one of the hotel shops or restaurants, you can get a voucher for free parking.

Kamakahonu & Ahuena Heiau

Kamakahonu, the beach at the north end of Kailua Bay, was the site of the royal residence of Kamehameha the Great. Shortly after his death here in 1819, Kamehameha's successors came to Kamakahonu and ended the traditional kapu system, sounding a death knell for the old religion.

The ancient sites are now part of the grounds of King Kamehameha's Kona Beach Hotel. A few thatched structures along with carved wooden *kii* (images) of gods have been reconstructed above the old stone temple.

Ahuena Heiau, which was once a place of human sacrifice, juts out into the cove and acts as a breakwater, offering protection to swimmers. The waters at Kamakahonu, which means 'Eye of the Turtle,' are the calmest in Kailua Bay.

The little beach in front of the hotel is the only downtown swimming spot. The hotel beach hut rents snorkels, kayaks, beach chairs and umbrellas.

King Kamehameha's Kona Beach Hotel

Be sure to take a stroll through the sprawling lobby of this hotel, which is full of museum-quality displays on various aspects of Hawaiian culture, including traditional foods, fishing methods, music, dress and more.

One display features Hawaiian musical instruments, including a nose flute, coconut-shell knee drum, shell trumpet, bamboo rattles and hula sticks. Others contain feather capes and leis, *kapa* (bark cloth) beaters, quilts, war clubs, calabashes and gourd containers. The displays have brief interpretive plaques, but if you ask at the activity desk in the lobby, you'll get a free brochure that describes them in greater depth.

Also, check out the interesting painting of King Kamehameha at Kailua Bay by Hawaiian artist Herb Kane. It's near the front desk.

The hotel offers free, guided historical tours that visit the indoor displays and take in the hotel's historic grounds; tours are usually given at 1:30 pm on weekdays, but it's best to check at the activity desk for the latest schedule.

Kailua Pier

Kailua Pier was long the center of sports fishing on Hawaii, but it simply got too crowded to handle all the action. Now Kona's charter fishing boats use the larger Honokohau Harbor north of town, and Kailua Pier is mainly used by dive boats and cruise ship tenders, though its hoist and scales are still put to use for weigh-ins during billfish tournaments.

Kailua Bay was once a major cattle shipping area. Cattle driven down from hillside ranches were stampeded into the water and forced to swim out to waiting steamers, where they were hoisted aboard by sling and shipped to Honolulu slaughterhouses. Kailua Pier was built in 1915, and cattle pens were still in place until the 1960s.

The tiny patch of sandy beach on the east side of Kailua Pier is known as **Kaiakeakua**, 'Sea of the Gods.' It once served as Kamehameha's canoe landing.

Pa o Umi Point

In the 16th century, the powerful King Umi moved his royal court from Waipio to Kona. The rocky lava outcropping on the northeast side of Kailua Bay where he is thought to have landed is called Pa o Umi, 'Umi's Enclosure.'

A seawall has been built over much of it, but when the tide is low, you can still see the tip of the lava point by looking over the wall in the area diagonally across the street from the Ocean View Inn.

Mokuaikaua Church

On April 4, 1820, Hawaii's first Christian missionaries landed at Kailua Bay, stepping out onto a rock that is now one of the footings for the Kailua Pier. When the missionaries landed, they were unaware that Hawaii's old religion had been abolished on this same spot just a few months before. Their timing couldn't have been more auspicious. Given a favorable reception from Kamehameha's successors, the missionaries established Hawaii's first Christian church on Kailua Bay, a few minutes' walk from Kamehameha's ancient heiau and house site.

The temporary church the missionaries erected was replaced in 1836 by the current Mokuaikaua Church, a handsome building with walls of lava rock held together by a mortar of sand and coral lime. The posts and beams, hewn with stone adzes and smoothed down with chunks of coral, are made from strong termite-resistant *ohia* wood, and the pews and pulpit are made of *koa*, a native hardwood. The steeple tops out at 112 feet, making the church still the tallest structure in Kailua.

From 9 am to 4 pm Monday to Saturday, an interpreter is often on site to talk about the church's history. An 8-foot model of the brig *Thaddeus*, the ship that brought those first Congregational missionaries to Hawaii, is also on display.

Hulihee Palace

Hulihee Palace, a modest two-story house, was built in 1838 by Governor 'John Adams' Kuakini as his private residence.

Kuakini was also the contractor of the Mokuaikaua Church, and both buildings were of the same lava-rock construction. The palace got its current look in 1885, when it was plastered over inside and out by King Kalakaua, who had taken to a more polished style after his travels abroad.

The palace belonged to a succession of royal owners until the early 1900s, when it was abandoned and fell into disrepair. The Daughters of Hawaii, a group founded in 1903 by daughters of missionaries, took it over and now operates the property as a museum.

Hawaiian royals were huge people, and everything inside the palace reflects their proportions, including a 7-foot-long bed.

Princess Ruth Keelikolani, who owned the palace in the mid-19th century, was indeed a lady of some presence and is said to have weighed more than 400 pounds. She was an earthy woman, preferring to live in a big grass hut on the palace grounds rather than being confined within the palace. After her death, the wooden posts that had supported her grass hut were carved with designs of taro, leis and pineapples and used as posts in one of the beds upstairs.

The palace is furnished with antiques, many picked up on royal jaunts to Europe. Some of the more Hawaiian pieces include a table inlaid with 25 kinds of native Hawaiian woods, some of which are now extinct, and an armoire that was made in China of Hawaiian sandalwood and inlaid with ivory. Some of Kamehameha the Great's personal war spears are also on display.

The palace is open 9 am to 4 pm on weekdays, 10 am to 4 pm on Saturday and Sunday. Admission, which costs $5 for adults and $1 for children under 12, includes a 40-minute tour.

There's no charge to visit the gift shop or take a look at the **fishpond** behind the palace. Though no longer stocked, the pond holds a few colorful tropical fish. It also has a curious history, having once served as a Queen's Bath and a canoe landing. The lava coastline adjacent to the fishpond is also interesting, with lots of sea urchins and scurrying black crabs camouflaged among the black rocks.

Hale Halawai Park

Hale Halawai is a quiet oceanfront park with a few shady trees. It's not a sunbathing spot – the coast is rocky and the sand full of coral chunks – but can be a fine place to sit and read the morning paper.

A prison and courthouse once stood at the site. Now you'll find a pavilion that's often used by seniors and other community groups; a county recreation office, which issues camping permits; and free parking for park users.

Kona Brewing Company

The Kona Brewing Company (☎ 334-1133), in a warehouse adjacent to the North Kona Shopping Center, is the Big Island's first microbrewery. Started a few years ago by a father and son from Oregon, this little family-run operation now ships its brew to the Neighbor Islands. The brewery's mainstay, Pacific Golden Ale, blends pale and honey malts to produce a traditional ale. If you prefer a little island flavor, try the Lilikoi Wheat, which has a light, passion-fruit bouquet. These handcrafted ales can be sampled at the conclusion of the free brewery tours, offered at 10:30 am and 3:30 pm Monday to Saturday. They're also served at the brewery's outdoor cafe and can be found in restaurants and grocery stores.

Old Kona Airport Beach Park

The old Kona Airport, which was replaced by the current Kona Airport in 1970, has been turned into a state recreation area and beach park. It's about a mile north of downtown Kailua-Kona, at the end of the Kuakini Hwy.

The old runway skirts a long sandy beach, but lava rocks run the length of the beach between the sand and the ocean. Although this makes for poor swimming conditions, it's ideal for fishing and exploring tide pools. At low tide, the rocks reveal an intriguing system of little aquarium-like pockets holding tiny sea urchins, crabs and bits of coral.

A couple of breaks in the lava, including one in front of the first picnic area, allow entry into the water.

A little cove, which can be reached by a short walk from the north end of the beach, is a good area for scuba divers and confident snorkelers. The reef fish are large and plentiful, and a steep coral wall in deeper waters harbors big moray eels and a wide variety of other sea creatures, such as lionfish and cowries.

When the surf's up, local surfers favor the offshore break. In high surf, though, it's too rough for other water activities.

While this local park is popular with families and picnickers, it's much too big to ever feel crowded. Facilities include rest rooms, showers and covered picnic tables on a lawn dotted with beach heliotrope and short coconut palms.

The old runway was once used by rowdy locals as a late-night drag strip; a gate now closes off that section of the park at 8 pm. The Kailua-Kona end of the park contains a gym, soccer and softball fields and four outdoor lighted tennis courts.

Directly behind the tennis courts is a break in the wall marked 'Shoreline Public Access.' A short path from here leads into an exclusive subdivision, but the beach fronting the subdivision, like all Hawaiian beaches, remains public. If you walk along the beach a few minutes toward downtown Kailua-Kona, you'll come to a sandy area with a big wading pool just a few feet deep – a great spot for children.

Saltwater Pool

One of Kona's best-kept secrets is a saltwater swimming pool in a little lava outcrop so close to the ocean that waves lap in over the side, carrying small tropical fish with them. It's as large as most condo pools – and it's open to the public.

The pool was originally part of a retired admiral's private estate. By the time it was sold to developers (Kona by the Sea condos are here now), all coastline had become public domain.

Kona by the Sea has put in four public-beach-access parking spaces at the side of its parking lot. A gravel path on the north side of the complex leads from the parking lot down to the pool.

The admiral had good taste. You float above the ocean and can glance over the edge and watch surfers riding into shore. Still, how tempting the pool water will be for swimming depends on whether big waves have washed through recently; algae tend to flourish when the water stands too long. Be careful getting into the pool, as the steps are slippery.

White Sands Beach Park

It's called White Sands, Magic Sands and Disappearing Sands, but it's all the same beach, midway between Kailua-Kona and

Keauhou. In winter when the surf is high, the sand can disappear literally overnight, leaving only rocks on the shore. But then it returns just as magically, creating a fine white-sand beach once again.

This is a very popular bodysurfing beach when the rocks aren't exposed. The facilities include rest rooms and a volleyball court.

Places to Stay

Hostels & B&Bs The cheapest place to stay in town is *Patey's Place* (☎ 326-7018, fax 326-7640, patey@mail.gte.net, 75-195 Ala-Ona Ona, Kailua-Kona, HI 96740). This hostel-style accommodation is in a rather congested residential neighborhood a 10-minute walk from the town center. Dormitory beds, which are four to six to a room, cost $17.50; semiprivate rooms with just two bunk beds cost $25 per person; and simple private rooms cost $31.50/41.50 for singles/doubles. Rates include tax. All rooms have ceiling fans, screens to let in the breeze, shared baths and access to a shared kitchen. The office is open 8 am to noon and 4 to 10 pm. There's an airport shuttle for $5 each way.

Anne's Three Bears Bed & Breakfast (☎/fax 325-7563, three.bears@pobox.com, 72-1001 Puukala St, Kailua-Kona, HI 96740) is a delightful cedar home 7 miles north of Kailua-Kona, off of Hwy 190. The home has a hillside location, sweeping views of the Kona Coast and good conditions for stargazing from the lanai. The two comfortable guest rooms have private baths, microwaves, refrigerators, toasters, coffeemakers and cable TV. Owners Anne and Art Stockel are active in environmental issues, speak fluent German and know the island inside out. For travelers with their own transportation, Three Bears would make a good base for exploring the Kona, Waimea and Waikoloa areas. Rates, which include breakfast fixings for the first two nights, are $60 a night for one room, $70 for the other. There's a four-night minimum stay. Anne also books other B&B accommodations in Hawaii.

Kiwi Gardens (☎ 326-1559, fax 329-6618, kiwi@ilhawaii.net, 74-4920 Kiwi St, Kailua-Kona, HI 96740) is a B&B about 3 miles north

of Kailua-Kona center. Ron and Shirlee Freitas, former San Franciscans, rent three rooms in their contemporary home. One room has a queen bed with a lanai and a sunset view, another is a smaller room with a twin bed and a double bed. Both these rooms share a bath and cost $65 as a double or $55 as a single. The third room is a master suite with a king brass bed, private bath and lanai for $75. There's a shared guest phone and a common area with '50s decor, complete with vintage soda fountain and juke box. Breakfast includes fresh-baked items, smoothies and seasonal fruits from the yard. If you're interested in deep-sea fishing, Ron has his own charter boat.

Condos In Kona, condos outnumber hotels many times over. Condos tend to be cheaper than hotels if you're staying awhile, although if you make advance reservations, which are recommended in the high season, you'll often have to deal with deposits and stiff cancellation penalties.

Many of Kona's condominiums can be booked through more than one rental agency. For condos with an address listed, you can write directly to the condo, as they either handle their own bookings or will pass correspondence on to the agents that do. For the rest, units are handled by at least one of the following agencies; each will send its latest listings and rates upon request. It's worth comparing the listings before booking.

Hawaii Resort Management
  (☎ 329-9393, 800-622-5348, fax 326-4137, kona@konahawaii.com, www.konahawaii.com)
  75-5776 Kuakini Hwy, suite 105C,
  PO Box 39, Kailua-Kona, HI 96740

Knutson & Associates
  (☎ 329-6311, 800-800-6202, fax 326-2178, knutson@aloha.net, planet-hawaii.com/knutson),
  75-6082 Alii Drive, suite 8,
  Kailua-Kona, HI 96740

SunQuest Vacations
  (☎ 329-6488, 800-367-5168 from the USA, 800-800-5662 from Canada, fax 329-5480, sqvac@sunquest-hawaii.com, www.sunquest-hawaii.com),
  77-6435 Kuakini Hwy, Kailua-Kona, HI 96740

Triad Management
  (☎ 329-6402, 800-345-2823, fax 326-2401),
  PO Box 4466, Kailua-Kona, HI 96745

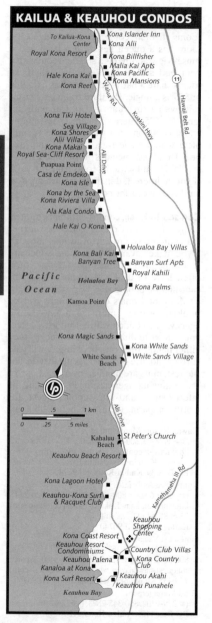

KAILUA & KEAUHOU CONDOS

To Kailua-Kona
Center
Royal Kona Resort
Kona Islander Inn
Kona Alii
Kona Billfisher
Malia Kai Apts
Hale Kona Kai
Kona Pacific
Kona Reef
Kona Mansions

Wailua Rd
Kuakini Hwy
Hawaii Belt Rd
11

Kona Tiki Hotel
Sea Village
Kona Shores
Alii Villas
Kona Makai
Royal Sea-Cliff Resort
Puapuaa Point
Casa de Emdeko
Kona Isle
Kona by the Sea
Kona Riviera Villa
Ala Kala Condo
Hale Kai O Kona

Alii Drive

Pacific
Ocean

Holualoa Bay Villas
Kona Bali Kai
Banyan Tree
Banyan Surf Apts
Royal Kahili
Holualoa Bay
Kona Palms

Kamoa Point

Kona Magic Sands

Kona White Sands
White Sands
Beach
White Sands Village

Alii Drive

0   .5   1 km
0   .25   .5 miles

Kahaluu
Beach
St Peter's Church
Keauhou Beach Resort

Kamehameha III Rd

Kona Lagoon Hotel

Keauhou-Kona Surf
& Racquet Club

Keauhou
Shopping
Center

Kona Coast Resort
Keauhou Resort
Condominiums
Country Club Villas
Keauhou Palena
Kona Country
Club
Kanaloa at Kona
Kona Surf Resort
Keauhou Akahi
Keauhou Punahele
Keauhou Bay

Most of Kona's condos are quite nice, have complete kitchens and are fully furnished with everything from linen to cooking utensils. The general rule is that the weekly rate is six times the daily rate and the monthly rate is three times the weekly. However, in the high season, if business is brisk, many places will offer only the daily rate, while in the off-season months of April, May and September you might be able to negotiate an even better deal.

Most rental agents typically require a three-day minimum stay, but Triad Management requires a five-day minimum stay in the low season and a seven-day minimum in the high season.

If you wait until you arrive in Kona to look for a place, you can sometimes find a good deal under 'Vacation Rentals' in the classified ads of *West Hawaii Today*. However, this is risky during the high season, when many of the better-value places book up well in advance.

All Kona condos listed here have swimming pools, unless otherwise noted.

The ***Kona Islander Inn*** (☎ 329-3181, 75-5776 Kuakini Hwy, Kailua-Kona, HI 96740) is an older development in the town center. Some of the ground-floor units can have a musty air, but others are fixed up nicely. Marc Resorts handles about two dozen of the 144 units and maintains a front desk. A hotel-style room with refrigerator costs $119 if you book from the mainland, though you can sometimes get a walk-in rate of around $59.

Most of the other Kona Islander Inn units are handled by Hawaii Resort Management, whose office is conveniently located at the side of the lobby. These units work out to be a significantly better deal, costing from $35 to $59 a day or $245 to $295 a week in the low season, and from $69 to $79 a day or $345 to $395 a week in the high season. The furnishings vary, but the rooms have TV, air-con, kitchenettes and phones with free local calls. Monthly rates start at $795/1000 in the low/high season.

Kona Billfisher (75-5841 Alii Drive) has 65 units that are well furnished with full kitchens, lanais, queen sofa beds in the living rooms, king beds in the bedrooms and both ceiling fans and air-con. They tend to have more consistent decor and better upkeep than other moderately priced complexes. All units are closed for maintenance on the 13th and 14th of each month. When booked through Triad Management, one-bedroom units cost $70/85 for the low/high season, two-bedroom units cost $90/105. Hawaii Resort Management also handles one-bedroom units here, and its prices are typically about $5 less. It's good value for this price range and within walking distance of town.

Alii Villas (☎ 329-1288, 75-6016 Alii Drive, Kailua-Kona, HI 96740) has 126 units and is a quiet place that attracts a fair number of seniors. The units are large and comfortable, each with a private lanai, cable TV and washer/dryer. Most have a phone and sofa bed. You can either contact Alii Villas directly or book through either of two agencies: Knutson & Associates, which has one-bedroom units starting at $60/75 in the low/high season; or SunQuest Vacations, which has one-bedroom units starting at $80 year-round.

Kona Makai (☎ 329-6488, 75-6026 Alii Drive), on the seaward side of Alii Drive next to Alii Villas, has air-con one-bedroom units that are fully equipped with everything down to a washer/dryer. Rates start at $90 a day through SunQuest Vacations. The complex has an exercise room and tennis courts.

Kona Riviera Villa (☎ 329-1996, 75-6124 Alii Drive) is a pleasant little complex right on the ocean. There are just 14 units, each with a full kitchen (including a microwave and dishwasher), a living room, a separate bedroom with a king or queen bed, and ceiling fans; most have a sofa bed in the living room. The complex has a pool and a coin laundry. Nine of the units are handled by Knutson & Associates, which charges a reasonable $75 for a garden view, $80 to $90 for an ocean view and $100 for an oceanfront unit. Rates drop $10 in the low season.

Casa de Emdeko (☎ 329-2160, 75-6082 Alii Drive) is rather standard fare, with one-bedroom units starting at $70/90 in the low/high season; book through Knutson & Associates, whose office is at the front of the complex. The units can feel a bit cramped, but they do have lanais and full kitchens. There are both freshwater and saltwater pools.

Kona Magic Sands Resort (☎ 329-3333, 77-6452 Alii Drive) is a small complex perched at the side of White Sands Beach. Fourteen of the 36 units are handled by Hawaii Resort Management. These are compact studio units, but they have full kitchens, TVs, phones, rattan furnishings and oceanfront lanais. Although it's an older building, the units have recently been upgraded, and it's a good value for being right on the water. Rates are $65 to $75 in the low season, $75 to $95 in the high season.

Kona White Sands (☎ 329-9393, 77-6467 Alii Drive) is a two-story building with eight bargain units, all with kitchens and lanais. A couple of these one-bedroom units can be booked through Hawaii Resort Management for $70/75 in the low/high season. There's no pool, but it's across the street from White Sands Beach.

Malia Kai Apartments (☎ 329-6402), inland from the Royal Kona Resort on Walua Rd, has 21 units, each with three levels. The bottom level has a carport and washer/dryer. The 2nd floor has a lanai, a kitchen and a living room with a sofa bed. The 3rd floor has one main bedroom with sliding shoji doors separating it from another room with a sofa bed. The complex has a garden courtyard with a small pool. The layout isn't perfect for everyone, but if you're with a few people it could be economical. Rates are $75/90 in the low/high season through Triad Management.

If you enjoy the sound of the surf, *Hale Kona Kai* (☎/fax 329-2155, 800-421-3696, 75-5870 Kahakai Rd, Kailua-Kona, HI 96740) is a pleasant find on the ocean just beyond the Royal Kona Resort. The 39 one-bedroom units aren't brand new, but they're comfortable and have full amenities like full kitchens and cable TV. All units have waterfront lanais with great ocean views. Rates start at $95 for up to two people. It's $10 more for a corner unit with a wraparound lanai and $10 more per person for additional guests. There's a three-day minimum on most units, a $150 security deposit and no Sunday or holiday check-in.

Kona Reef (☎ 329-2959, 800-367-5004, fax 329-2762, 75-5888 Alii Drive, Kailua-Kona, HI 96740) is a 130-unit condo complex run like a hotel by Castle Resorts & Hotels. The units have the usual amenities, including full kitchens, washer/dryers and private lanais. Rates begin at $155 for up to four people in a one-bedroom unit, which also has a sofa bed in the living room. It's cheaper, however, to book through SunQuest Vacations, which handles about a dozen units and charges $100.

Royal Sea-Cliff Resort (☎ 329-8021, 800-922-7866, fax 326-1887, 75-6040 Alii Drive, Kailua-Kona, HI 96740) is a modern 154-unit complex with some of the nicest condo units in Kona. They have large balconies, stylish furnishings, thermostatic air-con, modern kitchens and washers and dryers. There are tennis courts, a couple of pools and a sauna. The Aston chain runs it like a hotel with a front desk and there's no minimum stay. Studios cost $170/190 in the low/high season, while roomy one-bedroom units start at $190/210, two-bedroom units at $220/240. Various discount schemes are available, including 50% off for Entertainment and Encore travel club members.

Hotels One of the area's best hotel deals is the **Kona Tiki Hotel** (☎ 329-1425, fax 327-9402, 75-5968 Alii Drive, Kailua-Kona, HI 96740). This older three-story complex has 15 pleasant rooms, most with a queen and a twin bed and all with refrigerators and breezy oceanfront lanais. Squeezed on a narrow jut of land between the ocean and the road, the sound of the surf usually drowns out traffic noise. Amenities include a small seaside pool and complimentary coffee, juice and breakfast pastries. Rates are $58 for standard rooms, $65 for rooms with kitchenettes, plus $8 more for a third person. The hotel is very popular with return visitors and generally books up well in advance during the high season. Credit cards are not accepted.

Kona Seaside Hotel (☎ 329-2455, 800-367-7000, fax 922-0052, sandsea@aloha.net, 75-5646 Palani Rd, Kailua-Kona, HI 96740) has two sections. One's a modern six-story building with private lanais and rates of $95 and up. The older rear poolside wing is simpler and has walls that carry sound, making the $80 rate for those rooms a lesser value. You can usually get a cheaper local rate on both sections if you book within Hawaii; a package for $119 that includes a free Budget rental car and two nights' stay is perpetually advertised in the Sunday Honolulu paper. To get the best deal, skip the toll-free number and call the local booking desk (☎ 922-1228). You don't have to be a Hawaii resident to qualify for the cheaper rates, but the clerk may be loath to make the reservation if you call before you arrive in the islands or if you give a non-Hawaii mailing address. For more information, visit the hotel's website at www.sand-seaside.com.

For those who want to be right in the center of town, there's Uncle Billy's **Kona Bay Hotel** (☎ 329-1393, 800-367-5102, fax 935-7903, unclebillys@aloha.net, 75-5739 Alii Drive, Kailua-Kona, HI 96740). The older cinder-block buildings lack charm, but at $79 the place is relatively cheap and the rooms have TV, air-con, refrigerator and phones. There's a pool.

The 460-room **King Kamehameha's Kona Beach Hotel** (☎ 329-2911, 800-367-6060, fax 329-4602, reservation@hthcorp.com, 75-5660 Palani Rd, Kailua-Kona, HI 96740), at Kailua Bay, is on the only beach in town. Located at the site of King Kamehameha's former residence, it has a sprawling koa-wood lobby full of interesting Hawaiiana displays. Each of the comfortable rooms has two double beds, a lanai, thermostatic air-con, room safe, TV and phone. Other amenities include a pool, lighted tennis courts and free guest parking. Rates range from $120 to $195, depending upon the view. The hotel's website is at www.konabeachhotel.com.

The **Royal Kona Resort** (☎ 329-3111, 800-774-5662, fax 329-7230, cameron@royalkona .com, 75-5852 Alii Drive, Kailua-Kona, HI 96740), a former Hilton, has an oceanfront location on the edge of town. While it's lost a bit of its luster over the years, the 454 rooms have the expected amenities including TVs, coffeemakers, refrigerators and room safes.

The regular rates begin at $140, but better discount deals are available, including a room and car package for $109. There's no sandy beach, but there is a conventional swimming pool as well as a natural saltwater pool that's deep enough for swimming. The hotel also has tennis courts and a waterfront restaurant. For more information, visit the website www.konabeachhotel.com.

Places to Eat

Budget For a cheap meal on the run, try the *French Bakery*, at Kaahumanu Plaza in the industrial area, which makes crispy French bread, sticky buns and large muffins. The Tongan bread ($5), filled with cheese and spinach, makes a good lunch for two and can be microwaved on request. Hours are 5:30 am to 3 pm Monday to Friday, to 2 pm on Saturday.

The unassuming *Ocean View Inn*, on Alii Drive in the town center, is the best place for cheap local food. Complete breakfasts with coffee cost $3 to $6, while sandwiches are $2 to $5. You can get inexpensive Chinese, American and Hawaiian dishes, and it's a good place to try *lomi* salmon (which has been diced and marinated) or a side dish of *poi*, the Hawaiian taro paste. Breakfast is served 6:30 to 11 am, lunch 11 am to 2:45 pm, and dinner 5:15 to 9 pm. The Ocean View is closed on Monday.

Kona Mix Plate, in Kopiko Plaza, is a bustling eatery with counter service and good-value local fare. Cheeseburgers and *mahimahi* ('dolphin' fish) sandwiches served with fries cost $4.15, while most plate lunches, including a nice teriyaki chicken dish, cost $6. This spot is open 10 am to 8 pm Monday to Saturday.

Island Java Java, at Alii Sunset Plaza on Alii Drive, is a popular coffee shop with espresso, sandwiches and good homemade cinnamon rolls, muffins and pies – all at reasonable prices. You can linger over coffee at outdoor tables and listen to live music nightly. Island Java Java is open 6 am to 10 pm daily. If you prefer New York-style sandwiches, *A Piece of The Apple*, next door in the same complex, has good hearty sandwiches for around $6.

Another worthwhile option at Alii Sunset Plaza is *Thai Rin*, which has curries, pad Thai and stir-fry dishes for $6 to $8 at lunch, a bit more at dinner. Thai Rin is open 11 am to 2:30 pm Sunday to Friday and 5 to 9 pm daily.

If you're up for Chinese food, *Golden Chopstix*, at Kaahumanu Plaza in the industrial area, has long been the local favorite, despite its diner atmosphere. Lunch specials such as kung pao chicken or beef with broccoli cost $5 and come with soup, fried rice and tea, while main dishes at dinner cost $8. Golden Chopstix is open 11 am to 2:30 pm Monday to Saturday and 4:30 to 9 pm daily.

Jolly Roger, on Alii Drive just south of Waterfront Row, has a knockout ocean view right on the edge of the surf, though the food is uninspired. You can get breakfast items for around $5, lunchtime sandwiches or burgers with fries for $7 and chicken or mahimahi dinners for $14. Jolly Roger is open 6:30 am to 10 pm daily.

The 24-hour *Safeway* supermarket at the Crossroads Shopping Center is Kona's biggest supermarket and has a good bakery, deli and reasonably priced wines.

Kona Natural Foods, right next to Safeway, stocks organic wines and produce, along with a good variety of dairy and bulk food products. It also has an excellent little cafe serving veggie sandwiches and generous takeout salads starting at $4; a hearty meal of the day is just $6. The store is open daily 9 am to 9 pm (to 7 pm on Sunday), while the cafe closes about an hour earlier.

Kuz'ns, an ice cream place in the Kona Inn Shopping Village, sells Alta-Dena ice cream for $1.85 a single scoop and also makes fruit smoothies.

The Lanihau Center on Palani Rd has a large *Sack N Save* supermarket (open daily 5 am to midnight), a deli and bakery, an eatery that serves *saimin* (Japanese noodle soup), a simple Chinese restaurant, a *Baskin-Robbins* ice cream shop and a *KFC* (Kentucky Fried Chicken).

Kona also has *McDonald's, Pizza Hut, Taco Bell, Burger King* and *Wendy's* fast-food places and a *Starbucks* coffee shop.

Fresh island fruits, vegetables and flowers are available direct from the growers at the *farmers' markets* that set up opposite Waterfront Row from 6 am to 3 pm on Wednesday, Friday, Saturday and Sunday; and at Alii Gardens Market Place, on Alii Drive opposite the Kona Riviera Villa condominiums, 8 am to 4 pm on Wednesday, Friday, Saturday and Sunday.

Mid-Range *Bangkok Houses* (☎ 329-7764), in the King Kamehameha Mall, serves tasty Thai food at moderate prices. Lunch offerings include pad Thai, ginger chicken and flavorful curries, all just $5.50; at dinner, the same dishes cost $8. Lunch is served 11 am to 3 pm weekdays, and dinner is 5 to 9 pm nightly.

Su's Thai Kitchen (☎ 326-7808), nearby on Pawai Place in the industrial area, also has good Thai food. At dinner, 5 to 9 pm Monday to Saturday, most standard dishes such as beef, pork or chicken curry cost $9, while the house specialty, volcano chicken with a sweet and sour sauce, is $13. At lunch (11 am to 2:30 pm weekdays), you can get pad Thai or the curry of the day with rice for $6. The mood, like the food, is authentically Thai – the dining area is an informal outdoor lanai, lit by candles at night.

Rock music plays continuously and music memorabilia covers the walls at Kona's new *Hard Rock Cafe* (☎ 329-8866), on Alii Drive at the south end of town. The menu features the chain's standard salads, sandwiches and burger platters, all averaging $9. The splendid 2nd-floor ocean view may well be the best Hard Rock Cafe vista anywhere in the world. Hours are 11:30 am to 11 pm Sunday to Thursday, 11:30 am to 11:30 pm Friday and Saturday.

Kona Brewing Co (☎ 329-2739), at the back of the North Kona Shopping Center, has an outdoor cafe with good Greek, spinach and Caesar salads from $4 to $8 and creative pizzas for around $10 and up. Wash it all down with one of the fresh brews made on site. This spot is open 11 am to 10 pm Monday to Thursday, 11 am to midnight Friday and Saturday, 1 to 9 pm Sunday.

Sibu Cafe (☎ 329-1112), at Banyan Court, serves good Indonesian food in a casual cafe setting. A hearty gado gado salad costs $10,

and combination plates that offer three dishes (with choices like Balinese chicken, spicy Indian curry and shrimp satay) with brown rice cost $13 at dinner. On weekdays, the lunch specials make for a good deal at $6. The Sibu Cafe is open daily 11:30 am to 3 pm for lunch and 5 to 9 pm for dinner. Credit cards are not accepted.

Run by two Italian brothers, *Basil's Pizzeria Restaurante* (☎ 326-7836), on Alii Drive, is one of the busiest dining spots in the center of Kailua. It offers generous servings, good authentic Italian food and reasonable prices. Most dishes come with Caesar salad and garlic bread. Pizzas, pastas and eggplant parmigiana are priced around $11, seafood dishes a few dollars more. Meatball or chicken sandwiches, served with fries, go for $7. Basil's is open 11 am to 2 pm on weekdays and 5 to 9 pm nightly.

Pancho & Lefty's (☎ 326-2171), a large 2nd-floor restaurant at the Kona Marketplace, is a touristy place with standard Mexican fare. Burritos, enchiladas or fajitas served with rice and beans cost $9 to $15, a combination plate around $12. Until 6 pm, draft beer costs $1. It's open daily 11 am to 10 pm.

The *Sizzler* (☎ 329-3374), in the Kona Coast Shopping Center, has a good salad bar – with veggies, fresh fruit, soup and tortillas – that can be a meal in itself for $9 or included with a main course for $5. This family-style chain restaurant, open for lunch and dinner daily, specializes in standard steak and seafood dishes with prices beginning around $10.

Michaelangelo's (☎ 329-4436), on the upper floor of Waterfront Row, has only average Italian food but enjoys a pleasant waterfront setting. The usual pasta dishes cost $10 at lunch and around $15 at dinner. Thick-crust pizzas are around $10, but coupons frequently offer a 20% discount. Michaelangelo's is open for lunch 11 am to 4:30 pm and for dinner 4:30 to 10 pm.

Quinn's (☎ 329-3822), a bar on Palini Rd opposite King Kamehameha's Kona Beach Hotel, serves meals in its rear courtyard 11 am to midnight. The crowd is mostly longtime local residents who come for the consistently good fish and steak dinners. For the setting, prices aren't cheap – $9.25 for fish and chips or a fresh fish sandwich, $20 for an ahi dinner – but the portions are large. Burgers, soups and salads are also available.

King Kamehameha's Kona Beach Hotel (☎ 329-2911) offers a breakfast buffet from 6 to 10 am daily that costs $10 with hot dishes, $6.50 if you just want the cold dishes (fruit, pastries and cereal). On Sunday from 9 am to 1 pm, there's an elaborate champagne brunch for $22. On Friday and Saturday evenings, King Kamehameha's has a $20 seafood and prime rib buffet with everything from sashimi and crab legs to extensive salad and dessert bars, and on Monday there's a $14 Hawaiian buffet. On other nights, a more ordinary dinner menu is offered.

Top End The trendiest place in town is *Oodles of Noodles* (☎ 329-9222), at the Crossroads Shopping Center. Run by Amy Ferguson-Ota, former executive chef at one of the Kohala Coast resorts, the restaurant features noodles in all variations – from Vietnamese pho soup, pad Thai and Peking duck to grilled chicken fettuccine and a delicious wok-seared ahi noodle casserole. The menu also includes creative salads, calzones and gourmet pizzas. Most dishes are priced from $10 to $14. A recommendable appetizer is the veggie summer rolls for $6. Hours are 11 am to 9 pm Monday to Thursday, 11 am to 10 pm Friday and Saturday, 11 am to 7 pm Sunday.

Kona Inn (☎ 329-4455), in the center of town, opened in 1929 as the Big Island's first hotel. It's now a shopping center with a large water-view restaurant of the same name. Steak and seafood dinners are in the $15 to $25 range. Light meals, which are available from 11:30 am to 10:30 pm, include a chicken Caesar salad ($10) and steak sandwiches ($12).

Huggo's (☎ 329-1493), near the Royal Kona Resort, is a popular open-air restaurant right on the water's edge – a nice spot for a sunset drink. It attracts the biggest crowd at lunchtime on Tuesday and Thursday, when it features barbecued beef ribs served with baked beans and French bread for $9.50. At dinner the menu centers around steak and

fish dishes that are good but a bit pricey at around $25. Huggo's is open 11:30 am to 2:30 pm on weekdays and 5:30 to 10 pm nightly.

For authentic Greek food, try *Cassandra's Greek Taverna* (☎ 334-1066), in the Kona Plaza on Alii Drive. For around $15 you can get souvlaki, moussaka or a gyros plate, all served with rice. Appetizers, priced from $5 to $8, include Greek salad, hummus, calamari and pickled octopus. Cassandra's is open 11:30 am to 10 pm Monday to Saturday, 4 to 9 pm on Sunday.

Jameson's by the Sea (☎ 329-3195) is at Kona Magic Sands condos on White Sands Beach. The ocean-side tables are about as close as you can get to the surf without getting your feet wet, but the food is not as inspired as the setting. Dinner entrees typically range from $19 to $24 for fresh fish or steak. Lunch features sandwiches and salads for $8 to $11. Jameson's is open daily 11 am to 2:30 pm for lunch and 5 to 9:30 pm for dinner.

Entertainment

With numerous restaurants and bars lined up along Alii Drive, Kona has no shortage of sunset views and happy hours.

Huggo's (☎ 329-1493), near the Royal Kona Resort, has dancing to Top 40, reggae or Hawaiian music from 9 pm to at least midnight nightly.

Michaelangelo's (☎ 329-4436), at Waterfront Row, has dancing to a DJ starting at 10 pm, Wednesday to Saturday.

LuLu's (☎ 331-2633), on Alii Drive next door to the Hard Rock Cafe, boasts 13 TV monitors that plug into sports programs. *Jakes* (☎ 329-7366), in the same building, offers dancing to live music on most nights.

Uncle Billy's *Kona Bay Hotel* (☎ 329-1393), in the town center, presents a free hula show from 6 to 8 pm on Tuesday, Thursday and Sunday.

Cinemas Kailua-Kona has two multiscreen movie theater complexes: *Hualalai Theatres*, on Kuakini Hwy; and *Kona Marketplace Cinema*, in the center of town. The best deal is on Tuesday, when both theaters drop their rates from $6.50 to $4.

Luaus *King Kamehameha's Kona Beach Hotel* (☎ 326-4969) offers a popular luau every Sunday, Tuesday, Wednesday and Thursday on its beach in front of Ahuena Heiau. The luau begins with a shell-lei greeting at 5:30 pm, followed by torch lighting, a buffet dinner and a Polynesian dance show. The cost is $53 for adults, $20 for children six to 12, and free for children five and under. There's also limited seating at 7 pm, minus the dinner, which costs $28 for adults, $13.50 for children. If you stop by around 10 am on luau days, you can watch staff members bury the pig in the *imu* (underground oven) – they'll explain it all to you.

Shopping

The center of Kailua-Kona is thick with small shops selling trinkets, clothing, crafts and other tourist-related goods. King Kamehameha's Kona Beach Hotel has a Big Island Outlet store that features a wide variety of island crafts, food items, T-shirts and oddities like potted fuku bonsai trees.

You'll find good selections of Hawaiian music CDs and cassettes at Tempo Music in Kopiko Plaza and at Mele Kai Music in Kaahumanu Plaza.

The Kailua Candy Company, at 74-5563 Kaiwi St in the industrial area, makes delicious homemade chocolates using island fruits and nuts. The candies aren't cheap, but they make a nice souvenir. At the gift shop, open 8 am to 6 pm daily, you can get some free samples and take a peek through picture windows at the company's operations.

Getting Around

The Alii Shuttle (☎ 775-7121) makes 45-minute runs between Kailua-Kona and Keauhou nine times daily in each direction. The bus leaves the Kona Surf Resort in Keauhou at 8:30 am and every 1½ hours thereafter, with the last run at 8:30 pm. Stops are made at Keauhou Shopping Center, Keauhou Beach Resort, Royal Kona Resort, Kona Inn Shopping Village, King Kamehameha's Kona Beach Hotel and the Lanihau Center. In the southbound direction, buses leave the Lanihau Center every 1½ hours from 7:50 am to 7:50 pm. Among other

things, the shuttle makes a good option for getting to Kahaluu Beach Park (next to the Keauhou Beach Resort) if you're in Kailua-Kona without a car. The fare anywhere along the route is $2 each way, or you can get a day/week/month pass for $5/20/40.

KEAUHOU

Keauhou is the coastal area immediately south of Kailua-Kona. It starts at Kahaluu Bay and runs south beyond Keauhou Bay and the Kona Surf Resort.

Keauhou contains a planned community of three hotels, nine condo complexes, a shopping center and a 27-hole golf course, all neatly spaced out with a country club atmosphere. Bishop Estate, Hawaii's biggest private landholder, owns the land.

The area was once the site of a major Hawaiian settlement. Several historical sites can still be explored, although they now share their grounds with the hotels and condos.

Information

Inside the KTA Supermarket is a branch of the Bank of Hawaii, open 10 am to 7 pm on weekdays and 10 am to 3 pm on weekends. KTA also has a Bank of Hawaii ATM.

The local post office is at the Keauhou Shopping Center, on the corner of Alii Drive and Kamehameha III Rd. It's open 10 am to 4:30 pm on weekdays and 10 am to 3 pm on Saturday.

Keauhou Shopping Center contains a Longs Drugs, and KTA Supermarket has a small pharmacy.

St Peter's Church

The little blue and white church on the north side of Kahaluu Bay is St Peter's Catholic Church. It dates back to 1880, although it was moved from White Sands Beach to this site in 1912. Tidal waves and hurricanes have since attempted to relocate it on a couple of occasions.

St Peter's is Hawaii's most photographed 'quaint church' and is still used for weekend services and weddings.

Christians were not the first to deem the site a suitable place to worship the gods.

At the north side of the church, you'll find the remains of **Kuemanu Heiau**, a surfing temple. Hawaiian royalty, who surfed the waters at the north end of Kahaluu Bay, paid their respects at this temple before hitting the waves.

Locals keep up the surfing tradition here, although high surf usually generates dangerous northward rip currents, and it's not a good spot for beginners.

Kahaluu Beach

Kahaluu, which means the 'Diving Place' in Hawaiian, is the island's best easy-access snorkeling spot. The bay is like a big natural aquarium, loaded with colorful marine life. If you haven't tried snorkeling, this is a great place to learn. It's not even necessary to go out over your head to enjoy it!

Large rainbow parrotfish, schools of silver needlefish, brilliant yellow tangs, butterfly fish and colorful wrasses are among the numerous tropicals easily seen here.

The fish are tame enough to eat out of your hand, and if you bring along fish food, you'll be surrounded by frenzied swarms. There are lots of fish in the shallows, but generally the deeper the water, the better the coral and the larger the fish. At high tide, green sea turtles often swim into the bay to feed.

An ancient breakwater, said to have been built by the *menehune* (legendary 'little people'), is on the reef and protects the bay. Still, when the surf is high, Kahaluu can have strong currents that pull in the direction of the rocks near St Peter's Church, and it's easy to drift away without realizing it. Check your bearings occasionally to make sure you're not being pulled by the current. Before jumping in, take a look at the weathered display board by the picnic pavilion, which has information on water conditions.

THE BIG ISLAND

Green Sea Turtles

Green sea turtles are the most abundant of the three native species of *honu* (sea turtles) found in Hawaiian waters. Because green sea turtles feed on the algae that grows in the shallow waters of coastal reefs, they frequent some of the same beaches that snorkelers visit. Weighing upward of 200 pounds at maturity, these turtles are a thrilling sight to behold in the water.

The green sea turtle population in Hawaii has been on the increase in recent years, and sightings at places like Kahaluu Beach have become increasingly common. The turtles are not permanent residents of the main Hawaiian Islands. About once every four years, they return to their ancestral nesting grounds in the remote French Frigate Shoals, 700 miles east of the Big Island, where they mate and nest.

Hawaii's other two native sea turtles are the hawksbill, which is about the same size as the green sea turtle but far rarer, and the leatherback, a huge turtle that weighs up to a ton and is found in deep offshore waters.

A lifeguard is on duty daily, and a snack van sells burgers, sodas and ice cream. Another van rents silicone snorkel sets at $6 for two hours or $8 a day; it also sells fish food for $3 and disposable underwater cameras for $14.

The park has a salt-and-pepper beach composed of black lava and white coral sand. Facilities include showers, rest rooms, changing rooms, pay phones, picnic tables and grills. It's a popular place and often draws a crowd, particularly on weekends, so it's best to get there early.

Keauhou Beach Resort

The grounds of the Keauhou Beach Resort, immediately south of Kahaluu Beach, contain a number of easily explored historical sites. Ask at the front desk for a brochure and map of the sites.

The ruins of Kapuanoni, a **fishing temple**, are on the north side of the hotel. The reconstructed summer **beach house of King Kalakaua** is inland, beside a spring-fed pond once used as a royal bath. You can peek into the simple three-room cottage and see a portrait of the king in his European-style royal dress, a Hawaiian quilt on the bed and *lauhala* (pandanus-leaf) mats on the floor.

Other heiau sites are on the south side of the hotel. The remains of the seaside **Keeku Heiau**, just beyond the footbridge that leads to the now defunct Kona Lagoon Hotel, is thought to have been a luakini heiau.

The shelf of *pahoehoe* (smooth, ropelike lava) at the south side of the Keauhou Beach Resort holds some interesting **tide pools**, best explored when the tide is low. The pools contain numerous sea urchins, including spiny and slate pencil types, and small tropical fish.

When the tide is at its very lowest, you can walk out onto a flat lava tongue that is carved with numerous **petroglyphs**. The site is directly in front of the northern end of the Kona Lagoon Hotel, with most of the petroglyphs about 25 feet from the shore. Other than at low tide, the petroglyphs are submerged and cannot be seen.

The Keauhou Beach Resort grounds also contain a fertility pit, carved wooden god images, *kuula* stones sacred to fishers and an ancient house site or two.

Keauhou Bay

Keauhou Bay, which has a launch ramp and space for two dozen small boats, is one of the most protected bays on the west coast.

If you come by on weekdays in the late afternoon, you can watch the local outrigger canoe club practicing in the bay. There are rest rooms and showers.

In a small clearing just south of the harborside dive shacks, a stone marks the site where Kamehameha III was born in 1814. The young prince was said to have been stillborn and brought back to life by a visiting *kahuna* (priest/spiritual healer).

To get to the bay, turn *makai* (toward the ocean) off Alii Drive onto Kamehameha III Rd. Or, alternatively, drive down Kaleopapa Rd toward Kona Surf Resort, but continue to the end of the road instead of turning into the resort.

Manta Rays

If you're looking for something to do in the evening, you could go down to Kona Surf Resort and watch the manta rays that often gather in the late evening at the rocky outcrop below the resort's saltwater pool. They're attracted by the spotlights that shine down onto the ocean and thus make their best showings when there's no moon.

The wing tips of these impressive creatures measure up to 12 feet across. The manta rays cruise around in the surf, with their white underbellies flashing against the dark waters – it's hypnotic to watch.

Places to Stay

The 314-room ***Keauhou Beach Resort*** (☎ 322-7987, 800-922-7866, fax 322-3117, 78-6740 Alii Drive, Kailua-Kona, HI 96740) adjoins Kahaluu Beach Park and has interesting grounds that include historical sites and tide pools. The hotel has just reopened after a lengthy renovation and is now a member of the Aston chain. The rooms have minirefrigerators, TVs, lanais, and air-con. Rates range from $115 for a garden view to $175 for an oceanfront room. Aston offers a number of discounts ranging from 25% off for AAA auto club members to fifth-night-free deals.

Kona Surf Resort (☎ *322-3411, 800-367-8011, fax 322-3245, konasurf@ilhawaii.net, 78-128 Ehukai St, Kailua-Kona, HI 96740)* is a sprawling, 530-room hotel oriented to Japanese package tourists. It's been beset with financial problems in recent years, but the new owners have plans for a long-overdue renovation. Rather isolated on a rugged and rocky lava point on the south side of Keauhou Bay, the resort has a Polynesian decor, a little wedding chapel, tennis courts and both saltwater and freshwater pools. Rates range from $129 to $199.

Keauhou Resort Condominiums (☎ *322-9122, 800-367-5286, fax 322-9410, 78-7039 Kamehameha III Rd, Kailua-Kona, HI 96740)* has 48 units with full kitchens and washer/dryers. Although the units are about 30 years old, most are well maintained, and the property is the cheapest in Keauhou. One-bedroom units start at $70/97 in the low/high season with a garden view, $80/107 with an ocean view. Add about $25 more for a two-bedroom unit for up to four people. The minimum stay is five days. It's near the golf course and has a pool.

At the other end of the spectrum is ***Kanaloa at Kona*** (☎ *322-9625, 800-688-7444, reservations@outrigger.com, 78-261 Manukai St, Kailua-Kona, HI 96740),* with 100 condo units ranging from $205 for a one-bedroom apartment with a golf-course view to $290 for a two-bedroom unit with an ocean view. All units have lanais with wet bars as well as the standard amenities. The ocean-front units also have spas. There are three pools and two lighted tennis courts. The condo is a member of the Outrigger chain.

Other Keauhou condos are priced between the two and are largely booked through vacation rental agents. SunQuest Vacations (☎ *329-6488, 800-367-5168, 77-6435 Kuakini Hwy, Kailua-Kona, HI 96740)* handles units in most of them.

Places to Eat

Rocky's Pizza (☎ *322-3223)*, in the Keauhou Shopping Center, has average pizza, pastas and sandwiches. Eggplant parmigiana served with a salad and garlic bread or a small one-item pizza costs $9. Hours are 11 am to 9 pm daily.

Drysdale's Two (☎ *322-0070)*, in the Keauhou Shopping Center, specializes in sandwiches and burgers, most priced from $6 to $8. This is a hot spot for watching sports on TV. Food is served 11 am to midnight daily.

The Keauhou Shopping Center also has a ***KTA Supermarket***, open 7 am to 10 pm daily, a coffee shop, a doughnut shop, an ice cream stand and a ***Wendy's***.

Sam Choy at Keauhou (☎ *322-7987)*, in the Keauhou Beach Resort, has an open-air water-view setting and a kitchen run by Big Island native Sam Choy, who has a string of popular restaurants around Hawaii. A $16 breakfast buffet is offered from 6:30 to 10 am daily, and moderately priced salads and sandwiches are served from 11 am to 3 pm. Dinner, from 5 pm nightly, features fresh fish dishes prepared with a Hawaii Regional accent for around $25.

Entertainment

Kona Surf Resort has a free Polynesian dance show in its ***Nalu Terrace*** lounge from 5:30 to 7 pm on Tuesday and Friday.

The ***Keauhou Cinema***, a new multiscreen theater in the Keauhou Shopping Center, shows first-run movies.

Getting Around

Keauhou has a free on-call shuttle service (☎ 322-3500) that runs around the resort between 8 am and 4:30 pm every day.

HOLUALOA

Holualoa is a sleepy village perched in the hills, 1400 feet above Kailua-Kona. The slopes catch afternoon showers, so it's lusher and cooler than on the coast below.

Holualoa is an artists' community with craft shops, galleries and a community art center, all of which makes it a fun place to poke around.

This is pretty much a one-road village, with everything lined up along Hwy 180. There's a general store, a Japanese cemetery, an elementary school, a couple of churches and a library that's open a few days a week.

From Kailua-Kona, it's a scenic 4 miles up Hualalai Rd to Holualoa. The landscape is bright with poinsettia flowers, coffee bushes and fruit trees of all kinds.

While Holualoa remains off the beaten path, Kona's relentless development is creeping up this way. Older homes half hidden by jungly gardens are being joined by a jumble of new houses. It's an enviable location, with a fine view of Kailua Bay's sparkling turquoise waters below.

Kimura's Lauhala Shop

Kimura's Lauhala Shop (☎ 324-0053), at the intersection of Hualalai Rd and Hwy 180, sells items woven from lauhala, the *lau* (leaf) of the *hala* (pandanus) plant.

This was once an old plantation store that sold salt and codfish. During the Great Depression of the 1930s, Mrs Kimura started weaving lauhala hats and coffee baskets and taking them down to the plantations to sell.

Three generations of Kimuras still weave lauhala here. Their work is supplemented by the wives of local coffee farmers, who do piecework at home when it's not coffee season.

The hardest part, the Kimuras say, is preparing the lauhala, which is messy work, complicated by the sharp spines along the leaf edges. The easy part is the weaving. Once the lauhala is ready to weave, it takes a couple of hours to make a placemat, which sells for around $10.

The most common items are placemats, open baskets and hats of a finer weave. The shop is open 9 am to 5 pm Monday to Saturday.

Kona Arts Center

The soul of Holualoa is the Kona Arts Center, set in a ramshackle former coffee mill with a tin roof and hot-pink doors. Carol Rogers, who's been here since 1965, directs this nonprofit organization and teaches crafts, nurturing the spirit as much as the art.

This is a community scene and everyone's welcome to join; for a nominal monthly fee, you can participate in the workshops, which include pottery, batik, tie-dye, basketry, weaving and painting.

Visitors are free to drop in and look around; the center is open 10 am to about 3 pm Tuesday to Saturday. There's also a small display area with items for sale, including paintings, pottery and baskets made of natural fibers.

Galleries

Visiting galleries is the main thing to do in Holualoa.

A highlight is **Studio 7 Gallery**, which showcases the artwork of owner Hiroki Morinoue, who works in watercolors, oils, woodblock and sculpture. His wife, Setsuko, is a potter and the gallery's director. The gallery is like a little museum, and the Zen-like setting blends both Hawaiian and Japanese influences, with wooden walkways over lava stones.

The **Holualoa Gallery** has paintings with a Hawaiiana theme, including a few works by the noted Big Island artist Herb Kawainui Kane, and some creative raku pottery by gallery owner Matt Lovein.

Leaves from the hala plant make nice baskets.

The **Country Frame Shop** features watercolors and other paintings and also has a small collection of more affordable souvenirs. **White Garden Gallery** displays vivid watercolors with flora and fauna themes by gallery owner Shelly Maudsley White.

The old Holualoa post office building, opposite the Kona Arts Center, houses **Hale O Kula**, the workshop of goldsmith Sam Rosen, and **Chestnut & Company**, which features weavings by Peggy Chestnut and one-of-a-kind crafts and antiques.

Holualoa's galleries are open 10 am to 4 pm Tuesday to Saturday.

Places to Stay & Eat

Kona Hotel (☎ 324-1155, Hwy 180, Holualoa, HI 96725), an old wooden building in Holualoa center, retains the small-town character (and room rates!) of a bygone era. This old local hostelry has high ceilings and some nice views. Rooms are basic with just a bed and dresser, but they're clean and priced at only $20/26 for singles/doubles. Bathrooms are shared and down the hall. With only 11 rooms, the place is often full; getting a room is pretty much hit and miss, though it's generally easier on weekends.

Holualoa Inn (☎ 324-1121, 800-392-1812, fax 322-2472, inn@aloha.net, PO Box 222, Holualoa, HI 96725), run by Michael Twigg-Smith, is a beautiful upscale B&B perched atop 40 acres of sloping meadows with grand views of the Kona Coast. This contemporary house was built as a getaway by Michael's uncle, chairman of the *Honolulu Advertiser*, who at the time of construction owned a sawmill. The exterior is all western red cedar, and the interior floors are red eucalyptus from Maui. The 6000-sq-foot house has six guest rooms, each with private bath. They vary in size and decor, but all the rooms are spacious and have their own charm. If you're traveling with more than two people, go for the Bali suite; it has a bedroom with a king bed, a separate sitting room with a queen sofa bed, and absolutely unbeatable views. Guest amenities include a tile swimming pool, Jacuzzi, billiard table, rooftop gazebo, living room with fireplace, TV lounge and facilities for preparing light meals. Rates,

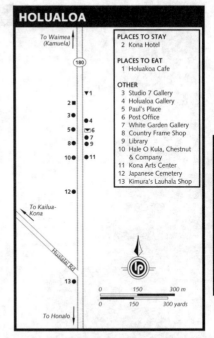

HOLUALOA

To Waimea (Kamuela)

To Kailua-Kona

Hualalai Rd

To Honalo

| PLACES TO STAY |
| 2 Kona Hotel |

| PLACES TO EAT |
| 1 Holuakoa Cafe |

| OTHER |
| 3 Studio 7 Gallery |
| 4 Holualoa Gallery |
| 5 Paul's Place |
| 6 Post Office |
| 7 White Garden Gallery |
| 8 Country Frame Shop |
| 9 Library |
| 10 Hale O Kula, Chestnut & Company |
| 11 Kona Arts Center |
| 12 Japanese Cemetery |
| 13 Kimura's Lauhala Shop |

0   150   300 m
0   150   300 yards

which include a continental breakfast with homegrown coffee and fruit, are $135 to $175 for up to two people and $30 more for a third person. You can view photos of the inn online at www.konaweb.com/hinn.

The **Holuakoa Cafe** has good pastries, bagels, espresso and herbal teas. It's open 6:30 am to 3 pm Monday to Saturday and has a pleasant courtyard where you can sit and relax.

You can pick up groceries at **Paul's Place**, the village's general store, which is open 8 am to 8 pm daily.

South Kona

Hwy 11 heads south out of Kailua-Kona through a number of small communities: Honalo, Kainaliu, Kealakekua, Captain Cook and Honaunau. These are unhurried upland towns surrounded by coffee farms and macadamia nut groves.

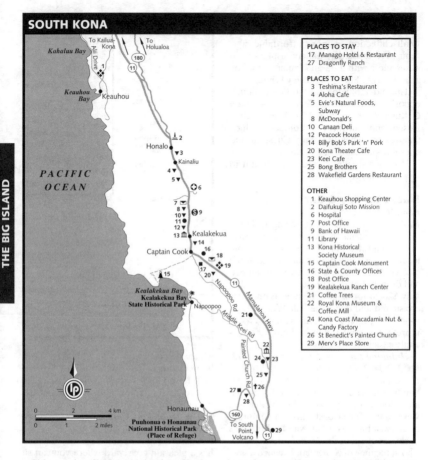

SOUTH KONA

To Kailua-Kona
Kahaluu Bay
Alii Drive
180
11
To Holualoa
1
Keauhou Bay   Keauhou

PACIFIC OCEAN

2
Honalo   3
Kainaliu
4
5
6
7
8
10
11
12
13   Kealakekua
14
Captain Cook   16
18
17   19
15
20
11
Kealakekua Bay
Kealakekua Bay State Historical Park   Napoopoo
21
22
24   23
25
27   26
28
Honaunau
160
Puuhonua o Honaunau National Historical Park (Place of Refuge)
To South Point, Volcano
11   29

Napoopoo Rd
Mamalahoa Hwy
Middle Keei Rd
Painted Church Rd

0   2   4 km
0   1   2 miles

PLACES TO STAY
17   Manago Hotel & Restaurant
27   Dragonfly Ranch

PLACES TO EAT
3   Teshima's Restaurant
4   Aloha Cafe
5   Evie's Natural Foods, Subway
8   McDonald's
10   Canaan Deli
12   Peacock House
14   Billy Bob's Park 'n' Pork
20   Kona Theater Cafe
23   Keei Cafe
25   Bong Brothers
28   Wakefield Gardens Restaurant

OTHER
1   Keauhou Shopping Center
2   Daifukuji Soto Mission
6   Hospital
7   Post Office
9   Bank of Hawaii
11   Library
13   Kona Historical Society Museum
15   Captain Cook Monument
16   State & County Offices
18   Post Office
19   Kealakekua Ranch Center
21   Coffee Trees
22   Royal Kona Museum & Coffee Mill
24   Kona Coast Macadamia Nut & Candy Factory
26   St Benedict's Painted Church
29   Merv's Place Store

Side roads off Hwy 11 lead to Kealakekua Bay, Puuhonua o Honaunau National Historical Park (also known as the Place of Refuge) and the villages of Hookena and Milo
lii. South Kona is short on beaches, but there are a couple of excellent spots for snorkeling and diving.

HONALO

Honalo is the small village at the intersection of Hwys 11 and 180.

Daifukuji Soto Mission, in the village center on the inland side of Hwy 11, is a big Buddhist temple with two altars, gold brocade,

large drums and incense burners. Visitors are welcome to view the inside. As at all Buddhist temples, leave your shoes at the door.

Teshima's Restaurant (☎ *322-9140*), on Hwy 11, is an unpretentious place serving authentic Japanese food. The best deal is the lunch teishoku of miso soup, sashimi, sukiyaki, tsukemono and rice, which costs $7.25 and is available 11 am to 1:45 pm. The same teishoku with the addition of fried fish costs $8.75 at dinner, which is served from 5 to 9 pm.

In a building out back, Teshima's has 10 rooms for rent, although most are booked on a monthly basis. These small rooms are very basic, each with a double bed, a private bathroom and a cabinlike ambience. The rate is $25/35 for singles/doubles.

KAINALIU

Kainaliu is a little town with positive energy. The focal point is the Aloha Cafe and the adjoining Aloha Theatre, home of the Aloha Community Players. Check the bulletin board next to the theater for the current performance schedule; you can often find long-term room rentals posted here as well.

The town is an interesting mix of old and new influences. Shops such as the Kimura Store, which has been selling traditional fabrics and dry goods here for generations, mingle with the likes of the Blue Ginger Gallery, which sells island crafts and New Age clothing, and Island Books, which has an up-to-date collection of used books.

The *Aloha Cafe* (☎ 322-3283), on Hwy 11, is the best place to eat in town and even has a distant ocean view from its outside terrace. The menu includes vegetarian dishes, good salads and fresh fish specials. A burrito or quesadilla with a side salad costs $7.25, while the most expensive dish, filet mignon, costs $17. You can also get fruit smoothies, fresh-squeezed juices, espresso and desserts. This spot is open 8 am to 3 pm Monday to Thursday, 8 am to 9 pm Friday and Saturday, and 8 am to 2 pm Sunday. Bring a sweater if you come for dinner in the winter, as it can get cool in the evenings.

A little farther south on the seaward side of Hwy 11 is *Subway*. Next to that is *Evie's Natural Foods*, which sells organic produce, fruit juices, dairy products, salads and sandwiches at reasonable prices.

KEALAKEKUA

Kealakekua means 'Path of the Gods,' a name commemorating the series of 40 heiaus that once ran from Kealakekua Bay north to Kailua-Kona.

These days, the town of Kealakekua is the commercial center for Kona's hill towns. The Kona Coast's hospital is on the north side of town, a quarter mile inland from Hwy 11. The post office is on the corner of Hwy 11 and Halekii Rd.

Kealakekua has a good library, which is open noon to 8 pm on Monday, 10 am to 5 pm Tuesday to Friday and 10 am to 1 pm on Saturday. Next door to the library is the coral mortar and lava-rock Kona Union Church, which dates back to 1854.

Kona Historical Society Museum

Kona Historical Society (☎ 323-3222) is on the seaward side of Hwy 11, just north of the Kealakekua Grass Shack gift shop. The stone and mortar building, built in the mid-19th century, was once a general merchandise store and post office. These days, it houses the society's office, archives and little museum.

The museum holds some interesting displays on the area's local history, illustrated with period photos, old bottles and other memorabilia. It's open 9 am to 3 pm Monday to Friday; admission is $2. The museum also sells some nice historical postcards.

Places to Stay

Merryman's Bed & Breakfast (☎ 323-2276, 800-545-4390, fax 323-3749, merry@manilhawaii.net, PO Box 474, Kealakekua, HI 96750), the home of former Alaskans Penny and Don Merryman, is in a quiet residential area in Kealakekua, a quarter mile above Hwy 11. The house is big and airy with ample windows, a large deck, lots of natural wood and exposed-beam ceilings. Two guest rooms share a bath and go for $75; two more have private baths and start at $95. All rooms are pleasantly furnished, and guests have use of a spacious common living area and a Jacuzzi. Full breakfast is included. For more information, visit the website at www.lavazone2.com/merrymans.

Reggie's Tropical Hideaway (☎ 322-8888, 800-988-2246, fax 322-7777, banana@ilhawaii.net, PO Box 1107, Kealakekua, HI 96750) consists of two naturist-friendly cottages on a small coffee farm near central Kealakekua. The two-bedroom cottage has high wooden ceilings, a full kitchen, a king bed in one bedroom, a queen waterbed in the other and a queen futon in the living room. It also has a sundeck with a Jacuzzi surrounded by privacy screens. The cost varies a bit with the season but is usually $100 per night for two persons, $125 for four and $150 for six. The one-bedroom cottage has a full kitchen, king bed, futon, deck and Jacuzzi; the cost is $85 to $125. Discounts are available for longer stays. Browse the Hideaway online at www .ilhawaii.net/~banana.

Places to Eat

Peacock House, on Hwy 11, offers inexpensive Chinese food but it's rather standard fare. You can get plate lunches from steamer trays for around $5 and a wide range of entrees for not much more.

Canaan Deli, on Hwy 11, serves reasonably priced eggs, pancakes and other breakfasts from 7 am daily. The lunch menu features sandwiches and burgers for around $6. *McDonald's* is also nearby on Hwy 11.

KEALAKEKUA BAY

Kealakekua Bay is a large bay, a mile wide at its mouth. At the south end of the bay is Kealakekua Bay State Historical Park, which encompasses Napoopoo Beach and Hikiau Heiau. The north end has a protected cove with one of the best snorkeling spots on the Big Island.

Kona Coffee

Missionaries introduced the first coffee trees to Hawaii in 1827, and by the turn of the 20th century, it was an important cash crop throughout the state. However, the erratic rise and fall of coffee prices eventually drove coffee farmers out of business on the other Hawaiian Islands. Only the Big Island's Kona coffee was of high enough quality to sell at a profit during gluts in world markets.

Coffee production in Hawaii had dropped dramatically by 1980, when a rising interest in gourmet coffee sparked sales of the highly aromatic Kona beans. Today, Kona coffee is the most commercially successful coffee grown in the USA. Almost the entire harvest comes from the upland towns of South Kona, from Holualoa in the north to Honaunau in the south. The coffee trees thrive in the rich volcanic soil and under the cloud cover that moves in nearly every afternoon.

A relative of the gardenia, coffee has fragrant white blossoms in the spring. In the summer, the trees have green berries, which turn red as they ripen.

The berries don't all ripen at once, so they must be picked by hand several times a season. The harvesting season begins in August. Coffee farmers at the lowest elevations may finish harvesting by December, while those at the 2000-foot level might harvest into March.

During the coffee season, buyers hang out signs announcing how much they'll pay for 'cherries,' the name given to the red coffee berries. In a good year, they may offer as much as a dollar a pound.

Steep sea cliffs prevent land passage between the two ends of the bay. The northern end is accessible only by sea or by a hike along a dirt trail beginning inland near the town of Captain Cook.

Kealakekua Bay is a state underwater park and marine life conservation district. Among the protected species here are spinner dolphins that frequently swim into the bay. Fishing is restricted, and the removal of coral and rocks is prohibited.

An obelisk monument on the north side of the bay marks the spot where Captain Cook died at the water's edge.

Kealakekua Bay State Historical Park

The 4-acre Kealakekua Bay State Historical Park is at the end of Napoopoo Rd, 4$\frac{1}{2}$ miles from Hwy 11.

This busy park's predominant feature is **Hikiau Heiau**, the large platform heiau above the beach. The park also has a boat landing, rest rooms, showers and a shack selling soft drinks and souvenirs.

Napoopoo Beach is rocky, and because it's small it often gets crowded. This is the less protected end of the bay, and it can have dangerous water conditions during *kona* (leeward) storms and at other times when the surf is high.

There's good snorkeling at Napoopoo, but the real prize is the cove at the northern end of the bay. Some people snorkel over to the cove from Napoopoo Beach when it's calm, but it's a long haul and only strong swimmers should consider it.

From the park, you can continue 4 miles south along a narrow road through scrub brush and lava to Puuhonua o Honaunau, the Place of Refuge. The road is little more than one lane, but paved and passable. Be careful if you pull over, as grasses conceal some roadside trenches.

Captain Cook Monument Trail

If you're up for a hardy hike, the trail to the Captain Cook Monument and the cove at the north end of Kealakekua Bay makes a good day outing. Although you'll no doubt work up a sweat, you'll be rewarded with

excellent snorkeling, a natural bath once reserved for royalty and some historic sites to explore.

The trail is not consistently maintained, so it's best suited for hikers who enjoy challenging conditions. At times this can be a jungly path through tall elephant grasses, while at other times the trail is kept clear by people who use it for horseback rides to the monument.

To get to the trailhead, turn off Hwy 11 onto Napoopoo Rd and go down about 250 yards, where you'll find a dirt road immediately after the second telephone pole on the right.

Start walking down the dirt road and after 200 yards it will fork – stay to the left, which is essentially a continuation of the road you've been walking on. The route is fairly simple and in most places runs between two rock fences on an old jeep road. When in doubt, stay to the left.

Eventually the coast becomes visible and the trail veers to the left along a broad ledge, goes down the hill and then swings left to the beach. Once you're at the water, the monument marking Cook's place of death is just a few minutes' walk to the left.

This area was once a Hawaiian village called Kaawaloa. Old lava-rock walls still go all the way out to **Cook's Point** at the north end of the bay, where a small light beacon stands sentinel.

Queen's Bath, a little lava pool with brackish spring-fed water, lies at the edge of the cove, a few minutes' walk from the Captain Cook Monument in the direction of the cliffs. The water is cool and refreshing, and this age-old equivalent of a beach shower is a great way to wash off the salt before hiking back – although the mosquitoes can get a bit testy here.

A few minutes beyond Queen's Bath, the path ends at the cliffs called **Pali-kapu-o-Keoua**, the 'cliffs sacred to the chief Keoua.' The cliffs' numerous caves were the burial places of Hawaiian royalty, and it's speculated that some of Captain Cook's bones were placed here as well.

A few lower caves are accessible, but they don't contain anything other than beer cans.

Captain James Cook

Captain James Cook, the first known Westerner to visit Hawaii, sailed into Kealakekua Bay at dawn on January 17, 1779. The beaches were lined with some 10,000 curious onlookers, and 1000 canoes sailed out to greet him.

Cook's tall ships with high sails appeared to fulfill a prophecy of the return of the god Lono, who was to arrive on a floating island covered with tall trees.

On his first evening ashore, Cook was brought to Hikiau Heiau, where the high priest performed a series of ceremonies recognizing Cook as the incarnation of Lono.

Eleven days later at the heiau, Cook performed a burial service for sailor William Whatman, who had died of a stroke. The inauspicious death of his mate raised a few questions among the islanders about Cook's own mortality as well.

On February 14, Cook was killed in a scuffle at the north end of the bay. Ironically, the world's greatest navigator was such a poor swimmer that he apparently stumbled into an angry crowd rather than swim a few yards out to a waiting boat.

The ones higher up are fortunately not as easy to get to and probably still contain bones. All are sacred and should be left undisturbed.

The hike on Captain Cook Monument Trail takes about an hour down and 1½ hours up. It's hot and largely unshaded, and it's an uphill climb all the way back. There are no facilities at the bottom of the trail. Be sure to bring your own drinking water and snorkeling gear.

Snorkeling

After working up a sweat on the Captain Cook Monument Trail, you can slip into the ocean from the rocks on the left side of the cement dock in front of the Captain Cook Monument. The water starts out about 5 feet deep and gradually deepens to about 30 feet. The cove is protected and usually very calm. Visibility is good, and both coral and fish are abundant.

Snorkeling tour boats (see the Activities section earlier in this chapter) pull into the bay in the morning, but they generally don't come ashore, and most leave by lunchtime. Anyway, the cove is big enough so it doesn't feel crowded.

CAPTAIN COOK

The town named for the Pacific navigator is on Hwy 11, above the bay where Cook met his untimely end. It's a small, unpretentious town with a few county and state offices, a shopping center, a hotel and a couple of restaurants. The Chevron gas station at the north side of town is open 24 hours a day.

As you continue south from town, you'll pass a handful of roadside coffee-tasting rooms that sell locally grown coffee and provide free freshly brewed samples.

If you just want to examine coffee trees, there's an unmarked pull-off for that purpose midway between the 107- and 108-mile markers, on the seaward side of the road. Coffee trees are planted in the front and macadamia trees beyond.

About a mile farther south is **Royal Kona Museum & Coffee Mill**, the latest incarnation of a complex that has undergone several transformations in recent years. The gift shop offers free coffee samples and displays interesting period photos. Out back there's a working coffee operation where you can observe the pulping mill, wash station and drying bins. There's also a walk-through lava tube and a few 'display' coffee trees. It's open 8 am to 5 pm daily.

Places to Stay

Manago Hotel (☎ *323-2642, fax 323-3451, Hwy 11, PO Box 145, Captain Cook, HI 96704)* is a family-run hotel that started in 1917 as a restaurant, serving bowls of udon to salespeople on the then-long journey between Hilo and Kona. Those wanting to stay overnight were charged $1 for a futon on tatami mats. These days, the basic rooms in the original roadside building show their age – the furnishings are spartan, the walls are thin, and the shared baths are down the hall – but the rates are just $25/28 for singles/doubles.

If you want comfort over character, go for one of Manago's 42 rooms in the newer wing at the rear. These motel-style rooms are ordinary but sufficient, with radios and private baths. The highlight is the unobstructed lanai view of Kealakekua Bay a mile below. Rates are $38 to $43 for singles, $41 to $46 for doubles; the higher rates are for better views. The hotel also has an atmospheric Japanese Room with tatami mats for $60. There's a common TV room near the restaurant. Although the flavor is purely local, Manago draws a fair number of international travelers.

Pomaikai Farm Bed & Breakfast (☎ *328-2112, 800-325-6427, fax 328-2255, nitabnb@ kona.net, 85-5465 Mamalahoa Hwy, Captain Cook, HI 96704)* is on Hwy 11 about 3 miles south of Captain Cook center. Host Nita Isherwood speaks fluent French. Accommodations are casual: two simple rooms in the main house for $50, a little converted coffee barn with an outdoor shower for $60 and an open-air duplex unit behind the house for $60. One of the rooms in the house has a shared bath, but the other units have private baths. There's a $10 charge for each guest beyond two and a $10 surcharge for stays of only one night. Guests have access to a refrigerator, microwave and barbecue grill. Rates include an all-you-can-eat breakfast with homegrown coffee and fruit, as well as macadamia nuts from the orchard out back. As the place is near the highway, expect some traffic noise. To see photos, go to wwte.com/hawaii/pomaikai.htm.

Cedar House (☎/fax *328-8829, cedrhse@ aloha.net, PO Box 823, Captain Cook, HI 96704)* consists of four guest rooms in the lovely contemporary home of Diana and Nik von der Luehe. Perched on a quiet 5-acre coffee farm a mile up from the town center, the house has lots of windows and natural wood, and a deck with a distant ocean view. The two pleasant rooms on the ground floor each have a king and a twin bed, private entrance, private bath and TV; one costs $80, while the other has a kitchenette and costs $90. The other two rooms, upstairs in the main house, are smaller but also comfortable; these have queen beds, TV and shared bath. They cost $65 with a garden view, $70 with an ocean view. Rates include a breakfast of fresh-baked items, fruit from the yard and homegrown coffee. Diana and Nik are friendly hosts who know the area well and can share tips on exploring; they also provide snorkel and beach gear. Nik speaks fluent German, as well as some French and Cantonese. The couple maintains a website at www.cedarhouse-hawaii.com.

Samurai House (☎ *328-9210, fax 328-8625, shubui@aloha.net, 85-5929 Mamalahoa, RR1, Box 359, Captain Cook, HI 96704)* is a B&B in a traditional Japanese house. Brought over piece by piece from Japan and re-erected in Captain Cook in the 1960s, the house has shoji doors, tatami mats, exposed cypress beams, a little carp pond and distant ocean views. Rooms include the Tatami Room, with a king bed and kitchenette for $85; a Westernized studio with a full kitchen for $75; and the Kimono Room, which has a refrigerator and rents for $65. All three have private lanais. A hot tub and TV/VCR are available. Samurai House, which is on Hwy 11 a mile south of the town center, is popular with the gay community but also welcomes straight clientele. For more information, visit the B&B's website at www.aloha.net/~shibui/public_html/index.html.

Places to Eat

The *Manago Restaurant* (☎ 323-2642), in the Manago Hotel, is a Japanese version of a meat-and-potatoes eatery. It's not health food, but the portions are large, and the old-style local atmosphere is fun. Pork chops are the specialty. Two big chops, rice, potato salad and side dishes such as tofu curd cost $8, while sandwiches are around $3. Breakfast is available 7 to 9 am, lunch 11 am to 2 pm, and dinner 5 to 7:30 pm. It's closed on Monday.

If you like tasty barbecued ribs and chicken, head for *Billy Bob's Park 'n' Pork* (☎ 323-3371), just south of the 111-mile marker, where a heaping plate of meat served with two side dishes such as chili and rice costs $10. The menu also offers chicken Caesar salads ($7) and prime rib ($10). Hours are 5 to 9 pm daily (to 8 pm on Sunday).

The Kealakekua Ranch Center on Hwy 11, about half a mile south of the Manago Hotel, has a *Sure Save* supermarket, a pasta place and a Chinese restaurant.

The *Kona Theater Cafe* (☎ 328-2244), in the renovated Kona Theater across from the Kealakekua Ranch Center, has espresso, pastries, bagels, Greek salads, sandwiches and tasty mango pie. It's open 7:30 am to 2 pm Tuesday to Sunday.

HONAUNAU

Honaunau's main attraction is Puuhonua o Honaunau National Historical Park, commonly called the Place of Refuge, but there are other things to see in this area as well.

Hwy 160 connects with Hwy 11 at the store Merv's Place, then leads down to the Place of Refuge, passing Painted Church Rd and some rural scenery with grazing horses, stone walls and brilliant bougainvillea.

Macadamia Nut Factory

The Kona Coast Macadamia Nut & Candy Factory, on Middle Keei Rd near Hwy 11, has a little display with a husking machine and a nutcracker. You can try it out, one macadamia nut at a time, and eat the final product.

The showroom overlooks the real operation out back, where nuts by the bagful are husked and sorted. The shop sells both raw and roasted macadamia nuts.

St Benedict's Painted Church

This church is noted for its painted interior done by John Berchmans Velghe, a Catholic priest who came from Belgium in 1899.

Father John painted the walls with a series of biblical scenes as an aid in teaching the Bible to natives who couldn't read. He designed the wall behind the altar to resemble the Gothic cathedral in Burgos, Spain.

When Father John arrived, the church was on the coast near the Place of Refuge. One of his first decisions was to move the church 2 miles up the slopes to its present location. It's not clear whether he did this as protection from tsunamis or just in an attempt to rise above – both literally and symbolically – the Place of Refuge and the old gods of 'pagan Hawaii.'

The tin-roof church still holds Sunday services, with hymns sung in Hawaiian. The church is on Painted Church Rd; turn north at the 1-mile marker on Hwy 160 and go a quarter mile – a small sign points the way.

Places to Stay

Dragonfly Ranch (☎ 328-2159, 800-487-2159, fax 328-9570, dfly@aloha.net, PO Box 675, Honaunau, HI 96726), on Hwy 160 near Painted Church Rd, is a cosmic New Age retreat with a gardenlike setting. Accommodation options include standard rooms in the main house for $85, a conventional studio adjacent to the main house for $150 and an open-air Honeymoon Suite for $200. The suite has a king-size bed on a platform deck without walls; netting keeps out the large but harmless spiders that share the gardens. Rates include a breakfast of organic coffee, fruit and baked items.

Places to Eat

Bong Brothers, on Hwy 11 just south of Middle Keei Rd, sells its own coffee as well as organic produce, smoothies and a few deli items. At lunchtime on Monday, Wednesday and Friday, a vegetarian chef cooks up homemade soups and healthy specials such as quinoa enchiladas for $5 or less.

Wakefield Gardens Restaurant (☎ 328-9930), on Hwy 160 just west of Painted Church Rd, has a relaxing open-air dining patio that makes for a pleasant lunch spot. Sandwiches, salads and vegetarian or meat burgers cost around $8, or get a cup of soup with a garden salad for $7. Wakefield Gardens is open 11 am to 3:30 pm daily.

Keei Cafe (☎ 328-8451), on Hwy 11 at the 106-mile marker, is a simple place with plastic chairs, but it has a credentialed gourmet chef who serves up the area's best dinners. The menu includes chalkboard specials such as delicious fresh ahi or *ono* (wahoo, a kind of mackerel), accompanied by a green salad with sun-dried tomato and goat cheese, for $19. Creative vegetarian selections and good homemade desserts are also available. The cafe is open 5 to 9 pm Tuesday to Saturday.

PUUHONUA O HONAUNAU NATIONAL HISTORICAL PARK

Puuhonua o Honaunau National Historical Park (☎ 328-2288) encompasses ancient temples, royal grounds and a *puuhonua*, a place of refuge or sanctuary. The park fronts Honaunau Bay, thus the tongue-twister of a name that simply means 'place of refuge at Honaunau.'

In old Hawaii, breaking any of the many kapus that strictly regulated all daily interactions was thought to anger the gods, who might retaliate with a natural disaster or two. To appease the gods, the offender was hunted down and killed.

Commoners who broke a kapu, as well as defeated warriors and ordinary criminals, could have their lives spared by reaching the sacred ground of the puuhonua.

This was more of a challenge than it might appear. Since royals and their warriors lived on the grounds immediately surrounding the refuge, kapu breakers were forced to swim through open ocean, braving currents and sharks, to get to the puuhonua.

Once inside the sanctuary, priests performed ceremonies of absolution that apparently placated the gods. Kapu breakers could then return home with a clean slate.

A Bitter Medicine

Medicinal plants played an important role in old Hawaii, and some of them can still be found growing on the grounds of Puuhonua o Honaunau National Historical Park.

One of the most curious is the *noni* tree, which has a pear-size, warty-looking fruit that somewhat resembles a mini-breadfruit. It grows well near the shore and was often planted adjacent to coastal homesites. The yellow fruit, which was eaten in times of famine, tastes as bad as it smells. Its more common usage was as a treatment for diabetes and high blood pressure.

❀❀❀❀❀❀❀❀❀❀❀❀❀

Hale o Keawe Heiau, the temple on the point of the cove, was built around 1650. The bones of 23 chiefs were buried there. It's thought that the *mana* (spiritual power) of the chiefs remained in their bones and added a spiritual power to those who came into the grounds. The heiau has been authentically reconstructed. The carved wooden kii that stand erect beside it are said to embody the ancient gods.

Leading up to the heiau is a large stone wall built around 1550. It's called the **Great Wall** and is more than 1000 feet long and 10 feet high. The west side of the wall contained the puuhonua, and the east side held the royal grounds.

A self-guided walk, detailed in the park brochure, passes by Hale o Keawe Heiau, two older heiaus, a petroglyph, legendary stones, a fishpond, lava tree molds and a few thatched huts and shelters. The canoe on display is hand-carved from koa wood.

There's also a stone board for *konane*, a Hawaiian game similar to checkers, which uses small stones of black lava and white coral. You can get a copy of the game rules at the park entrance and try your hand.

Also fun to explore are the **tide pools** in the pahoehoe lava at the south end of the park. The tiny black speckles dotting the

THE BIG ISLAND

shallow pools behind the heiau are *pipipi*, a kind of periwinkle. Even better are the tide pools near the picnic area farther south, which harbor coral, black-shelled crabs, small fish and eels, sea hares, and sea urchins with rose-colored spines.

Twenty-minute orientation talks, somewhat geared to people on tour buses who don't have time to see the whole park, are given at 10, 10:30 and 11 am and at 2:30, 3 and 3:30 pm daily.

Some of the rangers are native Hawaiians. You'll occasionally find one dressed in a *malo* (loincloth) or in *tapa* (clothing made of pounded bark), demonstrating traditional *pili* (bunchgrass) thatching or canoe or kii carving.

A program in Hawaiian studies is held monthly in the park's amphitheater, usually at 7:30 pm on the first Wednesday of the month. A festival with traditional displays and food, *hukilau* (net fishing) and a 'royal court' is held on the weekend closest to July 1.

Admission is $2 per person, or $4 per family, and is good for repeated visits over one week. Fees are generally collected between about 7:30 am and 5 pm, but visitors are free to enter and stroll the grounds from 6 am to 8 pm (to 11 pm on Friday and Saturday).

Beaches

Place of Refuge Swimming is allowed at Keoneele Cove inside the Place of Refuge. Shallow with a gradual decline, the cove was once the royal canoe landing. Snorkeling is best when the tide is rising, as the water is a bit deeper and the tide brings in fish. Sunbathing is discouraged.

South End of the Park Near the Place of Refuge visitor center, a road leads a quarter mile south to a beach park with picnic tables and some quiet sandy patches.

Winter surf can be rough in this area. Unless the sea is flat, it's best to stick to the Keoneele Cove area for swimming and snorkeling.

North End of the Park There's a terrific place to snorkel and dive just north of the Place of Refuge. From the park's parking lot, take the narrow road (marked with a 15mph sign) to the left and go down about 500 feet.

If you come by in the late afternoon, you'll see the Keoua Canoe Club practicing in the waters here. Incidentally, the little park on the inland side of the road was the original site of St Benedict's Painted Church.

Snorkelers step off a lava ledge immediately north of the boat ramp into about 10 feet of water. It then drops off fairly quickly to about 25 feet. Some naturally formed lava steps make it fairly easy to get in and out of the water, but there's no beach here, so the site is best suited for those who are comfortable jumping into deep waters.

Visibility is excellent, with good-sized reef fish and a fine variety of corals close to shore. The predatory 'crown of thorns' starfish can be seen here feasting on live coral polyps.

Wooden statues at Puuhonua

ERIC L WHEATER

THE BIG ISLAND

Divers can investigate a ledge a little way out that drops off about 100 feet. In winter, the water can get rough when the surf is high.

HOOKENA

Hookena was once a bustling village with two churches, a school, courthouse and post office. King Kalakaua sent his friend Robert Louis Stevenson here in 1889 to show him a typical Hawaiian village. Stevenson stayed a week with the town's judge and wrote about Hookena in *Travels in Hawaii*.

In the 1890s, Chinese immigrants began to move into Hookena, setting up shops and restaurants. A tavern and a hotel opened, and the town got rougher and rowdier.

In those days, Big Island cattle were shipped from Hookena's landing to market in Honolulu. When the circle-island road was built, the steamers stopped coming and the townspeople moved away. By the 1920s, the town was all but deserted.

These days, Hookena is a tiny fishing community with a small county beach park. The storm-beaten remains of the landing are in front of the park rest rooms.

Hookena is 2¼ miles down a narrow road from Hwy 11. The marked turnoff is between the 101- and 102-mile markers.

The beach has very soft black sand. The bay is backed by lava sea cliffs, and trees provide shade. When the winter surf is up, local kids with boogie boards hit the waves here.

When it's calm, you can snorkel straight out from the landing. It drops off pretty quickly, from 10 feet to about 30 feet, and there's lots of coral. Don't go too far out or you may encounter strong currents. Pygmy dolphins occasionally come into the bay, sometimes as many as a hundred at a time.

Hookena is a popular weekend picnic spot for Hawaiian families, and camping is allowed with a permit from the county. The beach park has toilets but no drinking water. For information on obtaining a camping permit, see Camping in the Accommodations section near the beginning of this chapter.

MILOLII

Milolii means 'fine twist.' Historically, the village was known for its skilled sennit twisters who used bark from the *olona* shrub to make fine cord and highly valued fishnets.

Milolii villagers still live close to the sea, and many continue to make a living from fishing. Some use an age-old form of aquaculture in which they sail out to feed papaya and taro to *opelu*, a type of mackerel. After months of this fattening and taming process, they return to net the fish.

While Milolii is one of the most traditional fishing villages in Hawaii, this is more in spirit than in appearance. Old fishing shacks have been replaced with modern homes, and fishers now zip out in motorized boats to do their fishing. The small village consequently holds little of direct interest to most visitors. Furthermore, Milolii residents generally prefer their isolation and are not enthusiastic about tourists poking around.

At Milolii Beach Park, past the village's little boat ramp, camping is officially allowed with a permit from the county. However, the beach park is right in the village, without a lot of space or privacy, and this is also the community's playground and volleyball court. All in all, it's not a recommendable place to camp for people who don't have ties with the village. For information on obtaining a camping permit, see Camping in the Accommodations section near the beginning of this chapter.

Milolii sits at the edge of an expansive 1926 lava flow that covered the nearby fishing village of Hoopuloa. The turnoff to Milolii is just south of the 89-mile marker on Hwy 11, from where it's 5 miles down a paved but steep and winding single-lane road that cuts across the lava flow. If you decide to make the drive, use a low gear, or your brakes will smoke on this one.

North Kona & South Kohala

Hwy 19 (Queen Kaahumanu Hwy) runs north 33 miles from Kailua-Kona up the Kona Coast to Kawaihae in the South Kohala district. This is hot, arid country with a lava landscape. Along the road, clumps of brilliant red bougainvillea look striking against the jet-black rock, but otherwise the vegetation is mainly sparse tufts of grass that survive the dry winds.

Here and there you'll notice the Big Island's unique version of graffiti – messages spelled out in white coral against a black lava background. And from much of this coast, you can look inland and see Mauna Kea, and to the south of it Mauna Loa, both of which are often snowcapped in winter.

Heading north out of Kailua-Kona, you'll first pass Honokohau Harbor and the new Kaloko-Honokohau National Historical Park, just a couple miles from town. Farther north is Kona Coast State Park, which now provides vehicle access to a nice undeveloped section of the coast. Many more beautiful secluded beaches and coves lie along this sparsely populated coastline, but they're hidden from the road and accessible only by foot. Once you hike in, you'll find white-sand beaches tucked between a sea of hardened lava and a turquoise ocean.

Continuing up the highway, you'll pass the turnoff to the Kona Village Resort, built on the site of a former fishing village. The shoreline between Kailua-Kona and Waikoloa was once dotted with tiny fishing villages, but most were wiped out by the tsunami of 1946.

At Waikoloa, home of the Big Island's fanciest resorts, you'll enter the South Kohala district. South Kohala was an important area in Hawaiian history, and today's visitors will find ancient trails, heiaus, fishponds, and petroglyph sites to explore. The resorts have wonderful drive-up beaches, as do the nearby Anaehoomalu and Hapuna Beach Parks.

Hwy 19 is flat and straight and easy to zoom along, but it's also a hot spot for radar speed traps, particularly on the stretch between the airport and Kailua. Be aware that most police cruise in their own unmarked cars – anything from Grand Ams to Explorers – so they're tough to spot.

The highway is part of the Ironman Triathlon route and has wide, smooth bike lanes bordering both sides of the road.

Cyclists should note that when the air temperature is above 85°F, reflected heat from asphalt and lava can edge the actual temperature above 100°F, and no drinking water or services are available along the road.

HONOKOHAU HARBOR

Honokohau Harbor was built in 1970 to take some of the burden off Kailua Pier. Most of the harbor's 155 slips are occupied by charter fishing boats, and these days almost all of Kona's catch comes in here. The harbor is about 2 miles north of Kailua-Kona on Hwy 19.

If you want to see the charter fishing boats pull up and weigh their catches of marlin and yellowfin tuna, drive straight in, park near the gas station and walk to the dock at the rear of the adjacent building. The best times to see the weigh-ins are generally around 11:30 am and 3:30 pm.

The harbor complex has a restaurant and bar serving frosted mugs of beer and reasonably priced fish and chips. There's also a fish market that sells fresh fish and smoked marlin by the piece.

The coconut trees that line the road down to the harbor were planted during a beautification project; in case you were wondering, the plaque in front of each tree names that tree's donor.

HONOKOHAU BEACH

Honokohau Beach, just north of the harbor, is part of the new Kaloko-Honokohau National Historical Park. For many years, this beach was a favorite haunt of nude sunbathers, but park rangers now patrol the area and swimsuits have become de rigueur.

The beach is composed of large-grained sand – a mix of black lava, white coral and rounded shell fragments. Walking along the sand gives a good foot massage. It's not a bad beach for swimming and snorkeling, although the bottom is a bit rocky.

To get there, turn onto the Honokohau Harbor road from Hwy 19, then turn right in front of the marina complex and follow the road a quarter mile. Pull off to the right after the dry dock boatyard. The trail begins at a break in the lava wall on the right, near the

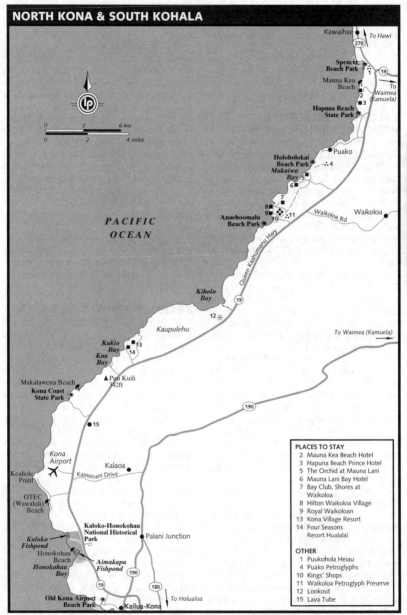

NORTH KONA & SOUTH KOHALA

Kawaihae
To Hawi
270
Spencer Beach Park
1
19
To Waimea (Kamuela)
Mauna Kea Beach
2
Hapuna Beach State Park
3
Puako
Holoholokai Beach Park
Makaiwa Bay
4
5
6
7
8
9
10
11
Anaehoomalu Beach Park
Waikoloa Rd
Waikoloa

PACIFIC OCEAN

Kiholo Bay
19
12

Kaupulehu

To Waimea (Kamuela)
190

Kukio Bay
13
14
Kua Bay

▲ Puu Kuili 342ft

Makalawena Beach
Kona Coast State Park

15

Kona Airport

Keahole Point

Kalaoa
Kaiminani Drive

OTEC (Wawaloli) Beach

190

Kaloko-Honokohau National Historical Park
Palani Junction
Kaloko Fishpond
Honokohau Beach
Honokohau Bay
Aimakapa Fishpond
190
180
To Holualoa
Old Kona Airport Beach Park
19
Kailua-Kona

0   3   6 km
0   2   4 miles

THE BIG ISLAND

PLACES TO STAY
2 Mauna Kea Beach Hotel
3 Hapuna Beach Prince Hotel
5 The Orchid at Mauna Lani
6 Mauna Lani Bay Hotel
7 Bay Club, Shores at Waikoloa
8 Hilton Waikoloa Village
9 Royal Waikoloan
13 Kona Village Resort
14 Four Seasons Resort Hualalai

OTHER
1 Puukohola Heiau
4 Puako Petroglyphs
10 Kings' Shops
11 Waikoloa Petroglyph Preserve
12 Lookout
15 Lava Tube

end of the road. It's a five-minute walk along a well-beaten path to the beach, although as development proceeds on the new park, access may change.

The only facilities at the beach are some pit toilets at the end of the trail. You might want to take along some insect repellent in case the gnats are feasting.

KALOKO-HONOKOHAU NATIONAL HISTORICAL PARK

Still in the developmental stages, Kaloko-Honokohau National Historical Park (☎ 329-6881) encompasses 1160 acres and includes Aimakapa and Kaloko Fishponds, ancient heiau and house sites, burial caves, petroglyphs, a *holua* (sled course), a Queen's Bath, the entire oceanfront between Kaloko and Honokohau Harbor, and a restored 1-mile segment of the ancient stone footpath known as the **King's Trail**, or Mamalahoa Trail.

There's speculation that the bones of Kamehameha the Great were buried in secret near Kaloko. This, combined with the fact that Aimakapa Fishpond is a habitat for endangered waterbirds, was enough to help squeeze the national park designation through Congress in 1978.

On the coast near the north end of the park is **Kaloko Fishpond**, acquired in 1986 from Huehue Ranch in exchange for 300 acres of federal land on the mainland. Before the park took over the land, mangrove had invaded the fishpond and spread rapidly, causing native birds to abandon the habitat. The park service eradicated the mangrove in a labor-intensive process that involved cutting and torching the trees, then tearing the new shoots up one by one and burning the roots. Native birds have now returned to Kaloko.

Aimakapa Fishpond, at the south side of the park just inland from Honokohau Beach, is the largest pond on the Kona Coast and an important bird habitat. Like Kaloko Fishpond, it had also been invaded by mangrove and required intensive eradication efforts. If you visit this brackish pond, you're likely to see the *aeo* (Hawaiian black-necked stilt) and *alae-keokeo* (Hawaiian coot), both

endangered native waterbirds that have made a significant return since the pond was cleared.

The **Queen's Bath** (called Kahinihiniula in Hawaiian) is a brackish spring-fed pool in the middle of a lava flow. Even though it's inland, the water level changes with the tide; at high tide, saltwater seeps in and the water in the pool rises. You can get there by walking inland from the north end of Honokohau Beach. The pool is marked by stone cairns as well as Christmas berries, always a dead giveaway that freshwater is nearby.

While most of the work within the park is still concentrating on natural restoration, trails are slowly being developed, and plans call for establishing a visitor center that will feature displays on Hawaiian culture and natural history.

The park entrance is on Hwy 19 at the 97-mile marker. The park gates are open 8 am to 3:30 pm daily, but there's also access from the harbor (see Honokohau Beach). A ranger is often on site to answer questions.

KEAHOLE POINT/OTEC BEACH

The turnoff leading to OTEC Beach and the Natural Energy Laboratory of Hawaii (NELH), a state hydroenergy research facility, is 1 mile south of the Kona Airport.

At Keahole Point, the seafloor drops steeply just offshore, providing a continuous supply of both cold water from 600-meter depths and warm water from near the surface. These are ideal conditions for ocean thermal energy conversion (OTEC).

The OTEC system operates like a steam turbine, with the difference in temperature between the cold and warm waters providing the energy source. Electricity has been successfully generated at the site, and research continues on ways to make this an economically viable energy source.

The nutrient-rich cold waters that are pumped up are also used in spin-off aquaculture projects, such as the farming of shrimp, oysters, seaweed and spirulina.

From the highway, it's about a mile in to OTEC (Wawaloli) Beach, where there are rest rooms and showers. This windswept lava coastline is rocky and not very good for swimming, although a large, naturally enclosed pool 200 yards south of the rest rooms is deep enough to wade in.

The rough dirt road that continues south from the beach leads half a mile to **Pine Trees**, one of the best surfing breaks in the Kona area.

ONIZUKA SPACE CENTER

The Astronaut Ellison S Onizuka Space Center (☎ 329-3441), opposite the car rental booths at the Kona Airport, pays tribute to the Big Island native who perished in the 1986 Challenger space shuttle disaster.

The little museum features exhibits and educational films about space and astronauts. Items on display include a moon rock, a NASA space suit and scale models of spacecraft. There's also a little space-themed gift shop. Admission is $3 for adults, $1 for children. It's open 8:30 am to 4:30 pm daily.

LAVA TUBE

A big open lava tube lies on the inland side of Hwy 19, north of the 91-mile marker and just before a speed limit sign. It's apt to seem rather tame if you've been to Hawaii Volcanoes National Park but interesting if you haven't.

The tube and the expansive lava flow surrounding the airport are both from the last eruption of Mt Hualalai, in 1801.

KONA COAST STATE PARK

The attractive sandy beach at Mahaiula Bay is open to the public as part of the recently established Kona Coast State Park. The park has shaded picnic tables, barbecue grills and portable toilets but is otherwise completely undeveloped. The facilities are at the south side of the beach, but the park's loveliest section is at the north end, about a five-minute walk away.

The inshore waters are shallow, and the bottom is gently sloping. Snorkeling and swimming are usually good, but during periods of high surf, which are not infrequent in winter, surfing is the sport of choice; it's best on the north side of the bay.

The road into the park, which begins 2 1/2 miles north of the airport off Hwy 19, is nearly as interesting as the beach. It runs for 1 3/4 miles across a seemingly endless lava flow that's totally devoid of trees and greenery, before depositing you at this little oasis. The road is passable in a regular car.

If you want to explore further, take the trail leading north from Kona Coast State Park about 1 1/4 miles to **Makalawena**, another beautiful stretch of beach. Makalawena is backed by sand dunes and contains some fine coves with good swimming and snorkeling.

On Wednesday, Kona Coast State Park is closed and the entrance gate is locked.

KUA BAY

Kua Bay, also known as Maniniowali, has a beautiful secluded beach with turquoise waters and gleaming white sands.

The beach has a gentle slope, and the waters are inviting for swimmers most of the year and for boogie boarders and bodysurfers in winter. Conditions are generally calm, but winter storms can generate currents in the bay and can also temporarily clear the beach of its sand.

The turnoff to the beach is just north of both the 88-mile marker and the grassy 342-foot Puu Kuili, the highest cinder cone on the seaward side of the highway. Look for the stop sign and gate at the head of the road.

The road is rough and over loose lava stones. Some people do drive down it about half a mile and then park near the roadside, but if you park near the highway it only takes about 20 minutes to walk in.

At the end of the road, a path crosses the rocks to the south end of the beach. There are no facilities.

KAUPULEHU

In ancient times, Kaupulehu was the site of a large fishing village, and a few Big Island fishers still lived along this shoreline until the tsunami of 1946 swept their homes away. The area, accessible only by boat, was then abandoned until the early 1960s, when a wealthy yachter who had anchored off Kaupulehu concluded this would be the perfect place for a hideaway hotel. The Kona

Village Resort opened in 1965. It was so isolated it had to build its own airstrip to shuttle in guests – the highway that now parallels the Kona Coast wasn't built for another decade.

The Kona Village Resort remains unique among Hawaii's getaway hotels in that its accommodations are in thatched Polynesian-style *hales* (houses) on stilts. The hales are spaced around a spring-fed lagoon and along the white sands of Kahuwai Bay. The resort limits nonguest access, but guided tours are given daily at 11 am.

In 1996, a second upscale hotel, the Four Seasons Resort, opened at Kaupulehu Beach, about a 10-minute walk south of Kona Village Resort. Originally begun as a multistory resort, the developers got so much resistance from island environmentalists that they dismantled the buildings halfway through the project and replaced them with low-rise, low-impact bungalows.

Four Seasons also opened up the shoreline, making the white-sand beach at **Kukio**

Bay and a string of pristine little coves to the south of it easily accessible to the public for the first time. Kukio Bay now has public beach access, showers, rest rooms, drinking water and visitor parking. A mile-long coastal footpath through the lava connects the Kukio Bay beach with the Four Seasons resort.

Places to Stay

The 125 freestanding cottages at the **Kona Village Resort** (☎ *325-5555, 800-367-5290, fax 325-5124, kvr@aloha.net, PO Box 1299, Kailua-Kona, HI 96745*) look like rustic thatched huts on the outside but are modern and comfortable inside, with high ceilings, rattan furnishings, ceiling fans and louvered windows. In keeping with the getaway concept, the units do not have phones or TVs. Daily rates range from $325 to $635 for singles, $425 to $735 for doubles, including meals and recreational activities. Despite the obvious irony of paying this kind of money to 'go native,' there seem to be few unhappy

---

Donkey Crossing

NED FRIARY

In the evenings, donkeys come down from the hills to drink at spring-fed watering holes and to eat seed pods from the *kiawe* (mesquite-like) trees along the coast between Kua and Kiholo Bays. The donkeys are descendants of the pack animals that were used on coffee farms until the 1950s, when they were replaced by jeeps.

Growers, who had become fond of these 'Kona nightingales,' as the braying donkeys were nicknamed, released many of the creatures into the wild rather than turning them into glue. The donkeys were largely forgotten until Hwy 19 went through in 1974.

The donkeys now need to cross the road for their evening feedings, and it's worth keeping an eye out for them at night, as they don't always pay attention to the 'Donkey Crossing' signs on the highway! They can sometimes be spotted feeding in the area immediately south of the two Kaupulehu resorts.

campers here. Visit the huts online at the website www.konavillage.com.

The *Four Seasons Resort Hualalai* (☎ *325-8000, 800-332-3442, fax 325-8100, PO Box 1269, Kailua-Kona, HI 96745)* takes a different approach, offering the pampering luxury of a posh country club. The 243 rooms, which are spread around three dozen low-rise buildings, are spacious, with large lanais, concealed TVs, fax lines and similar upscale amenities. Rates begin at $450 for a hotel room and top out at $5600 for the three-bedroom presidential suite. The resort has an 18-hole golf course, eight tennis courts, three oceanfront pools, a fitness club and spa, and interesting displays on Hawaiian art and culture.

Places to Eat

Pahuia (☎ *325-8000)*, at the Four Seasons Resort Hualalai, is an elegant oceanfront dinner restaurant that features reliably good Hawaii Regional cuisine, emphasizing local fish in a variety of preparations; entrees average $34 – a full meal about twice that. Pahuia is open 5:30 to 10 pm daily.

The Four Seasons' *Beach Tree Bar & Grill* (☎ *325-8000)* offers casual waterfront dining with good salads, sandwiches and grilled catch of the day for $10 to $15 at lunch, served until 5:30 pm.

The *Kona Village Resort* (☎ *325-8555)* is open for meals to nonguests, with advance reservations, except when the resort is at 100% occupancy. The daily outdoor lunch buffet, held from 12:30 to 2 pm, costs $30. And fine dining is available in the resort's *Hale Samoa*, a New Hebrides-style thatched building, where full meals cost $60 to $80, depending upon the entree selected. Dinner is served 6 to 8:30 pm daily.

KIHOLO BAY

Halfway up the coast, just south of the 82-mile marker, you'll come to a lookout that commands a great view of Kiholo Bay. With its intense blue waters and line of coconut trees, the bay appears like a little oasis in the midst of the lava.

An inconspicuous trail down to the bay starts about 100 yards south of the 81-mile marker. It follows a 4WD road, the beginning of which has been blocked off by boulders to keep vehicles out. The hike down takes about half an hour.

Kiholo Bay is almost 2 miles wide, and the south end of the bay has a lovely, large spring-fed pond called **Luahinewai**. It's refreshingly cold and fronted by a black-sand beach. There's also good ocean swimming when it's calm.

In ancient times, Kiholo provided a respite along the King's Trail, a stone footpath that ran along the coast. It was a fishing village famous for a large fishpond built by Kamehameha. The fishpond was filled in by an 1859 lava flow.

Cattle were shipped from here in the 1890s, and there was once a small hotel. Now the bay is ringed with a few private homes, including one owned by country singer Loretta Lynn.

WAIKOLOA BEACH RESORT

Just after crossing into the South Kohala district, a single turnoff leads to the Royal Waikoloan and Hilton Waikoloa Village hotels and to Anaehoomalu Beach Park. The road is just south of the 76-mile marker.

Waikoloa Petroglyph Preserve

As you travel down this road, a lava field etched with an impressive number of petroglyphs is off to the right, immediately before the Kings' Shops complex. If you park at the shopping complex, it's about a five-minute walk along a signposted path to the first of the etchings.

Many of the petroglyphs date back to the 16th century. Some are graphic (humans, birds, canoes), others cryptic (dots and lines). Western influences show up in the form of horses and English initials.

Although the footpath that leads through the petroglyphs is called the King's Trail, this section was actually a horse and cattle trail built in the late 19th century. The trail once connected Kailua-Kona with Kawaihae. It's possible to continue on the trail to a historical preserve at the Mauna Lani Resort, about 2 miles away, but it's a hot unshaded walk over lava.

Anaehoomalu Beach Park

Anaehoomalu Beach is a long, sandy beach that curves along an attractive bay. The waters are popular for swimming and windsurfing and have a gently sloping sandy bottom. Winter weather can produce rip currents, but most of the time the water is quite calm.

This is a fine beach for an outing if you're staying in Kona. The south end of the beach has public facilities, with showers, toilets, changing areas, drinking water and parking. The north end of the beach, which fronts the Royal Waikoloan hotel, has a little fitness area with swing ropes, chin-up bars and a volleyball net.

Both ends of the bay are composed of prehistoric lava flows from Mauna Kea, with *aa* (rough, jagged lava) to the north and smooth pahoehoe to the south.

Anaehoomalu was once the site of royal fishponds, and archaeologists from the Bishop Museum have found evidence here of human habitation dating back more than a thousand years.

Two large fishponds lie just beyond the line of coconut trees on the beach. A short footpath starts near the showers and winds by the fishponds, caves, ancient house platforms and a shrine. Interpretive plaques along the way explain the area's history.

The folks at the beach hut in front of the hotel can give you the latest on water conditions. They rent windsurfing equipment and snorkel sets and offer windsurfing lessons, beginning scuba lessons, boat dives, catamaran cruises and glass-bottom-boat rides.

A good spot for snorkeling at the north end of the beach is directly in front of the sluice gate. Here you'll find coral formations, a fair variety of tropical fish and, with a little luck, sea turtles. If you're not a snorkeler, you can still sometimes see the turtles by simply walking out onto the rock wall that encloses the sluice gate and looking down into the surrounding waters.

Hilton Waikoloa Village

The 62-acre Hilton Waikoloa Village is the most extravagant resort development on the Big Island. It has such the air of a sophisticated theme park that islanders nicknamed it 'Disneyland.'

The hotel had no beach, so it built its own, along with a 4-acre saltwater lagoon stocked with tropical fish, a dolphin pool, a 'river' with a current for rafting, and sprawling swimming pools with cascading waterfalls.

Guests navigate the grounds in canopied boats that cruise artificial canals and on a modernistic tram that looks like something straight out of downtown Tokyo. Because the complex is so large, both actually do function as public transport, and the novelty of using and waiting for them wears off quickly.

When it opened in 1988 at a cost of $360 million, the hotel billed itself as the world's most expensive resort. But despite all the excess, it's surprisingly casual, and anyone – guest and nonguest alike – is welcome to explore the grounds on the free boats and tram.

You can browse a multimillion-dollar **art collection** along a mile-long walkway that runs in both directions from the front lobby. The museum-quality pieces include extensive collections from Melanesia, Polynesia and Asia. It's particularly big on Papua New Guinea, with war clubs and spears, spirit boards, carved fighting shields and a partial replica of a ceremonial house. Other items on display include a collection of Han pottery that dates back 2000 years, antique dolls and Noh masks from Japan, 18th-century Burmese puppets and huge cloisonné vases. They've even managed to slip in a little Hawaiiana display with poi pounders and a few adze heads and koa bowls.

You can park free at the hotel or walk over from the Royal Waikoloan, a quiet 15-minute stroll away along the lava coast.

Places to Stay

The 545-room *Royal Waikoloan* (☎ 885-6789, 800-688-7444, fax 800-622-4852, reservations@outrigger.com, PO Box 5300, Waikoloa, HI 96743) is a former Sheraton hotel that's now part of the Outrigger chain. While this is the 'budget' hotel on Waikoloa's coast, the rooms are comfortable and the beachside location is far superior to that of the Hilton. Each room has either two double beds or one king bed, cable TV, phone, air-con and private lanai. The grounds include trails, a pool and a water-sports hut. And the Kings' Shops are within walking distance, so you're not captive to resort prices for all your meals. Rates currently begin at $140 for a garden-view room, but they'll probably go up after the impending $23 million renovation. Outrigger offers numerous discounts.

Hilton Waikoloa Village (☎ 885-1234, 800-445-8667, fax 885-2900, 1 Waikoloa Beach Resort, Waikoloa, HI 96743) is a megahotel with 1241 rooms and all the usual Hilton amenities. Rates start at $350/410 for garden/ocean views and go up to $4300 for the presidential suite.

Two upscale, fully equipped condominium complexes are in the area. Each has a pool, but they're both about a 15-minute walk from the beach. *The Bay Club* (☎ 886-7979, 800-305-7979, fax 886-7780, 5525 Waikoloa Beach Drive, Waikoloa, HI 96743) has one-bedroom units starting at $250 and two-bedroom units for $290 and up. Shuttle service to the beach and shopping center is provided.

The Shores at Waikoloa (☎ 885-5001, 800-922-7866, 5460 Waikoloa Beach Drive, Waikoloa, HI 96743) is an Aston-managed property. Rates start at $250/275 in the low/high season for a one-bedroom apartment, $290/320 for a two-bedroom apartment.

Places to Eat

The Kings' Shops has a little food pavilion, a couple of sit-down restaurants, and a small grocery store. The food pavilion, open daily until 9:30 pm, contains a *Subway*, with its standard menu of submarine sandwiches; a *Hawaiian Chili by Max*, serving chili and rice, hot dogs and chili dogs; a *Dairy Queen*; a pizza and plate-lunch eatery; and a coffee kiosk.

Also at the Kings' Shops is *Roy's Waikoloa Bar & Grill* (☎ 886-4321), a branch of the popular Roy's on Oahu. It has excellent Hawaii Regional cuisine and a changing menu of creative dishes. At lunch, salads, pastas and sandwiches average $11. At dinner, main courses such as rack of lamb in a *lilikoi* (passion fruit) cabernet sauce or

blackened ahi with pickled ginger average $25, while salads and appetizers are $7 to $10. Roy's is open daily 11:30 am to 2 pm and 5:30 to 9:30 pm.

Palm Terrace, in the Hilton (☎ 885-1234), offers good buffets for breakfast (6 to 11 am) and dinner (5 to 9:30 pm). Breakfast, which has a few Japanese touches as well as the standard American dishes and pastries, costs $17.50. Dinner, which features a different ethnic cuisine each night, is $23. The restaurant's pleasant and somewhat casual setting overlooks a pond with exotic waterbirds. Ask for a swan-view table.

The most highly regarded of the Hilton's fine-dining dinner restaurants is *Donatoni's* (☎ 885-1234), which features authentic Italian food. Look for starters like carpaccio for $10, followed by pasta dishes for around $20 and seafood or steak courses for $30.

Entertainment

The *Royal Waikoloan* (☎ 886-6789) has a poolside luau at 6 pm on Sunday and Wednesday. The cost of $53 for adults ($25 for children six to 12) includes a dinner buffet, an open bar and a Polynesian show.

The *Hilton Waikoloa Village* (☎ 886-1234) presents a 'Legends of the Pacific' dance show at 6:30 pm on Friday. The cost of $58 for adults and $25 for children five to 12 includes a dinner buffet and one cocktail. Also at the Hilton, a guitarist plays from 6 to 10 pm in the Kamuela Provision Company lounge.

WAIKOLOA

Waikoloa village, about 6 miles inland from the beach, is a modern residential development and bedroom community for workers in the nearby resorts. Although it offers little of interest for visitors passing through, the village does have condo complexes, a golf course, horse stables, a shopping center, a gas station and a bank. The 12-mile Waikoloa Rd connecting Hwys 190 and 19 runs through the village.

Elima Lani (☎ 883-8288, 800-551-5264, fax 883-8170, 68-3883 Lua Kula St, Kamuela, HI 96743) is a modern 216-unit condo complex beside the golf course. While it's not

THE BIG ISLAND

upscale, it's comfortable enough and the grounds have a couple of swimming pools. The units have two baths and the usual amenities, including microwave-equipped kitchens and washers and dryers. The rate is $110 for a one-bedroom unit, $131 for a two-bedroom unit. Up to four people are allowed at these rates, but note that the living-room sofas don't convert into beds.

The Waikoloa Highlands Shopping Center, on Waikoloa Rd, has a small *food court* with a deli, a pizzeria and a little sandwich and ice cream shop. The center also has a *grocery store* open 7 am to 9 pm daily.

MAUNA LANI RESORT

After a brief encounter with coconut palms and bright bougainvillea at the highway entrance, visitors turning down Mauna Lani Drive head through a long stretch of lava with virtually no vegetation. Halfway along there's a strikingly green golf course sculpted into the black lava. Mauna Lani Bay Hotel is at the end of the road. The Orchid at Mauna Lani hotel and Holoholokai Beach Park are to the north.

Mauna Lani Bay Hotel

This hotel is ritzy but still low-key – a modern open-air structure centered around a breezy atrium that holds waterways, orchid sprays and full-grown coconut trees. A saltwater stream that runs through the hotel and outdoors into the sun holds small black-tipped sharks and a variety of colorful reef fish. The atrium hosts live Hawaiian music and hula dancing at sunset nightly.

The hotel has good beaches and interesting historical sights, all open to the public. A free, self-guided trail map is available at the concierge desk.

Beaches The beach in front of the Mauna Lani Bay Hotel is protected but the water is rather shallow. Snorkelers might want to explore a coral reef beyond the inlet. Check at the hotel beach hut for current water conditions.

A less-frequented cove is down by the Beach Club restaurant, a 15-minute walk to the south.

An old coastal foot trail leads about a mile farther south to Honokaope Bay. It passes by a few historical sites, including a fishers' house site and other village remains. The southern end of Honokaope Bay is protected and good for swimming and snorkeling when the seas are calm.

Fishponds The ancient **Kalahuipuaa Fishponds** are along the beach just south of the hotel in a shady grove of coconut palms and *milo* (native shade trees).

The ponds are stocked, as they were in ancient times, with *awa* (Hawaiian milkfish). Water circulates from the ocean through traditional *makaha* (sluice gates), which allow small fish to enter but keep the older fattened ones from leaving. You might notice fish sporadically jumping into the air and slapping down on the water, an exercise that knocks off parasites.

The Kalahuipuaa ponds are among the few continuously working fishponds in Hawaii; the awa raised here have been used to provide stock for commercial fisheries.

Historic Trail The Kalahuipuaa Trail begins on the inland side of the Mauna Lani Bay Hotel, at a marked parking lot opposite the resort's little grocery store.

The trail, which is particularly pleasant in early-morning or late-afternoon light, offers a nice combination of historic sites and scenic views. It's also a good walk for spotting quail, northern and red-crested cardinals, saffron finches and Japanese white-eyes.

The first part of the trail meanders through a former Hawaiian settlement that dates from the 16th century, passing lava tubes once used as cave shelters and a few other archaeological and geological sites marked by interpretive plaques.

The trail then skirts fishponds lined with coconut palms and continues out to the beach, where you'll find a thatched shelter with an outrigger canoe and a historic cottage with a few Hawaiiana items on display. If you continue southwest past the cottage, you can loop around the fishpond and back to your starting point – a roundtrip of about 1 1/2 miles. A nice place to take a break en route is the attractive cove at the southern tip of the fishpond, where the swimming is good and a lunchtime restaurant offers simple fare.

Holoholokai Beach Park

Holoholokai Beach Park, north of The Orchid at Mauna Lani, has a rocky shoreline composed of coral chunks and lava. It's not a great bathing beach, but snorkeling is reasonably good when the waters are calm, and winter can bring good surf.

The park has showers, drinking water, rest rooms, picnic tables and grills and is open 6:30 am to 7 pm.

For those not picnicking, the main reason for visiting Holoholokai Beach Park is to walk the trail to the Puako petroglyphs. To get there, take Mauna Lani Drive and turn right at the rotary, then right again on the beach road immediately before the grounds of The Orchid.

Puako Petroglyphs With more than 3000 petroglyphs, the Puako petroglyph preserve has one of the largest collections of ancient lava carvings in Hawaii.

From the inland end of the beach parking lot, a well-marked trail leads three-quarters of a mile to the petroglyphs.

The human figures drawn in simple linear forms are some of Hawaii's oldest such drawings. Those with triangular shapes and curved forms are from more recent times.

The aging petroglyphs are fragile, as the ancient lava flow into which they're carved is brittle and cracking. Stepping on the petroglyphs can damage them, so be careful not to. The only safe way to record them is with a camera. If you want to make rubbings, use the authentically reproduced petroglyphs that have been created for that purpose; they're just a minute's walk down the trail from the parking lot. Bring rice paper and charcoal, or cotton cloth and crayons, and you can make your own souvenirs of 'old Hawaii.'

Because of the sharp thorns along the trail, flip-flops (thongs) are not appropriate footwear for the walk – the thorns can easily pierce their soft soles and your feet.

Places to Stay

The **Mauna Lani Bay Hotel** (☎ 885-6622, 800-367-2323, reservations@maunalani.com, 68-1400 Mauna Lani Drive, Kohala, HI 96743) is widely regarded as one of the finest resort hotels in the islands. All 350 rooms have TVs, phones, room safes, mini-bars, private lanais and bathrobes. Rates begin at $335 for a mountain-view room, $465 for an ocean view; from May through September rates drop about 10%, and a fifth-night-free deal is offered year-round. In addition to the rooms, the resort also has villas with full kitchens for $500 to $825, depending upon the number of bedrooms. The Mauna Lani can be booked internationally through the Pan Pacific Hotels chain. You can also make reservations online at www.maunalani.com.

The luxurious **Mauna Lani Point** (☎ 667-1666, 800-642-6284, fax 661-1025, info@classicresorts.com, 50 Nohea Kai Drive, Lahaina, HI 96761), a condo complex at the south side of the Mauna Lani Resort, is booked through Classic Resorts. One-bedroom units start at $250/280 in the low/high season, two-bedroom units at $315/365. See the condos online at www.classicresorts.com.

The Orchid at Mauna Lani (☎ 885-2000, 800-845-9905, fax 885-1064, 1 N Kaniku Drive, Kohala, HI 96743), on Pauoa Bay just north of the Mauna Lani Bay Hotel, is the Waikoloa area's newest hotel. It's a rather subdued place that originally opened as a member of the Ritz chain but more recently affiliated itself with Sheraton hotels. Rates for the 539 rooms start at $375 for a garden view, $525 for an ocean view. For more information, visit the hotel's website at www.orchid-maunalani.com.

Places to Eat

The open-air **Bay Terrace** (☎ 885-6622), at the Mauna Lani Bay Hotel, offers a pricey but otherwise tempting Sunday brunch with a sushi and sashimi table, waffles and omelettes to order, seafood dishes and a good variety of fruits, salads and desserts. The buffet is served 11:30 am to 2 pm and costs $39. A simpler breakfast buffet is offered 6:30 to 11:30 am daily and costs $22 (or $14.50 continental).

The *Canoe House* (☎ 885-6622), which fronts the beach beside the Mauna Lani Bay Hotel, is a romantic, open-air dinner restaurant that makes a good choice for a splurge night out. The menu blends Far East and Hawaiian influences, with an emphasis on seafood. Dishes such as Thai seafood curry or lemongrass swordfish with hearts of palm cost around $35 à la carte, while salads and appetizers will add another $10 to $20 to the tab. Dinner is typically served from 6 to 9 pm, though the hours vary a bit with the season.

The *Gallery* (☎ 885-7777), at the resort's golf clubhouse, serves good continental and Pacific Rim dishes. The fresh fish is a specialty; try the mouthwatering ahi, seared on the outside and sashimi-like inside, or the recommendable *onaga* (red snapper) with a macadamia crust. Most entrees cost $25 to $30, but as everything is strictly à la carte, expect dinner for two to edge up to $100. Dinner is served from 6 to 9 pm Tuesday to Saturday.

A bit easier on the wallet is the *Beach Club* (☎ 885-5910), a casual restaurant at the south end of Kaniku Drive overlooking a swimming cove. The menu includes an Oriental chicken salad or cheeseburger with fries for $8.75 and a fish sandwich for $11.50. The Beach Club is open 11 am to 4 pm daily.

PUAKO

Puako is a quiet one-road coastal village where everyone either lives on the beach or across the street from it. You can reach Puako via the marked turnoff from Hwy 19 or a bumpy side road from Hapuna Beach State Park.

The town is lined with giant **tide pools**, set in the swirls and dips of the pahoehoe lava that forms the coastline. Some of the pools are deep enough to shelter live coral and other marine life. Snorkeling can be excellent off Puako, although the surf is usually too rough in winter. A narrow beach of pulverized coral and lava lines much of the shore.

Hoku Loa Church, which dates back to 1858, is about half a mile beyond the Puako Bay boat ramp. A plain plastered building with a few simple wooden pews, it's still used for Sunday services, but at other times it's usually locked up tight.

You'll see several shoreline access signs, but the easiest beach access is at the south end of the village, just 150 yards before the road dead ends. Here a short dirt drive leads to the water. A couple of minutes' walk north along the beach will bring you to a few petroglyphs, a konane game board chinked into the lava and tide pools deep enough to cool off in.

HAPUNA BEACH STATE PARK

The long beautiful stretch of white sand along Hapuna Bay is the Big Island's most popular beach.

When it's calm, Hapuna Beach State Park has good swimming, snorkeling and diving. In the winter, it's a hot bodysurfing and boogie-boarding beach. The high winter surf can produce strong currents close to the shore and a pounding shorebreak. Waves over 3 feet should be left for the experts. Hapuna has had numerous drownings and many of the victims have been tourists unfamiliar with the water conditions.

A tiny cove with a small sandy beach lies about five minutes' walk north of the park. The water is a bit calmer there and in winter, less sand is kicked up by the waves.

The 61-acre state park includes the beach, A-frame cabins for overnight stays (see Camping in the front of this chapter) and a landscaped area with picnic facilities, showers, rest rooms, drinking water and pay phones. Lifeguards are on duty daily.

A snack bar, open 10 am to 4 pm daily, sells burgers, beverages, shave ice and ice cream. A window at the side rents boogie boards or snorkel sets for around $5 per half day.

Places to Stay

The 350-room *Hapuna Beach Prince Hotel* (☎ 880-1111, 800-882-6060, fax 880-3412, 62-110 Kaunaoa Drive, Kohala, HI 96743) is a new resort hotel at the northern end of Hapuna Beach. It largely gears its services to Japanese tourists who aren't taken aback by the sky-high room rates. A room with a garden view costs $325, one fronting the ocean is $495. The hotel has manicured lawns, a golf course, restaurants and a cocktail lounge.

MAUNA KEA BEACH

In the early 1960s, Laurance Rockefeller obtained a 99-year lease on the land around Kaunaoa Bay from his friend Richard Smart, owner of Parker Ranch. Five years later Rockefeller opened Mauna Kea Beach Hotel, the first luxury hotel on the Neighbor Islands, at the north side of this bay.

Kaunaoa Bay is a gorgeous crescent bay with a white-sand beach that has since come to be known as Mauna Kea Beach. It has a gradual slope and fine swimming conditions most of the year. There's good snorkeling on the north side when it's calm. The beach is open to the public, and parking spaces are set aside for beach visitors.

The hotel lobby and grounds have displays of Asian and Pacific artwork, including bronze statues, temple toys and Hawaiian quilts. The north garden holds the most prized possession, a seventh-century pink granite Buddha taken from a temple in southern India.

You can still stay at the *Mauna Kea Beach Hotel* (☎ 882-7222, 800-882-6060, fax 882-5700, 62-100 Mauna Kea Beach Drive, Kohala, HI 96743), which is affiliated with the Westin hotel chain. It recently underwent a major renovation and has all of the expected resort amenities, including a fitness center, tennis courts and an 18-hole golf course. The regular rates start at $325 for a mountain-view room and rise to $495 for ocean-view accommodations. To see pictures of the place, visit the hotel's website, www.maunakeabeachhotel.com.

SPENCER BEACH PARK

Spencer Beach Park, off Hwy 270 just south of Kawaihae, is a popular place for families with children, as the shallow sandy beach is protected by a reef and by the jetty to the north. If anything, it's a bit too protected – the water tends to get silty.

The rocky south end of the beach past the pavilion is better for snorkeling, although entry is not as easy.

Spencer is a popular beach park with a lifeguard station, picnic tables, rest rooms, showers, drinking water and both basketball and volleyball courts. Camping is allowed with a permit from the county. For information on obtaining a permit, see Camping in the Accommodations section near the front of this chapter.

PUUKOHOLA HEIAU

The Puukohola Heiau National Historic Site, which is off the side of the road that leads down to Spencer Beach, contains the last major temple built in Hawaii.

In 1790, after his attempt at a sweeping conquest of the islands was thwarted, King Kamehameha sought the advice of Kapoukahi, a soothsayer from Kauai. Kamehameha was told that if he built a temple to his war god here above Kawaihae Bay, then all of Hawaii would fall to him in battle. Kamehameha immediately began construction of Puukohola Heiau, completing it in 1791.

Kamehameha then held a dedication ceremony and invited his last rival on the Big Island, Keoua, the chief of Kau. When Keoua came ashore, he was killed and brought up to the temple as the first offering to the gods. With Keoua's death, Kamehameha took sole control of the Big Island and then went on to fulfill the soothsayer's prophecy by eventually taking control of the rest of the Hawaiian Islands.

Puukohola Heiau, terraced in three steps, was covered with wooden idols and thatched structures, including an oracle tower, an altar, a drum house and a shelter for the high priest.

After Kamehameha's death in 1819, his son Liholiho and powerful widow Kaahumanu destroyed the heiau's wooden images and the temple was abandoned. These days, only the basic rock foundation remains, but it's still an impressive site.

Puukohola means 'Hill of the Whales.' Migrating humpbacks can often be seen offshore during winter.

The visitor center (☎ 882-7218), open 7:30 am to 4 pm daily, has a few simple displays and someone on duty to provide a brief introduction to the park. A free brochure describes the historic sites spread over the park's 77 acres. There are no entrance fees.

A trail to the heiau starts at the visitor center and takes only two minutes to walk. If you arrive after hours, you can park at Spencer Beach Park and walk up to the heiau via an old entrance road that's now closed to vehicle traffic.

Just beyond Puukohola Heiau are the ruins of **Mailekini Heiau**, which predates Puukohola and was later turned into a fort by Kamehameha. **Hale o Kapuni Heiau**, a third temple dedicated to shark gods, lies submerged just offshore; nearby on land, you can see the stone leaning post where the high chief watched sharks bolt down the offerings he made.

The path continues down by the creek to **Pelekane**, the former site of the royal court. Warbling silverbills, doves and mosquitoes frequent the kiawe woods, but there's not much else to see.

The trail then leads across the highway to the site of **John Young's homestead**. Young, a shipwrecked British sailor, served Kamehameha as a military advisor and governor of the island. These days, all that remains of the homestead are the partial foundations of two of Young's buildings; there are plans to put up an interpretive board with drawings of what the site originally looked like.

KAWAIHAE

Kawaihae has the Big Island's second-largest deepwater commercial harbor. The harbor has fuel tanks, cattle pens and a little local beach park – not really much to attract visitors, most of whom stop in Kawaihae just long enough to eat and fuel up on their way to North Kohala.

Kawaihae Shopping Center on Hwy 270 has two restaurants, an ice cream and shave ice shop, a 7-Eleven convenience store, a quality Hawaiian crafts gallery and a dive shop.

Places to Eat

Cafe Pesto (☎ 882-1071), on the lower level of the Kawaihae Shopping Center, serves up good gourmet pizza, calzones, pastas and salads. Pizzas include a luau version with *kalua* pig (which has been roasted in an underground oven), sweet onions and pineapple and an Oriental pizza with sun-dried tomatoes, Japanese eggplant and roasted garlic. Both cost $10 for a 9-inch pizza, $17 for a 12-inch. At lunch, served until 4:30 pm, you can also get hot sandwiches for $8 to $10. The cafe is open 11 am to 9 pm on weekdays, to 10 pm on weekends.

There's more standard fare at *Tres Hombres Beach Grill* (☎ 882-1031), also in the Kawaihae Shopping Center. An enchilada, taco or tostada with rice and beans costs around $8; two-item combination plates are a few dollars more. Tres Hombres is open 11:30 am to 9 pm on weekdays, to 10 pm on weekends.

North Kohala

The northwest tip of the Big Island is dominated by a central ridge, the Kohala Mountains.

The leeward side of the ridge is dry and desertlike. The windward side is wet and lush with steep coastal cliffs and spectacular hanging valleys.

North Kohala is off the main track and often bypassed by travelers. But it has a couple of impressive historical sites, a few sleepy towns to poke around in and a lovely valley lookout at the end of the road.

There are two roads to North Kohala: an inland road and a coastal road. You can make a nice tour by going up one and down the other.

WAIMEA TO HAWI (HWY 250)

Hwy 250 (Kohala Mountain Rd) runs north for 20 miles from Waimea to Hawi. This is a very scenic drive along the upland slopes of the Kohala Mountains. The road goes past neat rows of ironwood trees and up through rolling green hills dotted with grazing cattle.

As you head north, Maui rises out of the mist, with the red crater of Haleakala capping the skyline. Mauna Kea and Mauna Loa are visible behind you. Expansive views of the coast and Kawaihae Harbor unfold

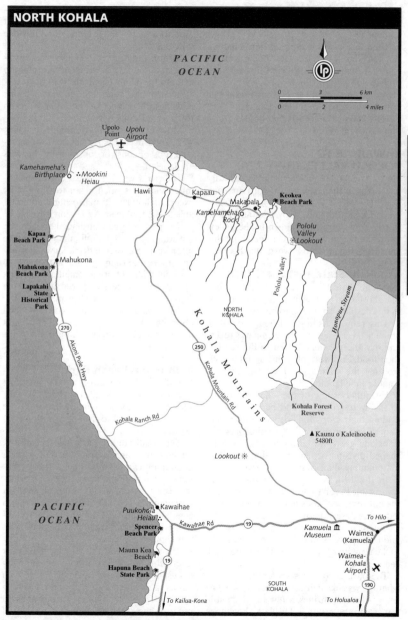

THE BIG ISLAND

below, and there's a roadside scenic lookout near the 8-mile marker where you can take it all in.

There are also a couple of new subdivisions up this way, the largest being Kohala Ranch. Kohala Ranch Rd runs through this private subdivision for 6 miles, connecting Hwys 250 and 270, but access to nonresidents is at the discretion of the gatekeepers.

Hwy 250 peaks at 3564 feet before dropping down into Hawi.

KAWAIHAE TO POLOLU VALLEY (HWY 270)

Hwy 270 (Akoni Pule Hwy) starts in Kawaihae, takes in the coastal sights of Lapakahi State Historical Park and Mookini Heiau and ends at a lookout above Pololu Valley. A trail runs from there down to the valley floor, but even if you're not up for a hike, the view from the lookout is worth the drive.

Lapakahi State Historical Park

Lapakahi State Historical Park has the feel of a ghost town – which it is. Even the visitors in this desolate spot tend to be few.

This remote fishing village was settled about 600 years ago; as the terrain was rocky and dry, the villagers turned to the sea for their food. Fish were plentiful, and the cove fronting the village provided a safe year-round canoe landing.

Eventually some of the villagers moved to the wetter uplands and began to farm, trading their crops for fish with those who had stayed on the coast. In the process, Lapakahi grew into an *ahupuaa*, a wedge-shaped division of land radiating from the mountainous interior out to the sea.

In the 19th century, Lapakahi's freshwater table began to drop. This, coupled with the enticement of jobs in developing towns, led to the desertion of the village.

Lapakahi was a big village, and this is a good-size park. A mile-long loop trail leads to the remains of stone walls, house sites and canoe sheds.

The park encourages visitors to imagine what life was like centuries ago. People worshipped at fish shrines, a few of which still remain on the grounds. Displays show how fishers used lift nets to catch opelu, a technique still practiced today, and how the salt used to preserve the fish was dried in stone salt pans.

Visitors can also try their hands at Hawaiian games. Game pieces and instructions are laid out for *oo ihe* (spear throwing), *konane* (Hawaiian checkers) and *ulu maika* (stone bowling), the object of the latter being to roll a round stone between two stakes.

Most of the tree varieties in the park were used by the early villagers for medicine, food or construction; many of the trees are labeled.

The park, which is just south of the 14-mile marker, is open 8 am to 4 pm daily except on holidays. Trail brochures are available at the trailhead. Admission is free.

The park is largely unshaded, so it can be hot walking around. While the park service often keeps a cooler of drinking water available, there's no running water in the park, so it's a good idea to bring something to drink.

Lapakahi's waters are part of a marine life conservation district. The fish are so plentiful and the water so clear that you can stand above the shoreline and watch yellow tangs and other colorful fish swim around in the cove below.

Mahukona Beach Park

Mahukona Beach Park, a mile north of Lapakahi and half a mile off Hwy 270, is the site of an abandoned landing that was once linked by railroad to the sugar mills on the north Kohala coast.

The small county park has rest rooms, picnic tables and a grassy camping area, although it can get a bit buggy. Those planning to camp should bring their own drinking water, as the park's water is unfit for consumption. For information on obtaining a camping permit, see Camping in the Accommodations section near the beginning of this chapter.

The area beyond the landing makes for interesting snorkeling and diving, although it's usually too rough in winter. Entry, via a ladder, is in about 5 feet of water. Heading north, it's possible to follow an anchor chain out to a submerged boiler and the remains of a ship in about 25 feet of water. Coral lines the bottom and visibility is good when it's calm. You'll find a shower near the ladder where you can rinse off.

Kapaa Beach Park

Kapaa Beach Park is 1¼ miles north of Mahukona and nearly a mile off Hwy 270. Its biggest selling point is its view of Maui.

Camping is allowed, but the park is rather dumpy and has neither a sandy beach nor much in the way of facilities. For information on obtaining a camping permit, see Camping in the Accommodations section near the beginning of this chapter.

MOOKINI HEIAU

Mookini is a massive heiau set atop a grassy knoll on the desolate northern tip of the Big Island. One of the oldest and most historically significant heiaus in Hawaii, it commands a clear view out across the ocean to Maui. This windswept site has a sense of timelessness and a certain eerie aura.

Chants date Mookini Heiau back to 480 AD. This was a luakini heiau, where the *alii* (chiefs) offered human sacrifices to the war god Ku.

According to legend, it was built in one night with basalt stones gathered in Pololu Valley and passed along a human chain stretching 14 miles.

A kapu that once prevented commoners from entering the heiau grounds wasn't lifted until recent times, and the site still remains well off the beaten path. Because so few people come this way, there's a good chance it will just be you, the wind and the spirits here.

The heiau is 250 feet long, with rock walls reaching a good 25 feet high. The entrance through the wall into the heiau itself is on the west side. The long enclosure on the right immediately before the heiau entrance was the home of the *mu*, or body catcher, who secured sacrificial victims for the heiau altar. The large scallop-shaped altar on the north end of the heiau is thought to have been added by Paao, a Tahitian priest who arrived around the 12th century and introduced human sacrifice to Hawaiian worship.

The current *kahuna nui* (high priestess), Leimomi Mookini Lum, is the most recent in a long line of Mookinis tracing their lineage back to the temple's first high priest.

To get there, turn north off Hwy 270 at the 20-mile marker and go 1¾ miles down to Upolu Airport. At the airport, turn left onto the road that runs parallel to the coast. Be aware, however, that this red dirt road is

Part of Mookini Heiau, once a site of human sacrifice

NED FRIARY

THE BIG ISLAND

rutted and bumpy and can get very muddy after heavy rains – it's not always passable in a standard car. After 1½ miles you'll come to a fork. The left road leads up to the heiau, a quarter mile farther.

Kamehameha's Birthplace

Kamehameha the Great was said to have been born on a stormy winter night in 1758 on this ruggedly desolate coast. If you continue straight ahead at the fork below the heiau for a third of a mile, you'll reach the stone enclosure that marks his birth site.

According to legend, Kamehameha's mother was told by a kahuna that her son would become a destroyer of chiefs and a powerful ruler. The high chief of the island didn't take well to the prophecy, and in a King Herod-like scenario, he ordered the newborn killed.

Immediately after birth, the baby was taken to Mookini Heiau for his birth rituals and then into hiding in the nearby mountains.

HAWI

Hawi (pronounced Hah-vee), with a population of less than 1000, is the largest town in North Kohala. It has a post office, grocery store, gas station, movie theater and a few galleries and restaurants.

North Kohala used to be sugar country, and Hawi was the biggest of half a dozen sugar towns. Kohala Sugar Company, which had incorporated all of the mills, closed down its operations in 1975. Hawi now has more storefronts than stores, and although some people are beginning to be drawn this way by the area's lower property values, it's still a very low-key place.

The park on Hwy 250 in front of the post office is cool and shady with giant banyan trees. Behind the park is the old sugar mill tower, a remnant of the town's former mainstay. You can still see the occasional strip of feral cane among the pastures outside town.

Places to Stay

Kohala Village Inn (☎ 889-0419, 55-514 Hawi Rd, Hawi, HI 96719), at the intersection of Hwys 270 and 250 in Hawi center, is an old-style hotel with 18 simple rooms. Over the years, the place has bounced between trying to attract tourists and being given over to long-term boarders, but its current owner has renovated it as a hotel again. A room with a double bed but no TV costs $47, while rooms with TV begin at $55. All rooms have private baths, but they don't have fans or air-con. If no one's at the front desk, walk around to the restaurant, which is managed by the same couple.

Cardinals' Haven (☎ 884-5550, PO Box 53, Hawi, HI 96719) is a homey place with a lovely rural setting 3 miles south of Hawi center. In the winter home of Peter and Sonja Kamber, the single guest unit consists of a bedroom with a comfortable queen bed and a living room with a small sofa bed that could accommodate a third person. It's all quite straightforward, but it does have a TV, microwave, hot plate, toaster, coffeemaker and mini-refrigerator. From the yard, you can look across cattle pastures clear out to Maui. The rental is open only from November 20 to May 10; you can make advance reservations when it's closed by calling ☎ 425-822-3120. The rate is $55 for two people, $60 for three, including food supplies to prepare your own breakfast, or $230 a week without food. Smoking is not allowed. Originally from Switzerland, the Kambers speak fluent German and French.

Places to Eat

Kohala Coffee Mill, on Hwy 270 in the town center, serves muffins, pastries, natural ice cream and fresh-brewed coffees.

Kohala Health Food, adjacent to Kohala Coffee Mill, sells vitamins, teas, juices and a few packaged health food items.

Bamboo (☎ 889-5555), on Hwy 270 in the village center, has excellent food and a pleasant tropical decor. Lunch items such as chicken satay with rice or a vegetarian black bean tostada cost around $8. At dinner, dishes such as chicken or teriyaki beef average $10. Save room for the good homemade desserts. Bamboo is open for lunch 11 am to 3:30 pm Tuesday to Sunday and for dinner 6 to 9 pm Tuesday to Saturday. There's sometimes live music on weekends.

Kohala Village Restaurant (☎ 889-0105), at the intersection of Hwys 270 and 250, also has good food at reasonable prices. Lunchtime favorites, which average $7, include chicken stir-fry, fried noodles and a chicken Caesar salad. At dinner, barbecued ribs, pastas and fresh fish cost around $15. This spot is open 8 am to 2 pm and 5:30 to 8:30 pm daily except Tuesday and Sunday.

KAPAAU

The statue of Kamehameha the Great on the front lawn of the North Kohala Civic Center may look familiar. Its lei-draped and much-photographed twin stands opposite the Iolani Palace in Honolulu.

The statue was made in 1880 in Florence, Italy, by American sculptor Thomas Gould. When the ship delivering it sank off the Falkland Islands, a second statue was then cast from the original mold. The duplicate statue arrived in the islands in 1883 and took its place in downtown Honolulu.

Later the sunken statue was recovered from the ocean floor and completed its trip to Hawaii. This original statue was then sent here, to Kamehameha's childhood home, where it now stands watching the traffic trickle along in quiet Kapaau.

Kapaau has a courthouse, police station and Kamehameha Park, which includes a large, modern gymnasium and everything from a ballpark to a swimming pool. The town also has a little library, a Bank of Hawaii and a few interesting shops.

Still, it's an aging town. The only crowd is at the senior center, which is part of the civic center. The senior citizens usually staff a table on the porch with visitor information.

Kalahikiola Church

Protestant missionaries Elias and Ellen Bond, who arrived in Kohala in 1841, built Kalahikiola Church in 1855. An earthquake damaged it in 1973, but it's since been restored and the church is still in use today.

If you want to take a look, turn inland off Hwy 270 onto a narrow road half a mile east of the Kamehameha statue, near the 24-mile marker. The church is half a mile up from the highway.

The land and buildings on the drive in to the church are part of the Bond estate, proof enough that missionary life wasn't one of total deprivation.

The church is sometimes paddle-locked shut, but the doors may seem to be locked even when they're not, as they don't push or pull, but rather slide open.

Kamehameha Rock

Kamehameha Rock is on the right side of the road, about 2 miles east of Kapaau, on a curve just over a small bridge. It's said that Kamehameha carried this rock uphill from the beach below to demonstrate his strength.

A road crew once attempted to move the rock to a different location; they managed to get it up onto a wagon, but the rock promptly fell off – an obvious sign that it wanted to stay put. Not wanting to upset Kamehameha's mana, the workers left the rock in place.

Tong Wo Society

Immediately around the corner from Kamehameha Rock is the colorful home of the Kohala Tong Wo Society, founded in 1886. Hawaii once had many Chinese societies, providing immigrants with a place to preserve their cultural identity, speak their native language and socialize. This is the last one remaining on the Big Island. The building is not open to the public.

Places to Eat

Jen's Kohala Cafe (☎ 889-0099), opposite the Kamehameha statue on Hwy 270, is the place to eat in town. Jen's has chicken Caesar salads, good chili and a recommendable Greek wrap sandwich with organic greens and feta cheese, all for $6 or less. Also on the menu are fresh fruit smoothies, deli sandwiches and soups. Jen's is open 10 am to 6 pm Monday to Friday, 11 am to 5 pm on Sunday.

MAKAPALA

The little village of Makapala has a few hundred residents, a beach park and a couple of places to stay. If you're hiking down to Pololu Valley, the town's little store is the last place to get a soft drink or snack.

Keokea Beach Park

Keokea Beach Park is on a somewhat scenic rocky coast but isn't a real draw for visitors, as there's no sandy beach and it's not great for water activities. Nevertheless, the park has covered picnic tables, rest rooms, showers, drinking water, barbecue grills and electricity.

Keokea is most active on weekends, and camping is allowed, with a county permit, on the grassy section below the pavilion. For information on obtaining a camping permit, see Camping in the Accommodations section near the front of this chapter.

The marked turnoff is about 1½ miles before the Pololu Valley Lookout. The park is about a mile in from the highway.

If you head this way, you'll pass an old Japanese cemetery on the way down to the park. Most of the gravestones are in kanji (Japanese script), and a few have filled sake cups in front of them.

Places to Stay

Don's Tropical Valley Hostel (☎ 889-0369, 877-889-6448, PO Box 1333, Kapaau, HI 96755) is an older three-bedroom home that's been converted to an unpretentious budget hostelry. The friendly owner, Kim Havens, lives in a separate house out back. There are two simple private rooms at $25/35 for singles/doubles, while the third room is set up as a dorm with four twin beds at a cost of $16 per bed. The house has a shared

bathroom and kitchen, and there's a small store next door selling snack foods, ice cream and a few grocery items. There's also a place to pitch tents in the backyard for $10 per site; campers have access to an outdoor shower and toilet. Don's is right on Hwy 270, a quarter mile west of the turnoff to Keokea Beach Park.

At *Kohala's Guest House* (☎ 889-5606, fax 889-5572, PO Box 172, Hawi, HI 96719), Nani and Don Svendsen rent two guest cottages near the start of the road down to Keokea Beach Park. Both are three-bedroom units; two of the rooms share a bath, while the other room has a private bath. These are modern places, though the bedrooms are simply furnished with just beds and a bureau. There's a shared living room with TV, VCR and stereo, as well as a kitchen with full facilities. The cost is $49 for a room, $125 for the whole house.

POLOLU VALLEY

Hwy 270 ends at a viewpoint that overlooks secluded Pololu Valley, with its scenic backdrop of steeply scalloped coastal cliffs spreading out to the east. The lookout has the kind of strikingly beautiful angle that's rarely experienced without a helicopter tour.

Pololu was once thickly planted with wetland taro. Pololu Stream fed the valley, carrying water from the remote, rainy interior to the valley floor. When the Kohala Ditch

---

Kohala Ditch

Kohala Ditch is an intricate series of ditches, tunnels and flumes that were built to carry water from the rugged wet interior of the Kohala Forest Reserve out to the Hawi area. The source of the water is the Waikoloa Stream, midway between the Pololu and Waipio Valleys.

The ditch was built in 1906 to irrigate Kohala sugarcane fields. The last Kohala cane was cut in the 1970s, but the ditch continues to be a source of water for Kohala ranches and farms.

It was engineered by a sugar man, John Hind, with the financial backing of Samuel Parker of Parker Ranch. Kohala Ditch runs 22½ miles and was built by Japanese immigrant laborers, who were paid about $1 a day for the hazardous work. More than a dozen of those laborers died during the construction.

Much of the ditch runs through 19,000 acres of Kohala land, which the agricultural giant Castle & Cooke sold a few years back to a developer. No development has yet occurred, but the owners have opened up the ditch to guided kayak tours (☎ 889-6922) that cost $75.

was built, it siphoned off much of the water and put an end to the taro production. The last islanders left the valley in the 1940s, and the valley slopes are now forest reserve land.

Pololu Valley Trail
The trail from the lookout down to Pololu Valley only takes about 20 minutes to walk. It's steep and can be hot walking, but it's not overly strenuous. You will need to be cautious with your footing since much of the trail is packed clay that can be slippery when wet.

Cattle and horses roam the valley; a gate at the bottom of the trail keeps them in.

The black-sand beach fronting the valley stretches for about half a mile and can make an enjoyable stroll. Driftwood collects in great quantities and on rare occasions glass fishing floats get washed up as well.

Surf is usually high in winter, and although it's a bit tamer in summer, there can be rip currents year-round.

Waimea (Kamuela)

Waimea has a pretty setting in the foothills of the Kohala Mountains at an elevation of 2670 feet. It's cooler than the coast, with more clouds and fog. The area has gentle rolling hills and frequent afternoon rainbows.

This is the headquarters of Parker Ranch, Hawaii's largest cattle ranch, which spreads across nearly one-ninth of the Big Island. Almost everything in Waimea is owned, run or leased by Parker Ranch.

Waimea has its cowboy influences, but it's rapidly growing and becoming more sophisticated. It's the main town serving the new subdivisions being developed on former ranches in the Kohala Mountains. While many of the newcomers are wealthy mainlanders, Waimea is also home to a growing number of international astronomers who work on Mauna Kea.

The WM Keck Observatory office in the town center has a short video and simple displays about the Mauna Kea telescopes. Visitors are welcome to stop by during business hours (8 am to 4:30 pm weekdays).

Waimea has a few good dining spots and galleries, but it's not a big tourist town with a lot of action or sightseeing attractions. The museums are good for a short visit and the green pastures are scenic, but for most visitors Waimea is just a stopover on the drive between Kona and Hilo.

Information
Waimea is also referred to as Kamuela, which is the Hawaiian spelling of Samuel. Although some say the name comes from an early postmaster named Samuel Spencer, most claim it's for Samuel Parker of Parker Ranch fame. The result is the same: confusion. Address all Waimea mail to Kamuela.

The post office, southwest of the Parker Ranch Center, is open 8 am to 4:30 pm on weekdays, 10 am to 1 pm on Saturday.

The Waimea-Kohala Airport, off Hwy 190, 1 3/4 miles south of the intersection of Hwy 19, is mainly used by private planes, although the small airline Pacific Wings flies here.

Parker Ranch Visitor Center
Parker Ranch Visitor Center (☎ 885-7655), in the Parker Ranch Shopping Center, is a small and not terribly dynamic museum of the ranch's history.

Exhibits include Parker family memorabilia, such as portraits, lineage charts, quilts and dishes; cowboy gear, including saddles and branding irons; and some Hawaiian artifacts – stone adzes, lava bowls, poi pounders, and tapa bed covers. Other Big Island museums have more extensive Hawaiiana collections.

Perhaps most interesting are the old photos and the 25-minute movie on Parker Ranch, which shows footage of cowboys rushing cattle into the sea and lifting them by slings onto the decks of waiting steamers.

The museum is open 9 am to 5 pm daily. Admission costs $5 for adults, $3.75 for children. A ticket that includes this museum and the Parker Ranch Historical Homes costs $10 for adults, $7.50 for children.

At the back of the shopping center, behind the parking lot, there's a picturesque view of Mauna Kea rising above an old wooden corral and pastures.

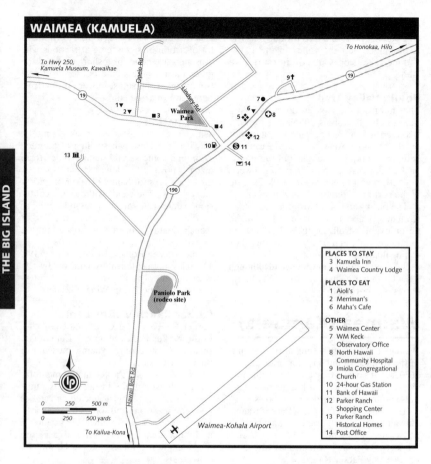

WAIMEA (KAMUELA)

To Hwy 250,
Kamuela Museum, Kawaihae

To Honokaa, Hilo

Opelo Rd

Lindsey Rd

Waimea Park

Paniolo Park
(rodeo site)

Hawaii Belt Rd

Waimea-Kohala Airport

To Kailua-Kona

PLACES TO STAY
3 Kamuela Inn
4 Waimea Country Lodge

PLACES TO EAT
1 Aioli's
2 Merriman's
6 Maha's Cafe

OTHER
5 Waimea Center
7 WM Keck
   Observatory Office
8 North Hawaii
   Community Hospital
9 Imiola Congregational
   Church
10 24-hour Gas Station
11 Bank of Hawaii
12 Parker Ranch
   Shopping Center
13 Parker Ranch
   Historical Homes
14 Post Office

Parker Ranch Historical Homes

At **Puopelu**, a mini-estate on the Parker Ranch, two historical homes are open to visitors. Grandest of the two is the estate's century-old manor, which holds an interesting collection of European art and antique Chinese vases. One room is French provincial, with chandeliers, skylights and walls hung with paintings by French impressionists, including works by Renoir, Degas and Pissarro.

Next door to the manor is the more modest **Mana Hale**, a re-creation of the original 1840s home that John Parker built in the hills 7 miles outside Waimea. Parker constructed his home in essentially the same saltbox style that was popular in his native Massachusetts. The exterior here is a replica, but inside it's the real thing; the original home's interior was dismantled board by board and rebuilt here at Puopelu. The house is simple and aesthetically striking, with walls, ceilings and floors made entirely of koa wood. It's decorated with period furnishings and interesting old photos of the hardy-looking Parker clan.

The turnoff to the homes is on Hwy 190, about three-quarters of a mile south of the intersection with Hwy 19. Hours are 10 am to 5 pm daily (last ticket sold at 4 pm); admission costs $7.50 for adults, $5 for children.

Church Row

Waimea's churches are lined up side by side in an area called Church Row. **Imiola Congregational Church** is the oldest, and the green-steepled church next to it is **Ke Ola Mau Loa Church**, an all-Hawaiian church. Buddhists, Baptists and Mormons also have places of worship in the row.

Waimea's first Christian church was a grass hut built in 1830. It was replaced in 1838 by a wood and coral structure, built with coral stones carved out of the reef and carried inland on the backs of Hawaiian Christians. They named it Imiola, which means 'seeking salvation.'

The current Imiola Congregational Church was constructed in 1857 and restored in 1976. The interior is simple and beautiful; it's built entirely of koa, most of it dating back to the original construction.

In the churchyard is the grave of missionary Lorenzo Lyons, who arrived in 1832 and spent 54 years in Waimea. Lyons wrote many of the hymns, including the popular 'Hawaii Aloha,' that are still sung in Hawaiian here each Sunday. Also in the garden is the church bell, too heavy for the church roof to support.

Kamuela Museum

There's a lot of history crammed into the Kamuela Museum (☎ 885-4724), at the junction of Hwys 19 and 250. Operated by octogenarian Harriett Solomon, a direct descendant of John Parker, the museum contains a treasure trove of Hawaiiana, including tapa beaters, 18th-century feather leis braided with human hair, fishhooks made of human bones, a stone knuckle duster and a dog-toothed death cup. Some items are very rare, and many once belonged to royalty; the museum houses Kamehameha the Great's sacred chair and tables of teak and marble from Iolani Palace.

There's a little bit of everything here – including a non-Hawaiian collection that ranges from a Tibetan prayer horn and stuffed moose heads from Canada to a piece of rope used on the Apollo 11 mission.

The museum is open 8 am to 5 pm daily. Admission costs $5 for adults, $2 for children under 12.

Parker Ranch

Parker Ranch claims to be the nation's largest privately owned ranch. It has 225,000 acres, 55,000 head of cattle and about 50 ranch hands. The ranch accounts for 80% of the livestock sold in Hawaii.

The first cattle arrived in Hawaii in 1793, a gift to King Kamehameha from British captain George Vancouver. To ensure the preservation of the herd, Vancouver convinced the king to place a 10-year *kapu* (taboo) on the killing of cattle.

The kapu worked, but the cattle ran wild and multiplied so quickly that they became an uncontrollable and destructive nuisance to both crops and native forests. Feral cattle still roam Mauna Kea today.

Parker Ranch owes its beginnings to John Palmer Parker, a 19-year-old from New England who arrived on the Big Island in 1809 aboard a whaler. He took one look at Hawaii and jumped ship.

Parker soon gained the favor of Kamehameha, who commissioned him to bring the cattle under control. Parker managed to domesticate some of the cattle and butchered others, cutting the herds down to size.

Later, Parker married one of Kamehameha's granddaughters and in the process landed himself a tidy bit of land. He eventually gained control of the entire Waikoloa *ahupuaa* (large land area) clear down to the sea.

Descendants of the Mexican-Spanish cowboys brought over to help round up the cattle still work the ranches today. Indeed, the Hawaiian word for cowboy, *paniolo*, is a corruption of the Spanish word *españoles*.

THE BIG ISLAND

Places to Stay

Waimea is upcountry, and if you equate Hawaii with beach life and constant sun, you may be disappointed making a base here. But if country scenery and open spaces are what you're looking for, the Waimea area can be an appealing choice.

Kamuela Inn (☎ 885-4243, 800-555-8968, fax 885-8857, kaminn@aloha.net, PO Box 1994, Kamuela, HI 96743) is in between an inn and a small hotel in both layout and atmosphere. There are 30 rooms with TV and private bath. Standard rooms cost $59 to $72; the cheaper rooms are comfortable, albeit small. Suites that have refrigerators and stoves and can sleep three or four people cost $89 to $99. Free pastries and coffee are provided in the morning. For more information, visit the inn online at www.hawaii-bnb.com/kamuela.

Waimea Country Lodge (☎ 885-4100, 800-367-5004, fax 885-6711, PO Box 2559, Kamuela, HI 96743) is a small motel with 21 rooms. All have private baths, phones, TVs and views of the Kohala hills out back; many also have pleasant open-beam ceilings. The main drawback is that there can be early morning noise from trucks unloading at the nearby shopping center. Rooms cost $98 with kitchenette, $84 without.

Waimea Gardens Cottages (☎ 885-4550, 800-262-9912, fax 885-0559, bestbnbs@aloha.net, PO Box 563, Kamuela, HI 96743), 2 miles west of town, are two charming cottages on the property of Barbara Campbell. Both have hardwood floors, French doors and a deck. The older unit, recently remodeled, has a full kitchen, Jacuzzi and private garden. The newer cottage has more limited cooking facilities, but also has many pleasant touches, including a working fireplace. Both come stocked with breakfast items. The rate is $135 to $150 single or double, $15 more for a third person; there's a three-day minimum stay. Barbara also runs an upscale B&B service called Hawaii's Best Bed & Breakfasts and can book other accommodations on the island in this price range.

Mountain Meadow Ranch (☎ 775-9376, fax 775-8033, wgeorge737@aol.com, PO Box 1697, Honokaa, HI 96727) offers a pleasant country setting a few miles east of Waimea. Located in a quiet eucalyptus grove off the Old Mamalahoa Hwy, this 7-acre estate would make a convenient base for exploring Waipio and the Hamakua Coast and is only about an hour's drive from Hilo. Amiable hosts Gay and Bill George have set aside the lower level of their redwood home for guests. There are two bedrooms, a large tiled bathroom, a dry-heat sauna and a lounge with a TV/VCR, microwave and refrigerator. One bedroom has a king bed and the other has a twin and a double bed. Only one party is booked at a time; that is, if you book one bedroom only, the other bedroom won't be rented out during your stay. The cost is $65/75 for singles/doubles; there's no minimum stay. There's also a pleasant cottage on the property that has two bedrooms with queen beds, a full kitchen and a living room with a TV, VCR, woodstove and queen sofa bed. The cottage would be a great place for a family; it costs $125/600 a day/week and has a three-day minimum. Credit cards are accepted. To see pictures of the accommodations, visit www.bnbweb.com/mountain-meadow/html online.

Places to Eat

Maha's Cafe (☎ 885-0693), at the north side of the Waimea Center, is a cheerful Hawaiian place serving home-style cooking. At breakfast, poi pancakes with coconut syrup cost $3.50. At lunch, you can get fresh fish with taro on local greens for $9 or sandwiches for $6.50. The cafe is inside Waimea's first frame house, built in 1852; a shop on the side sells Hawaii-made gifts. The cafe is open 8 am to 4:30 pm daily except Tuesday.

Aioli's (☎ 885-6325), in Opelo Plaza, is a popular little spot that bakes its own breads, cakes and pastries and offers good lunchtime sandwiches, salads and soups at reasonable prices. At dinner, there are full meals ranging from tofu curry for $12 to fresh catch and steaks for $16. The restaurant doesn't serve wine, but you can bring your own (no corkage fee). Aioli's is open 11 am to 8 pm Tuesday to Thursday, 11 am to 9 pm on Friday and Saturday and 8 am to 2 pm on Sunday.

Merriman's (☎ 885-6822), in Opelo Plaza, features Hawaii Regional cuisine, focusing on fresh products from Big Island farmers and fishers. A specialty is the delicious wok-charred ahi, blackened on the outside and sashimi-like inside. At dinner, there are a few vegetarian meals for $15, while most seafood and meat dishes cost $20 to $25. At lunch, there are salads, soups, sandwiches and a few hot grilled dishes, including a tasty coconut chicken with peanut sauce. Everything on the lunch menu is $10 or less. Merriman's is open 11:30 am to 1:30 pm weekdays, 5:30 to 9 pm nightly.

In the Parker Ranch Shopping Center, a branch of *Su's Thai Kitchen* (☎ 885-8688) features moderately priced Thai food, and the *Parker Ranch Grill* (☎ 887-2624) offers good steaks for around $20. Both are open daily for lunch and dinner.

The Waimea Center has *KTA Supermarket, Subway* and *McDonald's*, as well as a health food store, a bakery, a deli and Chinese and Korean restaurants.

You can buy produce at the *farmers' market* that sets up from 7 am to noon on Saturday at the Hawaiian Home Lands office, on the east side of town at the 55-mile marker.

Entertainment

Waimea's entertainment scene is limited, perhaps because cowboys rise at dawn and astronomers work all night!

Kahilu Theatre (☎ 885-6017), at the Parker Ranch Shopping Center, presents plays, classical music concerts, dance troupes and other productions.

Getting There & Away

Waimea is 40 miles from Kailua-Kona along Hwy 190. From Kona, the road climbs out of residential areas into a mix of lava flows and dry, grassy rangeland studded with prickly pear cactus. Along the way you'll see a little one-room church, broad distant coastal views, wide-open spaces and tall roadside grasses that have an incredible golden hue in the morning light.

If you come back on this road at night, the highway reflectors light up like an airport runway to guide you along.

AROUND WAIMEA
Waimea to Honokaa

Hwy 19 heads east from Waimea to Honokaa through rolling hills and cattle pastures, with views of Mauna Kea to the south.

For a peaceful, scented back road, turn right off Hwy 19 onto the Old Mamalahoa Hwy just west of the 52-mile marker. (If you're coming from Hilo, turn left at the 43-mile marker opposite Tex Drive Inn and then take the next immediate right.) This 10-mile detour winds through hill country, with small roadside ranches, old wooden fences and grazing horses. This is the part of Hawaii that tourists have yet to discover. Nobody's in a hurry on this road, if they're on it at all. It can make an interesting alternative route for cyclists, although you'll need to be cautious as the road is narrow and winding.

Mana/Keanakolu Rd

To get closer to Mauna Kea for photography or views, you could drive partway down Mana Rd, which leads around the eastern flank of Mauna Kea. It begins off Hwy 19 at the 55-mile marker on the eastern side of Waimea. After 15 miles, the road becomes Keanakolu Rd and continues about 25 miles before reaching Summit Rd (the road leading up Mauna Kea) near the Humuula Sheep Station.

Only the first part of the Waimea section is paved. The entire road is passable on horseback, on a mountain bike or in a 4WD vehicle, but a couple of dozen cattle gates must be opened and closed along the way. Be aware that it's mostly ranchers and hunters who come this way, and it's a long way from anywhere should you get stuck en route.

Keanakolu Rd passes along the new Hakalau Forest National Wildlife Refuge, which protects a portion of the state's largest koa-ohia forest. The forest provides habitat for the hoary bat and seven endangered bird species. Only very limited access is allowed into the refuge itself; call ☎ 933-6915 for information.

David Douglas Memorial A memorial to David Douglas, the Scottish botanist for whom the Douglas fir tree is named, is on

THE BIG ISLAND

The Death of David Douglas

The circumstances surrounding the death of famed botanist David Douglas in 1834 are somewhat mysterious, as his gored body was found trapped with an angry bull at the bottom of a pit on the slopes of Mauna Kea. Hunters commonly dug such pits and camouflaged them with underbrush as a means of trapping feral cattle, but the probability of both Douglas and a bull falling into the same hole seemed highly suspicious. Fingers were pointed at Australian Ned Gurney, an escaped convict from Botany Bay who had been hiding out in the area and had been the last person to see Douglas alive.

Hilo authorities, unable to solve the case, packed both Douglas' body and the bull's head in brine and shipped them to Honolulu for further investigation. By the time the body arrived in Oahu, it was so badly decomposed that they hastily buried Douglas' remains at the missionary church and the case was closed.

❀❀❀❀❀❀❀❀❀❀❀❀❀

Keanakolu Rd about halfway between Waimea and the Saddle Rd. Douglas died in 1834 at this spot.

Hamakua Coast

The Hamakua Coast, the northeastern coast of the Big Island, stretches 50 miles from Waipio Valley down to the city of Hilo.

From Waimea, it's 15 miles east on Hwy 19 to the town of Honokaa. From Honokaa, you can continue 9 miles northwest on Hwy 240 to reach Waipio Valley Lookout and one of the most spectacular valley views in Hawaii.

Much of the north end of the Hamakua Coast is idle agricultural land, with feral sugarcane growing in roadside fields. The rest of the coast is rugged, with luxuriant rain forests laced with streams and waterfalls.

The Hawaii Belt Rd (Hwy 19), which runs along the wet windward slopes of Mauna Kea, is an impressive engineering feat that spans deep green ravines with a series of sweeping cantilevered bridges.

Hwy 19 also passes small towns and unmarked roads leading down to unfrequented beach parks that can be fun to leisurely explore. If you're just whizzing through on your way between Kona and Hilo, at the very least make time for Waipio Valley Lookout, majestic Akaka Falls and the Pepeekeo 4-mile scenic drive.

HONOKAA

Honokaa's sugar mill opened in 1873, and sugar continued to be the mainstay of this town until the Hamakua Sugar Company closed down the mill in late 1994. After going through a bit of a recession, the town has begun to bounce back, though many Honokaa residents now commute to jobs in the Waikoloa resorts.

Most of the people living in Honokaa are descendants of immigrants brought here to work the sugar plantations. The Scots and English were the first to arrive. Then came the Chinese, Portuguese, Japanese, Puerto Ricans and Filipinos in turn.

While its boomtown days are but a dusty memory, quiet little Honokaa is still the biggest town on the Hamakua Coast – though these days the population is just 2200. Mamane St (Hwy 240), the main street through town, has an old-fashioned character, with most of its old wooden buildings dating to the 1920s. Among these aging storefronts are an increasing number of antique shops and crafts galleries that can make for good browsing.

Honokaa has a post office, library, banks, a grocery store, coin laundry, swimming pool and just about everything else you'd expect in a small town. The Honokaa People's Theater, built in 1930, has reopened and shows movies on weekends.

Places to Stay

Hotel Honokaa Club (☎ 775-0678, 800-808-0678, PO Box 247, Honokaa, HI 96727), on Mamane St in the town center, is an older hotel with 17 basic rooms. In an effort to attract budget travelers, it has cut the rates on a few of its rooms; visitors can share a dorm-style room for $15 or have a small private room with a sink and bed for $20/30 singles/doubles (the double room has only one double bed). These cheaper rooms share a shower and toilet in the hall, but they're at the quieter end of the hotel. There are also rooms with private baths for $45 to $65, with the more expensive room having a queen bed, TV and 2nd-floor view. For more information, visit the hotel's website at www .home1gte.net/honokaac.

Waipio Wayside B&B (☎/fax 775-0275, 800-833-8849, wayside@ilhawaii.net, PO Box 840, Honokaa, HI 96727), in between Hono-

kaa and Waipio, is a gracious older home in a setting of macadamia nut trees. This smoke-free B&B is pleasant and relaxed, with hammocks on the deck and a garden gazebo. There are five rooms, each with an upscale country decor. Rates, based on single or double occupancy, are $115 to $125 for the four rooms with attached private bath and $95 for the Moon Room, which has a private bath that's detached from the room. Owner Jackie Horne prepares a hearty breakfast that includes homegrown fruit and island coffee. Visit the B&B online at www .stayhawaii.com/wayside.html.

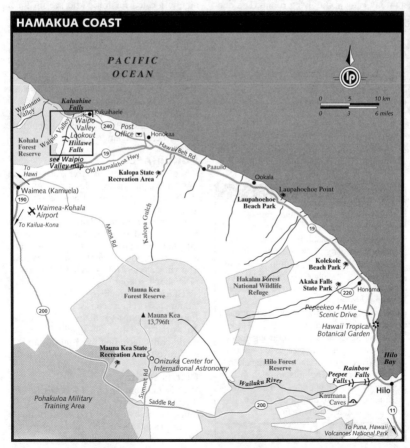

HAMAKUA COAST

Paauhau Plantation House (☎ 775-7222, fax 775-7223, PO Box 1375, Honokaa, HI 96727), off Hwy 19 just east of the Hwy 240 turnoff into Honokaa, is a classic 80-year-old plantation manager's house with plush period furniture, a billiard room, a fireplace, and so much historic character that you might expect ghosts to come out of the walls. The bedrooms in the house are furnished with antiques and have private baths. One of them rents for $100 a night, while a large master bedroom with king bed rents for $140. There are also three pleasant cottages with cooking facilities, separate bedrooms, and day beds in the living rooms. The one-bedroom cottage costs $110, while the two-bedroom cottages cost $140 for two, plus $15 for each additional person. There's a tennis court on the grounds.

Places to Eat

Most people staying in the area pick up groceries at the *TKS Supermarket* opposite the post office, but there are a couple of reasonable places to eat in town.

Simply Natural, on Mamame St just east of the post office intersection, serves Hilo Homemade ice cream and has chicken or tempeh sandwiches and both meat and vegetarian burgers for $5.50. Simply Natural is open 9 am to 4 pm daily. There's a bakery next door.

Taro Junction Natural Foods, a small health food store with dairy and juice products, is on Mamame St just west of Hotel Honokaa Club. It's open 10 am to 5:30 pm weekdays, 7:30 am to 3 pm on Saturday.

You can buy fruits, vegetables and tropical flowers from 6 am to 3 pm on Saturday at the *farmers' market* that sets up just west of the health food store.

Up on Hwy 19 is *Tex Drive Inn*, conveniently located for folks who are up for a quick bite during the drive between Waimea and Hilo. This unpretentious eatery makes the best and largest *malasadas* in Hawaii. Malasadas are Portuguese pastries made of sweet fried dough, rolled in sugar and served warm – like a doughnut without the hole. They cost 75¢ plain or $1 with a delicious papaya-pineapple filling. Tex also serves reasonably priced breakfast fare, sandwiches, burgers and plate lunches. Tex is open daily from at least 6:30 am to 8 pm.

KUKUIHAELE

About 7 miles beyond Honokaa heading toward Waipio Valley, a loop off Hwy 240 leads to the right and down to the tiny village of Kukuihaele.

Kukuihaele means 'Traveling Light' in Hawaiian and refers to the ghostly night marchers who are said to pass through this area carrying torches on their way to Waipio. The village is less than a mile from the Waipio Valley Lookout.

There's not much to Kukuihaele – its 'commercial center' consists mainly of the Last Chance Store and the Waipio Valley Artworks. The latter sells quality Hawaiian-made crafts, including dyed fabrics and an extensive selection of carved wooden bowls.

Places to Stay

Waipio Lookout Vacation Rentals (☎ 775-0585, PO Box 5149, Kukuihaele, HI 96727) rents out a contemporary two-story house on the ridge about 200 yards before the Waipio Valley Lookout. The house has a

---

A Hard Nut to Crack

Hawaii's first macadamia trees were planted in Honokaa in 1881 by William Purvis, a sugar plantation manager who brought seedlings from Australia. For 40 years the trees were grown in Hawaii, as in Australia, mainly for ornamental purposes, as the nut shells were considered too hard to crack.

Hawaii's first large-scale commercial macadamia orchard was planted in Honokaa in 1924 and is still producing today. Macadamia nuts have proven to be one of the most commercially viable agricultural crops in Hawaii. The nuts are high in fat, protein and carbohydrates and are a good source of calcium, phosphorous, iron, thiamine, riboflavin and niacin.

❀ ❀ ❀ ❀ ❀ ❀ ❀ ❀ ❀ ❀ ❀ ❀ ❀ ❀

one-bedroom apartment on the 1st floor that costs a reasonable $85 for up to four people and a two-bedroom apartment on the 2nd floor that costs $110 for up to six people. Both units have queen beds, full kitchens, washer/dryers, phones, TVs and lanais with valley views. Smoking is permitted on the lanais only. For more information, browse online at www1.interpac.net/~waipiohi.

Another option is the *Waipio Ridge Vacation Rental* (☎ 775-0603, *rlasko3343@ aol.com, PO Box 5039, Kukuihaele, HI 96727*), a one-bedroom cottage perched above Waipio Valley, just below the lookout. The kitchen has a refrigerator, microwave, toaster oven, coffeepot and a spectacular view of Waipio Valley from the dining table. There's a queen bed in the bedroom and a sofa bed in the living room, as well as a TV, VCR and private bath. The cost is $75 for two people, $15 more for additional guests; there's a $10 surcharge if you stay only one night. Owner Roger Lasko maintains a website at wwte.com/waipio.htm.

Places to Eat
Most people go into Honokaa to eat and get provisions, though there are a couple of simple options in Kukuihaele.

The village's *Last Chance Store* is just that, as no food or supplies are available in Waipio Valley. At this small grocery store you can get crackers, canned food, beer, water and wine. It's open 9 am to 5 pm Monday to Saturday.

The shop at the side of *Waipio Valley Artworks* sells Tropical Dreams ice cream, muffins, sandwiches and coffee at reasonable prices. It's open 8 am to 5 pm daily.

WAIPIO VALLEY
Hwy 240 ends abruptly at the edge of cliffs overlooking Waipio Valley. If you catch it on a day when it's not hazy, the view is glorious.

The largest and southernmost of the seven spectacular amphitheater valleys on the windward side of the Kohala Mountains, Waipio Valley is a mile wide at the coast and nearly 6 miles deep. Some of the near-vertical *pali* (cliffs) wrapping around the valley reach heights of 2000 feet.

Everything in Waipio Valley is lushly green, a mix of tangled jungle, flowering plants, taro patches and waterfalls. The mouth of the valley is fronted by a black-sand beach, which is divided in two by Waipio Stream.

History
Waipio means 'Curving Water,' and the valley is often referred to as the 'Valley of the Kings.' In ancient times, it was the political and religious center of Hawaii and home to the highest chiefs. Waipio was a very sacred place and the site of a number of important heiaus. The most sacred, Pakaalana, was also the site of one of the island's two major puuhonua.

Umi, the Big Island's ruling chief in the early 16th century, is credited with laying out Waipio's taro fields, many of which are still in production today. Waipio is also the site where Kamehameha the Great received the statue of his fearsome war god, Kukailimoku.

According to oral histories, at least 10,000 people – and possibly many times more – lived in Waipio before the arrival of Westerners. It was the most fertile and productive valley on the Big Island.

In 1823, William Ellis, the first missionary to visit the valley, guessed the population to be about 1300. Later in that century, immigrants, mainly Chinese, began to settle in Waipio. At one time, the valley had schools, restaurants and churches, as well as a hotel, post office and jail.

In 1946, the most devastating tsunami in Hawaii's history swept great waves far back into Waipio Valley. Afterwards, most people resettled 'topside' and Waipio has been sparsely populated ever since.

Today, taro remains important in Waipio. Many of the valley's 50 or so residents have taro patches, and you may see farmers knee-deep in the muddy ponds.

Other Waipio crops include lotus (for its roots), avocados, breadfruit, oranges and limes. There are *kukui* (candlenut) and mahogany trees, huge elephant ears, Turk's cap hibiscus, air plants, ferns and vines. Pink and white impatiens climb the cliffs along the road.

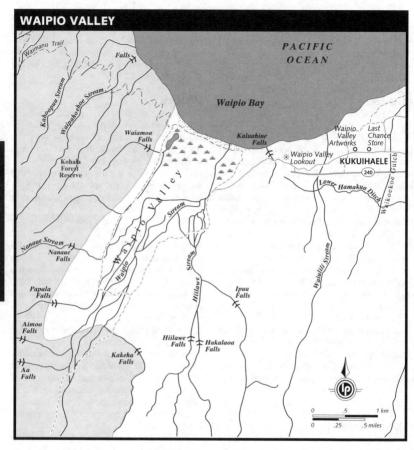

WAIPIO VALLEY

PACIFIC OCEAN

Waimanu Trail

Falls

Kahoonua Stream

Waipahoehoe Stream

Waipio Bay

Waiamoa Falls

Kaluahine Falls

Waipio Valley Artworks

Last Chance Store

Kohala Forest Reserve

Waipio Valley Lookout

KUKUIHAELE

240

Lower Hamakua Ditch

Waikoekoe Gulch

W a i p i o   V a l l e y

Waipio Stream

Hiilawe Stream

Waiulili Stream

Nanaue Stream

Nanaue Falls

Papala Falls

Ipuu Falls

Aimoo Falls

Hiilawe Falls

Hakalaoa Falls

Kakeha Falls

Aa Falls

0   .5   1 km

0   .25   .5 miles

Hiking

From the Waipio Valley Lookout at the end of Hwy 240, you can see the switchback trail that leads to Waimanu Valley on the opposite cliff face. The viewpoint also offers glimpses of the rugged coastal cliffs that stretch out to the northwest.

The narrow, paved, mile-long road that leads down into Waipio Valley is so steep (25% grade) that it's open only to hikers and 4WD vehicles. Two tour companies make the run daily, but the walk down is easier than it looks. There are rest rooms at the lookout, but the water there is unfit for drinking.

The hike from the lookout to the valley floor and back is not terribly difficult, although if you're not in good shape you may notice some forgotten muscles the next day. It takes about 30 minutes to walk down and about 45 minutes to hike back up. The road is carved into the cliffs at an angle that provides hikers with shade much of the way. Nevertheless, you can expect to work up a sweat; be sure to bring something to drink, as there are no public facilities.

From the bottom of the hill, if you walk to the left for about five minutes, there's a fair chance you'll see wild horses grazing along the stream. It's a picturesque scene set against the steep valley cliffs.

You'll also get a distant view of **Hiilawe Falls**, which is Hawaii's highest free-fall waterfall – a sheer drop of more than 1000 feet. According to legend, the god Lono looked down from the heavens and discovered Kaikilani, the beautiful woman who was to become his wife, sitting beside Hiilawe Falls. Lono slid down to the falls on a rainbow – definitely the preferred way to get there.

While hiking to Hiilawe Falls is not impossible, it is challenging, as there's no real trail and it's mainly bushwhacking. Keep in mind that many valley residents who are tolerant of visitors trekking down to visit the beach aren't keen on them exploring the valley interior – there are a lot of 'Private Property' signs and generally the farther back in the valley you go, the less friendly the dogs become.

Waipio Beach It takes about 10 minutes to walk to the beach from the bottom of the hill, although after heavy rains the road can be like a slippery mud pie.

Waipio Beach is lined with ironwood trees that act as an effective barrier against the strong winds that sometimes blow through here. It was an ancient surfing beach that occasionally still sees some action, but there are usually rip currents, and when the surf is high, the waters can be outright treacherous.

Walk along the beach toward the stream mouth for a good view of **Kaluahine Falls**, which cascade down the coastal cliffs to the east. They're easier to look at than to get to, however, as the coast between Waipio Beach and the falls is loose lava rock and rather rough walking. The surf sometimes breaks up over the uppermost rocks, so it can also be dangerous.

Local lore has it that ghost marchers periodically come down from the upper valley to the beach and march to Lua o Milu, a hidden entrance to the netherworld.

Switchback Trail to Waimanu Valley The switchback trail leading up the northwest cliff face of Waipio Valley is an ancient Hawaiian footpath. Although it looks arduous and is rated moderate-to-difficult, it really isn't all that bad if you're not carrying a heavy load. It's a well-beaten path, worn a few feet deep in places – almost like walking in a little trough. Those who are carrying a weighty backpack take note: Once you reach the ridge, the trail gets much easier.

Doing just part of the trail makes a nice day hike from Waipio. It takes about 1½ hours from the floor of Waipio Valley to the third gulch, where there are little pools and a small waterfall. The trail is used by hunters as well as hikers, and you might even come across old-timers on donkeys heading for the backwoods to hunt wild boar.

The trail continues up and down a series of ravines to Waimanu Valley. From Waipio Valley to Waimanu it's about 8 miles in all, and because of the numerous climbs you should allot about seven hours.

Waimanu is a smaller valley than Waipio, although it's similar in appearance. It too is a beautiful deep valley with steep walls, waterfalls, a lush green valley floor and a black-sand beach.

Waimanu Valley once had a sizable Hawaiian settlement and contains many ruins, including house and heiau terraces, stone enclosures and old taro ponds. In the early 19th century, Waimanu was inhabited by an estimated 200 people, but by the turn of the 20th century, only three families remained. Since the 1946 tsunami, the valley has been completely abandoned.

Because it represents an unaltered Hawaiian freshwater ecosystem, Waimanu Valley has been set aside as a national estuarine sanctuary, and the removal of any plant or aquatic life (except for freshwater prawns and ocean fish) is forbidden.

Water is available on this route from numerous gulches, but it must be boiled or otherwise treated before drinking.

Dangers & Annoyances During heavy rains, streams in Waipio Valley can swell to the point where they become impassable, usually for just a few hours at a time, although occasionally for longer periods. It's dangerous to try to cross such streams if the water reaches above your knees.

If you're planning on hiking to Waimanu Valley, keep in mind that heavy rains can make that route hazardous as well. There are a few creeks that cross the trail, as well as a stream in Waimanu Valley, all of which can become impassable torrents after rainstorms. These need to be treated as life-threatening obstacles; be patient and wait for the water to subside.

Because feral animals roam the area, precautions against leptospirosis are advisable (see the Health section in the Facts for the Visitor chapter). Taro farmers in Waipio have one of Hawaii's highest incident rates of this waterborne ailment.

Don't drink from any creeks or streams without first boiling or treating the water.

Organized Tours

Waipio Valley Shuttle offers 1½-hour tours via 4WD vans. These are essentially taxi tours for those who don't care to walk down, although the driver does point out waterfalls, identify plants and throw in a bit of history. Reservations (☎ 775-7121) can be made at Waipio Valley Artworks in Kukuihaele. It costs $35 for adults, $15 for children. The tours run between 8 am and 4 pm Monday to Saturday.

An alternative to the van tours is the 1½-hour jaunt through the valley offered by Waipio Valley Wagon Tours (☎ 775-9518), which transports guests in an open mule-drawn wagon. The tour guide gives commentary on the valley's history as he carts visitors along Waipio's rutted dirt roads and fords rocky streams. Tours leave from the Last Chance Store in Kukuihaele at 9:30 and 11:30 am and 1:30 and 3:30 pm Monday to Saturday. Passengers are taken by 4WD vehicle to the valley floor, where they transfer to the wagon. It costs $40 for adults, $20 for children.

A more adventurous possibility for touring the valley is on horseback. Waipio on Horseback (☎ 775-7291) offers a 2½-hour ride in the valley at 9:30 am and 1:30 pm for $75. Waipio Naalapa Trail Rides (☎ 775-0419) has a 2½-hour trail ride in the valley at 9:30 am and 1 pm, also for $75. There are no trail rides on Sunday or during bad weather.

Places to Stay

Limited camping is allowed in Waipio Valley, and backcountry camping is allowed in Waimanu Valley.

Bishop Estate, which owns most of Waipio Valley, allows camping inland from the beach. There are only four campsites, the maximum stay is four days, and you must fill out a permit application at least two weeks in advance of the first day of camping. The crux of the application is a liability waiver that each camper must sign. There are no facilities and campers are required to bring their own chemical toilets. The permits are free and can be obtained in advance by calling or writing the *Bishop Estate* (☎ 322-5300, fax 322-9446, 78-6831 Alii Drive, suite 232, Kailua-Kona, HI 96740). The office is in the Keauhou Shopping Center in Keauhou, just south of Kailua-Kona.

In Waimanu Valley, which is managed by the state, *camping* for up to six nights is allowed free by permit. Facilities include fire pits and a couple of composting outhouses. Camping reservations are taken no more than 30 days in advance by the Division of Forestry & Wildlife (☎ 974-4221, PO Box 4849, 19 E Kawili, Hilo, HI 96720). You can apply for the permit by phone, and if you do so at least two weeks before your camping date, the permit can usually be mailed to you. Otherwise, the actual permit can be picked up during office hours either at the forestry office in Hilo or at the state tree nursery on Hwy 190 in Waimea.

KALOPA STATE RECREATION AREA

Kalopa State Recreation Area is a few miles southeast of Honokaa and about 3 miles inland from the marked turnoff on Hwy 19.

This unfrequented park contains 100 acres of native rain forest as well as picnic sites and some pleasant cabins that hold up to eight people. At an elevation of 2000 feet, it's cooler than the coast and a bit wetter as well, averaging about 90 inches of rain a year.

The park has a pleasant hike leading to Kalopa Gulch in the adjoining forest reserve.

Begin the hike along Robusta Lane, which starts on the left between the caretaker's house and the campgrounds. It's about a third of a mile to the edge of the gulch through a thick forest of tall eucalyptus trees with mossy bark. The deep gulch was formed eons ago by the erosive movement of melting glaciers that originated at Mauna Kea. A trail continues along the rim of the gulch for another mile, and a number of side trails along the way branch off and head west back into the park.

Kalopa State Recreation Area also has a nature trail, beginning at the information board near the cabins, which loops for three-quarters of a mile through an ancient ohia forest where some of the trees are more than 3 feet in diameter. Kalopa's woods are habitat for the *elepaio*, an easily spotted native forest bird about the size of a sparrow. It's brown with a white rump, and it makes a loud whistle that sounds like its name.

The park offers tent camping in a pleasant, grassy area surrounded by tall trees. There are rest rooms and covered pavilions with electricity, running water, barbecue grills and picnic tables. If you enjoy cool nights and don't mind being off the beaten path, this rates as one of the Big Island's more recommendable camping options. For information on booking the campground or cabins, see Camping in the Accommodations section near the front of this chapter.

LAUPAHOEHOE POINT

Laupahoehoe Point is midway between Honokaa and Hilo. A highway sign marks the steep winding road that leads 1 1/3 miles down to the point. There are views of the coastal cliffs on the way down, and after heavy rains, waterfalls come to life in all directions.

Laupahoehoe means 'leaf of pahoehoe lava.' This flat peninsula-like point jutting out from the coastal cliffs was formed by a late eruption of Mauna Kea, which poured lava down a ravine and out into the sea.

Tragedy hit Laupahoehoe on April 1, 1946, when tsunami waves up to 30 feet high wiped out the schoolhouse on the point, killing 20 children and four adults. After the tsunami, the whole town moved uphill, although a few families have since settled back in. A monument on a hillock above the water lists those who died.

Laupahoehoe is a rugged coastal area and is not suitable for swimming. The surf is usually rough and pounding and can sometimes crash up over the rocks and onto the lower parking lot.

Interisland boats once landed here. Indeed, many of the immigrants who came to work the sugarcane fields along the Hamakua Coast first set foot on the Big Island at Laupahoehoe.

The county beach park on the point has rest rooms, campsites, showers, drinking water, picnic pavilions and electricity, and as it's off the highway, it's relatively secluded. All this makes it convenient for camping, but ideal for late-night partying, too. Campers should be aware that locals sometimes use the park as a drinking hangout and it can get fairly rowdy.

For information on obtaining a camping permit, see Camping in the Accommodations section near the front of this chapter.

KOLEKOLE BEACH PARK

This grassy park, beneath a big highway bridge, is at the side of Kolekole Stream, which flows down from Akaka Falls. There are small waterfalls, picnic tables, barbecue pits, rest rooms and showers, all of which make the park a popular weekend picnic spot for families. Locals sometimes surf here, but ocean swimming is dangerous. Camping is allowed with a permit from the county, although the park can be busy on weekends and in summer. For information on obtaining a camping permit, see Camping in the Accommodations section near the front of this chapter.

To get to the park, turn inland off Hwy 19 at the south end of the Kolekole Bridge, about three-quarters of a mile south of the 15-mile marker.

AKAKA FALLS

To get to Akaka Falls, turn inland off Hwy 19 onto Akaka Falls Rd (Hwy 220), midway between the 13- and 14-mile markers. The paved road passes through the town of Honomu and then climbs up through former cane fields, ending at the falls 3³/4 miles away.

Honomu

Honomu is an old sugar town that might have been forgotten, if not for its location on the route to Akaka Falls. As it is, things are pretty slow here, but among the village's handful of old wooden buildings, you'll find a shop selling vintage glass bottles, a used bookstore and two galleries.

Both galleries – Hawaii's Artist Ohana and the Akaka Falls Inn & Gift Gallery – have good collections of Big Island art and craft items, including fiber baskets, wooden bowls, pottery, jewelry, local fashions and paintings. On a rainy day, you can always have fun browsing even if you don't intend to buy.

Places to Stay & Eat Sonia Martinez, the owner of *Akaka Falls Inn & Gift Gallery* (☎ 963-5468, fax 963-6353, akakainn@gte.net, PO Box 190, Honomu, HI 96728), has two pleasant guest bedrooms in her home above the shop, which she rents for $55 and $65. Her son Anthony, a horticulturist, has revived some gracious old trees and gardens at the rear of the inn.

This is also the place to eat in town. The Martinezes, originally from Cuba, prepare quesadillas, chicken tamales, veggie or meat hoagies and organic salads – all priced from $4 to $6. The restaurant is typically open 11 am to 5 pm Tuesday to Sunday.

For travelers with a spiritual bent, there's *Akiko's Buddhist Bed & Breakfast* (☎/fax 963-6422, msakiko@aloha.net, PO Box 272, Hakalau, HI 96710), a mile north of Honomu. This rustic 85-year-old home has simple clean rooms, with futons on the floor and shared bath. Singles cost from $30 to $50, doubles from $45 to $65, with the price depending mostly on the room size. A breakfast of fruit from the yard, homemade bread and Kona coffee is included. Those staying a week or more get a slight discount and access to a kitchen. Guests are welcome to join Akiko for Zazen meditation, held

daily at 4:30 am. All in all, the place offers an appealing blend of New Age and old Hawaii. Akiko's maintains a website at www .alternative-hawaii.com/akiko.

Akaka Falls State Park

Akaka Falls State Park has the Big Island's most impressive, easy-to-view waterfall. It shouldn't be missed.

The waterfall lookout is along a delightful half-mile rain forest loop trail that takes about 20 minutes to walk. The paved trail passes through dense and varied vegetation, including massive philodendron vines, fragrant ginger, hanging heliconia, hillsides of bright impatiens and cool bamboo groves. Look up and you might even find orchids growing wild in the trees.

If you start the loop trail by going to the right, you'll first come to the 100-foot **Kahuna Falls**. It's a nice waterfall, but the real treat is still to come. Up ahead is **Akaka Falls**, dropping a sheer 442 feet down a ferndraped cliff. Its mood depends on the weather – sometimes it rushes with a mighty roar, and at other times it cascades gently. Either way it's always beautiful. With a little luck, you might even catch sight of a rainbow in the spray.

One legend says that whenever a branch of the lehua tree lands on a particular stone at the top of the falls, it will begin to rain. If so, there are apparently a lot of loose lehua branches upstream! You might want to bring an umbrella.

PEPEEKEO 4-MILE SCENIC DRIVE

Between Honomu and Hilo, there's a 4-mile scenic loop off Hwy 19 that makes for a delightful drive through a lush tropical jungle. The road crosses a string of one-lane bridges over little streams. In places it's almost canopied with African tulip trees, which drop their orange flowers on the road, and with passion fruit, guava and tall mango trees. The fruit can be picked up along the roadside in season.

The road is well marked on the highway at both ends, with the south end about 7 miles north of Hilo.

Hawaii Tropical Botanical Garden

If somehow the 4-mile scenic drive isn't enough, along the way there's also the Hawaii Tropical Botanical Garden (☎ 964-5233), a rain forest nature preserve with a lily pond, 1000 species of tropical plants and a couple of streams and waterfalls.

Buy your ticket at the yellow building on the inland side of the road, then walk down to the valley garden at nearby Onomea Bay. Note that it is a steep incline, so it may be a bit challenging for young children.

The nonprofit foundation that operates the garden charges a hefty admission fee of $15 for adults, $5 for children six to 16. After you're given a self-guided trail map, you may wander on your own for as long as you like. It's open daily 9 am to 5:15 pm, with the last entry down allowed at 4 pm.

Saddle Rd

True to its name, the Saddle Rd (see the Hamakua Coast map) runs between the island's two highest points, with Mauna Kea to the north and Mauna Loa to the south.

The road passes over large lava flows and climbs through a variety of terrains and climates. At sunrise and sunset, there's a gentle glow on the mountains and a light show on the clouds. In the early morning, it's crisp enough to see your breath, and if you take the spur road up to Mauna Kea, you'll reach permafrost.

Although most car rental contracts prohibit travel on the Saddle Rd, it's a paved road straight across. It's narrow, but it's no big deal – particularly by island standards. Locals looking for the rationale behind the car rental ban come up with things like military convoys or evening fog. The crux of the matter seems to be that the rental agencies just don't want to be responsible for the tow charge if your car breaks down on Hawaii's most remote road.

The Saddle Rd is 50 miles long and has no gas stations or other facilities along the way, so be sure to start out with a full tank of gas.

Crossing the island on the Saddle Rd is a bit shorter than taking the northern route of the Hawaii Belt Rd, but then again the Saddle Rd is also a bit slower; timewise there isn't much difference either way.

To the west, the Saddle Rd starts out in cattle ranch land with rolling grassy hills and planted stands of eucalyptus trees. It's beautiful, but like the rest of the western side of the island, it's changing. A new subdivision called Waikii Ranch has divided 3000 acres of the area's ranch land into million-dollar house lots and is marketing them to wealthy urban cowboys.

After about 10 miles, the land starts getting rougher and the pastures and fences fewer. The military takes over where the cows leave off, and you'll eventually come to the Quonset huts of the Pohakuloa Military Training Area. Most of the vehicles on the road are military jeeps and trucks, although in hunting season you'll come across a fair number of pickup trucks as well.

MAUNA KEA

Mauna Kea is Hawaii's highest mountain, and its 13,796-foot summit has a cluster of important astronomical observatory domes.

The unmarked Summit Rd, which climbs up Mauna Kea, begins off Saddle Rd at the 28-mile marker opposite a hunters' check station. It's a well-paved 6¼ miles to the Onizuka visitor center. The road winds up a few thousand feet in elevation. If you've got a small car, it's probably going to labor a bit, but it shouldn't be a problem making it up as far as the visitor center. A standard transmission is preferable.

Surprisingly, you don't really get closer views of Mauna Kea's peaks by driving up to the visitor center. The peaks actually look higher and the views are broader from Saddle Rd. But you'll find other nice vistas from Summit Rd and you can often drive up above the clouds. Mauna Kea doesn't appear as a single main peak but rather a jumble of peaks, some black, some red-brown, some seasonally snowcapped.

Summit Rd passes through open range with grazing cattle. It's easy to spot Eurasian skylarks in the grass, and if you're lucky you might see the *io*, an endemic Hawaiian hawk, hovering overhead. Both birds make their

grassy mountain slopes. Mauna
o home to the nene, as well as the
small yellow honeycreeper that lives
no ere else in the world.

One of the more predominant plants
here is mullen, which has soft woolly leaves
and shoots up a tall stalk. In spring, the
stalks get so loaded down with flowers that
they bend over from the weight of what
look like big yellow helmets. Mullen is not a
native plant but was inadvertently brought
in by ranchers as a freeloading weed in grass
seed.

For information on skiing on Mauna Kea,
see the Activities section at the beginning of
this chapter.

Onizuka Visitor Center

The Onizuka visitor center (☎ 961-2180,
www.ifa.hawaii.edu), officially the Onizuka
Center for International Astronomy, was
named for Ellison Onizuka, a Big Island
native and one of the astronauts who died in
the 1986 Challenger space shuttle disaster.

The center shows an interesting short
video on Mauna Kea's observatories and
has computers running astronomy programs.
It also has photo displays of the observatories,
information on discoveries made from
the summit and exhibits of the mountain's
history, ecology and geology.

The visitor center is currently open on
Thursday 5:30 to 10 pm; Friday 9 am to
noon, 1 to 4:30 pm and 6 to 10 pm; and Saturday
and Sunday 9 am to 10 pm. The hours
are subject to change, so it's a good idea to
call before making the trip.

Stargazing Program On Thursday to
Sunday evenings, 6 to 10 pm, the visitor
center offers a free astronomy program that
includes a presentation about Mauna Kea
and stargazing (weather permitting) using a
Meade LX-200 16-inch telescope and both a
14-inch and an 11-inch Celestron telescope.
You'll get a chance to view planets, galaxies,
star clusters, supernova remnants and planetary
nebulae. The instructor also points out
all of the constellations visible in Hawaii.
Children are welcome. Wear warm clothing,
as night temperatures can sometimes dip to
around freezing in winter and into the 40s
(°F) in summer.

Summit Tours The visitor center offers
Mauna Kea summit tours on Saturday and
Sunday. The tours visit one or two of the
summit telescopes, most commonly the University
of Hawaii's 88-inch telescope. The
tour is free, but you need to provide your
own 4WD transportation to the summit. If
you're lucky, you might be able to catch a ride
up with someone from the visitor center, but
you can't count on it. Pregnant women and
children under 16 are not allowed because
of altitude health hazards.

Check-in is at the visitor center at 1 pm;
the first hour is spent at the center watching
videos about astronomy on Mauna
Kea, which also provides an opportunity to
acclimatize. The tours usually last until 5 pm
and are subject to cancellation at any time
when there's inclement weather at the
summit.

For commercial tours to the summit, see
Organized Tours later in this section.

Summit Observatories

The summit of Mauna Kea has the greatest
collection of state-of-the-art telescopes on
earth and superior conditions for viewing
the heavens. Nearing 14,000 feet, the summit
is above 40% of the earth's atmosphere and
90% of its water vapor. The air is typically
clear, dry and stable.

Not only are the Hawaiian Islands isolated,
but Mauna Kea is one of the most
secluded places in Hawaii. The air is relatively
free from dust and smog. Nights are
dark and free from city light interference.

Eight out of 10 nights are good for
viewing. Only the Andes Mountains match
Mauna Kea for cloudless nights, although
air turbulence in the Andes makes viewing
more difficult there.

The University of Hawaii (UH) holds
the lease on Mauna Kea from the 12,000-
foot level to the summit, and UH receives
observing time at each telescope as one of
the lease provisions. Currently 10 telescopes
are in operation and a couple more are in
the making.

UH built the summit's first telescope in 1968 with a 24-inch mirror. The telescope sizes have been increasing by leaps and bounds ever since.

The UK Infrared Telescope (UKIRT), with its 150-inch mirror, was until the early 1990s the world's largest infrared telescope. It can be operated via computers and satellite relays from the Royal Observatory in England.

NASA's Infrared Telescope has measured the heat of volcanoes on Io, one of Jupiter's moons. The most active of Io's volcanoes is now named after the Hawaiian volcano goddess Pele.

Opened in 1992, the WM Keck Observatory, a project of the California Institute of Technology (Caltech) and the University of California, began operations with Keck I, the world's largest and most powerful optical/infrared telescope. In January 1996, the 390-inch Keck telescope discovered the most distant galaxy ever observed, at 14 billion light-years away. The discovery of this 'new galaxy,' in the constellation Virgo, has brought into question the very age of the universe itself, because the stars making up the galaxy seemingly predate the 'big bang' that is thought to have created the universe.

Keck featured a breakthrough in telescope design. Previously, the sheer weight of the glass mirrors was a limiting factor in telescope construction. The Keck telescope has a unique honeycomb design with 36 hexagonal mirror segments, each 6 feet across, that function as a single piece of glass.

A second Keck telescope (Keck II), a replica of the first, became operational in October 1996. The two telescopes are interchangeable and can function as one – 'like a pair of binoculars searching the sky' – allowing them to study the very cores of elliptical galaxies.

The Keck Observatory visitor gallery is open to the public 10 am to 4 pm Monday to Friday. It has an informative display, a 12-minute video, rest rooms and a viewing area inside the Keck I dome that allows you to see the telescope.

Just 150 yards west of Keck is Japan's new Subaru Telescope, which opened in 1999 after a decade of construction. Its $300 million price tag makes this the most expensive observatory yet constructed, and its 22-ton mirror, reaching 27 feet in diameter, is the largest optical mirror in existence. Incidentally, the telescope is named for the constellation Pleiades, which in Japanese is called Subaru.

Driving to the Summit

Visitors may go up to the summit in daytime, but vehicle headlights are not allowed between sunset and sunrise because they interfere with observation. What you'll see is mainly the outside of the observatory buildings, where the scientists are at work, although both the University of Hawaii 88-inch telescope and the WM Keck Observatory have visitor centers.

The road to the summit is paved only as far as Hale Pohaku, the buildings just above the Onizuka visitor center where the scientists reside. People en route to the summit should stop first at the Onizuka center for at least 30 minutes to acclimatize before continuing on.

The road from the Onizuka center to the summit is suitable for 4WD vehicles only; although people occasionally go up in standard cars, this is not recommended due to problems that can occur with poor traction on the slopes. Harper Car & Truck Rentals is the only car rental company that allows its vehicles (4WD jeeps) to be driven to the summit.

Dimming the Light

You might notice, as you tour around the Big Island, that the streetlights have an unusual orange glow. In order to provide Mauna Kea astronomers with the best viewing conditions possible, streetlights on the island have been converted to low-impact sodium. Rather than using the full iridescent spectrum, these orange lights use only a few wavelengths, which the telescopes can be adjusted to remove.

The drive takes about half an hour. You should drive in low gear and loosen the gas cap to prevent vapor lock. The upper road can become covered with ice during winter. Be particularly careful on the way down and watch out for loose cinder. Driving when the angle of the sun is low – in the hour after sunrise or before sunset – can create blinding conditions that make it difficult to see the road and oncoming cars.

About 4¹/₂ miles up is an area called **Moon Valley**, where the Apollo astronauts rehearsed with their lunar rover before their journey to the real moonscape.

At 5¹/₂ miles up, look to the left for a narrow ridge with two caves and black stones. That's **Keanakakoi**, 'Cave of the Adze,' an ancient adze quarry. From this spot, high-quality basalt was quarried to make adzes and other tools and weapons, which were traded throughout the islands. For people interested in archaeology, it's an impressive site. This is a protected area and nothing should be removed.

You can call ☎ 969-3218 for a recording on current road conditions.

Dangers & Annoyances The summit air has only about 60% of the oxygen available at sea level, and it's not uncommon for visitors to get altitude sickness. Not only is the height a problem, but also the fact that visitors often don't take the time to properly acclimatize.

Unlike Nepal, for instance, where great heights are generally reached only after days of trekking, here you can zip up from sea level to nearly 14,000 feet by car in just two hours.

Scuba divers who have been diving within the past 24 hours risk getting the bends by going to the summit. It's recommended that children under 16, obese people, pregnant women and those with a respiratory condition, or even a cold for that matter, do not go beyond the Onizuka visitor center. Because of the demand that the altitude puts on the heart, people with a heart condition should avoid the summit as well.

Even the astronomers who work up here never fully acclimatize and are always oxygen-deprived in the summit's thin air. Anyone who gets a headache or feels faint or nauseous should head back down the mountain. For more information, see Altitude Sickness under Health in the Facts for the Visitor chapter.

Bring warm clothing and be prepared for severe weather conditions, as temperatures can drop well below freezing. Mauna Kea can have snow flurries any time of the year, and winter storms can dump a couple of feet of snow overnight.

Lake Waiau

Lake Waiau is a unique alpine lake which, at 13,020 feet, is the third-highest lake in the USA. It sits inside the Puu Waiau cinder cone in a barren and treeless setting.

Lake Waiau is rather mysterious. It's a small lake, no more than 10 feet deep and set on porous cinder in desert conditions of less than 15 inches of rainfall per year. It's fed by melting winter snows and by permafrost, which elsewhere on Mauna Kea quickly evaporates. Lake Waiau has no freshwater springs and yet it's never dry.

Hawaiians used to bring the umbilical cords of their babies here and place them in the lake to give their children the strength of the mountain.

Mauna Kea Summit Trail

A 6-mile hiking trail to the top of Mauna Kea starts near the end of the paved road above the Onizuka visitor center. Instead of continuing on the main 4WD road, take the road to the left. The trail begins up through wooden posts and more or less parallels the summit road. It's marked with posts and stone cairns.

The trail starts at 9200 feet and climbs almost 4600 feet. Because of the altitude, the hike is quite strenuous and you can also easily get sunburned. Dress in layers of warm clothing and take sunscreen and plenty of water. Give yourself a full day for this hike – most people take four to five hours to get to the summit.

It's a difficult hike, as you're walking on cinders, but there are incredible vistas and strange moonlike landscapes. The trail passes through the **Mauna Kea Ice Age Natural Area Reserve**. There was once a Pleistocene glacier here, and scratchings on rocks from the glacial moraine can still be seen.

The ancient adze quarry Keanakakoi, at 12,400 feet, is two-thirds of the way up. Lake Waiau (see above) is a mile farther.

You might be tempted to hitch a ride from someone at the Onizuka visitor center who's going to the summit and then walk down. But if you haven't spent the previous night in the mountains, there's a danger in doing this, as you won't have as much time to acclimatize.

Organized Tours

Paradise Safaris (☎ 322-2366), PO Box A-D, Kailua-Kona, HI 96745, conducts sunset tours of Mauna Kea summit. The tour, which costs $135, includes stargazing from the company's own portable telescope and pickup in Kailua-Kona, Waikoloa or Waimea.

Waipio Valley Shuttle (☎ 775-7121), PO Box 5128, Kukuihaele, HI 96727, operates daytime tours that go to the summit of Mauna Kea and include an observatory visit. The tour, which costs $80, including lunch, leaves from Waimea and takes about six hours. There's a four-person minimum.

Arnott's Lodge (☎ 969-7097) in Hilo also offers a daytime outing to Mauna Kea; the cost is a reasonable $36 for people staying at Arnott's, $75 for nonguests.

See also Summit Tours, earlier.

Places to Stay

Mauna Kea State Recreation Area is 7 miles west of Summit Rd, near the 35-mile marker. The park has housekeeping cabins that are mostly used by hunters who hunt pigs, goats and game birds on the slopes of Mauna Kea. The cabins include basic kitchens, bathrooms, hot showers and bed space for up to six people. As most hunting is restricted to weekends, that's the most difficult time to book the cabins.

The park also contains picnic tables, rest rooms, a pay phone and 20 acres of shrub land. At an elevation of 6500 feet, the area commonly experiences cool days and cold nights.

Puu Poliahu

Just below Mauna Kea summit is the hill Puu Poliahu, home of Poliahu, the goddess of snow.

Poliahu is said to be more beautiful than her sister Pele. According to legend, during conflicts over men, Pele would get miffed and erupt Mauna Kea; Poliahu would cover it over with ice and snow. Then Pele would erupt again. Back and forth they would go. The legend is metaphorically correct. As recently as 10,000 years ago, there were volcanic eruptions through glacial ice caps here.

Because of its spiritual significance, Puu Poliahu is off-limits to astronomical domes, so you won't find observatories here.

Nearby military maneuvers can be noisy, but otherwise the park is a good base for those planning to hike Mauna Kea or Mauna Loa.

For reservations, contact the *Division of State Parks* (☎ 933-4200, PO Box 936, 75 Aupuni St, Hilo, HI 96721). Mauna Kea's rates are the same as those of other park cabins: $45 for one to four people, $5 more for each additional person.

MAUNA LOA'S NORTHERN FLANK

The road to Mauna Loa starts just east of Summit Rd and climbs 18 miles up the northern flank of Mauna Loa to a weather station at 11,150 feet. There are no visitor facilities at the weather station, so be sure to use the rest rooms before you set out.

The narrow road is gently sloping and passable in a standard car. As it's a winding, nearly single-lane drive with some blind spots, give yourself about 45 minutes to drive up. It might be wise to loosen your gas cap before you start in order to avoid vapor lock problems. Park in the lot below the weather station; the equipment used to measure atmospheric conditions is highly sensitive to vehicle exhaust.

The summit and domes of Mauna Kea are visible from here, and when conditions are just right you can glimpse the 'Mauna Kea shadow' at sunset. It's a curious phenomenon in which Mauna Kea sometimes casts a blue-purple shadow behind itself in the sky.

Observatory Trail

The weather station is the trailhead for the Observatory Trail, which connects up with the Mauna Loa Trail after 3 miles. From there it's 2½ miles around the western side of Mauna Loa's caldera, Mokuaweoweo, to the summit at 13,677 feet, or 2 miles along the eastern side of Mokuaweoweo Caldera to Mauna Loa cabin at 13,250 feet. The cabin marks the end of the 18-mile Mauna Loa Trail, which starts down in the main section of Hawaii Volcanoes National Park.

The Observatory Trail is very steep and difficult. If you haven't been staying in the mountains, altitude sickness is very likely. The hike to the cabin takes four to six hours for strong hikers. Anyone who is not in top shape shouldn't even consider it.

Overnight hikers need to register in advance with the Kilauea Visitor Center in Hawaii Volcanoes National Park. See Backcountry Hiking & Camping in the Hawaii Volcanoes National Park section for details.

Mauna Loa to Hilo

Heading eastward from the hunters' check station at the foot of Summit Rd, the terrain along Saddle Rd gradually becomes ohia-fern forest, shrubby at first, but getting thicker and taller as Hilo gets closer.

This section of road has been upgraded and the ride onward to Hilo is a fairly good one, but be cautious of oncoming drivers who take to the center of the road to cut curves.

About 4 miles outside Hilo, Akolea Rd leads off to the left and connects in 2 miles to Waianuenue Ave, which passes Peepee Falls, Boiling Pots and Rainbow Falls (see the Around Hilo section, later in this chapter). Alternatively, if you stay on Saddle Rd, you'll soon come to Kaumana Caves on the left. For information on all three of these sites, see the Hilo section that follows.

Hilo

Hilo, the county capital and commercial center, is situated along a large crescent-shaped bay and has Hawaii's second-largest port. With some 44,000 residents, Hilo accounts for nearly one-third of the Big Island's total population.

In terms of lush, natural beauty, Hilo beats Kona hands down any day – the only catch is in finding a sunny one. During an average year in Hilo, measurable rain falls on 278 days!

Although the rain dampens some spirits, it also feeds the area's waterfalls, junglelike valleys and lush gardens. Indeed, Hilo is the center of activity for Big Island nurseries growing orchids, anthuriums and other tropical flowers that are sent to florists around the world.

Hilo is ethnically diverse, with many residents of Japanese or Filipino descent. There's also an alternative community that's been filtering in since the '70s, attracted by Hilo's affordability and the windward coast's scenic appeal.

Hilo's numerous old buildings give it a period facade, but the town has had a precarious history. Hilo is a survivor. Natural forces have long been a threat to the city – tidal waves from one side, lava from the other. Two devastating tsunamis have hit Hilo in the post-WWII era, and as recently as 1984 a lava flow from Mauna Loa stopped short just 8 miles above town.

Hilo's reputation for wet weather has protected it from the invasive development that has spread elsewhere on the island. In many ways, Hilo is the last remaining Hawaiian city unaffected by mass tourism. Not that attempts haven't been made. In the 1970s, Hilo built a new airport and a few deluxe hotels and started a media blitz. The airlines began direct flights from the mainland, but the tourists never showed.

'America's rainiest city' just couldn't compete with the sunny Kona Coast. The mainland flights have all been dropped and some of the hotels have been turned into condos or cheap local housing. These days, the main

THE BIG ISLAND

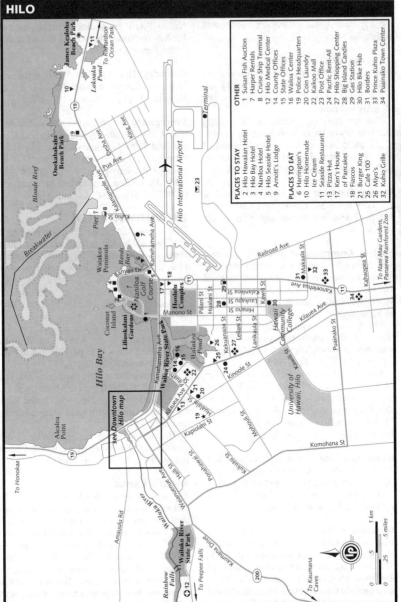

HILO

PLACES TO STAY
2 Hilo Hawaiian Hotel
3 Hilo Bay Hotel
4 Naniloa Hotel
5 Hilo Seaside Hotel
9 Arnott's Lodge

PLACES TO EAT
6   Harrington's
10 Hilo Homemade
    Ice Cream
11 Seaside Restaurant
13 Pizza Hut
17 Ken's House
    of Pancakes
18 Fiascos
21 Burger King
25 Cafe 100
26 Miyo's
32 Kuhio Grille

OTHER
1   Suisan Fish Auction
7   Harper Rentals
8   Cruise Ship Terminal
12 Hilo Medical Center
14 County Offices
15 State Offices
16 Wailoa Center
19 Police Headquarters
20 Coin Laundry
22 Kaikoo Mall
23 Post Office
24 Pacific Rent-All
27 Hilo Shopping Center
28 Big Island Candies
29 Gas Station
30 Hilo Bike Hub
31 Borders
33 Prince Kuhio Plaza
34 Puainako Town Center

growth in Hilo is not related to tourism but to the rediscovery of the city – and its reasonably priced real estate – by Honolulu businesses.

Information

Tourist Offices The Big Island Visitors Bureau (☎ 961-5797), on the corner of Haili and Keawe Sts, is open 8 am to 4:30 pm Monday to Friday.

Pick up camping permits at the County Department of Parks & Recreation (☎ 961-8311), at 25 Aupuni St, or the Division of State Parks (☎ 974-6200), at 75 Aupuni St. Both are near Wailoa River State Park.

Money The Bank of Hawaii has branches at 117 Keawe St, 120 Pauahi and 417 E Kawili. There are numerous other banks around town.

Post & Communications Hilo has two post offices. The main one, which is where general delivery mail is held, is on the road into the airport. It's open 8:15 am to 4:45 pm Monday to Friday and 8:30 am to 12:30 pm on Saturday.

The more convenient downtown post office is in the federal building on Waianuenue Ave. It's open 8 am to 4 pm Monday to Friday and 12:30 to 4 pm on Saturday.

You can check your email at PostNet (☎ 959-0066), at the Prince Kuhio Plaza on Hwy 11. The cost is $2.50 per 15 minutes, plus 25¢ per page to print. It's open 9 am to 7 pm on weekdays, 10 am to 6 pm on Saturday and 10 am to 4 pm on Sunday.

Travel Agencies Cut Rate Tickets (☎ 969-1944), at the Puainako Town Center on Hwy 11, sells discounted interisland air tickets.

Hawaiian Airlines (☎ 935-0858) has an office at 120 Kamehameha Ave.

Bookstores Basically Books (☎ 961-0144, reedbook@interpac.net), 160 Kamehameha Ave, is a book and map store specializing in Hawaiiana, including out-of-print books and Hawaiian literature. The store also has a good general travel section and USGS topographic maps of Hawaii and the Pacific.

There's a large new Borders bookstore on Hwy 11 immediately north of the Prince Kuhio Plaza. In addition, there are two bookstores, Waldenbooks and Book Gallery, in the Prince Kuhio Plaza.

Laundry Hilo Quality Washerette, 210 Hoku St, directly behind the 7-Eleven on Kinoole St, is open 6 am to 10 pm daily.

Emergency For police, fire and ambulance, dial ☎ 911. The hospital, Hilo Medical Center, is at 1190 Waianuenue Ave, near Rainbow Falls; for information, dial ☎ 974-4700, and for the emergency room, dial ☎ 974-6800. The police department headquarters (☎ 961-2213) is at 349 Kapiolani St.

DOWNTOWN HILO

Downtown Hilo is an interesting mishmash of classic old buildings from the early 1900s, many on the National Register of Historic Places, and aging wooden storefronts, some newly renovated, others falling apart.

This is a good area to explore on foot. One short walk that takes in historical sites and some interesting shops starts at the intersection of Kalakaua and Keawe Sts, goes northwest along Keawe, up Wailuku Drive, along Kinoole St past Kalakaua Park and back down Kalakaua St.

If you wander a little farther afield, you can explore the back streets, where there are little Japanese restaurants with faded kanji signs, barbershops with hand-pumped chairs and old pool halls.

The informative brochure *Walking Tour of Historic Downtown* is available free at the tourist office and some hotels.

Maui's Canoe

The walk along the north end of Keawe St will lead you past a couple of period buildings that have been painstakingly renovated. The Toyama Building, formerly the First Trust Building, on the corner of Keawe St and Waianuenue Ave, is an attractive Renaissance revival-style structure dating to 1908. The nearby Kulana Na Auao Building, which houses government offices, is of a similar style.

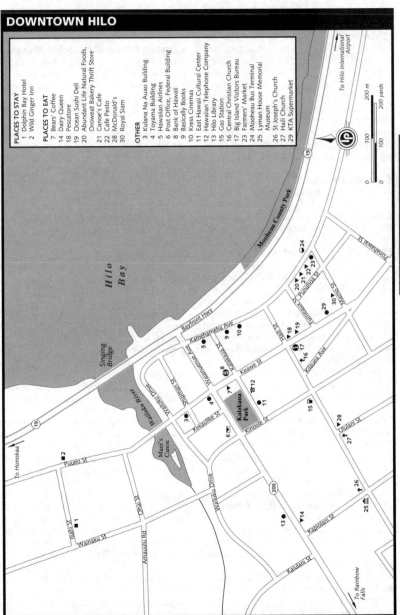

DOWNTOWN HILO

PLACES TO STAY
1 Dolphin Bay Hotel
2 Wild Ginger Inn

PLACES TO EAT
7 Bears' Coffee
14 Dairy Queen
18 Pescatore
19 Ocean Sushi Deli
20 Abundant Life Natural Foods,
     Oroweat Bakery Thrift Store
21 Canoe's Cafe
22 Cafe Pesto
28 McDonald's
30 Royal Siam

OTHER
3 Kulana Na Auao Building
4 Toyama Building
5 Hawaiian Airlines
6 Post Office, Federal Building
8 Bank of Hawaii
9 Basically Books
10 Kress Cinemas
11 East Hawaii Cultural Center
12 Hawaiian Telephone Company
13 Hilo Library
15 Gas Station
16 Central Christian Church
17 Big Island Visitors Bureau
24 Mooheau Bus Terminal
23 Farmers' Market
25 Lyman House Memorial
     Museum
26 St Joseph's Church
27 Haili Church
29 KTA Supermarket

THE BIG ISLAND

If you continue walking along Keawe St just beyond Wailuku Drive, you'll be on the Puueo St Bridge, which crosses over the Wailuku River. The large rock in the river upstream on the left is known as Maui's Canoe.

Legend has it that the demigod Maui paddled his canoe with such speed across the ocean that he crash-landed here and the canoe turned to stone. Ever the devoted son, Maui was rushing to save his mother, Hina, from a water monster who was trying to drown her by damming the river and flooding her cave beneath Rainbow Falls.

Kalakaua Park

In the late 19th century, King David Kalakaua established Hilo as the county seat. Kalakaua Park is a quiet downtown park with a statue of the king sitting beneath the shade of a banyan tree, holding a taro leaf and a hula drum. The park also has a sundial erected by the king in 1877, a war memorial and a pretty reflecting pool filled with some carp and water lilies.

A curious modern-day addition to Kalakaua Park is a capsule containing a collection of mementos buried during the total solar eclipse on July 11, 1991. It's intended to be opened on May 3, 2106, at the time of the next total eclipse.

The site of the king's former summer home, Niolopa, is opposite the park at the side of the now-closed Hilo Hotel.

Around Kalakaua Park

The **federal building**, opposite the park on Waianuenue Ave, was built in 1919 of neoclassical design with high columns and a Spanish-tile roof. It still houses the federal court and downtown post office.

On the other side of the park, on Kalakaua St, the **East Hawaii Cultural Center** has taken over the old police station (circa 1932). The center hosts quality art exhibits that change monthly. Admission is free and it's open 10 am to 4 pm Monday to Saturday. A performing arts center is upstairs.

Next to the cultural center is the **Hawaiian Telephone Company building**, designed by renowned Honolulu architect CW Dickey in the 1920s. It's of Spanish-mission influence with handsome tile work and a high-hipped roof.

Lyman House Memorial Museum

The Lyman House Memorial Museum (☎ 935-5021), 276 Haili St, is a first-class museum and a great place to spend a rainy afternoon.

You'll learn how adzes were made of volcanic clinker, how kukui nuts were skewered on coconut-frond spines to burn as candles, and about other aspects of life in ancient Hawaii. Exhibits include feather leis, tapa cloth and a house made of pili grass. Mana, kahunas and *awa* (kava) drinking are all succinctly explained.

The different lifestyles of those who came as indentured immigrants and stayed on to form Hawaii's multiethnic society are all given their due. Displays include costumes, cultural artifacts and insightful interpretive plaques. From Portugal there's a *braginha*, the forerunner of the ukulele.

The museum has a world-class mineral exhibit with thousands of rocks, crystals and gemstones. There are explanations of volcanic eruptions and lava formations with samples of spatter, olivine, Pele's tears and fine strands of Pele's hair.

The astronomy exhibit not only has celestial displays, but also gives visitors an introduction to the latest happenings in the world of astronomy via two computers linked to Mauna Kea summit observatories.

Adjacent to the museum is the **Mission House**, built by the Reverend David Lyman and his wife, Sarah, in 1839. The two missionaries had seven children of their own and in the attic boarded a number of island boys who attended their church school.

The docent-led Mission House tour will give you a good sense of the people who lived here. The house has many of the original furnishings, including Sarah Lyman's melodeon, rocking chair, china dishes and old patchwork quilts. The tours are given at 9:30, 10:30 and 11:30 am and 1, 2, 3 and 4 pm and are included in the museum admission price.

The museum is open 9 am to 4:30 pm Monday to Saturday. Admission costs $7 for adults, $3 for children six to 17.

An ancient royal compound on the Big Island

Nani Mau Gardens, near Hilo on the Big Island

Lava meeting the Pacific in Hawaii Volcanoes National Park on the Big Island

The black-sand beach Kehena Beach, in the Puna district of the Big Island

Palms along the Kohala Coast on the Big Island

Akaka Falls State Park on the Big Island

Bamboo grove in Oheo Gulch, Maui

Rustic Paia, along the Hana Hwy, Maui

Molokini crater, off Maui's southwest coast

Old-fashioned Hawaiian enterprise, on the Hana Hwy

Red Sand Beach (Kaihalulu Beach), in Hana, Maui

Windsurfers galore at Hookipa Beach, near Paia, Maui

A rare quiet moment on Lahaina's bustling Front St, Maui

Churches

Haili St was once called Church Row for the churches lined up along it. The three that remain, one Catholic and two Congregational, are worth a look if you happen to be in the neighborhood.

St Joseph's Church, on the corner of Haili and Kapiolani Sts, is an attractive pink church of Spanish-mission design that looks as if it came right out of Southern California. Built in 1919, it has stained-glass windows that open to the crosswinds and a columned entrance topped with angels.

Haili Church, at 211 Haili St, was built in 1859. With its straight lines and boxy square tower, it somewhat resembles a New England barn.

The **Central Christian Church**, on the corner of Kilauea Ave and Haili St, was built in the Victorian style by Portuguese immigrants in the early 1900s.

Hilo Library

Hilo has a good public library, at 300 Waianuenue Ave, that's open from 9 or 10 am to 5 pm daily except Sunday. It stays open to 8 pm on Wednesday and Thursday.

The two large stones on the library's front lawn are the Naha and Pinao Stones. The **Pinao Stone** was used as an entrance pillar to an old Hawaiian heiau. The **Naha Stone**, from the same temple grounds, is said to weigh 2½ tons. According to Hawaiian legend, any person who had the strength to budge the stone would also have the strength to conquer and unite all the Hawaiian Islands. Kamehameha I reputedly met the challenge, overturning the stone in his youth.

AROUND HILO
Wailoa River State Park

Wailoa River State Park (see the Hilo map), located on the grassy expanses where Shinmachi once stood, can be reached from Pauahi St. The park has two **memorials**, one dedicated to the tsunami victims and the other, an eternal flame, dedicated to the area's Vietnam War dead.

The Wailoa River flows through the park, and most of **Waiakea Pond** is within the park boundaries. This spring-fed estuarine pond has both saltwater and brackish water fish species, mostly mullet. There's a boat launch ramp near the mouth of the river; only motorless boats are allowed, and fishing licenses are required.

The park's **Wailoa Center**, near the memorials, is a state-run art gallery with multimedia exhibits that change monthly. An interesting photo presentation of the tsunami damage is on display downstairs. The center is generally open 8:30 am to 4:30 pm on Monday, Tuesday, Thursday and Friday and noon to 4:30 pm on Wednesday. It's best to arrive early, as the gallery staff sometimes locks up by 4 pm. Admission is free.

Banyan Drive

Banyan Drive (see the Hilo map) goes around the edge of the Waiakea Peninsula, which juts into Hilo Bay. The road skirts the Liliuokalani Gardens, the nine-hole Naniloa Country Club Golf Course and Hilo's bayfront hotels.

Banyan Drive is lined with large, sprawling banyan trees that were planted in the 1930s by royalty and celebrities. If you look closely, you'll find plaques beneath the trees identifying the planters – they include Babe Ruth, Amelia Earhart and Cecil B DeMille.

Suisan Fish Auction Local fishers sell their catch on weekday mornings at Suisan Fish Auction, near the intersection of Lihiwai and Banyan Drive, on the western side of the Waiakea Peninsula.

Although it's small scale, the auction is a lively local scene with the auctioneer running up the bids in Hilo's unique form of pidgin. It's open to the public with a roped-off sidewalk viewing area. Get there by 7:30 am before the auction bell rings, as the whole thing wraps up in a matter of minutes.

Next door there's a fish market with some of the freshest fish on the island and an outdoor snack shop where the fishers talk story over coffee following the auction.

Liliuokalani Gardens Hilo's 30-acre Japanese garden (see the Hilo map) takes its name from Queen Liliuokalani, Hawaii's last queen. This picturesque waterfront park is filled with ponds complete with mullet that jump clear out of the water, little Japanese pagodas, stone lanterns, arched bridges and patches of bamboo.

The gardens are a monument of sorts to the Japanese presence in Hawaii. Many of the lanterns and pagodas that dot the park were donated by Japanese regional governments and sister cities in honor of the 100th anniversary of Japanese immigration to Hawaii.

It's a pleasant place to walk around, although after heavy rain you'll need to stick to high ground.

Coconut Island Connected to land by a footbridge, Coconut Island (see the Hilo map) sticks out into the bay opposite the Liliuokalani Gardens. The island is a county park with picnic tables and swimming, but it's most popular as a recreational fishing spot. Hilo's Fourth of July fireworks display is shot off from the island, and the Eastertime Merrie Monarch Festival has its opening ceremonies here.

In ancient times, Coconut Island was called Moku Ola, 'Island of Life,' in part due to the powers of a healing stone on the island that was used by kahunas to cure the sick. Moku Ola also had pure spring water, which was said to bring good health, and a birthing stone that instilled mana in the children born on the island.

Little Tokyo & Big Tsunamis

On April 1, 1946, Hilo Bay was inundated by a tsunami that had raced its way across the Pacific from an earthquake epicenter in the Aleutian Islands. It struck at 6:54 am without warning.

Fifty-foot waves jumped the seawall and swept into the city. They tore the first line of buildings off their foundations, carrying them inland and smashing them into the rows behind. As the waves pulled back, they sucked much of the splintered debris and a number of people out to sea.

By 7 am the town was littered with shattered buildings as far as the eye could see. The ground was not visible through the pile of rubble. Throughout Hawaii the tsunami killed 159 people and racked up $25 million in property damage. The hardest hit was Hilo, with 96 fatalities.

Hilo's bayfront 'Little Tokyo' bore the brunt of the storm. Shinmachi, which means 'New Town' in Japanese, was rebuilt on the same spot.

Fourteen years later, on May 23, 1960, an earthquake off the coast of Chile triggered a tsunami that made a beeline for Hilo at a speed of 440 miles per hour. A series of three tidal waves washed up in succession, each one sweeping farther into the city.

Although the tsunami warning speakers roared this time, many people didn't take them seriously. The tiny tsunamis of the 1950s had been relatively harmless, and some people actually went down to the beach to watch the waves.

Those along the shore were swept inland, while others farther up were dragged out into the bay. A few lucky ones who managed to grab hold of floating debris were rescued at sea. In the end, this tsunami caused 61 deaths and property damage of over $20 million.

Once more the Shinmachi area was leveled, but this time, instead of being redeveloped, the low-lying bayfront property was turned into parks and the survivors were relocated to higher ground.

All along Kamehameha Ave you can still see the curbstone cuts that once led to streets or to the driveways of businesses that made up Shinmachi.

Beaches

Hilo is not a city that will hold much interest for beach bums. Still, there are some decent beaches along Kalanianaole Ave, a 4-mile-long coastal road on the eastern side of Hilo (see the Hilo map). The road, which is basically a continuation of Kamehameha Ave, starts in front of the Hilo Seaside Hotel.

Onekahakaha Beach Park First beach up is Onekahakaha, which is about a quarter mile north from Kalanianaole Ave.

The park has a broad sandy-bottomed pool formed by a large boulder enclosure. As the water's just a foot or two deep in most places, it's popular that have families with young children.

On the Hilo side of the park, an unprotected cove attracts some snorkelers on calm days, but be careful, as it has a seaward current. The park department cautions swimmers and snorkelers not to venture beyond the breakwater at any time. There are rest rooms, showers and a picnic area.

James Kealoha Beach Park Kealoha is a roadside county park known locally as 'Four-Mile Beach' because of the distance between the park and the downtown post office. The park, which is just before the Mauna Loa Shores apartments, has showers and rest rooms.

For swimming and snorkeling, most people go to the eastern side of the park, which is sheltered by an island and a naturally occurring rocky breakwater. It's generally calm there, with clean, clear water and pockets of white sand.

The Hilo side of the park is open ocean and much rougher. You can sometimes find people net fishing there. It's also a popular winter surfing spot, although there are strong rip currents running out to sea.

Richardson Ocean Park This park, just before the end of the road, has a small black-sand beach fronting Hilo's most popular snorkeling site. It's also favored by boogie boarders when the waves are right. The west side of the bay tends to be colder due to subsurface freshwater springs. On the east side,

AROUND HILO

the springs are less common and the snorkeling is better.

The eastern side of the park also has a lava shoreline that can be fun to explore, as it's pocketed with tiny inlets harboring black crabs and bright tropical fish. There are rest rooms, showers, picnic tables and a lifeguard.

Rainbow Falls

Rainbow Falls is on the western side of Hilo, off Waianuenue Ave just below the hospital.

Waianuenue, literally 'rainbow seen in water,' is the Hawaiian name for this pretty 80-foot waterfall. The huge cave beneath the falls is said to have been the home of Hina, mother of Maui. The falls are usually seen as a double drop, with the two streams flowing together before hitting the large pool at the bottom.

The best time to see rainbows is in the morning, although they're by no means guaranteed, as both the sun and mist need to be accommodating. You can get a straight-on view of the falls from the lookout in front of the parking lot.

For a little diversion, take the short loop trail that begins along the steps at the left side of the falls. The trail continues for about five minutes past a giant banyan tree and through a lush junglelike area before leading back to the parking lot.

Peepee Falls & Boiling Pots

Peepee Falls and Boiling Pots are up Waianuenue Ave, about 1½ miles past Rainbow Falls.

Peepee Falls drops over a sheer rock face. As the water runs downstream over a series of basalt depressions in the river, it swirls and churns into bubbling pools – hence the name Boiling Pots. The bubbling effect is most pronounced after periods of heavy rain, when the water runs strongest.

Kaumana Caves

The Kaumana Caves were formed by an 1881 lava flow from Mauna Loa. As the flow subsided, the outer edges of the deep lava stream cooled and crusted over in a tunnel-like effect. The hot molten lava inside then drained out, creating these caves.

The caves are wet, mossy and thickly covered with ferns and impatiens. If you have a flashlight, you might want to explore them, although they tend to be quite drippy.

The caves, which are signposted, are 3 miles up Kaumana Drive (Hwy 200) on the right.

Nani Mau Gardens

Nani Mau Gardens is a large commercial attraction on the tour bus circuit. The gardens encompass more than 20 acres of flowering plants, including a lovely orchid section, and much of the flora is identified with labels. Unlike many Hawaiian gardens, this one isn't terribly naturalized or charmingly overgrown. Instead, it's formally designed with sculpted plantings and wide asphalt paths. Narrated tram rides are available ($5 extra), and a restaurant is on the grounds.

Nani Mau is about 3 miles south of Hilo. The turnoff from Hwy 11 onto Makalika St is marked with a small sign. Admission is $10

for adults and $6 for children six to 17; the garden is accessible to the disabled. It's open 8 am to 5 pm daily.

Panaewa Rainforest Zoo

Panaewa Rainforest Zoo, the only tropical rain forest zoo in the USA, is in a forest reserve that gets 125 inches of rain annually.

Because of cuts in funding, the zoo has seen better days, but it's still good for an hour of strolling. There are monkeys, reptiles, a lowland tapir, a pygmy hippo, axis deer and feral pigs and goats. Plans call for a pair of tigers to arrive in the near future. You can also see some of Hawaii's endangered birds, such as the nene and the Hawaiian duck, hawk and owl. In addition to the 50 or so animal species caged here, free-roaming peacocks have the run of the place.

To get there, turn off Hwy 11 a few miles south of town at W Mamaki St, which almost immediately turns into the Stainback Hwy. The zoo is a mile west of Hwy 11. It's open 9 am to 4 pm daily; admission is free.

Mauna Loa Macadamia Nut Visitor Center

Mauna Loa Macadamia Nut Visitor Center is on Macadamia Rd off Hwy 11, about 5 miles south of Hilo. The 2½-mile road to the center cuts across row after row of macadamia trees, as far as the eye can see.

C Brewer Co, which owns the Mauna Loa Macadamia Nut operation, produces most of Hawaii's macadamia nuts. The large visitor center here caters to tour-bus crowds and is essentially just a gift shop and snack bar.

To the side is a working factory, which has an outside walkway with windows that allow visitors to view the large, fast-paced assembly line inside.

The little planted area behind the visitor center, with its labeled fruit trees and flowering bushes, is worth walking through if you've come this far. The center is open 8:30 am to 5 pm daily.

Places to Stay

Partially due to the weather, Hilo has no self-contained resorts. People don't come to Hilo to hang around a pool, but to visit the sights and then head on. Consequently, the 'vacation rental' condo market that's so common on the Kona Coast is virtually non-existent here.

Budget *Arnott's Lodge* (☎ 969-7097, fax 961-9638, info@arnottslodge.com, 98 Apapane Rd, Hilo, HI 96720) is a great place to connect with other travelers, if you don't mind being on the outskirts of town. This clean, friendly, hostel-style lodge has 36 dorm beds and 14 private rooms in a converted apartment building. It costs $17 for a bunk bed in a room with four people, $31 for a single room and $42 for doubles, all with shared baths and kitchen facilities. An adjacent house holds a two-bedroom unit that could accommodate up to five people and rents for $105. In addition, tenting is allowed in a small space adjacent to the hostel for $9 per person. There's a common TV/VCR room, a coin laundry, free airport pick-up and a scheduled daily shuttle service ($3 return) into town.

Arnott's offers a rotating schedule of well-run daily outings ($36 each), including visits to Puna, South Point and Green Sands Beach, Hawaii Volcanoes National Park, and Mauna Kea. Other extras include frequent barbecues ($7), an online computer ($2 per 15 minutes) and bike rentals for $10 a day. MasterCard and Visa are accepted. To get to Arnott's, go east 1½ miles on Kalanianaole Ave from Hwy 11 and turn left onto Keokea Loop Rd. The lodge is about 100 yards down the road. For more information, visit the hostel's website at www.arnottslodge.com.

The popular *Dolphin Bay Hotel* (☎ 935-1466, fax 935-1523, 333 Iliahi St, Hilo, HI 96720), on a hill just above downtown, is a friendly, family-run place. Not only is the hotel a good value, but it also welcomes travelers with children, unlike many other small inns. All 18 apartment-like units have full kitchens, TVs and bathrooms, and all except the standard rooms have sunken bathtubs. Fresh-picked fruit from the backyard is available in the lobby, along with free morning coffee. Standard rooms cost $59/66 for singles/doubles, while superior rooms cost

$69/76. Also available are four large one-bedroom units for $86 and a two-bedroom unit for $98, for either singles or doubles. It's $10 more for each additional person. There's an annex on the opposite side of the street with six rental units, each with a queen bed, kitchen and TV; these units rent by the week for $350. This is one of the few hotels in Hilo with a continuously high occupancy rate, so reservations are suggested.

The people at *Wild Ginger Inn* (☎ 935-5556, 800-882-1887, 100 Puueo St, Hilo, HI 96720) have taken a formerly rundown motel and given it a face-lift in pink and green Caribbean colors. Rooms in this nonsmoking inn are simple but quite adequate, and a breakfast of fruit and pastries is included in the price. The rooms have private baths and either a double or two twin beds; most also have small refrigerators. A wooded gulch behind the main wing provides many of the rooms with nice views of bamboo and a little stream. The cost is $39/44 single/double; for stays of three or more nights it drops to $35 for either singles or doubles.

Lihi Kai (☎ 935-7865, 30 Kahoa Rd, Hilo, HI 96720) is a B&B in Amy Gamble Lannan's home, perched on a cliff directly above Hilo Bay, 2 miles north of town. The two guest rooms – one with two twin beds, the other with a king bed – share a bath and a half. Amenities include a small heated swimming pool and a large living room with a wonderful ocean view. The rate of $55, single or double, includes breakfast. There's a three-night minimum stay or an extra $5 charge.

Mid-Range *Hilo Seaside Hotel* (☎ 935-0821, 800-367-7000, 126 Banyan Drive, Hilo, HI 96720) is a 145-unit complex of two-story motel-style buildings. The rooms are simple, with air-con, ceiling fans, turquoise carpets, louvered windows, TVs and small refrigerators. Avoid the rooms around the swimming pool and the streetside Hukilau wing, both of which can get a bit noisy. The nicest rooms are in the deluxe ocean wing and have balconies overlooking the hotel's carp pond and Reeds Bay. The usual room rates range from $60 to $88, but there are discounts if you book from within Hawaii (rather than toll-free from the mainland) and ask for the special – it's commonly $49 a day for a room only or $109 for a two-night package that includes a rental car.

Uncle Billy's *Hilo Bay Hotel* (☎ 935-0861, 800-367-5102, fax 935-7903, 87 Banyan Drive, Hilo, HI 96720) is a locally owned 130-room hotel with a touristy Polynesian theme. Rates range from a pricey $84 for a basic standard room to $104 for a much nicer oceanfront room.

Three miles north of Hilo off Hwy 19 is *Hale Kai Bjornen* (☎ 935-6330, fax 935-8439, 111 Honolii Pali, Hilo, HI 96720), a B&B in an attractive contemporary home with fine views across Hilo Bay. The five ocean-facing rooms, each of which has a private bath, cable TV and either a queen or king bed, range in price from $85 to $105, with breakfast included. Guests have use of a small swimming pool, a refrigerator and the living room.

Top End *Hilo Hawaiian Hotel* (☎ 935-9361, 800-367-5004, fax 961-9642, 71 Banyan Drive, Hilo, HI 96720), a 285-room high-rise near Coconut Island, is Hilo's best hotel. Rooms are comfortable with a pleasant though not distinguished decor, either a king or two smaller beds, air-con, TV and phone; most also have private lanais. Garden-view rooms, which look across the parking lot to the golf course, cost $107, while ocean-view rooms overlooking Hilo Bay cost $137. If you request it at the time of booking, you can often add a rental car at no extra cost.

Naniloa Hotel (☎ 969-3333, 800-367-5360, fax 969-6622, 93 Banyan Drive, Hilo, HI 96720) is a 325-room high-rise hotel – Hilo's largest. The rooms have air-con, TVs and phones but are rather straightforward for the rates, which range from $100 to $140 depending on the view. Only the top-end rooms have lanais. The Naniloa is popular with Japanese tour groups.

The *Shipman House Bed & Breakfast* (☎/fax 934-8002, 800-627-8447, bighouse@ bigisland.com, 131 Kaiulani St, Hilo, HI 96720), on a knoll above town, is a beautiful Victorian mansion that has been in the Shipman family since 1901; past visitors to the home have included Queen Liliuokalani and author Jack London. The congenial owners, Barbara-Ann and Gary Andersen, have thoroughly renovated the property, which is on the National Register of Historic Places. There are three B&B rooms in the main house; the downstairs room has two antique koa twin beds, while the two upstairs rooms both have queen beds. In addition, two more rooms are in the adjacent 1910 guest cottage. All have private baths, fans and small refrigerators. The cost is $130 to $150 for singles or doubles, breakfast included. Smoking is not allowed indoors. For more information, visit the inn's website at www.hilo-hawaii.com.

Places to Eat

Budget For a thoroughly local experience, head to *Cafe 100* (969 Kilauea Ave), a drive-in kind of place. It's a fun spot for cheap food, and it's perhaps the last eatery in Hawaii where you can get a 35¢ cup of coffee. Cafe 100 is the original home of loco moco (rice topped with a hamburger, a fried egg and a generous ladleful of brown gravy), which costs $2. It also has sandwiches for $2, full breakfasts for $3 and plate lunches for $4 and up. There are picnic tables at the side of the building where you can chow down. Cafe 100 is open 6:45 am to 8:30 pm daily (to 9:30 pm on weekends).

Bears' Coffee (106 Keawe St) is a nice place for a light lunch or breakfast. You'll find pastries, good Belgian waffles and egg dishes (until 11:30 am), and from 10 am on, there are deli sandwiches, burritos and 'designer' bagels with a choice of more than a dozen fillings. Almost everything costs $6 or less. Bears' is open 7 am to 5 pm Monday to Saturday, 8 am to noon on Sunday.

A casual little spot with good food is *Canoe's Cafe* (308 Kamehameha Ave), in the back of the S Hata Building, a classic 1912 edifice that once housed the city's main department store. Canoe's specializes in sandwiches with a choice of breads, including sourdough, focaccia, rye, pita and pocket wraps. A fresh fish grinder (a kind of submarine sandwich) with Maui onions, or a grilled chicken and Puna goat cheese sandwich cost

$6.50, a side of potato salad included. The cafe also has interesting fresh salads ($6.25), including sesame fish and Thai chicken versions that use local organic vegetables. Canoe's is open 9:30 am to 3 pm on weekdays and 10 am to 2 pm on Sunday and holidays; breakfast, which includes $3 Belgian waffles, is served until 10:30 am.

Soup or Roll (☎ 969-9907, 777 Kilauea Ave), a hole-in-the-wall at the east side of the Kaikoo Mall, is a friendly family-run place with good Vietnamese and Chinese food. The summer rolls ($3) make a tasty appetizer, and a wide range of curries and other main dishes run $5 to $6. From 10 am to 2:30 pm on weekdays, the restaurant offers a popular lunch buffet with a choice of two items for $4.15, rice or noodles included. Soup or Roll is open 9:30 am to 9 pm daily, but you may want to get there early at dinnertime, because there are only six tables.

Miyo's (☎ 935-2273, 400 Hualani St), in the back of the Waiakea Villas complex, is a charming home-style Japanese restaurant overlooking Waiakea Pond. The atmosphere is relaxed, the food good and the prices unbeatable. Many dishes can be ordered either with fish or meat, or vegetarian style. At lunch, you can get tempura, tonkatsu or sesame chicken – all served with rice, miso soup and salad – for around $6.50. A tempura and sashimi combination is just $7.50. The same meals at dinner cost a dollar or two more. Miyo's is open Tuesday to Saturday from 11 am to 2 pm and 5:30 to 8:30 pm.

You can get authentic Hawaiian food at *Kuhio Grille*, a casual eatery at the north side of the Prince Kuhio Plaza. It's owned by a couple of taro growers from Waipio Valley, and for $9.25 you can get a laulau plate made with local taro leaves, poi, lomi salmon and *haupia* (coconut pudding). The menu also includes omelettes, burgers, saimin and the usual plate meals, as well as local favorites like taro corned-beef hash. The Kuhio Grille is open 5 am to 9 pm Monday to Thursday and round-the-clock on weekends.

Hilo's best ice cream can be found at *Hilo Homemade Ice Cream* (1477 Kalanianaole Ave), on the road to Richardson Beach. Flavors include tasty *poha* (gooseberry),

zesty ginger and other island flavors like lilikoi, coconut cream and macadamia nut. It costs $1.40 for a single scoop, $2.40 for a double. Hours are 10:30 am to 5 pm daily.

Abundant Life Natural Foods (292 Kamehameha Ave) is a health food store with a variety of products including cheeses, yogurt, juices and bulk foods. It also has a simple deli and smoothie bar. The store is open 8:30 am to 6 pm weekdays, 7 am to 5 pm on Saturday and 11 am to 3 pm on Sunday; the deli has slightly shorter hours and is closed Sunday. Two doors away, *Oroweat Bakery Thrift Store* has slightly dated breads at discount prices.

If you're on Banyan Drive, you can pick up breakfast pastries and coffee at the *Hilo Hawaiian Hotel Bakery*, a kiosk in front of the hotel. Danish, raisin bran muffins, doughnuts or coffee all cost about $1. It's open 6 am to 6 pm daily.

Hilo has an abundance of fast-food restaurants spread around town. The biggest concentration is at the Puainako Town Center on Hwy 11, which has *McDonald's, Pizza Hut, Jack in the Box, Taco Bell, Little Caesar's, Subway* and *Baskin-Robbins*. *Ken's House of Pancakes* (1730 Kamehameha Ave) is open 24 hours daily.

KTA Supermarket (323 Keawe St), a convenient downtown grocery store, is open 7 am to 9 pm Monday to Saturday, to 6 pm on Sunday. There's a *Safeway* supermarket at the Prince Kuhio Plaza on Hwy 11 and a *Sack N Save* supermarket in the nearby Puainako Town Center. If you're heading for Volcano early in the morning, Sack N Save has coffee and doughnuts from 5 am. Hilo has a great *farmers' market* on Wednesday and Saturday mornings on the corner of Mamo St and Kamehameha Ave. You can usually pick up three or four papayas for $1, as well as Kau oranges and other island fruits, veggies and flowers direct from the growers at bargain prices.

Mid-Range *Royal Siam* (☎ 961-6100, 68 Mamo St) has good authentic Thai food at reasonable prices. There are salads, soups and noodle dishes, as well as a selection of tasty red, green and yellow curries that can be ordered mild to hot. Beef or chicken dishes cost $7, while most seafood dishes cost around $9; rice is an additional $2. The menu is extensive, with a page of vegetarian dishes priced around $6. Royal Siam is open 11 am to 2 pm and 5 to 9 pm Monday to Saturday.

Ocean Sushi Deli (☎ 961-6625, 239 Keawe St) is a perky place offering both traditional and contemporary sushi, with scores of creative options such as ahi-avocado, dynamite maki, Hilo roll and poke macnut. À la carte prices range from $1.20 to $6, depending on size and ingredients – or buy a mixed sushi box for around $10. Other items include inexpensive organic salads, miso soup and yakitori chicken. If you really want to splurge, there's all-you-can-eat sushi from 11 am to 4 pm for $16 and from 4 to 9 pm for $20.

Cafe Pesto (☎ 969-6640, 308 Kamehameha Ave), in the S Hata Building, is a popular restaurant serving creative pasta dishes and gourmet wood-fired pizzas and calzones. It also has some interesting salads including sesame poke with spinach and a ceviche pasta salad. The food is good, albeit a bit pricey, with the aforementioned items costing between $10 and $17 and dinner fish specials climbing to $25. Cafe Pesto is open 11 am to 9 pm Sunday to Thursday, to 10 pm on weekends.

Restaurant Miwa (☎ 961-4454, 1261 Kilauea Ave) is an authentic Japanese restaurant in the Hilo Shopping Center. It has a sushi bar, good sashimi and a full range of Japanese dishes at moderate prices. At lunch, a full-meal teishoku costs around $8, at dinner around $10, while more extensive dinner combinations cost $15. Although it's not gourmet, the food is good, with quality, price and decor comparable to a neighborhood restaurant in Japan. The restaurant is open 11 am to 2 pm Monday to Saturday and 5 to 9 pm daily.

Fiascos (☎ 935-7666, 200 Kanoelehua Ave) is a bustling place serving sandwiches, salads, pastas and an array of meat dishes at moderate prices. There's also a reasonably good soup-and-salad bar for $10 alone, $5 with a meal. Fiascos is open 11 am to 10 pm daily, to midnight on Friday and Saturday.

Top End ***Pescatore*** (☎ 969-9090, 235 Keawe St) has fine dining with attentive service and excellent Italian food. Lunch is a particularly good deal, with an array of pasta dishes ranging from $7 for spaghetti bolognese to $10 for scampi alfredo. At dinner, pasta dishes are about double the lunch prices, while meat and seafood main courses average $20. One recommendable item is the *fra diavolo*, a lightly spiced dinner dish combining fresh ahi, calamari and clams over pasta. Lunch is 11 am to 2 pm Monday to Saturday. Dinner is 5:30 to 9 pm daily.

Harrington's (☎ 961-4966, 135 Kalanianaole), perched on Reeds Bay, is a small waterfront restaurant with a fine view and standard steak and seafood dishes for around $20, salad included. Add another $8 for an appetizer such as shrimp cocktail or escargots It's mainly a dinner restaurant, open 5:30 to 9:30 pm nightly, but on weekdays from 11 am to 2 pm it also has a lunch menu of salads and sandwiches for around $9.

Seaside Restaurant (☎ 935-8825, 1790 Kalanianaole Ave), a family-run operation, has the island's freshest fish, served in a delightful setting. The unpretentious dining room is a simple open-air affair that sits pondside above the family's aquafarm. You can have your pick of fresh mullet, rainbow trout, perch or catfish, all of which are raised in the pond. The local favorite is steamed mullet wrapped in ti leaves, but there are other preparations to choose from. The meals, which include rice, salad, apple pie and coffee, cost a reasonable $17 and are served 5 to 8:30 pm Tuesday to Sunday. Call ahead for reservations, as meals are planned in advance.

Entertainment

Nighttime musical entertainment is not one of Hilo's strong points. *Fiascos*, on Hwy 11 near Banyan Drive, has country line dancing on Thursday evenings and jazz on Friday.

The lounge at *Hilo Hawaiian Hotel* sometimes has contemporary Hawaiian musicians, and the *Naniloa Hotel* has dancing to recorded music on weekends.

Uncle Billy presents a hula show during dinnertime, from 6 pm nightly, at the *Hilo Bay Hotel* restaurant.

Periodically there are community plays, dances and concerts at the **East Hawaii Cultural Center** on Kalakaua St; check the Hilo paper for the current schedule.

Cinemas *Kress Cinemas (174 Kamehameha Ave)*, in the meticulously renovated art deco-style Kress Building, is the most atmospheric place to take in a little celluloid. It shows standard first-run Hollywood films, as do the movie theaters at *Prince Kuhio Plaza*, on Hwy 11, and *Waiakea Shopping Plaza (88 Kanoelehua Ave)*, just south of Ken's House of Pancakes. Recorded information for all three theaters is available by calling ☎ 961-3456.

Shopping

Hilo has several shopping centers. The largest is Prince Kuhio Plaza, at the south side of town on Hwy 11, which has 75 stores, including Liberty House, Hilo Hattie, Sears, JCPenney, Longs Drugs, Safeway and a one-hour photo place.

Big Island Candies, 560 Kinanu St, sells chocolate-covered macadamia nuts, cookies and other sweet treats made on site. You can sample the products and sip a free cup of coffee while watching candy being hand-dipped in chocolate. It's open 8:30 am to 5 pm daily.

Puna

The Puna district is the diamond-shaped easternmost point of the Big Island. Its main attractions revolve around lava: black-sand beaches, lava tide pools, an ancient forest of lava tree molds and vast lava fields covering former villages.

Kilauea Volcano's active east rift zone slices clear across Puna. The most recent series of eruptions has been spewing lava since 1983. These days, the highway into Puna ends abruptly at the 1990 lava flow that buried the former village of Kalapana.

Not surprisingly, Puna has Hawaii's cheapest real estate – the closer to the rift, the greater the volcanic activity and the cheaper the land.

While a growing number of people are drawn to Puna by the idea of homesteading, many have found it tough making a living off a lava flow. For years, growing marijuana has been a potentially lucrative alternative, although changing public attitudes and mounting police pressures have made it an increasingly less appealing one. Paramilitary raids, intense herbicide sprayings and helicopters with infrared sensors that allow authorities to see into people's homes have sharply curtailed the growing. Nonetheless, the majority of all pot confiscated by Hawaii police is still taken in Puna.

Puna has the reputation, deserved or not, of being less than friendly. If you're traveling the main roads, you probably won't pick up on those vibes at all, but if you're cruising around off the beaten path, you may raise a suspicious eye.

Some crops take well to lava; Puna is a major producer of anthuriums, grows the best papayas in Hawaii, and grows many of the orchids that get credited to Hilo.

Puna is not known for its beaches, and for the most part waters along the coast here are subject to strong currents and riptides.

Orientation

Keaau is the entrance to Puna, where Hwys 11 and 130 intersect. From there, Hwy 130 goes south 11 miles to Pahoa and then continues on to the coast.

Maps that show Hwy 130 winding down through Puna and up the Chain of Craters Rd to Hawaii Volcanoes National Park were made obsolete in 1988 when a lava flow buried a large section of the road; active lava tunnels have continued flowing over that stretch of road to this day. Consequently, the national park can be entered only via the Hawaii Belt Rd (Hwy 11), which makes Puna more time-consuming to visit, as you need to backtrack out the same way you go in.

KEAAU

Keaau is the small town at the northern end of Puna. The main Puna sightseeing area is southeast of Keaau, but many of Puna's larger residential subdivisions are to the southwest. If you're heading toward

Hawaii Volcanoes National Park on Hwy 11, you'll pass through the villages of Kurtistown, Mountain View and Glenwood. Mountain View, 7 miles southwest of Keaau, has a hostel-style accommodation that could make a fun place to stay while also providing a glimpse of life in this rural slice of Hawaii.

Pineapple Park Hostel (☎ *968-8170, park@aloha.net, PO Box 639, Kurtistown, HI 96760*) is a good-energy budget place for those with their own transportation. The friendly owner, Annie Park, has a big contemporary house on 4 acres. There are separate dorms for men and women, with 18 beds that cost $16 each, bed linens included; four pleasant private rooms, with private baths, TV and VCR, for $50 to $65; and two two-bedroom bungalows with baths and kitchens that cost $100 for up to four people. The private-room rates include a full breakfast. Hostelers can add breakfast for $4, but it's easy to prepare your own meals in the big guest kitchen. Other amenities include a pool table, big-screen TV, laundry facilities, and lockers, and plans are in the works to add a swimming pool and hot tub. Mountain bikes rent for $10 a day and other transpor-

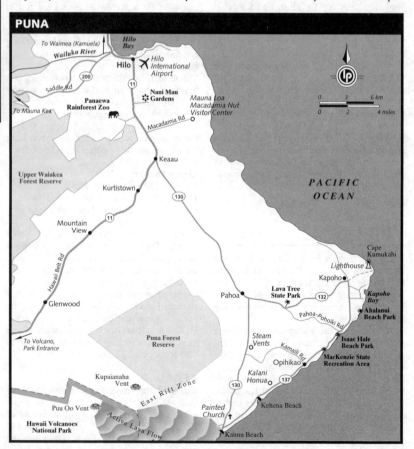

tation can sometimes be arranged. Annie's partner is converting some old buses into simple 'cabins' out back that will cost $35 and sleep up to four. You can also pitch a tent for $8 per person.

Pineapple Park is off the beaten track but could still be a convenient base for exploring the region, as it's less than a 30-minute drive from both Volcano and Hilo. From Keaau, head west on Hwy 11. After 6½ miles, pass the 13-mile marker and turn left onto S Kulani Rd. Turn right on Pohala St and left on Pikake St, then look for the sign. It's a total of 2½ miles from Hwy 11. For more information, visit the hostel's website at www.pineapple-park.com.

If you're hungry for a bite to eat, stop at the Keaau Shopping Center, at the intersection of Hwys 11 and 130, which has a supermarket, **Dairy Queen**, natural foods store and a couple of small local eateries. There's a **McDonald's** opposite the shopping center.

PAHOA

The heart of Puna is Pahoa, a little town with raised wooden sidewalks, cowboy architecture and an untamed edge. There are alternative influences from the '60s and '70s, but there are other more timeless ones as well. The Akebono Theater, which was built in 1917 and is one of the oldest theaters in Hawaii, has been renovated and once again features weekend movies and the occasional live concert.

If you'd like to take a look at life on a lava flow as you're driving around, stop by Pahoa Realty on Main St and pick up a free subdivision map and listings. Prices start as low as $2500 for a small lot (no electricity, water by catchment, gravel roads) on Kilauea's active east rift zone.

Wild orchids grow like weeds along the roadsides around Pahoa and throughout Puna. There are fields of cultivated orchids and lots of anthurium nurseries as well.

Places to Stay

The **Village Inn** (☎ 965-6444, PO Box 1987, Pahoa, HI 96778) has five 2nd-story rooms in a historic wooden building on Main St, adjacent to the theater. It's partly funky,

slanted hardwood floors and all, and partly classy, with rooms furnished with authentic Victorian-era antiques. All rooms have cable TV and mini-refrigerators. Rates are $30 for singles or doubles in rooms with shared bath, $40 for rooms with private baths. Credit cards are accepted.

The owner of **Pahoa Natural Groceries** (☎ 965-8322, fax 965-6263, PO Box 1546, Pahoa, HI 96778) is adding a few guest rooms above the new natural foods store, which is currently under construction. If things go according to plan, each room will have a private bath, TV and two double beds, and the cost will be between $50 and $60. The location, set back a bit from Main St, will probably make it the quietest place to stay in town.

The cheapest place to crash is the **Turn Around Inn** (☎ 965-5137), a small, simple boardinghouse above the shops at the east end of Main St in the town center. The rooms are very basic – a bed, TV and window fan – and share toilets, showers and a kitchen. Rooms are generally rented out only by the month, at $250, but the management occasionally will consider shorter-term rentals.

Places to Eat

Luquin's, on Main St in Pahoa's town center, has good, authentic Mexican food. A single taco or enchilada costs $2.50, while combination plates start at $6. Huevos rancheros with tortillas, rice and beans cost $5 and are served all day. Luquin's also offers American-style breakfasts and a good all-you-can-eat salad bar. It's open 7 am to 9 pm daily.

Huna Ohana, on Main St near Luquin's, is an incense-scented metaphysical bookstore and espresso cafe. Eggs with potatoes and toast, a Belgian waffle, tempeh burgers and various vegetarian lunches average $4 to $5. The shop also serves organic Kona coffee and makes good fruit smoothies. It's open 8 am to 5 pm Monday to Saturday.

Paolo's Bistro (☎ 965-7033), also on Main St in the town center, has genuine Northern Italian fare. Most pasta dishes, which are served with a cup of minestrone, cost $8 to $10, while the most expensive item on the menu, cioppino, costs $17. Add another $5 for a salad or tiramisu. Paolo's is open for dinner only, 5:30 to 9 pm Tuesday to Sunday.

Pahoa Natural Groceries, just off Main St at the west side of the town center, is a large well-stocked natural foods store with a dairy section, bakery items, inexpensive salads, healthy sandwiches and a hot-food bar. It's open daily 8 am to 8 pm (to 6 pm on Sunday).

Pahoa also has a **steak restaurant, Chinese and Thai restaurants** and an old **grocery store** where you'll find the local bulletin board.

You can buy fruits and vegetables, some of them organic, at the *farmers' market* that sets up in the theater parking lot from 7 am to 1:30 pm on Sunday.

Pahoa to the Coast

The usual route after Pahoa is a triangle that goes down Hwy 132 past Lava Tree State Park to Kapoho, then continues on Hwy 137 along the shore to the lava flow at Kaimu Beach and comes back to Pahoa via Hwy 130. Conveniently, Hwys 137 and 130 still connect, though they do so at the very edge of a lava flow.

From Pahoa, Hwy 132 passes through a tropical forest reserve. The area is very lush and junglelike, with ferns growing on the bark of trees and a thick ground cover of flowering impatiens. If you're short on time, a good alternative is Pahoa-Pohoiki Rd, which is also a nice rain-forest drive along a narrow road lined by old mango trees and papaya groves.

LAVA TREE STATE PARK

The lava tree molds at Lava Tree State Park were created in 1790, when this former ohia rain forest was engulfed in pahoehoe from Kilauea's east rift zone. The lava was free-flowing and moved quickly, like a river flooding its banks.

As the molten lava ran through the forest, some of it began to congeal around the moisture-laden ohia trunks, while the rest of the flow moved on through and quickly receded.

Although the trees themselves burned away, the molds of lava that had formed around them remained. Now, 200 years later, there's a ghost forest of lava shells.

A 20-minute loop walk winds around the 'lava trees.' Some are a good 10 feet high, while others are short enough to look down into, sheltering ferns within their hollows.

Be careful if you walk off the path, as in places the ground is crossed by deep cracks, some hidden by new vegetation. It's speculated that one deep fracture, which was caused by an earthquake at the same time as the flow, may have drained much of the lava back into the earth.

The park is on Hwy 132, 2$\frac{1}{2}$ miles east from its intersection with Hwy 130. The mosquitoes can be wicked.

KAPOHO

Hwy 132 heads east through orchards of papaya and long rows of vanda orchids to what was once Kapoho, a farming town of about 300 people.

On January 13, 1960, a fountain of fire half a mile long shot up in the midst of a sugarcane field just above Kapoho. The main flow of liquid pahoehoe lava ran toward the ocean but a slower moving offshoot of aa lava crept toward the town, burying orchid farms in its path.

Earthen barricades were built and fire hoses frantically pumped water onto the lava, but none of the attempts to harden or divert the flow worked.

On January 28 the lava entered Kapoho and buried the town. A hot springs resort and nearly 100 homes and businesses disappeared beneath the flow.

Then a bizarre phenomenon occurred when the river of lava approached the sea at **Cape Kumukahi**. Within a few feet of the cape's lighthouse, the lava parted into two flows and circled around the structure, sparing it from destruction. If you want to take a look, head 1$\frac{3}{4}$ miles down the dirt road that continues beyond the intersection of Hwys 132 and 137. However, while the parted lava flows are still visible, the old lighthouse has been replaced by a modern light. Cape Kumukahi, which means 'first beginning' in Hawaiian, is the easternmost point in the state.

Lava Surfing

The most dominant landscape feature in the Kapoho area is the Kapoho Crater, an ancient 420-foot cinder cone. The hill is lush green with thick vegetation and has a small crater lake on top of it.

One of the earliest legends of volcanic activity in Kapoho goes back to the 14th century. It seems that Kahavari, a young Puna chief, was holding a *holua* (sledding) contest on the slopes of Kapoho Crater. One of the spectators was an attractive woman who stepped forward and challenged the chief to a race.

Kahavari tossed the woman an inferior sled and charged down the hill, daring her to overcome him. Halfway down, he glanced over his shoulder and found her close behind, racing down atop a wave of molten lava. It was, of course, the volcano goddess Pele, who chased Kahavari clear out to sea, where he narrowly escaped in a canoe. Everyone and everything in Pele's path was buried in the flood of lava.

Hwy 137

Hwy 137 (Kalapana-Kapoho Beach Rd) is barely above water level and is bordered by invasive milo and hala trees that look as if they plan to reclaim the road. In a few places, it's so overgrown there's almost a tunnel effect, with just a lacy bit of light filtering in through the trees. The road sometimes floods during winter storms and high surf.

Kapoho Tide Pools

The Kapoho tide pools are in the Kapoho Vacationland subdivision, a mile south of the lighthouse. This network of tide pools is formed in lava basins, some of which are deep enough for swimming and snorkeling.

To get there, turn off Hwy 137 onto Kapoho Kai Drive, heading toward the ocean, and then turn left on Waiopai.

AHALANUI BEACH PARK

One of the few safe swimming spots on the Puna Coast is Ahalanui Beach Park, off Hwy 137 a mile north of Isaac Hale Beach Park. The star attraction is a lovely thermal spring-fed pool set in lava rock. It's roughly 60 feet in diameter and deep enough for swimming.

The water temperature averages about 90°F. The pool has an inlet to the ocean (which pounds upon the seawall rocks at one side of the pool), so the water stays clean.

On weekdays, it's generally a quiet spot, while on weekends, it's popular with families. The park has picnic tables, pit toilets and sometimes a lifeguard on duty. The pool is directly behind a long yellow house; parking is on the opposite side of the road, but don't leave anything valuable in your car, as break-ins are not uncommon here.

ISAAC HALE BEACH PARK

Isaac Hale Beach Park, on Pohoiki Bay along Hwy 137, has a shoreline of chunky lava rocks. This county park is small, but on weekends, there's usually a frenzy of local activity, including picnics and fishing.

The park has Puna's only boat ramp. Local kids like to swim near the ramp, which is somewhat protected by a breakwater, and there are sometimes surfers at the south side of the bay.

Camping is allowed, but it's not a very attractive option, as the camping area is virtually in the parking lot. For information on obtaining a camping permit, see Camping in the Accommodations section near the front of this chapter.

The park has toilets but no drinking water or showers.

MacKENZIE STATE RECREATION AREA

There's no beach at MacKenzie State Recreation Area but rather 40-foot sea cliffs and surging surf, which sometimes breaks three-

quarters of the way up the cliffs. Those who fish from the cliffs stand a good chance of catching *ulua*, a jack fish that favors turbulent waters.

This 13-acre park on Hwy 137 is quiet and secluded in a grove of ironwood trees. There's a soft carpet of needles underfoot. Both tent and trailer camping are allowed with a permit from the state, but the facilities, which include picnic tables and pit toilets, are run-down, and drinking water is unavailable. For information on obtaining a camping permit, see Camping in the Accommodations section near the front of this chapter.

An old Hawaiian coastal trail, called the **King's Trail**, passes through the park. It runs parallel to the ocean about 75 yards in from the cliffs. If you take it northeast from the parking lot for about three minutes, you'll come across the opening of a long **lava tube**, which is marked by a low thicket of ferns.

OPIHIKAO

The village of Opihikao is marked by a little Congregational church and a couple of houses.

Kalani Honua, a New Age conference and retreat center, is 2½ miles southwest of Opihikao village, midway between the 17- and 18-mile markers. The center hosts a wide diversity of workshops, including tai chi retreats, alternative health and fitness courses, heritage programs focusing on Hawaiian culture and weekend workshops geared to the gay and lesbian community. Visitors are welcome to stop by and take a look around.

Places to Stay & Eat

Kalani Honua (☎ 965-7828, 800-800-6886, kalani@kalani.com, RR2 Box 4500, Pahoa, HI 96778) caters mostly to groups but also welcomes individual travelers on a space-available basis.

There are 31 rooms, most in two-story cedar lodges with exposed-beam ceilings. Natural wood is used throughout, and a screened common area contains a shared kitchen. In the high season, singles/doubles cost $90/110 with a private bath, $75/95 with a shared bath. In the low season, singles/doubles cost $75/95 with a private bath,

---

Puna & Pele

In the Hawaiian language, there are several proverbial expressions that link Puna with the volcano goddess Pele. As an example, to express anger, someone might say *Ke lauahi maila o Pele ia Puna*, 'Pele is pouring lava out on Puna.' Equally common are both historic and modern stories of a mysterious woman traveling alone through Puna. Sometimes she's young and attractive, other times she's old and wizened, and often she's seen just before a volcanic eruption. Those who stop and pick her up hitchhiking or show some other kindness are protected from the lava flow.

After the 1960 lava flow destroyed the village of Kapoho, stories circulated about how the lightkeeper in the spared Kapoho lighthouse had offered a meal to an elderly woman who had showed up at his door on the eve of the eruption.

$65/75 with a shared bath. Also available are private cottages with one bedroom, bath and living room; the cost is $110/130 double in the low/high season.

Tents can be pitched on the grounds for $20/25 singles/doubles in the high season, $5 less in the low season. There's a sauna and a large swimming pool for guests.

The center has a work-scholar program that provides room and board in exchange for 30 hours of work per week; a three-month commitment is required. This could be an interesting budget option for a lengthy stay in Hawaii.

The dining room, which serves buffet-style vegetarian meals, is open to the public. Breakfast costs $7, lunch $8 and dinner $14. Dining room hours are short: 7:30 to 8:30 am for breakfast, noon to 1 pm for lunch and 6 to 7 pm for dinner. From 8 am to 8 pm you can also get sodas and simple snack items at the office.

For more information, visit Kalani Honua's website at www.kalani.com.

KEHENA BEACH

Kehena Beach, at the base of a cliff, is a black-sand beach created by a 1955 lava flow. Shaded by coconut and ironwood trees, the beach is a pleasant and free-spirited nude sunbathing spot.

When the water is calm, swimming is usually safe, but during periods of heavy surf there can be powerful currents and dangerous undertows. In winter, it's not unusual for dolphins to come close to the shore and swim with bathers.

Kehena is off Hwy 137, immediately south of the 19-mile marker. Look for cars parked at the side of the road and you'll find the start of the path down to the beach, a five-minute walk away. Don't leave valuables in your car.

KALAPANA

For years, the village of Kalapana sat precariously beneath Kilauea's restless east rift. When the current series of eruptions began in 1983, the main lava flow moved down the slope to the west of Kalapana. Much of the early flow passed through a series of lava tubes, which carried the molten lava down to the coast and into the sea. During pauses in the eruption in 1990, the tubes feeding lava to the ocean cooled long enough to harden and block up. When the eruption started again, the lava flow, no longer able to take its previous course, was redirected toward Kalapana. By the end of 1990 the entire village, including 100 homes, was buried.

Today the road (Hwy 137) ends abruptly at Kaimu Beach on the eastern edge of Kalapana. Kaimu, formerly the most famous black-sand beach in Hawaii, is now encased under a sea of hardened lava that flowed over the sandy beach and clear into the bay. Opposite the beach, the drive-in restaurant where the tour buses used to park was ironically spared – a reminder of the attraction that Kaimu once was. The rest of the coastal village is gone.

It's a 10-minute walk from the end of the road across the Kalapana lava flow, to where there's a new black-sand beach in the making. You'll need to watch your footing carefully, as there are cracks in the lava and potential thin spots, but it's an interesting walk that has become fairly well trodden. The lava has curious textures, unusual shapes and fissures where tiny ferns have already taken root.

If you're hungry for a bite to eat, **Verna's Drive-In**, at the end of the road, has recently reopened, hoping to catch enough business from lava-lookers to once more make a go of it here. It has ice cream, cheap burgers and omelettes, sandwiches, and plate lunches for under $5. Verna's is open 10 am to 6 pm on weekdays, 9 am to 5 pm on weekends.

KALAPANA TO PAHOA

From the edge of the lava flow at Kaimu Beach, a side road leads up to Hwy 130, which goes back to Pahoa. There are a couple of sights along the way.

You can also take a short detour on the eastern stub of the old national park road, which is now cut off by a lava flow a mile west of the Painted Church. Where the road meets the lava, you can usually see billowing steam clouds created by molten lava pouring into the sea a few miles away.

Painted Church

The Star of the Sea is a little white Catholic church noted for its interior murals painted in trompe l'oeil style to create the effect of being in a large cathedral. The painting style is primitive, but the illusion of depth is amazingly effective. The church also has a nice stained-glass window of Father Damien, who was with the parish before he moved to the leprosy colony on Molokai.

The church, which was in the town of Kalapana, was moved just before lava flows swept over the site. It now sits along Hwy 130 at the 20-mile marker.

Recently deconsecrated, the church is in the process of being turned into a cultural center by the Kalapana Ohana Association. Even if it's locked, you're free to walk up and take a look at the interior through the front windows.

Steam Vents

At the 15-mile marker, 3½ miles south of Pahoa, for some less than obvious reason a big blue highway sign marks a scenic view. While the scenery is not particularly special, if you look closely you'll notice steam rising from vents on the seaward side of the road.

Only a few minutes' walk away are some low spatter cones with hollowed out natural steam baths inside, perfect for a sauna. To get there, take the path leading down from the scenic lookout; when the path forks, bear right and walk to the cinder cone, which has a couple of pieces of wood inside that serve as seats.

Kau

The Kau district stretches from South Kona along the southern flanks of Mauna Loa, taking in the entire southern tip of the island all the way up to Hawaii Volcanoes National Park.

Kau is sparsely populated, with only about 5000 people and three real towns. Much of it is dry and desertlike. Indeed, the highest temperature ever recorded in the state was in Kau in the town of Pahala:

100°F in April 1931. However, Kau also has some lush areas in the foothills, where macadamia nuts and most of Hawaii's oranges are grown.

MANUKA STATE WAYSIDE PARK

Manuka State Wayside Park is an 8-acre arboretum off Hwy 11 just north of the 81-mile marker. The trees and bushes, planted here between the mid-1930s and the 1950s, include 48 native Hawaiian species and 130 introduced species. Many are labeled, some with both Latin and common names.

Camping is allowed by permit in the three-sided covered shelter, which has space for about five sleeping bags. In a pinch it might be okay for an overnight break between Hilo and Kona, but it feels a bit forlorn and it's quite close to the road. While camping under the trees looks tempting, it's prohibited. There are rest rooms and picnic tables, but no drinking water.

The park is in the midst of the 25,500-acre Manuka Natural Area Reserve, which reaches from the slopes of Mauna Loa clear down to the sea. The reserve takes in a couple of heiaus and other ruins.

The **Manuka Nature Trail**, a 2-mile interpretive loop, begins above the parking lot. The trail crosses ancient lava flows and goes through a varied mesic forest that contains both rain forest and dry lowland plants. A detailed brochure explaining the flora along the trail can be picked up from the state parks office in Hilo.

HAWAIIAN OCEAN VIEW ESTATES

A few miles east of Manuka there's a grocery store, a plate-lunch eatery, a pretty good pizzeria, a Texaco gas station, a post office and a hardware shop. This is the commercial center, such as it is, for Hawaiian Ocean View Estates and a couple of other isolated south-side subdivisions.

This area remains one of the last sunny expanses of land in Hawaii to be totally free of resorts. Controversial proposals for large developments occasionally pop up, but so far all have been defeated, to the relief of island environmentalists.

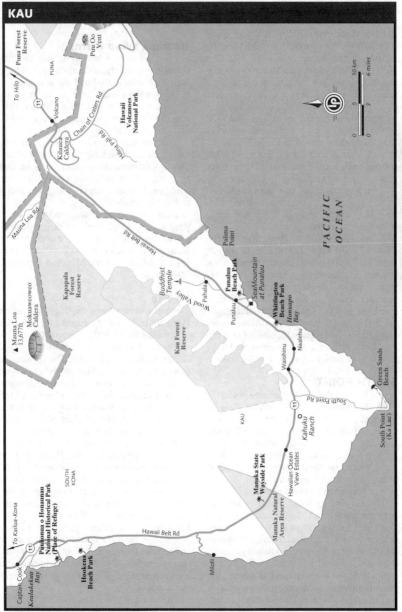

KAU

Puna Forest Reserve

To Hilo

PUNA

Puu Oo Vent

Volcano

Chain of Craters Rd

Hawaii Volcanoes National Park

Hilina Pali Rd

Kilauea Caldera

Mauna Loa Rd

▲ Mauna Loa 13,677ft

Mokuaweoweo Caldera

Kapapala Forest Reserve

Hawaii Belt Rd

PACIFIC OCEAN

Palima Point

Buddhist Temple

Wood Valley

Pahala

Punaluu

Punaluu Beach Park

Sea Mountain at Punaluu

Whittington Beach Park

Honuapo Bay

Kau Forest Reserve

Naalehu

Waiohinu

KAU

Green Sands Beach

Kahuku Ranch (Kai Lae)

South Point Rd

(11)

SOUTH KONA

Manuka State Wayside Park

Hawaiian Ocean View Estates

Manuka Natural Area Reserve

South Point (Ka Lae)

To Kailua-Kona

(11)

Puuhonua o Honaunau National Historical Park (Place of Refuge)

Kealakekua Bay

Captain Cook

Hookena Beach Park

Hawaii Belt Rd

Milolii

0   5   10 km
0   3   6 miles

THE BIG ISLAND

Despite the lack of resorts, there are still a couple of places to stay. **Bougainvillea Bed & Breakfast** (*☎/fax 929-7089, peaceful@interpac.net, PO Box 6045, Ocean View, HI 96704*), in the home of Martie and Don Nitsche, is in a quiet neighborhood in Hawaiian Ocean View Estates, on the seaward side of Hwy 11. This is a friendly, relaxed place with four comfortable rooms, each with private bath, private entrance and VCR (no TV reception, but there's a video library). Singles/doubles cost $55/65, breakfast included. There's a swimming pool and a hot tub set back behind the house; both make nice spots for stargazing. If you come by without a reservation, you can usually find Martie at the Texaco station, which she manages. The Nitsches also maintain a website at www.hi-inns.com/bouga.

South Point Bed & Breakfast (*☎ 939-7466, 877-939-7466, PO Box 6589, Ocean View, HI 96704*) is in Hawaiian Ocean View Estates, just inland from Hwy 11. There are three comfortable units, each with a private entrance and bath. Rates, which include a breakfast of fresh fruit, granola and pastry, are $60 a double for the two smaller rooms and $80 for the larger unit, which has a private lanai with a distant ocean view. All the rooms have a microwave and coffeemaker.

SOUTH POINT

South Point is the southernmost spot in the USA. In Hawaiian, it's known as Ka Lae, which means simply 'the point.'

South Point has rocky coastal cliffs and a turbulent ocean. It was the site of one of the earliest Hawaiian settlements and may have been where the first Polynesians landed. Much of the area is now under the jurisdiction of Hawaiian Home Lands.

The turnoff to South Point is midway between the 69- and 70-mile markers. South Point is 11 miles south of Hwy 11, at the end of a paved one-lane road. There are packed shoulders most of the way, allowing oncoming traffic to pass by without having to stop.

South Point Rd starts out in house sites and macadamia nut farms, which soon give way to grassy pastures. The winds are strong here, as evidenced by the trees, some bent almost horizontal with their branches trailing along the ground.

Kamaoa Wind Farms

As you go over a hill along this country drive, you suddenly come upon rows of huge high-tech windmills lined up in a pasture beside the road. With cattle grazing beneath, it's a surreal scene, and the unearthly whirring sound is what you might expect an alien invasion to sound like.

Each of these wind turbine generators can produce enough electricity for 100 families. It's thought, theoretically at least, that by using wind energy conversion, the state could produce more than enough electricity to meet its needs.

Four miles south of the windmills, you'll pass a few abandoned buildings wasting away. Until 1965, this was a Pacific Missile Range station that tracked missiles shot from California to the Marshall Islands in Micronesia.

Ka Lae

Ten miles down from the highway, South Point Rd forks and the road to the left goes to Kaulana boat ramp and a small cove.

The road to the right leads to the rugged coastal cliffs of South Point. The confluence of ocean currents just offshore makes this one of Hawaii's most bountiful fishing grounds. Locals fish from the cliffs, and many of the bolder ones precariously hang out over the edge of the steep lava ledges. Red snapper and ulua fish are particularly plentiful.

Ruins at Ka Lae include a heiau and a well-preserved fishing shrine. The outcrop on the west side of the fishing shrine is a good place to find some of the numerous canoe mooring holes that were long ago drilled into the rock ledges. Ancient Hawaiians used to anchor one end of a rope through the holes and tie the other end to their canoes. The strong currents would pull the canoes straight out to deep turbulent waters, where the enterprising Hawaiians could fish, still tethered to the shore, without getting swept out to sea.

The wooden platforms built on the edge of the cliffs have hoists and ladders that are used to get things to and from the small boats that anchor below.

There's a large unprotected hole in the lava directly behind the platforms where you can watch water rise and fall as the waves rush in. Keep an eye out for it, particularly if you have children with you, as it's not obvious until you're almost on top of it.

Walk down past the beacon and continue along the wall to get to the southernmost point in the USA. There are no markers here, no souvenir stands, just crashing surf and lots of wind.

Green Sands Beach

If you want to explore the area further, go back to the fork and take the road to Kaulana boat ramp. Beside the ramp you'll find pockets of green sand sparkling in the sun. These are olivine crystals worn from the lava cliffs by a relentless and pounding surf.

The highest concentration of green sand in Hawaii is at Green Sands Beach, a 2½-mile hike along the 4WD road heading northeast from the boat ramp. The walk is not difficult, though once you reach Green Sands you'll need to scramble down the cliffs to get to the beach. If you have a high-riding 4WD vehicle, you could consider driving in, but the road is rough and the drive takes about 25 minutes.

Pick a calm day to visit, as during periods of high surf the entire beach can be inundated. A couple of minutes beyond Kaulana boat ramp the trail passes the site of Kapalaoa, an ancient fishing village.

WAIOHINU

East of South Point Rd, Hwy 11 winds down into a pretty valley and the sleepy village of Waiohinu, which sits nestled beneath green hills.

The town's only 'tourist attraction' is a roadside monkeypod tree planted by author Mark Twain in 1866. The original tree fell in a typhoon in 1957, but hardy new trunks have sprung up and it's once again full grown. The tree is in the center of town, beside the restaurant named after Twain.

Also in the village center is Wong Yuen's Chevron gas station, which is open 7:30 am to 7 pm daily and has a small convenience store at the side.

Places to Stay & Eat

Shirakawa Motel (☎/fax 929-7462, PO Box 467, Naalehu, HI 96772), just off the highway in the very center of town, is a green, weather-beaten motel with a dozen basic units. The motel is plain but adequate, and the setting beneath the verdant hills is lovely. Rooms, which have private baths and twin beds, cost $30/35 for singles/doubles, $42 for a kitchenette unit.

Margo's Corner (☎/fax 929-9614, PO Box 447, Naalehu, HI 96772), at the home of Margo Hobbs and Philip Shaw, offers bicyclists and backpackers a place to pitch a tent and store gear while exploring the Kau area. Margo, who has a little co-op food store on site, enjoys meeting travelers from

Devastation Day

Kau was the center of devastation in the massive 1868 earthquake, the worst Hawaii has ever recorded. For five full days from March 27, the earth was rattled almost continuously by a series of tremors and quakes. Then, on the afternoon of April 2, the earth shook violently in every direction and an inferno broke loose from beneath the surface.

Those fortunate enough to be uphill watched as a rapidly moving river of lava poured down the hillsides and swallowed up everything in its path, including people, homes and cattle. Within minutes, the coast was inundated by tidal waves, and villages near the shore were swept away.

This deadly triple combination of earthquakes, lava flows and tidal waves permanently changed Kau's landscape. Huge cinder cones came crashing down the slopes, and one landslide buried an entire village. You can see the 1868 lava flow along the highway 2 miles west of the South Point turnoff. The old village of Kahuku lies beneath it.

THE BIG ISLAND

around the world. There are a couple of tent areas with pebbly mounds to allow drainage, or you can pitch your tent on the grass; tenters share a bathroom. No specific fee is charged, but the suggested donation is $25 per person, which includes breakfast and dinner with the family. Meals are vegetarian and incorporate produce from their organic garden.

There's also a new freestanding private cottage out back with a pentagon shape, cheery colors, private bath and queen bed; it costs $50/60 for singles/doubles, including two meals, with a two-night minimum. There are plans to add a wheelchair-accessible B&B room beneath the main house, which will be about the same price as the cottage. Smoking is not allowed. Margo's is on Wakea St, a couple of miles southwest of Waiohinu center, off Kamaoa Rd. Call ahead for reservations.

Macadamia Meadows Bed and Breakfast (☎/fax 929-8097, 888-929-8118, kaleena@ aloha.net, PO Box 756, Naalehu, HI 96772), half a mile south of Waiohinu center, is an upscale B&B on the 8-acre macadamia farm of Charlene and Cortney Cowan. Centered around an expansive contemporary home with open-beam ceilings, it has four guest rooms, all large with private entrance, lanai and cable TV. Rates range from $75 to $99, double occupancy, including a continental breakfast with homegrown fruit. A good choice at the lowest rate is the Mokupuni Room, which has a private bath, queen bed, microwave and refrigerator. There's a tennis court and a pool. For more information, visit the Cowans' website at www.stayhawaii.com/ macmed/macmed.html.

If you're hungry, *Mark Twain Square*, on Hwy 11 in the village center, is a reasonably priced restaurant that sits under the shade of Twain's monkeypod tree. The menu centers on hearty sandwiches, priced around $5. This spot is open 8:30 am to 6 pm on weekdays, 8:30 am to 4 pm on Saturday.

NAALEHU

Naalehu's claim to fame is being the southernmost town in the USA. It's 2 miles east of Waiohinu and a few inches to the south.

Modest as it is, Naalehu is the region's shopping center. It has a couple of grocery stores and eateries, a gas station, public library, post office, elementary school and the Kau police station.

Naalehu closes up early, so you shouldn't count on getting food or gas here if you're driving back to Kona from Hawaii Volcanoes National Park at night.

The best place to eat in town is the *Naalehu Fruit Stand* on Hwy 11, a reasonably priced produce stand, health food store, pizzeria and sandwich shop all in one. The food tastes good and everything sold here has been made on site. The ovens out back bake bread in the morning and pizzas to order ($8) starting at 11 am. The shop sells prepared sandwiches on homemade whole-wheat bread for $2.75, or you can get a submarine sandwich with the works for a bit more. Macadamia nut bars and other pastries cost about a dollar. The stand is open 9 am to 6:30 pm daily (to 5 pm on Sunday), and there are a few picnic tables near the front steps where you can eat.

WHITTINGTON BEACH PARK

Two miles beyond Naalehu there's a pull-off with a scenic lookout above Honuapo Bay. From the lookout you can see the cement pilings of the old Honuapo Pier, which was used for shipping sugar and hemp until the 1930s.

Honuapo Bay is the site of Whittington Beach Park; the turnoff is 1 mile from the lookout. Although there are tide pools to explore, there's really no beach at Whittington, and the ocean is usually too rough and dangerous for swimming. Endangered green sea turtles, which can sometimes be seen offshore, apparently have been frequenting these waters for a long time, as Honuapo means 'caught turtle' in Hawaiian.

Camping is allowed with a permit, and it's far enough from the highway to offer a little privacy. Overall, the park makes a pretty good choice for a county campground, but avoid setting up near the streetlight by the parking lot, as the light stays on all night and illuminates much of the lawn where tenting is allowed. Whittington has rest rooms and sheltered picnic tables, but there's no potable water.

For information on obtaining a camping permit, see Camping in the Accommodations section near the beginning of this chapter.

PUNALUU

Punaluu is a small bay with a black-sand beach. It was once the site of a major Hawaiian settlement, and in later days it became an important sugar port. The most popular section of the beach, the area fronting the now-closed Punaluu Black Sands Restaurant, is lined with coconut trees and backed by a duck pond. The ruins of the Pahala Sugar Company's old warehouse and pier are a short walk away at the north end of the beach. Sitting on a rise above it is the site of Kaneeleele Heiau.

Punaluu Beach Park, a county park just to the south, has rest rooms, showers, drinking water, picnic pavilions and camping. It's a flat, grassy area right on the beach and a nice place to camp, although it's very open with no privacy, and there can be a fair amount of activity here during the day. At night you can drift off to sleep to the sounds of crashing surf.

Be careful walking about, as the area's black sands are used as nesting sites by hawksbill turtles. Swimmers and snorkelers should be aware that the waters along the beach can have a strong undertow, and there's a dangerous rip current pulling out from the boat channel near the pier.

If heading east on Hwy 11, the first turnoff you'll reach in Punaluu is the entrance to SeaMountain, Kau's only condo complex. To get to the beach park, take the turnoff marked Punaluu Park, which is less than a mile farther along Hwy 11.

For information on obtaining a camping permit, see Camping in the Accommodations section near the beginning of this chapter.

Places to Stay & Eat

SeaMountain at Punaluu (☎ 928-6200, fax 928-8075, 800-344-7675, PO Box 460, Pahala, HI 96777) is a small condominium complex

with all the amenities you'd [...] a Kona condo, though there's [...] less to do in this area. The com[...] pool, tennis courts and a golf course.

The studios are big – almost as lar[...] one-bedroom units elsewhere – and som[...] of the one-bedroom units are two-level with cathedral ceilings. All have TVs and phones. Rates start at $90 for studios, $110 for one-bedroom units and $135 for two-bedroom units. Ocean views cost about $15 more, and all off-season rates are $10 lower. There's a two-day minimum stay.

Currently, the only place to eat at sleepy Punaluu is at the golf course pro shop at SeaMountain, which serves simple lunchtime sandwiches from 10:30 am to 2:30 pm. You're on your own for dinner.

PAHALA

Pahala, on the north side of Hwy 11, is really two little towns side by side. Down by the old mill is the original sugar town, with old dusty shacks, cars rusting in the yards and 'Beware of Dog' signs. In contrast, the north side of town has tract homes, gas stations, a hospital, a bank, a post office, a community center and a modern grocery mart.

Kau Agribusiness, which once had 15,000 acres of sugarcane planted for 15 miles in either direction from Pahala, closed its sugar mill in 1996. The company has now introduced groves of macadamia nut trees on much of the former cane land.

WOOD VALLEY

About 4 miles up the slopes from Pahala is remote Wood Valley and the Buddhist temple and retreat center of Nechung Dorje Drayang Ling. The temple, which has a quiet 25-acre setting, was built in the early 20th century by Japanese sugarcane laborers who lived in the valley.

In 1975 a Tibetan lama, Nechung Rinpoche, took up residence here, and in 1980 the Dalai Lama visited to dedicate the temple. Since that time, many Tibetan lamas have conducted programs here and the Dalai Lama himself returned to visit in 1994. In addition to its teachings of Buddhism, the center is also used by groups conducting

...her New Age
...'re interested,
... of upcoming

...*ng* (☎ 928-8539,
...ha.net, PO Box
... vns a two-story
building that has a .... ion hall and two
pleasant guest rooms on the upper floor. One
guest room has a queen platform bed and
Japanese decor, the other has a king bed and
Hawaiian decor; singles/doubles cost $40/50.
The ground floor also has a couple of simpler
rooms with twin beds for $5 less and a dor-
mitory for $25 a night. There's a two-day
minimum stay, and all rooms share a bath.
Guests must bring their own food; a kitchen
is available. There's a library of books on
Buddhist culture, and you're welcome to join
in morning services. For those seeking a
peaceful retreat, the temple is a special place.
To see pictures of the center, and gather
more information, visit www.planet-hawaii
.com/nechung.

PAHALA TO HAWAII VOLCANOES NATIONAL PARK

Hawaii Volcanoes National Park begins 12
miles from Pahala. Hwy 11 cuts across an 11-
mile stretch of the park. There's no charge to
drive through the park on the highway nor
to explore the Mauna Loa side of the park.

Kilauea's southwest rift zone runs through
this part of the Kau Desert, on the seaward
side of the road. The rift runs for 20 miles, all
the way from the summit of Kilauea down
to the coast.

You'll know you're getting closer to the
center of Hawaii Volcanoes National Park
when the signs start reading 'Caution, Fault
Zones. Watch for Cracks in Road.'

Before you reach the entrance to the
park, you'll pass Mauna Loa Rd. There are
tree molds near the turnoff, a hiking trail
through a native forest a mile farther up
and the trailhead to the Mauna Loa summit at the end of the road. All are detailed
in the following Hawaii Volcanoes National
Park section.

Hawaii Volcanoes National Park

Hawaii Volcanoes National Park is unique
among the US national parks. The huge
preserve contains two active volcanoes
and terrain ranging from tropical beaches to
the subarctic summit of Mauna Loa.

The centerpiece of the park is Kilauea
Caldera, the sunken center of Kilauea Volcano. This still-steaming crater, where molten
lava boils just beneath the surface, is said to
be the home of Madame Pele, goddess of
volcanoes. Both a foot trail and a paved road
circle the caldera's rim.

The park's landscape is awesome, with
dozens of craters and cinder cones, hills
piled high with pumice, and hardened rivers
of lava (complete with ripples and waves)
that have frozen rock-solid on the hillsides.
Here and there amid the seas of lava are
rain forests and fern groves that either have
been spared by lava flows or have since
grown over them. These islands of green
provide a protected habitat for a number of
native bird species.

The park is one of Hawaii's best places
for camping and hiking. It has 140 miles of
amazingly varied hiking trails and both drive-
up campsites and backcountry camping.

The park encompasses about a quarter
million acres of land – more than the entire
island of Molokai – and it's still growing.

Kilauea's southeast rift has been actively
flowing since 1983, destroying everything
in its path. The coastal road to Puna was
blocked by lava in 1988. The Wahaula Visitor Center on the south coast went under
the next year, and the entire village of Kalapana, with more than a hundred homes, was
buried in lava in 1990. Since that time, the
flows have crept farther west, engulfing
Kamoamoa Beach in 1994 and later claiming an additional mile of the road.

The current series of eruptions, which is
the longest in recorded history, has spewed
out more than 2 billion cubic yards of new
lava.

What you'll be able to see will depend on
the current volcanic activity. During the day,

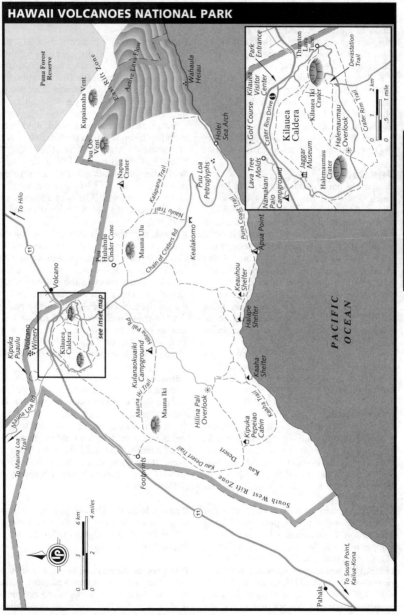

HAWAII VOLCANOES NATIONAL PARK

THE BIG ISLAND

Puna Forest Reserve

Kupaianaha Vent

East Rift Zone

Active Lava Flow

Wahaula Heiau

Puu Oo Vent

Napau Crater

Kalapana Trail

Naulu Trail

Puu Loa Petroglyphs

Holei Sea Arch

To Hilo

11

Puu Huluhulu Cinder Cone

Mauna Ulu

Chain of Craters Rd

Kealakomo

Apua Point

Puna Coast Trail

Volcano

Volcano Winery

see inset map

Keauhou Shelter

Halape Shelter

PACIFIC OCEAN

Kipuka Puaulu

Kilauea Caldera

Kaaha Shelter

Mauna Loa Rd

To Mauna Loa Trail

Kulanaokuaiki Campground

Mauna Iki Trail

Hilina Pali Rd

Kaaha Trail

Mauna Iki

Hilina Pali Overlook

Kipuka Pepeiao Cabin

Kau Desert

Footprints

Kau Desert Trail

South West Rift Zone

11

Pahala

To South Point, Kailua-Kona

N

6 km   4 miles
3   2
0   0

Inset map

Park Entrance

Thurston Lava Tube

Devastation Trail

Golf Course

Kilauea Visitor Center

Crater Rim Drive

Kilauea Iki Crater

Kilauea Caldera

Lava Tree Molds

Jaggar Museum

Namakani Paio Campground

Halemaumau Overlook

Halemaumau Crater

Crater Rim Trail

2 km   1 mile
1   .5
0   0

distant steam clouds from the vents can usually be seen clearly from the end of Chain of Craters Rd. After dark, the lava tubes on the mountainside glow red in the night sky, and lava lakes at the top of vents reflect light onto passing clouds.

Although many visitors expect to see lava fountains spurting up into the air, this is certainly the exception rather than the rule. But whenever Pele does put on one of her spectacular fireworks displays, cars stream in from all directions. In Hawaii, people generally run *to* volcanoes, not away from them.

Orientation

The park's main road is Crater Rim Drive, which circles the moonscape sights of Kilauea Caldera. It's possible to see the drive-up sites in an hour – and if that's all the time you have it's unquestionably worth it. Still, it's far better to give yourself a good three hours to allow time for a few short walks and stops at the visitor center and museum.

The park's other scenic drive is the Chain of Craters Rd, which leads south 20 miles to the coast, ending at the site of the most recent lava activity. Allow about three hours down and back to stop at all the scenic points along the way.

While you can get a good sense of the place in one full day, it would be easy to spend days, if not weeks, exploring this vast and varied park.

Information

The park's 24-hour hotline (☎ 985-6000) has recorded information on current volcanic activity and directions to the best viewing sites. If you have specific questions, you can speak to a staff member directly by calling the visitor center (☎ 985-6017) between 7:45 am and 5 pm.

You can obtain the main park brochure in advance, along with camping and hiking information if you specifically request it, by writing to Hawaii Volcanoes National Park, PO Box 52, Hawaii National Park, HI 96718. The park's website at www.nps.gov/havo also offers a wealth of information.

If you're interested in making a three-month commitment to work in the park, see Volunteer Programs in the Getting There & Away chapter in the front of the book.

Fees The park entrance fee of $10 per vehicle is good for multiple entries within a seven-day period. Visitors entering on foot or by bicycle through the check station are charged $5 each. The check station is staffed from about 8 am to 4:30 pm daily, although the park is open 24 hours.

National park passes are also sold here, including an annual pass for $50 that covers Haleakala on Maui and all other US National Park Service sites. US citizens with disabilities can obtain a free Golden Access pass, and those age 62 or older can buy a Golden Age pass for $10; both allow unlimited free access to all US National Parks.

Access for the Disabled Many of the park sites – including the Kilauea Visitor Center, Jaggar Museum, Volcano Art Center and Volcano House hotel – are wheelchair accessible. And many of the pull-ups along Crater Rim Drive and the Chain of Craters Rd are free of curbs. A few of the park's shorter trails, including Devastation Trail and an eastern section of the Crater Rim Trail near Waldron Ledge, have been converted to make them wheelchair accessible.

Climate The park has a wide range of climatic conditions that vary with elevation, and the weather can be moody as well. Rain and fog move in quickly, and on any given day it can change from hot and dry to cool and damp. Near Kilauea Caldera, temperatures average about 15°F cooler than in Kona. It's a good idea to wear clothing in layers. Get a recorded weather forecast by calling ☎ 961-5582.

Road Closures During periods of prolonged drought, both Mauna Loa Rd and Hilina Pali Rd are subject to closure due to fire-hazard conditions.

Dangers & Annoyances Hawaiian volcanoes are seldom violent, and most of the lava that flows from cracks in the rift zones is slow moving. The eruptions don't spew

Volcanic Formations

Hawaii's volcanoes are shield volcanoes, formed by repeated gentle eruptions. The mountains of lava build up over time, as thin layers are deposited one on top of another. As they get higher and wider, long cracks break open down their gently stretched slopes. These are called fault zones, or rift zones, and lava eruptions may come from these cracks (as is currently the case with Kilauea) as well as from the summit crater.

Craters are formed when volcanic hills release their lava and collapse back into themselves.

Pahoehoe and *aa* are Hawaiian words that are now used worldwide to describe the earth's two major types of lava. Pahoehoe refers to the rivers of lava that flow smooth and unbroken. When pahoehoe begins to harden, it twists into ropelike coils and swirls, as the outer skin cools and stiffens while the hotter lava underneath continues to move a little.

Aa is rough and jumbled lava that moves so slowly that the tip of the flow hardens. It's only the molten lava pushing from behind that keeps the flow moving, with the hard lava at the front piling up and falling over itself, slowing rolling and clunking its way along.

out a lot of ash or poisonous gases either, which is what accounts for most volcano-related deaths in other parts of the world.

There have been only two known violent explosions of Hawaiian volcanoes – both from Kilauea, in 1790 and in 1924. The only direct fatality from a volcanic eruption in the 20th century was during the 1924 explosion, when a boulder was tossed onto the leg of a photographer who then bled to death.

People with respiratory and heart conditions, pregnant women, infants and young children are advised to avoid the areas where sulfur fumes are most highly concentrated, including Sulphur Banks and the Halemaumau Overlook.

Other potential hazards include deep cracks in the earth and thin lava crust, which may mask hollows and lava tubes. If you stay on marked trails, you shouldn't have any problems. All park warning signs should be taken seriously.

CRATER RIM DRIVE

Crater Rim Drive is a field trip in vulcanology. This amazing 11-mile loop road skirts the rim of Kilauea Caldera and has marked stops at steam vents and crater lookouts. From roadside parking areas, short trails lead through various landscapes, including a lava tube, a native rain forest and a forest devastated by pumice. There are also trailheads for longer hikes into and around the caldera.

Natural forces have rerouted Crater Rim Drive on a few occasions. Earthquakes in both 1975 and 1983 rattled it hard enough to knock sections of the road down into the caldera.

The most interesting stops are at Jaggar Museum, Halemaumau Overlook, Devastation Trail and Thurston Lava Tube. If you take Crater Rim Drive in a counterclockwise direction, you'll start off at the visitor center.

Unlike the Chain of Craters Rd, Crater Rim Drive is relatively level, making it a good road for cyclists.

Kilauea Visitor Center

The visitor center is a good place to get oriented to the park. Rangers here have the latest information on volcanic activity, interpretive programs, guided walks, backcountry trail conditions and the like. They have free pamphlets for a few of the park trails and sell an excellent selection of books on volcanoes, hiking and park flora.

If you're traveling with children five to 12, ask about the junior ranger program, which offers a little self-guided project that children can work on as they tour the park.

The center contains a small theater where a 25-minute film on the geology of Kilauea is played on the hour from 9 am to 4 pm.

Although the films change periodically, footage usually includes flowing rivers of lava and some of the most spectacular lava fountains ever to be caught on film.

In addition, commercial videos of the most recent eruptions run continuously in the center's tiny museum, where you'll also find a few volcano-related exhibits. The center is open 7:45 am to 5 pm daily.

Volcano Art Center

The Volcano Art Center (☎ 967-7511), right next door to the Kilauea Visitor Center, sells island pottery, paintings, weavings, wood-work, sculpture and other arts and crafts. The pieces are of high quality, with many one-of-a-kind items, and it's worth a visit just to admire the solid workmanship, even if you're not up for shopping.

The center is in a former Volcano House lodge, built in 1877. The nonprofit organization that runs it offers workshops on crafts and hula and sponsors concerts, plays and other activities. It's open 9 am to 5 pm daily.

Sulphur Banks

The first stop beyond the art center is the Sulphur Banks, where the day-glo colors and piles of steaming rocks look like a landscape from another planet.

This is one of many areas where Kilauea lets off steam, releasing hundreds of tons of sulfuric gases daily. As the steam reaches the surface, it deposits sulfur around the mouths of the vents, giving them a froth of fluores-cent yellow crystals. The pervasive smell of rotten eggs is from the hydrogen sulfide wafting from the vents.

Steam Vents

There are a few open, nonsulfurous steam vents at the next pull-off, although they're not particularly remarkable. Rainwater that sinks into the earth is heated by the hot rocks below and rises back up as steam.

More interesting is the two-minute walk beyond the vents out to a part of the crater rim aptly called **Steaming Bluff**. The cooler it is, the more steam there'll be. A plaque on the rim tells a legend about the struggles between Pele and the pig-god Kamapuaa.

Jaggar Museum

This museum is worth a visit both for its dis-plays and for the fine view of Halemaumau Crater. Halemaumau sits within Kilauea Caldera and is sometimes referred to as the 'crater within the crater.' Detailed interpre-tive plaques at the lookout explain the geo-logical workings of volcanoes. When the weather is clear, there's also a good view of Mauna Loa to the west, 20 miles away.

The Jaggar Museum is open 8:30 am to 5 pm daily. It has photo displays, a section on Pele, seismographs, tiltmeters and printed updates showing the current status of vol-canic activity.

Drivers should be careful of the nene that congregate in the museum parking lot and at other tourist stops on the south side of the caldera. The nene move slowly and have a suicidal tendency of walking up to moving cars, looking for handouts. Feeding the nene contributes to the road-deaths of these endangered birds and is strictly prohibited.

After leaving the museum, you'll pass the **Southwest Rift**, where you can stop and take a look at the wide fissure slicing across the earth.

Halemaumau Overlook

The next attraction is Halemaumau Over-look, which is perched on the crater rim, just a five-minute walk from the parking area. For at least a hundred years (from 1823, when missionary William Ellis first recorded the sight in writing), Halemau-mau was a boiling lake of lava that alter-nately rose and fell, overflowing its banks and then receding.

This fiery lake attracted people from all over the world. Some observers compared it to the fires of hell, while others saw prim-eval creation. Mark Twain wrote of staring down at

circles and serpents and streaks of lightning all twined and wreathed and tied together....I have seen Vesuvius since, but it was a mere toy, a child's volcano, a soup kettle, compared to this.

In 1924, seeping water touched off a massive steam explosion that blew up the lava lake, causing big boulders and mud to rain down and setting off a lightning storm. When it was over, the crater had doubled in size and the lava activity had ceased. The crust has since cooled, although the crater still steams and the area is pungent with the smell of sulfur.

All of the Big Island is Pele's territory, but Halemaumau is her home. During special ceremonies, the hula is performed in her honor here, and throughout the year those wishing to appease Pele leave flowers, coins and other offerings at the crater rim.

The Halemaumau Overlook is at the start of the **Halemaumau Trail**, which runs 3 miles across Kilauea Caldera to the visitor center (detailed in the later Hiking Trails section). Although few people who aren't hiking the full trail venture past the overlook, it's an easy half-mile walk to the site of a 1982 lava flow that is well worth the 30 minutes it takes to walk there and back. The spewed lava along the trail has interesting textures and provides an eerie sense of the earth's raw power.

Devastation Trail

After the Halemaumau Overlook, Crater Rim Drive continues across the barren Kau Desert and then through the fallout area of the 1959 eruption of Kilauea Iki Crater. At that time, ash and pumice blown southwest of the crater buried a mile of Crater Rim Drive 8 feet deep, and the road had to be plowed by tractors, much like clearing snow after a blizzard.

The Devastation Trail is a half-mile walk across a former rain forest devastated by cinder and pumice from that eruption. Everything green was wiped out. What remains today are dead ohia trees, stripped bare and sun-bleached white, standing stark against the black landscape.

The trail is paved and has parking lots on each end. The prominent cinder cone along the way is Puu Puai, 'Gushing Hill,' formed during the 1959 eruption. The northeast end of the trail looks down into Kilauea Iki Crater.

Chain of Craters Rd intersects Crater Rim Drive opposite the west side parking area for the Devastation Trail.

Trickery & Tears

The Jaggar Museum is at Uwekahuna Bluff, the site of an infamous hut that once sat right on the edge of the crater. According to legend, a local *kahuna* (sorceror) is said to have tricked people into entering the building, where they slipped through a false-bottomed floor to the crater pit below. Tired of the trickery, locals burned the hut to the ground. When he saw the charred remains, the kahuna's eyes welled with *uwe* (tears), and henceforth the site was renamed Uwekahuna.

Thurston Lava Tube

On the east side of the Chain of Craters Rd intersection, Crater Rim Drive passes through the rain forest of native tree ferns and ohia that covers Kilauea's windward slope.

The Thurston Lava Tube Trail is an enjoyable 15-minute loop walk that starts out in ohia forest, passes through an impressive lava tube and then enters a fern grove. The cibotium tree ferns here grow to a height of 20 feet.

Lava tubes are formed when the outer crust of a river of lava starts to harden but the liquid lava beneath the surface continues to flow on through. After the flow has drained out, the hard shell remains. Thurston Lava Tube is a grand example – it's tunnel-like and almost big enough to run a train through.

You'll likely hear a lot of birdsong along this walk. The *apapane*, a native honey-creeper, is easy to spot at the upper end of the trail. It has a red body and silvery-white underside and flies from flower to flower, taking nectar from the yellow blossoms of the mamane tree and the red pom-pom-like flowers of the ohia tree.

Kilauea Iki Crater

When Kilauea Iki burst open in a fiery inferno in November 1959, the whole crater floor turned into a bubbling pool of molten lava. Its fountains reached record heights of 1900 feet, lighting the evening sky with a

Kilauea Meltdown

The Jaggar Museum, overlooking Kilauea Caldera, is named for Thomas A Jaggar, former head geologist at the Massachusetts Institute of Technology (MIT) and the first scientist to undertake in-depth studies of Kilauea. Jaggar led the group of geologists who lowered the first thermometer into Halemaumau's lava lake in the summer of 1911. The thermometer registered 1832°F before melting.

Today the Hawaiian Volcano Observatory, adjacent to the Jaggar Museum, has Kilauea completely wired, making it the most thoroughly studied volcano anywhere in the world. The observatory is not open to casual visitors, but you can view the goings-on at the observatory's website, www.hvo.wr.usgs.gov.

bright orange glow for miles around. At its peak, it gushed out 2 million tons of lava an hour.

From Kilauea Iki Overlook there's a good view of the mile-wide crater below. Today a trail runs across the crater floor. The hike is not unlike walking on ice – here, too, there's a lake below the hardened surface, although in this case it's molten lava, not water. For more information, see Hiking Trails later in this section.

CHAIN OF CRATERS RD

Chain of Craters Rd winds 20 miles down the southern slopes of Kilauea Volcano, ending abruptly at a lava flow on the Puna Coast. It's a good paved two-lane road, although there's no gas, food, water or other services along the way.

From the road you'll have striking vistas of the coastline far below, and for miles the predominant view is of long fingers of lava reaching down to the sea.

In some places the road slices through lava and elsewhere the lava's paved over it. You'll see both aa lava, which is crusty and rough, and pahoehoe lava, which is as shiny

and black as fresh tar. You can sometimes also find thin filaments of volcanic glass known as Pele's hair in the lava cracks and crevices.

In addition to endless lava expanses, the road takes in an impressive collection of sights, including a handful of craters that you can literally pull up to the rims of and peer into. Some are so new there's no sign of life, while others are thickly forested with ohia lehua, wild orchids and ferns.

Chain of Craters Rd once connected through to Hwys 130 and 137, allowing traffic between the volcano and Hilo via Puna. Lava flows closed the road in 1969, but by 1979 it was back in service, rerouted slightly. Flows from Kilauea's active east rift cut the link again in 1988 and have since buried a 9-mile stretch of the road.

Hilina Pali Rd

Hilina Pali Rd starts 2¼ miles down Chain of Craters Rd and leads 3½ miles to the new Kulanaokuaiki Campground. It's another 5½ miles to the end of the road and the site of Hilina Pali Overlook, a lookout at 2280 feet with a view of the southeast coast. The end of the road is the trailhead for the Kau Desert Trail and for the Kaaha and Hilina Pali Trails, which lead down to the coast. They are all hot, dry, backcountry trails.

Mauna Ulu

In 1969, eruptions from Kilauea's east rift began building a new lava shield, which eventually rose 400 feet above its surroundings. It was named Mauna Ulu, 'Growing Mountain.'

By the time the flow stopped in 1974, it had covered 10,000 acres of parkland and added 200 acres of new land to the coast.

It also buried a 12-mile section of Chain of Craters Rd in lava up to 300 feet deep. A half-mile portion of the old road survives, and you can follow it to the lava flow by taking the turnoff on the left, 3½ miles down Chain of Craters Rd. Just beyond this is Mauna Ulu itself.

The **Puu Huluhulu Overlook Trail**, a 3-mile roundtrip hike, begins at the parking area, crosses over lava flows from 1974 and

THE BIG ISLAND

climbs to the top of a 150-foot cinder cone, where there's a panoramic view that includes Mauna Loa, Mauna Kea, Kilauea and the east rift zone. Expect the hike, which is of moderate difficulty, to take about two hours roundtrip.

As you continue down Chain of Craters Rd, you'll be passing over Mauna Ulu's extensive flows.

Kealakomo

About halfway along the road, at an elevation of 2000 feet, is Kealakomo, a covered shelter with picnic tables and a superb ocean view. This would be a great place to unpack a lunch, at least on days when the wind's not whipping.

After Kealakomo, the road begins to descend along a series of winding switchbacks, some deeply cut through lava flows.

Puu Loa Petroglyphs

The Puu Loa Trail leads 1 mile to a field of petroglyphs carved into the lava by early Hawaiians. The site, which is along an ancient trail that once ran between Kau and Puna, has one of the largest concentrations of petroglyphs in Hawaii. A boardwalk runs along a large group of them and offers some fine photo opportunities. Puu Loa (Long Hill) was also a place where Hawaiians brought the umbilical cords of their babies in the hope that burying the cords here would bring their children long lives.

The marked trailhead begins on the Chain of Craters Rd midway between the 16- and 17-mile markers. It makes for an interesting, 75-minute roundtrip walk that's suitable for all ages.

Holei Sea Arch

About 2 1/2 miles after the petroglyphs and just before the 19-mile marker, look for the sign marking the Holei Sea Arch. This rugged section of the coast has sharply eroded lava cliffs, called Holei Pali, which are constantly being pounded by crashing surf.

The high rock arch carved out of one of the cliffs is impressive, although the wave action has numbered its days. The ocean, which is a strikingly deep blue, provides a picturesque backdrop to the scene.

End of the Road

Chain of Craters Rd ends at the coast, where hardened lava flows seal off the road. From around 1 to 7 pm, park rangers staff a simple station where you can get information. They also usually have inexpensive flashlights and bottled water for sale.

In recent times, most of the lava flowing from Kilauea's east rift has been coming out of the Puu Oo Vent. When the molten lava, which is carried down the hillsides in lava tubes, hits the ocean, it heats the water to a boil and produces an immense acidic steam plume.

Park rangers have marked a trail over the hardened lava to an observation point that offers a good, albeit somewhat distant, view of the billowing coastal steam cloud. After dark, surface flows and the steam cloud take on an orange glow. The trail is only about 300 yards, but give yourself about 30 minutes roundtrip. The walk is over crisp, shiny lava, and you need to watch your footing, as there are sharp jags as well as cracks and holes in the brittle surface. Wear sturdy shoes with good traction. If you plan to visit the area after dark to observe the red glow, you'll need a flashlight, as there are no artificial lights in the area.

For information on hiking even closer to the action, see the related boxed text.

MAUNA LOA RD

Mauna Loa Rd leads off Hwy 11 about 2 1/4 miles west of the visitor center. The road provides access to the eastern approach of Mauna Loa, the world's highest active volcano. Mauna Loa has erupted more than 18 times in the past century; the last eruption began in March 1984 and lasted 21 days.

The Mauna Loa Trail, which climbs the slopes of Mauna Loa, begins at the end of the road, 13 1/2 miles from Hwy 11. For further details, see Hiking Trails, below.

Near the start of Mauna Loa Rd there's a turnoff to some **lava tree molds**. These tube-like holes were formed when a lava flow engulfed the rain forest that stood here.

Getting Closer to the Flow

Giving in to visitor demands, the park service somewhat reluctantly allows people to hike from the end of Chain of Craters Rd to the active lava flow.

It's a long strenuous trek over hardened lava, and there's no established trail. As the coastline is unstable, hikers should stay about a quarter mile inland. The walk eventually leads close to the point where the lava flows into the sea, which is an impressive sight. For safety reasons, the park service suggests getting no closer to it than half a mile.

In all, the roundtrip hike covers a distance of about 6 miles and takes around 3½ to four hours. It's most interesting to begin late in the afternoon in order to view the orange glow after dark – however, it's inadvisable to be on the trail after sunset unless you have a knowledgeable guide. If you're interested in joining a guided trek, Arnott's Lodge makes the hike a couple of days a week; see Places to Stay in Hilo for contact information.

The trail is not only unmarked, it's unpatrolled and a potentially dangerous walk. During the day, the black lava reflects the sun's heat and the temperature commonly gets into the high 90s (°F); there's no shade along the way.

No matter how you do the hike, you'll need to be well prepared. The park service suggests that each person bring a minimum of 3 quarts of water, a flashlight (you can sometimes purchase them at the ranger's trailer), a first-aid kit in case of falls on jagged lava, sunscreen, sturdy boots and long pants.

It's also a good idea to bring a cotton handkerchief or bandanna to cover your mouth and nose for protection from the drifting steam clouds that can contain fine glasslike particles.

While the steam plumes are impressive to see from a distance, they are extremely dangerous to view up close. The explosive clash between seawater and 2100°F molten lava can spray scalding water hundreds of feet into the air and can throw chunks of lava up to a half mile inland.

The lava crust itself forms in unstable ledges called lava benches, which often collapse into the ocean without warning. Lava benches aren't just small coastal outcroppings – some as large as a city block have been known to break off, and a number of people have been hurt by attempting to get too close to the shoreline. In 1993, a collapsing lava bench sent one islander to his fiery death and burned more than a dozen people in the ensuing steam explosion. In March 1999, the scene almost repeated itself when seven onlookers scattered to safety after a series of explosions began blasting lava 'bombs' into the air and then collapsed the 25-acre lava bench they'd been standing on.

Volcanic activity and viewing conditions are always subject to change, so you should contact the park visitor center for the latest information.

Because the trees were so waterlogged, the lava hardened around them instead of burning them on contact. As the trees disintegrated, deep holes where the trunks once stood were left in the ground.

Some of the molds are very close to the parking lot, making it easy to get a quick glimpse.

Kipuka Puaulu

Kipuka Puaulu, a unique sanctuary for native flora and fauna, is about 1$1/2$ miles up Mauna Loa Rd. The mile-long **Kipuka Puaulu Loop Trail** runs through this 100-acre oasis of Hawaiian forest.

About 400 years ago, a major lava flow from Mauna Loa's northeast rift covered most of the surrounding area. Pele spared this bit of land when the flow parted, creating an island forest in a sea of lava. In Hawaiian, it's known as a *kipuka*.

Kipuka Puaulu is a tiny ecopreserve of rare endemic plants, insects and birds. The lava that surrounds the kipuka has served as a protective barrier against intruding foreign species.

Koa is the largest of the trees here. The young koa trees have fernlike leaves that are replaced with flat, crescent-shaped leaf stalks as the koa matures and rises above the forest floor. The tree provides a habitat for the ferns and climbing peperomia that take root in its moist bark.

Kipuka Puaulu is delightfully quiet, except for the chirping of birds. Native species include the inquisitive elepaio and three honeycreepers – the *amakihi*, *apapane* and *iiwi*. All of these birds are sparrow size and brightly colored. The honeycreepers have slender curved beaks that enable them to drink nectar from the flowers of native trees.

Also along the trail is a lava tube in the dark depths of which a unique species of big-eyed spider was discovered in 1973.

HIKING TRAILS

The park has an extensive network of hiking trails, rising from sea level to over 13,000 feet. The hikes range from short, easy walks to serious backcountry treks. Trails strike out in a number of directions – across crater floors, down to secluded beaches, across the Kau Desert, through native forests and up to snowcapped summit of Mauna Loa.

In addition to the hikes that follow, information on a number of shorter hikes – Devastation Trail, Thurston Lava Tube Trail, Puu Loa Trail, Puu Huluhulu Overlook Trail and Kipuka Puaulu Loop Trail – is given earlier in this section.

Crater Rim Trail

The Crater Rim Trail is an 11-mile hiking trail that runs roughly parallel to Crater Rim Drive. On the north side, the trail skirts the crater rim, while on the south side, it runs outside the paved road.

Because the vehicle road is designed to take in the main sights, you'll actually miss a few of them by hiking. If you have wheels of some sort, you might want to consider riding around the crater rim and saving your hiking legs for trails into areas inaccessible by car or bike.

Halemaumau Trail

Diagonally across the road from the visitor center are signs marking the way to a number of trails, including the Halemaumau Trail.

The first section of the Halemaumau Trail passes briefly through a moist ohia forest, with tall ferns and flowering ginger. It then descends about 500 feet to the floor of Kilauea Caldera and continues for 3 miles across the surface of this still-active volcano.

In ancient times, the caldera was much deeper, but in the past century overflows from Halemaumau Crater and eruptions from the caldera floor have built it up.

The process is easy to visualize, as the trail crosses flow after flow, beginning with one from 1974 and continuing over flows from 1885, 1894, 1954, 1971 and 1982, each distinguished by a different shade of black. The trail is marked with *ahu*, stone cairns created with piled lava rocks.

Shortly after breakfast on April 30, 1982, geologists at the Hawaiian Volcano Observatory watched as their seismographs and tiltmeters unexpectedly warned of an imminent eruption. The park service quickly closed off Halemaumau Trail and cleared

THE BIG ISLAND

Ohelo Berries

Ohelo, a bush about 2 feet high with clusters of bright red berries, is one of the early takers to lava. It can be found many places in the park, including near the Halemaumau Overlook. These low shrubs are from the heath family, related to blueberries and cranberries. Like their relatives, ohelo berries are tart but edible. In old Hawaii, the berries were said to personify Pele's sister Hiiaka and were sometimes presented as an offering to Pele.

hikers from the crater floor. Before noon a half-mile fissure broke open in the crater and began spewing out a million cubic meters of lava!

Although there hasn't been another major eruption here since 1982, on March 24, 1996, the tiltmeters again indicated that the caldera was inflating rapidly. However, that crisis ended the same day when the magma suddenly shifted downrift to the Puu Oo Vent, allowing Kilauea Caldera to subside without erupting.

Halemaumau Trail ends about 3½ miles from the visitor center at Halemaumau Overlook. Needless to say, there's no shade on the trail and it can be very hot. Take water with you, as there's none at the lookout.

Kilauea Iki Trail

When Kilauea Iki Crater exploded in 1959, its magnificent lava fountains set a new height record of 1900 feet. When the eruption finally settled, a huge expanse of the park southwest of the crater was buried deep in ash. Today, the crater floor is crossed by a popular hike.

Kilauea Iki Trail begins near the parking lot of the Thurston Lava Tube and descends 400 feet to the crater floor. From there it goes clear across the mile-long crater, passing the main vent on the way. The crater floor is still steaming, and there's molten lava beneath the hardened surface.

After you ascend the crater wall on the far side, you'll be on Byron Ledge, the ledge that separates Kilauea Iki from Kilauea Caldera. By looping around to the right, you can get back to the parking lot via the Crater Rim Trail, which skirts the north rim of Kilauea Iki. Altogether this loop hike is about 4 miles long, takes two to three hours to walk and is of moderate to challenging difficulty.

If you want to check it out before hiking, there's a drive-up lookout half a mile north of the Thurston Lava Tube.

Footprints Trail

The Footprints Trail is the beginning of the Mauna Iki Trail, which leads to a network of trails through the Kau Desert. The trailhead is between the 37- and 38-mile markers on Hwy 11, 9 miles southwest of Kilauea Visitor Center. The footprints are an easy three-quarter-mile hike in from the highway.

In 1790, a violent and massive explosion at Kilauea wiped out a regiment of warriors who were retreating to Kau after attacking Kamehameha's sacred Waipio Valley. The men were literally stopped in their tracks, suffocated by a rare cloud of poisonous gases. A shower of hot mud and ashes hardened around them, leaving a permanent cast of their footprints.

Two hundred years later, you can still count the toes in a few of the prints – although it takes some imagination these days, as most of the trailside footprints have been seriously damaged by vandals. Still, it's a pleasant walk.

Mauna Loa Trail

The Mauna Loa Trail begins at the end of Mauna Loa Rd, 13½ miles north of Hwy 11 and about an hour's drive from the visitor center. Overnight hikers are required to register at the visitor center, which also has the latest information on trail and cabin conditions.

This is a rugged 18-mile trail that ascends 6600 feet. The ascent is gradual, but the elevation makes it a serious hike and it takes a minimum of three days.

Two simple cabins are available to hikers on a first-come, first-served basis: Red Hill cabin has eight bunks with mattresses, and Mauna Loa summit cabin has 12.

The trail rises out of an ohia forest and above the tree line, climbing 7 miles to Red Hill at 10,035 feet. This leg of the hike takes four to five hours. From Red Hill there are fine views of Mauna Kea to the north and Haleakala on Maui to the northwest.

It's 11 miles and a full day's hike from Red Hill to the summit cabin at 13,250 feet. The summit has a subarctic climate, and temperatures normally drop to freezing at night year-round. Winter snowstorms can last a few days, bringing snow packs as deep as 9 feet. Occasionally, snow falls as low as Red Hill and covers the upper end of the trail.

It is important to acclimatize, as altitude sickness is not uncommon. Common symptoms are headache, nausea and shortness of breath. For minor symptoms, deep breathing brings some relief, as does lying down with your head lower than your feet. If the symptoms are more serious, get to a lower elevation immediately.

Hypothermia from the cold and wind is another hazard. A good windproof jacket, wool sweater, winter-rated sleeping bag and rain gear are all essential. Sunglasses and sunscreen will provide protection from snow glare and the strong rays of the sun that prevail in the thin atmosphere.

Backcountry Hiking & Camping

Hiking shelters and simple cabins are available along some of the park's longer backcountry trails. There's no fee to use them.

In addition to the two cabins along the Mauna Loa Trail, you'll find a small cabin at Kipuka Pepeiao along the Kau Desert Trail and primitive three-walled shelters on the coast at Keauhou, Halape and Kaaha. All have pit toilets and limited catchment water that should be treated before drinking. The

THE BIG ISLAND

Fragile Paradise

Halape was an idyllic beachfront campground bordered by coconut trees until November 29, 1975, when the strongest earthquake in 100 years shook the Big Island. Just before dawn, rock slides from the upper slopes sent most of the 36 campers running toward the sea, where the coastline suddenly sank. As the beach submerged beneath their feet, a series of tsunamis swept the campers up, carrying them first out to sea and then tossing them back up on shore. Miraculously, only two people died.

The earthquake left a fine sandy cove inland of the former beach, and despite its turbulent past, Halape is still a lovely spot. Swimming is good in the protected cove, but there are strong currents in the open ocean beyond.

Halape is one of only eight Big Island nesting sites for the endangered hawksbill sea turtle. The park service, which is trying to balance the need for protecting the turtles' habitat with visitor accessibility issues, has relocated the campsites east of the cove in an area that's unsuitable for nesting.

Campers should be careful not to set up tents in areas that are marked as turtle nesting sites; keep sites clean of food scraps, which attract cats and mongooses that prey upon turtle eggs and hatchlings; and minimize the use of night lighting, which can disorient the turtles. Hawksbill turtles also nest at the park's Keauhou and Apua Point backcountry camping areas.

current level of water at each site is posted on a board at the visitor center. Halape and Keauhou, the most popular of the coastal campsites, are about an 8-mile hike along the Keauhou Trail from the Chain of Craters Rd.

There are also two primitive camping areas that have pit toilets but no shelter or water. The seaside Apua Point campsite is along the Puna Coast Trail, about 6½ miles west of the Puuloa parking area off Chain of Craters Rd. The Napau Crater campsite, just 3 miles west of the erupting Puu Oo Vent, is reached via a 5¼-mile hike on the Naulu and Kalapana Trails.

All overnight hikers are required to register and obtain a free permit at the visitor center before heading out. Permits are issued on a first-come, first-served basis, beginning no earlier than noon on the day before your intended hike. There's a three-day limit at each backcountry camping site, and each site has a limit of eight to 16 campers.

Essential backpacking equipment listed by the park service for any of the backcountry trails includes a first-aid kit, a flashlight with extra batteries, a minimum of four quarts of water, an extra stash of food, a compass, a mirror (for signaling), broken-in boots, complete rain gear, a cooking stove with fuel (open fires are prohibited), sunscreen and a hat. Note that the desert and coastal trails can make for extremely hot hiking.

More information on backcountry hiking, including a basic trail map, can be obtained at the visitor center or by writing to Hawaii Volcanoes National Park, PO Box 52, Hawaii National Park, HI 96718.

VOLCANO

The village of Volcano, about a mile east of the park, has a couple of general stores, a place to gas up, a post office, a few eateries and a growing number of B&B-type places to stay.

There's also the little **Volcano Winery** at the end of the golf course road, a mile north of Hwy 11, which offers samples of Volcano's first wines. Although the winery is still in its infancy, the curious may want to stop by the tasting room to try its ambitious vintages, which come in flavors such as volcano blush and guava chablis. It's open 10 am to 5 pm daily.

Places to Stay

In Volcano *Holo Holo In* (☎ 967-7950, fax 967-8025, holoholo@interpac.net, 19-4036 Kalani Honua Rd, PO Box 784, Volcano, HI 96785), affiliated with Hostelling International, is a small hostel and lodge run by Yabuki Satoshi, a former backpacker who traveled the globe before settling in Volcano. The house has four large bedrooms. Two of the rooms have five beds each and are used as dorms; the dorm cost is $15 for hostel members and $17 for nonmembers. The other two are private rooms and cost $40 for two people and $15 more for each additional person. There's a shared kitchen, complimentary coffee and tea, a TV room, laundry facilities and a sauna that can be used for a small fee. Yabuki works during the day as an electrician, so it's best to call after 4:30 pm. Holo Holo is on Kalani Honua Rd; to get there, take Volcano Rd into the village center and turn north onto Haunani Rd near Volcano Store, then take the third left – the inn is right after the old Japanese school. For more information, visit the hostel's website at www.enable.org/holoholo.

At *My Island B&B* (☎ 967-7216, fax 967-7719, myisland@ilhawaii.net, PO Box 100, Volcano, HI 96785), Gordon and Joann Morse rent out three bedrooms with shared baths in their home starting at $45/65 singles/doubles, including breakfast. There are also a couple of $85 studio units adjacent to the house that have kitchens, TVs, phones and bathrooms. The B&B is a quarter mile east of Kilauea Lodge, on the left after Wright Rd. Gordon enjoys piling guests high with information on the Big Island – which he proclaims to be 'the *only* Hawaiian Island worth visiting' – and the living room is stacked with books on volcanoes, a few written by former guests.

Volcano Bed and Breakfast is an unpretentious B&B on Keonelehua Rd at the north side of the village center. It has six guest rooms, ranging from a small room with a double bed for $45 to larger rooms with queen beds for $65. Bathrooms are shared.

There's a common space with a fireplace, TV and VCR, and a kitchen that guests can use. The rates include a buffet-style continental breakfast. Check-in is at *Chalet Kilauea* (☎ 967-7786, 800-736-7140, fax 967-8660, *innkeeper@volcano-hawaii.com, PO Box 998, Volcano, HI 96785)*, an upscale B&B on Wright Rd, also in the village center. If you want to splurge, the Chalet's rooms are among the most luxurious in Volcano and cost from $135 to $395. For more information, visit the website www.volcano-hawaii.com.

Hale Ohia (☎ 967-7986, 800-455-3803, fax 967-8610, *info@haleohia.com, PO Box 758, Volcano, HI 96785)*, a B&B on an old estate, has pleasant grounds that include a hot tub in the backyard. There are seven rental units in all. Three of the units are in a two-story building (formerly the gardener's cottage) at the side of the main house. On the top floor there's a contemporary three-bedroom unit with a full kitchen ($115), while the 1st floor has two rooms ($85 each) with refrigerators and coffeemakers but no cooking facilities. There are also two guest bedrooms in the main estate house – a suite for $85 and a master bedroom for $125 – and two freestanding one-bedroom cottages with fireplaces and kitchenettes that cost $105. All rates, which include continental breakfast, are for doubles; add $15 more for each additional person. To view the accommodations online, go to www.haleohia.com.

Kilauea Lodge (☎ 967-7366, fax 967-7367, *stay@kilauea-lodge.com, PO Box 116, Volcano, HI 96785)*, on the main road in Volcano village, has a variety of accommodations, including four pleasantly renovated rooms in what was formerly a YMCA dormitory. These rooms cost $125 and have the sort of country comfort you'd find in a fine inn, with working fireplaces, quilts, high ceilings and bathrooms with tubs. A newer adjacent building has a common area with a large fireplace and seven cheery rooms at $110. Avoid room Nos 7 and 8, which are right off the common room and can get a bit noisy. The lodge also has a couple of cottages starting at $135. All rooms are nonsmoking, and prices include a full breakfast for two in the lodge's restaurant.

In the National Park The park has two drive-up campgrounds. Camping is free and the campgrounds are not usually crowded, although things can pick up in summer. There's no reservation system – it's simply on a first-come, first-served basis. Camping is officially limited to seven days per campground per year. Because of the elevation, nights can be crisp and cool at both Namakani Paio (4000 feet) and Kulanaokuaiki (3000 feet) Campgrounds. (For information on backcountry camping in the national park, see Backcountry Hiking & Camping at the end of the earlier Hiking Trails section.)

Namakani Paio Campground, the park's busiest campground, is just off Hwy 11, about 3 miles west of the visitor center. If you're on your way between Hilo and Kona, it's a convenient place to stop for the night. The open tent sites are in a small meadow that offers little privacy but is surrounded by fragrant eucalyptus trees. There are rest rooms, water, fireplaces and picnic tables. From the campground, it's about a 1-mile hike to the Jaggar Museum and Crater Rim Trail.

Kulanaokuaiki Campground, on Hilina Pali Rd, 3$^1/_2$ miles southwest of Chain of Craters Rd, is a new campground that is expected to open by late 1999. It's the less developed of the two campgrounds, but it has toilets, a water catchment system and picnic tables.

Namakani Paio Cabins are 10 dreary, windowless plywood cabins at the national park's Namakani Paio Campground. Each has one double bed, two single bunk beds and electric lights, but there are no power outlets or heating. There are communal showers and rest rooms. It can get cold at night, so bring a sleeping bag if you have one. (Or bring a tent as well and you can stay in the adjacent campground for free!)

You must book the cabins through Volcano House, where you pay and pick up your bag of linen. The rate is $40 for up to four people, and you'll also have to put up refundable deposits of $12 for keys and $20 for linen.

Volcano House (☎ 967-7321, fax 967-8429, *PO Box 53, Hawaii National Park, HI 96713)* is opposite the national park visitor center. Although it has an enviable location, perched right on the rim of Kilauea Caldera, many of the room views are disappointing. By and large, the lower-level rooms look out onto a walkway and even some of those on the upper floor have only a partial view of the crater. The rooms themselves are rather small but otherwise pleasant, with koa furnishings and a bit of character. The best, which cost a pricey $165 to $185, are the 2nd-story rooms in the main building, while the cheapest are in the annex and cost $85.

Places to Eat

If you're trying to see the park in a day, you can save time by bringing lunch and having a picnic wherever you are at noon. If you don't happen to be near the park entrance, it's a long haul from most points in the park out to a restaurant.

The only in-park public restaurant is at **Volcano House** (☎ 967-7321), which serves up a cafeteria-quality breakfast buffet from 7 to 10:30 am for $9.50 and a lunch buffet from 11 am to 2 pm for $12.50. The quality of the food is better at dinner (5:30 to 8:30 pm), with main courses ranging from $11 for pasta to $22 for shrimp scampi. While the dining-room view overlooking Kilauea Caldera is magnificent, it can be matched at much cheaper prices in the adjacent snack shop, which has chili, simple sandwiches, yogurt, juice and coffee. The snack shop is open 8:30 am to 4:30 pm.

You can pick up groceries and snack items at **Volcano Store** and **Kilauea General Store**, which are just a few hundred yards apart on Volcano Rd in the village center. One or the other is open 5 am to 7 pm daily.

Lava Rock Cafe, behind Kilauea General Store, is a pleasant little cafe and a favorite breakfast spot. Omelettes with home fries cost around $6, as do plate lunches. At dinner you can get fried chicken, lasagna or teriyaki beef, served with soup and salad, for $8 to $10. The cafe is open 7:30 am to 4 pm on Sunday, to 5 pm on Monday and Tuesday and to 9 pm on other days. The cafe also offers inexpensive Internet access.

Surt's (☎ 967-8511), adjacent to Volcano Store, offers an interesting fusion of Asian and European influences and such superb food that people drive all the way from Hilo just to eat here. At lunch, there are sandwiches or salads for around $7 and Thai dishes for a bit more. At dinner, the menu ranges from Indonesian curries to Italian pasta primavera and lobster ravioli – all dishes cost between $10 and $19, except for the daily fresh fish special, which is a few dollars more. Surt's is open 11 am to 9:30 pm daily.

Kilauea Lodge (☎ 967-7366) has an atmospheric dining room with high wooden ceilings, a stone fireplace and windows looking out onto a fern forest. Dinners of beef, seafood and chicken begin at around $20, and there's always at least one pasta dish on the menu for a few dollars less. The lodge is open 5:30 to 9 pm daily.

Getting There & Away

The park is 29 miles from Hilo and 97 miles from Kailua-Kona. If you didn't stop along the way, it would take about 45 minutes to drive from Hilo, 2 1/2 hours from Kailua-Kona.

The public bus running between Hilo and Waiohinu in Kau stops at the visitor center (and at Volcano village) once in each direction Monday to Friday. It leaves the visitor center for Hilo at 8 am and returns from Hilo at 2:40 pm. The ride takes about one hour and costs $2.25.

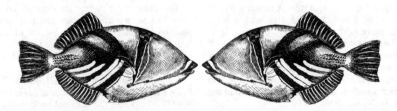

Maui

Maui has much to lure visitors, including superb scenery, diverse landscapes, world-class windsurfing and excellent conditions for most other water sports. The sunny west coast is lined with beautiful white-sand beaches. Maui's warm coastal waters are the main wintering grounds for North Pacific humpback whales, making it prime whale-watching country.

In the 1960s, Hawaii's first major resort development outside Waikiki was built on Maui. Since that time, Maui has become the most visited and the most developed of the Neighbor Islands. As might be expected, all resort action centers around the beaches of West Maui.

The main tourist destinations – Lahaina, the Kaanapali area and the Kihei strip – are urbanized experiences, complete with traffic and crowds. But Maui does have another side. It's quite easy to escape the touristed West Maui scene by heading to the east coast or the uplands. Staying in the small towns of Haiku, Kula or Hana is a totally different experience. Those towns sit beneath Haleakala, the massive mountain that provides the scenic backdrop to all of East Maui. Its slopes hold native rain forests, eucalyptus groves and open pastures with large cattle ranches.

Haleakala Crater, with a summit of 10,023 feet, is the centerpiece of Haleakala National Park. The crater is an extraordinary landscape of spewed red cinders and gray lava hills. Haleakala is the world's largest dormant volcano, its crater so big that an entire city could fit inside. Some incredible hiking trails cross the crater floor, and sunrise at the summit is awe-inspiring.

Kula, at a cool 3000-foot elevation on Haleakala's western slopes, is Maui's garden land. Flowers and vegetables that ordinarily don't have a chance in the tropics thrive up here. Upcountry also has the island's only winery.

The windward side of Haleakala is lush, wet and rugged. The famed Hana Hwy runs down the full length of it, winding its way above the coast through tropical jungle and past roadside waterfalls. It's the most beautiful coastal road in Hawaii.

HISTORY
Before Western contact, Maui had three major population centers: the southeast coast around Hana, the Wailuku area and the district of Lele (present-day Lahaina).

Highlights

- Watching the sun rise at the top of Haleakala

- Winding along the scenic cliffs of the Hana Hwy

- Windsurfing with the experts at Hookipa Beach

- Cruising through a pod of humpback whales

- Enjoying a drink at Lahaina's historic taverns

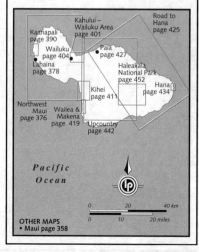

MAUI

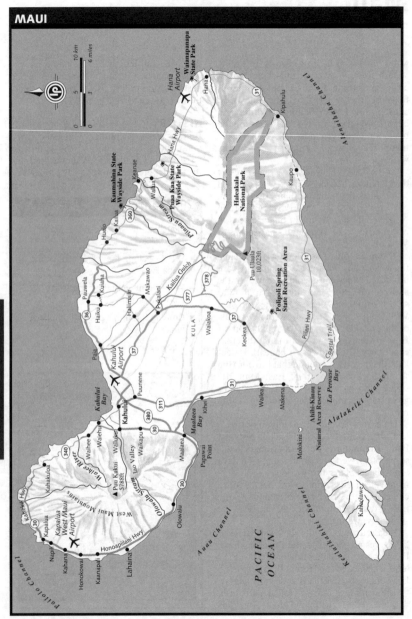

In the 14th century, Piilani, the chief of the Hana district, conquered the entire island. During his reign, Piilani accomplished some impressive engineering feats. He built Maui's largest temple, Piilanihale Heiau, which still stands today, as well as an extensive islandwide road system. Almost half of Maui's highways still bear his name.

The last of Maui's ruling chiefs was Kahekili. During the 1780s, he was the most powerful chief in Hawaii, bringing both Oahu and Molokai under Maui's rule.

In 1790, while Kahekili was in Oahu, Kamehameha the Great launched a bold naval attack on Maui. Using foreign-acquired cannons and the aid of two captured foreign seamen, Isaac Davis and John Young, Kamehameha defeated Maui's warriors in a fierce battle at Iao Valley.

An attack on his own homeland by a Big Island rival forced Kamehameha to withdraw from Maui, but the battles continued over the years. When Kahekili died on Oahu in 1794, his kingdom was divided. In 1795, Kamehameha invaded Maui again, and this time he conquered the entire island and brought it under his rule.

In 1800, Kamehameha established Lahaina as his main home and royal court. It remained the capital of Hawaii until 1845.

Whaling Days

Both the whalers and the missionaries arrived in Lahaina in the early 1820s. They were soon at odds.

Shortly after his arrival in 1823, William Richards, Lahaina's first Protestant missionary, converted Maui's governor, Hoapili, to Christianity. Under Richards' influence, Hoapili began passing laws against drunkenness and debauchery.

After months at sea, the whalers weren't looking for a prayer service when they pulled into port. Ready for grog and women, they didn't take kindly to the puritanical influences of New England missionaries. To most sailors, there was 'no God west of the Horn.'

In 1826, when English captain William Buckle of the whaler *Daniel* pulled into port, he was outraged to discover Lahaina had a new 'missionary taboo' against womanizing. Buckle's crew came to shore seeking revenge against Richards, but a group of Hawaiian Christians came to Richards' aid and chased the whalers back to their boat.

Following Captain Buckle's purchase of a Hawaiian woman, Richards wrote to Buckle's hometown newspaper reporting the details. A libel suit followed. Richards was summoned to Honolulu to be tried, but he was acquitted.

In 1827, after Governor Hoapili arrested the captain of the *John Palmer* for allowing women to board his ship, the *John Palmer* crew shot a round of cannonballs at Richards' house. The captain was released, but laws restricting liaisons between seamen and native women stayed.

After Governor Hoapili's death, laws prohibiting liquor and prostitution were no longer strictly enforced, and whalers began to flock to Lahaina. By the mid-19th century, two-thirds of the whalers coming into Hawaii landed in Lahaina, which had replaced Honolulu as the favored harbor. In 1846, almost 400 ships pulled into port.

By the 1860s, the whaling industry started to fizzle. The depletion of the last hunting grounds in the Arctic and the emergence of the petroleum industry spelled the end of the US whaling era.

Whaling had been the base of Maui's economy. After the whalers left, Lahaina became all but a ghost town.

Sugar

As whaling was declining, sugar was on the rise. Two of the first planters were Samuel Alexander and Henry Baldwin, sons of prominent missionaries.

In 1870, they began growing sugarcane on 12 acres in Haiku, and the next year they added another 500 acres. It was the beginning of Hawaii's biggest sugar company.

In 1876, the Alexander & Baldwin company began construction of the Hamakua Ditch, which carried water from the mountainous interior to the Haiku plantations 17 miles away. This system turned Wailuku's dry central plains into green sugar land. Sugar remained the backbone of the economy until tourism took over in the 1960s.

MAUI

GEOGRAPHY

Maui, the second-largest Hawaiian Island, arose from the ocean floor as two separate volcanoes. Lava flows and soil erosion eventually built up a valleylike isthmus between the two, linking them in their present form. The flat isthmus provides a fertile setting for fields of sugarcane and has given Maui the nickname 'The Valley Island.'

The eastern side of Maui, the larger and younger of the two, is dominated by Haleakala, which has a summit elevation of 10,023 feet. This dormant volcano has a massive craterlike valley containing numerous cinder cones and vents. Haleakala last erupted in 1790, which on the geological clock means it could just be snoozing.

The West Maui Mountains dominate West Maui, with Puu Kukui, at 5788 feet, the highest point.

The rainy northeast sides of both mountain masses are cut with deep ravines and valleys that lead down to the coast. White-sand beaches run along much of the island's western shoreline.

Maui's total land area is 728 sq miles.

CLIMATE

Maui's west coast is largely dry and sunny. The southeast coast and the Kula uplands receive more rain and commonly have intermittent clouds.

Temperatures vary more with elevation than season. The variance between winter and summer is only about 7°F in most places. The average August temperatures (over a 24-hour period) are 77°F in Hana, 78°F in Lahaina and Kihei, 79°F in Kahului and 50°F at Haleakala summit.

The lowest temperature ever recorded at the summit of Haleakala was 14°F, and temperatures hovering around freezing are common on winter nights. The mountain even gets an occasional winter snowcap.

Average annual rainfall is 69 inches in Hana, 13 in Kihei, 15 in Lahaina, 19 in Kahului and 44 at Haleakala summit.

Puu Kukui, the highest peak of the West Maui Mountains, gets 400 inches of rain a year. The peak is Maui's wettest spot, although it sits just 5 miles from the dry Wailuku plains.

FLORA & FAUNA

It's on Maui that you are most likely to see the endangered *nene* (Hawaiian goose) and the rare silversword plant. Haleakala is the habitat for both. Maui is also the best island for viewing humpback whales.

At least six birds native to Maui are found nowhere else in the world. These are the Maui parrotbill, the Maui *nuku puu*, the Maui creeper, the Maui *akepa*, the crested honeycreeper and the *poouli*, all of which are endangered. The poouli, quite amazingly, wasn't discovered until 1973, when it was sighted by a group of University of Hawaii students working in a secluded area of the Hana rain forest.

Maui also has feral pigs, goats and game birds, all of which are hunted both for recreational purposes and to control the damage that these introduced species cause to the habitat.

Humpback Whales

After spending their summers in Alaska, more than half of all humpback whales in the North Pacific come to Hawaii for the winter. The largest numbers are found in the shallow waters between Maui, Lanai and Kahoolawe.

Maui's Home

According to legend, the Polynesian demigod Maui was wandering the Pacific on a fishing expedition when his fishhook snagged the seafloor. He tugged with such a powerful force that the islands of Hawaii were yanked to the surface.

He then claimed the island of Maui and made it his home.

Humpbacks have tail flukes with distinctive individual markings, making them easy to identify. The Pacific Whale Foundation has counted more than a thousand humpback whales off Maui in recent seasons.

The peak season for humpbacks in Hawaii is the same as for tourists from cold-weather climates. Some whales arrive as early as November, and a few stay as late as May; most are in residence from January to March.

The western coastline of Maui from Olowalu to Makena (and the eastern shore of Lanai) are the chief birthing and nursing grounds for wintering humpbacks. Federal law protects these 'cow/calf waters' and prohibits boats and swimmers from approaching within 300 yards of the whales.

Humpbacks like to stay in shallow water when they have newborn calves, apparently as a safeguard against shark attacks. Maalaea Bay is a favorite nursing ground.

Humpbacks are highly sensitive to human disturbance and noise. Some activities, such as jet skis, are so disruptive that they are banned outright along the southwest coast of Maui from mid-December to mid-April.

Around Lahaina, where the waters are buzzing with activity, whales generally stay well offshore. The best bet for whale spotting if you're in the Lahaina area is to go south at least as far as Launiupoko Wayside Park. Maui's finest shoreline whale-watching spots are the stretches from Olowalu to Maalaea Bay and from Keawakapu Beach to Makena Beach.

GOVERNMENT

Maui County consists of the islands of Maui, Molokai, Lanai and uninhabited Kahoolawe. The county seat is in Wailuku. The county is governed by an elected mayor with a four-year term and nine council members with two-year terms.

ECONOMY

Maui's unemployment rate is 6%. The major industries are tourism, sugarcane and pineapple production, cattle grazing and diversified agriculture.

Surprisingly, more land on Maui is used for grazing dairy and beef cattle than for any other purpose. For every acre of sugar, there are 3 acres of ranch land.

Kula is one of the state's major flower- and vegetable-producing regions, accounting for more than half of the cabbage, lettuce, onions and potatoes grown in Hawaii and for almost all of the commercially grown proteas and carnations.

After Oahu, Maui captures the lion's share of Hawaii's tourist industry, accounting for roughly half the visitor accommodations on all the outer islands combined. Numbers, however, don't equate to bargains here. Maui has the highest room rates in Hawaii, averaging $155 a night, about 25% higher than the state average.

POPULATION & PEOPLE

Maui has a population of 106,000. The Wailuku district, which includes the sister towns of Wailuku and Kahului, is home to half of the island's residents.

Ethnically, 26% of the population is Caucasian, 16% Japanese, 15% Filipino and 2% Hawaiian. About one-third of Maui's residents consider themselves to be of 'mixed blood,' with two-thirds of these having some Hawaiian ancestry.

ORIENTATION

Most visitors to Maui land at the main airport in Kahului. From Kahului, it's 5 miles to Paia down Hwy 36 and another 45 miles to Hana.

The Upcountry area of Kula is 15 miles from Kahului on Hwy 37. From there, it's another 20 miles up to the summit of Haleakala.

It's about 10 miles to Kihei from Kahului along Hwy 311.

It's 25 miles from Kahului to Lahaina via Hwys 380 and 30, and 4 miles more from Lahaina to Kaanapali.

Be aware that most main roads are called 'highways' whether they're busy four-lane thoroughfares or just quiet country roads. What's more, islanders refer to highways by name, rarely by number. If you ask someone how to find Hwy 36, chances are they aren't going to know – ask for the Hana Hwy instead.

MAUI

Official Maui

Maui's nickname is 'The Valley Island.' Its official color is pink; its flower is the *lokelani*, a type of rose; and its unofficial slogan is *Maui no ka oi* – 'Maui is the best.'

Maps

The best map for getting around the island is the one published by the University of Hawaii (UH) Press. It not only covers the roads well, but shows beaches and major sights as well. You can buy it for a few dollars at convenience shops and bookstores around the island.

The free Maui Driving Map, available from the airport tourist office booth, is also a handy map and has useful town insets that show restaurants, shopping centers and places of interest.

INFORMATION
Tourist Offices

The Maui Visitors Bureau (☎ 244-3530, fax 244-1337) is headquartered at 1727 Wili Pa Loop, Wailuku, HI 96793, opposite the Wailuku post office. It's open 8 am to 4:30 pm Monday to Friday, but it's essentially an administrative office with a rack of brochures in the lobby; the same brochures are available at the tourist office booth in the airport arrival area. If you call ☎ 800-525-6284 before you go, the bureau will send its 'vacation planner,' a glossy 65-page magazine loaded with ads for vistors. You can also browse www.visitmaui.com for online information.

For details on Kaanapali, contact the Kaanapali Beach Resort Association (☎ 661-3271, 800-245-9229), 2530 Kekaa Drive, suite B1, Lahaina, HI 96761. For information on Wailea, contact Destination Resorts (☎ 879-1595, 800-367-5246, drh@maui.net), 3750 Wailea Alanui Drive, Wailea, HI 96753. Both organizations will mail out brochures on accommodations at their resorts.

Newspapers & Magazines

Maui's main newspaper, the *Maui News* (☎ 244-3981, 800-827-0347, www.mauinews.com), PO Box 550, Wailuku, HI 96793, has good coverage of local and off-island news and comes out daily except Saturday. The Sunday edition can be mailed to the US mainland for $8, postage included; it can be ordered by phone using a credit card.

There are several small community newspapers that focus on local issues and make interesting reading, including *Maui Time*, *Lahaina News*, *South Maui Weekly*, *Haleakala Times* and *Kihei Times*.

Free tourist magazines such as *This Week Maui* and *Spotlight's Maui Gold* are full of ads, discount coupons, simple maps and general sightseeing information. They're worth picking up at the airport and island hotels and restaurants.

Radio & TV

Maui has numerous radio stations, including KPOA (93.5 FM), which plays Hawaiian music most of the time.

All the major US mainland TV networks are available on cable. Cable TV Channel 7 has ongoing programs on Hawaii geared for visitors.

Bookstores

The island's largest bookstore, Borders, in the Maui Marketplace on Dairy Rd in Kahului, has an impressive collection of novels, travel guides, Hawaiiana books, magazines and international newspapers. Waldenbooks, which also has good selections of Hawaiiana and travel books, has branches in the Kukui Mall in Kihei, the Lahaina Cannery Mall in Lahaina and the Kaahumanu Mall and Maui Mall in Kahului.

Libraries

There are public libraries in Kahului, Wailuku, Lahaina, Hana, Makawao and Kihei. For information on Internet access through

Hawaii's public library, see the Libraries section in the Facts for the Visitor chapter.

Weather Hotlines

For the National Weather Service's recorded forecast of weather conditions on Maui, call ☎ 877-5111.

For a recreational forecast, including conditions at Haleakala and along the road to Hana, sunrise and sunset times and general marine conditions, call ☎ 871-5054. For a more extensive marine forecast, including surf conditions, winds and tides, call ☎ 877-3477.

Emergency

Dial ☎ 911 for police, ambulance or fire emergencies. The county crisis and help line is ☎ 244-7407.

Maui Memorial Hospital (☎ 244-9056), 221 Mahalani St, Wailuku, is a large facility with 24-hour emergency services.

ACTIVITIES
Swimming

Maui has lots of fine beaches, with plenty of good swimming spots. The northwest coast from Kaanapali up to Honolua Bay and the southwest coast from Maalaea down to Makena are largely fringed with white-sand beaches. This western side is dry and sunny, and water conditions are generally calmer than on the windward northern and eastern coasts.

Most of the west coast's best beaches are backed by hotel and condo developments – good if you're looking to stay right at the beach, not so good if you prefer seclusion. Still, the west coast does have some gorgeous undeveloped strands, the most notable being Makena's Big and Little Beaches, a short drive south of Kihei.

Swimming Pools The county maintains heated swimming pools open to the public in Wailuku, Lahaina and Pukalani. For current schedule information, call ☎ 243-7411 for the Wailuku pool, on the corner of Wells and Market Sts; ☎ 243-7394 for the War Memorial Pool, at Baldwin High School in Wailuku; ☎ 661-7611 for the Lahaina

Aquatic Center; and ☎ 572-1479 for the new pool at the Upcountry Swimming Complex in Pukalani.

Surfing

Maui has some unbeatable surfing spots, with peak surfing conditions from November to March. Hookipa Beach near Paia has surfing almost year-round, with incredible winter waves. When conditions are right, Honolua Bay on the northwest coast has the island's top action.

The Maalaea Pipeline, at the south side of Maalaea Bay, has a very fast break, best during south swells. However, this break, which *Surfer* magazine has described as one of the world's 10 best, could be seriously altered if a proposed expansion of Maalaea Harbor is allowed to go through.

A number of places give surfing lessons for beginners, including Andrea Thomas' Maui Surfing School (☎ 875-0625) in Lahaina, Nancy Emerson's School of Surfing (☎ 244-7873) in Lahaina, Lahaina Surfing School (☎ 671-8733) in Lahaina, Hawaiian Sailboarding Techniques (☎ 871-5423) in Kahului and Maui Mistral (☎ 871-7753) in Kahului.

Lessons typically last $1^1/2$ to two hours and cost $50 to $75. Most places guarantee that students of all ages will be surfing at the end of the lesson.

The most popular places for bodysurfing are Baldwin Beach Park in Paia, Fleming Beach Park in Kapalua and beaches in the Kihei area.

Both surfboards and boogie boards can be rented at numerous locations around Maui, including many of the windsurfing shops.

Hi-Tech Surf Sports (☎ 877-2111), 425 Koloa St, Kahului, rents entry-level surfboards for $14/80 a day/week and custom boards for $20/112. The branch of Hi-Tech Surf Sports (☎ 579-9297) at 51 Baldwin Ave in Paia rents boogie boards for $8/45 a day/week and entry-level surfboards for the same price as the Kahului shop.

Windrigger Maui (☎ 871-7753), 261 Dairy Rd, Kahului, rents boogie boards for $7/15 a day/week, surfboards for $20/95.

MAUI

Windsurfing

Maui is a mecca for windsurfers. Some of the world's best windsurfing is at Hookipa Beach in Paia, though it's suitable for experts only. Spreckelsville Beach in Paia is for intermediate and advanced windsurfers. Kanaha Beach in Kahului is good for beginners, as are parts of the Kihei coast.

In Maalaea Bay, conditions are good for advanced speed sailing; the winds are usually strong and blow offshore toward Kahoolawe. During the winter, on those occasions when kona winds blow, the Maalaea-Kihei area is often the only place windy enough to sail and becomes the main scene for all windsurfers.

Overall, Maui is known for its consistent winds, and windsurfers can find action in any month. Although trade winds can blow at any time of the year and flat spells could also hit anytime, generally the windiest time is June to September and the flattest from December to February.

The Maui Boardsailing Association has developed a 'sail safe' program with windsurfing guidelines; brochures with the guidelines are available at the windsurf shops.

Most windsurfing shops are based in Kahului. The following shops sell and rent windsurfing gear and either give lessons themselves or

through an affiliate that works out of the same shop.

Hawaiian Island Surf & Sport
(☎ 871-4981, 800-231-6958, www.hawaiianisland.com), 415 Dairy Rd, Kahului, HI 96732

Hi-Tech Surf Sports
(☎ 877-2111, 800-736-6284), 425 Koloa St, Kahului, HI 96732

Maui Windsurf
(☎ 877-4816, 800-872-0999), 520 Keolani Place, Kahului, HI 96732

Extreme Sports Maui
(☎ 871-7954, 800-328-8877, extreme@maui.net), 360 Papa Place F (entrance at the Dairy Center), Kahului, HI 96732

Second Wind
(☎ 877-7467, fax 877-0091), 111 Hana Hwy, Kahului, HI 96732

Windrigger Maui
(☎ 871-7753, 800-345-6284), 261 Dairy Rd, Kahului, HI 96732

Shops rent boards and rigs for about $50/285 a day/week, which usually includes swapping privileges that let you try different equipment. Some places, including Hi-Tech Surf Sports, will let you use the weekly rate on nonconsecutive days – hence you could sail for three days, take a couple of days off and then sail four more days for the same price it would cost to rent the gear for a week straight. Hawaiian Island Surf & Sport and Hi-Tech Surf Sports are both big operations with good reputations.

The business is very competitive, so if you ask about discounts and let it be known that you're getting price quotes with more than one company, you may be offered a better deal.

Windsurfing lessons, either one-day classes or multiday packages, can be arranged for any level. Introductory classes for beginners are usually held at Kanaha Beach or at the north side of Kihei, last two to three hours and cost around $60, equipment included.

Most of the Kahului shops also sell windsurfing equipment and can book package tours that include accommodations and windsurfing gear. Some can book vehicles, including vans or station wagons suitable for carting around gear.

Diving & Snorkeling

Some dive and snorkel boat tours go along the Maui shoreline, but the main destinations are the sunken volcanic crater of Molokini and the island of Lanai. Although a few dive boats take snorkelers, and some snorkeling tours take divers, as a rule you'll be better off going out on a tour that's geared for the activity you're doing.

For snorkeling from the beach, prime spots include Black Rock, at the Sheraton in Kaanapali; Olowalu, south of Lahaina; around the rocky points of Wailea and Makena beaches; and, in summer, at Honolua Bay and Slaughterhouse Beach on the northwest shore. Kapalua Bay is generally one of the calmest places for snorkeling year-round. Maui Dive Shop has a good free map that details the island's best diving and snorkeling spots.

Molokini Molokini, only a few miles off the southwest coast, is Maui's most popular snorkeling tour site. The fish are tame and numerous and the water is clear.

Morning is the best time to snorkel Molokini, as winds pick up in the afternoon. The fish are given their breakfast call by boat captains who drop in loaves of bread to start the action.

For divers, Molokini has walls, ledges, white-tipped reef sharks, manta rays, turtles and a wide variety of other marine life.

Although the snorkeling and diving is good, don't expect pristine conditions – dozens of tour boats crowd the islet every day, and all of the activity has taken a toll on the reef. Some sections have been permanently damaged, largely from dropped and dragged anchors that have carved swaths in the coral.

Black coral was once prolific in Molokini's deeper waters. However, most of it made its way into Lahaina jewelry stores before Molokini was declared a conservation district in 1977.

Lanai Lanai also has clear waters, but without the crowds. The most common destination is Hulopoe Bay.

Hulopoe is a big, beautiful beach that was once secluded but now has a luxury hotel at

Molokini

The largely submerged volcanic crater of Molokini lies midway between the islands of Maui and Kahoolawe. Half of the crater rim has eroded away, leaving a crescent moon shape that rises 160 feet above the ocean surface. Its land area is about 18 acres.

Molokini, which means 'many ties' in Hawaiian, is said to have been a beautiful woman who was turned to stone by a jealous Pele, goddess of volcanoes.

Today, Molokini draws scores of snorkelers and divers, who come here for its clear waters with abundant fish and coral.

Since 1977, Molokini has been set aside as a marine life conservation district, but it hasn't always been held in such high regard. During the WWII era, the US Navy shelled Molokini for target practice, and live bombs are still occasionally found on the crater floor. A decade ago, demolition experts removed three bombs that were in just 20 feet of water.

its northern end. The reef at the southern end harbors large schools of fish and is good for snorkeling.

For divers, the nearby Cathedrals site offers intriguing geological formations, including caves, arches and connecting passageways.

For more information, see the Lanai chapter of this book.

Dive Shops Maui has a number of dive operations. Maui Dive Shop, a five-star PADI operation, has the following branches around the island and can also be found on the Web at www.mauidiveshop.com.

Honokowai	
Honokowai Marketplace	☎ 661-6166
Kaanapali	
Whalers Village	☎ 661-5117
Kahana	
Kahana Gateway	☎ 669-3800

MAUI

Kihei
1455 S Kihei Rd	☎ 879-3388
Kamaole Center	☎ 879-1533

Lahaina
Lahaina Cannery Mall	☎ 661-5388

Wailea
Wailea Shopping Village	☎ 879-3166

Maui Dive Shop offers one-tank introductory dives for beginners for $70, two-tank beach dives for $65, two-tank boat dives for $110 at Molokini or elsewhere, and four-day certification courses from $300.

Lahaina Divers (☎ 667-7496, 800-998-3483, lahdivers@maui.net, www.lahainadivers .com), 143 Dickenson St, Lahaina, HI 96761, a long-established and well-regarded dive company, offers two-tank dives for $105 to either Lanai or Molokini, two-tank introductory dives for $95 and two-tank night dives for $105. A five-star PADI operation, the company also offers three-day certification courses for $295 and leads advanced drift and deepwater dives.

Smaller but also with a loyal following, Ed Robinson's Diving Adventures (☎ 879-3584, robinson@maui.net, www.mauiscuba .com), PO Box 616, Kihei, HI 96753, is operated by underwater photographer Ed Robinson, who offers two-tank boat dives for $105, two-tank night dives for $125 and two-tank Lanai dives for $125.

Snorkeling Tours & Rentals Numerous snorkeling cruises leave for Molokini daily from Maalaea Harbor. Boats are usually out from about 7 am to noon and average $40 to $60, including snacks and snorkeling gear. Competition is heavy, so deals and discount coupons are easy to come by. Tickets are sold at activity booths around the island.

Snorkeling gear can be rented at reasonable prices from most dive shops and at inflated prices from hotel beach huts.

Maui Dive Shop (see Dive Shops for locations) rents snorkel sets with silicone masks for $6/17 a day/week.

Maui Sports & Cycle (☎ 875-2882), with Kihei shops at Dolphin Plaza, 2395 S Kihei Rd, and Longs Center, 1215 S Kihei Rd, rents

cheap snorkel sets for as little as $2 a day and good quality silicone gear for $5 a day.

High-profile Snorkel Bob's has come-on rates of $9 a week for its cheaper snorkel gear, but you'll probably want better quality, and Bob's prices will rise accordingly. Maui locations include: 161 Lahainaluna Rd in Lahaina (☎ 661-4421), 34 Keala Place in Kihei (☎ 879-7449) and 5425 Lower Honoapiilani Rd at the Napili Village shopping complex in Napili (☎ 669-9603).

Kayaking

South Pacific Kayaks (☎ 875-4848, 800-776-2326, seakayak@maui.net), at the Rainbow Mall in Kihei, rents single kayaks from $25 a day and doubles from $35, including car racks, paddles and life vests. Three-hour guided kayak tours (some dubbed 'whale watch') are offered for $59. Five-hour outings around the La Perouse area cost $89, including snorkeling and lunch.

Kelii's Kayak Tours (☎ 874-7652) offers guided ocean kayak tours, with stops for snorkeling. Two tours – one running from Makena to the La Perouse area, and the other exploring the west shore's Olowalu area – cost $55 and last 2 1/2 hours. A five-hour tour along Maui's north shore, with lunch, costs $99.

Other Maui kayak operations include Maui Sea Kayaking (☎ 572-6299) and Tradewind Kayak Maui (☎ 879-2247).

Hiking

At Haleakala National Park, some extraordinary trails – from half-day walks to overnight treks – cross the moonscape-like Haleakala Crater. In the Oheo section of the park, which is south of Hana, a trail leads to two impressive waterfalls.

In Maui's Upcountry, Polipoli Spring State Recreation Area has an extensive trail system in cloud forest. One route, the Skyline Trail, leads up to Haleakala summit.

Several pull-offs along the Hana Hwy lead to short nature walks. There's also a pleasant coastal trail between Waianapanapa State Park and Hana Bay.

A nice choice north of Wailuku is the scenic Waihee Ridge Trail, which branches off the Kahekili Hwy. From La Perouse Bay, on the other side of the island, there's a strenuous coastline hike over a lava footpath. And, of course, Maui has many white-sand beaches perfect for strolls. Hikes are detailed in their respective sections.

Sierra Club The Maui branch of the Sierra Club leads hikes or service trips once or twice a month on weekends. The schedule is posted in the Community Events section of *Maui Time* and in the Datebook section of the *Maui News*.

The service trips sometimes involve helping to rid the island of invasive exotic plants, such as myconia and banana poka. The latter, a not-so-benign relative of the edible passion fruit vine, has run rampant over native forests on the Big Island and Kauai, but is kept relatively controlled on Maui thanks in large part to the Sierra Club. Their eradication tactics include bagging fruit and seedlings, pulling up vines and spraying herbicide on the roots.

Cycling
Each morning before dawn, groups of cyclists gather at the top of Haleakala for the thrill of coasting 38 miles down the mountain, with a 10,000-foot drop in elevation.

Companies offering this activity include Maui Downhill (☎ 871-2155, 800-535-2453), Maui Mountain Cruisers (☎ 871-6014, 800-232-6284) and Mountain Riders (☎ 242-9739, 800-706-7700). Generally, it's an all-day affair (eight to 10 hours), starting with hotel pickup at around 3 am, a van ride up the mountain for the sunrise and about 3½ hours of biking back down. It's not a nonstop cruise, as cyclists must periodically pull over for cars following behind, and the primary exercise is squeezing the brakes – you'll need to pedal only about 400 yards on the entire trip! The going rate is a steep $115, which includes bike, helmet, transportation and meals.

Bikes are generally modified with special safety brakes, and each group is followed by an escort van. Pregnant women, children under 12 and those less than 5 feet tall are usually not allowed to ride. Keep in mind that the road down Haleakala is narrow and winding with lots of blind curves, and there are no bike lanes.

Aloha Bicycle Tours (☎ 249-0911, 800-749-1564) offers a nonsunrise tour geared for stronger cyclists that begins with a glide down the Haleakala Crater Rd, but instead of continuing downhill to the coast, takes in various Upcountry sights before ending at the winery. The cost of $89 doesn't include hotel pick-up.

If you don't feel the need for a group outing or a guide to bring you back down the mountain, Upcountry Cycles (☎ 573-2888), 81 Makawao Ave in Pukalani, will rent you a 21-speed mountain bike with helmet, backpack, map and weather gear and give you a van ride up to Haleakala from the shop. The cost is $45 in the daytime, $65 in time for the sunrise.

Bicycle rentals are detailed in the Getting Around section, later in this chapter.

Horseback Riding
Maui has lots of ranch land and some of Hawaii's best opportunities for trail rides. The most unusual ride meanders down into Haleakala Crater via Sliding Sands Trail.

Pony Express (☎ 667-2200, ponex@maui .net, www.maui.net/~ponex) is in a eucalyptus grove on Haleakala Crater Rd, 2½ miles up from Hwy 377. The company's half-day Haleakala Crater ride leaves at 9:30 am, takes five hours and covers 7½ miles; it's open to novice riders and costs $130, including a picnic lunch on the crater floor. A full-day version covers 12 miles, goes to the Kapalaoa cabin and costs $160. Rides across the rolling meadows of Haleakala Ranch cost $40 for one hour, $65 for two hours.

Thompson Ranch (☎ 878-1910), in Keokea, offers 1½-hour trail rides for $50 and two-hour rides for $60.

Hana Ranch Riding Stables (☎ 248-8211) leads a guided trail ride along the Hana coast at 8 am, a ride in the hills at 10 am and a ride that combines both coast and woods at 2 pm. All rides last one hour, cost $35 and are scheduled Monday to Saturday.

Oheo Stables (☎ 667-2222, www.maui .net/~ray), a mile southwest of Oheo Gulch,

MAUI

offers a four-hour horseback ride within the Kipahulu district of Haleakala National Park. The ride departs at 10:30 am, moves at a casual pace, visits waterfalls, includes lunch and costs $119.

Makena Stables (☎ 879-0244), at the north end of La Perouse Bay in Makena, offers a variety of trail rides from Makena up the slopes to Ulupalakua Ranch. Available trips include a two-hour introductory ride for $99, a three-hour ride for $115 and a six-hour lunch ride that sometimes goes all the way up to the Tedeschi winery for $160.

Hang Gliding

Under the name Hang Gliding Maui (☎/fax 572-6557), German-born Armin Engert offers instructional tandem hang-gliding flights off the slopes of Haleakala, providing a scenic descent of nearly 10,000 feet down to the coast. The outing lasts about four hours and costs $250, including transportation from Pukalani, basic instruction and about 35 minutes of flight time in a tandem harness with Armin.

Armin also provides motorized hang-gliding instructional flights in an open-cockpit, ultralight aircraft for $100 and up.

Tennis

The county maintains tennis courts at: Lahaina Civic Center, Lahaina; Maluuluolele Park, Lahaina; Wells Park, Wailuku; War Memorial Complex, Wailuku; Kahului Community Center, Kahului; Kalama Park, Kihei; Hana Ball Park, Hana; Eddie Tam Memorial Center, Makawao; and Pukalani Community Center, Pukalani. County courts are free to the public on a first-come, first-served basis and are lit for night play.

Numerous hotels and condos have tennis courts for their guests. There are tennis courts open to the public on a fee basis at the Wailea Tennis Club (☎ 879-1958) in Wailea; Makena Tennis Club (☎ 879-8777) in Makena; Kapalua Tennis Garden (☎ 669-5677) in Kapalua; and the Maui Marriott (☎ 667-1200) and Royal Lahaina Tennis Ranch (☎ 661-3611) in Kaanapali.

Rates at the Makena Tennis Club are $18 per court per hour. At the Royal Lahaina,

the cost is $10 per person per day. At other resort clubs, rates are generally quoted at $10 to $12 per person 'per day,' although only the first hour of playing time is guaranteed, and the courts are subject to space availability after that. Rackets can be rented at all tennis clubs for $4 to $6 a day ($2.50 at Royal Lahaina); some clubs also rent tennis shoes.

Golf

Maui has 16 golf courses open to the public. They include, in order by listing, one municipal, five private and 10 resort courses. All are 18-hole, par-71, -72 or -73 courses except Maui Country Club, which is a nine-hole, par-36 course.

Grand Waikapu Country Club
(☎ 244-7888), in Waikapu, charges $200 for greens fees and cart.

Kaanapali Beach Resort
(☎ 661-3691) has two courses (North and South) in Kaanapali. At either course, greens fees and cart cost $100 for resort guests, $120 for nonguests; the twilight rate is $65.

Kapalua Golf Club
(☎ 669-8044) has three courses in Kapalua. Greens fees and cart total $95/140 for resort guests/nonguests at the Bay and Village Courses, $100/150 at the Plantation Course. All courses charge between $65 and $70 for twilight fees after 2 pm.

Makena Golf Course
(☎ 879-3344) has two courses (North and South) in Makena. Greens fees and cart cost $85/140 for resort guests/nonguests, but there's a $75 twilight rate after 2 pm.

Maui Country Club
(☎ 877-0616), in Spreckelsville, is open to the public on Monday only and charges $45, including a cart.

Pukalani Golf Course
(☎ 572-1314), in Pukalani, charges $63 for greens fees and cart if you tee off in the morning, $42 if you tee off after noon.

Sandalwood Golf Course
(☎ 242-4653), in Waikapu next to the Waikapu Country Club, charges $75 for greens fees and cart.

Silversword Golf Course
(☎ 874-0777), in Kihei, charges $69 for greens fees with shared cart and has a $44 twilight rate.

Waiehu Municipal Golf Course
(☎ 243-7400), north of Wailuku, charges greens fees of $25 on weekdays, $30 on weekends and holidays, plus $8 per person for a shared cart. Clubs rent for $15 a day. This is a busy little course, and reservations for starting times are taken up to two days in advance.

Wailea Golf Club
(☎ 875-7450) has three courses in Wailea. Greens fees with cart cost $95 for Wailea resort guests and $130 for the general public at the Gold & Emerald Courses, $80 for guests and $125 for nonguests at the Blue Course. Discounts are given for twilight play.

ORGANIZED TOURS
Bus & Van
It's possible for those without their own transportation to catch some of the island's main attractions by joining a day tour.

The largest company offering tours in English is Polynesian Adventure Tours (☎ 877-4242, 800-622-3011), which has tours of Hana for $69 and of Haleakala, central Maui and Iao Valley for $55. There's also a Haleakala sunrise tour for $52. Children under 12 are charged about 70% of the adult fare.

There are also a couple of smaller companies offering tours. Ekahi Tours (☎ 877-9775) has a more adventurous daylong Hana tour that continues south of Hana, visiting Oheo Gulch and Lindbergh's grave and taking the road through Kaupo up to Tedeschi winery and the Upcountry. The tour costs $75 for adults, $60 for children under 12.

Helicopter
Numerous helicopter companies take off from the heliport at Kahului Airport for trips around the island. Some cross the channel and tour Molokai's spectacular North Shore as well.

Most companies advertise in the free tourist magazines. Prices are competitive, with many places running perennial specials, offering free use of video cameras and the like.

Typical are 30-minute tours of the West Maui Mountains for around $100, 45-minute tours of Haleakala and Hana for $150 and one-hour circle-island tours for $200.

Helicopter companies operating on Maui include Sunshine Helicopters (☎ 871-0722, 800-544-2520), Blue Hawaiian (☎ 871-8844, 800-2745-2583), Hawaii Helicopters (☎ 877-3900, 800-994-9099), Air Maui (☎ 877-7005) and Alex Air (☎ 877-4354, 888-418-8457).

Cruises
Maui has enough dinner cruises, sunset sails, deep-sea fishing boats and charter sailboats to fill a book. Most leave from Lahaina or Maalaea, although a few depart from Kihei and Kaanapali.

You can get current rates and information from activity booths all around Maui or from the tourist magazines – or just go down to Lahaina Harbor, where the booths and the boats are lined up, and check out the scene for yourself.

Atlantis Submarines (☎ 667-7816, 800-548-6262) operates a 65-foot sub in the waters off Lahaina. The sub carries 48 passengers down to a depth of about 100 feet to see coral and fish. Tours leave from Lahaina Harbor via a catamaran every hour on the hour from 10 am to 2 pm daily. The cost is $79 for adults, $39 for children.

If you want a similar effect at half the price, take the semisubmersible *Nautilus* (☎ 667-2133), a glass-bottom boat with a submerged lower deck that has underwater viewing windows similar to those on the sub. It leaves Lahaina Harbor four times a day and costs $30 for adults, $16 for children six to 12 (free for children under six).

Whale Watching The peak humpback whale-watching season is from January to the end of March, though there are usually whales around Maui for a month or so on either side.

In season, whale-watching cruises are heavily advertised, and you'll have no trouble finding one. Whale-watch boats range from catamaran sailboats to large cruise vessels. Most leave from Maalaea or Lahaina Harbors, though a few leave from Kihei and Kaanapali. A two- to three-hour tour usually costs $25 to $40 for adults, half price for children. Some companies have hydrophones to hear whale songs, some claim to donate a

MAUI

portion of the ticket price to whale conservation groups and some guarantee whale sightings or give another tour free.

Many of the boats that take snorkelers to Molokini in the morning go out whale watching in the afternoon. During the season, there's a good chance of spotting whales on the snorkeling trip to Molokini itself.

The nonprofit Pacific Whale Foundation (☎ 879-8811, 800-942-5311) offers numerous daily cruises from both Maalaea and Lahaina for $31. The rate usually drops to just $21 for the first (7 am) and last (4:30 pm) boats out of Lahaina and for all afternoon departures from Maalaea. Children pay $15 on all cruises. The foundation uses a 50-foot sailboat from Lahaina and either a 36-foot motorboat or a 65-foot sailing catamaran from Maalaea. Some of the proceeds go to the foundation's marine conservation projects.

To Lanai Club Lanai (☎ 871-1144, 888-258-2526) sails a 149-passenger catamaran to secluded Kahalepalaoa Beach on Lanai's east coast. The cost of $89 includes all you can eat and drink and a few water activities. The boat leaves Lahaina Harbor's slip 4 at 7:30 am and returns at 3:30 pm.

Trilogy Excursions (☎ 661-4743, 800-874-2666) operates a day tour by catamaran from Lahaina to Lanai's Hulopoe Beach. The cost of $159 includes breakfast, a barbecue lunch, snorkeling and a brief land tour of Lanai.

In addition, some of Maui's dive shops offer dive or snorkel outings to Lanai. See also the Getting There & Away section of this chapter for information on the Lanai-Lahaina ferry, which deposits passengers at Manele Bay, a stone's throw from lovely Hulopoe Beach.

To Molokai Island Marine Activities (☎ 667-6165, 800-275-6969) operates the *Maui Princess*, a 118-foot boat that once provided daily commuter ferry service between Maui and Molokai. The commuter service is long gone, but the boat still cruises once a week to Kaunakakai, Molokai, carrying day visitors from Lahaina. It departs on Saturday from Lahaina Harbor's slip 3 at 6:15 am, arrives in Kaunakakai at 8 am, then

departs from Kaunakakai at 2 pm, arriving back in Lahaina at 3:30 pm. The roundtrip fare is $69 for adults, $35 for children. Once on Molokai you have a few options – you could explore Kaunakakai by foot or bicycle. Or, for $60 more per person, you can join a guided sightseeing tour by van that visits Kaunakakai and central Molokai. A third option is to rent a car and do a little exploring on your own – for $60, the boat company will arrange a car rental.

ACCOMMODATIONS

Other than camping, the cheapest places to stay on Maui are the Banana Bungalow and the Northshore Inn in Wailuku, both of which have dorm beds for $16.

Maui has some studio-style cottages and apartments that rent from about $60, with most of these found in the Haiku-Paia area. A number of B&Bs are spread throughout the island, offering some very pleasant places to stay for around $75.

Condos make up the bulk of the midrange accommodations. Kihei has the highest concentration, but you will also find mid-range rooms in Kahului, Lahaina and Honokowai. The lower end of this price range is around $75, but it's easy to spend over $100 a night for nothing special.

Maui's two biggest resort developments are Kaanapali Beach Resort and Wailea Resort, both of which have luxury hotels and condos. The beachfront hotels start around $175 in Kaanapali and $225 in Wailea, though the more exclusive hotels have room rates that are easily double that.

Overall, rates can be substantially lower during the low season (mid-April to mid-December), when you'll be able to pick and choose. During the high season, the better condo deals usually require reservations far in advance.

Camping

Maui has fewer camping options than the other islands. Waianapanapa State Park and Haleakala National Park are good choices for places to camp.

In addition to the federal, state and county campgrounds listed here, there's also a church-sponsored campground at Olowalu, which is described in that section.

State Parks Polipoli Spring State Recreation Area and Waianapanapa State Park, the only state parks on Maui with camping areas, both have tent sites and cabins. Permits are required. The maximum length of stay is five consecutive nights per month at each park, and tent camping is free.

, Polipoli, in Upcountry, has one primitive cabin (closed on Tuesday) and a primitive road into it, which usually requires a 4WD vehicle. Waianapanapa, on the coast near Hana, has 12 housekeeping cabins that are very popular and must be reserved well in advance. The cabin cost at either park is $45 for up to four people, $55 for six people.

For camping permits or cabin reservations, contact the Division of State Parks (☎ 984-8109), State Office Building, 54 High St, Wailuku, HI 96793. Office hours are 8 am to 4 pm weekdays.

County Parks Maui has only one county park that allows camping: Kanaha Beach Park, just north of the airport. While it's nice to be at the beach, the sites are directly beneath the flight path, so the airport noise – with flights scheduled from dawn to 11 pm – can be annoying.

Permits cost $3 per day (50¢ for children under 18), and camping is limited to three consecutive nights.

Permits are available by mail or in person from the Department of Parks & Recreation (☎ 243-7389), Camping Permit Office, 1580-C Kaahumanu Ave, Wailuku, HI 96793. The office is in the War Memorial Complex at Baldwin High School in Wailuku.

Haleakala National Park Tent camping is allowed at two free drive-up campgrounds in Haleakala National Park: at Hosmer Grove, which is at the main section of the park in the Upcountry, and at Oheo Gulch, on the coast south of Hana. They are both fine sites, though Oheo has no drinking water. No permits are required, and each campground has a limit of three days camping a month.

Backcountry camping is also allowed by permit inside the crater, and cabins are available as well. For full details, see the Haleakala National Park section, later in this chapter.

Condos

Maui has many more condominium units than hotel rooms. Some condo complexes are booked only through rental agents. Others operate more like a hotel with a front desk, though even in those places some of their units are usually handled by rental agents as well. Overall, the best rates are through the agents, but you'll have to deal with advance payments, and in some cases you might have to pay security deposits and cleaning fees.

Most agents require deposits within one to two weeks of booking, with full payment due 30 days prior to arrival. Cancellation policies vary, but expect a hefty charge (or no refund at all) for canceling within the last month. The minimum stay is usually four to seven days, depending on the place and season.

Each of the agents listed here handles a number of condo complexes and will send listings with rates, making it possible for you to compare values. The 800 numbers that follow can be called toll free from the continental USA, and most can also be called from Canada.

AA Oceanfront Condominium Rentals
(☎ 879-7288, 800-488-6004, fax 879-7500), 2439 S Kihei Rd, No 102A, Kihei, HI 96753

Bello Realty
(☎ 879-3328, 800-541-3060, fax 875-1483, pam@ bellomaui.com, www.bellomaui.com), PO Box 1776, 2395 S Kihei Rd, Kihei, HI 96753

Condominium Rentals Hawaii
(☎ 879-2778, 800-367-5242 in the USA, 800-663-2101 in Canada, fax 879-7825, crh@maui.net, www.crhmaui.com), 362 Huku Lii Place, No 204, Kihei, HI 96753

Hawaiian Apartment Leasing Enterprises
(☎ 714-497-4253, 800-854-8843, fax 714-497-4183), 479 Ocean Ave, suite B, Laguna Beach, CA 92651

Kihei Maui Vacations
(☎ 879-7581, 800-541-6284, fax 879-2000, www .kmvmaui.com), PO Box 1055, 2395 S Kihei Rd, Kihei, HI 96753

Klahani Resorts
  (☎ 667-2712, 800-669-0795, fax 661-5875), PO
  Box 11108, 505 Front St, Lahaina, HI 96761

Kumulani Rentals
  (☎ 879-9272, 800-367-2954, fax 874-0094, putt3@
  maui.net, www.maui.net/~putt3/kumulani), PO
  Box 1190, 1993 S Kihei Rd, Kihei, HI 96753

Maui Condominium & Home Realty
  (☎ 879-5445, 800-822-4409, fax 874-6144), PO
  Box 1840, 2511 S Kihei Rd, Kihei, HI 96753

Maui Network
  (☎ 572-9555, 800-367-5221, fax 572-8553), PO
  Box 1077, Makawao, HI 96768

ENTERTAINMENT

Maui's entertainment scene is second only to Oahu's, with a wide variety of music from rock and jazz to mellow Hawaiian guitar.

Casanova in Makawao sometimes has top-name musicians, and *Hapa's Brew Haus* in Kihei also has good live music. Otherwise, most of the action is in Lahaina and at the resort hotels, especially in Kaanapali and Wailea. See the relevant destination sections for more information.

The *Maui Arts & Cultural Center*, in Kahului, has two indoor theaters and a large outdoor amphitheater. It's the venue for performances by the Maui Symphony Orchestra, Maui Academy of Performing Arts and other community theater and cultural organizations. It's also one of the hottest places in Hawaii for big-name concerts – recent performers have included Pearl Jam, Ziggy Marley and Bonnie Raitt. For a current schedule of events, call the box office at ☎ 242-7469.

For Maui's gay community, Little Beach in Makena is a daytime meeting spot. There are no gay bars on Maui, but Hapa's in Kihei (especially on Sunday) and Casanova's in Makawao are gay-friendly evening spots. There's also an Upcountry social club that meets regularly for movies, dinner or other activities and welcomes visitors; for information, call *Camp Kula* (☎ 876-0000), a gay B&B in Kula.

The best source of current entertainment information is the *Maui News*, particularly the 20-page 'Maui Scene' insert in the Thursday paper. The free tourist newspapers and magazines – most notably *Maui Time* – also have some entertainment information.

Hawaiiana

Luaus are held regularly in Lahaina, Kaanapali and Wailea. All include a buffet dinner with Hawaiian foods and a Polynesian show, and all cost around $60. The Old Lahaina Luau in Lahaina puts on one of the more authentic productions.

The Napili Kai Beach Club in Napili has Friday dinner shows that feature hula dancing by local children. And free hula shows are often offered at shopping centers in Lahaina, Kaanapali and Wailea. Details on specific luaus and hula shows are given throughout the chapter.

SHOPPING

For local arts and crafts, some of the best deals are at the Lahaina Arts Society's gallery in Lahaina and at the Maui Crafts Guild in Paia. See the Lahaina and Paia sections for details.

Maui Blanc, Maui's own pineapple wine, is a decent-quality wine that makes a good gift. It sells for about $8 a bottle at liquor and grocery stores around the island.

Proteas are a Maui specialty. The best deal is to buy direct from the Upcountry farms where they are grown.

Several businesses sell food and flowers, including leis, proteas, papayas, pineapples, Maui onions and husked coconuts, which are agriculturally preinspected and delivered to the airport for you to pick up on your way out. Two such places are Take Home Maui (☎ 661-8067), 121 Dickenson St, Lahaina, and Airport Flower & Fruit (☎ 243-9367), 532 Keolani Place, Kahului.

GETTING THERE & AWAY
Air

The island's main airport is in Kahului. Maui also has two smaller commuter airports with scheduled air service: Kapalua West Maui Airport and Hana Airport.

For information on discounted tickets and air passes, see the Getting Around chapter in the front of the book.

Kahului Airport Hawaiian Airlines (☎ 800-882-8811) and Aloha Airlines (☎ 244-9071) fly directly to Kahului from Oahu, Kauai and the Big Island. Both airlines fly an average of twice hourly from Honolulu, with the first flight at 5:15 am; Aloha's last flight leaves Honolulu at 8 pm, followed by Hawaiian's last flight at 10 pm. From the Big Island, both airlines have three direct flights a day from Kona; Hawaiian Airlines also has two direct flights a day from Hilo. From Kauai, Aloha Airlines has two daily nonstop flights; all other Kauai-Maui flights go via Honolulu. One-way fares on either airline are $93, and roundtrip fares are double that.

Island Air (☎ 800-652-6541) flies to Kahului from Honolulu seven times a day, from Molokai four times a day, from Lanai three times a day and from Hana twice a day. One-way fares are $93.

Pacific Wings (☎ 873-0877, 888-575-4546), a small airline that recently relocated from Nevada, flies eight-passenger Cessna propeller planes between Kahului and Hana (once daily), Molokai's Kalaupapa Peninsula (once daily), Waimea (on the Big Island; once daily), Molokai's Hoolehua Airport (four times daily) and Honolulu (five times daily). The fare to Hana is $65; all fares to the other destinations are $75.

Airlines serving Kahului Airport from the US mainland include United, American, Hawaiian and Delta.

Kahului Airport has a lei stand, newsstand, restaurant, cocktail lounge, snack bar, car rental booths, visitor information booths and gift shops. It also has baggage storage ($2 per piece for 24 hours).

Kapalua West Maui Airport This is a small airport with a 3000-foot runway that's serviced by prop planes. The airport is between Kapalua and Kaanapali, about 2 miles from each.

Island Air (☎ 800-652-6541), the only scheduled carrier flying into Kapalua West Maui, has eight flights a day from Honolulu; the first leaves Honolulu at 7 am, the last at 4 pm. It also operates an afternoon flight from Kona. One-way fares are $93.

Hula dancer by 18th-century artist John Webber

Hana Airport Island Air flies to Hana twice daily from Honolulu, Kahului and Molokai. The fares are $93 one way. Pacific Wings flies once daily from Kahului for $65 one way.

Ferry

Expeditions (☎ 661-3756, 800-695-2624) runs a small ferry five times daily between Maui and Lanai. Not only is it much cheaper than flying, but if you take the boat in winter, you'll have a fair chance of seeing whales along the way. The boat leaves Lahaina Harbor from the public pier in front of the Pioneer Inn at 6:45 and 9:15 am and 12:45, 3:15 and 5:45 pm, arriving at Manele Boat Harbor in Lanai about an hour later. The boat leaves Lanai at 8 and 10:30 am and 2, 4:30 and 6:45 pm. The one-way fare is $25 for adults and $20 for children two to 11. Reservations can be made by phone in advance; tickets are purchased on the boat.

MAUI

GETTING AROUND
To/From the Airport

TransHawaiian (☎ 877-0380, 800-231-6984) has an airport shuttle bus to West Maui that leaves from the Kahului Airport every 30 minutes (on the hour and the half hour) from 9 am to 4 pm daily. It can drop passengers at the Pioneer Inn in Lahaina and at resort hotels in Kaanapali. Returning to the airport, shuttle buses leave the Whalers Village shopping center in Kaanapali every 30 minutes from 10:20 am until 5:20 pm. The cost is $13 if you're coming from the airport and $7 if you're going to the airport. Call ahead to make reservations on the return, as the shuttle will only stop at hotels where passengers are expected.

In addition, Speedi Shuttle (☎ 875-8070) has airport transfers on demand, with advance reservations. The price depends on the destination and the size of the group. For example, the cost for two people is $22 to Wailea, $31 to Lahaina, while a single person pays $20 and $26, respectively. There's a courtesy phone at the baggage claim area.

The TransHawaiian bus and the airport taxi dispatchers all have booths near the exit of the baggage claim area.

Bus

Maui has no public bus service, but a couple of private lines operate in the West Maui area and between West Maui and the Kihei and Wailea areas. While they can be used to get away for the day, these buses are geared more to shopping excursions than sightseeing. Schedules are subject to change, so it's wise to inquire before planning your day.

The Maui Ocean Center Trolley runs three times a day from major hotels in Wailea and Kihei to the Maui Ocean Center and then directly on to the Whalers Village shopping center in Kaanapali. To the Ocean Center, the cost is $7 from any point on the route. If you're going from the Kihei area to Kaanapali, the cost is $15 one way, but the return trip is free if you show a receipt for any purchase from one of the Whalers Village shops. Buses leave the Renaissance Wailea Beach Resort at 9 am and 12:15 and 3:30 pm, arriving at Whalers Village one hour later.

On the return, buses leave Whalers Village at 10:15 am and 1:30 and 4:45 pm.

The West Maui Shopping Express (☎ 877-7308) operates two shuttle routes from Kaanapali: one south to Lahaina and the other north to Kapalua. Both routes operate about once an hour throughout the day and cost $1. On the Kapalua route, the first bus heads southbound from the Ritz-Carlton in Kapalua at 9 am and northbound from the Whalers Village shopping center in Kaanapali at 9:15 am. The last southbound bus is at 8:20 pm, and the last northbound bus leaves at 8:50 pm. En route stops include the Embassy Suites, in Honokowai; the Sands of Kahana, in Kahana; and Napili Plaza, in Napili.

On the Lahaina route, the first southbound bus leaves the Whalers Village shopping center in Kaanapali at 9:55 am, and the last one leaves at 9:55 pm. Northbound, the first bus leaves the Wharf Cinema Center in Lahaina at 10:10 am, and the last one leaves at 10:10 pm.

In addition, Wailea and Kaanapali both have free resortwide shuttle services; see the respective destination sections for details.

For information on bus and van sightseeing tours, see Organized Tours in the earlier Activities section.

Taxi

Taxi fares are regulated by the county. The minimum flag-down fare is $1.75; the first mile totals around $3.50, and each additional mile is about $1.75.

Approximate one-way fares from Kahului Airport are: $5 to $10 to places around Kahului, $14 to Paia, $18 to $30 to Kihei, $45 to Lahaina, $50 to Kaanapali and $60 to Kapalua.

Car & Moped

Alamo (☎ 871-6235), Avis (☎ 871-7575), Budget (☎ 871-8811), Dollar (☎ 877-6526), Hertz (☎ 877-5167) and National (☎ 871-8851) all have booths at Kahului Airport.

Alamo, Avis, Budget, Dollar and National have offices on Hwy 30 in Kaanapali and will pick up at the Kapalua West Maui Airport. Dollar is the only rental agency serving Hana Airport.

More information on the national chains, including toll-free numbers, is in the Getting Around chapter in the front of the book.

Wheels R Us, which has branches at 741 Wainee St in Lahaina (☎ 667-7751) and 75 Kaahumanu Ave in Kahului (☎ 871-6858), rents older compact cars for $25/130 a day/week. Drivers under age 25 are charged $6 extra a day. If you don't have a credit card, a $300 cash deposit is required, and you must purchase the otherwise optional $9-a-day collision-damage waiver (CDW). Wheels R Us also rents mopeds for $26/130 a day/week.

Word of Mouth (☎ 877-2436, 800-533-5929, word@maui.net), 150 Hana Hwy, Kahului, rents old cars by the week for around $115 and newer cars (about six years old) for $135. Credit cards are required. The minimum age requirement for renters is usually 25, but the company will sometimes rent to younger drivers.

Good Kar-Ma Car Rentals (☎ 871-2911), 536 Keolani Place (the road into the airport in Kahului), has older cars but rents to people under age 25 without a surcharge. Vehicles range from compacts for $28/120 a day/week to windsurfing vans for $45/170.

Some of the windsurf shops can arrange reasonably priced car and van rentals for their customers.

Bicycle

Cyclists on Maui face a number of challenges: narrow roads, heavy traffic, an abundance of hills and mountains, and the same persistent winds that so delight windsurfers. The island's stunning scenery may entice hardcore cyclists, but casual riders hoping to use a bike as a primary source of transportation may well find such conditions daunting.

But getting around by bicycle within a small area can be a reasonable option for the average rider. For example, the tourist enclave of Kihei is largely level, and bicycle lanes – still a rarity on Maui – are now being added along its main beachfront drag, S Kihei Rd.

South Maui Bicycles (☎ 874-0068), 1993 S Kihei Rd, Kihei, rents quality mountain bikes for $30/110 a day/week and street cruisers for $17/79.

Maui Sports & Cycle (☎ 875-2882), with Kihei shops at Dolphin Plaza, 2395 S Kihei Rd, and at Longs Center, 1215 S Kihei Rd, rents mountain bikes for $19 to $31 a day depending upon the type of bike.

West Maui Cycles, with shops at 193 Lahainaluna Rd in Lahaina (☎ 661-9005) and on Lower Honoapiilani Rd in Kahana (☎ 669-1169), rents cruiser road bikes for $10/50 a day/week, hybrids for $19/79 and front-suspension mountain bikes for $25/110.

In Kahului, Island Biker (☎ 877-7744), 415 Dairy Rd, rents quality mountain bikes with your choice of knobby tires or road tires for $25/85 a day week. There are also a few full-suspension bikes available at $45 a day.

For information on cycle tours, see Cycling under Activities, earlier in this chapter.

Northwest Maui

Northwest Maui encompasses a large oval of land, from Kahului west to the coast and from Honokohau Bay south to Papawai Point. This region of the island contains both scenic coastal towns where rustic buildings survive from the 19th century and modern resort communities lined with condos. Behind it all, the dramatic West Maui Mountains dominate the landscape, with cliffs casting long shadows over old sugar cane fields.

MAUI

LAHAINA

In ancient times, Lahaina was a royal court for Maui chiefs and was the breadbasket, or, more accurately, the breadfruit basket, of West Maui. After Kamehameha I unified the islands, he set up his base in Lahaina, and the capital remained there until 1845. Hawaii's first stone church, first missionary school and first printing press were all in place in Lahaina by the early 1830s. The whaling years reached their peak in Lahaina in the 1840s, with hundreds of ships pulling into port each year. The town took on the whalers' boisterous nature, opening dance halls, bars and brothels. Hundreds of sick or derelict sailors, who had either been abandoned or jumped ship, roamed the streets. Among the

NORTHWEST MAUI

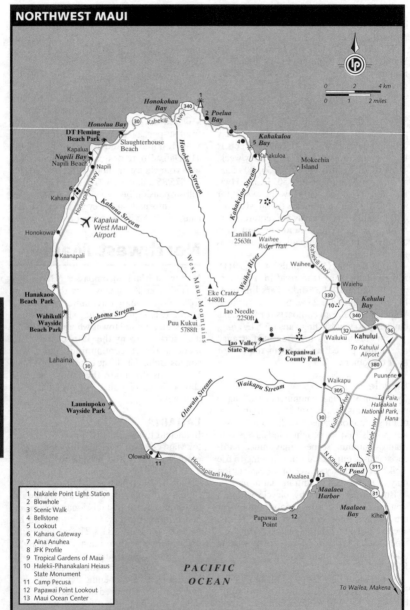

0   2   4 km
0   1   2 miles

Honokohau Bay
Poelua Bay
Honolua Bay
Kahekili
340
30
DT Fleming Beach Park
Slaughterhouse Beach
Kapalua
Kahakuloa Bay
Napili Bay
Napili Beach
Napili
Kahakuloa
Mokeehia Island
Honokohau Stream
Kahakuloa Stream
Kahana
Kahana Stream
Kapalua West Maui Airport
Honokowai
Lanilili 2563ft
Waihee Ridge Trail
Kaanapali
Waihee River
Waihee
Kahekili Hwy
Waiehu
330
Kahului Bay
Hanakaoo Beach Park
West Maui Mountains
Eke Crater 4480ft
340
Wahikuli Wayside Beach Park
Kahoma Stream
Iao Needle 2250ft
10
36
Puu Kukui 5788ft
Iao Valley State Park
Wailuku
Kahului
Lahaina
Kepaniwai County Park
To Kahului Airport
30
Waikapu
305
380
Puunene
Waikapu Stream
Launiupoko Wayside Park
Olowalu Stream
30
To Paia, Haleakala National Park, Hana
Mokulele Hwy
Kuihelani Hwy
Kealia Pond
311
Olowalu
Honoapiilani Hwy
N Kihei Rd
Maalaea
Maalaea Harbor
Papawai Point
Maalaea Bay
Kihei
31
To Wailea, Makena

PACIFIC OCEAN

1 Nakalele Point Light Station
2 Blowhole
3 Scenic Walk
4 Bellstone
5 Lookout
6 Kahana Gateway
7 Aina Anuhea
8 JFK Profile
9 Tropical Gardens of Maui
10 Halekii-Pihanakalani Heiaus
   State Monument
11 Camp Pecusa
12 Papawai Point Lookout
13 Maui Ocean Center

MAUI

multitudes that landed in Lahaina was Herman Melville, who later penned *Moby Dick*.

These days, Lahaina's streets are jammed with tourists. The old wooden shops that once housed saloons and provision stores are now crammed with boutiques and galleries.

While there are plenty of interesting historical sites to see, Lahaina is abuzz with commercial activity; if you're expecting something quaint and romantic, you may well be disappointed. The coastal setting and mountain backdrop *is* pretty, however, and it's easy to see why people have been drawn here. There are soft breezes off the water and fine sunset views of Lanai.

Orientation

Lahaina's chief attractions are 19th-century historical sites. Sightseeing spots include homes of missionaries, prisons for sailors and graveyards for both.

The focal point of Lahaina is its bustling small-boat harbor, which is backed by the old Pioneer Inn and Banyan Tree Square. Half of Lahaina's sights are clustered in this area, while the other half are scattered around town.

The main drag and tourist strip is Front St, which runs along the shoreline.

Information

The Bank of Hawaii branch in the Lahaina Shopping Center is open 8:30 am to 4 pm Monday to Thursday, 8:30 am to 6 pm on Friday. First Hawaiian Bank has a branch on the corner of Wainee and Papalaua Sts.

The post office substation in the Lahaina Shopping Center is open 8:15 am to 4:15 pm Monday to Friday. There's often a long wait for a parking space and a long queue inside. The main post office, where you pick up mail sent general delivery to Lahaina, is near the civic center, on Hwy 30 between Lahaina and Kaanapali. Hours are 8:30 am to 5 pm Monday to Friday, 10 am to noon on Saturday.

The Lahaina public library, 680 Wharf St, is open 9 am to 5 pm on Monday, Tuesday and Wednesday, noon to 8 pm on Thursday and 12:30 to 4:30 pm on Friday. It carries Maui, Honolulu and a few mainland newspapers.

Pioneer Inn

The old green-and-white Pioneer Inn is the most prominent landmark in town. It's got a whaling-era atmosphere, with swinging doors, ship figureheads and signs warning against womanizing in the rooms. The downstairs saloon is still a popular watering hole.

Actually, the two-story Pioneer Inn was built in 1901, long after the whaling boom had passed, but nobody seems to notice or care.

Banyan Tree Square

The largest banyan tree in the USA covers most of the space in the park next to the Pioneer Inn. It's so sprawling that it appears to be on the verge of pushing the old courthouse, which shares the square, clear off the block.

The tree was planted in 1873 to commemorate the 50th anniversary of the first missionary arrival in Lahaina. It has 16 major trunks and scores of horizontally stretching branches reaching across the better part of an acre. Local kids like to use the aerial roots to swing Tarzan-style from branch to branch. With its shaded benches and walkways, the square makes a nice spot to take a break from the crowds on Front St.

Old Courthouse & Lahaina Arts Society

Beyond the banyan tree is the old courthouse, built in 1859. It once served as the government center, housing customs, a post office and the governor's office.

The USA's largest banyan tree lives in Lahaina.

MAUI

LAHAINA

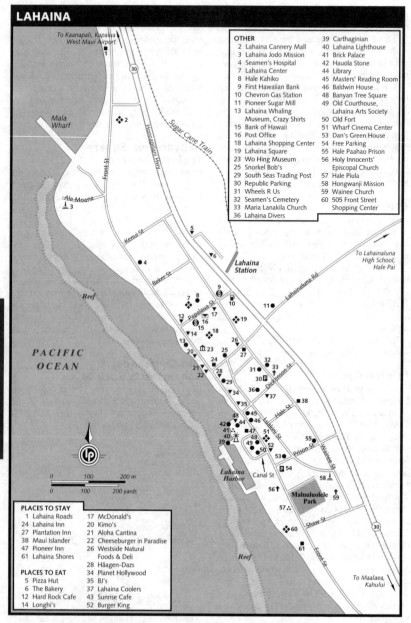

To Kaanapali, Kapalua
West Maui Airport

Mala Wharf

Ala Moana

Reef

PACIFIC
OCEAN

Front St
Honoapiilani Hwy
Sugar Cane Train
Kenui St
Baker St
Papalaua St

Lahaina
Station

To Lahainaluna
High School,
Hale Pai

Lahainaluna Rd

Dickenson St
Luakini St
Hale St
Prison St
Wainee St

Lahaina
Harbor

Canal St

Malululolele
Park

Shaw St
Front St

Reef

To Maalaea,
Kahului

0   100   200 m
0   100   200 yards

OTHER

2 Lahaina Cannery Mall	39 Carthaginian
3 Lahaina Jodo Mission	40 Lahaina Lighthouse
4 Seamen's Hospital	41 Brick Palace
7 Lahaina Center	42 Hauola Stone
8 Hale Kahiko	44 Library
9 First Hawaiian Bank	45 Masters' Reading Room
10 Chevron Gas Station	46 Baldwin House
11 Pioneer Sugar Mill	48 Banyan Tree Square
13 Lahaina Whaling	49 Old Courthouse,
Museum, Crazy Shirts	Lahaina Arts Society
15 Bank of Hawaii	50 Old Fort
16 Post Office	51 Wharf Cinema Center
18 Lahaina Shopping Center	53 Dan's Green House
19 Lahaina Square	54 Free Parking
23 Wo Hing Museum	55 Hale Paahao Prison
25 Snorkel Bob's	56 Holy Innocents'
29 South Seas Trading Post	Episcopal Church
30 Republic Parking	57 Hale Piula
31 Wheels R Us	58 Hongwanji Mission
32 Seamen's Cemetery	59 Wainee Church
33 Maria Lanakila Church	60 505 Front Street
36 Lahaina Divers	Shopping Center

PLACES TO STAY

1 Lahaina Roads	17 McDonald's
24 Lahaina Inn	20 Kimo's
27 Plantation Inn	21 Aloha Cantina
38 Maui Islander	22 Cheeseburger in Paradise
47 Pioneer Inn	26 Westside Natural
61 Lahaina Shores	Foods & Deli
	28 Häagen-Dazs
PLACES TO EAT	34 Planet Hollywood
5 Pizza Hut	35 BJ's
6 The Bakery	37 Lahaina Coolers
12 Hard Rock Cafe	43 Sunrise Cafe
14 Longhi's	52 Burger King

MAUI

Today the old jail in the basement is used by the Lahaina Arts Society, and the cells that once held drunken sailors now display artwork. The society is a nonprofit collective, with artists donating their time and paying a 30% commission to cover operating expenses. As that's roughly half of the commission charged by private galleries, you'll find some of the best prices in Lahaina here.

The exhibits are all by island artists and include paintings, jewelry, pottery, woodcarvings and some quality basketwork. Many of the baskets are composed entirely of fibers native to Maui, such as wattle, watsonia, philodendron, draco, ape and fishtail palm.

The society also sponsors community art classes, and a number of well-known Maui artists got their start here. It's open 9 am to 5 pm daily.

Old Fort

The Canal St corner of Banyan Tree Square has a reconstructed section of coral wall from a fort that was built in 1832 to keep rowdy whalers in line.

At the height of its use, the fort had 47 cannons, most salvaged from foreign ships that sank in Hawaiian waters.

Each day at dusk, a Hawaiian sentinel beat a drum to alert sailors to return to their ships. Those who didn't make it back in time ended up imprisoned in the fort. In 1854, the fort was dismantled and its coral blocks used as building materials for the new prison.

Canal St

Canal St, bordering Banyan Tree Square, used to be part of a canal system that ran through Lahaina. An enterprising US consul officer built this section of the canal in the 1840s to allow whalers easier access to freshwater supplies – for a fee, of course.

Because of problems with mosquitoes, most of the canal system was filled in long ago. Incidentally, Hawaii had no mosquitoes at all until the whalers brought them in from North America in their water barrels.

Lahaina Harbor

The four cannons on the waterfront opposite the old courthouse were raised from the wreck of a Russian ship that went down in Honolulu Harbor in 1816.

They now point directly at Lahaina's crowded small-boat harbor, which is filled with glass-bottom boats, windjammers, sportfishing boats, whale-watchers and sunset sailboats. Booths lining the edge of the harbor sell tickets for most of the cruises, as do the ubiquitous activity booths around town.

The Carthaginian

In 1972, the 960-ton *Carthaginian*, one of the last square-riggers in Hawaii, was on its way from Maui to Honolulu for repairs when it hit a reef outside Lahaina Harbor and sank. The wooden-hulled *Carthaginian* belonged to a class of swift brigantines that made freight runs between New England, Hawaii and China in the 19th century.

The ship that now sits in Lahaina Harbor is actually a steel-hulled vessel built in Kiel, Germany, in 1920, that has been converted into a replica of the original *Carthaginian*. After being brought to Lahaina in 1973, this 97-foot brig had to be completely restored and all the masts and yards handcrafted – a process that took a full seven years.

Although the most attractive view of the ship is from the outside, you can also go aboard for $3 ($5 for a family). Below deck, there's a tiny theater where films on whales are shown continuously. The ship is open 10 am to 4 pm daily.

Masters' Reading Room

The Masters' Reading Room, on the corner of Front and Dickenson Sts, is the office of the Lahaina Restoration Foundation (☎ 661-3262), the group most instrumental in preserving Lahaina's historical sites.

During the whaling years, the building was a reading room for sea captains. From here, they could keep an eye on happenings in the harbor across the road. The original construction of coral and stone blocks has been preserved.

Baldwin House

The Baldwin House, next door to the Masters' Reading Room, is the oldest building in Lahaina. Built in 1834, it was home to

MAUI

the Reverend Dwight Baldwin, a missionary doctor. The exterior of the coral and rock building once looked a lot like the Reading Room, but it has since been plastered over. The walls beneath the plaster are a full 24 inches thick, which keeps the house cool year-round.

It took the Baldwins 161 days to get to Hawaii from their native Connecticut. These early missionaries traveled neither fast nor light, and the house still holds the collection of china and furniture they brought with them around the Horn.

The entrance fee of $3 ($5 per family) includes a brief tour. It's open 10 am to 4:30 pm daily, with the last tour beginning at 4:15 pm.

Library Area

The entire area surrounding the Lahaina public library was once the site of a royal taro field. It was also the location of the first Western-style building in Hawaii, the **Brick Palace**, erected by King Kamehameha I so he could keep watch on arriving ships. Despite the grand name, this 'palace' was a modest two-story structure built around 1800 by two convicts. All that remains today is the excavated foundation, which can be found on the ocean side of the library.

The nearby **Hauola Stone** is a water-worn lava stone on the shoreline. To spot it, look to the right as you face the ocean – it's the middle stone. The Hawaiians believed this flat, seat-shaped stone emitted healing powers to those who sat on it.

In the same area, about 100 feet south of the Hauola Stone, stands the **Lahaina Lighthouse**, which claims to be the oldest lighthouse in the Pacific. It was commissioned in 1840 to aid whalers pulling into Lahaina, though the current building dates from 1916.

If you walk north down Front St past the library, you'll come to a row of interesting **historical buildings**, which date to the turn of the 20th century. The buildings are best appreciated from the seawall sidewalk.

Wo Hing Temple

The Wo Hing Temple, on Front St, was built in 1912 by the Chinese community in Lahaina. This two-story building functioned largely as a meeting hall, though for a period after WWII it was also used as a home for elderly Chinese men.

As Lahaina's ethnic Chinese population declined, so too did the building. It was restored and turned into a museum by the Lahaina Restoration Foundation in 1983. Inside you'll find cultural artifacts and period photos downstairs and a Taoist shrine upstairs.

The tin-roof cookhouse next door (built detached because of the danger of fire) has been set up as a little theater to show fascinating films shot by inventor Thomas Edison during his visits to the islands in 1898 and 1905.

Against the wall is a collection of little opium bottles found during the cleanup of the grounds. The museum is open 10 am to 4:15 pm daily. Admission is free, though donations are appreciated.

Lahaina Whaling Museum

Lahaina Whaling Museum is actually a display of whaling-era artifacts along one wall of the Crazy Shirts store at 865 Front St. It's an unusual setup for a museum, but it's authentic; free and open 9 am to 10 pm daily.

The collection includes antique harpoons, harpoon guns, scrimshaw and photos of the *Carthaginian* sinking outside Lahaina Harbor in 1972. The figurehead hanging from the ceiling in the front of the store was salvaged from the ship. It had been carved in 1965 to prepare the *Carthaginian* for its feature role in the movie *Hawaii*, the adaptation of James Michener's epic novel.

Out on the back porch are some period artifacts, including a rusty old cannon and anchor and a whaler's try-pot that was once used for boiling down blubber.

Hale Kahiko

At the rear of the Lahaina Center is Hale Kahiko, which consists of three *pili* (bunchgrass) houses, or *hale*, that replicate a slice of an old Hawaiian village. Despite the irony of being off to the side of a new shopping center's parking lot, the site does offer an interesting little glimpse of what life was like in Hawaii before Western development swept the landscape.

The buildings have been constructed in the old manner, using ohia-wood posts and native thatch and fiber lashings, and they're landscaped with a few of the native plants that Hawaiians used for food or medicinal purposes. Each hale had a different function; one was used as family sleeping quarters, another used to be a men's eating house (traditional *kapus*, or taboos, forced men and women to eat separately), and the third was a workshop where women made tapa. Inside the structures are gourd containers, woven baskets and a few simple everyday implements from the period.

It's open 9 am to 6 pm daily; admission is free.

Holy Innocents' Episcopal Church

The interior of Holy Innocents' Episcopal Church, 561 Front St, is decorated with a Hawaiiana motif.

Paintings on the front of the koa altar depict a fisher in an outrigger canoe and Hawaiian farmers harvesting taro and breadfruit. Above the altar is a Hawaiian Madonna and Child; a Lahaina mother and infant were the models for the painting.

Until the turn of the 20th century, the church property was the site of a vacation home belonging to Queen Liliuokalani, Hawaii's last reigning monarch.

Hale Piula

A couple of steps and a grassy building foundation between the Episcopal Church and the 505 Front St shopping center is all that remains of Hale Piula, Lahaina's half-hearted attempt at a royal palace.

Construction on the palace was started in the late 1830s but never completed – Kamehameha III preferred to sleep in a Hawaiian-style thatched house, and at any rate, he decided to move the capital to Honolulu halfway through the project. The building was used for a short time as a government office, but most of the stones were later carted away and used to build the harborside courthouse.

Maluuluolele Park

Maluuluolele Park, opposite Hale Piula, was once the site of a large pond containing a legendary *moo* (water dragon). An island in the center of the pond was home to Maui chiefs and at times to Kings Kamehameha I, II and III. Called Mokuula, which means 'sacred island,' it held an ornate burial chamber for royalty.

The park's present name means literally 'the breadfruit shade of Lele' ('Lele' was the ancient name for Lahaina).

In 1918, the island was leveled and the pond filled in. Today, the park has basketball courts, tennis courts, a baseball field and not a hint of its fascinating past.

Wainee Church

Wainee Church, 535 Wainee St, was built in 1832 as the first stone church in Hawaii. It's gone through a barrage of changes since. The steeple and bell collapsed in 1858. In 1894, the church was torched by royalists because its minister supported the annexation of Hawaii. A second church, built to replace the original, burned to the ground in 1947, and the third was blown away in a storm a few years later. One could get the impression that the old Hawaiian gods didn't take kindly to the house of this foreign deity!

The fourth version has been standing since 1953. It's now called Waiola Congregational Church and holds regular services.

The **cemetery** next door is more interesting than the church. Here lie several notables: Governor Hoapili, who ordered the original church built; Queen Keopuolani, once the highest-ranking woman in Hawaii and wife of Kamehameha I; and the Reverend William Richards, Lahaina's first missionary. Some of the old tombstones have interesting inscriptions and photo cameos.

Hongwanji Mission

The Lahaina Hongwanji Mission, 551 Wainee St, was built in 1927. It's usually locked, but the front doors are glass so you can glance in. Unlike Buddhist temples in Japan, this one has rows of wooden pews. Services are held each Sunday in English and once a month in Japanese.

Hale Paahao Prison

Hale Paahao ('stuck-in-irons house'), Lahaina's old prison, was built in 1852 by convicts, who dismantled the old harborside fort and carried the stone blocks here to construct these eight-foot-high prison walls.

Inside, one of the whitewashed cells has an authentic-looking 'old seadog' mannequin with a recorded story about 'life in this here calaboose.'

In another cell, you'll find a list of offenses and arrests for the year 1855. The top three offenses were drunkenness (330 arrests), adultery and fornication (111) and 'furious riding' (89). Others include profanity, aiding deserting sailors, drinking *awa* (kava moonshine) and giving birth to bastard children. Hawaiians could collect bounties by turning in sailors who jumped ship or fooled around with local women. There's also a copy of a 16-year-old seaman's diary, vividly describing his time spent in the prison. Admission is free.

Seamen's Cemetery

The Seamen's Cemetery on Wainee St is next to Maria Lanakila Church, the first Catholic church on Maui.

It's basically a local cemetery, with only one seaman's tombstone that can be identified. However, historical records indicate that numerous sailors from the whaling era were buried here, including a shipmate of Herman Melville's from the *Acushnet*.

Pioneer Sugar Mill

It's hard to think of tourist-jammed Lahaina as a sugar town, but it is. The Pioneer Sugar Mill has been a prominent part of Lahaina for 140 years, and its cane fields still stretch for 17 miles along the coast.

The dusty mill, which sits on both sides of Lahainaluna Rd on the slopes above the town center, stands in sharp contrast to all the tourist activity below.

Lahainaluna Seminary

Lahainaluna Seminary, established by Christian missionaries in 1831, was the first US educational institution west of the Rockies.

One of the school's original graduates was David Malo, a respected Hawaiian philosopher. He became Hawaii's first native-rights spokesperson, warning in his early writings in 1837 that Hawaii was about to be swallowed up by the masses of foreigners arriving on its shores. His book *Hawaiian Antiquities* is regarded as the preeminent published account of ancient Hawaiian history and culture.

Lahainaluna is now Lahaina's public high school, considered one of the finest in the state. Malo is buried on the hillside above the school.

The school is at the end of Lahainaluna Rd, $1\frac{1}{3}$ miles above the mill. There's a nice view of Lahaina with Lanai in the background from the school's lower parking lot.

Hale Pai, a printing house on Lahainaluna's grounds, was the site of the first printing press in Hawaii. Although the main purpose of the press was to make the Bible available to Hawaiians, it also was used to produce other works, including the first Hawaiian botany book and, in 1834, Hawaii's first newspaper.

Examples of early books are on display at Hale Pai. You can use a replica of the original Ramage press to hand print your own copy of a page from the first Hawaiian primer.

A limited corps of volunteers staff the building, so the hours are a bit flexible, but it's generally open 10 am to 3 pm weekdays. Admission is free but donations are appreciated.

Seamen's Hospital

In 1844, the building at 1024 Front St was leased by the US government and turned into a hospital for sick and abandoned seamen.

Officials at the hospital were notorious for embezzlement. Sailors who weren't sick and others long since dead were commonly signed onto the hospital books. A US warship with a board of inquiry was sent by the American government to investigate the corruption, but the ship and its findings mysteriously disappeared at sea on the return home!

The seamen's hospital has been completely restored and is now used as a private office. A huge anchor on the lawn marks the site.

Lahaina Jodo Mission

A large bronze statue of Buddha overlooks the compound of Lahaina Jodo Mission, off the north end of Front St, just before the bridge. The statue was put up in 1968 in celebration of the centennial of Japanese immigration to Hawaii. With its back to the mountains, the Buddha looks out over the Pacific toward Japan.

Just to the north is the long **Mala Wharf**, constructed in the 1920s to allow interisland ferries to land passengers directly ashore. It never made the grade. Rough seas prevented the ferries from pulling up alongside the pier, forcing them to continue shuttling passengers across the shallows of Lahaina Harbor in small boats.

The wharf is now crumbling and closed, though Mala does have a new launch ramp for small boats nearby.

Lahaina Beaches

Lahaina is not known for its beaches, which are largely shallow and rocky. The section near the Lahaina Shores is swimmable, but your best bet is to go north to Hanakaoo Beach Park or to Kaanapali.

Places to Stay

Camping The nearest campground is in Olowalu, 5 miles south of Lahaina. Details are in the Olowalu section.

B&Bs *Aloha Lani Inn* (☎ 661-8040, 800-572-5642, fax 661-8045, melinda@maui.net, 13 Kauaula Rd, PO Box 11475, Lahaina, HI 96761), about a two-minute walk south of Lahaina Shores, is a homey affordable option. Although it's a modest house, the accommodating owner, Melinda, has added a pleasant tropical decor, piled the living room with Hawaiiana books and made it all quite cozy. The three guest rooms have shared bath and cost $59/69 for singles/doubles. There's a two-night minimum. Breakfast is not included, but guests are allowed kitchen privileges and free coffee is available. To see photos of the accommodations, visit Melinda's website at www.maui-vacations.com/aloha.

The *Old Lahaina House* (☎ 667-4663, 800-847-0761, fax 667-5615, olh@oldlahaina.com,

A meditative moment in busy Lahaina

LEE FOSTER

PO Box 10355, Lahaina, HI 96761), also just a few minutes south of Lahaina Shores, consists of four guest rooms in the home of Sherry and John Barbier. Two rooms have king beds, private baths and refrigerators and rent for $95 for a double. The other rooms, which cost $69, each have two twin beds. All rooms have TV, phone and air-con, and there's a pool in the yard. Except on Sunday, a breakfast of pastries and fruit is included in the rates. For more information, visit the Barbiers' website at www.mauiweb.com/maui/olhouse.

The two B&Bs that follow are in a residential area about 4 miles north of Lahaina, just inland from Hwy 30 and about a 10-minute walk from Wahikuli Beach Park.

House of Fountains (☎ 667-2121, 800-789-6865, fax 667-2120, private@maui.net, 1579 Lokia St, Lahaina, HI 96761) is an attractive 7000-sq-foot contemporary residence with six pleasant rooms. All have TV/VCRs, air-con, ceiling fans, queen beds, private baths and mini-refrigerators. The smallest is $85 a day, while the largest, a commodious suite, costs $125. Guests share a large, well-equipped kitchen, laundry facilities, a pool and Jacuzzi. A full breakfast, which includes cold cuts and other European-style fixings, is served on the ocean-view deck. German is spoken. All in all, it's a real find for travelers looking for a touch of luxury in a personal

MAUI

setting. To see pictures of the inn, go to www .alohahouse.com online.

The GuestHouse (☎ 661-8085, 800-621-8942, fax 661-1896, guesthouse@compuserve .com, 1620 Ainakea Rd, Lahaina, HI 96761) is another upscale home serving as a B&B. It has four roomy suites, each with a private lanai, air-con, TV, VCR, ceiling fan, refrigerator, phone, queen bed and either a hot tub or a Jacuzzi. Three of the rooms also have a twin bed. Singles/doubles cost $105/115. Despite being a B&B, this spot offers plenty of privacy, and it would make a fun place for a honeymoon or other romantic getaway. There's a pool. Guests have access to laundry facilities and the use of beach gear, including boogie boards and snorkel sets. Breakfast is included in the rates.

Condos & Hotels   You couldn't be more in the middle of the action than at the **Pioneer Inn** (☎ 661-3636, 800-457-5457, fax 667-5708, 658 Wharf St, Lahaina, HI 96761). It can be noisy from the traffic, the tourists and the raucous bar, but this two-story, historic hotel has plenty of character. The funky old harborfront rooms for which the inn was best known are no longer available. Instead, it has 33 renovated rooms facing Front St, Banyan Square or the inn's courtyard. The rooms are small but comfortable, with period furnishings, queen beds, ceiling fans, air-con, phones and private baths. Considering the room size and the less-than-soundproof walls, the rates are pricey at $90 to $135. The hotel can be booked through Best Western.

Maui Islander (☎ 667-9766, 800-367-5226, fax 661-3733, 660 Wainee St, Lahaina, HI 96761) is a sprawling 372-unit hotel set back a few blocks from Front St. The hotel is standard fare without a great deal of character. Rooms have cable TV, air-con, ceiling fans and safes. There's a pool, a tennis court and a barbecue area. Rates are $99 for a room with a refrigerator, $125 for a studio with kitchen and $155 (for up to three people) for a one-bedroom suite. On stays of five nights, the fifth night is usually free.

The best-value condo in the Lahaina area is **Lahaina Roads** (☎ 661-3166, 800-624-8203, fax 661-5875, 1403 Front St, Lahaina,

HI 96761), north of the town center, near the Lahaina Cannery Mall. All of its 42 units are oceanfront, with full kitchens, lanais, TVs and phones with free local calls. There's an oceanside swimming pool. Roomy one-bedroom units have a sofa bed in the living room and cost $100 for up to four people. There's a 10% discount for seven nights or more. The minimum stay is three days.

The **Lahaina Inn** (☎ 661-0577, 800-669-3444, fax 667-9480, inntown@lahainainn .com, 127 Lahainaluna Rd, Lahaina, HI 96761) is a project of Crazy Shirts owner Rick Ralston, who spent over $3 million restoring this century-old 12-room hostelry. The rooms are small but delightfully atmospheric, and each has hardwood floors, floral wallpaper, antique furnishings and a lanai. Modern conveniences include air-con, private bath, telephone and piped-in classical music, but no TV. Room rates are $109 and $119, while suites are $169. Prices, which include continental breakfast, are the same for singles and doubles. Children under age 15 are not allowed. For more information, visit the inn's website at www.lahainainn.com.

The **Plantation Inn** (☎ 667-9225, 800-433-6815, fax 667-9293, inn@maui.net, 174 Lahainaluna Rd, Lahaina, HI 96761) is an elegant two-story Victorian-style inn with hardwood floors, antique furnishings, stained glass and a tiled pool. The 18 rooms and suites range from $135 to $215. Classy and comfortable, it's arguably the nicest place to stay in Lahaina. Prices include a continental breakfast at Gerard's, the restaurant at the front of the inn.

Lahaina Shores (☎ 661-4835, 800-642-6284, fax 661-1025, info@classicresorts.com, 475 Front St, Lahaina, HI 96761) is a 155-room condo run like a hotel. It's on the beach next to the 505 Front St shopping center, at the south side of town. Mountain-view studios cost $130/140 in the low/high season, one-bedroom units cost $165/195. Add on another $25/35 low/high for an ocean view.

Places to Eat

Budget *The Bakery* (991 Limahana Place), on the north side of town, is Lahaina's best bakery. In addition to freshly baked bread, you can get tempting sticky buns and huge muffins for under $2 and sandwiches made to order for $5. The bakery opens at 5:30 am daily, closing at 3 pm on weekdays, 2 pm on Saturday and noon on Sunday. To get there, turn *mauka* (inland) off Hwy 30 onto Hinau St at Pizza Hut.

Sunrise Cafe, in the town center opposite the library, is a casual little hole-in-the-wall with cinnamon rolls, bagels, pancakes, salads and sandwiches at reasonable prices. It's open 6 am to 6 pm.

Westside Natural Foods & Deli (193 Lahainaluna Rd) sells organic produce, yogurt, fresh juice and a variety of bulk trail mixes and granolas. The deli has a salad bar, a few hot vegetarian dishes for $6 a pound and cafe tables where you can sit and eat. Westside Natural foods is open from 7:30 am to 9 pm Monday to Saturday, from 8:30 am to 8 pm Sunday.

The *Maui Cafe*, at the 505 Front St Shopping Center, has the expected muffins, omelettes and sandwiches but also has top-notch Vietnamese food. It offers an unbeatable noodle dish with spring rolls and chicken on a bed of lettuce for $7, as well as authentic pho soups and Thai-style stir-fry dishes. As with most Vietnamese restaurants, there are a number of vegetarian offerings. It's open 7 am to 9 pm daily.

Lahaina has numerous fast-food restaurants, including *Burger King* (632 Front St), *McDonald's* (885 Wainee St) and *Pizza Hut* (Hwy 30). There are *Häagen-Dazs* ice cream shops fronting the Pioneer Inn and on Front St near Lahainaluna Rd.

The Wharf Cinema Center on Front St has a *Subway* sandwich shop, an *Orange Julius* and a few undistinguished ethnic restaurants.

Lahaina Square, off Wainee St, has a *Foodland* supermarket, a 24-hour *Denny's* restaurant, a *Maui Tacos* and *Local Boy's*, a good plate-lunch eatery.

Lahaina Cannery Mall, in a former pineapple cannery on the northern side of town between Front St and Hwy 30, has a 24-hour *Safeway* supermarket with takeout salads and good deli, produce and wine sections. The mall also has inexpensive Chinese and Greek food stalls, a moderately priced Mexi-

can restaurant and a cafe with fresh-ground coffee and deli fare.

Mid-Range *Lahaina Coolers* (☎ 661-7082, 180 Dickenson St) has good food at reasonable prices. The varied menu includes salads for $3 to $8 and creative pizza, pasta and Thai dishes, most priced from $10 to $12. You can also get burgers and fries for a few dollars less. Until 11:15 am daily, there's an extensive breakfast menu with egg dishes, pancakes and lox and bagels. It's open 8 am until midnight daily.

Kimo's (☎ 661-4811, 845 Front St) is a popular oceanfront restaurant with a sunset view. Lunch is mainly salads and sandwiches in the $6 to $10 range. Dinner features chicken, seafood and steaks for $15 to $20, including a Caesar salad and warm muffins. Lunch is served from 11 am to 3 pm and dinner from 5 to 10:30 pm daily.

Also on the water is *Cheeseburger in Paradise* (☎ 661-4855, 811 Front St), which offers pleasant open-air dining and Black Angus beef cheeseburgers. In addition, it serves salads, sandwiches, omelettes and vegetarian burgers. Most items are $7 to $8. It's open until 11 pm nightly.

The always-popular *Hard Rock Cafe* (☎ 667-7400, 900 Front St) also has good burgers and sandwiches, including a club sandwich, veggie burger or bacon cheeseburger for around $9, with fries. There are also a few hot dishes such as steak, grilled chicken and fajitas for $11 to $20. Food is served from 11 am to 10 pm daily.

Though its trendiness is on the wane, *Planet Hollywood* (☎ 667-7877, 744 Front St) still attracts hopeful star-watchers; the restaurant's Hollywood stockholders, such as Arnold Schwarzenegger and Sylvester Stallone, occasionally make cameo appearances when they're on the island. A Cajun chicken sandwich, California pizza or Asian salad costs $10; fajitas, ribs and pasta dishes are a few dollars more. You can also just go in and linger over a beer, taking in the celluloid decor. It's open 11 am to midnight, but meal service ends at 10:30 pm.

BJ's (☎ 661-0700, 730 Front St), a Southern California chain restaurant, serves good

MAUI

Chicago-style pizza. You can get a medium cheese pizza for $13 (add $2 for each topping) and sandwiches and pastas for $9 and up. Until 4 pm, a lunch special of a mini-pizza and salad costs $6.50. Take in the 2nd-floor ocean view while you eat. BJ's opens at 11 am and closes late at night daily.

Aloha Cantina (☎ 661-8788, 839 Front St) offers oceanfront dining and Tex-Mex food at moderate prices. A main dish, such as fajitas or tacos, with rice and beans costs $10 to $16. It's open for lunch and dinner from 11 am to 10 pm.

Maui Brews (☎ 667-7794, 900 Front St), in the Lahaina Center, is a lively sports bar/restaurant that features burgers or pizza for around $8 and ribs or steak for double that. It also has happy-hour specials and Lahaina's largest selection of draft beers. Meals are served from 10 am to 10 pm, and *pupus* (snacks) are available until 11:30 pm.

Top End *Pacific'O* (☎ 667-4341), at the 505 Front St Shopping Center, is Lahaina's top fine-dining spot, with beachside tables and good imaginative food at relatively reasonable prices. Appetizers include shrimp wontons or a hot calamari salad for around $10. Main courses, around $20 to $25, include mouthwatering offerings such as fresh fish tempura, sesame-crusted lamb, kiawe-grilled chicken in a ginger-coconut sauce and vegetarian tofu steak with shiitake mushrooms. The lunch menu offers simpler fare – goat-cheese salad, shrimp satay, fish and chips – for about $10. It's open 11 am to 4 pm and 5:30 to 10 pm daily.

Longhi's (☎ 667-2288, 888 Front St) is one of Lahaina's busiest upper-end restaurants. At lunch, sandwiches and pastas begin at around $8, while seafood dishes such as fresh ahi or prawns amaretto average $14. The same pasta and seafood dishes cost $18 to $25 at dinner. The restaurant also has an extensive wine list. Longhi's is open 7:30 am to 10 pm daily.

David Paul's Lahaina Grill (☎ 667-5117, 127 Lahainaluna Rd), in the historic Lahaina Inn, is a popular fine-dining spot with excellent Pacific Rim cuisine and an intimate setting. Main dishes, which average

$30, include lamb, fresh fish and the house specialty of spicy tequila shrimp with firecracker rice. Appetizers such as the Kona lobster-crab cakes or squid-ink ravioli cost around $15. It's open for dinner only, 6 to 10 pm nightly.

Gerard's (☎ 661-8939, 174 Lahainaluna Rd) serves traditional French country cooking in a pleasant setting at the Plantation Inn. The menu changes regularly, but rack of lamb and duck confit are house standards; à la carte entrees average $30. It's open for dinner only, 6 to 9:30 pm daily.

Entertainment

Front St is the heart of Lahaina's nightlife. The waterfront *Cheeseburger in Paradise* (☎ 661-4855, 811 Front St) usually has live music from 4:30 to 11 pm nightly, typically country-rock and folk-rock sounds. There's no cover charge.

The nearby *Aloha Cantina* (☎ 661-8788, 839 Front St) has live music on Thursday, Friday and Saturday nights, commonly Hawaiian or reggae, and there's no cover.

Maui Brews (☎ 667-7794, 900 Front St), at the Lahaina Center, has big-screen sports TV in the bar and dancing nightly in the adjacent club. The club presents a mix of DJ nights and live reggae, salsa, pop, jazz and swing bands. The cover charge depends on the music; some nights are free, others cost $5, and for a name band it's higher. Both the bar and the club have a good selection of beers on tap, including Pacific Golden Ale from the Big Island brewery.

Longhi's (☎ 667-2288, 888 Front St), which has an interesting koa-wood dance floor, presents live rock bands starting around 9:30 pm on Friday or Saturday. The cover charge is $5 to $10, depending on the band.

Overlooking the beach, *Pacific'O* (☎ 667-4341), at the 505 Front St Shopping Center, features live jazz from 9 pm to midnight on Thursday, Friday and Saturday, with no cover charge.

There are free *keiki hula shows* at 2 pm on Wednesday and 6 pm on Friday at the Lahaina Center at 900 Front St, as well as at 1 pm on Sunday at the Lahaina Cannery Mall.

Cinemas The *Lahaina Wharf Cinemas* at the Wharf Cinema Center and the *Front Street Theatres* at the Lahaina Center *(both ☎ 661-3347)* are multiscreen theaters showing first-run movies.

The *Hawaii Experience Domed Theater* *(☎ 661-8314, 824 Front St)* shows a 40-minute film about Hawaii on an enormous 180° screen. It starts every hour on the hour, 10 am to 10 pm daily, and costs $7 for adults, $4 for children four to 12.

Luaus The *Old Lahaina Luau (☎ 667-1998, 1251 Front St)*, on the beach behind the Lahaina Cannery Mall, has a buffet dinner with open bar, Hawaiian music and a show from 5:30 to 8:30 pm nightly. The cost is $65 for adults, $30 for children 12 and under.

Shopping

Lahaina has numerous arts and crafts galleries, some with high-quality collections and others with mediocre works. A good place to start is the Lahaina Arts Society, a Maui collective with an extensive gallery in the old harborside courthouse.

'Art Night,' held from 6 to around 9 pm on Friday, is the time when Lahaina galleries schedule their openings, occasionally with entertainment and hors d'oeuvres.

South Seas Trading Post, 780 Front St, stands apart from all the gaudy tourist shops on Front St. It sells Hawaiiana crafts, tapa cloth, Papua New Guinean face masks and items from Southeast Asia. The exact collection at any given time depends on the itinerary of the owner's last jaunt abroad, but it's always intriguing.

Dan's Green House, at 133 Prison St, sells *fuku-bonsai*, a quasi-bonsai effect created when the roots of the common houseplant schefflera (octopus tree) grow around a lava rock. The plants are treated for export and cost $25 and up.

Getting Around

Shuttle The West Maui Shopping Express *(☎ 877-7308)* operates a shuttle between the Wharf Cinema Center (pick up the bus at the rear of the center) in Lahaina and the Kaanapali resort, a ride of about 20 minutes.

The fare is $1. The bus runs in each direction once an hour; the first southbound bus leaves the Whalers Village shopping center in Kaanapali at 9:55 am, and the last leaves at 9:55 pm.

Parking Finding a space for your car in Lahaina can be a challenge. Front St has on-street parking, but there's always a line of cruising cars. Your best bet is the corner of Front and Prison Sts, where there's free public parking with a three-hour limit. There are also a few private parking lots, the biggest being Republic Parking on Dickenson St, which charges $3 for up to two hours, or $6 all day.

LAHAINA TO MAALAEA

The stretch between Lahaina and Maalaea has pretty mountain scenery, but during winter most people are craning their necks to look seaward as they drive along. This is a prime whale-watching road.

Launiupoko Wayside Park

Launiupoko Wayside Park, 2½ miles south of Lahaina, is most popular as a picnic spot and as a place to watch the sun set behind Lanai. The park has showers, toilets, picnic tables and changing rooms.

Olowalu

There's little to mark Olowalu other than Olowalu General Store and a seemingly misplaced expensive French restaurant named *Chez Paul*.

The Olowalu Massacre

Olowalu Beach was the site of an infamous massacre in 1790. After a skiff was stolen from the US ship *Eleanora* and burned for its iron nails and fittings, Captain Simon Metcalfe retaliated by tricking the Hawaiians into sailing out in their canoes to trade. He then mercilessly gunned them down with his cannons, killing an estimated 100 people.

MAUI

Braking for Whales

The popular bumper sticker 'I Brake For Whales' has particular significance along the stretch of Hwy 30 between Olowalu and Maalaea. Although they are usually spotted farther offshore, humpback whales occasionally breach as close as 100 yards from this coast. Forty tons of whale suddenly exploding straight up through the water can be a real show-stopper! Unfortunately, some of the drivers whose heads are jerked ocean-ward by the sight hit their brakes and others don't, making for high rear-ender potential.

❀❀❀❀❀❀❀❀❀❀❀❀❀❀❀

When the water is calm, there's good snorkeling around the 14-mile marker, south of the general store. The coral reef here is large and shallow, and there's a narrow sandy beach to lie on, though be careful of kiawe thorns.

Olowalu, which means 'many hills,' has a lovely setting, with cane fields backed by the West Maui Mountains.

Camping *Camp Pecusa (☎ 661-4303, 800 Olowalu Village, Lahaina, HI 96761)*, run by the Episcopal Church, has a low-profile 'tentground' available to individuals on a first-come, first-served basis. It's at the side of a cane field, half a mile south of the Olowalu General Store, on the *makai* (sea-ward) side of the road. Camping is in the shade and along a beach. The beach itself is not suitable for swimming, but there's good snorkeling farther out on the reef.

While the campground is basic, it does have a solar-heated shower, a couple of out-houses, drinking water and picnic tables. A caretaker lives on the grounds, making this the most secure place in Maui to camp. No alcohol is allowed, and there's a maximum stay of seven nights in any 30-day period. Reservations are not accepted, but space is usually available. The cost is $5 per person per night.

Papawai Point

The ocean between Olowalu and Makena is prime humpback cow/calf territory, and in the winter, whale watching can be fantastic from the shore.

A couple of inconspicuous roadside lookouts lie just south of the 10-mile marker, but they're both unmarked and difficult to negotiate in heavy traffic. Your best bet is to drive just a little farther to Papawai Point, a clearly marked scenic lookout with a big parking lot.

Because the point juts into the waters at the western edge of Maalaea Bay, a favored humpback nursing ground, it's a good whale-sighting spot. Papawai Point is also a good spot for sunsets, with Lanai, Kahoolawe and Molokini visible.

LAHAINA TO KAANAPALI

On the stretch from Lahaina to Kaanapali, the driving can be aggressive, and traffic often jams up, particularly during morning and late-afternoon rush hours.

Sugar Cane Train

The old train that once carried sugarcane from the fields to the mill has been restored and now takes tourists on a joy ride through the cane fields between Kaanapali and Lahaina.

At the Kaanapali end, board the train on the inland side of Hwy 30, off Puukolii Rd. To get to the Lahaina station, turn up Hinau St, off Hwy 30 at Pizza Hut.

The train (☎ 661-0089) makes the 6-mile journey eight times a day. The trip takes about half an hour each way and costs $14 roundtrip. Children three to 12 pay $7.50.

Wahikuli Wayside Beach Park

This wayside park occupies a narrow strip of beach between the highway and the ocean, 2 miles north of Lahaina. With a gift for prophecy, the Hawaiians named this coastal stretch Wahikuli, or 'noisy place.'

The beach is mostly backed by a black-rock retaining wall, though there's a small sandy area. If you don't mind the traffic noise, the swimming conditions are usually fine, and when the water's calm, you can snorkel near the lava outcroppings at the park's south end. There are showers, rest rooms and picnic tables.

Across the street from the beach are Lahaina's civic center, police station and main post office.

Hanakaoo Beach Park

Hanakaoo Beach Park is a long sandy beach just south of Kaanapali Beach Resort. As with all public beach parks, the parking here is free.

The park has full facilities and a lifeguard on duty daily. The beach has a sandy bottom, and water conditions are usually quite safe for swimming. However, southerly swells, which sometimes develop in the summer, can create powerful waves and shorebreaks, while the occasional kona storm can kick up rough water conditions in winter.

You can snorkel down by the second clump of rocks on the south side of the beach park or walk a few minutes north to the Hyatt and snorkel out by the green buoy.

Hanakaoo Beach is also called Canoe Beach, as local canoe clubs store their canoes here. You can see them paddling up and down the coast in the early mornings and late afternoons. It's a pretty scene.

KAANAPALI

Kaanapali is a high-rise resort community. Despite the opulence of some of its hotels, the overall development is rather generic – the influence is as much Southern Californian as Hawaiian.

In the late 1950s, Amfac, owner of the Pioneer Sugar Mill, earmarked 600 acres of relatively barren sugarcane land for development as the first resort outside Waikiki. The first hotels, the Royal Lahaina and the Sheraton Maui, opened in 1962. Now Kaanapali Beach is lined with six oceanfront hotels, each with its own shops and restaurants. The resort also includes six condominium complexes, two 18-hole golf courses, 40 tennis courts and the Whalers Village shopping center.

Kaanapali boasts 3 miles of sandy beach and pleasant views across Auau Channel to Lanai and Molokai.

While Kaanapali is not a 'getaway' in the sense of avoiding the crowds, it has its quieter niches. The north side of Black Rock, for instance, and the condos up around the golf course are less bustling than the central beach area.

Beach Walk

A mile-long beach walk runs between the Hyatt and the Sheraton. In addition to the coastal scenery, both the Hyatt and Westin have some striking garden artwork and landscaping worth a detour. In front of the Hyatt, the 17-foot-high bronze sculpture 'The Acrobats' is noteworthy and makes a nice photo silhouetted against the sunset. Created by Australian John Robinson, it's a copy of the one standing in front of the Tower of London.

If you stroll in the early evening, you'll often be treated to beachside entertainment, most notably in front of the Marriott, which holds its luau on the lawn beside the beach walk.

Hyatt Regency Maui The Hyatt's lobby and grounds contain a $2 million art collection, including Ming vases, Balinese paintings, Hawaiian quilts, ceremonial drums and New Guinean artifacts, storyboards and war shields.

Among the numerous noteworthy pieces: a bronze sculpture from Thailand of King Rama battling with the King of Demons; a large wooden Buddha, lacquered and gilded, from Mandalay; and a spirit figure from the Misingi village in Papua New Guinea.

Even if you're not into big hotels, it's hard not to be impressed by the lobby atrium with its lush tropical foliage. Outside are pools, waterfalls and gardens with swans and flamingos.

The concierge has a self-guided art tour booklet free for the asking. The Hyatt also offers its complimentary 'Art & Garden Tour' at 11 am on Sunday, Monday, Wednesday and Friday.

Westin Maui The Westin Maui is landscaped with five free-form pools, rushing waterfalls, water slides and a network of

MAUI

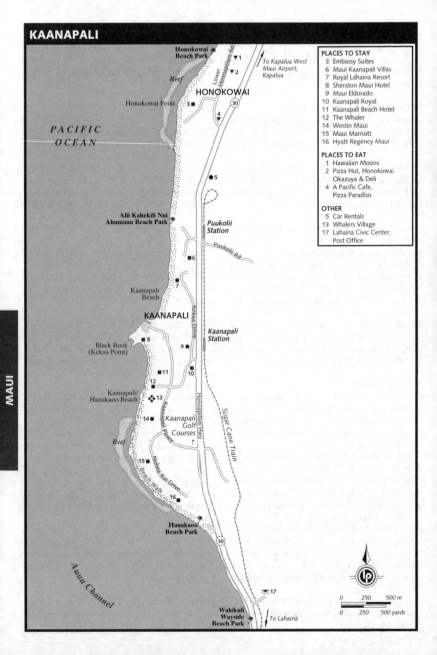

KAANAPALI

To Kapalua West Maui Airport, Kapalua

Honokowai Beach Park

Lower Honoapiilani Rd

Reef

HONOKOWAI

Honokowai Point

PACIFIC OCEAN

Alii Kahekili Nui Ahumanu Beach Park

Puukolii Station

Puukolii Rd

Kaanapali Beach

KAANAPALI

Kekaa Drive

Kaanapali Station

Black Rock (Kekaa Point)

Kaanapali/ Hanakaoo Beach

Honoapiilani Hwy

Sugar Cane Train

Kaanapali Pkwy

Kaanapali Golf Courses

Reef

Beach Walk

Nohea Kai Drive

Hanakaoo Beach Park

To Lahaina

Auau Channel

Wahikuli Wayside Beach Park

PLACES TO STAY
3 Embassy Suites
6 Maui Kaanapali Villas
7 Royal Lahaina Resort
8 Sheraton Maui Hotel
9 Maui Eldorado
10 Kaanapali Royal
11 Kaanapali Beach Hotel
12 The Whaler
14 Westin Maui
15 Maui Marriott
16 Hyatt Regency Maui

PLACES TO EAT
1 Hawaiian Moons
2 Pizza Hut, Honokowai Okazuya & Deli
4 A Pacific Cafe, Pizza Paradiso

OTHER
5 Car Rentals
13 Whalers Village
17 Lahaina Civic Center, Post Office

0   250   500 m
0   250   500 yards

MAUI

artificial streams and ponds with swans and crowned cranes.

Garden statuary, both Asian and European, is big here, with lots of Buddhas, vases and pairs of growling stone animals. The collection may seem a bit odd, especially the bronze dogs in menacing poses at the edge of the walkways.

Whalers Village

Whalers Village has three levels with more than 50 restaurants and shops, including upscale clothing stores, souvenir shops, a Fox Photo 1-Hour Lab and an ABC convenience store. In addition, a full skeleton of a sperm whale is on display at the entrance.

The high point of Whalers Village is its small but top-notch **whaling museum**. Period photos and detailed interpretive boards explain all aspects of whaling history, from how whales were hunted to the uses of whale oil.

A lot of the character of the whalers comes through, and you'll get a feel for how rough and dirty the work was. Wages were so low that sailors sometimes owed the ship money by the time they got home and had to sign up for another four-year stint just to pay off the debt.

There are harpoons, logs from whaling ships, all sorts of scrimshaw, a model of a whaling barque and a film on whales that plays continuously.

A newer wing of the museum has models of various whales, as well as displays of jawbones, teeth and baleen. It also has a small theater showing films on the present-day plight of whales and dolphins.

The museum is on the 3rd level of Building G and is open 9:30 am to 10 pm daily. Admission is free.

Kaanapali Beaches

Kaanapali can be considered two beaches, with Black Rock the dividing mark. The stretch south of Black Rock down to the Hyatt (and beyond to Hanakaoo Beach Park) is officially Hanakaoo Beach. The stretch from Black Rock north to Honokowai is Kaanapali Beach. Since the resort was built, however, the whole thing has generally been called Kaanapali Beach.

Kaanapali/Hanakaoo Beach The waters in front of the Hyatt have a shallow reef that makes for poor swimming but good snorkeling.

Much of the stretch between the Sheraton and the Hyatt can be dangerous, particularly on the point in front of the Marriott, where strong currents sometimes develop. As a general rule, waters are rougher in winter, though actually the worst conditions can occur in early summer if there's a southerly swell. Be careful in rough surf, as the waves can pick you up and bounce you onto the coral reef that runs from the southern end of the Westin down to the Hyatt. Check with the hotel beach huts for the day's water conditions before jumping in.

Black Rock Black Rock, also known as Kekaa Point, is the rocky lava promontory that protects the beach in front of the Sheraton. This is Kaanapali's safest and best spot for swimming and snorkeling.

You can snorkel along the southern side of Black Rock, where you'll find some nice coral and schools of fish that are used to being fed. The real prize, however, is the horseshoe cove cut into the tip of the rock, where there's more pristine coral, along with abundant tropical fish and the occasional turtle.

There's often a current to contend with off the point, which can make getting to the

MAUI

Souls Leap

According to traditional Hawaiian beliefs, Kekaa Point, the westernmost point of Maui, is a place where the spirits of the dead leap into the unknown and are carried to their ancestral homeland.

The rock itself is said to have been created during a scuffle between the demigod Maui and a commoner who questioned Maui's superiority. Maui chased the man to this point, killed him, turned his body into rock and cast his soul out to sea.

cove a little risky, but when it's calm you can swim right around into the horseshoe. Check with the Sheraton beach hut or snorkelers in the water regarding current conditions. Black Rock is also a popular shore-dive spot. If you want to see what the horseshoe cove looks like, you can peer down into it by taking the short footpath from the Sheraton beach to the top of Black Rock.

Alii Kahekili Nui Ahumanu This beach park at the north side of Kaanapali Beach is dedicated to Kahekili Nui Ahumanu, the last king of Maui. The park, which is on a nice section of the beach, has free parking, showers, changing rooms, toilets, a covered picnic pavilion and barbecue grills.

To get there from Honoapiilani Hwy, turn left onto Kai Ala Drive (opposite Puukolii Rd) and then bear right. The waters here are open ocean, but inshore it's usually calm and good for swimming.

This is a good walking beach. If you walk north for about 20 minutes, you'll come to a reef around Honokowai Point, where the clear waters are good for snorkeling when it's calm.

Places to Stay

All Kaanapali accommodations are either on the beach or within walking distance of it, and all have the expected amenities, including swimming pools.

Maui Kaanapali Villas (☎ 667-7791, 800-922-7866, fax 667-0366, mkv@tiki.net, 45 Kai Ala Drive, Lahaina, HI 96761) is an Aston property on the edge of Kaanapali, 200 yards south of Alii Kahekili Nui Ahumanu Beach Park. As is common with Aston properties, rooms are individually owned, and overall it's of a less meticulous standard than other Kaanapali properties. Hotel rooms with refrigerators cost $135/160 in the low/high season, and studios with kitchens start at $180/205.

Kaanapali Beach Hotel (☎ 661-0011, 800-262-8450, fax 667-5978, mauikbh@aloha .net, 2525 Kaanapali Pkwy, Lahaina, HI 96761) has an enviable beachside location near Black Rock. The hotel's 430 rooms are spread across a number of three- to six-story wings. While it's an older complex, it's pleasantly low-key. The rooms have lanais, refrigerators, safes and TVs. Prices start at $160 for a garden view, $210 for an ocean view. If you ask for the 'Free Ride' special, the rate includes a free rental car.

Maui Eldorado (☎ 661-0021, 800-688-7444, fax 667-7039, reservations@outrigger .com, 2661 Kekaa Drive, Lahaina, HI 96761) is a low-rise condo complex up the hill from the beach. It has a slower pace and a friendlier atmosphere than the big resort hotels. The units are individually owned, so they vary, but most are quite nicely furnished. The studios are big, with kitchens completely set apart from the bedrooms, and start at $175 for a garden view. One-bedroom units for four people start at $235. The hotel is managed by the Outrigger chain, which offers numerous discount schemes.

The Whaler (☎ 661-4861, 800-367-7052, fax 661-8315, 2481 Kaanapali Pkwy, Lahaina, HI 96791) is a 360-unit high-rise condo complex that looks rather boxy from the outside but is quite pleasant inside, with marble baths, private lanais and modern amenities. Studios cost $195 to $210. There are also one-bedroom units from $245 and two-bedroom units from $370.

Kaanapali Royal (☎ 667-7200, 800-676-4112, 2560 Kekaa Drive, Lahaina, HI 96761) is a low-rise complex with large two-bedroom condos. It has a hillside location near the golf course, a few minutes' walk from the beach. The units cost $200/220 in the low/high season for up to six people.

Royal Lahaina Resort (☎ 661-3611, 800-447-6925, fax 661-3538, 2780 Kekaa Drive, Lahaina, HI 96761) has 540 rooms on a broad stretch of beach on the north side of Black Rock. Standard rooms in the high-rise section cost $235 and up. Cottages, which are nicely clustered and spread out down to the beach, start at $295. The resort has 11 tennis courts and three pools.

The *Westin Maui* (☎ 667-2525, 800-228-3000, fax 523-3958, 2365 Kaanapali Pkwy, Lahaina, HI 96761) is a 762-room high-rise hotel with grounds featuring waterfalls, free-form pools and a garden full of statuary. The hotel itself is not as distinguished as the grounds, but then the Westin wasn't built from scratch – it's a remake of the old Maui Surf. Rates start at $265 for rooms in the old wing.

The *Maui Marriott* (☎ 667-1200, 800-228-9290, fax 667-8300, 100 Nohea Kai Drive, Lahaina, HI 96761) has 720 guest rooms in two long high-rises. Regular rack rates start at $290, but you can often get cheaper package deals that include breakfast and a car. It's pleasant enough, but not exceptional for the price.

The 815-room *Hyatt Regency Maui* (☎ 661-1234, 800-233-1234, fax 667-4714, 200 Nohea Kai Drive, Lahaina, HI 96761) has interesting artwork and a huge meandering swimming pool with a swim-through grotto and a 130-foot water slide. The rooms, which have standard Hyatt decor and amenities, begin at $275, or $375 with an ocean view.

The *Sheraton Maui Hotel* (☎ 661-0031, 800-782-9488, fax 661-0458, 2605 Kaanapali Pkwy, Lahaina, HI 96761) has the prime beach spot, behind Black Rock. Completely closed down and rebuilt in 1997 to the tune of $150 million, this 510-room hotel has rates ranging from $310 for a garden-view room to $3000 for a top-end suite.

Places to Eat

Hotels All of the Kaanapali hotels have restaurants, some formal and expensive, others more casual.

The cheapest spot to eat is the *Pizza Hut* at the Maui Marriott's poolside kiosk. It's open 11 am to 7 pm daily, and one-person pizzas cost $4.

The Marriott's *Moana Terrace* (☎ 667-1200) has a soup, (cold) pasta and salad buffet Monday to Thursday nights from 5 to 9 pm. The cost is $11.95 as a meal in itself or $4.95 with purchase of a sandwich or entree. On Friday night, the buffet includes prime rib and costs $15.95; on Saturday night, it features seafood dishes and jumps to $24.95; on Sunday, it's pasta and costs $14.95. Prices are reduced for children. Dining is either indoors or on the adjacent open-air terrace.

Nikko (☎ 667-1200), at the Marriott, is a Japanese restaurant specializing in *teppanyaki* (a style of cooking over an open grill).

Chefs prepare the authentic meals right at your table, while you enjoy the restaurant's ocean view and pleasant atmosphere. Complete dinners include miso soup, salad, rice and teppanyaki vegetables, all accompanying main dishes like sesame chicken ($22) and lobster tail ($37). Nikko is open for dinner only, 6 to 9 pm daily.

Whalers Village Whalers Village has three beachfront restaurants. The most interesting food is at the *Hula Grill* (☎ 667-6636), which has outdoor dining, a kiawe grill and a wood-fired pizza oven. Sandwiches with fries or pizzas are priced under $10, pasta dishes cost around $15, fresh fish $20.

The other two beachfront restaurants offer more standard fare. The *Rusty Harpoon* (☎ 661-3123) has burgers and sandwiches for around $10, chicken or barbecue rib dinners for $20 and pricier fresh fish meals. *Leilani's* (☎ 661-4495), next door, is a bit cheaper, with $7 burgers available at the ground-level dining area from 11 am to 11 pm. Upstairs, you can order chicken and steak dishes for $17.

Whalers Village also has a *Maui Yogurt* takeout shop with inexpensive sandwiches, salads and frozen yogurt; a *Häagen-Dazs* ice cream shop; and a small food court with a *McDonald's*, a *Korean eatery* with plate lunches, a *Japanese soba shop* and a stall selling pizza by the slice.

Breakfast Buffets Kaanapali has a number of breakfast buffets where you could easily while away the better part of a morning.

The *Hyatt Regency Maui* has an average spread of food in a superb setting at Swan Court. One side of the restaurant is in the open air and overlooks a large swan pond with artificial waterfalls and a Japanese garden. The buffet is served from 6:30 to 11:30 am, costs $19.50 and includes fresh fruit, pastries and an omelette station.

The *Maui Marriott* has a good breakfast buffet from 6:30 to 11 am daily at its Moana Terrace, with fresh fruit, yogurt, cereals, pastries, eggs Benedict and an omelette/waffle station. It costs $16.50 for a full breakfast or $13.50 for a continental breakfast, which

MAUI

consists of everything except the hot dishes. There's a pleasant garden patio but no ocean view.

The Westin's *Cooks on the Beach* also does a reasonably good breakfast buffet, from 6:30 to 11 am daily, but there's nothing special about the setting, and at $17.95 this is pricier than the more extensive Maui Marriott buffet.

The *Sheraton Maui Hotel* offers breakfast on an open-air veranda with a partial ocean view. It's not a grand spread but there are pastries, crepes, pancakes, sushi and omelettes made to order. Breakfast is available 6:30 to 11 am daily and costs $17.50.

The bargain of the breakfast buffets is at *Kaanapali Mixed Plate*, off the lobby of the Kaanapali Beach Hotel. Here you can get fresh pineapple, eggs, sausage, French toast, cereals and coffee. While not a notable culinary experience, you can eat your fill for $8.50. Breakfast is served from 6 to 10:45 am daily. There's also a reasonable lunch buffet for the same price from 11 am to 2 pm.

Entertainment

The Kaanapali hotels feature a variety of entertainment, including dance bands, pianists, Hawaiian music and Polynesian revues.

The *Hyatt Regency Maui* has a torch-lighting ceremony nightly at around 6 pm, followed by mellow Hawaiian music in its Lobby Bar.

In the courtyard of the *Kaanapali Beach Hotel* there's a free hula show from 6:30 to 7:30 pm nightly, followed by Hawaiian music until 9:30 pm.

The *Sheraton Maui Hotel* has a torch-lighting and cliff-diving ceremony at sunset nightly, with hula dancing at its Lagoon Bar.

The *Maui Marriott* has contemporary music from 5 to 11:30 pm nightly in its Makai Bar.

Whalers Village offers a free hula show at 7 pm on Monday, Wednesday, Friday and Saturday. There's often contemporary or Hawaiian music outdoors in the evening at one of the Whalers Village restaurants.

Luaus The Kaanapali luaus include an *imu* ceremony (when the pig is roasted in an underground oven), open bar, buffet dinner and Polynesian show with music and dance. Reservations are required. Most of the shows are held outdoors, so you can get a preview of them by walking along the beach.

The *Hyatt Regency Maui* (☎ 667-4420) holds its 'Drums of the Pacific' luau from

Enjoy some roast pig at a luau's imu ceremony.

5 to 8 pm most nights. The cost is $65 for adults, $27 for children.

The **Royal Lahaina Resort** (☎ 661-3611) puts on a luau starting at 5:30 pm nightly; $62 for adults, $28 for children.

The **Maui Marriott** (☎ 661-5828) has a luau from 4:30 to 8 pm nightly. The cost is $60 for adults, $25 for children.

Stargazing Visitors can look at the night sky through giant binoculars and a 15-inch telescope from the rooftop of the Hyatt Regency Maui. One-hour stargazing programs (☎ 667-3611) are offered at 8, 9 and 10 pm nightly and cost $20 for adults, $10 for children.

Getting Around
Shuttles A free shuttle runs between the Kaanapali hotels, Whalers Village shopping center, the golf course and the Sugar Cane Train's Kaanapali station about 20 times a day between 7:15 am and 10:15 pm.

For information on the shuttle between Kaanapali and Lahaina, see Getting Around in the Lahaina section. Other shuttle buses connect Kaanapali with Kapalua, south Maui and the airport; for details, see the Getting Around section near the front of this chapter.

Parking Free beach-access parking is available at many of the Kaanapali hotels, but the number of spaces is limited and they're earmarked strictly for beachgoers. The Hyatt also has free 'self parking' for hotel visitors at its south side. Otherwise, there's pay parking at the Whalers Village shopping center, which charges $2 an hour. If you make a purchase at Whalers Village of $10 or more, you can get three hours of free validated parking.

HONOKAWAI
North of Kaanapali, the road forks. The main road is Honoapiilani Hwy (Hwy 30), and the parallel shoreline road is Lower Honoapiilani Rd, which leads into Honokawai.

To the degree that Kaanapali is a planned community, Honokawai is an unplanned one, consisting mainly of a stretch of condos squeezed between the shoreline and Lower Honoapiilani Rd.

Many of these condos were intended to be year-round housing for island residents, but the growth in tourism makes daily and weekly rentals far more profitable. Indeed, the main reason most tourists are here is because the condos are relatively cheap compared to those at the nearby resorts.

If you just want to zip up to the beaches, bypassing the condos and resorts, stick to Hwy 30. Cyclists may want to come this way as well, as the highway has a wide shoulder lane marked as a bike route.

Honokowai Beach Park is largely lined with a submerged rock shelf and has poor swimming conditions with shallow water and a rocky bottom. Most people staying here head to Kaanapali Beach for swimming. For snorkeling, you can walk south to Honokowai Point (toward the pink Embassy Suites), where there's a reef marked by buoys in front of the hotel. Despite the rocky shoreline and mediocre swimming conditions at Honokowai, the area does have fine views of Molokai and Lanai.

Places to Stay
Honokowai Palms (☎ 667-2712, 800-669-0795, fax 661-5875, 3666 Lower Honoapiilani Rd, Honokowai, HI 96761) is a 30-unit, two-story, cinder-block building on the inland side of the road. It's a simple place, but it has a pool and relatively cheap rates. One-bedroom condo units cost $65 for up to four people, while two-bedroom units cost $75 for up to six people. There's a three-day minimum stay.

Kaleialoha (☎ 669-8197, 800-222-8688, fax 669-2502, 3785 Lower Honoapiilani Rd, Honokowai, HI 96761) is a pleasant 67-unit condo on the beach. The units have full kitchens, ceiling fans and washers and dryers. There's a swimming pool and barbecue area. Studios face the road and cost $75, while one-bedroom units with ocean views and lanais are $95 to $105. There's a three-night minimum.

Mahina Surf (☎ 669-6068, 800-367-6086, fax 669-4534, hawaii@gte.net, 4057 Lower Honoapiilani Rd, Honokowai, HI 96761) is

MAUI

between Honokowai and Kahana. This low-rise complex is nicely set around a large grassy yard with a heated pool in the center. All 56 units are spacious and have kitchens, VCRs, phones and lanais with ocean views. There's a three-night minimum. One-bedroom units cost $105 in the low season and $120 in the high season. It costs $25 more for a two-bedroom unit. If you're a member of AAA or AARP, be sure to ask for the 10% discount.

On the other end of the scale is *Embassy Suites* (☎ 661-2000, 800-669-3155, fax 667-5821, 104 Kaanapali Place, Honokowai, HI 96761), the pink giant on Honokowai Point, north of the Kaanapali resorts. Each of the 413 units is an 820-sq-foot suite with everything down to a 35-inch TV with VCR. Room rates start at $290 for up to four adults, including breakfast and evening cocktails, though promotions sometimes drop the rate to $200.

Places to Eat

Hawaiian Moons, across from Honokowai Beach Park, is an excellent health foods supermarket. It also has a deli (with cafe tables) that sells organic muffins, carrot cake, salads and a few hot dishes. Hawaiian Moons is open daily 7 am to 9 pm (to 7 pm on Sunday).

A small *Pizza Hut* in the shopping center just south of Hawaiian Moons has pizza for takeout only; it's open 11 am to 11 pm daily. In the same center is *Honokowai Okazuya & Deli*, which makes a good chicken Caesar salad and a delicious mahimahi dish with lemon, capers and rice – either for just $7. It's open 10 am to 2:30 pm and 4:30 to 9 pm Monday to Saturday.

If you want a more upscale setting and presentation, try the new *A Pacific Cafe* (☎ 669-2724), at the edge of the highway on the southern tip of the village. The menu is Hawaii Regional cuisine, and if it keeps to the same standards as the Kihei version of this restaurant, it should be very good. Expect dinner to run about $50. In the same complex as A Pacific Cafe is *Pizza Paradiso*, an Italian cafe that has standard breakfast offerings, big pizza slices and deli

sandwiches all priced around $5. It's open 7:30 am to 10 pm.

For fresh fruits and vegetables, visit the *farmers' market* that sets up south of the ABC store from 6:30 to 11:30 am Monday and Thursday.

KAHANA

Kahana is the high-rise stretch immediately north of Honokowai. It's more upscale than Honokowai, with condo and room rates averaging well above $100. Kahana is fronted with a sandy beach that has reasonable swimming conditions; for snorkeling, a good area is along the rocky outcropping at the north side of the Kahana Sunset condominium complex.

The Kahana Gateway shopping center, off Hwy 30 half a mile north of the Kapalua West Maui Airport, has a gas station, a Bank of Hawaii with an ATM, and a coin laundry that's open 6 am to 10 pm daily.

Places to Stay

Noelani (☎ 669-8374, 800-367-6030, fax 669-7904, noelani@maui.net, 4095 Lower Honoapiilani Rd, Kahana, HI 96761) has a friendly atmosphere and 50 nicely furnished units right on the beach. All have ocean-facing lanais, phones with free local calls, full kitchens, sofa beds and TV/VCRs; all but the studios have washer/dryers. There are two pools and a Jacuzzi. Studios cost $107, one-bedroom units $137. Two-bedroom, two-bath units cost $177 for up to four people, and three-bedroom units cost $207 for up to six people. Rates are $10 cheaper in the low season, and AAA and senior discounts are offered. There's a three-day minimum. All in all, it's a good deal for this area. To make reservations online, go to www.noelani-condo-resort.com.

Kahana Reef (☎ 669-6491, 800-253-3773, fax 669-2192, 4471 Lower Honoapiilani Rd, Kahana, HI 96761) is a four-story, 88-unit condo. All units are oceanfront, and most are nicely furnished. The small pool is on the ocean and has a great view of Molokai. The studios, which cost $115, are almost as large as one-bedroom units elsewhere; each has a single and a queen day bed, as well as a tiny second room with a single bed. For another $15, you can get a very large one-bedroom unit.

Royal Kahana (☎ 669-5911, 800-447-7783, marc@aloha.net, 4365 Lower Honoapiilani Rd, Kahana, HI 96761) is a Marc Resorts property. The units are spacious, modern and comfortable, with full kitchens, bathtubs, TVs, VCRs and phones. All but the studios have washer/dryers, and most have private ocean-facing lanais. Amenities include a heated pool, two tennis courts, a small fitness room and a sauna. The location is convenient, just a few minutes' walk from the Kahana Gateway shopping center. Low/high season rates begin at $159/179 for a studio, $199/219 for a one-bedroom unit and $249/269 for a two-bedroom unit. If you're a member of one of the travel clubs in which Marc participates, such as Entertainment, the rate drops 50%, making it a more appealing option. For details on special packages, visit the www.marcresorts.com website.

Places to Eat

The best bet for a meal is the Kahana Gateway shopping center. For cheap eats, the mall has a **McDonald's**; a frozen yogurt and ice cream shop; and the **Whalers General Store**, a small grocery store that's open 6:30 am to 11 pm daily and offers a few fast-food items.

The Kahana Gateway also contains **Roy's Kahana Bar & Grill** (☎ 669-6999), a branch of the renowned Roy's in Honolulu. Centered around a large exhibition kitchen, the restaurant features contemporary Hawaii Regional cuisine. Appetizers such as blackened ahi, Szechuan ribs or tandoori shrimp average $8 to $10. Main courses range from $17 for chicken dishes to $25 for fresh fish specials. Roy's also serves some of the island's most scrumptious desserts.

The adjacent **Roy's Nicolina** (☎ 669-5000), a sister restaurant, doesn't have the exhibition kitchen, and consequently it tends to be a bit quieter. Otherwise, the food and prices are essentially the same as at Roy's Kahana Bar & Grill. Often one of the two restaurants offers a special three-course meal for around $35. Either restaurant would make an excellent choice for a night out; both are open for dinner only, 5:30 to 9:30 pm nightly.

NAPILI

Napili Beach is a beautiful, curving, golden-sand beach, with excellent swimming and snorkeling when it's calm. Big waves occasionally make it into the bay in the winter, attracting bodysurfers but also creating strong rip currents. To get to the beach from Lower Honoapiilani Rd, turn down Hui Drive.

Napili Kai Beach Club, built in 1962, was the first hotel north of Kaanapali. To protect the bay, as well as their investment, Napili Kai organized area landowners and petitioned the county to create a zoning bylaw restricting all Napili Bay buildings to the height of a coconut tree.

The law was passed in 1964, long before the condo explosion took over the rest of West Maui, and consequently Napili is one of the more relaxed niches on the coast. It attracts a fair number of return visitors, the majority of them retirees escaping mainland winters.

Most of Napili's condos are on the beach and for the most part away from the road and the sound of traffic.

Places to Stay

Hale Napili (☎ 669-6184, 800-245-2266, fax 665-0066, halenapi@maui.net, 65 Hui Drive, Napili, HI 96761) is a well-maintained 18-unit condo on Napili Beach. The Hawaiian management is friendly, and the rooms are very pleasant and well equipped. All have full kitchens, queen and sofa beds, TVs, phones with answering machines, ceiling fans and lanais. Garden studios cost $98, oceanfront studios $128 and one-bedroom units $155, a bit less in the low season. It has a three-day minimum stay. There's no pool, but you're right on the ocean.

Napili Surf (☎ 669-8002, 800-541-0638, fax 669-8004, 50 Napili Place, Napili, HI 96761) is a motel-style, painted cinder-block place at the south end of Napili Bay. The 53 units are pleasant, the grounds are well kept, and there's a pool. Rates range from $109

MAUI

for studios with garden views to $229 for one-bedroom units with ocean views; during the low season, there are discounts of about 10% to 15% on weekly stays. There's a five-day minimum stay.

Napili Kai Beach Club (☎ 669-6271, 800-367-5030, fax 669-5740, 5900 Honoapiilani Rd, Napili, HI 96761) is a sprawling 165-unit hotel at the northern end of Napili Bay. The staff is friendly – almost pampering. The units are tasteful, with Polynesian decor and nice touches like Japanese shoji doors. The catch here is the price: rooms start at $170 without a kitchen, $185 with one.

Places to Eat

The Napili Plaza shopping center, at the junction of Napilihau St and Hwy 30, has a grocery store open 6:30 am to 11 pm daily; a *Subway* sandwich shop; the *Coffee Store*, which sells good pastries and coffees; and *Maui Tacos*, which serves healthy, inexpensive Mexican food. The plaza also has *Koho Grill & Bar*, a local sit-down restaurant with an extensive menu of hot dishes, sandwiches and burgers.

For a more appealing setting, head to the *Sea House Restaurant* (☎ 669-1500), at the Napili Kai Beach Club, which features open-air dining with a sunset view. The usual breakfast offerings and lunchtime burgers, sandwiches and salads range from $6 to $10. Dinners, which include fish and steak dishes, cost $15 to $25. The restaurant also has a worthwhile dinner show at 6:30 pm on Friday for $35, which features hula dancing by area children; reservations are required (☎ 669-6271) for the show. Restaurant hours are 8 to 11 am, noon to 2 pm and 6 to 9 pm.

The *Napili General Store*, in the Napili Village complex on Lower Honoapiilani Rd, sells groceries, liquor, wrapped sandwiches and a few mediocre fast-food items. It's open 7:30 am to 10 pm daily.

KAPALUA

The Kapalua resort development has the upscale Kapalua Bay and Ritz-Carlton hotels, some luxury condos, a few restaurants and three golf courses. It's a small, uncrowded development – the most exclusive in northwest Maui – but truth to tell, if you're not a well-to-do golfer, there's not a lot to do here.

Kapalua Beach Kapalua Beach, at Kapalua Bay, is a pretty white-sand crescent beach with a fine view of Molokai across the channel. The long rocky outcroppings at both ends of the bay make Kapalua Beach the safest year-round swimming spot on this coast.

There's good snorkeling on the right side of the beach, where you'll find lots of large tangs, butterfly fish, wrasses and orange slate-pencil sea urchins.

Take the unmarked paved drive immediately north of Napili Kai Beach Club to get to a parking area with about 25 beach access spaces, rest rooms and showers. A tunnel from the parking lot leads under the Bay Club restaurant to the beach.

DT Fleming Beach Park DT Fleming Beach Park, at the north side of Kapalua on Honokahua Bay, is a county beach park with rest rooms, picnic facilities and showers. The long sandy beach is backed by ironwood trees. There's good surfing and bodysurfing, with winter providing the biggest waves. The shorebreaks can be tough, however, and this beach is second only to Hookipa for injuries.

Take notice of the sign warning of dangerous currents – the beach has seen a number of drownings over the years. The reef out on the right is good for snorkeling, but only when it's very calm. There's a lifeguard on duty daily.

The Honokahua sand dunes just south of Fleming Beach were excavated in 1988 during the construction of the Ritz-Carlton hotel. After skeletal remains were found, construction was halted, the bodies were reinterred and the hotel site was relocated mauka of the seaside graves. The Honokahua burial ground is thought to contain the remains of over 1000 Hawaiians who were buried between 950 AD and the 18th century.

Places to Stay

Kapalua Bay Hotel (☎ 669-5656, 800-367-8000, fax 669-4690, 1 Bay Drive, Kapalua,

HI 96761) is a luxury complex with hotel rooms from $275. There are also one-bedroom condos with modern conveniences, full kitchens, living rooms and large lanais for $375.

One-bedroom condos in the same resort development can be rented from *Kapalua Ridge Rentals (☎ 669-9696, 800-326-6284, fax 669-4411, kapalua@microweb.com, 10 Hoohui Rd, suite 301, Kahana, HI 96761)* for $130/845 a day/week in the low season, $185/1210 in the high season. There are also two-bedroom, three-bath units for $195/1275 a day/week in the low season, $250/1700 in the high. Ridge Rentals has a five-day minimum stay.

The *Ritz-Carlton (☎ 669-6200, 800-241-3333, fax 669-3908, 1 Ritz-Carlton Drive, Kapalua, HI 96761)* has 550 rooms and suites with the usual upscale Ritz-Carlton standard and decor. Rates range from $265 for a garden-view room to $2000 for the presidential suite.

Places to Eat
Honolua Store is an old general store with a cafeteria-style deli serving local food such as stew and fried chicken. Plate lunches, available until 3 pm, are either 'hobo' style (a hot dish and rice) for $3.75 or a full plate for $5.50. Sandwiches cost around $5. Everything's takeout only. To get there, turn up Office Rd half a mile north of the Kapalua Bay Hotel.

Although the setting looks somewhat exclusive, the *Plantation House Restaurant (☎ 669-6299)* at the Plantation Course golf course is the best place in these parts for a reasonably priced sit-down brunch. From 8 am to 3 pm, eggs Benedict, salads and sandwiches cost about $7. Dinner, served from 5:30 pm, is a pricier affair with seafood, duck and steak main courses for $20 to $25. The restaurant has a fine view across the fairway clear down to the ocean.

The *Bay Club (☎ 669-8008)*, perched atop a promontory at the southern end of Kapalua Bay, has a beautiful view in an open-air setting. At lunch, creative salads and sandwiches go for around $10. At dinner, main courses such as seafood truffle risotto or filet

mignon cost $25 to $36. It's open 11:30 am to 2 pm and 6 to 9:30 pm daily.

HONOLUA & MOKULEIA BAYS
Kapalua marks the end of development on the West Maui coast. From there on, it's rural Hawaii, with golf carts giving way to pickup trucks and old cars with surfboards tied on top. The coast gets lusher, greener and more scenically rugged as you go along.

About a mile north of Fleming Beach are Mokuleia Bay (Slaughterhouse Beach) and Honolua Bay. The two bays are separated by the narrow Kalaepiha Point and together form the Honolua-Mokuleia Bay Marine Life Conservation District. Fishing is prohibited, as is collecting shells, coral, rock or sand. In the winter, both bays see heavy surf and sand erosion.

In winter, Honolua Bay has such perfect waves that it's made the cover of numerous surfing magazines. The bay faces northwest, and when it catches the winter swells, it has some of the best surfing to be found anywhere in the world.

Slaughterhouse Beach, named for the slaughterhouse that once sat on the cliffs above, is a hot bodysurfing spot during the summer when the rocks aren't exposed.

In summer, snorkeling is excellent in both bays. Both sides of Honolua Bay have good reefs with lots of different coral formations, while the midsection of the bay has a sandy bottom. Honolua Stream empties into the bay, and it can get quite murky after heavy rains. When it's calm, you can snorkel around Kalaepiha Point from one bay to the other.

Unfortunately, there's no designated parking area or easy land access. Beachgoers have traditionally parked their cars at a few pull-offs along the road, then scrambled along rough paths down to the beach. However, these paths cross private property, and until something is worked out between the state and the landowner, this is not officially allowed.

Kahekili Hwy
As you continue north beyond Honolua and Mokuleia Bays, the road climbs, offering

MAUI

some nice coastal views. The beaches along this section are open ocean with rough water conditions.

It's possible to continue around on this coastal road to Wailuku (see Kahekili Hwy at the end of the Kahului-Wailuku section). The last stop for gas and provisions on this side of Wailuku is at the Honolua Store in Kapalua.

KAHULUI-WAILUKU AREA

Kahului and Wailuku, Maui's two largest communities, flow together to form a single urban sprawl. This is where regular folks live, work and shop.

Kahului is the commercial center. The main road, Kaahumanu Ave, is a collection of stores, banks and office buildings and a mile-long strip of shopping centers. Kaahumanu Ave continues into Wailuku where it becomes W Main St. Wailuku, the county seat, is the more distinctive and less hurried end of it all. This is an older town with back-streets of curio shops, mom-and-pop stores and hole-in-the-wall ethnic restaurants.

Kahului Harbor, Maui's deepwater commercial port, services barges, cargo ships and the occasional cruise liner. This one's geared for work – there are no charming wharves or sailboats.

Maui's main airport is in Kahului. After landing, most people drive right out of town and don't come back until they're ready to leave. And, with a few exceptions (including mall shopping), there's really not much in Kahului for visitors.

Wailuku, which you'll pass through on the way to Iao Valley State Park, has a few historic places of interest and makes for a good lunch break and stroll. Wailuku also has some of Maui's cheapest places to stay.

Kahului

In the 1880s, Kahului became the headquarters of Hawaii's first railroad, which was built to haul sugar from the fields to the refinery and harbor. In 1900, an outbreak of bubonic plague hit Kahului, and in an attempt to wipe it out, the settlement that had grown up around Kahului Harbor was purposely burned to the ground.

The present-day Kahului is a planned community developed in 1948 by the Alexander & Baldwin sugar company. It was called 'Dream City' by cane workers, who dreamed of moving away from the dusty mill camps to a home of their own. These first tract homes are at the southern end of town.

Information Bank of Hawaii has a branch at 27 Puunene Ave and another in the Maui Marketplace.

The Kahului post office, on Puunene Ave, is open 8:30 am to 5 pm weekdays, 8:30 am to noon on Saturday.

The Coffee Store (☎ 871-6860), in the Kaahumanu Center, provides free Internet access but only has one computer, so you may have to wait.

The 24-hour Kinko's (☎ 871-2000), in the Dairy Center at 395 Dairy Rd, offers Internet access for 20¢ per minute, computer rentals, fax transmissions, photocopying and other business services.

There are two discount travel agencies a five-minute drive from the airport. Both sell air coupons for interisland flights for around $50. Cheap Tickets (☎ 242-8094) is in the Dairy Center at 395 Dairy Rd, while Cut Rate Tickets (☎ 871-7300) is on the next block at 333 Dairy Rd. The latter is open seven days a week and doesn't add a surcharge for using credit cards.

A large Borders bookstore is at the Maui Marketplace, and Waldenbooks has stores at both the Kaahumanu Center and the Maui Mall.

The Kahului public library, 90 School St, is open 10 am to 5 pm on Monday, Thursday, Friday and Saturday and 10 am to 8 pm on Tuesday and Wednesday.

Kanaha Pond Kanaha Pond is a wildlife sanctuary for the endangered black-necked stilt, a wading bird that feeds along the marshy edges of the pond. It's a graceful bird in flight, with long orange legs that trail behind. Even though the stilt population in all Hawaii is estimated at just 1500, the birds can commonly be spotted here.

Access to the pond is on Hwy 396, near the junction of Hwy 36. The parking lot is

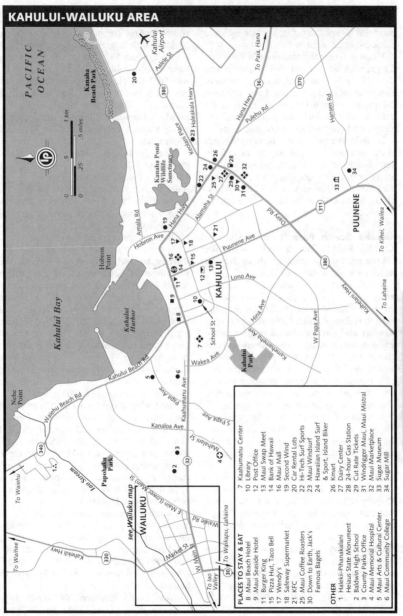

KAHULUI-WAILUKU AREA

PACIFIC OCEAN

Kanaha Beach Park

Kahului Airport

To Paia, Hana

Kanaha Pond Wildlife Sanctuary

Kahului Bay

Hobron Point

Nehe Point

Kahului Harbor

PUUNENE

To Kihei, Wailea

To Lahaina

Kahului Park

KAHULUI

WAILUKU

see Wailuku map

To Waihee

To Iao Valley

To Waikapu, Lahaina

PLACES TO STAY & EAT
8   Maui Beach Hotel
9   Maui Seaside Hotel
11 Burger King
15 Pizza Hut, Taco Bell
17 Wendy's
18 Safeway Supermarket
21 KFC
25 Maui Coffee Roasters
30 Down to Earth, Jack's
    Famous Bagels

7   Kaahumanu Center
10 Library
12 Post Office
13 Maui Swap Meet
14 Bank of Hawaii
16 Maui Mall
19 Second Wind
20 Car Rental Lots
22 Hi-Tech Surf Sports
23 Maui Windsurf
24 Hawaiian Island Surf
    & Sport, Island Biker
26 Kmart
27 Dairy Center
28 24-Hour Gas Station
29 Cut Rate Tickets
31 Windrigger Maui, Maui Mistral
32 Maui Marketplace
33 Sugar Museum
34 Sugar Mill

OTHER
1   Halekii-Pihanakalani
    Heiaus State Monument
2   Baldwin High School
3   County Parks Office
4   Maui Memorial Hospital
5   Maui Arts & Cultural Center
6   Maui Community College

marked with an HVCB warrior. An observation deck just beyond the parking lot is a good site for spotting stilts, coots, ducks and black-crowned night herons.

Upon entering the sanctuary, if you close the gate behind you and walk in quietly, you should be able to make sightings right there along the shoreline. The pond is a respite in the midst of suburbia, beneath the flight path for the airport and just beyond the highway where trucks go barreling along.

If you'd like to hike on the service roads in the sanctuary, it's possible to do so from September through March (when the birds aren't nesting) by obtaining a permit from the Division of Forestry and Wildlife (☎ 984-8100), State Office Building, 54 High St, Wailuku.

Kanaha Beach Park If you're stuck in Kahului, Kanaha Beach Park is okay for swimming, though most locals prefer the cleaner, clearer waters of Kihei.

Kanaha has a long white-sand beach, a roped-off swimming area, and a nice view of the West Maui Mountains all the way up the coast to Hakuhee Point. There are rest rooms, showers and pay phones, as well as picnic tables under the shade of hau, ironwood and kiawe trees. It's also the only county-run facility on Maui that allows camping. For information on obtaining a camping permit, see Camping in the Accommodations section near the beginning of this chapter.

Kanaha is a popular windsurfing spot, and when the wind is right, it draws a crowd. It's the best place in Maui for beginners, and most of the windsurfing shops give their lessons here.

The beach access sign is down by the car rental lots at the airport. Or from downtown Kahului take Amala Rd, the coastal road that runs makai of the Chevron storage tanks near the end of Kaahumanu Ave.

Places to Stay Kahului's two hotels are on the main commercial strip in an area that hardly conjures up images of vacationing in Hawaii.

Maui Seaside Hotel (☎ 877-3311, 800-367-7000 from the mainland, 800-560-5552 *in Hawaii, 100 Kaahumanu Ave, Kahului, HI 96732*) has two wings. The older wing has rooms for $68. The newer wing is a modern building with larger and more comfortable rooms costing $92. Rooms in both wings have air-con, cable TV and small refrigerators. With this Hawaiian-owned chain, you'll get much better rates if you book within Hawaii – look for discounted specials in Sunday's *Honolulu Advertiser* that include a room and car for less than the standard room rates.

Next door is the ***Maui Beach Hotel*** (☎ 877-0051, 800-367-5004, fax 596-0158), a Hawaiian Pacific Resorts property. It's an older facility with standard rooms that are pricey at $98. Free shuttle service is provided from the airport, but with advance reservations, you can often get a car/room package for the same price as the room alone.

Places to Eat The second level of the Kaahumanu Center has a food court with a handful of good fast-food ethnic eateries, including ***Yummy Korean BBQ***, ***Panda Express***, ***Edo Japan*** and ***Maui Tacos***, all of which have dishes for around $5. Also here are a ***McDonald's***, a coffee and pastry stall and a ***Papa Romero's***, which serves slices of pizza for $2.50. The best bet is just to walk around and see what catches your eye. The food court is open 11 am to 9 pm Monday to Saturday and 11 am to 6 pm on Sunday.

The Coffee Store, a casual little place on the ground level of the Kaahumanu Center, roasts its own coffee and serves it straight or as espresso or cappuccino. Salads, sandwiches and quiche cost $4 to $7, and there are tempting pastries such as baklava and raspberry cheesecake. The shop, which is open daily, has only a few cafe tables, so it gets crowded at lunchtime.

Pinata's Mexican Food (395 Dairy Rd), in the Dairy Center, has a fast-food atmosphere but serves up Mexican fare that's good for the price. A taco, enchilada, rice and beans plate costs $6, a single burrito $3. It's open 10:30 am to 7:30 pm Monday to Saturday.

Maui Coffee Roasters (444 Hana Hwy) serves its coffee-of-the-day for just 50¢ a cup or $1 for a large mug. It also has good cappuccino, scones, muffins and sandwiches. It's open 7:30 am to 6 pm on weekdays, 8 am to 5 pm on Saturday and 9 am to 2:30 pm on Sunday.

Jack's Famous Bagels (*333 Dairy Rd*), in the same complex as Cut Rate Tickets, specializes in bagels (75¢) but also has a few deli items and sandwiches. It's open from 6 am to 4 pm on weekdays and from at least 6:30 am to 3 pm on weekends.

Ba Le, inside the Maui Marketplace on Dairy Rd, has good, inexpensive French-Vietnamese fare, including a recommendable vegetarian sandwich (or various meat versions) on French bread for around $3. You'll also find flaky croissants, shrimp rolls, salads, plate lunches, Vietnamese pho soups and noodle dishes – all at $6 or less. It's open 8 am to 9 pm daily. Maui Marketplace also has a *Burger King* and a *Starbucks*.

Down to Earth (*305 Dairy Rd*), opposite the Maui Marketplace, is a large well-stocked natural foods store with reasonable prices, fresh organic produce and good dairy and juice sections. It also has a salad bar, a buffet with a few hot dishes for $5 a pound and a vegetarian deli with spring rolls, tofu-rice loaf and other creative items – all for takeout only. It's open 7 am to 9 pm daily (to 8 pm on Sunday).

Fast food is well represented in Kahului, with a *Pizza Hut*, *Taco Bell*, *Jack in the Box* and *Wendy's* lined up on Kamehameha Ave between Puunene Ave and Alamaha St; *Burger King* and *McDonald's* nearby on Puunene Ave; and a *KFC* (*144 Wakea Ave*).

You'll find a *Safeway* supermarket on Kamehameha Ave, a *Foodland* supermarket at the Kaahumanu Center and a *Star Market* at the Maui Mall.

Entertainment The main venue on Maui for theater, big-name concerts, foreign-film series and art exhibits is the *Maui Arts & Cultural Center* (☎ 242-7469), on Kahului Beach Rd. It's a great place to catch a performance; the indoor theaters are acoustically outstanding and the seats are very comfortable. For entertainment information, call the box office at the number listed above or go to the website at www.mauiarts .org. The art exhibits change on an ongoing basis; entry is free, though donations are appreciated. Free tours of the center are given at 11 am on Wednesday; call ☎ 242-2787 for tour reservations.

First-run movies are shown at the *Kaahumanu* multiscreen theater (☎ 244-8934), in the Kaahumanu Center.

Shopping The Kaahumanu Center, on Kaahumanu Ave, is the area's largest mall, with about 50 shops, including Liberty House, Sears, The Sharper Image and numerous clothing and shoe stores. You'll find a Longs Drugs and a couple of dozen other shops at the Maui Mall on Kaahumanu Ave. There's also a Kmart on Dairy Rd.

For some local flavor, try the Maui Swap Meet, held from 7 am to noon on Saturday on Puunene Ave, just south of the Kahului post office.

Puunene

Puunene is a working plantation village surrounded by sugarcane fields and centered around a mill run by the Hawaiian Commercial & Sugar Company. When the mill is in operation, the air hangs heavy with the sweet smell of sugar.

The power plant next to the mill burns residue sugarcane fibers (called bagasse) to run the mill machinery that extracts and refines the sugar. With a capacity of 37,000 kilowatts, it's one of the world's largest biomass power plants. Excess electricity is sold to Maui Electric.

Puunene's main attraction is the sugar museum opposite the mill.

Sugar Museum The Alexander & Baldwin Sugar Museum is a worthwhile little museum that tells the history of sugar in Hawaii. The displays, which explain how sugarcane grows and is harvested, include an elaborate working scale model of a cane-crushing plant.

Most interesting, however, are the images of people. The museum traces how Samuel Alexander and Henry Baldwin gobbled up vast chunks of Hawaiian land, how they fought tooth and nail with an ambitious Claus

MAUI

Spreckels to gain access to Upcountry water, and how they dug the extensive irrigation systems that made large-scale sugarcane plantations a possibility.

Representing the other end of the scale is a turn-of-the-20th-century labor contract from the Japanese Emigration Company stating that the laborer shall be paid $15 a month for working 10 hours a day in the field, 26 days a month (minus $2.50 banked for return passage to Japan). Interesting period photos and artifacts of plantation life are also on display.

The museum (☎ 871-8058), in the former home of the mill's superintendent, is at the intersection of Puunene Ave and Hansen Rd. It's open 9:30 am to 4:30 pm Monday to Saturday (and on Sunday in summer). Admission is $4 for adults, $2 for children six to 17.

Waikapu

The Honoapiilani Hwy (Hwy 30), which runs along the east side of the West Maui Moun-

tains, passes through the town of Waikapu just a couple of miles south of Wailuku.

Although Waikapu has a new golf course sitting above its pineapple fields, it remains quite rural. Its only sight is **Maui Tropical Plantation**, which features a touristy narrated tram ride past fields of sugarcane, pineapple and tropical fruit trees. The ride, which takes about 40 minutes, costs $9.

There's also a shop selling fresh fruit and a free-admission section that includes a nursery, a few taro plants and a couple of very simple exhibits on agriculture.

If you're driving by, you might want to make a quick stop, but it's not worth going out of your way. The plantation is open 9 am to 5 pm daily.

Wailuku

Wailuku sits beneath the eastern flank of the West Maui Mountains and is an interesting juxtaposition of old and new. While the central area serves as the county capital,

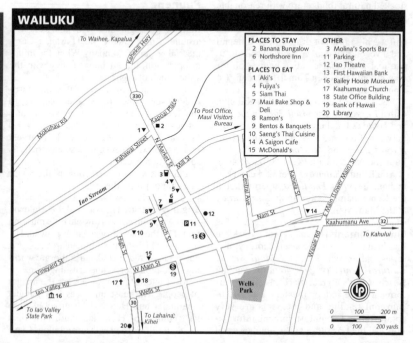

WAILUKU

PLACES TO STAY
2 Banana Bungalow
6 Northshore Inn

PLACES TO EAT
1 Aki's
4 Fujiya's
5 Siam Thai
7 Maui Bake Shop & Deli
8 Ramon's
9 Bentos & Banquets
10 Saeng's Thai Cuisine
14 A Saigon Cafe
15 McDonald's

OTHER
3 Molina's Sports Bar
11 Parking
12 Iao Theatre
13 First Hawaiian Bank
16 Bailey House Museum
17 Kaahumanu Church
18 State Office Building
19 Bank of Hawaii
20 Library

To Waihee, Kapalua
Kahekili Hwy
To Post Office, Maui Visitors Bureau
Mokuhau Rd
Kapoai Place
Kahawai Street
N Market St
Mill St
Iao Stream
Central Ave
Kaniela St
E Main/Lower Main St
High St
Church St
Nani St
Kaahumanu Ave
Waiale Rd
To Kahului
Vineyard St
W Main St
Wells St
Iao Valley Rd
Wells Park
To Iao Valley State Park
To Lahaina, Kihei

0   100   200 m
0   100   200 yards

complete with a few mid-rise government buildings, the backstreets are lined with a colorful hodgepodge of older shops and neighborhood restaurants. Wailuku is unabashedly local – there's nothing touristy in the whole town.

It's a fun town for strolling. Begin walking north from W Main St on N Market St, which has a handful of pawnshops, galleries and antique shops, some of them intriguingly cluttered affairs stocking a mishmash of Hawaiiana items, Asian handicrafts and lots of odds and ends.

Information The Maui Visitors Bureau (☎ 244-3530) is at 1727 Wili Pa Loop, near the post office. It's open 8 am to 4:30 pm Monday to Friday.

The State Office Building, where you can pick up permits for state park campgrounds, is on High St in downtown Wailuku. The county parks office, which issues county camping permits, is on Kaahumanu Ave at Baldwin High School.

Bank of Hawaii is at 2105 Main St, and First Hawaiian Bank is at 21 N Market St. Both have after-hours ATMs.

The Wailuku post office, 250 Imi Kala St, on the north side of town, is open 8:30 am to 5 pm on weekdays, 9 am to noon on Saturday.

Molina's Sports Bar (☎ 244-4100), 197 N Market St, has a computer with Internet access that you can use for $3.75 per half hour.

The Wailuku public library, 251 High St, is open 10 am to 8 pm on Monday and Thursday and 10 am to 5 pm on Tuesday, Wednesday and Friday.

Maui Memorial Hospital (☎ 244-9056), 221 Mahalani St, is the island's main hospital and has 24-hour emergency service.

Kaahumanu Church Kaahumanu Church, on the corner of W Main and High Sts, dates from 1837, making it the oldest Congregational church in Maui. The present building was erected in 1876 by missionary Edward Bailey.

The church was named in honor of Queen Kaahumanu, who cast aside the old gods and burned temple idols, allowing Christianity to flourish. She visited Wailuku in 1832 and in her ever-humble manner requested that the first church bear her name.

The old clock in the steeple was brought around the Horn in the 19th century, and it still keeps accurate time. Hymns are still sung in Hawaiian at Sunday morning services.

Bailey House Museum Bailey House, a five-minute walk up Iao Valley Rd from Kaahumanu Church, was home to the family of missionary Edward Bailey, who came to Wailuku from Boston, Massachusetts, in 1837.

The building, also called Hale Hoikeike, is the headquarters of the Maui Historical Society, which has turned the former mission house into a little museum.

There's a Hawaiiana section with stone adzes, tapa, bottle gourds, calabashes and the like, as well as period furnishings from the missionary days. Bailey was a painter and engraver, and many of his works are on display.

One of the most interesting sights is a surfboard used by Olympian Duke Kahanamoku; it's above the parking lot at the side of the shed. Compare it to today's sleek fiberglass boards – this six-footer is made of redwood and weighs in at a hefty 150lb!

Bailey House Museum is open 10 am to 4 pm Monday to Saturday. Admission is $4 for adults, $1 for children six to 12. The museum gift shop has quality crafts and a good Hawaiiana book selection.

Places to Stay In a funky old building right in the center of Wailuku, the *Northshore Inn* (☎ 242-8999, 800-647-6284, fax 244-5004, reservations@hostelhawaii.com, 2080 Vineyard St, Wailuku, HI 96793) is popular with international travelers. While it's certainly not fancy, by Hawaiian standards it's a decent budget accommodation. There are a few simple rooms with shared baths at $32/42 for singles/doubles and a handful of dorm rooms, which have two to six bunks to a room and cost $16 per bunk. Rates include sheets, a towel and a blanket. Shared amenities include a TV near the front desk, a group kitchen and free use of a computer for email. The inn is open only to travelers, and

MAUI

you might have to show a passport or airline ticket to book a room. For more information, visit the hostel's website at www .hostelhawaii.com.

Banana Bungalow (☎ 244-5090, 800-746-7871, bungalow@gte.net, 310 N Market St, Wailuku, HI 96793) is a larger hostel-type place catering to both international travelers and long-term boarders. Private rooms are simple but generally clean and cost $29/35 for singles/doubles. A bunk in one of the dorm rooms, which typically have three to four beds each, costs $16. Discounts and other arrangements can cut the cost for longer stays. Bedding is provided. All guests share community showers and toilets. Other common amenities include a TV room, group kitchen, Jacuzzi, coin laundry, a shed for storing windsurfing gear and a free shuttle to Kanaha Beach. The hostel maintains a website at home1.gte.net/bungalow.

Sunrise Garden (☎ 572-1440, fax 572-4612, sunrisegarden@pilialoha.com) is a cozy vacation rental in a pleasant neighborhood on the east side of Wailuku. Attached to the owner's home, this studio unit has a king bed, full bath, arbored patio, cable TV, VCR and a simple kitchenette with a microwave, coffeemaker and small refrigerator. Outside, the bay-view garden features an outdoor shower under a mango tree. Singles/doubles cost $80/85, and there's a two-night minimum stay. Some breakfast fixings are provided on arrival, but guests prepare their own meals. Smoking is allowed outdoors only. To see pictures of the accommodations, visit Sunrise Garden's website at www .pilialoha.com/sg1.html.

Places to Eat Wailuku has a nice range of good, reasonably priced restaurants. Within a few minutes' walk from the intersection of Vineyard and N Market Sts, you can sample Thai, Japanese, Mexican, Hawaiian and just plain local food. As this is the government center, plenty of weekday lunch deals are available, but most restaurants are closed at lunchtime on weekends.

In addition to the options listed below, Wailuku also contains some fast-food eateries, including a ***McDonald's*** at 2138 N Main St.

Saeng's Thai Cuisine (☎ 244-1567, 2119 Vineyard St) has a pleasant setting with open-air dining and a wide range of Thai dishes, including good curries. The dozen vegetarian offerings on the menu cost $7.50, while most meat and shrimp dishes are in the $9 to $12 range. Lunch features a handful of specials that include rice for $7. Saeng's is open 11 am to 2:30 pm on weekdays and 5 to 9:30 pm nightly.

Two blocks away is ***Siam Thai*** (☎ 244-3817, 123 N Market St), which has a more local atmosphere but food, prices and hours that are nearly the same as at Saeng's.

Bentos & Banquets (☎ 244-1124, 85 Church St) offers takeout lunch specials (available 10 am to 2 pm weekdays) that are quite popular with local businesspeople. The menu changes daily, though a few dishes like roast pork or teriyaki beef are standards. Most lunches cost around $6.

Maui Bake Shop & Deli (2092 Vineyard St), a small family-run operation, has a wide variety of good breakfast pastries and desserts, as well as soups, salads and sandwiches at reasonable prices. It's open 6 am to 5 pm on weekdays and 7 am to 2:30 pm on Saturday.

At ***Ramon's*** (☎ 244-7243, 2101 Vineyard St), you can get a Spanish omelette with rice for $6, an enchilada with rice and beans for $7 and standard Mexican combination plates for a few dollars more. It's open 10 am to 9 pm daily (to 10 pm on weekends).

Fujiya's (☎ 244-0206, 133 N Market St) has a sushi bar and also offers a wide variety of Japanese dishes for around $8. Hours are 11 am to 2 pm Monday to Friday and 5 to 9 pm Monday to Saturday.

Aki's (309 N Market St) serves Hawaiian food. Kalua pig with cabbage and salad costs $5.50, a small octopus with coconut milk is $3.80, and you can round it off with a side of poi for $1.90. It's a local experience. Hours are 11 am to 8 pm.

Hands down, the area's best restaurant is ***A Saigon Cafe*** (☎ 243-9560), on the corner of Main and Kaniela Sts, which offers superb Vietnamese food. The menu includes pho soup and various meat and vegetarian entrees for around $7. The curried lemongrass chicken with jasmine rice is excellent. Or go for the fun *banh hoi* ($9), a Vietnamese version of fajitas, with a plate of mint leaves, rice noodles, assorted vegetables and shrimp or tofu, which you roll up into rice-paper wraps. This restaurant doesn't have a sign and is a bit challenging to reach, but it's worth the effort; take Central Ave to Nani St and turn south on Kaniela St. It's open 10 am to 10 pm daily (to 9 pm on Sunday).

Entertainment Local theater groups present plays at the *Iao Theatre*, on Market St. Built circa 1928, the Iao has been restored after years of neglect. It's pleasantly casual, and cross breezes keep it cool and comfortable inside. For schedule information, call ☎ 244-8680.

Molina's Sports Bar (☎ *244-4100, 197 N Market St*), midway between the two hostels, has an 'international hostel night' once or twice a week with $2 beers and dancing to a DJ.

Iao Valley Rd

In 1790, Kamehameha I attacked Kahului by sea and quickly chased the defending Maui warriors up into precipitous Iao Valley. Those unable to escape over the mountains were slaughtered along the stream. The waters of Iao Stream were so choked with bodies that the area was called Kepaniwai, meaning 'Dammed Waters.'

Today, Iao Valley State Park encompasses much of the upper valley along the stream. Iao Valley Rd leads into the park, passing the following sights along the way.

Tropical Gardens of Maui If you're looking for a botany lesson, you'll enjoy Tropical Gardens of Maui; interpretive plaques identify many species among the widely varied flora displayed here. Even though it's a relatively new garden, the plantings have matured enough in the past few years to make this a worthwhile sight. It's open 9 am to 4:30 pm Monday to Saturday; admission is $3.

Kepaniwai County Park Kepaniwai County Park is dedicated to Hawaii's varied ethnic heritage. Like Hawaii itself, there's a little bit of everything mixed in, including a Hawaiian hale with a pili roof, a Filipino house, a New England missionary home and a Portuguese garden with a bubbling fountain and outdoor bread oven.

Most colorful are the Asian gardens, which hold stone pagodas, a carp pond and assorted pavilions. A Chinese pavilion, red and white with a green tile roof, houses the requisite statue of Sun Yat-sen. Not far away, a bronze statue of two Japanese sugarcane workers in traditional garb commemorates the centennial of Japanese immigration to the islands.

Iao Stream runs through the park and is bordered by picnic shelters with tables and barbecue pits.

Hawaii Nature Center At the west end of Kepaniwai County Park is the Hawaii Nature Center, a nonprofit educational facility that focuses on making children more aware of their natural environment. It has 30 exhibits, some interactive, that identify local birds, explain native stream life and the like. Although the center caters mostly to children on school outings, it's also open to the general public. Hours are 10 am to 4 pm daily; admission costs $6 for adults, $4 for children.

JFK Profile At a bend in the road half a mile after Kepaniwai Park, you'll likely see a few cars pulled over and their occupants staring off into Pali Eleele, a gorge on the right. One of the rock formations on the cliff face has an uncanny resemblance to John F Kennedy's profile. The profile is also rooted in Hawaiian traditions, having been associated with a powerful *kahuna* (priest/spiritual healer) who lived in the 1500s.

If parking is difficult here, just continue on to Iao Valley State Park, as it's only a couple of minutes' walk from there back to the profile viewing site.

Iao Valley State Park Three miles out of central Wailuku, Iao Valley State Park is nestled in the mountains at an elevation of 2250 feet. The valley is named for Iao, the beautiful daughter of Maui.

MAUI

Iao Needle, a rock pinnacle that rises 1200 feet from the valley floor, is said to be Iao's clandestine lover, captured by Maui and turned to stone.

Clouds often rise up the valley, forming a shroud around the top of Iao Needle. A stream meanders beneath the needle, and the steep cliffs of the West Maui Mountains form a scenic backdrop.

A two-minute walk from the parking lot, you'll reach a bridge where most people stop to photograph Iao Needle. However, just before the bridge, the walkway that loops downhill by the stream leads to the nicest photo angle – one that captures the stream, bridge and Iao Needle together.

Over the bridge, a short walkway leads up to a sheltered lookout with another fine view of Iao Needle.

The park is open 7 am to 7 pm daily; admission is free.

Halekii-Pihanakalani Heiaus

Halekii-Pihanakalani Heiaus State Monument marks one of Maui's most important historical sites.

Kahekili, the last ruling chief of Maui, lived here, and Keopuolani, wife of Kamehameha I and mother of Kamehamehas II and III, was born at this site. After the decisive battle of Iao in 1790, Kamehameha I came to these *heiaus* (temples) to worship his war god Ku, offering what is thought to have been the last human sacrifice on Maui.

The two adjoining heiaus sit atop a knoll and have a commanding view of the entire region, clear across the plains of central Maui and up the slopes of Haleakala. The temples were built with stones carried up from Iao Stream.

Halekii (literally 'House of the Idol'), the first heiau, has stepped stone walls and a flat grassy top. (Watch out for bullhead thorns if you're wearing flip-flops.) The pyramid-like mound of Pihanakalani Heiau is directly ahead, a five-minute walk away.

Pihanakalani, which means 'gathering place of supernatural beings,' is fairly overgrown with kiawe, wildflowers and weeds. Few people come this way, and doves fly up from the bushes as you approach.

Despite the state monument status, the government has been somewhat negligent in protecting the heiaus. This is one of the fastest-growing residential areas on Maui, and construction and gravel removal along both sides of the hill have been widespread – so much so that some conservationists fear the heiau site itself is being undermined.

Nevertheless, a certain spiritual essence still emanates from the site. To imagine it all through the eyes of the Hawaiians 200 years ago, ignore the industrial warehouses and tract homes and concentrate instead on the heiaus and the wide vistas. It must have been an incredible scene.

To get there from Waiehu Beach Rd, turn inland onto Kuhio Place, three-quarters of a mile south of the intersection of Hwys 340 and 330. Then take the first left off Kuhio Place onto Hea Place and drive up through the gates. The heiaus are less than half a mile from Hwy 340.

Kahekili Hwy

The Kahekili Hwy (Hwy 340) curves around the undeveloped northeastern side of the West Maui Mountains (see the Northwest Maui map). It's ruggedly scenic, with deep ravines, eroded red hills and rock-strewn pastures. The coastline is rocky lava sea cliffs and open ocean.

The route is pastoral and quiet, with a couple of waterfalls, blowholes and one-lane bridges. You'll likely spot cowhands on horseback and egrets riding the backs of lazy cows.

It's about 22 miles from the northern end of the road at Honokohau to the southern end at Wailuku (the Kahekili Hwy turns into Hwy 330 a few miles north of Wailuku). Like its counterpart to the south (the Piilani Hwy around the southern flank of Haleakala), the Kahekili is shown either as a black hole or an unpaved road on most tourist maps. The road, however, is paved its entire length – though much of the drive is very winding and narrow, with blind curves and the occasional sign warning of falling rocks.

The road between Honokohau and Kahakuloa is largely two lanes and easy going, while the section between Kahakuloa and

Waihee is mostly one lane (with two-way traffic) and has a few hair-raising cliffside sections without shoulders. While the posted speed limit on most of the road is 15mph, in some sections it's a mere 5mph. But taking it slowly is the whole point anyway.

Waiehu & Waihee Waiehu Beach Rd turns into Kahekili Hwy at the northern end of Wailuku and heads through the little towns of Waiehu and Waihee.

Waiehu Municipal Golf Course, down near the shore, is bordered by two county beach parks that have poor swimming conditions and limited appeal, other than for strolling and beachcombing.

The side road up to the Boy Scouts' Camp Mahulia is a pretty, winding drive through open pasture. It leads to the start of the **Waihee Ridge Trail**, a seldom-trodden route offering varied scenery and breathtaking views of the interior.

The one-lane paved road to the trailhead begins on the inland side of the highway just before the 7-mile marker. Be prepared to stop for cattle crossing the pavement. The trailhead is a mile up, on the left just before the camp. It's marked with a Na Ala Hele sign and a squeeze-through 'turnstile' through the fence. There's a little parking area to the left of the trailhead.

The well-defined trail is 3 miles one way and takes about three hours roundtrip. It crosses forest reserve land, and though it's a bit steep, it's a fairly steady climb and not overly strenuous. Consider packing a lunch, as there's a picnic spot with an unbeatable view at the end.

Starting at an elevation of 1000 feet, the trail climbs a ridge, passing from pasture to cool forest. Guava trees and groves of rainbow eucalyptus are prominent along the trail, and if you look closely, you can usually find thimbleberries. From the three-quarter-mile post, panoramic views open up with a scene that sweeps clear down to the ocean along the Waihee Gorge and deep into the interior valleys. The ridgetop views are similar to those you'd get from a helicopter, though the stillness along this route can only be appreciated by those on foot. The trail

ends at the 2563-foot peak of Lanilili, where you'll enjoy great views in all directions.

Waterfalls & Gardens Back on the highway, you'll pass a gentle waterfall on the left, rain permitting. For another waterfall view, stop at the pull-off a tenth of a mile north of the 8-mile marker and look down into the ravine below; you'll see a picture-perfect waterfall framed by double pools.

Shortly before reaching the 9-mile marker, a sign marks the driveway up to Aina Anuhea tropical gardens, a private estate offering a 20-minute walk through gardens with bromeliads and other labeled plants. The grounds also have two waterfalls, the largest with a 25-foot drop, and a shop selling crafts and a few simple snack items. The $4 admission includes a glass of pineapple juice.

Kahakuloa The village of Kahakuloa lies at the base of a small green valley. Although it contains only a few dozen simple homes, Kahakuloa ('Tall Lord') has two churches. The little tin-roof Catholic mission sits hillside at the southern end of town, just off the road, while the Protestant church, sporting a green wooden exterior and red-tile roof, hunkers down on the valley floor.

Up out of the valley, at the northern edge of town, a pull-off provides a good view of the village and the rugged coastline. The rise on the south side of Kahakuloa Bay is Kahakuloa Head, 636 feet high.

Bellstone Pohaku Kani is a large bellstone at the inland side of the road, just past the 16-mile marker.

If you hit the bellstone with a rock on the Kahakuloa side where the deepest indentations are, you might be able to get a hollow sound. It's pretty resonant if you hit it right, but it takes some imagination to hear it ring like a bell.

Pastures & Cliffs The wide turnoff about half a mile beyond the 16-mile marker looks down over a clifftop plateau with a rugged coast and crashing surf. The stretch of green turf practically invites you to take a scenic walk from the road down to the cliffs and out along the coastline. Although it's unshaded, it would be a fine place to break out a bottle of wine and a picnic lunch.

The surrounding terrain is hilly, with rocky cattle pastures punctuated by tall sisal plants. At a number of viewpoints and pulloffs, you can stop and explore.

Stone cairns are piled everywhere. They look like religious offerings, but most are just the creations of sightseers.

When the water is surging, a **blowhole** is visible from the road just past the 20-mile marker. It comes up after a sharp bend in the road. During the winter season, you can sometimes spot humpbacks breaching offshore in this area as well.

Nakalele Point Light Station About half a mile farther, a walk leads out to the light station at the end of Nakalele Point. The coastline here has interesting pools, arches and other formations worn out of the rocks by the pounding surf. As elsewhere in Maui, don't leave valuables in your car at the parking area. The smashed glass from broken windshields is indicative of the break-ins that take place here.

As you continue north along the road, Molokai comes into view, and the scenery is very lush on the way to Honokohau Bay.

Kihei

Kihei extends 6 miles along Maui's southwest coast, on the leeward side of Haleakala. Maalaea Bay is to the north, and the more exclusive Wailea resort is to the south.

Kihei is fringed with sandy beaches its entire length and has near-constant sunshine. It has long attracted sunbathers, boogie boarders, windsurfers and Kahului families on weekend picnics.

The beaches have views of Lanai and Kahoolawe as well as of West Maui, which because of the deep cut of Maalaea Bay looks like a separate island from here.

Thirty years ago, Kihei was a long stretch of undeveloped beach with kiawe trees, a scattering of homes and a church or two. But in the past couple of decades, develop-

ers have pounced on Kihei with such intensity that it has gained the dubious distinction of being Maui's fastest-growing community.

S Kihei Rd, which runs the full length of Kihei, is lined with condos, gas stations, shopping centers and fast-food places in such congested and haphazard disarray that it's the example most often cited by the anti-development forces on other Neighbor Islands. To them, Kihei is what no town wants to become.

While Kihei's 'condoville' character doesn't win any prizes for aesthetics, it has one advantage for visitors – the sheer abundance of condos means that Kihei's rates are among the cheapest in Maui. In addition, the infrastructure has begun to catch up with the rampant commercial growth; bike lanes are being added to S Kihei Rd, a library and other public facilities have been built, and steps have been taken to ameliorate some of the traffic problems.

Piilani Hwy (Hwy 31) parallels and bypasses the start-and-stop traffic of S Kihei Rd. Several crossroads connect the two.

Information

The Bank of Hawaii at Azeka Place II is open 8:30 am to 4 pm Monday to Thursday, 8:30 am to 6 pm on Friday. The bank has a 24-hour ATM that accepts MasterCard, Visa, American Express and JCB credit cards as well as Cirrus and Plus debit cards. Similar ATMs can be found in the Star Market and at the American Savings Bank in Longs Center.

The Kihei post office, at Azeka Place, is open 9 am to 4:30 pm weekdays, 9 am to noon on Saturday.

You can check your email for free at The Coffee Store (☎ 875-4244) at Azeka Place II.

The Fox 1-Hour Photo Lab at Azeka Place has on-site printing. If you're not in a hurry, Longs Drugs in the Longs Center offers send-out Fuji and Kodak processing services at cheaper prices; Longs is also a good place to pick up film.

There's a branch of the Waldenbooks chain in the Kukui Mall. Aloha Books, in the Kamaole Beach Center, sells both new and used books, including some Hawaiiana.

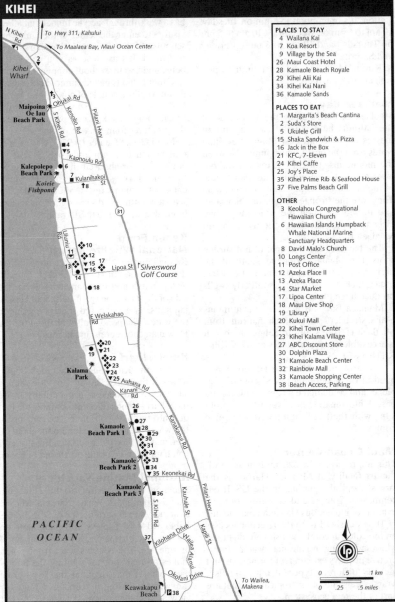

KIHEI

PLACES TO STAY
4 Wailana Kai
7 Koa Resort
9 Village by the Sea
26 Maui Coast Hotel
28 Kamaole Beach Royale
29 Kihei Alii Kai
34 Kihei Kai Nani
36 Kamaole Sands

PLACES TO EAT
1 Margarita's Beach Cantina
2 Suda's Store
5 Ukulele Grill
15 Shaka Sandwich & Pizza
16 Jack in the Box
21 KFC, 7-Eleven
24 Kihei Caffe
25 Joy's Place
35 Kihei Prime Rib & Seafood House
37 Five Palms Beach Grill

OTHER
3 Keolahou Congregational
   Hawaiian Church
6 Hawaiian Islands Humpback
   Whale National Marine
   Sanctuary Headquarters
8 David Malo's Church
10 Longs Center
11 Post Office
12 Azeka Place II
13 Azeka Place
14 Star Market
17 Lipoa Center
18 Maui Dive Shop
19 Library
20 Kukui Mall
22 Kihei Town Center
23 Kihei Kalama Village
27 ABC Discount Store
30 Dolphin Plaza
31 Kamaole Beach Center
32 Rainbow Mall
33 Kamaole Shopping Center
38 Beach Access, Parking

N Kihei Rd
To Hwy 311, Kahului
To Maalaea Bay, Maui Ocean Center
Kihei Wharf
Ohukai Rd
Kenolio Rd
Piilani Hwy
Maipoina Oe Iau Beach Park
S Kihei Rd
Kaonoulu Rd
Kalepolepo Beach Park
Koieie Fishpond
Kulanihakoi St
(31)
Uluniu Rd
Lipoa St
Silversword Golf Course
E Welakahao Rd
Kalama Park
Auhana Rd
Kanani Rd
Kamaole Beach Park 1
Kanakanui Rd
Kamaole Beach Park 2
Keonekai Rd
Kamaole Beach Park 3
Kauhale St
Piilani Hwy
S Kihei Rd
PACIFIC OCEAN
Kilohana Drive
Wailea Alanui
Kapili St
To Wailea, Makena
Okolani Drive
Keawakapu Beach
38

0   .5   1 km
0   .25   .5 miles

MAUI

Kihei has a modern public library on Waimahaihai St, directly behind the fire station. It's open noon to 8 pm on Tuesday, 10 am to 6 pm on Wednesday, 10 am to 5 pm on Thursday and 10 am to 6 pm on Friday and Saturday.

Kukui Mall has a coin laundry open 7:30 am to 8 pm daily.

Maalaea Bay

Maalaea Bay runs along the south side of the isthmus between the twin mountain masses of west and east Maui. Prevailing winds from the north, which funnel between the mountains straight out toward Kahoolawe, create strong midday gusts and some of the best windsurfing conditions on Maui. These are the strongest winds on the island, and in winter, when the wind dies down elsewhere, windsurfers still fly along in Maalaea Bay.

The bay also has a couple of hot surfing spots. The Maalaea Pipeline, south of the harbor, freight-trains right and is the fastest break in Hawaii. Summer's southerly swells produce huge tubes.

Maalaea Bay is fronted by a continuous 3-mile stretch of sandy beach that runs from Maalaea Harbor south to Kihei. The beach is accessible at several places along N Kihei Rd (Hwy 31).

The area near Maalaea Harbor has a handful of moderately priced condo complexes and could make a convenient central base. Unfortunately, however, it's had problems with theft and other visitor-targeted crimes.

Maui Ocean Center

This impressive new $20 million state-of-the-art facility at Maalaea Harbor is the largest tropical aquarium in the US. It encompasses 5 acres and contains some 60 exhibits of indigenous Hawaiian marine life.

The extensive 'Living Reef' section focuses on the colorful coral and fish you might see while snorkeling in Hawaiian waters. Interpretive displays explain reef formations and identify different types of butterfly fish, wrasses, eels and other tropical fish that are part of the reef ecosystem.

The most dazzling sight is the main tank, which holds 750,000 gallons of seawater and has a walk-through acrylic tunnel that allows visitors to enter the center of the tank while schools of fish and meandering sharks swim overhead. It's as close as you can get to being underwater without donning dive gear.

Other exhibits include interactive displays about whales, a couple of outdoor tanks that harbor sea turtles and stingrays, and a small touch pool where kids can examine some of the creatures found in tide pools.

Maui Ocean Center (☎ 270-7000) is open daily 9 am to 5 pm and costs $17.50 for adults, $12 for children three to 12 (under three free). The site is accessible by wheelchair. The center's restaurant has a pleasant sea-view setting and serves good salads and hot dishes in the $10 to $15 range.

Kealia Pond National Wildlife Refuge

Kealia Pond, on N Kihei Rd 2 miles south of the intersection of Hwys 31 and 30, is a saltwater marsh and bird sanctuary. From the side of the road, you can usually spot Hawaiian stilts, an endangered species, wading in the water. The pond is also a habitat for the Hawaiian coot, egrets and herons.

Kihei Wharf

In 1899, the Kihei Sugar Plantation built a wharf at the north end of Kihei for landing supplies. Sand accretion eventually made the wharf – which once jutted some 200 feet out into the bay – obsolete. The remains of the wharf, which now extend only about 30 feet, make a nice place to catch the sunset if you happen to be at the north end of Kihei.

National Marine Sanctuary

The new visitor center at the Hawaiian Islands Humpback Whale National Marine Sanctuary headquarters (☎ 879-2818), 726 S Kihei Rd, has displays and pamphlets on whales, sea turtles and other endangered marine life. The center's waterfront porch makes a great spot for sighting the humpback whales that frequent the bay during the winter season; a scope is set up for viewing. Ecology-oriented volunteers staff the facility, and it could make a good place to meet like-minded people. You can find more information about the sanctuary at www.t-link.net/~whale on the Web.

David Malo's Church

Another historic site at the northern end of Kihei is the church built in 1853 by David Malo, a noted philosopher and the first Hawaiian ordained to the Christian ministry. While most of the church was dismantled long ago, a three-foot-high section of the church walls still stands. Eighteen pews are lined up inside the stone walls, where open-air services are held on Sunday mornings. David Malo's Church is at 100 Kulanihakoi St, at the side of the Trinity Episcopal Church.

Another notable church in the area is the little green-and-white **Keolahou Congregational Hawaiian Church** at 131 S Kihei Rd, which was established in 1920. Many of the 1000 Tongans living on Maui belong to the congregation.

Beaches & Parks

Maipoina Oe Iau Beach Park Maipoina Oe Iau Beach Park, at the northern end of Kihei, has a long sandy beach and full facilities. Swimming and sunbathing are best in the morning before the wind picks up, while windsurfing is generally good in the afternoon; many people take windsurfing lessons here.

The park, whose name means 'forget me not,' is dedicated to Maui's war veterans.

Kalepolepo Beach Park The waters off Kalepolepo Beach Park offer only mediocre swimming, but this is one of the few places in Maui where you can see the remains of a fishpond.

Koieie Fishpond was built in the 16th century by King Umi and was used to raise mullet for the *alii* (royals). The 3-acre fishpond is now on the National Register of Historic Places.

Kalama Park Kalama Park, opposite Kihei Town Center, is a local park with ball fields, tennis and volleyball courts, a playground, picnic pavilions, rest rooms and showers. The

---

Koieie Fishpond

In a story with an unusual twist, the Koieie Fishpond at Kalepolepo Beach Park was said to have been built by regular-size Hawaiians. After the workers protested that the work couldn't be done properly without the help of the *menehune* (Hawaii's legendary little people), the chief in charge angrily ordered that when the job was finished the workers were to be cooked in an *imu* (underground oven). The night before the last rock was to be placed, the menehune came down from the mountains and carried away every stone. Only after the threats against the Hawaiian laborers were withdrawn did the menehune return with the stones and rebuild the fishpond.

---

park is long and grassy, but the beach is shallow and unappealing for swimming.

Kamaole Beach Park Kamaole Beach is one long beach divided into three sections by rocky points. All three are pretty golden-sand beaches, though sometimes powerful kona storms temporarily wipe out much of the sand.

Each section is along the roadside opposite condos and shopping centers. All three sections have full beach facilities and lifeguards.

Water conditions vary greatly with the weather, but there's usually good swimming. For the most part, these beaches have sandy bottoms with a fairly steep drop, which tends to create good conditions for bodysurfing as well.

For snorkeling, the southern end of Kamaole Beach Park 3 has some nearshore rocks harboring a bit of coral and a few tropical fish, though the Wailea beaches to the south are far better.

Keawakapu Beach Keawakapu Beach is bordered on its north end by the southernmost Kihei hotels and on its south end by

MAUI

Mokapu Beach and the Wailea resort area. More scenic and less crowded than the roadside Kihei beaches, Keawakapu is a sandy beach with a sandy bottom. Snorkeling is fairly good at the rocky outcrop at the southern end.

As there's no reef off Keawakapu, the state has been working to develop an artificial reef here for the past 30 years. The original drop consisted of piles of car bodies, but in recent years the state has switched to using 'fish shelters' made of old tires embedded in concrete; about 1000 of these shelters have been dropped some 500 yards offshore.

There's a fine view from the beach, and during the winter, whales cavort in the surrounding waters and sometimes come quite close to shore.

To get to Keawakapu, go south on S Kihei Rd until it ends. There you'll find 25 public parking spaces and an outdoor shower.

Places to Stay

B&Bs An excellent value is ***Dolphin House Bed and Breakfast*** (☎ 874-0126, 800-419-2521, fax 875-1799, info@dolphinhouse.com, 69 Kalola Place, Kihei, HI 96753), at the north end of Kihei, within walking distance of the beach. It consists of four pleasant rooms in the home of Ray Kashinski – a contractor who built the place himself using local woods and Victorian-style trim. All rooms have a queen bed and ceiling fan. The two with shared bath cost $45/55 for singles/doubles and have no minimum stay. The smaller of the two with private bath costs $65, while the larger – a lovely room with TV, VCR, refrigerator and king bed – costs $75. There's a two-night minimum stay on the rooms with private bath. In the morning, guests enjoy a breakfast of tropical fruit and muffins. For more information, visit the website www.dolphinhouse.com.

Wonderful World B&B (☎ 879-9103, amauibnb@maui.net, 2828 Umalu Place, Kihei, HI 96753), in a residential neighborhood about half a mile inland from Kamaole Beach Park 3, is in the contemporary home of Eva and Jim Tantillo. The ground floor contains three nicely furnished units: a one-bedroom unit with a full kitchen for $95, a simpler one-bedroom unit for $85 and a studio for $75. Each is amply sized and has a private entrance, private bath, cable TV, VCR, phone with free local calls and at least a microwave, refrigerator and toaster oven. In addition, there's an upstairs master bedroom that has a refrigerator, microwave and coffeemaker for $65. Guests have access to a washer and dryer. Rates include breakfast served on the ocean-view lanai. The Tantillos maintain a website, with photos, at www.thesupersites.com/wonderfulworld.

In a peaceful neighborhood convenient to the highway, ***Kokopelli Maui B&B*** (☎/fax 891-0631, 888-879-6064, 169 Keonekai Rd, Kihei, HI 96753) offers three rooms on the upper floor of a modern South Kihei home. The master bedroom has a private bath, private lanai, king bed and cable TV for $75; the two other bedrooms each have two twin beds and shared bath for $55. All rooms have ceiling fans. The three rooms share a large living room with a TV, a full kitchen, an ocean-view lanai and a phone. Continental breakfast is included. Although the rooms are already a good deal, you can usually work out a slightly cheaper price if you want to skip the breakfast or if you're staying any length of time. There's also a two-bedroom apartment on the ground floor that's rented by the week or month at reasonable rates. An Arizona-based Vietnam War veterans group runs the place; the manager lives downstairs.

Ann and Bob Babson (☎ 874-1166, 800-824-6409, fax 879-7906, babson@mauibnb .com, 3371 Keha Drive, Kihei, HI 96753) rent three bedrooms in their hillside home in the Maui Meadows area, about a mile above Wailea. The living room enjoys nice views of Kahoolawe, Molokini and Lanai. The master bedroom has a private deck, wraparound windows, a skylight and a Jacuzzi and costs $95. A smaller upstairs bedroom goes for $80, a larger one downstairs is $95, and a separate cottage adjacent to the house rents for $105. All have TVs, phones and private baths; prices include breakfast (except on Sunday) for all but the cottage, which has a kitchen. There's a four-day minimum stay.

For more details, visit the Babsons' website at www.mauibnb.com.

Condos Kihei is packed with condos but has few hotels. In many places along S Kihei Rd, the traffic will challenge you to get a good night's sleep, so when you book be sure to avoid rooms close to the road.

In addition to the following listings, scores of Kihei condos can be booked through rental agents; for details, see Condos under Accommodations in the front of this chapter.

Wailana Kai (☎ 877-5796, 34 Wailana Place) is a well-maintained little complex on a quiet cul-de-sac a block back from the beach at the 1-mile marker. It has a small pool and 10 pleasant units, each with cable TV, full kitchen, lanai and everything you'd expect in a more expensive condo except the price. One-bedroom units cost $60 in the low season and $70 in the high season. Two-bedroom units, which have two full baths, cost $80/90 low/high for up to four people. It can book up far in advance, particularly in winter. Credit cards are not accepted. For reservations, write to Mary Caravalho, 255 E Alamaha St, Kahului, HI 96732.

Village by the Sea (938 S Kihei Rd), also known as *Kauhale Makai*, is a six-story concrete-block complex with a pool, sauna and tennis court. About 50 of the 160 condo units are vacation rentals booked through *Maui Condominium & Home Realty* (☎ 879-5445, 800-822-4409, fax 874-6144, mchr@maui.net, PO Box 1840, Kihei, HI 96753). All units have lanais and the standard amenities such as kitchens, cable TV and phones, and while the location is not special, the interiors are on par with many of Kihei's pricier condos. Studios cost $70/85 in the low/high season, one-bedroom units $80/100, two-bedroom units $110/135. There's a four-day minimum stay.

Kihei Kai Nani (☎ 879-1430, 800-473-1493, fax 879-8965, 2495 S Kihei Rd, Kihei, HI 96753) is a friendly place with 180 low-rise apartments, about 40 of which are in the rental pool. All are one-bedroom units with full modern kitchens, ceiling fans, spacious balconies and phones with free local calls. The decor varies with the unit, but most are

quite pleasant for this price range. The hotel is opposite Kamaole Beach Park 2; the grounds have a pool, shuffleboard and barbecue grills, and there are restaurants and shops within easy walking distance. The rate is $65/89 in the low/high season; there's a three-day minimum stay. Between mid-April and mid-December, a monthly rate of $1100 is offered.

Kamaole Beach Royale (☎ 879-3131, 800-421-3661, fax 879-9163, 2385 S Kihei Rd, Kihei, HI 96753) is a well-managed, seven-story condo opposite Kamaole Beach Park 1 but set back from the road. It's quiet, with open rangeland behind and ocean views from the top floors. Units are spacious and well furnished with private lanais, modern kitchens, washer/dryers, TVs, phones with free local calls, VCRs and air-con. It's a particularly good value during the low season, when one-bedroom units cost $70, two-bedroom units $85. Both are $25 more in the high season. There's a cleaning charge of $50 for stays of five nights or less, and credit cards are not accepted.

Kihei Alii Kai (☎ 879-6770, 800-888-6284, fax 879-6221, Box 985, 2387 S Kihei Rd, Kihei, HI 96753), set back from the main road a two-minute walk from Kamaole Beach Park 1, is a 127-unit complex with a pool, sauna and tennis courts. The units are big, and most are quite nice for the money; all have a washer/dryer and cable TV. One-bedroom units cost $65/90 in the low/high season for up to two people, and two-bedroom units cost $90/115 for up to four people. The minimum stay is three days.

Koa Resort (☎ 879-3328, 800-541-3060, 811 S Kihei Rd, Kihei, HI 96753) is a pleasant place with 54 large, comfortable units spread over 5½ acres. All units are equipped with full kitchens, washer/dryers, lanais and cable TV. Other amenities include two tennis courts, a putting green, a spa and a large swimming pool. One-bedroom units cost $85/105 in the low/high season, while two-bedroom units cost $100/120. The minimum stay is four days.

Kamaole Sands (☎ 874-8700, 800-367-5004, vivmis@castle-group.com, 2695 S Kihei Rd, Kihei, HI 96753) is its own condo city

MAUI

with 440 units in 10 four-story buildings. The units are very large, and each has modern amenities – cable TV, full kitchen, lanai, washer/dryer, two bathrooms and a living room with a sofa bed – but the complex itself is big and impersonal. Kamaole Sands is directly opposite Kamaole Beach Park 3 and has a pool, Jacuzzi, tennis courts and a poolside restaurant. Castle Resorts, which handles the front desk, charges a steep $160 for one-bedroom units (for up to four people) and $215 for two-bedroom units (up to six people), but a number of available promotions and discount schemes can cut those rates by as much as half.

Hotels The *Maui Coast Hotel* (☎ 874-6284, 800-895-6284, fax 875-4731, 2259 S Kihei Rd, Kihei, HI 96753) is a modern seven-story hotel affiliated with the Canadian Coast Hotels chain. The 264 rooms are comfortable and pleasantly decorated, and all have air-con, ceiling fans, mini-refrigerators, coffeemakers, room safes, remote-control TVs, phones, lanais, sofa beds and either a king or two double beds. The hotel has complimentary washers and dryers, a heated pool, tennis courts and a restaurant. It's set back from the road, so it's quieter than most Kihei condos. Standard room rates begin at $129, suites at $149, but good discounts are usually available during the low season.

Places to Eat

These Kihei restaurants are listed in order from north to south. *Margarita's Beach Cantina* (☎ 879-5275, 101 N Kihei Rd), in Kealia Beach Plaza, has average Mexican food but a great sunset-facing deck overlooking the water. The usual combination plates with rice and beans go for $10 to $15. Or get a burger with fries for around $8. It's open 11:30 am to 11 pm daily. From 2:30 to 5 pm there's a happy hour with $2 margaritas.

The snack shop adjacent to *Suda's Store* (61 S Kihei Rd) has cheeseburgers and saimin for about $2.50 and also serves shave ice. On Tuesday and Friday from 1 to 5:30 pm, a farmers' market, with local fruits and vegetables, sets up in Suda's parking lot.

The *Ukulele Grill* (☎ 875-1188, 575 S Kihei Rd), in the open-air longhouse at Maui Lu Resort, has an old-fashioned Hawaiian atmosphere and good food. It's open 5:30 to 9 pm nightly and features island dishes such as guava-sesame chicken, imu-style ribs or fresh fish for $15 to $25. There's live Hawaiian entertainment nightly.

Stella Blues (☎ 874-3779, 1215 S Kihei Rd), a casual cafe and deli in the Longs Center, opens at 8 am daily and has coffees, desserts, kosher meat sandwiches and vegetarian options. Full breakfasts averaging $7 are served until 11 am. Most sandwiches, salads and burgers cost between $6 and $8. At dinner, which is served from 5 pm, you can also order hot dishes such as Cajun eggplant, spinach lasagna and Thai chicken for $12 to $15 with salad.

There's a *McDonald's* across from the Longs Center.

Azeka Place has a *Baskin-Robbins* ice cream shop, a *Taco Bell*, a *Pizza Hut* and an *International House of Pancakes*. On the south side of Azeka Place is a *Star Market* supermarket with a deli and bakery.

In Azeka Place II, opposite Azeka Place, is *Panda Express*, a fast-food chain Mandarin restaurant with about a dozen dishes, such as broccoli beef and spicy chicken with peanuts, served from steamer trays. The food is tasty, the servings generous, and the price a good value at $5 for any two dishes with rice or chow mein. You can eat in or order takeout. It's open 10:30 am to 9 pm daily.

The Coffee Store, in Azeka Place II, offers fresh-ground coffee for $1, as well as scones, Danish pastries and big veggie sandwiches at reasonable prices. It's open 6 am to at least 10 pm Monday to Saturday.

Azeka Place II also has *A Pacific Cafe Maui* (☎ 879-0069), an offshoot of chef Jean-Marie Josselin's Kauai restaurant. Despite its shopping center locale, this is *the* place for Pacific Rim food in Kihei. The menu changes nightly. Starters such as blackened ahi are around $10, while main dishes average $25 to $30. It's open 5:30 to 9:30 pm nightly.

Shaka Sandwich & Pizza (☎ 874-0331, 1295 S Kihei Rd), tucked back behind Jack in the Box, has good pizza. An 18-inch pizza costs $13 and up, while a single slice of cheese pizza is $1.65. Hoagie-style sandwiches cost $4.25. Shaka is open 10:30 am to 9 pm daily and offers delivery service with a $10 minimum order.

Adjacent to Azeka Place II is a **Jack in the Box** that has reasonably good fast food and is always offering some sort of discounted promotion.

The new **Mulberry St** (☎ 879-7790, 41 Lipoa St), in the Lipoa Center about 200 yards from S Kihei Rd, has an undistinguished location, but its Italian food is on par with pricey Wailea resorts. A specialty is the penne alla vodka ($14), which has onions, pancetta and shrimp in a flamed vodka sauce. The chef, who hails from Italy, also does an excellent job with the rack of lamb, which at $23 tops off the menu. The restaurant is open for dinner only, 5:30 to 9:30 pm Monday to Saturday. Call ahead, as this spot may relocate closer to the beach.

Kukui Mall has a **bakery** and a branch of the national chain restaurant **Tony Roma's**, which specializes in barbecued ribs.

There's a 24-hour **Foodland** supermarket at Kihei Town Center, and a **KFC** and a **7-Eleven** convenience store are immediately to the north.

Alexander's (☎ 874-0788, 1913 S Kihei Rd), at the north side of Village Marketplace, is the favorite spot for fish and chips, made with a choice of fresh mahimahi, ono or ahi for a reasonable $6.75. It's open daily 11 am to 9 pm. The food is prepared for takeout, but there are a few lanai tables where you can eat.

A good breakfast spot is **Kihei Caffe** (☎ 879-2230, 1945 S Kihei Rd), opposite Kalama Park, a casual little cafe with cappuccino, Kona coffee, homemade pastries and good karma. Fresh salads and sandwiches, as well as a range of breakfast offerings, including tempting banana macadamia-nut pancakes, are priced from $5 to $7. It's open 5 am to 3 pm daily.

Joy's Place (☎ 879-9258, 1993 S Kihei Rd), a small restaurant with a dozen cafe tables, has home-style food, mostly vegetarian. You can get organic salads, tortilla-wrapped sandwiches or chili with rice for around $5. It's open 7 am to 3 pm Monday to Saturday.

Jack's Famous Bagels (2395 S Kihei Rd), in the Dolphin Plaza, makes an inexpensive breakfast option with good 75¢ bagels, $1 coffee and an agreeable atmosphere. It's open 6 am to 4 pm on weekdays, and from at least 6:30 am to 3 pm on weekends. The Dolphin Plaza also has a hole-in-the-wall **taco shop**, a **sushi bar** and a takeout **Pizza Hut**.

Hawaiian Moons Natural Foods (2411 S Kihei Rd), in the Kamaole Beach Center, has an organic produce section, yogurts, juices, trail mix, bulk grains, granolas and a few organic wines. It also has a good salad bar for $5 a pound, as well as a juice and espresso bar. It's open 8 am to 8 pm Monday to Saturday, 8 am to 6 pm on Sunday.

Another decent cheap option in the Kamaole Beach Center is **Maui Tacos**, which serves tacos and burritos made with lard-free beans and fresh salsas. Everything can be made with or without meat, and most items cost from $2.50 to $5. You can either eat in or order for takeout.

Kihei Prime Rib & Seafood House (☎ 879-1954, 2511 S Kihei Rd) is a popular old standby with a water view and good steaks and fish. Regular dinners cost $18 for chicken and about $20 for fish or prime rib, including a salad bar. However, from 5 to 6 pm, you can get the same items as an early-bird special for $15. It's open 5 to 10 pm nightly.

The Kamaole Shopping Center, 2653 S Kihei Rd, has a **Denny's** family-style restaurant open 24 hours; **Canton Chef**, which offers a full range of moderately priced Chinese dishes; and **Cinnamon Roll Fair**, which sells warm goopy cinnamon rolls for $2.50.

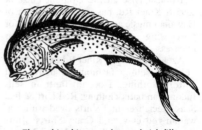

The mahimahi, a popular sandwich filler

A pleasant open-air spot for waterfront dining is *Five Palms Beach Grill* (☎ 879-2607, 2960 S Kihei Rd). Lunch, served from 11 am to 3 pm daily, ranges from a Caesar salad or artichoke hearts over angel-hair pasta for $9 to stuffed shrimp for $15, while dinner entrees, which feature steak and fish, average $20 to $30. Dinner is served from 4:30 to 9 pm daily.

Entertainment
While Kihei is not known for its entertainment scene, things have livened up a bit in recent years.

There's something happening nightly at *Hapa's Brew Haus* (☎ 879-9001, 41 Lipoa St), in the Lipoa Center. On some nights it has a DJ, and on others it offers live music by the likes of Willie K and the popular group Kapena.

The *Ukulele Grill* (☎ 875-1188, 575 S Kihei Rd) has live entertainment nightly, including a free keiki hula show at 6 pm on Sunday and a Polynesian show for $6 at 6 pm on Thursday. On most other nights, it hosts Hawaiian acoustic music.

The Sports Page Grill & Bar (☎ 879-0602, 2411 S Kihei Rd), in the Kamaole Beach Center, has big-screen TVs with sports broadcasts.

The Kukui Mall's *movie theater* (☎ 244-8934) features four screens.

Shopping
Kihei is overflowing with souvenir, gift and clothing shops of all sorts. Kihei Kalama Village, opposite Kalama Park, has a collection of stalls selling cheap T-shirts, swimwear, jewelry and souvenir items.

Tropical Disc, in the Dolphin Plaza at 2395 S Kihei Rd, has a good selection of Hawaiian music and a headphone setup for previewing some of the more popular releases.

Azeka Place on S Kihei Rd has a couple of shops selling fashionable lightweight cotton clothing: Tropical Tantrum sells Indonesian batik clothing; Red Dirt & Teal Seas specializes in T-shirts dyed with Hawaiian red clay; and Crazy Shirts offers more conventional T-shirts. Island Memories, also in Azeka Place, sells Hawaiian-made handicrafts.

Maui Dive Shop, whose main shop is at 1455 S Kihei Rd, sells reef walkers, boogie boards, snorkels, fins and wet suits. The ABC Discount Store, opposite Kamaole Beach Park 1, has liquor, cheap beach mats, suntan lotion and other practical items for visitors.

Wailea & Makena

At the end of the road south of Kihei lie the towns of Wailea and Makena, both a world away from the cluttered commercialism of Kihei. As soon as you enter Wailea, you'll be struck by the contrast with its northern neighbor – everything is green, manicured and precise. Makena has followed Wailea's lead, with a luxury hotel and golf course giving new life to this all-but-forgotten area.

WAILEA
Wailea has a few swank hotels on the beach, a number of low-rise condo villas, a shopping center, a trio of golf courses and a tennis club that's been nicknamed 'Wimbledon West.'

Wailea's lava-rock coastline is broken by attractive golden-sand beaches that lure swimmers, snorkelers and sunbathers. From Wailea and neighboring Makena, there are good views of Lanai, Kahoolawe and Molokini, and during winter there's superb shoreline whale watching.

Orientation
If you're heading to Wailea beaches from Lahaina or Kahului, be sure to take the Piilani Hwy (Hwy 31) and not S Kihei Rd. It's less than 10 minutes' drive this way, whereas the Kihei strip can be a tedious 30 minutes through congested traffic.

Wailea's main road is Wailea Alanui Drive, which turns into Makena Alanui Drive after Polo Beach and continues south to Makena.

Information
A free shuttle bus (☎ 879-2828) runs around the Wailea resort every 30 minutes from

6:30 am to 8:30 pm, connecting the hotels, condos, shopping center and golf courses.

Wailea Shopping Village, in front of the Outrigger Wailea Resort, has a First Hawaiian Bank, a couple of simple eateries, a little grocery store and a few boutiques.

Beaches

Wailea's beaches begin with the southern end of Keawakapu Beach and continue south with Mokapu, Ulua, Wailea and Polo Beaches. They are all lovely strands with free public access, parking, showers and rest rooms. Some also have picnic tables and barbecue grills.

While Wailea's beaches generally have good swimming conditions, occasional high surf and kona storms can create dangerous shorebreaks and rip currents.

Ulua Beach Ulua Beach is a little gem between the Outrigger Wailea Resort and the Renaissance Wailea Beach Resort. The first road south of the Renaissance leads to the beach parking lot.

When it's calm, Ulua Beach has the area's best snorkeling. There's coral at the rocky outcrop on the right side of the beach, and you can usually spot long needlefish, schools of goatfish, unicorn tangs and other tropicals. Snorkeling is best in the morning before the winds pick up. When the surf's up, forget snorkeling – in its place there's apt to be good bodysurfing.

During WWII, US Marines trained for the invasion of Tarawa off this beach, and consequently it was referred to locally as Tarawa Beach – but the developers of the Wailea resort area didn't think that conjured up holiday images, so they renamed it Ulua.

Wailea Beach Wailea is the largest and widest of Wailea's beaches. The sandy beach slopes gradually, making the inshore waters good for swimming. When the water's calm, there's good snorkeling around the rocky point on the south side of the beach. Divers entering the water at Wailea Beach can follow an offshore reef that runs down to Polo Beach. At times, there's a gentle shorebreak suitable for bodysurfing.

WAILEA & MAKENA

PACIFIC OCEAN

WAILEA

MAKENA

Makena Bay

Makena Golf Course

Wailea Blue Course

Wailea Gold & Emerald Courses

To Kihei
To Hwy 311, Kahului
Keawakapu Beach
Beach Access
Mokapu Beach
Ulua Beach
Wailea Ike Drive
Wailea Beach
Beach Access
Wailea Alanui Drive
Polo Beach
Kaukahi St
Makena Rd
Palauea Beach
Poolenalena Beach
Makena Alanui Drive
Maluaka Beach
Puu Olai 360ft
Little Beach
Big Beach
To Ahihi-Kinau Natural Area Reserve, La Perouse Bay

0   .5   1 km
0   .25   .5 miles

PLACES TO STAY
2 Renaissance Wailea Beach Resort
5 Outrigger Wailea Resort
7 Grand Wailea Resort
8 Four Seasons Resort
9 Kea Lani Hotel
11 Makena Surf
13 Maui Prince Hotel

PLACES TO EAT
3 Joe's Bar & Grill
10 Seawatch

OTHER
1 Parking
4 Wailea Tennis Club
6 Wailea Shopping Village
12 Keawalai Church
14 Makena Tennis Club

MAUI

Wailea Beach Walk

For a delightful stroll, take the shoreline path that runs for 1 1/4 miles from the Outrigger Wailea Resort to the Kea Lani, connecting the Wailea beaches and the resort hotels that front them. The path winds above the jagged lava points that separate the beaches and has an interesting landscape of native Hawaiian flora; some varieties are identified by plaques.

In winter, this is one of the best walks in all of Hawaii for spotting humpback whales – on a good day, you may be able to spot more than a dozen of them frolicking in the waters offshore.

Some of the luxury hotels you'll pass along the beach walk are also worth strolling through, most notably the Grand Wailea Resort, which has $30 million of artwork and some strikingly elaborate waterways and landscaping on its grounds.

Beach access is from the road running between the Four Seasons Resort and the Grand Wailea Resort, both of which front Wailea Beach.

Polo Beach Polo is fronted by a condo development and by the Kea Lani Hotel, but the south end is seldom crowded.

When there's wave action, boogie boarders and bodysurfers usually find a good shorebreak at Polo Beach. When the waters are calm, the rocks at the north end of the beach are good for snorkeling. At low tide, the lava outcropping at the south end of the beach has some interesting little tide pools that harbor spiny sea urchins and a few small fish.

To get to Polo Beach, turn down Kaukahi St after the Kea Lani Hotel. There's a large beach parking lot on the right, near the end of the road.

Palauea Beach Palauea Beach is along Makena Rd, a quarter mile south of Polo Beach. The kiawe brushland between the beach and the road is marked private property, though there are breaks in the fence where beachgoers cross. A fair number of people use the beach for surfing and bodysurfing. It's more secluded and less frequented than Polo Beach, but otherwise it's much the same, sans the development. You can walk to Palauea Beach from Polo Beach in less than 10 minutes.

Places to Stay

The **Outrigger Wailea Resort** (☎ 879-1922, 800-688-7444, fax 875-4878, reservations@outrigger.com, 3700 Wailea Alanui Drive, Wailea, HI 96753) has 516 rooms spread across a number of low-rise buildings and a mid-rise tower. For Wailea, it's an unpretentious, low-key operation. Although it's a relatively older hotel, the rooms have the usual resort-class amenities. Garden-view rooms cost $255, and ocean-view rooms cost an extra $90, but the Outrigger chain, which manages the hotel, often offers discounted promotions that can cut these rates substantially. For information on special deals, visit the chain's website at www.outrigger.com.

The **Renaissance Wailea Beach Resort** (☎ 879-4900, 800-992-4532, fax 879-6128, 3550 Wailea Alanui Drive, Wailea, HI 96753) is a tasteful resort hotel – upscale, but not as lavish and formal as its neighbors to the south. The grounds are lush, the 350 rooms are nicely furnished with rattan and wicker, and it's on a quiet beach. Regular rates start at $320 for garden views, $435 for ocean views, but there's a 'daily package' special that throws in a car and breakfast for about $100 less than the regular room rate.

The **Grand Wailea Resort** (☎ 875-1234, 800-888-6100, fax 874-5143, info@grandwailea.com, 3850 Wailea Alanui Drive, Wailea, HI 96753) is the most extravagant resort on Maui. The lobbies are filled with sculptures and artwork, while the grounds are given over to gardens, artificial waterfalls, a multimillion-dollar mosaic tile pool, fountains and the like. Some of it has an upscale Hawaiiana motif; all of it is unabashedly opulent. The 2000-foot-long system of pools, water slides and artificial grottos is Hawaii's most elaborate. All 761 rooms have three telephones, an ocean view, marble baths, a minimum of 640 sq feet and a daily rate of at least $380. The Grand Suite in the hotel's exclusive Napua Tower is the islands' most expensive night's sleep, setting you back (well, not *you*, perhaps, but setting *someone* back) a cool $10,000. One would hope the bed is comfortable.

The **Kea Lani Hotel** (☎ *875-4100, 800-882-4100, fax 875-1200, 4100 Wailea Alanui Drive, Wailea, HI 96753*) is a 450-suite resort hotel with fanciful Moorish-style architecture that resembles something out of *Arabian Nights*. Each suite has a lanai, a separate living room with a sofa bed, a phone with modem hookup, two TVs, a VCR, CD stereo, microwave and coffeemaker. One-bedroom suites cost from $295 to $570 for up to four adults, while oceanfront villas with private plunge pools begin at $1000.

While not as ostentatious as its neighbors, the 380-room **Four Seasons Resort** (☎ *874-8000, 800-332-3442, fax 874-2222, 3900 Wailea Alanui Drive, Wailea, HI 96753*) has open-air lobbies, lots of marble, a series of pools and fountains and the expected amenities. Rates begin at $305.

Destination Resorts (☎ *879-1595, 800-367-5246, fax 874-3554, drh@maui.net, 3750 Wailea Alanui Drive, Wailea, HI 96753*) books about 300 units in half a dozen complexes around Wailea and Makena. While they aren't cheap, most of the condos are quite nice and a far better value than Wailea's luxury hotels. Studio and one-bedroom condos in Wailea begin at $150, while the high end tops off with three-bedroom oceanfront units costing $600.

Places to Eat
Cafe Ciao (☎ *875-4100*), at the Kea Lani Hotel, has both a deli and an outdoor cafe. Takeout deli items include such things as muffins for around $3, thick sandwiches on specialty breads for $8 and cold tortellini or eggplant caponata for $10. The courtyard cafe, open 11 am to 10 pm, has pastas and wood-fired pizzas for around $15, as well as more expensive grilled items.

Joe's Bar & Grill (☎ *875-7767, 131 Wailea Ike Place*), overlooking the courts at the Wailea Tennis Club, is run by the owners of the popular Haliimaile General Store and has a reputation for reliably good food and service. Open for dinner from 5:30 to 10 pm, it offers American standards such as meat-loaf, lobster pie and a very popular New York steak. Entrees are priced from $17 to $30, while appetizers and salads cost from $6 to $13.

Seawatch (☎ *875-8080*), at the Gold & Emerald Course Clubhouse, is perched on a hillside with a great ocean view and offers both indoor and veranda dining. A breakfast favorite is the smoked-salmon eggs Benedict, while at lunch there are sandwiches, salads and stir-fried noodles – all averaging $8. Dinner features the likes of crispy duck or miso-glazed tiger prawns for $22 to $25. It's open 8 am to 3 pm daily for breakfast and lunch. Dinner starts at 5:30 pm.

Cafe Kula (☎ *875-1234*), in the Grand Wailea Resort, is an open-air cafe open 6 am to 2 pm daily. It has simple breakfast fare, including cinnamon rolls or muffins for $3 and muesli or granola for $4; add $2 for a cup of coffee. The hotel's **Bistro Molokini** has pizza and pastas for around $15 and is open 11 am to 10 pm daily. The Grand Wailea also has two expensive dinner restaurants: the **Kincha**, which has Japanese fare, and the **Humuhumu**, serving seafood and steaks in a Polynesian-style longhouse surrounded by carp ponds.

Pacific Grill (☎ *874-8000*), at the Four Seasons Resort, specializes in Pacific Rim cuisine with dishes such as ginger stir-fried mahimahi or mango-glazed duck breast for $25 to $30, appetizers for around half that. There's usually also a fixed-price menu for $37 that offers a choice of three different appetizers, entrees and desserts.

Entertainment
The Wailea hotels often have some sort of music in their restaurants and lounges. The Grand Wailea Resort's high-tech **Tsunami** nightclub has DJ dancing on Thursday, Friday and Saturday, typically with a $5 cover charge.

The **Wailea Shopping Village** presents a free Polynesian dance show at 1:30 pm

Tuesday and offers hula classes for children and adults on Wednesday (☎ 572-5864 for information). The *Outrigger Wailea Resort* has a luau on Monday, Tuesday, Thursday and Friday for $58 for adults, $26 for children. The *Renaissance Wailea Beach Resort* has a luau on Tuesday, Thursday and Saturday for $57 for adults, $27 for children. Both luaus start shortly before sunset.

MAKENA

Until recently, Makena was a sleepy and largely overlooked area at the end of the road. Its center was the abandoned Makena Landing, with its small and predominantly Hawaiian village.

In the 1980s, the Seibu Corporation bought up 1800 acres of Makena above the landing, and a development similar to Wailea is now in the making. So far, the resort contains a golf course, a tennis center, the Maui Prince Hotel and a new road to it all.

Makena's dominant shoreline feature is Puu Olai, a 360-foot cinder hill a mile south of the landing. Just beyond Puu Olai are two knockout beaches adjoining each other. They are commonly called Big and Little Beaches, or, together, Makena Beach.

Big Beach is a huge sweep of glistening sand and a prime sunset-viewing locale with straight-on views of Molokini and Kahoolawe. Little Beach is a secluded cove and Maui's most popular nude beach.

In the late 1960s, Makena was the site of an alternative-lifestyle camp that took on the nickname 'Hippie Beach.' The tent city lasted until 1972, when police finally evicted everyone on health code violations. More than a few of Maui's now-graying residents can trace their roots on the island to the camp at Makena Beach.

Makena Bay

To explore the older side of Makena, turn right down Makena Rd after the Makena Surf condo complex and go about a mile to Makena Bay.

In the 19th century, Makena was the busiest landing on this side of Maui. Cattle from Ulupalakua Ranch and other Upcountry ranches were brought down the hillsides

and shipped to market in Honolulu from **Makena Landing**. By the 1920s, interisland boat traffic had shifted to other ports on the island, and Makena lost its economic base.

Makena Landing is now a local recreational area with boat-launching facilities, showers and toilets. When seas are calm, there's good snorkeling along the rocks at the south side of the landing.

South of the landing is the **Keawalai Congregational Church**, which dates to 1832 and is one of Maui's early missionary churches. The current building was built in 1855 with three-foot-thick walls made of burnt coral rock. A small congregation still meets for Sunday services, which are held in a mix of Hawaiian and English. The church graveyard has a fine bayside view and old tombstones with interesting cameo photographs.

Makena Rd ends shortly after the church at a cul-de-sac on the ocean side of Maui Prince Hotel.

Maluaka Beach

At the southern end of Makena Bay is Maluaka Beach, a beige-sand beach fronting the Maui Prince Hotel. The beach, which slopes down from a low sand dune, has a sandy bottom in its center and rocky formations at each end that might provide decent snorkeling.

The showers and rest rooms opposite Keawalai Congregational Church not only serve beachgoers at Maluaka Beach, but they're also the nearest facilities to Big Beach.

Little Beach & Big Beach

Big Beach is the sort of scene that people conjure up when they dream of a Hawaiian beach – beautiful and expansive, with virtually no development on the horizon.

The Hawaiian name for Big Beach is Oneloa, literally 'Long Sand.' This golden-sand beach is well over half a mile long and as broad as they come, with clear turquoise waters. But the open ocean beyond Big Beach can have powerful rip currents and dangerous shorebreaks during periods of heavy surf.

The turnoff to the main parking area for Big Beach is exactly a mile past the Maui

Prince Hotel. A second parking area lies a quarter mile to the south. You can also park alongside the road and walk in, but thefts and broken windshields are commonplace in the area, and the parking lots are a safer bet. Watch for kiawe thorns in the woods behind the beach.

Little Beach is hidden by a rocky outcrop that juts out from Puu Olai, the cinder cone that marks the north end of Big Beach.

A trail over the rock links the two and takes just a few minutes to walk. From the top of the trail, there's a splendid view of both beaches.

Little Beach fronts a sandy cove that usually has a gentle shorebreak ideal for bodysurfing and boogie boarding. Snorkeling along the rocky point is good when the water is calm.

A trail continues for five minutes beyond Little Beach to an area where lava outcrops reach into the clear deep water like giant fingers. When it's very calm, divers and confident snorkelers sometimes explore these formations, which have caves and abundant marine life.

Little Beach, also known as Puu Olai Beach, is a popular nude beach, despite a rusty old sign to the contrary.

Makena Beach (the collective name for Little Beach and Big Beach) has recently become a state park, which may eventually lead to the addition of full beach facilities, but for now it remains in a natural state except for a couple of pit toilets and picnic tables.

South of Makena

Makena Rd continues as a narrow paved road for 2½ miles after Big Beach. The road goes through the Ahihi-Kinau Natural Area Reserve before ending at La Perouse Bay. Because of the road's narrow width and two-way traffic, it can be a very slow drive and is not really suitable for a quick sightseeing excursion.

Ahihi-Kinau The Ahihi-Kinau Natural Area Reserve covers 2045 acres and includes sections of Ahihi Bay and Cape Kinau.

Maui's most recent lava flow created most of the cape on its way to the sea in 1790. The reserve has lava tide pools, coastal lava tubes and all the *aa* (rough, jagged lava) you could ever want to see.

It has been designated a natural area reserve because of its distinctive marine life habitat and its unique geological features, including anchialine pools and *kipukas* ('islands' of land spared but surrounded by lava flows). The removal of any flora, fauna or lava is prohibited.

The remains of a coastal Hawaiian village – its old sites marked by walled and terraced platforms – sit between lava flows at Ahihi Bay.

A little roadside cove just one-tenth of a mile south of the first reserve sign offers good snorkeling. It's quite rocky and can be a bit challenging getting in, but the cove has lots of coral and fish.

La Perouse Bay The paved road ends just short of La Perouse Bay. Although it may be possible to drive all the way in on the 4WD road, you can also park where the asphalt ends and just walk down to the coast. A 10-minute foot trail leads over the lava and along the water, passing a few tiny coves with sandy patches before reaching La Perouse Bay. Keep an eye out for herds of spinner dolphins, which commonly come into the bay during the day to rest. La Perouse Bay is rather rocky and marginal for most water activities, other than advanced diving, but there are hiking possibilities in the area.

The Lost Explorer

In May 1786, the renowned French explorer Jean François de Galaup La Perouse became the first Westerner to land on Maui. As he sailed into the bay that now bears his name, scores of Hawaiian canoes came out to greet him and trade.

After leaving Hawaii, La Perouse mysteriously disappeared in the Pacific. While no one knows his fate, some historians speculate that he and his crew were eaten by cannibals in the New Hebrides.

MAUI

From La Perouse Bay, it's possible to continue on foot along the **King's Hwy Coastal Trail**. This ancient trail follows the coastline across jagged barren lava flows, so hiking boots are a good idea. It's a dry area with no water and little vegetation, and it can get very hot.

The first part of the trail is along the sandy beach at La Perouse Bay. Right after the beach, it's possible to take a spur trail for three-quarters of a mile down to the lighthouse at the tip of Cape Hanamanioa.

Alternatively, you could continue on the King's Hwy as it climbs up through rough aa lava inland for the next 2 miles before coming back to the coast at an older lava flow. In that area are a number of old Hawaiian house foundations and pebble and coral beaches.

Places to Stay

The *Maui Prince Hotel* (☎ 874-1111, 800-321-6284, fax 879-8763, 5400 Makena Alanui Drive, Wailea, HI 96753) turns inward in typical Japanese fashion. From the outside it looks like a fortress, but the interior incorporates a fine sense of Japanese aesthetics. The five-story hotel surrounds a courtyard with waterfalls, running streams, carp ponds and raked rock gardens. All 300 rooms have at least partial ocean views and rack rates from $260, though special promotions often undercut that.

Destination Resorts (see Places to Stay in the earlier Wailea section) handles condo rentals in Makena.

Places to Eat

Cafe Kiowai is the Maui Prince Hotel's only lunch spot, with salads, sandwiches and a few hot dishes from $7 to $15.

Hakone, at the Maui Prince, has kimono-clad waitresses and authentic Japanese food, including excellent sushi. There are a number of full meals with appetizer, rice and soup in the $25 to $35 range. It's open 6 to 9:30 pm Tuesday to Saturday.

The *Prince Court*, also at the Maui Prince, specializes in Hawaiian Regional cuisine, with main dishes priced from around $20 for the vegetarian option to $30 for lobster.

It's open 6 to 9:30 pm nightly. On Sunday from 9:30 am to 1 pm, the restaurant offers an indulgent champagne brunch featuring a splendid array of seafood dishes; the cost is $34.

Road to Hana

The Hana Hwy runs from central Maui to the village of Hana and beyond to the pools of Oheo Gulch. While all of the Hawaiian Islands have some incredible scenery, the Hana Hwy ranks as *the* most spectacular coastal drive in Hawaii. This road, which was built in 1927 using convict labor, is also very narrow; in many places, it's essentially 1½ lanes wide, with two-lane traffic!

The Hana Hwy is a cliff-hugger as it winds its way deep into lush valleys and back out above a rugged coastline, snaking around more than 600 twists and turns along the way.

One-lane bridges mark dozens of waterfalls. Some are tiny and Zen-like, others sheer and lacy. The 54 bridges to Hana have 54 poetic Hawaiian names taken from the streams and gulches they cross – names like Heavenly Mist, Prayer Blossoms and Reawakening.

The valleys drip with vegetation. African tulip trees add bright splashes of orange to the dense rain forests, bamboo groves and fern-covered hillsides.

It would take about two hours to drive straight through from Kahului to Hana. But this is not a drive to rush. If you're not staying over in Hana, get an early start to give yourself a full day. Those with time to explore will find short trails to hike, mountain pools to dip in and a couple of historic sites to check out, all just a few minutes beyond the road.

Remember to pull over if local drivers are behind you. They have places to get to and move at a different pace.

PAIA

Paia is an old sugar town with a fresh coat of paint. As part of the original Alexander & Baldwin sugar plantation, Paia in the early 20th century had a population of about

ROAD TO HANA

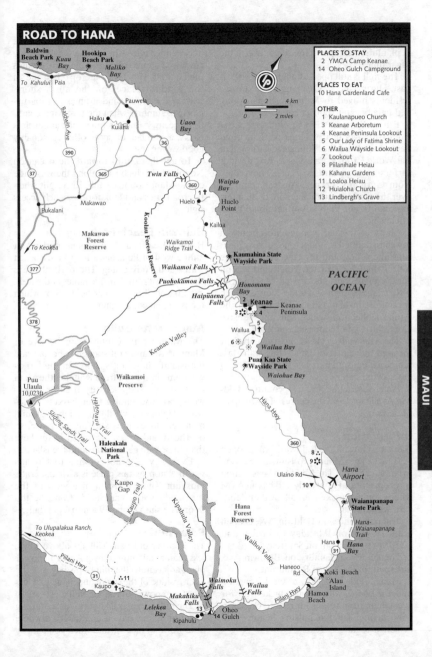

MAUI

PLACES TO STAY
2 YMCA Camp Keanae
14 Oheo Gulch Campground

PLACES TO EAT
10 Hana Gardenland Cafe

OTHER
1 Kaulanapueo Church
3 Keanae Arboretum
4 Keanae Peninsula Lookout
5 Our Lady of Fatima Shrine
6 Wailua Wayside Lookout
7 Lookout
8 Piilanihale Heiau
9 Kahanu Gardens
11 Loaloa Heiau
12 Huialoha Church
13 Lindbergh's Grave

8000, more than triple its present size. In those days, most of the town's residents lived in plantation camps on the slopes above the sugar mill.

The mill is still open, though its heyday is past. During the 1950s, many of the town's residents moved to Kahului, shops closed, and Paia began to collect cobwebs.

But in the early 1980s, windsurfers began to discover nearby Hookipa Beach, and Paia was dubbed the 'Windsurfing Capital of the World.' Today, Paia has as many windsurfers as sugarcane workers. They come from Germany, France, Australia and all over the world, giving Paia more of an international flavor than any other small town in Hawaii.

Many of the old wooden storefronts in town are painted in bright tones of rosy pink, sunshine yellow and sky blue, adding to the town's unique character. You'll find a good variety of restaurants, as well as some fun offbeat shops such as Hemp House, which specializes in hemp-fiber clothing, and the Aloha Collection, which sells inexpensive aloha shirts and Indonesian sarongs.

The Hana Hwy (Hwy 36) runs straight through the center of Paia – this is the last real town before Hana and the last place to gas up your car.

Paia is also a link to the Upcountry; Baldwin Ave leads from the center of town up to Makawao.

Information

Bank of Hawaii, on Baldwin Ave, is open 8:30 am to 4 pm Monday to Thursday, 8:30 am to 6 pm on Friday. The Minit Stop gas station stays open until 11 pm daily and has an ATM where you can make a credit-card or debit-card withdrawal.

The post office, on Baldwin Ave, is open 8 am to 4:30 pm Monday to Friday and 10:30 am to 12:30 pm on Saturday.

There's a coin laundry on Baldwin Ave, just south of the Vegan Restaurant.

Mana Foods, on Baldwin Ave, has a good bulletin board, with notices tacked up for everything from rooms for rent to classes in windsurfing, Tibetan pulsing healing and Ashanga yoga.

Spreckelsville Beach

Spreckelsville Beach, by the golf course between Kahului Airport and Paia, is a long stretch of shore composed of sandy strands punctuated with lava outcrops. It's one of the windiest places on the north shore, making it a prime windsurfing spot – particularly in summer when the best wind conditions occur. Although much of the beach is rocky, a number of spots offer reasonably good swimming.

To get there, turn toward the ocean on Nonohe Rd, which runs along the west side of the Maui Country Club. Turn right when the road ends and look for the beach access sign.

Baldwin Beach Park

Baldwin Beach Park, a big county park about a mile west of Paia, has a long sandy beach with good bodysurfing. The park also has showers, rest rooms, picnic tables and a well-used baseball and soccer field, all of which tends to make it a rather congested scene.

Maui Crafts Guild

The Maui Crafts Guild is a collective of Maui artists and craftspeople who operate the island's best crafts shop. On the left as you come into town from Kahului, the Maui Crafts Guild shop sells dyed cloth, woodwork, pottery, natural fiber baskets, beadwork, Japanese-style flutes and more. Guild members take turns staffing the place, so overhead and prices are much lower here than in private galleries around the island.

Even if you're not looking to buy, it's worth a stop, as this place is a virtual crafts museum. There's also a nice view of the surrounding sugarcane fields from the top floor. The shop is open 9 am to 6 pm daily.

Paia Mill

The century-old Paia Mill sits above town, less than a mile up Baldwin Ave. The power plant adjacent to the mill burns bagasse, the fiber residue of the sugarcane plant, producing steam power to run the mill.

The mill operates 24 hours a day, shutting down only four days a month. It's a whole little world of its own, and when you pass by

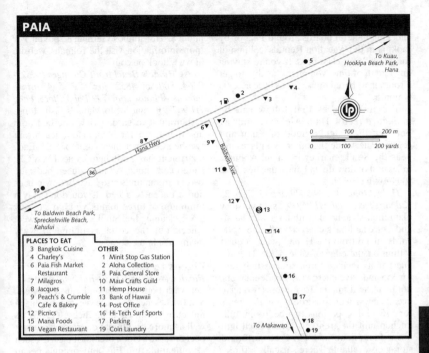

PAIA

To Kuau,
Hookipa Beach Park,
Hana

Hana Hwy

Baldwin Ave

36

To Baldwin Beach Park,
Spreckelsville Beach,
Kahului

0   100   200 m
0   100   200 yards

To Makawao

PLACES TO EAT	OTHER
3 Bangkok Cuisine	1 Minit Stop Gas Station
4 Charley's	2 Aloha Collection
6 Paia Fish Market	5 Paia General Store
Restaurant	10 Maui Crafts Guild
7 Milagros	11 Hemp House
8 Jacques	13 Bank of Hawaii
9 Peach's & Crumble	14 Post Office
Cafe & Bakery	16 Hi-Tech Surf Sports
12 Picnics	17 Parking
15 Mana Foods	19 Coin Laundry
18 Vegan Restaurant	

at night, it seems oddly surreal with its glowing lights and buzz of activity.

Rather than the more common process of squeezing sugarcane by rollers, the Paia Mill flushes juice out of shredded sugarcane in a process resembling that of a drip coffeemaker.

Mantokuji Buddhist Mission

Mantokuji, a circa-1921 Buddhist temple with an ocean view and a big gong in the yard, is on the Hana side of town. It's fronted by a graveyard with kanji-engraved stones, some decorated with colorful tropical flowers. During the summer, the Obon holidays are observed here with religious services and Japanese dances.

Hookipa Beach Park

Hookipa, which has long been one of Maui's prime surfing spots, has in more recent years established itself as Hawaii's premier windsurfing beach. It has good year-round action

for both – winter has the biggest waves for board surfers, and summer has the most consistent winds for windsurfers.

The beach attracts the world's top windsurfers and is the site of several international tournaments, including the Da Kine Hawaiian Pro Am in April and the Aloha Wave Classic in late October or early November.

Between the strong currents, dangerous shorebreak and razor-sharp coral, this is unquestionably an area for experts. As a spectator venue, it's great – if you come at the right time, you'll be watching some of the best action to be found anywhere.

Hookipa is just before the 9-mile marker; look for the line of cars on the lookout above the beach. The park has rest rooms, showers and picnic pavilions.

Places to Stay

While Paia has no hotels, it does have a number of smaller private places to stay. Most are rented out through B&B booking

MAUI

services, though you can also find rooms by checking bulletin boards around Paia or by looking in the 'Vacation Rentals' column of the *Maui News* classifieds. If you're staying any length of time, you might be able to get a room in a shared house for as little as $300 a month.

The three places that follow can be booked directly. Hale Aloha is midway between the neighborhood of Kuau and central Paia, while the other two places are near the 8-mile marker in Kuau. About 2 miles east of downtown Paia, Kuau lies close to Hookipa Beach.

Hale Aloha (☎ 579-9849 or 575-2726, 28 Kulani Place, Paia, HI 96779) is a two-story plantation-style house with large airy lanais and a nice laid-back character. It's about 500 yards inland from the Hana Hwy in a quiet setting on the edge of cane fields. The five guest units include three studios that rent for $55 and have microwaves, coffeemakers, hot plates and small refrigerators (two have ocean views); a one-bedroom unit that rents for $75; and a spacious two-bedroom, full-kitchen unit that rents for $125. Each unit has a fan, phone and TV. Free surfboard storage is available. There's usually a three-day minimum stay, though if things are busy, it can be as long as a week. Owner Steve Marachuk also rents an airy plantation-style one-bedroom cottage that he recently built next to his home in the village of Haiku; it goes for $110.

Hookipa Haven (☎ 579-8282, 800-398-6284, fax 579-9953, ttolman@maui.net, PO Box 108, Paia, HI 96779) consists of two units belonging to Terry and Margit Tolman. A one-bedroom apartment on the 1st floor of their home rents for $60. It has a queen bed, kitchen, bathroom, private entrance and a futon couch in the living room. There's also a fully furnished two-bedroom cottage on the grounds that costs $85 for two people or $95 for four; note that the walls are open at the ceiling, so there's no sound barrier between the rooms. Guests must put down a security deposit of $150 for the studio, $200 for the cottage. Margit runs a vacation rental service and books other accommodations in the Paia and Haiku areas, as well as else-

where on Maui, with daily rates starting at about $50 for studios. German is spoken. For more information, visit the Tolmans' website at www.hookipa.com.

At *Mama's Beachfront Cottages* (☎ 579-9764, 800-860-4852, fax 579-8594, info@ mamasfishhouse.com, 799 Poho Place, Paia, HI 96779), adjacent to Mama's Fish House restaurant, two garden-view one-bedroom apartments rent for $90, and four beachfront two-bedroom apartments rent for $225. Each apartment has a kitchen, cable TV, VCR, stereo and phone. All have queen beds; the two-bedroom units also have two twin beds and a queen sofa bed. If you don't stay a minimum of three nights, you have to pay a $35 cleaning fee. Smoking is not allowed. Check out the cottages online at www .mamasfishhouse.com.

Places to Eat

Picnics (☎ 579-8021, 30 Baldwin Ave) is a deli with both takeout and eat-in services. Sandwiches include a nice vegetarian spinach nut burger with cheddar cheese ($5.75), as well as more traditional offerings like roast beef or turkey. Good breakfast pastries, such as pineapple muffins and orange pecan scones, cost around $2 (only $1 after 1 pm). Picnics also has fruit and vegetable salads, cappuccino and espresso. There's a guide to the Hana Hwy on the back of the takeout menu, and you can get box lunches for the road. Hours are 7 am to 7 pm daily.

Peach's & Crumble Cafe & Bakery (☎ 579-8612, 2 Baldwin Ave) sells muffins, croissants and peach crumble squares for $1.50 to $2.50. Sandwiches, such as smoked salmon or an avocado veggie burger, go for around $5. The cafe also makes picnic lunches ($8) to go. It's open 6:30 am to 6 pm daily.

The *Vegan Restaurant* (☎ 579-9144, 115 Baldwin Ave) serves tasty vegetarian food at reasonable prices. It costs $5 for a vegan burger or various large salads. The menu also includes Mexican fare and daily specials – all under $10. As there are only a dozen small cafe tables, it's best to arrive early at dinner. It's open noon to 9 pm daily.

Milagros (☎ 579-8755), on the corner of Baldwin Ave and the Hana Hwy, is a popular

Tex-Mex cafe with good food and both indoor and sidewalk dining. Recommended are the fish tacos, which cost $8 at lunch or $14 at dinner, when they're served with a salad. Also on the menu are moderately priced sandwiches, salads, enchiladas and burritos. It's open 8 am to 9:30 pm daily.

Paia Fish Market Restaurant (☎ 579-8030), on the opposite corner of Baldwin Ave and the Hana Hwy, specializes in fresh fish, which you'll find on display in a refrigerated case at the counter. A good choice is the grilled fish sandwich on a whole-wheat bun, which costs $6 for either ono or mahi-mahi. Fish and chips cost $8 at lunch, $10 at dinner. It's open 11 am to 9:30 pm daily.

Charley's (☎ 579-9453, 142 Hana Hwy) is a popular place for a late breakfast. Both breakfast and lunch fare are served from 7 am to 2:30 pm, with omelettes, sandwiches and burritos all priced around $7.50. Dinner, available from 5 to 10 pm, includes pizza, pasta and calzones for around $10 and a few more elaborate dishes such as shrimp scampi for $15.

For authentic Thai food, the family-run *Bangkok Cuisine* (☎ 579-8979, 120 Hana Hwy) has a menu that includes curries, pad Thai and various shrimp, fish, meat and vegetarian dishes, most priced from $8 to $10. There's also a daily lunch special for $5. It's open 11 am to 3 pm and 5 to 9:30 pm daily.

Jacques (☎ 579-6255, 89 Hana Hwy) has a pleasant bistro atmosphere and serves top-end food at mid-range prices. Jacques, who did a stint as the personal chef of the Swedish king, specializes in Pacific regional dishes with a French accent. Appetizers, including grilled-chicken Caesar salad or Provençal-style mussels, cost $5 to $10, while most main dishes, such as Cajun-seared ahi or rack of lamb, average $16. The local favorite is the grilled fresh fish of the day, which is offered nightly for just $13. Dinner is served from 5 to 10 pm, but the bar stays open later.

Although pricey, *Mama's Fish House* (☎ 579-8488), along the Hana Hwy in Kuau, just east of Paia center, has excellent fish and a nice ocean view. The menu always offers three to five different types of fresh fish, priced at $24 for lunch and around $30 at dinner. Add another $6 for a salad, double that for an appetizer. It's open 11 am to 2:30 pm daily for lunch, 5 to 9:30 pm for dinner. Hawaiian residents get a 20% discount.

Mana Foods, on Baldwin Ave, is a large, down-to-earth health food store with a good variety of juices, yogurts, bulk nuts, granola, cheeses and organic produce. It also offers fresh-baked breads – including a loaf filled with tomatoes and feta cheese ($3) that makes a meal in itself – a fresh salad bar and a few inexpensive takeout hot dishes. Mana is open 8 am to 8 pm daily and, like most grocery stores in Hawaii, takes credit cards.

Entertainment

Jacques (☎ 579-6255, 89 Hana Hwy) has the island's longest monkeypod bar and is the most popular place in Paia to have a drink. If you want more action, *Casanova* (572-0220), in Makawao, is the best bet. For more information, see the Makawao section, later in this chapter.

Paia to Hwy 360

A couple of miles past Paia, the road passes Hookipa Beach and a clifftop vantage point of the surfing action.

After Hookipa, fields of sugarcane give way to long rows of pineapples. You'll pass through Haiku, but there's not much to see as it's a spread-out little town, most of it up the slopes.

Hwy 365, which leads up to Makawao and other Upcountry towns, comes in just after the 16-mile marker. At this point, the Hana Hwy changes numbers from Hwy 36 to Hwy 360 and the mile markers begin again at zero.

The road then changes dramatically, slicing through cliffs and becoming more of a mountain road than a highway. Hana is 35 scenic miles away.

HWY 360
Huelo

Huelo Rd, half a mile past the 3-mile marker, is a dirt road that leads down to Kaulana-pueo Church, a coral and stone church built in 1853. The church is likely to be locked, however, so if you're short on time, this one can be easily bypassed.

MAUI

Koolau Forest Reserve

After Huelo, the vegetation becomes increasingly lush as the highway snakes along the edge of the Koolau Forest Reserve.

Koolau, which means 'windward,' is the windward side of Haleakala and catches the rain clouds. The coast in this area gets 60 to 80 inches of rain a year, while a few miles up on the slopes the annual rainfall is an impressive 200 to 300 inches.

The reserve is heavily forested and cut with numerous gulches and streams. From here, there seems to be a one-lane bridge and a waterfall around every other bend.

Kailua

Kailua is home to many of the people who work for the East Maui Irrigation Company. They maintain the 75 miles of ditches and tunnels that bring water from the rain forests to the cane fields of dry central Maui. The century-old system is capable of carrying 450 million gallons of water a day.

Many of the dirt roads leading inland from the highway are the maintenance roads for the **Koolau Ditch**, which runs inland paralleling the highway.

If you want to take a closer look, stop at the small pull-off just before the bridge that comes up immediately after the 8-mile marker. Just 100 feet above the road you can see a section of the ditch – built of hand-hewn stone block – that meanders down the hillside and then tunnels into the rock face.

As you leave the village, you'll notice Norfolk pines up on the hillside, followed by a grove of painted eucalyptus trees with rainbow-colored bark, then a long stretch of bamboo and more painted eucalyptus.

Waikamoi Ridge Trail

This peaceful trail loops through tall trees with wonderful fresh scents. You're welcomed by a sign reading: 'Quiet. Trees at Work.'

Pull off at the unmarked turnoff half a mile after the 9-mile marker. The trailhead is up on the left beyond the covered picnic table.

This is an easy trail, three-quarters of a mile long. The grand reddish trees are *Eucalyptus robusta*. Note the huge climbing philodendron vines wrapped around them – the vines provide an apt illustration of the etymology of 'philodendron,' a Greek word meaning 'lover of trees'! The trail also passes lots of *hala* (pandanus), ferns and paperbark eucalyptus trees.

Especially if you're walking with children, keep an eye out for occasional metal spikes and tree roots that protrude along the path. From the ridge at the top, there's a good view of the winding Hana Hwy.

Waterfalls

Waikamoi Falls is at the bridge just before the 10-mile marker. One waterfall and a pool are near the road. It's possible to walk a short way up to a higher waterfall, but the rocks can be slippery, and the bottom waterfall is prettier anyway.

Past Waikamoi, bamboo grows almost horizontally out from the cliffs, creating a canopy effect over the road.

At the 11-mile marker, near Puohokamoa Bridge and just a few minutes' walk from the road, is **Puohokamoa Falls** – another attractive little waterfall. Because it has more parking space and a couple of picnic tables, Puohokamoa sees more visitors than the Waikamoi or Haipuaena waterfalls.

Haipuaena Falls, half a mile after the 11-mile marker, is a gentle little waterfall with a wonderful pool deep enough for swimming.

Most people don't know this one's here, as you can't see the pool from the road. If you're inclined to take a dip but don't have a proper bathing suit, this seems like a good choice.

There's space for just one or two cars, on the Hana side of the bridge. To reach the falls, walk upstream for a couple of minutes. Wild ginger grows along the path, and ferns hang from the rock wall behind the waterfall, making for a quite idyllic setting.

Kaumahina State Wayside Park

Kaumahina State Wayside Park is shortly after the 12-mile marker. A two-minute walk up the hill under the park's tall eucalyptus trees provides a broad ocean vista, with Keanae Peninsula to the southeast. The park has picnic tables and a large parking area.

Honomanu Bay

For the next several miles, the scenery is particularly magnificent, opening up to a new vista as you round each bend. If you're on this road after heavy rains, you can expect to see waterfalls galore crashing down the mountains.

Just after crossing the bridge at the 14-mile marker, an inconspicuous and very rough gravel road heads down to Honomanu Bay and a rocky black-sand beach used mostly by surfers and fishers. The water's usually too turbulent for swimming, though on very calm days it's possible to snorkel and dive there.

Keanae

Keanae is about halfway to Hana. The YMCA Camp Keanae is midway between the 16- and 17-mile markers. Within the next half mile, the Keanae Arboretum, the road to Keanae Peninsula and the Keanae Peninsula Lookout come up in quick succession.

Keanae Valley, which extends down from the Koolau Gap in Haleakala Crater, averages 150 inches of rain a year.

Keanae Arboretum This informal arboretum, three-quarters of a mile past the 16-mile marker, has 6 acres of trees and numerous ornamental and food plants. Introduced tropical plants seen here include painted eucalyptus trees and golden-stemmed bamboo, whose green stripes look like the strokes of a Japanese *shodo* artist.

A short trail leads up past heliconia, ti, banana, guava, breadfruit, ginger and other fragrant plants. The higher ground has dozens of varieties of Hawaiian taro in irrigated patches.

Keanae Peninsula The road that leads down to Keanae Peninsula is just beyond the arboretum.

Lanakila Ihiihi o Iehova Ona Kaua (Keanae Congregational Church) is an attractive old (1860) stone church about half a mile down. This is one church made of lava rocks and coral mortar whose exterior hasn't been covered over with layers of whitewash. And rather than locked doors, you'll find a guest book and a 'Visitors Welcome' sign.

Keanae is a quiet little village with colts and goats roaming freely. At the end of the road is a scenic coastline of jagged rock and pounding waves. The rock island down the coast is Mokumana Island, a seabird sanctuary.

Keanae Peninsula Lookout There's a good view of Keanae village, with its squares of planted taro fed by Keanae Stream, at an unmarked pull-off just past the 17-mile marker. Look for the mailbox under the tsunami speaker.

Keanae Peninsula was formed by a later eruption of Haleakala that flowed through Koolau Gap down Keanae Valley. Outlined by its black lava shores, the peninsula still wears its birthmark around the edges. It's very flat, like a leaf floating on the water.

Places to Stay The *YMCA Camp Keanae*, on a knoll overlooking the coast, has guest cabins that can sometimes fill with groups on weekends. Otherwise, they're usually available to individual travelers as hostel-style dorms for $10 per person. The cabins have bunk beds, but you have to bring your own sleeping bag, food and cookware. Kitchen facilities are not available, but the cabins have simple outdoor grills. If you prefer to set up a tent, you can do that instead of staying in the cabins. There's no pool, but you can take a dip in nearby Ching's Pond. Because of space limitations, advance reservations are required, and there's a three-night limit. Reservations are made through the *Maui YMCA office* (☎ 242-9007, 250 Kanaloa Ave, Kahului, HI 96732).

Wailua

Shortly after the Keanae Peninsula Lookout, you'll pass a couple of **fruit stands** along the road selling drinks and snacks. One, Uncle Harry's, is run by the family of the late Harry Kunihi Mitchell, a native Hawaiian-rights advocate who wrote the popular 'Mele o Kahoolawe' (Song of Kahoolawe).

Take Wailua Rd seaward immediately after Uncle Harry's to get to **Our Lady of Fatima Shrine**. This little white-and-blue chapel, built in 1860, is also known as the Coral Miracle

MAUI

Church. The coral used in the construction came from a freak storm that deposited coral rocks onto a nearby beach. Before this, men in the congregation had been diving quite deep but were only able to bring up a few pieces of coral at a time. After the church was completed, another rogue storm hit the beach and swept all the leftover piles of coral back into the sea. Or so the story goes.

The chapel has just half a dozen little pews. The current congregation now uses St Gabriel's Mission, the larger and newer church out front.

From Wailua Rd, you can also get a peek of the long cascade of **Waikani Falls**, which is just to the left of the Wailua Lookout up on the Hana Hwy.

Wailua Rd dead-ends half a mile down, though you might not want to go that far, as driveways blocked off with logs and milk crates prevent cars from turning around.

Wailua Wayside Lookout

Back on the Hana Hwy, just before the 19-mile marker, Wailua Wayside Lookout comes up on the right. It has a broad view into Keanae Valley, which appears to be a hundred shades of green. You can see a couple of waterfalls, and if it's clear, you can look up at Koolau Gap, a break in the rim of Haleakala Crater.

If you climb up the steps to the right, you can get a good view of Wailua Peninsula, but there's a better view of it at a large paved turnoff a quarter mile down the road.

Puaa Kaa State Wayside Park

Halfway between the 22- and 23-mile markers is Puaa Kaa State Wayside Park, where a tranquil waterfall empties into a pool before flowing down into a ravine.

The park has rest rooms, a pay phone, shaded streamside picnic tables and a pool large enough for swimming. The only disadvantage to the site is a pack of stray cats that might pester picnickers.

Kahanu Gardens

Kahanu Gardens, a 122-acre botanical garden on Kalahu Point, a few miles north of Hana, is under the jurisdiction of the National Tropical Botanical Garden. This nonprofit group is involved in the propagation and conservation of rare and medicinal plants, and Kahanu Gardens features ethnobotanical collections of numerous Polynesian trees. Here in one place you'll see kukui, hala, hau and the Pacific's largest known collection of breadfruit cultivars, as well as many other species.

The Kahanu grounds are also the site of **Piilanihale Heiau**, the largest heiau on Maui, which has a stone platform that stretches 415 feet in length. It was built by Piilani, the 14th-century Mauian chief who is also credited with construction of many of the coastal fishponds and taro terraces in the Hana area.

Kahanu Gardens can only be visited on guided tours, which are given by reservation Monday to Friday; the cost is $10 per person. For information, call ☎ 248-8912 weekdays between 10 am and 3 pm.

Waianapanapa State Park

The road into Waianapanapa State Park is immediately after the 32-mile marker, half a mile south of the turnoff to Hana Airport. This 122-acre park has 12 cabins, tent camping, picnic pavilions, rest rooms, showers and drinking water.

The road ends at a parking lot above Pailoa Bay, which is surrounded by a scenic coastline of low rocky cliffs. There's a natural lava arch on the right side of the bay. A short path from the parking lot leads down to the small black-sand beach, which is unprotected and usually has strong rip currents. When it's very calm, the area around the arch is said to be good for snorkeling. Check it out carefully, though, as people have drowned here.

Caves Two impressive lava-tube caves are just a five-minute walk from the parking lot along a loop path. On the outside, the caves are covered with ferns and flowering impatiens. Inside, they're dripping wet and cool.

Waianapanapa means 'glistening waters,' and should you be tempted to take a dip in the cave pools, the clear mineral waters will leave you feeling squeaky clean.

On certain nights of the year, the waters in the caves turn red. Legend says it's the blood of a princess and her lover who were killed in a fit of rage by the princess's jealous husband after he found them hiding together here. Less romantic types attribute the phenomenon to swarms of tiny bright red shrimp called *opaeula*, which occasionally emerge from subterranean cracks in the lava.

Hana-Waianapanapa Trail A coastal trail that parallels the ancient King's Hwy leads south about 2 miles from the park to Kainalimu Bay, just north of Hana Bay. Some of the original smooth lava stepping stones are still in place along the trail.

Beyond the park cabins, the trail passes blowholes and the ruins of a heiau. Gorgeous coastal views take in endless expanses of cobalt blue water below craggy black lava outcrops. Hala and beach naupaka are the predominant flora along the trail; the naupaka has delicate white flowers that look as if they've been torn in half.

From the end of the trail, it's about a mile farther to the center of Hana.

Camping Tent camping is free with a permit. The housekeeping cabins, which book up months in advance, cost $45 for up to four people, $5 for each additional person. Make reservations (or obtain a camping permit) through the Division of State Parks (☎ 984-8109), State Office Building, 54 High St, Wailuku, HI 96793.

HANA

Separated from Kahului by 54 bridges and almost as many miles, the isolated town of Hana has thus far avoided development. And even though a line of traffic passes through each day, not many visitors stay on.

Hana sits beneath the rainy slopes of Haleakala, surrounded by green pastures and a jagged black coastline. In ancient times, it was the heart of one of Maui's largest population centers. The village itself was thought to have been reserved for the alii.

In the late 19th century, Chinese, Japanese and Portuguese laborers were brought in to work the newly planted sugarcane fields, and

Hana became a booming plantation town. A narrow-gauge railroad connected the fields to the Hana Mill. In the 1940s, Hana could no longer compete with larger sugar operations in central Maui, so the mill shut down.

In 1943, San Francisco businessman Paul Fagan, who owned Puu O Hoku Ranch on Molokai, purchased 14,000 acres in Hana. Starting with 300 Herefords, Fagan converted the cane fields to ranch land.

A few years later, Fagan opened a six-room hotel as a getaway resort for his well-to-do friends. Geographically and economically, Hana Ranch and the hotel became the hub of town.

Today, Hana Ranch still has a few thousand head of cattle worked by Hawaiian cowhands. When the cattle are ready for Oahu stockyards, they're trucked all the way up the Hana Hwy to Kahului Harbor. Visitors to the ranch can play *paniolo* (cowboy) by going for a ride on horseback.

Hana is not a grand finale to the magnificent Hana Hwy, and people expecting great things are often disappointed. While the setting is pretty, the town itself is simple and sedate. What makes Hana special is more apparent to those who stay on. There's an almost timeless rural character, and though 'Old Hawaii' is an oft-used cliché elsewhere, it's hard not to think of Hana in such terms.

Hana is one of the most Hawaiian communities in the state. Many of Hana's 1900 residents have Hawaiian blood and a strong sense of *ohana*, or extended family. If you spend time around here you'll hear the words 'auntie' and 'uncle' a lot.

People in Hana cling to their traditional ways and have largely been successful in warding off the changes that have altered much of the rest of Maui. In the latest round, they beat down a plan by outside developers to build a golf course and luxury homes on the pasturelands.

A small community of celebrities, including George Harrison and Kris Kristofferson, have long had homes in the Hana area.

Information

Hana Ranch Center is the commercial center of town. It has a post office, open 8 am to

MAUI

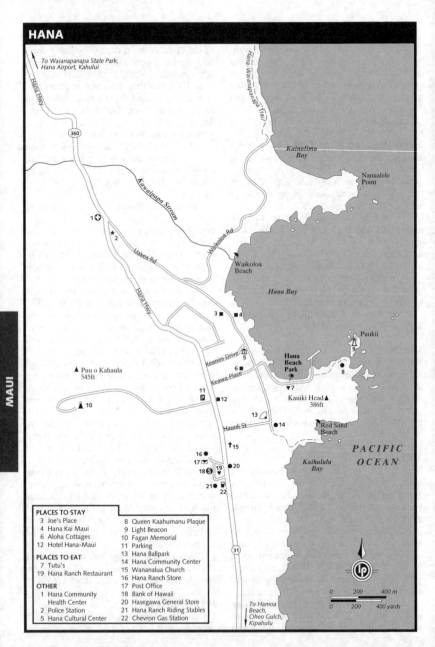

HANA

To Waianapanapa State Park,
Hana Airport, Kahului

360

Kawaipapa Stream

Uakea Rd

Hana Hwy

Hana Hwy

Waikoloa Rd

Hana-Waianapanapa Trail

Kainalimu
Bay

Nanualele
Point

Waikoloa
Beach

Hana Bay

Puukii

1

2

3

4

Keanini Drive

5

6

Keawa Place

11

12

13

14

Hauoli St

15

16

17

19

18

20

21

22

Puu o Kahaula
545ft

10

Hana
Beach
Park

7

9

8

Kauiki Head
386ft

Red Sand
Beach

PACIFIC
OCEAN

Kaihalulu
Bay

31

To Hamoa
Beach,
Oheo Gulch,
Kipahulu

0   200   400 m
0   200   400 yards

PLACES TO STAY
3 Joe's Place
4 Hana Kai Maui
6 Aloha Cottages
12 Hotel Hana-Maui

PLACES TO EAT
7 Tutu's
19 Hana Ranch Restaurant

OTHER
1 Hana Community
   Health Center
2 Police Station
5 Hana Cultural Center

8 Queen Kaahumanu Plaque
9 Light Beacon
10 Fagan Memorial
11 Parking
13 Hana Ballpark
14 Hana Community Center
15 Wananalua Church
16 Hana Ranch Store
17 Post Office
18 Bank of Hawaii
20 Hasegawa General Store
21 Hana Ranch Riding Stables
22 Chevron Gas Station

MAUI

4:30 pm weekdays; a tiny Bank of Hawaii, open 3 to 4:30 pm Monday to Thursday and 3 to 6 pm on Friday; and the Hana Ranch Store, which sells groceries, liquor and general supplies and is open 7 am to 7 pm daily.

Hasegawa General Store has an ATM. There are community bulletin boards outside the post office and the two grocery stores.

Hana closes up early. If you're going to be heading back late, get gas in advance – the Chevron station, which has the longest hours, usually closes at 6 pm (5:30 pm on Sunday).

The ballpark has public tennis courts.

Hasegawa General Store
The old Hasegawa General Store, Hana's best-known sight, burned to the ground in 1990. After a brief hiatus, it relocated under the rusty tin roof of the old theater building in the town center. While some of its character was inevitably lost along with its eclectic inventory, the store is still packed with just about everything from bags of poi and aloha dolls to fishing gear and machetes. It also has clothing, groceries, hardware, newspapers and the record that immortalized the store in song. The business has been in the Hasegawa family since 1910. The store is open 8 am to 5:30 pm Monday to Saturday, 9 am to 4:30 pm on Sunday.

Fagan Memorial
When Paul Fagan died in 1959, his family erected a memorial on Lyon's Hill, which was Fagan's favorite spot for watching the sunset. The huge hilltop cross is now Hana's most dominant landmark.

A trail up Lyon's Hill starts opposite the Hotel Hana-Maui. The trail is often used by cyclists and joggers, and it takes about 15 minutes to walk up the hill. If you want to drive up, ask at the hotel front desk to borrow the gate key.

Wananalua Church
The Wananalua Congregational Church, south of the Hotel Hana-Maui, looks like an ancient Norman church. On the National Register of Historic Places, the current church was built in 1838 with thick walls of lava rock and coral mortar to replace the congregation's original grass church. There's a little cemetery at the side with graves randomly laid out rather than lined up in rows. Even at rest, Hana folks like things casual.

Hana Cultural Center
The Hana Cultural Center is a small museum displaying quilts, Hawaiian artifacts, wooden carvings, period photographs and a couple of reconstructed thatched hales of the type once found in traditional Hawaiian villages. It's a friendly community-run operation and a good place to get a sense of Hana's roots.

The same grounds contain the old Hana district police station and three-bench courthouse, which dates to 1871. Although it looks like a museum piece, the court is still used a couple of times a month; a judge shows up to hear minor cases such as traffic violations, sparing Hana residents the need to drive all the way to Wailuku. The museum is open 10 am to 4 pm daily; admission is $2.

Hana Beach Park
Hana Beach Park, at the southern end of Hana Bay, has a black-sand beach, snack bar, showers, rest rooms, a small boat ramp and picnic tables.

Hana folks occasionally come down here with ukuleles, guitars and a few beers for impromptu evening parties. With luck, you may even find one of Hana's celebrities joining in.

When water conditions are very calm, snorkeling and diving are good out in the direction of the light beacon. Currents can be strong, and snorkelers shouldn't go beyond the beacon.

Surfers head to Waikoloa Beach, at the northern end of the bay.

Kauiki Head
Kauiki Head, the 386-foot cinder hill on the south side of Hana Bay, is said to have been the home of the demigod Maui and was the site of an ancient fort.

The islet at the tip of the point, which now holds a light beacon, is Puukii or 'Image Hill.' The name can be traced to a huge idol that the great king Umi erected here in

MAUI

the 16th century to ward off invaders. In 1780, the Mauian chief Kahekili successfully fought off a challenge by Big Island chiefs at Kauiki Head.

Queen Kaahumanu, the favorite wife of Kamehameha I and one of the most powerful women in Hawaiian history, was born in a cave here in 1768. It was Kaahumanu who ended the ancient kapu system and freed women from restrictive taboos.

A trail to a plaque noting the queen's birth starts along the hill at the side of the wharf at Hana Beach Park. It leads through ironwood trees toward the light beacon, passing by a tiny red-sand beach. The walk to the rock where the plaque is mounted is only mildly interesting, but then again it takes just five minutes. Watch where you step, as some of the trail is a bit crumbly.

Red Sand Beach

Red Sand Beach (Kaihalulu Beach), on the south side of Kauiki Head, is favored by nude sunbathers. It's a gorgeous little cove with sand eroded from the red cinder hill and beautiful turquoise waters.

Although the cove is partly protected by a lava outcrop, the currents can be dangerous if the surf is up. Water drains through a break on the left side, which should be avoided.

The path to the beach is at the end of Uakea Rd beyond the ballpark. It starts across the lawn at the lower side of the Hana Community Center, where a steep trail continues down to the beach, less than 10 minutes away.

The curious can also find an interesting overgrown Japanese cemetery – a remnant of the sugarcane days – just two minutes' walk east from the community center.

Places to Stay

Camping There's tent camping and cabins at Waianapanapa State Park, just north of Hana (see the earlier Road to Hana section), and tent camping at Oheo Gulch, 10 miles south of Hana (see the Hana to Kipahula section, later in this chapter). If you plan to camp at Oheo, you'll need to stock up on food and water in Hana.

Guest Houses, Condos & Hotels *Joe's Place* (☎ 248-7033, PO Box 577, Hana, HI 96713), in town on Uakea Rd, has eight rooms that cost $45 with a shared bath, $55 with a private bath, for either one or two people. Most rooms have two single beds, though a few have double beds. Rooms are small and basic, but they're clean and comfortable enough. Guests have access to a community kitchen, a TV room and a phone.

Aloha Cottages (☎ 248-8420, PO Box 205, Hana, HI 96713) is on Keawa Place, opposite the Hotel Hana-Maui. Run by Fusae Nakamura, the cottages include one studio with twin beds and a hot plate, toaster and refrigerator for $62; and three two-bedroom cottages, each with full kitchen, a queen bed and two twin beds for $82 for two people, $10 for each additional person. All the units are straightforward; none has a phone, but messages are taken.

Tradewinds Cottages (☎ 248-8980, 800-327-8097, twt@maui.net, PO Box 385, Hana, HI 96713) are two pleasant cottages on the 5-acre tropical flower farm of Michael and Rebecca Buckley. One is a studio with a queen bed and a sofa bed. The other is a two-bedroom cottage with a queen bed, two twin beds and a sofa bed. Both have full kitchens, cable TV, ceiling fans and covered decks with hot tubs and fine views. The cottages are separated from the main house, giving you the feeling of being in your own private garden; guests are free to pick papayas, bananas and avocados. The cost is $100 for the studio and $125 for the two-bedroom for two people; add $10 for each additional person. There's a two-night minimum stay, but if the Buckleys have a gap in the schedule, they'll sometimes take a last-minute booking for just one night. Tradewinds is a couple of miles north of town, near the start of the airport road. Visit the website at www.maui.net/~twt/cottage .html.

Hana Kai Maui (☎ 248-8426, 800-346-2772, fax 248-7482, hanakai@tiki.net, PO Box 38, Hana, HI 96713), at the north side of town, is a modern, though not fancy, 17-unit condo. Units have full kitchens and lanais, most with fine ocean views of Hana Bay and within earshot of the breaking surf. Studios cost $125 to $135 double occupancy; one-bedroom units are $145 to $165 for up to four people. For more information, visit the website www.hanakai.com.

The **Hotel Hana-Maui** (☎ 248-8211, 800-321-4262, fax 248-7202, Hana Hwy, Hana, HI 96713) is one of Maui's more exclusive getaway hotels, though it's lost a little of its luster over the years. On 23 acres in the center of town, the Hana-Maui is low profile, more like a plantation estate than a luxury hotel. Everything's very airy and open, with Hawaiian accents from local art to quilt bedspreads. The 77 rooms are mostly in single-story row cottages that have bleached hardwood floors, tiled baths, a view over a private garden and French doors opening to trellised patios. Pampering has its price – rates range from $395 to $795.

Vacation Rentals A couple of vacation rental agencies handle cottages and houses in the Hana area. As the properties can vary greatly in quality and maintenance, it's recommended that you get specific details before sending a deposit.

Hana Alii Holidays (☎ 248-7742, 800-548-0478, fax 248-8595, info@hanaalii.com, PO Box 536, Hana, HI 96713) manages more than a dozen private homes and cottages. Daily rates range from a studio condo at $95 to an estate home for $295. You can see pictures of the properties online at www.hanaalii.com.

Hana Plantation Houses (☎ 923-0772, 800-228-4262, fax 922-6068, info@hana-maui .com, PO Box 249, Hana, HI 96713) rents a dozen houses. At the low end, there's a little Japanese-style studio with an efficiency kitchen for $80; at the high end, a two-bedroom two-story house with hot tub and garden setting rents for $150. The houses are about 10 minutes outside town, and all have cooking facilities. Rates are for up to two people; add $10 for each extra person. For more information, visit the website www .hana-maui.com.

Places to Eat

Tutu's, a fast-food grill at Hana Beach Park, is open 8 am to 4 pm daily, though the grill closes 15 minutes earlier. Hamburgers and veggie sandwiches or mahimahi burgers cost $3.75. Tutu's also has $6 plate lunches and ice cream.

A good lunch stop is the **Hana Gardenland Cafe** (☎ 248-7340), 3 miles north of town on the Hana Hwy, which runs with the motto: 'nothing even close to a hamburger.' Here you'll find a garden setting and a menu that emphasizes locally grown produce. For breakfast, try a waffle topped in coconut-guava syrup. At lunch, you can get a green salad or choose from a list of sandwiches, including turkey, albacore and vegetarian versions. Most items cost $5 to $8. Fresh-squeezed juices, fruit smoothies, espresso and desserts are also available. It's open 9 am to 5 pm daily.

The **Hana Ranch Restaurant** (☎ 248-8255), at the Hana Ranch Center, is open for lunch 11 am to 3 pm daily, with a buffet that includes a simple salad bar and a few hot dishes for $11. At dinner on Friday and Saturday (6 to 8 pm), pasta or steak meals range from $15 to $25, salad bar included. On Wednesday night, pizza and pasta are served at moderate prices.

A takeout counter at the side of the restaurant is open 6:30 am to 4 pm on Wednesday, Friday and Saturday and until 7 pm on other days. It offers standard breakfast fare for around $5, plate lunches for $6.75 and saimin, burgers and sandwiches for a bit less. There are picnic tables outside where you can chow down.

The **Hotel Hana-Maui** (☎ 248-8211) serves only dinner, and the food tends to be straightforward despite the setting. Seatings are from 6 to 8:30 pm. Main courses include pasta and chicken for $22 and catch of the day for $29, with salads and appetizers an additional $9 to $15. There's live Hawaiian music in the hotel bar on most nights from 6:30 to 9 pm, with no cover charge.

Bring groceries from Kahului if you plan to stay awhile, as the Hana grocery stores have only a limited selection.

Getting There & Around

Hana Airport is 3½ miles north of town. Dollar Rent-A-Car (☎ 248-8237) has a branch office at the airport.

MAUI

HANA TO KIPAHULU

From Hana, the road continues on to Kipahulu, passing Oheo, the southern end of Haleakala National Park. This incredibly lush stretch is perhaps the most beautiful part of the entire drive down from Paia. As it continues south from Hana, the road changes its name to the Piilani Hwy.

From Hana to Oheo, the road is narrow and winding. Between the hairpin turns, one-lane bridges and drivers trying to take in all the sights, it's a slow-moving 10 miles.

You'll get extra coastal views by detouring along the 1½-mile Haneoo Rd loop, which runs past Koki and Hamoa Beaches and a couple of ancient shoreline fishponds. The turnoff is half a mile south of Hana Ranch headquarters.

Koki Beach is at the base of a red cinder hill less than half a mile from the start of the loop. Most of Koki's sand washes away in winter, leaving a rocky shoreline. Local surfers who know the coastline sometimes surf here, but rocks and strong currents make it hazardous for newcomers.

The offshore rock topped by a few coconut trees is **Alau Island**, a seabird sanctuary. The trees were planted years ago by a couple of Hana residents so that they'd have coconuts to drink while fishing off the island.

A little farther is **Hamoa Beach**, a nice gray-sand beach that's used by the Hotel Hana-Maui but is accessible to everyone. When the surf's up, there's good surfing and bodysurfing, though be aware that rip currents can sometimes be present. When seas are calm, swimming in the cove is good. Public access is down the steps below the hotel's bus-stop sign.

As you continue south, you'll see waterfalls cascading down the cliffs, orchids growing out of the rocks, and lots of breadfruit and coconut trees. There's even a statue of the Virgin Mary tucked into a rock face on the side of the road.

Wailua Falls, 3 miles before Oheo, is particularly attractive, with its 100-foot drop visible from the road. At the waterfall pull-off, you might find a couple of vendors selling hand-painted T-shirts and the like.

Oheo Gulch

Oheo Stream dramatically cuts its way through Oheo Gulch in a lovely series of waterfalls and wide pools, each one tumbling into the next one below. In fair weather, the pools make good swimming holes. A 2-mile trail runs up the streambed.

A large Hawaiian settlement once spread throughout the Oheo area, and the stone remains of more than 700 structures have

Kipahulu Valley

In the 1960s, 11,000 acres of Kipahulu Valley were jointly purchased by the Nature Conservancy and the state of Hawaii for preservation. The valley, which borders the main body of Haleakala National Park and stretches southeast to the coast, was turned over to the US Department of the Interior and added to the national park in 1969. The coastal Oheo Gulch area is part of the Kipahulu Valley property.

The upper Kipahulu Valley is a pristine rain forest that provides refuge for endangered native plants and birds. The Maui parrotbill, whose sole population lives in this valley, has a habitat range of just over 8 miles. Fewer than 500 of the birds survive. Also in Kipahulu Valley is the entire population of the Maui *nuku puu*, Hawaii's most endangered honeycreeper – about 30 birds in all. The parrotbill and nuku puu are both beautiful forest birds, about 5 inches long, with bright yellow underbellies.

The upper part of the valley gets up to 300 inches of rain a year and is swampy with dense vegetation. In an effort to protect the habitat, no public access is allowed.

been identified. The early villagers cultivated taro and sweet potatoes in terraced gardens.

One of the expressed intentions of Haleakala National Park is to manage the Oheo area 'to perpetuate traditional Hawaiian farming and *hoonanea*' – a Hawaiian word meaning to pass the time in ease, peace and pleasure.

Not so long ago, Oheo Gulch was dubbed the 'Seven Sacred Pools' in a tourism promotion scheme. There are actually 24 pools from the ocean all the way up to Waimoku Falls, and they were never sacred (although it was kapu for menstruating women to bathe in them).

The park's ranger station (☎ 248-7375) is staffed from 9 am to 5 pm daily. Programs here include occasional Hawaiian-culture demonstrations and short ranger-led walks. A three-hour guided hike to Waimoku Falls is usually offered on Saturday at 9:30 am, as long as the weather is accommodating and at least four people want to go. Rest rooms are available – they're near the visitors' parking lot – but drinking water and food are not.

Lower Pools A 20-minute loop trail runs from the Oheo Gulch parking lot down to the lower pools and back, passing interpretive signs along the way. The ranger station is near the start of the trail. A few minutes down, you'll come to a broad grassy knoll with a beautiful view of the Hana coast. On a clear day, you can see the Big Island, 30 miles away across Alenuihaha Channel. This would be a fine place to break out a picnic basket.

The large freshwater pools along the trail are terraced one atop the other and are connected by gentle cascades. They're usually calm and great for swimming, though the water's brisk. The second big pool below the bridge is a favorite.

If it's been raining heavily and the water is flowing too high and fast, the pools are closed and signs are posted. Still, heavy rains falling on the upper slopes can bring a sudden torrent here at any time. If the water starts to rise, get out immediately. People have been swept out to sea from these pools by flash floods. The ocean below is not

Climbing Fish

Oheo Gulch is home to a rare goby called *oopu*, a bottom fish that spends the first stages of its life in the ocean but, as it reaches maturity, returns to breed in the upper stream. The fish, which has a face that resembles a frog, works its way out of the ocean and up the chain of pools and waterfalls by using its front fins as suction cups on the rocks. After spawning, the eggs flow downstream into the sea, where the cycle begins again.

inviting at all – the water is quite rough, and gray sharks frequent the area!

Actually, most of the injuries that occur here come from falls on slippery rocks. Also hazardous are submerged rocks and ledges in some of the pools; check carefully before diving in.

Waterfall Trails Opposite the parking lot is a trail leading up to Makahiku Falls (half a mile) and Waimoku Falls (2 miles). Along the path, you'll pass large mango trees and lots of guava before coming to a fork after about 10 minutes. **Makahiku Falls**, a long bridal-veil waterfall that drops into a deep gorge, is just off to the right. Thick green ferns cover the sides of 200-foot basalt cliffs where the fall cascades. The scene is quite rewarding for such a short walk.

To the left of the overlook, a path continues up to the top of the falls, where there's a popular skinny-dipping pool. Around midday the pool is quite enjoyable, but by late afternoon the sun stops hitting it and the mosquitoes move in. Rocks above the falls will keep you from going over the edge as long as the water level isn't high; a cut on one side lets the water plunge over the cliff. But if the water starts to rise, get out immediately – a drop over this sheer 184-foot waterfall could obviously be fatal!

Waimoku Falls is a thin, lacy 400-foot waterfall dropping down a sheer rock face. The walk to the falls is made all the more

MAUI

special by three thick bamboo groves. When you come out of the first grove, you'll see the waterfall in the distance. By the time you emerge from the third thicket, you're there.

It takes about an hour to hike the 1½ miles to Waimoku Falls from the Makahiku Falls viewpoint. The upper part of the trail is muddy, but boardwalks cover some of the worst sections. Ancient farm sites with abandoned taro patches can be seen along the way, although it takes a keen eye to recognize them. Mosquitoes thrive along the streambed.

The pool under Waimoku Falls was partially filled in by a landslide during a 1976 earthquake, so it's not terribly deep. At any rate, swimming is not recommended due to the danger of falling rocks.

If you want to take a dip, you'll find better pools to swim in along the way. About 100 yards before Waimoku Falls, you'll cross a little stream. If you go left and walk upstream for 10 minutes (there's not really a trail; just walk alongside the stream), you'll come to an attractive waterfall and a little pool about neck deep. There's also a nice pool in the stream about halfway between Makahiku and Waimoku Falls.

Places to Stay The national park maintains a primitive campground about half a mile southeast of the main Oheo Gulch visitor's area. The campground is Hawaiian-style: free and undeveloped – just a huge open pasture. There are some incredible places to pitch a tent on grassy cliffs right above the coast and the pounding surf. Not only is the scenery stunning, but the camping area is set amid the ruins of an old Hawaiian village, making this quite a powerful place to be.

In winter, there are usually only a handful of tents here. It gets quite a few campers in summer, but even then it's generally large enough to handle everyone who shows up. Facilities include pit toilets and a few picnic tables and grills but *no* water. Permits aren't required, though camping is officially limited to three nights each month.

Kipahulu

The village of Kipahulu is less than a mile south of Oheo. At the turn of the 20th century, Kipahulu was one of several sugar plantation villages in the Hana area. It had a working mill from 1890 to 1922. Following the closure of the mill, unsuccessful attempts were made to grow pineapples. Then ranching took hold in the late 1920s.

Today, Kipahulu has both exclusive estates and more modest homes. Fruit stands are set up here and there along the roadside; some are attended by elderly women who string leis and sell bananas, papayas and woven *lauhala* (pandanus-leaf) hats. This is the end of the line for most day visitors who have pushed beyond Hana.

Lindbergh's Grave The Hana area was home to aviator hero Charles Lindbergh during the last years of his life. He began visiting in the 1960s, built a cliffside home in Kipahulu in 1968 and died of cancer in Maui in 1974.

Lindbergh is buried in the graveyard of Palapala Hoomau Congregational Church. His simple grave is surrounded by a chain and marked with little American flags.

Would-be visitors sometimes get the location mixed up with St Paul's Church, which sits on the highway three-quarters of a mile south of Oheo; the dirt drive down to Palapala Hoomau Church is a quarter mile beyond that, on the seaward side of the road. Turn in at the gate just past the wooden cistern at the end of the field.

Palapala Hoomau Church, with its 26-inch-thick walls and simple wooden pews, dates from 1864. The church is known for its window painting of a Polynesian Christ dressed in the red and yellow feather capes worn only by Hawaii's highest chiefs.

The churchyard is a peaceful place, with sleepy cats lounging around, waiting for a nice warm car hood to sprawl out on.

Getting There & Away

A lot of people leave the Oheo Gulch area in midafternoon to head back up the Hana Hwy. Some of them, suddenly realizing what a long trek they have ahead, become very impatient drivers.

You might want to consider leaving a little later, which would give you more time to sightsee and allow you to avoid the rush. Getting caught in the dark on the Hana Hwy does have certain advantages. You can see the headlights of oncoming cars around bends that would otherwise be blind, and the traffic is almost nonexistent.

There are no shortcuts back, but sometimes there is another option.

From Kipahulu, the Piilani Hwy (don't be misled by the term 'highway' – there's barely a road in places!) heads west through Kaupo up to Keokea in Kula. It's usually passable, but not always, and it shouldn't be done in the dark.

The Oheo Gulch ranger station can give you the latest information on road conditions. Another option is to drive to the south end of Kipahulu and talk to people coming from the Kaupo direction. Most likely they've either just driven down from Kula or else have started up the road from Kipahulu, found road conditions bad and turned around.

For more details on the drive, see the Piilani Hwy section, later in this chapter.

Upcountry

Upcountry, the highland area of East Maui on the western slopes of Haleakala, has some of Maui's finest countryside, with rolling hills, grazing horses and green pastures. You have to drive through Upcountry to get to Haleakala National Park, but the region is well worth visiting for its own sake.

Upcountry is uncrowded and dotted with small towns. A fair chunk of the area is occupied by ranches; Haleakala Ranch covers vast spreads to the north, while Ulupalakua Ranch encompasses thousands upon thousands of acres to the south.

Kula, in the center of it all, boasts rich farmland where most of Maui's vegetables and flowers are grown. On the mountainside above Kula are the delightful cloud forests of Polipoli. Upcountry sightseeing spots include landscaped gardens and a winery with a tasting room.

From Upcountry, you can look across the central plains to the West Maui Mountains

and get a good view of the Maui coastline and the neighboring islands. Daytime temperatures are cooler in Upcountry than on the coast, and nights can be downright brisk.

PAIA TO MAKAWAO

Baldwin Ave (Hwy 390) runs 7 miles from Paia up to Makawao. It starts amid sugarcane, passes the Paia Mill and then runs up through pineapple fields interspersed with little open patches where cattle graze.

There are two churches along Baldwin Ave. The **Holy Rosary Church**, with its memorial statue of Father Damien, comes up first on the right, and the attractive **Makawao Union Church**, a stone-block building with stained-glass windows, is farther along on the left. The latter, built in 1916, is on the National Register of Historic Places.

On the left just after the 5-mile marker is Kaluanui, the former 9-acre plantation estate of sugar magnates Harry and Ethel Baldwin, which now houses the **Hui Noeau Visual Arts Center**. The two-story plantation home with Spanish-style tile roof was designed by famed Honolulu architect CW Dickey in 1917. Maui's first mule-powered centrifugal sugar mill was once on the site.

The nonprofit group Hui Noeau (☎ 572-6560) offers community classes in printmaking, weaving, batik and dozens of other visual arts at the center. The main house features changing exhibits and a gift shop, while the stables at the back have been turned into a ceramics studio. The gallery and gift shop are open 10 am to 4 pm Monday to Saturday.

Haliimaile

Haliimaile is a little pineapple town on the edge of an expansive cane and pineapple plantation. The main attraction is the old general store, built circa 1918, which has been converted into one of the better upscale restaurants on this side of Maui.

Places to Stay *Peace Of Mind* (☎ 572-5045, 888-475-5045, pom@maui.net, 1290 Haliimaile Rd, Makawao, HI 96768) is a great down-to-earth budget option in the large contemporary home of John and Tammi Cadman, who live with their four

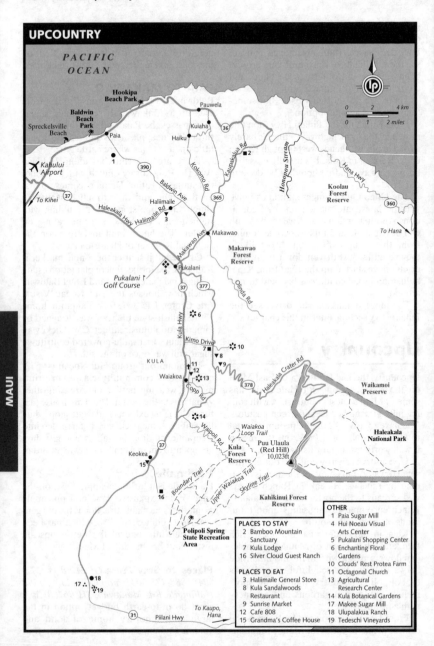

UPCOUNTRY

PACIFIC OCEAN

0   2   4 km
0   1   2 miles

Hookipa Beach Park

Baldwin Beach Park

Spreckelsville Beach

Paia

Pauwela

Kuiaha

36

Haiku

Kahului Airport

To Kihei

37

390

Baldwin Ave

Haleakala Hwy Haliimaile Rd

Haliimaile

365

Kokomo Rd

Kaupakulua Rd

2

Homopou Stream

Koolau Forest Reserve

360

To Hana

3

4

Makawao Ave

Makawao

Makawao Forest Reserve

Olinda Rd

5

Pukalani Golf Course

Pukalani

37

377

6

Kula Hwy

Kimo Drive

7   10

8

9

11

12

Waiakoa

13

Copp Rd

378

Haleakala Crater Rd

KULA

Waikamoi Preserve

14

Waipoli Rd

Waiakoa Loop Trail

Kula Forest Reserve

Puu Ulaula (Red Hill) 10,023ft

Haleakala National Park

Keokea

37

15

16

Boundary Trail

Upper Waiakoa Trail

Skyline Trail

Kahikinui Forest Reserve

Polipoli Spring State Recreation Area

17   18

19

31

Piilani Hwy

To Kaupo, Hana

PLACES TO STAY
2 Bamboo Mountain Sanctuary
7 Kula Lodge
16 Silver Cloud Guest Ranch

PLACES TO EAT
3 Haliimaile General Store
8 Kula Sandalwoods Restaurant
9 Sunrise Market
12 Cafe 808
15 Grandma's Coffee House

OTHER
1 Paia Sugar Mill
4 Hui Noeau Visual Arts Center
5 Pukalani Shopping Center
6 Enchanting Floral Gardens
10 Clouds' Rest Protea Farm
11 Octagonal Church
13 Agricultural Research Center
14 Kula Botanical Gardens
17 Makee Sugar Mill
18 Ulupalakua Ranch
19 Tedeschi Vineyards

MAUI

sons on the 2nd floor. On the 1st floor are six guest rooms – one with a king bed, three with queen beds and two with bunk beds. All rooms have TV and a small refrigerator; bathrooms are shared. Guests share a full kitchen, a large living room, a phone, a barbecue grill and a place to store surfboards. Breakfast is not included, but Tammi provides complimentary homegrown fruit. The rooms cost $35 for up to two people. There's also a pleasant one-bedroom cottage with two twin beds (which can be arranged as a king), a full kitchen, a queen futon in the living room and a deck with a distant ocean view for $65. The property is on a quiet 2-acre homestead at the east side of Haliimaile village. If you have a car, the location is convenient, just five minutes from Makawao and 10 minutes from Paia. For more information, visit the Cadmans' website at www.maui.net/~pom/index.html.

Places to Eat With high ceilings and plantation-era decor, ***Haliimaile General Store*** (☎ 572-2666) features a mix of Hawaiian and Asian cooking influences. At dinner, served from 5:30 to 9:30 pm, main dishes ($17 to $30) include barbecued ribs, blackened chicken with banana-rum sauce, and a tasty Szechuan barbecued salmon. Lunch, from 11 am to 2:30 pm, features salads and sandwiches from $7 to $10.

To get there from Paia, turn right onto Haliimaile Rd, 5 miles up Baldwin Ave. From Kahului, turn left onto Haliimaile Rd, about 4½ miles up Hwy 37.

MAKAWAO

Makawao is billed as a paniolo town. Despite a recent spurt of growth, it's still bordered by ranch land, and the false-front wooden buildings in the town center retain a certain Old West appearance. The town's main events are a couple of big-time rodeos.

All that aside, Makawao is a town in flux. In the past decade, a sizable amount of alternative culture has seeped in: the health food store has set up down the street from Makawao Feed & Garden, and the gun shops have given way to storefronts specializing in crystals, Chinese herbs and yoga therapy.

Makawao has some interesting upscale galleries, including those at The Courtyard, at 3620 Baldwin Ave. Most notable here is Hot Island Glass, where you can watch glassblowers at work every day until 4:30 pm.

Check the bulletin board at the health food store if you want to know what's happening in the community – you'll find listings for such things as spiritual healing, belly dance classes and mantra meditation.

Makawao is an enjoyable town, and poking around is easy; nearly everything is within a few minutes' walk from the intersection of Hwys 365 and 390 (Baldwin Ave).

Places to Stay
The bulletin board at the health food store often has ads for rooms and studios that can be rented on a monthly basis.

For a weekly rental, one option is ***Hale Lani*** (☎ 572-0020, halelanimaui@hotmail.com, PO Box 1527, Makawao, HI 96768), run by Paul Santos. Its three attractive rental units occupy a quiet residential neighborhood on the south side of Makawao. The largest unit is a comfortable three-bedroom, two-bath house with an open-beam living room, deck, hot tub and stereo; one bedroom has a king bed, the others have queen beds. If you use only the master bedroom, the rate is $700 a week; if you use all three, it's $1200. Another unit is an attractive one-bedroom, one-bath cottage with a queen bed, deck and hot tub for $630 a week. And adjacent to the house is a smaller one-bedroom unit with a queen bed for $400 a week. All have cable TV, VCRs, phones, well-appointed kitchens and washer/dryers, and they all share a heated above-ground swimming pool.

Makawao Oceanview Cottage (☎ 572-6437, vrentals@shaka.com, 1179 Kehau Place, Makawao, HI 96768) is a pleasant, modern studio cottage within easy walking distance of the town center. Attached to the side of Mark and Susie Dubois' home, it has a full kitchen, microwave, cable TV, phone, ceiling fan, queen bed and queen sofa bed. The large private deck has a gas grill and a distant ocean view. You can pick your own oranges, lemons, bananas and grapefruit in season, and you have free use of a washer and dryer. It's a good value at $55 a day, $1175 for 28 days.

Places to Eat

Cafe Makawao, at the intersection of Hwys 365 and 390, is a casual place with a predominantly vegetarian menu. The breakfast fare, veggie sandwiches, tempeh burgers and salads are priced around $6. The cafe also makes salads and sandwiches using fish and free-range poultry. It's open 7 am to 8 pm on weekdays, 8 am to 10 pm on Saturday and 7 am to 2 pm on Sunday.

Across the street is the *Casanova Deli*, a popular Italian delicatessen with salads, sandwiches and pastas for around $6. It also has coffees, desserts and bagels. There are cafe tables where you can eat if you're not ordering takeout. Hours are 7:30 am to 6 pm Monday to Saturday, 8:30 am to 5 pm Sunday.

Casanova Restaurant, next to the deli, has good crispy-crust pizza baked in a kiawe-fired brick oven, as well as creative pastas for $10 to $15 and fish and meat dishes for around $22. At lunch, from 11:30 am to 2:30 pm, hot sandwiches and pastas cost $8 to $10. Dinner is served 5:30 to 9:30 pm daily.

Polli's, at the intersection of Hwys 365 and 390, is a reliable old standby serving good Tex-Mex food. The usual dinner combos start at $12; a fajita plate is $14. At lunch, an enchilada with rice and beans or huevos rancheros costs $7. Vegetarians can order dishes with tofu instead of meat. It's open 11 am to 10 pm daily.

Kitada's Kau Kau Korner, in a funky old building on Baldwin Ave, opposite The Courtyard galleries, has been making saimin here for generations. The servings are generous and the prices cheap – you can slurp down a large bowl for just $4. It's open 6:30 am to 1:30 pm Monday to Saturday.

Down to Earth Natural Foods, on Makawao Ave across from Casanova, has organic produce, bulk and packaged foods, a dairy section, juices, sandwiches, a good salad bar and a few hot takeout items. The store is open 8 am to 8 pm daily.

The *Komoda Store & Bakery*, on Baldwin Ave just south of the intersection of Hwys 390 and 365, is a family-run place that bakes tempting cream puffs, cinnamon rolls and other pastries. It opens at 7 am, and the bakery items typically run out by noon.

Entertainment

Casanova (☎ 572-0220) is East Maui's hottest music spot, bringing in mainland performers as well as some of Hawaii's top musicians. The typical schedule features a DJ on Wednesday and Thursday and live bands – anything from rock and reggae to Jawaiian and jazz – on weekends. The cover charge is usually $5 to $8 for local bands, $20 to $25 for big names.

Cafe Makawao sometimes hosts acoustic music or poetry readings.

HAIKU

Scenic back roads head out in all directions from Makawao, and almost any one you choose to explore will make a prime country drive.

Some of those roads lead through Haiku, a scattered community that stretches north from Makawao down the slopes to the Hana Hwy. From Makawao, take Kaupakalua Rd (Hwy 365) north. After a mile, turn left onto Kokomo Rd, which passes through pineapple fields before reaching the modest village that marks the center of Haiku.

Alexander & Baldwin grew their first 12 acres of sugarcane near Haiku, and the village once had both a sugar mill and a pineapple cannery. Today, the old cannery houses a few local eateries, a grocery store and a hardware store.

Haiku is seeing a bit of a revival. Its rural character and its proximity to Makawao and Hookipa have attracted a number of new residents, including windsurfers, artists and New Age folks. The area has some interesting places to stay and makes a fairly convenient base for exploring the whole island.

Places to Stay

Bamboo Mountain Sanctuary (☎ 572-5106, fax 573-2281, zendo1@gte.net, 1111 Kaupakalua Rd, Haiku, HI 96708) makes an interesting place to stay if you're looking for a meditative experience. Tucked backed in the woods a few miles from the coast, it occupies a rustic plantation house on the grounds of a New Age retreat center. The five clean, simple rooms have wood floors and either a queen, a double or two twin beds. Showers are in the hall. The cost is $45/60 for singles/doubles; the seventh night is free on weekly stays. The setting is serene, with verandas overlooking the surrounding forest, and guests have access to a kitchen, a living room with a video library and a meditation room; massage and yoga can be arranged. The sanctuary maintains a website at home1 .gte.net/zendo1.

Lanikai Farm (☎ 572-1111, fax 572-3498, lanibb@maui.net, 100 S Lanikai Place, PO Box 797, Haiku, HI 96708), run by Margaret and Achim Koebke, is a contemporary home in a residential neighborhood about a 10-minute drive from Hookipa Beach. The house has three guest rooms, each with a queen bed and a small refrigerator. A common room contains a TV, VCR and microwave, and there's a squash court on the premises. Two of the rooms share a bath and cost $70/75 for singles/doubles; the other has a private bath and costs $100. Also available is a two-bedroom apartment with queen beds, a fireplace, kitchen and lanai for $90. Rates for the three guest rooms include breakfast every morning; rates for the apartment include breakfast only the first morning. Both English and German are spoken. There's a two-night minimum stay.

Pilialoha (☎ 572-1440, fax 572-4612, machiko@pilialoha.com, 2512 Kaupakalua Rd, Haiku, HI 96708) is a delightful cottage in upcountry Haiku, about 2 miles from the center of Makawao. Owned by Machiko and Bill Heyde, the cottage is set in a eucalyptus grove and has oak floors, sliding glass doors, a deck, a bedroom with a queen bed and a second room with a single bed. Other amenities include a fully equipped kitchen, washer/dryer, phone and a living room with cable TV, VCR, CD player and queen sofa bed. Machiko, an artist, has quilted and painted the pillows and adds other charming touches, such as roses cut daily from her garden. The cost is $100 for one or two

people, $120 for three. There's a three-day minimum stay, and smoking is allowed outdoors only. Kona coffee, tea, fruit and homemade granola and breads are provided for breakfast; if you don't eat sugar, Machiko will bake with honey. For more details, visit the website www.pilialoha.com.

Halfway to Hana House (☎ 572-1176, fax 572-3609, gailp@maui.net, PO Box 675, Haiku, HI 96708) is not actually in Haiku, but about 5 miles southeast of it, on the road to Hana. It consists of a cozy studio unit at the side of the home of Gail Pickholz, a friendly host who prepares the room for guests with tropical flower arrangements. The studio has a private entrance and bath, a double bed, microwave, hot plate, toaster oven, coffeepot and an unobstructed view across treetops to the ocean. The cost is $60/70 for singles/doubles with breakfast, $55/65 without. There's a three-night minimum; smoking is not allowed. You can see photos of the house at Gail's website, www .maui.net/~gailp.

PUKALANI

Pukalani, on the way to Haleakala, is a residential community with a population of 6000, making it the biggest Upcountry town.

Pukalani is 2 miles from Makawao along Hwy 365. If you're coming from Kahului, take the Haleakala Hwy (Hwy 37), which climbs for 6 miles through cane fields before reaching Pukalani. If you just want to go to Haleakala or Kula, take the new bypass that skirts Pukalani; if you want to visit the town, stay on Hwy 37.

The Pukalani Terrace Shopping Center, south of the intersection of Hwys 365 and 37, has a coin laundry and a bank with an ATM. A couple of gas stations are on Hwy 37 in the center of town; the Minit Stop station, next to McDonald's, is open 4 am to 11 pm daily.

Places to Eat

The Pukalani Terrace Shopping Center has a *Foodland* supermarket with a deli and bakery, open 5 am to midnight daily, a *Pizza Hut* with takeout service only, a *Subway* and a *Chinese restaurant*.

MAUI

McDonald's is a little farther up the highway, next to a convenience store that sells fried chicken and giant steak fries by the piece.

Pukalani Terrace Country Clubhouse (☎ 572-1325) is where Pukalanians head when they want to go out. It's above the golf course, three-quarters of a mile past the shopping center on Pukalani St. The $9.25 lunch buffet offers hot dishes like teriyaki chicken and mahimahi, as well as a salad and soup bar. Complete Hawaiian plates, which include kalua pig, lomi salmon, poi and haupia, cost about $8, while chicken and beef dishes are a few dollars more. Standard breakfast fare is around $5. The dining room has a good view down to the ocean and is open 8 am to 2 pm and 5 to 9 pm daily. Things can be a bit hectic at lunch, as the restaurant is a popular stop for Japanese tour buses.

KULA

The Kula region, perched at an average elevation of 3000 feet, is the agricultural heartland of Maui. Crops such as lettuce, tomatoes, carrots, cauliflower and cabbage thrive in Kula's warm days, cool nights and rich volcanic soil. No gourmet cook in Hawaii would be without sweet Kula onions.

During the California gold rush in the mid-19th century, Hawaiian farmers in Kula shipped so many potatoes off to the miners that the area became known as 'Nu Kaleponi,' the Hawaiian pronunciation for New California. In the late 19th century, Portuguese and Chinese immigrants moved in to farm the Kula area after they had worked off their contracts on the sugar plantations.

Kula grows most of Hawaii's proteas, large bright flowers with an unusual flair. Some, like the pincushion varieties, are very delicate, and others have spinelike petals. Almost 90% of the carnations used in leis throughout Hawaii are grown in Kula, as are many of the chrysanthemums. In spring, you'll find a burst of color right along the roadside as well, as the purple blossoms of the jacaranda tree and the yellow flowers of gold oak bloom in profusion.

Hwy 377 (Haleakala Hwy) and Hwy 37 (Kula Hwy) are both scenic. Take your pick, or go up one and down the other.

Gardens

All of Kula is a garden, but if you want to take a closer look, you can visit several established walk-through gardens.

Clouds' Rest Protea Farm, a mile off Hwy 377 along Upper Kimo Drive, has a little garden area with plants identified by plaques. You can stroll through it for free from 8 am to 4:30 pm daily. Cut proteas are on sale at rock-bottom prices at the farm and at more typical prices by mail order.

Sunrise Market, on Hwy 378 on the way to Haleakala, has a free roadside garden with a small but select group of proteas.

Kula Botanical Gardens is a mature garden, pleasantly overgrown and shady, with walking paths that wind past a wide variety of tropical plants. It's on Hwy 377, three-quarters of a mile up from the southern intersection of Hwys 377 and 37. The garden is open 9 am to 4 pm daily, and admission is $4 for adults, $1 for children.

The more recently established **Enchanting Floral Gardens** is sunny, open and orderly, with both tropical and cool-weather flowers. It has a colorful collection, and most plants are labeled in both Japanese and English. It's on Hwy 37 at the 10-mile marker and is open 9 am to 5 pm daily. Admission is $5 for adults, $1 for children.

The University of Hawaii maintains a 20-acre **Agricultural Research Center** in Kula. It's there that Hawaii's first proteas, natives of Australia and South Africa, were established in 1965. You can walk through rows of their colorful descendants, as well as dozens of new hybrids under development. The protea has more than 1400 varieties and is named after the Greek god Proteus, who was noted for his ability to change form.

There are now more than 50 protea farms in Hawaii, supplying freshly cut flowers to florists in the US, Japan and Europe. The nearest is just across the street from the research center.

Some sections of the research center garden are used for experiments in plant pathology and are thus closed to visitors, but the rest of the garden is open to the public until 3:30 pm Monday to Thursday (Friday is the day set aside for pesticide spraying).

The research center is about a half mile above town; to get there, follow Copp Rd (between the 12- and 13-mile markers on Hwy 37) and turn left on Mauna Place.

Octagonal Church
The octagonal Holy Ghost Church is a hillside landmark in Waiakoa village. This distinctive white building has a roof that glints silver in the sun and is easily visible from the highway. Built in 1897 by Portuguese immigrants, the church features a beautifully ornate interior that looks like it came right out of Portugal, and much of it did. Because of problems with termites, the church was dismantled and completely renovated in 1992.

Places to Stay
Kula View Bed & Breakfast (☎ 878-6736, 140 Holopuni Rd, PO Box 322, Kula, HI 96790) is less than a mile east of Hwy 37 in Waiakoa. Occupying the 2nd floor of Susan Kauai's home, the B&B offers a pleasant studio room with nice views of the garden and distant ocean. The room has a queen bed, mini-refrigerator, toaster oven, coffeepot, dining table, desk, private entrance and bath. The rate of $85 includes a breakfast of homemade muffins, juice, local fruit and coffee. Smoking is not allowed. There's a two-night minimum stay.

Kula Lodge (☎ 878-2517, 800-233-1535, fax 878-2518, RR1 Box 475, Kula, HI 96790), on Hwy 377, has five cottages in the same complex as its restaurant. All have private decks and are pleasant but not notably special for the money. Cheapest is a studio without a view for $110. Other units include two cottages for $135, each with a queen bed and a small loft with two futons; and two larger cottages for $165, with a similar setup but with twin beds in the loft and the addition of gas fireplaces. It costs $10 more for each occupant beyond two. There are no TVs or phones, and breakfast is not included in the rates.

Camp Kula (☎ 876-0000, camper@maui .net, PO Box 111, Kula, HI 96790) is a gay bed and breakfast on 7 secluded acres with views of central Maui. There are three guest rooms. The Prince Kuhio Room has a single bed and a shared bath for $42 to $50, depending on the season. The Queen Emma Suite has a king bed, TV, VCR and private bath, while the King Kamehameha Room has a double bed, TV, VCR, private lanai and shared bath; each of these rooms costs $52/65 for singles/doubles in the low season, $62/78 in the high season. The rates include a breakfast of herbal teas, homegrown fruits and baked goodies. HIV-positive guests are welcome.

Places to Eat
The venerable *Kula Lodge*, on Hwy 377 less than a mile north of Haleakala Crater Rd, has wraparound windows and a fine view of central Maui and the ocean beyond. Alas, the food is less inspired. Breakfast, served from 6:30 to 11:15 am, features pancake and egg dishes for $7 to $10. At lunch, burgers and sandwiches cost around $10, while the dinner menu features pricey pastas and steaks. The Kula Lodge serves dinner until 8:30 pm daily.

You'll find a similar view and better food at the family-run *Kula Sandalwoods Restaurant*, just past Kula Lodge on the inland side of Hwy 377. Breakfast, which is served until 11 am, includes waffles, omelettes and a superb eggs Benedict, while lunch features hearty sandwiches and fresh salads. Most items cost $5 to $10. It's open 6:30 am to 2 pm daily (to noon on Sunday).

Sunrise Market is a quarter mile up from the intersection of Hwys 378 and 377 on the way to Haleakala. You can pick up your morning coffee here along with bakery items, wrapped sandwiches and fresh and dried fruits. The store is open 7:30 am to 4 pm daily.

Cafe 808, a quarter mile south of the Octagonal Church in Waiakoa, is a popular local eatery. From 6 to 11 am, you can order either banana pancakes, an omelette with home fries or loco moco (rice topped with hamburger, egg and gravy) for around

$5. At lunch and dinner, the cafe serves inexpensive sandwiches, burgers and plate lunches. It's open until 8 pm daily. There's a small *grocery store* across the street.

POLIPOLI SPRING STATE RECREATION AREA

Polipoli Spring State Recreation Area is high up in the Kula Forest Reserve on the western slope of Haleakala. The park is in a coniferous forest and has picnic tables, camping and a network of trails. It's not always possible to get all the way to the park without a 4WD, but it's worth driving even part way up for the view.

Waipoli Rd, the road to the park, is off Hwy 377 just under half a mile before its southern intersection with Hwy 37. The turnoff is marked with a Na Ala Hele sign.

Waipoli is a narrow, switchbacking one-lane road through groves of eucalyptus and open rangeland (watch for cattle on the road). Layers of clouds often drift in and out; when they lift, you'll get panoramic views across green rolling hills to the islands of Lanai and Kahoolawe.

Few people venture up this way, and, except for the symphony of bird calls, everything is still.

When the clouds are heaviest, visibility is measured in feet. The road has some soft shoulders, but the first 6 miles are paved. The road then enters the forest reserve and turns to dirt. When it's muddy, the next 4 miles up to the state park are not worth trying in a standard car.

The whole area was planted during the 1930s by the Civilian Conservation Corps (CCC), a Depression-era work program. Several of the trails pass through old CCC camps. There are stands of redwood, ash, cypress, cedar and pines. It all looks somewhat like the Northern California coast.

Waiakoa Loop Trail

The trailhead for the Waiakoa Loop Trail starts at the hunter check station 5 miles up Waipoli Rd. Walk three-quarters of a mile down the grassy spur road on the left to a gate marking the trail. The hike, which starts out in pine trees, makes a 3-mile loop. You can also connect with the Upper Waiakoa Trail at a junction about a mile up the right side of the loop.

Upper Waiakoa Trail

The Upper Waiakoa Trail is a maintained 7-mile trail that's been reconstructed in recent years by the Na Ala Hele group. The trail begins off Waiakoa Loop at an elevation of 6000 feet, climbs 1800 feet, switchbacks and then drops back down 1400 feet. It's stony terrain, but it's high and open, with good views. Bring plenty of water.

The trail ends on Waipoli Rd between the hunter check station and the campground. If you want to start at this end of the trail, keep an eye out for the trail marker for Waohuli Trail, as the Upper Waiakoa Trail begins across the road.

Boundary Trail

The 4-mile Boundary Trail is a marked and maintained trail that begins about 200 yards beyond the end of the pavement. Park to the right of the cattle grate that marks the boundary of the Kula Forest Reserve.

This is a steep downhill walk that crosses gulches and drops deep into woods of eucalyptus, pine and cedar, as well as a bit of native forest. In the afternoon, the fog generally rolls in and visibility fades.

Skyline Trail

This 6½-mile trail is the major link in a hiking route that begins at 9750 feet near the summit of Haleakala and leads down to Polipoli campground at 6200 feet, a total distance of 8½ trail miles.

Starting at the top, in Haleakala National Park, go past the summit and take the road to the left just before Science City. The Skyline Trail, a dirt road used to maintain the state park, starts in open terrain made up of cinder and craters.

After 3 miles, you'll reach the tree line (at an elevation of 8500 feet) and enter a native mamane forest. In the winter, mamane is heavy with clusters of delicate yellow flowers that look like sweet-pea blossoms.

Skyline Trail eventually merges into Haleakala Ridge Trail, which then connects with Polipoli Trail, a half-mile spur to the campground.

There's solitude on this walk. And if the clouds treat you kindly, you'll have broad views all the way beween the barren summit and the dense cloud forest.

Places to Stay

Tent camping is free with a permit from the state, but facilities are limited. There are rest rooms, but no showers or drinking water.

Polipoli also has one housekeeping cabin that rents for $45 for up to four people. Unlike the other state cabins, this one has gas lanterns and a wood-burning stove but no electricity or refrigerator. For reservations, contact the Division of State Parks (☎ 984-8109), State Office Building, 54 High St, Wailuku, HI 96793.

Come properly prepared, as this is cold country; winter temperatures frequently drop below freezing at night. Fellow campers are likely to be pig hunters.

For information on obtaining a camping permit, see Camping in the Accommodations section near the beginning of this chapter.

KEOKEA

Around the turn of the 20th century, Keokea was home mainly to Hakka Chinese who farmed the remote Kula region.

Although there's not much to it, Keokea is the last real town before Hana if you're swinging around the southern part of the island. It has a coffee shop, gas pump and two small stores: the Fong Store and the Ching Store.

The village's green-and-white St John's Episcopal Church was built in 1907 to serve the Chinese community. 'St John's House of Worship' is still written in Chinese above the door.

On a clear day, you'll enjoy good views of West Maui and Lanai from the church and elsewhere along the roadside.

Places to Stay

Moonlight Garden Bed & Breakfast (☎ 878-6977, *mauimoon@maui.net, 213 Kula Hwy, Kula, HI 96790*) consists of two lovely freestanding cottages adjacent to the home of Anne and Marvin Miura. The place is quiet and secluded despite being within walking distance of the Keokea village center. The grounds are gardenlike with fruit trees and bamboo, and the hosts are friendly and knowledgeable. The one-bedroom cottage, which is spacious and has a fireplace, costs $95. The two-bedroom cottage, which has a queen bed in one bedroom and two twins in the other, costs $105. Both options have full kitchens, TVs, phones, washer/dryers, pleasant Hawaiian decor and large decks that enjoy splendid sunset views clear out to the sea. Prices are for double occupancy; add $20 per person for additional guests. Breakfast items, including fresh fruit, muffins, granola and Kona coffee, are supplied daily; vegan diets can be accommodated. Smoking is permitted outside only.

Bloom Cottage (☎/fax 878-1425, RR2 Box 229, Kula, HI 96790) is a two-bedroom freestanding cottage in town. It has a kitchen, TV, VCR, front porch and a fireplace to ward off evening chills. The rate is $115 for doubles, $20 for each extra person, with breakfast fixings provided. There's a two-night minimum stay, and smoking is not allowed.

Silver Cloud Guest Ranch (☎ 878-6101, 800-532-1111, fax 878-2132, slvrcld@maui .net, RR2 Box 201, Kula, HI 96790) is a former ranch turned B&B. It's on Thompson Rd, in a country setting just over a mile from central Keokea. The atmospheric plantation home has six guest rooms, all with private baths. The cheapest room ($85) is small and simple, while the most expensive ($125) is large and airy with a private porch and a fine ocean view. The house has a formal living room with hardwood floors, a fireplace, a piano and lots of upholstered chairs and love seats that invite lounging.

In addition, the bunkhouse out back has been converted into five small studios, each with a kitchenette and French doors leading to a little porch; a couple of them have nice ocean views. Rates are $105 to $145, but, as might be expected, the bunkhouse is not as refined as the plantation house. There's also a separate cottage with a wood-burning stove and covered lanai for $150. Breakfast

MAUI

is included in all rates; trail rides are available. For more information, visit the ranch's website at www.maui.net/~slvrcld.

Places to Eat

Upcountry folks gravitate to **Grandma's Coffee House** (☎ 878-2140), on Hwy 37, for homemade pastries and fresh dark-roasted Maui coffee. This cheery little place also has sandwiches and a few lunch items for around $6. Grandma's is open 7 am to 5 pm daily.

The family that owns Grandma's has been growing coffee beans on the slopes of Haleakala since 1918. If you want to see what coffee trees look like, just walk out to the side porch.

You can pick up a few simple grocery items next door at **Fong Store**.

ULUPALAKUA RANCH

From Keokea, Hwy 37 winds south through ranch country with good views of Kahoolawe and the little island of Molokini. Even on overcast days, you can often see below the clouds to sunny Kihei on the coast.

Tedeschi Vineyards, in the middle of Ulupalakua Ranch, is 5¹/₂ miles south of Keokea.

In the mid-19th century, Ulupalakua Ranch was a sugar plantation owned by whaling ship captain James Makee. The 25,000-acre ranch has been owned by Pardee Erdman and family since 1963. It's a working ranch with about 6000 head of cattle, 600 Merino sheep and 150 head of Rocky Mountain elk.

Ulupalakua Ranch Store, opposite the ranch headquarters, is a small local store selling cowboy hats, T-shirts, souvenirs, snack items, sandwiches and ice cream. It's open 9 am to 5 pm daily. Be sure to check out the wooden cowboys on the front porch; they were carved by the late artist Reems Mitchell, who lived on the ranch.

Tedeschi Vineyards

Tedeschi Vineyards (☎ 878-6058) planted its first grapes in 1976. While waiting for the vines to mature, the vineyard began producing Maui Blanc, a pineapple wine that is surprisingly light and dry.

Tedeschi now makes a variety of wines from grapes – sparkling wine, red, rosé and blush zinfandel – which you can try out in the tasting room from 9 am to 5 pm daily. Free winery tours are given between 9:30 am and 2:30 pm.

Opposite the winery, you can see the remains of the three stacks of the Makee Sugar Mill, built in 1878.

PIILANI HWY

The Piilani Hwy (Hwy 31) curves along the southern flank of Haleakala. From Tedeschi Vineyards, it's 25 rugged miles to the town of Kipahulu, near Oheo Gulch, the southern end of Haleakala National Park.

Someday, in an asphalt future, this may well be a real highway with cars zipping along in both directions. For now, it's an unspoiled adventure. Signs such as 'Motorists Assume Risk of Damage Due to Presence of Cattle' and 'Narrow Winding Road, Safe Speed 15mph' give clues that this is not your standard highway.

The hardest part is finding out if the road is currently open and passable. Many tourist maps mark it as impassable, and car rental agencies say that just being on it is a violation of their contract.

There are a couple of possibilities for getting the latest on road conditions. While the best is word of mouth from other drivers, you can also call the Oheo Gulch ranger station (☎ 248-7375) daily between 9 am and 5 pm or the county public works department (☎ 248-8254) weekdays between 6:30 am and 3 pm.

The trickiest section of the drive is around Kaupo, where the road goes over a couple of rocky creek beds. These are usually dry and pose little problem. But after hard rains, streams flow over the road, making passage difficult, if not dangerous. Flash floods sometimes wash away portions of the road, making it impossible to get through until it's repaired.

The best way to approach the drive is with an early morning start. Take something to munch and plenty to drink, and check your oil and spare tire. It's a long haul to civilization if you break down, and the tow charge is said to be around $400. If all goes well, you could be soaking in one of Oheo's pools by early afternoon.

The road between the winery and the Kaupo area has been upgraded in recent years and is now in pretty good condition. After that, there are 5 unpaved miles continuing east toward Kipahulu; depending on when this section of road was last graded, you might face a couple of torturous climbs over rocky riverbeds.

A 4WD, or at least a high-riding car with a manual transmission, will make for the easiest going and minimize your chances of bottoming out.

Keokea is the last place on the Kula side to get gas and something to eat. In the Oheo Gulch area, you might find a fruit stand, but drinking water, gas stations and other services are nonexistent until you reach Hana.

Tedeschi Vineyards to Kaupo

South from Tedeschi Vineyards, groves of fragrant eucalyptus trees soon give way to a drier and scrubbier terrain. It's open rangeland here; cattle graze right beside the road and occasionally mosey across in front of you.

A few miles south of the winery, the road crosses an expansive lava flow dating from 1790, Haleakala's last eruption. This flow, which is part of the Kanaio Natural Area Reserve, is the same one that covers the La Perouse area of the coast south of Makena. It's still black and barren all the way down to the sea.

Just offshore is the crescent island of Molokini with Kahoolawe beyond. The large grassy hills between here and the sea are volcanic cinder cones.

Painters sometimes set up their easels along the roadside to paint scenes of the grassy rock-strewn hills and the distant ocean. There's such a wide-angle view that the ocean horizon is noticeably curved.

As the road continues, it runs in and out of numerous gulches and crosses a few bridges, gradually getting closer to the coast. Around the 28-mile marker, keep an eye out for a natural lava sea arch. As you continue, you'll pass a few black-sand beaches.

Kaupo

Kaupo Gap is a deep and rugged valley providing the only lowlands on this section of coast. The village of Kaupo is around the 35-mile marker. However, don't expect a developed village in any sense of the word, as Kaupo is spread out and there's really not much to see. This is home for the scattered community of paniolos – many of them third-generation ranch hands – who work the Kaupo Ranch.

Kaupo General Store, on the east side of the gap, is 'the only store for 20 miles' and sells snacks, beer and wine. Officially, the hours are from around 9:30 am to 5 pm Monday to Saturday, but they can be a bit flexible, so it's best not to count on it being open. At the west side of the store, Auntie Jane commonly sets up an afternoon lunch wagon selling burgers and sandwiches.

Kaupo was once heavily settled. It has three heiaus from the 18th century and two churches from the 19th century. Loaloa Heiau, the largest, is a registered national historical monument. All three heiau sites are mauka of Huialoha Church.

Huialoha Church, which is less than a mile east of Kaupo General Store, is on the rocky black-sand Mokulau Beach. The attractive whitewashed church, built in 1859 and restored in 1978, is surrounded by a stone wall and a few windswept trees. Mokulau, which means 'many small islands,' is named for the rocks just offshore. The area was an ancient surfing site.

From here the road curves in and then out, at which point it's well worth stopping and looking back for a picturesque view of the church across the bay. There used to be a landing in the bay for shipping Kaupo Ranch cattle, and you can still see steps leading down into the water on a rock jutting out into the ocean. This area is cool and forested, with sisal plants on the hillsides.

As the road winds into Kipahulu, it skirts the edge of rocky cliffs and the vegetation picks up. First you'll see increasing numbers of hala and guava trees. Then as you return to civilization, the road is shaded with big mango trees, banyans, bougainvillea and wiliwili trees with red tiger-claw blossoms. For details on Kipahulu, see the end of the Hana to Kipahulu section, earlier in this chapter.

Haleakala National Park

Haleakala, the world's largest dormant volcano, is 7½ miles long and 2½ miles wide. It last erupted 200 years ago.

Haleakala National Park centers around the volcano's crater, an awesome geological wonder. The crater resembles the surface of the moon, its seemingly lifeless floor dotted with high majestic cinder cones. The park offers impressive views from the rim and hikes across the crater floor.

In Hawaiian, Haleakala means 'House of the Sun.' The volcano has long been considered Maui's soul, and its summit is thought to be an energy vortex, a natural power point for magnetic and cosmic forces.

In ancient times, it was a spiritual center for Hawaiian kahunas.

Whether it's the lingering mana of the gods who once made their home here or the geological forces of the earth that still release an occasional tremor, Haleakala does emanate a sense of omnipresent power.

The requisite pilgrimage to witness the sunrise at the rim of the crater can be an experience that borders on the mystical. Mark Twain referred to it as 'the sublimest spectacle' he'd ever seen.

Morning is usually the best time for viewing the crater. Later in the day, warm air generally forces clouds higher and higher until they pour through the two gaps in the crater's rim and into the crater itself.

Although sunrises get top billing, sunsets can be impressive too. Sometimes there's a high, thin layer of cirrus clouds and a lower layer of fluffier clouds, with the sunset reflecting colors on both levels. At other times, however, it's completely clouded over.

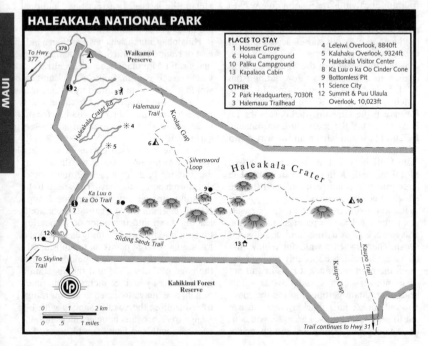

HALEAKALA NATIONAL PARK

PLACES TO STAY
1 Hosmer Grove
6 Holua Campground
10 Paliku Campground
13 Kapalaoa Cabin

OTHER
2 Park Headquarters, 7030ft
3 Halemauu Trailhead

4 Leleiwi Overlook, 8840ft
5 Kalahaku Overlook, 9324ft
7 Haleakala Visitor Center
8 Ka Luu o ka Oo Cinder Cone
9 Bottomless Pit
11 Science City
12 Summit & Puu Ulaula Overlook, 10,023ft

Haleakala National Park stretches from Haleakala Crater down to the pools of Oheo Gulch on the coast south of Hana. There are separate entrances to both sections of the park, but there's no passage between them. For information on the Oheo Gulch area, see the Hana to Kipahulu section earlier in this chapter.

Geology

In its prime, Haleakala probably reached a height of 12,000 feet before water erosion began to carve two large river valleys out of the rim. The valley gaps, Koolau Gap on the northwest side and Kaupo Gap on the southeast, are dominant features in the crater wall.

Later eruptions have added numerous cinder cones to the floor of Haleakala Crater. The yellow colors visible on the cinder cones are from sulfur, while the reds are from iron oxide.

Information

It's a good idea to check on weather conditions (☎ 871-5054) before driving up. It's not uncommon for it to be cloudy at Haleakala when it's clear on the coast. A drizzly sunrise is a particularly disappointing nonevent after getting out of bed at 4 am. The *Maui News* prints a sunrise schedule.

For information on scheduled activities, camping and general park conditions or to request a park brochure in advance, call ☎ 572-4400. You can also browse www.nps.gov/hale on the Web.

The park never closes. The pay booth at the park entrance opens after dawn, but you can drive through before that. Entrance passes, good for seven days, cost $10 per car. If you walk or cycle through, the cost is $5 per person. National park passes are valid and can be purchased at the gate, as can a $20 annual Haleakala pass.

Park headquarters, less than a mile from the park boundary, is open 7:30 am to 4 pm daily. The office has brochures, provides camping permits and sells books on geology and flora and fauna. A few silverswords grow in front of the building, and occasionally a pair of nene wander around the parking lot.

House of the Sun

Legend says that long ago, the goddess Hina was having problems drying her *tapa* (bark) cloth because the days were too short. Her son Maui, the prankish demigod for whom the island is named, decided to take matters into his own hands.

One morning, he went up to the mountaintop and waited for the sun. As it came up over the mountain, Maui lassoed the rays one by one and held on until the sun came to a halt. When the sun begged to be let go, Maui demanded that as a condition for its release it hereafter slow its path across the sky.

The sun gave its promise, the days were lengthened and the mountain became known as Haleakala, 'House of the Sun.' There are about 15 more minutes of daylight at Haleakala than on the coast below.

No food is sold in the park. Bring something to eat, particularly if you're going up for the sunrise; you don't want a growling stomach to rush you all the way back down the mountain before you've had a chance to explore the sights.

Haleakala Crater Rd

Haleakala Crater Rd (Hwy 378) runs 11 miles from Hwy 377 up to the summit. It's a good paved road, but it's steep and winding. You don't want to rush it.

The drive to the summit takes about 1¼ hours from Paia or Kahului, two hours from

Lahaina. If you need gas, fill up in Pukalani, as there are no services on Haleakala Crater Rd.

On your return from the summit, you'll see much of Maui unfolding below, with sugarcane and pineapple fields creating a patchwork on the valley floor. The highway snakes back and forth, and sometimes as many as four or five switchbacks are in view all at once.

Hosmer Grove Hosmer Grove, three-quarters of a mile before park headquarters, has a pleasant half-mile loop trail that begins in the campground. The trail starts in a forest of introduced trees and then passes into native Hawaiian shrub land.

The exotics in Hosmer Grove were introduced in 1910 in an effort to develop a lumber industry in Hawaii. They include incense cedar, Japanese sugi, Douglas fir, eucalyptus and various pines. Although the trees adapted well enough to grow, they didn't grow fast enough at these elevations to make tree harvesting practical. Thanks to this failure, today there's a park here instead.

Native plants include ohelo, pukiawe, mamane, pilo and sandalwood. There are wonderful scents and lots of bird calls along the trail.

Walking through either Hosmer Grove or the nearby Waikamoi Preserve, you might see the native iiwi or apapane, both fairly common sparrow-size birds with bright red feathers. The iiwi has a very loud squeaking call, orange legs and a curved salmon-colored bill. The apapane is a fast-moving bird with a black bill, black legs and a white undertail. It feeds on the nectar of ohia flowers.

You might also see the melodious laughing thrush, also called the spectacle bird for the circles around its eyes that extend back like a pair of glasses, and the greenish Japanese white-eye, also with eye circles. These two are nonnative species.

Waikamoi Preserve Waikamoi Preserve is a 5230-acre reserve adjoining Hosmer Grove. In 1983, Haleakala Ranch conveyed the land's management rights to the Nature Conservancy.

The area contains native koa and ohia rain forest and is a habitat for Hawaiian forest birds, including a number of rare and endangered species. The yellow-green Maui creeper and the crested honeycreeper, while both endangered, are more common than some of the others. The crested honeycreeper is a beautiful but aggressive bird that often dive-bombs apapane and chases them off branches.

The Nature Conservancy offers guided hikes on the second Saturday of each month

The Nene – Hawaii's State Bird

The native *nene*, Hawaii's state bird, is related to and resembles the Canada goose. It has been brought back from the verge of extinction (only 30 birds remained in 1951) by a captive breeding and release program.

Currently, Haleakala's nene population is holding steady at about 250. The birds generally nest in high cliffs surrounded by rugged lava flows with sparse vegetation.

Nene are rather curious. Many hang out where people do, from the crater floor cabins to park headquarters. Unfortunately, they don't do well in an asphalt habitat, and many have been run over by cars.

for a suggested donation of $15 ($5 for members). Reservations are required and can be made by calling the organization's office at ☎ 572-7849. The National Park Service offers free guided hikes that enter the preserve from Hosmer Grove campground at 9 am on Monday and Thursday.

Leleiwi Overlook Leleiwi Overlook, at an elevation of 8840 feet, is midway between park headquarters and the visitor center. From the parking lot, it's a five-minute walk out to the overlook, from where you can see the West Maui Mountains and both sides of the isthmus connecting the two sides of Maui. You also get another angle on Haleakala Crater.

In the afternoon, if weather conditions are right, you might see the Brocken specter, an optical phenomenon that occurs at high elevations. Essentially, by standing between the sun and the clouds, your image is magnified and projected onto the clouds. The light reflects off tiny droplets of water in the clouds, creating a circular rainbow around your shadow.

Kalahaku Overlook Kalahaku Overlook, elevation 9324 feet, is about a mile above Leleiwi Overlook. The lower section has a fenced enclosure containing lots of silversword, from seedlings to mature plants.

The upper section has an observation deck looking down into Haleakala Crater. With the help of the deck's information plaque, you can clearly identify seven cinder cones on the crater floor below.

For photography, afternoon light is best. In the early morning, you can get more favorable light by walking a few minutes down an unmarked path to the left of the observation deck.

Haleakala Visitor Center The visitor center, on the rim of the crater, is the main sunrise-viewing spot. It's open from shortly before sunrise to 3 pm daily.

The center has displays on geological and volcanic evolution and a recording explaining what you see on the crater floor 3000 feet below. Books on geology, plants and the national park are for sale here, and a ranger is usually on duty.

Summit The Puu Ulaula (Red Hill) Overlook, at 10,023 feet, is Maui's highest point. The summit building at the overlook has wraparound windows, and on clear days you can see the Big Island, Lanai, Molokai and even Oahu. The summit building is half a mile uphill from the visitor center.

The 37-mile drive from sea level to the summit of Haleakala is said to be the highest elevation gain in the shortest distance anywhere in the world.

Science City On the Big Island's Mauna Kea, scientists study the moon. Here at Haleakala, appropriately enough, they study the sun.

Science City, just beyond the summit, is outside park headquarters and off-limits to visitors. It's under the jurisdiction of the University of Hawaii, which owns some of the domes and leases other land for a variety of private and government research projects.

In addition to UH's solar observatory, the university's Institute of Astronomy operates a lunar ranging facility. Purdue University and the University of Wisconsin jointly operate a gamma ray telescope.

Defense-related projects include laser technology related to the 'Star Wars' project, satellite tracking and identification and a deep-space surveillance system. The newest military telescope, which became operational in 1997 and cost $123 million to build, is capable of identifying a grapefruit-size object flying in space thousands of miles away.

Activities

Natural or cultural history talks that last around 20 minutes are held at the summit building at 9:30, 10:30 and 11:30 am daily.

Park rangers lead a moderately strenuous two-hour hike that goes about a mile down Sliding Sands Trail into the crater; meet at the trailhead at 9 am on Tuesday and Friday.

Guided 3-mile hikes into the Waikamoi Preserve leave from Hosmer Grove campground at 9 am on Monday and Thursday and last about three hours.

MAUI

The Sunrise Experience

Sunrise at Haleakala is an unforgettable experience. As you drive up the mountain in the dark, the only sights are twinkling lights: a sky full of stars, scattered city lights resembling a large connect-the-dots drawing, and a distant fishing boat or two on the dark horizon.

About an hour before sunrise, the night sky begins to lighten and turn purple-blue, and the stars fade away. Interesting silhouettes of the mountain ridges appear.

Plan to arrive 30 or 40 minutes before the actual sunrise. The gentlest colors show up in the moments just before dawn. The undersides of the clouds lighten up first, accenting the night sky with pale silvery slivers and streaks of pink.

About 20 minutes before sunrise, the light intensifies on the horizon in bright oranges and reds, much like a sunset. Turn around for a look at Science City, whose domes turn a surreal pink.

Temperatures hovering around freezing and a cold wind are the norm at dawn. There's often a frosty ice in the top layer of cinders, which crunch underfoot.

If you don't have a winter jacket or sleeping bag to wrap yourself in, bring a warm blanket from your hotel. This will give you the option of sitting outside in a peaceful spot to take it all in rather than huddling for heat inside the crowded visitor center.

Everyone comes out for the grand finale. The moment the sun appears, the earth awakens and everything glows.

Every morning is different, but once the sun is up, the silvery lines and the subtleties disappear. The best photo opportunities occur before the sun rises.

Other activities take place less frequently. For example, guided hikes along the 12-mile Sliding Sands-Halemauu Trail are led once or twice a month, and evening stargazing programs and full moon hikes are occasionally offered in summer. All park programs and guided hikes are free.

Bicycle tours down Haleakala via the park road and horseback rides into the crater are detailed in the Activities section near the front of the Maui chapter.

Places to Stay

Camping Free tent camping is allowed at three campgrounds in the Upcountry section of the park and at one campground on the coast at Oheo Gulch. For information on the Oheo Gulch area, see the Hana to Kipahulu section earlier this chapter.

Hosmer Grove has a *drive-up campground* immediately after the park entrance. It includes picnic tables, grills, toilets and drinking water. Permits are not required, though there's a three-day camping limit per month. It's busier in summer than in winter and is often full on holiday weekends. Located at the 6800-foot elevation, Hosmer Grove tends to be cloudy and a bit wet.

Two *backcountry campgrounds* lie inside Haleakala Crater. One is at Holua, 4 miles down the Halemauu Trail, and the other is at Paliku, at the trail's end. Both are below steep cliffs, though Holua is dry and barren while Paliku is lush and wet.

Permits are required for backcountry camping at Haleakala National Park. They are issued at park headquarters on a first-come, first-served basis between 8 am and 3 pm on the day of the hike. Camping is limited to three nights in the crater each month, with no more than two consecutive nights at either campground.

Each campground is limited to 25 people. Permits can go quickly if large groups show up, a situation that is more likely to occur in summer.

The backcountry campsites have pit toilets and limited nonpotable water supplies. Fires are prohibited, and you'll need to carry out all your trash.

MAUI

Cabins Three primitive cabins lie along trails in the crater. The cabins – one each at Holua, Kapalaoa and Paliku – were built by the CCC in the 1930s, and each has a wood-burning stove, some cooking utensils, 12 bunks with sleeping pads (but no bedding), pit toilets and a limited supply of water and firewood. Hiking distances to the cabins from the crater rim range from 4 to 10 miles.

Cabin fees are $40 per night for a group of one to six people, $80 for seven to 12 people. There's a three-day limit, with no more than two consecutive nights in any cabin. Each cabin is rented to only one party at a time.

The problem here is the demand, which is so high the park service actually holds a monthly lottery to award reservations! To enter, your reservation request must be received two months prior to the first day of the month of your proposed stay (for example, requests for cabins on any date in July must arrive before May 1). Your chances are increased if you list alternate dates within the same calendar month and if you choose weekdays rather than weekends. A separate request is needed for each month.

Only written reservation requests are accepted (no phone or fax). You can send for a form or just submit the information on a regular sheet of paper; include your name, address, phone number, specific dates and cabins, and the number of people in your group. Mail it to: Cabin Lottery Request, Haleakala National Park, PO Box 369, Makawao, HI 96768.

Do not send money with your request form. If you are selected in the lottery, you will be notified, at which point the fees will have to be paid in full at least three weeks prior to the reservation date. They can be paid by Visa, MasterCard, check or money order.

Cancellations occasionally occur, creating last-minute vacancies. Calls regarding cancellations are accepted only between 1 and 3 pm daily, and you'll need to have a credit card available to secure the cabin if there is a vacancy.

HIKING THE CRATER

Hiking the crater floor offers a completely different angle on Haleakala's lunar landscape. Instead of peering down from the rim, you're looking up at the walls and towering cinder cones. It looks so much like a moonscape that US astronauts trained here before going to the moon.

The crater floor is a very still place to walk. The sound of cinders crunching underfoot is often the only noise to reach your ears.

The trails inside the crater connect with each other and are marked at junctions.

The weather at Haleakala can change suddenly from dry, hot conditions to cold, windswept rain. Although the general rule is sunny in the morning and cloudy in the afternoon, fog and clouds can blow in at any time.

No matter what the weather is like at the start of a hike, be prepared for temperatures that can drop into the 50s (°F) during the day and the 30s at night, at any time of year. Hikers without proper clothing risk hypothermia.

The climate also changes radically as you walk across the crater floor. In the 4 miles between the Kapalaoa and Paliku cabins, rainfall varies from an annual average of 12 inches to 300 inches. December to May is the wet season.

With the average elevation on the crater floor at 6700 feet, the relatively thin air means that hiking can be quite tiring. The higher elevation also means that sunburn is more likely. Take sunscreen, rain gear, a few layers of clothing and plenty of water.

Sliding Sands Trail

Sliding Sands, the summit trail into the crater, starts at the south side of the visitor center parking lot. The trail leads 9¾ miles to the Paliku campground and cabin, passing the Kapalaoa cabin at 5¾ miles. The first 6-mile segment of the trail follows the south wall of the crater.

From Kapalaoa to Paliku, the descent is gentle and the vegetation gradually increases. Paliku (6380 feet) is beneath a sheer cliff at the eastern end of the crater. In contrast to the crater's barren western end, this area

MAUI

Silversword

The strikingly beautiful silversword, with its pointed silver leaves, is a distant relative of the sunflower. The plant grows for four to 25 years before blooming just once.

In its final year, it shoots up a flowering stalk sometimes as high as 9 feet. During the summer, the stalk flowers with hundreds of maroon and yellow blossoms. When the flowers go to seed in late autumn, the plant dies.

The silversword, found only in Hawaii, was nearly wiped out in the early 20th century by grazing feral goats and by people who took them for souvenirs. It's making a comeback thanks to efforts by the park service staff members, who have fenced in sections of the park to protect the plants.

LEE FOSTER

receives heavy rainfall that makes for grassy campsites, with ohia forests climbing the slopes.

Sliding Sands-Halemauu Trail

One of the most popular day hikes for people in good shape is the 12-mile hike that starts down Sliding Sands Trail and returns via Halemauu Trail. It's a strenuous full-day outing.

Sliding Sands starts out at 9740 feet and descends steeply over loose cinders down to the crater floor. If you hike it after catching the sunrise, you'll walk directly into a gentle warmish wind and the rays of the sun. There are great views on the way down, but except for a few shrubs, there's no vegetation in sight.

Four miles down, after an elevation drop of 2500 feet, a spur trail leads north about 1½ miles to the Halemauu Trail.

Once on the Halemauu Trail, it's possible to take a short loop to the **Bottomless Pit**. Legends say the pit leads down to the sea, though the park service says it's just 65 feet deep. It's basically a large hole in the ground of limited interest.

About 1½ miles along the Halemauu Trail, the short **Silversword Loop** passes by silversword plants in various stages of growth. If you're here in summer, you should be able to see plants in bloom.

About a mile farther along Halemauu Trail you'll come to the Holua cabin and campground. A large **lava tube** here is worth exploring. At 6940 feet, this is one of the lowest areas along this hike, and you'll see impressive views of the crater walls rising a few thousand feet to the west. From the cabin, it's 4 miles to the Halemauu Trailhead.

Because of its steep descent, Sliding Sands Trail makes a better entry trail into the crater than a return trail. The Halemauu Trailhead, at an elevation of 8000 feet, is an easier exit.

Halemauu Trailhead is on Hwy 378, 6 miles below the visitor center (and the trailhead to Sliding Sands) and 3½ miles above park headquarters. If you haven't either arranged to be picked up or left a car at the trailhead, you could try your luck hitchhiking.

Halemauu Trail

If you're not up for a long hike, you might try doing just part of the Halemauu Trail. Even hiking in the first mile to the crater rim gives a fine view of the crater with Koolau Gap to the east. It's fairly level up to this point.

If you were to continue on the trail and hike down the switchbacks to the Holua cabin and back, the 8-mile roundtrip would be a fine day hike and a good workout. From the trailhead to the bottom of the cliffs, the trail descends 1400 feet. Once on the floor of the crater the trail follows the west wall for about a mile to the Holua cabin at 6940 feet. The trail continues another 6 miles to the Paliku cabin.

Halemauu Trailhead, 3½ miles above park headquarters, is marked. There's a fair chance you'll find nene in the parking lot.

Ka Luu o ka Oo Trail

Two miles down the Sliding Sands Trail (a descent of 1400 feet), a spur trail leads up the Ka Luu o ka Oo cinder cone, about half a mile to the north.

Midway along Ka Luu o ka Oo Trail are some silversword plants. From the visitor center to the cinder cone and back, it's a strenuous three-hour hike. Because of the uphill

climb back, this is a good hike to do early in the morning so as to avoid the midday heat.

Kaupo Trail

From the Paliku campground on the eastern edge of the crater floor, it's possible to continue another 8½ miles down to Kaupo on the southern coast. The first 3½ miles of the trail drops 2500 feet in elevation before reaching the park boundary. It's a steep rocky trail through rough lava and brushland. The last 5 miles pass through Kaupo Ranch property on a rough jeep trail as it descends to the bottom of Kaupo Gap, exiting at the east side of the Kaupo General Store. There are fine coastal views along the way.

The 'village' of Kaupo is a long way from anywhere, with very little traffic. Still, what traffic there is – largely sightseers braving the circle-island road – moves slow enough along Kaupo's rough road to start conversation. If you have to walk the final stretch, it's 10 miles to Oheo Gulch and what will seem like hordes of people and traffic.

This is a strenuous hike, and because of the remoteness and the ankle-twisting conditions, it's not advisable to hike it alone. The National Park Service publishes a Kaupo Trail brochure that people considering the hike should pick up in advance.

MAUI

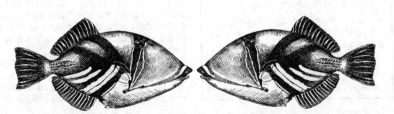

Molokai

Molokai is the last stronghold of rural Hawaii. It manages to survive in a sort of time warp: no packaged Hawaiiana, no high-rises, more farmers than tourists.

If you're looking for lots of action, this isn't the place. Instead, you can walk along Hawaii's largest beach with barely another soul in sight, or take the cliffside mule trail down to the old leprosy colony of Kalaupapa. Molokai offers quiet hikes, spectacular valleys and a handful of historical sites.

Molokai is the most Hawaiian of the main islands, with almost 50% of its population claiming native Hawaiian ancestry. It's only sparsely populated, with but a handful of small towns.

According to ancient chants, Molokai is a child of Hina, goddess of the moon. This is a place to get in touch with basics. In the morning, you can sit on the edge of an 800-year-old fishpond and watch the sun rise over Haleakala on distant Maui. In the evening, you can watch the sun set behind the silhouette of Molokai's royal coconut grove.

Molokai retains so much small-town character that at times it seems more like some forgotten outpost in the South Pacific than the island that lies between the high-rises of Maui and Oahu.

HISTORY

Molokai had powerful sorcerers whose reputations were well respected throughout the islands. Through carvings of poisonwood idols and other elaborate rituals, they were able to keep potential invaders at bay. For centuries, the battling armies of Maui and Oahu were careful to bypass Molokai.

By the 18th century, magic alone wasn't enough to protect the island from outside influences. Internal dissent among the *alii* (royal chiefs) of Molokai, largely over access to valuable fishing grounds at Moomomi, led the rulers to align themselves with chiefs from other islands. Oahu, Maui and the Big Island all got involved in the ensuing power struggle.

Eventually the king of Oahu, Peleioholani, established his rule over Molokai. When the daughter he left on Molokai was captured and killed by Molokai chiefs, Peleioholani hastily returned to the island and struck back with a vengeance. Those Molokai chiefs who were unable to flee to Maui were captured and roasted alive.

Oahu continued to rule over Molokai until 1785. Over the next decade, Maui and the Big Island, which were at war with each other, took alternate turns ruling Molokai until Kamehameha the Great finally united all the islands in 1795.

The first detailed description of the island was recorded by Captain George Vancouver, a British navigator, who anchored off Molokai in 1792. His estimate placed Molokai's population at around 10,000.

When the missionaries first arrived in the 1830s, they did a more detailed count, estimating Molokai's total population at 8700.

Molokai's largest settlements were on the rainy south coast of the eastern half of the island. The shallow waters and coastal indentations there were ideal for the construction of fishponds, and in the valley wetlands, taro patches flourished.

The missionaries found the densest populations between Kamalo and Waialua, and it is in this area that they established their first missions. Some of the churches still stand.

Highlights

- Riding a mule down the cliffs to Kalaupapa, the historic leper colony
- Strolling along Papohaku, Hawaii's longest beach
- Soaking up Kaunakakai's small-town atmosphere
- Enjoying the view at picturesque Halawa Valley

MOLOKAI

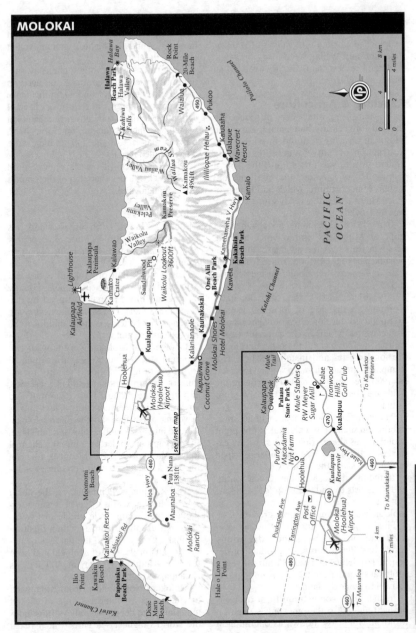

MOLOKAI

Kalaupapa Peninsula held the island's other major settlement, with about 2500 people. The North Shore valleys of Halawa, Pelekunu and Wailau were also populated. Molokai's central plains and dry western half were only lightly settled.

Ranching & Agriculture

Cattle and sheep, which were introduced in the mid-19th century, had a major impact on Molokai. Grazing resulted in widespread destruction of native vegetation, causing upland soils to wash down into the coastal fishponds. As a result, the centuries-old system of aquaculture, which had long provided Hawaiians with a ready source of food, was destroyed.

In the 1850s, Kamehameha V acquired the bulk of Molokai's arable land, forming Molokai Ranch. After his death, the ranch became part of the Bishop Estate, which sold it off to a group of Honolulu businesspeople in 1897.

A year later, in 1898, the American Sugar Company, a division of Molokai Ranch, attempted to develop a major sugar plantation in central Molokai. The company built a railroad system to haul the cane, developed harbor facilities and installed a powerful pumping system to draw up water. However, by 1900 the well water used to irrigate the fields had become so saline that the crops failed.

The company then got into honey production on such a big scale that at one point Molokai was the world's largest honey exporter. In the mid-1930s, an epidemic wiped out the hives and the industry.

In the meantime, Molokai Ranch continued its efforts to find 'the crop for Molokai.' Cotton, rice and numerous grain crops all took their turn biting Molokai's red dust.

Finally, pineapple took root as the crop most suitable for the island's dry, windy conditions. Plantation-scale production began in Hoolehua in 1920. Within 10 years, Molokai's population tripled as immigrants arrived to work the fields.

In the 1970s, competition from overseas brought an end to the pineapple's reign on Molokai. Dole closed down its operation in 1976, and the other island giant, Del Monte, later followed suit. These closures brought hard times and the highest unemployment levels in the state.

Then cattle raising, long a mainstay, suddenly collapsed. In a controversial decision in 1985, the state, after finding an incidence of bovine tuberculosis, ordered every head of cattle on Molokai to be destroyed. Molokai Ranch has since restocked some of its herd, but the majority of the 240 smaller cattle owners called it quits.

Molokai Ranch still owns about one-third of Molokai, or more than half of the island's privately held lands.

GEOGRAPHY

Molokai is Hawaii's fifth-largest island. It is 38 miles long, 10 miles wide and roughly rectangular in shape, with a land area of 264 sq miles.

The western half of Molokai is dry and arid, with rolling hills and the gradually sloping range of Maunaloa (1381 feet), capped by Puu Nana (1381 feet). The island's highest point, Kamakou (4961 feet), is in the middle of a rugged eastern half.

Geologically, Molokai is a union of two separate shield volcanoes that erupted to form two distinct islands. The lofty mountains of eastern Molokai acted like a screen, capturing the clouds. Heavy rainfall and stream erosion then cut deep valleys into its towering north face. Dry western Molokai formed into more modest hills and tableland. Later eruptions spilled lava into the channel that separated the two volcanoes, forming the Hoolehua Plains and creating present-day Molokai.

The Kalaupapa Peninsula, on the north side of Molokai, seems to have been an afterthought by Madame Pele, goddess of volcanoes. An eruption from the then-offshore Kauhako Crater created the flat lava peninsula long after the rest of Molokai had been formed. Kauhako Crater, at 400 feet, is Kalaupapa's highest point.

Molokai's North Shore, from Kalaupapa to Halawa, is a wilderness area of coastal mountains and deeply cut valleys. It includes the world's highest sea cliffs, which reach heights of 3300 feet with an average gradient of 58°. Hawaii's highest waterfall, Kahiwa Falls (1750 feet), drops from these cliffs.

The North Shore is spectacular, but for the most part its steep slopes and rain forests are virtually impenetrable. The main way to get into the valleys is by boat, but rough winter seas restrict that to the summer season.

CLIMATE

At Kaunakakai, the average daily temperature is 70°F in winter, 78°F in summer. The average annual rainfall is 27 inches.

FLORA & FAUNA

The two most dominant tree types on Molokai are *kiawe* in the drier areas and *ohia lehua* in the wetter. Along the banks of streams, which were once heavily cultivated with taro, forests of *kukui* (also called the candlenut tree) and guava now dominate. For more information on these plants, see the Facts about Hawaii chapter at the beginning of this book, as well as the Glossary at the back of the book.

The axis deer that run free in Molokai are descendants of eight deer sent from India in 1868 as a gift to King Kamehameha V. Feral pigs, introduced by the early Polynesian settlers, still roam the upper wetland forests, and feral goats inhabit the steep canyons and valley rims. All three wreak havoc on the environment and are hunted game animals.

Native water birds include the common moorhen, Hawaiian coot and black-necked stilt, which are all endangered. Molokai also has five native forest birds, mostly in the undisturbed upland forests, and the Hawaiian owl.

Humpback whales spend winters cavorting in the waters between Molokai, Lanai and Maui. In season, look for the whales off Molokai's southeast coast.

GOVERNMENT

Kalaupapa Peninsula is a quasi-county unto itself, called Kalawao, which is essentially administered by the state Department of Health. The rest of Molokai, along with neighboring Lanai, is swallowed up in the mire of Maui County.

Molokai Plan

In the 1980s, a Maui County Committee was appointed to create a community plan to address development issues on Molokai. The committee conducted hearings and surveys on Molokai, and much to the surprise of Molokai residents – who were used to being bullied by Maui's prodevelopment forces – the recommendations put forth in the final plan were tuned in to their own feelings on growth.

The Molokai Plan calls for the preservation of Molokai's rural lifestyle and the maintenance of agriculture as the basis of the island's economy. It also calls for all resort development to be limited to the West End and to be low-rise. The Molokai Plan has been widely accepted as the guiding code for land use on Molokai and is referred to whenever there are disputes over development – which is often.

You can pick up on a lot of local anti-development sentiment simply by noticing bumper stickers on Molokai pickup trucks, which bear such slogans as 'Molokai Is Too Small To Be Big' and 'Keep Molokai Molokai.'

MOLOKAI

Most administrative decisions affecting Molokai are made on Maui. Since many community planning and development issues are decided at a county level, the island of Maui, with 12 times Molokai's population, has the clout.

ECONOMY

Molokai has chronically high unemployment that hovers around 16% – roughly triple the state average.

After the huge pineapple plantations left Molokai in the late 1970s, islanders began to develop small-scale farming more intensely.

Molokai has rich soil, and some feel the island may have the potential to be Hawaii's 'breadbasket.' Significant crops include watermelons, dryland taro, macadamia nuts, sweet potatoes, string beans and onions.

On the southern shore, the Kaunakakai area has some of the world's best growing conditions for seed corn. Hawaii's climate makes it possible to produce three generations of hybrids each year versus only one on the mainland. Corn for seed has been raised in Hawaii since the late 1960s, and much of the corn produced in the USA can trace its roots to Molokai.

In 1991, coffee trees were planted on formerly fallow pineapple fields in Kualapuu and now cover some 600 acres.

POPULATION & PEOPLE

Molokai has a population of 6800. Outside of Niihau, Molokai is the most Hawaiian of the islands, with almost 50% of its people claiming Hawaiian or part-Hawaiian ancestry. Filipino is the next largest ethnic group, followed by Japanese and Caucasian.

The large Hawaiian population is in part due to the Hawaiian Homes Act of 1921, which awarded 40-acre blocks of land to people with at least 50% Hawaiian ancestry. The purpose of the act was to encourage homesteading among native Hawaiians, who had become the most landless ethnic group in Hawaii. The first settlements under the act were made on Molokai.

ORIENTATION

Molokai lies midway in the Hawaiian chain, 26 miles southeast of Oahu and 9 miles northwest of Maui. Lanai is 9 miles directly south.

The airport is on the island's flat central plains, more or less in the center of Molokai. As you leave the airport parking lot, turn right to reach Hwy 460. At the highway, either turn left to proceed to Kaunakakai, the main town, 7 miles away; or turn right and drive 13 miles to Kaluakoi Resort on the West End.

This one highway is Molokai's main road, stretching from east to west. From Kaunakakai westward, it's called Hwy 460 (Maunaloa Hwy). From Kaunakakai eastward, it's Hwy 450 (Kamehameha V Hwy).

Maps

The best map of Molokai, albeit not perfect, is the Molokai-Lanai map published by the University of Hawaii Press; it's sold in shops around Kaunakakai.

Exploring Molokai

Molokai is not the place to explore dirt roads just to see what's there. People on the island spend a lot of time outdoors, and their yards are extensions of their homes. Many dirt paths that seem like they could be roads are just driveways into someone's backyard. In addition, as on other islands, there's still a bit of *pakalolo* (marijuana) growing here and there. All in all, folks aren't too keen on outsiders cruising around on their private turf.

On the other hand, if there's a fishpond you want to see and someone's house is between the road and the water, it's usually easy to stop and strike up a conversation. Molokai people are generally receptive and friendly. If you ask permission first, they'll often let you cross their property. If you appear interested, they might even share a little local lore and history – the old-timers in particular can be fascinating to listen to.

INFORMATION
Tourist Offices
The Molokai Visitors Association (☎ 553-3876, fax 553-5288, mva@molokai-hawaii.com), Box 960, Kaunakakai, HI 96748, distributes tourist information about Molokai. From the US mainland and Canada, call ☎ 800-800-6367 (toll-free); from within Hawaii, call ☎ 800-553-0404; or visit the association online at molokai-hawaii.com.

Money
There are half a dozen banks and credit unions on the island; the Bank of Hawaii on Hwy 460 in Kaunakakai is the largest.

Post
The main post office is in downtown Kaunakakai; there are also post offices in Hoolehua, Kualapuu, Maunaloa and Kalaupapa.

Newspapers
Molokai's two weekly newspapers, both distributed free around the island, provide a glimpse of island life. *The Dispatch* (☎ 552-2781, www.aloha.net/~mkkdisp), Box 96, Maunaloa, HI 96770, is published each Thursday. The *Molokai Advertiser-News* (☎/fax 558-8253, molokaiman@flex.com), HC 01, Box 770, Kaunakakai, HI 96748, is published each Wednesday.

You can pick up a copy of the *Honolulu Advertiser* at C Pascua Store in Kaunakakai and at the airport.

Weather Hotlines
For recorded weather and marine forecasts by the National Weather Service, call ☎ 552-2477.

Emergency
Dial ☎ 911 for police, ambulance and fire emergencies. The Molokai General Hospital (☎ 553-5331) in Kaunakakai has 24-hour emergency service. The Molokai Helpline (☎ 553-3311) provides crisis counseling.

ACTIVITIES
Swimming
Papohaku Beach on the west coast is the broadest and longest sandy beach in all of Hawaii. Although it's a great walking beach, it's not safe for swimming. However, just a few miles south of Papohaku is Dixie Maru Beach, a popular family beach with a small protected bay.

If you're looking for something quieter, Kawakiu Beach, north of Kaluakoi Golf Club, is a beautiful crescent beach with fine coastal views and good swimming when seas are calm. Moomomi Beach, on the north coast, is another secluded coastal stretch, this one backed by expansive dunes.

In terms of swimming, the Kaunakakai area is a dud, with a coastline of silty, shallow waters. Most Kaunakakai visitors drive to the southeastern end of the island, where the beach around the 20-mile marker offers some of Molokai's best swimming and snorkeling. Rock Point, not far north of there, and Halawa Bay, at the northern end of the road, are popular surfing spots.

There are other beaches in remote places, but Molokai is about the last place you'd need to torture yourself with washed-out roads or trips through jungle growth simply to get away from it all. Those who have ever fantasized about having a vast secluded beach to themselves can simply drive up to the miles of gleaming sand at Papohaku.

Official Molokai

Molokai's official flower is the white *kukui* blossom, its official color is green and its nickname is 'The Friendly Island.'

MOLOKAI

Swimming Pools The Mitchell Pauole Center in Kaunakakai has a 25-meter pool free to the public from 8:30 am to 4:30 pm daily except on Thursday and Sunday, when it opens at 1 pm. It's not uncommon to have the pool to yourself, particularly in winter, when islanders consider the pool water to be cold.

Snorkeling

Molokai's snorkeling options are limited. The waters off 20-Mile Beach in East Molokai present the best opportunities for seeing some colorful fish.

Molokai Fish & Dive, on Ala Malama St in Kaunakakai, rents snorkel sets for $9 a day; you can buy a mask and snorkel for $30.

Kayaking

Phillip Kikukawa, the owner of Molokai Bicycle (☎ 553-3931, 800-709-2453 within Hawaii, molbike@aloha.net, www.bikehawaii .com/molokaibicycle), at 80 Mohala St in Kaunakakai, offers daily kayak rentals for $30 (single kayak) or $40 (double kayak). The shop's open 9 am to 2 pm Saturday and 4 to 7 pm Tuesday and Thursday, but you can arrange to pick up a kayak at other times.

Hiking

Molokai offers a handful of hiking opportunities. The Nature Conservancy's Kamakou Preserve features unique rain forest hikes in the island's rugged interior and out to scenic valley overlooks. The Palaau State Park area has a couple of good hiking options. One, the hike down the mule trail to Kalaupapa, not only offers fine views but also provides a way to reach the peninsula without dishing out a lot of money. A less frequented trail from the Kalaupapa Overlook provides a pleasant hour-long hike through a forest of fragrant eucalyptus and ironwood.

On the west side of the island, there's an easy hike to secluded Kawakiu Beach from the Kaluakoi Golf Course. The expansive white sands of the Papohaku Beach and Moomomi Beach offer fine walks as well.

Cycling

Molokai Bicycle (☎ 553-3931, 800-709-2453 within Hawaii, molbike@aloha.net), 80 Mo-

hala St in Kaunakakai, is a small operation run by Phillip Kikukawa, a local schoolteacher. He rents out mountain bikes with front suspension ($20 for the first day and $15 for subsequent days) and rigid-frame bikes ($15/14). Road bikes are also available for $24/20. Rentals include helmet, lock and water bottle; pick-up and drop-off services from the airport or elsewhere can be arranged. The shop hours are limited to 9 am to 2 pm on Saturday and 4 to 7 pm on Tuesday and Thursday, but it's possible to make advance arrangements to pick up a bike at other times. The shop's website is www.bikehawaii.com/molokaibicycle.

Horseback Riding

Molokai Ranch (☎ 552-2741, 800-254-8871) offers 2½-hour guided horseback rides for $90. The rides cross ranch pasture, providing views of the ocean and Lanai. For the more adventurous, the ranch can also organize a 'paniolo (cowboy) roundup,' complete with barrel racing, pole vending and cattle herding, as well as a 'cattle trail drive' geared to those who want to play cowhand while riding on the range.

Molokai Horse & Wagon Ride (☎ 558-8132) offers guided horseback rides that visit Iliiliopae Heiau and include both beach and mountain riding. The rides last about 1½ hours, cost $40 and are available every morning at 10 am.

Tennis

The Mitchell Pauole Center in Kaunakakai has two lighted tennis courts near the pool. There's no charge, and you can reserve a court in advance by calling ☎ 553-3204. Like everywhere else in Molokai, you're not likely to find a crowd waiting.

Golf

The Kaluakoi Golf Course (☎ 552-2739, 888-552-2550) is an 18-hole par 72 course open 7 am to 6:30 pm. There's also a driving range, a putting green and a pro shop. The cost for 18 holes, including a cart, is $45 for resort guests, $65 for nonguests. Clubs can be rented for $22, shoes for $10.

Although most tourists stick to the resort golf course, the Ironwood Hills Golf Club

(☎ 567-6000) in Kalae is the course of choice by islanders and is a real test of skill. It's open 7 am to 5 pm daily. Fees are $10 for nine holes or $14 for 18 holes, plus $7 to $14 for carts.

ORGANIZED TOURS
Van Tours
Kukui Tours & Limousines (☎ 552-2282) has three-hour island tours for $30 per person; these tours include the towns of Kaunakakai and Maunaloa, Kaluakoi Resort, Purdy's Macadamia Nut Farm and the Kalaupapa Overlook. Seven-hour tours, which add on a ride through eastern Molokai, cost $50. There's a three-person minimum. Kukui also has sightseeing vans that can be chartered at an hourly rate of $79 with a two-hour minimum.

Friendly Isle Tours (☎ 552-2218) has similar tours at similar prices.

Molokai Off-Road Tours & Taxi (☎ 553-3369) offers 4WD tours, including a 'rain forest adventure' of the interior forests for $53 with a four-person minimum.

Wagon Rides
If you're interested in the coffee biz, Coffees of Hawaii (☎ 567-9023, 800-709-2326) offers mule-drawn wagon tours through its coffee fields every weekday at 10 am and 1 pm, weather permitting. As nothing on Molokai is exactly bustling, it's best to call ahead to let the guides know you're coming, but reservations aren't required. The tours leave from the Espresso Bar, cost $14 ($7 for children under age 14) and last about an hour – a bit less if there aren't many questions for the guide.

Molokai Horse & Wagon Ride (☎ 558-8132, wgnride@aloha.net), Box 1528, Kaunakakai, HI 96748, is a small local operation that provides a horse-drawn wagon ride from the beach at Mapulehu to Iliiliopae Heiau. The cost is $35 (adults or children), and the company usually requires at least seven participants in order to operate the ride.

Water Activities
Molokai Charters (☎ 553-5852), Box 1207, Kaunakakai, HI 96748, offers a $40 two-hour sunset sail and a $50 four-hour sail that includes whale watching in season. There's also a full-day trip to Lanai that includes snorkeling and lunch for $90. All tours leave Kaunakakai aboard *Satan's Doll*, a 42-foot sloop. The boat goes out with a minimum of four people.

Bill Kapuni's Snorkel & Scuba Adventures (☎ 553-9867, bk@molokai-aloha.com, www.molokai-aloha.com/kapuni), Box 1962, Kaunakakai, HI 96748, has a 22-foot Boston whaler that can be used for snorkel and dive tours. The cost is $85 for a two-tank dive, $45 for snorkeling. Whale-watching, sunset, fishing and North Shore charters can be arranged.

Joe Reich (☎ 558-8377), Box 825, Kaunakakai, HI 96748, has a 31-foot boat, the *Alyce C*, that can be chartered for fishing trips, whale-watching jaunts and inter-island runs.

ACCOMMODATIONS
Molokai has a total of two hotels, five condo complexes and a handful of B&Bs.

The Kaunakakai area has one hotel, the Hotel Molokai, and one condo, Molokai Shores. Both front a beach with a good view of Lanai, but with waters unsuitable for swimming; each place does, however, have a swimming pool.

Molokai's only resort is Kaluakoi, on the west coast, which has one hotel, a golf club, three condo complexes and attractive white-sand beaches.

The only other development, the Wavecrest Resort condo complex, is 13 miles east of Kaunakakai, on Molokai's wetter, lusher eastern side.

Unless otherwise specified, the rates given in this chapter are the same for both singles and doubles.

Camping
Camping is allowed at Palaau State Park and Waikolu Lookout, at the county beach parks of Papohaku and One Alii, at the Kapuaiwa Coconut Grove and at the Waialua Pavilion and Campground.

State Parks Camping is free at Palaau State Park and at Waikolu Lookout, the latter a remote and primitive site just outside

MOLOKAI

Kamakou Preserve. There's a five-day maximum stay at each site. Permits, which are required, may be obtained at the Department of Land & Natural Resources office (☎ 567-6891), in the Molokai Water Systems building, which is just south of the post office on Puupeelua Ave (Hwy 480) in Hoolehua. It's open 7:30 am to 4 pm Monday to Friday. For Palaau State Park, you can also pick up permits directly from the state park caretaker, whose residence is immediately north of the mule stables on the road to Palaau State Park.

County Parks The Department of Parks & Recreation (☎ 553-3204) at the Mitchell Pauole Center in Kaunakakai issues camping permits for Papohaku and One Alii Beach Parks. The office is open 8 am to 4 pm Monday to Friday. Permits cost $3 per adult and 50¢ per child (age 17 and under) per day and can be obtained by mail (Box 1055, Kaunakakai, HI 96748) or in person. Permits are limited to three consecutive days; if you want to camp longer, you must return to the county parks office every three days for a new permit. Both parks have rest rooms, drinking water, showers and picnic areas.

Kapuaiwa Coconut Grove The Department of Hawaiian Home Lands (☎ 567-6296), Box 198, Hoolehua, HI 96729, on Puukapele Ave in Hoolehua, issues permits for only one group each night for camping at Kapuaiwa Coconut Grove, on the shore just west of Kaunakakai and east of Kalanianaole. The cost is $5 per night for the entire site. While it's usually booked by groups for parties, reunions and the like, individual travelers can stay when it's available. The site has electricity, water, picnic tables, rest rooms and showers.

Waialua Pavilion & Campground The Waialua Congregational Church operates this informal campground (☎ 558-8150, fax 558-8520, vacate@aloha.net), HC 1, Box 780, Kaunakakai, HI 96748, on the east side of Molokai. It's located in Waialua, just past the 19-mile marker. For $15 per night per person, campers are welcome to pitch a tent in the church's seaside picnic grounds, which are enclosed by a chain-link fence. There's a shower, toilet and picnic tables here. JoAnn Simms, a member of the congregation, lives nearby and handles the reservations. Groups occasionally book the grounds, so you should contact JoAnn in advance to confirm that space is available.

SHOPPING
Just about every shop in Kaunakakai has an assortment of T-shirts proclaiming Molokai's rural pride, with slogans such as 'Keep Hawaiian Lands in Hawaiian Hands' and 'Molokai Mo Bettah.' For other distinctive, local-color gifts, visit the Big Wind Kite Factory, which sells handmade kites, in Maunaloa.

Molokai-grown coffee is now being commercially harvested, and it can be purchased at the Coffees of Hawaii center in Kualapuu and in grocery stores around the island. Or you could take back the same stash islanders do when they leave Molokai: an island-grown watermelon and some fresh-baked Molokai bread from the Kanemitsu Bakery in Kaunakakai.

GETTING THERE & AWAY
Air
Island Air (☎ 800-652-6541 on the Neighbor Islands, 484-2222 in Oahu) flies directly to Molokai nine times per day from Honolulu, four times from Kahului and twice from Hana on Maui. One-way fares are $93.

Hawaiian Airlines (☎ 800-882-8811 on the Neighbor Islands, 838-1555 in Oahu) flies direct to Molokai twice daily from Honolulu at 6 am and 3:50 pm. There's a flight once daily from Kahului to Molokai at 2:50 pm. One-way fares are $93.

The Molokai Air Shuttle (☎ 567-6847 in Molokai, 545-4988 in Oahu) flies a five-passenger Piper airplane between Honolulu and Molokai on demand about half a dozen times a day. Unlike other commuter airlines, it doesn't hit up tourists for higher prices than it charges islanders. The cost is just $50 one way, $55 roundtrip. The catch is that you'll need to have your own car (or take a taxi) on the Honolulu side, as the Air

Shuttle is located at the back side of the airport, off Lagoon Drive.

Pacific Wings (☎ 888-575-4546), which flies eight-passenger Cessna 402s, offers four scheduled flights a day to Molokai from both Honolulu and Kahului, though pilots generally only stick to their schedule if they have advance bookings on the flight. The fares are $75 one way for tourists and $45 for Hawaii residents.

Paragon Air (☎ 800-428-1231) flies six-seater prop planes on demand to Molokai from both the Kahului and Kapalua West Maui airports. Paragon typically flies over to Molokai in the morning and back in the afternoon, but there's no regular schedule, and you may have to be flexible. On the plus side, Paragon charges a reasonable $50 one way and $89 roundtrip.

Information on flights to and from Kalaupapa is in the Kalaupapa section, later in this chapter.

For more information on air travel, including discounts and air passes, see the Getting Around chapter in the front of this book.

Molokai Airport Molokai Airport, also called Hoolehua Airport, contains car rental booths, a snack bar, a liquor lounge, a *lei* (garland) stand, rest rooms, pay phones and a visitor information booth that is occasionally staffed. The Molokai newspapers can be picked up free, and off-island papers are for sale.

The snack bar, which is open from 6:30 am to 6 pm daily, sells breakfast and lunch plates for around $7, cheeseburgers for $3, and carries loaves of Molokai bread.

Sea

Island Marine Activities (☎ 667-6165, 800-275-6969) operates the *Maui Princess*, a 118-foot boat that once provided daily commuter service for Molokai residents heading to jobs on Maui. Cutbacks in state funding brought an end to the commuter service, but the boat still cruises once a week to Kaunakakai carrying day visitors from Lahaina on Maui. It departs from Lahaina Harbor's Slip 3 at 6:15 am on Saturday, arrives in Kaunakakai at 8 am, then departs from Kauna-

kakai at 2 pm, arriving back in Lahaina at 3:30 pm. The roundtrip fare is $69 for adults, $35 for children.

You can take the boat one way, but the cost is the same. It may also be possible to go from Maui to Molokai one week and return the next week for the cost of a roundtrip ticket, but the return is on a space-available basis. One more caveat: Since the boat can be chartered privately by people who may want to use it on a Saturday, the day of the week it visits Molokai occasionally changes.

GETTING AROUND
Car

Renting a car on Molokai is just about essential if you intend to explore the island thoroughly. However, as there are currently only two major companies operating on Molokai, it's best to book well in advance, especially if you're planning on going over on a weekend.

Budget (☎ 567-6877) and Dollar (☎ 567-6156) both base their operations at the airport. Keep in mind that rental vehicles are officially not allowed to be driven on dirt roads, and with Dollar there can be restrictions on camping as well. See the Getting Around chapter in the front of this book for general rental information and toll-free reservation numbers.

There are gas stations in Kaunakakai and Maunaloa.

Taxi

There aren't any metered taxis on Molokai, but a couple of companies do provide taxi services for set fees. The taxis occasionally meet incoming flights, but to be assured of a ride from the airport, you should make advance reservations.

From the airport, Kukui Tours & Limousines (☎ 552-2282) charges $9 per person (with a two-person minimum) to the Kaluakoi Resort on the West End or to the Kaunakakai area, including Molokai Shores or Hotel Molokai.

Friendly Isle Tours (☎ 552-2218) also offers taxi services and airport transfers by pre-arrangement; with a three-person minimum, Friendly Isle charges $7 per person to the

Kaluakoi Resort and $9 per person to the Kaunakakai area.

Bicycle

For bicycle rentals, see Cycling in the earlier Activities section.

Kaunakakai

Kaunakakai, Molokai's biggest town, takes much of its character from what it doesn't have. There's not a single traffic light, no shopping centers and no fast-food chains.

Most of Molokai's businesses are lined up along Ala Malama St, the town's broad main street. The stores have aging wooden false fronts that give Kaunakakai the appearance of an old Wild West town. There are a couple of restaurants, a bakery, a post office, a pharmacy and one of just about everything else a small town needs. The tallest point is still the church steeple.

Kaunakakai is a town that hasn't changed its face at all for tourism. It has an almost timeless quality and a nice slow pace.

Information

The Molokai Visitors Association (☎ 553-3876), at the corner of Hwy 450 and Kaunakakai Place can give you brochures and the lowdown on what's happening around the island. The office is open 8:30 am to 4:30 pm Monday to Friday.

The Bank of Hawaii, on Ala Malama St, is open 8:30 am to 4 pm Monday to Thursday,

---

> ### Walking on Water
>
> In Kaunakakai, if you're down at the beach at night, you may spot what looks like ghosts walking out on the water. There's no need to be spooked – these are actually local fishers who walk far out onto the shallow coastal reef carrying lanterns. The fishing is good at night, when the wind dies down, and lantern light stuns the prey.
>
> ❀❀❀❀❀❀❀❀❀❀❀❀❀

8:30 am to 6 pm on Friday. There's a 24-hour ATM out front.

The post office, on Ala Malama St, is open 9 am to 4:30 pm Monday to Friday and 9 to 11 am on Saturday.

Friendly Isle Travel, on Ala Malama St, can assist with travel arrangements.

Molokai Drugs, the local pharmacy on Ala Malama St, sells film, magazines, maps and Hawaiiana books. It's open from 8:45 am to 5:45 pm Monday to Saturday.

Kaunakakai's good public library, on Ala Malama St, is open 9 am to 5 pm on Monday, Tuesday and Friday; noon to 8 pm on Wednesday; 11 am to 5 pm on Thursday. You can browse through several newspapers there, including the *Wall Street Journal*, *USA Today* and the *Honolulu Advertiser*.

Since Molokai doesn't have a daily newspaper, bulletin boards around Kaunakakai are the prime source of news and announcements. The board next to the Bank of Hawaii is the most extensive.

The coin laundry behind Outpost Natural Foods is open 7 am to 9 pm daily. It costs $1 to wash and about $1 to dry. There's another coin laundry on Kamoi St opposite the Molokai Drive Inn.

Kaunakakai Harbor

Gone are the days when pineapple was loaded from Kaunakakai Wharf, but a commercial interisland barge still pulls into the harbor a couple of times a week with supplies. The harbor also has mooring facilities for small boats.

Molokai was the favorite island and playground of King Kamehameha V, who built a large vacation house of thatched grass on the shores of Kaunakakai Harbor. The house was called Malama, which today is the name of the main road leading from the harbor through town. All that remains of Kamehameha V's home is the stone foundation, now overgrown with grass. It's on the right side of the road before the wharf, near the canoe shed.

Fishponds

Molokai's southeast coast is dotted with the largest concentration of ancient fishponds in

MOLOKAI

KAUNAKAKAI

To Kapuaiwa Coconut Grove,
Molokai (Hoolehua) Airport

Mitchell
Pauole
Center

Kaunakakai
Harbor

Kaunakakai
Wharf

PLACES TO EAT
3 Outpost Natural Foods
5 Rabang's Restaurant
7 Kanemitsu Bakery
18 Kamoi Snack-N-Go
23 Mrs K
26 Molokai Drive Inn
29 Molokai Pizza Cafe

OTHER
1 Molokai General Hospital
2 Coin Laundry
4 Molokai Fish & Dive
6 Molokai Wines & Spirits
8 C Pascua Store
9 Police Station
10 Department of Parks &
Recreation

11 Tennis Courts
12 Public Pool
13 Friendly Isle Travel
14 Misaki's
15 Friendly Market
16 Post Office
17 Molokai Drugs
19 Softball Field
20 Baseball Field

21 Gas Station
22 Library
24 Bank of Hawaii
25 Molokai Bicycle
27 Coin Laundry
28 Molokai Visitors
Association
30 Kamehameha V
House Site
31 Pau Hana Inn

Hawaii. Grazing by cattle and sheep introduced in the mid-1800s resulted in widespread erosion, and the clay that washed down from the mountains choked out the ponds. Over the years, efforts have been made to revive a few of the fishponds, although without much commercial success.

One of the most impressive and easily visited is the **Kalokoeli Fishpond**, behind Molokai Shores condos.

Kapuaiwa Coconut Grove

The coconut grove a mile west of the main part of town has 10 oceanside acres of coconut palms planted by Kamehameha V around 1860. Kapuaiwa means 'mysterious taboo.' The grove is under the management of Hawaiian Home Lands today. If you bring a car to the grove, be careful where you park, because falling coconuts can act like aerial bombs.

Across the highway is **Church Row**, where a quaint white church with green trim sits next to a quaint green church with white trim and so on down the line. Any denomination that attracts a handful of Hawaiian members receives its own little tract of land to put up a church.

MOLOKAI

One Alii Beach Park

One Alii, 3 miles east of Kaunakakai, is the beach park nearest to town. As the water is shallow and swimming conditions are poor, the park is used mainly for picnics, parties and camping. Two memorials erected in the park commemorate the 19th-century immigration of Japanese citizens to Hawaii.

Places to Stay

Camping Camping is allowed with a county permit at *One Alii Beach Park*, a roadside park on a shallow beach 3 miles east of Kaunakakai. While the campsites are near the water, they have little privacy, and because the park is close to town, it tends to be busy.

A second camping option that's sometimes available in the Kaunakakai area is at *Kapuaiwa Coconut Grove*, on Hawaiian Home Lands property just west of town. However, this spot is often booked up far in advance, as camping permits are issued to just one group at a time and priority is given to native Hawaiians.

For booking information for both campgrounds, see Camping under Accommodations, earlier in this chapter.

B&Bs, Condos & Hotels *Ka Hale Mala* (☎/fax 553-9009, cpgroup@aloha.net, 7 Kamakana Place, Box 1582, Kaunakakai, HI 96748) is a delightful three-room apartment about 4 miles east of Kaunakakai. Occupying the ground level of the contemporary home of Jack and Cheryl Corbiell, a friendly Canadian couple, Ka Hale Mala stands as the best accommodation value on the island. The spotless 850-sq-ft apartment has exposed beam ceilings and a *lanai* (veranda) overlooking the garden. There's a living room with two twin beds, TV and stereo, a separate dining room with a fully equipped kitchen, a private bathroom with a tub and a bedroom with two twin beds. Guests are free to borrow snorkeling gear and mountain bikes and to pick fruit from the garden. Cheryl cooks a full breakfast that includes specialties such as taro pancakes or poi muffins. The rate is $70 for two people and $15 more for each additional person. If you prefer to prepare your own breakfast, the price is $5 less per person. The Corbiells have

their own website at www.molokai-aloha.com/kahalemala.

A'ahi Place Bed & Breakfast (☎ 553-5860, mitty@aloha.net, Box 528, Kaunakakai, HI 96748) is 1½ miles east of Kaunakakai, uphill from Molokai Shores. Owned by Meridith Smith, an amiable former Alaskan, the rental is a casual cedar cottage detached from the main house. It has a full kitchen, a bedroom with two double beds, a bath and a lanai. The entire cottage is essentially a single open space that's best suited for one or two people. There's a washing machine and a clothesline, and guests enjoy access to a phone and TV, both of which are on the covered deck below the owner's house. The rate is $75, with a continental breakfast of Molokai coffee, fresh bread and local fruit included. Smoking is not allowed. There's a two-night minimum stay. To see pictures of the accommodations, visit the website www.molokai-aloha.com/aahi.

Molokai Shores (☎ 553-5954, 800-535-0085, fax 553-5954, marc@aloha.net, Box 1037, Kaunakakai, HI 96748), about 1½ miles east of town, has 100 condo units, 25% of which are in the rental pool. Most are decorated nicely, and each has a kitchen, sofa bed, cable TV, lanai and ceiling fans. Ask for a unit on the 3rd floor, where the units have high cathedral ceilings. The one-bedroom condos cost a pricey $144 for up to four people, and two-bedroom units cost $189 for up to six people, but discount schemes can cut the rates substantially. There's a pool and coin-operated laundry on the premises. Molokai Shores belongs to the Marc Resorts chain, which offers online booking and occasional discounts at www.marcresorts.com.

The closest hotel to the town center, the *Pau Hana Inn*, closed in early 1999 after going through management changes and failing to make ends meet as an operation run by the community. Prior to closing, it had the cheapest rooms in Molokai, so it will be missed by budget travelers. Whether it will reopen remains to be seen. For more information, contact the Molokai Visitors Association.

Hotel Molokai (☎ 553-5347, 800-367-5004, fax 553-5047, Box 546, Kaunakakai, HI 96748), about 2 miles east of town, has recently reopened after an extensive restoration to repair termite damage and modernize the rooms. The hotel has a Polynesian design of sorts and a laid-back atmosphere that's well-suited to the character of Molokai. The rooms, which are in clusters of two-story buildings, feature private baths, cable TV, phone and modem hookups. If you're sensitive to traffic noise, request a room away from the road; in any unit, rooms on the 2nd floor are generally quieter than those on the lower floor. Room rates range from $75 to $125, depending on the size and view; kitchenette units are available for $130. There's an oceanfront pool, as well as top-notch sunsets and stargazing from the shore.

Places to Eat

Kanemitsu Bakery, on Ala Malama St, makes *the* Molokai bread that is shipped around the islands, as well as a variety of Danish pastries and doughnuts. The cinnamon apple crisp ($1) is a favorite. The restaurant in the back of the bakery is the island's most popular breakfast spot. Eggs, toast, ham and coffee go for $5.25, sandwiches and burgers for $2.50 and plate lunches for about double that. The restaurant is open from 5:30 am to 1 pm (to noon on Sunday), the bakery from 5:30 am to 6:30 pm; both are closed on Tuesday.

Outpost Natural Foods sells health food, including bulk granola, dried fruit, yogurt, vitamins and fresh produce, some of it organic. The *Juice Bar* inside the store makes good burritos and sandwiches for $3.50 and salads for $5. There's also a daily special, such as a veggie enchilada or a tofu quiche and salad for around $6. The juice bar is open 10 am to 3 pm Sunday to Friday, and there's a picnic table out back where you can eat. The store is open 9 am to 6 pm Monday to Thursday, 9 am to 4 pm on Friday and 9 am to 5 pm on Sunday.

Kamoi Snack-N-Go, on Kamoi St behind the post office, is a combination convenience store and ice cream shop that's open daily from 9 am to 9 pm (from noon on Sunday). It sells about 30 different flavors of the gourmet, Honolulu-made Dave's Ice Cream at a reasonable $1.60 for a one-scoop cone – a welcome bargain on a hot day.

Molokai Pizza Cafe (☎ 553-3288), in a small complex behind the Molokai Visitors Association, is open 11 am to 10 pm Sunday to Thursday, 11 am to 11 pm on Friday and Saturday. The pizza is good, with single-topping versions priced at $10 for a medium (12 inches) that's big enough for two – although if you're really hungry, the large is only $2 more. Other items include sub sandwiches, lasagna and spaghetti with meat balls, all priced around $7.50. On most evenings, as long as the local fishers did well, the restaurant also features a recommendable fresh catch of the day for around $10, and each Wednesday there's a Mexican food special.

Molokai Drive Inn, on the Maunaloa Hwy, has inexpensive hamburgers, breakfasts and $5 plate lunches. The food is takeout, but there are picnic tables at the side where you can chow down. This place used to be a Dairy Queen, but Molokai wasn't quite ready for a fast-food chain, so the sign came down. The Drive Inn is open 6 am (6:30 am on weekends) to 10:30 pm.

Another option for inexpensive food is *Mrs K*, a hole-in-the-wall just north of the Bank of Hawaii. Sample sandwiches for $3 and plate lunches for $6. Mrs K is open 7 am to 5:30 pm Monday to Saturday.

Rabang's Restaurant, a simple local eatery on Ala Malama St, has Filipino lunch plates like turkey tail adobo for around $6, as well as burgers and shave ice. Rabang's is open 7 am to 10 pm daily.

The open-air restaurant at *Hotel Molokai* (☎ 553-5347) sits right on the beach, with a prime sunset view of both Lanai and waves lapping at the shore. At lunch, served from 11:30 am to 2 pm, you can order burgers, teriyaki chicken or *mahimahi* ('dolphin' fish) sandwiches for around $7.50, while at dinner, fresh fish and steaks are under $20.

Misaki's and *Friendly Market*, both on Ala Malama St, are the island's two major grocery stores and are open 8:30 am to 8:30 pm Monday to Saturday. Misaki's, which is also open 9 am to noon on Sunday, has the island's cheapest wine prices, though the selection is limited.

Molokai Wines & Spirits carries a good assortment of imported beers and a wide

MOLOKAI

selection of wine at reasonable prices. The shop, open 9 am to 10 pm daily, also carries Häagen-Dazs ice cream and a few food items.

Entertainment

There's not much standard evening entertainment around Kaunakakai. The best bet is to check with **Hotel Molokai** (☎ 553-5347), which occasionally features local musicians playing mellow Hawaiian guitar.

Other than this, the baseball field in Kaunakakai is the most active spot on the island. For some local flavor, you could go down and cheer on the Molokai Farmers as they compete against their high school rivals, the Lanai Pinelads.

East Molokai

The 28-mile drive from Kaunakakai to Halawa Valley is along the Kamehameha V Hwy (Hwy 450) and takes about 1½ hours one way. It's a good paved road from start to finish. Check your gas gauge before starting off on the trip, as there are no gas stations after Kaunakakai.

The road edges the ocean for much of the drive, with the mountains of East Molokai rising up to the north. The terrain starts out relatively dry and becomes greener and lusher as you head east. It's all quite pastoral, with small homes tucked into the valleys, horses grazing at the side of the road and silver waterfalls dropping down the mountainsides.

The beaches along this stretch are mostly shallow and silted and not particularly good for swimming until you reach the 20-mile marker. The last part of the road is narrow, with lots of hairpin bends and scenic coastal views, as you wind up to a clifftop view of Halawa Valley.

KAWELA

The **Kakahaia Beach Park**, a grassy roadfront park in Kawela, shortly before the 6-mile marker, has a couple of picnic tables but little other reason to stop. This park is the only part of the **Kakahaia National Wildlife Refuge** open to the public. Most of the 40-acre refuge is inland from the road. It includes marshland, with a dense growth of bulrushes and an inland freshwater fishpond that has been expanded to provide a home for endangered birds like the Hawaiian stilt and coot.

Farther inland is the **Kawela Puuhonua**, a place of refuge that was used in ancient times by those running from the law or hiding from personal enemies. The stone ruins are on a high ridge separated by deep gulches and nearly impossible to reach.

In 1795, Kamehameha the Great invaded Molokai with such a large force that his war canoes were lined up for a full 4 miles along this coast. He quickly brought Molokai under his command and then went on to invade Oahu, the last battle in a campaign that eventually would unite all of the Hawaiian Islands.

KAMALO

The biggest attraction in Kamalo, a small village some 10 miles east of Kaunakakai, is the roadside **St Joseph's Church**.

Only two of the four Molokai churches that the island's most famous missionary, Father Damien, built outside of the Kalaupapa Peninsula are still standing, and one of them is St Joseph's in Kamalo. This simple, one-room wooden church built in 1876 has a steeple and bell, five rows of pews and some of the original wavy glass panes. A statue of Damien and a little cemetery are at the side of the church. Only the yellow tsunami-warning speaker brings the scene into the 20th century.

Just over three-quarters of a mile after the 11-mile marker, a small sign on the *makai* (seaward) side of the road notes the **Smith-Bronte Landing**, the site where pilot Ernest Smith and navigator Emory Bronte safely crash-landed their plane at the completion of the world's first civilian flight from the US mainland to Hawaii.

The pair left California on July 14, 1927, coming down on Molokai 25 hours and two minutes after taking off. Oahu was the intended destination. A little memorial plaque is set among the kiawe trees and grasses, in the spot where they landed.

Places to Stay

The **Kamalo Plantation Bed & Breakfast** (☎/fax 558-8236, kamaloplantation@aloha .net, HC 1, Box 300, Kaunakakai, HI 96748) is in a fruit orchard opposite St Joseph's Church. There's a bedroom in the main house with TV, refrigerator, microwave, coffeemaker, king-size bed and private bath for $75. The other option is an adjacent studio-style cottage with a king bed, a sofa bed and a full kitchen; it costs $85 and would be quite suitable for a couple with a child. Guests enjoy a breakfast of homemade breads and homegrown fruits. The grounds have the stone foundation of an ancient *heiau* (temple) and the owners, Glenn and Akiko Foster, can point out little-known hiking trails in the area. The Fosters have a website at www .molokai.com/kamalo.

Kumueli Farms Bed & Breakfast (☎ 558-8281, fax 558-8284, dcurtis@aloha.net, Box 1829, Kaunakakai, HI 96748) is a guest room in the upscale home of David and Dorothe Curtis. The house is on a quiet 8-acre estate of tropical palms and fruit trees, not far from St Joseph's Church. The room has a private entrance, mountain views and a bathroom that opens to a sundeck. There's a queen bed, ceiling fan, microwave, refrigerator, coffeemaker, TV and VCR. Guests also have access to the 75-foot lap pool. The rate is $100, and there's a two-night minimum stay. The Curtises maintain a website at www.visitmolokai.com/kumueli.

UALAPUE

The Wavecrest Resort, a condo development, is at the 13-mile marker in Ualapue.

Shortly beyond Wavecrest, you'll spot **Ualapue Fishpond** on the seaward side of the road. Molokai once had more than 60 productive fishponds, constructed from the 13th century onward. Built of lava rock upon the reefs, their slatted sluice gates allowed small fish into the pond, where the fledgling fish were fed and fattened, while preventing the mature fish from swimming back out. A ready supply of fish could then be easily scooped up with a net as needed. The Ualapue Fishpond was restored a few years ago and restocked with mullet and milkfish,

two species that had been raised there in ancient times.

Beyond this, look for the defunct Ah Ping Store and its old gas pump at the roadside. This classic building of faded green wood with a red tin roof was a Chinese-owned grocery store in the 1930s.

If you're looking for a place to stay, the **Wavecrest Resort** (☎ 558-8103, 800-367-2980, fax 558-8206, marc@aloha.net, HC 1, Box 541, Kaunakakai, HI 96748) is a 126-unit condo complex that has about a dozen units in the rental pool. The condos vary depending upon the owners' taste, but all are spacious and most are pleasantly decorated. Each has separate bedrooms, a roomy living room with a sofa bed, a full kitchen, TV and lanai. Breezes blow right through the oceanfront units, which enjoy great views of Maui and Lanai from the lanai. Maximum occupancy is four people in the one-bedroom units, which cost $119 to $149, depending upon the view. There are also two-bedroom units that can accommodate up to six people for $189. Weekly discounts are

St Joseph's Church in Kamalo

NED FRIARY

MOLOKAI

available, and since Wavecrest is a member of Marc Resorts, there are other discounts as well. The resort has a pool, tennis courts, coin laundry and a small food shop that's open Tuesday to Saturday.

KALUAAHA

The village of Kaluaaha is about 2 miles past Wavecrest. The ruins of Molokai's first church are here, a bit off the road and inland but (barely) visible if you keep an eye out. **Kaluaaha Church** was built in 1844 by Molokai's first missionary, Harvey R Hitchcock. There had been talk of rebuilding the church, but the rusting old steel rods in the original structure thwarted the plan.

Our Lady of Sorrows Church is a quarter of a mile past the Kaluaaha Church site. The present Our Lady of Sorrows is a 1966 reconstruction of the original wood-frame building, constructed in 1874 by the missionary Father Damien.

From the church parking lot, a fine view of an ancient **fishpond** and the high-rise-studded shores of West Maui provide an incongruous backdrop.

ILIILIOPAE HEIAU

Iliiliopae is the largest and best-known heiau on Molokai and is thought to be the oldest as well. Approximately 300 feet long and 100

feet wide, the heiau is about 22 feet high on the east side and 11 feet high at the other end. It is strikingly level. Historians believed the heiau may have originally been three times its current size, reaching out beyond Mapulehu Stream.

The path to the heiau is on the inland side of the highway, nearly half a mile past the 15-mile marker, immediately after a little bridge. It starts on a dirt drive on the east side of the creek. After a 10-minute walk, a footpath leads off to the left, opposite a house. The heiau is two minutes farther.

Although once a site of human sacrifice, Iliiliopae is today silent except for the chittering of birds. African tulip trees line the trail to the site, a peaceful place whose stones still seem to emanate vibrations of a powerful past. A good place to sit and take it all in is on the north side, up the steps to the right of the heiau.

Visiting the heiau is usually straightforward, but since it is on private property, it's advised that you check with the tourist office to see if you need permission in advance.

PUKOO

The village of Pukoo was once the seat of local government – complete with a courthouse, jail, wharf and post office – until the plantation folks built Kaunakakai and cen-

---

Iliiliopae Sacrifices

Legend says Iliiliopae Heiau was built in one night by *menehune* (legendary 'little people') who brought *iliili* (stones) over the mountains from Wailau Valley. In return for their efforts, they were each given one *opae* (shrimp) – hence the temple's name.

Lono, the god of harvest, and Ku, the god of war, were both worshipped here. Human sacrifices were made at this *heiau* (temple), always on the eve of a full moon. Drums were beaten to call all males to the temple where, upon the priest's direction, all fell prone, and the victims to be sacrificed were brought to the platform. Amid chanting and rituals, these victims, always male, were strangled to death and their bodies later burned.

One local legend tells of a man, Umoekekaua, who lost nine of his 10 sons to sacrifice at Iliiliopae. He became so outraged that he went with his only remaining son to Pelekunu Valley to enlist the aid of Kauhuhu, the shark god. Kauhuhu sent a torrent of rain, flooding the heiau and washing the priests responsible for the sacrifices into Pukoo Harbor, where they were duly eaten by sharks.

tered everything there. The population shifted away from Pukoo, and it's been a sleepy backwater ever since. Now, bit by bit, islanders are beginning to move back to the Pukoo area, and while it's not exactly suburbia, you'll notice a handful of newer homes as the road continues.

You can stay overnight at **Honomuni House** (☎ 558-8383, HC 1, Box 700, Kaunakakai, HI 96748), a pleasant guest cottage just beyond the Honomuni Bridge, about a mile northeast of Pukoo. The guest cottage is studio-style, with a kitchen, bath and outdoor deck and shower. The living room area has a sofa bed, a TV and a small dining table made of wood from the monkeypod tree, which grows on the grounds. Rates are $85 for two, plus $10 for each additional adult. There's no extra charge for children. Breakfast is not included, but bananas and other seasonal fruits are provided. Host Patty McCartney and her family live in a large house on the same grounds.

If you're hungry for a bite to eat, the **Neighborhood Store 'N' Counter**, near the 16-mile marker, is not only a well-stocked little grocery store but also the only place to get a meal on the east side. The grill at the side of the store offers decent food, including omelettes, burgers and $6 plate lunches that sometimes include fresh fish specials. Try the hearty teri-chicken sandwich, which comes topped with a slab of tomato and costs $3.75. There are picnic tables at the side. The grill is open 8 am to 6 pm daily except Wednesday; the store is open 8 am to 6 pm daily.

WAIALUA

Waialua is a little roadside community around the 19-mile marker. The attractive little Waialua Congregational Church, which marks the center of the village, was built of stone in 1855. The church also owns nearby property that it makes available to campers (see Camping in the front of this chapter). The nearby Waialua Beach is the site of Molokai's *keiki* (child) surf competitions.

Sugar Mill Remains

Three-quarters of a mile after the 19-mile marker, begin looking for the remains of a stone chimney, a remnant of the Moanui Sugar Mill, which processed sugar from a nearby plantation until the mill burned down in the late 1800s. The ruins are about 50 feet inland from the road, just before a stand of tall ironwood trees.

Twenty-Mile Beach

A stretch of white-sand beach pops up right along the roadside at the 20-mile marker. There are places where you can park just beyond that. During the winter, when other Molokai beaches are rough, this is the area everyone directs you to for swimming and snorkeling.

However, when the tide is low, the water is sometimes too shallow for snorkeling inside the reef. Snorkeling is much better beyond the reef, but unless it's very calm the currents can be dangerous.

Rock Point

The point of rocks sticking out as the road swings left before the 21-mile marker is called, appropriately enough, Rock Point. This is a popular surf spot where local competitions sometimes take place.

Waialua to Halawa

After the 21-mile marker, the road starts to wind upwards. Tall grasses just at the edge seem to be trying to reclaim the road, while ironwood trees and the spindly spikes of sisal plants dot the surrounding hills.

It's a good paved road – the only problem is there's not always enough of it. In places, including some cliff-hugging curves, this road is really only wide enough for one car, and you'll need to do some horn tooting. The road levels out just before the 24-mile marker, where there's a view of the small island of Mokuhooniki, a seabird sanctuary.

The fenced grassland in this area is part of the Puu O Hoku Ranch, Molokai's second-largest cattle ranch. A grove of sacred kukui trees on the ranch property marks the grave of Lanikaula, a famous *kahuna* (wise person) of the late 16th century. Over the years, many islanders claim to have seen the night lanterns of ghost marchers bobbing along near the grove.

MOLOKAI

After passing the 25-mile marker, the jungle begins to close in, and the scent of eucalyptus fills the air. One and a quarter miles after the 25-mile marker, there's a turn-off with a great panoramic view of Halawa Valley – if the viewpoint is overgrown, just park and walk down the road a little farther to reach a clearing. In the winter, this is also a good place to watch for whales breaching off the coast.

There are lots of 'beep as you go' hairpin bends on the one-lane road that leads down to the valley, but the road is in good condition and the incline is reasonably gradual.

HALAWA VALLEY

Halawa Valley once had three heiaus, two of which are thought to have been used for human sacrifice. Little remains of the sites. In the mid-19th century, the fertile valley had a population of about 500 people and produced most of Molokai's taro as well as many of its melons, gourds and fruits. Taro production declined over the years, coming to an abrupt end in 1946, when a massive tsunami swept up Halawa Valley, wiping out the farms and much of the community. A second tsunami washed the valley clean in 1957. Only seven families now remain in Halawa. Sunday services are still occasionally held in Hawaiian at the valley's little church.

Halawa Beach Park

Halawa Beach was a favored surfing spot for Molokai chiefs and remains so today for local kids. This beach has double coves separated by a rocky outcrop, with the north side a bit more protected than the south. When the water is calm, there's good swimming, but both coves are subject to dangerous rip currents when the surf is heavy. There can also be strong currents whenever Halawa Stream, which empties into the north cove, is flowing heavily.

Halawa Beach Park has rest rooms and running water; the water, which is piped down from the upper valley, does not meet health standards and should be treated before drinking. The old building before the park is the remains of a village church that burned down a few decades ago.

Central Molokai

Central Molokai takes in the Hoolehua Plains, which stretch from windswept Moomomi Beach in the west to the former plantation town of Kualapuu. The central part of the island also has forested interiors leading to Kamakou Preserve, a unique rain forest that includes the island's highest mountain, Kamakou (4961 feet). On the north side of central Molokai is Kalaupapa Peninsula, the site of Hawaii's infamous leprosy colony.

The most trodden route in central Molokai is the drive up to the Kalaupapa Overlook, where you'll find one of the prettiest views on Molokai. It takes about 15 minutes to drive the 10 miles from Kaunakakai, on the southern shore.

Turning north off Hwy 460 onto Hwy 470 (Kalae Hwy), the road starts in dry grasslands and climbs past a coffee plantation, the town of Kualapuu, a restored sugar mill, a mule stable and the trail down to the Kalaupapa Peninsula. The road ends at Palaau State Park, site of the Kalaupapa Overlook.

KUALAPUU

Kualapuu is the name of both a 1017-foot hill and the village that has grown up north of it.

At the base of the hill is the world's largest rubber-lined reservoir. It can hold up to 1.4 billion gallons of water, which is piped in from the rain forests of eastern Molokai and is presently the source of water for both the Hoolehua Plains and the dry West End.

Del Monte set up headquarters here in the 1930s, and Kualapuu developed into a plantation town. The center of Del Monte's activities covered the spread between Kualapuu and the nearby Hoolehua homesteads.

In 1982, Del Monte decided to phase out its Molokai operations, and the economy came tumbling down. Old farm equipment rusted in overgrown pineapple fields for a decade before Coffees of Hawaii leased out the abandoned fields and replanted them with coffee saplings. Rows of coffee trees now extend down the slope from the town center. Kualapuu is banking on this new crop to spur its revival, and indeed the operation has grown into the town's largest employer, with some 30 people working there year-round and about 65 during the harvest season of September to January.

If you want to try out the final product, stop by Coffees of Hawaii, in the village center, where there's a little cafe with free coffee samples and a gift shop selling packaged coffee and a few local handicraft items. There are also mule-drawn wagon tours of the coffee fields for $14 (see Activities in the front of this chapter).

Places to Eat

The *Espresso Bar* at Coffees of Hawaii sells fresh-ground coffee and espresso, bagels, smoothies and sandwiches – all priced at $3 or less. It's open 7 am to 3 pm weekdays and 10 am to 3 pm weekends.

The *Kualapuu Cookhouse* (☎ 567-6185) is a busy place for such a small town. There are breakfast omelettes and plate lunches for $7 to $8. You can also order chili, *saimin* (Japanese noodle soup), burgers or sandwiches for around $4. Homemade pies are a specialty – for sheer indulgence, try a slice of the chocolate macnut pie. The restaurant is open 7 am to 9 pm Monday to Saturday.

KALAE
RW Meyer Sugar Mill

Four miles north of Hwy 460, in Kalae, is the sugar mill built by Rudolph W Meyer, an industrious German immigrant.

Meyer was on his way to the California gold rush when he dropped by Hawaii, married a member of Hawaiian royalty and in the process landed a tidy bit of property. He eventually found his gold in potatoes, which he grew and exported to the Californian miners. He also served as overseer of the Kalaupapa leprosy settlement and as manager of King Kamehameha V's ranch lands.

In the 1850s, Meyer established his own ranch and exported cattle from Palaau village. In one infamous incident, after finding his herd declining, he had all the men of Palaau charged with cattle rustling and sent off to a jailhouse in Honolulu.

In the late 1870s, when a new reciprocity treaty gave Hawaiian sugar planters the right to export sugar duty-free to the US, Meyer turned his lands over to sugar and built this mill. The sugar mill operated for about 10 years.

A lot of time and money has gone into authentically restoring the mill, including the complete rebuilding of a 100-year-old steam engine and other rusting machinery abandoned a century ago. The mill, which is on the National Register of Historic Places, is the last of its kind. If you're into sugar mills, antique steam engines and that sort of thing, you'll certainly find it interesting.

The sugar mill (☎ 567-6436) is open 10 am to 2 pm Monday to Saturday. Admission is $2.50 for adults, $1 for students.

A building behind the sugar mill contains a small display of Molokai's history through period photos and a few Hawaiiana items. Meyer and his descendants are buried in a little family plot out back.

Ironwood Hills Golf Club

There are no polo shirts here. Ironwood Hills is a delightfully casual golf course, with crabgrass growing in the sand pits and local golfers who actually look like they're having fun. The course is down the red dirt road at the tree-lined edge of the pasture immediately south of Meyer Sugar Mill.

Originally built by Del Monte for its employees, the course was maintained by Molokai residents after Del Monte left and is now open to all. For more information, see the Activities section in the front of this chapter.

PALAAU STATE PARK

Palaau State Park is at the northern end of Hwy 470. The park's main sight, the Kalaupapa Overlook, is just a couple of minutes' walk from the parking lot. In the opposite direction, a five-minute trail through a grove of ironwoods leads to a phallic-shaped rock. Both trails are marked and easy to follow. The park has campsites, picnic areas and lovely stands of paperbark eucalyptus.

Kalaupapa Overlook

The Kalaupapa Overlook provides a scenic overview of the Kalaupapa Peninsula from

MOLOKAI

the edge of a 1600-foot cliff. It's like an aerial view without the airplane.

Interpretive plaques identify the landmarks below and explain Kalaupapa's history as a leprosy colony. The village where all of Kalaupapa's residents now live is visible, but Kalawao, the original settlement and site of Father Damien's church and grave, cannot be seen from here.

The **lighthouse** at the northern end of the peninsula once boasted the most powerful beam in the Pacific. The 700,000-candlepower Fresnel crystal lens cast its light until 1986, when it was taken down and replaced by an electric light beacon.

Kalaupapa means 'Flat Leaf,' an accurate description of the lava slab peninsula that was created when a low shield volcano poked up out of the sea long after the rest of Molokai had been formed. The dormant Kauhako Crater, visible from the overlook, contains a little lake that's more than 800 feet deep.

Kalaupapa residents use the term 'topside' to refer to all of Molokai outside their peninsula. Seen from the overlook, the reason is obvious.

Whether or not you get down to Kalaupapa itself, a visit to the overlook is a must. Because of the angle of the sun, the best light for photography is usually from late morning to mid-afternoon.

Hiking There's an old trail that continues directly beyond the last plaque at the overlook. For a pleasant forest walk, simply follow this trail for about 30 minutes. Few people go this way, and it's very peaceful – if you're lucky, you may even spot deer crossing the trail.

The path, on a carpet of soft ironwood needles, passes through a thickly planted forest of ironwood and eucalyptus, dotted here and there with Norfolk pines. These diagonal rows of trees were planted during a Civilian Conservation Corps (CCC) reforestation project in the 1930s. The trees create a canopy over the trail, and, as is generally true under ironwood and eucalyptus trees, there's little undergrowth to obscure the way.

There's no destination – the joy here is the woods. Eventually, the trail winds down into a gully and peters out a little while after that.

Phallic Rock

Kauleonanahoa, literally 'the penis of Nanahoa,' is Hawaii's premier phallic stone, poking up in a little clearing inside an ironwood grove. Nature has endowed it well, but it's obviously been touched up by human hands.

Although it's said that women who bring offerings and spend the night here will return home pregnant, there apparently is no danger in just going to have a look.

Places to Stay

Camping is free at Palaau State Park. The camping area is in a grove of eucalyptus and ironwood trees that make everything cool and shady in summer, although the area can feel dark and damp at other times of the year, especially when it's rainy. In winter, you may well have the place to yourself, and even in the summer you're unlikely to find a crowd. The camping area is usually quite peaceful, with the only sounds coming from roosters and the braying of mules from the nearby stables.

There are rest rooms, cement picnic tables, fireplaces and an outdoor shower, but the tap water is not fit for drinking.

KALAUPAPA PENINSULA

Kalaupapa Peninsula seems both strikingly beautiful and strikingly lonely. At the base of majestic and formidable cliffs, it has been a leprosy settlement for more than a century. The trip to the peninsula – accessible only by mule, on foot or by small plane – is one of Molokai's major attractions. It's also a pilgrimage of sorts for admirers of Father Damien (Joseph de Veuster), the Belgian priest who devoted the latter part of his life to helping people with leprosy, before dying of the disease himself.

Kalaupapa Peninsula is a national historical park jointly managed by the Hawaii Department of Health and the National Park Service. It is unique among historic parks in that many of the people whose lives are being interpreted are still living on the site.

Kayaking near the steep cliffs of Molokai's North Shore

View of Kalaupapa Peninsula from Kalaupapa Overlook, Molokai

The colorful underwater life off the coast of Lanai

Kauai's Kalalau Valley

ANN CECIL

LEE FOSTER

Wailua Falls, Kauai

ERIC L WHEATER

Waimea Canyon, Kauai

Taro fields in Hanalei Valley, Kauai

Na Pali Coast shrouded in fog, Kauai

Lumahai Beach on the North Shore of Kauai

Old state laws that require everyone who enters the settlement to have a 'permit' and to be at least 16 years old are no longer a medical necessity, but they continue to be enforced in order to protect the privacy of the patients. There's no actual paper permit. A reservation with either Damien Tours or Molokai Mule Ride (see the Getting There & Around section, later in this chapter) is considered a permit.

Only guests of Kalaupapa residents are allowed to stay overnight. There are no stores or other public facilities for visitors.

History

Ancient Hawaiians used Kalaupapa as a refuge when caught in storms at sea. The peninsula held a large settlement at the time of early Western contact, and the area is rich in archaeological sites.

In 1835, doctors in Hawaii diagnosed the state's first case of leprosy, one of many diseases introduced by foreigners (probably Chinese laborers, in this case). Alarmed by the spread of the disease, King Kamehameha V signed into law an act that banished people with leprosy to Kalaupapa Peninsula, beginning in 1865.

It was a one-way trip. Kalaupapa Peninsula is surrounded on three sides by some of Hawaii's roughest and most shark-infested waters and on the fourth by the world's highest sea cliffs. Once the afflicted arrived on Kalaupapa Peninsula, there was no way out, not even in a casket. Hawaiians called leprosy *mai hookaawale*, which means separating sickness, a disease all the more dreaded because it tore families apart forever.

Father Damien arrived at Kalaupapa in 1873. He wasn't the first missionary to come, but he was the first to stay.

Damien nursed the sick, wrapped bandages on oozing sores, hammered coffins and dug graves. On average, he buried one person a day. He put up more than 300 houses – each little more than four walls, a door and a roof, but still a shelter to those cast here. Damien was a good carpenter. Some of the solid little churches he built earlier around the Big Island and Molokai still stand today.

The original settlement was in Kalawao, at the wetter eastern end of the peninsula. Some of the afflicted arrived in boats, whose captains were so terrified of the disease that they would not land but instead dropped patients overboard into the bay. Those who could, swam to shore.

Early conditions were unspeakably horrible. Before modern medicine, leprosy manifested itself in dripping, foul-smelling sores. Eventually, patients experienced loss of sensation and tissue degeneration that could lead to fingers, toes and noses becoming hideously deformed or falling off altogether.

In 1888, Damien installed a water pipeline to the sunnier western side, and the settlement moved to where it is today. Over the years, some 8000 people have come to the Kalaupapa Peninsula to die. During Damien's time, lifespans here were almost invariably short.

Yet, even in Damien's day, leprosy was one of the least contagious of all communicable diseases. All in all, more than 1100 volunteers have worked with patients at Kalaupapa, but only Damien contracted leprosy. He died in 1889 at the age of 49. In 1995, Damien was beatified by Pope John Paul II and is now a candidate for sainthood.

Father Damien, hero of Kalaupapa

MOLOKAI

Damien's work inspired others. Brother Joseph Dutton arrived in 1886 and stayed 44 years. In addition to his work with the sick, he was a prolific writer who kept the outside world informed about what was happening in Molokai. Mother Marianne Cope arrived a year before Damien died. She stayed 30 years, helping to establish a girls' home and encouraging patients to live life to the fullest. She is widely considered to be the mother of the hospice movement.

In 1909, a fancy medical facility called the US Leprosy Investigation Station opened at Kalawao. However, the hospital was so out of touch – requiring patients to sign themselves in for two years, live in seclusion and give up all Hawaiian-grown food – that even in the middle of a leprosy colony it attracted only a handful of patients. It closed four years later.

Although sulfone antibiotics have been used successfully to control leprosy since the 1940s, the isolation policies in Kalaupapa weren't abandoned until 1969.

Today, fewer than 100 patients live on Kalaupapa Peninsula, the vast majority of them over 50 years old. Some of the elderly have become blind or weakened. Others fish or tend gardens, although lots of people just stay glued to their TVs.

Current residents are free to leave, but Kalaupapa is the only home most of them know. They have been given guarantees that they can remain on Kalaupapa Peninsula throughout their lifetimes.

While the state of Hawaii officially uses the term 'Hansen's Disease' for leprosy, many Kalaupapa residents consider that to be a euphemism that fails to reflect the stigma they have suffered and continue to use the old term.

Things to See & Do

On typical tours, the village looks nearly deserted. The sights are mainly cemeteries, churches and memorials. Places where residents go to 'talk story' – the post office, store and hospital – are pointed out, but no stops are made. Visitors are not allowed to photograph the residents. Kalaupapa is a tourist attraction, but its people are not.

The tours make stops in town at **memorials** for Father Damien and Mother Marianne and at a simple **visitor center** where photographs of the original settlement are on display and books are for sale. The tours then travel across the peninsula to Kalawao.

St Philomena Church (better known as 'Father Damien's Church') in Kalawao was built in 1872. You can still see where Damien cut open holes in the floor so that the sick who needed to spit could attend church and not be ashamed. The graveyard at the side contains Damien's gravestone and original burial site, although his body was exhumed in 1936 and returned to Belgium.

The view from Kalawao is one of the island's finest. You can look out on the *pali* (cliffs) of the northeast coast, each successive cliffside jutting out behind the one in front, each looking more like a shadow in the mist. The park boundaries include the Waihanau, Waialeia and Waikolu Valleys, east of the peninsula.

The **rock island** just offshore is the legendary home of a giant shark. From some angles, it looks like a shark's head coming straight up out of the water, while from other angles it looks like a dorsal fin.

Getting There & Around

The switchback mule trail down the pali is the only land route to the peninsula; the other option for getting to Kalaupapa is by air. No matter how you get there, you cannot wander around Kalaupapa Peninsula by yourself. By law, you must take a guided tour, which are offered Monday to Saturday.

Hiking The 3-mile hike along the mule trail takes about 1¼ hours going down, a bit longer going up. It's best to begin hiking by 8 am, before the mules start to go down, to avoid walking in fresh dung. The narrow trail is rutted in places and can be slippery and muddy if it's been raining, but otherwise it's not terribly strenuous.

The trail starts on the east side of Hwy 470 just north of the mule stables. Don't be intimidated by the 'Unauthorized Persons Keep Out' sign at the start of the path. If you have tour reservations, this is the trail in.

Air Kalaupapa has a little air strip at the edge of the peninsula and air service via small prop planes. Passengers must first book a tour with Damien Tours or Molokai Mule Ride before buying air tickets.

For the cheapest airfare, contact Molokai Air Shuttle (☎ 567-6847), which offers a 9 am flight from the Molokai (Hoolehua) Airport every day but Sunday as long as there are at least two passengers booking the flight. The return flight leaves at 2 pm. The cost is $50 roundtrip.

Island Air (☎ 800-652-6541 on the Neighbor Islands, 484-2222 in Oahu) flies daily between Honolulu and Kalaupapa via the Molokai (Hoolehua) Airport. The flight leaves Honolulu at 7:30 am and arrives in Kalaupapa at 8:25 am. The return flight leaves Kalaupapa at 3:05 pm. The fare is $93 each way between Molokai and Kalaupapa, $95 between Honolulu and Kalaupapa; roundtrip fares are double.

Pacific Wings (☎ 888-575-4546) flies between Honolulu and Kalaupapa via the Molokai Airport. The flight leaves Honolulu at 8:20 am and arrives in Kalaupapa at 9:15 am. The return flight leaves Kalaupapa at 2:05 pm. There's also a flight from Kahului on Maui to Kalaupapa that operates on the same schedule. Fares from Kahului or Honolulu are $75 each way; roundtrip fares are double. You can also pick up the flight from Molokai to Kalaupapa for $100 roundtrip.

Mule Rides One of the best-known outings in the islands is the mule ride down the pali to Kalaupapa.

The tour begins at the mule stables at 8 am with a short riding instruction. At around 8:30 am, riders hit the trail, which begins opposite the stables. The mules arrive in Kalaupapa around 10 am, and shortly thereafter a bus tour of the peninsula begins. The tour, which costs $150, includes lunch. Expect to return to the stables at around 3:30 pm. Wear loose trousers, closed shoes and a windbreaker.

While the mules move none too quickly – actually, hiking can be faster – there's a certain thrill in trusting your life to these sure-footed beasts while descending 1600 feet on 26 narrow cliffside switchbacks.

Rides take place daily except Sunday. Because the tour is limited to 15 riders, it can fill up quickly. Make reservations well in advance, particularly on weekends, by calling Molokai Mule Ride (☎ 567-6088, 800-567-7550, fax 567-6244, muleman@aloha.net), Box 200, Molokai, HI 95757. You can make reservations online at www.muleride.com.

Organized Tours Damien Tours (☎ 567-6171 or 567-6675), Box 1, Kalaupapa, HI 96742, does land tours for people who come to the Kalaupapa Peninsula on foot or by plane. Richard Marks, who runs Damien Tours, is a wonderful storyteller, an oral historian and the third generation of his family to be banished to Kalaupapa. Reservations must be made in advance, and the cost is $30. Bring your own lunch. The tours pick up visitors at both the airport and the bottom of the trail.

Molokai Mule Ride can also organize land tours for those who fly in or hike down on their own; the tour price ($40) includes lunch.

KAMAKOU
The mountains that form the spine of Molokai's east side reach up to Kamakou, the island's highest peak (4961 feet). Over half of Molokai's water supply comes from the Kamakou rain forest.

Hawaiian women used to hike up to the top of Kamakou to bury the afterbirth of their babies. According to folklore, this ritual would lead the newly born children to reach great heights in life. These days, islanders come to the forest to pick foliage for leis as well as to hunt pigs, deer and goats.

The Nature Conservancy's Kamakou Preserve is a near-pristine forest that is home to more than 250 native plants and some of Hawaii's rarest birds. With its mountaintop perch, Kamakou offers some splendid views of the North Shore valleys that unfold below. Just before the preserve entrance, Waikolu Lookout features a full panoramic view of remote Waikolu Valley, while a hike inside the preserve leads to another lookout, this one into the spectacular Pelekunu Valley.

MOLOKAI

Kamakou is a treasure, but it doesn't come easy. It is protected in its wilderness state in part because the rutted dirt road leading to it makes it a challenge to reach.

Start the journey to Kamakou Preserve by driving north from Kaunakakai on Hwy 460. Turn right three-quarters of a mile after the 3-mile marker, immediately before Manawainui Bridge. The paved road ends shortly at the Kalamaula hunters' check box. The 10-mile drive from the highway to Waikolu Lookout takes about 45 minutes, depending on road conditions. During the rainy season, vehicles leave tracks and the road tends to get progressively more rutted until it's regraded in the summer.

A 4WD is recommended and may be essential. In dry weather, some people do make it as far as the lookout in a car, but if it's been raining heavily, it's not advisable to try. In places where the road is narrow, one car that gets stuck can block the whole road.

From the Kalamaula hunters' check box, the road starts out fairly smoothly but deteriorates as it goes along. Bear left at the first fork, about five minutes' drive up the dirt road, and from there just follow the main road all the way.

Although there's no visible evidence of it from the road, the Kalamaula area was once heavily settled. It was here that Kamehameha the Great knocked out his two front teeth in grieving the death of a female high chief whom he had come to visit.

The landscape starts off shrubby, dry and dusty, later turning to woods of eucalyptus with patches of cypress and Norfolk pines. The trees were planted in the 1930s by the CCC to stem the erosion and watershed loss caused by the free-range cattle policies of earlier times.

The Molokai Forest Reserve starts about 5½ miles down the main road. A short loop road on the left leads to a former Boy Scout camp that's now used by the Nature Conservancy. After another 1½ miles, there will be an old water tank and reservoir off to the left. Just past this, a sign marked 'Kakalahale' points to the right. (This is one of several 4WD roads – mainly used by hunters – that lead south to the coast or to Kaunakakai. Once the roads leave forest reserve land, they run across private property, often with closed gates along the way.) It's 2 miles more to the Sandalwood Pit and a mile past that to the Waikolu Lookout and the Kamakou Preserve.

Sandalwood Pit

Lua Moku Iliahi, or Sandalwood Measuring Pit, is a hull-shaped grassy depression on the left side of the road. It takes a little imagination to see the whole picture, as over the years water erosion has rounded the sides.

The sandalwood pit was dug in the early 19th century, shortly after the lucrative sandalwood trade began. In the frenzy to make a quick buck to pay for alluring foreign goods, the alii forced the *makaainana* (commoners) to abandon their crops and work the forest.

The pit was dug to the exact measurements of a 75-foot-long ship's hold and filled with fragrant sandalwood logs cleared from the nearby forest. When the pit was full, the wood was strapped onto the backs of the laborers, who hauled it down to the harbor for shipment to China. The sea captains made out like bandits, while Hawaii lost its sandalwood forests.

After all the mature trees were cut down, the makaainana pulled up virtually every new sapling in order to spare their children the misery of another generation of forced harvesting.

Waikolu Lookout

Waikolu Lookout, at 3600 feet, provides a spectacular view into Waikolu Valley and out to the ocean beyond. Even if you're not able to spend time in Kamakou Preserve, the lookout is a fine destination in itself. If it's been raining recently, you'll be rewarded with numerous waterfalls streaming down the sheer cliffsides. Waikolu means 'Three Waters' – presumably named for the three drops in the main falls. Morning is the best time for views, as afternoon trade winds commonly carry clouds to the upper level of the canyon.

The steep mountains effectively prevent rain clouds from entering Molokai's central plains. In 1960, a 5½-mile tunnel was bored into the western side of Waikolu Valley. It now carries up to 28 million gallons of water each day down to the Kualapuu Reservoir.

A grassy camping area is directly opposite the lookout. If you can bear the mist and cold winds that sometimes blow up from the canyon, this could make a base camp for hikes into the preserve. The site has pit toilets but no water supply or other amenities. For more information, see the Camping section in the front of this chapter.

Kamakou Preserve

In 1982, Molokai Ranch conveyed to the Nature Conservancy of Hawaii the rights to manage the Kamakou Preserve, which starts immediately beyond the Waikolu Lookout. Its 2774 acres of native ecosystems include cloud forest, bogs, shrub land and habitat for many endangered plants and animals.

Much of the preserve is forested with *ohia lehua*, a native tree with fluffy red blossoms whose nectar is favored by native birds. The forest is home to two rare birds that live only on Molokai (Molokai creeper and Molokai thrush) and also to the bright red *apapane* (Hawaiian honeycreeper), the yellow-green *amakihi* (a type of native bird) and the *pueo* (Hawaiian owl). Other treasures include tree ferns, native orchids and silvery lilies.

The road deteriorates quickly from the preserve entrance. Don't even think about driving it without a 4WD vehicle. Even with a 4WD, if you're not used to driving in mud and on steep grades, it can be challenging. There are a few spots where it would be easy to flip a vehicle.

The Nature Conservancy asks visitors to sign in and out at the preserve entrance. Check out the sign-up sheet, where visitors write short entries on everything from car breakdowns to trail conditions and bird spottings.

Occasionally, portions of the preserve are closed. At such times, notices are posted at Kaunakakai's post office, Kalamaula hunters' check box and the preserve entrance.

Hiking As Kamakou is a rain forest, trails in the preserve can be very muddy. Rain gear is a good idea, and you should bring along an ample supply of drinking water.

The best hiking trail is the **Pepeopae Trail**, which goes east 1 mile to an overlook with a stunning view of Pelekunu Valley. The trail runs along a raised wooden boardwalk over Pepeopae Bog. The extensive boardwalk allows hikers access to this unique area while protecting the fragile ecosystem from being trampled. Pepeopae is a nearly undisturbed Hawaiian montane bog, a mysterious miniature forest with stunted trees and dwarfed plants. The area receives about 180 inches of rain each year, making it one of the wettest regions in the Hawaiian Islands.

There are two ways to reach the Pepeopae Trail. The easiest method is to walk from Waikolu Lookout about 2½ miles along the main jeep road to the Pepeopae Trailhead. This is a nice forest walk that takes just over an hour. There are some side roads along the way, but they're largely overgrown and it's obvious which is the main road. You'll eventually come to the 'Pepeopae' sign that marks the start of the trail, which branches to the left.

The second and far rougher way is to take the **Hanalilolilo Trail**. This trail, which is muddy and poorly defined, begins on the left side of the road about five minutes' walk past the Waikolu Lookout, shortly after entering the preserve.

The Hanalilolilo Trail climbs 500 feet through a rain forest of moss-covered ohia trees and connects with the Pepeopae Trail after 1½ miles. Turn left on the Pepeopae Trail, and it's about a half-mile walk up to the summit overlooking Pelekunu Valley.

From the Pelekunu Valley Overlook, you'll enjoy a view of majestic cliffs, and if it's not too cloudy, you can see down the valley out to the ocean.

Pelekunu Valley is also under the stewardship of the Nature Conservancy. The Pelekunu Valley Preserve includes nearly 6000 acres, extending from sea level up to a height of almost 5000 feet at the valley's upper rim. This inaccessible valley contains one of the few remaining perennial streams in Hawaii. It's an important habitat for gobies and river shrimp, which return from the ocean each year to swim up and lay their eggs in the fresh water of Pelekunu Stream.

Give yourself a good half day to do the entire hike from the Kamakou Preserve entrance and back. If you'd like to shorten the walk, consider one of the **guided hikes** led by the Nature Conservancy; these group outings enter the reserve in 4WD vehicles and start the hike at the Pepeopae Trailhead. Tour guides offer insights into the history and ecology of the preserve.

The conservancy's hikes are conducted monthly, usually on the first Saturday of the month. The cost and reservation information is the same as for Moomomi hikes; see the end of the Moomomi Beach section, later in this chapter, for more details.

HOOLEHUA

Hoolehua is the dry plains area that separates eastern and western Molokai. Here, in the 1790s, Kamehameha the Great trained his warriors in a year-long preparation for the invasion of Oahu. Hoolehua was settled as an agricultural community in 1924 as part of the Hawaiian Homes Act, which made public lands available to native Hawaiians. The land was divided into 40-acre plots. By 1930, more than half of Molokai's ethnic Hawaiian population was living on homesteads.

The first homestead was attempted closer to the coast, at Kalanianaole, but it failed when the well water pumped to irrigate crops turned brackish. Many of those islanders then moved north to Hoolehua, where homesteaders were already planting pineapple, a crop that required little water. As the two giant pineapple companies established operations in Molokai, homesteaders found it increasingly difficult to market their own pineapples and were eventually compelled to lease their lands to the plantations.

These days, there is a reliable water supply and more diversified crops, including coffee, sweet potato, papaya and fresh herbs.

Orientation & Information

Three roads run east to west, with minor crossroads going north to south. The post office and the adjacent Department of Land & Natural Resources office are on Puupeelua Ave (Hwy 480), just south of where it intersects with Farrington Ave.

Mail Home Some Aloha

Postmaster Margaret Keahi-Leary of the Hoolehua post office stocks baskets of unhusked coconuts that you can address and mail off as a unique (and edible!) 'postcard.' These coconuts, which Margaret gathers on her own time, are free for this 'post-a-nut' purpose, and she keeps a few felt pens on hand so you can jot down a message on the husk. Priority mail postage to anywhere in the USA costs $4 for an average-size coconut. The Hoolehua post office is open 7:30 to 11:30 am and 12:30 to 4:30 pm Monday to Friday.

Farrington Ave is Hoolehua's main street, with a fire station, Episcopal church and Molokai's high school. The Hawaiian Home Lands office is up on Puukapele Ave.

Puukapele Ave leads westward and then merges into another paved road that deceptively appears to be a find, heading beachward, but the road ends at the Western Space & Missile Center, a radio receiving station for the US Air Force. Here, a bunch of odd metal towers and wire cables make it look as if grown-up kids have been playing with a giant Erector Set.

MOLOKAI

Purdy's Macadamia Nut Farm

Tuddie Purdy runs the best little macadamia nut farm tour in all of Hawaii. Everything is done in quaint Molokai style: You can crack open macadamia nuts on a stone with a hammer and sample macadamia blossom honey scooped up with slices of fresh coconut.

Unlike tours on the Big Island that focus on processing, Purdy takes you into his orchard and explains how the nuts grow. A single macadamia tree can simultaneously be in different stages of progression – with flowers in blossom, tiny nuts just beginning and clusters of mature nuts. Purdy's 1½ acres of mature trees are nearly 75 years old and grow naturally: no pesticides, herbicides, fertilizers or even pruning.

Admission to the farm is free. Macadamia nuts (roasted or raw) and honey are for sale. To get to the farm, head north on Hwy 470 and turn left onto Farrington Ave. After 1 mile, turn right onto Lihi Pali Ave, just before the high school. The farm is a third of a mile up, on the right.

The hours are a bit flexible, but you might find Purdy there from 9:30 am to 3:30 pm Monday to Friday and 10 am to 2 pm on Saturday.

MOOMOMI BEACH

Moomomi Beach, located on the western edge of the Hoolehua Plains, is ecologically unique. It stands as one of the few undisturbed coastal sand dune areas left in Hawaii. Among its native grasses and shrubs are at least five endangered plant species that exist nowhere else on earth. It is one of the few places in the populated islands where green sea turtles still find a habitat suitable for breeding.

Evidence of an adze quarry and the fossils of a number of long-extinct Hawaiian birds have been unearthed here, preserved over time by Moomomi's arid sands. In 1988, the Nature Conservancy purchased 921 acres of Moomomi from Molokai Ranch and established Moomomi Preserve. Moomomi is not lushly beautiful, but windswept, lonely and wild.

To get there, turn off Hwy 460, east of the airport, onto Hwy 480. Then turn left onto Farrington Ave and head west. The paved road ends after about 3 miles. From there, it's 2½ miles farther along a red dirt road that is in some areas quite smooth and in others deeply rutted. In places, you may have to skirt the edge of the road and straddle a small gully. The road condition varies, depending on when it's last been graded, and it could be difficult going if it's muddy. Still, it's ordinarily passable in a standard car, although the higher the vehicle the better. It's best if you have a 4WD.

A little over 2 miles after the paved road ends, the road forks. Bear to the right and follow this road half a mile down to the beach. If it gets too rough, there's a spot halfway down this last stretch where you can pull off to the right and park.

At the end of the road is Moomomi Bay and a little sandy beach used by sunbathers. The rocky eastern point that protects the bay provides a perch for fishers. This area is part of the Hawaiian Home Lands.

The lovely beach that people refer to as Moomomi is not here, but at Kawaaloa Bay, a 20-minute walk to the west. Kawaaloa is a broad white-sand beach. The wind, which picks up steadily each afternoon, blows the sand into interesting ripples and waves.

The high hills running inland are actually massive sand dunes. The coastal cliffs, which have been sculptured into jagged abstract designs by wind and water, are made of sand that has petrified due to Moomomi's dry conditions.

The narrower right side of Kawaaloa Bay is partially sheltered; however, the whole beach can be rough when the surf is up, and swimming is discouraged. Visitors are not allowed to take any natural objects, including flora, rocks and coral.

There's a fair chance you'll have Kawaaloa to yourself, but if you don't you can always walk farther on to one of the other sandy coves along the shore. Most of the area west of here is open ocean with strong currents.

Because of the fragile ecology of the dunes, visitors should stay along the beach and on trails only. Foot access is allowed without a permit via the route described, although visitors with a 4WD vehicle can also get a gate key from the Nature Conservancy and drive directly to Kawaaloa Bay. To do that, a permit application and $25 key deposit are required.

The Nature Conservancy leads monthly guided hikes of Moomomi, usually on the third or fourth Saturday of the month. The cost of $15 for conservancy members and $25 for nonmembers includes transportation to and from the preserve. As it's common for hikers to fly over from other islands to join in, the pick-up run includes Molokai Airport. Reservations are required and must usually be made well in advance.

For a hike schedule or for reservations, contact the Nature Conservancy of Hawaii (☎ 553-5236), Molokai Preserves, Box 220, Kualapuu, HI 96757. If you're writing, include a self-addressed, stamped envelope.

West End

The Maunaloa Hwy (Hwy 460) heads west from Kaunakakai, passes Molokai Airport, and then climbs into the high grassy rangeland of Molokai's arid western side.

Hwy 460 is about 17 miles long, and the drive takes about half an hour from its start in Kaunakakai to its end at Maunaloa. It's a good paved road all the way, as are the roads to and around Kaluakoi Resort and down to Papohaku and Dixie Maru beaches. Most other West End roads, however, are privately owned dirt roads that are locked off to the public.

Molokai Ranch owns most of the land on this side of the island. Access is at the whim of the ranch but generally requires special permission.

From Molokai's West End beaches, the twinkling lights of Oahu are just 26 miles away. The view is of Diamond Head to the left, Makapuu Point to the right.

West End Development

In the 1970s, Molokai Ranch joined with Louisiana Land & Exploration Company to form the Kaluakoi Corporation, which proposed developing western Molokai into a major suburb of Honolulu, complete with a ferry service. The plan called for 30,000 private homes on the heretofore uninhabited west coast. A vocal anti-growth movement boomed quicker than the buildings could, however, and the plan was scrapped.

In its place, a somewhat more modest master plan was drawn up for the development of Kaluakoi Resort. The new scheme called for 1100 hotel units, 1200 condo units, 1000 single-family homes and a 15-acre shopping center.

Only 200 of the condo units, one 18-hole golf course and one of the four planned hotels have been built thus far. The 290-room hotel never really took off and the occupancy rate has been so low that part of it has been turned into condos. The house lots have been subdivided, but as of yet fewer than 100 houses have been built, mostly exclusive homes scattered along the edge of the beach and up on the bluff.

MAUNALOA

The long mountain range that comes into view on the left past the 10-mile marker is Maunaloa, which means 'Long Mountain.' Its highest point is Puu Nana at 1381 feet. In addition to being the site of Hawaii's first hula school and one of the Hawaiian Islands' most important adze quarries, Maunaloa was also once a center of sorcery.

The name Maunaloa not only refers to the mountain range but also to the town at the end of the road. Built in the 1920s by Libby, McNeill & Libby, this little plantation town was the center of the company's pineapple activities on Molokai. Dole, which acquired Libby, McNeill & Libby in 1972, closed down operations in Maunaloa in 1975.

These days, about 400 people live in the area, most working for Molokai Ranch or at Kaluakoi Resort.

Maunaloa is currently a town in flux. Molokai Ranch, which owns the land that the town sits on, is replacing many of the old plantation-era cottages with modern housing and adding new conveniences, including a business center and movie theater. Some of the housing is for local residents, but the town is also being targeted for growth, with plans for about 200 new house lots in all.

Information

The Molokai Ranch Outfitter Center is on the right as you enter town.

The little rural post office, opposite the grocery store, is open from 8 am to 4:30 pm Monday to Friday.

The village gas station, the only one on the West End, is open 7 am to 5 pm on weekdays, 9 am to 5 pm on Saturday and noon to 4 pm on Sunday.

Places to Eat

All of Maunaloa's businesses, including restaurants, lie along the Maunaloa Hwy, the town's main street. The most popular spot is the *Village Grill* (☎ 552-0012), which offers a simple lunch menu of salads, stew or sandwiches (around $7) from 11 am to 2 pm and good steak and fish dishes ($16 to $20) from 6 to 9 pm. The Village Grill also serves pizza at dinner, but the pies are pricey at $9 to $15.

For cheap eats, there's a small *KFC* at the side of the new movie theater, with the usual fried chicken offerings. It's not memorable, but you can get a meal of chicken, potatoes and biscuits for just $5; KFC is open 11 am to 8 pm daily (to 9:30 pm on weekends).

Otherwise, pick up supplies at the *Maunaloa General Store*, which is open 8 am to 6 pm Monday to Saturday and has a reasonable grocery selection, plus wine and beer.

Shopping

The Big Wind Kite Factory (☎ 552-2364), 120 Maunaloa Hwy, sells kites of all shapes and styles. Owner Jonathan Socher's kites have a reputation for their creative flair. Many of them, which have tropical fish and other island-influenced designs, are made on-site, and if you're lucky, you can watch the process. An extension of the kite factory is the eclectic gift shop next door, which has wood carvings from Bali, Fijian war clubs, scrimshaw carvings from Molokai deer, books and jewelry. Both are open 8:30 am to 5 pm Monday to Saturday and 10 am to 2 pm on Sunday.

Molokai Sorcery

According to legend, fire gods who roamed the heavens as shooting stars landed on Maunaloa, where they inhabited a grove of trees. Unsuspecting men who tried to cut down the possessed trees were poisoned upon touching the wood, until at last one of the gods explained to a *kahuna* (sorcerer) how to cut the trees down. The kahuna was then able to carve the poisoned wood into images that harnessed the force of the gods. During the 17th century it became a powerful sorcery that could be sent off into the night to wreak vengeance upon enemies. It was potent stuff, and none of Molokai's neighbors dared to violate Molokai's sovereignty in those days.

MOLOKAI RANCH

The 54,000-acre Molokai Ranch, headquartered in Maunaloa, has tried a number of things over the years to draw income from tourism. Until recently, it operated a small safari wildlife park in which exotic animals ranged freely while tourists were carted around in vans to feed the creatures and snap pictures. Some of the animals also served as targets for trophy hunters willing to pay $1500 to shoot an African eland or blackbuck antelope.

In the late 1990s, the safari park was closed, making way for a new tourist operation that focused more on the property's ranch character. With 6000 head of cattle, Molokai Ranch is the second largest working cattle ranch in the state.

Molokai Ranch now has three guest camps on its property: one near the village of Maunaloa, another in a more rugged corner of the ranch and a third on the beach at Kaupoa. Each camp has at least 20 'tentalows' – a canvas framed tent or yurt pitched on an elevated platform. Each tentalow has a queen-size bed, lights, ceiling fan, shower, deck and ice chest. The camps are equipped with pavilions where meals are prepared

MOLOKAI

buffet-style, not surprisingly with an emphasis on grilled meats.

A visit to Molokai Ranch is very much a packaged tour. Ranch staff pick up guests at the airport, check them in at the ranch's Maunaloa headquarters and then take them by van along the ranch's red dirt roads to the selected camp. Although the ranch offers visitors a chance to relax in a remote space and play a bit of paniolo, guests generally don't see much of Molokai outside the ranch gate. The cost, which includes meals, ranges from $128 to $245 per person per day, depending on whether the price covers activities. The activities include kayaking, mountain biking, horseback riding and a 'city slicker' cattle drive. Make reservations through **Molokai Ranch** (☎ 552-2741, 877-726-4656, Box 259, Maunaloa, HI 96770).

KALUAKOI RESORT

Off Hwy 460 at the 15-mile marker, a road leads down to Kaluakoi Resort. The 6700-acre development includes Kaluakoi Hotel & Golf Club, the condominium complexes of Kaluakoi Villas, Paniolo Hale and Ke Nani Kai, private house lots and a beautiful windswept coast. Overall, it's a low-key and unobtrusive development that's pleasantly quiet and uncrowded.

Kepuhi Beach is the white-sand beach in front of Kaluakoi Hotel. During the winter, the surf breaks close to shore, carrying a tremendous amount of sand to and fro. Experienced surfers take to the northern end of the beach.

Swimming conditions are often dangerous here. Not only can there be a tough shore-break, but strong currents can be present even on calm days.

A five-minute hike up to the top of **Kaiaka Rock**, a 110-foot-high promontory at the south end of Kepuhi Beach, rewards strollers with a nice view of Papohaku Beach. To get there, turn off Kaluakoi Rd onto the golf course road (Kaiaka Rd), proceeding a half mile to the road's end. At the top, you'll find the remains of a pulley that was once used to carry cattle down to waiting barges for transport to Oahu slaughterhouses. There was also a 40-foot heiau on the hilltop until 1967,

when the US Army bulldozed it. There have been on-again, off-again plans to build a luxury hotel at Kaiaka Rock.

Places to Stay
Kaluakoi Hotel & Golf Club (☎ 552-2555, fax 552-2821, kaluakoi@juno.com, Box 1977, Maunaloa, HI 96770) has rooms that are fairly standard for a resort hotel, although they're wearworn and on the small side. The cost is $105 for a garden-view room, $130 for ocean-view accommodations. There are also condo-style units that start at $155 for a studio, $170 for a one-bedroom. The hotel's amenities include an 18-hole golf course, tennis courts, a pool, a restaurant and a couple of small stores.

About 60 units of the Kaluakoi Hotel are under separate management and are booked as **Kaluakoi Villas** (☎ 552-2721, 800-525-1470, fax 552-2201, Box 350, Maunaloa, HI 96770). The units each have a private lanai, a TV and a kitchenette with refrigerator, coffeemaker and four-burner stove. While the walls are on the thin side and the decor varies with the unit, most are pleasant, and they can be a good value if you get a discounted rate – such as the 50% Entertainment discount (see the boxed text 'Travel Clubs' in the Facts for the Visitor chapter, earlier in this book). Standard rates are $125 to $150 for studio units, $150 to $180 for one-bedroom units. Ask for a 2nd-floor unit, as these have cathedral ceilings; many offer a peek of the ocean.

Paniolo Hale (☎ 552-2731, 800-367-2984, fax 552-2288, Box 190, Maunaloa, HI 96770) is a 77-unit condominium. The units are airy and each has a kitchen, ceiling fans, TV, washer/dryer and screened lanai. In the low season, studios cost $95, one-bedroom units with two baths cost $115 and two-bedroom units cost $145. In the high season, all rates are $20 more. Up to two people can stay in the studios and four in the other units. The minimum stay is usually three nights, although a couple of the units sometimes allow a two-night stay. There's a 10% weekly discount. The complex has a pool and barbecue grills. The office is open only from 8 am to 4 pm Monday to Saturday.

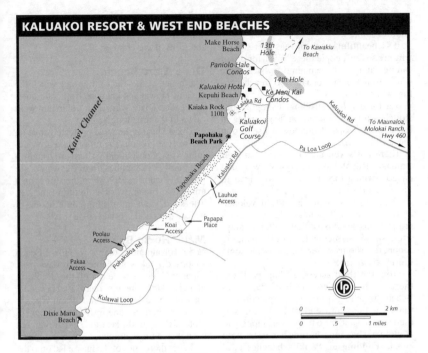

KALUAKOI RESORT & WEST END BEACHES

Ke Nani Kai (☎ 552-2761, 800-535-0085, fax 552-0045, marc@aloha.net, Box 126, Maunaloa, HI 96770) is a 120-unit condominium, 40 of which are in the rental pool. Units are individually owned so they vary significantly in upkeep and decor. Each has a full kitchen, lanai, washer/dryer and TV; most have a sofa bed in the living room. The units on the 2nd floor have high, exposed-beam ceilings, and the best of them are arguably the nicest on Molokai. Rack rates are $149 for up to four people in a one-bedroom unit, $179 for up to six people in a two-bedroom, two-bath unit. Those with ocean views are $20 more, but it's a distant and partial view. There's a pool and two tennis courts. Various discount schemes can cut the rack rates by as much as half.

Places to Eat
The only restaurant at the resort is the ***Ohia Lodge*** (☎ 552-2555), in the Kaluakoi Hotel. The dining room is pleasant, and the food is

reasonably good. Expect a standard breakfast of french toast or eggs to cost around $7, while the dinner prices range from $16 for chicken stir-fry to $24 for steak and shrimp. The restaurant is open 6:30 to 10:30 am and 6 to 9 pm daily.

Lunch is served at the hotel's ***snack bar***, which sells simple fare like burgers for $4 and teriyaki chicken plates for $5.50. The snack bar is open 11 am to 4:30 pm daily.

The hotel also has a ***sundries shop***, with wine, beer and a few convenience foods at inflated prices.

WEST END BEACHES
Papohaku Beach
Papohaku Beach lays claim to being Hawaii's largest beach. It's 2½ miles long and vast enough to hold the entire population of Molokai without getting crowded, although that would be an unlikely scenario. There's seldom more than a handful of beachgoers, even on sunny days, and at times

MOLOKAI

you can walk the shore without seeing another soul.

It's a beautiful beach and easy to reach, so why are so few people there? Well, for one, it can be windy. But the main drawback is the water itself, which is usually too treacherous for swimming.

Yet for barefoot strolling, it's a gorgeous stretch, with soft golden sands gleaming in the sun and wisps of rainbows tossed up in the crashing surf.

There are seven beach access points off Kaluakoi Rd; all have outdoor showers and paved parking lots. The first three lead to Papohaku Beach.

The first access point, the most developed of the seven, is Papohaku Beach Park, a grassy landscaped park that contains campsites, showers, picnic facilities, changing rooms, rest rooms, water fountains and some thorny kiawe trees.

From the third access, off Papapa Place, there's a broad view of all of Papohaku Beach, stretching north. The large concrete tunnel at the south end of the beach was used to load sand onto barges for shipping to Honolulu. The sand was used in construction and in building up Waikiki beaches until environmental protection laws put a halt to the sand mining operation in the early 1970s. This beach is a good place to find the small puka shells that islanders make into necklaces. It's also a great place to catch the sunset.

The next three beach accesses lead to rocky coastline, more suitable for fishing than other water activities.

Places to Stay Papohaku Beach Park is a choice site for camping – beautiful and quiet, with the surf lulling you to sleep and the birds waking you up. The tent sites are grassy and level. Secure your tent carefully, as the wind sometimes blows with hardy gusts. The camping area has two sections; they are watered by timed sprinklers on different days of the week, so pay attention to the sign that tells which days each area is scheduled for watering – there's nothing more depressing than finding your tent and belongings soaked!

For information on obtaining a permit, see Camping in the Accommodations section at the front of this chapter.

Dixie Maru Beach

The beach at the end of the road, which the ancient Hawaiians knew as Kapukahehu, is now called Dixie Maru after a ship that went down in the area long ago.

Dixie Maru is the most protected cove on the west shore and the most popular swimming area. Consequently, there are usually a fair number of families here. The waters are generally calm, except when the surf is high enough to break over the mouth of the bay. The sand is an interesting confetti mix of waterworn coral bits and small shells.

Make Horse Beach

Make (pronounced mah-kay) Horse Beach supposedly takes its name from days past, when wild horses were run off the cliff north of here. *Make* means 'dead' in Hawaiian. This pretty little white-sand beach is more secluded than the one in front of Kaluakoi Hotel. It's a good place for sunbathing, but it's not safe for swimming.

To get there, turn off Kaluakoi Rd onto the road to Paniolo Hale condos and then turn left toward the condo complex. It's best to park just beyond the condos and walk the last quarter-mile down to the golf course, though some people brave the deeply rutted dirt road to its end, where there's a little spot to park. Once at the golf course, cross a narrow stretch of fairway, and you're on the beach.

Kawakiu Beach

Kawakiu, north of the Kaluakoi Resort complex, is a broad crescent beach of white sand and bright turquoise waters.

In 1975, Kawakiu was a focus of Molokai activists, who began demanding access to private, and heretofore forbidden, beaches. The group, Hui Alaloa, marched to Kawakiu from Moomomi in a successful protest that convinced Molokai Ranch to provide public access to this secluded West End beach.

To get there, turn off Kaluakoi Rd onto the road to the Paniolo Hale condos, but instead of turning left down to the condos, continue straight towards the golf course. Where the paved road ends, there's space to pull over and park just before crossing the greens. There are rest rooms and drinking fountains here, at the 14th hole. It's the last chance to get water.

The red dirt road that continues down to the beach is rocky and rutted and not likely to be passable in anything but a 4WD. But anyway, why bother driving when it's a pleasant half-hour hike down to the beach?

After the golf course, the road passes through ranch land with kiawe trees. Trees that died during the mid-1980s drought now stand bleached white by the sun, making interesting silhouettes against the blue sky.

You'll come first to a rocky point at the southern end of the bay. Before descending to the beach, scramble around up here for a scenic view of the coast, south to the sands of Papohaku Beach and north to Ilio Point.

When seas are calm, Kawakiu is generally safe for swimming, although that's more common in summer than winter. When the surf is rough, there are still areas where you can at least get wet. On the southern side of the bay, there's a small, sandy-bottomed wading pool in the rocks. The northern side has an area of flat rocks over which water slides to fill up a shallow shoreline pool.

On weekends, there are often a few families picnicking under the kiawe trees, but at other times you may well have the place to yourself.

Locals occasionally camp here as well, but there are no facilities.

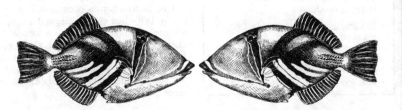

MOLOKAI

Lanai

Until recently, Lanai was a one-crop, one-company, one-town island. The latter two still hold true.

For over half a century, Castle & Cooke, the company that owns 98% of Lanai, ran the island as its own private pineapple plantation. For a time, nearly one-fifth of the world's pineapples came from Lanai, but competition from more cheaply produced Costa Rican and Philippine pineapples gradually eroded the profitability of the Lanai crop.

Castle & Cooke has now ceased its commercial pineapple operations completely and is turning rural Lanai into an exclusive tourist destination. In the past decade, the company has opened two luxury resorts, both with 18-hole golf courses, and built some of the island's first million-dollar vacation homes.

Until 1990, Lanai had only one little hotel with just 10 rooms. The few visitors who came this way were largely hunters, hikers and independent travelers trying to avoid the tourist scene on the other islands. Now, with its two new resorts, which are among the most expensive ever built in Hawaii, Castle & Cooke is gambling that enough wealthy visitors in search of seclusion will show up to make it all pay off.

On the surface, the hotels, with 350 rooms combined, haven't altered things all that radically. The center of Lanai remains Lanai City – not a city at all, but merely a little plantation town of tin-roofed houses and small shops. It's still home to all but a few dozen of Lanai's 3000 residents, most of whom work for the Lanai Company, the non-agricultural subsidiary of Castle & Cooke.

Lanai has bright red earth, dry and dusty gullies, forested ravines, white-sand beaches and cool, foggy uplands. The island also has some obscure archaeological sites and petroglyphs and the last native dryland forest in Hawaii.

Although Lanai can be interesting to explore, many of the sights are a good distance from town, along rutted dirt roads that require a 4WD vehicle.

Not surprisingly, Lanai can be quite expensive to visit. One of the easiest ways to get a glimpse of it is to take the ferry over from Maui in the morning, snorkel at Hulopoe Bay, which has the island's finest beach, and then take the boat back in the afternoon.

HISTORY

Archaeological studies indicate Lanai was never heavily settled. Villages were relatively small and scattered throughout the island.

Since ancient times, Lanai has been under the rule of its more dominant neighbor, Maui. In 1778, when the Big Island chief Kalaniopuu was routed in a failed attempt to invade Maui, he decided to take his revenge on tiny Lanai and sent warriors under the command of Kamehameha the Great.

Kamehameha's troops were brutal. They killed everyone they found and virtually depopulated Lanai. When English explorer George Vancouver sailed by Lanai in 1792, he saw no villages and noted that the island might at best be only sparsely populated.

Due to treacherous ocean swells, which by the 1820s had already claimed a couple of foreign ships, would-be visitors were dissuaded from landing on Lanai's shores. In 1823, a missionary named William Ellis became the first Westerner to step ashore. He guessed the island's population to be around 2000.

Highlights

- Snorkeling in the pristine waters off Hulopoe Beach

- Strolling through historic Lanai City, an old plantation town

- Spotting whales from the ferry between Maui and Lanai

- Beachcombing on Shipwreck Beach

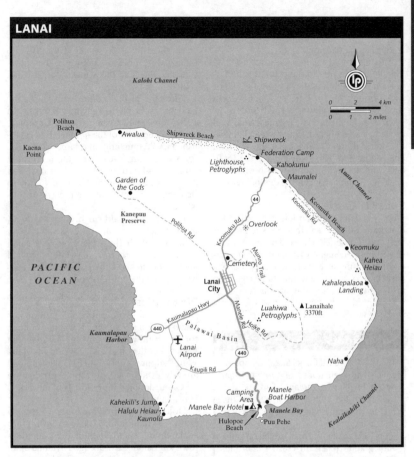

LANAI

Kalohi Channel

Polihua Beach

Kaena Point

Awalua

Shipwreck Beach

⚓ Shipwreck

Federation Camp

Lighthouse, Petroglyphs

Kahokunui

Maunalei

Garden of the Gods

Kanepuu Preserve

Polihua Rd

(44)

Keomuku Rd

Anau Channel

Keomuku Rd

Keomuku Beach

Overlook ☀

PACIFIC OCEAN

Munro Trail

Cemetery

Lanai City

Keomuku

Kahea Heiau

Kahalepalaoa Landing

Luahiwa Petroglyphs

▲ Lanaihale 3370ft

Kaumalapau Hwy

(440)

Kaumalapau Harbor

Palawai Basin

Manele Rd

Hoike Rd

Lanai Airport

✈

(440)

Naha

Kaupili Rd

Kahekili's Jump

Halulu Heiau

Kaunolu

Camping Area

Manele Bay Hotel ▲

Manele Boat Harbor

Manele Bay

Hulopoe Beach

Puu Pehe

Kealaikahiki Channel

0   2   4 km
0   1   2 miles

Although the early missionaries didn't spend much time on Lanai, they still had an influence. They introduced the heretofore unknown concept of adultery to Hawaii, and in the 1830s Maui women accused of that criminal offense were banished to the barren northwestern side of Lanai as punishment.

Mormons

In the 1850s, the Mormons moved in and set up a community at Palawai Basin, south of present-day Lanai City. Their intention was to establish a 'City of Joseph' in Hawaii.

The community floundered until 1861, when a new charismatic elder, Walter Gibson, arrived. Mormons from around the islands poured in, as did money to buy Palawai Basin. At the height of it all, there was one Mormon for every Lanaian.

Gibson, a shrewd businessman, handled the financial matters for the community – including the acquisition of land. Things got sticky when it was discovered that he had made the land purchases in his own name, rather than in the church's. In 1864, after refusing to transfer the title of his Lanai holdings to the mother church in Salt Lake City, he was excommunicated by church leader Brigham Young.

This apparently suited Gibson just fine. Unable to gain title to the property, the Lanai congregation faded away and the 300 or so Mormons left for Laie on Oahu's north shore, where their church is still based today.

Gibson held onto the prime Lanai real estate he had cornered. Equally calculating in the political arena, Gibson became a friend and confidant of King Kalakaua in the 1880s and came to hold a number of positions in Kalakaua's cabinet, including that of premier.

Sugar & Cattle

Upon his death, Gibson left the land to his daughter, Talula Lucy. In 1888, she and her husband, Frederick Hayselden, established the Maunalei Sugar Company and developed a landing at Kahalepalaoa on Lanai's east coast. A water pumping station went up at nearby Keomuku, the surrounding area was planted with sugarcane and the whole shebang was connected by a little railroad.

Sugar Roots

The short-lived Maunalei Sugar Company, which had high hopes of turning Lanai into a bustling sugarcane plantation at the end of the 19th century, was not the first try at establishing the sugar business on Lanai.

In 1802, a Chinese man landed on Lanai with granite rollers to crush sugarcane, which had been growing freely on the islands since the arrival of the first Polynesians. Using iron pots, he boiled the crushed cane down into a sugary syrup. Although his name has been lost to history, this man is commonly credited with being the first person to attempt commercial sugar production in Hawaii. This particular enterprise was a failure, but it was such Chinese know-how that became the basis for the Maunalei Sugar Company and other sugar mills throughout Hawaii.

❀ ❀ ❀ ❀ ❀ ❀ ❀ ❀ ❀ ❀ ❀ ❀ ❀ ❀

More than 400 Japanese laborers were brought in to work the fields. The sugar days were short-lived, however. By 1901, the pumps were drawing saltwater, the sugarcane had died and the whole enterprise had folded.

After the dismal failure with sugar, the land was sold off to ranching interests. In 1910, the newly formed Lanai Company consolidated most of the holdings and established cattle ranching on a larger scale. The following year, New Zealander George Munro was hired to manage the ranch, and a landing was established at Manele Bay so that the company could ship cattle to off-island markets.

In 1917, the Baldwin brothers, sons of missionaries from Maui, purchased the Lanai Company. With the exception of a small ranch held by other *haole* (white men) and about 500 acres held by Lanaians, the Baldwins owned the entire island.

Pineapples

In 1922, Jim Dole paid $1.1 million for Lanai, a mere $12 an acre. It was just enough for the Baldwins to buy the Ulupalakua Ranch that they had long coveted on Maui. With the purchase of Lanai, Dole, who had already established pineapple production on Oahu, doubled his holdings of cultivable Hawaiian land.

Dole's Hawaiian Pineapple Company poured $4 million into Lanai to turn it into a plantation island. It built the plantation town of Lanai City, dredged Kaumalapau Bay to make it a deepwater harbor, put in roads and water systems, cleared the land and planted pineapples. By the end of the 1920s, production was in full swing.

Dole had marketed his pineapples well and was producing bumper crops – the future looked rosy. Then the Great Depression hit the mainland, and sales plummeted. The newly popular canned pineapples had become an exotic extra, one that most Americans could easily do without in hard times.

Following an $8 million loss in 1932, a reorganization took place. Castle & Cooke purchased much of the stock and eventually gained a controlling interest in Dole; the

Spirits in the Night

According to legend, Lanai was a land of *akua* (spirits), and they alone roamed the island until the 15th century.

It was at this time that Kaululaau, the young prince of Maui, lived in what is today the town of Lahaina on Maui. He was a mischievous child. After he had torn out breadfruit trees that his father had just planted, the elders decided to banish him to uninhabited Lanai, an almost certain death.

Not one to be easily intimidated, Kaululaau learned to trick the evil spirits of Lanai. During the day, the akua would see him on the beach and ask where he spent his nights, hoping to ambush him in his sleep. He convinced them that he slept in the surf, though when darkness fell he slipped off to the shelter of a cave.

Night after night, the akua returned to the beach and rushed out to look for Kaululaau in the waves. The longer they searched, the more exhausted they got, until finally the pounding surf overcame them. Kaululaau continued his pranks until all 400 of Lanai's akua had either perished or fled to Kahoolawe.

Kaululaau's family had given him up for dead when Mauians noticed a light from a fire across the Auau Channel, which separates Maui and Lanai. When they went over to investigate, they found Kaululaau alive and well and the island devoid of spirits. Kaululaau was brought back to Maui a hero.

company has been the dominant force on Lanai ever since.

GEOGRAPHY

Lanai is the sixth-largest Hawaiian island. It's 18 miles long, 13 miles wide and shaped like a teardrop. It has an area of 140 sq miles.

Lanai lies 9 miles south of Molokai and 9 miles west of Maui. The name Lanai means 'hump.' When viewed from Maui, it looks somewhat like the back of a whale rising out of the water. The island was formed by a single volcano, Palawai, now long extinct. The large flat basin of Palawai crater contains most of Lanai's arable land.

Lanai's terrain and climate are dominated by a ridge running from the northwest to the southeast. It reaches a height of 3370 feet at Lanaihale. From there, a series of gulches radiate down to the east coast, ending at a strip of coastal flats.

The western side of the ridge is a cool central plateau, which includes Lanai City at 1620 feet.

The southwest coast has sheer sea cliffs, some higher than 1000 feet. Northwest Lanai is dry and barren and slopes gently down to the coast.

CLIMATE

Lanai City has a mild climate. The lowest temperature on record is 46°F; the highest is 88°F. Average temperatures range from 73°F in the summer to 66°F in the winter. Evenings can be brisk, with temperatures commonly dipping down to around 50°F in winter.

Lanai is rather dry. Molokai to the north and Maui to the east draw much of the rain out of the moisture-laden trade winds before they reach Lanai.

Annual rainfall averages 37 inches in Lanai City and 10 to 15 inches along most of the coast. The difference is great enough that when it's overcast in Lanai City, chances are that Shipwreck Beach or Manele Bay will be sunny.

As in the rest of Hawaii, October to April is the rainiest season. Even the island's drier areas can get soaked with heavy rainfall during winter storms. The summer months see much lighter precipitation.

LANAI

FLORA & FAUNA
Lanai has suffered the greatest loss of native forests, plants and birds of any of the main Hawaiian islands, thanks to drastic overgrazing.

Lanai has about 8000 axis deer, descendants of a herd of eight brought to Molokai from India in 1868. The deer were introduced to Lanai in 1920 and are more prolific than on Molokai, the only other Hawaiian island where they roam free.

Mouflon sheep were introduced to Lanai in 1954 and inhabit the island's gullies and ridges. Both the deer and sheep are hunted.

Lanai has no mongooses, which eat the eggs of ground-nesting birds, so introduced game birds thrive. Ring-necked pheasants, francolin and chukar partridges, quails, doves and wild turkeys are all common.

However, the island has only two endemic birds remaining – the *pueo* (Hawaiian owl) and the *apapane* (native honeycreeper) – and they are scarce.

After a long period of decline, green sea turtles have been making a comeback in recent years, especially along Lanai's remote northeastern shore. The most abundant of the three native turtle species found in Hawaiian waters, the green sea turtle weighs upwards of 200 pounds at maturity.

The most noticeable types of vegetation are thorny *kiawe* (a relative of mesquite) trees, common in Lanai's dry coastal areas, and stately Norfolk Island pines, which abound around Lanai City. Lanai has a unique native dryland forest, under the protection of the Nature Conservancy.

GOVERNMENT
Lanai is part of Maui County, but control of the island is largely in the hands of Castle & Cooke, which owns all but 2% of Lanai. Total county and state land accounts for just over 100 acres. Beaches on Lanai, as elsewhere in Hawaii, are in the public domain under state jurisdiction.

ECONOMY
About 80% of Lanai's 1200 workers are employed by the Lanai Company, mostly in its resort operations. Lanai has an unemployment rate of 4.5%, which is lower than the statewide average.

Although visitors will see a couple of high-profile pineapple fields, these small patches are only 'show fields' – the last commercial pineapple harvest was in 1992. Some of the former pineapple fields have been given over to forage crops and cattle raising, but the importance of agriculture and ranching is secondary at best.

Lanai's transition from a plantation economy to a tourism-oriented service economy hasn't been entirely smooth. The resorts initially mounted millions of dollars in operating losses, but occupancy rates climbed after the opening of a second golf course in 1994.

Around that same time, Bill Gates, the Microsoft founder who has become the wealthiest of the world's rich and famous, selected Lanai as the site for his marriage, creating a publicity shower for the resorts. In the past few years, the Lanai hotels have seen a steady growth in visitors despite slowdowns at top-end resorts elsewhere in the Hawaiian Islands.

In the next stage of development, the Lanai Company intends to build hundreds of luxury homes geared for wealthy, second-home owners who have bypassed Lanai up to now. If it all develops according to plan, Lanai's population could more than triple to 10,000 in the next decade.

POPULATION & PEOPLE
Lanai has seen some dramatic rises and declines in its population. It had dropped well below 200 when Dole arrived in 1922.

Lanai's current population has risen to 3000, but that's still about 10% less than it was during pineapple's heyday in the 1950s. All but a few dozen of Lanai's residents live in Lanai City. The largest ethnic group is Filipino (51%), followed by Japanese (18%), Caucasian (11%) and part-Hawaiian (9.2%).

Approximately a third of the people living on Lanai were born in the Philippines; Filipino immigrants came to the island to work on Dole's pineapple plantation in the mid-20th century.

ORIENTATION

Lanai has only one town, Lanai City, which is smack in the center of the island. The town is laid out in a sensible grid pattern, which makes it easy to find your way around.

Outside Lanai City there are only three paved roads: Keomuku Rd (Hwy 44), which heads northeast towards Shipwreck Beach; Kaumalapau Hwy, which heads west to Kaumalapau Harbor; and Manele Rd, which goes south to Manele and Hulopoe bays. Both Kaumalapau Hwy and Manele Rd are marked Hwy 440, even though they are two distinct roads.

The airport is on Kaumalapau Hwy, $3^1/_2$ miles southwest of town.

Maps

As Lanai has so few roads and relatively few visitors, it may come as no surprise that there's no proliferation of road maps. The University of Hawaii's joint Molokai-Lanai map shows Lanai's topography as well as geographical and archaeological sites. The Lanai Company distributes a simpler fold-out map that shows Lanai City, the grounds of the two resorts and the island's main roads; it can be picked up free at the hotels.

Dirt Roads

Most roads on Lanai are dirt roads, many of them built to service the pineapple fields of yesteryear; their conditions vary from good to impassable, largely as a result of the weather.

If you rent a 4WD vehicle and plan to travel these roads, ask the rental agency for the current best routes to out-of-the-way sights – often there are a few alternatives, and the agencies know which roads are washed out and which are passable. If you do go off the beaten path and get stuck, it can be a long walk back to town, and you can expect to pay a lot for the towing and repair fees.

INFORMATION

There's no local daily newspaper, but community notices, including ads about rental housing and the movie theater schedule, are posted on bulletin boards outside the post office and at grocery stores.

Official Lanai

Until recently Lanai had the nickname 'The Pineapple Island,' but the latest promotional slogan is 'The Secluded Island.' Lanai's official color is yellow and its official flower is *kaunaoa*, a thin, yellow-orange parasitic vine.

Money

There are two banks in Lanai City, both on Lanai Ave. The First Hawaiian Bank is near 7th St and the Bank of Hawaii is on the opposite side of the post office, near 8th St. The banks are both open 8:30 am to 4 pm Monday to Thursday and 8:30 am to 6 pm on Friday. Both banks have 24-hour ATMs that accept major bank cards and credit cards.

Post & Communications

Lanai's post office, at the east side of Dole Park in Lanai City, is open 9 am to 4:30 pm on weekdays and 10 am to noon on Saturday.

Libraries

Lanai's library is on Fraser Ave in Lanai City, adjacent to the Lanai Elementary and High School. It doubles as the school library and hence is fairly large. There's a good collection of newspapers, including the *Wall Street Journal*, the *Honolulu Advertiser* and other Neighbor Island papers. The library is open 2 to 8 pm on Wednesday, from 8 am to 5 pm on other weekdays and 10 am to 3 pm on Saturday. There's a computer with Internet access, but a Hawaii state library card is required to use the computer. (For more information, see Libraries in the Facts for the Visitor chapter, earlier in this book).

Laundry

There's a coin laundry, open 6 am to 9 pm daily, on 7th St in Lanai City.

Weather Hotlines

For recorded weather forecasts and water conditions, call ☎ 565-6033.

LANAI

Emergency

For all emergencies, call ☎ 911. Lanai Community Hospital (☎ 565-6411), on 7th St in Lanai City, offers 24-hour emergency service.

ACTIVITIES

There's a public recreation center in Lanai City, next to the school and the library, with a 75-foot-long pool, a basketball court and a couple of lighted tennis courts.

Both the Manele Bay Hotel and the Lodge at Koele have 18-hole designer golf courses complete with dress codes and $125 greens fees ($175 for nonguests), cart included.

The Cavendish Golf Course, a local nine-hole course on the north side of Lanai City, is the only free golf course in Hawaii and a popular recreation spot for islanders. Anyone can play; simply bring your clubs and begin. There are no dress codes and no fees, though there is a donation box where you can make an anonymous offering.

Lanai Ecoadventure Centre (☎ 565-7737), PO Box 1394, Lanai City, HI 96763, offers a kayak and snorkel tour along the northeast side of the island, as well as mountain-bike tours to destinations like the Munro Trail and the Garden of the Gods. Tours cost $69 for a half-day outing or $119 for a full-day trip.

The two resort hotels offer a variety of activities, including tennis, diving and horseback riding; however, fees are generally quite high, and many of the activities are limited to hotel guests.

GETTING THERE & AWAY
Air

Island Air (☎ 565-6744, 800-652-6541) flies to Lanai from Honolulu 10 times a day and from Kahului on Maui three times a day. Hawaiian Airlines (☎ 565-7281) flies to Lanai from Honolulu once a day on weekdays, twice daily on weekends, and from Molokai and Kahului to Lanai once daily. On both airlines, the one-way fare is currently $93; for the same price, you can fly between Lanai and any other island, with connections via Honolulu.

For information on discounted tickets and air passes, see the Getting Around chapter, near the front of this book.

Ferry

Expeditions (☎ 661-3756, 800-695-2624) operates a small passenger ferry between Lahaina on Maui and Manele Boat Harbor on Lanai. The boat departs Lahaina at the dock in front of the Pioneer Inn at 6:45 and 9:15 am and 12:45, 3:15 and 5:45 pm daily. The boat departs Manele at 8 and 10:30 am and 2, 4:30 and 6:45 pm daily. The trip takes 45 minutes to one hour. One-way fares are $25 for adults and $20 for children ages two to 11. Reservations can be made in advance; tickets are purchased on the boat.

This is a great way to get to Lanai. Although the ride can be jolting when the seas are rough, it's usually quite pleasant, and there's a good chance of seeing whales during the winter. Migrating humpbacks often pass through the waters between Maui and Lanai.

Organized Tours

For details on diving, snorkeling and sailing tours to Lanai from Maui, see the Activities section in the Maui chapter.

GETTING AROUND
To/From the Airport

The Lodge at Koele and the Manele Bay Hotel have a shuttle bus that meets hotel guests at the airport; the same shuttle will also drop guests off at Hotel Lanai, though officially you're supposed to arrange this in advance when you book your room. Lanai City Service provides taxi service from the airport, and if you have reservations for a rental car, the company provides free transfers to its in-town office, an affiliate of Dollar Rent A Car.

Car

Only one international car rental company operates on Lanai, and consequently the rates are high.

Lanai City Service (☎ 565-7227, 800-367-7006), on Lanai Ave in Lanai City, handles rentals for Dollar Rent A Car. Unlike its affiliates on other islands, Dollar's Lanai branch requires a one-day deposit to make a booking, and there are no discounts available. Compact cars rent for $60 a day, 4WD Jeep Wranglers for $119.

While there are many dirt roads in fine condition, Lanai City Service restricts all its cars to paved roads – the 4WD jeeps may be driven on most dirt roads. The jeeps are usually available on short notice, but the cars can be in short supply and sometimes need to be booked a week or more in advance.

The other possibility is renting a vehicle from Red Rover (☎ 565-7722, fax 565-7377), a small company that has 4WD Land Rovers for $109 to $149 per day; discounts are available for Hawaiian residents. The agency is on Lanai Ave, across the street from Lanai City Service.

Shuttle

The resorts run a free shuttle bus between the Manele Bay Hotel and the Lodge at Koele for their guests. The bus runs about every 30 minutes throughout the day, stops en route at the Hotel Lanai, and operates late enough for you to catch dinner at either resort and still get back to your own hotel.

Taxi

Lanai City Service (☎ 565-7227) provides a limited taxi service. The cost is $5 per person between the airport and town and $10 per person between Manele Bay and town. If you're flying in, it's best to call and make arrangements in advance. Otherwise, once you arrive you'll have to call to see if someone is available to come and get you; you'll find a courtesy phone in the airport's baggage claim area.

If you're coming from Maui by ferry, Lanai City Service operates a shuttle van that usually meets the ferries.

Around Lanai

LANAI CITY

Lanai City is nestled among Norfolk pines on a cool central plateau beneath the slopes of Lanaihale mountain. For an old plantation town, it's a tidy little place. Houses are brightly painted, and many have lovely front gardens with flowering plants and trees.

The center of town is **Dole Park**, a large grassy park lined with lofty Norfolk pines.

The park stretches six blocks from Fraser Ave to Lanai Ave, the two main roads in town.

The two local-style eateries lie on the north side of the park; the deli/health food store and the grocery stores are on the south side. To the east of the park you'll find the post office, hospital and Hotel Lanai. To the west are the school and recreation center, with houses spread out for half a dozen blocks on either side – and that's about it.

At sunset, walking through the town and looking at the pines silhouetted against the crimson sky can be a delight. On Sunday mornings, a stroll by the **Hawaiian Church** on the corner of 5th and Gay Sts will treat you to fine melodies of choir music.

While the new resorts have brought some changes, this is still a place where you can unwind. All in all, it's hard to imagine a town less hurried than Lanai City.

Places to Stay

Dreams Come True (☎ 565-6961, 800-566-6961, fax 565-7056, hunters@aloha.net, 547 12th St, Lanai City, HI 96763) is a B&B in a period plantation house furnished with Asian antiques. There are three guest bedrooms: One has a king bed, while the other two each have a four-poster queen bed and one single bed. Each has its own private bath – though it may be across the hall. There's a common room with cable TV. Rates, which include a continental breakfast of homemade breads and fresh fruit, are $61/75 for singles/doubles. There's a $25 surcharge on stays of less than two nights. The owners, Michael and Susan Hunter, also rent out a nearby rustic three-bedroom home and a new two-bedroom home with a queen sofa bed in the living room; both houses can sleep up to six for $190 a day. There are a couple of Jeep Cherokees that guests can rent for $100 a day (no insurance).

Hotel Lanai (☎ 565-7211, 800-795-7211, fax 565-6450, hotellanai@aloha.net, PO Box 520, Lanai City, HI 96763) was built by Dole in 1923 to house plantation guests. It still maintains an engaging mountain lodge ambiance that's a throwback to an earlier era. The 10 restored rooms are pleasant, with

LANAI

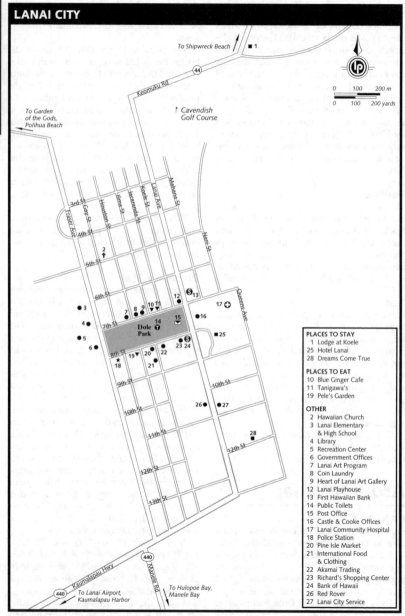

LANAI CITY

To Shipwreck Beach ■ 1

44

Keomuku Rd

↑ Cavendish
Golf Course

To Garden
of the Gods,
Polihua Beach

0   100   200 m
0   100   200 yards

3rd St
Fraser Ave
Gay St
Houston St
Ilima St
Jacaranda St
Koele Ave
Lanai Ave
Mahana St

4th St

5th St   2 ✝

Nani St

6th St   12   ⓢ13
                         17 ✛

● 3   7 8 9 10 11   Queens Ave
4 ●   ▼▼   15 ✉
5 ●   14 ☎   ● 16
7th St   Dole
         Park   ■ 25
6 ●   ⓢ
8th St   19▼ 20   23 24
18 ★   21 22
9th St

10th St   10th St

26 ● ● 27

11th St   28 ■

12th St   12th St

13th St

440

Kaumalapau Hwy
440
To Lanai Airport,
Kaumalapau Harbor

Manele Rd

To Hulopoe Bay,
Manele Bay

PLACES TO STAY
1 Lodge at Koele
25 Hotel Lanai
28 Dreams Come True

PLACES TO EAT
10 Blue Ginger Cafe
11 Tanigawa's
19 Pele's Garden

OTHER
2 Hawaiian Church
3 Lanai Elementary
  & High School
4 Library
5 Recreation Center
6 Government Offices
7 Lanai Art Program
8 Coin Laundry
9 Heart of Lanai Art Gallery
12 Lanai Playhouse
13 First Hawaiian Bank
14 Public Toilets
15 Post Office
16 Castle & Cooke Offices
17 Lanai Community Hospital
18 Police Station
20 Pine Isle Market
21 International Food
   & Clothing
22 Akamai Trading
23 Richard's Shopping Center
24 Bank of Hawaii
26 Red Rover
27 Lanai City Service

hardwood floors, pedestal sinks, bleached pine furnishings, patchwork quilts and painted wooden walls that are anything but soundproof. There are various bed options, ranging from twin and queen bed combinations to one king bed. Each room has a private bathroom and costs $95 to $105; the more expensive rooms include front porches overlooking Lanai City. There's also a one-bedroom cottage in the rear that has a separate sitting room with a sofa bed for $135 a night. Rates include continental breakfast. To see pictures of the accommodations, visit the hotel's website at www.onlanai.com.

The *Lodge at Koele* (☎ 565-7300, 800-321-4666, fax 565-4561, reservations@lanai-resorts.com, PO Box 774, Lanai City, HI 96763) is a low-rise, 102-room hotel with the character of an overgrown plantation estate. The hotel maintains a genteel image, complete with afternoon tea, lawn bowling and croquet. Its lobby, called the Great Hall, is stuffed with an eclectic collection of antiques, artwork and upholstered furnishings and boasts Hawaii's two largest stone fireplaces. Guest rooms are nicely appointed with four-poster beds, private *lanais* (verandas), marble bathrooms, VCRs and the like. The service is attentive and the hotel has received a number of accolades, including being named 'Best Resort in the USA' by the Zagat survey. Pampering comes at a price, however, with rooms costing $325 to $485; suites, which include butler service, start at $600.

Places to Eat

The *Blue Ginger Cafe* (☎ 565-6363), an unpretentious little bakery and cafe with cement floors and plastic chairs, makes decent muffins and turnovers, in addition to dishing up three square meals a day. At breakfast, pancakes and waffles cost less than $5. The cafe also serves inexpensive hamburgers and *saimin* (Japanese noodle soup) and $7 plate lunches. At dinner, specials such as shrimp tempura or fresh *mahi-mahi* ('dolphin' fish) cost around $13. The cafe is open 6 am to 9 pm daily, with breakfast served until 11 am.

Tanigawa's (☎ 565-6537) has the most popular burgers on Lanai – you can get one with the works for a mere $2. The restaurant, which has an old-style counter where you can sit over coffee and watch the bacon sizzle on the grill, offers breakfast dishes and lunch plates for around $6. Tanigawa's is open 6:30 am to 1 pm daily except Wednesday, when it's closed.

A good alternative spot is *Pele's Garden* (☎ 565-9629), a combination deli and health food store on 8th St. The store, which is open 9:30 am to 6:30 pm Monday to Saturday, has vitamins, packaged foods and a tiny produce and frozen food section. The deli, open 11 am to 7 pm Monday to Saturday, has sandwiches for around $6, including an excellent turkey and avocado version. It also offers cheese and free-range turkey by the pound, deli-style, as well as fresh-squeezed juices, most made from local produce (some organic). There are cafe tables on the front porch where you can sit and watch the Lanai City traffic trickle by.

The most bustling dinner spot is *Henry Clay's Rotisserie* (☎ 565-4700) at the Hotel Lanai, where the chef shows off his New Orleans roots. The dining room features a fireplace, high ceilings and hardwood floors. Main dishes include Creole eggplant pasta or Louisiana-style pork ribs for $17 and country French duck confit for $24. Starters include New England chowder or a Caesar salad for around $8 to $10. Henry Clay's is open 5:30 to 9 pm nightly, though the bar stays open until midnight as long as there are still customers.

At the Lodge at Koele, the lobbyside *Terrace Dining Room* (☎ 565-7300) overlooks the hotel gardens. Breakfast menu items like hotcakes or salmon omelettes, as well as lunchtime salads and sandwiches, average $10 to $14. At dinner, main courses, such as clams on polenta 'pizza' or grilled fish, are $16 to $24. Breakfast is served from 7 to 11 am, lunch from 11 am to 6 pm and dinner from 6 to 9:30 pm.

The Lodge's *Formal Dining Room* (☎ 565-7300), which is open for dinner only, is the most highly rated restaurant on Lanai. It features à la carte entrees (such as rack of lamb, Maine lobster or venison from Lanai axis deer) for $35 to $40. While prices are steep, the food and service generally live up to the bill. As the name implies, a jacket is required of men, but it can be borrowed from the front desk.

The island's largest grocery stores, *Richard's Shopping Center* and *Pine Isle Market*, are near each other on 8th St. Richard's is open 8:30 am to 6:30 pm Monday to Saturday, and Pine Isle's hours are 8 am to 7 pm Monday to Saturday. In addition to groceries, both stores stock a varied collection of items from sandals and hardware to beer and wine. Although its selection is much smaller, *International Food & Clothing*, nearby on Ilima St, is open on Sunday from 8 am to 1:30 pm; other days, it's open 8 am to 6 pm.

Entertainment
People go to bed early in Lanai, and there's no real nightlife, although the *Lodge at Koele* usually has mellow Hawaiian music from 7 to 10 pm in its Great Hall lobby.

The *Lanai Playhouse* (☎ 565-7500), the island's cozy little movie theater on 7th St, shows first-run feature films every day but Thursday.

Shopping
The Lanai Art Program, on 7th St, is the site of the community arts program and the place to purchase locally made arts and crafts. The items, all made by Lanai residents, include watercolors, painted T-shirts, batik scarves and simple ornaments. Hours can be a bit irregular, but you'll often find someone there during the day from Monday to Saturday.

The Heart of Lanai Art Gallery, a few doors east on 7th St, offers more upscale items, including paintings, wooden bowls and pottery, from artists throughout Hawaii. It's open 1 to 6 pm Monday to Saturday.

Akamai Trading, on 8th St, sells Lanai-motif T-shirts and a few local paintings.

Gifts With Aloha, at the rear of Pele's Garden on 8th St, also carries some local art, jewelry, wooden bowls, aloha shirts and Hawaiian-print skirts.

SHIPWRECK BEACH & KEOMUKU
Hwy 44 runs 8½ miles from town to the northeast coast. The highway is narrow but well paved. To get to Hwy 44, head north on Lanai Ave and bear right on Keomuku Rd (Hwy 44).

The road heads into hills and pastures with grazing cattle. The uplands here are often cool, with fog and cloud cover drifting in and out. The Lodge at Koele lies along Hwy 44, a mile above town.

A mile past the lodge is a paved road on the right that leads to the Munro Trail (for trail information, see the Munro Trail heading later in this chapter). The road to the trailhead, which is lined with Norfolk pines, ends in half a mile at a cemetery with gravestones in Japanese and Filipino. Mourners have placed sake offerings at some of the Japanese graves, while pinwheels and toys adorn a few sites where Filipino children are buried.

Back on Hwy 44, 3 miles out of town, there's an overlook to the right with a beautiful vista. Straight ahead is the undeveloped southeast shore of Molokai and its tiny islet of Mokuhooniki, while the view to the right is of Maui and the Kaanapali high-rises.

From the overlook, the road slopes down to the coast. The scenery is punctuated by interesting rock formations sitting atop the eroded red earth, similar to those found at Garden of the Gods (see separate heading, later in this chapter). Farther along the road, a shipwreck comes into view.

The paved road ends near the coast. A dirt road off to the left leads to Shipwreck Beach and a former lighthouse.

Shipwreck Beach
Shipwreck Beach is the name that's been given to 9 miles of Lanai's northeast shore. It starts in the area known as Kahokunui at the end of Hwy 44 and stretches up to Polihua Beach on the northwest shore. True to its name, there are a couple of shipwrecks, as well as a coastline that's good for beachcombing.

The dirt road that heads left from the highway ends after 1¾ miles at the site of a former lighthouse on a lava-rock point. Only the cement foundations of the lighthouse remain.

When it's dry, the road is usually passable by car, but you'll miss the beach walk. An alternative is to hike (or drive) in about half a mile from the end of the paved road, cut down to the beach and walk to the lighthouse from there. You can walk back by the road, which is quicker.

Lots of driftwood washes up on this windswept beach. Some of the pieces are identifiable as sun-bleached timbers from shipwrecks – hulls, side planks, perhaps even a gangplank if your imagination is active. There are also fishing nets, ropes and the occasional glass float.

It's likely to be just you and the driftwood, although about 20 minutes up the beach, there's a cluster of small wooden beach shacks called Federation Camp, which is sometimes used by local fishers. The lighthouse is 10 minutes farther.

The beach sand is a bit soft and sinks underfoot, making this a good walk for your calves. The sand gradually changes colors as you walk along. In some places, it's a colorful, chunky mixture of rounded shells and bits of rock that look like some sort of beach confetti.

A low rock shelf lines much of the shore, and the shallow, murky waters are not good for swimming or snorkeling.

Up on the slopes, some of the beach *pohuehue* (morning glory) is entwined with an air plant that looks something like yellow-orange fishing line. This is Lanai's official flower, a leafless parasitic vine called *kaunaoa*.

Petroglyphs From the lighthouse foundations, markings lead directly inland to some small petroglyphs a short walk away. The simple figures are etched on large boulders on the right side of the path, down the slope past the 'Do Not Deface' sign.

The rocky path is through ground cover of flowering golden *ilima* and pink and yellow lantana. The former is native, while the latter was introduced to Hawaii just 50 years ago and has escaped from cultivation

to become a major pest throughout the islands.

Keep your eyes open for wild animals – sightings of mouflon sheep on the inland hills are not uncommon. The males have curled-back horns, and the more dominant ones travel with a harem of females.

Shipwrecks It's about 15 minutes farther up the beach to a rusting WWII Liberty ship that washed up on the reef. You can see the shipwreck clearly from the lighthouse.

This is the point where most people turn around and head back, but it's possible to walk another 6 miles to **Awalua**, which long ago was the location of a north shore landing. There's another shipwreck at Awalua but not much else. The beach is generally windy, and the hike is hot and dry, although the farther down the beach you go, the prettier it gets.

Keomuku Beach
Keomuku Beach is the stretch of shore that runs from Kahokunui, at the end of Hwy 44, south to Kahalepalaoa Landing.

The dirt road is likely to be either dusty or muddy, with deep ruts, though if you're lucky enough to catch it after it's been graded, it's not so bad. Still, it's a 4WD road. This uninhabited coast is not particularly attractive, and there's not much to see, other than a few marginal historical sites, scattered groves of coconuts and lots and lots of kiawe.

Real diehards can go the full 12 miles down to **Naha**, at the end of the road. It can take as long as two hours one way when the road is rough, half of that when the road conditions are good.

Less than a mile down the road is **Maunalei**. An ancient *heiau* (temple) that once sat there was taken apart by Frederick Hayselden, who used its stones to build a cattle fence. Soon after, he lost his shirt in the ill-fated Maunalei Sugar Company – islanders believed it was the temple desecration that had caused the wells to turn salty and kill off the sugarcane Hayselden had planted.

Keomuku, 5¾ miles south of Hwy 44, was the center of Hayselden's short-lived sugarcane plantation. There's little left to see other than the reconstructed Ka Lanakila o Ka Malamalama Church, originally built in 1903 after Maunalei Sugar collapsed. The ruins of a couple of fishponds lie along the coast, but they're not easily visible.

Another heiau at **Kahea**, 1½ miles south of Keomuku, was also dismantled by Maunalei Sugar Company, this time to build a railroad to transport the sugar to Kahalepalaoa Landing. Kahea, meaning 'red stains,' was a *luakini* heiau, where human sacrifices were made.

Kahalepalaoa Landing, just south of Kahea, has the best beach on this end of the island – a popular destination for Club Lanai, which operates day outings from Maui. The road onward to Naha really doesn't offer much more scenery for the effort, but should you want to continue, it's about 4 miles farther. Naha is occasionally used by local fishers but is not a good place for swimming.

MANELE BAY & HULOPOE BAY

To reach Lanai's best beach, Hulopoe, drive 20 minutes down Manele Rd, a paved road that starts just south of town. The beach is 7½ miles south of the intersection of Manele Rd and Kaumalapau Hwy.

About 1½ miles down Manele Rd, you'll come across an unusually wide dirt road on the left. This is Hoike Rd, which leads to the Munro Trail and the Luahiwa Petroglyphs.

After 4 miles, Manele Rd veers to the left, and a mile farther, there's a small pull-off with a pretty coastal view of both Manele Bay to the left and Hulopoe Bay to the right. The island beyond is Kahoolawe.

Manele Boat Harbor

Manele Harbor is a scenic, crescent-shaped natural harbor backed by sheer cliffs. Lanai folks like to fish from the stone breakwater that sticks out into the mouth of the bay.

Manele is a very protected harbor and a popular sailboat anchorage. Lanai is one of the easier islands to sail to from Honolulu (although 'easy' is a relative term – the waters can be quite rough).

In the early 20th century, cattle were herded down to Manele Bay for shipment to Honolulu. To see the remains of a cattle chute, which was used to load the animals directly onto ships, walk around the point to the right at the end of the parking lot.

Stone ruins from a Hawaiian fishing village and concrete slabs from the days of cattle ranching are up on the hill above the parking lot, though the ruins are now largely overgrown with kiawe and ilima.

Inside Manele Bay, coral is abundant near the cliffsides, where the bottom quickly slopes off to about 40 feet. Beyond the western edge of the bay, near the rock called Puu Pehe, is Cathedrals, a popular dive site. Off the parking lot are rest rooms, showers, drinking water, picnic tables and a little harbormaster's office. If you arrive by boat, it's a 10-minute walk from Manele Bay to Hulopoe Beach.

Hulopoe Beach

Hulopoe Beach is a gently curving white-sand beach. It's long and broad and protected by a rocky point to the south. On the north side of the bay, the Manele Bay Hotel sits on a low seaside terrace.

Even with the hotel, this is a pretty quiet beach. Generally, the most action occurs when the boats from Maui pull in with snorkelers.

For some of Lanai's best snorkeling, head to the left side of the bay, where there are lots of colorful coral and reef fish.

Also on that side, just beyond the sandy beach, there's a low lava shelf with tide pools worth exploring. One area has been blasted out, making a protected pool for children. Cement steps lead down to the pool from the rocks. It looks as if all the children on Lanai rushed down to scrawl their names in the cement when it was poured in August 1951.

Hulopoe Beach includes a landscaped park with solar-heated showers, rest rooms, picnic tables, pay phones, drinking water fountains and campsites.

Both Manele and Hulopoe bays are part of a marine life conservation district, which prohibits the removal of coral and rocks and restricts many fishing activities. Water activities can be dangerous during *kona* storms, when leeward winds produce strong currents and swells.

Puu Pehe Cove

From Hulopoe Beach, a short path leads south to a point with interesting coastal formations. The peninsula of land separating Hulopoe and Manele Bays is a volcanic cone that's sharply eroded on its southerly seaward edge. Here on the point, the lava has rich rust-red colors with swirls of gray and black in fascinating patterns. The texture is bubbly and brittle – so brittle that huge chunks of the point have broken off and fallen onto the coastal shelf below. There's a small sea arch below the point.

Puu Pehe is the name of the cove to the left of the point as well as the sea stack just offshore. This islet, also called Sweetheart's Rock, has a tomblike formation on top that figures into Hawaiian legend.

Places to Stay

Camping Surprisingly, even with the luxury hotel nearby, camping is still allowed at six campsites just a short stroll from Hulopoe Beach.

As long as the ***Lanai Company*** (☎ 565-3982, PO Box 310, Lanai City, HI 96763) continues issuing permits, here's how it goes: There's a $5 registration fee per campsite plus $7 per person per night. The maximum length of stay is seven consecutive days. Reservations can be made by mail or phone. Fees must be paid within five days of confirmation of the reservation.

Sometimes you can get permits without advance reservations if the campground's not full, but keep in mind that it's commonly booked up weeks in advance during the summer and on weekends throughout the rest of the year. Pick up permits at the Lanai Company, in the Castle & Cooke offices on Lanai Ave opposite the post office.

Hotels The 250-room ***Manele Bay Hotel*** (☎ 565-7700, 800-321-4666, fax 565-3868, reservations@lanai-resorts.com, PO Box 774, Lanai City, HI 96763), overlooking Hulopoe Beach, features spacious, partially open-air lobbies adorned with artwork and antiques. There's a reading room with a dark-wood decor and leather-bound books, lots of Italian marble floors and a central lounge with

Puu Pehe

According to local lore, an island girl named Pehe was so beautiful that her lover decided to make their home in a secluded coastal cave, lest any other young men in the village set eyes on her. One day the lover was up in the mountains fetching water when a *kona* (leeward) storm suddenly blew in. He rushed down the mountain, but by the time he arrived, the waves had swept into the cave, drowning Pehe.

The islanders brought a *tapa* (bark) cloth and prepared to bury the girl in the village. But Pehe's lover slipped off with her body at night and carried it out to the top of a nearshore islet, where he erected a tomb and laid her to rest within. Immersed in grief, he then jumped into the surging waters below and was dashed back onto the rock. The islanders recovered his body, wrapped it in the tapa they had prepared for Pehe and buried him in the village.

sofas, elegant chairs and a grand piano. As might be expected, guest rooms are quite pleasant, all with four-poster beds, lanais and marble baths. Rates are $275 for a room without a view, $525 for an oceanfront room and $650 and up for suites.

Places to Eat

The Manele Bay Hotel serves breakfast in its ***Hulopoe Court*** (☎ 565-7700) from 7 to 11 am. The setting has a bit of everything: high ceilings with showy chandeliers, ornate Chinese vases and a view of the ocean. There's a full breakfast buffet for $18 or a continental version with fruit, pastries and cereals for $12. You can also order à la carte, but expect to run up a similar tab. The restaurant also serves dinner from 6 to 9:30 pm, with dishes such as ginger barbecued chicken or blackened *ahi* (tuna) priced from $24 to $28.

The ***poolside grill***, open from 10 am to 6 pm, is the main lunch venue, with light eats such as fresh fish sandwiches or a variety of salads for around $12.

The *Club House* (☎ 565-7700) at the hotel golf course has sandwiches, salads and fish & chips for $10 to $15. It's open from 11 am to 9 pm Monday through Saturday, 11 am to 5 pm on Sunday.

The hotel's open-air *Ihilani Dining Room* (☎ 565-7700), which is elegant and quite pleasant, serves fine French food at dinner. Appetizers include lobster chowder and ahi carpaccio for $20 to $25, with entrees such as fresh fish, Maine lobster or local venison for around $45.

KAUNOLU

Kaunolu was the site of an early Hawaiian fishing village that was abandoned in the mid-19th century. It boasts the greatest concentration of ruins on Lanai.

Kaunolu was a vacation spot for Kamehameha the Great, who went there to fish the prolific waters of Kaunolu Bay. Kamehameha also held tournaments and sporting events at Kaunolu and had a house up on the bluff on the eastern side of the bay.

Kaunolu Gulch separates the two sides of the bay. Most of the house sites sit on the eastern side. The now-overgrown **Halulu Heiau**, on the western side, once dominated the whole scene. The heiau included a *puuhonua* (place of refuge), where renegade *kapu* (taboo) breakers could be absolved from their death sentences. There are a number of petroglyphs, including some on the southern side of the heiau.

Beyond the heiau ruins, the Palikaholo sea cliffs rise more than 1000 feet. Northwest of the heiau, there's a high natural stone wall along the perimeter of the cliff. Look for a break in the wall at the cliff's edge, where there's a sheer 90-foot drop. This is **Kahekili's Jump**, named after a Lanaian chief. There's a ledge below it that makes diving into the ocean here a bit death-defying. Apparently, Kamehameha used to amuse himself by making upstart warriors leap from this cliff.

The late Dr Kenneth Emory of Oahu's Bishop Museum did an extensive survey of Kaunolu in 1921 and counted 86 house sites, 35 stone shelters and a number of grave markings, pens and gardens. These days, most of the sites are simply too overgrown with kiawe even to recognize.

There are a couple of ways to get to Kaunolu. The easiest is to go south from Lanai City down Manele Rd. At three-quarters of a mile past the 9-mile marker, there's a sharp bend in the road. Rather than follow Manele Rd as it bears left to Manele Bay, go straight ahead onto an access road that begins as pavement but soon turns to dirt. Just before reaching a painted water pipe, a sign marks the turn-off to Kaunolu; turn left onto this dirt road, which leads south in the direction of the lighthouse. If the road hasn't been washed out by rain recently, you may be able to make it most of the way down with a 4WD vehicle, but odds are, you'll have to walk the last mile or so.

KAUMALAPAU HARBOR

Kaumalapau, Lanai's commercial harbor, is 6½ miles west of Lanai City, at the end of the airport road. The harbor was built for shipping pineapples; now that the industry is gone, it's a rather sleepy place. These days, the main traffic here is the cargo boat that arrives weekly from Oahu.

You can often find people fishing from the boulder jetty for *awa* (milkfish), a tasty fish that's a common catch in the bay. Scuba divers sometimes use the bay as well, as the deep waters at Kaumalapau are extremely clear.

As along most of the southwest coast, Kaumalapau has sheer coastal cliffs.

NORTHWEST LANAI

To reach sights in the northwest part of Lanai, head north on Fraser Ave in Lanai City and, shortly after it turns to dirt, turn right onto Polihua Rd. This dirt road passes along former pineapple fields and the Nature Conservancy's Kanepuu Preserve before reaching the Garden of the Gods after about 5½ miles.

The section of road leading up to the Garden of the Gods is a fairly good, albeit dusty, route that usually takes about 20 minutes from town. To travel from the Garden of the Gods to Polihua Beach is another matter, however, as the road down to the beach is rocky and narrow and is suitable only for a 4WD. Depending on when the road was last graded, the trip could take anywhere from 20 minutes to an hour.

Kanepuu Preserve

The Nature Conservancy manages 462 acres at Kanepuu, a diverse native dryland forest that is the last of its kind in all of Hawaii. Native plants include *iliahi* (Hawaiian sandalwood), *olopua* (an olive), *lama* (in the persimmon family), a morning glory, a native gardenia and fragrant vines of *maile* and *huehue*.

Native dryland forests once covered 80% of Lanai and were also common on the leeward slopes of other Hawaiian islands, but feral goats and cattle made a feast of the foliage. Credit for saving this forest goes to naturalist and former ranch manager George Munro, who realized the need to protect this ecosystem and fenced hoofed animals out in the 1920s.

The Kanepuu Preserve is about 6 miles northwest of Lanai City. Castle & Cooke retains title to the land but has given the Nature Conservancy an easement to the forest in perpetuity.

Garden of the Gods

There's no garden at the Garden of the Gods, but rather a dry and barren landscape of strange wind-sculpted rocks in rich shades of ocher, pink and brown. The colors change with the light and are much gentler in the early morning and late afternoon.

How godly the garden appears depends on what you're looking for. Some people just see rocks, while others find the formations hauntingly beautiful.

Polihua Beach

Polihua Beach, on the northwestern tip of the island, is a broad, 1½-mile-long white-sand beach. It offers a great view of the entire south coast of Molokai. Although it's a gorgeous beach, strong winds kicking up the sand often make it uncomfortable, and water conditions are treacherous all year round.

Polihua means 'eggs in the bosom' and refers to the green sea turtles that used to nest here en masse. After a long hiatus, the now-endangered turtles are beginning to return.

MUNRO TRAIL

The Munro Trail is an 8½-mile dirt road that can either be hiked or negotiated in a 4WD vehicle. On foot, it's a full day's hike. If you're driving and the road is in good condition, it takes about 11 hours. However, be aware that the road can become very muddy (particularly in winter and after heavy rainstorms) and jeeps occasionally get stuck. Drivers also need to watch out for sheer drops; the road can be quite dangerous when wet. All in all, it's best to consider this as a fair weather outing only.

To start, head north on Hwy 44, the road to Shipwreck Beach. About a mile past the Lodge at Koele, turn right onto the paved road that leads to a cemetery half a mile down.

The Munro Trail starts at the left of the cemetery. It passes through sections planted with eucalyptus and climbs up along the ridge, where the path is draped with ferns and studded with Norfolk pines.

The trail is named after naturalist George Munro, who planted the trees along this trail and elsewhere around the island in order to provide a watershed. He selected species that draw moisture from the clouds and fog, both of which are fairly common in the high country (more so in the afternoon than in the morning).

Before the Munro Trail was upgraded to a dirt road, it was a footpath. It's along this trail that islanders tried to hide from Kamehameha the Great when he went on a rampage in 1778. Hookio Battleground, where Lanaians made their last stand, is just above Hookio Gulch, about 2½ miles from the start of the trail.

The Munro Trail looks down upon a series of deep ravines that cut across the eastern flank of the mountain, and it passes Lanaihale, which at 3370 feet is the highest point on Lanai. On a clear day, you can see all of the inhabited Hawaiian Islands except Kauai and Niihau from various points along the route. The trail ends on Hoike Rd, which is a little more than 1½ miles south of the intersection of Manele Rd and Kaumalapau Hwy.

Luahiwa Petroglyphs

The Luahiwa Petroglyphs have been carved onto about three dozen boulders spread over 3 acres. Lanai's highest concentration of petroglyphs includes a wide variety of forms

thought to have been carved during different eras. There are lots of dogs in various poses, linear and triangular human figures and a canoe or two. Unfortunately, many of the petroglyphs are quite weathered.

It's a little challenging to get to this spot, but basically you turn onto Hoike Rd and then head for the water tower on the ridge. The boulders are near the head of a ravine north of the road, below the trees.

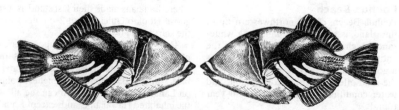

Kahoolawe

Kahoolawe, the uninhabited island 7 miles off the southwest coast of Maui, was used by the US military as a bombing target from WWII until 1990. Although the bombing has now stopped, the island remains off limits due to the stray ammunition that peppers Kahoolawe and its surrounding waters.

Kahoolawe played an important role in Hawaiian history. The channel between Lanai and Kahoolawe, as well as the westernmost point of Kahoolawe itself, is named Kealaikahiki, meaning 'pathway to Tahiti.' When early Polynesian voyagers made the journey between Hawaii and Tahiti, they lined up their canoes at this departure point.

More than 500 archaeological sites have been identified on Kahoolawe. They include several *heiaus* (temples) and many *koa* (hardwood) shrines and *kuula* (fishing shrine) stones dedicated to the gods of fishers. Puu Moiwi, a large cinder cone in the center of the island, contains one of Hawaii's largest ancient adze quarries.

In 1981, Kahoolawe was added to the National Register of Historic Places as a significant archaeological area. For nearly a decade, the island had the ironic distinction of being the only such historic place that was being used by its government for bombing target practice.

Kahoolawe became a symbol of the separation of native Hawaiians from their land and a focal point in the growing Hawaiian rights movement.

HISTORY
Prisoners & Opium

Since ancient times, Kahoolawe has been under the rule of Maui.

From 1830 to 1848, Kaulana Bay, on the island's northern side, served as a place of exile for Maui men accused of petty crimes. (Female outcasts were sent to Kaena Point on the northwestern tip of Lanai.)

Kahoolawe proved to be less of a 'prison isle' than intended. In 1841, some of the prisoners managed to swim to the Makena area of Maui, where they stole both food and canoes and paddled back with their booty. Later raids included a journey to Lanai, where they picked up female prisoners and brought them back to Kahoolawe.

Kahoolawe's secluded southwestern side was used for decades by smugglers importing Chinese opium. To avoid detection, they'd unload their caches at Hanakanaea Bay (commonly known as Smugglers Bay) on arrival from China and return later in small fishing boats to pick up the illicit goods.

In more recent times, Smugglers Bay was the site of a US military base camp.

Agriculture

Kahoolawe was once a green and forested island. It is now largely barren, and *pili* grass and *kiawe* trees are the main forces in keeping the dry red soil from blowing away completely.

RC Wyllie, the Scotsman who developed a sugar plantation at Princeville on Kauai, made the first attempt at ranching in 1858. Wyllie leased the entire island of Kahoolawe from the territory of Hawaii, but the sheep he brought over were diseased and the venture failed. Those sheep that survived were left to roam freely, causing serious damage to native plants.

Over the years, the territory granted a series of leases to other ranchers. Cattle were first brought over around 1880, and sheep were also tried again. Land mismanagement was the order of the day.

By the early 1900s, feral goats, pigs and sheep had dug up, rooted out and chewed off so much of Kahoolawe's vegetation that the island was largely a dust bowl.

Kahoolawe Ranch

Angus MacPhee, the former manager of Maui's Ulupalakua Ranch, ran Kahoolawe's most successful ranching operation, which lasted from 1918 to 1941.

When MacPhee got his lease from the territorial government in 1918, Kahoolawe was overrun with goats and looked like a wasteland. MacPhee rounded up 13,000 goats, which he sold on Maui, and built a fence across the width of the entire island to keep the remaining goats at one end. He then brought in large redwood tanks to store water and planted grasses and ground cover. Once the land was again green, MacPhee created Kahoolawe Ranch Company in partnership with Harry Baldwin, a sugar plantation owner. Cattle were brought over and raised for the Honolulu market. Ranching Kahoolawe was not easy, but MacPhee, unlike his predecessors, was able to make it profitable.

Inez MacPhee Ashdown, Angus' daughter, has written her story in *Kahoolawe* (Topgallant Publishing Co, Honolulu, 1979). The book includes legends of Kahoolawe, as told to her by native Hawaiians, as well as the ranch's history.

A Bombing Target

In 1939, Kahoolawe Ranch subleased part of the island to the US Army for bombing practice and moved the cattle and ranch hands over to Maui.

After the attack on Pearl Harbor in 1941, the US military took control over all of Kahoolawe and began bombing the entire island. Ranch buildings and water cisterns were used as targets and reduced to rubble.

Of all the fighting that took place during WWII, Kahoolawe was the most bombed island in the Pacific – even though the 'enemy' never fired upon it.

After the war, civilians were forbidden to return to Kahoolawe; MacPhee was never compensated for his losses.

In 1953, a presidential decree gave the US Navy official jurisdiction over the island, with the stipulation that when Kahoolawe was no longer 'needed,' the live ammunition would be removed and the island would be returned to the territory of Hawaii.

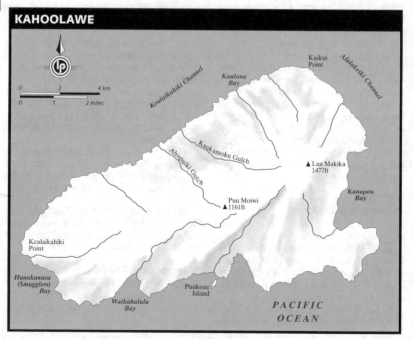

Kahoolawe Movement

In the mid-1960s, Hawaii politicians began petitioning the federal government to cease its military activities and return Kahoolawe to the state of Hawaii. In 1976, a small group of Hawaiians set out in boats and occupied the island in an attempt to attract greater attention to the bombings. There were a series of occupations, some lasting more than a month.

During one of the 1977 crossings, group members George Helm and Kimo Mitchell mysteriously disappeared in the waters off Kahoolawe. Helm had been an inspirational Hawaiian-rights activist, and with his death the Protect Kahoolawe Ohana movement sprang up. Helm's vision of turning Kahoolawe into a sanctuary of Hawaiian culture and identity became widespread among islanders. In June 1977, two group members, Walter Ritte Jr and Richard Sawyer, were tried for trespassing on Kahoolawe and sentenced to six months in jail.

In a letter to President Jimmy Carter asking that the two men be pardoned, Daniel Inouye, US senator from Hawaii, wrote:

...it was a form of protest against, what was to them, the unconscionable desecration of the land by the Navy's continued bombing of Kahoolawe. *Aloha aina*, love for the land, is an important part of the Native Hawaiian religion and culture.... Kahoolawe has become a symbol of the resurgence of the Hawaiian people, a movement formulating for many Hawaiians a renewed respect for their culture and their history.

Kahoolawe Today

In 1980, in a court-sanctioned consent decree, the Navy reached an agreement with Protect Kahoolawe Ohana that allowed the Ohana regular access to the island. The decree also required the Navy to preserve archaeological sites, eradicate goats and control soil erosion.

Although the bombing continued, the decree restricted the Navy from using live munitions on part of the island and from bombing historic sites. In 1982, the Ohana began to go to Kahoolawe to celebrate *makahiki*, the annual observance that honors Lono, god of agriculture and peace.

In 1982, Maui County, of which Kahoolawe is part, adopted a planning document calling for a 20-year phaseout of the military and the development of Kahoolawe as a historical and cultural site, with Protect Kahoolawe Ohana as the steward of the land. The Navy refused to recognize the document.

In what many Hawaiians saw as the ultimate insult to their heritage, the US military offered Kahoolawe as a bombing target to foreign nations during biennial Pacific Rim exercises. But in an unanticipated backlash against the military, the exercises brought recognition of what was happening in Kahoolawe into a broader arena. An international movement against the bombing, led by both environmentalist and union groups in New Zealand, Australia, Japan and the UK, resulted in those countries withdrawing from the Kahoolawe exercises. With only the US and Canada willing to participate, the plan was scrapped.

In the late 1980s, Hawaii's first native Hawaiian governor, John Waihee, and other state politicians became more outspoken in their demands that Kahoolawe be returned to Hawaiians. In October 1990, as Hawaii's two US senators, Daniel Inouye and Daniel Akaka, were preparing a congressional bill to stop the bombing, President Bush issued an order to halt military activities. The senators' bill, which became law the next month, required the island to be cleared of munitions and restored to a prewar condition. It also established a federally funded Kahoolawe Conveyance Commission to prepare recommendations on terms for the transfer of the island to the state of Hawaii.

On May 7, 1994, in a ceremony marked by Hawaiian rituals, chants and prayers, the US Navy signed over control of Kahoolawe to Governor Waihee and the state of Hawaii. Following the signing, 100 native Hawaiians dressed in traditional *malo* (loincloth) and *tapa* (bark-cloth) cloaks went to Kahoolawe to perform sunrise rituals honoring the return of the island. Among the ceremonies was the placing of leis at memorial plaques for Helms and Mitchell.

One enormous obstacle that remains is the cleaning up of live munitions from the

KAHOOLAWE

island. The federal government has established a $400 million fund for that purpose, but the cleanup now underway will take many years to complete. In the meantime, a new state entity, the Kahoolawe Island Reserve Commission, has taken over administration of the island and is in the process of developing a new master plan. Proposals for the island's future range from establishing a marine sanctuary to making the island the center for a new Hawaiian nation.

GEOGRAPHY

Kahoolawe is 11 miles long and 6 miles wide, with a land area of 45 sq miles. With the help of a vivid imagination, its shape can be seen as a crouching lion facing eastward.

A ridge runs diagonally across the island, and the terrain is gently sloping. The highest point is the 1477-foot Lua Makika, at the site of the caldera that formed the island. Kahoolawe is a dry, arid island with only 10 to 20 inches of rainfall annually.

Because of the red dust in the air, Kahoolawe often appears to have a pink tinge when viewed from Maui, particularly in the afternoons, when the breezes pick up. At night, it's pitch black, devoid of any light.

GETTING THERE & AWAY

There's no public access to the island unless you're a member or guest of the Ohana, who make occasional trips to the island to celebrate makahiki, clean up historic sites and work on revegetation projects.

Two weekends every month, offshore waters 20 fathoms (120 feet) or deeper are open to local fishers, but at all other times boats are prohibited from going within 2 miles of Kahoolawe. As the island and its nearshore waters are still dangerous, due to unexploded ammunition, shoreline access is expected to remain off limits to the public until the final stages of the cleanup, which is currently scheduled to continue for a while, until November 2003.

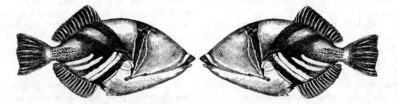

Kauai

If you're looking for lush scenery, Kauai is a great choice – the island is so richly green that it's nicknamed 'The Garden Island.'

Kauai is the oldest of the main Hawaiian landmasses and arose from the sea as a high, smooth island. Over time, heavy rains have eroded deep valleys, while pounding waves and falling sea levels have cut steep cliffs.

The island's central volcanic peak, Mt Waialeale, is the wettest place on earth and feeds seven rivers, including Hawaii's only navigable one. A deep north-south rift slices the western end of the island, creating the impressive Waimea Canyon.

The North Shore is lush and mountainous, with waterfalls, beautiful beaches and stream-fed valleys. The northwest coast is lined by the steeply fluted Na Pali sea cliffs, Hawaii's foremost hiking destination.

Moviemakers looking for scenery bordering on fantasy have often found it in Kauai. *South Pacific* and *Raiders of the Lost Ark* were both filmed on Kauai's North Shore. The remote Honopu Valley on the Na Pali Coast was the jungle home of King Kong, while both the Hanapepe and Lawai Valleys served as locations for Steven Spielberg's *Jurassic Park*.

Kauai is the least developed of the four major islands, and most of its interior is made up of mountainous forest reserve. The Alakai Swamp is poised on a high, cliff-bound plateau, about 1000 feet below rainy Mt Waialeale. There, clouds and mist that rarely lift support a unique ecosystem where trees grow knee high.

Kauai is dry and sunny on its southern and western sides, with long stretches of white-sand beaches. Sugarcane fields cover large portions of the island just inland from the coast in a semicircle from the northeast to the west.

Kauai's main attraction is its stunning natural beauty; hiking trails lead into some incredible places.

HISTORY

Kauai was probably settled between 500 and 700 AD by Polynesians who migrated from the Marquesas Islands. Archaeological finds, including ring-shaped poi-pounding stones found both in Kauai and the Marquesas, support the connection.

While Hawaiian lore makes no direct references to the Marquesan culture, Kauai is often referred to as the home of a race of little

---

Highlights

- Trekking along the dramatic cliffs of the Na Pali Coast
- Soaking up rays at Poipu's sunny resorts
- Kayaking down quiet, meandering rivers
- Sighting rare seabirds at Kilauea Point
- Gazing into the deep chasms of Waimea Canyon

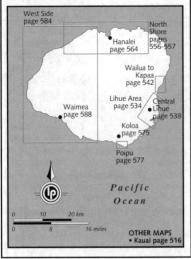

West Side page 584

North Shore pages 556-557

Hanalei page 564

Wailua to Kapaa page 542

Lihue Area page 534

Central Lihue page 538

Waimea page 588

Koloa page 575

Poipu page 577

Pacific Ocean

0   10   20 km
0   8   16 miles

OTHER MAPS
• Kauai page 516

KAUAI

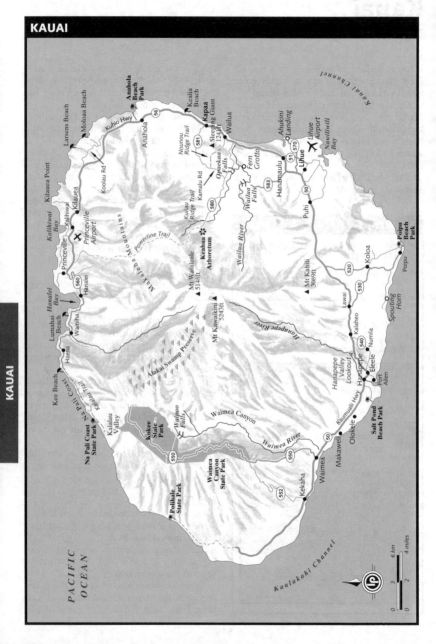

KAUAI

Kauai Channel

Anahola Beach Park
Moloaa Beach
Larsens Beach
56
Kuhio Hwy
Anahola
Koolau Rd
Kealia Beach
Kapaa
Sleeping Giant 1241ft
Wailua
Ahukini Landing
Lihue Airport
Nawiliwili Bay

Kilauea Point
Kilauea
Kilauea
Kalihiwai
Kalihiwai Bay
Princeville Airport
Nounou Ridge Trail
581
Opaekaa Falls
Kamalu Rd
Fern Grotto
51
570
Lihue
583
Hanamaulu

Powerline Trail
Kuilau Ridge Trail
580
Wailua Falls
Wailua River
Puhi
50

Princeville
Hanalei Bay
Hanalei
560
Haena
Lumahai Beach
Waimea
Makaleha Mountains
Keahua Arboretum
Mt Waialeale 5148ft
Mt Kahili 3089ft
Lawai
Koloa
520
530
Spouting Horn
Poipu Beach Park
Poipu

Kee Beach
Na Pali Coast
Kalalau Trail
Na Pali Coast State Park
Kalalau Valley
Kokee State Park
Waipoo Falls
Alakai Swamp Preserve
Mt Kawaikini 5243ft
Hanapepe River
Kalaheo
Kalaheo
540
Numila
Eleele
Port Allen
Hanapepe
Salt Pond Beach Park

Waimea Canyon
Waimea River
Waimea Canyon State Park
550
550
Kekaha
Waimea
Makaweli
Olokele
50
Kaumualii Hwy
Hanapepe Valley Lookout

Polihale State Park
552

PACIFIC OCEAN

Kaulakahi Channel

6 km
4 miles
0 3
0 2

people called *menehune*. Legend after legend tells of happy, Disney-like elves coming down from the mountains to produce great engineering works in stone.

It seems likely that when the first wave of Tahitians arrived in about 1000 AD, they conquered and subjugated the Marquesans, forcing them to build the temples, irrigation ditches and fishponds now attributed to the menehunes.

The Tahitian term for 'outcast' is *man-ahune*. And the diminutive social status the Marquesans had in the eyes of their conquerors may have given rise to tales of a dwarf-size race.

The menehunes may have created the temples, but the Tahitian settlers created the legends. While the stonework remains, the true identity of Kauai's 'little people' is lost.

During a subsequent wave of Tahitian migration, around the 12th century, a high chief named Moikeha arrived at Wailua with a fleet of double-hulled canoes. There, inside the royal court, Moikeha was received by Kauai's aging *alii-nui* (high chief), Puna.

Puna gave his daughter to Moikeha in marriage, and upon Puna's death Moikeha became the alii-nui of Kauai. Moikeha introduced taro and sweet potatoes to Kauai and sent his son Kila back to Tahiti to fetch the *pahu hula*, a sharkskin drum essential for use in hula temples. This type of drum is still used in hula performances today.

Early Settlements

Kauai is the most isolated of the major islands, lying 72 miles from Oahu, its nearest neighbor. It was never conquered by invaders from another Hawaiian island, and its history is one of autonomy.

Kauai was settled most intensively along river valleys near the coast, such as Wailua, Waimea and Hanalei. Even valleys that were difficult to reach, like Kalalau and Nualolo on the Na Pali Coast, had sizable settlements. When winter seas prevented canoes from landing on the northern shore, trails down precipitous ridges and rope ladders provided access.

When Captain Cook landed on Kauai in 1778, he estimated the island had 50 villages

and a total population of about 30,000. Missionaries in the 1820s estimated the population to be closer to 10,000. Historians tend to side with the missionaries and discredit Cook's estimates, but considering the deadly diseases Cook's men left behind, it's possible both were correct.

Kaumualii

Kaumualii was the last chief to reign over an independent Kauai. Although he was a shrewd leader and Kauai's warriors were fierce, it was apparently the power of Kaumualii's *kahunas* (priests) that protected him from the advances of Kamehameha the Great.

In 1796, Kamehameha, who had conquered all the other islands, sailed with an armada of war canoes toward Kauai. A mysterious storm suddenly kicked up at sea, compelling him to turn back to Oahu, and he never reached Kauai's shores.

During the next few years, both Kamehameha and Kaumualii continued to prepare for war by gathering foreign weaponry and trying to ally foreign ships to their causes.

In 1804, Kamehameha and his warriors again massed on the shores of Oahu, ready to attack Kauai. However, on the eve of the invasion, an epidemic of what was probably cholera struck the island of Oahu, decimating the would-be invaders and forcing yet another delay.

While Kamehameha's numerically superior forces had Kaumualii unnerved, Kaumualii's uncanny luck had a similar effect on Kamehameha. In 1810 they reached an agreement that recognized Kaumualii as the alii-nui of Kauai but ceded the island of Kauai to the Kingdom of Hawaii.

It was essentially a truce, and the plotting continued, with Kaumualii never fully accepting Kamehameha's ultimate authority.

Russian Presence

In January 1815, a Russian ship loaded with seal skins was wrecked off the coast near Waimea, and Kaumualii confiscated the cargo. In November, the Russian-American Company sent Georg Anton Schaeffer to retrieve the skins.

KAUAI

When Schaeffer arrived in Hawaii, he saw opportunity in the rift between Kaumualii and Kamehameha. In Kauai, he exceeded his authority by entering into an agreement with Kaumualii in which he claimed the Russians would provide a ship and military assistance for the invasion of Oahu. In return, Kaumualii offered the Russians half of Oahu plus all the sandalwood on Oahu and Kauai. In September 1816, Hawaiian laborers under Schaeffer's direction began to build forts in Waimea and Hanalei.

Later that year, when Russian naval explorer Otto von Kotzebue visited Hawaii, he informed Kamehameha that the Russian government did not endorse Schaeffer's alliance. Kamehameha, tired of all the scheming, ordered Kaumualii to kick the Russians out or face the consequences. In May 1817, Schaeffer was escorted to his ship and forced to leave Kauai.

The End of a Kingdom

When Kamehameha died in 1819, he was succeeded by his son Liholiho, who didn't trust Kaumualii's loyalties any more than his father had. In 1822, Liholiho set off for Kauai in an 83-foot luxury schooner he had purchased from Western traders in exchange for sandalwood.

In Kauai, Liholiho tricked Kaumualii into going out for a cruise. He then kidnapped him and took him to Oahu, where Kaumualii was forced to marry Kamehameha's widow, Kaahumanu. In the grand scheme of royal design, this served to bring Kaumualii into the fold. When Kaumualii passed away in 1824, so too did the Kingdom of Kauai.

GEOGRAPHY

Shaped like a slightly compressed ball, Kauai is 33 miles from east to west and 25 miles from north to south. The highest elevation is Mt Kawaikini, at 5243 feet.

The fourth largest of the Hawaiian Islands, Kauai has an area of 558 sq miles.

Kauai arose as a single volcano, of which Mt Waialeale is the eastern rim. Moisture-laden trade winds blow into the deep North Shore valleys, which channel the winds up to the top of Mt Waialeale. Near the mountain's 5148-foot summit, cooler temperatures cause the moisture to condense, creating the heaviest rainfall on earth.

CLIMATE

Kauai's temperature varies more with location than season. The average coastal temperatures are 70°F in February and 77°F in August. At Kalalau Beach, the temperature seldom drops below 60°F, while a few thousand feet above, at Kokee State Park, it dips into the 30s during winter nights. Kokee averages a crisp 55°F in February and 65°F in August.

Kauai's average annual rainfall is about 40 inches, but the variances are extreme. Waimea, on the southwest coast, averages 21 inches, while Princeville, in the north, averages 85 inches. And Mt Waialeale in the swampy interior averages a whopping 486 inches, the world record.

Summer trade winds keep the humidity from becoming oppressive and bring in refreshing showers.

Winter is far less predictable. It's quite possible to have fairly continuous downpours for a week at a time in midwinter. Then again, it might be all blue skies and calm seas.

FLORA & FAUNA

Kauai boasts the largest number of native bird species in Hawaii. It is the only major island free of mongooses, which prey upon the eggs of ground-nesting birds.

The greatest concentration of Kauai's native forest bird species can be found in the remote Alakai Swamp. Many of these species are endangered, some having fewer than 100 birds remaining.

The Kauai oo, the last of four species of Hawaiian honeyeaters, was thought to be extinct until a nest with two chicks was discovered in Alakai Swamp in 1971. However, the call of the oo – that of a single male – was last heard in 1987.

Alakai Swamp is unique in that it has 10 times more native birds than introduced birds. (Elsewhere in Hawaii, introduced birds outnumber the natives many times over.) Not only is the swamp inhospitable to exotic bird species, but due to its high elevation it is one of the few places in Hawaii where mosquitoes, which transmit avian diseases, do not flourish.

The *ao*, or Newell's shearwater, is a threatened seabird with a call that sounds like a braying donkey. Though it once lived on all major Hawaiian Islands, today the ao nests almost exclusively in the mountains of Kauai. This rare species digs earthen burrows and lays just one egg each year. And because it flies only between dusk and dawn, the ao often fails to see utility wires strung across its path to the sea. Despite a forestry program that recovers some of the birds that crash-land, hundreds of ao still die in this way each year.

One nonnative bird you're apt to see is the *moa*, a jungle fowl that early Polynesian settlers brought to Hawaii. The colorful species now survives solely on Kauai. Not shy of people, the birds congregate in parking lots looking for handouts.

Hawaii has two native mammals. The hoary bat lives in Kokee State Park, and the Hawaiian monk seal occasionally hauls out on Kauai beaches. You'll never know where the monk seals will show up, but they don't necessarily avoid people – they've appeared in such heavily touristed areas as Poipu Beach Park and the Coconut Plantation beach in Wailua. When you observe these endangered creatures, give them a wide berth so as not to disturb them.

Wild pigs, goats and black-tailed deer are nonnative mammals that are hunted on the island.

The most common tree in Kauai forests is the *ohia lehua* (look for its red pom-pom

Hurricane Iniki

On September 11, 1992, Hurricane Iniki, the most powerful storm to strike Hawaii in a century, made a direct hit on Kauai. Packing gusts of 165 miles per hour, Iniki felled thousands of trees and caused serious damage to an estimated 50% of the buildings on Kauai. A combination of powerful gusts and abrupt changes in atmospheric pressure caused some buildings to literally shatter, as if hit by a bomb blast. Although nearly 100 people were injured by flying debris, only two people were killed.

Even though Kauai is small and lightly populated, the total value of the damage to the island was $1.6 billion, making Iniki the third-costliest disaster in US history. In all, 5000 homes were damaged and 1300 were totally destroyed. Particularly hard hit were Kauai's two main resort areas – Poipu and Princeville – and some beachfront hotels had entire wings wiped out by 30-foot waves. Hotels that did survive were turned into temporary housing for aid workers and Kauai's 8000 newly homeless residents. Tourism, which was brought to a standstill, has only recently returned to pre-Iniki levels.

As for the natural environment, Kauai is again lushly green, and to the casual eye there's not much to indicate the hurricane ever took place. Nevertheless, some sections of the native *koa* (hardwood) forest have failed to recover and are now overrun by opportunistic exotic plants such as guava, blackberry and banana poka. In addition, a couple of Kauai's endangered native bird species have not been spotted on the island since Iniki.

KAUAI

The ao, or Newell's shearwater

flowers). *Koa*, *kiawe* and *kukui* (candlenut) are also plentiful, along with guava trees. For more information on Hawaiian vegetation, see the Facts about Hawaii chapter.

GOVERNMENT

Kauai County is composed of the islands of Kauai and Niihau. The elected mayor serves a four-year term, and the seven county council members serve two-year terms.

ECONOMY

Since Hurricane Iniki hit in 1992, Kauai has experienced high unemployment. Although it's recently improved a bit, at around 9% the unemployment rate is still 50% higher than the state average.

Kauai's labor force is 29,500. The service industry, including hotels, accounts for 42% of all workers. It is followed by wholesale and retail trade at 21%, government at 12% and agriculture at 4%.

The sugar industry still cultivates 30,000 acres on Kauai, but mechanization has streamlined the industry's labor force to fewer than a thousand employees. Other sizable crops grown commercially are guava, taro and papaya. Attempts to diversify as sugar production declines have resulted in the introduction of new crops, including seed corn, sunflower seeds and coffee.

POPULATION & PEOPLE

The population of Kauai is 56,100. People of Hawaiian and part-Hawaiian ethnicity make up 25% of Kauai's population; those of mixed ethnicity other than part-Hawaiian comprise 19%, followed by Japanese (18%), Caucasian (18%) and Filipino (17%).

ORIENTATION

Kauai is roughly circular. A belt road runs three-quarters of the way around the island, from Kee Beach, near Haena in the north, to Polihale in the west. (The paved portion of the road ends just north of the Barking Sands Pacific Missile Range Facility, several miles south of Polihale State Park.)

Travelers arrive at the main airport in Lihue, the county capital, on the east coast. From Lihue, the road runs north past Wailua and Kapaa, continuing up to the Princeville Resort and Hanalei before ending at the eastern edge of the Na Pali cliffs.

South of Lihue, a side road leads down to the resort beaches at Poipu, while the main road continues west to Waimea. In Waimea, one 'highway' goes west to the arid Barking Sands region and another heads north up Waimea Canyon into Kokee State Park.

Maps

The tourist office distributes a decent free map with town insets; it's produced by the Kauai Chamber of Commerce. The best road map of the island is *Hawaii, Maui & Kauai* produced by Compass Maps and sold for $2.50 at bookshops and other stores around the island.

For hiking and mountain biking, pick up a quality foldout topographical map of Kauai at the Division of Forestry & Wildlife office, 3060 Eiwa St, room 306, Lihue, HI 96766. The free map shows the island's network of trails. You can also request one by mail; enclose a self-addressed 10-by-13-inch manila envelope with 99¢ postage on it (no checks or cash) for addresses in the USA. For foreign addresses, include enough international reply coupons for a 3½ oz letter.

INFORMATION
Tourist Offices

The Kauai Visitors Bureau (☎ 245-3971) is at 4334 Rice St, suite 101, Lihue, HI 96766; you can browse www.kauaivisitorsbureau .org for online information.

KAUAI

A hotline that can answer visitor-related questions about Kauai (☎ 245-6920, 800-262-1400) operates from 5 am to 5 pm Monday to Friday and 6 am to 2 pm Saturday. You can also call this number to request a free 'vacation planning kit.'

Be aware that the tourist office is not affiliated with the various commercial visitor information booths found in busy tourist locales. These commercial ventures are set up to sell activity packages and to lure tourists in to hear time-share sales pitches. Some of these can be quite deceptive – and if you book a tour through the agents and don't attend the time-share sales pitch, you may be charged a fee on your credit card.

Money

The Bank of Hawaii has branches in Lihue, Kapaa, Princeville, Hanalei, Hanapepe and Waimea. First Hawaiian Bank has branches in Lihue, Kapaa, Koloa, Princeville, Eleele and Waimea. Automatic teller machines (ATMs) can be found in many of the bank branches as well as in most grocery stores.

There are Western Union money transfer stations at Star Market in the Kukui Grove Center in Lihue and at Foodland markets in Waipouli and Princeville.

Newspapers & Magazines

Kauai's main newspaper, the *Garden Island* (☎ 245-3681, www.planet-hawaii.com/gardenisland), 3137 Kuhio Hwy, Lihue, HI 96766, publishes Monday to Friday and on Sunday.

Free tourist magazines such as *This Week Kauai*, *Spotlight's Kauai Gold* and *Kauai Beach Press* can be picked up at the airport, hotels and major shopping centers. All are loaded with ads and activity information. Also worth picking up is the free *Menu Magazine*, which prints menus of many of Kauai's restaurants.

Kauai Magazine, a full-color quarterly magazine with articles about island life and attractions, is sold in bookstores for $5.

Radio & TV

Kauai has three AM and three FM radio stations. Kauai's community radio station, KKCR (90.9 FM and 91.9 FM) often plays Hawaiian music, especially in the mornings.

Commercial and public TV stations are relayed from Honolulu, and cable TV is available in most communities. KVIC, on cable channel 3 or 18, is a visitor information channel that shows continuous videos on sightseeing attractions, with ads for restaurants and tourist activities.

Bookstores

The Borders bookstore in Lihue, behind the Kukui Grove Center, is Kauai's biggest bookstore and has comprehensive collections of novels, travel guides, Hawaiiana books, magazines and foreign newspapers.

The Waldenbooks chain, which contains travel and Hawaiiana sections, has a store in the Kauai Village shopping center in Waipouli. The Kauai Museum in Lihue also sells Hawaiiana books.

Libraries

You'll find public libraries in Lihue, Hanapepe, Kapaa, Koloa and Waimea.

Official Kauai

Kauai's nickname is The Garden Island. Its flower is the *mokihana*, which blooms on a small tree of the citrus family found only on Kauai. Tiny anise-scented mokihana berries are commonly combined with twists of fragrant *maile* leaves as a ceremonial *lei* (garland). Kauai's color is purple.

KAUAI

Weather Hotlines

The National Weather Service provides recorded local weather information (☎ 245-6001) and marine forecasts (☎ 245-3564).

Emergency

Dial ☎ 911 for police, ambulance and fire emergencies.

The main hospital, Wilcox Memorial Hospital (☎ 245-1100) at 3420 Kuhio Hwy in Lihue, and the smaller West Kauai Medical Center (☎ 274-3901), off Waimea Canyon Drive in Waimea, have 24-hour emergency-room services.

ACTIVITIES
Swimming

There are respectable beaches all around Kauai. For swimming, the North Shore is tops in summer, the South Shore in winter.

Hanalei Bay on the North Shore is the island's most popular summer beach, while Poipu, on the South Shore, has a string of beautiful white-sand beaches that swimmers flock to in winter.

To the west, Salt Pond Beach Park is a popular family beach with protected swimming. Farther west, Kekaha, Barking Sands and Polihale have expansive white-sand beaches, though with open ocean and often treacherous water conditions.

The beaches around Lihue and Kapaa are generally not great for swimming. The safest one is Lydgate Beach Park in Wailua, a large family park with a boulder retaining wall that creates a protected year-round swimming pool.

Many beaches have rough water conditions at various times of the year, so it pays to be cautious. Kauai has an average of nine drownings a year, about half of those on the North Shore between October and May.

Lifeguards are on duty year-round at Salt Pond Beach Park, Poipu Beach Park, Lydgate Beach Park and Hanalei Bay.

Swimming Pools The county has free swimming pools open to the public in Kapaa at Kapaa Beach Park (☎ 822-3842) and in Waimea (☎ 338-1271) next to the high school.

Surfing

Kauai has 330 named surfing sites. Generally, the best surfing is on the north coast in winter, the south coast in summer and the east coast during transitional swells.

Hanalei Bay tends to be a very good spot for North Shore surfing, as well as boogie boarding and bodysurfing. Tunnels and Cannons are two other popular North Shore surf spots.

The area around the Sheraton at Poipu Beach is a top summer surf spot. Pakalas, a surf break at the east side of Makaweli, and Majors Bay at Barking Sands are two West Side favorites.

When the breaks are on the East Side, Kealia and the Wailua Bay area opposite Coco Palms can have good surf conditions.

Margo Oberg (☎ 742-8019), a former World Cup surfing champion, gives surfing lessons at Poipu Beach. The cost is $45 for a 1½-hour class.

Nukumoi Beach & Surf Company (☎ 742-8019), near Poipu Beach Park, rents surfboards for $5 an hour, $20 a day or $60 a week. Seasports Divers (☎ 742-9303), at Poipu Plaza, rents surfboards for $20 a day, $100 a week.

Kayak Kauai, in Hanalei (☎ 826-9844) and Wailua (☎ 822-9179), rents soft surfboards for $15/60 a day/week and fiberglass boards for $20/75. Surfing lessons cost $35 per hour.

Hanalei Surf Company (☎ 826-9000), in the Hanalei Center in Hanalei, rents soft surfboards for $12/50 a day/week, fiberglass boards for $15/65 and wet suit tops for $4/17.

Windsurf Kauai (☎ 828-6838) offers 1½-hour surfing lessons in winter at Hanalei Bay for $60, including all-day use of the board.

Boogie Boarding

For boogie boarding, Brennecke's Beach and Shipwreck Beach in Poipu are hot spots, while Hanalei Bay on the North Shore can see some good action.

Boogie boards can be rented at lots of places. Most of the beach huts at the resort hotels charge about $5 an hour, while in-town shops are much more reasonable.

Hanalei Surf Company (☎ 826-9000), in the Hanalei Center in Hanalei, rents boogie boards with fins for $7/22. Pedal & Paddle (☎ 826-9069), in the Ching Young Village in Hanalei, charges similar prices.

Kayak Kauai, in Hanalei (☎ 826-9844) and in Wailua (☎ 822-9179), rents boogie boards for $6 the first day and $4 each additional day, or $20 a week.

Seasports Divers (☎ 742-9303), at Poipu Plaza in Poipu, charges $4 to $8 a day or $15 to $25 a week, the exact price depending on the type of equipment.

Nukumoi Beach & Surf Company (☎ 742-8019), conveniently located opposite Poipu Beach Park, rents boards for $5/15 a day/week.

Windsurfing

Beginner windsurfers usually start off at Anini Beach Park on the North Shore or at Nawiliwili Bay in Lihue. Tunnels Beach in Haena, Mahaulepu Beach on the South Shore and Salt Pond Beach Park in Hanapepe attract more advanced windsurfers, although Anini is also a top-notch place for speed sailing when the wind is up.

At Anini Beach, Windsurf Kauai (☎ 828-6838), PO Box 323, Hanalei, HI 96714, and Anini Beach Windsurfing (☎ 826-9463), PO Box 1602, Hanalei, HI 96714, offer lessons for all levels year-round. Both charge $65 for a three-hour lesson and rent boards for $25 an hour and around $60 a day.

True Blue (☎ 246-6333), at the Kauai Marriott on Nawiliwili Bay, PO Box 1722, Lihue, HI 96766, rents windsurfing equipment for $20 an hour and gives two-hour lessons for $85.

Diving

Popular summer diving spots on the North Shore include Kee Beach, Tunnels Beach and Cannons Beach, all shore dives in the Haena area. Cannons is particularly special; it's a wall dive, with crevices and lava tubes sheltering all sorts of marine life.

Koloa Landing and Poipu Beach Park in Poipu are easy beach dives. On those rare days when *kona* (leeward) winds blow from the south, east-side diving is good and Ahukini Landing becomes a favored site. A

number of offshore boat dives are available as well, including dives around Niihau.

Dive shops sometimes give a free introductory scuba lesson at resort hotel pools; for information, check at the hotel beach huts or call the dive shops.

Most dive shops offer two-tank dives with equipment for around $90 for shore dives, $100 for boat dives. Most also offer night dives for around $75, introductory dives for beginners for around $85 and certification courses for around $400.

Dive Kauai and Fathom Five Divers are the island's five-star PADI operations.

Four recommendable dive operations are:

Dive Kauai
  (☎ 822-0452, email@divekauai.com), 976 Kuhio Hwy, Kapaa, HI 96746
Fathom Five Divers
  (☎ 742-6991, 800-972-3078, fathom5@fathom-five .com), 3450 Poipu Rd, PO Box 907, Koloa, HI 96756
Seasports Divers
  (☎ 742-9303, 800-685-5889, seasport@pixi.com), at Poipu Plaza in Poipu, PO Box 638, Koloa, HI 96756
Sunrise Diving Adventures
  (☎ 822-7333, 800-695-3483, doctrox@aloha.net), 4-1435 Kuhio Hwy, Kapaa, HI 96746

Snuba If you'd like to slip underwater without loading yourself down with dive equipment, you might consider snuba, in which you breathe through an air hose attached to a tank that floats on the water surface. Snuba Tours of Kauai (☎ 823-8912) offers snuba from Lawai Beach in Poipu for $55. The whole thing, including outfitting and orientation, takes 1½ hours; the time in the water is about 45 minutes.

Snorkeling

On the North Shore, Kee Beach has good snorkeling most of the year. Nearby Tunnels Beach offers excellent snorkeling in summer, but be cautious of currents.

On the South Shore, the section of Poipu Beach that's just west of Nukumoi Point is one of Kauai's best snorkeling spots for beginners. Another good snorkeling spot in Poipu is Koloa Landing. On the West

Side, you can try Salt Pond Beach Park near Hanapepe.

Lots of places rent snorkeling gear. The beach huts at the resort hotels usually charge much higher prices than the in-town shops. A snorkel set at most of the beach huts goes for about $5 an hour.

Hanalei Surf Company (☎ 826-9000), in the Hanalei Center in Hanalei, rents snorkel sets (including corrective masks) for $5/20 a day/week and snorkel vests for $4/17. Pedal & Paddle (☎ 826-9069), in the Ching Young Village in Hanalei, has similar equipment at similar prices.

Kayak Kauai, in Hanalei (☎ 826-9844) and Wailua (☎ 822-9179), rents snorkel sets for $8 the first day and $4 each additional day, or $20 a week.

Snorkel Bob's, at 4-734 Kuhio Hwy in Kapaa (☎ 823-9433) and 3236 Poipu Rd in Koloa (☎ 742-2206), rents basic snorkel sets for $2.50 a day and good ones for $6.50. Weekly rates range from $9 to $29.

Seasports Divers (☎ 742-9303), at Poipu Plaza in Poipu, rents snorkel gear for $4 to $8 a day or $15 to $25 a week, depending on the type of equipment.

Nukumoi Beach & Surf Company (☎ 742-8019), conveniently located opposite Poipu Beach Park, rents snorkel sets for $5/15 a day/week.

Kayaking

With all its waterways, Kauai has some of Hawaii's best kayaking.

The most popular route is up the Wailua River, where you can stop at the Fern Grotto or take a mile-long side hike to a 200-foot waterfall. The whole kayak route is about 7 miles roundtrip. It's got the advantage of being convenient – the launch site, near the mouth of the river, is central, and you can rent a kayak right there at the boat ramp. On the downside, this is also the busiest route. On a sunny weekend day, there can be hundreds of people on the Wailua River, mostly kayakers, but also local motorboaters and water-skiers, not to mention the Fern Grotto tour boats with their blaring loudspeaker commentary.

If you prefer a quieter scene, one appealing option is the Hanalei River, which goes through the Hanalei National Wildlife Refuge and meanders deep into Hanalei Valley. The riverfront is lush and beautiful, in places canopied by overhanging trees. The journey is about 6 miles roundtrip, though just how far you'll be able to go depends on the water level in the river, which varies with the rainfall.

Another pleasant kayaking place on the North Shore is the Kalihiwai River up the scenic Kalihiwai Valley, though it's a fairly short route. Other good kayaking spots include the Huleia Stream in the Lihue area and the Hanapepe and Waimea Rivers on the southwest side of the island.

Wailua Kayak & Canoe (☎ 821-1188) is right on the water at the Wailua River State Park boat ramp. Single kayaks rent for $25, double kayaks for $50. If you don't want to set off on your own, there's a three-hour guided tour to the Fern Grotto for $60 and a five-hour tour that includes the waterfall hike for $80.

Kauai Water Ski & Surf Company (☎ 822-3574) and Wailua Kayak Adventures (☎ 822-5795), both near the Kintaro restaurant on the Kuhio Hwy in Wailua, will deliver kayaks to the Wailua River. Both charge around $25/50 for single/double kayaks, but they'll sometimes discount that a bit.

One way to kayak the Wailua River while avoiding congestion near the river mouth is to rent a kayak from Kamokila Hawaiian Village (☎ 823-0559), a sightseeing spot 1½ miles up Hwy 580. The village has its own landing site at a bend in the river, not too far

from the Fern Grotto. The kayak rental fee of $25 per person includes the village tour and admission fee.

If you have a car and don't mind carting your own kayak, you could try one of a number of rental places along the Kuhio Hwy on Kauai's East Side (from Wailua to Kapaa); prices average around $20/40 for single/double kayaks. Shops include Chris The Fun Lady (☎ 822-7759), opposite the Waipouli Town Center, a shopping plaza.

Pedal & Paddle (☎ 826-9069), in the Ching Young Village in Hanalei, rents single kayaks for $20 a day and double kayaks for $35 a day.

Kayak Kauai, in Hanalei (☎ 826-9844, www.kayakkauai.com) and at the Coconut Marketplace in Wailua (☎ 822-9179), rents single kayaks for $25 a day, double kayaks for $48 a day. As the Hanalei shop is on the Hanalei River, you can set the boat in the river and paddle right from the shop. In addition to rentals, Kayak Kauai also offers guided tours. A three-hour tour of either the Hanalei River or the Wailua River costs $55. In summertime, a full-day guided sea-kayaking tour along the Na Pali Coast costs $130; in winter, a similar trip along the South Shore costs $105.

In the Poipu area, Outfitters Kauai (☎ 742-9667, www.outfitterskauai.com), at Poipu Plaza, rents single kayaks for $30 a day and double kayaks for $45 a day. Guided 2-mile, 3½-hour kayak outings along the South Shore are available year-round, and cost $65. In the summer, Outfitters Kauai also offers full-day guided tours along the Na Pali Coast for $135.

Island Adventures (☎ 245-9662) leads 2½-hour guided kayak trips from Nawiliwili Harbor along the Huleia Stream past the Menehune Fishpond and Huleia National Wildlife Refuge. Tours cost $48 for adults, $24 for children under 12.

Kayak prices typically include paddles, life vests and a car rack setup when necessary.

Fishing

For deep-sea sport fishing, True Blue Charters (☎ 246-6333) and Sea Lure Fishing Charters (☎ 822-5963) take boats out of Nawiliwili Harbor. Anini Fishing Charters (☎ 828-1285) and Robert McReynolds Fishing Charters (☎ 828-1379) are based at Anini Beach.

Kauai has largemouth and smallmouth bass in some of its private freshwater reservoirs. Two guide services provide freshwater charters: JJ's Big Bass Tours (☎ 332-9219) and Cast & Catch (☎ 332-9707).

Rainbow trout inhabit several streams and reservoirs in Kokee State Park. The season begins on the first Saturday in August and runs for 16 days, usually continuing on weekends and holidays through September. A valid state freshwater license is required (on Kauai, call ☎ 274-3344).

Hiking

Kauai has some excellent hikes. The best known is the spectacular 11-mile Kalalau Trail, which hugs the rugged Na Pali Coast.

Kokee State Park is also a hiker's paradise, with the largest concentration of trails on Kauai. Some of these trails lead to splendid views of the Na Pali Coast. Others include short nature walks, mountain stream trails and a muddy trek through the unique Alakai Swamp.

South of Kokee, backcountry trails lead down into the picturesque Waimea Canyon, forking into abandoned river valleys.

The Kapaa-Wailua area also offers some pleasant hiking opportunities, including a trail that goes across the chest of the Sleeping Giant mountain. Keahua Arboretum near Wailua is the trailhead for a couple of scenic ridgetop trails, including the Powerline Trail, which goes all the way to Princeville, and the shorter Kuilau Ridge Trail.

These hikes are all detailed in their respective sections.

Guided Hikes The Kauai division of the Sierra Club (www.hi.sierraclub.org/kauai/kauai.html) offers guided hikes, usually on weekends, that range from strolls up the Sleeping Giant to overnighters in Waimea Canyon. Advance registration is sometimes required, and a donation of $3 is suggested. For a hike schedule, send a self-addressed stamped envelope to the Sierra Club, PO Box 3412, Lihue, HI 96766. Once in Kauai, you can find the Sierra Club hikes listed in the free *This Week Kauai* tourist magazine and in the 'Calendar' section of Sunday's *Garden Island*.

Mountain Biking

Mountain biking is becoming increasingly popular on Kauai, and many of the island's forest reserve trails, including the 13-mile Powerline Trail from Wailua to Princeville, are open to mountain bikers. The Division of Forestry & Wildlife (☎ 274-3433), 3060 Eiwa St, room 306, Lihue, HI 96766, has a free leaflet that lists the open trails. The pamphlet should be used in conjunction with the forestry's free topographical map (see the earlier Maps section).

The following companies provide guided group tours.

Kauai Coasters (☎ 639-2412, coast@aloha.net, www.aloha.net/~coast) leads cyclists down the Waimea Canyon road, starting at sunrise from the Kalalau Lookout. The 12-mile ride takes about 1½ hours, mostly coasting downhill. The entire outing lasts four to five hours, depending on your pick-up point, and costs $70, including a continental breakfast.

If you're interested in a downhill bicycle tour of Waimea Canyon, Outfitters Kauai (☎ 742-9667, www.outfitterskauai.com), at Poipu Plaza in Poipu, offers one for $70.

Kauai Cycle and Tour (☎ 821-2115, www.bikehawaii.com/kauaicycle), 1379 Kuhio Hwy in Kapaa, offers daylong mountain-biking tours into Kauai's rugged interior. The cost is $75, lunch included.

For information on renting bicycles, see the Getting Around section, later in this chapter.

Horseback Riding

CJM Country Stables (☎ 742-6096) has some enjoyable rides in the Mahaulepu Beach area. There's a three-hour breakfast ride for $75 and two-hour morning or afternoon rides for $60. A 3½-hour afternoon ride, which includes time for a swim and a picnic on the beach, costs $90. The stables are in Poipu, 1½ miles east of the Hyatt Regency Kauai.

Princeville Ranch Stables (☎ 826-6777), along Hwy 56 near the Princeville Airport, offers a four-hour ride ($110) across ranch

lands to a waterfall for a picnic and swim; a three-hour ride ($95) to Anini Beach, with a break for a swim; and a 1½-hour ($55) ride along a bluff with ocean views.

Both stables are closed on Sunday.

Tennis

County tennis courts, which are free and open to the public, are available at the following locations: Wailua Houselots Park and Wailua Homesteads Park, both in Wailua; Hardy St, near the Convention Hall in Lihue; opposite Kauai Community College in Puhi; Kapaa New Park in Kapaa; Knudsen Park in Koloa; Kalawai Park in Kalaheo; near Hanapepe Stadium in Hanapepe; and on the corner of Hwys 552 and 50 in Kekaha.

Several hotels have tennis courts available for their guests.

The following places are open to the general public. All rent rackets for $5.

The Kauai Lagoons Racquet Club (☎ 246-6000), adjacent to the Kauai Marriott in Lihue, has seven courts. The cost is $20 per court per hour, but there are also cheaper clinics and round-robins.

The Kiahuna Tennis Club (☎ 742-9533), in Poipu, has 10 courts and charges $10 per person per hour. There are $5 round-robins on Wednesday.

The Hyatt Regency Kauai (☎ 742-1234), at 1571 Poipu Rd in Poipu, has four courts and charges $20 per court per hour.

The Princeville Tennis Club (☎ 826-3620), at 5380 Honoiki Rd in Princeville, has six courts and charges $13 per person, which allows at least 1½ hours of play.

The Hanalei Bay Resort Tennis Club (☎ 826-6522), in Princeville, has eight courts and a full tennis program, charging $6 per person per hour.

Golf

Kauai has nine golf courses. Major tournaments are hosted at Princeville's Prince course and at the Poipu Bay Resort. The Kauai Lagoons' Kiele course in Lihue and Princeville's Makai course are also top-rated.

The Wailua County Golf Course (☎ 241-6666), an 18-hole par-72 course off Hwy 56 north of Lihue, is a well-regarded public course that's very heavily played. Reservations for morning tee times are taken up to seven days in advance. Greens fees are $25 on weekdays and $35 on weekends and holidays. After 2 pm, the greens fees drop in half and play is on a first-come, first-served basis. Cart rentals cost $14, club rentals $15.

Kauai's newest course is the 10-hole Grove Farm Golf Course (☎ 245-8756), south of the Kukui Grove Center in Lihue. Greens fees are $35, including a cart, and club rentals cost $15.

The Kauai Lagoons Golf Club (☎ 241-6000, 800-634-6400), north of the Kauai Marriott in Lihue, has two 18-hole par-72 courses. The Kiele course costs $123, the Lagoons course $83, with cheaper off-peak rates. Clubs rent for $30.

On the North Shore, the Princeville Resort (☎ 826-2727, 800-826-1105) has two courses: the 18-hole par-72 Prince and the 27-hole par-72 Makai. Greens and cart fees for the Makai course are $97 for guests staying in Princeville and $115 for non-guests. The fees for the Prince course are $124/155. There are 'matinee discounts' at both courses if you wait until the afternoon to tee off. Club rentals cost $32.

On the southern part of the island, the Kukuiolono Golf Course (☎ 332-9151) in Kalaheo is a nine-hole par-36 course on an old estate with a grand hilltop view and an earthy appeal. Greens fees are just $7, and pull carts cost $2 more.

In Poipu, the Kiahuna Golf Club (☎ 742-9595), an 18-hole par-70 course run by the Sports Shinko Group, charges $75 in the early morning, $55 after 11 am, cart included. Clubs rent for $15 to $30.

Also on the South Shore, the Poipu Bay Resort Golf Course (☎ 742-8711, 800-858-6300), an 18-hole par-72 course adjacent to the Hyatt Regency Kauai, charges Hyatt guests $100, nonguests $145. Prices drop to $95 after noon, $50 after 3 pm. Carts are included in the rate; club rentals start at $40.

ORGANIZED TOURS
Van
In Kauai, most sightseeing tour prices vary with the pick-up point.

Polynesian Adventure Tours (☎ 246-0122, www.polyad.com) offers full-day van tours that include Wailua, Fern Grotto, Koloa, Poipu, Waimea, Waimea Canyon and Kalalau Lookout for $60 with pick-up in Lihue or Wailua, $65 from Poipu, $73 from Princeville. Half-day North Shore tours that take in Hanalei, Haena and Kee Beach cost $33 from Lihue or Wailua, $28 from Princeville, $43 from Poipu. Half-day Waimea Canyon tours cost $39 from Lihue or Wailua, $43 from Poipu, $59 from Princeville. Full-day outings that squeeze in both Waimea Canyon and the North Shore cost $60 from Lihue or Wailua, $65 from Princeville or Poipu.

TransHawaiian (☎ 245-5108) and Roberts Hawaii (☎ 245-9101) offer similar tours at comparable prices.

In addition, Kauai Paradise Tours (☎ 246-3999, fax 245-2499) specializes in tours narrated in German. Eight-hour sightseeing tours cost $88, including a picnic lunch.

Kauai Mountain Tours (☎ 245-7224, 800-452-1113) visits Waimea Canyon and Kokee State Park in 4WD vans that are capable of detouring from the beaten path to take in sights along forest dirt roads. Tours last six to seven hours and cost $84, lunch and hotel pick-up included.

All tour companies offer discounted prices for children.

Helicopter
Many wilderness hikers resent the intrusion of helicopters into otherwise serene areas, and local environmentalists have successfully stopped copter landings on Na Pali Coast beaches. However, these 'Kauai mosquitoes' that are an irritant to people on the ground no doubt offer some pretty spectacular views as they swoop down into Waimea Canyon, run along the Na Pali Coast and seek out hidden waterfalls.

Several helicopter companies offer flights around Kauai. The free tourist magazines advertise most of them and often have discount coupons.

The going rate is about $125 for a 45-minute 'circle-island tour' that zooms by the main sights. There's usually some sort of 'ultimate splendor' tour that can add on 20 minutes and run up another $50 to $75. Most of the helicopter offices are either in central Lihue, near the corner of Hwy 56 and Ahukini Rd, or at the side of Lihue Airport.

Cruises

Like the other islands, Kauai has its fair share of catamaran picnic sails, sunset cruises and the like. It also has something the other islands don't: the spectacular Na Pali Coast.

Several boat companies run cruises down the Na Pali Coast, but with the recent closure of the Hanalei launch site, all Na Pali cruises – at least temporarily – depart from the western side of Kauai. This tends to make the tours both longer and pricier than they have been in the past.

Typical of the Na Pali Coast cruises is the one offered by Holo Holo Charters (☎ 246-4656), which departs from Port Allen near Hanapepe, takes six hours and costs $119, including snorkeling, breakfast and lunch.

Other companies include Na Pali Explorer (☎ 335-9909) and Na Pali Eco Adventures (☎ 826-6804), both of which depart from Port Allen, and Liko Kauai Cruises (☎ 338-0333), which departs from Kikiaola Harbor in Kekaha.

The smoothest rides are generally in the summer. For most of the winter, the seas are too rough on the Na Pali Coast for nearshore activities, and on some days it's simply too rough for the boats to go out at all. A few companies then switch to the calmer southern shore for snorkeling cruises and whale-watching tours.

ACCOMMODATIONS

Three areas in Kauai – Poipu, Princeville, and the strip from Lihue to Kapaa – contain almost all of the island's hotels and condos.

For the most part, Kauai's beach hotels are a bit expensive. The cheapest begin around $85, although the majority are nearly double that. Condos have a similar price range but tend to be a better deal, particularly if you're traveling in a group.

The best accommodations deals on the island are found in the scattering of B&Bs that have sprung up in recent years. The Wailua area has the greatest concentration

of B&Bs, with prices from around $50/60 for singles/doubles. Many are in fine homes that are comfortable and situated in a scenic location, a few miles up the slope from the coast. Wailua also makes a good base for exploring, as it's midway between the North Shore and Kokee State Park.

A couple of hostel-style places in Kapaa shore up the bottom end with dorm beds for $16 to $20 per person. For $30 to $40, there are basic cabinettes at Kahili Mountain Park near Koloa and rooms at spartan in-town hotels in Lihue.

Camping

Kauai has some fine camping spots. Some are drive-up beach parks, some are in dense forest and others are at the end of daylong hikes into remote valleys.

There are camping areas at three state parks, seven county parks and at forest reserve trailside camps in Waimea Canyon and the nearby Kokee area.

State Parks Camping is allowed at Kokee, Polihale and Na Pali Coast State Parks. Permits are required and are free. They are issued from 8 am to 4 pm Monday to Friday at the Division of State Parks (☎ 274-3444), 3060 Eiwa St, room 306, Lihue, HI 96766, and at state park offices on other islands. Up to 10 people may be listed on each permit, but the person applying for the permit must show an ID (such as a driver's license or passport) for each person.

You can also obtain a permit by mail by sending the state park office either a completed official application form or a regular sheet of paper specifying the park(s) at which you want to stay and the exact dates you wish to stay at each park. For Na Pali Coast State Park, you'll also have to specify which campground you're requesting on which night. Along with this application include a photocopy of each camper's ID (with the ID number and birth date clearly readable).

You can apply for a permit as early as a year in advance. During the busy summer period of May to September, Na Pali Coast campsites are often completely booked up many months ahead, so apply for your permit as far in advance as possible. If you change your mind about camping once you get the permit, be sure to cancel, as otherwise you'll be tying up an empty space and preventing someone else from camping.

At each state park, you may camp for up to five consecutive nights within a 30-day period. At the Na Pali Coast State Park, this means a maximum of five nights on the entire Kalalau Trail, with the additional restriction that you may not spend two consecutive nights at either Hanakapiai or Hanakoa Valley.

The Milolii Valley section of Na Pali Coast State Park, accessible only by small boat, is open May to September and has a three-day limit. Although the service was temporarily suspended at press time, two companies – Captain Zodiac (☎ 826-9371) and Hanalei Sea Tours (☎ 826-7254) – usually can drop campers off at Milolii for a roundtrip fee of around $150. On rare occasions when the surf gets too high, the pick-up service may be delayed, so campers should carry extra provisions.

County Beach Parks Camping is allowed at Haena, Hanalei, Anini, Anahola, Hanamaulu, Salt Pond and Lucy Wright Parks. The camping areas at Haena, Anini and Salt Pond are all on nice beaches and are good choices. Camping is allowed at Hanalei Beach Park on Friday, Saturday and holidays only.

All county campgrounds have showers and rest rooms, and most have covered picnic pavilions and barbecue grills. There's a typical Hawaiian laissez-faire style to the campgrounds, so don't expect to find numbered sites or caretakers.

Permits, which are required, are $3 per adult per night (no fees for children under 18 or Hawaii residents). There's a limit of seven days at each campground and a limit of 60 days of camping a year.

Permit applications can be made by mail if a completed form and payment are received at least one month in advance. Otherwise, pick up the permits in person from 8 am to 4:15 pm Monday to Friday at the Divi-

sion of Parks & Recreation (☎ 241-6 4444 Rice St, suite 150, Lihue, HI 96766, the Lihue Civic Center, at the corner of Hwys 50 and 56.

You can also just set up camp and wait for the ranger to come around and collect, but if you do this the fee jumps to $5 per person. Be aware that rangers sometimes wake up campers late at night or as early as 5 am to collect fees, and if they determine that the camping area is too full, campers without permits can be asked to move.

In 1999, the county instituted a new policy of closing each campground one day a week. So Haena and Lucy Wright are closed on Monday, Anini and Salt Pond are closed on Tuesday, Hanamaulu is closed on Wednesday and Anahola is closed on Thursday. If the closure day happens to coincide with a public holiday, the park will remain open.

Waimea Canyon The Division of Forestry & Wildlife allows backcountry camping at four sites along trails in Waimea Canyon and at two sites (Sugi Grove and Kawaikoi) in the Kokee State Park area. Camping is limited to four nights in the canyon and three nights in the Kokee area within a 30-day period.

Camping permits, which are required and are free, can be picked up in person between 8 am and 4 pm weekdays at the forestry office, 3060 Eiwa St, room 306, Lihue, HI 96766. You can also get the permits mailed to you in advance by writing (or by calling ☎ 274-3433); simply list the name and address of each camper, the camping area in which you want to stay and the dates you plan to camp.

Cabins Cabins run by a private concessionaire are available in Kokee State Park. Cabins in a mountain setting are in Kahili Mountain Park, north of Koloa. See the relevant sections for more information.

Camping Supplies Pedal & Paddle (☎ 826-9069), in Ching Young Village in Hanalei, rents two-person dome tents for $10/30 a day/week, backpacks for $5/20, daypacks for $3/10 and light blankets, trail stoves and

h for $4/12. The shop also
plies it rents.
oth in Hanalei (☎ 826-9844)
22-9179), rents two-person
tents or backpacks for $8/30 a day/week,
camping stoves or sleeping bags for $6/20,
sleeping pads for $3/10 and daypacks for
$4/15.

All three shops are open daily, from at
least 9 am to 5 pm.

ENTERTAINMENT

Most of Kauai's entertainment scene is at the
larger hotels. The main place to go dancing is
Gilligan's, inside the Outrigger Kauai Beach
hotel in Lihue. On the North Shore, the main
dance venue is Sushi & Blues in Hanalei's
Ching Young Village.

You can listen to live Hawaiian music at
some of the resorts' poolside bars, in Duke's
Canoe Club at the Kauai Marriott in Lihue,
and on the North Shore at the Hanalei
Gourmet in Hanalei and the Hanalei Bay
Resort in Princeville.

Luaus take place at Kauai Coconut
Beach Resort and Smith's Tropical Paradise
in Wailua, at the Hyatt Regency Kauai in
Poipu and at the Princeville Hotel on the
North Shore.

Free hula shows are presented at the
Coconut Marketplace in Wailua, the Kukui
Grove Center in Lihue and the Hyatt Re-
gency Kauai in Poipu.

There are movie theaters in the Kukui
Grove Center in Lihue and the Coconut
Marketplace in Wailua.

For more details on specific venues, see the
relevant town sections in this chapter. Check
the local paper or the free tourist magazines
for the latest entertainment schedules.

SHOPPING

Popular souvenir items include Niihau shell
leis, oil paintings of Kauai landscapes and
island-made products such as soap and
coconut-oil lotions. While the early harvests
of Kauai-grown coffee have not been as
highly regarded as the gourmet Kona coffee,
the price is a relative bargain; some of the
best prices on both coffees can be found at
discount stores such as Longs Drugs.

Good places to look for locally made arts
and crafts include the Kilohana Plantation
in Puhi, Ching Young Village in Hanalei, the
Kauai Museum in Lihue and shopping
centers around the island.

Kauai's largest shopping center, the
Kukui Grove Center in Lihue, has a Kauai

Sunshine Markets

For island-grown fruits and vegetables that are both fresher and cheaper than grocery store
produce, try to catch one of the farmers' markets, known locally as Sunshine Markets. Not
only will you find bargain prices on fruits like papayas, oranges and avocados, but you'll also
find items such as passion fruit and guava that aren't sold in supermarkets at all.

The organizers keep the markets on a fixed schedule, but occasionally there are adjust-
ments; call ☎ 241-6390 for the latest information.

The current schedule is: at Knudsen Park, on Maluhia Rd in Koloa, at noon on Monday; on
Hwy 560 just west of Hanalei at 2 pm on Tuesday; at Kalaheo Neighborhood Center in
Kalaheo at 3:30 pm on Tuesday; at Kapaa New Town Park in Kapaa at 3 pm on Wednesday;
at Hanapepe Town Park in Hanapepe at 3:30 pm on Thursday; at Kilauea Neighborhood
Center, opposite Kong Lung Center in Kilauea, at 4:30 pm on Thursday; at Vidinha Stadium
in Lihue at 3 pm on Friday; at Kekaha Neighborhood Center in Kekaha at 9 am on Saturday.

Get there early. As a matter of fact, it's best to be there before the starting time, as once
the whistle blows there's a big rush and people begin to scoop things up quickly. Depending
on the location, it can all wrap up within an hour or so.

Products Store that sells a full range of Kauai-made items, from expensive jewelry and koa-wood bowls to papaya-seed dressing and taro chips. The nearby Borders bookstore stocks an excellent selection of Hawaiian music and has a nifty headphone setup that enables you to preview CDs.

GETTING THERE & AWAY
Air
All scheduled passenger flights to Kauai land at Lihue Airport.

Hawaiian Airlines (☎ 245-1813, 800-882-8811) flies nonstop from Honolulu to Lihue about once an hour from 5:45 am to 8 pm. Aloha Airlines (☎ 245-3691, 800-241-6522) flies the same route an average of once every 45 minutes from 5:30 am to 8 pm. Aloha also has a couple of nonstop flights between Lihue and Kahului (Maui), as well as several daily flights between Lihue and Kona (Big Island) that require a stop in Honolulu but no change of planes. One-way fares are currently $93 on either airline.

United Airlines (☎ 800-241-6522) has a daily nonstop flight to Lihue from Los Angeles; fares vary with the time of year and promotions, but the cheapest tickets typically hover around $450 roundtrip.

Kauai also has a small airport in Princeville on the North Shore, but it no longer has scheduled service.

For more information on air travel, including discounts and air passes, see the Getting Around chapter in the front of this book.

LIHUE AIRPORT
Lihue Airport's modern terminal includes an agricultural inspection station for passengers returning to the mainland, a restaurant, cocktail lounge, flower shop, gift shop and newsstand. You'll find well-stocked racks loaded with activity and accommodations brochures, as well as Kauai's free tourist magazines, in the baggage claim area.

GETTING AROUND
Kauai has a limited public bus service, and while it connects most towns on the island, it's not geared for visitors and won't take you off the beaten path or out to major destinations like Kilauea Lighthouse, Waimea Canyon or Kokee State Park. Consequently, renting a car is almost essential for exploring the island in depth.

Kauai's main roads are straightforward and easy to follow, but if you plan on doing a lot of exploring, consider picking up a good road map, such as the *Hawaii, Maui & Kauai Map of the Neighbor Islands* by Compass Maps.

Surprisingly, Kauai does have rush-hour traffic jams, especially in central Lihue and on the highway between Lihue and Kapaa. To reduce the rush-hour congestion, temporary cones are sometimes set up on Hwy 56 in the Wailua area to create 'contra-flow' lanes; reversing the direction of traffic flow in one of the lanes on the uncongested side of the road opens an additional lane in the congested direction.

To/From the Airport
The public bus does not stop at Lihue Airport. Taxis can be picked up curbside in front of the arrival area. Car rental booths are lined up on the other side of the street, opposite the arrival and departure gates.

Bus
The public bus has two main routes, both originating in the county capital of Lihue and operating eight times a day on weekdays and four times a day on Saturday. One route heads north to Hanalei, stopping along the way at the Coconut Marketplace in Wailua, the library in Kapaa, the intersection of Kolo Rd and Hwy 56 in Kilauea, and the Princeville Shopping Center. The second route runs between Lihue and Kekaha, Kauai's westernmost town, making stops in Kalaheo, Eleele, Hanapepe and Waimea; once a day in each direction, the bus swings down through Koloa and Poipu as well.

In addition to those routes, the service includes a bus that shuttles between Lihue and Kapaa four times a day on weekdays, and a local Lihue bus that runs between Lihue's shopping centers once an hour on weekdays.

In Lihue, the buses can be boarded on Eiwa St, near the Old County Building. Buses

KAUAI

are white with a green sugarcane motif and are marked 'Kauai Bus.' Destinations are posted in the front window. The fare on all routes is $1 per ride; have the exact fare ready as drivers are not allowed to make change. There's also a $25 monthly pass. You can get more information on the bus by calling ☎ 241-6410 from 7 am to 5 pm Monday to Saturday.

If you plan to use the bus, keep in mind that there's no service on Sunday or holidays. Carry-on bags have a size limit of 7-by-14-by-22 inches; boogie boards are not allowed and nothing can be stored in the aisles.

You can pick up a bus schedule from most bus drivers, at the library in Kapaa and in room 103 of the Old County Building, at 4396 Rice St in Lihue.

For information on commercial sightseeing bus tours, see Organized Tours in the Activities section, earlier in this chapter.

Car & Motorcycle

Budget (☎ 245-1901), Hertz (☎ 245-3356), Avis (☎ 245-3512), Alamo (☎ 246-0645), Dollar (☎ 245-3651) and National (☎ 245-5636) have car rental booths at Lihue Airport. For more information, including toll-free numbers, see the introductory Getting Around chapter in the front of this book. Chris The Fun Lady (☎ 822-7759), opposite the Waipouli Town Center in Waipouli, has Yamaha Razz motorbikes for $8.50/35 an hour/day and Honda Elites for $10/50. Both are 49cc but the Hondas are peppier, reaching cruising speeds of 30 to 35mph.

Taxi

Taxis charge $2 at flag-fall and then $2 a mile, metered in 25¢ increments. The fare from Lihue Airport is about $17 to Coconut Plantation in Wailua, $20 to Kapaa and $30 to Poipu.

Taxi companies are Akiko's Taxi (☎ 822-7588), in the Lihue-Kapaa area; North Shore Cab (☎ 826-6189), based in Princeville; and Poipu Taxi (☎ 639-2044), for service on Kauai's south side.

Bicycle

Kauai's roads are generally narrow, shoulders are often nonexistent, and traffic can be a little heavy in places – all safety concerns for cyclists. The hilly terrain is another challenge: Expect a hefty workout, especially if you cycle into interior areas. All said and done, unless you're a seasoned cyclist accustomed to difficult conditions, don't plan on touring the island extensively by bike.

Bicycle rentals generally include use of a helmet, lock, water bottle and car rack, though some places charge an extra $5 for the car rack.

Kayak Kauai, in Hanalei (☎ 826-9844) and at the Coconut Marketplace in Wailua (☎ 822-9179), rents mountain bikes for $20/75 a day/week and beach cruisers for $15/60.

Pedal & Paddle (☎ 826-9069), in the Ching Young Village in Hanalei, rents mountain bikes for $20/80 a day/week and beach cruisers for $10/50.

Outfitters Kauai (☎ 742-9667), in the Poipu Plaza in Poipu, rents beach cruisers for $20 a day and road bikes for $30. Mountain bikes cost $25 to $33 a day, with the higher prices for full-suspension models. Discounts are available on rentals of more than three days.

Kauai Cycle and Tour (☎ 821-2115), 1379 Kuhio Hwy in Kapaa, rents mountain bikes with front suspension for $20/95 a day/week and full-suspension bikes for $35/150.

See Mountain Biking in the earlier Activities section for information on cycling outings.

East Side

The commercial heart of Kauai, the East Side includes the island's largest city, Lihue, as well as Wailua, Waipouli and Kapaa – three small towns with hotels and condo complexes, shopping centers and restaurants. Despite the density of businesses here, though, you'll hardly encounter any traffic jams on the Kuhio Hwy, the main route through the area. Many visitors to Kauai choose to stay in the relatively inexpensive accommodations of the East Side; its central location makes it a convenient base for exploring the lush river valleys of the North Shore and the sunny beaches to the south.

LIHUE

Lihue is the county capital, the island's commercial center and the arrival point of virtually all visitors to Kauai. Nevertheless, it's small (with a population of only 5500) and rather ordinary. Essentially a grown-up plantation town with no special charm, Lihue contains inexpensive local hotels and restaurants and the island's main shopping mall but only a few sights of interest.

Information

The Kauai Visitors Bureau (☎ 245-3971), at 4334 Rice St, suite 101, in the Watumull Plaza, is open 8 am to 4:30 pm Monday to Friday. If you're looking for brochures and printed information, however, the racks at the airport are better stocked.

The Bank of Hawaii, on Rice St, is open from 8:30 am to 4 pm Monday to Thursday, from 8:30 am to 6 pm on Friday and 9 am to noon on Saturday. It also has a 24-hour ATM.

The post office is opposite the Kauai Museum on Rice St, next to the Bank of Hawaii. Post office hours are 8 am to 4:30 pm Monday to Friday, from 9 am to 1 pm on Saturday.

Mokihana Travel (☎ 245-5338), 3016 Umi St, suite 3, sells interisland flight tickets at reasonable prices.

The Lihue Public Library, 4344 Hardy St, is open 10 am to 8 pm on Monday and Wednesday; 9 am to 5 pm on Tuesday, Thursday and Friday; and 9 am to 1 pm on Saturday.

If you need to wash any clothes, there's a coin laundry in the Rice Shopping Center, on Rice St in the center of town.

Kauai Museum

A few hours at the Kauai Museum (☎ 245-6931), 4428 Rice St, should give you a good overview of the island's history.

The displays begin with Kauai's volcanic genesis from the ocean floor, then move on to describe the island's unique ecosystems. The 1st floor covers early Hawaii, with displays of hula instruments, poi pounders and tapa-making tools.

Upstairs, the sugarcane workers and missionaries arrive on the scene. A replica of a plantation worker's spartan shack sits opposite the spacious bedroom of an early missionary's house, furnished with a four-poster koa bed and Hawaiian quilts. It is to these folks that Hawaii traces its multiethnic roots and vastly unequal distribution of land and wealth. The displays are accompanied by well-written interpretive presentations of life in old Kauai.

The gift shop has a good selection of Hawaiiana books and a small collection of koa bowls and other handicrafts. If you only want to visit the gift shop, which is inside the museum lobby, you can enter without paying.

The museum is open 9 am to 4 pm Monday to Friday and 10 am to 4 pm Saturday. Admission is $5 for adults, $3 for children 13 to 17 and $1 for children six to 12. If you run out of time, ask for a free reentry pass when you leave.

Lihue Sugar Mill

The conveyer belt that crosses over Hwy 50 just south of its intersection with Hwy 56 transports crushed sugarcane to the Lihue Sugar Mill. The mill produces raw sugar crystals that are shipped to California to be refined. Molasses is also made here, and if you happen by on one of those days, you'll find the air laden with the sweet, thick smell of the syrup.

Old Lutheran Church

From the outside, the oldest Lutheran church in Hawaii is just one more quaint Hawaiian church. From the inside, it's much more interesting.

German immigrants styled their church to resemble the boat that brought them from their homeland to Hawaii in the late 19th century. The floor has been built to slant like the deck of a ship, the balcony resembles a captain's bridge and ship lanterns hang from the ceiling. The current building was actually constructed in 1983, but it's an almost exact replica of the original 1885 church that was leveled by Hurricane Iwa in 1982.

The immigrants themselves now lie at rest in the church cemetery on a knoll overlooking the cane fields in which they toiled.

The church is a quarter of a mile up Hoomana Rd, which is just west of the intersection of Hwys 56 and 50.

KAUAI

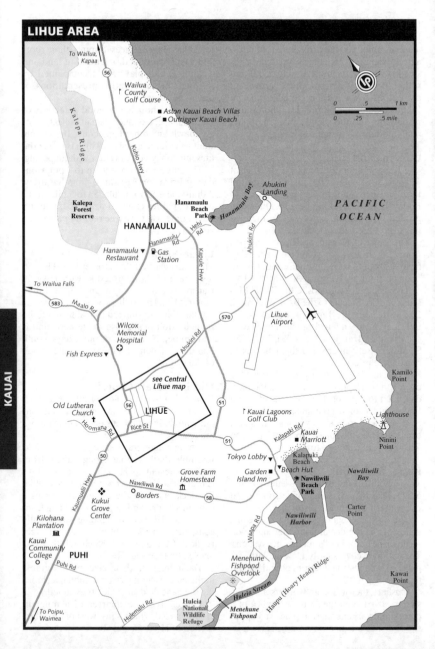

LIHUE AREA

To Wailua, Kapaa

56

Wailua County Golf Course

Kalepa Ridge

■ Aston Kauai Beach Villas
■ Outrigger Kauai Beach

Kalepa Forest Reserve

Kuhio Hwy

0   .5   1 km
0   .25   .5 mile

Ahukini Landing

PACIFIC OCEAN

Hanamaulu Beach Park

HANAMAULU

Hanamaulu Bay

Hehi Rd

Hanamaulu Rd

Hanamaulu Restaurant ▼

Gas Station

Ahukini Rd

To Wailua Falls

583   Maalo Rd

Kapule Hwy

570

Lihue Airport

Wilcox Memorial Hospital

Fish Express ▼

Ahukini Rd

Kamilo Point

see Central Lihue map

Old Lutheran Church ✝

56   LIHUE

51

↑ Kauai Lagoons Golf Club

Lighthouse ⚠

Rice St

Hoomana Rd

51

Ninini Point

50

Kalapaki Rd

Kauai Marriott ■

Kaumualii Hwy

Nawiliwili Rd

Tokyo Lobby ▼

Kalapaki Beach

Beach Hut ▼

Nawiliwili Bay

Grove Farm Homestead 🏛

Garden Island Inn ■

Nawiliwili Beach Park

Borders ○

58

Kukui Grove Center

Kilohana Plantation 🏛

Kauai Community College ○

PUHI

Waapa Rd

Nawiliwili Harbor

Carter Point

Puhi Rd

Menehune Fishpond Overlook ✳

Haupu (Hoary Head) Ridge

Kawai Point

To Poipu, Waimea

Hulemalu Rd

Huleia Stream

Huleia National Wildlife Refuge

Menehune Fishpond

Wailua Falls

Wailua Falls is a scenic 80-foot waterfall that's just north of Lihue. To get there from Lihue, follow Hwy 56 north and turn left onto Maalo Rd (Hwy 583), a narrow paved road that weaves through sugarcane fields. The road ends at the falls at precisely 3.94 miles – as the highway marker fastidiously proclaims.

Wailua, which means 'two waters,' is usually seen as two falls. However, after heavy rains, it becomes one wide rushing waterfall and you can watch fish being thrown out beyond the powerful waters for a flying dive into the pool below.

This is not a waterfall to explore from the top. A sign at the parking lot near a closed path reads, 'Slippery rocks at top of falls. People have been killed.' There are plenty of stories told of people sliding off the rocks, some miraculously grabbing roots and being rescued and others not so lucky.

A third of a mile before the road's end, at a large dirt pull-off, an eroded trail leads to the base of the falls. The steep part of the trail leading down to the river can be very slippery when wet, if not outright hazardous. And the part that follows the riverbed to the base of the falls commonly floods over, which makes it barely discernible after heavy rains. However, when all's said and done, local kids do sometimes manage to scramble their way through the overgrowth to the waterfall. If you decide to give it a try, expect to work up a sweat; it can be humid enough along the riverbed to steam up eyeglasses.

Back on the road, keep an eye out for wood roses – bright yellow flowers shaped like morning glories and commonly used in dried floral arrangements. The vines bearing the flowers are especially thick around the bridge that's half a mile down the road from the waterfall.

Hanamaulu

Hanamaulu is a little village between Lihue and Wailua along Hwy 56. It's significant in Hawaiian folklore as the birthplace of Kauai's legendary hero Kawelo, depicted in folktales as a skillful warrior and champion spear thrower. Today, Hanamaulu is a sleepy town with just a few businesses, including an old-fashioned Japanese restaurant, a hole-in-the-wall post office and a doughnut shop that closes each day as soon as the doughnuts are gone.

Three-quarters of a mile from the village center, **Hanamaulu Beach Park** lies at the inside of Hanamaulu Bay, a deep protected bay with a boulder breakwater part way across its mouth. The park has campgrounds with full facilities, but it's more of a local hangout than a visitor destination. The waters are occasionally off limits because of pollution. For information on obtaining a permit to camp, see Camping in the Accommodations section, near the beginning of this chapter.

From Hwy 56, turn *makai* (seaward) onto Hanamaulu Rd at the 7-Eleven store. After a quarter mile, turn right onto Hehi Rd. As you enter the park, you'll first go under the highway bridge and then the arched trestle of an abandoned railroad bridge.

Ahukini Landing

If you've got some time to kill before your flight, you could drive to the end of Hwy 570 to see Ahukini Landing, 1½ miles beyond the airport. The road runs through cane fields and crosses a series of narrow-gauge railroad tracks that were once used to bring sugarcane down to the landing. *Ilima* (a native ground cover) and chain-of-love flowers grow along the road.

Ahukini State Recreation Pier, at the end of the highway, consists largely of cement pillars and the decaying framework of the old pier. A wooden walkway runs out across the pier, providing a prime locale for pole fishing. At the head of the bay is Hanamaulu Beach Park.

Ninini Point

The lighthouse on Ninini Point stands 100 feet above the shore, marking the northern entrance to Nawiliwili Bay. The road down to the lighthouse begins off Hwy 51, a little over half a mile south of the intersection with Hwy 570. Although you'll have to go through a guard gate and cross the Kauai

KAUAI

Lagoons Golf Course property to get to the coast, access is free to visitors.

The 2½-mile drive from the gatehouse to the lighthouse passes between the airport fence and the golf course. After 2 miles, the pavement ends and the road continues as dirt; this section is sometimes too rough to pass in a low-slung car, and you may have to hike the last 10 minutes of it.

Not only is there a fine view from the lighthouse, but nearby is one of the few sections of accessible shore in the area. Here, Hawaiians can still fish, pick *opihi* (a kind of mollusk) and gather *limu* (seaweed) as they've done for generations.

Kalapaki Beach
Lihue's best beach is Kalapaki Beach, a sandy strand sheltered by points and breakwaters at Nawiliwili Bay. The beach, off Hwy 51, lies in front of the Kauai Marriott but is open to the public.

Swimming is usually good, even in the winter, unless storms kick the surf up. The beach hut here rents snorkel gear, surfboards and kayaks.

There's free beach parking close to the water at the north side of the hotel.

Nawiliwili Beach Park
Nawiliwili Beach Park is largely a parking lot facing an ocean retaining wall. From here, you can look across to the light beacon on Kukui Point, and at the far end of the parking lot, you can also see the lighthouse on the more distant Ninini Point.

There's no beach at Nawiliwili Beach Park, but there is a footbridge that crosses Nawiliwili Stream to Kalapaki Beach.

Right at the mouth of the stream under ironwood trees is an old shelter with a wooden sign reading 'Pine Tree Inn' – it's an impromptu neighborhood open-air bar of sorts. Old-timers gather here during the day with ice chests of beer to 'talk story' and play music.

Nawiliwili Harbor
Nawiliwili Harbor is a deepwater port with a commercial harbor and an adjacent small-boat harbor. Several deep-sea fishing boats are based at the small-boat harbor, which has a picturesque setting backed by the edge of Haupu (Hoary Head) Ridge.

Waapa Rd runs southwest past the harbor and then connects with Hulemalu Rd, which leads up to an overview of the Menehune Fishpond.

Menehune Fishpond Overlook
Half a mile up Hulemalu Rd there's a lookout on the left with a view of Alakoko Fishpond, more commonly called Menehune Fishpond. In the background is misty Haupu Ridge.

The fishpond, created by a stone wall that runs along a bend in Huleia Stream, was said to have been built in one night by menehunes (see the History section, earlier in this chapter). The stone wall is now covered by a thick green line of mangrove trees. Morning is a good time for viewing as in the afternoon you look into the sun.

The **Huleia National Wildlife Refuge** lies along the north side of Huleia Stream. Once planted with taro and rice, the area now provides breeding and feeding grounds for endemic waterbirds. The refuge is not open to the public.

If you continue about a mile past the fishpond overlook and then turn right onto Puhi Rd, you'll arrive at Hwy 50, opposite Kauai Community College.

Grove Farm Homestead
The Grove Farm Homestead Plantation Museum along Nawiliwili Rd (Hwy 58), 1¾ miles from Waapa Rd, is a preserved farmhouse built in 1864 by George Wilcox, son of missionaries Abner and Lucy Wilcox. A bit musty and filled with memories, it's somewhat like the house of an old aunt. Rocking chairs sit on a covered porch. One room is lined with bookshelves stuffed with a home library, with koa-wood bowls and a small model ship on top. In one corner, a card table is set up, waiting for a foursome to sit down to a wild game of cribbage.

Two-hour tours begin at 10 am and 1 pm on Monday, Wednesday and Thursday. Reservations are required (☎ 245-3202); space sometimes fills up a week or so in advance.

The cost is $5 for adults, $2 for children ages 12 and under.

Kilohana Plantation

Kilohana, 1½ miles south of Lihue on Hwy 50, is the 1930s sugar plantation estate of Gaylord Parke Wilcox, once head of Grove Farm Homestead. The Tudor-style mansion built by Wilcox was the most distinguished house on Kauai in its day.

The home has been restored, with most of the rooms now turned into shops that sell artwork, antiques and handicrafts. It's a nice way to preserve the old estate, and you can have a look around without being charged an admission fee.

Visitors are free to wander through rooms full of antiques. The hallways hold cases of stone poi pounders, koa bowls and a few other Hawaiian artifacts, while Oriental rugs grace the hardwood floors. If you're hungry, try Gaylord's restaurant, which occupies the U-shaped courtyard surrounding the lawn.

Many island galleries rent space at Kilohana, giving it one of the widest collections of arts and crafts on Kauai. On the 1st floor, a former cloakroom is now the Hawaiian Collection Room, which sells finely strung Niihau shell leis and scrimshaw.

The upstairs bedrooms have likewise been turned into shops, with displays even in the bathrooms and closets. The works include jewelry, dolls, wood carvings of whales and dolphins, and contemporary paintings by local artists.

Behind the main house, on the lawn just east of Kilohana Clayworks pottery shop, there's a little screenhouse full of fluttering monarch butterflies. You can stroll through for free.

Kilohana (☎ 245-5608) is open 9 am to 9:30 pm Monday to Saturday, 9 am to 5 pm on Sunday. The 35-acre grounds are still part of a working farm; 20-minute tours in old-fashioned carriages pulled by Clydesdale horses cost $8 for adults and $4 for children under 12.

Queen Victoria's Profile

The rock profile of Queen Victoria, part of Haupu (Hoary Head) Ridge, can be seen from a marked 'scenic view' pull-off in front of Kauai Community College along Hwy 50 in the town of Puhi.

It takes some imagination, but here's how to find it: Position yourself midway in the pull-off facing the mountains to the south. Look across the highway at the phone pole, then over to the metal light pole in the background to the right. The queen's crowned head is under the arch of the lamp – the crown is the high part at the right, her chin lower and to the left.

Supposedly, she's shaking her thin pointy finger at an imaginary William, saying 'Na, Willy, Willy,' hence the harbor's name.

Places to Stay

Budget Lihue has some of Kauai's cheapest hotels, though they're generally drab places and, except for Motel Lani, are filled mostly with local residents.

The family-run *Motel Lani* (☎ 245-2965, *4240 Rice St, PO Box 1836, Lihue, HI 96766)* is the best budget choice, though it sits at a

Princess Hina's Profile

Long before Europeans decided that the vague rock profile on the Haupu Ridge looked like Queen Victoria, the Hawaiians had their own story. They call the rock Hina-i-uka.

Long ago, Peleula, a princess from Oahu, sailed to Kauai to check out rumors that the island had the most handsome men in Hawaii. Hina, a Kauai princess, welcomed her with a royal banquet. At the banquet was Kahili, a young chief from Kilauea, who caught the fancy of both women. To compete for his affections, they danced the hula.

Peleula's dance was stunning. But Hina, who was perfumed with the scent of Kauai's endemic mokihana berries, was absolutely mesmerizing, and she became Kahili's lover. The people of Kauai then carved one ridge of the Haupu Mountains into the image of Hina, with her finger up to warn off women from other islands.

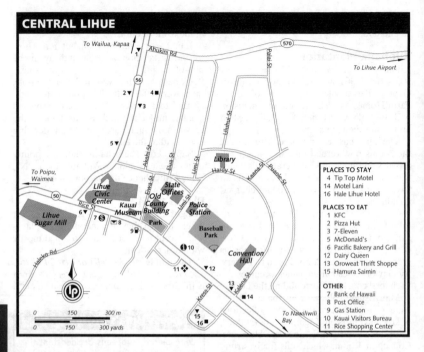

CENTRAL LIHUE

PLACES TO STAY
4 Tip Top Motel
14 Motel Lani
16 Hale Lihue Hotel

PLACES TO EAT
1 KFC
2 Pizza Hut
3 7-Eleven
5 McDonald's
6 Pacific Bakery and Grill
12 Dairy Queen
13 Oroweat Thrift Shoppe
15 Hamura Saimin

OTHER
7 Bank of Hawaii
8 Post Office
9 Gas Station
10 Kauai Visitors Bureau
11 Rice Shopping Center

busy intersection. There's a long cinder-block building with six $32 rooms that are basic but clean and have private baths, air-con and mini-refrigerators. There are also a couple of 'deluxe' rooms (around $50) that are larger and have TVs. There's a two-day minimum stay or a $2 surcharge.

Hale Lihue Hotel (☎ 245-2751, 2931 Kalena St, Lihue, HI 96766) has 20 rooms for $24.50/27.50 for singles/doubles. Rooms have two twin beds and private baths, but are quite spartan with zilch for atmosphere.

Tip Top Motel (☎ 245-2333, fax 246-8988, 3173 Akahi St, PO Box 1231, Lihue, HI 96766) has a couple dozen rooms in two-story cinder-block buildings. Rooms are basic, with twin beds, air-con and louvered windows, but they do have TV and private baths. The rate is $44 single or double.

Mid-Range & Top End The *Garden Island Inn* (☎ 245-7227, 800-648-0154, garden@ aloha.net, 3445 Wilcox Rd, Lihue, HI 96766)

is an older three-story hotel that has been extensively renovated. The 21 rooms are compact but tidy and modern with TVs, ceiling fans, mini-refrigerators, microwaves and coffeemakers. The rate is $59 for ground-floor rooms and $69 for rooms on the 2nd floor, which have air-con and small lanais. The hotel is near an industrial area and at the side of a rather busy road, so expect to hear some traffic noise. On the plus side, it's within walking distance of Kalapaki Beach and restaurants such as Tokyo Lobby and the Beach Hut.

Banyan Harbor Resort (☎ 245-7333, 800-422-6926, fax 246-4776, banyan@aloha.net, 2411 Wilcox Rd, Lihue, HI 96766) is a large condominium complex adjacent to the Garden Island Inn. It has modern units, each with a full kitchen, a sofa bed in the living room, either one or two compact bedrooms and a washer and dryer. The regular rates are $110/140 for one/two bedrooms, but there's a cheaper room-and-rental-car deal that costs just $99/119, and unlike most places there's no restriction on the number of people in the room. Up to four people could squeeze into the one-bedroom unit, and a family of six might get by in a two-bedroom unit. There's a tennis court and swimming pool.

A few miles north of downtown Lihue is the **Outrigger Kauai Beach** (☎ 245-1955, 800-688-7444, fax 246-9085, reservations@ outrigger.com, 4331 Kauai Beach Drive, Lihue, HI 96766), which has 341 rooms that range from $155 (a mountain view) to $210 (an ocean view). The hotel was originally built as a Hilton and has the standard design and amenities you'd expect of that chain, including tennis courts and large, free-form swimming pools. For further information, visit the hotel's website at www.outrigger.com.

On the same beachfront propperty as the Outrigger, **Aston Kauai Beach Villas** (☎ 245-7711, 800-922-7866, 4330 Kauai Beach Drive, Lihue, HI 96766) features one-bedroom condos at $185 for up to four people and two-bedroom units at $255 for up to six people. Rates are $20 cheaper in the low season. To make reservations online, go to www.aston-hotels.com.

The 356-room **Kauai Marriott** (☎ 245-5050, 800-228-9290, fax 241-6025, Kalapaki Beach, Lihue, HI 96766) is an upmarket hotel with an interesting history. Originally built as the Kauai Surf, the island's first multistory resort spawned a successful campaign to limit the height of new buildings on Kauai. Now, no new structures can be taller than a coconut tree. In the late 1980s, the resort was transformed into a luxury hotel with a multimillion-dollar art collection, marble lobbies and acres of artificial lagoons stocked with exotic wildlife. After the devastation of Hurricane Iniki, it reopened as a more scaled-down resort, though it still has a grand pool with spouting fountains, a health spa and fitness center, tennis courts, a golf course and restaurants. Room rates range from $259 for a garden view to $365 for an ocean view, though cheaper promotions are usually available.

Places to Eat

Budget The **Fish Express** (3343 Kuhio Hwy), just south of Wilcox Memorial Hospital on Hwy 50, makes superb fresh fish lunches for takeout. On weekdays from 10 am to 2 pm, you can get the fish of the day with a choice of several preparations, including grilled with passion-guava sauce or blackened in ginger curry, along with rice and fresh veggies for just $7. Or opt for a fish sandwich with fries for $5, an excellent ahi stir-fry for $6 or Hawaiian specialties like *lomi* salmon (marinated raw salmon) and *laulau* (pork or beef with salted fish wrapped in leaves). Outside of lunch hours, you can still buy from the deli case: Generous sashimi trays are $4.50, and tasty *poke* (marinated fish sliced into cubes) is sold by the pound. The market is open 10 am to 7 pm daily.

At **Hamura Saimin** (2956 Kress St) in central Lihue, you can get a bowl of freshly made *saimin* (a Japanese noodle dish) for $3.50 and tasty skewers of barbecued chicken for just a dollar. This little second-generation family-run operation is a throwback to an older Kauai. There are no tables, just a winding saimin bar where visitors and locals rub elbows as they slurp bowls of steaming hot saimin. The one rule of etiquette is written on the menu board – 'Please do not stick gum under counter!' Hamura Saimin is open daily from 10 am until business dies down, typically 10 pm on weekdays and midnight on weekends.

Pacific Bakery and Grill (4479 Rice St), opposite the Lihue Civic Center, is a pleasantly casual place with the same owner as the upscale A Pacific Cafe in Waipouli. At breakfast, served from 7 to 11 am, macadamia nut pancakes or an avocado and mushroom omelette cost $5. At lunch, from 10 am to 3 pm, soup and an organic green salad are $4.25, and burgers with fries or island-style plate lunches cost around $6. The bakery also carries apple turnovers, muffins and other pastries.

The **Beach Hut**, near Kalapaki Beach, is a popular fast-food place with an ocean view. Pancakes, French toast and other breakfast standards cost around $4. At lunch, the two hottest items are the bacon burger and the mahi fish sandwich, each $5.75. The Hut is open 7 am to 7 pm daily.

Cafe Kauai, an espresso cafe inside the Borders bookstore on Nawiliwili Rd, has sandwiches, pastries and a variety of newspapers that you can read while sipping your coffee. It's open from at least 8 am to 9:30 pm daily, except on Sunday, when it closes at 7:30 pm.

Vim N Vigor, housed in the Rice Shopping Center in central Lihue, is a small health food store that carries vitamins, granola and other standard products. The *Oroweat Thrift Shoppe*, on the corner of Rice and Kalena Sts, has day-old bakery products at discounted prices, and there's a *Dairy Queen* nearby, on Rice St.

A *McDonald's, Pizza Hut, KFC* and *7-Eleven* are clustered together on Hwy 56, and a *Burger King* and *Taco Bell* are off Hwy 50 just north of the Kukui Grove Center. *Star Supermarket*, inside the Kukui Grove Center, is open every day from 6 am to 11 pm.

Mid-Range & Top End Hanamaulu Restaurant (☎ 245-2511), on Hwy 56 in Hanamaulu, has many faces: a sushi bar with a little carp pond, tatami-matted tearooms in a garden setting and a no-frills dining room. A dinner teishoku (Japanese fixed-plate meal) that includes tempura, sushi and sashimi costs $14. A better deal is the special plate meal of miso soup, rice, shrimp tempura and teriyaki for $8 at lunch, $9.50 at dinner. Average Chinese dishes are available at similar prices. The restaurant is open 10 am to 1 pm Tuesday to Friday and 4:30 to 8:30 pm daily except Monday.

Tokyo Lobby (☎ 245-8989), in the Pacific Ocean Plaza, is a thoroughly authentic Japanese restaurant in terms of both atmosphere and food. The lunch menu includes noodle dishes, donburi and chicken teriyaki plates for around $8 and good sushi and sashimi for a bit more. At dinner, there's a wide range of meals with soup, salad and rice for $12 to $15. Tokyo Lobby is open 11 am to 2 pm Monday to Friday and 4:30 to 9:30 pm nightly.

Duke's Canoe Club (☎ 246-9599), at the Kauai Marriott, is a recommendable beachside restaurant. It has a pleasant atmosphere and a selection of fresh fish with half a dozen different preparations for $20, a good salad bar included. There are also chicken, pasta and steak dishes starting at $15, and a $5 children's menu. Duke's is open for dinner from 5 to 10 pm. If you come by car, the most convenient place to park is in the lot behind the Beach Hut eatery, where a footbridge crosses the stream to Duke's.

Gaylord's (☎ 245-9593), at the Kilohana Plantation, enjoys a pleasant, open-air estate setting, though the food is ordinary and pricey. Lunch is served from 11 am to 3 pm daily except Sunday, with sandwiches and salads for $9. Dinner, from 5 pm nightly, features chicken and steak entrees that range from $17 to $24. On Sunday, there's a brunch from 9:30 am to 3 pm, with dishes starting at $10.

Entertainment

Kauai's main nightclub is *Gilligan's* (☎ 245-1955), at the Outrigger Kauai Beach, which has dancing and a DJ on Friday and Saturday nights. There's a small cover charge.

A good place to hang out on Friday is *Duke's Canoe Club* (☎ 246-9599), at the Kauai Marriott, where the popular local duo Shilo plays contemporary Hawaiian music from 4 to 6 pm and then returns with a backup band from 9 to 11 pm. Duke's also has live music from 9 to 11 pm on Thursday. There's no cover charge.

Cafe Kauai, inside Borders bookstore in Lihue, occasionally features live music on weekends, often spotlighting islanders who are promoting their latest CDs.

There's a free *hula show* at 6 pm on Friday at the Kukui Grove Center.

The fourplex *Kukui Grove Cinema* (☎ 245-5055), in the Kukui Grove Center, shows standard Hollywood movies.

WAILUA

The 3-mile stretch of the Kuhio Hwy (also known as Hwy 56) from Wailua to Kapaa is largely a scattering of shopping centers, restaurants, hotels and condos. Wailua doesn't really have a town center. Most of its sights are clustered around the Wailua River.

Long ago, Wailua was the site of Kauai's royal court, with 'Seven Sacred Heiaus' running from the mouth of the Wailua River up to the top of Mt Waialeale. Six of these *heiau* (temple) sites are within a mile of the river mouth. Five are visible, while the sixth is abandoned in a sugarcane field on the northern side of the Wailua River. All date back to the early period of Tahitian settlement and are considered to be of typical menehune construction. (For more information, see the History section, earlier in this chapter.) **Wailua River State Park** encompasses a hodgepodge of sites, including most of the heiaus, sections of the Wailua River's bank, the Fern Grotto, the riverboat basin and a public boat ramp.

The Wailua River, 11¾ miles long, is the only navigable river in Hawaii. It's long been popular with packaged tourists on riverboat tours, as well as local water-skiers, and in recent years it's become thick with kayakers as well.

Lydgate Beach Park

Lydgate Beach Park is a popular family beach, with protected swimming and snorkeling in a large seawater pool created with stone walls. It's fun for kids but deep enough for adults to swim in as well. The open ocean beyond often has strong currents, and there have been many drownings on both sides of the Wailua River mouth, just north of Lydgate. The park, which is on Leho Drive near the Holiday Inn, has a lifeguard, changing rooms, rest rooms, showers, drinking water, picnic pavilions and playground facilities.

Hikina A Ka La Heiau This long, narrow heiau is aligned directly north to south at the far end of the Lydgate Beach parking lot. Hikina A Ka La means 'rising of the sun.'

The heiau is thought to have been built around 1200 AD. Boulders still outline the shape, but most of the stones have long since been removed.

At the northern end of the heiau, a bronze plaque on a large stone reads: 'Hauola, City of Refuge.' The mounded grassy area behind the plaque is all that remains of this former refuge for *kapu* (taboo) breakers.

Ten feet to the left of the plaque, the stone with the bowl-shaped depressions is an adze grinding stone. While it's easy to recognize, the stone hasn't always been in this upright position; to grind a correct edge, it would have had to be flat. There are also a couple of flat stone salt pans on the grounds.

If you look straight out across Wailua Bay, you can see the remains of Kukui Heiau on Alakukui Point. Only its foundation stones are discernible, as that heiau site has been landscaped over in a carpet of condo grass. In ancient times, torches were lit on the point at night to help guide outrigger canoes.

If you walk straight down to the beach while looking toward Alakukui Point, you may find a few ancient stones with petroglyphs carved into the rock, though they're usually hidden under shifting sands.

Malae Heiau

Malae Heiau is in a thick clump of trees growing on the edge of a sugarcane field, a mere 40 feet *mauka* (inland) of the highway, across from the Holiday Inn. Although this is the largest heiau on the island, covering 2 acres, it's thickly overgrown with grasses and Java plum trees and almost impossible to explore.

In the 1830s, the missionaries converted Deborah Kapule, the last Kauaian queen, to Christianity, and she converted the interior of Malae Heiau into a cattle pen. Except for these alterations, it's relatively well preserved, thanks largely to its impenetrable overgrowth. The stone walls, which encompass an altar, reach up to 10 feet high and extend 8 feet wide.

The heiau is on state property, and there are plans to incorporate it eventually into Wailua River State Park.

Fern Grotto

Kauai's busiest tourist attraction is the riverboat tour up the Wailua River to the Fern Grotto, complete with corny jokes and packaged sentimentality to the tune of Elvis' 'Hawaiian Wedding Song.'

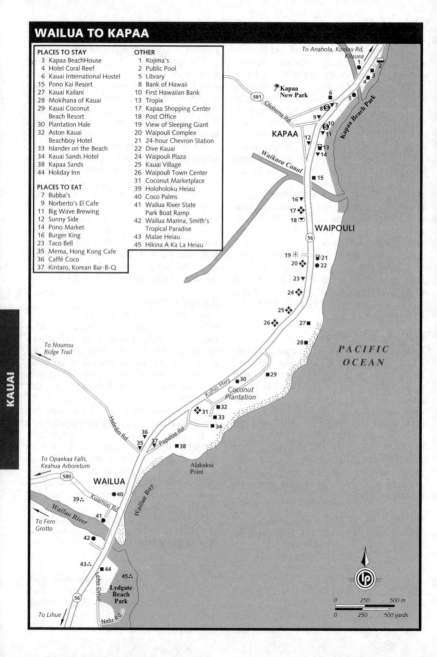

WAILUA TO KAPAA

PLACES TO STAY
3 Kapaa BeachHouse
4 Hotel Coral Reef
6 Kauai International Hostel
15 Pono Kai Resort
27 Kauai Kailani
28 Mokihana of Kauai
29 Kauai Coconut
 Beach Resort
30 Plantation Hale
32 Aston Kauai
 Beachboy Hotel
33 Islander on the Beach
34 Kauai Sands Hotel
38 Kapaa Sands
44 Holiday Inn

PLACES TO EAT
7 Bubba's
9 Norberto's El Cafe
11 Big Wave Brewing
12 Sunny Side
14 Pono Market
16 Burger King
23 Taco Bell
35 Mema, Hong Kong Cafe
36 Caffé Coco
37 Kintaro, Korean Bar-B-Q

OTHER
1 Kojima's
2 Public Pool
5 Library
8 Bank of Hawaii
10 First Hawaiian Bank
13 Tropix
17 Kapaa Shopping Center
18 Post Office
19 View of Sleeping Giant
20 Waipouli Complex
21 24-hour Chevron Station
22 Dive Kauai
24 Waipouli Plaza
25 Kauai Village
26 Waipouli Town Center
31 Coconut Marketplace
39 Holoholoku Heiau
40 Coco Palms
41 Wailua River State
 Park Boat Ramp
42 Wailua Marina, Smith's
 Tropical Paradise
43 Malae Heiau
45 Hikina A Ka La Heiau

To Anahola, Koolau Rd,
Kilauea

Kapaa
New Park

Olohena Rd

Kapaa Beach Park

KAPAA

Waikaea Canal

WAIPOULI

PACIFIC
OCEAN

To Nounou
Ridge Trail

Kuhio Hwy

Coconut
Plantation

Haleilio Rd

Papaloa Rd

To Opaekaa Falls,
Keahua Arboretum

Alakukui
Point

WAILUA

Kuamoo Rd

Wailua Bay

Wailua River

To Fern
Grotto

Leho Drive

Lydgate
Beach
Park

Nalu Rd

To Lihue

KAUAI

0   250   500 m
0   250   500 yards

The riverboats are big with wide, flat bottoms – very simple, like covered barges. Some people compare them to cattle boats even before they pack the tourists on. The grotto, a large musty cave beneath a fern-covered rock face, is pretty enough but not a must-see sight.

Smith's Motor Boat Service (☎ 821-6892) and Waialeale Boat Tours (☎ 822-4908) both charge $15 for adults and $7.50 for children under 12, and one or the other leaves the Wailua River Marina about every 30 minutes between 9 am and 3:30 pm.

Smith's Tropical Paradise

Smith's Tropical Paradise (☎ 821-6895), at Wailua Marina, has a loop trail through theme gardens, open from 8:30 am to 3:30 pm daily. Admission is $5 for adults, $2.50 for children under 12. Three evenings a week, there's a luau and Polynesian show; see Entertainment, later in this section, for details.

Coco Palms

The Coco Palms resort was built on the site of Kauai's ancient royal court, in the midst of a historic 45-acre coconut grove. The hotel at this site – which was devastated by Hurricane Iniki and never repaired – looked a bit like a movie set, with lagoons, thatched cottages and torchlit paths. In fact, the hotel's outdoor chapel was originally built in 1954 for the movie *Sadie Thompson* with Rita Hayworth. The highest-profile wedding that took place at Coco Palms was that of Elvis Presley and Joan Blackman in *Blue Hawaii*, after which thousands of mainland couples flocked to the chapel to take their own wedding vows.

Hwy 580

Also known as Kuamoo Rd, Hwy 580 begins at the traffic light on Hwy 56 at Coco Palms. It passes heiaus, historical sites, Opaekaa Falls and Wailua Homesteads before reaching Keahua Arboretum, the starting place for a couple of backcountry trails.

Holoholoku Heiau Holoholoku, a luakini heiau (a temple used for human sacrifices), is a quarter mile up Hwy 580 on the left.

Like all the Wailua heiaus, this one was of enclosure-type construction, with its stone walls built directly on the ground rather than on terraced platforms.

This whole area used to be royal property, and on the west side of the grounds, against the flat-backed birthstone, queens gave birth to future kings. This stone is marked by a plaque reading 'Pohaku Hoohanau.' Another stone a few yards away, marked 'Pohaku Piko,' was where the *piko* (umbilical cords) of the babies were left.

Above the temple where Hawaiian royals were born, steps lead to a hilltop cemetery where later-day Japanese laborers lie at rest.

Poliahu Heiau Poliahu Heiau, perched high on a hill overlooking the meandering Wailua River, is named after the snow goddess Poliahu, one of Pele's sisters. This relatively well preserved heiau is thought to have been of the luakini type.

Poliahu Heiau is immediately before the Opaekaa Falls lookout, on the opposite side of the road.

Bellstone Immediately south of Poliahu Heiau, on the same side of Hwy 580, look for a 'Falling Rocks' sign that marks a short and rutted dirt drive leading to a bellstone. Because of the road's angle, it's easiest to approach coming downhill from Poliahu.

In old Hawaii, the Wailua River was a naval entrance, and the bellstone at this lookout was thought to have been used by sentries to warn of attacks as well as to ring out announcements of royal births.

There are actually two stones at the end of the drive, one with an all-too-perfect petroglyph whose age is suspect. Archaeologists question just which stone may have been the bellstone. Although you can find depressions in the stones, they may well be the result of modern-day poundings by people trying to check out the resonance for themselves.

A short path down from these rocks leads to a vista of the river, where you can commonly see cattle grazing on the banks below and hear the amplified narration from the passing riverboats.

Opaekaa Falls Opaekaa Falls is a high, broad waterfall that usually flows as a double cascade, though after a heavy rain the two sides often merge. The peaks of the Makaleha Mountains form a scenic backdrop, and white-tailed tropicbirds can often be seen soaring in the valley below the falls. The marked turnoff to the viewpoint is 1½ miles up Hwy 580 from Wailua. For the best angle, walk up the sidewalk past the parking lot toward the bridge.

Kamokila Hawaiian Village Situated along the shores of the Wailua River, this re-created Hawaiian village is comprised of grass huts, an assembly house, a women's house and various other structures that were once common to native communities. This is a small down-home operation: Tour guides describe the function of each building, explain the traditional uses of the native plants that grow on the grounds, demonstrate the hula, weave ti-leaf bracelets, and husk drinking coconuts for guests – all for a $5 donation. The hour-long tour provides a nice sense of aloha that is lost in many larger, mass-produced operations elsewhere.

Incidentally, if you saw the 1995 Dustin Hoffman movie *Outbreak*, the round huts in the village center may look familiar – they were used as a set for the disease-ravaged African village that was burned to the ground in that film.

Kamokila (☎ 823-0559) is on the south side of Hwy 580, opposite Opaekaa Falls, at the end of a narrow half-mile-long paved road. It's open 8 am to 5 pm Monday to Saturday. You can also kayak from Kamokila; for details, see Kayaking in the Activities section earlier in this chapter.

Wailua Homesteads

In the Wailua Homesteads area, on the west side of the Sleeping Giant mountain, the government once offered 160-acre parcels to people willing to work the land. Most early homesteaders used the land to graze cattle, though at one point Dole grew pineapples in the area. Today, Wailua Homesteads is largely a mix of spacious residential lots and pastoral countryside reminiscent of Pennsylvania Dutch farmland.

The main through-road is Hwy 581 (Kamalu Rd), which connects with Hwy 580 at its southern end and with Olohena Rd at its northern end. Together, Kamalu Rd and Olohena Rd form Hwy 581.

Nounou Ridge (Sleeping Giant) Trail

The Nounou Ridge Trail climbs up the Sleeping Giant to a summit on the giant's upper chest, affording views of both the east coast and the highland valleys. It's a well-maintained trail that takes 1½ to two hours roundtrip. Because the trail is somewhat steep, it provides a hardy workout.

There are two trailheads, both marked. The trail on the western side is a shaded forest trail of tall trees and moss-covered stones. The trail on the eastern side, which is more exposed and a bit longer, begins at a parking lot a mile up Haleilio Rd in the Wailua Houselots neighborhood.

The trail up the western side of the mountain starts on Kamalu Rd (Hwy 581), near house No 1068. Walk through a metal gate marked as a forestry right-of-way and up along a small cattle pasture to the trailhead. If you have a car, note that you can't park at the trailhead, but you can park and access the trail at the end of Lokelani Rd, which is off Kamalu Rd a bit farther north. If you pick up the trail there, it will deposit you on the same pasture but closer to the woods.

This is a wonderful trail to do early in the morning, when it's relatively cool and you can watch the light spread across the valley below. The packed trail can get slippery when wet; look for a walking stick, which hikers sometimes leave near the trailhead.

The eucalyptus trees at the trailhead soon give way to a tall, thick forest of Norfolk pines that were planted in a Civilian Conservation Corps (CCC) reforestation program during the 1930s. About five minutes into the woods, right after the Norfolk pines begin, there's a fork. Veer left up the path with the large rock beside it.

The trail passes through thick strawberry guava bushes that can grow up to 15 feet high; in places, the guava creates a canopied, tunnel-like effect. Strawberry guava has a small red fruit that's eaten whole and is considered the sweetest of any guava.

A few minutes below the summit, the eastern and western trails merge on the ridge. Continue up to the right past some *hala* (pandanus) trees. On the summit is a picnic table shelter that offers protection from the rain. Passing showers can create some incredible valley rainbows. To the west, there's a 180-degree view of Wailua and the Makaleha Mountains.

Below, to the east, you can see Kapaa, sugarcane fields, Wailua Houselots, Coco Palms and the Wailua River. To the right of the riverboat docks and inland from the Holiday Inn, there's a square, dark green area in the sugarcane field. This is Malae Heiau, now overgrown with Java plums.

If you go south across the picnic area, the trail continues. About five minutes up, there's a rocky area where you can sit and enjoy the view. The ridge continues up the giant's chin. Should it tempt you, size it up carefully. It's sharp, and loose rocks and slides are visible.

Kuilau Ridge Trail

For the effort, the Kuilau Ridge Trail is one of the most visually rewarding trails on the island. The marked trailhead is on the right just before Hwy 580 crosses the stream at the Keahua Arboretum, 3.9 miles up from the junction of Hwys 580 and 581. Don't leave anything of value in your car.

The trail starts up a wide dirt path also used by horses and the occasional renegade dirt biker. Along the way, birdsong emanates from the dense native vegetation, which includes koa trees, ohia lehua and thickets of ti. In the upper reaches, the lush, fern-covered hillsides provide broad vistas of the mountains. Guava trees and wild thimbleberries grow along the path.

The hike climbs to a broad ridge offering views into valleys on both sides and clear down to the coast. You can see Kapaa to the east and the island's uninhabited central region to the west. It takes about 35 minutes to walk the 1¼ miles up to a grassy clearing on

the ridgetop, where you'll find a couple of picnic tables and a view of Mt Waialeale.

Beyond the clearing, to the right past the picnic area, the Kuilau Ridge Trail continues as a narrow footpath offering even more spectacular views. It ends in about a mile at the Moalepe Trail. If you don't want to go that far, at least walk a little of it, as some of the best vistas are along the next half mile of the trail.

If you go left at the connection with the Moalepe Trail, you'll come to a viewpoint after about 10 minutes. If you go right on Moalepe, you'll come out on Olohena Rd in Wailua Homesteads after about 2¼ miles.

Coconut Plantation

Back on Hwy 56 heading north, you'll reach Coconut Plantation, a resort development with four hotels, a condominium and a shopping center. It fronts a half-mile-long beach partially shaded by ironwood trees.

Water activities are restricted due to the low lava shelf that runs along most of the beach and the strong currents that prevail beyond. The best section for swimming is in front of the Kauai Sands Hotel, where you'll find a beachside shower and a break in the lava shelf.

While water conditions are mediocre, the beach makes for good strolling. Its sand is unique, each grain polished to a high gloss. The large field between the Kauai Coconut Beach Resort and the Kauai Coast Resort at the Beachboy is popular with golden plovers and other migratory birds.

The resort's shopping center, Coconut Marketplace, has numerous stores, including Liberty House, Fox Photo (with one-hour processing), art galleries, boutiques and gift shops. All are open 9 am to 9 pm Monday to Saturday, 10 am to 6 pm Sunday.

Places to Stay

B&Bs & Cottages Though they're not on the beach, the following Wailua B&Bs represent some of the best values on Kauai. The listings in this section are all in the Wailua Homesteads area, about 3 miles from the coast in a rural setting. All are within a mile or so of the intersection of Hwys 581 and 580.

KAUAI

Rosewood B&B (☎ 822-5216, fax 822-5478, rosewood@aloha.net, 872 Kamalu Rd, Kapaa, HI 96746) is a beautifully restored 90-year-old plantation home belonging to Rosemary and Norbert Smith. Upstairs in the home is a pleasant guest room with a king bed, a tiled bath with sunken tub, and a view of mountains and grazing cattle. The rate is $85 for a double, breakfast included.

Also on the grounds are two guest cottages, both of which come with a basket of breakfast fixings. The charming Victorian cottage ($115) is light and airy, with high ceilings and natural oak floors. Its spacious layout includes a full kitchen, a master bedroom with a king bed, and an upstairs loft with two twin beds. Amenities include ceiling fans, cable TV and a phone. The second cottage ($85) is simpler and studio-style, with coconut-frond thatching on the roof and screened windows all around that open to a garden with birdsong. It has a king bed, queen-size futon, kitchenette, ceiling fans, indoor toilet, outdoor hot shower and barbecue grill.

A third building, the Bunkhouse, has three straightforward but comfortable rooms geared for budget travelers. Each has its own sink, coffeemaker, microwave, toaster and small refrigerator. All share an indoor toilet and an outdoor shower that's set in a garden. Rates, without breakfast, are $40 for the two smallest rooms – one of which has two single beds and the other a double – and $50 for the largest, which has a double bed in the loft and a queen sofa bed on the lower level. All accommodations are nonsmoking. Guests are allowed to check their email on the office computer. Rosewood also handles other vacation rentals around Kauai, including an $85 condo unit at Plantation Hale. For more information, visit the website www.rosewoodkauai.com.

The *House of Aleva* (☎ 822-4606, 5509 Kuamoo Rd, Kapaa, HI 96746) is a B&B in the home of Ernest and Anita Perry, right on Hwy 580, 2 miles up from Coco Palms. Ernest is a retired merchant seaman, and Anita is a retired nurse who reads palms and makes ceramic Hawaiiana sculptures. The two upstairs guest rooms ($55) share a bath.

Each has a queen bed with comfortable mattress, as well as a phone, TV, mini-refrigerator and microwave. The smaller downstairs room has a twin bed and rents for $40. Rates include breakfast. Photos of past guests, which line one wall, include a fair number of European travelers.

Inn Paradise (☎ 822-2542, mcinch@aloha.net, 6381 Makana Rd, Kapaa, HI 96746) has three delightful units with nice touches like Persian carpets, rattan furnishings and quality Hawaiiana wall prints. Each has a phone, cable TV, refrigerator, microwave, toaster, coffeemaker and private entrance. The three units are in a guest house that stands separate from Major and Connie Inch's contemporary home. All share a lanai with an unspoiled view of pasture and mountains. The Prince Kuhio room, which has a king bed, costs $60. The Queen Kapule suite, which has a king bed and a separate living room with a Murphy bed, costs $75; additional guests beyond two are $10 more. The King Kaumualii unit, which is equipped like a small house, has two bedrooms, one with a king bed, the other with two twins, and a full kitchen; it costs $100 for up to four people. There's a two-night minimum; rates include breakfast provisions and use of a washer and dryer.

Hale Kahawai (☎ 822-1031, fax 823-8220, bandbkauai@aol.com, 185 Kahawai Place, Kapaa, HI 96746) is a B&B that's popular with gay and lesbian travelers. Owned by Arthur Lucas and Thomas Hart, this pleasant contemporary home has lovely mountain views from the rear deck, where there's a hot tub. Guests have access to a kitchen and a spacious living room with a 35-inch TV. Two small rooms with queen beds and shared bath cost $60/70 for singles/doubles, while a third upstairs room with king bed and private bath is $10 more. There's also an apartment on the ground level with a kitchenette, full bath, queen bed and sofa bed for $90. Rates include a breakfast of fruit, cereal and Thomas' homemade bread. To see pictures of the accommodations, visit the website members.aol.com /bandbkauai.

Royal Drive Cottages (☎ 822-2321, fax 822-7537, sand@aloha.net, 147 Royal Drive, Kapaa, HI 96746) consists of two studio cottages on a quiet street just off Hwy 580. The cottages have a pleasant Hawaiian simplicity that's wholly adequate. Each has two twin beds, a phone, refrigerator, microwave, hot plate and coffeemaker. One of the units also has a screened lanai and cable TV. The cottages do have corrugated metal roofs and this is a wet island – some people find the sound of rain on tin romantic, while it may keep others awake. The rate for either cottage is $80. The future of the place is a bit iffy, however, as the property is up for sale.

Hale Lani (☎ 822-5216, fax 822-5478, 5780 Lokelani Rd, Kapaa, HI 96746) is an immaculate two-bedroom cottage that would make an ideal home away from home. Built by a Seattle couple as a future retirement residence, it has oak floors, cathedral ceilings, a washer/dryer, ceiling fans, a fully equipped kitchen and a living room with a stereo system, TV and VCR. There's a queen bed in one bedroom, a king bed in the other. The price is $125 for up to four people, plus a $75 cleaning fee. This is a nonsmoking property in a quiet neighborhood at the base of the Sleeping Giant Trail.

Condos & Hotels Wailua's condos and hotels all have swimming pools and the usual standard resort facilities.

Kauai Sands Hotel (☎ 822-4951, 800-367-7000, sandsea@aloha.net, 420 Papaloa Rd, Kapaa, HI 96746) is part of the Hawaiian-owned Sand & Seaside hotel chain. The rooms, which are in a series of two-story buildings that mostly surround the lawn and pool, are plainer than those in neighboring hotels, but it's a good value if you book at the rates commonly advertised within Hawaii: around $60 for a room only, $139 for two nights with a car. Otherwise, the rate quoted to people who call from the mainland using the toll-free number is $85 for standard rooms, $120 for rooms with kitchenettes. Each of the spacious rooms has two double beds, air-con, a TV, mini-refrigerator and lanai.

Kapaa Sands (☎ 822-4901, 800-222-4901, fax 822-1556, 380 Papaloa Rd, Kapaa, HI 96746) has 20 condo units set up in either duplexes or fourplexes. All have kitchens, lanais, louvered windows to catch the breeze, and at least a partial ocean view. While the complex is an older one, the units were renovated a few years ago and are a relatively good value at $85 for studios for one or two people and $114 for two-bedroom units for up to four people. Oceanfront units cost $15 more. There's a three-day minimum stay in the low season and a seven-day minimum in winter. For photos of the accommodations, visit www.kapaasands.com online.

Islander on the Beach (☎ 822-7417, 800-847-7417, fax 822-1947, islander@aloha.net, 484 Kuhio Hwy, Kapaa, HI 96746) is a pleasant hotel with 195 rooms in half a dozen three-story buildings. Each room has a king bed or two double beds, a refrigerator, coffeemaker, air-con, TV, room safe and lanai. Rates range from $110 for a garden-view room to $150 for an oceanfront room. There's a poolside bar. For more information about the accommodations, visit the hotel's website at www.islander-kauai.com.

The **Kauai Coast Resort at the Beachboy** (☎ 822-3441, fax 822-0843, 484 Kuhio Hwy, Kapaa, HI 96746) is a modern beachfront hotel with 243 rooms in blocks of three-story buildings. Although undistinguished, the rooms are pleasant enough and each has either one king or two double beds, air-con, a lanai, TV, mini-refrigerator and room safe. Rates range from $120 to $155, depending on the view, As we go to press, the hotel's new owner is planning some ambitious renovations, due to be completed in late 2000.

Holiday Inn (☎ 823-6000, 800-823-5111, fax 823-6666, info@holidayinn-kauai.com, 3-5920 Kuhio Hwy, Kapaa, HI 96746) is adjacent to Lydgate Beach Park. Recently reopened after a thorough renovation, the hotel features rooms that are modern and comfortable, though they vary significantly in size. Request the Pikake wing, which has larger rooms, each furnished with two queen beds, a big-screen TV, desk, refrigerator and a phone with free local calls. Room rates range from $150 for a garden-view unit to

KAUAI

$175 for ocean-view accommodations. The hotel commonly offers discount schemes, including a perennial 'Great Rate' deal that knocks 20% off the above rates – so ask about promotions when booking. You can also find out about special deals online, at www.holidayinn-kauai.com.

Closer to the highway side of Coconut Plantation is **Plantation Hale** (☎ 822-4941, 800-775-4253, fax 822-5599, ph@aloha.net, 484 Kuhio Hwy, Kapaa, HI 96746), a member of the Best Western chain. The complex has 160 spacious and modern one-bedroom units, each with either two double beds or one king bed in the bedroom, a queen sofa bed in the living room, a full kitchen, air-con, ceiling fans and two TVs. The rate of $125/135 in the low/high season is the same for up to four people, which makes this spot a reasonable value for small groups. The hotel maintains a website at www.plantation-hale.com.

Kauai Coconut Beach Resort (☎ 822-3455, 800-222-5642, fax 822-1830, PO Box 830, Kapaa, HI 96746), a former Sheraton, is a 309-room hotel at the quieter north end of Coconut Plantation. The rooms are comfortable, with either two doubles or a king bed, TV, room safe, mini-refrigerator, coffee-maker and a tiny lanai that can barely fit two people. The 4th-floor rooms are the nicest, as they have high ceilings that make the rooms feel a bit larger. Published rates are pricey at $165 for a standard room, $215 for an ocean view, but there's often a $115 special that combines a standard room with a buffet breakfast for two.

Places to Eat

Caffé Coco (☎ 822-7990, 4-369 Kuhio Hwy) is a casual spot serving generous portions of tasty, healthy food. The emphasis is on locally grown produce, vegetarian fare and fresh fish. At breakfast, you can order egg dishes or homemade granola with fresh fruit for less than $5. At other times, there are organic salads and creative sandwiches, including a delicious seared ahi sandwich on focaccia for $8.50, as well as full meals for around $13. Caffé Coco is open 9 am to 9 pm Tuesday to Sunday. The restaurant,

which is set back a bit from the highway, doubles as an art gallery and has a covered courtyard with tables out back.

Although it's declined in recent years, **Mema** (☎ 823-0899, 4-361 Kuhio Hwy) still has a pleasant decor and reasonable Thai food. Chicken, beef and pork dishes cost around $9, while shrimp or fish dishes go for $11; most dishes can also be prepared vegetarian. The shrimp rolls, served on a bed of fresh lettuce and mint leaves, make a nice appetizer. Mema is open 11 am to 2:30 pm weekdays and 5 to 9:30 pm daily.

A more casual option is the **Hong Kong Cafe** (☎ 822-3288), in the same complex as Mema. The inexpensive Chinese food includes plate lunches with items such as lemon chicken, roast duck or teriyaki beef for $4 to $6; combination plates are around $6. The Hong Kong Cafe is open 10:30 am to 9:30 pm weekdays, 2:30 to 9:30 pm on weekends.

On the opposite side of the street, **Korean Bar-B-Q** (☎ 822-6744, 4-356 Kuhio Hwy) has good Korean food at honest prices. A plate lunch with two scoops of rice and four vegetable side dishes costs $5.50 with barbecued chicken, $6.50 with a beef and chicken combination. It's open from 10 am to 9 pm Wednesday to Monday and from 4:30 to 9 pm on Tuesday.

Near Korean Bar-B-Q, **Kintaro** (☎ 822-3341, 4-370 Kuhio Hwy) is widely regarded as the best Japanese restaurant on the island. It has a good sushi bar as well as a teppanyaki room, where the chef prepares food on an iron grill at your table – all done with much ado and some fancy knife work. Although the tempura is easy to pass up, the food is otherwise consistently good. Dinners are priced from $14 to $20. Kintaro is open 5:30 to 9:30 pm Monday to Saturday.

A handful of food kiosks are in the Coconut Marketplace. The best are **Aloha Kauai Pizza**, with good, moderately priced calzones and pizzas, including a tasty artichoke-garlic version; the **Fish Hut**, with fresh fish sandwiches for $7 and fish and chips for $8; and **Harley's Ribs-N-Chicken**, which has Cajun chicken sandwiches for $5 and a Caesar salad with lemon-pepper chicken for $6.25. The Coconut Marketplace also has a couple of sit-down restaurants, an average cafe/bakery and a small convenience store that sells snacks and liquor. All are open from 11 am to 8 pm, at least.

Entertainment

Coconut Marketplace Cinemas (☎ 821-2324), in the Coconut Marketplace, is a two-screen theater showing first-run movies.

Free hula shows take place at the *Coconut Marketplace* a few days a week; call ☎ 822-3641 for the current schedule.

Kauai Coconut Beach Resort (☎ 822-3455) holds its own luau at 6 pm nightly. It includes an open bar, dinner and a rather standard Polynesian revue. The cost is $52 for adults, $30 for children 12 to 17, and $20 for children three to 11. You can catch a glimpse of the festivities from the hotel parking lot. If you're interested in seeing the *imu* (oven) preparation, you can watch the pig being stuffed with hot rocks and buried at 10:45 am.

Smith's Tropical Paradise (☎ 821-6895), at Wailua Marina, has a luau with cocktails, dinner and musical show at 6 pm on Monday, Wednesday and Friday. It costs $52 for adults, $27 for children seven to 13 and $18 for children three to six.

WAIPOULI

Waipouli is the mile-long strip between Coconut Plantation and Kapaa. Its biggest draw is its assortment of shopping centers, which are not only the area's largest, but also contain some of Kauai's best places to eat.

In Kauai Village, Waipouli's largest shopping center, you'll find the **Kauai Heritage Center**, which displays handmade wood carvings, feather leis, bamboo nose flutes and other traditional Hawaiian crafts. The center also offers one-day craft workshops for those who would like to learn more.

Information

American Savings Bank, inside the Foodland supermarket in the Waipouli Town Center, is open 9 am to 7 pm weekdays, 9 am to 5 pm on Saturday and 11 am to 4 pm on Sunday.

The Kapaa post office, in the Kapaa Shopping Center, is open 8:30 am to 5 pm Monday to Friday, 10 am to 2 pm on Saturday.

There's a coin laundry in the Kapaa Shopping Center that's open 7:30 am to 9:30 pm daily.

Sleeping Giant

From a marked viewpoint just north of the Waipouli Complex, look for the outline of the Sleeping Giant atop Nounou Ridge.

According to legend, the friendly giant fell asleep on the hillside after eating too much poi at a luau. When his menehune friends needed his help, they tried to awaken him by throwing stones. But the stones bounced from the giant's full belly into his open mouth. As the stones lodged in the giant's throat, he died in his sleep and turned into rock. Now he rests eternally, stretched out on the ridge with his head in Wailua and his feet in Kapaa.

A hiking trail runs across the ridge, connecting Wailua Houselots and Wailua Homesteads (see the Wailua section). At an elevation of 1241 feet, the giant's forehead is the highest point on the ridge.

Places to Stay

Mokihana of Kauai (☎ 822-3971, 796 Kuhio Hwy) is a time-share complex that rents to nonmembers on a space-available basis. It has 79 studio units on the beach, and while they're rather plain, each has twin beds, a hot plate, a refrigerator and a lanai with an ocean view for $65.

The front desk at Mokihana also handles the 58 two-bedroom time-share units at nearby *Kauai Kailani*. These units have full kitchens, two twin beds in one room and a queen in the other, and cost $65 in the inland wing and $75 in the oceanside building; rates cover up to four people.

Don't expect anything elaborate, as the units have a strictly economy feel. They're adequate, however, and the price is a bargain, particularly during the high season. You can also make advance reservations through *Hawaii Kailani* (☎ 360-676-1434, 800-640-4786, fax 360-676-1435, 1201 11th St, suite 100, Bellingham, WA 98225).

KAUAI

Places to Eat

Papaya's Natural Foods, in the Kauai Village shopping center, is a well-stocked health food store with a little cafe serving wholesome salads, sandwiches and simple meals. Veggie burgers cost $5, while full-meal specials, such as fish tacos with brown rice and salad, are around $8. The cafe is open 9 am to 7 pm; the store stays open until 8 pm.

The *King & I* (☎ 822-1642), in the Waipouli Plaza, has good Thai food at reasonable prices. The spring rolls make a nice starter, while the green curry, which gets its nice color from fresh basil, lime leaves and lemongrass, is an excellent choice for an entree. The curries, like most other dishes on the menu, cost $6.50 for meat varieties, $9 for shrimp or fish. All can be prepared mild, medium or hot. The restaurant has both sticky Thai rice and brown rice, and numerous dishes can be ordered vegetarian. The King & I is open 4:30 to 9:30 pm daily (to 10 pm on Friday and Saturday).

The *Bull Shed* (☎ 822-3791, 796 Kuhio Hwy), at the Mokihana of Kauai condo complex, is a steak house that receives mixed reviews, but those looking for a big slab of prime rib ($20) that comes with a salad bar – along with a great ocean view – will likely be happy here. Chicken and fish dishes are also available. The Bull Shed is open from 5:30 to 10 pm nightly.

A Pacific Cafe (☎ 822-0013), in Kauai Village, is a bustling, high-energy restaurant serving excellent Pacific Rim cuisine. French chef Jean-Marie Josselin offers a creative menu with dishes like fresh fish in Thai curry sauce and Chinese roast duck with ginger-pineapple glaze. Starters and soups range from $7 to $10, and main dishes are $20 to $25. A Pacific Cafe is a class act, with artful presentation and attentive service – if you're saving one night for a splurge, this is a top choice. It's open 5:30 to 10 pm nightly; reservations are usually essential.

At the opposite end of the gastronomic scale are the numerous local fast-food eateries, including *Taco Bell*, north of Waipouli Plaza on the Kuhio Hwy; *Subway*, in Kauai Village; *Burger King*, at the Kapaa

Shopping Center; and *McDonald's* and *Pizza Hut*, in the Waipouli Town Center.

A good alternative to fast food is the 24-hour *Safeway* supermarket, in Kauai Village, which has a deli counter with fried chicken and salads, a bakery with tempting Danish pastries and chocolate croissants, and a fish counter with a variety of poke, including a delicious sesame-ahi variety. In addition, the store has a good, reasonably priced wine selection – though if you're willing to go with the weekly sale items, the island's best alcohol prices are often found at the adjacent *Longs Drugs*.

The area's other large supermarket, *Foodland*, is in the nearby Waipouli Town Center. Open daily from 6 am to 11 pm, it has a good selection of doughnuts and cheap hot coffee in a variety of sizes and brews.

KAPAA

Kapaa is an old plantation town with a small commercial center that is half-local, half-tourist oriented. As unimposing as it appears, Kapaa is one of the island's largest towns. However, most of the residential area is well inland of the center, and you can walk the main drag in just 10 minutes.

While many of Kapaa's historic buildings were leveled by Hurricane Iniki, most of the reconstruction has been in keeping with the town's original character rather than adopting the shopping mall appearance that predominates to the south of Kapaa. The town has a handful of budget accommodations, a few restaurants and a couple of sports and clothing shops.

Information

Bank of Hawaii and First Hawaiian Bank have branches on the Kuhio Hwy in the town center. Both are open 8:30 am to 4 pm Monday to Thursday, 8:30 am to 6 pm Friday.

Bubba's (☎ 823-0069), a burger joint on Hwy 56 in the center of Kapaa, allows customers to check their email for free.

Kapaa Public Library, 1464 Kuhio Hwy, is open 9 am to 5 pm on Monday, Wednesday and Friday; noon to 8 pm on Tuesday and Thursday.

Kapaa Beach Park

Kapaa Beach Park begins along the north side of Kapaa, where there's a ball field, picnic tables and a public swimming pool. The beach continues south for about a mile; the section fronting the Pono Kai Resort, a condo complex, has one of the nicer sandy areas. Along the length of the beach, there's a shoreline foot and bicycle path that follows a former cane-rail line and passes over a couple of old bridges. If you're staying in the area, the path makes an appealing alternative to walking along the highway to and from town.

Places to Stay

Kauai International Hostel (☎ 823-6142, 4532 Lehua St, Kapaa, HI 96746) is a casual, private hostel conveniently located in the center of Kapaa. There are about 30 dorm beds, four to six to a room, and five simple private rooms with double beds. The dorm beds cost $16, the private rooms $40. All rooms, including the private ones, have shared bathrooms. The hostel has a common dining room, kitchen, pool table, TV room and coin laundry. Bags can be stored while you're hiking, and day trips ($40) are available about twice a week if enough people are interested. Note that there's a no-refund policy, so if you're going to be paying for several days in advance, make sure that this is where you want to be for that entire period.

Kapaa BeachHouse (☎ 822-3424, nvb@ hawaiian.net, 1552 Kuhio Hwy, Kapaa, HI 96746) is an old oceanfront property that's in the early stages of being renovated into a hostel-style guest house. One room has eight bunks, each with a double mattress and a curtain that can be drawn for some privacy; these cost $20/35 for singles/doubles. There is also a private room for $45. Currently, there are only two toilets and one shower for all to share. Guests have use of kitchen facilities, a washing machine, an ocean-view deck and a combination TV/weight room. Current ambitious plans call for adding more dorm space, private rooms and a rooftop hot tub. For more information, visit the website www.kauai-blue-lagoon.com.

Mahina's Guest House (☎ 823-9364, mahinas@hawaiian.net, 4433 Panihi Rd, Kapaa, HI 96746) is a casual, three-bedroom private home near the beach on the south side of Kapaa. It provides accommodations for women travelers. One room is shared, with two single beds, at $20 per person. Another room has one double bed and costs $30/40 for singles/doubles. The third room is larger, has a king bed and costs $40/50 for singles/doubles. Guests share kitchen, bathroom and laundry facilities. Owner Sharon Gonsalves takes efforts to keep allergens low; there are no pets and smoking is not allowed.

KK Bed & Bath (☎ 822-7348, 800-615-6211 ext 32, sugi@aloha.net, 4486 Kauwila St, Kapaa, HI 96746) has a convenient location in the town center and just a short walk from the beach. It consists of two identical units in a converted storehouse behind the home of owner Richard Sugiyama. Though Richard refers to them as a budget alternative, the units are comfortable, each with a queen bed, private bath, refrigerator, TV, phone, small table and ceiling fans. A portable barbecue is available, and the place is wheelchair accessible. The rate is $30/50 for singles/doubles. You can book online at www.aloha.net/~sugi/b&b.html.

Hotel Coral Reef (☎ 822-4481, 800-843-4659, fax 822-7705, 1516 Kuhio Hwy, Kapaa, HI 96746) is a small, family-run hotel with two sections. The main building contains a handful of $59 rooms with private bath, TV and either one queen or a double and twin bed. Rooms in the seaside building are a bit larger and have lanais overlooking the ocean, but they're also more expensive at $89. Complimentary coffee and homemade breads are available at breakfast time in the lobby. There's no pool, but the hotel is right on the beach.

Keapana Center (☎ 822-7968, 800-822-7968, keapana@aloha.net, 5620 Keapana Rd, Kapaa, HI 96746) is a relaxing, New Age B&B with a scenic hilltop location 3 miles above Kapaa center. There are three rooms with shared bath at $40/55 singles/doubles and two rooms with private bath at $65/70. The rooms are small and suitably simple; the

KAUAI

rates include continental breakfast and use of the hot tub. Guests also share use of a refrigerator and microwave, as well as a large, airy lounge and a platform for sunrise stretching with a splendid view of the Anahola Mountains. Metaphysical books are loaned free, and massage is available for a fee. No preteen children are allowed. The Center has a website at www.planet-hawaii .com/keapana.

The beachfront *Pono Kai Resort (4-1250 Kuhio Hwy, Kapaa, HI 96746)* is a well-maintained 219-room condominium at the south side of Kapaa, within walking distance of the town center. Each of the roomy, well-equipped units has a full kitchen with dishwasher and microwave, and a living room with a queen sofa bed. Additional amenities include air-con, ceiling fans, cable TV, VCRs and lanais. On the grounds are tennis courts, a pool and a beach. Although most people book through *Marc Resorts (☎ 800-535-0085)*, which manages some of the units here, its rates begin at a steep $179 for a one-bedroom unit and $229 for a two-bedroom two-bath unit. For a better deal, contact *RCIM (☎ 822-9831, fax 822-9054, ponokai@hawaiian.net)*, which handles the majority of Pono Kai's units as time-share properties. RCIM commonly has a few unoccupied units that it rents out to the general public at $129/189 for one-/two-bedroom condos and offers a 25% discount on stays of a week or more.

Places to Eat

The eateries that follow are within a few minutes' walk of each other on the Kuhio Hwy (Hwy 56), near its intersection with Olohena Rd.

Bubba's, near the Kauai International Hostel, has hot dogs, chili dogs, fish and chips and a range of burgers, including tempeh burgers and fish burgers, all priced under $5. It's open 10:30 am to 8 pm daily.

Big Wave Brewing (☎ 821-2337) is a new microbrewery with a 2nd-story view of downtown Kapaa. It specializes in German-style wheat and amber beers – a 12oz glass costs $2.50. The food menu includes sandwiches, burgers and baby back ribs for around $6, as well as pizza by the slice. At dinner, you can more fully appreciate the chef's Louisiana roots by ordering meals that blend Hawaiian and Creole influences, such as Jawaiian blackened chicken or a tasty shrimp jambalaya for $17. The wave theme extends to the bar, which is shaped like a rippling blue wave, and to the big-screen TV that plays continuous surfing footage. Big Wave Brewing is open from 11:30 am to around midnight.

Norberto's El Cafe (☎ 822-3362), Kauai's original Mexican restaurant, offers hearty portions of decent Mexican fare, with full dinner plates that include soup, rice and beans for $12 to $15 and mini-plates for a few dollars less. You can wash everything down with margaritas or Mexican brews. This spot is open 5:30 to 9 pm Monday to Saturday.

Pono Market, a small food store, has good takeout sushi, including a recommendable California roll for $3.25. It also has some Hawaiian foods, such as laulau and poke. If you're looking for a full-size grocery store, the nearest to Kapaa center is *Kojima's*, opposite the public pool.

Fresh fruit and vegetables are sold at *Sunny Side*, a large produce stand in Kapaa center.

Tropix, a gay-friendly bar, features $1 domestic draft beer during its happy hour, held 2 to 5 pm daily.

KAPAA TO KILAUEA

The drive north from Kapaa heads through fields of sugarcane in varying stages of growth, from newly planted seed cane to mature stalk. Beyond the fields, the jagged peaks of the Anahola Mountains cut their way through the clouds. In the other direction, you'll catch glimpses of bright blue ocean and distant bays.

A couple of scenic lookouts just north of Kapaa offer views. Sunsets can be particularly nice at low tide, when waves break over the shallows and fishers are out with their throw nets.

The long, pretty beach at the 10-mile marker is **Kealia Beach**. During transitional swells, Kealia can become a good place for surfing. There are no facilities here.

After rainstorms, the beach tends to be heavily littered with tree limbs carried down Kealia Stream, which empties at the south side of the beach.

Anahola

Anahola is a small, scattered village, much of it spread out along Anahola Bay. This wide bay, which is fringed with a sandy beach, was an ancient surfing site, and its break is still popular with surfers today.

Anahola Beach Park, a county park on Hawaiian Home Lands, sits at the south side of the bay. To get there, turn off Hwy 56 onto Kukuihale Rd at the 13-mile marker, drive a mile down and then turn onto the dirt beach road. For information on obtaining a permit to camp at the beach park, see Camping under Accommodations, near the beginning of this chapter.

Anahola's modest commercial center consists of the Anahola post office, a burger stand and a small general store grouped together at the side of Hwy 56, just south of the 14-mile marker.

Just to the north, on the inland side of the road, the quaint **Anahola Baptist Church** is backed by a picturesque mountain setting.

Places to Stay & Eat On Anahola Bay, *Mahina Kai* (☎/fax 822-9451, trudy@ aloha.net, 4933 Aliomanu Rd, PO Box 699, Anahola, HI 96703), a B&B in a contemporary home, has Asian-Pacific touches such as shoji doors and a swimming pool and hot tub in a Japanese garden. It's a quiet place to relax. There are three rooms with private bathrooms at $100/125 singles/doubles, breakfast included, as well as a two-bedroom apartment with kitchenette that costs $150 for two people, $200 for four.

Ono Char Burger, on Hwy 56, sells good sandwiches and burgers for $4 to $6. The best deal is the basic burger, which comes with lettuce and tomato – more expensive burgers basically add a dollop of sauce or cheese on top. You can chow down at some outdoor picnic tables. Ono's is open from 10 am to 6 pm daily (from 11 am on Sunday).

Whalers General Store, next door to the burger stand, has hard-boiled eggs for a quarter, hot dogs for a dollar and cold beer. It's open from 6:30 am to 9:30 pm daily.

Hole in the Mountain

Although the Hole in the Mountain, once an obvious sight, was largely filled in by a landslide in the 1980s, a speck of it is still visible. Slightly north of the 15-mile marker, look back at the mountain, down to the right of the tallest pinnacle, and you'll be able to see a shimmer of light coming through a small opening in the rock face.

Legend says the original hole was created when a giant threw his spear through the mountain, causing the water stored within to gush forth as waterfalls. Incidentally, after the landslide closed the hole, Hawaii began to experience one of the worst droughts in its history.

Koolau Rd

Koolau Rd is a peaceful drive through rich green pastures with white egrets and a smattering of bright wildflowers. Take it as a scenic loop off the highway or as a way to get to Moloaa Beach or Larsens Beach. Both the road and the beaches are well off the tourist track. Neither beach has any facilities.

Koolau Rd connects with Hwy 56 half a mile north of the 16-mile marker and again one-tenth of a mile south of the 20-mile marker.

Moloaa Beach To get to Moloaa Beach from the south, turn right onto Koolau Rd, and after 1¼ miles, turn right onto Moloaa Rd. The road ends three-quarters of a mile down at a few beach houses. As the road near the beach is narrow, finding a place to park can be quite challenging.

Moloaa is rural, with horses grazing on the hills above the crescent-shaped bay. The northern end of the beach before the rocky outcrop is somewhat protected for swimming, though it's not all that deep. The whole bay can have strong currents when the surf is rough.

Larsens Beach Larsens is a long golden-sand beach, good for solitary strolls and beachcombing. Although it's a bit shallow for swimming, snorkeling can be good when the waters are very calm, which is generally in the summer only. Beware of a current that runs westward along the beach and out through a channel in the reef.

Often the Holstein cattle that graze the hills above the beach are the only company you'll encounter. However, if the tide is low, you may well see a few Hawaiian families on the outer edge of the reef collecting an edible seaweed called *limu kohu*. The seaweed found at Larsens is considered to be some of the finest in all of Hawaii.

The turnoff to Larsens Beach is on Koolau Rd, a little more than a mile down from the north intersection of Koolau Rd and Hwy 56, or just over a mile north of the intersection of Moloaa and Koolau Rds. Turn toward the ocean on the dirt road there and then take the immediate left. It's one mile to the parking area and then a five-minute walk downhill to the beach.

North Shore

Kauai's North Shore enjoys an unhurried pace and incredible scenery. Here you'll find deep mountain valleys, rolling cattle pastures, ancient taro fields, white-sand beaches and the rugged Na Pali Coast.

The North Shore is lush and often wet. In winter, that can mean rain for days on end, but in summer it usually means brief showers followed by rainbows. On bright full-moon nights, you may even see a moonbow – a rainbow colored with moonbeams.

Rainy days can be almost dreamlike. The tops of the mountains become shrouded in clouds that alternately drift and lift, revealing a series of waterfalls that plunge down the mountainsides.

A drive along the North Shore takes in the seabird sanctuary at Kilauea and a couple of small coastal villages before reaching the resort community of Princeville, with its condos and golf courses.

But it's the area beyond, from Hanalei Bridge to Kee Beach at road's end, that best embodies the North Shore spirit. This is a part of Hawaii that has resisted mass tourism and has stalled development. Its appeal is not in creature comforts but in stunning natural beauty. It attracts people who are tuned in to the environment. Over the years, musicians like Graham Nash and Buffy Sainte-Marie and other alternative-minded folks have made Kauai's North Shore their home.

KILAUEA

Kilauea is a former sugar plantation town whose main attractions are a picturesque lighthouse and a seabird sanctuary, both at Kilauea Point. The sanctuary is the most visited site on the North Shore and shouldn't be missed.

Kolo Rd, the main turnoff into Kilauea, is a third of a mile beyond the 23-mile marker on Hwy 56. On Kolo Rd, you pass a gas station, a mini-mart and an Episcopal church, all in quick succession. Kilauea Rd starts opposite the church and ends 2 miles later at Kilauea Point.

Episcopal Church

The little Christ Memorial Episcopal Church attracts attention because of its striking lava-rock architecture. It was built in 1941, but the interesting lava-rock headstones in the churchyard are much older, dating back to when the original Hawaiian Congregational Church stood on this site.

Kilauea Bay

If you're looking for someplace new to explore, you might try Rock Quarry Beach at Kilauea Bay. Also known as Kahili Beach, it's a nice sandy beach and the site of an abandoned rock quarry and steamer landing. This remote beach is mostly used by local fishers, but when the surf is unusually high, surfers also take to these waters. Swimmers should be aware of strong nearshore currents when the surf is up.

Public access is via Wailapa Rd, which begins midway between the 21- and 22-mile markers on Hwy 56. Follow Wailapa Rd north for a half mile beyond Hwy 56 and then turn left on the unmarked dirt road that begins at a yellow water valve. The dirt road, which continues for a half mile before

Crater Hill Hikes

The 568-foot Crater Hill, a protected seabird nesting site just east of the wildlife refuge at Kilauea Point, is now accessible to visitors on guided hikes led by US Fish and Wildlife Service volunteers. A 100-acre cliffside site acquired by the refuge a decade ago, Crater Hill offers fine scenery and a chance to see nature up close.

The trail to the top of the hill is about 1¼ miles long and moderately strenuous. Plan on wearing good walking shoes as well as long pants for protection against thorny trailside vegetation. The guides provide insights into the flora and fauna found along the way; with any luck, you'll see a red-footed booby or two. At the top, visitors enjoy a splendid view of the North Shore.

The hikes leave the visitor center at 10 am daily, take about two hours and are limited to 15 participants. There's no fee to join the hike, other than the refuge's $2 admission charge. Reservations are required (☎ 828-0168), and the hikes typically book up a few days to a week ahead.

The red-footed booby

---

ending at the beach, is usually in fairly good shape and passable in a car.

Kilauea Point

Kilauea Point (☎ 828-1413), a national wildlife refuge, is the northernmost point of the inhabited Hawaiian Islands. Topped by a lighthouse built in 1913, it's picture-postcard material.

Four species of birds come to Kilauea to nest. Most of these birds leave after their young have been hatched and reared. Red-footed boobies, the most visible, are abundant on the cliffs to the east of the point, where they build nests of sticks and leaves in the trees. Boobies nest from February to September, with their peak egg laying occurring in spring.

Wedge-tailed shearwaters arrive by April and stay until November, nesting in burrows that they dig into Kilauea Point. Another readily spotted species is the red-tailed tropicbird, which nests along the cliff edges from March to October. If you're lucky, you'll spot a pair flying in loops, performing their courtship ritual.

Laysan albatross are at Kilauea from about November to July. Some nest on Mokuaeae Rock, straight off the tip of the point. Other albatross nesting sites lie on the grassy clearing to the west of Kilauea Point. If you look out beyond this clearing, you can also see Secret Beach, divided into three scalloped coves by lava fingers.

Great frigate birds nest on the Northwestern Hawaiian Islands, not Kauai, though these aerial pirates do visit Kilauea Point to steal food from other birds. Great frigate birds can be spotted circling above Kilauea Point year-round. You won't see the distinctive red throat balloon that the male puffs out to attract females, though, as they're not here for courtship. The frigate birds, which have a wingspan of 7 feet and a distinctive forked tail, soar with a mesmerizing grace.

Some of Kauai's estimated 100 *nene*, the endangered Hawaiian goose that was reintroduced to Kauai in 1982, can also be spotted in the refuge.

While birds are certainly the main attraction at Kilauea Point, with a little luck you may also spot sea turtles swimming in the cove at the base of the cliffs. During winter, it's not unusual to see whales pass by the point.

The refuge is open from 10 am to 4 pm daily, except on federal holidays. Admission is $2 for adults, free for children under 16.

KAUAI

You can borrow binoculars for free from the visitor center near the lighthouse. Volunteers are usually available to answer questions, and if you want to delve deeper, there's a collection of books on flora and fauna for sale.

Even when the refuge is closed, it's worth driving to the end of Kilauea Rd for the picturesque view of the lighthouse and point.

Guava Kai Plantation

The Guava Kai Plantation (☎ 828-6121) cultivates 480 acres of guava trees that produce juice for Ocean Spray and a handful of other juice companies. A visitor center doles out small samples of guava juice and sells guava products. A path leading through a garden planted with tropical flowers makes for a nice short stroll.

To get there, turn inland onto Kuawa Rd from Hwy 56, just north of the 23-mile marker and a quarter mile south of the Kolo Rd turnoff to Kilauea. The visitor center,

which is open 9 am to 5 pm daily, is about a mile from the highway.

As you go up the road past rows of guava trees, it may seem as if the fruit is too big to be the same guava that grows wild elsewhere on the island – in fact these guava trees are hybrids whose fruit grows to half a pound, twice the normal size.

Places to Eat

The *Farmer's Market*, a grocery store with a good deli, is in the Kong Lung Center, half a mile up Kilauea Rd from Hwy 56. The deli has a variety of sandwiches on whole-wheat bread, good hummus rolls and salads. The store is open daily from 8:30 am to 8:30 pm (to 7:30 pm on Sunday); the deli hours are 10 am to 3 pm.

Kilauea Bakery & Pau Hana Pizza (☎ 828-2020), tucked in the back of the Kong Lung Center, sells breakfast pastries, pizza and breads. At lunchtime, you can get a slice of pizza with a salad for $6. Whole pizzas cost

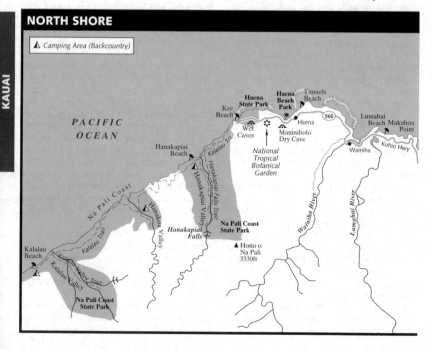

NORTH SHORE

⚠ Camping Area (Backcountry)

PACIFIC OCEAN

Na Pali Coast

Kalalau Trail

Kalalau Beach

Kalalau Valley Trail

Kalalau Valley

Na Pali Coast State Park

Hanakoa Valley

Hanakoa Trail

Hanakapiai Beach

Hanakapiai Valley

Hanakapiai Falls Trail

Hanakapiai Falls

Na Pali Coast State Park

▲ Hono o Na Pali 3330ft

National Tropical Botanical Garden

Kalalau Trail

Wet Caves

Kee Beach

Haena State Park

Haena Beach Park

Maniniholo Dry Cave

Tunnels Beach

Haena

560

Lumahai Beach   Makahoa Point

Kuhio Hwy

Wainiha

Wainiha River

Lumahai River

$11.25 for a 12-inch cheese version; extra toppings include pepperoni, feta cheese and soy-based 'tofurella.' This spot is open from 6:30 am to 9 pm daily except Sunday, with pizza available from 11 am. There are tables on the lawn where you can eat.

A good place for a sit-down meal in these parts is the ***Roadrunner Cafe*** (☎ 826-8226, *2430 Oka St*), a right turn off Kilauea Rd one block before the Kong Lung Center. This family-run operation is a combination bakery and cafe, with hearty breads, healthy salads and Mexican fare. Try the pair of fish tacos served with rice and beans for $8 or the ahi salad with fresh tuna and local organic greens for $9. Items can also be ordered in meat, tofu or vegan versions. The Roadrunner is open 7 am to 8:30 pm Monday to Saturday.

For a down-home treat, stop at ***Banana Joe's***, the bright yellow shack on the inland side of Hwy 56, just north of the Kolo Rd turnoff to Kilauea. Joe dishes up a nice fruit frosty, made solely of frozen fruit that is squeezed through a processor until it comes out as smooth as ice cream. The papaya and pineapple flavors are the best. A bowl of this ($2.50) and a granola bar ($1.25) make a nice snack. You can also buy dried banana and jackfruit strips and a few fresh fruit items grown on the adjacent 6-acre plot. The stand is open from 9 am to 6 pm daily.

KALIHIWAI

Kalihiwai Rd was a loop road going down past Kalihiwai Beach, connecting with the highway at two points, until the tidal wave of 1957 washed out the Kalihiwai River bridge. The bridge was never rebuilt, and now there are two Kalihiwai Rds, one on each side of the river.

Kalihiwai Rd, just half a mile west of Kilauea, leads down a mile to **Kalihiwai Beach**. At the very end of the road, you can still see the pillars that once supported the bridge. The river empties out into a wide, deep bay. The broad, sandy beach is a popular spot for

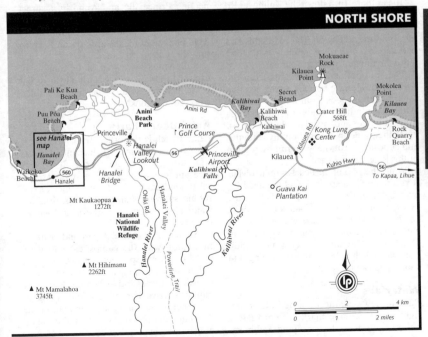

all kinds of activities, including picnicking, swimming, boogie boarding, bodysurfing and, when the northwest swells roll in, some daredevil surfing along the cliff at the east end of the bay. The river is popular with kayakers. The beach has no facilities.

As you take Kalihiwai Rd back up to the highway, look to the left as soon as you see the 'Narrow Bridge' sign; you'll spot a picturesque waterfall that's partially hidden in a little valley.

Secret Beach

Secret Beach is a gorgeous golden-sand beach backed by sea cliffs and junglelike woods. The beach is well off the beaten path, and access to it has changed frequently over the years, so few visitors discover it. Secret Beach is frequented mostly by Kauai's alternative community and nude sunbathers, and even though tourists aren't exactly welcomed, unobtrusive visitors who can blend in are unlikely to encounter any problems.

To get there, turn down the Kalihiwai Rd a half mile west of Kilauea and then turn right onto the first dirt road, which is a tenth of a mile from Hwy 56. The road ends at a parking area a third of a mile down. Don't leave anything of value in your car.

The well-defined trail begins from the parking lot along a barbed-wire fence that separates the woods from a horse pasture. After two minutes, it leads downhill through ironwood trees and mixed jungle growth. All in all, the trail only takes about five minutes and deposits you at the westernmost section of this long, sandy beach.

While this part of the beach is quite idyllic, if you're up for a stroll or feel the need for even more privacy, you can walk along the beach in the direction of Kilauea Lighthouse.

The beach has open seas, with high winter surf and dangerous currents prevailing from October to May. In summer, water conditions are much calmer, and swimming and snorkeling can be good.

Waterfalls

Back on Hwy 56, there's a pull-off on the right at the 25-mile marker, immediately before you cross the sweeping Kalihiwai

Bridge. A brief stop will treat you to views of three waterfalls and the lovely Kalihiwai Valley.

The highest and most distant waterfall is **Kalihiwai Falls**, seen by crossing the road (beware of fast-moving traffic), walking a third of the way onto the bridge ahead and looking up into the valley.

You can see a bit of another waterfall by simply walking to the side of the pull-off and looking down over the edge. For the third, you must walk back along the road a minute or two toward Lihue. The waterfall is just above the road.

ANINI

The area known as Anini has a long beach that's fronted by vast reef flats and backed by a beach park. To get there, cross Kalihiwai Bridge, turn onto the second Kalihiwai Rd and then bear left onto Anini Rd. It's about 1½ miles from the highway to the beach.

Over the years, there's been talk of connecting Princeville and Anini by a direct coastal road, but local resistance to the plan has kept the road at bay. For now, Anini's dead-end street means little traffic, keeping this area unhurried and quiet.

Still, Anini is growing, and a number of exclusive homes have been built in recent years, including some by people with Hollywood connections.

Anini Beach Park

Anini Beach Park borders the shoreline for more than a mile and is divided into day-use, windsurfing and camping areas. It's a very pleasant spot, with gentle breezes and tropical almond shade trees. Facilities include rest rooms, showers, changing rooms, drinking water, picnic pavilions, barbecue grills and a pay phone.

Anini has a good campground right on the water, with the campsites shaded by trees. It's pretty spacious for a beach park, although the camping area gets a little more crowded on weekends, when locals (mostly families) arrive. For information on obtaining a permit to camp, see Camping in the Accommodations section, near the beginning of this chapter.

You can swim and snorkel in the day-use area and in front of the camping area; conditions are best when the tide is high. A pretty good spot is opposite the midpoint of Kauai Polo Club's fence.

Past the western end of the park, Anini Channel cuts across the reef. While some people use the channel for water activities when the seas are calm, waters flowing off the reef create dangerous rip currents in the channel. The protected lagoon west of the channel provides safer water conditions.

At the far end of Anini, you can sometimes see people walking way out onto the shallow reef of Anini Flats, picking opihi, net fishing and catching octopus.

PRINCEVILLE

Princeville, Kauai's biggest development, traces its *haole* (Caucasian) roots to Robert Wyllie, a Scottish doctor who later became foreign minister to Kamehameha IV. In the mid-19th century, Wyllie bought a large coffee plantation in Hanalei and began planting sugar.

When Queen Emma and Kamehameha IV came to visit in 1860, Wyllie named his plantation and surrounding lands Princeville in honor of their young son, Prince Albert. The plantation later became a cattle ranch, and in 1968 ground was broken for the Princeville Resort.

Today, Princeville is a planned community spread over 11,000 acres on a promontory between Anini Beach Park and Hanalei Bay. It has a dozen condo complexes, a luxury hotel, hundreds of private homes, a couple of championship golf courses, restaurants, tennis courts, a shopping center and even its own little airport.

While Princeville may seem out of place on the North Shore, and it certainly stands in sharp contrast to the free-spirited communities that lay beyond, its manicured grounds are spacious, the condos are low-rise and the development is uncrowded compared to its counterparts on other islands.

Information

Princeville Center has a supermarket, small medical clinic, one-hour photo shop, ice cream shop, two banks with ATMs and a few restaurants and boutiques. There's a post office inside the Foodland supermarket and a large new public library at the east side of the complex.

Also at the Princeville Center is the Princeville Chevron gas station, open 6 am to 9 pm daily. If you're heading toward Kee Beach at the end of the road, this is the last place to buy gas.

Kuhio Hwy changes from Hwy 56 to Hwy 560 at the 28-mile marker in front of Princeville Center. The 10-mile stretch from here to Kee Beach at the end of the road is one of the most scenic drives in all of Hawaii.

Princeville Hotel

The Princeville Hotel offers a splendid view of Hanalei Bay and the Bali Hai mountains. The luxury hotel was erected amid a great deal of controversy in 1985. Locals, who were miffed at losing one of their favorite sunset spots, nicknamed the bluffside building 'The Prison.' The hotel was indeed dark and inward-looking, and it so failed to incorporate its surroundings that the owners closed it down in 1989. Over the next two years, the hotel was gutted and virtually rebuilt. The current Princeville Hotel has a lobby with floor-to-ceiling windows offering 180-degree views of Bali Hai. It also has marble floors, posh furniture, pools of flowing water and a smattering of antiques and artwork, but the real attraction is the view.

The site of **Fort Alexander,** a short-lived Russian fortress, can be found on a grassy knoll at the northwest side of the hotel. The interpretive display, housed in a shelter, points out a couple of stones that were once part of the fort's foundation, but there's little else to see from that era.

Princeville is not known for its beaches, but there's a reasonably large one, **Puu Poa Beach,** between the Princeville Hotel and the mouth of the Hanalei River. On the opposite side of the hotel, below the Puu Poa condos, **Pali Ke Kua** (also called Hideaways) is a secluded, sandy pocket of beach that has good swimming and snorkeling when it's calm. High surf, common in winter, can generate dangerous currents at both beaches.

KAUAI

Powerline Trail

In the 1930s, electric transmission lines were run along the mountains, and a 13-mile maintenance route now known as the Powerline Trail was created. There is occasional talk of turning it into a real inland road connecting Princeville to Wailua, but environmental concerns make it unlikely to happen anytime soon.

To get to the trailhead, take the paved road going uphill from Princeville Ranch Stables, a third of a mile after the 27-mile marker on Hwy 56. The pavement ends at a water tank 1¾ miles up; even if you don't plan to hike the trail, the road makes for a pretty drive, offering fine mountain views and glimpses of Hanalei Bay.

The trail continues from the end of the pavement along a rutted 4WD dirt road used mainly by hunters and the power company. It's a full day's walk to its end at the Keahua Arboretum and is recommended only in dry weather.

Places to Stay

Some of Princeville's condo complexes are perched on cliffs, while others are by the golf course. While all of the complexes have some units that are vacation rentals, many units are occupied as year-round housing.

Sometimes you can find residents renting out bedrooms in their condos or homes for about $50 a day. Most people who do this list their rooms on the bulletin board outside the Foodland supermarket in Princeville Center, though occasionally someone will run an ad in the newspaper.

Most condo complexes are represented by a number of different rental agents. While agents offer cheaper prices than direct bookings at a front desk, be aware that there may be cleaning fees, minimum stays and other restrictions. The following agents have fairly extensive Princeville rental listings:

Kauai Paradise Vacations
   (☎ 826-7444, 800-826-7782, fax 826-7673, kpv1@ aloha.net), PO Box 1080, Hanalei, HI 96714
Oceanfront Realty
   (☎ 826-6585, 800-222-5541, fax 826-6478, ori@aloha.net, www.oceanfrontrealty.com), PO Box 3570, Princeville, HI 96722

Pacific Paradise Properties
   (☎ 826-7211, 800-800-3637, fax 826-9884), PO Box 3195, Princeville, HI 96722
North Shore Properties
   (☎ 826-9622, 800-488-3336, fax 826-1188, hnsp@ aloha.net, planet-hawaii.com/visit-kauai), PO Box 607, Hanalei, HI 96714

Sealodge is an older complex, and the quarters can be a bit cramped, but it's high on a cliff and many of the 86 units have great sunrise views across the expansive coral reef of Anini. If you leave the windows open, the surf is guaranteed to give you nautical dreams. One-bedroom units can be booked through the rental agents listed above for around $100.

Pali Ke Kua, a pleasant upscale property near the Princeville Hotel, can be booked through **Marc Resorts** (☎ 922-9700, 800-535-0085, fax 922-2421, marc@aloha.net), which maintains an office at the complex. Rates range from $179 for a one-bedroom garden-view unit to $229 for a two-bedroom ocean-view unit. There's a two-night minimum stay. The same Marc Resorts office also handles a couple of simpler units for $119 in the nearby **Hale Moi** complex, though most are occupied by long-term residents. Marc offers various discount schemes that can cut rates by 20% to 50%, at which times the properties can be a good deal.

The **Cliffs at Princeville** (☎ 826-6219, 800-622-6219, fax 826-2140) is an older complex with one of the more ordinary settings, but its units have been refurbished and it remains relatively inexpensive for pricey Princeville. The units are large and have one bedroom, front and rear lanais, two bathrooms and all the usual condo amenities. The Cliffs is adjacent to the golf course, and there's a pool. Rates if booked through the front desk are $155, but you can often find a unit for around $100 through an agent.

Hanalei Bay Resort (☎ 826-6522, 800-367-5004, fax 826-6680, 5380 Honoiki Rd, Princeville, HI 96722) has both hotel-style rooms and condo units. The hotel rooms range from $165 for a mountain-view unit to $235 for ocean-view accommodations. Studios begin at $175, one-bedroom condos at $300 and two-bedroom condos at $390.

The units are pleasant, and the grounds feature a couple of swimming pools (including a large free-form one), eight tennis courts and fine views of Hanalei Bay. The rates listed above apply to the units managed by Castle Resorts, which runs the front desk and handles 190 of the 280 units at Hanalei Bay Resort. But you can find better prices through the condo rental agents listed in this section. A good one to start with is Kauai Paradise Vacations, which handles several Hanalei Bay Resort units, with rates starting at $110/130 for rooms/studios. For more information on the Castle Resorts properties, visit the website www.castle-group.com.

The *Princeville Hotel* (☎ 826-9644, 800-325-3589, fax 826-1166, 5520 Ka Haku Rd, Princeville, HI 96722), a Sheraton property, has 252 luxury rooms with king beds, marble bathrooms and modern amenities that run the gamut from original oil paintings with dimmer-controlled spotlights to liquid-crystal windows between the bedroom and bath that can be turned from opaque to clear with the flick of a switch. Rates are $360 for a garden-view room, $510 for an ocean-view unit and $3500 for the royal suite. To see photographs of the accommodations, browse www.princeville.com online.

Places to Eat

The *Foodland* supermarket in the Princeville Center has a bakery section with cheap doughnuts and pastries and a deli with take-out items. The deli's tasty fried chicken breasts are the area's best value at $1.29 – grab a can of fruit juice and you've got yourself a cheap lunch. The store is open from 6 am to 11 pm daily.

Hale Java, in the Princeville Center, has cafe food, including breakfast items, soups, sandwiches and deli salads at moderate prices. There are also pizzas from $10 to $20, depending on the size and toppings. It's open from 6:30 am to about 9:30 pm.

Chuck's Steak House (☎ 826-6211), in the Princeville Center, has standard fare such as burgers and sandwiches for $4 to $8 at lunch and a dinner menu that ranges from $17 for chicken to $28 for a steak and fresh fish combo. Lunch is served from 11:30 am to

The root of the taro plant yields poi.

2:30 pm weekdays only; dinner runs from 6 to 10 pm nightly.

Princeville Restaurant & Bar (☎ 826-5050), at the Prince Golf Course, a half mile west of the Princeville Airport, has a broad view, a country club setting and reasonable prices. At breakfast, from 8 to 11 am (Sunday until 2 pm), a Belgian waffle or banana pancakes with bacon cost around $6.50. At lunch, from 11 am to 3 pm, there are sandwiches, salads and good daily specials for $8 to $10.

Bali Hai Restaurant (☎ 826-6522), in the Hanalei Bay Resort, has open-air dining with a wonderful view of Hanalei Bay and the Bali Hai mountains. At breakfast, from 7 to 11 am, you can get a 'taro patch breakfast' of two fried eggs, Portuguese sausage, poi pancakes and taro hash browns for $8.25 or 'macnut' (macadamia nut) waffles for $6.75. At lunch, from 11:30 am to 2 pm, sandwiches with fries average $10. At dinner, from 5:30 to 9:30 pm, à la carte entrees range from $16 for chicken stir-fry to $29 for Black Angus steak. The food's okay, but the view's the real attraction.

Cafe Hanalei (☎ 826-2760), in the Princeville Hotel, has a striking view of Hanalei Bay, but expect to pay a premium for it.

There's a breakfast buffet with waffle and omelette stations, pastries, fruit and a few hot dishes for $21, while at lunch, sandwiches are priced from $12 to $17. The breakfast buffet lasts from 6:30 to 10:30 am Monday to Saturday and to 9:30 am on Sunday. Lunch is from 11 am to 2 pm Monday to Saturday. From 10 am to 2 pm on Sunday, the elaborate brunch spread costs $32.

La Cascata (☎ 826-2761), also in the Princeville Hotel, has a lovely view of Bali Hai and specializes in upscale Italian food, with à la carte pasta, seafood or meat dishes averaging $28. It's open from 6 to 10 pm nightly.

Entertainment
At the Hanalei Bay Resort's *Happy Talk* lounge, there's live Hawaiian guitar music from 5 to 8 pm on Sunday and from 6:30 to 9:30 pm other nights.

Amelia's (☎ 826-9561), at the Princeville Airport, features a good blues band on Sunday.

The *Princeville Hotel* (☎ 826-2788) stages a luau at 6 pm on Monday and Thursday; the cost of $52 for adults and $30 for children includes an imu ceremony, Hawaiian food and live music and dance.

HANALEI VALLEY
Just beyond Princeville, the Hanalei Valley Lookout provides a spectacular bird's-eye view of the valley floor with its meandering river and spread of patchwork taro fields. Be sure not to miss it.

The Hanalei National Wildlife Refuge encompasses 917 acres of the valley, stretching up both sides of the Hanalei River. The wetland taro farms in the refuge produce two-thirds of Hawaii's commercially grown poi taro, while at the same time serving as habitat for endangered waterbirds.

Prior to Western contact, the valley was planted in taro, but in the mid-1800s, rice farming was introduced into Hanalei Valley to feed the Chinese laborers who worked the sugarcane fields. The rice grew so well that by the 1880s it became a major export crop. Now taro once again predominates.

From the lookout, to the lower right you can see the North Shore's first one-lane bridge, which opened in 1912. Visible to the south are the twin peaks of Hihimanu, which in Hawaiian means 'beautiful.'

Hanalei Bridge
The Hanalei Bridge and six other one-lane bridges between the Hanalei River and the end of the road not only link this part of the North Shore to the rest of the island, they also protect it from runaway development.

Big cement trucks and heavy construction equipment are beyond the bridges' limits. Even large package-tour buses are kept at bay.

Over the years, developers have introduced numerous proposals to build a two-lane bridge over the Hanalei River, but North Shore residents have successfully beaten them all down.

While it's not a frequent occurrence, during unusually heavy rains the road between the taro fields and the river can flood and the Hanalei Bridge remains closed until the water subsides.

After the Hanalei Bridge, the valley widens. Buffalo belonging to Hanalei Garden Farms graze in the pastures to the right. Having shed their thick woolly fur for a short tropical coat, these creatures are raised for their meat and are the source of the buffalo burgers and kebabs found on Kauai menus.

Ohiki Rd
If you want to head into Hanalei Valley, turn left onto Ohiki Rd immediately after the Hanalei Bridge. The scenic drive parallels the Hanalei River, starting in taro fields and later passing banana trees, bamboo thickets, *hau* (hibiscus) trees, ferns and wild ginger. It dead-ends after 2 miles.

This is a great place for bird watching. From the roadside, you can commonly spot snow-white egrets and night herons as well as some of the endangered Hawaiian waterbirds that reside in the valley, including the Hawaiian coot, the Hawaiian stilt, the Hawaiian duck and the cootlike Hawaiian gallinule with its bright red bill.

HANALEI
After the Hanalei Bridge, Hwy 560 runs parallel to the Hanalei River. The mile before

Hanalei village is a pastoral scene of taro patches and grassland. There's no development of any kind and no buildings in sight. Take away the telephone poles and asphalt road, and this is how the area has looked for centuries.

Hanalei has a pleasant low-key village center. The village took a severe battering during Hurricane Iniki, losing many old wooden buildings. Fortunately, most of the reconstruction has been done in a period style matching the original character of the town.

Hanalei is friendly, casual and slow. If you're in a hurry, you're in the wrong place.

Information

There's a Bank of Hawaii ATM inside the Foodland market in the Ching Young Village shopping center.

The Hanalei post office, on Hwy 560 in the village center, is open 7:30 am to 4 pm Monday to Friday, 9 am to noon on Saturday.

Hanalei contains several shops geared to outdoor sports. Kayak Kauai specializes in kayak rentals and tours, but also rents bicycles, camping gear, surfboards and snorkel sets. Pedal & Paddle, in the Ching Young Village, rents kayaks, bicycles, camping gear and snorkel sets. Hanalei Surf Company, in the Hanalei Center, rents surfboards, boogie boards and snorkel sets.

Ching Young Village

The old Ching Young Store, the North Shore's main general store since the late 19th century, has evolved into the larger Ching Young Village shopping center. The original Ching Young Store now houses Evolve Love, a gallery with hand-painted silk clothing, jewelry, paintings, woodwork and other handicrafts by local artisans.

Opposite Ching Young Village is the old Hanalei elementary school, which has been renovated and turned into the Hanalei Center complex, with a restaurant and a couple of shops. The building is on the Hawaii Register of Historic Places.

Waioli Huiia Church

Hanalei's first missionaries, the Reverend and Mrs William Alexander, arrived in 1834 in a double-hulled canoe. Their church, hall and mission house are in the middle of town, set on a huge manicured lawn with a beautiful mountain backdrop. These folks knew how to pick property.

The picturesque Waioli Huiia Church is a favorite subject for local watercolorists. The green wooden church retains an airy Pacific feel, with large windows that open outward and high ceilings. The doors remain open during the day, and visitors are welcome to go inside. A Bible printed in Hawaiian circa 1868 is on display on top of the old organ. The Waioli Church Choir, the island's best, sings hymns in Hawaiian at the 10 am Sunday service.

Waioli Mission Hall, to the right of the church, was built in 1836. The hall, which originally served as the church, was built of coral lime and plaster with a distinctive steeply pitched roof to handle Hanalei's heavy rains. An old church graveyard is beside the hall.

Waioli Mission House Museum

The Waioli Mission House is behind the church and hall. The Alexanders spent their first three years living in a grass hut on these grounds, but they couldn't adjust to living Hawaiian-style, so they built this big New England house. It was home to other missionaries over the years, most notably Abner and Lucy Wilcox, whose family became the island's most predominant property holders.

The main part of the house, built in 1837, has period furnishings, including braided rugs, lanterns, a spinning wheel and simple straight-backed chairs.

The house has old wavy glass panes, some nice simple woodwork and several other interesting architectural features. For instance, the upstairs porch slopes, not from settling but because it was constructed to allow water to run off during the valley's frequent torrential rains.

The Mission House (☎ 245-3202) is open 9 am to 3 pm on Tuesday, Thursday and Saturday; there's no admission fee, but donations are appreciated. The inconspicuous parking lot is just past the church. To get there, turn inland immediately before Hanalei School

KAUAI

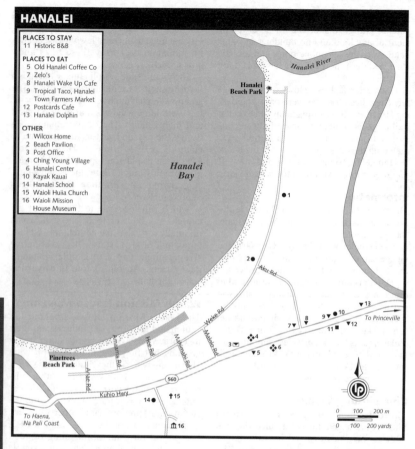

HANALEI

PLACES TO STAY
11 Historic B&B

PLACES TO EAT
5 Old Hanalei Coffee Co
7 Zelo's
8 Hanalei Wake Up Cafe
9 Tropical Taco, Hanalei
   Town Farmers Market
12 Postcards Cafe
13 Hanalei Dolphin

OTHER
1 Wilcox Home
2 Beach Pavilion
3 Post Office
4 Ching Young Village
6 Hanalei Center
10 Kayak Kauai
14 Hanalei School
15 Waioli Huiia Church
16 Waioli Mission
   House Museum

Hanalei River

Hanalei
Beach Park

*Hanalei
Bay*

Aku Rd

To Princeville

Weke Rd

Anaeana Rd

Hee Rd

Malihini Rd

Malolo Rd

Pinetrees
Beach Park

Kuhio Hwy

560

Anae Rd

To Haena,
Na Pali Coast

0   100   200 m
0   100   200 yards

and then left on the dirt driveway opposite the water hydrant.

Hanalei Bay

Hanalei means 'Crescent Bay,' and that it is – a large, perfectly shaped bay, and one of the most scenic in all Hawaii. Weke Rd, which runs a mile along the bay between Waioli Stream and the Hanalei River, can be reached by turning off Hwy 560 at Aku Rd.

Just after turning right onto Weke Rd from Aku Rd, there's a public beach with a picnic pavilion. The more appealing Hanalei Beach Park is about half a mile farther, at the end of Weke Rd. Pinetrees Beach Park is in the opposite direction.

Each of the three beaches has rest rooms, showers, drinking water, picnic tables and grills. Hanalei Beach Park is the best place for catching the sunset, as you can see Bali Hai from there. It's also a popular summer anchorage for sailboats.

On the opposite side of the road, midway between the pavilion and Hanalei Beach Park, the big brown house with the wrap-around porch is the old **Wilcox Home**, which traces its roots to early Hanalei missionaries Abner and Lucy Wilcox.

Incidentally, if the road names sound familiar, it means you're beginning to learn the names of Hawaiian fish – each road along the beach is named after a different one.

Hanalei Beach Park Hanalei Beach Park, one of the North Shore's most frequented beach parks, has a grassy area and a long beach shaded by ironwood trees. The beach has a sandy bottom and a gentle slope, but dangerous shorebreaks and rip currents are common during periods of high surf. While surfing is good in winter, swimming and snorkeling are good in summer, when the water is calm.

The remains of a narrow-gauge railroad track, used a century ago to haul Hanalei rice, still lead up to the long pier that juts out into the bay.

The mouth of the Hanalei River and a small boat ramp are at the eastern end of the park. That part of the beach is called Black Pot, after the big iron pot that was once hung there by local fishers for impromptu cookouts. Camping is allowed on Friday, Saturday and holidays with a permit from the county. For information on obtaining a permit, see Camping under Accommodations, near the start of this chapter.

Pinetrees Beach Park Pinetrees Beach Park, named by surfers, is actually shaded by ironwood trees.

From Weke Rd, turn onto either Hee Rd where there's a bigger parking lot, or Amaama Rd, which has the rest rooms and showers. This section of the beach is also known locally as Toilet Bowls. Pinetrees has some of the bay's highest winter surf and is the site of various surfing contests.

Places to Stay

The *Historic B&B* (☎ 826-4622, PO Box 1662, Hanalei, HI 96714) occupies the oldest Buddhist temple on Kauai, built in Lihue in 1901 and moved to the center of Hanalei in 1985. Operated by Jeff and Belle Shepherd, this is a pleasant little place, with tasteful decor that includes antique furniture and Jeff's own artwork. There are three guest rooms with shoji sliding doors; two rooms

have bamboo four-poster queen beds with canopied mosquito nets, while the other has twin beds. The rate, which includes breakfast, is a reasonable $59/68 for singles/doubles, with a two-night minimum. Credit cards are accepted. Because sound travels easily through the shoji doors, small children are not allowed.

Bed, Breakfast & Beach (☎ 826-6111, PO Box 748, Hanalei, HI 96714) is in a large, contemporary three-story house, a two-minute walk from the beach pavilion section of Hanalei Bay. There are four nicely decorated rooms, each with TV; the 'Honeymoon Suite' has a king bed, while the others have queen beds. All have a private bath, either attached or just outside the room. The house has a wraparound 2nd-floor lanai, hardwood floors and a common living room. Rates range from $70 to $125, breakfast included. The minimum stay is two or three nights, depending on the unit. There's also a two-bedroom house nearby that can be rented by the week for $775, plus $10 per day each for a third or fourth person. Visit the Bed, Breakfast & Beach online at www.bestofhawaii.com/hanalei.

Just across the street, Mary and Dave Cunning rent *Ohana Hanalei* (☎/fax 826-4116, PO Box 720, Hanalei, HI 96714), a pleasant studio unit attached to the side of their home. The daily rate is $70; for stays of a week, the seventh night is free. The unit has its own entrance and bath, a king bed, refrigerator, microwave, coffeemaker, cable TV and a phone with free local calls.

Bali Hai Realty (☎ 826-7244, 800-404-5200, fax 826-6157, c/o Hanalei Trader, 5-5016 Kuhio Hwy, PO Box 930, Hanalei, HI 96714) books vacation rental homes in the Hanalei area, as well as in Haena, Princeville and Anini. Rates begin at around $700 a week.

North Shore Properties (☎ 826-9622, 800-488-3336, fax 826-1188, hnsp@aloha.net, PO Box 607, Hanalei, HI 96714) also books a number of vacation rentals, including singer Graham Nash's four-bedroom Hanalei Bay beachfront house for around $4500 a week and Nash's two-bedroom 'tree house cottage' for $1200 a week. For more information,

KAUAI

browse online at www.planet-hawaii.com /visit-kauai.

Places to Eat
Budget *Tropical Taco*, which parks its old green van in the parking lot adjacent to Kayak Kauai, dishes out decent $5 burritos and other simple Mexican fare from about 11 am to 3:30 pm daily except Monday. There are a couple of picnic tables where you can sit and eat. *Hanalei Town Farmers Market*, a truck selling fresh fruit, sets up shop at the same site from Tuesday to Sunday. A truck with shave ice usually parks in the same lot, too.

Hanalei Gourmet, in the Hanalei Center, has both a deli and a restaurant. Sandwiches range from $6 for turkey to $8 for roasted eggplant on focaccia. The offerings also include pasta salads, green salads and sandwich meats sold over the counter, so you can put together your own picnic. The deli is open from 7 am to 9 pm, the restaurant from 10 am to 10:30 pm daily.

Old Hanalei Coffee Co, west of Hanalei Center, has a relaxed setting and good home-made pies, cakes and pastries, as well as fresh brewed coffee. It's open 7 am to 6 pm daily.

For surfers and other early risers, the *Hanalei Wake Up Cafe*, on Aku Rd, is open daily by 6 am. The menu features omelettes, custard French toast or half a papaya with yogurt and granola for $5 to $7.

For inexpensive hot dogs, corn dogs and hamburgers, there's *Bubba's*, at the west side of Hanalei Center, open from 10:30 am to 6 pm daily.

Pizza Hanalei (☎ 826-9494), at Ching Young Village, has good pizza at reasonable prices. A 10-inch cheese pizza on either traditional white or whole-wheat crust topped with sesame seeds is $9.40, plus $1.35 per topping. The spicy calzone-style pizzarittos, loaded with cheese and veggies, make a good meal for $5. At lunchtime, you can also buy slices of pepperoni or pesto pizza for $2.85. Pizza Hanalei is open 11 am to 9 pm daily.

Next door, the little *Hanalei Natural Foods* sells juices, a few organic vegetables, vitamins and other health food items. It's open from 9 am to 7 pm daily.

Zababaz, a vegetarian deli at the back of Evolve Love at Ching Young Village, has salads, Lappert's ice cream and $5 plate lunches that usually have a Mexican or Thai theme. The deli's open from 10 am to around 5:30 pm daily.

Big Save supermarket, at Ching Young Village, is open 7 am to 9 pm daily and has a *Subway* fast-food counter inside.

Mid-Range & Top End Zelo's (☎ 826-9700) is the most bustling sit-down restaurant in Hanalei. At lunch, it has good burgers with fries for $6 and omelettes or blackened fresh fish sandwiches for $8. At dinner, there are various pastas for around $15 and steak or fresh fish for about $23. Zelo's serves meals from 11 am to 3:30 pm and from 5:30 to 9:30 pm daily.

Postcards Cafe (☎ 826-1191), a vegetarian (and seafood) restaurant, is pricey but good, and most items are organic. Dinner, served from 6 to 9:30 pm, features the likes of Thai coconut curry with tempeh for $16, fish pasta in a sherry sauce for $22 and fresh fish at market prices. Appetizers such as summer rolls, grilled prawns or taro fritters with papaya salsa cost around $10.

Hanalei Dolphin (☎ 826-6113), at the east side of the village on the Hanalei River, is a steak-and-seafood restaurant. At lunch, served from 11 am to 3:30 pm, you can get fish burgers, sandwiches or salads for $6 to $8 and eat outdoors at the side of the river. At dinner, from 5:30 to 10 pm, meals range from chicken or frozen mahimahi for $16 to king crab and filet mignon for $26. For cheaper eats, visit the fish market, at the rear of the restaurant, which has takeout chowder, sushi rolls and poke.

Entertainment
Sushi & Blues (☎ 826-9701), in the Ching Young Village, has a dance floor and live bands playing reggae, blues, funk or rock from 9:30 pm to 12:30 am on Friday and Sunday, with a $5 cover charge. There's Hawaiian music, with no cover, from 4 to 6 pm on Sunday.

Hanalei Gourmet (☎ 826-2524) has live jazz, rock or other contemporary music from 8:30 to 10:30 pm nightly and Hawaiian music from 3:30 to 8 pm on Sunday. There's no cover charge.

HANALEI TO WAINIHA
Waikoko Beach
The western part of Hanalei Bay, called Waikoko Beach, has a sandy bottom, is protected by a reef and is shallower and calmer than the middle of the bay. There are beachside places to park under ironwood trees around the 4-mile marker, but there are no facilities.

Winter surfing is sometimes good off Makahoa Point, the western point of the bay, called Waikokos by surfers.

Lumahai Beach
Lumahai is the gorgeous mile-long stretch of beach where Mitzi Gaynor promised to wash that man right out of her hair in the 1958 musical *South Pacific*. It's a broad white-sand beach with lush jungle growth on one side and tempestuous open ocean on the other.

This is always a good beach for walking and exploring. Around some of the lava outcrops you can find green sand made of the mineral olivine.

There are two ways onto Lumahai. The first and more scenic is a three-minute walk that begins at a pull-off along a stone retaining wall three-quarters of a mile past the 4-mile marker. Park in the direction of the traffic flow to avoid a ticket. The trail to the beach starts at a 'No Lifeguard' sign and goes down the slope to the left.

The lava point at this eastern end of the beach offers protection from the winds that often blow from the Princeville direction. These rocks are a rather popular place for sunbathing and for being photographed, but size it up carefully, as people have been washed away by high surf and rogue waves. Lumahai has dangerous shorebreaks and is not a beach to turn your back on. It's particularly treacherous in winter, though there are strong currents year-round. Because of the numerous drownings that have occurred here over the years, Lumahai has been nicknamed Luma*die* by locals.

Back on the road, there are a couple of lookouts with views down onto Lumahai.

The first is at the 5-mile marker, though the next one that pops up around the bend has a better angle.

The other access onto Lumahai Beach is along the road at sea level at the western end of the beach, just before crossing the Lumahai River Bridge. The beach at this end is lined with ironwood trees. Across the road is the Lumahai Valley, open and flat with grazing horses and cattle.

Wainiha
Wainiha has a tiny general store that's the last place where you can buy groceries and beer before the end of the road. It's open 9:30 am to 6:30 pm daily.

Ancient house sites, heiau sites and old taro patches reach deep into Wainiha Valley. This valley is said to have been the last hideout of the menehune. In fact, as late as the mid-19th century, 65 people in the valley were officially listed as menehune on the government census!

For a glimpse into an older Hawaii, take a side trip up the **Wainiha Powerhouse Rd**, which begins off Hwy 560 shortly before the 7-mile marker. It leads to Wainiha Valley, a narrow valley with steep green walls.

This narrow road is lined with simple tinroof homes, old rusting pickup trucks and sleeping dogs. At 1½ miles up, an incongruous manicured estate with a cool blue stream meandering through the property suddenly comes into view. Shortly after, you arrive at the Wainiha hydroelectric plant, built in 1906 by McBryde Sugar Company and still pumping out juice today. Beyond the powerhouse, the road turns to dirt and begins to feel more private.

HAENA
Haena has houses on stilts, little beachfront cottages, a few vacation homes, the YMCA camp, large caves, campsites and beautiful sandy beaches. It also has the only condo complex and restaurant beyond Hanalei.

Tunnels Beach
Tunnels is a big horseshoe-shaped reef that has great diving and snorkeling when the water is calm, which is generally limited to

the summer. There's a current as you head into deeper water. When conditions are right, you can start snorkeling near the east point and let the current carry you westward. It's more adventurous than Kee Beach, and the coral is beautiful.

Tunnels was not named after the caves and other crevices in the underwater walls but for its tubular winter surf break at the outer corner of the reef. The beach is popular with both windsurfers and board surfers, though dangerous rip currents that prevail from October to May make it suitable for experts only.

To get there, look for cars parked at the side of the road near phone pole No 144, midway between the 8- and 9-mile markers opposite the beach access road. Or you can park at Haena Beach Park and walk along the beach to Tunnels.

Haena Beach Park

Haena Beach is a beautiful curve of white sand. To the right, you can see the horseshoe shape of Tunnels outlined by breaking waves. To the far left is Cannons, another good dive spot. Haena itself is not protected by reefs and has very strong rip currents and some powerful shorebreaks from October to May.

The county beach park has campsites, covered picnic tables, rest rooms, showers and a pay phone. There are usually a few hikers from the Kalalau Trail camping here. It's a bit over a mile to the trailhead, and this is a safer place to park a car than the end of the road if you're going on to Kalalau.

For information on obtaining a permit to camp, see Camping in the Accommodations section at the front of this chapter.

Maniniholo Dry Cave

Three large sea caves, which were part of the coast thousands of years back, are on the inland side of the road between Haena and Kee Beach. One is dry, and two are wet.

According to legend, the caves were created when the goddess Pele dug into the mountains looking for a place on Kauai's North Shore to call home.

Maniniholo Dry Cave, across the road from Haena Beach Park, is a deep broad cave that you can walk into. Dry is a relative term, as the dripping water that constantly seeps from the cave walls keeps the interior of Maniniholo damp and humid.

National Tropical Botanical Garden

Most of Limahuli, the last valley before the start of the Na Pali Coast, is still lush, virgin forest. The National Tropical Botanical Garden, a nonprofit organization that preserves and propagates rare native plants, owns 1000 acres of the valley. The Limahuli garden contains collections of Hawaiian ethnobotanical and medicinal plants and other endangered native species. There are also ancient stone terraces planted with taro. Endemic trees include the endangered Kokio hauheleula, which has a red hibiscus-like blossom, and the equally beautiful but more common ohia lehua tree.

The garden starts at a concrete driveway on the inland side of the highway, just before the stream that marks the Haena State Park boundary.

It's open from 9:30 am to 4 pm Tuesday to Friday and on Sunday. It costs $10 to walk through the garden on your own, on a three-quarter-mile loop trail, or $15 to join a two-hour guided tour (call ☎ 826-1053 for reservations).

Wet Caves

Haena State Park includes the two wet caves as well as Kee Beach. The caves are near each other, less than a quarter mile from the end of the road. The first, Waikapalae Wet Cave, is just a few minutes' walk uphill from the main road along a rutted dirt drive opposite the visitor parking overflow area. The second, Waikanaloa Wet Cave, is easier to spot, as it's right on the south side of the main road.

Both caves are big, deep, dark and dripping, with pools of very cold water. Divers sometimes explore them, but the caves can be dangerous and it's certainly best to go with an experienced local diver.

Kee Beach

Kee Beach is commonly called 'the beach at the end of the road,' which it is.

On the left side of the beach is the distinctive 1280-foot cliff that marks the start of the Na Pali Coast. Almost everyone calls it Bali Hai, its name in *South Pacific*. The Hawaiian name is Makana, which means 'gift.' A heiau and ancient hula school site are at its base.

Snorkeling is good at Kee Beach, which has a variety of tropical fish. A reef protects the right side of the cove, and except on high surf days, it's usually calm. The left side is open and can have a powerful current, particularly in winter.

When it's really calm – generally only in summer – snorkelers cross the reef to the open ocean where there's great visibility, big fish, large coral heads and the occasional sea turtle. It makes the inside of the bay look like kid's stuff, but check it out carefully because breaking surf and strong currents can create dangerous conditions.

When the tide's at its lowest, you can actually walk a great distance out on the reef without getting your feet wet and peer down into tide pools.

Showers, drinking water, rest rooms and a pay phone are tucked back in the woods behind the parking lot.

There are several ways to see views down the Na Pali Coast from Kee Beach. One way is to walk the first 30 minutes of the Kalalau Trail (detailed in the following Na Pali Coast section). Another is to take the short walk out around the point at the left side of the beach.

Or, simply walk down the beach to the right for a few minutes and look back as the cliffs unfold, one after the other.

Kaulu Paoa Heiau To make the five-minute walk out to Kaulu Paoa Heiau, take the path on the western side of the beach. The walk is shaded by tropical almond trees, which drop their edible nuts along the trail. Follow the stone wall as it curves uphill, and you'll reach the heiau almost immediately.

The overgrown section at the foot of the hill is one of the more intact parts of the heiau, but don't stop there. Instead, continue walking up the terraces toward the cliff face. Surf pounding below, vertical cliffs above – what a spectacular place to worship the gods!

Beneath the cliff face, large stones retain a long flat grassy platform. A thatched-roof *halau* (a longhouse used as a hula school) once ran the whole length of the terrace. Here, dances to Laka, the goddess of hula, were performed. In ancient Hawaii, this was Kauai's most sacred hula school, and students aspiring to learn hula came from all of the islands to Kaulu Paoa.

Fern wreaths, rocks wrapped in ti leaves, leis and other offerings to Laka are still placed into the crevices of the cliff face. The site is sacred to native Hawaiians and should be treated with respect. Night hula dances are still performed on special occasions.

Lohiau's House Site Lohiau's house site is just a minute's walk above the parking lot at Kee Beach. At the Kalalau Trail sign, go left along the barely discernible dirt path to a vine-covered rock wall. This overgrown level terrace runs back 54 feet to the bluff

---

Taylor Camp

If you walk down Kee Beach about 15 minutes to the northeast, you'll come to a stream and the site of the former Taylor Camp.

In the late 1960s, a little village of tents and tree houses sprang up on property owned by actress Elizabeth Taylor's brother. Reports of drugs, orgies and pipe organ music in the middle of the night eventually prompted the authorities to crack down on the camp. When state officials tried to evict everyone on public health grounds, the campers challenged them in court, claiming squatters' rights. The 'squatters' eventually lost, and the property was condemned and incorporated into the state park system. Taylor Camp remains part of North Shore folklore, though there's nothing left to see.

and is said to have been the home of Lohiau, a 16th-century prince.

Legend says that the volcano goddess Pele was napping one day under a hala tree on the Big Island when her spirit was awakened by the sound of distant drums. Her spirit rode the wind in the direction of the sound, searching each island in turn until she finally arrived at Kee Beach. Here above the heiau she found Lohiau beating a hula drum, surrounded by graceful hula dancers.

Pele took the form of a beautiful woman and captured Lohiau's heart. They became lovers and moved into this house. In time Pele had to go back home to the Big Island, leaving the lovesick Lohiau behind. His longing quickly got the better of him, and on this site he died from his grief.

Places to Stay & Eat
Kauai YMCA-Camp Naue (☎ 826-6419 or 246-9090, fax 246-4411, PO Box 1786, Lihue, HI 96766), in Haena, just before the 8-mile marker on Hwy 560, has simple beachside bunkhouses, each with screened windows, cement floors and six to 14 bunks. The camp is geared to groups but sometimes accepts individual travelers. It costs $12 for one of the 50 bunks, which have vinyl mattresses but no linen or blankets. To pitch a tent costs $10 for the first person and $7 for each extra person. There are hot showers, but the kitchen is reserved for large groups only. The Y doesn't accept reservations, but you should still call ahead, as there are specific check-in policies and on occasion the camp shuts down completely. Also, in summer and some other holiday periods the camp is commonly booked by children's groups, at which times it's closed to individual travelers. The camp is a 10-minute walk from Tunnels Beach.

Hanalei Colony Resort (☎ 826-6235, 800-628-3004, fax 826-9893, hcr@aloha.net, PO Box 206, Hanalei, HI 96714) is an older but renovated low-rise condo complex on the east side of Haena. Each of the 52 units has a full kitchen, a lanai and two bedrooms, although one of the bedrooms is really a sitting area with two twin beds that's separated from the rest of the living room by sliding doors. The complex is right on the beach and has a swimming pool and barbecue area. This is a place to listen to the surf: there are no TVs, radios or room phones. Rates range from $130 for a garden-view room to $215 for an oceanfront room in the low season, $150 to $240 in the high season. The rates are the same for up to four people, and for weekly stays, the seventh night is free.

The only restaurant past Hanalei is a new beachside steak and fish restaurant at the Hanalei Colony Resort.

NA PALI COAST
In Hawaiian, *na pali* means simply 'the cliffs.' Indeed, these are Hawaii's grandest.

The Na Pali Coast is the rugged 22-mile stretch between the end of the road at Kee Beach in the north and the road's opposite end at Polihale State Park in the west. It has the most sharply fluted coastal cliffs in Hawaii.

Kalalau, Honopu, Awaawapuhi, Nualolo and Milolii are the five major valleys on the Na Pali Coast. These deep river valleys once contained sizable settlements.

In the mid-19th century, missionaries established a school in Kalalau, the largest valley, and registered the valley population at about 200. Influenced by Western ways, people gradually began moving to towns, and by the end of the century the valleys were largely abandoned.

The Na Pali valleys, with limited accessibility and abundant fertility, have long been a natural refuge for people wanting to escape one scene or another. While Koolau the Leper is the best known, there have been scores of others.

Kalalau Trail
Kalalau is Hawaii's premier trail. Here, it's common to come across hikers who have trekked in Nepal or climbed to Machu Picchu. The Na Pali Coast is similarly spectacular, a place of singular beauty.

The Kalalau Trail is basically the same ancient route used by the Hawaiians who once lived in these remote north coast valleys. The trail runs along high sea cliffs and winds up and down across lush valleys before it finally ends below the steep fluted pali of Kalalau. The scenery is breathtaking, with sheer green cliffs dropping into brilliant turquoise waters.

While hikers in good shape can walk the 11-mile trail straight through in about seven hours, it's less strenuous to break it up and spend a night camping in one of the two valleys along the way.

In winter, there are generally only a few people at any one time hiking all the way in to Kalalau Valley, but the trail is heavily trodden in summer. As it's a popular hike for islanders as well as visitors, weekends tend to see the most use.

The hike can be divided into three parts: Kee Beach to Hanakapiai Valley (2 miles); Hanakapiai to Hanakoa Valley (4 miles); and Hanakoa to Kalalau Valley (5 miles).

The first 2 miles of the hike make for a popular day trip, and hiking permits are not required for those going only as far as Hanakapiai Valley. Even if you're not planning to stay overnight, a permit is officially required to continue on the Kalalau Trail beyond Hanakapiai; day-use hiking permits are available free from the Division of State Parks (☎ 274-3444), 3060 Eiwa St, room 306, Lihue, HI 96766.

The trail is within Na Pali Coast State Park. Camping is allowed in all three valleys but is limited to five nights total, with no two consecutive nights in Hanakapiai or Hanakoa Valley. At press time, Hanakoa was closed to campers because new pit toilets were needed, but the state expects this to be only a temporary situation. State camping permits are required. (For details on obtaining permits, see Camping in the Accommodations section at the start of this chapter).

Kee Beach to Hanakapiai The 2-mile trail to Hanakapiai Valley is a delightfully scenic hike. Morning is a good time to be going west, and the afternoon to be going east, as you have the sun at your back and good light for photography.

The trail weaves through kukui and ohia trees and then back out to clearings with fine coastal views. There are purple orchids, wildflowers and a couple of tiny Zen-like waterfalls. The black nuts embedded in the clay are kukui, polished smooth by the scuffing of hundreds of hiking shoes.

Just a quarter mile up the trail, you can catch a fine view of Kee Beach and the surrounding reef. After 30 minutes, you get your first view of the Na Pali Coast. Even if you weren't planning on a hike, it's well worth coming this far.

Hanakapiai has a sandy beach in the summer. In the winter, the sand washes out,

Koolau the Leper

Koolau was a *paniolo* (cowhand) who contracted leprosy in 1893. Rather than accept separation from his family and banishment to Molokai's leprosy colony, as was the law at the time, Koolau hiked down into Kalalau Valley, taking along his wife and young son. Shortly after, a sheriff and deputy showed up to clear the valley of renegade lepers. Koolau was the only resister. That night, in the light of a full moon, the sheriff snuck up the valley hoping to take Koolau in his sleep. In self-defense, Koolau shot the sheriff.

When word reached Honolulu, a shipload of soldiers was sent to land on Kalalau Beach. As they marched up the valley, they met Koolau's gunfire. After two of the soldiers were shot off the ridge and a third accidentally killed himself, they switched strategies. Just before dawn, they blasted Koolau's hideaway with cannon fire, not knowing he had slipped through their lines the night before. From a nearby waterfall, Koolau watched as the soldiers loaded up and set sail. They never returned, and Koolau lived the rest of his days in the valley undisturbed.

Eventually the son, and then Koolau, died of leprosy. Both are buried on a valley hillside. When Koolau's wife, Piilani, left the valley, she found Koolau had largely been forgotten. A decade later, a visiting reporter, John Sheldon, recorded her story. Jack London later wrote *Koolau the Leper*, a more fictionalized account.

KAUAI

and it becomes a beach of boulders, some of them sparkling with tiny olivine crystals. The western side of the beach has a small cave with dripping water and a miniature fern grotto.

The ocean is dangerous here, with unpredictable rip currents year-round. It's particularly treacherous during winter high surf conditions, but summer trades also bring powerful currents. Hanakapiai Beach is matched only by Lumahai for the number of drownings on Kauai.

If you're just doing a day hike and want to walk farther, it makes more sense to head up the valley to Hanakapiai Falls than it does to continue another couple of miles on the coastal trail.

Hanakapiai Falls The 2-mile hike from Hanakapiai Beach to Hanakapiai Falls takes about 2½ hours roundtrip. Because of some tricky rock crossings, this trail is rougher than the walk from Kee Beach to Hanakapiai Beach. Due to the possibility of flash floods in the narrow valley, the Hanakapiai Falls hike should only be done in fair weather.

The trail itself is periodically washed out by floodwaters, and sections occasionally get redrawn, but the path is not that difficult to follow, as it basically goes up the side of Hanakapiai Stream. The trail is not maintained, and in places you may have to scramble over and around tree trunks and branches.

There are trails on both sides of the stream, but the main route heads up the stream's western side. About 50 yards up, there are old stone walls and guava trees. If the guavas are ripe, it's a good place to stock up. There are also some big old mango trees along the way.

Ten minutes up from the trailhead, you'll find thickets of green bamboo interspersed with eucalyptus. Also along the trail is the site of an old coffee mill, although all that remains is a little of the chimney.

The first of four or five stream crossings is about 25 minutes up, at a sign that warns: 'Hazardous. Keep away from stream during heavy rainfall. Stream floods suddenly.'

Be particularly careful of your footing on the rocky upper part of the trail. Some of the rocks are covered with a barely visible film of slick algae. It's like walking on glass.

Hanakapiai Falls is spectacular, with a wide pool gentle enough for swimming. Directly under the falls; the cascading water forces you back from the rock face – a warning from nature, as rocks can fall from the top.

This is a very peaceful place to spend a little time meditating. It's a beautiful lush valley, though it's not terribly sunny near the falls because of the incredible steepness.

Hanakapiai to Hanakoa Just 10 minutes up the trail running from Hanakapiai Valley to Hanakoa Valley, there's a nice view of Hanakapiai Beach, but from there the trail goes into bush, and the next coastal view is not for another mile. This is the least scenic part of the trail.

The camping site at Hanakoa is tucked into the valley about half a mile inland. Of the three camping areas, Hanakoa is the wettest. It also tends to have the largest number of mosquitoes.

The valley is lovely and Hanakoa Stream has pools perfect for swimming. There's a waterfall about a third of a mile up the valley, but it's rough getting up there as the path is overgrown. The valley was formerly settled by farmers who grew taro and coffee, both of which still grow wild.

Hanakoa to Kalalau This is the most difficult part of the trail, although without question the most beautiful. Make sure you have at least three hours of daylight left.

About a mile out of Hanakoa Valley, you'll reach the coast again and begin to get fantastic views of Na Pali's jagged edges. There are some very narrow and steep stretches along this section of the trail, so make sure your gear is properly packed and be cautious of your footing. A little past the halfway mark, you'll get your first view into Kalalau Valley.

The large valley has a beach, a little waterfall, a heiau site, some ancient house sites and some interesting caves that are sometimes dry enough to sleep in during the summer.

An easy 2-mile trail leads back into the valley to a pool in Kalalau Stream with a natural water slide. If you have a quick hand, you might try your luck at catching prawns that live in the stream.

Valley terraces where Hawaiians cultivated taro until 1920 are now largely overgrown with bitter Java plum and edible guava and passion fruit. Feral goats scurry up and down the crumbly cliffs and drink from the stream.

Kalalau Valley has fruit trees, including mango, papaya, orange, banana, coconut, guava and mountain apple. During the 1960s and '70s, people wanting to get away from it all tried to settle in Kalalau, but forestry rangers eventually routed them out. Even today, rangers occasionally swoop in unexpectedly by helicopter to check camping permits; those without permits are forced to hike back out immediately, and those suspected of being repeat offenders commonly have their gear confiscated.

Warnings & Information The Kalalau Trail is a hike into rugged wilderness and hikers should be well prepared. In places, the trail runs along steep cliffs that can narrow to little more than a foot in width, which some people find unnerving. However, hikers accustomed to high-country trails generally enjoy the hike and don't consider it unduly hazardous. The Sierra Club, which occasionally leads hikes into Kalalau, classifies the trail as moderate to strenuous. Like other Hawaiian trails, the route can be muddy and slippery if it's been raining – at such times, a walking stick makes a good companion.

Accidents are not unknown. Most casualties along the Kalalau Trail are the result of people trying to ford swollen streams, walking after dark on cliff-edge trails or swimming in treacherous surf. Keep in mind that the rock the cliffs are composed of is loose and crumbly; don't try to climb the cliffs, and don't camp directly beneath them, as goats commonly dislodge stones that tumble down the cliff walls. Still, for someone who's cautious and aware, this can be a hike into paradise.

There's no shortage of water sources along the trail, but all drinking water must be boiled or treated.

Bring what you need, but travel light. You won't want to have extra shifting weight on stream crossings or along cliff edges. Shoes should have good traction; it's certainly not a trail for flip-flops. If you bring a sleeping bag, make it a light one.

The state parks office in Lihue can provide a Kalalau Trail brochure with a map. There is also information posted at the Kee Beach trailhead.

Break-ins to cars left overnight at Kee Beach are all too common. Some people advise leaving cars empty and unlocked to prevent smashed windows. It's generally safer to park at the campground at Haena Beach Park. Whatever you do, don't leave valuables in a locked car.

Kayak Kauai (☎ 826-9844) in Hanalei lets hikers park cars in the shop's lot for $5 a day and stores bicycles, backpacks or suitcases for $3 a day. North Shore Cab (☎ 826-6189) charges about $20 for a taxi from Hanalei to Kee Beach.

You can also usually arrange to leave extra luggage wherever you've been staying. Other possibilities include Lihue Airport, where baggage storage can be arranged through the airport porters for $3 per bag per day, and the general store in Wainiha (☎ 826-6251), on Hwy 560 en route to Kee Beach, which stores bags for $2 to $3 a day, depending on the size.

Getting There & Away
Precarious trails once led from the upland Kokee area down to the valley floors along the Na Pali Coast. In some places, footholds were gouged into cliffs, and in others rope ladders were used. These trails no longer exist.

Only the Hanakapiai, Hanakoa and Kalalau Valleys can still be reached on foot, solely along the 11-mile Kalalau coastal trail.

The only other access is by boat. Landings are limited to the Kalalau, Nualolo and Miloliii Valleys and are largely restricted to summer, when the seas are calm. Milolii, part of Na Pali Coast State Park, has primitive camping. For more information on Milolii, see the Camping section at the start of this chapter.

For years, Captain Zodiac (☎ 826-9371, www.planet-hawaii.com/zodiac) has been licensed to drop off and pick up backpackers in Kalalau Valley during the summer months, giving people the option of hiking the Kalalau Trail just one way. In 1998, however, the governor, in response to concerns about pollution and traffic issues near the Hanalei boat ramp, suspended all commercial boat operations out of Hanalei – which has the only launch site on the North Shore. Consequently, the boat service to Kalalau remains suspended, but there are some indications that it might resume. If it does, expect the service to cost around $75 per passenger, or $35 if you want to just send off your backpack on the boat and hike the route pack-free. If you're considering this option, there is one caveat: Rough surf at Kalalau has been known to prevent landings for several days in a row.

In addition to approaching the Na Pali Coast from the North Shore, you can also look down into the Na Pali valleys from Kokee State Park. The park has a drive-up lookout right on the rim of Kalalau Valley, as well as strenuous hikes out to clifftops that offer gorgeous views into Awaawapuhi and Nualolo Valleys (for details, see Kokee State Park in the West Side section, later in this chapter).

South Shore

Poipu is Kauai's main beach resort area. It's typically sunny, and for the larger part of the year, including winter, it has calm waters good for swimming and snorkeling. During the summer, the surf kicks up, and it becomes a surfers' haunt.

The village of Koloa, 3 miles inland from Poipu, was the site of Hawaii's first sugar plantation. This sleepy town could have doubled for Dodge City before it got caught up in Poipu's boom. Now most of its shops are geared for tourists, and it catches the overflow from neighboring Poipu.

Poipu and Koloa are about 10 miles south of Lihue. To get there, take Hwy 50 (Kaumualii Hwy) and turn off onto Hwy 520 (Maluhia Rd).

Tree Tunnel

Immediately after turning down Maluhia Rd, you enter the Tree Tunnel, a mile-long stretch of road canopied by swamp mahogany trees, a type of eucalyptus. Originally, the tree tunnel was more than double this length, but when Hwy 50 was rerouted to the south, most of the tunnel was lopped off.

In 1992, Hurricane Iniki brought down many of the branches, temporarily destroying the tunnel effect, but by and large it has filled back in nicely.

The cinder hill to the right about 2 miles down Maluhia Rd is Puu o Hewa. From its top, the ancient Hawaiians raced wooden *holua* (sleds) down paths covered with oiled *pili* (bunchgrass). To add even more excitement to this popular spectator sport, the Hawaiians crossed two sled paths near the middle of the hill. The paths were about 5 feet wide, and if you strain your eyes you might be able to see the X on the hillside where they crossed.

Hewa means 'wrong' or 'mistake.' The hill's original name was lost when a surveyor jotted 'Puu o Hewa' (wrong hill) on a map he was making, and it mistakenly went off to the printer like that.

The two grassy hills to the left of the road are known as Mauna Kalika, or Silk Mountain. Two American entrepreneurs introduced Chinese silkworms here in the 1830s in an attempt to develop a Hawaiian silk industry. The climate proved unsuitable for the silkworms, so the hills, like the rest of the surrounding area, were eventually given over to sugarcane.

KOLOA

Hawaii's first sugar plantation was started in Koloa in 1835. The raw materials had arrived long before; sugarcane came with the original Polynesian settlers, and the earliest Chinese immigrants brought small-scale refinery know-how. However, large-scale production did not begin until William Hooper, an enter-

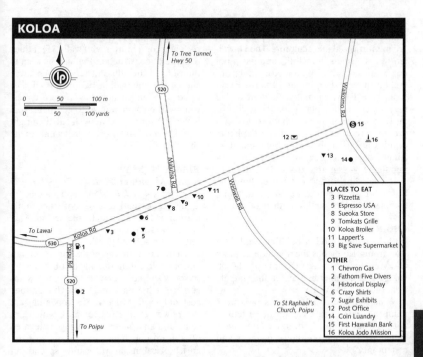

KOLOA

| 0 | 50 | 100 m |
| 0 | 50 | 100 yards |

To Tree Tunnel,
Hwy 50

520

Waikomo Rd

Maluhia Rd

Weliweli Rd

Koloa Rd

Poipu Rd

530

520

To Lawai

To Poipu

To St Raphael's
Church, Poipu

⑧ 15

⏚ 16

▽ 13   14 ●

12 ✉

7 ●   ▽ 11

▽ 10

▽ 9

▽ 8

● 6

▽ 3   ● 5

● 4

▣ 1

● 2

PLACES TO EAT
3 Pizzetta
5 Espresso USA
8 Sueoka Store
9 Tomkats Grille
10 Koloa Broiler
11 Lappert's
13 Big Save Supermarket

OTHER
1 Chevron Gas
2 Fathom Five Divers
4 Historical Display
6 Crazy Shirts
7 Sugar Exhibits
12 Post Office
14 Coin Laundry
15 First Hawaiian Bank
16 Koloa Jodo Mission

prising 24-year-old Bostonian, arrived in Kauai and made inroads with the *alii* (local chief).

With financial backing from Honolulu businesspeople, he leased land in Koloa from the king and paid the alii a stipend to release commoners from their traditional work obligations. He was then free to hire Hawaiians as wage laborers, and Koloa became Hawaii's first plantation town.

Koloa Rd (Hwy 530), which runs between Koloa and Lawai, is the best way to leave Koloa if you're heading west – it's a pleasant drive through pastures and cane fields.

Information
The First Hawaiian Bank, on Waikomo Rd, is open 8:30 am to 3 pm Monday to Thursday, 8:30 am to 6 pm on Friday. The branch also has an ATM machine.

The post office on Koloa Rd, which serves both Koloa and Poipu, is open 9 am to 4 pm Monday to Friday, 9 to 11 am Saturday.

Espresso USA, on Hwy 530, has a computer with Internet access that costs $3 per half hour; it's open 8 am to 4 pm on weekdays, 8:30 am to 2:30 pm on weekends.

There's a coin laundry on Waikomo Rd, behind the Big Save supermarket.

Sugar Exhibits
Any sugarologists in the crowd? The field at the intersection of Hwy 520 and Koloa Rd is for you.

In a tiny garden, a dozen varieties of **sugarcane** are labeled with faded interpretive markers. Some are noted for their high tonnage, others for high sucrose and some for their good ratooning abilities, though the different varieties have all grown to twist and clump together. Who knows, maybe there's a great new hybrid sprouting up among the tangles!

The **stone smokestack** in another corner of the field is a relic from one of Koloa's early mills and dates back to 1841.

KAUAI

In the center of the field, the principal ethnic groups that worked the plantations are immortalized in a **sculpture**. The Hawaiian wears a *malo* (loincloth) and has a poi dog by his side. The Chinese, Korean, Japanese, Portuguese, Filipino and Puerto Rican groups are likewise in native field dress. You may notice that the plaque on the wall curiously makes reference to a haole overseer – present-day islanders found the depiction of this Caucasian plantation boss seated on a high horse so unacceptable that at the last minute he was omitted from the sculpture.

If you want to find out more about the history of sugar, you can read the informative plaques at the sculpture display.

Old Koloa

With its aging wooden buildings and false storefronts, Koloa has the appearance of an Old West town. It was a thriving plantation village and commercial center that largely went bust after WWII.

While its history is sugar, its present is unmistakably tourism. The former fish markets, barber shops, bathhouses and beer halls have become boutiques, galleries and restaurants.

The building that houses Crazy Shirts was, until recently, the Yamamoto General Store. Moviegoers would line up at Yamamoto's for crack seed (a local snack) and soft drinks until the theater across the street burned down. On the sidewalk in front of the store are a couple of sculptures by the late Maui artist Reems Mitchell. In the courtyard behind the store, you'll find the site of the former town hotel, along with a little **historical display** that includes a Japanese bath and some period photos.

At the east side of town is the **Koloa Jodo Mission**, which dates back to 1910. The Buddhist temple on the left is the original, while next to it is a newer and larger temple where services are now held. During services, the smell of incense and the sound of beating drums fills the air.

St Raphael's Catholic Church

St Raphael's, the oldest Catholic church on Kauai, is the burial site of some of the first Portuguese immigrants to Hawaii. The original church, built in 1854, was built from lava rock and coral mortar with walls 3 feet thick – a type of construction that can be seen in the ruins of the adjacent rectory. When the church was enlarged in 1936, it was all plastered over, and it now has a more typical whitewashed appearance. To get there from Koloa Rd, turn onto Weliweli Rd, then right onto Hapa Rd and proceed half a mile to the church.

Places to Stay

Kahili Mountain Park (☎ 742-9921, PO Box 298, Koloa, HI 96756) is only a mile up a sugarcane road just beyond the 7-mile marker on Hwy 50. Run by the Seventh Day Adventist church, it enjoys a beautiful setting beneath Mt Kahili.

There are four categories of accommodations. Old cabinettes, at the bottom end, are very simple structures on cement slabs and are rather dark and dank, though they cost only $30. Much more appealing are the newer cabinettes for $40, which are clean and airy one-room cottages elevated off the ground. There are also two categories of cabins, all pleasantly spread out around the grounds: eight older rustic cabins that cost $50 and five newer ones that cost $60. The new cabins, while not as quaint in appearance, are larger, spiffier and have screened porches that serve as a second room.

All categories have bed linens, a two-burner gas stove, pots and pans, a sink and a refrigerator; cabinettes have shared showers and toilets, while cabins have private bathrooms. Cabinettes hold five people, cabins hold four to six. The rates quoted above cover up to two people, with each additional person charged $10. It's an unbeatable value and only about a 20-minute drive to the beaches in Poipu. As Kahili Mountain Park commonly books up during the high season, advance reservations are advised.

Places to Eat

The following places to eat, as well as a *Lappert's* ice-cream shop, are on Koloa Rd

(Hwy 530) near its intersection with Maluhia Rd (Hwy 520).

The snack shop at the side of the **Sueoka Store** sells burgers, cheese sandwiches and saimin for $1.50 each and plate lunches for $4. It's open 10 am to 3 pm Monday to Saturday.

Espresso USA has island coffee, muffins and pastries at reasonable prices.

Pizzetta (☎ 742-8881) is a decent little pizzeria where a generous slice of cheese pizza costs $2.75, and a whole pizza is $12. It's open 11 am to 10 pm daily.

Tomkats Grille (☎ 742-8887) is a popular lunch spot with a pleasant courtyard and good sandwiches, ranging from a veggie burger for $6.25 to a grilled mahimahi sandwich for $8.50. At dinner, there are also seafood, chicken and steak dishes for $11 to $15. Tomkats is open from 11 am to 10 pm daily.

Koloa Broiler (☎ 742-9122) is in a funky old tin-roof wooden building that used to be a soft drink bottling plant. The 'menu' is a display case of raw meat and fish. Diners get to be cooks, preparing their own orders over a communal gas grill. Dishes range from $7 for a burger to around $12 for chicken or steak and $15 for fresh fish, with a simple buffet of rice, beans and salad included. Koloa Broiler is open 11 am to 10 pm daily.

POIPU
Poipu is about 3 miles south of Koloa down Poipu Rd. Other than the lovely sandy beaches, Poipu's most popular attraction is the Spouting Horn blowhole. To get to Spouting Horn, turn right off Poipu Rd onto Lawai Rd, just past Poipu Plaza, and continue for 1¾ miles.

Prince Kuhio Park
Prince Kuhio Park is about half a mile down Lawai Rd, across from tiny Hoai Bay. Here you'll find **Hoai Heiau** and a monument honoring Prince Jonah Kuhio Kalanianaole, the Territory of Hawaii's first delegate to the US Congress. It was Prince Kuhio who spearheaded the Hawaiian Homes Commission Act, which provided homesteads for native Hawaiians. The remains of a fishpond and an ancient Hawaiian house platform are also on the grounds.

Baby Beach
A protected swimming area just deep enough for children is off Hoona Rd, east

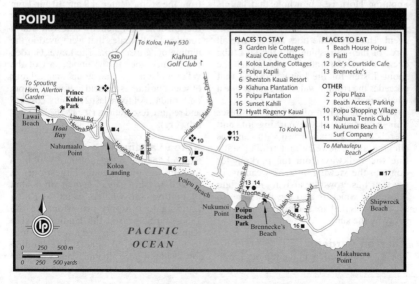

PLACES TO STAY	PLACES TO EAT
3 Garden Isle Cottages, Kauai Cove Cottages	1 Beach House Poipu
4 Koloa Landing Cottages	8 Piatti
5 Poipu Kapili	12 Joe's Courtside Cafe
6 Sheraton Kauai Resort	13 Brennecke's
9 Kiahuna Plantation	
15 Poipu Plantation	**OTHER**
16 Sunset Kahili	2 Poipu Plaza
17 Hyatt Regency Kauai	7 Beach Access, Parking
	10 Poipu Shopping Village
	11 Kiahuna Tennis Club
	14 Nukumoi Beach & Surf Company

of Prince Kuhio Park. Look for the beach access post that marks the pathway between the road and the beach. Adults may want to walk west down the beach to reach a sandy break with fewer rocks and deeper water.

Lawai Beach

Lawai Beach is west of Prince Kuhio Park, opposite Lawai Beach Resort. It's a little rocky, but during winter the water is usually quite clear and snorkelers will find an abundance of tropical fish. When the surf's up in summer, the beach is always inundated with surfers.

Across from the beach, you'll find rest rooms, a shower and public parking.

Kukuiula Bay

Kukuiula Bay, about a half mile east of Spouting Horn, is a small boat harbor maintained by the state and mostly used by fishing and diving boats. The beach is rocky and more suitable for pole fishing than other water activities. There are nine mooring spaces, a launch ramp and a concrete wharf.

Spouting Horn Beach Park

Spouting Horn is a blowhole that has its days. Sometimes it has a fairly impressive spout, while at other times it's simply a non-event. The waves, the tides and the overall force of the sea rushing into the lava tube decide how much water surges through the spout. Listen for the low whooshing that precedes the rushing water – it sounds like a whale breathing.

During the height of the day, tour buses pull in and out of the parking lot, and there's often a small crowd with cameras clicking away. Jewelry and trinket stalls line the walkway from the parking lot down to the viewing area. You can avoid the tour bus crowd by arriving in the late afternoon, which is also the best time to see rainbows that are sometimes cast in the spray by the sun.

Allerton Garden

The Allerton Garden, in the remote Lawai Valley east of the Spouting Horn area, was

started in the 1870s by Queen Emma, who built a summer cottage on the site. Chicago industrialist Robert Allerton bought the property in the late 1930s and significantly expanded the decorative gardens in the 100-acre estate.

In 1971, the site became part of the National Tropical Botanical Garden, which propagates tropical and endangered plant species and does research in ethnobotanical and medicinal plants. The organization, which owns much of the Lawai Valley and allows entrance via guided tours, maintains a visitor center across from Spouting Horn Beach Park.

Surrounding the visitor center are some newly planted exhibition gardens – one with native Hawaiian plants, another with the varieties of fruit trees and vegetables grown around cane workers' homes – and an agricultural garden with plantings of sugar, pineapple, macadamia trees and coffee. The center, which also has a gift shop filled with Hawaii-made items, is open 8:30 am to 5:30 pm Monday to Saturday. There's no admission fee.

The Allerton Garden tour, which takes in the lower part of the Lawai Valley, departs from the visitor center at 9 am, 10 am, 1 pm and 2 pm Tuesday to Sunday. This tour visits the gardens designed by Allerton and a couple of valley sites that were used in the filming of *Jurassic Park*. The Lawai Garden tour, which goes to the upper part of the valley and is more of an ethnobotanical tour of scientific interest, is held at 9 am and 1 pm on Monday. All tours last 2½ hours, cost $25 and require reservations (☎ 742-2623, tours@ntbg.org).

Koloa Landing

Koloa Landing, at the mouth of Waikomo Stream, was once Kauai's largest port. It served to ship sugar grown on Koloa Plantation, and whalers called at Koloa Landing to resupply provisions. In the 1850s, farmers used the landing to ship Kauai-grown oranges and sweet potatoes to California gold miners. The landing lost its importance after an island wide road system was built, and it was abandoned in the 1920s. Other than a small county boat ramp, there's nothing left to see.

Beneath the water, it's another story. Koloa Landing is a popular snorkeling and diving spot. Its protected waters reach depths of about 30 feet, and it's generally calm all year, although kona winds can sometimes create rough water conditions. The area has some underwater tunnels and a good variety of coral and fish. Sea turtles are commonly seen, and monk seals make occasional appearances. For the best sights, swim out to the right after entering the water.

Poipu Beach

The long stretch of white sand running from the Sheraton Kauai Resort east to Poipu Beach Park is generally referred to as Poipu Beach. It's actually three attractive crescent beaches separated by narrow rocky points. The turquoise waters are often good for swimming, bodysurfing, windsurfing, board surfing and snorkeling.

Cowshead, the rocky outcropping at the west end of the beach near the Sheraton, has Poipu Beach's best boogie boarding and bodysurfing breaks. Top surfing spots are Waiohai, which is off the east side of Poipu Beach, and First Break, offshore in front of the Sheraton. Slow, gentle waves more suitable for beginners can be found inshore along the beach.

Poipu Beach Park

Poipu Beach Park, at the end of Hoowili Rd (off Poipu Rd), has a lifeguard station, shallow nearshore waters and safe swimming, making it one of the most popular weekend destinations for families on the South Shore.

Nukumoi Point extends into the water at the western side of the park. At low tide, you can walk out on the point and explore tide pools that shelter small fish and sea urchins. You'll find the best snorkeling at the west side of the point, where there are swarms of near-tame fish.

Beach facilities include rest rooms, showers and picnic tables. Snorkel sets, boogie boards, beach chairs and umbrellas can be rented across the street at Nukumoi Beach & Surf Company.

Brennecke's Beach

Brennecke's has good shorebreaks that make it the South Shore's best spot for bodysurfing and boogie boarding. However, it breaks very close to shore and is suitable only for the experienced. While it's best when surf is highest, which is generally in the summer, there's some respectable action in winter as well. Beware of strong rips that are present with high surf. The beach is only a small pocket of sand and the waters can get crowded. For safety reasons, fins are not allowed and surfboards are prohibited.

Brennecke's is off Hoone Rd, just east of Poipu Beach Park.

Shipwreck Beach

Shipwreck Beach, the pleasant golden-sand beach fronting the Hyatt Regency Kauai, also sees some top bodysurfing and boogie boarding conditions. A couple of challenging nearshore surf breaks attract local board surfers as well. The water conditions here are not for novices, and the pounding shorebreak and high surf make for treacherous swimming conditions along the entire beach.

Mahaulepu Beach

Secluded Mahaulepu Beach, just a couple of miles beyond Shipwreck Beach, has lovely white sands, sheltered coves, tide pools, petrified sand dunes and sea cliffs. At various times of the year, Mahaulepu is good for surfing, windsurfing, boogie boarding and snorkeling.

Before the arrival of white Westerners, the area was heavily settled, and many important historic sites lie buried beneath the cane fields and shifting beach sands. Along the beach, people still claim to see ghost marchers coming in from the sea at night.

The property is owned by Grove Farm, which allows beach access from 7:30 am to 6 pm in winter and to 7 pm in summer. To get there, drive past the Hyatt Regency Kauai and continue on the cane road for 1½ miles, at which point the road will be blocked by a gate. Turn right, continue past the gravel plant, and after a third of a mile, you'll come to a gatehouse; from there, it's half a mile to the beach parking area at the end of the road. A short trail to the beach begins at the right side of the parking area. This will bring you to a popular windsurfing spot and a convenient place from which to explore.

One striking geological feature in the area is a **cinder cone** with a cave; you can wander deep inside. To get there, walk west along the beach for about a third of a mile. After crossing a little stream, the trail going inland leads to the cave, a couple of minutes away. In the cave's center, you'll find an opening looking straight up to the heavens – it feels like you're sitting in a little volcano.

Or, instead of heading to the cave, walk east along the beach for about 10 minutes to reach scenic **Kawailoa Bay**, which is surrounded by sand dunes to the west and protected by jutting sea cliffs to the east. The bay has a lovely beach, and it's not uncommon to find a few Hawaiians net-fishing in the waters along the shore.

Places to Stay

Budget Koloa Landing Cottages (☎ 742-1470, 800-779-8773, fax 332-9584, dolfin@ aloha.net, 2704B Hoonani Rd, Poipu, HI 96756) is comprised of five cottages across the street from Koloa Landing. All cottages have TVs, phones and full kitchens. Studio units, which have queen beds, cost $60. Full cottages, which have both a queen bed and two twins, range from $70 for two people in a smaller unit to $110 for four people in the largest unit. A cleaning fee of $20 for the studios, $40 to $60 for the cottages, is tagged on to the bill. Reserve as far in advance as possible, as the place is often booked solid. For more information, visit the website www.planet-hawaii.com/koloa.

Poipu Plantation (☎ 742-6757, 800-634-0263, plantation@poipubeach.com, 1792 Pee Rd, Poipu, HI 96756) consists of nine condo-style units and a 1930s home with three B&B rooms. The best deals are the condos, which are modern and comfortable with tropical rattan furniture, air-con, TVs and full kitchens. One-bedroom units start at $95, and two-bedroom units at $120. While not as spacious, the B&B accommodations are pleasant enough, have private baths, include breakfast and cost $85 for a room in the back with either a queen or a king bed, or for the front room with a king bed. There's a hot tub, as well as a barbecue area and coin-operated washers and dryers.

Perched above Koloa Landing, *Garden Isle Cottages (☎ 742-6717, 800-742-6711, fax 742-1933, vacation@oceancottages.com, 2666 Puuholo Rd, Poipu, HI 96756)* is a friendly place that has seven pleasant units. Oceanfront studios with both a double and single bed, refrigerator and coffeemaker cost $102. One-bedroom apartments with ocean-view lanais, queen beds, kitchens and roomy living rooms start at $128. Extra guests (more than two per room) are $10 each. All the units have TVs, ceiling fans and abstract paintings and sculpture by owner/artist Robert Flynn. There are no phones in the units, but a pay phone is out front. Garden Isle also rents a studio ($92) and a large suite ($159) in a separate house with a lap swimming pool near Poipu Crater. You can make reservations online at www.oceancottages.com.

The nearby *Kauai Cove Cottages (☎ 742-2562, 800-624-9945, info@kauaicove.com, 2672 Puuholo Rd, Poipu, HI 96756)* consists of three comfy new studio units. Each is pleasant, with hardwood floors, queen bed, 25-inch TV, CD player, full kitchen with a standard oven and a microwave, phone, ceiling fans and a little patio with a gas barbecue. The rate is $85. The only drawback is that the place is near the road, but it is a relatively quiet street. To see pictures of the accommodations, go to the website www.kauaicove.com.

Sunset Kahili (☎ 742-1691, 800-827-6478, fax 742-6058, sunsetk@aloha.net, 1763 Pee Rd, Poipu, HI 96756) is an older, well-maintained five-story condo. Each of the 36 units has an ocean view, a washer/dryer, cable TV and lanai. Rates are $125 for up to two people in a one-bedroom unit and $155 for up to four people in a two-bedroom unit. Off-season rates are $10 less. The minimum stay is three nights. Sunset Kahili can be difficult to book from January through March, particularly if you're looking for a longer stay, as a lot of retirees return each year to spend the winter.

Top End *Poipu Kapili* (☎ 742-6449, 800-443-7714, fax 742-9162, aloha@poipukapili .com, 2221 Kapili Rd, Poipu, HI 96756) is a 60-unit condominium complex. The units are large and nicely furnished, with ceiling fans, full kitchens, ocean views and a queen-size sofa bed in the living room. One-bedroom units, which have either a queen or king bed, start at $185. The two-bedroom units typically have a king bed in the master bedroom and two twins in the second bedroom and begin at $230. There's a three-day minimum, though it's waived when things are slow. There are two tennis courts and a swimming pool. For more information, visit the website www.poipukapili.com.

The *Kiahuna Plantation* (☎ 742-6411, 800-688-7444, fax 742-1698, reservations@ outrigger.com, 2253 Poipu Rd, Poipu, HI 96756) is a 333-unit condo complex spread across acres of quiet, garden-filled grounds between Poipu Rd and Poipu Beach. The units are pleasant, each with a full kitchen, a living room with a sofa bed and a large balcony. Prices mainly reflect the distance from the water: $175 for a one-bedroom garden-view unit that sleeps four people, $400 for a one-bedroom oceanfront unit. Two-bedroom condos cost $315 to $450 for up to six people. If you book at the lower end, request a 3rd-floor unit, as some have glimpses of the ocean despite being in the garden-view category. The Outrigger chain, which manages the property, offers numerous promotions that can cut the rates by as much as half. You can make reservations online at www.outrigger.com.

Gloria's Spouting Horn Bed & Breakfast (☎/fax 742-6995, 4464 Lawai Beach Rd, Poipu, HI 96756) is an upscale oceanside B&B just a few minutes' walk from Spouting Horn. The three comfortable guest bedrooms all front the ocean. Each has a refrigerator, microwave, phone, TV, VCR, a bath with a deep soaking tub and a seaside balcony. Rates, which include breakfast, are $200 for singles or doubles; there's a three-day minimum stay.

Sheraton Kauai Resort (☎ 742-1661, 800-782-9488, fax 742-9777, 2440 Hoonani Rd, Poipu, HI 96756), an upmarket hotel on Poipu Beach, has recently reopened after extensive rebuilding and repairs following Hurricane Iniki. In addition to the standard resort hotel amenities, all 413 rooms have lanais. Room rates range from $265 for a garden view to $400 for oceanfront accommodations. There are two swimming pools, three tennis courts and a couple of restaurants. The resort maintains a website at www.sheraton-hawaii.com.

Poipu's most exclusive hotel is the 600-room *Hyatt Regency Kauai* (☎ 742-1234, 800-233-1234, fax 742-1557, 1571 Poipu Rd, Poipu, HI 96756). It's all quite elegant, with airy lobbies adorned with antiques, and its central building nicely incorporates the ocean view into its design. There are also extensive artificial lagoons and waterways spread around the resort grounds. Garden-side rooms start at $310, while the best suites climb to $3000. The Hyatt has restaurants, a health spa, tennis courts and a golf course.

Vacation Rentals The *Poipu Beach Resort Association* (☎ 742-7444, fax 742-7887, info@poipu-beach.org, PO Box 730, Poipu, HI 96756) has a brochure listing most of Poipu's accommodations. For more information, visit the website www.poipu-beach.org.

The following vacation rental companies book condos and private homes in Poipu:

Suite Paradise
    (☎ 742-6464, 800-367-8020, fax 742-9121, mail@ suite-paradise.com), 1941 Poipu Rd, Poipu, HI 96756
Grantham Resorts
    (☎ 742-7220, 800-325-5701, fax 742-9001, gresort@aloha.net),
    PO Box 983, Poipu, HI 96756
R&R Realty & Rentals
    (☎ 742-7555, 800-367-8022, fax 742-1559, randr@ aloha.net), 1661 Pee Rd, Poipu, HI 96756
Kauai Vacation Rentals
    (☎ 245-8841, 800-367-5025, fax 246-1161, aloha@ kvrre.com), 3-3311 Kuhio Hwy, Lihue, HI 96766

Places to Eat

Budget Taqueria Nortenos, in the Poipu Plaza, is popular for its takeout Mexican food. The meatless burrito is a good value at $2.85, while two enchiladas with rice and beans cost $4.50. The food is fine for the price. Taqueria Nortenos is open 11 am to 10 pm daily except Wednesday.

Joe's Courtside Cafe, at the Kiahuna Tennis Club, is the local favorite for breakfast. You can get half a papaya for $3, a bowl of delicious homemade granola for $4 and various breakfast standards like pancakes and omelettes for around $7. Joe's is open 7 to 11 am for breakfast and 11 am to 2 pm for lunch, which features salads, sandwiches and burgers for $6 to $8.

Poipu Shopping Village, at the corner of Poipu Rd and Kiahuna Plantation Drive, has a few simple eateries, including *Amigo's*, a Mexican restaurant with $8 plates that include rice and beans, and *Shipwreck Subs*, a sandwich stand.

Keoki's Paradise (☎ 742-7535), in the Poipu Shopping Village, has an open-air Polynesian motif with artificial waterfalls, lit torches and hanging vines. While it's a bit contrived, it somehow all works nicely. The food is reasonably good, and dishes, which come with a Caesar salad, include vegetarian lasagna for $11, Balinese chicken for $15 and the catch of the day for $20. Keoki's Paradise is open for dinner from 5:30 to 10 pm daily. A simpler cafe menu of burgers, sandwiches and *pupus* (snacks), including a good $4 fish taco, is offered near the bar from 11 am to 11:30 pm.

Brennecke's (☎ 742-7588), a touristy restaurant and bar opposite Poipu Beach Park, has an ocean view and good but pricey fish dishes. A fresh fish sandwich costs $10 at lunch, while beef or vegetarian burgers are a bit cheaper. For the salad bar, add $2.50. Dinner dishes, which include the salad bar, range from chicken stir-fry for $16 to the fresh catch for $22. Brennecke's is open 11 am to 10 pm daily.

Top End *Piatti* (☎ 742-2216) has a pleasant setting overlooking the gardens at Kiahuna Plantation. The restaurant features good Italian food with Polynesian influences. In addition to Mediterranean salads, carpaccio, pizza and pasta, you can also order baby back ribs in a ginger-apple sauce, fresh local seafood and a coconut-milk bouillabaisse. Appetizers and pizzas cost $6 to $12, pasta and meat dishes $14 to $25. Be sure to request a table on the veranda. Piatti is open 5:30 to 10 pm nightly.

In the Poipu Shopping Village is *Roy's Poipu Bar & Grill* (☎ 742-5050), a branch of the famed Roy's on Oahu. It has excellent Hawaii Regional cuisine, a changing menu of creative dishes and good service. Appetizers, such as coconut-crusted shrimp or duck and strawberry salad, cost $6 to $8. Main courses range from $16 for lemongrass chicken to $24 for fresh fish. The hot chocolate soufflé makes an indulgent dessert. Roy's is open for dinner only, from 5:30 to 9:30 pm nightly.

The *Beach House Poipu* (☎ 742-1424), on Lawai Rd, offers similar fare to Roy's at slightly higher prices but with a waterfront setting right on Lawai Beach. Operated by chef Jean-Marie Josselin, who also owns A Pacific Cafe in Waipouli, this is a great place to dine at sunset. Appetizers, such as shrimp and scallop *gyoza* (Japanese-style dumpling) or grilled fish nachos with passion-fruit sauce, are around $10, while main courses, which include the likes of rack of lamb, pistachio-crusted salmon or mango-ginger roast duck, cost $20 to $26. The Beach House is open 5:30 to 10 pm nightly.

The most interesting restaurant at the Hyatt Regency Kauai is *Tidepools* (☎ 742-6260), which has a romantic setting with open-air thatched huts overlooking a sprawling carp pond. Appetizers, such as sashimi or shrimp cakes, cost around $10, while entrees include prime rib or charred ahi for $25 and Maine lobster for $36. Tidepools is open 6 to 10 pm nightly.

Entertainment

The *Hyatt Regency Kauai* is the main entertainment venue in Poipu. There's live Hawaiian music and hula dancing from 6 to 8 pm nightly in the open-air *Seaview Terrace*, just off the lobby; on most nights, the entertainment includes a picturesque torch-lighting ceremony at sunset. It's free, though for the price of a drink and an early arrival you can get yourself a front-row table.

There's live jazz from 8 to 11 pm nightly in the Hyatt's **Stevenson's Library** lounge and bar. The Hyatt also hosts a **luau** from 6 to 8:30 pm on Thursday and Sunday; the evening costs $60 for adults, $40 for teens and $30 for children six to 12.

Poipu Shopping Village presents a free Polynesian dance show at its center stage from 5 to 5:45 pm on Monday and Thursday.

West Side

The top destinations on Kauai's West Side are Waimea Canyon and Kokee State Park, both with ruggedly spectacular scenery.

It's 38 miles along the Kaumualii Hwy (Hwy 50) from Lihue to Polihale State Park, the farthest accessible point on the West Side. This is sugar country, with cane lining the roadside much of the way.

KALAHEO
Kalaheo, an old sleepy Portuguese community, is quintessentially local in flavor. Pig hunting remains popular in this town, which accounts for all the hunting dogs in tiny backyard cages.

The town's main shops are clustered around the intersection of Hwy 50 and Papalina Rd. They include a couple of food marts, the post office and Kalaheo's restaurants.

While Kalaheo is off the main tourist track, it has some reasonably priced accommodation options, is within driving distance of Poipu Beach and could make a convenient base for exploring Kauai's splendid West Side sights.

Kukuiolono Park
Kukuiolono Park (☎ 332-9151) is an unassuming little golf course with gardens and scenic views. Kukuiolono means 'light of Lono,' referring to the torches that Hawaiians once placed on this hill to help guide canoes safely to shore.

From Hwy 50, turn left onto Papalina Rd in Kalaheo. Just short of a mile, turn right onto Puu Rd and then make an immediate right, which takes you through an old stone archway and up into the park. A neat little Japanese garden is at the far end of the parking lot.

The park gates are open from 6:30 am to 6:30 pm. The nine-hole golf course is open to the public on a first-come, first-served basis. Greens fees are a mere $7. The little clubhouse has an inexpensive snack shop and a fine view clear down to the coast.

Puu Rd Scenic Drive
Puu Rd is a scenic loop with small ranches, grand mango trees and fine coastal views. It's a winding country road, only one lane with some blind curves, but nothing tricky if you drive slowly. And it's so quiet, you may not even encounter another car.

After leaving Kukuiolono Park, turn right onto Puu Rd to start the drive. It's just over 3 miles back to Hwy 50 this way. About halfway along, you'll look down on Port Allen's oil tanks and the town of Numila, with its old sugar mill.

Down the slope on the west side of the road are coffee trees, part of a total of 4000 acres that have been planted between Koloa and Eleele. The coffee, on McBryde Sugar Company property, is one of that company's grander schemes for diversifying crops on land formerly planted solely in sugarcane.

Places to Stay
Kalaheo Inn (☎ 332-6023, 888-332-6023, chet@aloha.net, 2711 Milo Hae Loop, Koloa, HI 96756) enjoys a central location on Papalina Rd behind the Kalaheo Steak House. Chet and Tish Hunt have taken an old local motel and thoroughly renovated it into an inviting, reasonably priced place to stay. There are nine pleasant units; each has a kitchen with microwave, coffeemaker, toaster and refrigerator, a living room with a TV and VCR, a private bath and a bedroom with a queen or two twin beds. Six of the units also have a sofa bed in the living room. Rates are $55 in the three smallest units and $65 in the larger ones; add an extra $10 per person beyond two people. For those who plan on staying a month, the rate drops to

KAUAI

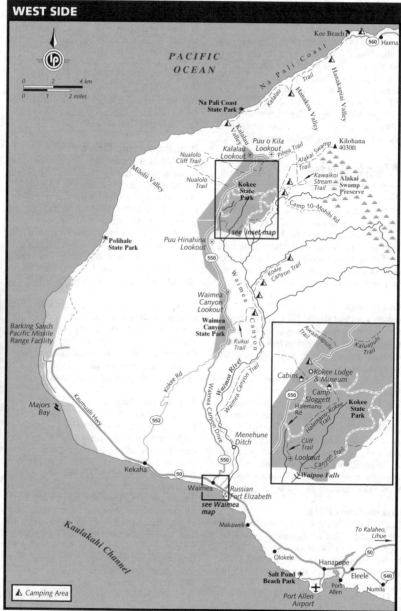

WEST SIDE

PACIFIC OCEAN

Na Pali Coast

Kee Beach
560 Haena

Kalalau Trail
Hanakoa Valley
Hanakapiai Valley

Na Pali Coast State Park

Kalalau Valley
Puu o Kila Lookout
Kalalau Lookout
Pihea Trail
Kilohana 4030ft
Alakai Swamp Trail

Nualolo Cliff Trail
Kokee State Park
Kawaikoi Stream Trail
Alakai Swamp Preserve

Nualolo Trail
see inset map
Camp 10-Mohihi Rd

Miloli Valley

Polihale State Park

Puu Hinahina Lookout

550

Koaie Canyon Trail

Waimea Canyon Lookout
Waimea Canyon

Waimea Canyon State Park

Barking Sands Pacific Missile Range Facility

Kokee Rd

Kukui Trail

Waimea River

Waimea Canyon Trail

Awaawapuhi Trail
Kaluapuhi Trail

Cabins
Kokee Lodge & Museum

Camp Sloggett
550
Halemanu Rd
Kokee State Park
Halemanu-Kokee Trail

552

Majors Bay

Kaumualii Hwy

Waimea Canyon Drive

Cliff Trail
Lookout
Canyon Trail
Waipoo Falls

Menehune Ditch

550

Kekaha
50
Waimea
see Waimea map
Russian Fort Elizabeth

Kaulakahi Channel

Makaweli

To Kalaheo, Lihue
50

Olokele
Hanapepe
Eleele
540

Salt Pond Beach Park
Port Allen
Numila
Port Allen Airport

△ Camping Area

$40 a day. For more information, visit the inn's website at www.kalaheoinn.com.

Kalaheo Plantation Estates *(☎/fax 332-7812, 888-332-7812, kalaheo1@gte.net, 4579 Puu Wai Rd, PO Box 872, Kalaheo, HI 96741)* is an attractive B&B within walking distance of the town center. Stained-glass artist James Hargraves and his Japanese-born wife LeeAnn have made this 75-year-old plantation home a cheery place. There are four units, each with private bath and cable TV. The cheapest, the Blue Ginger room, is perfectly adequate with two twin beds that can be arranged as a king, a refrigerator, toaster, microwave and coffeemaker; it costs $55/300 a day/week. A delightful mid-range room is the Magnolia suite, which has a king bed, a screened lanai overlooking a quiet garden, both a shower and a bathtub, and a well-equipped kitchenette; it costs $69/400. The other two units have more beds and full kitchens and cost $75 for two people, $10 more for a third or fourth person. There's a two-night minimum or a $10 surcharge. A continental breakfast can be arranged for an additional $5 per person.

Classic Vacation Cottages *(☎ 332-9201, fax 332-7645, clascot@hawaiian.net, PO Box 901, Kalaheo, HI 96741)* is in Kalaheo, half a mile up from Hwy 50. Two appealing options are the studio ($75), which includes a queen bed, a skylight and French doors that lead to a little porch, and the one-bedroom unit above the studio, which has high ceilings, a lanai and a peek at the ocean for the same price. There are also two ground-level units at the side of the main house for $75. All have sofa beds, kitchens and cable TV. You can also rent the main house, a large and fully equipped contemporary home with one bedroom, a full kitchen, a den with a futon and a living room with a sofa bed for a reasonable $85. For additional guests beyond two, add $10. To see pictures of the accommodations, go to www.hawaiian.net/~clascot online.

Places to Eat

The ***Bread Box***, on Papalina Rd, sells good whole-grain breads, tasty macnut rolls for $1.30 and coffee for just 25¢. It's open 4 am to noon, or until the bread sells out, from Tuesday to Saturday.

Kalaheo Coffee Co, on Hwy 50 at the side of the Menehune Food Mart, is a friendly cafe with good coffee, espresso and pastries. At breakfast you can get a bowl of Anahola granola, a Belgian waffle or an omelette for $4 to $6. Lunch features sandwiches, burgers, vegetarian tortilla wraps and salads for $5 to $8. This spot is open 6 am to 4 pm Monday to Saturday, 7 am to 2 pm Sunday.

Another good spot for lunch is the ***Camp House Grill***, on Hwy 50 in the town center, which has generous chicken-breast sandwiches for $5. It also has reasonably priced breakfast and dinner options and is open 6:30 am to 9 pm daily.

The popular ***Brick Oven Pizza*** *(☎ 332-8561)*, on Hwy 50, is a bit pricey but good. Small (10-inch) pizzas start at $10, large ones (15-inch) at $20. The pizzas are made with your choice of whole-wheat or white crust. The restaurant also has sandwiches, salads, wine and beer. It's open 11 am to 10 pm daily except Monday.

Kalaheo Steak House *(☎ 332-9780)*, on Papalina Rd (off Hwy 50), has excellent steaks in sizes to quell the most voracious of appetites. Red meat dishes range from 12oz sirloin steaks ($16) to 24oz cuts of prime rib ($25). There are also chicken, seafood and pork dishes. All come with a nice fresh salad and bread. The Kalaheo Steak House is open 6 to 10 pm nightly.

HANAPEPE VALLEY LOOKOUT

The scenic lookout that comes up shortly after the 14-mile marker offers a view deep into Hanapepe Valley. The red clay walls of the cliffs are topped by bright green cane like a sugar frosting.

The same Robinson family that owns the island of Niihau also has substantial landholdings in these parts, including a hideaway estate deep in Hanapepe Valley.

While old king sugar may dominate the scene surrounding Hanapepe Valley, if you glance toward the opposite side of the road from the lookout, you'll see Kauai's newest commercial crop – coffee trees.

KAUAI

ELEELE, NUMILA & PORT ALLEN

Eleele is largely a residential area of limited interest to visitors. It does have a shopping center at the 16-mile marker with a Big Save supermarket, bank, post office, coin laundry, a McDonald's and a pretty good Thai restaurant.

Hwy 540 is an alternate route that leads off Hwy 50 just after Kalaheo and connects back to Hwy 50 at Eleele. It passes through fields of coffee trees and swings by Numila, a former cane town with tin-roof wooden houses surrounding a defunct sugar mill. On Hwy 540, at the southwest edge of Numila, the **Kauai Coffee Company** has a little visitor center, open from 9 am to 5 pm daily, with simple displays on the company's operations, a gift shop and free samples of their brews.

Port Allen, immediately south of Eleele on Hanapepe Bay, is both a commercial harbor and one of Kauai's busiest recreational boat harbors. The state-run small craft harbor here is protected by breakwaters and has launch ramps, berthing and mooring spaces.

Glass Beach

Glass Beach, just east of Port Allen, is a cove piled high with colorful bits of glass that have been worn into smooth pebblelike pieces. The glass comes from a long abandoned dump site nearby, and its weathering is the result of decades of wave action. At certain times of the year, the glass is deep enough to scoop up by the handful, while at other times it's largely washed out to sea.

To get to the little cove, take the last left before entering the Port Allen commercial harbor, go past the fuel storage tanks and then curve to the right down a rutted dirt road that leads 100 yards to the beach.

HANAPEPE

Before Hurricane Iniki hit, Hanapepe was one of the best-preserved historic towns in Hawaii. Parts of the popular TV miniseries *The Thorn Birds* were filmed here because Hanapepe bore such a close resemblance to the dusty Australian outback of days past.

While the hurricane wreaked havoc on the town's old wooden buildings, claiming about half of them, Hanapepe still has lots of character and a nice unhurried pace that invites lingering.

Hanapepe Rd, the town's main street, retains a decidedly period face, with small local stores and several **art galleries**. Two of the more interesting are Koa Wood Gallery, which occupies the former bowling alley and specializes in wood crafts, and Kauai Fine Arts, which has a collection of antique maps and prints, including some works related to Captain Cook's explorations.

Be sure to take a stroll over the swinging bridge, which crosses the Hanapepe River; the path begins opposite the Koa Wood Gallery. Its funky old predecessor fell victim to Iniki, but in a community-wide effort this new bridge was erected in 1996.

The turnoff into Hanapepe is marked by a sign on Hwy 50.

Salt Pond Beach Park

Kauai has long been known for its *alae* salt, a sea salt with a red tint that comes from adding a bit of iron-rich earth. The salt is made by letting seawater into shallow basins called salt pans and allowing it to evaporate. When dry, the salt crystals are scraped off. Native Hawaiians still make salt this way down on the coast south of Hanapepe.

Salt Pond Beach Park is just beyond the salt ponds. It has a sandy beach, campsites, covered picnic tables, barbecue grills, a pay phone, showers and a lifeguard on duty daily. Water in the cove gets up to 10 feet deep and is good for swimming laps – four times across equals half a mile. Both ends of the cove are shallow and good for kids.

For information on obtaining a permit to camp, see Camping in the Accommodations section, near the beginning of this chapter.

To get to Salt Pond Beach Park, turn left just past the 17-mile marker onto Lele Rd, then right onto Lokokai Rd; the beach is about a mile from the highway.

Places to Eat

Hanapepe Cafe (☎ 335-5011), in the town center on Hanapepe Rd, is a good cafe-style restaurant specializing in vegetarian fare. Breakfast, served from 8 to 11 am, includes multigrain pancakes or waffles topped with macnuts and real maple syrup for $5.25, as well as scones and pastries made on site. Lunch, from 11 am to 2 pm, includes garden burgers, sandwiches, and a pasta special or baked frittata served with a Caesar salad – all for under $8. Dinner is available from 6 to 9 pm Wednesday to Saturday only (reservations suggested) and features creative pasta meals priced from $16 to $19, accompanied by a slack key guitarist. The restaurant is closed on Sunday and Monday.

There are also several places to eat on Hwy 50, the most interesting being the new *Camp House Grill & Cantina* (☎ *335-5656*), which has good burgers and sandwiches for around $5, reasonably priced breakfast fare, and Mexican food either à la carte (fish tacos for $4) or full meals such as *chiles rellenos* with rice and beans for $13. The Camp House Grill is open 6:30 am to 9 pm daily.

OLOKELE

Olokele exists only for the Olokele Sugar Company. Of the company's 220 employees, mostly field laborers, 200 live in Olokele.

The road to the sugar mill, which comes up immediately after the 19-mile marker, is shaded by tall trees and lined with classic, century-old lampposts. Taking this short drive offers a glimpse into real plantation life. Everything is covered with a layer of red dust from the surrounding sugarcane fields and mill. Rather than fight it, many of the houses are painted in beige-red tones.

MAKAWELI

Makaweli is headquarters for Gay & Robinson, Niihau Ranch and Niihau Helicopters, all enterprises of the Robinson family, the owners of Niihau. Quite a few native Niihauans live in this area, many of them working for the Robinsons. Once or twice a week, an old military landing craft makes the 17-mile trip between Niihau and Makaweli Landing.

RUSSIAN FORT ELIZABETH

The remains of Russian Fort Elizabeth stand above the east bank of the Waimea River. Hawaiian laborers started building the fort in 1816 under the direction of Georg Anton Schaeffer, a representative of the Russian-American Company. The alliance between the Russians and Kauai's King Kaumualii proved to be a short-lived one, and the Russians were tossed out in 1817, the same year the fort was completed.

You can take a short walk through this curious period of Kauai's history. The most intact part of the fort is the exterior lava-rock wall, which is 8 to 10 feet high in places and largely overgrown with scrub and colorful wildflowers. The seaward side was designed like the points of a star, but it takes close observation to appreciate the effect.

The fort, which is under state jurisdiction, has a good view of the western bank of the Waimea River, where Captain Cook landed. Bear right down the dirt road that continues past the parking lot and you'll find a vantage point above the river mouth with a view of Waimea Pier and the island of Niihau. There are rest rooms and a pay phone in the parking lot.

WAIMEA

Waimea (which means 'reddish water') was the site of an ancient Hawaiian settlement. It was at Waimea, on January 19, 1778, that Captain Cook first came ashore on the Hawaiian Islands. In 1820, the first wave of missionaries to Hawaii also selected Waimea as a landing site. In 1884, Waimea Sugar moved in, and Waimea developed into a plantation town. The old sugar mill, now abandoned, sits along the highway on the west side of town.

Today, Waimea remains the biggest town on this side of the island. It has a number of small wooden buildings, some with false fronts. The dominant building by the square is the First Hawaiian Bank, built in 1929 in neoclassical style.

If you're on your way to Waimea Canyon or out to the coastal beaches, it probably doesn't make sense to give Waimea too much time. Most people just stop to eat and then move on.

Waimea Canyon Drive (Hwy 550) heads north from town to Kokee State Park.

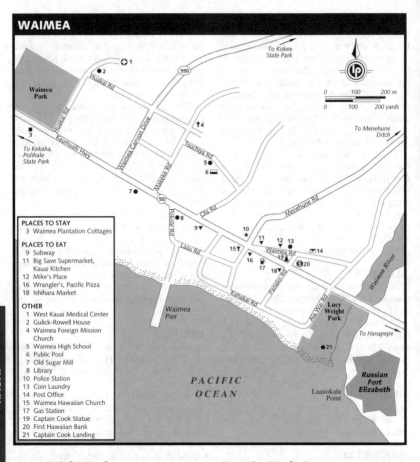

WAIMEA

To Kokee
State Park

550

Waimea
Park

Huakai Rd

To Menehune
Ditch

Waimea Canyon Drive

Huakai Rd

Kaumualii Hwy

To Kekaha,
Polihale
State Park

Tsuchya Rd

Makeke Rd

Olia Rd

Menehune Rd

50

Pokole Rd

Waimea River

PLACES TO STAY
3 Waimea Plantation Cottages

PLACES TO EAT
9 Subway
11 Big Save Supermarket,
    Kauai Kitchen
12 Mike's Place
16 Wrangler's, Pacific Pizza
18 Ishihara Market

OTHER
1 West Kauai Medical Center
2 Gulick-Rowell House
4 Waimea Foreign Mission
   Church
5 Waimea High School
6 Public Pool
7 Old Sugar Mill
8 Library
10 Police Station
13 Coin Laundry
14 Post Office
15 Waimea Hawaiian Church
17 Gas Station
19 Captain Cook Statue
20 First Hawaiian Bank
21 Captain Cook Landing

Laau Rd

Waimea Rd

Panako Rd

Kahakai Rd

Ala Wai Rd

Waimea
Pier

Lucy
Wright
Park

To Hanapepe

*PACIFIC
OCEAN*

Laauokala
Point

*Russian
Fort
Elizabeth*

KAUAI

Lucy Wright Park

The Cook landing site is noted with a simple plaque on a nondescript rock on the western side of the Waimea River. The plaque is on the beach at Lucy Wright Park, on Ala Wai Rd, as soon as you cross the Waimea Bridge. This county park also has a ball field, picnic tables, rest rooms and showers. Camping is allowed on a flat grassy area, but it's at the side of the road in town and doesn't have much appeal. For information on obtaining a permit to camp, see Camping in the Accommodations section, near the beginning of this chapter.

Captain Cook Statue

The statue of Captain Cook in the center of town is a replica of the original statue by Sir John Tweed that stands in Whitby, England. The Pacific's greatest navigator, clutching his charts and all decked out in his finest captain finery, now watches over traffic on Hwy 50.

Waimea Pier

Until Port Allen was built, Waimea served as the region's main harbor. It was a major port of call for whalers and traders during the mid-19th century, and plantations started exporting sugar from Waimea later on in the century.

Waimea Pier, off Pokole Rd, is now used primarily for pole fishing, crabbing and picnicking.

Waimea Churches

The **Waimea Foreign Mission Church**, at the corner of Huakai and Makeke Rds, was originally a thatched structure built in 1826 by the Reverend Samuel Whitney, the first missionary to Waimea. Whitney and his wife are buried in the churchyard. The present church was built of sandstone blocks and coral mortar in 1858 by another missionary, the Reverend George Rowell.

In 1865, Reverend Rowell had a spat with some folks in the congregation and went off and built the **Waimea Hawaiian Church**, on Hwy 50, a wooden frame church that was downed in the 1992 hurricane but has since been rebuilt.

It was Rowell who finished building the **Gulick-Rowell House**, at the end of Huakai Rd. Construction began in 1829, making it the oldest house still standing in Kauai. The two-story stone-block house is now privately owned and not open to the public.

Menehune Ditch

The Menehune Ditch is a stone and earthen aqueduct constructed prior to Western contact. Kauai's legendary little people, the menehune, are said to have built the ditch in one night. The ditch was an engineering masterpiece, with rocks carefully squared and joined to create a watertight seal.

When Captain Vancouver visited Waimea at the close of the 18th century, he walked up the river valley atop the wall of this ditch, which also served as a footpath. He estimated the walls to be a full 24 feet high. These days most of the ancient waterway lies buried beneath the road, but one section about 2 feet high can still be seen. Even today, the ditch continues to divert water from the Waimea River along, and through, the cliff to irrigate the taro patches below.

To get there, turn at the police station onto Menehune Rd and go about 1⅓ miles

up the Waimea River. The ditch is along the left side of the road after a very small parking area.

On the drive up to the ditch, notice the scattered holes in the cliffs to the left. These are Hawaiian burial caves. One group of seven caves behind the Waimea Shingon Mission was explored by Wendell Bennett of the Bishop Museum in the 1920s. At that time, each of the caves held a number of skeletal remains, some in canoe-shaped coffins and others in hollowed-out logs.

Places to Stay & Eat

Waimea Plantation Cottages (☎ 338-1625, 800-992-4632, fax 338-2338, 9600 Kaumualii Hwy, Waimea, HI 96796) is a collection of nearly 50 plantation workers' homes that date to the early 1900s. The wooden cottages, which are clustered around a coconut grove, are cutesy-rustic right down to their tin-roof porches. They've been thoroughly restored and pleasantly furnished with appropriately simple decor. Rates are pricey, ranging from $195 for a one-bedroom cottage that sleeps two to $295 for a three-bedroom cottage that can sleep five.

Wrangler's, in the center of Waimea on Hwy 50, has a varied menu and average food. At lunch, which is available weekdays until 5 pm, you can get a chicken dish, an enchilada or a burger for $6.75, each accompanied with selections from a simple soup and salad bar. Dinner, served from 5 to 9 pm Monday to Saturday, features steaks for around $17. Adjacent to Wrangler's is **Pacific Pizza**, which has calzones and sandwiches starting at around $5 and pizzas for double that. Pacific Pizza is open 11 am to 9 pm daily.

Kauai Kitchen, inside the Big Save supermarket on Waimea Rd, has standard plate lunches for $6. The best grocery store, however, is **Ishihara Market**, on Hwy 50 at Panako Rd, which has a nice deli selling inexpensive takeout sushi, green salads and a delicious somen salad ($4); it's open from 6 am (7 am on weekends) to 8:30 pm daily.

Early risers looking for a caffeine fix can find it at **Mike's Place**, on Waimea Rd in the center of town. This little coffee shop opens at 5 am on weekdays and 7 am on weekends. There's a **Subway** sandwich shop on Hwy 50 on the west side of town.

The new **Waimea Brewing Co**, at Waimea Plantation Cottages, lays claim to being the westernmost microbrewery in the USA. The flagship drink at this popular open-air brewpub is Waialeale Ale, a light golden brew with a slightly dry character, but there are always a couple of seasonal ales as well. You can get a 16oz mug for $3.25 or a taster of four different brews for $5. The pub menu features salads, sandwiches, noodle soups and snacks such as quesadillas or fried calamari for around $6 to $8. The Waimea Brewing Co is open 11 am to 11 pm daily.

KEKAHA

Kekaha has great beaches, or rather it has one long glorious stretch. Hwy 50 follows the beach for about 2 miles, with roadside parking all along the way. This is open ocean, and when the surf is high there can be dangerous currents; when there's no swell, you can usually find swimmers here. Niihau and its offshore island, Lehua, are visible from the beach.

There's a very inconspicuous shower just inland from the highway between Alae Rd and Amakihi Rd; rest rooms and picnic tables are nearby.

A few blocks inland from the beach is Kekaha Rd, the main village street, which runs parallel to the highway. It has a grocery store, a post office and the last gas station before the end of the road. The village's most dominant feature is its working sugar mill, which is visible from the highway.

On its eastern end, Kekaha Rd comes out to Hwy 50 near the Kikiaola Small Boat Harbor. This state harbor has one launch ramp and eight mooring spaces.

Kekaha is Kauai's westernmost town, and as you continue on toward Polihale, it's a rural scene, with the inland cliffs getting higher and the ravines deeper. Corn and sunflowers, which are planted for seed production, grow in fields along the road. Cattle and cattle egrets feed in the pastures.

Places to Stay & Eat

Mindy's (☎ 337-9275, mindys@hgea.org, 8842 Kekaha Rd, PO Box 861, Kekaha, HI 96796) is the only accommodations alternative beyond Waimea (other than camping) and would make a good base for exploring Kokee and the southwest coast. Mindy and Dave Heri rent a pleasant 2nd-story apartment above their home, with a large deck, a full kitchen and a living room with a double sofa bed. The bedroom has a double bed and a cane-field view. The place is modern and comfortable, with ceiling fans throughout, TV, phone, radio and a shower/tub combination in the bathroom. The rate is $55 for one person, $5 for each additional person up to four; add $10 more if you're staying for just one night. Complimentary fruit and coffee are provided.

On Kekaha Rd at the base of Hwy 552, there's a small center with a **Menehune Food Mart**, which has limited groceries, wrapped sandwiches and only a few simple hot items, and **Waimea Canyon Snack Shop**, which sells Lappert's ice cream, chili with rice, and hot dogs.

BARKING SANDS

Barking Sands Pacific Missile Range Facility, a US Navy base, usually has at least one stretch of its beach open to the public. For a recorded message on current access, dial ☎ 335-4229.

The road in is at the 'Pacific Missile Range Facility' sign, less than half a mile after the 32-mile marker. At the gate, military personnel will ask to see your driver's license and then explain where you can go, which is usually the beach about 2 miles south of the gate; locals call this beach **Majors Bay** and the military refers to it as RecArea No 3.

This broad, curving sweep of fine golden sand is a good sunbathing and walking beach, though it's open and hot. The scrub brush behind the beach offers no shade, but it hardly matters, as the vegetation line is the DMZ line and you're forbidden to go beyond it anyway.

In winter, Majors Bay is a popular surfing spot, although as with all West Side beaches, the waters can be dangerous. There are no facilities. The purple-tinged island of Niihau can be seen on the horizon.

On very sunny days, when the wind is blowing off the water just right, the moving sands make sounds similar to barking dogs – hence, the area's name.

The missile range facility at Barking Sands provides the above-ground link to a sophisticated sonar network that tracks more than 1000 sq miles of the Pacific. Established during WWII, it's been developed into the world's largest underwater listening device. The equipment is sensitive enough to pick up the songs of wintering humpback whales, and the base has gathered the most comprehensive collection of humpback whale soundtracks ever recorded.

POLIHALE STATE PARK

Polihale is near-desert. When it's raining everywhere else, beachgoers head this way.

The beautiful long white-sand beach here is washed with aqua-colored water that often comes to shore in huge explosive waves. Expert surfers occasionally give Polihale a try, but strong rip currents make the waters treacherous for swimming.

Polihale State Park is about 5 miles from the Barking Sands military base. Turn left three-quarters of a mile north of the base entrance onto a wide dirt road that passes through sugarcane fields. The road is a bit bumpy but passable. Set your odometer at zero here.

After 3⅓ miles, at a large spreading tree in the middle of the road, a turnoff leads to the only safe swimming spot in the area. To get there, turn left at the tree, and then after a quarter mile, follow the road up the hill to the right to the base of the dunes. Walk a couple of minutes to the north along the beach and you'll come to **Queen's Pond**, where a large semicircle of reef comes almost to shore, creating a protected swimming pool. When the seas are relatively calm, the reef blocks the ocean currents. But when surf breaks over the reef and into the pool, a dangerous rip current runs toward an opening at the southern end of the reef. The rest of the beach is bordered by open sea.

To get to the state park facilities, go back to the tree at the main cane road, turn left and continue another mile. A turnoff on the left leads to a camping area with rest rooms, outdoor showers, drinking water and a picnic pavilion. Farther down, other camping areas are in the dunes just above the beach amid thorny kiawe trees. For information on obtaining a permit to camp, see Camping in the Accommodations section, earlier in this chapter.

At the very end of the beach is Polihale Cliff, marking the western end of the Na Pali Coast. Combined with the untamed ocean and vast expansive beach, it's a magnificent sight. Sunsets here can be a meditative experience.

There's a terraced **heiau** toward the base of the cliff. It was originally on the beach, but over the years ever-shifting sands have added a 300-foot buffer between the heiau and the sea. The heiau is so overgrown that even after you tramp into the brush and find it, it's really hard to get a perspective on it. Wasps are another obstacle – if you're allergic to stings, forget about exploring this one.

WAIMEA CANYON

Waimea Canyon is nicknamed the 'Grand Canyon of the Pacific.' This may sound like promotional hype, but it's not a bad description. Although it's smaller and 200 million years younger than the famous Arizona canyon, Waimea Canyon is certainly grand.

The canyon's colorful river-cut gorge is 2785 feet deep. The river that runs through it, the Waimea-Poomau, is 19½ miles long, Kauai's longest. All in all, it seems incredible that such an immense canyon could be tucked inside such a small island.

The view of the canyon is usually a bit hazy. The best time to be there is a sunny day after it's been raining heavily – at such times, the earth's a deeper red and waterfalls cascade throughout the canyon, providing unbeatable scenery.

Waimea Canyon Drive

Waimea Canyon Drive (Hwy 550) starts in downtown Waimea. The road is 19 miles long, ending at lookouts with terrific views into Kalalau Valley on the Na Pali Coast.

The views start about a mile up from Waimea and get better and better as the road climbs. There are plenty of little scenic lookouts where you can stop to take it all in. The one at 1¾ miles looks down on the Waimea River and the taro patches that are irrigated by the Menehune Ditch. About 2½ miles up, there are good views across cane fields to Kekaha Beach with Niihau in the background. From there on, it's all canyon views.

WAIMEA CANYON STATE PARK

The southern boundary of Waimea Canyon State Park is about 6 miles up the road. Waimea Canyon Drive and Kokee Rd merge nearby. Kokee Rd (Hwy 552), which climbs up from Kekaha, also has scenic views, but not of the canyon.

Iliau Nature Loop

The marked trailhead for the Iliau Nature Loop comes up shortly before the 9-mile marker. (This is also the trailhead for the longer Kukui Trail, described in the following Waimea Canyon Trails section.) Near the start of the trail, there's a bench with a scenic view, though for the best angle, take a two-minute walk to the left, where you'll be rewarded with a top-notch vista into Waimea Canyon. After heavy rainfall, waterfalls explode down the sheer rock walls across the gorge.

Iliau Loop takes only about 10 minutes to walk. The trail is named for the *iliau*, a plant endemic to the West Side of Kauai, which grows along the trail and produces stalks up to 10 feet high. Like its cousin the silversword, iliau grows to a ripe old age. Then for a grand finale it bursts open with blossoms and dies.

Scenic Lookouts

The most scenic of the lookout points along this stretch, **Waimea Canyon Lookout** is clearly signposted a third of a mile north of the 10-mile marker. The lookout offers a sweeping view of Waimea Canyon from a perch of 3400 feet. The prominent canyon running in an easterly direction off Waimea

is Koaie Canyon, which is accessible to back-country hikers.

As you continue up the road, the 800-foot **Waipoo Falls** can be seen from a couple of small unmarked lookouts before the 12-mile marker and then from a lookout opposite the picnic area shortly before the 13-mile marker. The picnic area has barbecue pits, rest rooms, drinking water, a pay phone and Camp Hale Koa, a Seventh Day Adventist camp.

Puu Hinahina Lookout, at 3640 feet, is at a marked turnoff between the 13- and 14-mile markers. There are two lookouts close to the parking lot. One has a fine view down Waimea Canyon clear out to the coast, while the other has a view of Niihau.

Waimea Canyon Trails

For serious hikers, there are trails that lead deep into Waimea Canyon. The trailhead for the **Kukui Trail** is shortly before the 9-mile marker. This trail continues from the Iliau Nature Loop at a sign-in box. From there, the Kukui Trail makes a steep 2000-foot descent down the western side of Waimea Canyon, 2½ miles to the Waimea River. Wiliwili Camp is at the end of the trail.

The **Koaie Canyon Trail** begins at Kaluahaulu Camp, half a mile up the Waimea River from the end of the Kukui Trail. From there, it runs east for 3 miles along the southern side of Koaie Canyon. If you'd like to cool off, there are some good swimming holes in the stream along the way and at the end of the trail. This trail should be avoided during stormy weather due to the danger of flash flooding.

The canyon's fertile soil once supported an ancient Hawaiian settlement, and the long-abandoned remains of a heiau and some house sites are still discernible. The Koaie Canyon Trail passes Hipalau Camp and ends at Lonomea Camp.

All four camps on these trails are part of the forest reserve system. Although they have simple open-air shelters, there are no facilities, and the stream water needs to be treated before drinking. For information on permits, see Camping under Accommodations, near the beginning of this chapter.

A third trail in this area is the 8-mile **Waimea Canyon Trail**, which runs south from Wiliwili Camp to the town of Waimea, ending on Menehune Rd. Much of the trail is along a 4WD road that leads to a hydro-electric power station. While there's public access along the route, the trail passes over private property, so no camping is allowed. There are a number of river crossings, making the trail best considered only during periods of dry weather.

During weekends and holidays, all of these trails are fairly heavily used by pig hunters.

KOKEE STATE PARK

The Kokee State Park boundary starts beyond the Puu Hinahina Lookout. After the 15-mile marker, you'll pass park cabins, Kokee Lodge, a museum and a campground one after the other. Kokee Lodge, incidentally, is not an overnight lodge but a restaurant and the concessionaire station for the nearby cabins.

The ranger station in Kokee hasn't been staffed for years, but the helpful people at the Kokee Museum can provide a little assistance, including basic information on current trail conditions. And outside the museum you'll find an information board and a posted trail map.

Kokee Museum

A good place to learn about Kauai's ecology is the Kokee Museum (☎ 335-9975), which features displays of local flora and fauna, climate and geology, along with detailed topographical maps of the area and a glass case of poi pounders, stone adze heads and other historic artifacts. Quality koa bowls, a good selection of books and inexpensive trail maps are for sale. The museum is open from 10 am to 4 pm daily. Admission is free, though a $1 donation is suggested.

Ask at the museum for the brochure to the short nature trail out back. The brochure, which can be borrowed for free or purchased for $1.50, offers interpretive information corresponding to the trail's numbered plants and trees, many of them native Hawaiian species.

Meadow Spirits

According to legend, Kanalohuluhulu Meadow, opposite Kokee Museum, was once a forested hideout for an evil *akua* (spirit) who enjoyed harassing people passing through on their way to Kalalau Valley. Distraught travelers appealed to the great god Kanaloa to protect them from the akua. Kanaloa responded by ripping out all the trees and declaring that they were never again to grow here, thus destroying the akua's hiding place. These days the meadow is full of good vibes and makes a nice place for kids to play.

By the way, the chickens that congregate in the museum's parking lot are not the common garden variety but moa, or jungle fowl. Early Polynesian settlers brought moa to Hawaii, and they were once common on all the main islands. Now the moa remain solely on Kauai, the only island that's free of the mongoose, an introduced mammal that preys on the eggs of ground-nesting birds.

Kalalau Lookouts

The two Kalalau Valley lookouts at the end of the road are not to be missed.

The first, the **Kalalau Lookout**, is at the 18-mile marker. From a height of 4000 feet, you can look deep into the green depths of the valley and straight out to the sea. When the weather is cooperative, late-afternoon rainbows sweep so deeply into Kalalau Valley that the bottom part of the bows curve back inward. Bright-red *apapane* birds feed from the flowers of the ohia lehua trees near the lookout railings.

Kalalau Valley was once the site of a large settlement and was joined to Kokee by a very steep trail that ran down the cliffs. These days the only way into the valley is along the coastal Kalalau Trail from Haena on the North Shore.

The cone-shaped pinnacles along the valley walls look rather like a row of sentinels standing at attention. One legend says that rain has sculpted the cliffs into the

KAUAI

shapes of the proud chiefs who are buried in the mountains.

The mushroom-shaped white dome and satellite dishes visible on the hill as you walk back to the parking lot are part of the Kokee Air Force station.

The paved road continues another mile to **Puu o Kila Lookout**, but you'll need to follow the road on foot for 15 minutes or so to get there – the road is currently closed to vehicle traffic 100 yards beyond the Kalalau Lookout. This is the last leg of the aborted Kokee-Haena Hwy, which would have linked Kokee with the North Shore, thus creating a circle-island road. One look at the cliffs at the end of the road, and you'll understand why the scheme was scrapped. The Pihea Trail that climbs the ridge straight ahead runs along what was to be the road.

From this lookout, you can enjoy another view into Kalalau Valley and a glance inland toward the Alakai Swamp Preserve. A sign here points to Mt Waialeale, the wettest spot on earth.

Kokee State Park Trails

Kokee State Park is the starting point for about 45 miles of trails, some maintained by the Division of State Parks, others by the Division of Forestry & Wildlife. Pig and goat hunters use some of these trails during the hunting season, so it's a good idea for hikers to wear brightly colored clothing.

Three of the trails – Nualolo, Awaawapuhi and Pihea – offer clifftop views into valleys on the Na Pali Coast. A couple of trails go into the swampy bogs of Alakai Swamp, while others are easy nature trails.

Halemanu Rd Trails Halemanu Rd, the starting point for several scenic hikes, is just north of the 14-mile marker. Whether or not the road is passable in a non-4WD vehicle often depends on whether it's been raining recently. Keep in mind that the clay roads provide no traction when wet, and even if you're able to drive a car in, should it begin to rain, driving out can be another matter!

The first hike is **Cliff Trail**, where a short walk leads to an overlook into Waimea Canyon. From there, you can continue on the **Canyon Trail**, a rather strenuous 1¾ miles one way that follows the canyon rim, passes Waipoo Falls and ends at Kumuwela Lookout with views down the canyon to the ocean beyond. On both trails, there's a good chance of spotting feral goats scrambling along the canyon walls.

A little farther down Halemanu Rd is the start of **Halemanu-Kokee Trail**. This easy 1¼-mile (each way) nature trail passes through a native forest of koa and ohia trees that provide a habitat for native birds, including the *iiwi, apapane, amakihi* and *elepaio*. One of the common plants found on this trail is banana *poka*, a member of the passion fruit family and a serious invasive pest. It has pretty pink flowers, but it drapes the forest with its vines and chokes out less aggressive native plants.

Nualolo & Awaawapuhi Trails The Nualolo and Awaawapuhi Trails each go out to the very edge of sheer cliffs, allowing you to peer down into valleys that are otherwise accessible only by boat. The valley views are extraordinarily beautiful.

The Nualolo and Awaawapuhi Trails connect via the Nualolo Cliff Trail. You can combine the three trails to make a strenuous day hike of about 10 miles. Then you'll have to either hitch a ride or walk an additional 2 miles back down the road to where you started.

Bring plenty of water, as there's none along the way. Edible plants along the trail include blackberries, thimbleberries, guava and passion fruit.

Wild goats, prolific in the North Shore valleys, are readily spotted along the cliff walls. Capable of breeding at five months of age, the goats have no natural predators in Hawaii, and their unchecked numbers have caused a fair amount of ecological damage.

The 3¾-mile Nualolo Trail starts between the cabins and Kokee Lodge. The trail begins in cool upland forest and descends 1500 feet, ending with a fine view from Lolo Vista Point, a lookout on the valley rim. There's a USGS survey marker at the lookout, at an elevation of 2234 feet.

The trailhead for the Awaawapuhi Trail begins at a parking area just after the 17-mile marker. The trail descends 1600 feet, ending after 3¼ miles at a steep and spectacular pali overlooking Awaawapuhi and Nualolo Valleys. The hike starts in an ohia forest. About half a mile down the trail, the forest becomes drier, and koa begins to mix in with the ohia. Awaawapuhi means 'valley of ginger,' and *kahili*, a pretty yellow ginger, can be seen along the way.

The 2-mile Nualolo Cliff Trail is very scenic and offers numerous viewpoints into Nualolo Valley. There's even a picnic table where you can break for lunch. The Nualolo Cliff Trail connects at the Nualolo Trail near the 3¼-mile mark and at the Awaawapuhi Trail a little short of the 3-mile mark.

Kawaikoi Stream Trail This trail begins in between the Sugi Grove and Kawaikoi Campgrounds, off Camp 10-Mohihi Rd. This is a scenic mountain stream trail of about 3 miles roundtrip. It starts out following the southern side of Kawaikoi Stream, then heads away from the stream and makes a loop, coming down the northern side of the stream before reconnecting with the southern side. If the stream is running high, don't make the crossings.

Kawaikoi Stream is popular for rainbow trout fishing, which is allowed during an annual open season in August and September. Fishing licenses are required.

Camp 10-Mohihi Rd is up past the Kokee Museum on the right. Like many of the dirt roads in Kokee, when it's dry, it can accommodate ordinary cars, at least part way. However, on those occasions when the road is really wet and rutted, even 4WD vehicles can have difficulty.

Pihea Trail The Pihea Trail starts from the Puu o Kila Lookout and combines coastal views with an opportunity to see some of the Alakai wilderness. The beginning of the trail was graded in the 1950s, before plans to make this the last leg of the circle-island road were abandoned.

The first mile of the trail runs along the ridge, offering fine views into Kalalau Valley,

before coming to the Pihea Lookout, a view-point that requires a steep scramble to reach. The Pihea Trail then turns inland through wetland forest and, at about 1¾ miles, crosses the Alakai Swamp Trail. If you turn left there, you can continue for about 2 miles through Alakai Swamp to Kilohana Lookout. If you go straight instead, you'll reach the Kawaikoi Campground in about 2 miles.

Alakai Swamp Trail The Alakai Swamp Preserve is inaccessible enough that even invasive plants haven't been able to choke out the endemic swamp vegetation, and native bird species still have a stronghold.

Parts of the swamp receive so little sunlight that moss grows thick and fat on all sides of the trees. Most people that see this swamp see it from a helicopter, but it's possible to walk through a corner of it by taking the Alakai Swamp Trail.

This rough 3½-mile trail starts off Camp 10-Mohihi Rd and goes through rain forest and bogs before reaching Kilohana Lookout, perched on the rim of Wainiha Pali. If it's not overcast – and that's a big 'if' considering this is the wettest place on earth – hikers will be rewarded with a sweeping view of the Wainiha and Hanalei Valleys to the north. While most of the trail has been spanned with boardwalks, this can still be an extremely wet and slippery trail, and in places you can expect to have to slog through mud. It's certainly a trail that's best suited for hiking in the relatively drier summer season.

If your car can't make it down Camp 10-Mohihi Rd, parking near the Kalalau Lookout and approaching the Alakai Swamp Trail via the Pihea Trail is probably your best bet.

Kaluapuhi Trail The Kaluapuhi Trail, a forest trail leading to a plum grove, is about 2 miles long. The trailhead starts at the highway a quarter mile past the 17-mile marker. In midsummer, lots of islanders come to pick the wild plums.

Places to Stay
Camping The most accessible camping area is the Kokee State Park campground, which is north of the meadow, just a few

KAUAI

minutes' walk from Kokee Lodge. The sites are in an uncrowded grassy area beside the woods and have picnic tables, drinking water, rest rooms and showers. Camping is free and allowed for up to five nights, but state camping permits must be obtained before arriving in Kokee.

If you want to go farther off the main track, Kawaikoi and Sugi Grove Campgrounds are about 4 miles east of Kokee Lodge, off the 4WD Camp 10-Mohihi Rd in the forest reserve adjacent to the state park. Each campground has pit toilets, picnic shelters and fire pits. You'll need to carry in your own water or treat the stream water before drinking it. These forest reserve campgrounds have a three-night maximum stay and also require obtaining camping permits in advance.

The Kokee area campgrounds are at an elevation of almost 4000 feet, and nights are crisp and cool. This is sleeping-bag-and-warm-clothing country.

For more information on camping permits, see Camping in the Accommodations section, near the beginning of this chapter.

Lodges *Kokee Lodge* (☎ 335-6061, PO Box 819, Waimea, HI 96796) manages the 12 cabins in Kokee State Park. The oldest cabins are a little tired and have just one large room but are a bargain at $35. Newer and spiffier are the two-bedroom cedar cabins for $45. Every cabin, old and new, has one double and four twin beds and a kitchen equipped with a refrigerator and oven, as well as linens, blankets, a hot-water shower, and a woodstove that can be fired up on cool evenings. One of the cedar cabins, No 2 Lehua, is particularly comfortable and has a wheelchair ramp. State park rules limit stays

to five days. The cabins are often booked up well in advance, but cancellations do occur, and you can occasionally get a cabin at the last moment if you're flexible.

The YWCA's *Camp Sloggett* in Kokee State Park has a lodge that sleeps 10 people, a hostel-style bunkhouse that holds 40 and a cement slab platform for tent camping. A bed in the bunkhouse costs $20; guests must provide their own bedding and towels, but there's a kitchenette and bathrooms with hot showers. Tent campers, who pay $10 per person, have a barbecue pit for cooking and use of the showers and toilets in the bunkhouse. For the bunkhouse and tent sites, call the caretaker (☎ 335-6060) to check availability. The lodge is rented to only one group at a time; the per-person rate is the same as the bunkhouse, with a minimum charge of five people on weekdays and eight people on weekends. Bookings for the lodge are made through the *YWCA* (☎ 245-5959, 3094 Elua St, Lihue, HI 96766). Camp Sloggett is about half a mile east of the park museum down a rutted dirt road that's usually passable in an ordinary car.

Places to Eat
Kokee Lodge is the only place to eat north of Waimea. Open from 9 am to 3:30 pm daily, the restaurant serves Portuguese bean soup, quiche, chili, salads and sandwiches for $7 or less and lilikoi pie for $3.50. If you're only hungry for a snack, the gift shop in front of the restaurant sells candy bars and soft drinks; it's open till 4 pm.

If you're staying in the cabins or campgrounds, be sure to bring ample provisions, as the nearest stores (and gas station) are in Waimea, 15 miles away.

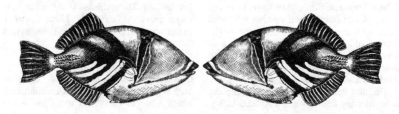

Niihau

Niihau has long been closed to outsiders, thereby earning itself the nickname 'The Forbidden Island.'

No other place in Hawaii has more successfully turned its back on change than Niihau. There are no paved roads, no airport, no island-wide electricity and no telephones.

Niihau is a native Hawaiian preserve and is the only island in the state where the primary language is still Hawaiian. The entire island, right down to the church, belongs to the Niihau Ranch, which is privately owned by the non-Hawaiian Robinson family. The Robinsons are highly protective of Niihau's isolation.

Most of Niihau's 190 residents live in Puuwai, a settlement on the dry western coast. Each house in the village is surrounded by a

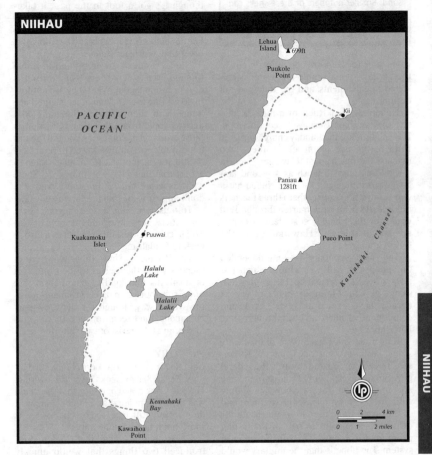

NIIHAU

Lehua Island

▲ 699ft

Puukole Point

Kii

PACIFIC OCEAN

Paniau ▲ 1281ft

Kuakamoku Islet

Puuwai

Pueo Point

Halulu Lake

Halalii Lake

Kaulakahi Channel

Keanahaki Bay

Kawaihoa Point

0   2   4 km
0   1   2 miles

Niihau Shell Leis

Niihauans create fine handcrafted necklaces made of tiny seashells painstakingly strung in spiral strands and intricate patterns. These Niihau shell leis are Hawaii's most highly prized – and priced – leis. They are sold in fine jewelry shops and craft galleries on the other islands, some for well over $1000.

The shells used in the necklaces come mainly from beaches on Niihau, where they're collected by sifting through the sand. Smaller numbers of these shells can also be found on Kauai.

stone wall to keep grazing animals out of the gardens. It's a simple life; water is collected in catchments, and the toilets are in outhouses.

Niihauans speak their own melodic dialect of Hawaiian. Business is conducted in Hawaiian, as are the Sunday church services. Both of the two Robinson brothers who manage the ranch speak Hawaiian fluently.

Children learn English as a second language when they go to school. Niihau has a two-room schoolhouse where three teachers hold classes from kindergarten through 12th grade for the island's 55 students. Courses are taught solely in Hawaiian up to the fourth grade.

The island economy has long depended on sheep and cattle ranching, which has always been a marginal operation on windswept Niihau. Major droughts in recent decades have taken a toll on the herds, and consequently Niihau has been through some hard times.

Ranch activities have been dramatically scaled back in recent years, and the Robinsons have been looking towards the federal government as a potential source of income and employment. They are now negotiating with the US Navy to lease the southern end of the island to be used as a launch site for drone target missiles, as part of the testing program for a new US ballistic defense system. The hope is that the military would

be such a secretive tenant that it wouldn't interfere with the rest of Niihau's affairs.

Niihau is 17 miles from Kauai and is connected by a weekly supply boat that travels between the two islands. The boat, an old WWII military landing craft, docks in Kauai at Makaweli, headquarters of Niihau Ranch and the Robinson family. Makaweli is also home to a settlement of Niihauans who prefer to live on Kauai, though many of them still work for the Robinsons.

Niihau is by no means a living-history museum of Hawaiians stuck in time. Although it's got a foot in the past, it takes what it wants from the present. The supply boat brings soda as well as *poi* (a staple Hawaiian food), and the island has more dirt bikes than outrigger canoes.

Niihau residents are free to go to Kauai to shop, have a few beers (Niihau itself is dry) or just hang out. What they are not free to do is bring friends from other islands back home with them. Those Niihauans who marry people from other islands, as well as those whom the Robinsons come to see as undesirable, are rarely allowed to return.

Still, for the most part, Niihauans seem to accept that that's the way things are. Some who leave are critical, but those who stay don't appear to be looking for any changes.

To outsiders, Niihau is an enigma. Some romanticize it as a pristine preserve of Hawaiian culture, while others see it as a throwback to feudalism.

The Robinsons view Niihau as a private sanctuary and themselves as the protectors of it all. It's that kind of paternalism that often rubs outside native Hawaiian groups the wrong way, though for the most part Niihauans don't seem to share those sentiments, and they resist outside interference.

HISTORY

Captain Cook anchored off Niihau on January 29, 1778, two weeks after 'discovering' Hawaii. Cook noted in his log that the island was lightly populated and largely barren, a description still true today. His visit was short, but it had a lasting impact.

It was on little Niihau that Cook first introduced two things that would quickly

NIIHAU

change the face of Hawaii. He left two goats, the first of the grazing animals that would devastate the native flora and fauna. And his men introduced syphilis, the first of the Western diseases that would decimate the Hawaiian people.

In 1864, Elizabeth Sinclair, a Scottish widow who was moving from New Zealand to Vancouver when she got sidetracked in Hawaii, bought Niihau from King Kamehameha V for $10,000 in gold. He originally tried to sell her the 'swampland' of Waikiki, but she passed it up for the 'desert island.' Interestingly, no two places in Hawaii today could be further apart, either culturally or in land value.

Mrs Sinclair brought the first sheep to Niihau from New Zealand and started the ranching operation that her great-grandsons continue today.

GEOGRAPHY
Niihau is the smallest of the inhabited Hawaiian Islands. It is 18 miles long and 6 miles wide, with a total area of 70 sq miles. It has 45 miles of coast, and the highest elevation is 1281 feet, at Paniau. The island is semi-arid, in the lee of Kauai.

Niihau's 860-acre Halalii Lake is the largest in Hawaii, though even during the rainy winter season, it's only a few feet deep. In the summer, it sometimes dries up to a mud pond. About 50% of Hawaii's endangered coots breed on Niihau – when there's enough water.

GETTING THERE & AWAY
Although outsiders are not allowed to visit Niihau, the Robinsons have 'opened up' the island – at least to a degree – via expensive helicopter flights.

Niihau Helicopters (☎ 335-3500), Box 370, Makaweli, HI 96769, has no set schedule; tours should be arranged well in advance. The tours, which last about three hours and take off from Port Allen Airport in Kauai, cost $250 per person. The helicopter generally makes one of two stops, either at Puukole Point on the northern end of the island, or at Keanahaki Bay, on the southern end of the island, where Captain Cook landed. The pilot flies over much of Niihau but avoids Puuwai village, where people live.

The helicopter was purchased for emergency medical evacuations, and the tours are given in an effort to defray the cost.

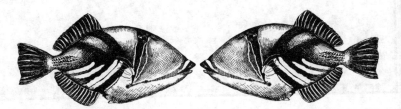

Northwestern Hawaiian Islands

The Northwestern Hawaiian Islands, also called the Leeward Islands, stretch from Kauai nearly 1300 miles across the Pacific in an almost straight northwesterly line.

Volcanic in origin, the islands once jutted up high above sea level as the main Hawaiian Islands do now. However, they are slowly slipping back into the sea as a result of a sagging of the ocean floor and the ongoing forces of erosion. Where the mountains once raised their heads, coral reefs now appear like flower *leis* (garlands) left floating on the water.

There are 10 island clusters in all. Together, the clusters encompass 33 islands, all of which are small. They include atolls, each with a number of low sand islands formed on top of coral reefs, as well as some single-rock islands and a reef that is mostly submerged.

Listed from east to west, the clusters are Nihoa Island, Necker Island, French Frigate Shoals, Gardner Pinnacles, Maro Reef, Laysan Island, Lisianski Island, Pearl and Hermes Atoll, Midway Islands and Kure Atoll.

The total land area of all the Northwestern Hawaiian Islands together is just under 5 sq miles, though the atoll lagoon areas add up to a hundred times that.

All the islands except Kure Atoll (a state seabird sanctuary) and the Midway Islands are part of the Hawaiian Islands National Wildlife Refuge. Established in 1909 by US President Theodore Roosevelt, it is the oldest and largest of the national wildlife refuges. In 1988, the Midway group was given

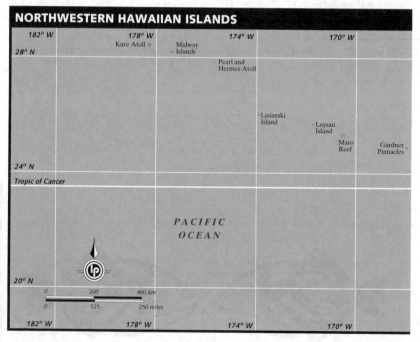

NORTHWESTERN HAWAIIAN ISLANDS

Kure Atoll
Midway Islands
Pearl and Hermes Atoll
Lisianski Island
Laysan Island
Maro Reef
Gardner Pinnacles

PACIFIC OCEAN

Tropic of Cancer

182° W · 178° W · 174° W · 170° W
28° N · 24° N · 20° N

0 · 200 · 400 km
0 · 125 · 250 miles

a separate refuge status as the Midway Atoll National Wildlife Refuge.

With the exception of Midway, visitors are not allowed on the Northwestern Hawaiian Islands unless they have permits, and these are granted only in the rarest of circumstances. Human activities are simply too disturbing to the fragile ecosystem. The only human habitation in the Hawaiian Islands National Wildlife Refuge is at Tern Island, and that is for wildlife researchers.

The Northwestern Hawaiian Islands come under the political, though not the practical, jurisdiction of the City & County of Honolulu.

FAUNA
The Northwestern Hawaiian Islands are home to around 15 million seabirds, all of which find room for at least a foothold. Endangered Hawaiian monk seals, green sea turtles and four endemic land birds also live there.

Seabirds
Eighteen seabird species nest on these islands, feeding on the abundant fish that live around the submerged reefs. The avian population includes frigate birds, boobies, albatrosses, terns, shearwaters, petrels, tropicbirds and noddies.

The sooty terns are the most abundant, numbering several million. These screeching black-and-white birds also nest on the offshore islets of Oahu's windward coast.

Shearwaters and petrels lay their eggs in burrows that the birds dig in the sandy soil. The roofs of the burrows can easily collapse under the feet of unobservant walkers, which is one reason why visitors are discouraged.

Land Birds
The Laysan duck, Laysan finch, Nihoa finch and Nihoa millerbird, endemic to Laysan and Nihoa Islands respectively, are all listed as endangered or threatened species.

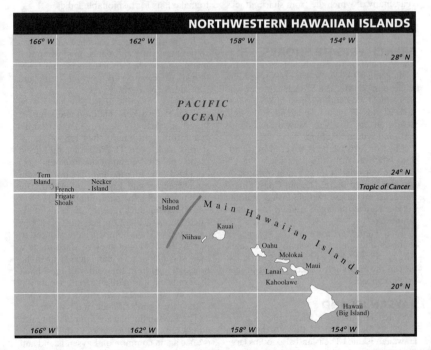

NORTHWESTERN HAWAIIAN ISLANDS

This is not because their numbers are declining, but because these species exist in only one place on earth and are therefore susceptible to the introduction of new diseases and predators or the disruption of their habitat. One rat from a shipwrecked boat, weed seed from a hiker's boot or an oil slick washing ashore could mean the end of the species.

Monk Seals

The endangered Hawaiian monk seal, which exists only in Hawaii, uses Kure Atoll, the French Frigate Shoals and Laysan, Lisianski, Nihoa and Necker Islands for its pupping grounds. The seals are easily disturbed by human contact.

In the 19th century, the seals were hunted nearly to extinction. Military operations in the area during and after WWII also resulted in a decline.

Fewer than 200 seal pups are born each year, many of which die from shark attacks. The total species population is estimated to be about 1300.

FRENCH FRIGATE SHOALS

The French Frigate Shoals consist of 13 sand islands and a 135-foot rock, La Perouse Pinnacle, named after the French explorer who was almost wrecked on the reef. One of the sand islands, 37-acre Tern Island, is the field headquarters for the Hawaiian Islands National Wildlife Refuge.

Most of Tern Island is covered by an airfield left over from the days when the US Coast Guard had a loran (radio navigation system) station there. The old Coast Guard barracks now house two US Fish & Wildlife Service refuge managers and up to a dozen volunteers.

Tern Island is home to 17 species of seabirds and many Hawaiian monk seals. Ninety percent of the green sea turtles that nest in the Hawaiian Islands nest at French Frigate Shoals.

LAYSAN ISLAND

Despite its small area (1.45 sq miles), Laysan ranks as the biggest of the Northwestern Hawaiian Islands. The island also looms large

as a classic example of how human interference can wreak havoc on island ecology.

Prior to the 19th century, millions of birds lived on Laysan – mostly Laysan albatrosses, otherwise known as gooney birds. From 1890 to 1904, though, human settlers mined Laysan for guano, the phosphate-rich bird droppings used as fertilizer. This endeavor led to the construction of new houses, the introduction of mules (which served as pack animals) and the docking of large ships – all of which compromised the birds' habitat.

In addition to guano mining, people once exploited the island's natural resources by collecting hundreds of thousands of albatross eggs and extracting the albumen, a substance used in photo processing. As each albatross lays just one egg a year, an 'egging' sweep could destroy an entire year's hatch. Hunters also took a toll. In one six-month period alone, 300,000 birds were killed for their feathers, which were used by milliners to make hats for fashionable ladies.

There are now about 160,000 pairs of Laysan albatrosses on the island, still one of the world's largest colonies. Albatrosses sometimes court and dance for five annual mating seasons before actually mating. Once they do mate, pairs stay together for life and sometimes live for 30 years.

Rabbits, introduced to Laysan first as pets for the workers' children and later for breeding, virtually destroyed the island's vegetation, and where they left off sandstorms took over. The loss of native food plants spelled the end of the three endemic land birds: the Laysan flightless rail, Laysan honeycreeper and Laysan millerbird. The rabbits were finally exterminated in 1923.

The Laysan duck reached the brink of extinction as a result of the activities of rabbits and hunters. Their numbers were reduced to just six by 1911, but they've since made a modest comeback. Laysan ducks swim in the brackish lagoon in the center of the island, their only habitat. With a current population of about 300, the Laysan ducks rank as one of the rarest kinds of duck in the world.

The Laysan finch, whose population once numbered only 100 (thanks to the rabbits), is once again common on Laysan Island and has also been introduced to Pearl and Hermes Atoll. Unlike its honeycreeper cousins on the main Hawaiian Islands, which feed on nectar, the Laysan finch has become carnivorous and feeds on seabird eggs, as well as the carcasses of dead seabirds.

More than 1 million sooty terns nest on Laysan.

NECKER & NIHOA

Necker and Nihoa, the two islands closest to the main Hawaiian Islands, were probably settled more than a thousand years ago. Archaeological remains of stone temple platforms, house sites, terraces and carved stone images suggest that the early settlers on these islands were from the Marquesas Islands in French Polynesia.

Necker and Nihoa are not coral atolls but rugged, rocky islands, each less than a quarter of a square mile in area. Nihoa is the tallest of the Northwestern Hawaiian Islands, with sheer sea cliffs and a peak elevation of 910 feet.

Two land bird species live only on tiny Nihoa and nowhere else.

With a population of a few thousand, the Nihoa finch is hanging in there. (Like the Laysan finch, the Nihoa finch is a scavenger that devours other birds' eggs.) In 1967, biologists attempted to develop a backup colony in case something happened to the birds on Nihoa, but the strategy failed when all 42 finches sent to the French Frigate Shoals died.

The gray Nihoa millerbird, related to the Old World warbler family, is rare and secretive. It wasn't even discovered until 1923 and was so named because it eats miller moths. Approximately 400 birds remain.

MIDWAY ISLANDS

The Midway Islands, best known as the site of a pivotal WWII battle between Japanese and American naval forces, is the only place in the Northwestern Hawaiian Islands open to tourism.

Midway, which in the postwar era served as a naval air facility with some 3000 personnel, was one of several military bases targeted for closing at the end of the Cold War.

In 1996, the military transferred jurisdiction of Midway to the US Fish & Wildlife Service and then began an extensive environmental cleanup program to remove contaminants that resulted from the military occupation and to rid Midway of nonnative plants.

When the Fish & Wildlife Service took over the islands, the agency initiated a unique management policy that blends wildlife protection with low-impact tourism. The Fish & Wildlife Service maintains a limited presence on Midway, but a private company handles most of the atoll's operations. This company, Midway Phoenix Corporation, has been granted the right to develop the island for ecotourism purposes and also has a contract to maintain Midway's airfield, which is used for refueling and fisheries-enforcement operations by the US Coast Guard.

Midway Phoenix spent half a million dollars renovating former officers' quarters into hotel rooms and installing a satellite cellular phone system. The atoll is now open to tours geared for naturalists and divers. Access to some of Midway's white-sand beaches is limited in order to minimize disturbance to Hawaiian monk seals, and diving and other activities can only be done with guides.

Because of the environmental impact, no more than 100 visitors are allowed on Midway at any one time. Initial assessments indicate that tourism has not significantly disturbed the wildlife, and the money generated from tourism helps defray the $4 million cost of operating the refuge.

More than a million seabirds nest on Midway, including the world's largest colony of Laysan albatrosses, which are so thick during the months of November through July that they virtually blanket the ground. Fourteen other seabird species pass through Midway, including red-tailed tropicbirds, Bonin petrels, wedge-tailed shearwaters, brown noddies and both grey-backed and sooty terns.

Sand Island, where the facilities lie, is the largest island in the three-island Midway Atoll, measuring about 2 miles in length and a mile across. In addition to its dense colonies of seabirds, Sand Island contains a smattering of early 20th-century relics, including the remains of a transpacific cable station that dates to 1903, as well as WWII-era bunkers and anti-aircraft guns. The surrounding waters harbor coral gardens, unusual tropical fish and schools of spinner dolphins.

Getting There & Away

Most people visit Midway on a guided tour, but the atoll is open to individual travelers as well. Roundtrip airfare on one of the twice weekly flights from Honolulu is $750, and the cheapest room-and-meal plan costs $150 a day. Most flights are aboard a 19-passenger turboprop plane, but occasionally an Aloha Airlines jet is chartered for one of the weekly flights. For independent travel, contact Midway Phoenix Corporation (☎ 770-387-2000, 888-643-9291), 100 Phoenix Air Drive, Cartersville, GA 30120.

For ecology tours with an emphasis on birds and spinner dolphins, contact Oceanic Society Expeditions (☎ 415-441-1106, 800-326-7491, fax 415-474-3395), Fort Mason Center, Bldg E, San Francisco, CA 94123. A weeklong package begins at $1930, including activities, accommodations, meals and airfare to and from Honolulu. Participants help in ongoing research projects, such as mapping seabird nests and monitoring chick hatching, and partake in discussions on island ecology and seabird biology.

Those interested in dive tours should contact Midway Sports and Diving (☎ 770-254-8326, 888-244-8582), Box 217, Newnan, GA 30264. A weeklong package, including diving, accommodations, meals and airfare to and from Honolulu, begins at $2600. Because of water conditions, the dive tours are available only from April through October.

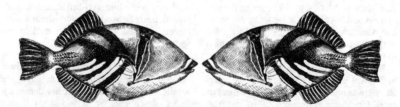

Glossary

aa – type of lava that is rough and jagged
ahi – yellowfin tuna
ahu – stone cairns used to mark a trail; or an altar or shrine
ahupuaa – traditional land division, usually in a wedge shape that extends from the mountains to the sea
aikane – friend
aina – land
akamai – clever
aku – skipjack tuna
akua – god, spirit, idol
akule – bigeye mackerel
alii – chief, royalty
aloha – the traditional greeting meaning love, welcome, good-bye
aloha aina – love of the land
amaama – mullet
amakihi – small, yellow-green bird; one of the more common native birds
ao – Newell's shearwater (a seabird)
apapane – bright-red native Hawaiian honeycreeper
au – marlin
aumakua – ancestral spirit helper
auwe – Oh my! Alas!
awa – kava, made into an intoxicating brew; milkfish
awapuhi – wild ginger

bento – the Japanese word for a box lunch

crack seed – snack food, usually dried fruits or seeds; can be sour, salty or sweet

elepaio – a brownish native bird with a white rump, common to Oahu forests

gyoza – a grilled dumpling made of minced pork and garlic

hala – pandanus plant; the leaves are used in weaving mats and baskets
hale – house
hana – work; a bay, when used as a compound in place names

haole – Caucasian; literally, 'without breath'
hapa – half; person of mixed blood
hau – indigenous lowland hibiscus tree whose wood is often used for outrigger canoes
haupia – coconut pudding
Hawaii nei – all the Hawaiian Islands taken as a group
heiau – ancient stone temple, a place of worship in Hawaii before the arrival of Westerners
Hina – Polynesian goddess (wife of Ku, one of the four main gods)
holoholo – to walk, drive or ramble around for pleasure
holoku – a long dress similar to the *muumuu*, but more fitted
holua – sled or sled course
honu – turtle
hoolaulea – celebration, party
huhu – angry
hui – group, organization
hukilau – fishing with a seine (a large net), involving a group of people; the word can also refer to the feast that follows
hula – traditional Hawaiian dance
hula halau – *hula* school or troupe
humuhumunukunukuapuaa – rectangular triggerfish

iiwi – a bright red forest bird with a curved, salmon-colored beak
iliahi – Hawaiian sandalwood
iliili – stones
ilima – native plant, a ground cover with delicate yellow-orange flowers
imu – underground earthen oven used in traditional *luau* cooking

kahili – a feathered standard, used as a symbol of royalty
kahuna – wise person in any field; commonly a priest, healer or sorcerer
kahuna nui – high priest
kaiseki ryori – a formal Japanese meal consisting of a series of small dishes

kalo – see *taro*

kalua – traditional method of baking in an underground oven *(imu)*

kamaaina – native-born Hawaiian or a longtime resident; literally, 'child of the land'

Kanaloa – god of the underworld

kane/Kane – man; also the name of one of four main Hawaiian gods

kapa – see *tapa*

kapu – taboo, part of strict ancient Hawaiian social system

kaunaoa – a thin, parasitic vine

kava – a mildly narcotic drink made from the roots of *Piper methysticum*, a pepper shrub

keiki – child, children

ki – see *ti*

kiawe – a relative of the mesquite tree introduced to Hawaii in the 1820s, now very common; its branches are covered with sharp thorns

kii – image, statue

kipuka – an area of land spared when lava flows around it; an oasis

ko – sugarcane

koa – native hardwood tree often used in woodworking of native crafts

kohola – whale

kokua – help, cooperation

kona – leeward; a leeward wind

koolau – windward side

Ku – Polynesian god of many manifestations, including god of war, farming and fishing (husband of Hina)

kukui – candlenut tree and the official state tree; its oily nuts were once burned in lamps

kuleana – an individually held plot of land

kupuna – grandparent, elder

kuula – fishing shrine

Laka – goddess of the hula

lanai – veranda

lauhala – leaves of the *hala* plant used in weaving

laulau – wrapped package; bundles of pork or beef with salted fish that are wrapped in leaves and steamed

lei – garland, usually of flowers, but also of leaves or shells

lilikoi – passion fruit

limu – seaweed

lio – horse

lolo – stupid, crazy

lomi – to rub or soften; *lomi* salmon is raw, diced salmon marinated with tomatoes and onions

lomilomi – massage

Lono – Polynesian god of harvest, agriculture, fertility and peace

loulu – native fan palms

luakini – a type of *heiau* (temple) dedicated to the war god Ku and used for human sacrifices

luau – traditional Hawaiian feast

mahalo – thank you

mahele – to divide; usually refers to the missionary-initiated land divisions of 1848

mahimahi – also called 'dolphin,' but actually a type of fish unrelated to the marine mammal

maile – native plant with twining habit and fragrant leaves; often used for *leis*

makaainana – commoners; literally, 'people who tend the land'

makaha – a sluice gate, used to regulate the level of water in a fishpond

makahiki – ancient annual four-month-long winter harvest festival dedicated to Lono

makai – toward the sea

makaku – creative, artistic *mana*

malasada – a fried dough served warm, similar to a doughnut

malihini – newcomer, visitor

malo – loincloth

mana – spiritual power

manini – convict tang (a reef fish); also used to refer to something small or insignificant

mano – shark

mauka – toward the mountains; inland

mele – song, chant

menehune – the 'little people' who built many of Hawaii's fishponds, *heiaus* and other stonework, according to legend

milo – a native shade tree with beautiful hardwood

moo – water spirit, water lizard or dragon

mu – a 'body catcher' who secured sacrificial victims for the *heiau* altar

muumuu – a long, loose-fitting dress introduced by the missionaries

naupaka – a native shrub with delicate white flowers

Neighbor Islands – the term used to refer to the main Hawaiian Islands outside of Oahu

nene – a native goose; Hawaii's state bird

nisei – people of Japanese descent

noni – Indian mulberry; a small tree with yellow, smelly fruit that is used medicinally

nuku puu – a native honeycreeper with a bright yellow underbelly

ohana – family, extended family

ohelo – low-growing native shrub with edible red berries related to cranberries; said to be sacred to the goddess Pele

ohia lehua – native Hawaiian tree with tufted, feathery, pom-pom-like flowers

okole – buttocks

olo – surfboards used by Hawaiian royalty

onaga – red snapper

ono – delicious; also the name of the wahoo fish

opae – shrimp

opakapaka – pink snapper

opihi – edible limpet

pahoehoe – type of lava that is quick and smooth-flowing

pakalolo – marijuana; literally, 'crazy smoke'

pali – cliff

palila – native honeycreeper

paniolo – cowboy

pau – finished, no more

Pele – goddess of fire and volcanoes; she's said to live in Kilauea Caldera

pho – a Vietnamese soup of beef broth, noodles and fresh herbs

piko – navel, umbilical cord

pili – a bunchgrass, commonly used for thatching houses

pilikia – trouble

pipikaula – salted, dried beef that is served broiled

poha – gooseberry

pohaku – rock

poi – a gooey paste made from *taro* roots; a staple of the Hawaiian diet

poke – chopped raw fish marinated in soy sauce, oil and chili pepper

Poliahu – goddess of snow

pua aloalo – a hibiscus flower

pueo – Hawaiian owl

puhi – moray eel

puka – any kind of hole or opening

pupu – snack food, hors d'oeuvres; shells

puu – hill, cinder cone

puuhonua – place of refuge

saimin – a Japanese noodle soup

tabi – Japanese reef-walking shoes

talk story – to strike up a conversation, make small talk

tapa – cloth made by pounding the bark of the paper mulberry tree, used for early Hawaiian clothing (*kapa* in Hawaiian)

taro – a plant with green heart-shaped leaves; cultivated in Hawaii for its edible rootstock, which is mashed to make *poi* (*kalo* in Hawaiian)

teishoku – Japanese word for fixed-plate meal

teppanyaki – Japanese style of cooking with an iron grill

ti – common native plant; its long shiny leaves are used for wrapping food and making *hula* skirts (*ki* in Hawaiian)

tutu – aunt; used out of respect for any older woman

ukulele – a stringed musical instrument derived from the 'braginha,' which was introduced to Hawaii in the 1800s by Portuguese immigrants

ulu – breadfruit

ulu maika – ancient Hawaiian game

wahine – woman

wana – sea urchin

wikiwiki – hurry, quick

Acknowledgments

THANKS

Many thanks to the travelers who used the last edition and wrote to us with helpful hints, useful advice and interesting anecdotes:

Robin Adlerblum, Nate Anderson, Connie Baker & John Sabo, Magdalena Balcerek, Rolf Ballmoos, Anna Banerji, Jane Battersby & Neil Griggs, Nano Beivi & Iris Dietisheim, Vincent Boisvert, Monique Bonoo, Helen Bottrill, Dave Brown, Alexandra Brucker, Mike Buckley, Anne Burgess, Andrea Caloini, Gayle M Campbell, Andrea & Edward Canapary, Katherine Carroll, Alessandra Cassar, Deivy Centeio, Sumeet Chhibber, Danielle Clode, Matt Collier, Marisa & Andrea Daniele, James Davis, Mark Davis, Juli Dent, Andre Desjardins, Sam & Osa Detrick, Ava Dolan, Mark Domroese, Kylie Duthie, Greg & Juli Edward, Andrew & Louise Edwards, Jesse Elliott, Justin Farley, Marietta Fedder, Pam Feinstein, Dan Fowler, Sheila Freita, Phyllis Frey, Chirag Gandhi, Will Gardner, Annemone Goldschmied, Lori Gonder, Gerd Gopel, James Gordon, John Gropp, Nadine Guitton, Anja Hansen, W John Harker, TS Heaton, Jack & Linda Hibbard, Lori Higa, Chuck & Nancy Hooper, Lee Howard, Beverley Jennings, Stig Jepsen, Brian L Jester, Liz Jones, Lloyd Jones, Sarah Kettley, Min Kim, Olliemarie Kingston, Marge & Tom Kinney, J Kosowski, Thomas Krahenmann, Ann Krumboltz, Dr Angela Kung, Larry Kwiatkowski, Frances Kwok, Hau Boon Lai, Karen Latter, Rosemary & Randy Leach, Gavin Lock & John Dyer, Barbara Lohoff, Francine Marshall, Simon McHugh, E McRae, Anne Marie McTrowe, Joan & Bill Meikle, Russ Michaels, Ann Miya, Roz Morris, Frank Murillo, Chris Murray, Trish & Bruce Murray, Anna Mya, Anja Niewolik, Ken & Joyce Norris, Kevin P O'Connell, David & Sharyn Olive, Nort Petrovich, Karen White Pettigrew, Bill Pollington, Joel & Maria Teresa Prades, Tom Regan, Graham Rivers & Tess Camfield, Forrest Roberts & Heather Martin, K Rogers, Kristen Rogers & John Kosowski, Herwig Rombauts, Dan Sabath, Michael Schuette, Janna Scopel, Darren Scott, Terri Scott, Dawn Sentance & Padraig Eochaidh, Jacob Siboni, Andrew Sinclair, Christos Siopis, Teresa Sivilli, Catherine Smith, Dawn Smith, Michelle Smith, Sue Smith, Matthew Staley & Craig Foss, Sandra Starke, Alexandra Stern, Charlie Stokes & Kay Lamier, Kevan & Cindy Strube, Tim Sturge, Tammy Svoboda, Eleanor Swain, Giselle Sweet-Escott, Mike Tailor, Kathleen Thomas, Mike Tuggle, Judith Uhart, Anne Vaile, Erwin & Diana van Engelen, Maggie & Martin Varco, Amanda & Ian Vernalls, Jim R Walker, S Bruce Warthman, Catherine Watkins, Mary Wells, Dörte Wendlandt, Jodie Wesley, Arvis & Ken Willetts, Ann Wilson-Wilde, Milse Wolbe, Simon Wood, Hannah & Bart Wright, Erin Zoski

LONELY PLANET

Phrasebooks

Lonely Planet phrasebooks are packed with essential words and phrases to help travellers communicate with the locals. With colour tabs for quick reference, an extensive vocabulary and use of script, these handy pocket-sized language guides cover day-to-day travel situations.

- handy pocket-sized books
- easy to understand Pronunciation chapter
- clear & comprehensive Grammar chapter
- romanisation alongside script to allow ease of pronunciation
- script throughout so users can point to phrases for every situation
- full of cultural information and tips for the traveller

'... vital for a real DIY spirit and attitude in language learning'
— *Backpacker*

'the phrasebooks have good cultural backgrounders and offer solid advice for challenging situations in remote locations'
— *San Francisco Examiner*

Arabic (Egyptian) • Arabic (Moroccan) • Australian *(Australian English, Aboriginal and Torres Strait languages)* • Baltic States *(Estonian, Latvian, Lithuanian)* • Bengali • Brazilian • British • Burmese • Cantonese • Central Asia *(Uyghur, Uzbek, Kyrghiz, Kazak, Pashto, Tadjik • Central Europe (Czech, French, German, Hungarian, Italian, Slovak)* • Eastern Europe *(Bulgarian, Czech, Hungarian, Polish, Romanian, Slovak)* • Ethiopian (Amharic) • Farsi (Persian) • Fijian • French • German • Greek • Hebrew • Hill Tribes • Hindi & Urdu • Indonesian • Italian • Japanese • Korean • Lao • Latin American Spanish • Malay • Mandarin • Mediterranean Europe *(Albanian, Croatian, Greek, Italian, Macedonian, Maltese, Serbian, Slovene)* • Mongolian • Nepali • Pidgin • Pilipino (Tagalog) • Portugese • Quechua • Russian • Scandinavian Europe *(Danish, Finnish, Icelandic, Norwegian, Swedish)* • South-East Asia *(Burmese, Indonesian, Khmer, Lao, Malay, Tagalog Pilipino, Thai, Vietnamese)* • South Pacific Languages • Spanish (Castilian) *(also includes Catalan, Galician and Basque)* • Sri Lanka • Swahili • Thai • Tibetan • Turkish • Ukrainian • USA *(US English, Vernacular, Native American languages, Hawaiian)* • Vietnamese • Western Europe *(Basque, Catalan, Dutch, French, German, Greek, Irish, Italian, Portuguese, Scottish Gaelic, Spanish (Castilian), Welsh)*

Lonely Planet Guides by Region

Lonely Planet is known worldwide for publishing practical, reliable and no-nonsense travel information in our guides and on our Web site. The Lonely Planet list covers just about every accessible part of the world. Currently there are 16 series: Travel guides, Shoestring guides, Condensed guides, Phrasebooks, Read This First, Healthy Travel, Walking guides, Cycling guides, Watching Wildlife guides, Pisces Diving & Snorkeling guides, City Maps, Road Atlases, Out to Eat, World Food, Journeys travel literature and Pictorials.

AFRICA Africa on a shoestring • Botswana • Cairo • Cairo City Map • Cape Town • Cape Town City Map • East Africa • Egypt • Egyptian Arabic phrasebook • Ethiopia, Eritrea & Djibouti • Ethiopian Amharic phrasebook • The Gambia & Senegal • Healthy Travel Africa • Kenya • Malawi • Morocco • Moroccan Arabic phrasebook • Mozambique • Namibia • Read This First: Africa • South Africa, Lesotho & Swaziland • Southern Africa • Southern Africa Road Atlas • Swahili phrasebook • Tanzania, Zanzibar & Pemba • Trekking in East Africa • Tunisia • Watching Wildlife East Africa • Watching Wildlife Southern Africa • West Africa • World Food Morocco • Zambia • Zimbabwe, Botswana & Namibia
Travel Literature: Mali Blues: Traveling to an African Beat • The Rainbird: A Central African Journey • Songs to an African Sunset: A Zimbabwean Story

AUSTRALIA & THE PACIFIC Aboriginal Australia & the Torres Strait Islands •Auckland • Australia • Australian phrasebook • Australia Road Atlas • Cycling Australia • Cycling New Zealand • Fiji • Fijian phrasebook • Healthy Travel Australia, NZ & the Pacific • Islands of Australia's Great Barrier Reef • Melbourne • Melbourne City Map • Micronesia • New Caledonia • New South Wales • New Zealand • Northern Territory • Outback Australia • Out to Eat – Melbourne • Out to Eat – Sydney • Papua New Guinea • Pidgin phrasebook • Queensland • Rarotonga & the Cook Islands • Samoa • Solomon Islands • South Australia • South Pacific • South Pacific phrasebook • Sydney • Sydney City Map • Sydney Condensed • Tahiti & French Polynesia • Tasmania • Tonga • Tramping in New Zealand • Vanuatu • Victoria • Walking in Australia • Watching Wildlife Australia • Western Australia
Travel Literature: Islands in the Clouds: Travels in the Highlands of New Guinea • Kiwi Tracks: A New Zealand Journey • Sean & David's Long Drive

CENTRAL AMERICA & THE CARIBBEAN Bahamas, Turks & Caicos • Baja California • Belize, Guatemala & Yucatán • Bermuda • Central America on a shoestring • Costa Rica • Costa Rica Spanish phrasebook • Cuba • Cycling Cuba • Dominican Republic & Haiti • Eastern Caribbean • Guatemala • Havana • Healthy Travel Central & South America • Jamaica • Mexico • Mexico City • Panama • Puerto Rico • Read This First: Central & South America • Virgin Islands • World Food Caribbean • World Food Mexico • Yucatán
Travel Literature: Green Dreams: Travels in Central America

EUROPE Amsterdam • Amsterdam City Map • Amsterdam Condensed • Andalucía • Athens • Austria • Baltic States phrasebook • Barcelona • Barcelona City Map • Belgium & Luxembourg • Berlin • Berlin City Map • Britain • British phrasebook • Brussels, Bruges & Antwerp • Brussels City Map • Budapest • Budapest City Map • Canary Islands • Catalunya & the Costa Brava • Central Europe • Central Europe phrasebook • Copenhagen • Corfu & the Ionians • Corsica • Crete • Crete Condensed • Croatia • Cycling Britain • Cycling France • Cyprus • Czech & Slovak Republics • Czech phrasebook • Denmark • Dublin • Dublin City Map • Dublin Condensed • Eastern Europe • Eastern Europe phrasebook • Edinburgh • Edinburgh City Map • England • Estonia, Latvia & Lithuania • Europe on a shoestring • Europe phrasebook • Finland • Florence • Florence City Map • France • Frankfurt City Map • Frankfurt Condensed • French phrasebook • Georgia, Armenia & Azerbaijan • Germany • German phrasebook • Greece • Greek Islands • Greek phrasebook • Hungary • Iceland, Greenland & the Faroe Islands • Ireland • Italian phrasebook • Italy • Kraków • Lisbon • The Loire • London • London City Map • London Condensed • Madrid • Madrid City Map • Malta • Mediterranean Europe • Milan, Turin & Genoa • Moscow • Munich • Netherlands • Normandy • Norway • Out to Eat – London • Out to Eat – Paris • Paris • Paris City Map • Paris Condensed • Poland • Polish phrasebook • Portugal • Portuguese phrasebook • Prague • Prague City Map • Provence & the Côte d'Azur • Read This First: Europe • Rhodes & the Dodecanese • Romania & Moldova • Rome • Rome City Map • Rome Condensed • Russia, Ukraine & Belarus • Russian phrasebook • Scandinavian & Baltic Europe • Scandinavian phrasebook • Scotland • Sicily • Slovenia • South-West France • Spain • Spanish phrasebook • Stockholm • St Petersburg • St Petersburg City Map • Sweden • Switzerland • Tuscany • Ukrainian phrasebook • Venice • Vienna • Wales • Walking in Britain • Walking in France • Walking in Ireland • Walking in Italy • Walking in Scotland • Walking in Spain • Walking in Switzerland • Western Europe • World Food France • World Food Greece • World Food Ireland • World Food Italy • World Food Spain **Travel Literature:** After Yugoslavia • Love and War in the Apennines • The Olive Grove: Travels in Greece • On the Shores of the Mediterranean • Round Ireland in Low Gear • A Small Place in Italy

Lonely Planet Mail Order

onely Planet products are distributed worldwide. They are also available by mail order from Lonely Planet, so if you have difficulty finding a title please write to us. North and South American residents should write to 150 Linden St, Oakland, CA 94607, USA; European and African residents should write to 10a Spring Place, London NW5 3BH, UK; and residents of other countries to Locked Bag 1, Footscray, Victoria 3011, Australia.

INDIAN SUBCONTINENT & THE INDIAN OCEAN Bangladesh • Bengali phrasebook • Bhutan • Delhi • Goa • Healthy Travel Asia & India • Hindi & Urdu phrasebook • India • India & Bangladesh City Map • Indian Himalaya • Karakoram Highway • Kathmandu City Map • Kerala • Madagascar • Maldives • Mauritius, Réunion & Seychelles • Mumbai (Bombay) • Nepal • Nepali phrasebook • North India • Pakistan • Rajasthan • Read This First: Asia & India • South India • Sri Lanka • Sri Lanka phrasebook • Tibet • Tibetan phrasebook • Trekking in the Indian Himalaya • Trekking in the Karakoram & Hindukush • Trekking in the Nepal Himalaya • World Food India **Travel Literature:** The Age of Kali: Indian Travels and Encounters • Hello Goodnight: A Life of Goa • In Rajasthan • Maverick in Madagascar • A Season in Heaven: True Tales from the Road to Kathmandu • Shopping for Buddhas • A Short Walk in the Hindu Kush • Slowly Down the Ganges

MIDDLE EAST & CENTRAL ASIA Bahrain, Kuwait & Qatar • Central Asia • Central Asia phrasebook • Dubai • Farsi (Persian) phrasebook • Hebrew phrasebook • Iran • Israel & the Palestinian Territories • Istanbul • Istanbul City Map • Istanbul to Cairo • Istanbul to Kathmandu • Jerusalem • Jerusalem City Map • Jordan • Lebanon • Middle East • Oman & the United Arab Emirates • Syria • Turkey • Turkish phrasebook • World Food Turkey • Yemen **Travel Literature:** Black on Black: Iran Revisited • Breaking Ranks: Turbulent Travels in the Promised Land • The Gates of Damascus • Kingdom of the Film Stars: Journey into Jordan

NORTH AMERICA Alaska • Boston • Boston City Map • Boston Condensed • British Columbia • California & Nevada • California Condensed • Canada • Chicago • Chicago City Map • Chicago Condensed • Florida • Georgia & the Carolinas • Great Lakes • Hawaii • Hiking in Alaska • Hiking in the USA • Honolulu & Oahu City Map • Las Vegas • Los Angeles • Los Angeles City Map • Louisiana & the Deep South • Miami • Miami City Map • Montreal • New England • New Orleans • New Orleans City Map • New York City • New York City City Map • New York City Condensed • New York, New Jersey & Pennsylvania • Oahu • Out to Eat – San Francisco • Pacific Northwest • Rocky Mountains • San Diego & Tijuana • San Francisco • San Francisco City Map • Seattle • Seattle City Map • Southwest • Texas • Toronto • USA • USA phrasebook • Vancouver • Vancouver City Map • Virginia & the Capital Region • Washington, DC • Washington, DC City Map • World Food New Orleans **Travel Literature**: Caught Inside: A Surfer's Year on the California Coast • Drive Thru America

NORTH-EAST ASIA Beijing • Beijing City Map • Cantonese phrasebook • China • Hiking in Japan • Hong Kong & Macau • Hong Kong City Map • Hong Kong Condensed • Japan • Japanese phrasebook • Korea • Korean phrasebook • Kyoto • Mandarin phrasebook • Mongolia • Mongolian phrasebook • Seoul • Shanghai • South-West China • Taiwan • Tokyo • Tokyo Condensed • World Food Hong Kong • World Food Japan **Travel Literature:** In Xanadu: A Quest • Lost Japan

SOUTH AMERICA Argentina, Uruguay & Paraguay • Bolivia • Brazil • Brazilian phrasebook • Buenos Aires • Buenos Aires City Map • Chile & Easter Island • Colombia • Ecuador & the Galapagos Islands • Healthy Travel Central & South America • Latin American Spanish phrasebook • Peru • Quechua phrasebook • Read This First: Central & South America • Rio de Janeiro • Rio de Janeiro City Map • Santiago de Chile • South America on a shoestring • Trekking in the Patagonian Andes • Venezuela **Travel Literature**: Full Circle: A South American Journey

SOUTH-EAST ASIA Bali & Lombok • Bangkok • Bangkok City Map • Burmese phrasebook • Cambodia • Cycling Vietnam, Laos & Cambodia • East Timor phrasebook • Hanoi • Healthy Travel Asia & India • Hill Tribes phrasebook • Ho Chi Minh City (Saigon) • Indonesia • Indonesian phrasebook • Indonesia's Eastern Islands • Java • Lao phrasebook • Laos • Malay phrasebook • Malaysia, Singapore & Brunei • Myanmar (Burma) • Philippines • Pilipino (Tagalog) phrasebook • Read This First: Asia & India • Singapore • Singapore City Map • South-East Asia on a shoestring • South-East Asia phrasebook • Thailand • Thailand's Islands & Beaches • Thailand, Laos & Cambodia Road Atlas • Thai phrasebook • Vietnam • Vietnamese phrasebook • World Food Indonesia • World Food Thailand • World Food Vietnam

ALSO AVAILABLE: Antarctica • The Arctic • The Blue Man: Tales of Travel, Love and Coffee • Brief Encounters: Stories of Love, Sex & Travel • Buddhist Stupas in Asia: The Shape of Perfection • Chasing Rickshaws • The Last Grain Race • Lonely Planet ... On the Edge: Adventurous Escapades from Around the World • Lonely Planet Unpacked • Lonely Planet Unpacked Again • Not the Only Planet: Science Fiction Travel Stories • Ports of Call: A Journey by Sea • Sacred India • Travel Photography: A Guide to Taking Better Pictures • Travel with Children • Tuvalu: Portrait of an Island Nation

Notes

Index

Abbreviations

BI – Big Island
K – Kauai
Kah – Kahoolawe

L – Lanai
M – Maui
Mol – Molokai

N – Niihau
NHI – Northwestern Hawaiian Islands
O – Oahu

Text

A

accommodations 75-80. *See also individual islands*
  B&Bs 78-9
  cabins 78
  camping 76-8
  condos 79
  hostels 78
  hotels 79-80
  reservations 76
  travel club discounts 76
agricultural inspection 99
Ahalanui Beach Park (BI) 333
Ahihi-Kinau (M) 423
Ahuena Heiau (BI) 252
Ahukini Landing (K) 535
AIDS. *See* HIV/AIDS
air travel 93-101, 103-5
  interisland 103-5, **103**
  international 93-101, **100**
  to/from US mainland 98-9, **100**
Akaka Falls (BI) 309-10
akua 497, 593
Ala Moana Beach (O) 144
Ala Moana Center (O) 142, 144, 155-6
Alakai Swamp (K) 518-9, 595
Alexander, Samuel 136, 403-4
Alexander & Baldwin Sugar Museum (M) 403-4
alii 13
Alii Kahekili Nui Ahumanu (M) 392

Aliiolani Hale (O) 134-5
Allerton Garden (K) 578
Aloha Tower (O) 137
altitude sickness 63
American Automobile Association 68
Anaehoomalu Beach Park (BI) 284
Anahola (K) 553
Anini (K) 558-9
annexation 25
antiques 140-1
aquariums 169-70, 195, 412
Arizona 26, 186, 187-8
art 41, 140, 170, 266-7, 285
ATMs 53

B

Baby Beach (K) 577-8
backpacking. *See* hiking & backpacking
Bailey House Museum (M) 405
Baldwin, Henry 136, 359, 403-4, 512
Baldwin Beach Park (M) 426
Baldwin House (M) 379-80
B&Bs. *See* accommodations
Banzai Pipeline (O) 222
Barking Sands (K) 590-1
Battle of Nuuanu 111
beaches 56. *See also individual beaches*
  Big Island 238
  Kauai 522
  Maui 363
  Molokai 465, 491-3, **491**
  Oahu 117, 164-8

Bellows Field Beach Park (O) 196
bicycling. *See* cycling; mountain biking
Big Beach (M) 422-3
Big Island 231-356, **232-3**
  accommodations 245-7
  activities 238-44
  beaches 238
  climate 235-6
  entertainment 247
  flora & fauna 236
  geography 235
  Hamakua Coast 302-11, **303**
  Hawaii Volcanoes National Park 342-56, **343**
  Hilo 316-29, **317**, **319**, **323**
  history 233-5
  Kau 336-42, **337**
  Kona 249-67
  North Kohala 290-7, **291**
  North Kona & South Kohala 277-90, **279**
  population 237
  Puna 329-36, **330**
  Saddle Rd 311-6
  shopping 247
  South Kona 267-77, **268**
  tours 244-5
  transportation 247-9
  Waimea (Kamuela) 297-302, **298**
birds 34, 57
  Big Island 236, 351
  Kauai 518-9, 555
  Lanai 498

Bold indicates maps.

Maui 360
Molokai 463
Oahu 111, 114
Northwestern Hawaiian
Islands 601-3
birthstones, royal 214
Bishop, Princess Bernice
Pauahi 23, 151, 204
Bishop Museum (O) 150-1
Black Rock (M) 391-2
boats. See cruises; ferries
bodysurfing 118, 195, 579
Boiling Pots (BI) 324
boogie boarding 118, 167,
522-3, 579
books 56-9
Bowfin Park (O) 187-8
breakfast 180
Brennecke's Beach (K) 579
buses 105-6, 108
Bushnell, OA 58
business hours 72
Byodo-In (O) 204

C

cabins. See accommodations
camping 76-8
Big Island 245-7, 308,
355-6
Kauai 528-30, 595-6
Lanai 507
Maui 370-1, 433, 456
Molokai 467-8, 472, 480,
492
Oahu 124-5, 189, 210
Captain Cook (BI) 272-4
cars 106-8. See also individual
islands
Cathedral of Our Lady of
Peace (O) 134
caves 228, 314, 324, 433-4,
568
Central Waikiki Beach (O) 165
Chain of Craters Rd (BI) 348-9,
350
children, traveling with 67
Chinatown (O) 138-42, 158-9,
139
ciguatera poisoning 64
Circle Pacific tickets 95, 98
climate 31-3

Coconut Island (BI) 322
Coconut Island (O) 204
Coconut Plantation (K) 545
coconut 'postcards' 486
coffee 270, 467, 478-9
condos. See accommodations
cone shells 70
consulates 51
Contemporary Museum (O)
148
Cook, Captain James 16-8,
34, 233, 272, 517, 587,
588, 598-9
coral 64, 69
costs 53-4
county parks 77-8. See also
individual parks
crack seed 82
crafts 41, 84
Crater Hill (K) 555
Crater Rim Drive (BI) 345-8
creation myth 31
credit cards 52-3
crime 71
cruises 101-2, 109, 123, 244,
369, 528
culture 41-2, 58
currency 52
customs 52
cycling 56, 108. See also
mountain biking
Big Island 241-2, 249
Kauai 532
Maui 367, 375
Molokai 466
Oahu 129

D

Damien, Father 58, 133, 169,
336, 474, 480-2
Damien Museum (O) 169
Diamond Head (O) 190, 192
disabled travelers 66-7, 98
diving 56, 87, 88
Big Island 239-40
Kauai 523
Lanai 506
Maui 365-6
Oahu 119, 193
Dixie Maru Beach (Mol) 492
documents 48-9, 52

Dole, James 26, 496
Dole, Sanford 24, 25, 135
Dole Pineapple Pavilion (O)
214
dolphins 37-8
donkeys 282
Douglas, David 301-2
drinks 83-4
DT Fleming Beach Park (M)
398

E

Earthjustice Legal Defense
Fund 33, 67
economy 39-40
education 40, 144-5
eels 70
Ehukai Beach Park (O) 222
electricity 60-1
Eleele (K) 586
email 55-6
embassies 50
emergencies 71-2
Big Island 238
Kauai 522
Lanai 500
Maui 363
Molokai 465
Oahu 117
Emma, Queen 23, 111, 197,
578
Emory, Kenneth 'Keneti' 58,
508
employment 75
entertainment 84
environment 33-4
groups 33-4, 67
tours 102
exchange rates 52

F

Fagan, Paul 433, 435
farmers' markets 530
fauna. See wildlife
fax 55
Fern Grotto (K) 541, 543
ferries 108
films 59
fish
ciguatera poisoning 64
guides 57

species of 81, 439
stings from 70
fishing 89, 241, 525
fishponds
Big Island 253, 280, 286
Kauai 536
Maui 413
Molokai 470-1, 475, 476
flora 34-5, 57. *See also
individual species*
Big Island 236
Kauai 518-20
Lanai 498
Maui 360
Molokai 463
Oahu 111, 114
food 80-3
Fort DeRussy (O) 168-9
Fort DeRussy Beach (O) 165
Foster Botanical Garden (O)
141-2
French Frigate Shoals (NHI)
602
fruit, tropical 80, 82-3
fungal infections 63

G

games, ancient 15, 292
Garden of the Gods (L) 509
gays & lesbians 65-6
geography 30
geology 30-1
Gibson, Walter 495-6
Glass Beach (K) 586
glass-bottom boats 245, 369
gliding 122-3
gods 14
golf 34
Big Island 242-3
Kauai 526-7
Lanai 500
Maui 368-9
Molokai 466-7, 479
Oahu 122
government 38-9
Gray's Beach (O) 165
Great Mahele 22-3
Green Sands Beach (BI) 339

grocery stores 82-3
Grove Farm Homestead (K)
536-7
guavas 83, 556

H

Haena (K) 567-70
Haiku (M) 444-5
Haipuaena Falls (M) 430
Halalii Lake (N) 599
Halape (BI) 353
Hale Halawai Park (BI) 253
Hale Kahiko (M) 380-1
Hale o Keawe Heiau (BI) 275
Hale Paahao Prison (M) 382
Hale Piula (M) 381
Haleakala National Park (M)
31, 33, 452-9, **452**
Haleiwa (O) 32, 217-20, **218**
Haleiwa Alii Beach Park (O)
219
Haleiwa Beach Park (O) 219
Halemaumau (BI) 346-7,
351-2
Haliimaile (M) 441, 443
Hallekii-Pihanakalani Heiaus
(M) 408
Halona Blowhole (O) 194
Hamakua Coast (BI) 302-11,
303
Hamoa Beach (M) 438
Hana (M) 433-7, **434**
Hana Cultural Center (M) 435
Hana Hwy (M) 424-41, **425**
Hanakaoo Beach (M) 389,
391
Hanakapiai (K) 571-2
Hanakoa (K) 572
Hanalei (K) 562-7, **564**
Hanalei Valley (K) 562
Hanamaulu (K) 535
Hanapepe (K) 586-7
Hanauma Bay Beach Park (O)
192-3
hang gliding 368
Hapuna Beach State Park (BI)
288-9
Hasegawa General Store (M)
435
Hauula (O) 208-9

Hawaii. *See* Big Island
Hawaii Maritime Center (O)
137-8
Hawaii Nature Center (M) 407
Hawaii Theatre (O) 136-7, 160
Hawaii Tropical Botanical
Garden (BI) 311
Hawaii Volcanoes National
Park (BI) 342-56, **343**
accommodations 354-6
Chain of Craters Rd 348-9,
350
Crater Rim Drive 345-8
hiking 351-4
Mauna Loa Rd 349, 351
restaurants 356
Hawaiian Electric Beach (O)
224
Hawaiian Home Lands 28, 29
Hawaiian Islands National
Wildlife Refuge (NHI) 600-1
Hawaiians, native
early 13
declining population of 21,
25, 40
sovereignty for 28-30
Hawaii's Plantation Village
(O) 188-9
Hawi (BI) 294-5
Healing Stones (O) 213
health issues 61-4
emergencies 71-2
medical kit 62
problems & treatment 61-4
heat, effects of 62-3
Heeia State Park (O) 204
heiaus 14-5. *See also individual temples*
helicopter tours 109, 244,
369, 527-8, 599
herbalists 142
Hiilawe Falls (BI) 307
Hikina A Ka La Heiau (K) 541
hiking & backpacking 56,
89-91
Big Island 241, 271-2,
306-8, 314-5, 316, 350,
351-4
Kauai 525-6, 545, 555,
560, 570-4, 592-5
Lanai 509-10

Bold indicates maps.

Maui 366-7, 433, 439-40, 448-9, 455-6, 457-9
Molokai 466, 480, 482-3, 485-6
Oahu 120-1, 145-6, 151, 189, 190, 208-9, 229-30
Hilo (BI) 316-29, **317, 319, 323**
    accommodations 324-6
    beaches 323
    climate 32
    entertainment 328-9
    restaurants 326-8
    shopping 329
Hilton Waikoloa Village (BI) 284
Hina (goddess) 13, 453
Hina (princess) 537
history. *See also individual islands*
    early 13-5
    after 'discovery' by West 16-25
    as US territory 25-8
    as US state 28-30
    books 57
hitchhiking 108
HIV/AIDS 49, 63-4
Hole in the Mountain (K) 553
Holei Sea Arch (BI) 349
holidays 72-5
Holoholokai Beach Park (BI) 287
Holoholoku Heiau (K) 543
holua races 15
Holualoa (BI) 265-7, **267**
Honalo (BI) 268-9
Honaunau (BI) 274-5
Honokaa (BI) 302-4
Honokawai (M) 395-6
Honokohau Beach (BI) 278, 280
Honolua Bay (M) 399-400
Honolulu (O) 129-61, **130, 132**
    accommodations 151-4
    Ala Moana & University area 142-5, **143**
    Chinatown 138-42, 158-9, **139**
    climate 32
    downtown 130-8, **132**
    entertainment 154-60
    history 129-30
    restaurants 154-60
    shopping 140-1
Honolulu Academy of Arts (O) 137
Honolulu International Airport (O) 93-4, 126-7
Honolulu Zoo (O) 170
Honomanu Bay (M) 431
Honomu (BI) 310
Hookena (BI) 277
Hookipa Beach Park (M) 427
Hoolehua (Mol) 486-7
Hoomaluhia Park (O) 203-4
Hopper, Pegge 41, 140
horseback riding 122, 242, 367-8, 466, 526
Hosmer Grove (M) 454
hostels. *See* accommodations
hotels. *See* accommodations
Hualalai (BI) 31
Huelo (M) 429
hula 40, 170, 372, 394, 569
Hulihee Palace (BI) 253
Hulopoe Bay (L) 506-8
Hulopoe Beach (L) 506
human sacrifices 13, 221, 293, 476
humpbacks 36-7, 89, 360-1
Hurricane Iniki 519

I

Iao Valley State Park (M) 407-8
Iliiliopae Heiau (Mol) 476
ILWU 27
immigration 21-2, 25
Inouye, Daniel 27, 513
insects 64
insurance
    car 107-8
    travel 49
international transfers 53
Internet access & resources 55-6
Iolani Palace (O) 131, 133
Ironman Triathlon (BI) 91, 243
Isaac Hale Beach Park (BI) 334

J

Jaggar Museum (BI) 346, 347, 348
James Kealoha Beach Park (BI) 323
jellyfish 69
Jensen, Rocky Kaiouliokahi-hikoloehu 41
jet lag 63
jogging 91-2

K

Ka Lae (BI) 338-9
Ka Lahui Hawaii 28-9
Kaaawa (O) 206-7
Kaahumanu 19-20, 234, 289, 518
Kaanapali (M) 389-95, **390**
Kaena Point State Park (O) 217, 229-30
Kahakuloa (M) 409
Kahalepalaoa Landing (L) 506
Kahaluu Beach (BI) 263-4
Kahana (M) 396-7
Kahana Valley (O) 207-8
Kahanamoku, Duke 58, 165, 166-7, 405
Kahanamoku Beach (O) 165
Kahanu Gardens (M) 432
Kahe Point (O) 224
Kahekili 111, 359
Kahoolawe 511-4, **512**
Kahoolawe Ranch (Kah) 511-2
Kahuku (O) 210-1
Kahului-Wailuku area (M) 32, 400-10, **401**
Kaiaka Beach Park (O) 219
Kaikilani 15, 307
Kailua (M) 430
Kailua (O) 198-203
Kailua Pier (BI) 252
Kailua-Kona (BI) 249-62, **250**
    accommodations 255-9, **256**
    entertainment 261-2
    restaurants 259-61
    shopping 262
Kainaliu (BI) 269
Kalae (Mol) 479
Kalahaku Overlook (M) 455
Kalaheo (K) 583, 585

Kalahikiola Church (BI) 295
Kalakaua, King David 19, 23-4, 131, 264, 277, 496
Kalakaua Park (BI) 320
Kalalau Trail (K) 570-4
Kalalau Valley (K) 593-4
Kalama Park (M) 413
Kalanianaole, Prince Jonah Kuhio 27, 29, 577
Kalaniopuu 17, 233-4, 494
Kalapaki Beach (K) 536
Kalapana (BI) 335
Kalaupapa Overlook (Mol) 479-80
Kalaupapa Peninsula (Mol) 480-3
Kalepolepo Beach Park (M) 413
Kalihiwai (K) 557-8
Kaloko-Honokohau National Historic Park (BI) 280
Kalopa State Recreation Area (BI) 308-9
Kaluaaha (Mol) 476
Kaluakoi Resort (Mol) 490-1, **491**
Kamakahonu (BI) 252
Kamakou (Mol) 483-6
Kamalo (Mol) 474-5
Kamaoa Wind Farms (BI) 338
Kamaole Beach Park (M) 413
Kamehameha the Great 13, 18-9, 110-1, 129, 135, 233-4, 252, 289, 294, 295, 359, 494, 517-8
Kamehameha II (Liholiho) 19, 20, 23, 133, 206, 234, 289, 518
Kamehameha III 19, 21, 22, 135
Kamehameha IV 19, 20, 23, 134
Kamehameha V 19, 23, 134, 151, 462, 470, 599
Kamokila (K) 544
Kamuela. See Waimea (BI)
Kamuela Museum (BI) 299
Kanaha Beach Park (M) 402

Kanaha Pond (M) 400, 402
Kanaloa 14, 593
Kane 14
Kane, Herb Kawainui 41, 266
Kaneaki Heiau (O) 227
Kaneana Cave (O) 228
Kaneohe (O) 203-5
Kanepuu Preserve (L) 509
Kapaa (K) 550-2, **542**
Kapaa Beach Park (BI) 293
Kapaa Beach Park (K) 551
Kapaau (BI) 295
Kapahulu Groin (O) 167
Kapalua (M) 398-9
Kapiolani Beach Park (O) 167-8
Kapiolani Park (O) 169-70
Kapoho (BI) 332-3
Kapuaiwa Coconut Grove (Mol) 468, 471
kapus 13, 19, 233, 234, 275
Kau (BI) 336-42, **337**
Kauai 515-96, **516**
   accommodations 528-30
   activities 522-7
   beaches 522
   climate 518
   East Side 532-54
   entertainment 530
   flora & fauna 518-20
   geography 518
   history 515, 517-8
   North Shore 554-74, **556-7**
   population 520
   shopping 530-1
   South Shore 574-83
   tours 527-8
   transportation 531-2
   West Side 583-96, **584**
Kauai Museum (K) 532
Kauiki Head (M) 435-6
Kaulu Paoa Heiau (K) 569
Kaululaau 497
Kaumahina State Wayside Park (M) 430
Kaumalapau Harbor (L) 508
Kaumana Caves (BI) 324
Kaumualii 517-8
Kaunakakai (Mol) 470-4, **471**
Kaunolu (L) 508
Kaupo (M) 451-2

Kaupulehu (BI) 281-3
Kawaiahao Church (O) 135
Kawaihae (BI) 290
Kawakiu Beach (Mol) 492-3
Kawela (Mol) 474
kayaking 87, 89
   Big Island 240-1
   Kauai 524-5
   Maui 366
   Molokai 466
   Oahu 120
Keaau (BI) 329-31
Keaau Beach Park (O) 228
Keahole Point (BI) 280-1
Keaiwa Heiau State Park (O) 189
Kealaikahiki (Kah) 511
Kealakekua (BI) 269-70
Kealakekua Bay (BI) 270-2
Kealia Beach (K) 552-3
Keanae (M) 431
Keauhou (BI) 262-5, **256**
Keawakapu Beach (M) 413-4
Kee Beach (K) 569, 571
Kehena Beach (BI) 335
Kekaa Point (M) 391
Kekaha (K) 590
Kennedy, John F 407
Keokea (M) 449-50
Keokea Beach Park (BI) 296
Keomuku Beach (L) 505
Keoua 234, 289
Kepaniwai County Park (M) 407
Kepuhi Beach (Mol) 490
Kihei (M) 410-8, **411**
Kiholo Bay (BI) 283
Kilauea (BI) 30, 31, 342, 345-6
Kilauea (K) 554-7
Kilauea Iki (BI) 347-8, 352
Kilohana Plantation (K) 537
King Kamehameha's Kona Beach Hotel (BI) 252
Kipahulu (M) 440
Kipahulu Valley (M) 438
Kipuka Puaulu (BI) 351
kites 489
Kodak Hula Show (O) 170
Kohala Ditch (BI) 296
Kokee Museum (K) 593
Kokee State Park (K) 593-6

Bold indicates maps.

Koki Beach (M) 438
Koko Crater (O) 194
Koko Head Regional Park (O) 193-5
Kolekole Beach Park (BI) 309
Kolekole Pass (O) 212-3
Koloa (K) 574-7, **575**
Koloa Landing (K) 578-9
Kona (BI) 249-67
Kona Arts Center (BI) 266
Kona Brewing Company (BI) 254
Kona Coast State Park (BI) 281
Kona Historical Society Museum (BI) 269
Koolau 571
Koolau Forest Reserve (M) 430
Ku 13-4, 15, 476
Kua Bay (BI) 281
Kualapuu (Mol) 478-9
Kualoa Ranch (O) 206
Kualoa Regional Park (O) 206
Kuhio Beach Park (O) 167
Kukailimoku 13-4, 233, 234
Kukuihaele (BI) 304-5
Kukuiolono Park (K) 583
Kukuiula Bay (K) 578
Kula (M) 32, 446-8
Kunia (O) 212

L

La Perouse Bay (M) 423-4
Lahaina (M) 375, 377-87, **378**
  accommodations 383-4
  climate 32
  entertainment 386-7
  restaurants 384-6
  shopping 387
Lahaina Jodo Mission (M) 383
Lahaina Whaling Museum (M) 380
Lahainaluna Seminary (M) 382
Laie (O) 209-10
Lanai 494-510, **495**
  accommodations 501, 503, 507
  activities 500
  climate 497
  entertainment 504

flora & fauna 498
geography 497
history 494-7
population 498
restaurants 503-4, 507-8
shopping 504
transportation 500-1
Lanai City (L) 501-4, **502**
land ownership 22, 28, 29
language 42-5, 59
Lanikai (O) 200
Lapakahi State Historical Park (BI) 292
Larsens Beach (K) 553-4
lauhala weaving 84, 266
laundry 61
Laupahoehoe Point (BI) 309
lava 345
Lava Tree State Park (BI) 332
lava tubes 281, 334, 347, 432-3, 458
Lawai Beach (K) 578
Laysan Island (NHI) 602-3
Leeward Islands. *See* Northwestern Hawaiian Islands
legal matters 72
leis 41, 58, 85, 598
Leleiwi Overlook (M) 455
leprosy settlement (Mol) 480-2
leptospirosis 61-2
lesbians. *See* gays & lesbians
libraries 68
lighthouses 195, 332, 380, 410, 480, 505, 535-6
Liholiho. *See* Kamehameha II
Lihue (K) 32, 533-40, **534, 538**
Liliuokalani 19, 24-5, 57, 131, 133, 134, 217, 219
Liliuokalani Church (O) 217, 219
Liliuokalani Gardens (BI) 321-2
Lindbergh, Charles 440
literature. *See* books
Little Beach (M) 422-3
Lohiau 569-70
Loihi 30
Lono 14, 15, 16, 307, 476
Lua Makika (Kah) 514
Luahiwa Petroglyphs (L) 510

luaus 80-1
  Big Island 247, 262
  Maui 372, 394-5
  Oahu 125
Lucy Wright Park (K) 588
Lumahai Beach (K) 567
Lunalilo 19, 23, 135
Lydgate Beach Park (K) 541
Lyman House Memorial Museum (BI) 320
Lyon Arboretum (O) 146

M

Maalaea Bay (M) 412
macadamia nuts 39, 274, 304, 324, 487
MacKenzie State Recreation Area (BI) 334
MacPhee, Angus 511-2
magazines 59-60
Mahaulepu Beach (K) 579-80
Mahukona Beach Park (BI) 292-3
mail 54
Maili (O) 226
Maipoina Oe Iau Beach Park (M) 413
Makaha (O) 226-8
makahiki festival 15
Makahiku Falls (M) 439
Makalawena (BI) 281
Makapala (BI) 295-6
Makapuu Point (O) 195-6
Makawao (M) 443-4
Makaweli (K) 587
Make Horse Beach (Mol) 492
Makena (M) 422-4, **419**
Makiki Valley (O) 146-9, **147**
Makua Valley (O) 228
Malae Heiau (K) 541
Malaekahana State Recreation Area (O) 210
Malo, David 382, 413
Maluuluolele Park (M) 381
Manele Bay (L) 506-8
Maniniholo Dry Cave (K) 568
Manoa Falls (O) 149, **147**
man-of-war 69, 200
manta rays 264
Mantokuji Buddhist Mission (M) 427

Manuka State Wayside Park (BI) 336
maps 46-7
marijuana 237, 329
Marquesans 13, 515
Maui 357-459, **358**
  accommodations 370-2
  activities 363-9
  beaches 363
  climate 360
  entertainment 372
  flora & fauna 360-1
  geography 360
  Haleakala National Park 452-9, **452**
  Hana Hwy 424-41, **425**
  history 357, 359
  northwest 375-418, **376**
  population 361
  shopping 372
  tours 369-70
  transportation 372-5
  Upcountry 441-52, **442**
  Wailea & Makena 418-24, **419**
Maui (god) 360, 453
Maui Crafts Guild (M) 426
Maui Ocean Center (M) 412
Mauna Kea (BI) 30, 31, 32, 33, 235, 301, 311-5
Mauna Kea Beach (BI) 289
Mauna Lani Resort (BI) 286-8
Mauna Loa (BI) 30, 31, 33, 235, 315-6, 349, 351, 352-3
Mauna Ulu (BI) 348
Maunaloa (Mol) 488-9
measurement system 61
medical care. See health issues
medicinal plants 275
Menehune Ditch (K) 589
menehunes 13, 517
Midway Islands (NHI) 603-4
military 39-40
Mililoli (BI) 277
Mission Houses Museum (O) 135-6
Missouri 188

Moana. See Sheraton Moana Surfrider
Moanalua (O) 151
Mokuaikaua Church (BI) 253
Mokuauia (O) 210
Mokuleia (O) 216
Mokuleia Bay (M) 399-400
Moloaa Beach (K) 553
Molokai 460-93, **461**
  accommodations 467-8
  activities 465-7
  beaches 465, 491-3, **491**
  climate 463
  flora & fauna 463
  geography 462-3
  history 460, 462, 481-2
  population 464
  shopping 468
  tours 467
  transportation 468-70
Molokai Ranch (Mol) 462, 488, 489-90
Molokini 365
money 52-4
Mookini Heiau (BI) 293-4
Moomomi Beach (Mol) 487-8
mopeds 128-9
motion sickness 63
motorcycles 249, 532
mountain biking 56, 92. See also cycling
  Big Island 241-2, 249
  Kauai 526
  Maui 367, 375
  Molokai 466
movies 59
mule rides 483
Munro, George 496, 509
Munro Trail (L) 509-10
music 40-1, 84-5

N

Na Ala Hele 90
Na Pali Coast (K) 570-4
Naalehu (BI) 340
Nakalele Point Light Station (M) 410
Nanakuli (O) 224, 226
Nanaue 228
Nani Mau Gardens (BI) 324
Napili (M) 397-8

national parks 38, 77
  Haleakala National Park (M) 452-9, **452**
  Hawaii Volcanoes National Park (BI) 342-56, **343**
National Tropical Botanical Garden (K) 568
Nature Conservancy of Hawaii 33-4, 67, 438
Nawiliwili Beach Park (K) 536
Nawiliwili Harbor (K) 536
Necker Island (NHI) 603
nene 34, 236, 360, 454, 555
newspapers 59-60
Nihoa Island (NHI) 603
Niihau 597-9, **597**
Ninini Point (K) 535-6
nisei 26-7
noodle factories 142
North Kohala (BI) 290-7, **291**
North Kona (BI) 277-90, **279**
North Shore Surf & Cultural Museum (O) 217
Northwestern Hawaiian Islands 600-4, **600-1**
Numila (K) 586
Nuuanu Pali Drive (O) 197

O

Oahu 110-230, **112-3**
  accommodations 123-5
  activities 117-23
  beaches 117, 164-8
  central 211-4
  climate 111
  entertainment 125
  flora & fauna 111, 114
  geography 111
  history 110-1
  Honolulu 129-61, **130**, **132**
  North Shore 215-24, **215**
  Pearl Harbor area 186-9
  population 114
  shopping 125-6
  southeast coast 190-8, **191**
  tours 123
  transportation 126-9
  Waianae Coast 224-30, **225**
  Waikiki 161-86, **162-3**
  windward coast 198-211, **199**

Bold indicates maps.

Oahu Market (O) 140
observatories 297, 312-3, 455
ocean safety 68-71
ohelo berries 83, 352
Oheo Gulch (M) 438-40
Old Kona Airport Beach Park
   (BI) 254
Olokele (K) 587
Olowalu (M) 387-8
One Alii Beach Park (Mol) 472
Onekahakaha Beach Park (BI)
   323
Onizuka Space Center (BI)
   281
Onizuka Visitor Center (BI)
   312
Opaekaa Falls (K) 544
Opihikao (BI) 334-5
OTEC Beach (BI) 280-1

P

Pa o Umi Point (BI) 252
Paao 13, 233
packing 47
Pahala (BI) 341, 342
Pahoa (BI) 331-2
Paia (M) 424, 426-9, **427**
Palaau State Park (Mol) 479-80
Palauea Beach (M) 420
Pali Hwy (O) 196-8
Panaewa Rainforest Zoo (BI)
   324
Paniau (N) 599
Papawai Point (M) 388
Papohaku Beach (Mol) 491-2
Parker Ranch (BI) 297-9
passports 48-9
Pauahi, Princess Bernice. See
   Bishop, Princess Bernice
   Pauahi
Pearl City (O) 188
Pearl Harbor (O) 26, 186-9
Peepee Falls (BI) 324
Pele 14, 31, 315, 333, 334,
   342, 570
Pepeekeo Scenic Drive (BI)
   310
petroglyphs 14, 58
   Big Island 264, 283, 287,
      349
   Lanai 505, 510

phones 54-5
photography 60
pidgin 44-5
Piilani 359
Piilani Hwy (M) 450-2
Pili 13
pineapples 26, 39, 82, 214,
   496
Pinetrees Beach Park (K) 565
plane tours 244
planning 46-7
plant life. See flora
Poipu (K) 577-83, **577**
Pokai Bay Beach Park (O) 226
Poliahu 14, 315
Poliahu Heiau (K) 543
Polihale State Park (K) 591
Polihua Beach (L) 509
Polipoli Spring State Recreation
   Area (M) 448-9
politics 38-9, 57
Polo Beach (M) 420
Pololu Valley (BI) 296-7
Polynesian Cultural Center
   (O) 209
population 40
Port Allen (K) 586
Portuguese man-of-war 69,
   200
postal services 54
pottery 84
Pounders Beach (O) 209-10
Prince Kuhio Park (K) 577
Princeville (K) 32, 559-62
Protect Kahoolawe Ohana
   movement 28, 513
Puaa Kaa State Wayside Park
   (M) 432
Puako (BI) 288
Puako petroglyph preserve
   (BI) 287
Pukalani (M) 445-6
Pukoo (Mol) 476-7
Puna (BI) 329-36, **330**
Punaluu (BI) 341
Punaluu (O) 208
Punchbowl (O) 149-50
Puohokamoa Falls (M) 430
Pupukea Beach Park (O) 222
Puu Loa petroglyphs (BI) 349
Puu o Mahuka Heiau (O) 222

Puu Pehe Cove (L) 507
Puu Poliahu (BI) 315
Puu Rd (K) 583
Puu Ualakaa State Park (O)
   147-8
Puuhonua o Honaunau
   National Historical Park (BI)
   275-7
Puukohola Heiau (BI) 289-90
Puunene (M) 403-4

Q

Queen Emma Summer Palace
   (O) 197
quilting 41

R

radio 60, 116
Rainbow Falls (BI) 323-4
Red Sand Beach (M) 436
religion
   early 13-4, 19
   modern 42
restaurants 80-1. See also
   individual islands
Richards, William 359
Richardson Ocean Park (BI)
   323
rip currents 68
rogue waves 68-9
Round-the-World (RTW)
   tickets 94-5
Royal Hawaiian Hotel (O)
   166, 168, 178
Royal Mausoleum State
   Monument (O) 150
running 91-2, 121, 243-4
Russian Fort Elizabeth (K) 587

S

Sacred Falls State Park (O) 208
Saddle Rd (BI) 311-6
safety issues 68-71
   crime 71
   hiking 90-1
   hitchhiking 108
   ocean 68-71
   tsunamis 71
Salt Pond Beach Park (K) 586
Sand Island (O) 138
sandalwood 18-9, 484

Sandy Beach (O) 194
Sans Souci Beach (O) 168
Science City (M) 455
scorpions 64
scuba diving. See diving
Sea Life Park (O) 195-6
sea urchins 70
seals, Hawaiian monk 35-6,
   519, 602
Secret Beach (K) 558
senior travelers 67
shaka sign 43
sharks 70-1
shave ice 82
Sheraton Moana Surfrider (O)
   166, 178
Shipwreck Beach (K) 579
Shipwreck Beach (L) 504-5
shopping 84-5. See also
   individual islands
shorebreaks 68
Sierra Club 33, 67, 90, 367
silversword 458
skiing 243
skydiving 122-3
slack-key guitar 40-1
Sleeping Giant (K) 544-5, 549
snacks 81
snorkeling 56, 87
   Big Island 240, 263-4, 272,
      276, 284
   Kauai 523-4, 569
   Lanai 506
   Maui 365-6, 419
   Molokai 466
   Oahu 119-20, 193
snowboarding 243
snuba 87, 119, 523
South Kohala (BI) 277-90, 279
South Kona (BI) 267-77, 268
South Point (BI) 338-9
sovereignty movement 28-30
special events 72-5
Spencer Beach Park (BI) 289
spiders 64
sports
   ancient 15
   spectator 84

Spouting Horn Beach Park (K)
   578
Spreckelsville Beach (M) 426
St Andrew's Cathedral (O)
   134
St Benedict's Painted Church
   (BI) 274
St Joseph's Church (Mol) 474,
   475
St Peter's Church (BI) 262-3
St Raphael's Catholic Church
   (K) 576
State Capitol (O) 133
state parks 67, 77. See also
   individual parks
statehood 28
steam vents 336, 346
steel guitar 40-1
submarine rides 245, 369
sugar 20-1, 25, 39, 359, 382,
   403-4, 479, 496, 533,
   574-6
sunburn 62
Sunset Beach Park (O) 223
surfing 56, 86
   Big Island 238
   history 15, 166, 263
   Kauai 522
   Maui 363, 399, 427
   Molokai 478
   museum 217
   Oahu 117-8, 216, 219, 222
swimming. See also beaches;
   ocean safety
   Big Island 238, 254
   Kauai 522
   Maui 363
   Molokai 465-6
   Oahu 117

T

Tantalus (O) 146-9, 147
taxes 54
taxis 108
Taylor Camp (K) 569
tea ceremonies 185
Tedeschi Vineyards (M) 450,
   451
telephones 54-5
tennis 122, 242, 368, 466, 526
theft 71

theme parks 209, 221
tidal waves. See tsunamis
time zone 60
tipping 54
tourist offices 47-8
tours 102, 108-9. See also
   individual islands
trails. See hiking & backpacking
transportation 93-109
   air travel 93-101, 103-5,
      100, 103
   bicycle 108
   boats 101-2, 108, 109
   buses 105-6
   cars 106-8
   hitchhiking 108
   taxis 108
travel clubs 76
travel insurance 49
traveler's checks 52
Tree Tunnel (K) 574
triathlon 91, 243
Tropical Gardens of Maui (M)
   407
tsunamis 71, 322
Tunnels Beach (K) 567-8
turtles 263, 353
TV 60, 116
Twenty-Mile Beach (Mol) 477

U

Ualapue (Mol) 475-6
ukuleles 41
Ulua Beach (M) 419
Ulupalakua Ranch (M) 450
Ulupo Heiau (O) 198-9
undertows 68
unionization 27
University of Hawaii (O)
   144-5, 143
Upcountry (M) 441-52, 442
Upper Manoa Valley (O) 145-6
US Army Museum of Hawaii
   (O) 168-9

V

Valley of the Temples (O) 204
Vancouver, George 18, 221,
   224, 299, 460, 494, 589
Victoria, Queen 537
video 60

Bold indicates maps.

visas 48-9
vog 235
Volcano (BI) 354-6
volcanoes 30-1, 345. *See also*
    Hawaii Volcanoes National
    Park (BI)
volunteer programs 102

W

wagon rides 467
Wahiawa (O) 213-4, **213**
Wahikuli Wayside Beach Park
    (M) 388-9
Waiahole (O) 205-6
Waialeale, Mt (K) 515, 518
Waialua (Mol) 477
Waialua (O) 216
Waianae (O) 226
Waianae Coast (O) 224-30,
    225
Waianapanapa State Park (M)
    432-3
Waiau, Lake (BI) 314
Waiehu (M) 409
Waihee (M) 409
Waikamoi Falls (M) 430
Waikamoi Preserve (M) 454-5
Waikane (O) 205-6
Waikapu (M) 404
Waikiki (O) 161-86, **162-3**
    accommodations 170-9
    beaches 164-8
    entertainment 184-6
    history 166
    restaurants 179-84
    shopping 186
Waikiki Aquarium (O) 169-70
Waikiki Beach Center (O)
    165-7
Waikoko Beach (K) 567
Waikoloa (BI) 285-6

Waikoloa Beach Resort (BI)
    283-5
Waikoloa petroglyph preserve
    (BI) 283
Waikolu Lookout (Mol) 484-5
Wailea (M) 418-22, **419**
Wailoa River State Park (BI)
    321
Wailua (K) 540-9, **542**
Wailua (M) 431-2
Wailua Falls (K) 535
Wailua Falls (M) 438
Wailuku (M) 404-7, **404**
Waimanalo Bay Beach Park
    (O) 196
Waimanalo Beach Park (O)
    196
Waimea (BI) 32, 297-302,
    298
Waimea (K) 587-90, **588**
Waimea (O) 220-4
Waimea Bay Beach Park (O)
    221
Waimea Canyon (K) 591-3
Waimea Valley Adventure
    Park (O) 221
Waimoku Falls (M) 439-40
Wainee Church (M) 381
Wainiha (K) 567
Waiohinu (BI) 339-40
Waioli Huiia Church (K) 563
Waioli Mission House
    Museum (K) 563-4
Waipio Beach (BI) 307
Waipio Valley (BI) 305-8, **306**
Waipouli (K) 549-50
Wananalua Church (M) 435
Washington Place (O) 134
weather forecasts
    Big Island 238
    Kauai 522

    Lanai 499
    Maui 363
    Molokai 465
    Oahu 117
weddings 66
whale watching 89, 244,
    360-1, 369-70, 388, 467
Whalers Village (M) 391, 393
whales 36-7, 89, 360-1
whaling 20, 129, 359, 380,
    391
White Sands Beach Park (BI)
    254-5
Whittington Beach Park (BI)
    340-1
Wilcox Rebellion 24
wildlife 34-8, 57. *See also
    individual species*
    Big Island 236
    dangerous 64, 69-71
    Kauai 518-20
    Lanai 498
    Maui 360
    Molokai 463
    Northwestern Hawaiian
        Islands 601-2
    Oahu 111, 114
windsurfing 86
    Big Island 238-9
    Kauai 523
    Maui 364, 412, 427
    Oahu 118-9, 223
Wo Hing Temple (M) 380
women travelers 65
Wood Valley (BI) 341-2
work 75
World War I 26
World War II 26-7

Z

zoos 170, 324

Boxed Text

'Agricultural' Golf Courses 34
Agricultural Inspection 99
Air Travel Glossary 96-7
Attending University 145
A Bitter Medicine 275
Braking for Whales 388
Breakfast Ideas 180
Captain James Cook 272
Climbing Fish 439
Considerations for Responsible Diving 88
Crater Hill Hikes 555
The Creation Myth 31
The Death of David Douglas 302
Devastation Day 339
Dimming the Light 313
Donkey Crossing 282
Embassies & Consulates 50-1
Everyday Health 61
Exploring Molokai 464
Fish 81
Fragile Paradise 353
From Swamp to Resort 166
Getting Closer to the Flow 350
Green Sea Turtles 263
H-3 203
A Hard Nut to Crack 304
Hawaiian Home Lands 29
Hawaiian Sports & Games 15
Hawaiian Weddings 66
Hawaii's Alii 19
Herbs & Noodles 142
Hitchhiking Weeds 120
HIV & Entering the USA 49
House of the Frigate Bird 219
House of the Sun 453
Human Sacrifices 221
Hurricane Iniki 519
Iliiliopae Sacrifices 476
Ironman Triathlon 91
Kaena Point Legends 229
Kilauea Meltdown 348
Kipahulu Valley 438
Kohala Ditch 296
Koieie Fishpond 413
Kona Coffee 270
Koolau the Leper 571
Lava Surfing 333
Lava Wasteland? 248

Little Tokyo & Big Tsunamis 322
The Lost Explorer 423
Mail Home Some Aloha 486
Maui's Home 360
Meadow Spirits 593
Medical Kit 62
Molokai Plan 463
Molokai Sorcery 489
Molokini 365
Na Ala Hele 90
Nanaue the Shark Man 228
The Nene – Hawaii's State Bird 454
Niihau Shell Leis 598
North Shore Water Conditions 216
Official Hawaii 38, 238
Official Kauai 521
Official Lanai 499
Official Maui 362
Official Molokai 465
Official Oahu 116
Ohelo Berries 352
The Olowalu Massacre 387
Parker Ranch 299
Petroglyphs 14
Princess Hina's Profile 537
Puna & Pele 334
Puu Poliahu 315
Rolling Sweet Potatoes 148
Sacred Ground 206
Shaka Sign 43
Silversword 458
Souls Leap 391
Spirits in the Night 497
Sugar Roots 496
The Sunrise Experience 456
Sunshine Markets 530
Taylor Camp 569
Tea Ceremony 185
Travel Clubs 76
Trickery & Tears 347
Tropical Fruit 82-3
Vog 235
Volcanic Formations 345
Wailea Beach Walk 420
Walking on Water 470
Whale Songs 37
Where's the Highway? 107

MAP LEGEND

BOUNDARIES

- ·—·—·—· International
- ···—···— State
- — — — — County

HYDROGRAPHY

- Water
- Reef
- Coastline
- Beach
- River, Waterfall
- Swamp, Spring

ROUTES & TRANSPORT

- Freeway
- Toll Freeway
- Primary Road
- Secondary Road
- Tertiary Road
- Unpaved Road
- Pedestrian Mall
- Trail
- Walking Tour
- Ferry Route
- Railway, Train Station
- Mass Transit Line & Station

ROUTE SHIELDS

- (H1) Interstate Freeway
- (11) State Highway

AREA FEATURES

- Building
- Cemetery
- Forest
- Golf Course
- Park
- Plaza

- ✪ NATIONAL CAPITAL
- ◉ State, Provincial Capital
- ● LARGE CITY
- ● Medium City
- ● Small City
- ● Town, Village
- ○ Point of Interest

- ■ Place to Stay
- ▲ Campground
- ⛺ RV Park
- ⛺ Shelter

- ▼ Place to Eat
- ■ Bar (Place to Drink)
- ☕ Café

MAP SYMBOLS

- ✈ Airfield
- ✈ Airport
- ∴ Archaeological Site, Ruins
- $ Bank
- ⚾ Baseball Diamond
- ⚑ Beach
- ⚏ Buddhist Temple
- ⛟ Bus Depot
- ✝ Cathedral
- ⌒ Cave
- ✝ Church
- ⚓ Cruise Ship Terminal
- ✇ Dive Site
- ◎ Embassy
- ⋈ Footbridge
- ✾ Garden
- ⛽ Gas Station
- ✚ Hospital, Clinic
- ❶ Information
- ⛓ Lighthouse
- ※ Lookout

- ▲ Monument
- ▲ Mountain
- 🏛 Museum
- ← One-Way Street
- ⚘ Park
- Ⓟ Parking
-)(Pass
- ⋔ Picnic Area
- ★ Police Station
- 🏊 Pool
- ✉ Post Office
- ❶ Public Toilet
- ⛩ Shinto Shrine
- ❖ Shopping Mall
- 🏛 Stately Home
- ⚐ Surfing
- ☯ Taoist Temple
- ☎ Telephone
- ⚐ Trailhead
- ⚘ Winery
- 🐾 Zoo

Note: Not all symbols displayed above appear in this book.

LONELY PLANET OFFICES

Australia
Locked Bag 1, Footscray, Victoria 3011
☎ 03 8379 8000 fax 03 8379 8111
email: talk2us@lonelyplanet.com.au

USA
150 Linden St, Oakland, CA 94607
☎ 510 893 8555 TOLL FREE: 800 275 8555
fax 510 893 8572
email: info@lonelyplanet.com

UK
10a Spring Place, London NW5 3BH
☎ 020 7428 4800 fax 020 7428 4828
email: go@lonelyplanet.co.uk

France
1 rue du Dahomey, 75011 Paris
☎ 01 55 25 33 00 fax 01 55 25 33 01
email: bip@lonelyplanet.fr
www.lonelyplanet.fr

World Wide Web: www.lonelyplanet.com *or* AOL keyword: lp
Lonely Planet Images: lpi@lonelyplanet.com.au